Modern Fruit Science

Orchard and Small Fruit Culture

NORMAN FRANKLIN CHILDERS

Adjunct Professor of Fruit Crops, University of Florida, Gainesville, 32611
Formerly M.A. Blake Professor and Research Specialist of Horticulture
Rutgers University — The State University of New Jersey
Assistant Director and Senior Plant Physiologist
United States Department of Agriculture Experimental Station in Puerto Rico
Associate in Horticulture, Ohio Agricultural Experiment Station
Assistant Professor in Horticulture, The Ohio State University
Instructor, Cornell University

PLEASE ORDER ADDITIONAL BOOKS FROM:

HORTICULTURAL PUBLICATIONS
3906 NW 31 Place
Gainesville, Florida 32606

i

NORMAN F. CHILDERS, Author

Adjunct Professor of Fruit Crops, University of Florida, Gainesville 32661

The Cover

These college students, son and daughter of prominent fruit growers, are Rick Breeden from Illinois who went to the University of Wisconsin, River Falls, majoring in business, and Mary Edwards also of Illinois, who attended Michigan State University, East Lansing, majoring in pomology. Both assisted in orchard duties at home and took part in operating their roadside markets to help them finance their college training.

ii

Dr. Wayne B. Sherman (above) discusses the fruit breeding program with peaches at the University of Florida, Gainesville, with undergraduates and graduate students working toward advanced degrees. Dr. Paul M. Lyrene (below) discusses blueberry breeding for the milder climates. Students trained in temperate and tropical and subtropical fruits have the advantage of being qualified for a wider scope of jobs on graduation. (Photographs courtesy Steve Hiss, University of Florida).

The Pick-Your-Own (PYO) method of harvesting both tree and small fruits has become popular, particularly where there are plenty of people and competition among local growers is not serious. The grower gets 100% of the consumer's dollar immediately. (Mark Robson, Rutgers University).

Contents

An orchard in full bloom is a beautiful sight. This scene is in Bucks County, Pennsylvania.

This is a deciduous fruit growing region in West Germany. Vineyards are contoured on the river banks. Fruit trees on the level area are largely on dwarfing stocks. (Courtesy the late F. Hilkenbaumer, Institut Fur Obstbau der Universitat der Bonn, Germany.)

Copyright Editions:

Ninth, Copyright 1983
(complete revision)

Eighth, Copyright 1981
(reprinted)

Eighth, Copyright 1978
(complete revision)

Seventh, Copyright 1976
(slight revision)

Sixth, Copyright 1975
(slight revision)

Fifth, Copyright 1973
(complete revision)

Fourth, Copyright 1972
(reprinted)

Fourth, Copyright 1969
(complete revision)

Third, Copyright 1966
(slight revision)

Second, Copyright 1961
(complete revision)

First, Copyright 1949
(J.B. Lippincott Co., Chicago)

(second printing, 1950)

(third printing, 1952)

(fourth printing, 1954)

By
Norman F. Childers, Publisher

U.S. Library of Congress
Catalogue Card Number 80-8347
ISBN Number 0-938378-01-5

Labrusca or "fox" type grapes are produced heavily in the Finger Lakes region of New York. This is Keuka Lake in mid winter. Concord is the leading cultivar. (Courtesy J. William Moffett, Editor, Eastern Grape Grower and Winery News)

These scenes are in the area of Cashmere and Wenatchee, Washington. Most of the orchards are located along the river bottom land or low plateaus near water. This is east of the Cascade Mountains. Much of the irrigation water comes from the Wenatchee, Okanagan and Columbia Rivers in this general apple growing area. High sunlight, adequate water and cool nights near harvest aid in the production of the highest quality and colored fruits, mainly Delicious and Golden Delicious.

California leads in fruit growing in the United States. The strawberry crop is grown on raised beds with poly mulch and drip irrigation. Muddy walk-rows are avoided, the berries are kept clean with less disease problems at harvest. (Courtesy Bill Uyeki, The Packer.)

(Above) Main fruit regions of New Zealand are: Auckland (extreme north); Hawkes Bay (above; east side of North Island); Nelson (north end of South Island); and Central Otago (southern South Island), each producing 18-24% of total fruit crop. New Zealand is one of the finest and most picturesque fruit growing regions of the world. (Below) This is a high-density apple orchard in bloom and on dwarfing stock in the Huon Valley, Tasmania. This is an important island ("The Apple Isle") of deciduous fruit growing off the southeast corner of Australia. (Courtesy the late E. Cole, Div. of Hort., Dept. of Agric., Victoria, Australia.)

In the Swiss Alps, these are individual gardens for the adjoining homes, some vegetables - mostly grapes and short-season bush fruits. (Courtesy Geigy Company, Ardsley, New York 10502.)

Preface

This book has been prepared primarily for undergraduate *fruit and nut growing courses in colleges*. The author has made a special attempt, however, to make the book not only complete and technically accurate but interesting and easy-to-read so that it can be used as a text or reference in *technical courses and in home gardens*. In addition, it is hoped that the book will be of value to the *grower* of deciduous fruits and nuts who desires to keep abreast with new ideas, trends and research developments.

While considerable information and research data are given in this text, it is left largely to the teacher to challenge the students with additional research data, theories, depth of discussion and assignments, depending upon their experience and scholastic level. A special effort has been made to present the subject material in an attractive logical manner, using numerous photographs and charts to keep the attention and interest so that the reader will not become bored and later fail to take active part in class discussions.

The subject matter presentation is different from most fruit growing texts. The first and third chapters generally refer to all deciduous tree fruits to be discussed. The early few chapters are devoted to the apple since it is grown widely, and, being important, it has the most and best research background. The apple chapters cover in detail the important subjects from planting to marketing. Thus, the student has an opportunity to become acquainted with the scientific principles upon which the different practices in apple growing are based and with this foundation he can grasp quickly the practices peculiar to the other tree fruits in subsequent chapters. Actually, for all practical purposes, there are few basic differences among fruit and nut crops with regard to their growth processes, fruiting responses and cultural requirements.

Then, following, there are two general chapters covering irrigation, pest and frost control. Each of the important small fruits or groups of small fruits then is covered in a single chapter complete in itself.

The plan of presentation in this book should lend itself to certain regions where some fruits are of little or no importance. For example, much less time would be devoted to cherries in Maine than in Michigan. The cranberry merely would be mentioned in Missouri whereas it is of outstanding importance in New Jersey, Massachusetts, Washington and Wisconsin. The subject matter is readily available to the fruit grower specializing in but one or two fruits. If a peach grower desires information on pruning, soil management, harvesting and other practices he finds it all in one chapter and thus it is not necessary for him to use the index and thumb through general chapters on each orchard management phase to pick out those particular practices relating to the peach.

The appendix at the back of the book gives the reader detailed information that cannot be found in other books, such as a list of world publications carrying pomological information, cost-of-production data, and a list of books, nurseries and U.S. and Canadian experiment stations and universities experimenting with and teaching deciduous fruits. The appendix also includes a glossary and a listing of sources of equipment and materials used in fruit growing.

There is much variation in methods of teaching pomology and results obtained. The teacher's organization and *method of presentation* of material appear to be the most important factors governing student interest. Actually, the professor is probably more than 50 percent responsible for the success of his course; I often have thought 75 percent responsible. But the teacher obviously should not try to carry most of the weight; he must call upon and stimulate his students to contribute since by this approach they will retain more information and generate more interest.

Each teacher has a personal pattern of presentation. The system which works well for one may make a poor showing for another. In the author's experience the above system of presenting a full picture of one important fruit at a time seems to be less confusing to unacquainted students than when several pruning methods for a wide variety of fruits are jumbled together in one or two lectures. When such a discussion is concluded most students cannot seem to recall what practice is used on which fruit and why. If a student studies and thinks only one fruit from the time the cultivars are selected until the product is sold, the entire picture unfolds as a story with a beginning and an end and experience seems to indicate that he retains much more basic information about that fruit during and after the final examination.

Pomology teachers should gradually build a file of 2 x 2 color slides for each lecture and laboratory to break the monotony of straight lectures. An opaque projector is

(Above) The Chinese were the first to use contour plantings. (Below) Origin of many of the cultivated fruits, including the peach (Sian area) was in China over 4000 years ago. This is an apple orchard on *Malas baccata* seedlings in Liaoning Province in northeastern China, interplanted with peanuts. It is an experimental block at the Research Institute of Pomology, Chinese Academy of Agricultural Sciences. (Courtesy Szcepan A. Pieniazek, Institute of Pomology, Skierniewice, Poland.)

good to reflect bulletins and books, 8-1/2 x 11 inches or smaller, tables, pictures, and live material on the screen (Chas. Besler Co., Photo Proj. Equip., E. Orange, N.J. Write for information.)

The portable-overhead-transparency projector with equipment to copy charts and tables on transparencies enables the teacher to operate the equipment on his desk in front of the class, pointing to numbers, bars on a graph, etc., and to draw diagrams while the class watches. The chart and pencil are reflected on a standard projection screen against the front wall. (Minnesota Mining and Manufacturing Co., Visual Products, 2501 Hudson Rd., St. Paul, Minn. 55119.)

The college course in which this book is used really should be four-hours credit to do justice to the subject in lectures and laboratories. A three-hour course is a bit too time-limited.

Today, there is a shortage of trained pomologists in the fruit industry and profession. Professors of pomology *must* increase their efforts to attract promising young people to this field. Colleges and universities now are falling far short of meeting the needs for well-trained capable pomology graduates. It is hoped that this book will help attract more of the better students to pomology.

Many specialists in the field of pomology have assisted in the revisions of this book over the past 35 years. Many have retired or passed on. These distinguished people have been cited in previous editions. Those who have assisted more recently in one way or another with the individual chapters are cited with the respective chapters. Others have made suggestions by mail or personally to the author while travelling the world. They include: S.A. Pieniazek, Poland; Hayao Iwigaki, Japan; Tsuin Shen, China; Robert Wertheim, Holland; Peter Greef, South Africa; Donald McKenzie, New Zealand; R.E.C. Layne, Ontario, Canada; Shimon Levee, Israel; Filberto Loreti, Italy; Romero Ortega and Michael Borys, Mexico; Stephan Wagner and Andre Botar, Romania; Dusan Stankovic, Yugoslavia; V. Kolesnikov, Russia; Bonifacio Nakasu, Brazil; Tony Wiley, Chili; Tony Preston, England; Abdul Kamali, Lebanon; and Richard Lowe, Australia.

Many pomologists in the USA have helped, including: George M. Darrow, Maryland; James N. Moore and Justin R. Morris, Arkansas; Gene J. Galletta and Miklos Faust, USDA; Warren C. Stiles, Gene H. Oberly and Richard L. Norton, Cornell; E. L. Proebsting, Jr., Ronald B. Tukey and Robert A. Norton, Washington; Jerry Hull, George M. Kessler and Robert F. Carlson, Michigan; Delbert D. Hemphill, and Robert Denney, Missouri; Ernest G. Christ and Paul Eck, New Jersey; David W. Buchanan, Wayne Sherman, Paul Lyrene and Michael J. Burke, Florida; Robert G. Hill and David C. Ferree, Ohio; Roy K. Simon, Illinois; Walter E. Ballinger, North Carolina; Robert E. Gough, Rhode Island; James A. Beutel, California; Robert L. Stebbins, and W. Ardeen Sheets, Oregon; Elden J. Stang, Wisconsin; John A. Barden, Virginia; Tara Auxt and Steve H. Blizzard, West Virginia; Jean Overcash, Mississippi; and Frank Emerson and Jules Janick, Indiana.

C. Palmer Bateman, Jr., and his able staff, Somerset Press, Inc., Somerville, New Jersey, have been very helpful over the years in publishing this and other books. Particular thanks go to Gordon Davies, Walter Lech and Kenny Fredericks in the Somerset Press Inc. Thanks also go to my wife, Alma, who has been a real asset and afforded much encouragement and help in continuing to revise this book. Steven Hiss, Fruit Crops, University of Florida is responsible for converting many of my 2 x 2 color slides collected over the world to black and white prints useable in this text. Thank you, Steve, for a fine job. All of these people gave more of their help than I probably should have accepted. I appreciate it.

August 1983   Norman F. Childers

TEN COMMANDMENTS FOR A GOOD TEACHER

(1). PREPARE YOUR LESSON WELL. A lack of proper preparation is the unpardonable sin of a teacher. Nothing will inspire the confidence of his class so quickly as the teacher who makes adequate preparation of his lesson.

(2). BE PRESENT WHENEVER POSSIBLE. Unnecessary absences will not teach your students to be regular in their attendance, and will hinder interest and progress in your class. When it is necessary to be absent, always advise your substitute in sufficient time for him to make necessary preparation.

(3). BE ON TIME. Negligence and indifference on the part of the teacher will soon be absorbed by the class. Be present several minutes before the time set for the class to begin.

(4). BE PERSONALLY INTERESTED IN EACH MEMBER OF YOUR CLASS. Call members by their names. Be interested in the limitations and problems of each member of your class, and willingly give such attention or assistance to those problems as you can.

(5). BE ATTENTIVE OF THE PHYSICAL CONDITIONS OF YOUR CLASSROOM. Before beginning the lesson, make necessary adjustment of the lights, ventilation, window shades, seating arrangements, maps, charts, blackboard, etc.

(6). BEGIN AND CLOSE PROMPTLY. Do not wait for late comers, and do not extend the lesson beyond the time set to end the class. A violation of either of these points will distract interest from your class. Your promptness will beget promptness in your pupils.

(7). DO NOT DO ALL THE TALKING. Do not make your lesson a lecture, as it takes a near genius to give an interesting lecture. Encourage class discussion. Never tell anything you can get your class to tell.

(8). DO NOT PERMIT ARGUMENTS IN YOUR CLASS. Nothing will kill interest more quickly. Permit discussions of differences, but when they turn into arguments, pass on to the next question or point of discussion.

(9). REALIZE YOUR SERIOUS RESPONSIBILITIES. Be as serious as possible about your teaching. Realize that what and how you teach may lead your pupils to fuller understanding and appreciation, or discourage their acceptance of the facts presented.

(10). BE INTERESTED IN YOUR CLASS. Consider your students, and be wise in your teaching. A good slogan for teachers is: "If the student hasn't learned — the teacher hasn't taught."

By Victor H. Wolford

(Above) In heavily populated areas where land values escalate, some fruit growers have converted all or a part of their orchards into fairways and organized golf clubs. This is Apple Ridge Country Club in northern New Jersey near Ramsey, owned and operated by Clinton D. Carlough, formerly one of the largest apple growers in the area. He maintains the remaining trees for beauty and profit.

(Below) This is the entrance to Apple Ridge Country Club of over 2000 members on land formerly a part of a 400-acre orchard. Recreation of many fruit growers is golfing, thus enabling Clinton Carlough, the owner, to continue his hobby. Fruit growers are essentially plantsmen — horticulturists — as the landscaping here so well indicates.

CHAPTER I

Introduction

It is interesting to note that the origin of the many delicious fruits we grow, eat, prepare as drinks and ferment today have originated in many different countries around the world. *Abyssinia:* gave us coffee; *Afghanistan:* the pear, apple, and walnut; *Brazil - Paraguay:* cocoa, pineapple, Brazil nut, cashew, and passion fruit; *China:* the peach, apricot, orange, and mulberry; *Mexico:* the guava; *North America:* cultivated blueberry, cranberry, pecan; *Persia:* cherry, plum, grape, almond, fig, date, persimmon, pistachio nut, and pomegranate; *Peru:* the papaya; and *Siam-Malaya-Java:* banana, coconut, and pomelo.

The early world travellers, traders and settlers carried with them many of these fruit plants and seeds from native lands. The different kinds and cultivars[2] of fruits, many of which are commercially important today, were rapidly propagated and distributed in new territories by religious workers, travelers, pioneer farmers, and such well-known characters as Johnny Appleseed. Gradually, interested individuals and later the governmental agricultural experiment stations, through chance selection or scientific breeding, enlarged the list of high-quality cultivars commercially grown today.

[1]Dr. Arthur H. Thompson, University of Maryland, assisted in revision of this chapter, with William G. Doe, grower-commercial sales, Harvard, Massachusetts. Mr. Doe also made many suggestions from an engineer's and fruit grower's standpoint throughout the text.

[2]The terms "cultivars" and "varieties" are used interchangeably.

Figure 1. In British Columbia, Canada, to the right are orchards on bench land overlooking Okanagan Lake. In recent years there has been encroachment of housing and industrial developments on this prime orchard land and sites. This trend over the world should be slowed considerably if we continue to maintain the present quality fruit production.

TABLE 1. RELATIVE WORLD DECIDUOUS FRUIT PRODUCTION IN THOUSANDS OF METRIC TONS[1] EARLY 1980s.

Crop	U.S.A.	Canada	Mexico	South America[2]	Western Europe[3]	Central and Eastern Europe (Socialistic)[4]	Oceania[5]	Asia[6]	Africa[7]	World (approx.)
Almond	275	—	—	0.2	447	8	0.2	132	47	909
Apples	3,700	450	275	1400	13,000	6400	530	7,900	455	34,110
Apricot	107	—	8	35	600	120	35	420	170	1,495
Blueberry	45	12	—	—	21	—	1	—	—	78
Cherries (all)	80	12	18	8	1200	—	12	150	—	1,480
Cranberry	98	7	—	—	—	—	—	—	—	105
Currant	43	—	—	—	389	53	12	—	—	486
Fig	30	—	14	37	550	—	—	280	165	1,076
Filbert	13	—	—	—	151	4	—	311	—	480
Grape	4,560	72	476	—	4,861	39,480	6,500	800	7,120	66,069
Gooseberry	—	—	—	85	65	—	3	—	—	153
Peach, Nectarine	1,500	35	185	575	3,073	252	100	1,170	240	7,130
Pear	800	38	44	254	3,693	660	150	2,7600	219	8,620
Persimmon	9	—	—	—	4	—	—	50	0.5	63
Plums, Prunes	683	7	76	100	3,012	542	27	825	58	5,330
Pistachio	9	—	—	—	4	—	—	50	.05	63
Raspberry	13	8	—	—	115	72	2	—	—	210
Strawberry	315	26	90	13	891	8	8	305	0.1	1,660
Walnuts	191	—	5	8	243	68	0.2	300	6	821

[1]   U.S. ton is 2000 lbs.; metric ton is 2204.6. Figures given here approximate productive capacity of the country. These data are from FAO Production Yearbook, Vols. 35 & 36, Rome, Italy headquarters.

[2]   Includes: Argentina, Bolivia, Brazil, Chile, Colombia, Equador, Guyama, Paraguay, Peru, Surinam, Uruguay, Venezuela.

[3]   Includes: Albania, Austria, Belgium (Lux.), Bulgaria, Czechoslovakia, Denmarkl, Finland, France, German (DR), Germany (FR), Greece, Hungary, Ireland, Italy, Malta, Netherlands, Norway, Poland, Portugal, Romania, Spain, Sweden, Switzerland, UK, Yugoslavia.

[4]   Includes: Australia, New Zealand.

[5]   Includes: Afghanistan, China, Cyprus, India, Iran, Iraq, Israel, Japan, Korea (Rep.), Lebanon, Pakistan, Syria, Turkey.

[6]   Includes: Algeria, Egypt, Libya, Madagascar, Morocco, Reunion, South Africa, Tunisia.

The technique of growing fruits has undergone a marked change the past seventy-five years. In the early 1900's, fruit growing was rather simple as compared with the many steps and different types of machinery involved today. Where formerly little or no spray material was applied, now as many as eight to ten sprays are applied to apples in one season. The need for more spraying was brought about by an increase in number of insects and diseases and greater resistance of some species to standard spray materials.

Also, today we are using Integrated Pest Management (IPM), monitering insects, their predators, and diseases and spraying only when necessary, not on a set schedule as formerly. Much of the apple crop was formerly harvested and sold directly out of the orchard with comparatively little grading and packing. Now, most of the commercial crop is carefully brushed or washed, graded, sized, and packed with the aid of specialized machinery. A large part of the crop may be placed in storage for weeks or months before being sent through established marketing channels. Obviously, the amount of labor and equipment required to grow and prepare fruit for sale has increased. About 20 times as many bushels of apples are required to pay the annual wages of a hired person as the amount required in the early 1900s. Although modern machinery has made it possible to increase our efficiency in output, this gain often has been passed on to labor in awarding higher wages. Thus, the fruit grower must be increasingly more efficient in the use of his labor if he is to continue to enjoy profits above wages paid.

Shortly after 1940, great advancements were made in new machinery designed to reduce high labor costs in fruit growing. An example is the modern power sprayer which requires only one or two people to spray a large orchard, whereas formerly five to seven or more people were needed to do the same job in triple the period of time. Although the initial cost of such machinery is relatively high, the greater output and long-time saving in labor costs justify its use. It should be pointed out, however, that only those growers who can obtain *high production per acre of high-quality* fruit will be able to adopt the improved but more expensive production machinery and methods.

Some economic principles. A chief concern of the person who desires to plant or buy an orchard is the future likelihood of profits. Obviously, no one can predict accurately the profits of an orchard due to so many variables. There are, however, some economic principles which frequently hold and which may be considered.

The most important factor influencing cash returns to fruit growers is the general price level, which is usually going up or down, as history has shown. Major rises in price level have been correlated with six wars: the War of 1812, the Civil War, World War I, World War II, and the Korean - Vietnam Wars (Figure 2). These price reactions to wars are similar worldwide. Foreign imports of fresh and processed fruits also influence domestic prices and

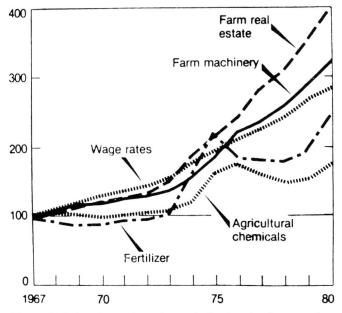

Figure 2. Prices have risen dramatically for the farmers since 1967 (the left figures refer to percent of 1967), the most notable being farm land. As farm land becomes more scarce, its value rises, provided there is continuing temptation for the small farmer to sell his land for a substantial profit. (USDA)

movement of fruit.

In present-day agriculture, the fruit grower must buy supplies on the market to produce and sell his products. When prices are falling, the fruit growers, as with all farm operators, are at a disadvantage because they must pay a higher price for things they buy than the price they receive for things they sell. Before you make a long-term investment in an orchard, it would be well for you to determine if the price level is high or low, and if it is going up or down. There undoubtedly will be less foreclosures in the next 10 to 20 years if fruit growers will remember that rising prices at one time mean falling prices at some later date. The profitability of an orchard set in 1985 will be determined by prices obtained for fruit products and the cost of things from 1990-2010. With small fruits such as strawberries and full-dwarf trees that bring full crops in 2-5 years after planting, the grower is in a better position to take full advantage of peak-price-return periods by increasing acreage accordingly.

The fruit industry. Generally speaking, the USA will account for about 25 percent of the combined world crops of apples, pears, peaches, plums, prunes, oranges, grapefruit, lemons, limes and other citrus (Table 1). Of the individual fruits, the United States produces about the following percentages; apples, 11; pears, 9; peaches, 21; plums and prunes, 12; oranges and tangerines, 26; other citrus, 20. When we consider total value of all fruits and nuts in the USA, citrus accounts for about 25 to 30 percent and nuts around 10 percent. Per capita consumption of various fruits in the U.S. is shown in Table 2.

TABLE 2. Per Capita Consumption of Fresh Fruits (fresh weight basis), U.S. Ann. Av. 1982 in lbs.

Bananas	21.4	Avocados	1.1
Apples	17.3	Nectarines	1.2
Oranges	13.4	Pineapples	1.4
Grapefruit	8.5	Cherries	0.6
Peaches	5.3	Cranberries	0.1
Pears	2.3	Apricots	0.07
Grapes	3.3	All fresh fruits	84.6
Strawberries	2.2	All citrus	26.5
Plums & Prunes	1.6	All non-citrus	57.5

Note: Peaches compete well (major volume in 20 wks.) with other fruit sold year round.

Regions in which fruits and nuts are grown in large commercial quantities in the United States are shown in Figure 3. The heaviest producing areas are located in the Far West and the eastern half of the United States. The densely speckled areas in the Northwest and Northeast can be largely attributed to apples, whereas those in the southeastern states, with the exception of central Florida, largely represent peaches and pecans. In Florida, southern Texas, and southern California (Figure 3), the concentrated areas are principally citrus.

California is the leading fruit state, producing over one-fourth of the total United States fruit and nut crop.

TABLE 3. Relative Production and Importance of Fruits and Nuts in the United States

	Fruit Crops*	Commercial Production (1979-1982)	Trend
		Short Tons (1000)	
1.	All citrus (5)	10,050	Down
2.	Grapes (14)	5,000	Up
3.	Apples (34)	4,070	Up
4.	Peach (34)	1,410	Steady
5.	Pears (11)	880	Up
6.	Plums and Prunes (5)	250	Down
7.	Strawberries*(23)***	350	Up
8.	Cherries, all (12)	120	Down
9.	Almonds (1)	300	Up
10.	Walnuts, English (2)	220	Up
11.	Apricots (3)	120	Down
12.	Nectarines (1)	180	Up
13.	Avocados (2)	180	Up
14.	Cranberries (5)	130	Up
15.	Pecans, all types (11)	125	Up
16.	Olives (1)	70	Steady
17.	Blueberries (5)**	45	Steady
18.	Figs, all (1)	40	Steady
19.	Bushberries	30	Steady
20.	Dates (1)	20	Steady
21.	Papayas (1) Hawaii	25	Up
22.	Filberts (2)	15	Up
23.	Macadamia nuts (1) Hawaii	15	Up
24.	Pomegranates (1)	10	Up
25.	Persimmons (1)	2.3	Steady

* Numbers in ( ) are commercial states involved. U.S. ton is 2000 lbs. or "short ton". These data are survey which give you an estimate only — the best data we have.

** Blueberry data are for wild and cultivated types total. They include Canada. Breakdown is 25.2T cultivated; 16.5T wild.

*** Strawberry imports from Mexico are significant: Fresh - 32,200 tons; frozen - 88,100 tons.

Figure 3. Fruits are grown in every state of the Union, but there are definite well suited areas where each fruit reaches peak production. The particular fruit or fruits involved in the concentrated areas shown above are pointed out in subsequent chapters. (USDA)

Almost every kind of fruit and nut produced in the United States can be grown in California due to its many climates, fertile soils, and elaborate irrigation systems. California produces both temperate fruits, such as the apple and peach, and tropical and subtropical fruits, such as citrus, avocados, figs, dates and olives.

On a tonnage basis, the leading deciduous fruit grown in the United States is grapes, as indicated in Table 3. It is closely followed by apples and then, in order, by peaches, pears, prunes, strawberries, cherries and apricots.

In the last 20 years all fresh fruit in the USA has dropped about 8% and stands at about 81 lbs. consumption per capita. Processed fruit is up 15% to 58 lbs./capita. Much of this is due to orange juice which has risen 90%. Wine and grape juice consumption is on the increase. All processed foods are increasing due to less home cooking, more women in industry and by more people eating out. See Figure 4 for trends of non-citrus fruits in the USA.

In the past over fifty years, the production of citrus has increased rapidly until the orange leads all other fruits in tonnage, with grapefruit and lemons also ranking high. On the other hand, the production of apples has increased somewhat while peaches have remained at about the same level.

Fruits, particularly strawberries, have a relatively high value on the basis of amount of land occupied. Some crops, such as hay, wheat, and oats, on the other hand, have a comparatively low value. Also, the value and tonnage of apples and peaches are closely related, but the value of grapes is much less than that of apples and peaches on a tonnage basis. Cultivated blueberries, on the other hand, have a high value per land unit.

During and after World War II, record crops of many of the deciduous fruits were attained, due to the great world need for food and to the high prices being paid for fruits.

The increased production was largely attained by over-all better care of plantings, by renovating old orchards and vineyards, and new plantings. Inasmuch as general over-all increases in fruit acreage are attended with some risk, the individual grower may well exercise caution in increasing his own acreage during such periods.

Trends in fruit growing. Those people who believe in the philosophy of "an unfinished world" are constantly looking to the future and making plans. The following trends in fruit growing may help to assess the situation.

Production costs have reached a point where a fruit grower *must increase production by increasing acreage or by using high-density compact plantings to reduce costs/ton.* Also, he must keep careful cost accounting of each block of fruit to be sure it is profitable. Computer analysis is being adopted by many growers, personally or by contract, to keep accurate and up-to-date cost/profit records on various operations and blocks of fruit to save labor and increase profits. There also has been a trend toward grower owned corporates that manage large acreages such as walnuts in California and grapes in western New York. But there always will be a place for the small and medium acreage fruit growers.

In the past, many fruit growers have made it a practice to devote full time to raising only one fruit such as apples. Some growers are continuing this practice with good success. But there is a trend toward diversification giving better year-round use of labor, a wider and more profitable market outlet, and better distribution of cash returns for the year as a whole. Perhaps everyone should not diversify, but some growers may find it to their advantage to raise several kinds of fruits or some vegetables, bees, nursery stock or livestock, such as beef, depending upon local opportunities and markets. It would be well to exercise caution, however, and not expand these activities to the point where the fruit business suffers.

During recent years there has been an increasing tendency of the apple grower to rotate his orchard with respect to age. This gives him opportunity to plant new cultivars, try new crops. Also, young or smaller trees with good orchard care tend to produce a better quality product at less cost. With this system, the land available for orcharding is planned so that a new block of trees is set every five to ten years and an old block removed when for one reason or another it is not paying a decent profit.

Several valuable new chemicals are being introduced to control growth, flowering, fruit set, and size, color, maturation, and quality of the fruit. Alar, gibberellin, cytokinin and ethephon are examples showing promise, serving to give a better product at reduced cost. And, as indicated, Integrated Pest Management is now an accepted successful program.

In spite of the best orchard management, there will always be a certain amount of low-grade fruit. This fruit

4

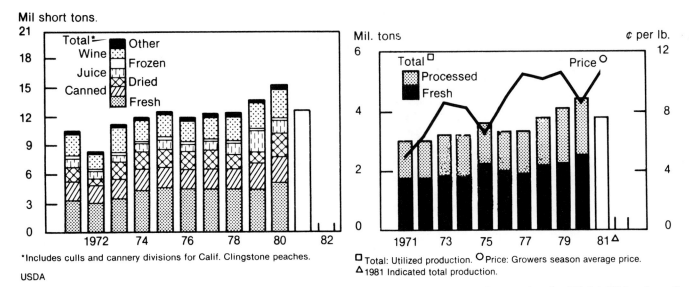

Mil short tons.

*Includes culls and cannery divisions for Calif. Clingstone peaches.

USDA

□ Total: Utilized production. ○ Price: Growers season average price.
△ 1981 Indicated total production.

Figure 4. (Left) Noncitrus Fruits: Fresh fruits, wine and juices have shown an increase over the past decade. (Right) USA prices of apples have risen the past decade but inflation has been a factor. Note the increase in commercial processing, with fewer wives doing home cooking and more people eating out. (USDA).

should be processed, but today considerable *good* fruit also is processed by demand. Fruit processing will no doubt undergo considerable future expansion. The importance of this field is emphasized by the fact that about half of the deciduous fruits produced are processed. A slight increase was noted in fruit processing during World War II and this increase is continuing (Figure 4) in light of the growing interest in wines, juices and the blending of pure fruit juices, the latter of which will furnish increasing competition for synthetic drinks. It is probable that dehydrated fruits will receive more attention, and it is certain that some kind of new fruit products will be devised as a result of the research being conducted in this field (Figure 6).

Much needs to be done in improving transportation and marketing systems for deciduous fruits, all of which are more or less perishable. The importance of the fruit marketing field is evidenced by the fact that over 60 cents of the consumer's dollar for apples goes into marketing channels, and the remaining 40 cents goes to the grower. Fruits that unquestionably find the quickest sales at the highest prices are those that are tree-ripened, of high quality and undamaged. In the past, the merchandiser and the fruit grower have blamed each other for bruised unattractive fruit, but this does not solve the problem for the consumer who wants a top product and is usually willing to pay a good price. The handling of fruit from tree to table needs increasingly more study and careful attention by the grower, experiment station worker, and by the merchandiser. Definite advancements are being made in fruit grading and sizing machinery and in special packaging to reduce bruising. There is also a trend toward more storages on farms in which the ripening processes of

harvested fruit can be quickly reduced to a minimum. Controlled atmosphere storage has shown a marked increase in most apple sections, helping to extend the supply to consumers and processors, thus stabilizing prices. Precooling and better refrigeration conditions for fruit in transportation are receiving more widespread use. Air freight is growing rapidly in quick long-distance transportation of some fruits such as strawberries at the "eating-ripe" stage.

A mechanization trend is strong and use of materials such as herbicides to cut labor costs. All-red mutations of standard apple varieties and "spur-type" sports are being widely planted. There is a strong trend toward direct sales by small suburban and large-acreage growers directly to

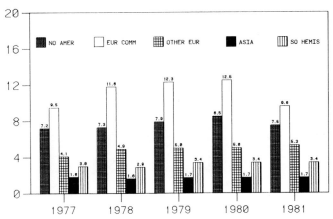

Figure 5. Shown in this graph is the relative production of deciduous fruits in regions of the world. The leaders are North America and the European Community (West). Southern hemisphere countries produce only a fraction of the world deciduous fruits in comparison with the northern hemisphere countries. In millions of metric tons. (USDA-Foreign Estimates)

5

Figure 6. This Eastern Regional Laboratory at Philadelphia, Pennsylvania (there are four in the United States) is an indication of the great research effort being made by the U.S. Department of Agriculture to find new and better uses for fruit and other agricultural by-products. (USDA).

consumers at roadside sales, in city-assigned lots, and in public-pick-your-own fruit.

The field of consumer education is in need of more attention. It is surprising how little the general public knows about the proper buying and use of fruits. Cooking advice on TV, radio, and in news media teaches families how to buy the different cultivars of fruit in season and for specific uses. Also, a more widespread educational program for retail dealers is needed on handling and displaying deciduous fruits, which are unlike citrus. Most chefs have lost the art of baking *good* fruit pies. But in spite of this, the apple pie is still the national favorite pie according to a Gallup poll: 27% desired pie, 23% ice cream and 19% cake; those who preferred pie named apple pie 27%, cherry 12% and lemon meringue 10%.

And last but not least, there is an increasing shortage of young trained fruit growers and professional pomologists available for the jobs. This is particularly true with professional pomologists. During the 1970s and early 1980s there have not been enough pomologists to fill the

Figure 7. This is one of the large orchards in socialist Yugoslavia owned and operated by the State. Rows may be several miles long. Fruit production in Yugoslavia and Romania and shipping to neighboring countries is concerning marketers from free enterprise countries.

opening positions, resulting in many of the jobs being filled by candidates not trained in pomology and not really oriented to this field. So those of you interested in the fruit business should be encouraged to further your training.

The fruit grower. In spite of great advancements in ways and means of growing fruit and in the amount of scientific knowledge available, the most important factor in successful fruit growing is the grower himself. To make a good living today, a fruit grower or any business person must have first a thorough and well-rounded practical knowledge of the business which comes with experience. If a good practical knowledge then can be reinforced with college training or its equivalent in such subjects as botany, horticulture, plant pathology, plant physiology, chemistry, entomology, and agricultural economics and engineering, the grower is in a much better position to lead and compete with the best operators in the business. A technical training in fruit growing is becoming increasingly important because of the many technical problems arising in what has become a scientific business. Among numerous other things, the fruit grower must understand the complicated mechanisms of harvesters and spray machines; he must be a semi-expert on refrigeration; he must understand the fundamental physiology and anatomy of his plants, the chemistry of his spray materials and the physics of their applications; and he must be acquainted with the life cycles of the important insects and diseases in fruit plantings. Furthermore, he must have a basic knowledge of the economics and marketing of his fruit and use computers and their data efficiently. Hence, a good fruit grower today is as keen a business person as anyone in the city.

Growers, to keep abreast, must spend a lot of time reading and developing a collection of bulletins, books, professional magazines, and weather and crop reports. In addition, growers should make it a practice to attend and take part in local and state horticultural society meetings (Figure 7). Such meetings not only provide an opportunity to study new developments in fruit growing, but to compare notes with other growers, and to discuss special problems with professional and commercial people. Horticultural meetings, as well as competitive exhibitions of fruit, have the fine quality of stimulating ambition

Figure 8. Growers should make a special effort to attend and take part in local and national fruit meetings. If only one new idea is obtained, it is well worth your time. This is a New Jersey fruit meeting to which Fred W. Burrows, retired, International Apple Institute, Inc., is speaking. (Below) Blueberry meeting, North Florida.

among growers to go home and do a better job of producing higher quality fruit.

In every group of growers, there are invariably some who are outstandingly more successful than the group as a whole, even during the most trying years. True, they may have a large established physical unit and sufficient capital to back the business, but there are other key reasons in the final analysis. Among other qualities, including those suggested above, the successful grower is a steady hard worker and thinker. He is systematic in performing every job from pruning and spraying to keeping an accurate account of expenses, cash income, and net returns. And above all, he is a good administrator in picking able assistants and laborers, keeping harmony among them, and in accomplishing the maximum amount of work with the labor and facilities at hand. He is open to new developments, but usually seeks first the advice of qualified professional people, then experiments cautiously in his own orchard before discarding the old and tried methods for the new.

An interesting business. Most everyone has a certain leaning toward country life and some kind of farming. Young people raised on a fruit farm often continue their life work as fruit growers if the business is bringing satisfactory returns. The city student who desires to specialize in fruit growing must recognize at the outset that he is at a disadvantage among young people raised on the farm. It requires hard work for the city people entering college to acquire the practical knowledge of fruit growing and at the same time gain a technical training in college. Young students from the city who want to specialize in fruit growing should make every effort to get practical orchard experience during summer vacations or by taking a full year off from college if necessary before attempting to enter the fruit growing business. Practical experience is equally essential before entering the fields of research, teaching, or the commercial sales and handling of materials used in fruit growing. Thus, the young city student who becomes interested in fruit growing while attending educational institutions should by no means be discouraged from continuing with this field for life work. People succeed best where their talents and main interests lie.

It may be of interest to cite some figures regarding the fruit growing business. According to the U.S. Census, about 2 per cent of the farms in the United States are devoted principally to production of fruits and nuts. In comparison with other farms, the value of the land and buildings on fruit farms is more than twice as great as on the average farm. The expenditure for labor in an orchard is about three times as much. Also, on the average there are more automobiles, motor trucks, and tractors on fruit farms. There are more dwellings which are lighted with electricity and considerably more fruit farms with telephones. This analysis from the Census is an index of the cultural development of orchard folk. In fact, probably no one has a better vocation, a more delectable product, or more desirable associates than the fruit grower. A good home with all modern conveniences, which sets his family off as a cultured, comfortable group, is fully in the picture, together with good vacations and job improvement trips to fruit growing areas around the world.

Review Questions

1. List four deciduous fruits and indicate where they originated.
2. Considering present economic conditions, would you recommend expansion in fruit plantings in your area? Why?
3. How does your country rank in world production of your main fruits?
4. Briefly describe where the main fruit regions of the world are located.

7

5. How do wars over the years affect the fruit grower?
6. List the five leading deciduous fruits grown in the world.
7. How does citrus production compare over the years with the production of leading deciduous fruits?
8. What is the relative importance of the processing field in deciduous fruit growing?
9. Discuss briefly qualifications of a successful fruit grower.
10. Discuss 5 of the most important trends in the fruit growing business today.

Suggested Collateral Readings

THE ABCs of borrowing money. U.S Small Business Administration Bul. MA-170. Wash., D.C. Request recent publ.

ALLEGER, D.E. Retirement income and expectations of rural southerners — a survey in Florida and the rural south. Fla. Agr. Exp. Sta. Bull. 729. 26 pp. (ask for recent edition).

ANONYMOUS. Farm Economics. Dept. of Agr. Econ., Cornell University, Ithaca, N.Y. This is a bulletin issued several times a year, keeping all types of farmers up-to-date economically.[1]

ANONYMOUS. "Crop report for fruits," "The fruit situation," and other fruit crop data. U.S. Department of Agr., Agricultural Marketing Service. Washington, D.C. (Issued several times a year).[1] Fruit production in foreign countries is available through this source in "World Agricultural Production and Trade." Statistical Report.[1]

EXEC. SEC'Y. International Apple Institute Special Letters. Bi-weekly to monthly. (Must be a member to receive them). P.O. Box 657, 6707 Old Dominion Dr. Suite 210, McLean Va. 22101.

COREY, Fred P. 1975. Thank You Johnny Appleseed. Fruit Varieties Journal 29:71-72.

CROWE, A.D. Apple Growing in Eastern Canada. Res. Sta., Kentville, Nova Scotia. Publ. 1553. 1975.

DEARBORN, C.H. Apples for southcentral Alaska. Agroborealis. Univ. of Alaska, Fairbanks. 38-9. 1979.

EMERSON, R.D. and L. POLOPOLUS. Unemployment Insurance and Agriculture. Gainesville: Agricultural Experiment Stations, University of Florida, September 1975. (ask for recent edition).

FRUIT CROPS RESEARCH (issued annually). Ohio Agr. Exp. Sta., Wooster. 44691.

---

[1] Fruit growers, teachers, and commercial distributors of fruit growing equipment and materials may be interested in having their names placed on the mailing list to receive these fruit crop data, now priced.

GOUGH R.E. and V.G. SHUTAK. Apple Trees for the Homeowner. Univ. of R.I. Coop. Ext. Serv. Bul. 201, 12 p. 1974.

HOOFNAGLE, W.S. Conversion factors and weights and measures for agricultural commodities and their products. Statistical Bull. 362. USDA/ERS. 87 p. (ask for recent edition).

KOLBE, M.H. Tree Fruit Production for Home Use. The No. Carolina Extension Service. Reprint. 1978.

LOUGHEED, E.C. *et al.* Fruit and Vegetable Production and the Energy Shortage. HortSci. 10(5):459-462, 1975.

MARIS, T.L. and R.L. MATHIS. Staffing a small business, U.S. Small Bus. Admin. Bul. MA-238. Wash., D.C. Request an up-date.

NAPIER, E. (ed.). Fruit Present and Future. Volume II. The Royal Horticultural Society, London. 175 p. 1973.

PAWLICK, J.E. Estate Planning for Pennsylvania families. Cir. 557. 20 p. (ask for recent edition) 1973.

REED, A. D. Business organization for modern farms. Univ. of Calif. Agri. Ext. Serv. AXT-49 Rev. (Feb.) (ask for recent edition)

SWALES, J.A. Commercial apple growing in British Columbia. Dept. of Agric.(BC) Victoria. 127 p. 19702.

U.S.D.A. Part-Time Farming Farmers' Bull. 2178. Washington, D.C. 14 p. (ask for recent edition).

VAVILOV, N.I. Origin, variation, immunity and breeding of cultivated plants. (Translated to English by K.S. Chester). Chronica Botanica Co., Waltham, Mass. USA. 364 pp. 1935, 1949/50.

United States agricultural economics depts. who are contributing regularly to fruit growing production and costs-and-returns data are New York at Cornell Univ., Michigan, Washington, U.S. Dept. of Agr., Ohio, Pennsylvania, Georgia and Florida. (See appendix for addresses).

The National Junior Horticultural Association is helping young people gain skills in horticulture. Contact NJHA through ASHS, 701 N. St. Asaph St., Alexandria, VA. 22314.

(See additional references in former book editions.)

A LABORATORY MANUAL for the MODERN FRUIT SCIENCE book is available, containing over a dozen exercises which supplement information given in this book. The MANUALS also are available from Horticultural Publications, 3906 N.W. 31st Place, Gainesville, Florida 32606.

TWO GREAT HORTICULTURISTS. Younger horticulturists should be aware of these two leaders who made significant contributions in establishing professional horticulture and pomology as of today. To the left is Liberty Hyde Bailey, 1858-1954, and on the right, William Henry Chandler, 1878-1970, of Cornell University and University of California, respectively. Dr. Chandler also was associated with the University of Missouri and Cornell University. These two men lived highly productive lives to 96 and 92 years, respectively.

CHAPTER II

Apple Regions, Production, and Cultivars

The apple has been cultivated in Europe for over two thousand years. Seed and grafted trees of the better European cultivars were brought to North America and planted by the earlier settlers. Seed from these trees were disseminated westward by the Indians, traders, missionaries and the well known Johnny Appleseed (John Chapman).

There are natural forests of fruit and nut trees, including apples, still covering millions of acres of the Caucasus Mountains of southern Asia. This is a fruit breeders paradise to search for desired new characters of growth, fruiting, season of ripening, resistance to pests and diseases, tolerance of adverse soils and drouth, and resistance to cold, heat, nematodes and other problems. These new characters, when found, can be bred into our already quality fruits to improve them further.

Today, it is interesting to note that most of the deciduous fruit growing regions of the world have been determined largely on the basis of apple growing. It is true, however, that some plants, particularly commercial peaches, will not thrive in all apple sections due to low winter temperatures.

The relative importance of each world area in apple production has been shown in Table 1, Chap. 1. The leaders are: Western Europe, USA, Eastern Europe, Canada, Japan, Australia, and Argentina. Leading states, USA, in millions of lbs are: Washington, 2774; New York, 978; Michigan, 740; California, 580; Pennsylvania, 501; Virginia, 436; North Carolina, 382; West Virginia, 235; Ohio, 125; and New Jersey, 105.

Figure 2 shows the percent production of apple trees by region in the United States. This map has been divided into six regions mainly on the basis of climate and cultivars[1] grown. It is apparent that over 90 percent of the apple crop is obtained from the Northeastern (I), Central Atlantic (II), and West Coast states (VI). During the 1940-50's there was a slight shift of the apple crop from the Midwest to the Eastern and Western sections of the United States. The sections in Figure 2 will be described separately to emphasize the important factors governing apple regions and some of their respective problems. There is a definite trend toward compact, ultimately semi- and full-dwarf trees in all regions.

---

[1] "Cultivar" as a term is preferred over "variety", but they are used interchangeably.

Northeastern section (I). About 30 per cent of the apple crop in the United States is produced in this area. Temperatures during the growing season are moderately cool, ranging between 65 and 70° F. from June to August, inclusive. Along the southern boundary of this section, the time from apple bloom in spring to the first freeze in fall allows the use of apple varieties which will mature within 155 to 160 days. In the northern regions where the growing season is shorter, as well as across the border in Canada, cultivars maturing in 140 to 150 days are used. In western New York 60 percent plus of the crop is processed. Varieties being suggested are: McIntosh, Cortland, Empire and Delicious. For Processing: Twenty Ounce, Spy, Rhode Island Greening and for dual purpose Wayne, Golden Delicious, Idared and Rome. For eastern New York and New England where the crop is stored largely and packed out: McIntosh, Cortland and Delicious for upper New England. For lower New England and Hudson Valley: fewer McIntosh, with more emphasis on Empire, Delicious, Idared and Rome. Other varieties performing well are Jerseymac, Tydeman, Paulared and Spartan. Cortland seems to be trending slightly upward in recent years. Varieties in Michigan are: Jonathan, McIntosh, Delicious, N. Spy, Golden Delicious, Stayman, and R.I. Greening.

Rainfall in N. England and E. New York is about 45 inches, in the western area, 30-35, annually. Half the rainfall comes during the growing season between April and September, inclusive, and it is unusually dependable — more so than in any other major apple section in the United States. In orchards on moderately deep and well-drained soil, there is little danger of serious moisture shortage. This is due to a combination of dependable rainfall conditions and cool growing season. The Great Lakes have an important moderating effect on the temperature.

Central Atlantic section (II). This section produces about 28 percent of the crop, showing a big jump (Fig. 2) mainly in the 1960s-70s. The average summer temperatures are about five degrees higher than in the Northeastern section, (I), ranging between 70 and 75° F. Some orchards are planted as high as 2000 feet above sea level in the Appalachian Mountains, and the temperature at this height ranges between 65 and 75° F. Relatively few apples are grown in the area of South Carolina and southward

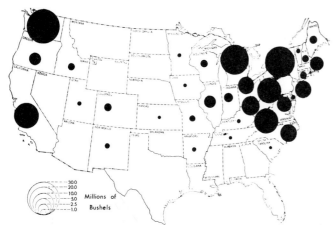

Figure 1. The relative production of apples by state in the United States. See Appendix for world apple distribution map.

due to warmer temperatures, averaging above 75° F. Most of the apples grown in the southern parts of this section necessarily are located at higher altitudes in the Appalachian Mountains. Winter freezing of trees is hardly a factor in this region due to the fact that minimum temperatures rarely go below -10 to -15°. In the mountainous areas, there are many orchard sites that permit good air drainage where there is less possibility of spring frosts.

With the increasing migration of people from the northern tier of states to the South, there is developing interest in the low-chilling apple cultivars such as Anna and Dorsett Golden which are being planted in home gardens and small commercial plantings. These cultivars are being grown as far south as southern Florida.

Rainfall ranges between 40 and 45 inches for most of the section with the exception of the Potomac Valley where it is somewhat lower. From April to September, inclusive,

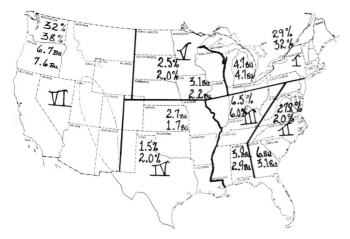

Figure 2. This map is divided into six regions on the basis of climate, varieties, and other factors. The percentage production indicated in each region. Upper number in each case is for recent yrs.; lower for 1950s, showing shifts. Yield per tree rose in Region II, remained about the same in other areas.

about 22 inches of rain fall, but long periods of drouth seem to occur more frequently than in the Northeastern section (I). Soils that permit deep rooting and cultural methods for conservation of moisture are necessary. Irrigation is being used increasingly.

Cultivars should be selected for the northern part that require 165 days or less for maturity. Varieties requiring longer periods of development can be grown in the southern section. Processing varieties are gaining favor. York (leads in W. Va.) is widely grown for processing but may show cork. The York-like apple, 'Nittany', is said not to cork. Delicious and Golden Delicious have been widely planted. Stayman, Jonathan and Rome are declining in the north; Winesap is losing favor. North Carolina has shown a sharp rise in production. The early Mollie Delicious is being planted in southern areas; it can have a blight problem in "blight" areas.

The Ohio Basin section (III). About 6.5 percent of the apple crop in the United States is produced in this region. The June to August temperature averages about 75° F. The length of the growing season is approximately the same as that in the Central Atlantic section (II) for the northern and southern areas. Along the Ohio River where many apple orchards are located the annual precipitation is around 40 inches with about 20 inches occurring during the growing season. In the southern section, rainfall may reach 50 inches. However, due to the fact that temperatures are higher during the growing season, there is greater need for water than in northern sections of the United States. The drouth periods under these conditions tend to be more injurious to the trees. If the orchards are in soils of good water-holding capacity to a depth of three to four feet, serious damage is not likely to occur. Irrigation is on the increase.

Several varieties are popular throughout the region; namely, Golden Delicious, Delicious, Rome Beauty, Grimes Golden, Jonathan, and Stayman. In Tennessee, early summer varieties, Yellow Transparent and Early Harvest, also are widely planted in commercial orchards. In Illinois, Golden Delicious, Jonathan and Delicious are most important with Rome taking a poor fourth place. This is almost 100% of the commercial varieties.

Southwestern section (IV). About 1.5 percent of the apple crop is produced in this section. The temperature between June and August is high, averaging between 75 and 80° F. The growing season is relatively long. Most of the rainfall occurs in Arkansas, with an annual precipitation of 45 to 50 inches; in southern Missouri, 40 to 45 inches; in northern Missouri and eastern Kansas, 35 to 40 inches; and in Nebraska, western Kansas, and western Oklahoma, below 35 inches. In regions where precipitation is under 30 inches per year, relatively few apples have been planted.

Jonathan is important and Golden Delicious and

Delicious are being widely planted. Other varieties are Stayman, Grimes Golden, York Imperial and Wealthy. Mollie Delicious is being planted.

Northcentral section (V). About 2.5 percent of the apples are produced here. Through most of the section, summer temperatures range from 65 to 75° F. In the southern section, however, the range is between 70 and 75°. In northern Wisconsin, it is relatively cool, or under 65°. Cultivars with moderately long growing seasons can be grown in the southern section, whereas in the northern areas, it is necessary to plant cultivars which are outstandingly resistant to low winter temperatures. Rainfall in the apple sections is relatively low, ranging from 25 to 35 inches. In the western part, rainfall is less, and apples are grown primarily in home plantings. In general, less water is needed, however, due to the lower mean temperatures. Extreme winter cold is the main hazard. States in this region are conducting breeding programs for winter resistant cultivars.

In southern Iowa and along Lake Michigan in Wisconsin, cultivars commonly grown are McIntosh, Wealthy, Cortland, Viking and summer varieties such as Oldenburg and Yellow Transparent. Delicious, Jonathan, and to some extent Stayman Winesap are grown. Special cold resistant varieties have been developed; namely, the Harlson, Honeygold, Red Baron and Regent. In Minnesota, Joan, Sector in Iowa, Anoka in South Dakota.

Western section (VI). This section grows 32 percent of the entire apple crop and based on new high-density plantings will rise markedly. The apple regions are concentrated in scattered areas which usually occur in valleys surrounded by mountains. Commercial apple production for the region as a whole has increased rapidly during the past 45 years; it is characterized by a relatively high production per tree and per acre. The production from one year to the next has been relatively uniform due, primarily, to the clear almost cloudless days throughout the summer, regular water supply from irrigation, and less trouble from spring frosts and freezes. The production for this area on an acre basis is generally higher than for other apple sections of the United States. In Washington State, the average yield is over seven bushels per bearing tree which, for an average of all orchards in a state is considered good. Size and color of the apples also are generally good. Circled area (Fig. 2) has a lower per tree yield. Winter freezes have killed many older trees in recent years.

It is true that western fruit usually sells for better prices than the eastern fruit, but the freight cost-returns to the western grower on a box basis have been generally less than that obtained by the eastern growers, especially when apple prices are low. However, with high apple prices in recent years, the good productiveness of the western orchards has resulted in good returns.

It appears that Washington will average 45 million boxes

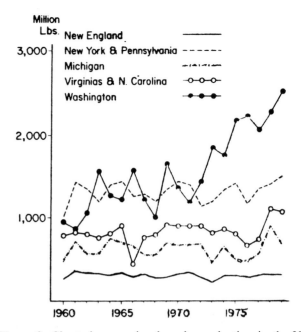

Figure 3. Chart shows regional apple production in the USA. Washington is showing a marked increase in production since 1960. New England region has shown no change, whereas other regions have shown slight trends upward. (USDA)

in the immediate future.

The *Wenatchee district* is in northcentral Washington along bench land of the Columbia River and tributaries. Spring frosts are rare, summer temperatures are 65 to 70° F, nights cool, precipitation 7 to 10 inches annually and mostly in winter as snow, soils deep and irrigation extensively practiced using 40 to 45 inches.

The *Yakima* district lies along the Yakima River about 100 miles south of the Wenatchee district, ranking second to it in Washington. Frosts may occur in low wide areas, and irrigation timing is important due to light rather shallow soils.

Delicious and Golden Delicious make up over 95% of Washington's crop. The remaining percentage is largely Rome and Jonathan, a few Stayman and Yellow Newtowns. The lower-quality Winesap has dropped appreciably with CA storage holdings of better quality apples.

In Oregon, the *Hood River* Valley in the northcentral area is important. Winter injury is a problem, but production is relatively good. Summer temperatures are around 65° F. Delicious, Golden Delicious and Yellow Newtown are the leading cultivars with Rome, Jonathan, Gravenstein of minor importance.

Apple trees have been replaced by pear trees in the Rogue River Valley and the nonirrigated Willamette Valley because the climate is more favorable for pears.

California ranks high in apple production, rising fast in recent years. The Sebastapol area is north of San Francisco where it is cool, rainfall about 40 inches and irrigation

11

rarely needed. Gravenstein is harvested in July and the best apples are distributed widely throughout the United States as an early summer apple; most Gravenstein, however, are processed to sauce and other products. Approximate rank of cultivars is: Delicious, Yellow Newtown, Gravenstein, Rome, Golden Delicious, and some Jonathan.

Another district is south of San Francisco in the Watsonville area. Rainfall is 25 to 30 inches and some irrigation is practiced. Main variety is Yellow Newtown, which is largely placed in CA storage. Yellow varieties are used because of fogginess and poor coloring of red varieties, although red strains of Delicious are being planted.

Idaho orchards are located at 700 to 3000 feet altitude along the tributaries of the Snake River near the Oregon line. Summer temperatures average about 70° F. Frost is a factor in the broad valley floors. High water table, also, has been a detrimental factor. Leading cultivars are: Delicious, Rome, Jonathan and Golden Delicious.

Utah orchards are located adjacent to the Great Salt Lake on the south and southeast shores. Production is limited. Altitude is about 4500 feet; average summer temperature is 70° F. Frosts and irrigation water are limiting factors. Delicious, Rome, Jonathan and Golden Delicious with some McIntosh and Lodi make up the cultivar list.

Western Colorado apple regions are in the valley of the Colorado River and its tributaries. Orchards are being planted at higher elevations (Mesas) to overcome poorly drained soils in the valleys. Delicious, Golden Delicious, Jonathan, and Rome are popular.

In *Montana* the winter hardy McIntosh is planted along the Bitterroot River. In *New Mexico,* planted along the San Juan River, are Delicious, Rome, Jonathan and Golden Delicious.

In *Canada,* most of the apples are grown in British Columbia and Ontario. Varieties grown in approximate order are McIntosh, Red and Golden Delicious, N. Spy and Spartan. Production is around 20 to 30 million pounds.

World Apple Regions. A map in the Appendix gives a quick view of where apples are grown in the world. In western Europe, which dominates, production in round figures is as follows in 1000s of metric tons: Italy, 1900; West Germany, 1600; France, 1800; Netherlands, 450; United Kingdom, 450; Spain, 750; Yugoslavia, 400; Belgium-Luxembourg, 250; Greece, 200; Austria, 200; Denmark, 75; Switzerland, 100; Norway, 50; and Sweden, 50.

Production in other areas where approximate data are available: *South America* — Argentina, 550; Chile, 90; in *Africa,* 300; in *Oceania:* Australia, including Tasmania, 400; New Zealand, 150. In *Asia:* Japan, 1000; Turkey, 800 and Lebanon, 125. In *China* no data are available but the

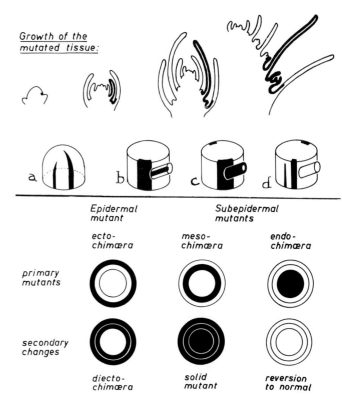

Figure 4. This is how mutations or "sports" arise in fruit trees. A vegetative cell mutates (black, upper row left) in a growing point of a shoot and continues dividing to right to "a" (second row left). Limb "b" carries only part of mutant and fruits developing on limb are variable for the standard and mutant character, as, e.g., scarlet red skin of fruit. At "c" mutant redder fruits on this limb will be alike. Side limb at "d" bears fruits like parent tree. (lower chart) Different types of periclinal (circular) chimaera mutants are shown on cross-cut spurs or limbs. Some of these apple color mutants revert back to the initial skin coloring due to mixed tissue and are referred to as unstable. A few color mutants of Delicious, Rome and Stayman are examples. (The late Nils Nybom, Sweden)

two main regions are: (a) Liaoning Province, southern Manchuria and (b) in the loesslands of Shansi, Shensi and Kansu provinces, southwest of Peking. In the *USSR* apples are grown in Moldavia, Ukraine and northern Caucasia with production increasing to over 8 million tons, 30% in home gardens, the rest in state-owned co-operatives. In upper *Mexico,* production is upward, (about 3M trees). Data are unavailable for *Eastern Europe,* covering Poland, Rumanina, Bulgaria, Hungary, Czechoslovakia and the German Deomocratic Republic. Iran was planting heavily and Afghanistan was increasing modest plantings but has been disrupted in recent years by war. Northernmost *India* has modest plantings. Apples and pears in Oceania are termed "pips".

Temperate seasons are opposite above and below the Equator; when it is summer weather above, it is cold weather below, and vice-versa. *Argentina* grows apples in the Neuquen (largest), Mendoza and Buenos Aires-Santa

TABLE 1. TREND AND IMPORTANCE OF APPLE CULTIVARS IN THE UNITED STATES
(DATA FOR ORCHARDS OF 100 OR MORE TREES)

Cultivars Listed By Importance 1979-82	Production (Millions of Lbs)[1]						Probable Trend
	1942-48	1949-55	1961-67	1969-71	1975-77	1979-82	
1. Delicious	940.4	1074.1	1494.6	1846.2	2498	3166	Marked Inc.
2. G. Delicious	115.5	161.5	510.1	814.8	1171	1462	Marked Inc.
3. McIntosh	414.9	580.9	721.4	693.2	629	681	Slight Inc.
4. Rome	313.5	336.5	442.3	510.6	515	589	Slight Inc.
5. Jonathan	350.5	331.9	394.5	424.4	364	411	Steady
6. York Imp.	253.6	239.7	289.3	352.1	262	334	Slight Inc.
7. Stayman W.	235.1	198.2	277.4	299.8	207	232	Steady
8. Winesap	534.7	502.5	343.5	207.8	169	140	Decrease
9. Y. Newtown	202.8	207.5	190.6	173.1	148	184	Steady
10. Cortland	69.2	119.9	157.1	160.6	136	139	Slight Inc.
11. R.I. Greening	87.6	113.7	141.6	151.4[2]	121	128	Steady
12. N. Spy	78.4	101.4	140.1	137.8[2]	93	108	Steady
13. Gravenstein	124.5	133.7	104.7	108.4[2]	90	68	Decrease
14. Baldwin	147.5	147.5	84.7	51.3[2]	Idared	90	Increase
15. Grimes G.	96.8	96.8	38.5	30.6[2]	G. Smith	16	Increase
16. B. Davis, Gano	101.4	87.6	39.0	.7[2]	—	—	Decrease
17. Wealthy	96.8	92.2	49.5	21.8[2]	—	—	Decrease
18. Others	567.0	497.9	412.2	543.9	692	522	Slight Dec.
19. Total	—	—	—	—	—	8206	Increase

[1] In 1967 USDA Crop Reporting Service changed from bushels to pounds for apples due to so many different containers; e.g. 12 3-lb. poly bags in a carton weigh 38 lbs; 12 4-lb. bags in a carton weigh 50 lbs. A tray pack carton of apples weighs 42 lbs. USDA is using the figure 46.1 lbs. for one bushel of apples.

[2] Data for these varieties for 1971 and later are included under "miscellaneous." Other varieties include: Esopus Spitzenburg, Wagener, Stark, Winter Banana, King David, Limbertwig, Tompkins King, Yellow Bellflower, and recently named varieties that have not been fully evaluated for wide planting.

Fe areas. Most apples in *Chile* are grown about 500 miles above and below Santiago, a few around Lima, *Peru* and limited in other areas of South America. *Tasmanian* apple production has almost halved (6 mil. bu) by shipping ocean freight rates and other problems. Australian apples are grown below Perth and east of Adelaide to the coast up to Brisbane. Apples are grown in extreme northwest and southern *Africa*.

Trend in apple trees and production. Since 1910, U.S. apple tree numbers have decreased markedly with little decrease in production since 1930 due to better sites, soils and cultural practices and elimination of marginal orchards. There likely will be a modest rise in production in the future. While population is increasing, the per capita consumption of apples has been decreasing due to sales competition with other fruits, such as citrus, melons and tomatoes. Per capita consumption of apples is around 18 lbs, citrus approaching twice as much at 30 lbs.

Trend in cultivars. Since the 1920s, consumers are trending toward higher quality dessert apples. Table 1 shows the U.S. trend in cultivars since 1942. Of the 17 varieties only Delicious and Golden Delicious have shown a marked increase while the poorer-quality long-storage Winesap has dropped with expanding CA storage space. Many varieties, formerly important, such as Baldwin, Grimes, Spy and Wealthy have fallen into the "miscellaneous" class. Delicious and Golden Delicious, in fact, have shown a spectacular increase in planting in the

U.S. and in most apple regions of the world. Jonathan also is widely favored and leads in some countries, as Hungary, with the bright red mutations in demand.

Red Delicious, half of which is produced in Washington, accounts for about 40% of the U.S. crop and is rising; McIntosh, 8% with 45% in New York and 32% in New England; Golden Delicious, 18%; Rome 7%; Jonathan, 5%; and the York, 4%. These six cultivars account for 80% of the U.S. crop. About 90% of the U.S. crop is winter cultivars; 8-9% fall and 2-4% summer cultivars.

A national survey by Washington Apple Commission showed United States housewives preferred in order: Delicious and Golden Delicious, with Jonathan and McIntosh preferred over Winesap. Market demand and prices for Delicious have been good, but there is always a danger of over-planting it; also, many growers complain of shy yields.

With the holding of high quality fresh apples in controlled atmosphere storage most months of the year, the number of leader varieties may be reduced, for the most part, to only three to four as e.g., Delicious, Golden Delicious, McIntosh, and Jonathan. Possibly one or two summer varieties may be included since they can be produced economically, spread the season, and are sold quickly with little storage. With more apples being processed, it is possible that such varieties as York, Northern Spy, Idared, Rome Beauty and Rhode Island Greening will continue to show increased planting, as

TABLE 2. SOME FRUIT CHARACTERISTICS OF THE MORE IMPORTANT WORLD APPLE CULTIVARS.

Variety	Where Mostly Grown[1]	Days Bloom to Picking	Fruit[2] Size	Fruit[3] Color	Fruit[4] Shape	Acidity[5]	Dessert or Cooking	Cold Storage Season Days[8]	Scald[6] Tendency	Age of Bearing (Yrs.)	Ann. or Blen. Bearing Tendency	Standard Tree Size[7]
Y. Transparent	US, USSR, WG	70- 95	S-M	Y	Co	H	Cooking	0 (90)	None	4-6	Bien.	M-S
Oldenburg	US	90- 95	M	SR	Ro-Ob	H	Cooking	0- 30(90)	Sl	4-6	Intermed.	M
Tydeman E.	WE, US	90- 95	M	R	Ro-Ob	M	Dessert	30- 90	—	4-5	Ann.	L.
Paulared	US	105-115	M	SBR	Ro-Ob	M	Both	0- 30(90)	—	5-6	Ann.	M
Jerseymac	US, Ca	90- 95	M+	RBl	Ro-Ob	M	Dessert	0- 30(60)	Sl	4-5	Ann.	L.
Gravenstein	US, N	110-115	M	SBR	Ob-Ang	M-H	Cooking	0- 30(90)	Sl	6-8	Ann.	M-L
Anna	W	110-120	S-M	Bl	Co	M	Dessert	30- 30(90)	Sl	2-3	Ann.	S
Dorsett Golden	W	110-120	S-M	Y	Co	M	Dessert	30- 50(90)	Sl	2-3	Ann.	S
James Grieve	C, WE, N, S, At, NE	110-120	M-L	YRS	Ro-Co	M	Dessert	60- 90	Sl	4-6	Ann.	M-S
Antonovka	USSR	110-120	M	Y	Ro-Co-Ang	H	Cooking	60- 90	M	4-6	Bien.	M
Wealthy	US, P	120-125	M	MR	Ro-Ob	M-H	Both	0- 30(90)	Sl	4-6	Bien.	M-S
Winter Banana	US	120-125	M-L	YBl	Ro-Co	M-L	Both(fair)	90-120(150)	Sl	4-6	Intermed.	M
Cortland	US	125-130	M-S	MR	Ob	M	Both	90-120(150)	M	4-6	Ann.	M
McIntosh	US, USSR, P	125-130	M	MR	Ro-Ob	M	Both	60- 90(150)	Sl[9]	4-6	Ann.	L
Goldpairmain	C, WE, Sw, B, USSR, C	125-135	M-S	YRS	Co	M	Both	100-120	M	4-6	Intermed.	M
Ingrid Marie	D, S, NE, WG	130-140	M	G-Y,R	Co	M-L	Dessert	90-120	Sl	5-7	Intermed.	M
Landsberger R.	EE,C	130-140	M-L	YMR	Co	H-M	Both	120-140	Sl	4-6	Intermed.	M
Cox's Orange	S, EE, WE, D, H, UK,SA,C,At,NE	130-150	S-M	YSR	Ro	M-L	Dessert	90-120(150)	Sl	4-6	Intermed.	M-L
Idared	US	135-145	M	R	Ro-Co	M	Both	90-120(150)	Sl	5-6	Ann.	M
R.I. Greening	US, USSR	135-145	M-S	GY	Ro-Ob	M-H	Cooking	90-120(180)	Sev.	6-8	Intermed.	M-L
Bramley's Se.	UK, Be	135-145	L	GYS	Ro-Ob-Co	H	Cooking	150-180	Sev.	5-7	Bien.	L-M
Landsberger Rtte.	EE, ME	130-150	M-L	Y	Ob-Ang	H	Cooking	30- 60(90)	—	6-8	Intermed.	L
Ralls	J, K, Ch	—	M-S	R	Ro-Co	M	Dessert	120-150(250)	M	6-8	Bien.	M
Kidd's Orange Red	NZ	140-150	M	BSR	Co	M-L	Dessert			5-8		M
Mollie Del.	US	140-145	M	SBl	Co	L	Dessert	120-150(180)	—	4-5	Ann.	M
Go. Delicious	W	140-145	M-L	Y	Co	M	Both	90-120(150)	Sl	4-6	Intermed.	M
Grimes Golden	US	140-145	M-S	Y	Ro-Ob	M	Both	60- 90(150)	Sev.	4-8	Intermed.	M-L
Jonathan	W	140-145	M-S	UBR	Ro-Co	M-H	Both	60- 90(120)	Sl[9]	4-6	Ann.	L
Empire	US	140-145	M	R	Ro-Ob	M	Dessert	90-100(180)	Sl	5-6	Ann.	M
Mutsu	J, US	140-145	L	Y-BR	Ro-Co	M	Both	150-180(240)	—	4-6	Ann.	L
Delicious	W	140-150	M-L	MR	Ob-Co	L	Both	90-100(180)	Sl	5-8	Intermed.	M-L
Spartan	Ca, US	145-150	ML	R	Ro-Ob	M	Both	100-120(150)	—	5-6	Ann.	M
Esopus Spitzen.	US	145-150	M-L	BR	Ob-Co	M	Both	90-120(180)	Sl	6- 8	Intermed.	L
Boskoop	C,WE,D,Sw, NE, UK	145-155	L	G-Y M-R Ob-Ro		H / M	Both	120-140(180) / 120-150(180)	Sl / Sl	8-10 / 10-14	Intermed. / Intermed.	L / M-L
No. Spy	US	145-155	L	BSR	Ro-Co	H	Dessert	140-170	Sl	5- 8	Ann.	L
Bancroft	P	145-155	M-S	RS	Ro	L	Cooking	180-210	Sev.	8-10	Bien.	L
Ayvanya	B	145-155	S	Y	Ro-Co	H-M	Both	120-140	Sl	4- 6	Intermed.	S
Ontario	EG	150-160	L	YS	Ob-Co	H	Dessert	150-180	—	6- 8	Bien.	M
Glockenapfel	S,WG	150-165	M-L	Y	Ro-Co	M	Cooking	120-150(180)	Sev.	6- 8	Bien.	L
York Imperial	US	155-165	M-L	LR	Ob-Obl	H	Both	120-150	—	8-10	Intermed.	L
Roter Boskoop	WE	160-170	L	G-Y,R	Ro	M-L	Cooking	120-150(210)	M	4- 6	Ann.	M-S
Rome Beauty (Imperatore)	US, I	160-165	L	MR	Ro-Ob	M-H	Both	150-180(240)	Sl	8-10	Bien.	M
Yellow Newtown	US	160-165	M	Y	Ro-Ob	M	Both	150-210(240)	M	6- 8	Intermed.	M
Winesap	US	160-170	M-S	DR	Co	M	Both	120-150(180)	Sev.	4- 6	Ann.	L
Stayman	US	160-165	M-L	MR	Ro-Co	M	Both	180-200				M
Sturmer Pip.	B, P, USSR, Au	160-165	M-L	YG MR	Ro-Co	M	Both	120-150(180)	Sev.	8-10	Bien.	L
Black Twig (Paragon)	US	165-170	M-L	MDR	Ro-Ob	L-M	Both	150-180(210)	Sev.	5- 7	Ann.	M-L
Granny Smith	A, Au, NZ, Chile US, SA	180-200	M-L	Green	Ob-Ro	M-H	Dessert	150-180(240)	Sl	8-10	Intermed.	M
Democrat	Au	190-195	L	R	Ob							

Symbols:

1 Abbreviations for countries. (Where a country is listed for a variety, neighboring countries, or those of similar environment, also may grow it.) Dr. S.A. Pieniazek of Poland, Dr. M. Zwintzscher of Germany, and Dr. J. R. Magness, USA, furnished data for this table. A-Argentina; At-Austria; Au-Australia; B-Bulgaria; Be-Belgium; C-Czechoslovakia; Ch-China; D-Denmark; EE-Eastern Europe; EG-Eastern Germany; H-Hungary; I-Italy; J-Japan; K-Korea; M-Mexico; ME-Middle Europe; N-Norway; Ne-Netherlands; NZ-New Zealand; P-Poland; S-Sweden; SA-South Africa; Sw-Switzerland; UK-United Kingdom; US-United States; USSR-Russia; W-of fairly world wide importance; WE-Western Europe; WG-Western Germany

2 S-small; M-medium; L-large.
3 Y-yellow, S-striped; R-red; B-bright; M-medium; D-dull; Bl-blush.
4 C-conic; Ob-oblate; R-round; Obl-oblique; Ang-angular.
5 M-medium, H-high; L-low.
6 Sl-slight; M-medium; Sev-severe.
7 L-large; M-medium; S-small.
8 Maximum storage days in parenthesis.
9 Susceptible to soft scald.

indicated in Table 1. Winesap, a former leader and good keeper, is gradually losing to better quality CA stored varieties. About 50 percent of the U.S. crop is processed and up to 70 percent in some areas; processing probably will continue to increase.

Granny Smith is drawing increasing interest from buyers and growers in the USA. Washington has taken the lead with over 50,000 trees in the early 1980s. The cultivar has a long growing season and cannot be planted successfully with a growing season of less than about 180 days.

Desired characterstics. The most important characteristics of an apple cultivar to consider when making a selection are these: it should be an *annual bearer,* good to very good in dessert quality, very attractive in appearance, relatively pest-resistant, productive, and hardy. If the fruit is of good storage and good handling quality, and a good processor, the value of the variety is greatly increased. Some of the important characteristics which should be considered in the selection of a variety are given in Table 2. Also indicated is the region or areas of the world where the variety is popular.

Color strains. There are a number of "bud sports" of popular varieties which are supposedly the same as the parent except they are redder, less russetting, etc. (See Fig. 4). However, a considerable degree of caution should be taken in the use of any or all color strains. There are some cases where they have been propagated with relatively little preliminary trial. Although the best color strains of the red apple varieties appear to have considerable merit, there is no assurance that these strains are identical in every respect except color, etc., to the parent variety. The size, storage quality of the fruit, and other factors also may be different. In some cases, the shade of color in the strain appears to be deeper than the parent, and, in fact, so deep that the color is dull and unattractive. Thus, it is important that the prospective grower of such color strains make every effort to see bearing trees of the strain under his conditions and make his own decision if it is better than the parent. Red color is important in good sales appeal. Most of the apple trees now being planted are red strains, a few have been grown rather extensively under commercial conditions and can be evaluated briefly as follows:

Delicious strains. Let's compare, e.g., Starking and Richard. Starking reddens about two weeks ahead of the standard Delicious, but the date of maturity of the fruit is the same; hence, one must be careful not to pick the variety too soon, which has been a problem with red strains. At picking time the Starking develops a dark maroon red when it is fully mature. Richared does not color as early as Starking and at picking time it is more completely colored than the standard variety.

See above for tentative evaluation by Washington state specialists of the better of over 100 strains introduced. There is a spread in ripening as, e.g., in New Jersey, in

Figure 5. Delicious is the most widely planted apple variety in the world. It accounts for 27% of the U.S. crop. This is because it has a good combination of tree characters and popular high-quality fruit.

order: Red King, Ryan Red, Royal Red, Redspur, Starking and Starkrimson, aiding in harvest, etc.

Rome Beauty strains. Gallia Beauty is a seedling, apparently, and Cox Red Rome is of bud sport origin. Both strains have a bright attractive red color more uniform than the standard Rome Beauty. The fruits are smaller, earlier maturing, and possibly not quite so good in storage quality as the standard Rome Beauty, although more experimental data are needed to verify this.

Stayman Winesap strains. Stamared and C & O Stayman are popular. Their color is apparently similar to that of Stayman except they average somewhat brighter color at maturity. Both strains may crack.

Jonathan Strains. Jonard and Blackjon are the earlier strains. Jonard appears to have a somewhat brighter color. Jonee, Jonamac Jonagold show promise. Frumos de Voinesti (Boskoop x Jonathan) from Romania is larger, no "spot," better quality, less mildew, no fireblight yet observed.

Spur Strains. These are usually preferred when available; about ¾ size tree, at least 20% less pruning, more upright and open with long limbs with many fruiting spurs, apparently mutations. Some Golden Delicious spurs may russet more; do well on seedling or size-control stocks; "dead-spur" disease may be a problem on Delicious strains, not yet understood. Delicious strains apparently more susceptible are: 'Chelan Red', 'Earlistripe', 'Red Prince', 'Royal Red', 'Ryan', 'Sharp Red', and 'Top Red'. There now is a Rome and a McIntosh spur strain.

Other varietal strains. There are red color strains of other red apple varieties, such as York Imperial, Northern Spy, McIntosh, Esopus Spitzenburg, Gravenstein, and Oldenburg.

The original and earlier trees of the McIntosh variety

15

GROUP I (Lowest Color)			GROUP II (Intermediate Color)			GROUP III (Greatest Color)		
Variety	Color Pattern	Type of Growth	Variety	Color Pattern	Type of Growth	Variety	Color Pattern	Type of Growth
Earlired	Stripe	Standard	Wellspur	Blush	Spur	Top Red	Stripe	Standard
Hi Red	Blush	Standard	Red Rich (Scacco)	Blush	Standard	Starkrimson (Bisbee)	Blush	Spur
Starking (Old)	Stripe	Standard	Hardispur	Blush	Spur	Red Prince	Stripe	Standard
Wood	Stripe	Spur	Starking (Franks)	Stripe	Standard	Cheland Red	Blush	Standard
			Harrold	Stripe	Standard	Ryan Red	Stripe	Standard
			Redspur	Blush	Spur	Hi Early	Stripe	Standard
			Huebner	Stripe	Standard	Houser Red	Blush	Standard
			Imperial	Blush	Standard	Red Queen	Stripe	Standard
			Royal Red	Blush	Standard	Redchief	Blush	Spur
			Red King	Stripe	Standard & Spur			

The general rule of thumb was to choose from Group III if in a poor coloring area and Group II or I if in a good coloring area. Growers and researchers have been on the lookout for a high-color striped spur, considered desirable. The spur-type trees are more upright and open with long limbs with numerous fruiting spurs; apparently they are mutations.

apparently were of a good solid red type of color. However, in recent years there have been mutations to a striped type which is not very attractive. It would be well to avoid the striped strain.

Golden Delicious. This is one of the highest quality apples. The main problems are russeting, shrivelling in storage and obtaining a bright yellow at harvest. Many substitutes have been suggested. Mutsu (Golden Delicious x Indo) or Crispin from Japan; Smoothee (Hilltop Nursery), Spigold (Red Northern Spy x Golden Delicious) from New York are being planted and tested. VPI No. 8, Missouri A-3071 and A-2071; Sundale Sturdy Spur,

Figure 6. There is increased world planting of high-density orchards. Cion wood is of high-color strains of standard varieties or of "spur-growth-type" strains grafted on stocks of various degrees of dwarfing. The earlier-bearing spur strains on seedling roots form a three-quarter size tree and, hence, also are being close-plated. Above is a high-density orchard of Delicious and Golden Delicious near Ashville, North Carolina.

PrimeGold (B. Hoekman, Wash.) and Stark's Blushing also are under test. Smoothee shows the least russet.

Promising New Varieties. It takes about 40 years to evalute fully an apple from the time of the cross to when it has been accepted commercially. The following varieties are being planted commercially. It would be well for you to check your specialist on local performance. *Early Varieties.* Puritan (McI. x R. Astra.) from Mass.; and Viking (Jon., Del., E. McI. +) Wisc.; Jerseymac, Vista Bella (Julyred, Melba +) N.J., look promising. Tydeman (Worchester Pearman x McIntosh) from England shows promise, Mollie's Delicious (mix of Golden Delicious, Edgewood, Red Gravenstein, Close) from N.J. and Paulared (Mich. seedling) are commercially planted. *Later Varieties.* Prima (G. Del. x Rome +), N.J. scab-resistant; Idared (Jon. x Wag.) Idaho, widely planted in apple regions; Wayne (Northwestern Greening x Red Northern Spy), Macoun (McIntosh x Jersey Black) and Monroe (Jonathan x Rome) all from New York are being planted generally in regions where their parents are grown. Melrose (Jonathan x Delicious) from Ohio is planted in the midwest area. Spartan (McIntosh x Yellow Newtown) from British Columbia shows promise in the northern tier of states and the northwest. Crandall (Rome x Jonathan) from Illinois is being planted in the midwest. Regent (Daniels Red, Duchess x Delicious) from Minnesota is hardy, late, dessert, processor. A1379 (Cox x Jonathan), England looks good, W. Europe; Empire (McI. x Del.) N.Y., looks very good. Fuji (Ralls Janet x Delicious) is "taking over", Japan.

Granny Smith is being planted in NW USA and in milder longer-growing season regions; Penn State Univ. has a "cork-resistant" York, Nittany. Bright McIntosh (mutant), Sinta (G. Del. x Grimes) and Spencer (McI. x G.

Del.) look good in Ontario; Redwell in So. Dak. and Minn.; Elstar in Holland with close runner Jonagold and Karmijin; Summerland (E. Blenheim) in B.C.; Jonamac and Jonagold are liked, west N.Y.

Low-Chilling Cultivars. For subtropical regions with 50 to 200 hrs below 45° F, the Anna (Israel), Dorsett Golden (Florida) and Ein Schemer (Israel) are grown. With good altitude in the tropics and subtropics and about a month drouth to break the rest, many of the temperate zone apples can be grown.

"Fingerprinting" Fruit Trees. The tree and leaf samples are homogenized in a blender into a "pea soup", the liquid clearified, placed in a gel in a test tube and placed in an electrophoresis unit. The unit separates the proteins into bands that are different for each fruit strain. The technique is helpful to nurseries in patents, identifying rootstocks, and keeping cultivars properly grouped when and if mutations occur, plus other benefits.

Review Questions

1. List key factors to consider in selecting an apple variety for ready sale and good profits year after year.
2. List the main weaknesses of the Red Delicious and Golden Delicious.
3. How do you account for the fact that apple production in the East in recent years is more uniform from year to year than in earlier years; Why is production in Wenatchee district of Washington higher per tree and per acre than in the eastern districts?
4. What is the general trend of apple trees and apple production since 1910; how do you account for this?
5. Explain how an all-red mutation of a bright red strain of a striped-fruit apple variety will appear on some limbs of a tree and not on others.
6. What apple varieties are showing increase in popularity, how do you account for this?
7. What is the general situation and recommendations regarding the planting of color strains of standard varieties?
8. Discuss in general the world apple variety situation.
9. Point out the apple regions of the world.
10. What is meant by "spur" strains of apple?

Suggested Collateral Readings

ALDERMAN, W.H. Fruit breeding — past, present, and future. Proc. ASHS 51, 670, 1948.

ALDWINKLE, H.S. and R.C. LAMB. Controlling apple diseases without chemicals, N.Y. Food and Life Sci. Vol. 10. No. 2, 1977.

ANONYMOUS. Agricultural Outlook Charts, Agr. Marketing Service, U.S. Dept. of Agr., Washington, D.C.

ANONYMOUS. Foreign Crops and Markets. Office of Foreign Agricultural Relations, Circular, U.S. Dept. of Agr., Washington, D.C.

ANONYMOUS. Monthly crop report for fruits and supplemental publications on production, use and value of noncitrus fruits in the U.S. and world. U.S. Dept. of Agr., Agricultural Marketing Service. Washington, D.C.

APPLES, Bull. 207, British Ministry of Agriculture, request latest edition, (contact E. Malling Res. Sta., Maidstone, Eng.) Priced.

BEACH, S.A. Apples of New York. Vols. I & II, N.Y. Agr. Exp. Sta. 1903. (Out of print).

BERTI-PETROVICI, I, *et al.* Apple variety and tree descriptions (Pomologia II) 1007 pp. Editura Academici Repub. Populare Romine. 1964.

BRADT, O.A., A. HUTCHINSON, S.J. LEUTY and C.L. RICKET-SON. Fruit Varieties — A Guide for Commercial Growers. Ministry of Agri. and Food, Ontario. Publ. 430. 1978.

BROOKS, Reid M. and H.P. OLMO. Register of New Fruit and Nut Varieties List 31. HortSci. 13(5): 522-532. 1978.

CHANDLER, Craig K. Bregger Student Award Paper (1979): Polyploin Breeding: A Valuable Tool for Fruit Crop Improvement. Fruit Varieties Journal 34(2): 43-45. 1980.

CROCKER, T.E. and W.B. SHERMAN. Apples for Florida. Fruit South. 156-158. July 1978.

FISHER, D.V. and D.D. KETCHIE. Literature survey on red strains of 'Delicious.' Wash. State Bull. 0898. 17 p. 1981.

HANSCHE, Paul E., and William BERES. Genetic Remodeling of Fruit and Nut Trees to Facilitate Cultivar Improvement. HortScience 15(6): 710-715, 1980.

HOUSER, Jean A. Bregger Student Award Paper (1979): Origin of the Macoun Apple Cultivar. Fruit Varieties Journal 34(2): 45-48. 1980.

LAMB, R.C., H.S. ALDWINCKLE, R.D. WAY, and D.E. TERRY. 'Liberty' Apple. HortScience Vol. 14(6): 757-758. Dec. 1979.

LORD, William J., *et al.* A Comparison of Tree Size, Productivity, and Fruit Quality of 'Delicious' Strains. J. ASHS 105(6): 883-887. 1980.

MULLINS, C.A. and David W. LOCKWOOD. Performance of Selected New Late Season Apple Cultivars in Tennessee. Fruit Varieties Journ. 34(1): 8-10. Jan. 1980.

OMURA, M., Y. SATO, and K. SEIKE. Long Term Preservation of Japanese pear seeds under extra-low temperatures. Long Term Preservation of Favourable Germ Plasm in Arboreal Crops. Fruit Tree Res. Sta. MAF, Japan 1978.

ROM, R.C. and G.R. MOTICHEK. Jonathan, Jonnee, Jonadel and Jonalicious Apples: A Quality Comparison. Fruit Varieties Journal, Vol. 35, No. 1, January 1981.

SETH, J.N., S.D., LAL, S.S. SOLANKI and R.P. KUKSAL. Chaubattia Anupam, an Early Sweet Apple. Fruit Varieties Journal, Vol. 35, No. 2, April 1981.

WATERWORTH, H.E. Scionwood of Apple Cultivars, Rootstocks and Species Available from the Plant Introduction Station. Fruit Varieties Journal 34(2): 27-33. 1980.

WAY, Roger. Apple varieties for New York. N.Y. Life & Sci. Bul. 78. 15 pp. 1979.

(See additional references in former book editions.)

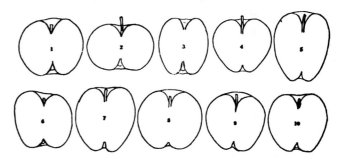

SHAPES OF APPLES USED IN IDENTIFICATION (1) Wealthy, round. (2) Wagner, oblate. (3) Spitzenburg, oblong. (4) Golden Delicious, conic. (5) Chenango, oblong-conic. (6) York, oblique. (7) Mother, ovate. (8) Rhode Island Greening, round-oblate. (9) Twenty Ounce, round-conic. (10) Baldwin, round-oblate. (Hendrick, Systematic Pomology, Macmillan, 1925)

CHAPTER III

Establishing the Fruit Planting

LOCATING THE ENTERPRISE

It is a serious mistake to locate an orchard improperly. An error in planting annual crops can be corrected the following year, but with fruit trees it is a long-time investment. Careful orchard planning at the beginning pays dividends later. In the early 1900's during boom periods, orchards were indiscriminately planted, many on sites where climate and soil were not suited to fruit growing, and, as a result, these orchards proved unprofitable and sooner or later were abandoned. Today, commercial fruit growing is limited to definite regions which have proven over many years to be adapted to profitable fruit growing.

Before selecting a region for fruit growing, it is important to make a careful study of the transportation and marketing facilities, winter and spring temperatures, moisture, soil and site conditions, and suitability of a certain kind of fruit for a given region and site. There are many advantages in locating the fruit enterprise in a region where fruit growing is well established and where there are big centers of population. The advantages are:

1. There are definite savings in co-operative purchasing of supplies and equipment on a large scale.

2. Repairs for machinery and general orchard supplies are readily available from near-by dealers.

3. In well-established regions, there is considerable local interest and inspiration to be gained from intelligent and alert fellow workers.

4. There is a more stable market with efficient selling organizations where buyers of quantity are available to fill their requirements.

5. Shipping charges to distant markets are held to a minimum.

6. Commercial storage space, processing plants for fruits, and outlets for the by-products are likely to be favorable.

7. Broad and heavily traveled roads near large cities afford excellent sites for roadside markets, rent-a-tree or pick-your-own operations.

8. Transportation facilities in and out of the region, when needed, are usually adequate and rapid.

9. In general, a grower gets more return on his tax money in better quality and more extensive public services from recognized agencies, such as the experimental stations, agricultural college, county agricultural agents, and large commercial firms dealing in orchard equipment and supplies.

There always will be scattered orchards away from centers of population and fruit growing, and they have their advantages. Such growers usually manage smaller acreages and enjoy a more or less independent local market where fruit prices are often better than in heavily supplied general markets, provided the business is not overdone. Good fruit land in such areas is often less expensive and carries less taxes, which makes for better profit in production. Furthermore, there is less danger from insect and disease contamination from neighboring unkept orchards, or from buildup in certain insect populations such as mites and codling moth.

Climatic factors. *Temperature* is the most important climatic factor affecting the geographic distribution of fruits and their cultivars. Man has little control over temperature and, therefore, it is wise to check carefully with local growers, horticultural extension service specialists, and the government weather station regarding frequency of hail, frosts and extreme temperatures in past years. An increase in altitude results in lower temperatures the same as a change in latitude from the equator northward or southward. Very cold winters where the temperature falls to -20° to -40°F (-7° to -40°C) or wide fluctuations from relatively warm temperatures in winter to extremely cold temperatures are not desirable for deciduous fruits. Long hot dry summers are not favorable to successful fruit growing. Adequate hours of temperature below 45°F (7.2°C) must occur to break the *rest period* for specific fruits and their cultivars (Table 1).

Spring frosts or freezes shortly before, during, or after bloom constitute one of the most important hazards in fruit growing. They are far more destructive to the fruit industry than autumn frosts. The possibility of an occasional frost is a hazard on which many fruit growers take a chance regardless of how successful a given region may be in fruit production. It is hard to find orchards that do not suffer from them at one time or another. Dwarfs being low should be planted on the higher sites. The average peach grower in the midwestern states expects an average of three good crops of peaches in five years, with two entirely or partially lost to spring frosts or winter freezes. Large deep bodies of water will temper spring frost damage a mile or so from the shores. Also, a northern

Northern papaw	100-1800	Sour cherry	600-1400
American plum	700-1700	Sweet cherry	500-1300
Domestic plum	900-1700	Blueberry	150-1200
Apple****	250-1700	Peach	250-1100
Raspberry	800-1700	Kiwi	600-800
Filbert	800-1700	Apricot	300-900
Pear	200-1500	Blackberry	200-400
Currant and		Quince	100-400
Gooseberry	800-1500	Almond	100-400
Walnut	400-1500	Persimmon	100-400
Japanese plum	300-1200	Grape*	100-1500
Peach (Florida)	50- 400		
Peach (Texas)	350- 950		
Peach (General)	800-1200	Strawberry	200-300
Pecan***	300-1000	Fig**	0-300

Some data were taken from Chandler *et al.* Ca. Agr. Exp. Sta. Bull. 611. 1937. Breeders are seeking lower chilling germplasm for many of the fruits. Cultivars are being bred with lower chilling requirements than indicated above. Contact Dr. Wayne Sherman, IFAS, Univ. of Fla., Fruit Crops, Gainesville, 32611 for latest information on a given crop.
* Grapes require very little chilling and some tropical cultivars required hardly any, but most cultivars start better in spring with moderate chilling.
** Figs are almost evergreen but grow well with moderate chilling.
***Pecans perform better with 500 or better hours chilling but the Stuart does fairly well with as low as 300 hrs.
****Anna and Dorsett Golden apple flower and fruit at least 5 mi. below Miami, Florida, 25°N latitude with chilling less than 50 hrs.

exposure will hold back bud development.

Wind machines work best under quiet air conditions by mixing warm air above the trees (so-called temperature inversion) with colder air among the trees. *Firing* is of two types: (a) burns as open flame (petroleum bricks, logs, rubber tires, etc.) and (b) heats metal objects, such as stacks that radiate heat (Figure 1 and also Chapter 19). Firing is effective if enough fuel is burned to keep the plant and air temperatures above danger levels. Heating is more effective in big orchards with large trees, which tend to hold the heat in the orchard. Freezing of tissue reaches the danger point around 28°F, so that heating or wind machines should start at around 32°F. *Sprinkling* by water or prebloom misting retards spring bud-swell and on freezing releases heat (heat of fusion), holding the plant temperature at around 32°F as long as water is applied. Tree breakage, of course, can be a problem with big trees but not so much with dwarfs, and particularly those on a trellis. Icicles indicate an adequate application rate. Florida Circular 287, California Circlar 400, and USDA Farmers' Bull. 1588, cover these subjects. Michigan has a bulletin on sprinkling; Utah on pre-bloom tree misting. There is a switch to sprinkling with higher fuel costs.

Figure 1. (Left) A California dual "Tropic Breeze" machine for drawing warmer air from above and spreading it over up to 20 acres of the orchard floor to prevent frost damage. Helicopters are serving a similar role. (Right) Orchard heaters are most effective in a large orchard and where air is fairly quiet. Coldwater misting of trees in spring may hold back bud development 2 weeks or more (Utah tests). Tests in California indicate that control of two types of bacteria in orchards by zinc sprays in spring may slow ice nucleation and allow super-cooling of bloom tissue by several degrees without freeze damage. With high-priced fuel, under- and over-tree sprinkling increases. (Chap. 19).

Figure 2. Windbreaks may be desirable in areas where wind blows more or less continuously from one direction. Consult the local forester. This popular windbreak grew to 50 feet in 18 years and is backed by slower-growing red pines. Located near Peru, N.Y., it improves bee activity, reduces bruised fruit, winterkill, and windfallen fruit. In West Europe, the European alder (*Alnus cordata*) is often used as a windbreak, planted two yrs. before the orchard, at 400-500 ft. intervals, no nitrogen.

Heavy winds blowing more or less continuously over a site are definitely undesirable. It is difficult to do a good job of spraying when the wind blows continuously from one direction. Dry winds during the blossoming period affect the fruit set and may result in frequent reductions in the fruit crop. Also, there is a tendency for young trees to grow one-sided and lean with the prevailing wind. This more or less develops a tree off balance and may cause it to break apart with a heavy crop. Windbreaks help (Figure 2).

Amount of *sunshine* is important in governing the rate of food manufacture by fruit-tree leaves which, in turn, affects the size and amount of color of fruit and the regularity with which the tree bears from year to year. For example, in regions of Washington State where sunshine is relatively abundant, fruit production per acre tends to be greater and alternate bearing of heavy and light crops of fruit is less pronounced than in Eastern states where there is more cloudiness during the growing season.

Hail is a hazard in fruit growing but is less likely to be destructive than spring frosts. There are some areas in fruit growing regions, however, which experience hail more frequently than others. Local growers, the Weather Bureau and hail insurance companies are probably better informed on the susceptible areas. Hail can be destructive to the fruit, reducing it in grade or almost destroying it completely if the stones are large. It shatters the leaves and is also destructive to the bark, bruising and splitting it, as well as stunting growth in general (Figure 3). Hail insurance for fruit is available and some growers in regions

20

with history of hail have found it worthwhile. A fungicidal (sulfur) spray after a hail storm helps reduce loss from rots. A public-pick-your-own program has helped salvage hail fruit. See appendix for discussion of hail insurance.

Size of planting. If the grower intends to serve a large and general market, he might consider a large enterprise of 100 to 200 acres or more. This will enable him to ship in truck loads and thus receive greater consideration from large marketing agencies. If he intends to serve the local market, his business may be large or small, depending upon the size of the population to be served in the neighborhood. For example, near Cleveland, Ohio, one grower is managing 200 acres from which he sells almost his entire apple crop to the Cleveland trade. If the local market consists of scattered small towns, such a neighborhood usually will not absorb as large a quantity of fruit at a given time. However, it will purchase a continuous supply in small quantities throughout the season. Grower-owned cold storages have made it possible for fruit growers away from concentrated population centers to give a small continuous supply of fruit to a limited local market.

The fact should not be overlooked that if you intend to grow standard size tree crops, there is a period of five to ten years when the orchard will be largely an expense, and the trees will pay back little. Compact trees, however, bring quicker returns, or you can consider diversifying your business by growing other crops such as small fruits or vegetables, and perhaps some livestock. Cultivation of small fruits or vegetables between trees, especially stone fruit trees, such as peaches, cherries, and plums, is beneficial to the trees, as well as to the intercrop. The same equipment and facilities in general are required for both the tree and the intercrops and, therefore, the initial cost for equipment is no greater. With modern commercial closer-planted compact earlier-fruiting trees, intercropping is uncommon.

The profit from small orchards of 10 to 20 acres is usually not adequate support for an average-size family, and it is necessary for the operator to have outside interests. There are increasing cases, however, where you can handle a small acreage, preferably diversified, together with a pick-your-own operation, or a roadside market, purchasing additional produce to supply the trade. It is much to *your* advantage to be on a well-travelled highway.

Selection of site. It is important to select a good orchard site with *favorable elevation*. Upland rolling or sloping fields which are not too steep for efficient orchard operations are the most desirable sites (Figure 4). River bottoms or flat valley floors are usually undesirable. Cold air settles in these areas and frequent frost or freezing injury is possible. Cold air should move out of the orchard into land and valleys located at a lower level. On a slope, trees should not be planted lower than about 50 feet above the base of the slope, especially where cold air drains slowly from the valley floor. Under such conditions, a difference of 100 feet in elevation may make a difference of 5° to 10°F in the minimum temperature encountered. In some

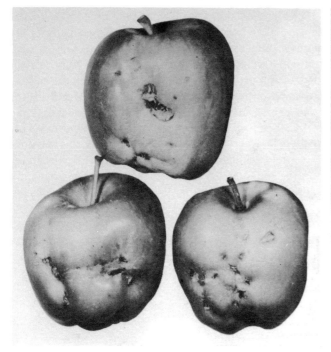

Figure 3. A hail storm while the fruit is developing results in bruised, malformed fruit, most of which must be classified as culls or for cider. The trees also may be severely damaged. Sites where hail storms are known to occur frequently should be avoided. Spring hail damage may afford fire blight entry paticularly on pear. A funcidal spray following reduces rots.

21

Figure 4. An excellent orchard site located near the heavily populated region of Columbus, Ohio. Peaches are shown in the foreground, apples in the background, with the residence, storage, and machinery sheds located in the center of the orchard next to a hard-surfaced road. Note rotation of different ages of trees in background.

seasons, such differences would make the difference between a full crop and a crop failure. Level land is not objectionable if frosts are not a problem or if located within a mile or so from large bodies of *deep* water, so that there is a tempering effect of the water.

Where there is a thick woods nearby, it is unwise to plant closer than within about 75 feet of it because the timber tends to harbor cold air and compete with the fruit plants for light, water, and nutrients. Woods on a slope below an orchard may retard movement of cold air downward, but this can be remedied to some extent by cutting 75-foot swaths through the woods at 100-yard intervals.

Although an orchard should be located on an elevated site to secure good air drainage, sites on top of ridges may be unsatisfactory because of exposure to winds, and generally drier and less fertile soil conditions. The direction of slope of the land usually has little effect upon the fruit crop. However, in case of persistent prevailing winds, an orchard planted on the leeward slope would be the more desirable, especially if the winds continue during extremely cold weather. Such winds will increase freezing damage at a given temperature. It is true that north slopes tend to retard bud development in the spring, whereas south slopes accelerate it, and east and west slopes fall between in this respect. But there is little evidence on crop yeilds in favor of one slope over the other.

The location of an orchard on very steep slopes presents a number of problems. On steep hillsides, spraying may be a problem. This can be managed by installing a central stationary spray plant and piping the orchard. The trend, however, is to pick better sites where modern air-blast spraying can be used. Cultivation of steep hillsides may be impractical because of the danger of erosion. It is for-

tunate, however, that the apple and pear will thrive well under permanent or semipermanent sod systems on slopes as steep as 20° to 30° (e.g., 20' drop in 100'), which is too steep for satisfactory growing of peaches, cherries, and plums. Many orchard operations, such as pruning, thinning, harvesting, and hauling fruit are much more difficult on steep hillsides than on gentle slopes. With *compact* trees, however, orchard machinery will be smaller and better adapted to rolling or sloping land.

Selection of soil. The *first requirement* of a good orchard soil is proper *water drainage* which permits good aeration and extensive root development. The subsoil is probably more important than the upper layer of soil in growth and production of an orchard. When the subsoil is hard and impervious, trees may grow satisfactorily for a few years, but when the tops and crops demand more water, they may become weak, and if a dry year, very wet year, or a severe winter occurs, they may die (Figure 5). Fruit trees will not tolerate wet soils during the growing season. The roots can withstand some submergence during the winter dormant period, provided the water drains away by the time growth starts in the spring. Submergence of the root system for even a few days during the growing season, when temperatures are high, usually results in eventual death of the roots. Another period when waterlogging is disastrous is during the spring months when the buds are opening and the shoots developing.

A soil on which water stands for more than a week after a heavy rain is considered unfit for fruit growing. In most orchards, it is not unusual to find a wet spot here and there in depressed areas. These can be avoided, drained by tile, or made into ponds for water supply in spraying. There are instances where entire orchards have been drained by tile

Figure 5. The soil beneath this Schmidt sweet cherry tree near Ithaca, N.Y. is underlain with rock 18 inches below the surface. As a result of shallow rooting, the tree is dying during an extended drought. Fruit trees generally perform best with a 4-to-6-ft. rooting depth.

carry the trees through the same period of drought. Today, however, most commercial fruit growers figure at the outset on some form of irrigation for their trees, even in humid regions where periods of drouth during the growing season are likely. Drip irrigation is popular.

Level of the *ground water table* during the growing season, especially at blossoming time, is an important criterion of a good orchard soil. The soil is said to be unsatisfactory for orchard purposes if the water table remains within six inches or a foot of the soil surface for a week after a heavy spring rain, or within three feet of the surface for several weeks after growth starts. It is good practice to make a survey of the water table and drainage conditions previous to planting because some soils may be deceiving on the surface; also the subsoil may vary considerably within a horizontal distance of 50 to 100 feet. The survey can be made by boring about four random holes per acre, using a tractor-driven or hand digger. The holes should be about four feet deep, into which a galvanized drain pipe or four-inch tiles are placed. The water table should be studied about three weeks before and after bloom. In case of the better fruit soils, the ground water may exist within a few inches of the soil surface for an hour or so after heavy spring rains, but it falls rapidly and within a day or two, it drops to three or four feet below the surface. It is important that readings be taken at three-day intervals during spring months. In case of a poorly drained soil, the water table will remain a foot or two below the surface for a week or so after heavy rains.

but such a practice is expensive. It is better to select land that does not need such preparation.

It is not a recommended practice to dynamite a hardpan to improve drainage unless the hardpan is underlain with well-drained sandy soil. Otherwise, a heavy soil will further compact with the blast. In Australia and New Zealand, a shallow soil is scraped into ridges on which trees are planted and drip irrigated, with surface drainage provided by a graded furrow between ridges (Figure 6).

The *rooting area* for a fruit tree should be at least four to five feet in depth, but this depends somewhat on the region and soil type. Where rainfall is plentiful and well distributed over the growing season as in some sections of West Virginia, a soil three feet deep may be satisfactory for fruit. In New York, fruit trees live longer and are more profitable on well-drained, even-textured, sandy or gravelly loam soils that permit root penetration to eight to nine feet than on heavy clay soils where root penetration is but three feet. In Nebraska where there is likelihood of long summer droughts and where deep loess soils are available, wider tree spacing in soils deeper than nine feet is being recommended. Generally speaking, about twice the rooting depth of soil is necessary in a medium sandy soil than would be necessary in a heavier silt loam soil to

Figure 6. Where the top soil is only 12-18 inches deep with a poorly drained tight subsoil, as in some areas of New Zealand and Australia (Scoresby Experiment Station, above, below Melbourne), the top soil is scraped to ridges on which the trees are planted, in this case Granny Smith apples. Plums and pears, which are more tolerant of damp soil conditions, may also be handled in this manner.

Special surface preparation of the soil will be needed if some sections of this type site are to be used (Fig. 6).

Roots must have *good aeration* in order to function properly. This is the reason that drainage is so important. Under optimum rooting conditions in the soil, the pore space should be occupied 50 percent with water and 50 percent with air. If the soil is poorly drained, the greater percentage of the pore space will be occupied by water. The inclusion of sand, gravel or organic material in soil tends to lighten it, enables it to absorb rain or irrigation water faster, gives it better drainage, and has a tendency to make it warm. Clay gives the soil body, but when it is present in considerable amounts, it makes the soil difficult to work when wet and it cracks when dry. Presence of a certain amount of clay (20 to 40 per cent) is desirable because it contains available nutrient elements and assists in retaining moisture. Decaying vegetation and humus are also valuable in a soil because they, too, help make nutrients available, greatly increase water penetration, and assist in giving the soil good tilth.

Fruit plants have a wide tolerance to *soil pH*. Good apple orchards have been found on soils from quite acid to very alkaline (pH 8.5; neutral is pH 7.0). Most pomologists arbitrarily have set the optimum soil pH at 6.5 to 7.0 because most intercrops and cover crops grow best in slightly acid soils. Also, laboratory research with potted fruit plants and field observations and data indicate that this pH range is most favorable.

Soil fertility from the standpoint of an orchard is not as important as the points discussed previously. Many of the fruit growing soils around the world, except the very sandy soils, are supplied with the necessary elements for tree growth, except for nitrogen. This can be applied to the soil or as a spray to the foliage in the form of nitrogen fertilizers. Other elements which may be deficient in some soils, such as boron, potassium, magnesium phosphorus, iron, and zinc, also can be supplied. Hence, the fertility of a soil is relatively less important than its physical characteristics and its location or site.

The soil shows orchard possibilities if it will grow a good crop of weeds and if the native trees are large and vigorous. Poor weed growth and trees showing dieback in the tops indicate an infertile or tight soil with shallow rooting area. A Washington grower is using second-hand earth-moving equipment in low-labor periods to move the top soil of bottom land to hillsides for orchard plantings, and growing soil-improving legumes on the scalped land.

Agricultural experiment stations are giving valuable soil survey service, working through county agricultural agents, to assist fruit growers in choosing good orchard soils and sites.

PLANTING PLANS

When to plant. Early spring planting as soon as the soil can be worked is generally the best time to plant in the deciduous fruit growing areas of the world. When spring begins to break rapidly, a difference of two weeks in the date of planting often results in obviously better growth of the earlier planted trees. New roots will develop when the soil temperature is above 45°F (7.2°C) if the trees are planted as soon as the frost is out of the ground, some root development will occur before the leaves appear. This early root development is highly important in getting the trees off to a good start. Occasionally, there are periods of three or four weeks in spring when the weather is unduly dry. Many trees may be lost if one of these dry periods follows shortly after planting. It may be necessary to haul water to the field in a spray machine, or in a large tank mounted on a truck. It may make the difference between a 100 or a 50 percent stand. (Figure 7).

In the milder climatic sections, if the temperature is not likely to fall below 0°F., trees may be planted any time the ground is not frozen in fall, winter, or early spring. However, it should be noted that the roots are more tender than the tops and may be killed by temperatures 20° to 24°F (-6.7° to -4.4°C). Consider this fact in shipping and handling trees during the winter months.

Fall planting in the colder zone can be done more successfully with apples, pears, sour cherries, and European varieties of plums than with peaches, sweet cherries, and Japanese plums. The advantages of fall planting are (1) the soil may be in better condition than in spring, (2) weather conditions are more favorable in fall than spring, (3) there are usually fewer windy days, (4) nursery stock is less likely to become overheated in transit, and (5) a fall-planted tree starts growth at the earliest time

Figure 7. If a spring drouth occurs, or if it occurs later, watering the trees at the critical time can make the difference between heavy replanting the next year or little or no replanting.

the following spring, usually earlier than spring-planted trees. In the milder zone where peach trees are often planted in the fall, a common practice is to pile soil about the base of the tree to protect it from crown damage during the winter. The land should be well drained when fall planting to prevent soil heaving. North-south hedgerows have better sunlight distribution and seem to bear better than east-west orientation.

Cultivars. The cultivar is the keystone of American fruit growing. Probably more attention has been given to cultivars than to any other phase of fruit growing. In spite of the accumulation of much information, however, the selection of the proper cultivars for a given location or condition needs serious study. Study the market to be served to determine which cultivars bring the higher prices. Good size and quality Golden and Red Delicious have been bringing the better prices in USA. The standard Red Delicious may bring one to two dollars less per bushel than the double red cultivars; Extra Fancy fruit may bring two dollars per bushel more than Fancy fruit.

Quality of the fruit is becoming of utmost importance in the final selection of a cultivar. It is too often true, however, that high-quality fruits have shortcomings which limit the extent to which they should be planted. These shortcomings may consist of susceptibility to disease, insect and cold injury, light or tardy bearing, short life, special soil requirements, uneven ripening, high proportion of low-grade fruit, fruit easily bruised, poor storage qualities, and others. Rome Beauty, in spite of its inferior quality, is a moneymaker because of its tendency *to bear annually, a most important character!*

Cross-pollination. Some varieties of fruits will not set fruit when planted alone or with certain other varieties of the same fruit. It is important to match varieties to get cross-fertilization. As a general statement, it is unwise to plant a single variety in a large plot. Plant two to four rows of a given variety and alternate with two to four rows of another variety with the same, or an overlapping blooming period. The pollinizer variety should not be farther away than two tree rows and this holds also for full-dwarf trees since bees tend to fly down the rows. Do not mix varieties in a row. See Chapter VI, other respective fruit chapters.

Picking date. It is well to select about five good varieties of a fruit which ripen successively over a period of from one to three months, depending upon the kind of fruit. This facilitates many of the major orchard operations such as spraying, thinning, and especially picking and packing. The crews can spray, thin or pick continuously, shifting from one variety to the next as the trees successively bloom, the fruit increases in size, and ripens. It has been a common mistake to plant too many varieties; one should rarely plant more than ten unless for season-spread for roadside market or pick-your-own.

Planting systems. There are several systems for planting

an orchard and the selection will depend upon the topography of the land, kind and cultivar of fruit, the soil management practices, rootstock used and if fillers will be used. Apple, pear, and quince will grow and produce satisfactorily in permanent or semipermanent sod. On the other hand, peaches, cherries, and plums are more satisfactory under a cultivation system. The sod system of management can be used in regions of the country where annual rainfall is greater than 35 inches. If rainfall is below 35 inches and irrigation is not available, herbicides or cultivation with or without cover crops or mulch will be necessary for moisture conservation for all tree fruits. Contour planting with or without terraces is a system adapted to rolling or sloping land but it is being less used in most areas of the world. In the Socialist East European countries there has been a tendency to use contour planting on upland for orchards and save the fertile more level lowland for grain and soybeans.

The *square* system was the most common for large trees in which a tree stood in each corner of the square; it is easy to cultivate and spray. The *quincunx* system of planting is essentially the square system with a filler tree in the middle of the square. In the *triangular* or hexagonal system, all trees are equidistant on the triangle. About 15 percent

Figure 8. At the Long Ashton and East Malling Stations in southern England, a number of orchard designs are under test directed at high populations of trees per acre and mechanical means of handling the crops. This is the so-called "Meadow Orchard" with trees planted 12 x 18 inches in blocks on MM. 106 bearing a crop every other year, then cut back, growth managed with Alar the next year before another crop the following year. (Long Ashton Research Station, Long Ashton, England.)

more trees can be planted per acre than in the square system, using the same planting distance. In the *rectangular* system, a tree is planted in each corner of a rectangle. The trend over the world is toward compact trees, free standing, staked or trellised.

Contour planting with or without terraces has some advantages, and a few disadvantages. Soil and rain water are conserved, resulting in better growth and production of the tree over a longer period of time. The terrace channels are convenient for irrigation. There is more economical operation of orchard machinery on the more or less level contour runways, as compared with operating on a slope. One disadvantage is the difficulty of spraying at different angles of the wind. (See Fig. 18).

The *hedgerow* is the most efficient management system since it is well adapted to mechanical harvesting and other modern machinery and practices. At maturity, trees are side by side in rows spaced wide enough to accommodate machinery and management. Hedgerow planting is used also for peaches, set about 14 feet apart in rows 22 feet apart. The system is adaptable to other tree fruits, and particularly to compact trees, staked, free-standing or trellised. Rows should run North and South for better light penetration.

Meadow or Bed Orchard. In England, the E. Malling (Maidstone) and Long Ashton Research Stations (Bristol) are testing apple varieties, self-rooted, or on MM-106 or EM-27 root-stocks. Nursery trees or stocks budded "in situ" are spaced 12 x 18 inches apart, either in beds with isle-ways or solid-planted with sprinkler heads through which may be applied hormones, fertilizers, herbicides, pesticides and water for drouth and frost control. Early work indicated cropping every other year (20 T/A) but cropping every year may be possible by judicious pruning and management of the bed system trees. A single shoot/tree or multi-shoots for vigorous varieties (Bramley's Seedling) may be used (Fig. 8). Meadow planting has worked well for peaches in the climate of Israel, but in the long growing season of the southeastern USA and other areas tested, there is doubt of its commercial success under present conditions.

New Zealand Lincoln Canopy System. System is shown in Figure 9. It is adapted to compact trees planted 8 ft. apart in rows 13 ft. apart or about 416 trees/A. This leaves about 5.2 ft. between canopies. Key advantages are excellent light exposure; good fruit coloring and quality; pruning, tying and fruit thinning done from the ground; good spray coverage with small equipment; well adapted to mechanical harvesting as shown in Chapter X where the fruit drops only a few inches to a canvas and shows no more, or less, damage than with hand picking. Details of trellis construction and tree training are found in N.Z. Ext. Bul. 10, 20 p., "Apple Production for Mechanized Harvesting on The Lincoln Canopy System" Oct. 1981.

Seek latest suggestions. M. Stolp, Lincoln College, Canterbury, S. Island, N.Z.

Planting distances. The proper distance for planting a given fruit has never been definitely settled. Distance of planting will depend upon the region, soil type, cultural care, and the variety to be grown. Fruit trees grow larger in some sections than in others. On a deep fertile soil in the New England area, a McIntosh tree may have a spread of 50 feet at maturity, whereas on a more shallow less fertile soil, it may occupy only 30 feet. Some varieties are naturally small and do not require as much space as other varieties. Small varieties are Wealthy, Jonathan, Yellow Transparent, G. Delicious, spurs, and Rome B. Varieties which tend to grow larger are Stayman, Cox's Or., McIntosh, Bramley's, and Delicious. A Montmorency cherry needs more space than a Morello, a sweet cherry more than a tart. The planting distances suggested for standard size fruit and nut trees and for compact trees are given in Table 2.

The number of plants or trees required to plant an acre may be determined by multiplying the distance they stand apart both ways and dividing the figure into the number of square feet in an acre (43,560). For plants or trees per hectare, multiply this figure by 2.47. To convert feet into meters, there are 3.28 ft. in a meter. Thus, if plants are 1.5 meters apart in the row, this is equivalent to about 5 ft. apart in the row (1.5 x 3.28).

Figure 9. The Lincoln Canopy training system using here Delicious on MM. 106 for mechanical harvesting for fresh market is receiving world interest. Summer mower pruning, winter snipping, hand fruit thinning, and pest control can be done conveniently. Light exposure is excellent, crops are regular and yields high. Trees eventually cover entire fence-wire space. See harvesting equipment in Chap. X (John S. Dunn, Lincoln College, Canterbury, N. Zealand.)

ORDERING AND CARE OF NURSERY STOCK

Trees should be ordered from a nursery as far in advance as possible, at least by the fall previous to planting. Nurseries become overloaded with last-minute orders in late winter and may not get your trees to you until after spring breaks and this is too late; trees in shipment at this time may be damaged by over-heating. Also, late-placed orders may find the desired cultivars exhausted. Buy the better-grade larger plants in a given age. One-year whips of apple, pear, and certain other fruits can be used, but nurserymen are being encouraged to grow "feathered" (branched) trees. Whips must be cut back to about 30 inches to induce branching for laterals selection.

Standard cultivars[1] of fruit do not come true to seed. It is necessary to bud or graft wood of desired cultivars onto selected roots, or use own-rooted trees which are being extensively studied. Nurserymen are planting seed of Delicious, McIntosh, Rome, or Delcon (superior germination, uniformity at Mich.) in wooden flats, layered in wet peat moss and given special temperature treatment during winter. In spring they are germinated and grown for a year in beds, then transplanted to the nursery row. These seedlings may be (1) budded in the field to desired varieties the following mid to late summer, cut back the next spring above the bud, and allowed to grow in the nursery a year for one-year trees and two years for two-year trees, or, (2) the seedlings may be dug in the fall and the roots cut into

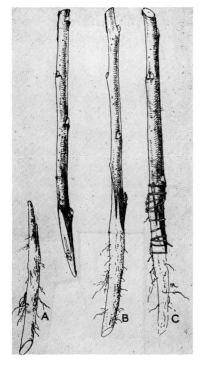

Figure 10. Varieties of fruit trees do not come true to seed. During the dormant season, pieces of shoot wood are removed from the desired variety and whip-grafted on roots or clones of the same or a closely related fruit. Above system of propagation can be used for apples and pears.

[1]"Cultivars" and "Varieties" are used interchangeably, the former now preferred.

TABLE 2. PLANTING DISTANCES SUGGESTED FOR FRUIT AND NUTS TREES[1]

STANDARD SIZE TREES

FRUIT	RANGE (FT.)	FRUIT	FEET
Apple	35-45	Filbert	18
Pear	25-35	English Walnut	40
Plum	20-24	Black Walnut	50
Peach	20-24	Hickory	40
Apricot	20	Pecan	70
Cherry, sour	20-25	Chestnut	40
Cherry, sweet	25-30		
Quince	18-22		

COMPACT APPLE TREES[2][3]

SPACING IN ROWS AND BETW. ROWS (FT.)	TREES PER ACRE	CLONAL ROOTSTOCK	COMMENTS
			Any Variety[4]
		EM IX, M26	Rome, York, Jonathan
6 x 14	518	EM VII, MM106	G. Del., Del., Jon., Spy
8 x 16	340	EM VII, MM106, EM II	Stay., McIn., Jon., Spy
10 x 18	242	EM VII, MM106, EM II	Rome, York, Jon. Spurs
12 x 20	182	MM 104, MM111	G. Del., Delicious
14 x 22	141	MM 104, MM111	Stayman, McIntosh
16 x 24	114	MM 104, MM111	Canadian Varieties
18 x 26	93	Robusta 5 (Hardy)	Any Variety
18 x 26	93	MM109, EM XVI,	
20 x 28	78	seedling	

COMPACT TREE SIZE BY VARIETY[3]

30' W x 20' Hi. EM 16; Std. Seedling.	25' W x 17' Hi. MM 109, 111, EM XII	22' W x 17' Hi. MM104, EM II		15' W x 10' Hi. MM 106, EM VII	
Jonathan	Jonathan	Jan.	Rome	G. Del.	N. Spy
	Spur. Del.	G. Del.	York	Mc In.	Idared
	Rome	Mc I.	Stay.	Del.	Beacon
	York	Sp. Del.	N. Spy	·Stay.	S. Rambo

[1]Distances are greater with large-size varieties with favorable soil and climatic conditions, less with reverse situation, "Spur" strains are 3/4ths std. size; std. strains may attain std. size on MM stocks under good growing conditions.

[2]See respective chapter for dwarfing stocks for other tree fruits.

[3]Adapted from tables by L. P. Batjer and C. M. Ritter.

[4]Growers are tending toward free-standing semi-dwarf trees in hedgerows. Use of trellis and stakes with full-dwarf root-stocks in hedgerows has been governed, more or less, by cost. M.26 may be satisfactory free-standing in good soil, using spur strains. Trellis permits tying down limbs for early bearing, although some staked varieties that normally bear early may not need tying down. Spur Delicious is preferred.

See Figure 14 for relative dwarfing capacity of apple stocks.

sections onto which shoots of desired varieties are whip-grafted (Figure 10). This is done indoors during the winter, generally mid to late winter, when work is slack. The grafts are then stored in the cellar in cool moist peat moss or sawdust until the following spring when they are set about 12 inches apart in nursery rows spaced three feet apart. After one season's growth in the nursery, they are cut back and allowed to grow another season, after which they are dug (Fig. 11) and sold in the spring as one-year trees. If growth is weak, they may be cut back, grown another year and sold as two-year trees.

Some growers contract with a reputable nurseryman a year or so in advance of planting, furnishing budwood from their own orchard-proven trees, or, they may produce their own trees. Large-acreage growers usually buy from reputable nurseries.

Piece-root grafting in apple and pear propagation, as described in Figure 10, may be used instead of budding. Advantages of this system are that in case of cold-resistant varieties, they have their grafted seedling roots which may be tender to cold, deeper in the soil and thus better protected from cold, as compared with budded stock. Robusta 5 is used for stocks in eastern Canada and Aluarp 2 in Sweden. Where clonal dwarfing roots are used, the coin wood must not touch soil to avoid its rooting.

Double-worked trees. The tree consists of wood from three different cultivars. With apple the root may be Delicious seedling, the trunk Robusta 5, and the top McIntosh. The tree has been grafted twice, or double-worked. The McIntosh so-grafted bears earlier, is hardier, and also will tolerate heavy soils and more moisture. Another example would be a MM.111 root, EM IX interpiece and a an Empire top. Hibernal is used for the same purpose, and such trees are giving good results with certain variety combinations in New Jersey; trees are three-quarter size.

Interstem trees usually take two years to develop. They can be developed in one year by summer budding the desired cultivar at 15-18 cm intervals on interstem wood, then the following spring cut the pieces apart just above the buds and graft them on the desired clonal root. (Fig. 12). Interstems may vary in length from 3 to 9 inches with 6 inches being the more common. The longer the interstem

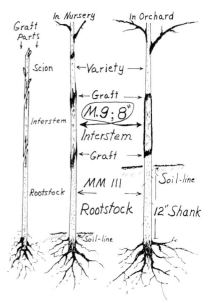

Figure 12. To develop a stronger deeper root system, horticulturists are testing full-dwarfing interstems (6-8 in. is common) such as virus-free M.9 on root-stock MM.111. The development of this type tree is shown above on (a) the grafting bench, (b) in the nursery and finally (c) in the orchard. Note depth of orchard planting for better anchorage, less suckering, other reasons. Interstem trees are more expensive but may be justified for some sites, soils and climates. Richard Norton, N.Y. Ag. Ext., suggests 10'' interstem for Jonathan, Rome and 12'' for more vigorous cultivars McIntosh, Cortland, Paulared, Macoun. An 85-95% take with nursery budding is average, with spurs somewhat less. Stark Nursery in Missouri has considerable experience with interstems. MM 106 w/9 interstem shows promise in W. New York.

the more the dwarfing effect.

Certified trees. Most nurseries sell certified trees which means that the trees have been checked and identified by state inspectors as true to name. This is valuable service to the customer because it protects him against planting undesirable varieties. Inspectors can identify varieties by the leaf, bark, and general growth characteristics of the

Figure 11. This is nursery tree-digging equipment used by a large midwest nursery. As the equipment passes down the nursery row, it lifts and loosens the trees so they can be lifted out easily by hand. This equipment explains in part why millions of dollars are invested in the nursery business alone.

28

tree. (See K. Lapins reference; also J. K. Shaw.)

Pedigreed trees or bud-selected stock means that the nurseryman has selected buds or scion wood from special highly colored or "high-yielding strains." Such "strains" may be trees that are growing on particularly fertile or well-drained soil, or that might have been growing on seedling stocks that were especially congenial. Thus, the more desirable characteristics of such trees are due to environmental influences and not to characters inherent in the scion wood from the tree. Pedigreed trees, therefore, may not have the virtues implied by the name.

Bud sport (Mutation). On a named variety of tree in the orchard, occasionally a spur, limb, or larger portion of the tree may show a distinct variation in the fruit or growth as compared with the rest of the tree. These are known as bud spots and can be perpetuated by grafting the wood of this limb upon desired stocks or roots. An example of a bud sport is spur-type Red Delicious which is a mutation of the ordinary strain of Delicious. Other well-known sports are the Starking, Richared, Jonared, Starkrimson, Gallia Beauty, and Blackjon. It is well for the orchardist to be on the look-out for these improved bud mutations in his own orchard.

Not all varieties are obtained from bud variations. Some are developed by scientific breeding to obtain new varieties superior to the parents. Examples of varieties which have been developed by breeding programs are the Cortland apple, Fredonia grape, Tioga strawberry, Coville blueberry, and the Redhaven peach.

Clonal stocks are vegetative pieces from a desired parent plant and are propagated by mound layering or tissue culture. (See Chap. 8, Grafting, etc.). (See also Figure 13). A rooted stock is planted in spring, cut back the next spring, and soil mounded around shoots as they develop. Shoots rooted at bases are removed at end of the season, bench-grafted to a desired scion variety in winter, stored, planted in a nursery row the next spring, grown for that year and sold; or the rootstock is lined out in a nursery and budded to a scion variety in summer, grown for the next year and sold.

Spur-type apples together with numerous higher colored fruit mutations (sports) largely from the Northwest, were named for the most part in the 1950-60's, although a few were named earlier as, e.g. Okanoma (spurred Delicious) in 1921. These are inherent and apparently permanent and can be propagated vegetatively. Spur-type trees are characterized by long limbs with few side branches but many spurs. Trees are more open and restricted in tree size to about 3/4 of the standard trees. In the Northwest, they are being planted by hedgerow on seedling roots, clonal and dwarfing stocks; MM 111 and 106 looked good in the

---

1970s. Examples are Goldspur (Golden Delicious) and Wellspur (or Bisbee from Starking) and a Macspur. Spurs are not available as yet for some cultivars. They may ripen later and require 80% less pruning. "Dead-spur" on Delicious is a problem disease in some orchards.

Compact trees. Only in recent years has there been world-wide interest in planting of dwarf and semidwarf tree fruits. Dwarfing stocks, of course, have been used for over 50 years in Europe where they originated but other countries, particularly the United States and Canada, have turned to them because of the many advantages over the large trees of (a) reduction in labor and production costs per bushel, (b) higher production per acre, (c) earlier bearing, and (d) improvement in color and marketability of the fruit, together with several lesser advantages. See Figure 13 for clonal propagation.

Richard L. Norton of Cornell Ext. Service says, "The orchard of the future must be oriented to a tree size ranging from 6 to 10 ft. tall and as wide. The reason is clear — overwhelming economic and efficiency advantages

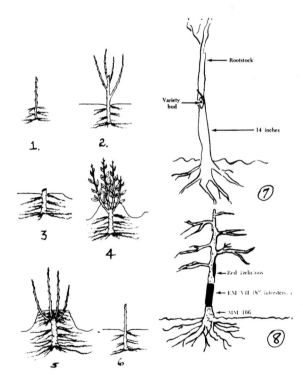

Figure 13. How dwarf trees are propagated. (1) Rooted clonal (e.g. EM 26) branch or root is spring planted in field bed. (2) After one season's growth, the cutting is (3) cut back the next spring. (4) Rooted cutting is mounded with soil when shoots are 12 in. tall and still tender; mounded again a few weeks later to depth of 12-15 in. of soil. (5) Roots develop on new shoots the second spring; rootstock cut off at the original base, and (6) rooted cuttings are lined out in nursery row for summer budding of (7) desired variety scion or (8) interstock. At (8) double-grafting or budding is shown to get interstock effects, as well as clonal rootstock effects on the size and performance of Red Delicious top. (R.F. Carlson, Michigan State Univ., E. Lansing)

---

¹"Scion" or "Cion", spelling is correct either way. "Stion" is sometimes used to denote a stock/cion combination.

29

compared with large trees. It is time to focus our attention on proper use of rootstocks and cultivars in the optimum planting system. Only minor gains will be made elsewhere in profits.''

TABLE 2. RELATIVE INITIAL PLANTING COSTS WITH PROFITS FIRST 10 YRS. FOR 4 ORCHARD DENSITIES
(After Cummins and Norton, N.Y. Agr. Exp. Sta., Bull. 41, Geneva, 1974).

Densities	Trees/A	Planting* Costs/A	Relative Cumm. Profits, to 10th yr.*
Low	121	100	100
Medium	218	157	128
High	454	436	203
Ultra-high	792	725	403

**Low desity trees - 100%.

Because of the rather limited experience with stion stock/scion combinations of compact trees under a broad set of conditions, suggestions on their use should be accepted with reservation. Growers should convert from standard to compact trees gradually if the practice continues to look good. The MM and EM rootstocks (except EM 26) may be winter damaged in colder apple regions or prove not well adapted to warmer climates. Breeders are testing and developing dwarfing stocks for specific climates and soil conditions.

A fruit tree is dwarfed to various degrees by grafting a cion variety on a clonal interstock (stem piece) or rootstock which has a dwarfing influence. In some cases there may be little or no dwarfing but there is the advantage of the trees being more uniform in character, size and fruiting. Where an interstock is used, the amount of dwarfing is proportionate to the length of the interstem which may be 3-12''. The nurseryman should so-label the trees. "EMLA" heat-treated virus-free clonal roots from England require less fertilizer and appear to remain virus-free, bearing 20% more fruit. On good soil, however, some growers complain of too much growth.

EM, (or M) refers to clonal stocks developed at the East Malling Research Station, Kent, England and MM refers to the Malling Merton series, developed as a cooperative breeding program between the John Innis Horticultural Institute, Merton, England, and the E. Malling Station above. See the late Dr. H.B. Tukey's book for more details.

M.27. More dwarfing than EM IX, nonsuckering, more easily propagated, less susceptible to fire blight, commercially available but of doubtful value except for interstems.

M.9. Wood brittle, must be staked or trellised, requires best soil in orchard, needs mulching and/or irrigation, suckering reduced by high budding and deep planting,

must maintain central leader, resistant to crown rot (*P. cactorum.)*[1]. There has been a heavy world demand, mostly virus-free good production to 25-30 yrs.[2].

M.26. Showing considerable commercial promise in U.S., may use as filler tree, brittle roots, usually staked or trellised. Stock overgrows cion as M.9 and has thicker bark, judged more winter resistant in north. (See Figure 14). Blight susceptible apples (York, Jonathan) may blight badly on EM 26 in blight years. May succeed free-standing in good soils.

M.7. Commercially productive, popular in USA, trees uniform, propagates easily, must be high-budded and planted deep to reduce suckering, some trees may need staking, susceptible to crown rot, 50% dwarfing 150+ trees/A, McIntosh, Spartan, Red Rome, Golden Delicious suited; Delicious questionable in some sites. Trees may attain standard size in very good soils.

MM.106. A popular stock, early bearing, well anchored, non-suckering, productive, check crown rot[1] problem in your area, worse on late-maturing cion cultivars as Delicious and Paulared. In as much as MM. 106 tends to induce late maturing, some crown rot could be due to winter damage in the colder regions.[2]

M.2 Does not propagate as easily as EM 7 or the MMs, does best in moisture retaining loam and not a heavy clay in which it tends to lean, fairly resistant to crown rot, suited to Delicious, Cortland, Spy, Jonathan, McIntosh. Smaller tree than on MM.111; nematodes may be a problem.

MM.111. Drouth tolerant, aphis resistant, good anchorage, vigorous varieties tend to uprightness; rootstock being used for interstem trees.

MM.104. More vigorous than MM.111, but cion variety as Delicious produces a more spreading tree, requires well-drained soil, susceptible to crown rot, good for Golden Delicious and Spur Delicious.

MM.109. Trees almost as large as on EM 16 (similar to seedling stock), well anchored, may lean after summer gale in wet soil and with heavy crop, productive, best in well-drained soils, does not sucker.

M.4. Semi-dwarf to semi-standard, early bearing, heavy producer, was used widely in Denmark, Holland, Germany, leans in exposed areas but adapted to spindle bush with no staking, resistant to crown rot, liked in British Columbia.

Alnap 2 (A-2). From Sweden, winter hardy, dwarfing like MM.111 or M.2, well anchored, good tree form, all-purpose stock, 90% used in Sweden, being tested as interstem in trees in the U.S.

[1]See Calif. Agric. 30(8):8-9. 1976 for effective control.
Crown rot may be controlled by soil drench at trunk base with 1 lb./100 gal. maneb or ferbam. Problem, however, could be more winter damage with late-maturing. Dr. Mike Ellis, Oh. St. Univ., also has controls.
[2]Burr knots (root initials) near graft unions are controlled by painting with "Gallex" (Ag-Biochem, Inc.)

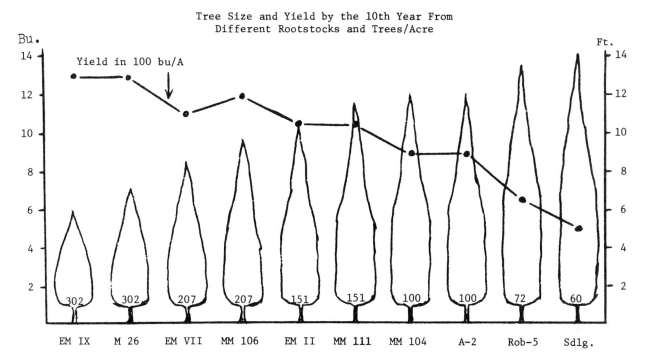

Tree Size and Yield by the 10th Year From
Different Rootstocks and Trees/Acre

Bu.

14

Yield in 100 bu/A

12

10

8

6

4

2

302   302   207   207   151   151   100   100   72   60

EM IX   M 26   EM VII   MM 106   EM II   MM 111   MM 104   A-2   Rob-5   Sdlg.

Ft.

14

12

10

8

6

4

2

Figure 14. At least 10 dependable rootstocks are available. Relative yielding capacity of cion variety is shown by receeding curve (See Table 2), bu/tree on left, trees per acre within tree diagram, and height in ft. on right. M.27, not shown, is more dwarfing than M.9. (Courtesy R.F. Carlson, Mich. State Univ.)

Robusta 5. Winter hardy, using about two feet of trunk, dwarfing in East Canada area particularly in lighter soil types. Antanovka and McIntosh are used similarly in colder regions.

In Australia and New Zealand, Granny Smith and Jonathan on MM. 104, 109 and on N. Spy vegetatively propagated are used. M.793 is popular below the Equator, gives a semi-dwarf tree in medium to low fertility soils, propagates easily, resistant to woolly aphids and bears early and well.

Buy one-year trees well "feathered" (branched) where available. Order as early as possible, no later than the fall before spring planting. It is unwise to buy nursery trees older than two years. They are either so large that the shock of transplanting is too great, or, they are inherently slow-growing and ultimately may be small and weak.

When the nursery stock is opened and separated, all varieties should be checked as to number, variety and grade, and those trees rejected which show crown gall[1], severe aphid injury on the roots, or winter killing as indicated by brittleness of wood and discoloration of the inner tissues. Since most trees are shipped in moss, sawdust or shavings and are in plastic-covered bundles to reduce evaporation of water, they can be placed in cold storage, sprinkled to keep moist, not wet, or dunked in pond, drums of water over night if arrive a bit dry. *Do not store with fruit*, which gives off ethylene, causing buds to break. As soon as the soil can be worked, the trees should be planted.

Figure 14A. A 3-wire trellis can be used for apple on EM9 or 26 (see chap. XX), and for dwarf pears although not as much trellis strength is needed vs grapes. Lighter wires and wider post spacing can be used. Bagging for pest protection sometimes is used in Japan and France where this photo was taken (Ernest G. Christ, Rutgers University.)

PLANTING THE TREES

Preparation of the soil. Plant fruit trees in tilled strips, regardless of the type of soil management followed later. If the land has been in sod, fall plowing is preferable to permit the soil to settle and the sod to decompose during winter. If the land is plowed in spring, do it as early as possible so that the ground can settle and absorb rainfall. Trees will need this moisture. Subsoiling in fall to a depth of 20 inches in the row and 3-4 ft. on either side when soil is dry and cracks is good practice.

Staking the field. Building laths cut in half and sharpened on one end make satisfactory stakes. Where the land is rolling, full lengths of the lath can be nailed together to give greater height in low places. Tips of the stakes can be seen at greater distances and in hollows by dipping the ends in whitewash or by wrapping a white cloth around the tops. If timber poles are used, the bark can be peeled off the tops to expose the light colored sapwood.

Determine your tree spacing between and in the rows, use a straight base line such as a road or fence line, then measure and stake your tree locations for the key outside row trees and sight-in the inside trees in the block. If the field is large or hilly, run a stake line across the center or divide the field and stake separately.

A plow, drag-chain or subsoiler can be used to mark a tree-row line, sighting on a distant stake. Hedgerow plantings need lining only in one direction.

Trellis design. The design should be picked which is economical and still does a lasting job. Somewhat less strength is needed here as compared with a grape trellis since tree trunks support some of the weight. As an example, a trellis for Golden Delicious on EM IX may have these specifications: 3 wires of No. 9 galvanized wire, bottom wire 18 inches from ground, treated posts 2 to 3 inches diameter at top, 9 to 10 ft. long, 3 ft. in ground end posts, 2 to 3 ft. depth between end posts, all 6 to 7 ft. above ground with dead man at end (sunken post in concrete, with screw-type powerline anchor) to hold the wire taut. posts are set 30-35 ft. apart, about 5 trees between posts; trellis gadgets are in nursery catalogues (See Appendix addresses); cedar, locust posts, dipped in low-caustic (to trees) preserver; obtainable with wire from farm fence-post sources.

Trellis posts with one lower wire can be installed the first or second year, other wires as needed. Full-dwarf trees should be staked immediately. When soil is moist, posts can be pushed into soil with down-pressure of tractor PTO lift or backhoe. See Chapter 20 for grape trellis design.

Planting trees. The PTO back-hoe is better than the tractor drill to dig holes; the latter may leave packed walls that must be chopped on sides with a shovel. On sandy soils, plow out a furrow and set trees with a garden shovel. Trees can be trucked to the field in 50-gallon drums one-third full of water. *Keep roots moist* until planted. They must not dry excessively at any time. Trim off broken or injured roots. Set standard-size trees about the same depth as they grew in the nursery (you can see the soil line). In very sandy and dry soils it may be desirable to set the trees deeper than they grew in the nursery. High-budded trees on dwarfing stock should be set a foot to a foot and a half deeper than grown in the nursery to get good root anchorage, but not so deep that the cion variety can root. Place the bulk of the roots toward the prevailing wind. If possible, place the "bud crook" and the lowest good scaffold limb toward the prevailing wind. Put the topsoil in the bottom of the hole mixed with a little peat moss if available (Figure 15). Tromp the soil solidly, leaving no air pockets (Figure 16). Apply 0.05 lb. actual nitrogen (e.g. ¼ lb. ammonium sulphate or ½ lb. 10-10-10) in a ring on the surface one foot from the trees.

Dr. A. P. Preston, England, has planted dwarf nursery trees with side roots removed with little difference in "take" (for rapid machine planting; Fig. 17). See reference.

Contour planting. In contour planting on sloping land, all trees in any one row are in the soil at about the same level with slight incline to one end of the row to drain excess water. With this planting system, cultivation is done on the contour between the rows and not up and down the

Figure 15. (Left) The hole should be large enough to accommodate the root system. Cut back broken and long roots; set tree as deep as it grew in the nursery or if high-budded on clonal dwarfing stock, set deeper for better anchorage. (Right) In heavier soils, better tree growth is obtained if a three-gallon pail of wet peat moss is mixed with the soil as it is sifted about the roots. Lift and lower the tree slightly while filling the hole; tamp soil thoroughly as roots are covered. Where anchor posts are used, set them on the leeward tree side.

Figure 16. After the tree has been sighted in place, tamp the soil solidly about the roots with topsoil replaced first and sub-soil last. Tree is leaned slightly toward the prevailing wind.

hill. Thus, cultivation tends to build up slight ridges or natural low terraces at the tree row which reduces the tendency of the water to run down the slope and increases soil absorption. Obviously, the tree rows will not be equally spaced in all parts of the orchard. On the slight slopes, the rows will be somewhat closer together; but on the almost level areas, they will be farther apart. In some places, a given row may be so far from another row that it

is possible to insert what is known as a "spur" row. On steeper parts of the orchard, it may be necessary to discontinue parts of rows to prevent the trees from becoming too close.

Today, there is a tendency away from contour terracing of orchards. There have been problems in maintaining unbroken terraces (washouts), getting "lost" among the taller trees, "fighting" a wind as the sprayer moves around contours, moving across the terraces with equipment and getting fruit out of the orchard at harvest. See previous editions of this book or references for details on laying out contour orchards where land is limited and contouring is the only alternative. Also see Clemson University, So. Car., Bull. 97, revised.

AN ANALYSIS OF SOME DWARFING ROOTSTOCK PROBLEMS

The following discussion is largely based on comments by James N. Cummins and Richard L. Norton in their N. Y. Agr. Exp. Sta. (Geneva) Bulletin No. 41. As indicated earlier, the field of dwarfing rootstocks is changing rapidly, there are problems, and the experiment station staffs as well as the growers are working together to get the highest early yields of marketable fruit per unit of ground. Dwarf trees show so many advantages over the large standard-size trees, that there is feverish work all over the fruit growing world to seek, breed, and test new and old rootstocks for the many fruits, varieties of fruits,

Figures 17. With the trend toward many more fruit trees to the hectare, machinery is being perfected to set these trees quicker and with less expense per tree. This USDA designed planter with three laborers can plant trees eight times faster than conventional methods with five people, or 500 trees/hr. (Dr. Bernard R. Tennes, USDA, Mi. St. University, E. Lansing 48824.)

soil types and climates. It is a whole new "ball game" that will demand increased research in all phases of fruit growing from the agronomists to the horticulturists, breeders, engineers, growers, and economists to the sales people. Among the key advantages of the smaller trees are:

1. Reduces pruning costs per hundred weight of fruit by half or more.
2. Requires less spray material per unit fruit weight, doing a more thorough job.
3. Permits use of smaller and much less expensive orchard equipment.
4. Extends the spectrum of labor available. (Labor prefers to work with small trees.)
5. Tends to produce more top-quality fruit per unit of ground, especially during the first decade of the planting. This enables the grower to get his investment money back earlier, as well as building profits earlier.
6. Cuts harvesting costs almost in half as compared with climbing up and down ladders.
7. Should enable growers to use more kinds of mechanical equipment to get jobs done easier with less expense.
8. Low trees, in summary, are easier and less expensive to manage in nearly all operations.

The Assets of Seedling Rootstocks. Most seedlings came from the Pacific Northwest, suggesting that almost all have Red Delicious as one parent. They are somewhat tolerant of fire blight, collar rot, and woolly apple aphids (WAA), and reasonably winter hardy. By selection, we have tended to get fairly uniform trees despite genetic diversity. In the orchard, we frequently get some scion rooting with good anchorage in a wide variety of soil types. Both the nurseryman and orchardist liked seedling rooted trees because of numerous advantages with our past orchard technology.

With the clonal rootstocks, there are potential problems with fire blight, collar rot, woolly apple aphids, root suckering, viruses, and nematodes. If these difficulties are recgonized, they can be prevented or reduced.

Fireblight. Change to clonal rootstocks has brought these problems: (1) Trees on clonal stocks may begin bearing when the tree is small so that a single canker on the rootstock can girdle and kill it. (2) Fire blight may develop from infected flowers on low-trunk spurs and extend to kill much of the tree. (3) Bees tend to work down a row, distributing innoculum more efficiently. (4) Most serious, some clones are extremely susceptible to fire blight. M.9 and M.26 are susceptible even though the scion variety is resistant; MM.106 moderately, while M.7 and MM. 111 are relatively resistant. It is important to control M.9 root suckers. (Use a 1.5-2 percent NAA when suckers are young, tender). Lesions on suckers of M.7 and MM.111 usually terminate well above the main root. A careful fire blight control program in dwarf trees is most important.

Suckers also can be trimmed lightly, well above ground level, inducing several relatively weak shoots, which lignify earlier than vigorous suckers and are susceptible to fire blight for a shorter time. Severity of fire blight on the *fruiting scion* varies with the rootstock.

1. Most clonal stocks, especially M.9, M.26, and MM.106, accelerate the onset of scion flowering, courting earlier infection.
2. The downward extension of a fire blight lesion is limited, in part, by "hardening" of the stem. Shoots of MM.106 grow later and "harden" weeks after trees on M.9.
3. Empire, McIntosh, Idared, Monroe, and Jonathan produce fruit buds on 1-year-old spurs. When they are grown on M.9, M.26, and (sometimes) on MM.106, many lateral shoot buds differentiate into fruit buds that open 3 to 7 days later than the normal spur buds, extending the flowering season. Additional blight sprays may be needed when considerable lateral flowering occurs.

Collar Rot. This term should refer to a set of symptoms caused by *Phytophthora cactorum*; unfortunately, a number of other causes may be involved: fire blight, winter injury, girdling by wire (rodent) guards, and girdling by field mice. Except on the worst sites, *true* collar rot has not been a significant rootstock problem with standard trees, although very susceptible scion varieties such as Grimes Golden, York, and Twenty Ounce have taught us the need for resistant trunks.

Most tree losses commonly attributed to collar rot really may be more related to soil management and drainage. The late-maturing of trees on MM.106 is accentuated when the fruiting variety is also late maturing causing the tree in colder zones to go into winter tender to temperature extremes. For example, on a site that is moderately to poorly drained, after a wet autumn, the following tree losses were recorded, spring 1973:

Twenty Ounce (late maturing)	60%
Red Rome (late maturing)	40
Idared (intermediate)	0
Golden Delicious (early)	0
McIntosh (early)	0

Rootstocks rank in about the following order of susceptibility to root rot: M.9 (resistant); M.2 and MM.111 (moderately resistant); M.7, MM.106, M.26, and domestic seedlings (susceptible); MM.104 (very susceptible).

Burr Knots can be a problem in warm moist climates on the MM and EM stocks. Knots are a bunching of aerial roots forming under these conditions which may be subject to rot entrance.

Wooly Apple Aphids (WAA). Under present spray programs, WAA have been a minor problem on the large,

34

poorly pruned tree. On smaller trees, WAA are rarely seen above ground.

With a pest program for only major pests, WAA can build up on fruiting parts so that pickers find it difficult to work. Special sprays, particularly of systemic materials, may be required.

Malling-Mertons are highly resistant to WAA race(s) in New York, but a resistant stock does not impart resistance to the fruiting variety. M.9, M.26, and M.7 are highly susceptible to WAA. A large WAA population on the roots may stop tree growth.

Replant Problems. Shallow-rooted rootstocks such as M.9 and M.26 benefit more from preplant soil fumigation than deep-rooted stocks such as M.7. This appears to be due to more of the M.7 root system being below the level of maximum nematode infestation.

Neither M.9 nor M.26 has performed well without irrigation on a nematode-prone site without preplant fumigation.

If you are planning to set clonal stocks in light soil, you should remove all possible roots from the proposed site, have the soil analyzed and apply the indicated nutrients, grow a good local cover crop, perhaps sudan grass, for at least one season, and fumigate the fall before planting. Fumigation may confer benefits in addition to nematode control.

Viruses. Most of the apple varieties in commercial cultivation are infected with one or more viruses, yet ill effects are seldom seen. Similarly, the older clonal rootstocks, especially M.7 and M.9, are infected with four or more latent viruses. Lack of apparent orchard effects from such a complex of viruses suggests that the fruiting varieties, the older clonal rootstocks, and the seedling stocks have tolerance for these common viruses. M.26, MM.106, and MM.111 also appear to be highly tolerant of the common viruses.

A few varieties are sensitive. Golden Delicious crops may be significantly reduced by rubbery wood virus (M.7 and M.9 stocks carry rubbery wood virus; the strains vary in virulence. (Dr. Bob Wertheim, Netherlands, has a "virus-free" strain somewhat more vigorous and producing 20% more fruit). We have some instances of Idared/M.7 trees infected with flat limb, transmitted to the Idared from the infected but tolerant M.7 roots. "Virus-free" heat-treated, selections of both fruiting varieties and rootstocks are rapidly becoming available. "Virus-free" strains of M.9 appear to be somewhat more difficult to root than the standard, virus-infected M.9 strains. Trees budded on "virus-free" M.9 are somewhat more vigorous than those on infected M.9 roots. If further tests confirm this tendency of "clean" trees to be more vigorous, then this could be regarded as a liability.

MANAGEMENT PROBLEMS WITH CLONAL STOCKS

Anchorage. With the size-control rootstock, anchorage can become a major problem. Rootstock anchorage problems must fit the orchard site and soil. Many free-standing M.7 trees at Geneva, New York on a deep well-drained soil have shown no "leaners" during 18 years of heavy production of McIntosh/M.7, Delicious/M.7, and Cortland/M.7. On other sites they have shown many "leaners." But the trees may become standard-size on good soils.

Regardless of soil type, apparently only MM.111 will produce a well-anchored tree. For M.9, tree support is commercially necessary. On certain soils and/or with certain varieties, it is necessary to support M.26 and M.7.

Four different types of support systems can be considered:

1. *Temporary basal support* may be needed on the M.7. A stake 2 feet in the ground, with a foot or more above, is adequate to prevent "pocket formation" (due to wind) around the lower trunk and stabilize the root system.

2. Permanent basal support should be provided trees of vigorous varieties on M.26 roots on strong soils. A 6-foot treated (against rot) pole can be cut into two excellent 3-foot stakes.

3. Permanent *poles or stakes* are only economically practical, if at all, for about 500 or more trees/A on M.9 roots, as in the "slender spindle" of the Dutch; such a program also may be appropriate for trees on M.26 roots. This 8- or 9-foot pole supports the crop during years when the developing central leader lacks diameter for structural strength. The tree top is pruned out each year, and a *weak lateral* is used as the leader and tied to the support, preventing an overgrowth of the top.

4. Another support for M.9 trees is *wire trellis* which supports the bearing scaffolds and makes it easier to keep scaffolds in a narrow row. The trellis *requires substantially smaller capitalization* per hectare than does the pole system; the trellis may be especially attractive with very vigorous cultivars, such as Mutsu on M.9.

Soils. In general, two types of soil problems are accentuated with clonal stocks: (1) All of the common clonal rootstocks, except M.13, are sensitive to "wet feet", M.26 and MM.106 appear to be sensitive. (2) A hardpan 12 to 24 inches below the surface stops the downward extension of the root system; M.7 is especially sensitive to such a barrier.

Several glacial outwash and beach soils are excellent for all stocks if irrigation is supplied. Even with irrigation, though, truly droughty types are not suitable for M.9, M.26, and M.7. MM.111 is the more tolerant. A soil with a shallow hardpan barrier should never be planted to M.7, which has a tap-root tendency. Thus, the MM.111 rootstock with a full-dwarfing interstem looks promising.

On shallow-rooting soils, as in Australia, the top soil is graded into ridges one to three feet high on which the trees are planted. This system also can be used for sites that tend to be "damp". Drainage is arranged for row middles. (Fig. 6)

Variety/Rootstock Interactions. Poor anchorage has commonly been reported for Delicious/M.9 and Delicious/M.7 trees on marginal sites, while McIntosh is well anchored. Earlier cropping on McIntosh seems to stem growth of the top with more strength going to root development.

Most reported cases of stock/scion incompatibility are now known to have been virus-related. Of the stem pitting, rubbery wood, trunk-twisting types, Golden Delicious and Spartan may show this.

Clean breaks at the union have been observed in Wayne/M.9 and Wayne/M.26 plantings due to disoriented vascular tissues of genetic incompatibility. It seldom appears in trees more than 4 or 5 years old. Breaks are rare in supported trees.

Longevity and Rotation. Under proper management, orchards on these clonal stocks are long-lived. At Geneva, there are trees on M.9 45 years old, near Wooster, Ohio, 27 yrs. old, McIntosh/M.2, 29 years, and Red Delicious, Cortlandt, McIntosh, and Monroe on M.7, 18 years old. But with dwarfs, blocks can be replanted and into production in 3 to 4 years.

Winter Hardiness. In most western New York orchards, e.g., that lie near a lake, dependable and persistent snow cover greatly lessens the likelihood of winter injury to the rootstock. On most hilly sites, though, orchards are often swept completely free of snow.

Of the commercial clonal stocks available, M.26 is the hardiest; M.7 the least; and MM.111, M.9, and MM.106 intermediate. Still hardier clonal stocks include Ottawa 3, Hibernal, and Antonovka. Robusta 5 is very resistant to mid-winter cold, but starts activity too early in the spring. Breeding for cold-resistant and better rootstocks is underway in the U.S., Poland, Russia and England.

Tree Senescence. With very dwarfing rootstocks, such as M.9, and a precocious variety, as Idared and Jonathan, symptoms of aging may occur within 6 to 10 years.

There is a razor-edge balance between fruit production and tree growth for a few of the precocious varieties on precocious stocks. In high density systems, heavy early cropping of such trees can cause an initial loss in tree vigor so that future yields and fruit quality may be sacrificed. Invigorative pruning is necessary to maintain a reasonable balance between fruitfulness and growth; this will not only prevent senescence but will also contribute to better fruit quality and to avoidance of alternate bearing.

Tree Training and Pruning. In medium density orchards, especially those on M.2, MM.106, and MM.111, spring-type clothespins or circular wood toothpicks can be used to establish good crotch angles during the first two summers when shoots are tender, 4-8 inches. Early limb selection and encouragement helps to induce heavy, early fruiting and bring the tree spread to desired limits.

Full-dwarf trees are set close together to induce high early production. Much less attention to tree structure is required in the early years as compared with the big seedling-stock trees. The diminished pruning of the tree on dwarfing stocks leads to earlier fruit bud formation and much heavier production during the early years. With densities of 500 to 800 trees per acre, the grower cannot rely on pruning to correct overcrowding, because heavy pruning reduces yield. High density systems favor top growth which must be carefully removed each year; a 2-year-old scaffold is tied up to the post to serve as a new leader. The treatment minimizes growth response in the top of the tree and stimulates a modest growth in the lower parts. *Pruning emphasis is on renewal and on slowing the growth of the central leader.* The high density orchard (on M.9) requires far less pruning time per bushel; 8 hrs/A vs. 20 hrs. for MM.106 vs. 31 hrs. for seedling-rooted trees. Almost all the cuts are made with hand shears, so no elaborate pruning machinery is needed, and brush disposal is not a problem.

In high density plantings, miscalculation in spacing can ruin the production potential in a few years. If the trees are too close, more pruning is done that stimulates more growth and reduces yield. Spacing of Delicious/M.9 trees frequently has been too close because Delicious bears later and grows vigorously in early years. Golden Delicious, Jonathan and Idared on M.9 begin bearing very early, and the trees grow but little after the fourth or fifth year. On a given soil, Golden Delicious/M.9 and Idared/M.9 may do quite well at a 5-foot x 12-foot spacing, while Delicious/M.9 might require a 10-foot x 18-foot space. *Ringing* the trunks a month after bloom and/or Alar sprays should assist in inducing Delicious to bear earlier. Propping downward and tying limbs to trellis is effective.

High Investment Requirement. As the apple industry continues to move toward higher density plantings of smaller trees, with wire or pole support, the initial cost per acre will increase dramatically. However, this high initial capitalization is rapidly amortized in the well-managed high-density orchard. Rapid amortization increases in importance as land values and interest rates continue to rise.

During the early years of an orchard, high density plantings produce much more per hectare than do low density plantings. Throughout the life of the orchard, production costs per bushel are substantially lower for small trees because the big labor users — pruning, harvesting, and pest control costs — are lower. Gross profits during the first 10 years are directly related to orchard density.

Pollination. In orchards with definite row patterns and one-directional travel, the honey bees tend more to fly down the row, rather than across the rows. Unless there are *pollinator trees located within the row,* the chances of a bee encountering a pollinator tree are definitely diminished and pollination efficiency is decreased. There is twice as much crossing by bees from one row to another with a 10-foot alleyway down the row as with a 15-foot alley, so it is advisable to avoid excessive spacing between rows.

Spring Frost Hazards. A high percentage of the total bearing surface of a slender spindle tree on M.9 is near ground level. Usually, the frost hazard decreases as height above ground level increases.

If, for compelling reasons, a grower should elect to plant on a site on which spring frosts do occur, then the income potential of the high-density planting fully justifies the additional investment in a frost protection system.

Loss of a crop due to frost in the third or fourth growing season makes tree size control much more difficult throughout the life of the planting, and loss of two crops in succession virtually guarantees a permanent overcrowding problem. Overcrowding, in turn, leads inevitably to a depression in yield and a reduction in fruit quality.

The "Umbrella Effect". Trees on MM.106, M.7, M.26, and M.9 stocks usually set fruit on the central leader before it has enough girth to support the crop. This results in the leader being carried over to the side, with the branches assuming a weeping form. *Care should be exercised to limit the amount of fruit carried by the developing leader.* A petalfall spray of napthalenacetic acid + Sevin applied at low pressure with a light hand gun is very effective and will not remove the crop from the rest of the tree. Training the leader to a post or trellis wire also is effective.

Rootstocks in the Future. New rootstocks are becoming available. From the USSR, Budagovsky #118 appears a worthy competitor for M.7, especially where winter hardiness is a major factor. Ottawa 3 may be superior to M.26 for resistance to collar rot, to fire blight, and possibly to winter cold. The most promising candidate to replace M.9 appears to be the hardy Budagovsky 9, which is, unfortunately, infected with a considerable number of viruses and will not be commercially available until the clone is suitably sanitized. From England, the very dwarfing M.27 is in commercial channels. Compared with M.9, it is more dwarfing, nonsuckering, more easily propagated, less susceptible to fire blight, but otherwise similar. Tests are mainly as an interstock.

Rootstock breeding programs are receiving major emphasis at Geneva, East Malling, the USSR, and in Poland. The goals are resistance to critical diseases,

hardiness in the prevailing climate, tree-size control, good nursery behavior, and induction of early and heavy production. At Geneva, major resistance objectives are fire blight, collar rot, and WAA, with mildew a low priority. The free-standing M.7 dwarfing range is top priority.

General Management of Dwarf Trees. As the apple industry moves toward the intensive planting systems, good mangement is becoming critically important, compared with management using seedling-rooted trees at wide spacings. As orchard densities increase, greater consideration must be given to all the items that affect ultimate tree growth. Soil, rootstock, variety, and cultural practices, if not arranged and conducted in correct balance with the higher density systems, can cause the failure of a planting. Excessive growth, encouraged by a strong soil, or too long a non-fruiting period caused by poor cultural practices or late spring frosts, can throw such a planting system out of harmony. The seedling-rooted orchard could tolerate mistakes, yet only one such error might spell disaster to the high density system employing size-controlling rootstocks. The high density orchard on M.9 demands intensive management, but, paradoxically, fewer man-hours per bushel and per acre are required.

When a semi-dwarf tree is being shaken with an inertial shaker, the observer gains the impression that the tree has little chance of surviving. Rather wide experience has shown that there is little damage to the trees or future crops.

Wildlife Problems. Mice find the thick bark of close-planted M.9 trees, compared with seedling rootstocks or other vigorous growing rootstocks, a real "delicacy." Trees on M.9 must be protected with mouse guards and extra care given to other control procedures.

Pheasants, snails and ground pests may destroy much of the crop by feeding on low hanging fruit on M.9 trees. Wire trellising helps this to some extent. Also, deer feeding on M.9-rooted trees retards their growth and may spread fire blight.

Root Suckers. With knapsack sprayer, apply in midsummer 0.5% NAA alone or at 0.25% with adjuvant, as a "stretcher and spreader", at 0.5%.

Note: For references and other details, specific photographs, see the N. Y. Bull. No. 41 (Geneva) by Cummins and Norton and/or request recent material being issued.

Readers are encouraged to join the International Dwarf Fruit Tree Association, headquarters Horticulture Department, Michigan State University, East Lansing, 48823, USA, to receive regular newsletters, booklets, summaries, announcements of meetings, etc. Cost was $5 in 1982. Try to attend the three-day annual meetings in March and summer tours.

Review Questions

1. List 5 advantages of locating the fruit enterprise in a region where fruit growing is well established near large centers of population.
2. What is the most important climatic factor to consider in selecting a region for fruit growing? Why?
3. How do large deep bodies of water influence temperature conditions along the shore line?
4. What set of conditions would encourage adapting the planting to pick-your-own or roadside marketing or both?
5. What are the qualifications of a good orchard site?
6. What are the characteristics of a good orchard soil?
7. In colder regions, what tree fruits can be planted in spring or fall with about the same degree of success?
8. Discuss planting systems today for fruit trees.
9. What are the advantages and disadvantages of contour planting with terraces?
10. What factors govern the planting distance of fruit trees?
11. What type nursery tree for apple is desired today?
12. What is a double-worked tree? What are its advantages?
13. Define a certified tree, a clonal stock, an interstock, a "spurred" Red Delicious.
14. What are the advantages of semi-dwarf trees grafted on vegetatively uniform rootstocks? Discuss trends.
15. Briefly list the steps in properly planting a fruit tree.
16. What are the advantages and disadvantages of M.9, M.26, MM. 106, M.7 and MM. 111 as rootstocks and/or interstems. Set in table form if you wish.
17. What technique would you use to switch an orchard of standard large trees to one of semi-dwarfs?
18. Compare dwarf and standard size trees with respect to (a) disease, (b) insect, and (c) animal pest problems.

Suggested Collateral Readings
Sites, Rootstocks, Propagation (Chap. III)

ANON. Trees against wind (windbreaks). Pacific NW Bulletin No. 5. 38 pp. Contact Wash., Ore., or Utah Agr. Exp. Sta. for copy. Jan. 1962.

APPLES, Ministry of Agriculture, Fisheries and Food. Bull. 207. Her Majesty's Stationery Office, London. 200 p. 1972.

ATKINSON, David. Distribution and effectiveness of tree crop roots. Horticultural Reviews. Avi. Publ. Co. 2:424-90. 1980.

BALBOA-ZAVALA, ORLANDO and F.G. DENNIS, Jr. 1977. Abscisic acid and apple seed dormancy. J. Amer. Soc. HortSci. 102(5):633-637. 1977.

BARK, L. Dean. When to expect late-spring and early-fall freezes in Kansas. Kansas Agr. Exp. Sta. Bull. 415, 23 pp. December 1959.

BARDEN, J. A., and D. C. FERREE. Rootstock effects on photosynthesis, dark respiration, leaf weight, and transpiration of apple. J. Amer. Soc. HortSci. 104(4):526-528. 1979.

BENNETT, R. G. and W. G. NEWMAN. Rootstocks for fruit trees. Min. of Agri. and Food. Ontario, Can. Publ. 334. 1976.

BOTTS, R.R. Insurance for farmers. U.S.D.A. Farmers Bull. 2016. Request recent Bull.

CAMPBELL, A. I. Growth comparison young apple trees on virus-infected, healthy rootstocks. Jour. of HortSci. Vol. 46 No. 1 pages 13-16, Jan. 1971.

CAMPBELL, A. I. and R. A. GOODALL. Rootstocks for standard cider trees. Long Ashton Res. Sta., Rept. p. 219. 1977.

CARLSON, R. F. Root temperature effects on MM, Delicious seedlings. Proc. ASHS 86:41-45. 1965.

CARLSON, R. F. The Mark apple rootstock. Fruit Var. Jl. 35: 2. April 1981.

CARLSON, R. F. Int. Dw, Fr. Jr. Ass'n. (IDFTA) Proc. by year now avail. At Hort. Dept., Mi. St. Univ., E. Lansing, 48824. Members receive annual copies of proceedings.

CARLSON, R. F. Status and performance of 'M.26' Rootstock. Fruit Var. Journ. 28:71-72. 1974.

CHALMERS, D. et al. Productivity and mechanization of the Tatura trellis orchard. HortSci. 13(5):517-521. 1978.

CUMMINS, J.N. and H. S. ALDWINCKLE. Fire blight susceptibility of fruiting trees of some apple rootstock clones. HortSci. 8 (3):176. June 1973.

CURTIS, O. F. Jr. and J. N. CUMMINS. Simazine for production of rooted stoolshoots of MM.106. HortSci. 16:(4) 524-5. Aug. 1981.

CURTIS, O. F., Jr. D. R. RODNEY. Ethylene injury to nursery trees in cold storage. Proc. A.S.H.S. 60, 104, 1952.

CUTTING, C. V. and H. B. S. MONTGOMERY (eds.). More and better fruit with EMLA (virus-free wood). Long Ashton Res. Sta., Bristol, England, 29. p. 1973.

DOLL, C. C. Rabbit damage to interstem trees. Frt. Var. J. 32: 3. 67. July 1978.

DOWNY, Rob et al. Economics of high-density apple systems in W. New York. Cornell University, New York, 31 pp. 1974.

DOZIER, A. J., C. A. KOUSKOLEKAS, and E. L. MAYTON. Susceptibility of certain apple rootstocks to black root rot and woolly apple aphids. HortSci. 9(1):35. 1974.

DWARF fruit trees. Agricultural Research Service, Hort. Crops Research Branch. U. S. Dept. Agr. Leaflet 407. 1975.

EDMUNDSON, R. Hail on peaches, Fruit So. 1:(4) 120. May 1975.

FAUST, MIKLOS and C. B. SHEAR. Fine structure of the fruit surface of three apple cultivars. J. ASHS 97(3):351. May 1972.

FERREE, D. C. Rootstocks, propagation method, and transplanting on growth and flowering of young apple trees. J. Amer. Soc. HortSci. 101(6): 676-8. 1976.

FERREE, D. C. Performance of six cultivars on M.26. Fruit Var. 33(4):110-114. 1979.

FERREE, D. C. Apple interstems in 10 states. Fruit Var. J. 36:1 Jan. 1982.

FERREE, D. C. 15 apple cultivars on MM106, M26. Fruit Var. J. *32:2*. 40-2. 1978.

FOGLE, H. W. Identification of clones within four tree fruit species by pollen exine patterns, J. Amer. Soc. HortSci. 102(5):552-560. 1977.

FORSHEY, C.G. and D. C. ELFVING. Planting, early care of apple orchard. N.Y. St. Coll. of Agr. and Life Sci. Inform. Bull. 65. 19 pp. 1973.

FRITH, H. J. Frost protection in orchards using air from temperature inversion. Aust. J. Agr. Res. 2, 24, 1951.

GARDNER, R. G., et al. Fire blight resistance in the Geneva Apple Rootstock Breeding Program. J. ASHS 105(6):907-12; 912-16. 1980.

GOONEWARDENE, H. F., et al. Leaf pubescence in 'Delicious' Apple Strains. HortSci. 13(3):252-253. 1978.

HAMILL, A.S., R.E.C. LAYNE, and F.G. VON STRYK. Weed control in fruit tree nursery with herbicide-impregnated string. HortSci. 10:587-588. 1975.

HAUT, I. C. After ripening and germination of fruit-tree seed. Maryland Agr. Exp. Sta. Bull. 420, 1938.

HEINICKE, D. R. High-density apple orchard management, etc. USDA Ag. Hndb. 458, 34 p. 1975.

HUTCHINSON, ALECK. Dwarf Apple Trees on EMIX Rootstock: 30 year trial. Ann. Rpt. Hort. Res. Inst., Vineland, Ontario. 1970.

HUTCHINSON, A. A. 13-year study with certain Malling Merton and other apple rootstocks. Ontario Dept. of Agric. & Food, Vineland Sta., Reports, 1968. 1970.

HUTCHINSON, ALECK. Rootstocks for fruit trees. Canada Vineland Station. Min. of Agr., Ontario, Can. Publ. 334. 1976.

INTERNATIONAL Horticulture Congress Proceedings. See particularly 1962, '66, '70, '74 and subsequent proc. for dwarf trees, growth regulators, etc., and World Research in these areas. Meeting (every 4 yrs.) in Hamburg, Germany 1982; in Davis, Ca. 1986.

JACKSON, J. E. Light interception and utilization by orchard systems. Hort. Rev., Avi. Publ. Co. 2:208-67. 1980.

KAYS, S.J. and C.W. NICKLOW. Plant competition: Influence of density on water requirements, soil gas composition and soil compaction. HortSci. 99 (2): 166. March 1974.

KERR, A. Soil microbiological studies on agrobacterium radiobacter and biological control of crown gall. Soil Sci. 118:168-172. 1974.

KOLESNIKOV, V.A. The root system of fruit plants. In English, very good. Mir Publishers, Moscow USSR, 269 pages, 1971.

LAMB, R.C. The N.Y. State Fruit Testing Coop. Ass'n. — 60 years of new fruit varieties. Fruit Var. J. 33(3):91-94. July 1979.

LAPINS, K.O. Inheritance of compact growth type in apple. J. of Amer. Soc. for HortSci. 101(2):133-5. Mar. 1976.

LARSEN, F. E. and G. D. LOWELL. Tree Fruit Nursery Stock Defoliation. HortSci. 12(6):580-2. 1977.

LARSEN, F. E. Branching stimulation in nursery stock with ethyl 5-(4)chlorophenyl)-2H-tetrazole-2-acetate. J. Amer. Soc. HortSci. 102(6):770-773. 1979.

LARSEN, F. E. Stimulation of leaf abscission of tree fruit nursery stock with ethephon — surfactant mixtures. J. ASHS 98(1):34. 1973.

LARSEN, Fenton E. The relation of apple scion and rootstock to longitudinal trunk bark cracking. HortSci. 7(6):564. 1972.

LUCKWELL, L. C. Hormone production by the developing apple seed. J.H.S. 28, 14, 1953.

MARTIN, D. Variation among apple fruits. Aust. J. Agr. Res. 4, 235, 1953; Between trees, 5, 9, 1954.

MORI, H., Editor. Science of apple growing (Ringo Saibai Zensho). Asakura Co., Tokyo (in Japanese). 1958.

MULLINS, C. A. and D. W. LOCKWOOD. Selected new summer apple cultivars in Tenn. Fruit Var. J. 33(3):94-96. July 1979

NAGASAWA, K. Modern fruit growing (Kajyu Engei Shinsetsu). Asakura Co., Tokyo (in Japanese). 1953.

NELSON, S. H. and H. B. TUKEY. Temperature responses of apple rootstocks. J. H. S. 31, 55, 1956.

NORTON, RICHARD L. Western N.Y. Coop. Ext. Spec. High-Density Apple Planting Using Clonal Rootstocks. N.Y. (Cornell) Agr. Exp. Sta., 1971 (Several spot reports) contact Co. Agr. Agts. Office, Rochester, N. Y. for latest rpts.

PARTRIDGE, N. L. and J. O. VEATCH. The relationship between soil profile and root development of fruit trees. Mich. Agr. Quar. Bull. Vol. XIV. 1932.

PLICH, H. and E. S. HEGAZI. Induction of "feathers" in apple trees in the nursery. Fruit Sci. Reports. Skierniewice, Poland IV: (2). 1977 11-21. 1977.

PRESTON, A. P. Malling-Merton rootstocks. J.H.S. 30, 25, 1955.

PRESTON, A.P. Tree growth on clonal stocks planted with and without roots. J. HortSci. 47: 329-35, 1972.

PROCTOR, J. T. A. Planning and planting the orchard. University of Guelph, Ontario, Canada. Publ. 528. 1979.

PROEBSTING, E. L. Soil temperature and root distribution. Proc. A.S.H.S. 43, 1, 1943.

ROACH, S. C. AND G. E. DAVIS. Height at which trunks should be measured, Ann. Rpt. E. Mall. Res. Sta. 1953 ('54).

ROACH, W. A. Rootstocks and mineral nutrition. Ann. Rept. East Malling Res. Sta. for 1946.

ROGERS, W. S., and M. S. Parry. Effects of deep planting on anchorage and performance of apple trees. J. Hort. Sci. 43, 103-6, 1968.

ROGERS, W. S. Growth and cropping of clonal-root apple trees on five soils. J. Pom. and H. S. 22, 209, 1946.

ROOSJE, G. S. Experiences in handling high-density apple orchards. Res. Sta. for Fr. Growing. Wilhelminadorp, Netherlands. Write Dr. Roosje for publ. list. 1960's-70's.

ROM, Roy C. and S.A. BROWN. Cultivar and interstem on apple rootstock sprouting: control with NAA. Fruit. Varieties Journal. Vol. 31, July 1977, No. 3, pp. 54-56. 1977.

ROM, R. C. and S. A. BROWN. Factors affecting burrknot formation on clonal Malus rootstocks. HortSci. 14(3):231-232. June 1979.

ROSS, N. W. and J. L. MEYER, orchard preplant land preparation; new and replant sites. California Agriculture (June): 12-14. 1975.

SAX, KARL. Interstock effects in dwarfing fruit trees. Proc. A.S.H.S. 62: 201-204, 1953.

SAX, K. STOCK and scion relationship in graft incompatibility. Proc. Amer. Soc. Hort. Sci. 64: 156-158. 1954.

SCOTT, K. G. and A. R. BELCHER. Living windbreaks: a review of work at Long Ashton. Long Ashton Research Station, Report. p. 204. 1977 England.

SEELEY, E. J., et al. Influence of rootstock and strain on performance of 'Delicious' and 'Golden Delicious' apple. J. ASHS 104(1):80-83. 1979.

SHAW, J. K. Malling rootstocks and American apple trees. Proc. A.S.H.S. 48, 166, 171, 1946.

SIMONS, ROY. Frost injury on Golden Delicious apples — morphological and anatomical characteristics of russeted and normal tissue. A.S.H.S. 69: 48-55. 1957.

SNIR, Iona, and Ammon Erez. In Vitro propagation of Malling Merton apple rootstocks. HortSci. 15(5):597-598. 1980.

SNYDER, D.P. Enterprise analysis: a guide for determining fruit crop costs and returns. N.Y. State Coll. of Agric. and Life Sci. (Cornell) Mar. 1976.

STOUFFER, R. F. et al. The 'Nittany' Apple resistant to York spot. HortSci. 13(3):306-7. 1978.

STUSHNOFF, CECIL, GERALD HARRIS. An electronic system for acquisition and evaluation of fruit breeding data. Hort. Science 9(1):16. 1974.

THOMPSON, W. K., D. G. NICHOLS, and D. L. JONES. Chilling requirements of the apple 'Stoke Red'. Aust. J. of Exp. Agr. and Animal Husb. 14:702-704. 1974.

TISCORNIA, J. R. and F. E. LARSEN. Rootstocks for apple and pear — a literature review. Wash. Agr. Exp. Sta. Cir. 421. 45 pp. mimeo. July, 1963.

TUKEY, H. B. and K. D. BRASE. The dwarfing effect of an intermediate stem-piece of Malling IX apple. Proc. Am. Soc. Hort. Sci. 42:357-364, 1943.

TUKEY, R. B., et al. Malling rootstocks during 12 years. Proc. A.S.H.S. 64, 146, 154.

TUKEY, H.B. Sr. Dwarfed fruit trees. The Macmillan Book Co., New York City. 562 pp. 1964. 1978. (Reprint, 1964).

UTERMARK, H. Growing, mkting. apples, Elbe River Valley, W. Germany. 38-48. 10:Intern. Dw. Fr. Tr. Ass'n. June 1977.

VALLI, V. J. F. Freeze Prevention in Appalachian Fruit Region. The Mountaineer Grower, Martinsburg, W. Va. No. 283, pp. 3-22. 1970.

WERNER, E. M. and A. A. BOE. In Vitro propagation of M7 Rootstock. HortSci. 15:(4):509. Aug. 1980.

Note: Agricultural Experiment Stations with considerable experience in dwarfing rootstock studies are: E. Malling Res. Sta. (ask for publication list), Kent, England; Long Ashton Res. Sta., Bristol, England; Mich. State University (E. Lansing); New York (Geneva); British Columbia (Summerland); Pennsylvania (Univ. Park), and Res. Sta. for Fruit Growing, Wilhelminadorp, The Netherlands.

(See additional references in former book editions.)

Pruning Apple Trees

Annual pruning, and we emphasize *annual,* is probably the most important operation in the orchard to get good size, color and quality fruit. Annual pruning also reduces the need for thinning fruit. It provides for better spray and light penetration, improving fruit quality and annual cropping.

Much of the apple tree acreage over the world is still of the standard size trees of about 28 to 60 trees/acre, but the newer plantings are largely high-density compact trees of around 75-500-1,000 or more trees/acre. Hence the discussion of tree training and pruning in this chapter is still more or less slanted toward the standard trees, although, actually the principles discussed are applicable to either the standard or compact trees. Machine management of both standard and compact trees is dictating a shift in the tree spacing designs, the training of young trees and the ultimate pruning of the mature trees. With compact spur-type trees kept in good bearing starting at 2 to 3 yrs. of age, pruning is reduced by as much as 80% compared with standard size trees.

The new approach, of course, is to reduce labor costs and problems, and still get a profitable marketable product either for the fresh or the processing trade. As the "bugs" are gradually worked out of machine management of fruit trees, it is quite likely that as good or a better quality product can be placed on the market. Use of this more expensive equipment, however, will be limited for the most

part to the large-acreage growers. Medium to smaller acreage growers are using pole pruners, loppers and chain saws. Some are contracting the pruning job annually.

The kind and amount of pruning to be done on a tree will depend upon (1) the age, (2) existing framework, (3) condition of bark and wood, (4) growth characteristics, and (5) fruiting habits of the variety.

Season for pruning. Most of the tree pruning has been done during the dormant season (no leaves) for the following reasons: (1) The branches can be seen easily at that time; (2) other orchard operations are less pressing; (3) there is less danger of pulling the bark away from pruning wounds; and (4) pruning goes well with cool weather. Dr. A. P. Preston, England, and H. Utermark, W. Germany, have shown that mid to late summer pruning has many benefits without inducing late growth.

The best time to start the pruning will depend upon the size of the job and amount of labor available. It is more hazardous to prune in late fall and early winter than later in the dormant season, because evidence has shown that extremely cold temperatures following the pruning operation, even within hours, are likely to result in serious freezing injury to the trees. It is better, if the situation will permit, to wait until late winter when there is less danger of extremely cold temperatures. The mature apple trees should be pruned first and the young trees last, because the latter are more succulent and somewhat more subject to freezing injury. Actually, pruning wounds heal best if the cuts are made at about the time when active growth begins in the spring, but the job can be done this late only when

---

[1]Dr. William J. Lord made suggestions for revision of this chapter, from Univ. of Mass., Amherst.

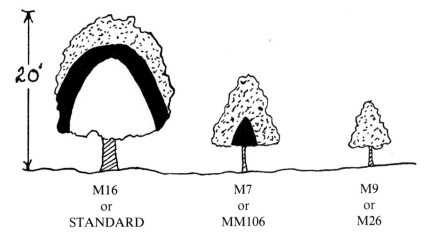

Figure 1. (left) On large standard-size fruit tree (a) speckled area is productive, (b) black is partly productive, (c) white is unproductive "cordwood." Center tree is semi-compact showing productive and partly productive areas, no unproductive volume. Right tree is full dwarf showing total productive area. Densely planted full-dwarf trees are generally the most productive/A. Good sunlight penetration is main factor influencing productiveness, marketable fruit quality and profitableness of compact trees. About 50% or more light penetration throughout the tree is needed. (After Don Heinicke, Ione, Wash.; R. L. Norton, Cornell Univ.) Grower trend in the USA is toward semi-dwarf apple on seedling or clonal stocks with spur tops, freestanding.

M16 or STANDARD   M7 or MM106   M9 or M26

Figure 2. Among the pruning tools used in the orchard are those pictured above plus hand-operated hydraulically powered clippers on portable scaffolds, "squirrels" on the ground. Lightweight hand tools used may be, "A", pole saws or, "G", pole pruners; "B", loppers for peach or apple; "C", mini-loppers for grapes, bushes, small trees; hand shears "D" or "E" for small-wood cuts or "F", a folding pull saw. ("B-F," Corona Clipper Co., P. O. B. 730, Corona, Calif., 91720; "A," A. M. Leonard & Son, Piqua, O., 45356; "G," Seymour Smith & Son, Oaksville, Conn., 06779; below, Miller-Robinson, P.O.B. 2886, Santa Fe Springs, Calif., 90670. Orchard Equipment Co., Conway, Ma. 01341 has one of the better pole pruners.

there is a limited number of trees. Generally, it is better to play safe and start early so that the job is completed and the brush removed before spraying starts. Pruning can be performed through and shortly after the blossoming period in an emergency.

With young or compact trees it may be advisable to do a small amount of summer training or power-mower pruning to assist the tree in assuming a better shape and to prevent it from making unnecessary growth in undesired places. During periods of severe labor shortage, a certain amount of pruning can be done at apple thinning time by using pole pruners and loppers and removing with medium cuts the excessive twig growth along with some apples. At this season, the nonfruiting and weak wood can be spotted easily and removed. In early summer, it is good practice to "mop-off" the succulent water sprouts that arise on the trunks and main limbs of mature trees. This reduces aphid accumulation and the added need for nutrients and water. This can be done by hand, using leather gloves.

Some mid-summer detail pruning is being studied and used by growers to admit more light for fruit coloring, route calcium into fruit rather than shoot tips, and reduce bitter pit and corking. Hand shears and small loppers are used and some mower trimming. Summer pruning is common in West Europe. Research indicates some loss in fruit sugars at harvest.

Pruning equipment. The skill with which an operator uses pruning tools is probably more important than the tools he uses. However, the fact cannot be overlooked that good tools in first-class condition and which can be handled nimbly will offer the workmen every possible advantage in doing a rapid and high quality job with less

effort. For young trees, light maneuverable loppers and a "half-moon" saw are usually sufficient (Figure 2). For older trees, the same equipment can be used plus pole pruners or long-handled motor-driven 6"-8" circular saws on maneuverable squirrels (Figures 2 and 3).

In commercial practice the compressed-air or pneumatic pruners with portable scaffold or a squirrel are becoming common equipment for cutting labor costs to about one-third[1]. Squirrels speed the pruning, picking, etc., up to 50% faster (medium-small orchards).

Buy better quality pruning tools that are strong, lightweight, stay sharp longer, and are less tiring. Experienced contract teams are using light pole pruners (aluminum with cable inside tube) doing most of work from the ground. Trend is to "work" the taller trees down so most of the pruning can be done from the ground or 6-8 ft. step ladders. Wear rubber sole/heel boots to reduce limb scarring, if climbing trees (Figure 6).

Making the cut. Use sharp tools at all times to make cuts clean and smooth. Ragged cuts heal slowly and often poorly. In removing large branches, make the cut close and parallel to the supporting limb (Figure 4). Large stubs do not heal and result in decay which may eventually enter the trunk of the tree and weaken the entire structure. Small stubs left on the periphery of the tree, however, have caused no serious problem.

[1]Contact Dept. of Agr. Eng., Cornell Univ., Ithaca, N.Y. 14850 for plans for building scaffolds; for squirrels, Inland Industries, 16166 SW 72 Ave., Portland, Ore. 97223 or 279 Ortley Dr., NE, Atlanta, Ga. 30324; for pneumatic tools, Robinson Industries, 11845 Burke St., Santa Fe Springs, Ca. 90670 or see July issue of American Fruit Grower magazine, 37841 Euclid Av., Willoughby, Oh. 44094.

Figure 3. So-called "squirrel" equipment can speed pruning up to 50% faster on the taller trees. However, tall trees should be "worked" down in two or three years to a height accessible with an 8-ft. ladder. See Figure 5.

Use both hands wherever possible. Cut with one hand and hold the limb to be removed with the other, steadily pushing the limb away from the blade as the cutting proceeds. Less "fist" strength is required with hand shears when the cutting is done in this manner. In using hand or lopping shears, place the cutting blades at the side or below the crotch (but not in the crotch) to secure the best cut. Never wiggle the shears left and right (up and down is okay) through a cut. This results in a ragged wound and may "spring" the shears.

If the orchard has been trained properly from the beginning, there is little or no need for removing large limbs, which is a practice to be avoided as much as possible. However, there are times when this must be done and the following procedure is recommended. Use a saw, making three separate cuts. Small and/or medium size light-weight chain saws are quick with little effort if many cuts are to be made. The first shallow cut is made on the lower side of the limb about eight inches from the base of the limb. Thence, cut from above, starting about two inches closer to the base of the limb than the lower cut and continue until the limb falls. This prevents the limb from tearing bark or splitting down the trunk. The third cut is made close to the supporting limb to remove the stub.

Types of Cuts. Shoot and spur growth is stimulated around a cut, but growth elsewhere in a mature tree is little affected. The cut at "a" in Figure 5 (right) is called a *"heading-back cut"* and is used (a) on nursery whips about two feet above ground to force out laterals to form tree framework if the nursery tree is not already "feathered" (with side branches) and (b) on young and compact trees to correct long "leggy" growth at the periphery of the tree.

Thinning-out and bulk pruning. The term "thinning-out" in pruning is used where entire branches are removed. If these branches are large limbs, such pruning is termed "bulk" pruning. The principle behind this pruning is to admit more light and to remove unproductive branches which are producing few if any desirable fruit. See Figure 6 for a system of opening large apple trees to admit light and lower the tree to 10-12 ft. over 2-3 yrs. so most of the work can be done from the ground or short step ladders.

Bear in mind that poor flowering and fruiting on lower limbs is due to inadequate light reaching them. Try to provide for good light throughout the tree by thinning out the top.

Thin-wood pruning. The term "thin-wood" pruning has been used by the Michigan Agricultural Experiment Station, and it refers to the removal of slow-growing, weak, underhanging branches or spurs which are either not fruiting or producing fruit of low quality. Such wood is classified arbitrarily as any four-year-old apple wood less than one-quarter-inch in diameter at the base of the fourth-year annual "ring" (a group of bud scale scars where growth started each spring). The wood is said to be intermediate in vigor if it is four years old, has a diameter between one-quarter- and three-eighths-inch in diameter; and it is productive or thick in diameter if over three-eighths-inch near the base. Data from Michigan show that the thick apple branches produce at least ten times as many desirable apples as the thin-wood branches. Varieties differ in the amount of thin-wood they should be allowed to support. It will vary, also, with the location of this wood

Figure 4. This close smooth cut is made properly. Note that it is healing satisfactorily. Avoid leaving stubs when removing the larger branches. Small stubs left over the tree are not important.

Figure 5. (Left) A small maneuverable chain saw can be used by one man ahead of pruning crew to remove dead and undesirable large limbs, or to disect a bulldozed-out tree. (Right) Heading-back cut was made at "a" the year preceding, resulting in several side shoots. Used on nursery whips to force laterals for tree framework and on dwarfs to subdue undesirable growth or dwarf a shoot competing with the leader limb and to subdue the leader once it has reached its desired height. (Homelite, P.O. Box 7047, Charlotte, N.C. 28217; Ohio State Univ., resp.). See Figure 20 for effect of placement of heading-back cut on subsequent shoot and spur development.

on the tree, and other conditions.

The brush pile should consist mostly of thin-wood and branches which are "fruited out" and poorly located. Thin-wood usually develops on the oldest wood in the center of the tree and on branches nearest the ground. Thin wood can be detected best by standing next to the tree trunk at harvest and looking upward and outward and studying which type of wood is carrying the small poor-quality fruit.

Cutting to lateral branches. Many of the cuts in pruning are of this type. A limb is shortened by cutting to a lateral branch, making the cut in line with the side branch, as shown in Figure 8. The main objective of this type of pruning is to keep the sides of the tree within bounds and to lower the tops of tall trees so that they are within easy and more economical range for pruning, spraying, thinning and harvesting. Also, branches that droop to the ground, or, those which grow closely parallel on top of other limbs are often cut back by this method to an upward or outward-growing lateral. Such cuts do not dwarf the branch as much as heading-back cuts, nor do they induce many side branches to appear, and this is par-

Figure 6. Expensive-to-manage large apple trees can be lowered to 10-12 ft. by removing one or two large limbs from the center over a 2-3 yr. period. Other limbs also are gradually removed to admit light and bring lower limbs into fruiting, as Eric Gunn of England is doing here at the Annual Dwarf Fruit Tree Meeting, Grand Rapids, Mich. A small chain saw is used and wounds are sprayed with an NAA compound to discourage sprouts. (Courtesy The Great Lakes Fruit Grower News, Sparta, Mich.)

Correction of weak crotches. Figure 7 shows an apple tree split apart as a result of three limbs of equal size being allowed to develop with narrow-angled crotches. It is important that no side or scaffold branch be permitted to develop as fast as the central leader limb. If a fast-growing side branch has a wide angle in the crotch, is properly located, and worth keeping, its rate of growth can be checked by pruning it back and thinning out the remaining laterals. Such pruning will assist in dwarfing it to a lateral, and permitting the leader limb to grow upward and a few inches ahead of all side limbs.

Summer pruning. In Western Europe, Dr. Hellmut Utermark (see reference) lists advantages of summer pruning: (1) Better illumination of leaves and improved assimilation in center of trees, (2) better illumination of fruits and better fruit color; (3) better fruit quality and storage; (4) slower total growth of trees; (5) less wood production; (6) less total pruning effort and improved work efficiency in summer; (7) possibility of reducing crown volume of tree, better utilization of space, more trees per acre; less need for restraining rootstocks; and (8) less danger of winter injury by frost cracks on stems. Dr. Utermark places emphasis on winter pruning by saw and summer pruning by hand shears. He prunes in early August by cutting back to fruiting spurs, causing little or no regrowth. After system is established, they take 10 hrs/acre in winter and 40 hrs in summer at a slack work period. Summer pruning induces earlier flowering by

Figure 7. An apple tree split three ways with a heavy crop because of equal-size branches arising at the same point on the trunk. This is the result of improper training methods when the tree was young. (Cornell University.)

ticularly true if the lateral shown at "L" in Figure 8 is almost the same size as the branch removed. It is poor practice to remove a relatively large limb back to a weak growing lateral. But with *compact* trees it is highly important to cut back to *weak side limbs* at the periphery of the tree to discourage the tree from becoming too big and to slow extension growth.

Detail pruning. This is a common practice and refers to the removal of small branches (not necessarily thin-wood) with the cuts well distributed over the length of limb. Both cuts in Figure 8 are classified under detail pruning. The main purpose is to prevent the small limbs, especially on the outer portion of large limbs, from becoming thick, crowded, and forming a canopy more or less over the center of the tree, shading it too much. A special advantage of detail pruning during the dormant season is that excessive flower buds and leaf buds are removed, thus improving the size and color of fruit developing from the remaining fruit buds. This pruning is particularly valuable when done in advance of an expected heavy crop. To some extent it takes the place of hand thinning of fruit in early summer. Popular varieties which tend to respond well to detail pruning are Yellow Transparent, Golden Delicious, Rome Beauty, Jonathan, Wealthy, Cortland.

Figure 8. A limb is shortened by cutting to a strong lateral, as shown at L. This type of cut is used to keep a tree from becoming too tall or too wide. (Ohio State Univ.) Cuts are made back to weak side limbs on the leader of compact trees to control height.

about 3 days. Research in Virginia shows less fruit sugar on summer-pruned trees.

Treating pruning wounds and cankers. Wound dressings are needed only for cuts larger than about two inches in diameter. The sun is probably as good a disinfectant as any for the smaller cuts. There are several good wound dressings on the market which should be applied only to the exposed wood and *not* to the bark or healing area. Water asphalt emulsions, used for roofing paint, are inexpensive and effective, but take caution against toxic ingredients as creosote. "Tre-Hold" by AmChem Co. or black latex paint with 2% NAA sprayed on wounds inhibits sprouts, encourages healing (Fig. 6).

In case of large diseased cankers on limbs and trunks, make a cigar-shaped or pointed cut which reaches live bark on all sides. Cuts through the bark should be vertical, not sloping; the latter retards healing. Wound dressings should be made during the dormant season, preferably in late dormancy together with necessary top-working and bridge-grafting.

In case of cankers of fire blight, bitter rot, and black rot, those limbs should be removed which are dead or have been two-thirds or more girdled by the disease. Such diseases are easily spread from one tree to the next by carry-over cankers. Remove blighted limbs 6 to 8 inches below diseased areas. Leave small cankered areas and treat both with antiseptic solution[1].

Some growers "cook" the canker with a blow-torch to the "bubbling" stage a few inches above and below "blight line" to cauterize limbs, with reportedly good success.

Effects of pruning on growth and production of young trees. There is a close relationship between the activities of the roots and the activities of the leaves of fruit plants which must be considered to understand the results from pruning. The raw materials used by the leaves in manufacturing the tree's food supply come from the soil and from the air. The water and essential mineral nutrients are absorbed from the soil by the roots. From the air the leaves absorb carbon dioxide through the open stomata (Figure 10). In the leaves, largely among the mesophyll cells, the carbon dioxide from the air and the water from the soil combine in the presence of sunlight and green coloring (chlorophyll) to form starches and sugars. This process is known as photosynthesis. The mineral nutrients from the soil then combine with the carbohydrates to form the proteins and other plant foods which are used in the growth processes of the tree. The greater the amount of healthy leaf surface on a young tree, the faster it is capable of growing, gaining the desired size and carrying an early crop of fruit.

Pruning has a dwarfing effect on young trees. The greater the amount of pruning, the greater the dwarfing effect on the tree. This has been demonstrated clearly by many experiment stations (Figure 11) and has been readily seen in the orchards by commercial fruit growers. It is true that one gains the impression that pruning stimulates shoot growth, but this will occur only near the cut. Under these

---

[2]Apply the following antiseptic solution to fire blight cankers, using a small paint brush: Add one quart of hot water to four tablespoons of concentrated hydrochloric acid in an enamel kettle, and in this mixture, dissolve nine pounds of dry zinc chloride powder. Commercial grades of these chemicals can be secured at the local drug store. Add sufficient red or blue coloring, or any good dye, so that diseased areas can be checked for good coverage. After cooling, pour the above solution into seven pints of denatured alcohol and mix well. Store in tightly stoppered glass bottles or jugs to prevent evaporation.

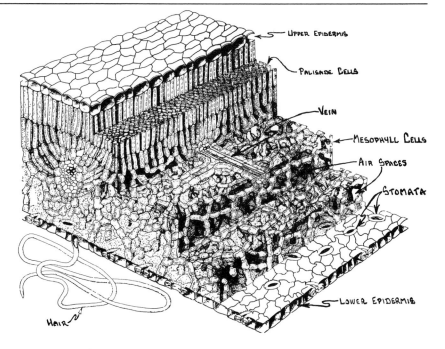

Figure 10. A cross section of an apple leaf magnified many times, showing the principal parts. Food materials for tree growth and fruit production are manufactured in the leaves. Heavy pruning should be limited. It reduces the "manufacturing centers" (leaves) of the tree.

UPPER EPIDERMIS

PALISADE CELLS

VEIN

MESOPHYLL CELLS

AIR SPACES

STOMATA

LOWER EPIDERMIS

HAIR

Figure 11. Pruning is a dwarfing process. These 27-year Stayman Winesap trees show different growth responses following variations in pruning. The large tree at the left has never been pruned, the tree in the center has received moderate pruning, while the tree at the right has been given heavy annual pruning. Average yield in pounds per tree for the ten-year period, 1933-1942, was for the unpruned tree — 533, for the lightly pruned tree — 606, and for the heavily pruned tree — 467. Fruit from the unpruned (left) tree was small with a large percentage in the low grades. In recent years increased trees per acre have necessitated heavier pruning to keep trees in bounds and to get a greater percentage of large extra fancy fruit. (Ohio Agr. Exp. Sta.)

conditions, the top has been reduced in comparison with the roots and there is relatively more nutrients and water available to the remaining shoots. Experiments have shown that the total shoot growth for all terminals over a pruned tree, however, is less than if the tree had not been pruned. This effect is accumulative and after a period of four or five years with young trees, it is clearly evident that the unpruned trees are larger than the pruned trees, depending upon how much pruning was done. Light annual pruning, only for the purpose of training the tree, however, has little effect in delaying bearing.

The best way to induce early bearing of trees is to bend the limbs outward by trellis or on free-standing trees by use of spreaders made from stiff wire or wood splints with headless sharpened nails driven in the ends. Splints can be prepared inside on rainy or bad days and set in place in the crotches later. This requires hand labor but it is worth it.

TRAINING YOUNG APPLE TREES

The ideal tree. It is generally agreed among horticultural specialists and growers that the *modified-leader type* of tree is the strongest and easiest to manage for free-standing standard-size orchard trees. It consists of a central trunk around which scaffold or side branches, of the desired number and spacing, can be arranged with wide-angle crotches. It is difficult to point out an ideal tree-framework in the orchard since each variety and tree tends to grow differently. There are three to five scaffold branches arising from the central leader trunk. This is about the right number of scaffold limbs for a mature bearing tree. The central leader is then "modified," or cut to a side limb, at about 5 ft. above the ground so that it no longer grows straight up but has been diverted outwardly. By so doing, the tree will be kept relatively lower and within better reach from the ground. Also, the top center of the tree has been thinned out for light to enter

throughout the inside and lower portions of the tree. For machinery usage the lowest limb is about 18-24 inches from the ground and the other scaffold limbs are spaced vertically about six to 10 inches apart around the trunk so that each has a definite section of the tree into which it can grow. In developing a tree, keep in mind the need for open areas in the sides of the tree to place step ladders for pruning and harvesting. The entire system is adapted to shake-catch machine harvesting and to chemical weed and mouse control.

Jonathan, McIntosh, Cortland and Stayman have a spreading growth habit. Some varieties such as Delicious, Rome and Northern Spy tend to grow upright and it is somewhat more difficult to attain the desired framework. Delicious in Washington have produced longer on large trees where about three main limbs form the tree, ac-

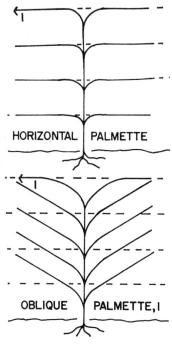

Figure 12. Low-wire trellis training of full-dwarf trees (on EM IX or 26) by horizontal palmette gives maximum growth suppression. Oblique palmette training fits natural growth pattern of tree. Both induce early bearing, are resistant to wind and heavy-crop damage, and are suitable for commercial and particularly the home planting. Use spur-type cions on fertile ground. (L. D. Tukey, Penn State University).

HORIZONTAL PALMETTE

OBLIQUE PALMETTE,I

46

Figure 12a. Spring-type clothes pins can be applied to tender shoots destined for main side limbs on the central leader limb, as shown. They hold limb at wide angle in formative stage to make the crotch strong, induce early fruiting. Round toothpicks, wires, stakes, etc., also can be used. Remove props as soon as limb is "set". (R.L. Norton, Cornell Univ.)

cording to the late John C. Snyder, pomologist. With semi-dwarf trees where crop leverage is less on the shorter limbs, more side limbs can be left.

Training Dwarf Trees. The smallest dwarfs (on e.g. M.9) are staked or trained on a trellis by any one of several systems. Semi-dwarfs, usually planted in a hedgerow, may be trained also by one of several methods. In dwarf trees, it is important that the *leader limb* be maintained ahead of other limbs. Research is showing that compact trees should be allowed to start fruiting as early as possible with any needed fruit thinning to prevent over-fruiting for their size. Forcing limbs to the horizontal or down encourages early fruiting. Wire trellis or use of clothes pins on tender shoots (Fig. 12a.) or splints with spiked ends aids in spreading branches out and down.

Hedgerows or Tree Walls. Hedgerow trees usually are trained to a *central leader* til they reach the desired height, then pruned back to a *weak* lateral each season. Ad-

Figure 13. Palmette training, common in upper Mediterranean countries, is essentially intermeshed fan-shaped trees with a leader and side limbs tied to and interwoven, using Canna poles and wire trellis w/posts. Management is facilitated. (Courtesy E. G. Christ, Rutgers University).

vantages are: (a) provides maximum trees per acre, (b) affords use of mechanical equipment for pruning, fruit thinning, and harvesting, and (c) easier and more efficient spray application. Adequate space must be provided between tree rows to operate machinery. Plant rows north and south for better light where feasible.

There are two types of hedgerows: (a) trees supported by individual posts or by a trellis. Where standard seedling or semidwarfing stocks on good soils are used for hedgerows, the best cion selection where available may well be the three-quarter size spur-type strains. (b) Trees are un-supported. This refers to cions on better-rooted stocks like M. 2, 7A, or 795 (below Equator), or MM 106, 104 or 111. M. 26 free-standing may be satisfactory w/some varieties on the stronger soils.

The so-called *"spindle bush"* is trained with (dwarfs) or without (semi-dwarfs) support posts with a central leader, straight, and with many small fruiting side branches. These branches are bent out and down by spreaders to induce early fruiting and wide crotches. Tree spread is controlled by cutting back ½ to ¾ths of the length of the shoots or back to weak laterals as in renewal peach pruning.

"Pillar" pruning consists of a central leader tree, un-supported on semidwarfing stock. Leader is cut back, part way each year for stiffening and forcing laterals. After 3 or 4 years growth and one fruiting year on a lateral, it is removed back to a stub. Hence, when mature, tree should have about an equal number of one, two, three, and four-year laterals. System works best when growth is carefully controlled by fertilizer and water since heavy cutting is stimulating.

Palmette pruning is used mostly in upper Mediterranean countries and consists of more or less interlocking hedgerow trees trained to trellis, fan shape, with tree row width a few feet thick, using poles interlaced with the limbs (Fig. 13). Branches lower than 18'' above ground are removed, leader is kept dominant by removing or heading back competitors, vigorous limbs are tied down (important for slow-bearing Delicious, Winesap, Newtown, and Tydeman's Early), overly vigorous leader is cut back to a weak lateral to force laterals below. See also training suggestions in Chap. III for dwarf trees.

Pruning one-year nursery trees at planting. Most of these trees come as whips with no branches except for a few varieties like York, Bramley's Seedling and Jonathan. With compact trees, today's nurserymen are being encouraged to provide "feathered" (branched) trees.

Tall whips are cut back to about 30 in., shoots are all allowed to attain 6-8 inches when the leader is cut back to a strong lateral, and the best wide-angle crotch shoots or limbs around the trunk are retained, the rest removed. On full-dwarf trees, side limbs may be needed at 15-18 inch level, necessitating cutting back leader to force out side limbs for the first tellis wire.

Figure 14. Two-yr. standard size apple tree before and after pruning at planting. The largest and best of two central limbs was retained for the leader and cut back to about 50 inches above ground. The tree was planted with the best wide-angled lateral toward prevailing wind; lateral was cut back two-thirds. All other laterals were removed because they arose too close together. (Ohio State University).

Deshooting one-year nursery trees. Some attention has been given to training one-year nursery trees by the deshooting method. After planting, the one-year trees are cut back as described above. When the leafy side shoots are about six inches long in early summer, select well-spaced, wide-angled shoots which will develop into a desirable scaffold system. Remove the undesired shoots. It is preferable to have the lowest branch on the southwest side or toward the prevailing winds. Where possible, the second branch is preferred on the southeast side; the third on the northwest; and the fourth continuing the trunk into the northeast section. This provides a main scaffold branch for each quarter of the tree. Try to leave eight to twelve inches of vertical distance between the wide-angled scaffold branches. It may take longer than one year to select the main scaffold limbs for a desirable system. With careful attention the first two or three years, some excellent scaffold systems can be developed by using this training method. With some varieties subject to weak crotches, this method of training may result in some narrow-angled crotches. Under these conditions, narrow-angled crotches are spread with wires, toothpicks or clothespins when in their "tender" stage.

Pruning two-year (std.) nursery trees at planting. The 2-year apple trees have been headed back in the nursery to about 24 inches above the ground and they come to the grower as branched trees. There are usually several branches arising close together near the point where the tree was headed. Two or more of the branches may already be competing for the leadership, as shown in Figure 14. Select the best and usually the most vigorous branch for the leader and cut it back. Remove the other competing leader if its crotch is narrow; otherwise, cut it back one-third and reserve it for a scaffold limb if properly placed. If additional side branches are available around the tree at distances of six to twelve inches apart, they can be retained and pruned likewise. However, one rarely finds more than two desirable side branches on a two-year nursery apple tree. Remove all side branches which form narrow angles or which are too close to other scaffold limbs. A side limb does not move upward from the ground as the tree develops. It is true, however, that as two neighboring limbs increase in circumference, they gradually come closer to each other. This is sufficient reason for wide spacing of scaffolds on young trees. See Figs. 12 and 15 for handling full-dwarf trees.

Pruning after one year of growth in the orchard. You must continually bear in mind that *narrow-angled crotches* should be eliminated early, particularly on semi-dwarf and standard trees. You must visit each tree at least once a year until the frameworks are fully established. Whorls of branches arising at about the same point on the leader should be reduced to one limb. The result of too many limbs arising at one place on the trunk is shown in Figure

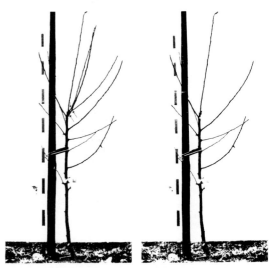

Figure 15. Two-year Boskoop tree after one season in orchard, on M.9 full-dwarfing stock. Nursery tree at planting had no side limbs (feathers), and was cut back to force side limbs. (Right) Same tree after pruning after one year in orchard. Because extension twig of central leader is not strong, cutting back is not needed. See Figure 16, noting handling of leader as it develops. (S. J. Wertheim, The Netherlands).

Figure 16. (Left) Nine-year Golden Delicious on M.9 roots, trained to "slender round spindle". Central leader zig-zags a bit due to regular heading back to a weak lateral to keep growth at the upper level moderate. Same tree at right after pruning with 21 cuts. Note shortened side branches, lowered top leader and thinning out of fruiting branches. Planting distance in row is 4.1 ft. (1.25 M), for medium-small frame on good soil. (S. J. Wertheim, Fruit Exp. Sta., Wilhelminadorp, The Netherlands).

8. Double and multiple leaders must be eliminated. This can be done by heavy pruning or removal of the limbs not selected for the single leader. Head back lateral limbs about one-fourth into last yr's. growth. Remove all water sprouts or limbs appearing at odd places on the trunk and at the base of the scaffold limbs. In general, little pruning should be done on the secondary or side branches that arise from the scaffold limbs. In this manner, pruning can be kept light and still accomplish the training. Compact trees, particularly on trellis, can carry more wood on and near the leaders and strength of the crotch angle is important. (Figure 16).

Subsequent pruning of young apple trees. For the first few years, one should concern himself primarily with the main scaffold and leader development of a tree. Use a limb-spreading technique to encourage early bearing. Leave the small branches and spurs on the young trees; they are the wood upon which the first fruit will develop.

Since every tree presents a different problem in pruning, nothing will substitute for common sense judgment in making cuts. For the beginner, study the tree carefully before cutting. After a little experience, pruning becomes more or less second nature. Actually, it is a fascinating game.

The following suggestions are given for making the cuts on young apple trees:

1. Remove first the dead, cankered, broken or diseased limbs.

2. Remove as soon as possible (if they can be spared) branches which leave the leader at a narrow angle. These limbs are unsatisfactory scaffolds.

3. Scaffold limbs may be found crowding each other. Remove one.

4. Scaffold limbs may be found growing closely parallel, one above the other. Remove the weaker, preferably the lower limb. If there are three limbs parallel one above the other, remove the middle one, or if still too close, remove

two. There should be a spacing of about 4 feet between scaffold limbs on large standard trees.

5. Correct double leaders or whorls of limbs on the main leader and scaffold branches.

6. Remove water sprouts, unless they are needed to develop scaffold limbs in open areas of the tree.

Figure 17. Holland growers tend toward ultra-high density plantings on M.9 to increase fruit production/man hour, using high-income varieties Beauty of Boskop, Golden Delicious, Jonathan, and Cox's Orange Pippin. "Spur-types" are used on MM stocks due to overgrowth of non-spur types. This planting is in its 5th year, 3¾x10 ft., staked, slender-spindle-trained and pruned. Orchards should attain 90 lbs. fruit/man-hour average, with Goldens most productive and Cox's less. There has been a shift away from stakes due to expense. (R.S. Roosje, former Director, Proefstation, Voor de Fruitteelt, Wilhelminadorp, Holland).

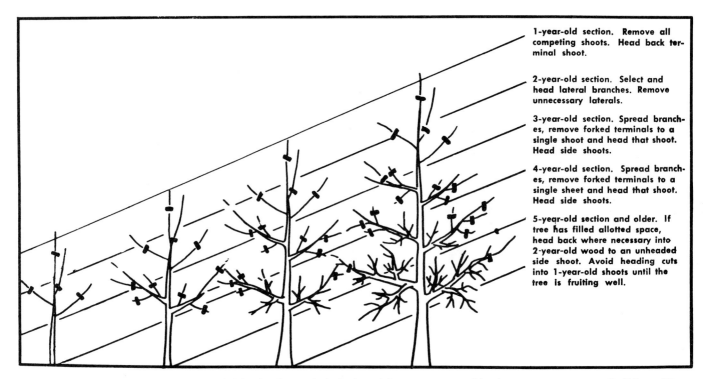

1-year-old section. Remove all competing shoots. Head back terminal shoot.

2-year-old section. Select and head lateral branches. Remove unnecessary laterals.

3-year-old section. Spread branches, remove forked terminals to a single shoot and head that shoot. Head side shoots.

4-year-old section. Spread branches, remove forked terminals to a single sheet and head that shoot. Head side shoots.

5-year-old section and older. If tree has filled allotted space, head back where necessary into 2-year-old wood to an unheaded side shoot. Avoid heading cuts into 1-year-old shoots until the tree is fruiting well.

Figure 18. This chart shows how Dr. Heinicke develops a 1, 2, 3, 4, and 5-yr. tree, central leader compact tree spur Delicious. Heavy marks show where pruning cuts were made to encourage stout branched spurred main laterals. He also uses spreaders not shown here, to get lateral limbs positioned at about 45° angles. Secure a copy of USDA Agr. Handbook No. 458 on "Planning, training, pruning high-density orchards" by Dr. Don R. Heinicke, Supt. of Documents, Wash. D.C. for further details.

7. Keep the central leading limb growing about six to ten inches above lateral limbs. At 4 to 5 yrs. on semi-dwarf trees, modify the leader and begin to open the top by cutting the leader back to a lateral. This should be done only after 4 to 5 strong scaffold limbs have developed. Remove fruit from a willowy leader until established.

8. Remove side branches on scaffolds closer than 1 ft. to trunk on big trees, 4-6 in. on compacts. Space other side branches on scaffold limbs so that they ultimately will not interfere with each other. The less desirable branches are those growing toward the ground, straight up or into the tree center; remove these first when thinning is needed.

9. The lower limbs on the younger trees, being the oldest, come into bearing first and should be retained for fruit production as long as the fruit quality is satisfactory.

Bending or tying down branches. Northern Spy, Yellow Transparent, Rome, Delicious, and other upright growing varieties are difficult to train because almost every main limb tends to grow upright. Crotch angles can be widened easiest while the branch is young and willowy (Figure 9). Wood spreaders can be used (see below). Trellis wires assist in tying limbs horizontal or downward for early fruiting. Trunk ringing or scoring with a knife also can be used to induce flowering on stubborn varieties as Delicious and Spy.

The Heinicke System. Dr. Don Heinicke, former university extension and USDA staff member, now a commercial orchardist in Washington state has developed a successful system of training and pruning apple trees in compact high-density orchards (semi-dwarf spur strains on seedling roots or semi-dwarfing rootstocks). Among his principles are pruning to admit an abundance of light, heading back cuts on developing scaffolds to encourage spurring on essentially a central leader tree. The leader is cut to a lateral after four or five good laterals have developed to open the top to light, or it can be topped higher to a weak lateral, provided the character of the tree is admitting good light to the lower center area. Wooden props are inserted (Fig. 19) to spread the limbs for earlier bearing. Nails pointed at both ends are inserted in the ends of the props (nails available from fence distributors or manufacturers). The Heinicke technique encourages earlier bearing of quality good size fruit on spur strains such as Delicious. Limb spreading reduces amount of pruning needed. (See Figs. 18 to 21).

PRUNING BEARING APPLE TREES

What are the reasons for pruning a mature apple tree and what are the ultimate effects upon the tree? The purpose is to increase the quantity of high-grade marketable fruit and to keep the tree within height and width bounds for economical management. Pruning improves color, increases size of fruit, keeps the fruiting

Figure 19. (Upper left) Spur Delicious before Heinicke Pruning. (Upper right) Same tree, no pruning, but tree opened with spiked wood spreaders. Note big change in tree with admittance of light to lower limbs. (Lower) Limbs have been pruned out to reduce competition, admit more light. Note small amount of prunings at left. This tree was loaded the next season with well sized and spaced fruit easy to harvest mostly from the ground. Spaces should be left in the tree to insert the step ladder.

wood vigorous on old trees, and assists in controlling insects and diseases. With some varieties such as Jonathan, McIntosh, and Rome Beauty, the detail and thin-wood pruning will largely take care of the need for fruit thinning in July, and at less cost per tree.

Shoot growth. Shoots are defined as the leafy new growths on a tree; when the leaves on these shoots are lost in autumn, they then become "twigs." It is interesting to note that terminal and lateral shoot growth on a bearing tree are often completed within a few weeks after growth starts in spring (Figure 22). As the tree becomes older and begins to bear, there is a tendency for the growth in length and diameter of the shoots to become less each year. Pruning, together with fruit thinning and a desirable soil management program, then become necessary to control the kind and amount of fruiting wood to maintain production of marketable fruit. In case of young trees, about 24 inches or more per year is desirable, but at the same time properly ripen and mature the wood for winter

(wood growing vigorously into autumn is likely to winter kill). With bearing trees, plump terminal shoot growth of 10 to 15 inches is desirable on fruiting branches, with the longer 15-inch terminals desired for such light setting varieties as Delicious and Stayman Winesap.

Fruit spurs. The term "spur" refers to the numerous short growths which are abundant over the fruit tree and upon which most of the fruit is borne (Figure 22, 23). Large thick spurs well-supplied with leaves will produce large well colored fruit. Well distributed cuts over older trees are needed every year to keep spurs vigorous. *Spur leaves must have good light!* "Spur type" trees tend to grow openly with an abundance of spurs well exposed to light and are preferred over standard strains (Fig. 23).

The apple fruit bud, which contains both flowers and leaves, is usually terminal on the spur and when it sets a fruit, the new shoot growths are forced out from the sides as shown in Figure 22 and 23. This explains why a fruiting spur has a zig-zag growth. A nonfruiting spur, on the other hand, grows straight year after year because the terminal bud is always a leaf bud. Some varieties bear fruit terminally and/or laterally on last year's shoot growth, in addition to bearing on spurs. Examples are Jonathan, Wealthy, and Rome Beauty.

An apple fruit spur usually bears fruit every other year. Pruning reduces the total number of blossoming spurs on trees which are heavily supplied with them, thus reducing the tendency to overload with fruit and inducing a more regular bearing habit from one year to the next. When an excessive number of growing points blossom and fruit at the same time, conditions are unfavorable for fruit bud

Figure 20. Dr. Heinicke suggests cutting back laterals about one-fourth early in their development to get well developed side limbs with many spurs. (Left) limb not headed back. Spurs will bear early but with few side limbs yields will drop. (Center) Limb cut back one fourth. Note develoment of both spurs and side limbs for continued fruiting. (Right) Limb cut back one-half. Note fewer spurs and many spurless branches. (Courtesy Don Heinicke, Ioni, Washington)

Figure 21. Dr. Don Heinicke gave this neglected 7-yr. spur Delicious tree rather heavy corrective pruning before a group of Colorado growers. He has opened the tree to abundant light in the center and lower limbs, thinned out dense branches, left a leader, subdued others by pruning to weak or moderately weak laterals, used spiked-wood spreaders to push lower limbs outward at 45° angle for more light to induce fruiting, nipped back lateral limbs and last year shoots to induce laterals and spurs, and left 2 or 3 spaces in tree side to insert 8 ft. ladder.

formation during the early summer of the overload period.

Good light must reach the leaves on the fruit spur, for these leaves will manufacture a large part of the carbohydrates that go to form the neighboring fruit. Heavily shaded spurs with two or three small leaves rarely develop well colored and good-sized fruit. Also, spurs will be thin and weak or eventually die. Thinning out pruning is needed, spread over 2 to 3 years if heavily matted.

The varieties which respond well to thin-wood pruning on mature trees include Rome Beauty, Stayman Winesap, Golden Delicious, Delicious, McIntosh, Cortland, Yellow Transparent, Jonathan, Wealthy, Rhode Island Greening, Northern Spy and York Imperial.

BENEFITS OF PRUNING MATURE TREES

Pruning increases fruit color. Sunlight must reach the inner leaves on a tree and the fruit to obtain good fruit color. With proper pruning over the tree, sunlight will be admitted to all fruits and leaves. Leaves thus can carry on a higher rate of food manufacture. Sugars resulting from this manufacture are used in the development of highly colored fruit. During the ripening period, fruit must be well supplied with carbohydrates, principally sugars, beyond other requirements. Apples that are red on one side and greenish on the other indicate inadequate pruning to admit light to the center of the tree. This explains overall high fruit color on dwarf and some semi-dwarf trees.

Pruning increases size of fruit. Judicious dormant pruning promotes the rapid sizing of fruit, starting immediately after fruit set in spring. Dormant pruning is more effective in obtaining size improvement in fruits than fruit thinning in early summer because by this time nutrients and carbohydrates will have gone into the fruits that are knocked to the ground by chemical or hand thinning. Thin-wood and detail pruning prevent this wastage of nutrients and food materials by diverting them to the better located apples. Pruning must be interrelated with other practices, especially thinning, use of fertilizers, and soil management to secure the greatest response in fruit size improvement. However, when pruning is carried to extremes, it reduces yields.

Pruning keeps fruiting wood young and vigorous. Every orchardist has noticed the large size, good color, and fine quality of fruit which is borne on young trees when they

Figure 22. Vigorous spur in early summer with terminal buds formed at A and B; scar of dropped apple at E; scars of dropped flowers at D; cluster base formed in spring at C; last years growth at F, and spring growth started at G (Cornell Univ.).

52

Figure 23. These are 22-year-old spurs from (left) an original "spur type" Delicious tree and (right) a standard type Delicious tree. Note difference in flowering points. "Spur type" strains of standard varieties are about ¾ size trees whether on seedling or clonal stocks. The "spur type" strains are preferred by growers except on full-dwarfing stock where they too may be preferred on naturally vigorous varieties and on good soils. (A..H. Thompson, Univ. of Md.)

come into bearing. Pruning must be performed on mature trees in such a way as to keep the fruiting wood similar to the ideal growth conditions found in the young bearing trees. Essentially, this means that well-placed new growths should be encouraged, pruning them for a few years while vigorous and productive and then eliminating them when they become old, underhanging, and weak.

Pruning assists in controlling insects and diseases. If the tree is kept open, it is much easier to direct spray material into and through the tree. Effective spraying is highly

Figure 24. This is a spur strain Red Delicious on seedling stock trained to the central leader system with a number of scaffold limbs. This tree was selected by Pomology Extension Specialist Ernest G. Christ, Rutgers University, as a desirable free-standing semi-dwarf apple tree. Note vigorous spur development, bloom coming and well distributed limbs for good light penetration.

important because it represents up to half the cost of growing apples. The tree should dry rapidly after rains. A dense matted condition of limbs prevents this rapid drying and encourages diseases and spray injury (particularly on sensitive-skin varieties as Golden Delicious and Jonathan) and such important apple diseases as scab, blotch, bitter rot, Brooks spot, and sooty fungus. Cover the fruits on all four sides with sprays, not just one side, to control scab, codling moth, apple maggot, bitter rot and aphids. Compact trees, particularly full dwarfs, have the advantage in getting *good spray coverage.*

STEPS IN PRUNING BEARING APPLE TREES

One of the chief objects in pruning mature trees, in addition to increasing the amount of quality fruit, is to keep the trees within height and width bounds. In recent years, there has been a tendency to maintain the tree tops low at about 10 to 12 ft. or less. Low trees are much easier and less expensive to spray, thin, pick, prune and manage Fig. 1. One of the common faults in pruning bearing apple trees is to leave a shell of unpruned branches around the outside of the tree and to remove too much inside and lower fruiting wood because it is the easiest to reach. Platform and pneumatic pruning have resulted in better pruning attention in these neglected areas on big trees.

The following suggestions are for mature semi-dwarf and standard trees:

1. Start at the top of the tree and work downward, cutting upward-growing limbs back to weak laterals, removing the crowding branches, and thin-wood pruning the remaining limbs. Start at the tips of the limbs and prune back to the base, leaving the vigorous fruiting wood well spaced along the length of the limbs. By working from the top downward, it is possible to remove the brush from the tree as you work downward. A stepladder will be needed to prune the high side branches and keep the top open if a platform is not used. Pole pruners or hydraulically operated "squirrels" are useful here (Fig. 3).

2. Remove dead, broken, and diseased wood. Dead wood harbors and disseminates such diseases as bitter rot and black rot (frog-eye).

3. Remove or dwarf by heavy pruning any large limbs that are crowding other limbs, growing parallel with them, or resting upon them. Use judgment, however, in making large cuts so that direct afternoon sunlight on hot days in summer will not sunscald exposed limbs or apples. This can be a problem south of the Equator.

4. Remove water sprouts, except an occasional one that will fill a vacant space in the tree.

5. To thin a thick side branch, the first cuts should be made on the under side of the limb where the weakest wood is. Next, thin out the "thin-wood" or badly placed interfering branches growing upward from the top of the

Figure 25. Orchards of the future may be within the tree-size range at right. M.27 is being studied in the so-called "Bed" orchard under test at the East Malling Research Station, Maidstone, England. EM9A may attain 6 to 8 ft. EM-26 about 8-10 ft. height depending upon soil fertility, other factors. Trees are 6 yrs. old, Cox's orange variety. (A. P. Preston, retired, E. Malling Research Station).

M27   M9a   M26

limb. Then, thin the poorer wood arising from either side of the limb. Divert branches to open areas and away from other branches by pruning back to laterals. Be careful not to overprune. See Figure 25 for special pruning on full-dwarf Delicious.

6. Bearing trees are kept in best condition by annual pruning. This promotes regular annual bearing. If it is impossible to give the orchard a light pruning each year, the next alternative is to arrange the pruning so that it will be done preceding the expected heavy-crop years to control blossom and fruit overloads.

7. If pruning is irregular, or at intervals of three or four years, many trees will grow out-of-bounds and develop irregular bearing with undesirable excessive loads of fruit that further exhaust the tree. An annual bearing tree is much easier to keep within bounds because a good crop of fruit tends to compete with and reduce vegetative growth.

8. There is much less risk from winter injury when pruning is done in late winter or early spring.

9. See subsequent topic, "Adapt Pruning to Variety" for special variety requirements.

THINNING AN OVERPLANTED BLOCK

If trees have been planted too closely, usually semi-dwarfs, for the fertility level of the soil and need to be thinned, this can be done by removing every other tree in a hedgerow, or, if planted on the square, remove the trees on a diagonal through the orchard. Another alternative is to "fan" the trees to be removed by gradually cutting back the limbs that are crowding the neighboring trees then eventually removing the trees. Fruit on the fanned trees will be of better size and well colored. There is the temptation to leave the fanned trees too long. Scoring the tree trunks 3 or 4 weeks after bloom each year will encourage fruit bud formation. See Chapter VI for method of ringing, scoring.

REJUVENATING AND REPLANTING OLD OR NEGLECTED ORCHARDS

Growers sometimes can take over a neighboring neglected orchard by only paying the taxes for the owner. Neglected trees have dwarfed matted lower limbs and because of little cropping, the top-most limbs grow upward until out of economical reach. Cut back top limbs to weak laterals, gradually bringing the trees down to about 10 to 12 ft. if large trees. Thin out dead and matted limbs to open remaining spurs to light and sprays. Spread the pruning over 3 to 4 years (see Fig. 6). Ten lbs. of sodium nitrate or equivalent in humid regions (ammonium sulfate in arid regions) per standard tree before growth starts helps to set a good crop, size the fruit and invigorate the tree.

Probably the best way to renew an old orchard is to bulldoze it out one fifth to one fourth a year and replant until the entire block is replanted. Avoid planting new trees in old-tree holes unless holes are filled with trucked-in top soil. If the new planting is on dwarfing stocks, the first block will be bearing in a few years. Soil fumigation of old apple land has induced markedly better growth of young replanted apple trees in the Northwest U.S.A. (Fig. 1, Ch. 5).

ADAPT THE PRUNING TO THE VARIETY

There are many differences in growth habits, wood color, hairiness, and other characters which enable the workmen to identify one dormant apple variety from another. Because of these differences, it is necessary to emphasize a certain type of pruning on one variety and perform little or none of it on another.

Delicious and Strains. These trees may have weak crotches and grow many limbs from the same point on a branch, forming whorls. Young trees must be visited once a year for the first three to five years to correct fast-growing, narrow-angled crotches and to reduce the number of limbs in a whorl. Trees will develop numerous medium-sized branches and eventually become dense unless removal of some of these limbs is done. One must be

Figure 26. Power-take-off heavy-duty mowers or hammer-type shredders are widely used to shred brush that has been windrowed. This operation returns organic matter to the soil, is better than burning the brush. Thick wood is removed for firewood.

careful, however, not to overprune. Since these varieties are more profitable when grown as fancy apples eaten out of hand, it is important to get good branch spacing to admit sunlight, and that this be followed by removal of underhanging thin-wood. It pays in earlier cropping to prop the side limbs outward with wood splints (Figs. 18-21).

The trees have a weakness in setting light crops, which this type of pruning will assist in correcting. An interrelated program of pruning, fruit thinning, and use of adequate nitrogen should be maintained to obtain about 15-inch terminal growths.

With the advent of spur strains of Delicious, the trees naturally are more open, admit more light, require less pruning and tend to bear annually a better grade of fruit than the non-spurs. The spur strains are a tremendous improvement in growing Delicious but there remains a question if the fruit quality is as good as the non-spurs. Washington state specialists claim it is a matter of harvesting at the proper time.

Jonathan. Due to the development of numerous branches and twigs on Jonathan trees, the lower limbs may become shaded soon after the trees begin to bear. Jonathan responds better to thinning-out than to heading-back cuts. It is best to remove undesired branches entirely and then distribute small cuts on the remaining branches. With good thinning-out and detail pruning, Jonathan will

For brush choppers, windrowers, etc., see recent July issue of Amer. Fruit Grower Magazine.

require little or no hand thinning of fruit. This variety is susceptible to fire blight; avoid heavy pruning. Tree openness for fast drying of spray chemicals reduces russeting, a Jonathan problem.

McIntosh. The general growth habit of McIntosh is good. It is easy to train when young. Open-prune the trees so spray can enter the trees freely to control scab to which McIntosh is readily susceptible. Also, keep the tops low to facilitate spraying in these areas where much of the crop is borne. Attention to detail pruning is needed to get Fancy fruit.

Stayman Winesap. Under good soil management, this variety develops many long leggy branches with poorly spaced scattered laterals. On young trees, heading-back is necessary to produce laterals on long terminal growths. Stayman is an open grower. It is not necessary to make many large cuts except to avoid double leaders or weak crotches which tend to split easily. This variety must be kept in vigorous condition by over-all annual detail pruning and a good soil management program.

Rome Beauty. Young Rome Beauty trees are discouraging to the pruner because most of the limbs tend to grow straight up, making a dense crowded situation. *Annual attention* to training young Rome Beauty trees is highly important. As the young trees begin to bear fruit, however, the weight of the fruit pulls the limbs out and the tree gradually assumes a spreading habit. Avoid over-pruning young trees to get a desired shape. Rome wood is willowy and fairly resistant to breaking. Limb spreaders will give better crotches and earlier bearing of quality fruit.

Rome Beauty bears much of its fruit terminally on rather long twigs at the ends of the limbs and branches. Numerous small cuts must be used on mature trees to remove the excess amount of twiggy growth which develops toward the outside of the tree. Attention must be given to thin-wood pruning. Start at the outer end of the branches and work toward the base, scattering the cuts evenly. It is a common mistake to start at the base of a large limb and prune outward, taking off branches and leaving a "cow tail" situation with unpruned busy twigs at the ends of the branches.

Yellow Transparent, Wealthy. Trees become dense by producing an excess of small and medium-size branches. A portion of these branches should be removed. Remaining branches should be detail and thin-wood pruned. Relatively little topping of the outward-growing laterals is needed. Both cultivars have a tendency to alternate-year bear. Prune heavier in advance of an expected heavy crop. In addition, trees must be fruit-thinned by hand or chemicals. Both fruit thinning and pruning are important to obtain good-sized fruit. Request Wash. State Bull. 146.

Golden Delicious. This variety has the weakness of developing forks and narrow-angled crotches. Its long leggy branches are brittle and break easily with the first heavy load of fruit. Annual attention is important while the trees are young to get well-spaced scaffold limbs each of which is of good diameter and strong. Golden Delicious bears early and training cuts are not likely to retard bearing. Goldens are like Delicious in having a higher nitrogen need, but carefully regulated to get full harvest-yellow fruit.

Head-back or modify the leader at a height of six feet; the leader can be pulled to a side by removing the small branches on the side toward the prevailing wind. Fruit on the other side of the leader, with the help of the wind, will pull this branch to the side. Thin-wood pruning is highly important to attain large size fruit. Chemical fruit thinning is a standard practice with this variety to get annual cropping. Open the trees for good air movement, quick drying and high-finish fruit. Open-growing *spur* Goldens are being widely planted.

Yellow Newton and York Imperial. These varieties bear biennially if allowed to over-set fruit. In spite of all precautions, they tend to alternate heavy and light crops. As trees enter the light-crop year, save as many blooming spurs as possible. But as trees enter the heavy-crop years, reduce the blooming spurs by heavier pruning. Distribute pruning over the entire tree and keep the tops fairly open.

HURRICANE DAMAGE

Trees in leaf and in soggy ground are blown over easily by high winds and are damaged much more than trees after leaf fall. Most hurricanes occur before leaf drop and during or following heavy rains. It probably is best to leave the medium-to-large trees leaning and gradually prune and train them to upright trees with a leaning trunk. The larger trees pulled upright by tractor may lose many feeding roots and it takes them years to regain vigor, if they do. Young trees or mature trees leaning slightly may be straightened and braced immediately as in Figure 27 while the ground is still soggy.

CHEMICALS TO RETARD GROWTH AND WIDEN CROTCHES

With high-density orchards there may be a need for "Bio-Regulants" or chemicals to retard growth and keep trees within bounds. A chemical which may be used is succinic acid 2, 2-dimethylhydrazide known as Alar (Uniroyal Co., Naugatuck, Ct. 06770) applied at 2000 ppm in the spray tank about two weeks after bloom time. Terminal growth will stop on Delicious soon after application whereas growth will continue to August on young trees. A spray must be applied each year for continued effect. Trees are more compact with trunk diameter little affected. Alar has many benefits, one being to induce earlier and more flowering the year after application.

Figure 27. Triangle tree brace made from 1-1½x4 inch rough lumber is simple, easily placed, effective, and nonharmful to tree. Good for moderately leaning trees due to high wind, which have been pulled upright by tractor. Badly leaning tree probably should be left as is and gradually trained to upright tree with leaning trunk.

TIBA (tri-idobenzoic acid) 1000 ppm is used on young trees for wide-angle crotches, but is not recommended for bearing trees (causes fruit cracking, early dropping, cork, other problems). PP333, a fungicide with strong growth inhibition at 1000 ppm, may have strong carryover effects the next year. A spray of cytokinin and GA also can be used to widen crotches. Since use of these chemicals and similar ones are in the developmental stages, it is well to check with extension specialists in fruit and with the manufacturers for the latest developments and usage.

REMOVING OLD TREES

Studies at Pennsylvania State University indicate that medium to large apple trees can be removed quickest with a large bulldozer of about D-6 size. Time required to uproot a tree is about a minute. One small D-2 tractor with a twenty-five foot cable can wiggle out most trees with some maneuvering, whereas two D-2 tractors, one pushing and the other pulling is quicker. Cost for removing a tree will vary, depending upon size of tree, depth of rooting, number of trees involved, type of soil, and whether the tractors are available on the farm or have to be rented and transported. Chain saws are convenient for sectioning the trees.

WILD GAME CONTROL

In some orchards deer may cause considerable damage to young and old fruit trees by browsing the new growth and by rubbing their antlers against the bark. Unfortunately, there is as yet no economical or completely satisfactory method for solving the deer problem. Any kind of human hair, about a handful in old stockings tied to outside trees and spaced about 10 ft. apart have been effective for up to six months. Cooperation with barber shop owners is needed. Z.I.P. is used by some growers. Cloth bags of tankage hung on trees should repel deer for several weeks.

An eight-foot high fence around the orchard is another method for controlling deer. Some state governments will supply the fencing. For young trees, three fence posts placed 1½ to 2 feet apart in an equilateral triangle around the trees will prevent bucks from rubbing their antlers against the bark. The Dupont spray repellant Arasan (thiram) has been fairly effective on deer and for rabbits and mice on above-ground trunks of young trees. Helicopters are used to herd elk and antelope out of Washington orchards.

University of California, Davis, has a bulletin on gophers. Woodpeckers may "hammer" a circle of holes in particularly McIntosh trunks, causing some ringing effects. Baboons can be a problem in Zimbabwe, bears in cherry trees in Idaho, both breaking off sizeable limbs. There is no suggested control, except perhaps the gun.

For mouse control, see Chapter V.

Review Questions

1. What factors influence the kind and amount of pruning needed by an apple tree?
2. Discuss dormant season pruning vs. summer pruning.
3. Discuss the trend in size and training of trees and the relationship to machine management.
4. What type of pruning cuts are used to keep a compact and standard-size apple tree within height and width bounds; explain how the cuts are made?
5. Pruning is a dwarfing process! Or is it? Explain.
6. Describe the arrangement of limbs on an apple tree trained to the modified leader, central leader, palmette, spindle bush and hedge-wall.
7. What is meant by the "deshooting" system of training newly planted apple trees?
8. Why should the small twigs be left on the lower branches of young trees?
9. Describe a weak and vigorous apple spur; why do some apple spurs grow a zigzag fashion?
10. How can you recognize a flower bud and a leaf bud on dormant apple wood?
11. List the benefits of pruning mature bearing apple trees.
12. When is "fan" type pruning and training used?
13. How does the pruning of a bearing Golden Delicious tree differ from the pruning of a bearing Red Delicious tree?

Suggested Collateral Readings

BADIZADEGAN, M. and R.F. Carlson. Effect of N⁶ benzyladenine on seed germination and seedling growth of apple. ASHS 91. 1-8. 1967.

BARDEN, J.A. et al. Photosynthesis, respiration of apple not affected by shoot detachment. HortSci. 15(5):595-597. 1980.

BARDEN, J.A. Light on photosynthesis, respiration, leaf weight, growth of young apple trees. J. ASHS. 99:547-551. 1974.

BARDEN, J.A. Apple tree physiology as affected by continuous and intermittent shade. J. Amer. Soc. HortSci. 102(4):391-394. 1977.

BRADT, O.A. et al. Pruning and training fruit trees. Agric. Can. Publ. 1513. 1973.

BYERS, R.E. Hand baits, ground sprays on pine voles, HortSci. 10:122-123. 1975.

BYERS, R.E. Chemical control of vegetative growth and flowering of non-bearing 'Delicious' apple trees. HortSci. 11(5):506-7. 1976.

CARLSON, R.F. Intermediate stem effects on apple. ASHS 87:21-28. 1965.

CARLSON, R.F. Compact Fruit Tree Proc. International Dwarf Fruit Tree Association. Growers should belong to this Ass'n. to attend meetings, among the best, and receive proceedings. Write Dept. of Hort., Mich. State Univ., E. Lansing. 44823.

CHEMICAL regulations of plant processes. A symposia. HortSci. 4(2): 1969.

CUTTING, C.V. and L.C. Luckwill. The physiology of tree crops. Proceedings of a symposium held at Long Ashton Research Station, University of Bristol, 392 pp. 1969. 1970.

DOUD, D.S. and D.C. Ferree. Light levels on fruiting of Delicious apple. ASHS 105(3) 325-28. 1980. Same authors. Effect of reflectants and shade on light in Delicious apple trees. ASHS 105(3). 397-400. 1980.

DOZIER, W.A., Jr. and J.A. Barden. Shoot growth of young apple trees as influenced by ethephon. J. ASHS 98(3):244. 1973. J. ASHS 98(3):239. 1973.

EDGERTON, L.J. et al. Persistence of daminozide residues in apple spurs under different climatic conditions. HortSci. 12(3):242-44. 1977.

EDGERTON. L.J. and W.J. Greenhalgh. Absorption, translocation and accumulation of labeled (Alar) in tissues. ASHS 91:25-30. 1967.

FERREE, D.C. Heading height of newly planted apple trees on growth. Ohio Agric. Res. and Dev. cen. Res. Cir. 239. 5-8. July 1978.

FERREE, D.C. Canopy and yield of Golden Delicious in four orchard management systems. ASHS 105(3). 376-80. 1980.

FERREE, D.C. et al. 16 yrs. of Delicious strains, other cultivars on intersterms, rootstocks. Fruit Varieties Journ. 36:(2) 37-47. 1982.

FERREE, D.C. and A.N. Lakso. Dormant pruning techniques in a hedgerow apple orchard. ASHS 104(6):736-739. 1979.

FERREE, D.C. and F.R. Hall. Physical stress on apple leaf activity. ASHS 106:3:348-51. May 1981.

FISHER, D.V. Spur-McIntosh strains. Offset 8pp. Summerland, B.C. 1970.

Figure 28. Planes can be used for quick distribution of chemicals in orchards. A deer repellant (Z.I.P.) is being applied here in a Washington apple orchard. Biplanes give a better down-draft coverage than monoplanes. (Courtesy Wenatchee Daily World.)

FORSHEY, C.G. Alar on vigorous McIntosh apple trees. J. ASHS 95(1):64-67. Jasn. 1970.

FORSHEY, C.G. and M.W. McKee. Production efficiency of large vs. small McIntosh trees. HortSci. 5:164-5. 1970.

FUNT, R.C. Training and pruning fruit trees. Ohio Coop. Ext. Serv. Bul. 528. 1982.

GERDTS, M.H. et al. Chemical defoliation of fruit trees. Calif. Agr. Apr. 1977. pp. 19.

HAMZAKHEYL, N., D.C. Ferree, and F.O. Hartman. Effect of lateral shoot orientation on growth and flowering of young apple trees. HortSci. 11(4):393-5. 1976.

HATCH, A.H. Response of mechanically-topped apple trees to SADH applied to the top. HortSci. 8(3):179. June 1973.

HEINICKE, A.J. and N.F. Childers. The daily rate of photosynthesis, during the growing season of 1935, of a young apple tree of bearing age. Cornell Univ. Agr. Exp. Sta. Memoir 201, 1937.

HEINICKE, D. High-density apple orchards - planning, training and pruning. U.S.D.A. Agr. Handbook 458. 34 pp. 1975. (Your County Agent may have a copy).

HEINICKE, D.R. Characteristics of McIntosh and Red Delicious apples as influenced by exposure to sunlight during the growing season. ASHS 89:10-13. 1966.

HEINICKE, D.R. The micro-climate of fruit trees. III. The effect of tree size on light penetration and leaf area in Red Delicious apple trees. ASHS 85:33-41. 1964.

JACKSON, J.E., et al. Shade effects on apple fruit size, color, storage quality. J. HortSci. 46(3):277-287. July 1971.

KENDER, W.J. and S. Carpenter. Stimulation of lateral bud growth of apple trees by 6-Benzylamino purine. J. ASHS 97(3):377. May 1972.

KETCHIE, D.O. et al. "Dead-spur" disorder of 'Delicious' apple. HortSci. 13(3):282-3. 1978.

LAKSO, A.N. et al. Conversion of central leader apple trees for improved mechanical harvest. J. ASHS 103(2):284-287. 1978.

LAKSO, A.N. Fisheye photography and canopy structure, light, climate, and biological responses to light in apple. ASHS 105(1):43-36. Jan. 1980.

LAKSO, A.N. Light studies in apple trees. N.Y. Food & Life Sci. 8:6-8. 1975.

LAPINS, K.O. Spur-type growth habit in 60 apple progenies. J. ASHS 99:568-572. 1974.

LEE, J.M. and N.E. Looney. Branching habit and apical dominance of compact and normal apple seedlings as influenced by TIBA and GA3. J. Amer. Soc. HortSci. 102(5):619-622. 1977.

LETHAM, D.S. and M.W. Williams. Regulators of cell division in plant tissues. VIII. The cytokinins of the apple fruit. Phys. Plantarum Vol. 22. p. 925-936. 1969.

LORD, William J. et al. Flowering of young apple trees following summer pruning. ASHS. 104(4):540-544. 1979.

LOUGHEED, E.C. and E.W. Franklin. Air flow rates influence CO_2 production of apple fruits, potato tubers and onion bulbs. HortSci. 10:388-390. 1975.

LOVE, J.M. and J.A. Barden. Ethyl 5- (4-chlorophenyl)-2H- tetrazole-2-acetate on net photosynthesis, stomatal resistance, transpiration in apple. HortSci. 14(4):515-516. August 1979.

LOVE, J.M. and J.A. Barden. "Pinching" agent on net photosynthesis of apple. HortSci. 13(3):281-2. 1978.

MANDAVA, N.B. Plant growth substances. Amer. Chem. Soc., Wash. D.C. 310 pp. 1979.

MARTIN, G.C. and M.W. Williams. Breakdown products of C^{14} labeled N- Dimethylaminosuccinamic acid (Alar) in the apple tree. ASHS 89:1-9. 1966.

MILLER, S.S. Stub-cut summer pruning young trees. Fruit South a:(4) 122-4. May 1977.

MILLER, S.S. Controlling roosuckers on apple trees. HortSci. 12(6):577-8. 1977.

MULLINS, M.G. and W.S. Rogers. Effects of stem orientation, bud position on apple shoot growth. J. HortSci. 46(3):313-321. July 1971.

NEELY, D. Healing of tree wounds. J. ASHS. 95(5):536-540. 1970.

NORTON, R.L. High-density apple plantings (good paper). N.Y. (Albion) St. Hort. Sco. Newsletter (Suppl.) Apr. 1970. Request recent public.

PELLETT, H. et al. Metal compounds as root pruning agents. HortSci.

15(3):308-309. 1980.

PORPIGLIA, P.J. and J.A. Barden. Seasonal trends in photosynthetic potential, respiration, and leaf weight of apple as affected by canopy position. ASHS 105(6):920-923. 1980.

POWELL, L.E. Effect of photoperiod on endogenous abscissic acid in *Malus* and *Betula*. HortSci. 11(5):498-9. 1976.

PRESTON, A.P. Results from pruning experiments with apples at E. Malling. bull. de l'Institut Agron, et des. Sta. de Res. de Gambloux (Belgium). Hors Serie (in English). Vol. III:1053-62. 1960.

PROCTOR, J.T.A., W.J. Kyle, and J.A. Davies. Penetration of Global Solar Radiation into Apple Trees. J. ASHS. 100:40-44. 1975.

PROCTOR. J.T.A., et al. Carbon budget of young apple tree. J. Amer. Soc. Hort. Sci. 101(5):579-582. 1976.

RAESE, J.T. Sprout control apple and pear trees with NAA. HortSci. 10:396-398. 1975.

ROBITAILLE, H.A. Stress ethylene production in apple shoots. A. Amer. Soc. Hort. Sci. 100:524. 1975.

SACHS, R.M., J. DeBie, T. Kretchun, and T. Mock. Comparison of commercially available maleic hydrazide on Plant Species. HortSci. 10:366-367. 1975.

SACHS, R.M., H. Hield, and J. DeBie. Dikegulac: Promising foliar-applied growth regulator for woody species, HortSci. 10:367-369. 1975.

SEELEY, E.J., et al. Apple tree photosynthesis: A coordinated review. ASHS. 13(6):640-652. 1978.

STEBBINS. R.L. Training and pruning apple and pear trees. Pacific Northwest Ext. Publ. 156. 15pp. Oct. 1976. (Ore. State Univ.)

STEMBRIDGE, G.E. and M.E. Ferree. Immediate and residual effects of Alar on young Delicious apple trees. A.S.H.S. 94:6:602-604. 1969.

STOHR, J.V., Dufkova, and L. Chvojka. Mixtures of CCC. B-995. Fractions of plant oils on apple-tree growth. Rostlinna vyroba 18:751-755. 1972.

STORER, T.I. Control of field rodents in California. Calif. Agr. Ext. Serv. Cir. 138. (Request revised edition).

SUCKLING, P.W. et al. Global and photosynthetically active radiation within a dwarf apple orchard. Can. Journ of Bot. 53:14, 1428-1441. 1975.

TAYLOR, B.H. and D.C. Ferree. Summer pruning on leaf activity, abscission, dry weight of apple. ASHS 106:3:389-92. May 1981.

TROMP, J. and J. Oele. Growth and composition of apple leaves and fruit as affected by relative humidity of air. Plant Physio. 27:253-258. 1972.

TUKEY, H.S. Dwarfed Fruit Trees. The MacMillan Co., New York City. 1964.

UTERMARK, H. Summer pruning to control growth fruiting, in mature apple trees in West Germany. Compact Fruit Tree of IDFTA Proceedings 10:86-90. June 1977. Contact Dr. R. F. Carlson. Mi. St. Univ., E. Lansing 48824 for annual copies.

VERNER. L. Hormone and apple tree training. Idaho Agr. Exp. Sta. Res. Bull. 28, 1955.

WERTHEIM, S.J. Training slender spindle apple trees. Proefstation Voor De Wilhelminadorp. No. 10, Netherlands. Nov. 1970. Request recent work. Wertheim (1973).

WERTHEIM, S.J. and J.J. Lemmens. Planting systems for apple and pear. Fruit Res. Sta. Wilhelminadorp. Netherlands. (Eng. and Dutch) 77 pp. No. 12. 1973.

WERTHEIM, S.J. and J.L. Baarends. Light in relation to fruit color. De Fruitteelt 64:228-230. (In Dutch).

WEST, D.W. and D.F. Gaff. An error in the calibration of xylem-water potential against leaf-water potential. J. of Exp. Botany 22:342-346. (Reprint) 1971.

WESTWOOD, M.N. and A.N. Roberts. Relationship between trunk cross-sectional area and weight of apple trees. J. ASHS Vol. 95:1.28-30. Jan. 1970.

WILLIAMS, M.W. and J.D. Billingsley. Increasing apple crotch angles with cytokinins and GA. ASHS 95(5):649-651. 1970.

WILLIAMS, M.W. Induction of spur and flower bud formation in young apple trees with chemical growth retardants. J. Amer. Soc. Hort. Science. Vol. 97, No. 2. March 1972 P. 210.

YOUNG, L.C.T., J.T. Wineberger, J.B. Bennett. Growth of resting Buds. J. ASHS 99(2):146. March 1974.

See previous book editions for earlier pertinent literature.

CHAPTER V

Soil Management for Apples

No one cultural program can be recommended for all orchards. A program that is satisfactory for one orchard under one set of climatic and soil conditions may be undesirable for another under a different set of conditions. Good tree performance often may be obtained under any of several different systems of management. The cultural program selected, however, must be interrelated with the pruning, fertilization, fruit thinning, and the spraying programs to obtain good shoot growth, moderate over-all tree vigor, and high production of marketable fruit. It is generally known that fruit trees respond more or less directly to the soil type in growth and yield; the more favorable the soil, the less important is the particular cultural program to be followed.

Many orchards have been planted on rolling or relatively steep land in order to secure good air drainage and freedom from frost damage. These orchards are subject to soil erosion, and special care must be exercised in the cultural program to minimize erosion as much as possible. If the slope of the land is less than 10 per cent, contour planting with or without terracing is effective in conserving both soil and moisture. However, if the slope is greater than about 10 per cent, the orchardist is almost forced to keep his land in a sod program in humid regions.

An orchard soil management program should meet the following objectives:

1. Provide a *favorable moisture supply* to the trees throughout the growing season.

2. Minimize or *prevent soil erosion.*

3. *Increase,* or at least *maintain,* the *organic matter* by use of cover crops or mulching or herbicides and sod.

4. Supply necessary *nutrients.*

5. *Loosen the soil* for good *aeration* and *water penetration* and correct machinery compaction. Latter may be corrected with fall sub-soiling.

It is generally agreed that the young or dwarf trees require a different type of soil management than large-size apple trees (Figure 1). This is because the small trees are shallow-rooted and are more likely to suffer from a limited supply of nutrients and water. The large trees, on the other hand, are less subject to competition with sod for water and nutrients. Their root systems penetrate the soil to a greater width and depth; also, they have greater food

Dr. Paul Larsen, Utah State University, Logan, helped revise this Chapter.

reserves in the bark and wood tissues to tide them over periods of stress.

Soil Management: Young and Compact Trees. These trees should make 15-30 inches annual terminal growth. Preplant soil fumigation should be considered (Figure 1 and Figure 2). Some system of cultivation and/or use of herbicides around the trees is needed. The world trend is to use an early shallow cultivation (after bloom) with rototiller-type equipment (tree hoes) to a 2-inch depth

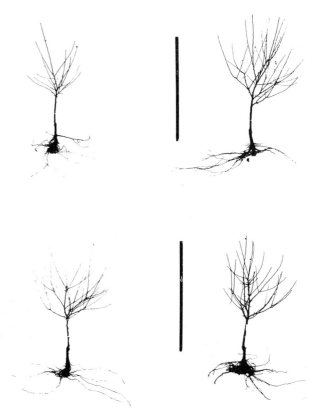

Figure 1. Photos show Cox's Orange Pippin on M. 26 in England after three seasons growth; trees 8 ft. apart in rows 14 ft. apart. Middles and 4 ft. square areas around trees were treated as follows: (top left) grass, with 4 ft. sq. grassed; (top right) grass, with 4 ft. sq. mulched; (lower left) cultivated with 4 ft. sq. hoed; (lower right) grass, with 4 ft. sq. treated with herbicide sprays. Mulched trees were most vigorous but herbicide-treated trees grew as well as cultivated trees. Grassed trees grew least. Tree size at end of first year controls size of tree next few years. (Courtesy G.C. White and R.I.C. Holloway, E. Malling Res. Sta., Kent, England.)

Figure 2. Replanting fruit trees on old orchard sites can be a problem, worldwide. Preplant soil fumigation is economically sound whether the problem is nematodes or unknown. Above, apple trees on right on an old site which has been fumigated, and left, no treatment. Methyl bromide has been shown to increase yields 2 to 3x in 6-8 yrs. (Wash. Agr. Res. and Educ. Center, Wenatchee).

about 4 ft. on either side of the trees (Figure 3) followed with a herbicide program for the balance of the season. The middles are left in a grass sod strip (Figure 3 and 4) such as red fescue, Alta (K-31 Figure 5) fescue or bahia grass (tropics, sub-tropics). In humid regions the Alta fescue, which was bred for childrens' playgrounds, is a tough sod that "squeezes" out weeds such as dandelions and can withstand heavy orchard traffic (Figure 4). A broadcast of a light NPK fertilizer mix every other year

Figure 3. The rototiller-type equipment has largely replaced the disc in the orchard, cultivating the soil to a depth of about 2 inches to avoid harming the roots, in spring after bloom and followed with or without a herbicide program. Middles are left in mowed sod.

should maintain the sod. Periodic mowing is needed to reduce competition for water and nutrients with the trees. Some form of irrigation, possibly drip or microjet, is good insurance in regions subject to drouth to get the trees well established. A dry period shortly after the trees are planted can result in loss of many trees and replanting the next spring. While irrigation is a *must* in arid regions, spring drouths occur often enough in humid regions to encourage orchardists to install irrigation at the start for insurance (Figure 4).

Formerly, with wide-spaced low-density trees, cash crops such as strawberries, grain, soybeans and vegetables were grown to make the land pay while the trees were coming into bearing. This still can be done with closer-planted trees but only for a few years until the trees occupy the space. Commercially, however, few orchardists grow intercrops with compact trees. On a small scale, possibly.

With the use of specialized machinery, most orchards are being planted on semi-level to rolling sites. If an orchard is planted on a 10 percent slope (10 ft drop in 100 ft), too steep for terrace management, it is dubious to perform any kind of cultivation, except to use tractor-hoeing around the trees or spot herbicides. Mulching can be used but it must be maintained 6-8 inches deep by bringing mulch in or mowing the middles and raking the mulch about the trees, with or without drip or microjet irrigation. This system is adaptable to small plantings or in the backyard. Double nitrogen application will be needed to help the bacteria decompose the mulch the first year. If mulch is maintained regularly thereafter, little or no fertilizer may be needed.

There are several advantages of mulching where the grower or the home gardener can and wishes to use it:

1. Less fluctuation of moisture under the trees with reduced evaporation from the soil, grass and weeds.

2. Availability of nutrients from the decomposing mulch is favorable to tree growth. Legumes decompose faster than grain straw and provide some nitrogen causing the straw to decompose faster in a mixture of legume and straw.

Figure 4. This is a 3-yr apple orchard on M. 26 rootstock, trellised, with drip irrigation installed at the outset, and strip-weed-control down the row with middles sowed to Alta fescue in New Jersey, sandy loam soil.

60

Figure 5. This a 6-ft. power-take-off (PTO) seeder-compacter being used to sow Alta (K-31) fescue in a New Jersey orchard of compact trees. Fescues are seeded about 40-50 lbs/A, usually late summer or early spring.

Figure 6. Two species of mice injurious to fruit trees. (Top) The pine mouse has a small body, short tail, Roman nose, sunken eyes, brownish fur and tail as short or shorter than hind leg; burrows deep, damages roots. (Bottom) Meadow mouse has a large body, long tail, prominent eyes; dark-grayish fur, tail longer than hind leg; makes surface marks. (U.S. Dept. of Interior).

3. Organic matter is higher under mulch by as much as one percent, and 2-3% higher than under cultivation.

4. Mulch will act as a cushion for dropping apples, thus affording a better sales price.

5. For mature trees, mulching affords as good or better growth and production than other systems of management. Less water and fertilizer will be needed. Color and quality of the fruit is as good or better.

There are limitations of mulching:

1. Mulch and dry grass are a fire hazard. Fires are difficult to control in an orchard; keep spray equipment full of water during drouths.

2. Mulch may harbor insects, diseases, rodents.

3. Mulch some seasons may extend growth in the fall with reductions in fruit quality.

4. Cost of mulch may make practice prohibitive. Spoiled hay left in the field is often available free for hauling.

Mice can be a problem in almost any orchard regardless of the soil management program. The field or meadow mouse (*Microtus pennsylvanicum,* Figure 6) works on the soil surface or a few inches below the surface. Most of the damage is bark injury to the tree near the soil surface. In some regions, as southern New York, the Virginias, and regions of similar climates, the pine mouse (*Pitymys pinetorum scalopsoides,* Figure 6) is a serious pest, causing bark damage on the roots, as shown in Figure 7. Damage is serious because it is difficult to detect before it is too late to save the tree. It is also inconvenient and difficult to correct by bridge-grafting, as can be done for damage by the meadow mouse. (For methods on bridge-grafting, see Chapter VIII.)

For mouse control, a milder short-life chemical such as Remek Brown is preferred by FDA vs endrin, although endrin is still used and effective in some areas. There is some shift to (a) baiting and (b) the encouragement of

forage for mice in the row middles such as orchard, blue and quack grasses, perennial forbs and bulb and rhizome plants. Ground under trees should be kept clean by frequent mowing, shallow off-set PTO rototilling, or by herbicides. Also plastic or wire-mesh trunk guards 18″ high and cinders around the tree base can be used, particularly on young trees.[1]

In grassy areas apply poison bait by hand or by "trail-builder"[2] (cuts labor, time; cannot use on rocky ground) in the fall during good weather and before hard freezes. Sprinkle 1 level teaspoon of zinc phosphide rodenticide (1 oz. can treats 20 qts.; covers 8-10 acres) over each quart of cubed apples; tumble the cubes. Broadcast and/or place bait in fresh mouse runs or under fertilizer bags, etc. Use both apple cubes and zinc-phosphide or strychnine oats or wheat for pine mice. Use 10 lbs./A broadcast or 3 lbs./A trial bait. Waterproof tubes (mouse can enter) with poisoned grain glued to inside walls are available in quantity (Prolin Mouse Tubes, Niagara Chem. Co.). Important: Do not apply bait during harvest and do not apply bait to bare ground. Before broadcasting bait by plane or machine, check with the State Fish and Game Dept., required by some states. Spread bait when 3-5 days

---

[1]Obtain up-to-date recommendations from manufacturer, your government specialist, or Dr. Ross Byers, Hort. Dept., VPI, Winchester, Va. 22601, who has a continuing research program. Contact U.S. Fish and Wild Life Serv., Dept. of Interior, Rodent Control, Wash., D.C., USA for "trail-builder" recommendations.

Figure 7. Injury to apple tree roots by the pine mouse (*Pitymys pinetorum scalopsoides*) is difficult to detect before it is too late to save the tree. A regular poisoning program is effective in preventing this damage in areas where these mice are known to exist. (U.S. Dept. of Interior).

of clear weather are likely to follow.

Mice seem to girdle M.9 Delicious stocks readily, pheasants may destroy low-hanging fruit and deer browsing may transfer fire blight. Natural enemies of mice such as skunks, dogs, weasels, hawks, owls and foxes can be encouraged. Mow the orchard and remove dropped apples before baiting. Mice tend to develop resistance to almost any poison used against them. There is continued research to keep "ahead of them" with new chemicals and approaches.

Porcupines, active in cold weather, may girdle trees. Traps, poison or a low electric fence are controls.

Chemical Weed Control. Chemical control of weeds in the tree row has several advantages: (1) Reduces mouse injury to trees by destroying their harboring places; (2) the ground is undisturbed and prevents weed seed germination; (3) prevents bark injury from discing and also root injury from deep discing; and (4) pickers do not have to fight their way through weeds and poison ivy to get to the fruit. Dropped fruit can be picked up more easily.

Herbicides must be handled very carefully with *strict rate control*. They can harm the trees and reduce yields if applied improperly.

Most herbicides are applied at 30 lbs pressure and 40-60 gal/A. The boom type sprayer is used with the outer nozzle offset to spray close to the trunk but avoid hitting it. Other nozzels are fan-shaped. One or two flood-jet tips at 4-inch

Figure 8. Poison ivy can be a problem, particularly to the harvest crew. Ammate-X, 2, 4-Dand Roundup. (Courtesy Ernest G. Christ, Rutgers University).

spacing 12 inches off the ground can be used. The herbicides can be blocked on either side of the tree (less expensive) or sprayed in continuous strips to about 4 ft out on one side of the row at a time. Locate the boom to the side and in front for visibility (See "Weed Control" Chapter XVIII).

Types of Herbicides. Residual herbicides stay in the soil and inhibit seed germination or kill the young plants. These include Princep, Sinbar, Casaron, Karmex, Surflan and Enide. *Knockdown with little residual activity* type herbicides include Paraquat, Roundup, Dowpon and orchard formulations of 2, 4-D. Combinations of these herbicides with residual herbicides controls existing weeds and prevents further seed germination during the season.

Suggestions. Do not continue to use the same herbicide, causing weeds to develop resistance to it. Combine and/or rotate herbicides. We need to know more about use of herbicides on dwarfed trees; start by using only on a few trees for awhile. Work with your extension specialist to keep up-to-date on new herbicides and combinations for best control. Most experiment stations publish up-to-date weed control recommendations every year.

Poison Ivy and Virginia Creeper. These weeds are a pest, particularly at harvest and there is really no completely effective control. Using a hand gun and spot treating, some growers have had some success with Ammate-X (AMS) at 60 lbs./A, treating in spring after leaves have dropped. Avoid hitting trunk and apple leaves or fruit. Ammate corrodes sprayers which need a good cleaning afterward. 2, 4-D is effective for poison ivy, not Virginia Creeper; avoid hitting trunk, leaves, fruit. Roundup controls poison ivy and suppresses Creeper; follow label directions (Figure 8).

Before planting the trees, weeds on the site should be controlled the previous season by applying Amitrol, Roundup, Dowpon or 2, 4-D according to label directions. For *young trees*, Surflan, Glyphosate and Paraquat are suggested.

Table 1 gives typical herbicide information and suggestions for the soil and climatic conditions of western New York.

Soil Management: Low-density Bearing Trees. In most regions of the world the horticulturists and agronomists are generally agreed that a program of continuous cultivation with or without cover crops throughout the life of the orchard is detrimental both to the soil and to the trees. Figure 9 shows the subtle damage that can be done to trees over many years of clean cultivation. Hence, with widely planted trees or with closer-planted compact trees of bearing age, the trend is a continuation of the system used for young trees — mowed sod middles with strip cultivation and/or herbicides under the trees. Some form of irrigation is suggested from the beginning, even in humid regions where over the years drouths occur suf-

TABLE 1. SOME HERBICIDES FOR TREE FRUITS, RELATIVE COST, RATES, COMMENTS. (AFTER RICHARD L. NORTON, CORNELL UNIVERSITY, 1980s). ADJUST PRICES FOR CURRENT PRICE LEVEL.

Herbicides, which fruits,[1] Rates/A:	Relative Cost/ Unit	Relative Cost/ Acre	Comments
Karmex (diuron 80% WP) 2 - 4 lbs. (1, 2, 3)	$ 4.95/lb.	$ 9.90 - 19.80	Apply early spring, can use with Paraquat, one + yrs. tree age, 3 + yrs peach, low rate on light, shallow soils, not on sand, gravelly soils. Don't treat trees on shallow full dwarfing root stocks as M.9.
Princep (simazine 80% WP) 2.5 - 5 lbs. (1, 2, 3, 4, 5)	4.25/lb.	10.63 - 21.25	Late fall or early spring, can be used with Paraquat, trees one + yrs; low rate light or shallow soils and under plums; extreme caution on cherries.
Sinbar (terbacil 80% WP) 1 - 2 lbs. (1, 2)	18.00/lb.	18.00 36.00	Early spring, trees 3 + yrs; low rate shallow or light soils, don't use sandy, gravelly soils; for quack, orchard grass, nutsedge.
Casoron G-4 100 - 150 lbs. (1, 2, 3, 4, 5)	1.30/lb.	130.00 - 195.00	Volatilizes w/warm temperature, very early spring or late fall.
Dalapon 74% (Dowpon) 5 - 10 lbs. (1, 3)	2.50/lb.	12.50 - 25.50	Young weeds less than 10 in.; repeat regrowth; don't spray bark less than 2 yrs old, apply guards to trunk bark beforehand; use with residual herbicide.
Paraquat (2 lbs./gal.) 1 - 2 qts. (1, 2, 3, 4, 5)	51.10/gal.	12.75 - 25.50	
Ammate X (60 lbs./100 gals.) (1, 3)	1.00/lb.	60.00	Can be used on poison ivy
Round-up 2 - 5 qts. (1, 3, 5)	90.00/gal.	45.00 - 112.50	Poison Ivy
Dacamine 40 (4 lbs./gal.) 1 - 2 qts. (1, 3)	20.50/gal.	5.13 - 10.25	Poison Ivy
Devrinol 50% WP (napropamide) 8 lbs. (1, 2, 3, 4, 5)	8.45/lb.	67.60	Late fall, very early spring before weeds; mix w/Paraquat or follow; safer than simazine for plum; apply before or in rain.
Surflan 75% WP (1, 2, 4, 5) 2⅔ - 5⅓ lbs.	12.20/lb.	31.75 64.66	One of safer herbicides on young trees, stone fruits.

[1] 1-apple; 2-pear; 3-peach; 4-plum; 5-cherry.

ficiently often to make the practice pay. Drip or microjet method of application of water is the growing trend.

A word of caution should be given against mechanical injury to young and mature trees by orchard implements. Broken branches and patches of bark knocked off the trunk are serious injury to young and mature trees by orchard implements. The most valuable preventative of injuries to trees is a *skillful* and *careful* driver. A moment's

Figure 9. These apple trees are in neighboring plots receiving different soil management programs. (Left) Typical tree under cultivation with cover crops for 22 years; trunk circumference was 31 11/16 inches. (Right) Tree under sod-mulch plus additional mulch for 21 years (cultivated with cover crop the first year); trunk diameter was 34 13/16 inches. Compare heights of the two trees with 20-foot pole in center of trees. Experiment demonstrated that clean cultivation with cover crops over a 22-year period was detrimental to soil structure and to size and yield of trees. Hence, with widely planted trees or with closer-planted compact trees of bearing age, the trend is a continuation of the system used for young trees - mowed sod middles with strip cultivation and/or herbicides under the trees. (Michigan State University).

Figure 10. Heavy machinery used in orcharding packs soil in the rooting area. Periodic breaking of sod is needed. (Top) Tool bar to loosen soil before planting. (Bottom left) Killifer subsoiler blade loosening dry soil in fall. (Bottom right) Good soil break-up for better aeration and moisture penetration. Soil shatters best in fall when dry.

carelessness may cause an injury that will take years to heal or, in fact, threaten the life of the tree.

Subsoiling. Heavy orchard machinery packs the soil between the trees. Some growers use the subsoiler blade to a depth of twenty inches on either side of the tree row at the branch spread of low-density trees to get better drainage and storage of water (Figure 10). The blade is run one direction one autumn, and at right angles the next, or in the hedgerow middles every 3-4 yrs.

Another practice is to loosen the sod after bloom with a spring tooth harrow. Some growers do this every three to five years. It helps to correct a more or less "sod bound" condition, discourages mice, stimulates growth of the sod, and loosens the soil for better absorption and penetration of rainfall. This "set-back" to the sod also reduces the water and nitrogen requirements by the grass at a time when they are most needed by trees. Grass soon recovers and by winter, it is well established to prevent erosion. A

light broadcast of NPK fertilizer should speed recovery of the sod.

Orchard Cover Crops. With the advent of more closely planted compact trees the use of cover and intercrops has almost ceased, with the excepton of pecans, e.g. for which no satisfactory dwarfing stocks have been found. The cover crops that have been satisfactory for orchards, if and when used, consist of legume and non-legume and summer and winter covers. The legumes have the advantage of contributing nitrogen to the soil, which is worth considering with the high price of nitrogen but modern orchardists prefer to use chemical nitrogen where they can control the availability to the tree by season and obtain better quality fruiting. Among the legumes that have been used for summer cover are: soybeans, cowpeas, lespedeza, and alfalfa (permanent sod), while non-legumes include millet and buckwheat. Winter cover legumes are winter vetch, crimson and red clover, sweet clover, crotolaria and alfalfa (permanent sod). Winter cover non-legumes are rye, wheat, oats (killed by first heavy frost in cold climates), field brome, and "weeds." Recommendations for growing these crops can be gotten from agronomy departments at state universities or your farm advisor.

FERTILIZING THE APPLE ORCHARD

The nutrients in the soil are first dissolved in the soil water and then absorbed by the fruit trees mainly through the fine root hairs at the tips of the root-lets. Nutrients also can be absorbed by the leaves and bark when dissolved and applied as sprays. Among the more important elements

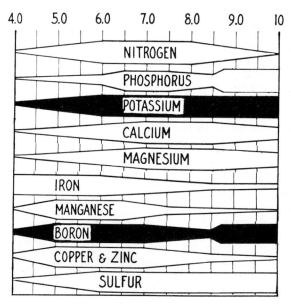

Figure 11. Number at top of chart represent pH (4.0 is very acid; 10 is very alkaline). Maximum availability of a nutrient is where the lines are widest apart. The pH under fruit trees in a humid region should be maintained at 6.5 to 7.0 by liming, according to research from Pa. State Univ. (After E. Troug, Univ. of Wis.)

absorbed are nitrogen, phosphorous, potassium, magnesium, calcium, sulphur, and iron. Boron, zinc, manganese, copper, chlorine and molybdenum are considered of lesser importance though highly important when deficient.

Lime Requirement, Bearing Orchards: The pH of the soil should receive first attention. In humid regions, the general recommendation is to maintain the pH at between 6.0 and 7.0 by liming. Research from Pennsylvania State University indicates that for calcium shortage (cork and bitter pit), the pH should be held at 6.5 to 7.0, using dolomite if magnesium also is low. In arid regions and marl soils a naturally high soil pH of 7.0 and above can create problems. As indicated from the Figure 11, high soil pH tends to cause most trace elements and some major elements to be less available to the tree roots. Applications of calcium sulphate and use of ammonium sulfate may improve availability of a nutrient such as iron. See comments on "Soil and Leaf Analysis", this chapter.

Nutrients Needed in Fruit Plantings and Deficiency Correction. The key nutrient for deciduous fruits over the world is unquestionably nitrogen. There are a few sections of the world, such as the arid San Joaquin Valley in California, where thirty-year orchards have never had a pound of nitrogen, only zinc sprays, but these areas are limited.

In regions where rainfall is at least fifteen to twenty inches, and particularly if the soil is sandy, there is sufficient leaching of the soil to reduce the available nitrogen supply to the deficient level for most fruits. Commercially, nitrogen is the key nutrient used to control growth and fruiting. The other nutrients, such as potash, magnesium, zinc, and boron, are supplied, if needed, in adequate quantities to prevent deficiencies from occurring. Excess boron is a problem where irrigation water carries too much boron. Excess sodium in some arid regions can be a problem. Be aware that some pesticides contain nutrients such as zinc, copper, sulphur, iron and manganese which may be enough to prevent deficiencies, particularly for the trace elements. These elements also may be impurities in NPK fertilizers.

Magnesium is becoming more widely recognized as a deficient nutrient in deciduous orchards in humid areas. Nitrogen, potassium, magnesium, and boron are all readily soluble and thus tend to be leached in areas where annual rainfall is at least moderate — thirty to fifty inches. Boron may be found to be deficient in some areas, however, where rainfall is no more than ten inches a year. The deficiency is created by a relatively high pH of the soil which tends to tie up the boron, making it unavailable to the trees. This also can happen with other trace elements, such as zinc, iron, and manganese. As yet there has been no report of molybdenum deficiency in deciduous orchards but this is not to say that the deficiency does not

exist. Trees have responded to copper in former corral areas and in sandy low-organic soils.

If zinc and manganese deficiencies occur in fruit trees growing in sandy soils in humid areas, they can be corrected either by applying sulfate forms to the soil (slow acting, if on high pH soils), or quicker response can be obtained by sprays. A spray of two to five pounds of manganese sulfate such as Techmangan (Tennessee Corp., Atlanta, Ga.) is applied preferably when foilage is young to medium age.

Zinc is generally caustic to foliage and it is usually applied as a dormant spray at from 6 to 40 pounds per hundred gallons just before the buds break, depending upon severity of deficiency and the crop. Zinc deficiency is more difficult to correct on sweet cherry than apple. In desert areas where soil pH is moderately high and these nutrients are "tied up in the soil", either dormant or foliar spraying or daubing the pruning cuts (grapes) is the best approach for deficiency correction, following the local government station's and extension service suggestions.

Iron chelate spray is partly effective for correcting iron deficiency in arid regions. In severe cases trunk injections have been used. Use ammonium sulfate if soil pH is high. In humid areas where organic matter content is low, or in sandy or overlimed soils the major elements, such as

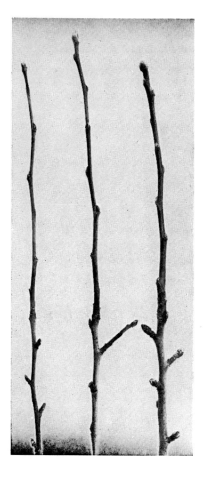

Figure 13. Shoot thickness is as important as shoot length in judging vigor of trees. Note the thick shoot and the plump fruit buds on the spurs of the Delicious wood at the right. Thin weak wood and spurs which contain mostly leaf buds are shown at the left. Wood of intermediate vigor is shown in the middle. Nitrogen fertilization would probably benefit growth of the trees from which the two left twigs were taken. (Rutgers University).

nitrogen, potassium, and magnesium also are likely to be limited.

Does the Orchard Need Fertilizer? Fruit trees are in good vigor if the leaves are large, plentiful, dark green, and the shoot growth is thick and relatively long for the age of the tree (Figure 13), and the fruiting is regular and satisfactory in size and quality. With a mature bearing apple tree, shoot growth at the tips of the branches should be at least six to ten inches annually, preferably 12 to 14 inches. Terminal growth for young nonbearing apple trees should be from 15 to 30 inches with the longer growths on the younger trees. The trunk and scaffold limbs should be thick and stocky with a dark greenish-brown color and only a moderate amount of scaliness of the bark. Amount of growth and number of leaves on the spurs are important indications of tree vigor. The nonbearing spurs in good condition should make from one-half- to three-fourths-inch length growth and should have from six to ten healthy leaves.

It should be stressed that pruning and nutrition are closely interrelated. Annual pruning throughout the tree tends to reduce fertilizer problems.

If the trees under question do not meet the above qualifications for good vigor, the difficulty may be due to a limited supply of one of the following nutrients, deficiency symptoms of which are briefed below. See also Figure 14 and color insert Chap. XVIII. It should be emphasized that by the time "eye-ball" deficiencies appear, considerable damage already may have occured to the tree and crop.

Low nitrogen. Shoot growth short and thin; leaves small, erect and light green or yellowish in color, dropping early, and showing somewhat more red color in the veins in autumn; bark light brown to yellowish orange in color; fruit small and highly colored, good storage quality, with crop relatively light, and tree alternate bearing.

Low potassium. Marginal and tip burning of the leaves; failure of lateral buds to unfold; short thin shoot growth; reduced size, color, and quality of the fruits. Potassium deficiency is more likely to occur on light soils, or shallow poorly drained soils, or in old orchards where the soil has been exploited by roots. Grain straw mulch is high in K.

Low phosphorus. Dark grayish-green foliage and stems, restricted shoots, leaf size; buds die; dull unattractive fruit lacking firmness, reduced yields. Rare in most orchards; there is a problem in New Zealand and Australia, resembling zinc deficiency in many respects (Figure 15).

Low magnesium. The leaves show some chlorosis and an interveinal scorch which may extend to the margins. This may appear suddenly in mid-summer and progress rapidly from the base toward the tip of the shoots. The basal leaves usually absciss in late summer while the tip leaves persist. Excess potash may induce deficiency. Leaf scorch is more uniform on old trees (Figure 14). Fruit drops early, but size, yield, and quality are less affected.

Low calcium. Restricted root growth, brown root tips; death of the growing shoot tips; chlorotic browning and breakdown of large spots in leaf centers; tip shoot leaves curled upward, yellowish; fruit with large lenticels, cracking, storage breakdown, more "sunscald," cork, scald, bitter pit. Ca sprays are beneficial. Low leaf zinc, small crop, accompanies low Ca. Summer pinching or

Figure 14. Three mineral deficiences that are common in some apple sections. Upper photos show cracked and misshapen McIntosh from British Columbia on the left, as compared with fruit receiving adequate boron; right photos show a flatter Delicious with no points, internal cork and badly misshapen fruit. (Lower left) Rosetted small narrow zinc deficient leaves with some chlorosis and wavy margins. (Lower right) Magnesium deficiency on apple showing interveinal chlorosis on upper leaves grading into interveinal necrosis in mid and lower leaves. Both symptoms occur on apple, depending upon variety and growing conditions. See color insert, Chap. XVIII.

Figure 15. Years of research finally revealed that the problem above in western Australia was due to phosphorus deficiency in soils that seem to "tie up" the P. There is poor growth and dying throughout the top; on close inspection the growth characters resemble zinc deficiency. It took the above tree about 15 yrs to develop the condition.

mowing of shoots may reduce fruit problems. See additional calcium comments at end of this chapter.

Low boron. Water-soaked exuding spots occur in the bark near the growing tips where they enlarge, turn brown and girdle the tips, causing death of leaves beyond the girdle; bark eventually becomes rough, cracks, and has corklike patches; some shoots develop leaf "rosettes"; poorly developed root system; fruit shows sunken corky areas near the skin and core, falls prematurely (Figure 14). B excess resembles B shortage.

Low zinc. Small mottled abnormally shaped leaves near the shoot tips with wavy margins which bunch together and form rosettes (Figure 14); reduced number of fruit buds, some "dieback" of shoots. Fruits small, misshapen, running high in percentage culls, and with reduced yields (Figure 14).

Low iron. Leaves near shoot tips show complete straw yellow or a fine network of green veins on yellowish green. Some leaves may show marginal burn. Yields reduced, fruit poorly colored, flat flavor.

Low manganese. Tip and mid-shoot leaves have herringbone appearance, with yellowish-green areas between main veins which are surrounded with a deeper green. The leaf size is not much affected; yields reduced; Mn excess in acid soils is associated with bark "measles," corrected by liming.

Low sulphur. Even yellowing of tip leaves first, whole tree if severe; reduced growth, fruiting and quality. Found in areas away from industry, or where pesticides and fertilizers do not contain S and irrigation water contains less than 0.75 ppm S.

Low copper. Dieback of shoots, black leaves resembling fire blight, yellowing of tip leaves; shoots tender, drooping in "S" pattern; reduced fruiting of poor quality; susceptible to winter injury; early leaf drop. Leaves curled, ragged edges.

Low molybdenum. Soil pH generally low; interveinal yellowing of tip leaves; marginal scorching lower leaves; rare.

Note: Deficiency correction techniques vary so much with soil, crop and climatic conditions, it is probably best for you to contact your government official for local recommendations. The book, *"Fruit Nutrition — Temperate to Tropical,"* Hort. Publ., 3906 NW 31 Pl., Gainesville, FL. 32606, USA, is a complete treatise on this subject with 100 8" x 10" pages of photographs, 888 pp total. Covers 20 key crops ($25).

Soil or Leaf Analysis? In regard to soil tests it should be stated that insofar as fruit tree crops are concerned, about the only value of soil analysis is to indicate the pH and whether the potash, magnesium, and phosporus, (calcium, boron, others when analyzed) are excessively high or low for the trees and particularly the ground cover.

The main difficulty is getting a representative sample of soil in an orchard. With perennial trees which are deeply rooted, even as deep as thirty feet in loess soil, the roots will be feeding at much lower depths than that from which the soil sample is taken. It is true that eighty to ninety per cent of the roots are in the upper foot of soil, but where a deficiency occurs, the lower feeding roots apparently pick up needed nutrients from lower depths.

It appears that our best indication of nutritional needs by trees and other deep-rooted plants is, in addition to soil tests, a chemical analysis of the leaves and perhaps the fruit. We do need more information on critical levels of nutrients in *fruit,* particularly *calcium.* Latter service is available from government stations or private consultants for interested growers at an added cost.

In collecting leaf samples from blocks, whether a problem or not, and having them analyzed in a soil or leaf analysis laboratory, it is well to bear some basic considerations in mind (thanks to Dr. Warren C. Stiles, Cornell University, Pomology, Ithaca, N.Y. 14850).

1. Method and time of sample collection should be uniform if samples are to be compared. Specifying the sampling time, i.e., 60 to 70 days after bloom, and location of leaves to be sampled is helpful in comparing results to standards. Collect about 50 leaves/block at random in a paper bag at breast height, mid growing season from middle portion of current season growth.

2. The leaf sample analysis indicates the amounts of various elements in the sample as submitted. Leaf analysis does not distinguish the amount of an element that is physiologically active from the amount that may be present as contamination.

3. Varieties, rootstocks, growth status and cropping levels, as well as soil variability and weather conditions during the growing season, influence leaf contents of elements in various ways and must be considered in interpreting leaf analysis results. When growth is severely limited by deficiency of some elements, the concentrations of all elements including the deficient one(s) may appear to be normal. In such cases diagnosis of the actual cause of the problem may require much additional information, or even cooperative farmer-researcher field trials of suspected elements. Some of these types of relationships will be illustrated as individual elements are considered below.

4. Leaf analysis can be used for various purposes such as diagnosing possible causes of a problem, or, preferably, to monitor nutrient status year to year so that corrections can be made before a problem becomes serious. In practice, both approaches are usually involved.

Standards for Apples

Nitrogen. Optimum N varies with cultivar and purpose for which it is grown. Usually the optimum values fall within an overall range from 1.8 to 2.4%. Values below 1.8% N are usually associated with reduced growth, smaller fruit size, and greater tendency toward biennial bearing. Annual removal of N *by fruit* is in the range of 30 to 40 lbs. per acre. An additional 30 to 60 pounds may be required for tree growth, to build reserves, and to support grass growth under the trees. Eliminating grass competition by herbicides reduces the rate of N applications required by approximately 30 to 40 pounds per acre per year. Excessive tree vigor resulting from excessive N applications can be partially compensated for by late summer pruning. This has two main effects: it improves fruit color by improving light distribution, and tends to limit root growth. Fruit size and sugars may also be reduced by summer pruning (Va. Poly. Tech. St. Univ. results).

Phosphorous. Leaf concentrations of P may range from 0.08 to over 0.30%. McIntosh tends to accumulate less P than Delicious. High levels of P in leaf samples indicate the possibility that tree growth has been stunted by lack of N, drought, competition from grass, root and/or trunk injuries, or because of other nutrient deficiencies.

Potassium. Optimum K levels usually fall between 1.2 and 1.8%. Cultivars such as Delicious appear to be more efficient in taking up K than others such as McIntosh. K levels should be considered in relation to N levels, with N/K ratios of 1.25 to 1.50 indicating reasonable balance. Levels below 1.2% indicate possible need for additional application of K; those below 0.8% indicate deficiency. The form of K applied should be related to Mg levels. If both K and Mg are adequate the use of muriate of potash or other forms may be appropriate.

Calcium. Ca levels below approximately 1.24% should be considered low, those below 1.00% deficient. Low levels of Ca may indicate insufficient soil levels of Ca (particularly as indicated by the subsoil), and/or low pH, but may be the result of shortages of other elements such as N or boron (B) or of other factors that limit the ability of the tree to absorb and translocate Ca. Leaf Ca levels normally show a direct positive relationship with leaf N concentrations. Liming and correcitng soil pH should be the first step in dealing with low Ca levels. If additional corrective treatments are required these might include soil applications of calcium sulfate (gypsum) if pH is too high, and/or foliar applications of calcium chloride. Fruit content of Ca has been related to keeping quality. Large fruit usually contain lower concentrations of calcium. Foliar sprays and/or post-harvest application of $CaCl_2$ may be needed on such fruit.

The Pennsylvania and New Jersey recommendations for *bitter pit* are 2 lbs $CaCl_2$/100 gal + wetting agent, 3 sprays with last spray 2 wks before harvest. Another treatment of 50 lbs $CaCl_2$ in 500 gal in the scald dip (includes DPA, 5 lbs captan, 1¼ lbs Benlate) helps reduce *bitter pit* developing in storage. For *cork* control, 1½ lbs $CaCl_2$ is used in each cover spray until 18-24 lbs/A are applied. This also helps with bitter pit control.

Additional Comments on Calcium. At a calcium conference held at U.S. Dept. of Agriculture, Beltsville, Md. the following summary notes may be of interest.

1. Ca moves mostly in young wood under bark. Growing shoot tips have highest affinity for CA, over and above the fruit. During a drouth, shoot tips remove both water and Ca from developing fruit, favoring pit or cork.

2. Any cultural practice inducing more shoot growth may increase cork/pit problem, such as too much N, heavy winter pruning, heavy fruit thinning, light crop, big fruit and inherent cultivar vigor. Hormone TIBA seems to hamper Ca movement to fruit.

3. Application of $CaCl_2$ sprays, summer pruning and post-harvest Ca dips help to increase Ca in fruit. Late sprays are more effective than early sprays for pit control. Fruit dips with a surfactant, as 0.35% Keltral and 4% $CaCl_2$ can increase Ca from, e.g. 200 ppm to 400-500 ppm in fruit and forego or greatly reduce pit development in storage. J.L. Mason of Summerland, B.C. recommends a surfactant both in sprays and dips.

4. $CaCl_2$ may move down rapidly when applied to the soil but little or no Ca increase occurs in tree leaves the first season, according to Dr. Mason.

5. Heavy N applications to the soil decrease Ca uptake more than it decreases K or Mg.

6. Most Ca uptake is near the root tips. Suberization on older root sections reduces Ca absorption.

7. Small apples have higher Ca content. Fruit on trees

with moderate to heavy crops show less cork and bitter pit, possibly due to the heavy crop holding back shoot growth.

8. A single rather concentrated spray of CaCl₂ (5%) about two weeks before harvest has given a 50% increase in fruit calcium (with some foliar burn). This may be adequate under British Columbia conditions.

9. Physiological disorders corrected other than pit and cork by calcium sprays are scald and internal break down. Firmness and storage life also are improved.

10. Between 1000 and 2000 ppm of Ca in the fruit is needed to get firmer fruit and hold firmness in storage.

11. Some cultivars as York, Baldwin, R.I. Greening and Spy are more susceptible to Ca disorders as pit. Less susceptible are Delicious, Golden Delicious, Rome and McIntosh.

12. Most of the Ca on the surface of a dipped apple goes into the outer flesh the first 2 wks. It takes 8-16 weeks to reach the inner flesh and core.

13. Storage humidity has a small effect on Ca movement into fruit. About 90% humidity is suggested for best penetration.

14. Vacuum forced infiltration of Ca helps speed movement into fruit. About 90% humidity is suggested for best penetration.

15. Withholding K over 10 yrs. to apple trees boosted Ca in leaves from 1.8 to 3.6%

16. Pear cork spot will respond to CaCl₂ sprays and dips as the apple. With Old Home rootstock no pear cork spot developed in Washington State whereas Bartlett, *Calleryana* and Winter Nelis seedling roots induced appreciable cork in fruit.

17. Over-tree irrigation reduces cork spot. It was suggested we try giving the Ca a different electrical charge than the leaf and fruit, perhaps causing Ca to move into the fruit better. This is being done with pesticide spray particles to make them stick to the tree better.

Magnesium. Optimum levels of Mg fall in the range of 0.30 to 0.45%. Rapidly growing young trees and trees bearing heavy crops of fruit are most susceptible to Mg deficiency. Low Mg supply in the soil is the major limiting factor. High-Mg dolomitic lime and applications of Mg salts such as kieserite or langbeinite (Sulpomag) are usually required to overcome this problem. Raising soil pH with calcitic lime may give a partial and temporary improvement in Mg availability but does not correct the basic Mg shortage. Response to soil applications of Mg salts may be slow (2-5 years). Inclusion of Epsom salts in the petal fall, first and second cover sprays is usually necessary until soil Mg levels are corrected. Epsom salts should be applied at a rate of 45 lbs. per acre in each of these 3 sprays if Mg levels in leaf samples are less than 0.3%.

Figure 16. Rotary mowers with swingout head are being used in low-and high-density sod orchards to keep the floor clean, particularly before mouse control treatment. (Courtesy R. Van Delft, Marwald, Ltd., Waterdown Rd., Burlington, Ont., Canada.)

Boron. Optimum leaf concentrations of B are in the range of 35 to 50 ppm. B sprays are effective in meeting fruit requirements and avoiding cork formations and early drop associated with B deficiency in apple. However, B is also necessary for root development. Annual applications of B in the fertilizer or applied separately *plus* foliar sprays may be required to meet the needs of high-producing apple orchards on size-controlling rootstocks. Using annual soil applications of 1¼ to 2 lbs. actual B per acre (equivalent to 6¼ to 10 lbs. of a 20% fertilizer grade borate) should meet the approximate annual needs but may require 1 or 2 foliar sprays of Solubor (total of 2 to 6 lbs. depending on tree size and planting density) to fully meet the boron requirements. Half this amount may give needed response on light sandy low-organic soils, pH 6.0 - 7.0.

Zinc. Optimum Zn leaf levels are similar to those of B, i.e., 35 to 50 ppm. Leaf concentrations below 15 ppm should be considered deficient. Varieties that accumulate higher levels of P appear to have higher Zn requirements than those that accumulate less P. Annual requirements for Zn are approximately 2 lbs. per acre if applied as inorganic salts in dormant sprays or approximately 0.2 to 0.3 lb. of actual Zn applied as foliar sprays of EDTA chelates (3 to 5 lbs./acre). Amounts of Zn required to correct severe deficiencies may be 4 to 5 times these amounts. Zn-containing fungicides provide some benefit but are not adequate to supply the total need. Leaf samples from trees sprayed with Zn-containing fungicides may contain 150 ppm to 500 ppm Zn but most of this is not active. In such cases, P contents of the samples and tree growth and fruiting are usually more indicative of the Zn status.

Manganese. The optimum levels of Mn range from 35 to 50 ppm. Mn deficiency may be associated with high soil pH, K deficiency, or in some cases may be associated with long-term effects of certain herbicide programs. It is easily supplied by using Mn-containing fungicides in the petal fall, first and second cover sprays, or by applying manganese sulfate (2 to 4 lbs. per 100 gallons dilute rate equivalent) at first cover. Leaf samples from trees sprayed with these materials may contain high levels of Mn, but much of this represents inactive contamination.

Copper. Optimum levels of Cu are in the range of 7.5 to 12 ppm. Leaf concentrations below approximately 3.5 ppm are deficient. High soil pH and/or high P levels may aggravate Cu deficiency. Cu can be added to the fertilizer but this is usually less effective and more expensive than a spray of a fixed-copper fungicide applied between greentip and ¼-inch green. Delaying this spray to ½-inch green may cause fruit russeting. (See bud development, color, Chapter XVII).

Iron. Fe is not usually a problem in humid regions and leaf concentrations vary considerably depending on several factors. Levels of 50 ppm appear to be adequate under most circumstances. High levels of Fe in relation to Mn may be used as an indicator of Mn deficiency, i.e. if Fe/Mn ratios approach or exceed 2.0. Iron sulfate can be added 30 lbs./T for sandy or gravelly soils in humid regions, but correction techniques are changing. Contact your government service for latest effective approach.

Sulfur is not included in most leaf analyses but requirements are believed to fall in a range between those for P and those for Mg, i.e. approximately 0.2% leaf content. Responses obtained from soil applications of gypsum, or sulfate of potash magnesia, or foliar sprays of Epsom salts suggest that at least a part of the response to such treatments may be related to sulfur. Until more definite information, pro or con, about sulfur requirements is developed, it would appear appropriate to rely on sulfate forms of other nutrients in sprays and ferlitizers to supply this element.

Combinations of Deficiencies

It is common to find two or more elements involved in a particular orchard nutrition problem. These combination problems may involve low K *plus* low Mg, low B *plus* low Zn; low Mg *plus* low Zn; high P *plus* low Zn *or* low Cu among others. In a few such cases, the cause of the problem may be a matter of imbalance, but in most instances the amounts of each of the elements available to the trees can be considered independently.

If both K and Mg, for example, are in short supply, application of both will be required. The apparent aggravation of a Mg shortage by increased application of K indicates a need for increasing the supply of Mg rather than limiting the supply of K.

Another common problem involves B and/or Zn shortages. Young trees that are flowering heavily for the first time or that bore their first heavy crop during the previous season may show varying degrees of shoot dieback resembling winter injury. Examination of these trees usually shows that the cambium has not been damaged by cold.

Prompt application of B and Zn sprays usually enables such trees to recover before dieback occurs. Left untreated, however, the same trees may lose a high percentage of terminal shoots and leaders, with the damage extending considerable distances back into older wood. As is the case with deficiencies of most micro-nutrients, this type of injury may be evident only on some branches and not as a general condition throughout the tree.

Summary. The nutritional status of an orchard should be evaluated by thoroughly analyzing soil test results, leaf sample analysis and observations of tree performance on a block to block basis. Varietal, cultural, soil and weather factors must be considered. After this has been done, a preventive fertilizer program can be developed and applied. This approach should minimize the adverse effects of nutrient shortages and optimize the production of high-quality fruit.

Amount of fertilizer needed. It should be stressed that fertilizer will not overcome fundamental difficulties of poor drainage, injury by rodents, nematodes, viruses, pesticides or herbicides which may cause low vigor and low fruit production. The amount of fertilzer to apply to an orchard will depend upon the amount of shoot growth obtained, the yield and quality of fruit, the soil type, permanent sod, cultivaton or chemical weed control, and the type spray chemicals being used. Each orchard presents a different problem. Trees on the lighter sandy type of soil require more fertilizer and usually more nutrients in the fertilizer than trees on the heavier soils. Orchards with sod growing beneath the trees will require more fertilizer, especially nitrogen, than trees under mulch or cultivation. For a bearing apple tree with a 40-footspread, ½ to 1 extra pound of actual nitrogen will be needed for the grass in addition to that required by the tree. The nitrogen stored in the green grass is readily available to the tree if the sod is cut frequently.

Under sod conditions, the average amount of fertilizer for apples per year, using ammonium nitrate, is based on the thickness of the trunk. Diameter of the trunk is divided by three which gives the approximate number of pounds of ammonium nitrate to apply. For example, an apple tree measuring six inches in trunk diameter would receive 2 pounds of ammonium nitrate, or equivalent in another form of nitrogen. Mixed fertilizers are applied on the basis of actual nitrogen desired per tree or acre and the percent N in the mix, e.g. a 16-16-16 has 16% N (16 lbs. N/100 lbs.

mix); ammonium nitrate has 33.5% actual N (33.5 lbs. N/100 lbs.) or about twice as much N as in the 16-16-16 mix.

Other sources of nitrogen used in orchards and percent N in each are: Urea (Nugreen is trade name for spray form), 45%; ammonium sulfate, 20%; nitrate of soda, 16%; nitrate of potash, 13% N, 44% K_2O; nitrate of soda-potash, 13% N, 15% K_2O; calcium nitrate, 15% N, 20% ws. Ca; and ammo-phos, 11% N, 48% phosphoric acid. Cost per lb. of actual N, of course, is important. Sodium nitrate is quickly available but more expensive per unit of N. Ammonium sulfate is slower acting, lowers pH in upper soil layer, is desirable in high pH soils, but can be counteracted in humid areas by liming, based on soil tests every other year or every three or four years.

Since the last World War when nitrate of soda and sulfate of ammonia were scarce or unavailable, ammonium nitrate and urea sprays have been used on orchards. Both proved stisfactory. Urea is conveniently placed in the tank with or without pesticides and applied at three pounds per hundred gallons before bloom and five pounds after. This may supplement soil applications of N, or provide the sole source. Urea applied as a spray has the advantage of the nitrogen entering the tree within a few hours. Urea is frequently used in an emergency, when in early spring it is apparent that inadequate nitrogen has been applied to the soil for a heavy bloom and fruit set, as judged by foliar color and shoot growth. Urea sprays probably should not be applied after about the second cover spray.

Urea applied directly to the soil must be "rained in" almost immediately. Otherwise the urease enzyme in the soil will change it to ammonium carbonate, thence evaporated to the air as ammonia and carbon dioxide. Urea applied to recently-limed soil also will cause the nitrogen to be evaporated. Urea is the most economical form of N per lb but can be the most expensive if handled improperly.

Continued applications of ammonium nitrate to the soil tend to increase soil acidity. For each hundred pounds of fertilizer applied, about fifty-eight pounds of lime are required. It is advisable to have samples of the soil checked every few years by state or dealer agencies, and then apply the recommended lime to raise the pH to between 6.5 and 7.0, to benefit trees and the sod. Accumulation of sulfur in the soil from sprays is also a factor in increasing soil acidity. High-magnesium lime (dolomite) is best when soil test shows a Mg need.

Some apple varieties require more nitrogen than others. Delicious, Jonathan, Stayman and Winesap usually respond well to more nitrogen than Golden Delicious, McIntosh, and Rome. The latter three varieties in sod require about a pound of actual nitrogen per big tree. Varieties that respond better to about half this amount are

English Codling, Twenty Ounce, and Starr.

Manure of any kind is usually classified as a nitrogenous fertilizer, although it carries about as much potash as nitrogen, and is low in phosphorus. Manure used in field experiments at Pennsylvania State University was computed to carry the equivalent of 9.8 pounds of nitrogen, 2.82 pounds of phosphorus, and 7.14 pounds of potassium per ton. These figures vary for different manures and other factors. It requires about 20 times as much manure by volume to furnish the same amount of nitrogen as in sulfate of ammonia. Also, nitrogen in manure becomes available to the trees more slowly than the commercial forms and, for this reason, it seems advisable to make a light application of manure in early spring or late fall in combination with sufficient soluble nitrogen in spring to meet the requirements.

As for phosphorus, there are only limited data (except in Australia and New Zealand) indicating a response by fruit plants other than strawberries to phosphorus applications. Nevertheless, in humid areas it is a common practice to use an N-P-K base mix. For fruit plantings in general, a 1-1-1 ratio seems to be the most widely used, however, where the soil is quite sandy, a 1-2-2 ratio of N-P-K is used and may be needed, although there are insufficient experimental data to back this suggestion.

On sandy soils in *humid* regions an N-P-K base mix is generally advisable. If organic matter is low, other nutrients may give response if included on an insurance basis. If this is desired, a magnesium oxide content in a complete mix should be about the same as the nitrogen percentage; for example, if a 5-10-10 is used, about four to five per cent magnesium oxide should be included. Borax can be included so that no more than about five pounds per acre per year is applied. In a 5-10-10 mix this would be about ten pounds of borax per ton. Peaches are very sensitive to excessive use of boron, whereas apples will tolerate up to a pound per mature low-density tree, provided it is applied only every third year.

Bitter pit in apples and *cork spot,* can be reduced by calcium foliar sprays. Addition of B and a spreader to calcium spray also has reduced cork (Contract Dr. G. Greene, Pa. State Sub-Sta., Biglerville, 17307.) Avoid *heavy* pruning. Avoid fruit thinning, temporarily, on problem trees. Summer mowing of shoots may help reduce cork and bitter pit.

In the above base mix and on a ton basis, the following nutrients also may be included; twenty pounds each of manganese and zinc sulfate, ten pounds of copper sulfate, thirty pounds of iron sulfate, and one pound of sodium or ammonium molybdate. There are proprietary trace element mixes on the market, such as FTE (Ferro Corporation, Cleveland, Ohio) and Esminel (Tennessee Corporation, Atlanta, Ga.), which can be mixed with N-P-K-Mg base mixes at 50 to 100 lbs/T. A liquid complete

71

Figure 17. A snowball bloom creates a heavy drain on both stored food and nutrients, dwarfing the foliage (right) at a period of the year when rapidly enlarging leaves are very important. Proper pruning, fruit thinning, and fertilization, are effective in attaining the ideal bloom shown at left.

fertilizer mix with chelated trace elements and herbicide is in use in New Jersey (See Childers' references).

Annual Bearing, Quality Fruit. No one is a better judge than the grower himself as to how much nitrogen to apply to his trees each year based on their performance in the past. Growers should go through their orchard several times a season and particularly at harvest. Too little nitrogen will result in the trees becoming "hard", foliage light green in color at harvest, yields down, but color, eating and storage quality of a high order. If too much nitrogen is being used, trees will become too green and healthy appearing, fruit production will be upped but fruit color will be less and the eating and storage quality likely lowered. It is true, however, that growers contracting their crop to processors will use more nitrogen for better yields and reduce the spray program since fruit finish and full color are not as important for processing.

Trees on seedling roots will vary as to the amount of nitrogen required. Some trees in the row will be smaller and need more fertilizer, others may be getting too vigorous. When growing fruit for the fresh market, it is wise to check the crop at harvest and tag overly-vigorous trees that need less fertilizer with a plastic colored label. Trees on clonal stocks are more uniform vs seedling roots. The entire orchard may be showing less need for nitrogen, in which case it should be cut slowly, not eliminated entirely as too often done. Cut it to three-fourths or half. Complete omission of fertilizer for two or three years may result in alternate bearing and be difficult to get the trees back into annual bearning. Temporary use of a major-trace element fertilizer on medium-low fertility soils in New Jersey has brought trees to uniform vigor.

If a heavy crop is expected, both the pruning (reduce bloom points) and fertilizer may be increased modestly so that adequate nitrogen will be available to the heavy bloom to set the apples, and at the same time develop big leaves to supply food to size the apples (See Figure 17). An excessive bloom and fruit set draws heavily on the same ingredients it takes to size the leaves. Once leaves have attained a small size early, they never become larger later. If a heavy crop is set, which is likely, then use of chemical thinners to remove the excess crop will enable the subsequently formed leaves to size better.

As indicated in the pruning Chapter IV, annual pruning probably is the most important practice in a bearing apple orchard. On soils of moderate native fertility in New Jersey, some growers have reduced their fertilizer applications to little or nothing over several years and compensated for it by *annual* pruning, which also has increased the quality and color of the fruit. This practice, however, must be checked carefully to start adding a little fertilizer if yields begin to drop. Annual pruning also will reduce the cost of thinning the fruit, harvesting, and help eliminate the growing and handling of cull fruit.

Old orchards which have lost vigor frequently can be brought back to good production by good pruning practice (spread over 2-3 years), by doubling or quadrupling the fertilizer applications, particularly nitrogen, and by use of trace elements if known to be deficient in the area, until vigor is restored. Borax at one half to one pound per mature apple tree the first year may help. On the other hand, it may be better to pull old trees block by block and replant with high-density trees.

Figure 18. For backyards and in small orchards, applying fertilizer by hand may be the best approach. Most feeding roots are in a band just under the outside drip of the branches. The tree gets most of the fertilizer if applied in a 2- to 3-ft. band at least a month before buds swell in spring. (Penn. State Univ., University Park 16802.)

Figure 19. This is a power-take-off tractor-operated fertilizer or lime spreader for quick broadcast of dry fertilizer.

Medium- and Low-Density Trees. The amount and kind of fertilizer to use varies with the variety and basic fertility of the soil. Recommendations for the kind of fertilizer to use in this chapter for low-density trees more or less hold for medium and high-density trees. Amount per tree is based on trunk diameter. For example, if a bearing low-density Golden Delicious tree in sod with a 10-inch trunk requires 1 lb. actual N (or 10 lbs. 10-10-10 or 3 lbs. am. nitr. or 5 lbs. am. sulfate), a dwarf Golden Delicious with a 2 in. trunk would require about 1/5 this amount. One-fourth to one-third less fertilizer may be needed where in-row shallow rototillng or herbicides are used. Here again, rate of fertilizer should be adjusted according to color, quality and yield of fruit the previous year or years.

If in doubt of the amount of fertilizer to use, it is best to apply at the lower rate and gradually make any adjustments needed in subsequent years.

Time for application. Nitrogen fertilizer will do the most good if applied at least three to four weeks before the buds begin to swell in spring. This gives the nitrogen ample time to be dissolved by rain or irrigation, absorbed and transferred to the spurs and shoots, resulting in early development of large leaves, good shoot growth, good set of fruit, and rapid development in fruit size.

If a heavy bloom occurs, supplemental nitrogen in urea sprays may be needed to size the leaves and carry the heavy fruit set. A heavy bloom and fruit set tend to dwarf leaves in early spring (Figure 17).

Experimental evidence has shown little or no diffrenece in tree response with fall or spring applications of fertilizer. In fall it should be applied about a month after leaf drop to avoid trunk cold injury in low-temperature areas. Some fertilizer may be leached below the rootzone if soils are light and sandy, but the saving in price of fall delivered fertilizer and better labor availability may justify fall application. Do not apply when the ground is frozen or icy. Rains and thawing may carry much of it away.

Method of application. Former commercial method was to apply fertilizer by hand in a band around the tree under the spread of the branches (Figure 18). No fertilizer was applied within two or three feet of the trunk. Few feeding roots are in this area. Method is effective in saving of fertilizer but laborious.

Where feasible, application of fertilizer by machinery is more rapid and labor saving than by hand. Fruit growers report satisfacotry results with endgate distributors, lime drills, and grain drills. With endgate distributors, the dealer truck or PTO tractor-attached unit is driven up the row middles broadcasting over the entire area, or thrown to the right or left, one side only, directly under the trees (Figure 19). Where the land and tree spacing is suitable, some growers apply in one direction one year and in the cross direction the next.

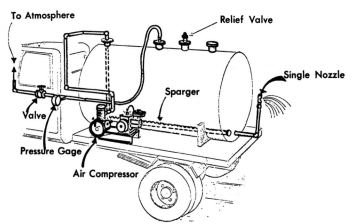

Figure 20. With deciduous fruit trees, fertilizers should be applied at least a month before buds break. This can be in dry or liquid form. It can be spread over the orchard floor which takes more fertilizer (left) or directed in a circle under the tree (right), using only enough to feed the tree. Left equipment spreads the fertilizer in an adjustable swath up to 40 ft. from one jet nozzel at 20-30 lbs/sq. in from a small compressor.

If liquid fertilizer is used, spray application equipment can be designed or built by the grower (Figure 20). Time and labor can be saved, and with this job greatly reduced, only the best days need be picked. Liquid fertilizer with or without chelated trace elements also is being strip-applied by tank-truck booms or through overhead permanent irrigation pipes and in drip irrigation (fertigation) with careful timing.

Orchard irrigation. Orchard irrigation is increasing for apples in world orchards and particularly the more shallow-rooted compact-tree orchards. Most of the commercial orchards in the USA are being irrigated. Heavy mulching and other practices for conserving moisture on the better soils, however, may be more economical in tiding the trees over dry periods, but one severe drouth in 5-10 yrs., e.g., may so-damage the trees that it takes yrs for them to recover, in which case it would have paid to provide irrigation at the outset.

Irrigation should be considered in heavy shallow-rooting soils or in sandy soils if, in spite of mulching, fruit thinning, and other standard practices, the trees are making less than eight to ten inches annual terminal growth and producing small-size, poor-quality fruit. It would be well to study local U.S. Weather Bureau rainfall records, speak to local farmers and determine the frequency of droughts for the region.

The first requisite in orchard irrigation is a plentiful supply of water from a deep well, river or stream which does not go dry during the most extensive drought. There is increasing switch to drip or microjet irrigation in many areas. See Chapter 19 for irrigation systems being used, amount of water needed, other details.

Review Questions

1. Why does a young or dwarf apple orchard require different soil management than a low-density bearing orchard?
2. Outline a soil management program for dwarf (indicate stock(s), cultivar) apple trees planted in hedgerows on gently rolling, relatively heavy soil.
3. Outline a soil management program for dwarf (indicate stock(s), cultivar) apple trees in hedgerows on gently rolling sandy-gravelly soil.
4. What are the advantages of sod mulch with additional mulch for mature bearing apple trees? Disadvantage?
5. Discuss a control program for mice.
6. What is the value of a subsoiler in orchards?
7. Discuss a control program for deer or an animal pest peculiar to your area.
8. Select 2 of the following orchard nutrient deficiencies and describe symptoms: nitrogen, potassium, calcium, zinc, iron and boron.
9. Discuss the interrelationship between pruning, fertilization, irrigation, fruit thinning, cultivation and/or sod as they affect fruit color and quality.
10. In apple orchards, what nutrient receives most attention in the fertilization program, and why?
11. How much fertilizer would you apply to a 20-year apple tree growing in medium-heavy soil in sod and making annual terminal growth of from 2 to 3 inches?
12. What percentage nitrogen do the following fertilizers contain: sulfate of ammonia, nitrate of soda, urea, and ammonium nitrate?
13. What effect do continued applications of the above fertilizers have on soil acidity in the upper few inches of soil?
14. Discuss briefly orchard irrigation in your region? When needed, how applied.
15. Discuss soil and leaf analysis in determining lime and fertilizer needs in your area.

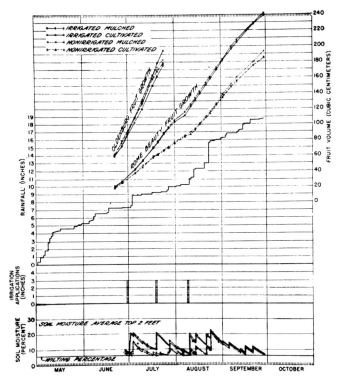

Figure 21. This chart shows the effect of soil moisture level on rate of fruit growth of an early ripening apple, Oldenburg, and a late ripening variety, Rome Beauty in Maryland. Effect of mulching, cultivation, and irrigation on size of apples was greater for the late-ripening Rome than for the early ripening Oldenburg (Courtesy John R. Magness, USDA).

Suggested Collateral Readings

ALLEN, M. Apple leaf uptake of inorganic sprays (Cu, Mg). Pesticide and Science 1:152-5, 1970.

BARKER, A.V. and H.A. MILLS. Ammonium and nitrate nutrition in horticultural crops. Hort. Rev. Avi Publ. Co. 2:395-423. 1980.

BATJER, L.P., et al. Nitrogen intake of dormant apple trees at low temperature. Proc. ASHS 42, 69, 1943.

BEATTIE, J.M. High nitrogen for Baldwin apples. Proc. ASHS 63, 1, 1954.

BENSON, N.R. and R.P. COVER, Jr. Response of apple seedlings to zinc fertilization and mycorrhizal innoculation. Hort. Sci. 11(3):252-3. 1976.

BENSON, N.R., et al. Sulfur deficiency in deciduous tree fruits. ASHS 83:55-62. 1963.

BENSON, N. Soil fumigation helps replants in old apple orchards. Wash. State Hort. Ass'n. Proc. 90-95. 1974.

BENSON, N.R. and R.P. COVEY, Jr. P nutrition of young apple trees in gravel culture. J. ASHA. 104(5):682-685. 1979.

BENSON, N.R., et al. Apple replant problem. Washington Stat. J. ASHS 103(2):156-158. 1978.

BERNSTEIN, L. Salt tolerance of fruit crops. USDA Agr. Inf. Bull. No. 292. 8 pp Aug. 1965.

BLACK, F. "Daily flow" irrigation for fruit trees, row crops. Leaf H191 (request recent ed.) Scoresby Fruit Res. Sta., Ferntree, Victoria, 3156 Austr. (Pioneer in drip irrigation)

BLACK, J.D.F. Development of impermeable layer under straw mulch in a soil management trial, Aust. J. of Exp. Agr. and Animal Husbandry 3:101-104. 1963.

BLACK, J.D.F. and P.D. MITCHELL. Soil water use from an apple orchard under various soil management systems. Aust J. of Exp Agr. and Animal Husb. 10:209-213. 1970.

BLANPIED, G.D. and G.H. OBERLY. Ca and Mg in annual rings of apple wood. J. ASHS. 103(5) 638-640. 1978.

BLANPIED, G.D. Artificial rain, pH and Ca Conc on Ca and K in apple leaves. Hort. Sci. 14(6):706-708. Dec. 1979.

BOLLARD, E.G., P.M. ASHWIN, and H.J.W. MCGRATH. 1962. Leaf Analysis in the Assessment of Nutritional status of Apple Trees. N.Z. Jour. of Agri. Res. 5(5&6):373-88.

BOON, J. van der and A. POWER. Bitter pit in James Grieve apples and nitrogen, calcium nitrate sprays, fruit thinning, picking time. Haren. Institute for Soil Fertility. Rapport 3-74 (in Dutch) 1974.

BOULD, C., et. al. Grass and uptake of P by trees. J.H.S. 29, 301, 1954.

BOULD, C., and A.I. CAMPEBELL. Virus, fertilizer and rootstock effects on young apple trees. Jour. Hort. Sci. Vol. 45, No. 3. 287-294. July 1970.

BOYNTON, D. Magnesium nutrition of apple trees. Soil Sci. 63, 53, 1947.

BOYNTON, D., et al. Hay mulch and N supply. Proc. ASHS 59, 103, 1952.

BOYNTON, D., et al. N metabolism in McIntosh apple trees sprayed with Urea. Proc. ASHS 62, 135, 1953.

BOYNTON, D. and O.C. COMPTON. Oxygen concentration and new root formation. Proc. ASHS 42, 53, 1943.

BYERS, R.E. Rodenticides for Control of Pine Voles, Orchards. J. ASHS 103(1):65-9. 1978.

BYERS, R.E., and R.S. YOUNG. Cultural Management for Pine Voles. HortSci. 9:445-446. 1974.

CARROLL, E.T. Control of Apple Measles. Queensland Agricultural Journal 100:29, 1974.

CHANDLER, W.H., D.R. HOAGLAND and J.C. MARTIN. Zinc and copper deficiency in corral soils. Proc. ASHS 47, 15, 1946.

CHAPLIN, M.H. and A.R. DIXON. Analysis of Plant Tissue by Direct Reading Spark Emission Spectroscopy. App. Spectro. Vol. 28, No. 1. 1974. pp. 5-6. 1973.

CHILDERS, N.F. Liquid major-trace-elements soil fertilizer mix. Hort. News (Cook Coll., New Bruns., N.J. 08903) Nov. 1970.

CHILDERS, N.F. Fruit nutrition-temperature to tropical. Horticultural Publications, 3906 NW 31Pl., Gainesville, FL. 32606. Over 900 pp. 1966. $22.

CHUNTANAPARB, N., and G. CUMMINGS. Seasonal trends in conc. of N, P, K, Ca, Mg in leaves. Apple, Blueberry, Grape and Peach. J. ASHS 105(6):933-935. 1980.

COOPER, R.E. and A.H. THOMPSON. Solution culture investigations of the influence of manganese, calcium boron, and pH on internal bark necrosis of 'Delicious' apple trees. J. ASHS 97(1):138. Jan. 1972.

CROCKER, T.E., and A.L. KENWORTHY. Investigation of internal bark necrosis in 'Delicious' apple trees. J. ASHS 98(6):559. Nov. 1973.

DELVER. P. Soil factors in relation to bitter pit. De Fruitteelt 64:542-545 (in Dutch). 1974.

DEVYATOV. A., et al. Sand as mulch in your apple orchards. Fruit Sci. Reports. Vol. III, Nov. 4. 1976 Skierniewice, Poland. 1976.

DINAUER, R.C., Ed. et al. P in agriculture. (Book) Am. Soc. Agric., Univ. of Wis., Madison. 910 pp. 1980.

DOMOTO, P.A. and A.H. THOMPSON. Interactions of Calcium, Potassium and Manganese on Delicious Apple as Related to Internal Bark Necrosis. J. ASHS 101:44-47, 1976.

DORAN, S.M. Cost removing, replacing fruit trees. Wash. Farm Bus. Mgmt. Rpts EM 4298. Nov. 1977.

DRAKE, M., W.J. BRAMLAGE, and J.H. BAKER. Calcium in 'Baldwin' Apples and Tree Yield, Physiological Disorders, J. ASHS 99:379-380. Also, J. ASHS, 99:376-8. 1974.

EATON, G.W., and C.N. MEEHAN. The effect of interstock on the mineral nutrition of young trees of four apple cultivars. J. ASHS 7(5):496. 1972.

EGGERT, D.A. and A.E. MITCHELL. Russeting of Golden Delicious apples, physiological and biochemical literature review. Bot. Rev. 34:441-469. 1968.

FAUST, M., and J.D. KLEIN. Levels and sites of metabolically active calcium in apple fruit. J. ASMS 99(1):L93. Jan. 1973.

FAUST, M. and C.B. SHEAR. Corking disorders of apples, physiological and biochemical literature review. Bot. Rev. 34:441-469. 1968.

FAUST, M., et al. Calcium accumulation in fruit of certain apple crosses. HortSci. 6(6):542. Dec. 1971.

FAUST, M. and C.B. SHEAR. Ca on apple respiration. J ASHS:97-4. 437-9, 1972.

FERNANDEZ, C.E. and N.F. CHILDERS. Molybdenum deficiency of apple. Proc. Amer. Soc. Hort. Sci. 75:32. 1960.

FERREE, D.C., and A.H. THOMPSON. Bark necrosis of apple as influenced by Ca placement and soil Mn. Md. Ag. Exp. Sta. Bull. A-166, June 1970.

FERREE, D.C., and G.A. GAHOON. N nutrition of apple on M9 roots. Oh. Agric. Res. and Devel. Cen.; Res. Cir. 239. 9-p12. July 1978.

FISHER, E.G. and D.R. WALKER. Apple leaf absorption of Mg and P applied to lower surface. Proc. ASHS 65, 17, 1955.

FORD, E. M. Epsom salt sprays on apple trees on two rootstocks. J. Hort. Sci. 43, 505-17. 1968.

FORD, H.W., et al. The effect of iron chelate on root development of citrus. Proc. ASHS 63, 81, 1954.

FRITH, G.J.T. Light stimulated activity of nitrate reductase in apple roots. Plant & Cell Physiol. 15:153-155. 1974.

GEIGY CHEMICAL CORPORATION, Ardsley, N.Y. 10502. Contact for latest weed control chemicals for fruits and for chelated trace elements for fruits.

GERGELY, I., et al. Polyethylene glycol induced water streess; Effect on apple seedlings. II. ⁴⁵Ca Uptake. J. ASHS 105(6):858-861. 1980.

GILBERT, F.A. The place of sulfur in plant nutrition. Bot. Rev. 17, 671, 1951.

GRASMANIS, V.O. and G.R. EDWARDS. Flower Initiation in Apple by Short Exposure to Ammonium Ion. Aust. J. Plant Physiol. 1:99-105. 1974.

GRAY, A.S. Sprinkler irrigation handbook. Latest edition. Rain Bird Sprinker Mfg Corp., Glendore, Calif.

GREEN, G.M. Calcium applications and cork spot control. Pennsylvania Fruit News. April, 1974.

GREENHAM, D.W.P. Long-term manurial trial on apple trees. J. Hort. Sci. 40 213-35, 1965.

GREENHAM, D.W.P. and G.C. WHITE. Effects of grass sward, straw mulch, cultivation on Laxton's Superb trees. Rpt. E. Maill. Res. Sta. for 1967 (1968) 121-8.

HALLER, M.H. and P.L. HARDING. Relation of soil moisture to firmness and storage quality of apples. Proc. Amer. Soc. Hort. Sci. 36:205-211. 1938.

HAMMOND, W., and S.D. SEELEY. Spring bud development of Malus and Prunus species and soil temperature. J. ASHS. 103(5):655-657. 1978.

HARLEY, C.P., et al. Nutrients from a mulch. Proc. ASHS 57, 17, 1951.

HEWITT, E.J. Metal interrelationships in plant nutrition. J. Exp. Bot. 4, 59, 1953; and 5, 110, 1954.

HIMELRICK, D.G., and J.E. POLLARD. Effect of daminozide on nutrient accumulation in apple fruits. HortSci. 13(5):540-541. 1978.

HIMELRICK, D.G., and M. INGLE. Ionselective electrode determination of Ca in apple fruits. HortSci. 15(2):156-157. 1980.

HIMELRICK, D.G. Total and ionic Ca in apple leaf and fruit. ASHS J. 106:5. 619-21.

HIMELRICK, D.G. and J.E. POLLARD. Effect of Sampling Date and Daminozide on the Nutrient Composition of 'McIntosh' Leaves. J. ASHS 102(1):97-100. 1977.

HOLLAND, D.A. Estimating leaf area on a tree. Rpt. East Malling Res. Sta. for 1967, pp. 101-104. 1968.

HUBERTY, M.R. and H.E. PEARSON. Some effects of water rather high in sodium. proc. ASHS 53, 62, 1949.

KELLEY, W.P., et al. Soil salinity in relation to irrigation. Hilgardia. 18, 635, 1949.

KETCHIE, D.O. and M.W. WILLIAMS. A method for feeding

chemicals into young apple trees. J. ASHS 7(5):491. 1972.

KIRBY, A.H.M. and T.M. WARMAN. Influence of Mg50₄ on physiochemical properties of orchard pesticides. Rpt. E. Mall. Res. sta. 1966 (1967), 177-80.

KLAREN, C.H., and D.O. KETCHIE. Nutritional and metabolic aspects of 'Delicious' apple with "dead spur." HortSci. 14(5):594-595. Also 596-7. 1979.

KOCH, B.L., et al. Growth of apple, pear seedlings on pear soil fumigation with chloropicrin. HortSci. 15(5):598-600. 1980.

KOCH, B.L., et al. Soil fumigation on early growth, production of 'Delicious' Apple. J. ASHS 105(6):887-890. 1980.

KOTZE, W.A.G., C.B. SHEAR, and J. FAUST. Nitrogen Source and Aluminum on Growth and Mineral Nutrition of Apple and Peach Seedlings. J. ASHS 102(3):279-282. 1977.

LATIMER, L.P. and G.P. PERCIVAL. Sawdust, hay, and seaweed mulch. Proc. ASHS 50, 23, 1947.

LEECE, D.R. (ed). Fertilizers and the Environment. Aust. Inst. of Agr. Sci., Sydney. 132 p. 1974.

LEWIS, T.L., et al. A sheltered environment on mineral element composition of Merton Worcester apple fruits and leaves and on the incidence of bitter pit at harvest. J. Hort. Sci. 52:401-407. 1977.

LEWIS, T.L. and D. MARTIN. Longitudinal distribution of applied calcium, and of naturally occuring calcium, magnesium, and potassium, in Merton apple fruits. Aust. J. Agric. Res. 24:363-71. 1973.

LIDSTER, P.D., et al. Storage relative humidity on calcium uptake by 'Spartan' apple. J. Amer. Soc. Hort. Sci. 102(4):394-396. 1977.

LIPECKI, J., and W. MARTYN. Effect of ethylene on fungal spores of fruit rot. Fruit Sci. Rpts. Skierniewice, Poland. Vol. IV:(1) 25-29. 1977.

LORD, W.J., et al. Liming and N on Sturdeespur Delicious apple. ASHS J. 106:5. 616-4. 1981.

LORD, W.J., et al. Accumulation of simazine in mulch residue under apple trees. Hort. Sci. Vol. 5. No. 4, August 1970.

LORD, W.J., et al. Phytotoxicity of soil-incorporated 2. 6-Dichloro-Benzonitrile to clonal apple rootstocks. J. ASHS 97(3):390. 1977.

LORD, W.J., L.F. MICHELSON and D.L. FIELD. Response to irrigation and soil moisture by McIntosh apple trees in Massachusetts. Mass. Agr. Exp. Sta. Pub. 537. 23 pp. November 1963.

LORD, W.J. and D.W. GREENE. Apple Tree Response to Dichlobenil. HortSci. 10:395-396. 1975.

LUNDERGAN, C., and J. JANICK. Low temperature storage of in vitro apple shoots. HortSci. 14(4):514. Aug. 1979.

MAGNESS, J.R., E.S. DEGMAN, and J.R. FURR. Soil moisture and irrigation investigations in Eastern apple orchards. USDA. Tech. Bull. 491. 1935.

MAHAN, J.N. The fertilizer supply. 1972-73. USDA Leaflet, Washington, D.C. April 1973. (The bulletin should be available annually from the Agricultural Stabilization and Conservation Service).

MARINI, R.P., and J.A. BARDEN. Apple flowering, growth affected by summer pruning. J. ASHS 107:1. 34-9. 1982.

MARINI, R.P., and J.A. BARDEN. Light entering trees, leaf weight and summer, dormant pruning. J. ASHS 107:1. 39-43. 1982.

MARONEK, D.M., et al. Mycorrhizal fungi, importance in horticultural crop production. Hort. Rev. 3; 172-213. Avi. Publ. Co., Westport, Ct. 1981.

MARTIN, D., et al. Tree Sprays of Calcium, Boron, Zinc and Naphthaleneacetic Acid, on Storage Disorders in Merton Apples. Aust. J. Agric. Res. 1976. 27, 391-98.

MARTIN, D., et al. Calcium sprays on stored Sturmer apples. Field Station Record, Div. of Plant Indus. CSIRO. (Aust.); Vol. 7, p 10-21. 1971.

MARTIN, D., et al. Tree sprays to control bitter pit, scald. Fld. Sta. Res. Rpt., Div. Pla. Ind. CSIRO. (Aust.); 45-64. 1969.

MARTIN, D., et al. High levels of N on disorder incidence in Jonathan. Comm. Sci. Ind. Res. Org., Australia 1970.

MASON, J.L., and J.M. MCDOUGALD. Calcium in Nutrient Solution on Breakdown and Uptake in 'Spartan' Apple. J, Firmness and Ca Conc. in 'Spartan' Apple Fruits J ASHS. 99:318-321. 1974.

MASON, J.L., B.G. DROUGHT, and J.M. MCDOUGALD. Effect of a Calcium Chloride Dip on Breakdown, Firmness and Ca Conc. in 'Spartan' Apple. HortSci. 9:596. 1974.

MASON, J.L. and B.G. DROUGHT. Penetration of Calcium into 'Spartan' Apple Fruits from a Post-Harvest Calcium Chloride Dip. J. Amer. Soc. Hort. Sci. 100:413-415. 1975.

MAYNARD, D.N., and A.O. LORENZ. Controlled-release fertilizers for horticultural crops. Hort. Rev. 1:79-140. Avi. Publ. Co., Westport, Ct. 1979.

MCSORLEY, R. Parasitic nematodes on tropical and subtropical fruits. Fla. Agr. Sta. Bul. 823. July 1981.

MERSON, M.H., and R.E. BYERS. Commercial zinc phosphide baits on control of meadow and pine voles. HortSci. 16(1):49-51. 1981.

MICHELSON, L.F., et al. Response of apple trees to soil injections of lime. Hort. Sci. Vol. 4 (3) 251-252. 1969.

MILLIKAN, C.R. and B.C. HANGER. Distribution of Zn in pear trees following bark injection. Reprint Aust. J. Agric. Res. 18:85-93. 1967.

MISIC, P. and M. GRAVRILOVIC. Effects of Malling Rootstocks on some apple varieties. Jour. for Sci. Agric. Res. (Yugoslavia) 20:68, 2-28. 1967.

MOON, H.H., et al. Early-season symptoms of magnesium deficiency in apple. Proc. ASHS 59, 61. 1952.

MORESHET, S., G. STANHILL, and M. FUCHS. Aluminum mulch increases quality and yield of 'Orleans' Apples. HortSci. 10:390-391. 1975.

MORTVEDT, J.J. et al. (eds). Micro-nutrients in agriculture — Zn, Fe, B, Mo, Cu, Mn. Soils Sci. Soc. of Amer., Madison, Wisconsin. 665 p. 1972.

OBERLY, G.H. and C.G. FORSHEY. Cultural Practices in the bearing Apple Orchard. N.Y. St. Coll. of Agr. and Life Sci. Ext. Bull. 1212, 26 p. 1974.

OBERLY, G.H. Effect of 2, 3, 5-triiodobenzoic acid on bitter pit and calcium accumulation in 'Northern Spy' apples. J. ASHS 98(3):269. 1973.

ORCHARD MANAGEMENT. Several states issue annual recommendations for spraying, fertilizing, rootstocks, other key practices. Contact the Washington, Michigan, Ohio, New York, Penna., Virginia or N.J. experiment station hdqtrs.

ORGANIC GARDENING in South Carolina. Clemson Cir. 541. Clemson Univ. 24 pp. Sept. 1973.

PARISH, C.L. Graft-transmission of blister bark and internal bark necrosis in Delicious apple. HortSci. 16(1):52-54. 1981.

PEARSON, K. and C.G. FORSHEY. Pine vole on tree vigor. Yield. N.Y. Apples. Hort Sci. 13(1):56-7. Feb. 1978.

PERRING, M.A. and A.P. PRESTON. Orchard factors on chemical composition of apples. III. Some effects of pruning and nitrogen application on Cox's Orange Pippin fruit. J. Hort. Sci. 49:85-93. 1974.

POUWER, A. Fruit analysis for prediciton of bitter pit. Acta Hort. 45:39-43. 1974.

POWELL, L.E. and S.D. SEELEY. Abscisic Acid into a Water Soluble Complex in Apple. ASHS 99:439-441. 1974.

PRESTON. A.P. and M.A. PERRING. Summer pruning and nitrogen on growth, cropping, and storage quality of Cox's Orange Pippin apple. J. Hort. Sci. 49:77-83. 1974.

RAESE, J. Leaf Ca and sorbitol in 'Delicious' apple as influenced by herbicides and N levels. HortSci. 15(2):154-156. 1980.

RATKOWSKY, D.A. and D. MARTIN. Multivariate analysis of disorder and mineral element content in apples. Aust. J. Agric. Res. 25:783-90. 1974.

REASE, J.T. and M. W. WILLIAMS. Fruit Color of 'Golden Delicious', N Content and Leaf Color. J. ASHS 99:332-334. 1974.

REIL, W.O., et al. Trunk injection corrects iron and zinc deficiencies in pear trees. Ca. Agr. 22-23. Oct. 1978. See June 1979 also.

RILEY, R.G. and P.E. KOLATTIKUDY. Treatment with Calcium Ion-Containing formulations on the Firmness of 'Golden Delicious' Apples. HortSci. 11(3):249-51. 1976.

ROACH, W.A. Mineral Nutrition and the rootstock-scion effect. (Appendices on methods of analysis by A.C. Mason and F.H. Vanstone). Rep. E. Mall. Res. Sta., 1946 (1947), 88-94.

ROGERS, E. Iron-Manganese relations of 'Starking Delicious' apples in Western Colorado. J. ASDHS 97(6):726. 1972.

ROWE, R.N. and D.V. DEARDSELL. Waterlogging of Fruit Trees. Hort. Abst. 43:534-544. 1973.

SADOWSKI, A., et al. Mg nutrition of apple trees III. Comparison of different methods of Mg fertilization. *Acta agrobooanica* 29, (2):201-17. 1976.

SCHNEIDER, G.W., et al. Apple rootstock, tree spacing, cultivar on fruit and tree. J. ASHS 103(2):230-232. 1978.

SENTI, F.R. and R.L. RIZEK. Nutrient Levels in Horticultural Crops. HortScience 10:243-246. 1975.

SEQUESTRENE MICRONUTRIENT CHELATES — coating on granular fertilizer. Ciba-Geigy Tech. Bull. Ciba-Geigy Corp., Ardsley, N.Y. 10502. 1972.

SHANNON, L.M. Internal bark necrosis of the Delicious apple. Proc. ASHS 64, 165, 1954.

SHEAR, C.B., and M. FAUST. Nutritional ranges in deciduous tree fruits and nuts. Hort. Rev. 2:142-63. Color deficiencies. Avi. Publ. Co., Westport, Ct. 1980.

SHEAR, C.B. Ed. Calcium Nutrition of economic crops, Internat. Symp. Comm. in Soil Sci. and Plant Anal. P.O.B. 11305, Church St. Sta. N.Y. 10249. 500 pp. 1979.

SHEAR, C.B. Calcium Deficiency on Leaves and Fruit of 'York Imperial' apple. ASHS Vol. 96, No. 4. July 1971. pp. 415.

SHEAR, C.B., et al. Nutrient balance and leaf analysis. Proc. ASHS 51, 319, 1948.

SHELTON, J.E. Placement of Phosphorus Fertilizer and Lime on Growth of 'Delicious' and 'Golden Delicious' Apple Trees. J. Amer. Soc. Hort. Sci. 101(5):481-485. 1976.

SHIM, K.K., J.S. TITUS, and W.E. SPLITTSTOESSER. The utilization of post-harvest urea sprays by senescing Apple leaves. J. ASHS 97(5):592. 1972.

The utilization of post-harvest urea sprays supplied to roots of apple trees. J. ASHS 98(6):523. Nov. 1973.

SHIM, K.K., J.S. TITUS, and W.E. SPLITTSTOESSER. The utilization of post-harvest urea sprays supplied to roots of apple trees. J. ASHS 98(6):523. Nov. 1973.

SMOCK, R.M. and D. BOYNTON. The effects of differential nitrogen treatments in the orchard on the keeping quality of McIntosh apples. Proc. Amer. Soc. Hort. Sci. 45: 77-86. 1944.

SMOCK, R.M. Apple fruit respiration off the tree. J. ASHS: 97-4, 509-11. 1972.

SODERLUND, R.O., and B.C. HANGER. Ca free nutrient solution and demineralized water on movement of previously deposited Ca in roots of apple seedlings. J. ASHS 105(6): 769-773. 1980.

STAHLY, E.A. and N.R. BENSON. Calcium Levels of 'Golden Delicious' Apples as influenced by Calcium Sprays. 2, 3, 5-triodobenzoic Acid, and Other Regulator Sprays. J. ASHS 101(2):120-2. March 1976.

STAHLY, E.A. and M. WILLIAMS. TIBA-induced pitting of Golden Delicious. Hort. Sci. Vol. 5 (1):45-46. February 1970.

STEBBINS, R.L. and D.H. DEWEY. Transpiration on Ca45 in apple. J. ASHS:97-4.471-7. 1972.

STEBBINS, R.L., D.H. DEWEY and V.E. SHULL. Calcium crystals in apple stem, petiole and fruit tissue. J. ASHS 7(5):492. 1972.

STEWART, I. and C.D. LEONARD. Molybdenum deficiency. Proc. ASHS 62, 111. 1953.

STORER, T.I. and E.W. JAMESON, Jr. Field rodents on California farms. Calif. Ext. Serv. Circ. 535, 55 pp. 1965.

TESKEY, B.J.E. and K.R. WILSON. Tire Fabric Waste as Mulch for Fruit Trees. J. Amer. Soc. Hort. Sci. 100-153-157. 1975.

TOENJES, R., R.J. HIGLOW and A. L. KENWORTHY. Soil moisture used by orchard sods. Mich. Agr. Expt. Sta. Article 39-34. 1956.

TOENJES, W. The first twenty years' results in a Michigan apple orchard, cultivation cover-crop versus sod-mulch culture. Mich. State Coll. Special Bull. 313. 1941.

TROMP, J. and J.C. OVAA. Spring mobilization of protein nitrogen in apple bark. Plant Physiol. 29:1-5. 1973.

TROMP, J. Temperature on growth, mineral nutritiion on apple fruits. — Spec. Ref. to Calcium. Physiol. Plant. 33:87-93. 1975.

TROMP, J. and J.C. OVAA. Time of nitrogen application on amino-nitrogen composition of roots and xylem Sap of Apple. Physiol, Plant. 37:29-34. 1976.

UNRATH, C.R. Cooling effects of sprinkler irrigation on Apples. J. ASHS 97(1):55. Jan. 1972. Quality of apples as affected by sprinkler irrigation. J. ASHS 97(1):58. Jan. 1972.

VEIHMEYER, F.J. and A.H. HENDRICKSON. Essentials of irrigation and cultivation of orchards. Calif. Agr. Exp. Sta. Cir. 486. 22 pp. 1960.

VERNER, L., W.J. KOCHAN, D.O. KETCHIE, A. KAMAL, R.W. BRAUN, J.W. BERRY, JR., and M.E. JOHNSON. Trunk growth as a guide in orchard irrigation. Idaho Agr. Exp. Sta. Res. Bull. No. 52. 32 pp. October 1962.

WALLACE, A., et al. Behavior of chelating agents in plants. proc. ASHS 65, 9. 1955.

WALSH, C.S., and W.J. KENDER. Ethylene evoluton from apple shoots and spur buds. J. ASHS 105(6):873-877. 1980.

WANDER, I.W. and J.H. GOURLEY. Potassium penetration from mulch. Proc. ASHS. 46, 21 1945.

WEEKS, W.D., et al. Soil nutrients 10 years after heavy mulch. Proc. ASHS 56, 1. 1950.

WHITE, G.C. and R.I.C. HOLLOWAY. Grass, cultivation, mulch, herbicide treatment and growth of Cox's orange on M. 26. Jour. Hotr. Sci. 42:377-89. 1967.

WIGGANS, C.C. Depletion of Subsoil moisture by apple trees and other woody species. Neb. Agr. Exp. Sta. Res. Bull. 216. 32 pp. April 1964.

WIGHTMAN, K., et al. Ca., B. and NAA sprays on cork spot. ASHS 95(1):23-27. January 1970.

WILDUNG, D.K., C.J. WEISER, and H.M. Pellett. Temperature and moisture effects on hardening of apple roots. HortScience 8(1):53. 1973.

WILLIAMS, J.M. and A.H. THOMPSON. P, N and daminozide on growth and first fruiting of dwarf apple. HortSci. 14(6):703-704. Dec. 1979.

WILLIAMS, M.W. and H.D. BILLINGSLEY. Effect of nitrogen fertilizer on yield, size and color of 'Golden Delicious' apple. J. ASHS 99(2):144. March 1974.

YAMAZAKI, T., H. MORI, H. YOKOMIZO and H. FUKUDA. Relation of bitter pit to mineral nutrition of apples. Effects of calcium and nitrogen supplies. Bull. of Tohoku Nat. Agr. Exp. Sta. No. 23. Pages 152-196. Jan. 1962.

ZEIGER, D.C. and J.E. SHELTON. Leaf chlorosis and twig discoloration in 'Delicious' apple trees having Mn-induced internal back necrosis. J. ASHS 7(5):494. 1972.

Note: For information, assistance on irrigation techniques and equipment, see a recent July issue of American Fruit Grower, 37841 Euclid Av., Willoughby, Ohio 44094.

(See additional references in former book editions.)

CHAPTER VI

Flowering, Pollination, Fruit Set in Apple

Time and manner of flower-bud formation. In temperate zones, the flower buds of fruit trees are more or less well developed the season *previous* to their unfolding into blossoms. The exact time when initiation of flower buds occurs in the apple varies somewhat with growth pattern, region and the cultivar. The gradual development of an apple flower bud is shown in Figure 1, starting in late spring or early summer of one year and reaching completion at spring bloom the following year. In general, the outside parts of the flower bud develop first, and the inside last.

The observations of A.W. Drinkard on flower-bud development in Virginia are similar to those diagrammed here. The cultivar of apple which he used was the early-season ripening Duchess of Oldenburg. First indication of flower-bud primordia was noticed between June 15 and 30; calyx lobes were seen, June 30 and July 7; anthers, July 1 and 14; pistils, August 7 and 14; cavities of the ovaries where the ovule is located, September 15 and 30; flower petals near base of calyx, November 15, ovules did not appear until March; mature pollen was evident in March; and differentiation of the flower was complete by April 1 shortly before it opened into a blossom.

Thus, in Virginia, U.S.A., for that year, June to July was the period during which it was determined whether an apple bud will be a flower bud or a "vegetative" growing point without flowers. Any cultural treatment to induce flower-bud formation should be done the previous spring or fall. Flower-bud initiation usually coincides with the post-bloom vegetative flush but can occur anytime following.

Factors affecting flower-bud formation. From a physiological standpoint, it has not been well established as to the exact factors associated with flower-bud formation in the apple and other pomological fruits. Many horticulturists and plant physiologists have explained flower-bud formation on the basis of relative amounts of carbohydrates and nitrogen in the plant tissues. While this theory appears to be a logical explanation in that a certain balance between carbohydrates and nitrogen has been found to be correlated with flower-bud differentiation, there is insufficient clear-cut evidence at this time to fully substantiate it as a sole relationship. The concept has

developed largely on the basis of work done with the tomato by E.J. Kraus and H.R. Kraybill who show by extensive chemical data the effects of different carbohydrate-nitrogen relationships in tissues on fruit setting but not on flower-bud formation. In the original work four classes were designated into which a tomato plant may be placed according to its vegetative and fruiting responses. These classes may be repeated arbitrarily for the apple, as shown in Table 1. An apple tree which has been heavily fertilized with nitrogen would be placed in Class II, whereas a neglected tree growing in sod would probably fall in Class IV. Note that high carbohydrates and high nitrogen are symbolized respectively by large "C" and large "N", whereas low carbohydrates and low nitrogen are designated respectively with a small "c" and "n". Intermediate amounts are symbolized by letters intermediate in size.

There is increasing evidence that auxins are important in flower-bud formation. In fact, scientists in this field of research are inclined to place more emphasis on auxins or growth substances as a factor inducing flower-bud initiation than on the carbohydrate-nitrogen concept, although the importance of the latter still may not be

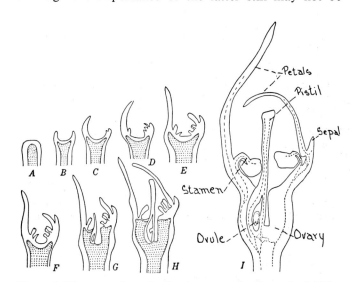

Figure 1. Diagrams show the development of a flower bud of the apple, beginning 6 to 8 weeks after bloom at (A) and extending to the following spring bloom period at (I). The outer parts of the flower appear first, the inner parts last. In Virginia, U.S.A. (Hayward "The Structure of Economics Plants". The Macmillan Co., New York City)

[1]Dr. L. J. Edgerton, Cornell University, and Dr. C. Richard Unrath, N. Car. St. Univ., Raleigh, assisted in revision of this chapter.

TABLE 1. The Influence of Different Amounts of
Carbohydrates and Nitrogen in Tree Tissue on the
Growth and Fruiting

Class	Relative Amounts of "C" & "D"	Amount of Vegetative Growth	Amount of Fruit	Situation Due to
I	$\dfrac{C}{N}$	poor	Few, bitter pit, large punky	Defoliation by insects, diseases, sprays, or continued excessive summer pruning.
II	$\dfrac{C}{N}$	rank	limited	Too much nitrogen fertilization or too heavy pruning, or both.
III	$\dfrac{C}{N}$	moderate	good	Judicious fertilization, pruning, fruit thinning, soil management, and spraying.
IV	$\dfrac{C}{N}$	poor	reduced	Insufficient nitrogen often found under sod management with little or no attention to nitrogen applications.

revealed fully. These growth substances, the chemical nature of which is not well understood, are apparently formed in the leaves and transported to and concentrated in the regions of the plant where flower buds are formed. Future research may indicate more clearly the exact nature of these substances which together with the carbohydrate food supply are influential in the initiation of flower buds. The fact still remains, however, that flowers and their end products, such as fruit and seed, are composed largely of the products of photosynthesis and of the organic nitrogen complexes. Thus, the green leaves are no doubt of utmost importance in governing flower-bud formation and should be guarded against injury from insects and diseases, caustic sprays and agents that lower their efficiency. Flower-bud initiation will compete with shoot growth for the carbohydrate food supply from leaves (Figure 1a).

There are several environmental factors known to stimulate or depress flower-bud formation. These are discussed below.

Under natural conditions, *light intensity* is the most important environmental factor governing the rate of carbohydrate manufacture in leaves. It is important especially from the standpoint of amount of light reaching the foliage in the center of trees. With dense trees, low light intensity is one of the chief reasons for few flowers in the tree centers. Use of full-dwarf trees and opening the top of trees by *pruning*, therefore, admits light to the centers and tends to increase flower-bud formation in this region. On the other hand, *excessive pruning* reduces the foliage to such an extent that the roots are able to supply relatively large quantities of nutrients and water to the remaining portion of the top, resulting in considerable shoot growth and water-sprouts with little or no flower-bud formation. *Root pruning,* or any injury to the roots as a result of cold, excessive moisture, deep plowing, subsoiling, or rodent injury, tends to increase flower formation temporarily. Root pruning reduces the root system and thus, limits the amount of water and nutrients available to the top, resulting in reduced shoot and spur growth. Such a retardation in top growth is usually associated with in-creased flower-bud formation. Root pruning is an amateur practice in Europe with the purpose of inducing young vigorous trees to bear earlier. *Summer pruning* tends to halt shoot growth and divert needed substances for flower-bud formation and development. *Chemical hormonal sprays,* as Alar, TIBA, CCC, GA and ethephon, tend to increase or decrease flower-bud formation.

It is known that ethylene develops in the fruit before it drops, but it is not certain if the ethylene forms because the fruit is preparing to drop or that the formation of ethylene is causing the fruit to drop.

Removal of leaves or defoliation due to injury by in-sects, diseases, or caustic sprays results in reduced flower-bud formation, especially if defoliation occurs prior to the

Figure 1a. Shown here is the effect of ringing the trunks in late spring (June, the smaller trees) of every other Northern Spy tree on flowering and growth the following spring. Northern Spy has the tendency to come into bearing late (12-year delay). (Courtesy Michigan State University, E. Lansing).

period of flower-bud differentiation. In principle, this is due to a reduction in the needed substances available to the buds in the axils of the injured or dropped leaves. A *deficiency of water* during the period when flower buds are forming may stimulate flower-bud formation intensely. However, if water deficiency is severe and the tree is already in weak condition due to poor cultural management or other reasons, flower-bud formation may be affected adversely. Excessive application of *nitrogen fertilizers* to young apple trees results in rank vegetative growth and tardy bearing. On the other hand, moderate nitrogen applications to low-vigor trees usually increase flower-bud formation. Zinc, copper, and boron are key deficiencies that tend to reduce normal flowering and performance.

In summary, there appears to be the need for a delicate balance among hormones, carbohydrates, nutrients and the climate to trigger flower bud formation.

Bending of limbs often results in increased flower formation beyond the bend. Back of the bend, however, new and vigorous shoot growth may be induced. The theory involved is that the bend restricts the movement of carbohydrates and auxins from the outer portion of the limb toward the roots. An accumulation of carbohydrates and slowing down of growth beyond the bend is, therefore, assumed to be favorable to flower-bud formation. Back of the bend, less carbohydrates are available, but more water and nutrients from the roots are present, resulting in vigorous shoot growth in this area. Thus, bending or propping (35-45° angle without bending) will induce young apple/pear trees to flower earlier. *Dwarfing rootstocks* for standard cultivars usually cause the trees to bear much earlier in life. The dwarfing stocks reduce the rate of shoot and spur growth, probably by restricting uptake of soil moisture and nutrients, and together with a physical bending out and down of limbs induce early flowering.

Ringing is a special commercial practice that usually causes increased flower formation. Ringing is defined as the removal of a thin strip of bark from around the trunk or at the base of main limbs. "Scoring" has a similar effect and consists of making two or more cuts to the sapwood around the trunk or limbs, but no bark is removed. Driving nails into the trunk or cutting out notches below buds influence flowering more or less the same as ringing. Likewise, injuries to the limbs, crotches, trunk, or roots due to low temperature, cankers, disease, hail, fire, or rodents result in increased flower formation. If a wire label is left attached to a young tree, it becomes taut and eventually rings or constricts the tree, causing carbohydrates to accumulate above the wire; the top becomes weakened, and flower-bud formation takes place.

Ringing is a practice used occasionally to increase flower formation on fast growing young trees tardy in bearing, as Delicious. It is also practiced commercially along with rather heavy pruning on filler trees which are beginning to crowd the permanent trees. Ringing is done about three to four weeks after petal fall or before flower-bud formation. The entire trunk may be ringed but it seems preferable to ring a few main branches one year and the rest the next year. The wounds should be covered with roofing or horticultural asphalt free of creosote or like materials harmful to the tissues. Shoots developing near the ring must be removed immediately to prevent entrance of the fire blight organism (*Erwinia anylovora*). See Figure 1a.

The ringing should not be performed on very young trees, small limbs, more or less defoliated trees, trees in very low vigor, or on peaches, apricots, cherries, or plums. The ringing of alternate bearing trees early in the "on" year may or may not induce fruit production in the following predicted "off" year, depending upon the vigor of the tree and other factors.

Use of *Alar* (succinic acid 2-2, dimethyl hydrazide) spray about three weeks after bloom on apples at 4-8 lbs./A or 1000-2000 ppm has increased return bloom (Fig. 2). It does not seem to affect fruit set. Some fruit size reduction may result if high rates of Alar are used on trees bearing fruit.

Figure 2. (Left) Young Golden Delicious tree was sprayed the previous season with Alar. (Right) No spray. (Courtesy late L.P. Batjer, USDA, Wenatchee, Wash.)

Use high rates only on non-bearing trees. Ethrel (ethephon) (2-chloro-ethyl phosphonic acid) applied shortly after bloom at 250-1000 ppm also increases return bloom on young trees. Some fruit abscission (thinning) may result at the time of application on bearing trees. The strongest chemical treatment for increasing flower bud initiation is an Alar-Ethrel mix on non-bearing trees where fruit thinning or fruit size are not a concern. Scoring, crotch-spreading and/or chemicals are particularly useful in bringing a young orchard into production.

By modern radio-active tracer technique, molecules of NAA can be "tagged" and, thus, are thought to be directly responsible for greater flower-bud formation on trees that have been thinned with NAA. Hence, this could, in part, account for better annual bearing of apple trees fruit-thinned with NAA and other hormones.

POLLINATION AND FRUIT SET

In discussing pollination, it is important to know first the essential parts of the flower. The stamen, or male organ, consists of two parts (Figure 3): (a) the anther, which is made up of two sacs containing the pollen grains and (b) the filament, or stalk which supports the anther. The three parts of the pistil, or female organ, are (a) the basal part or ovary which contains the young ovules and which, along with other parts, develops into the fruit, (b) the styles which are attached to the ovary and bear at their apexes the receptive sticky surfaces known as (c) the stigmas upon which the pollen grains are caught and germinate.

Once the flower has opened in the spring, pollination must take place to induce the fruit to "stick" to the tree and begin to develop. If limited or no pollination occurs, the flower will drop, or develop into a small fruit that drops early. *Pollination* is defined as the transfer of the pollen grains from the anther to the stigma. If the transfer is from anther to stigma on the same flower or to the stigma of another flower of the same cultivar, it is known as *self-pollination*. If the transfer is from an anther of one cultivar to a stigma of another cultivar, it is known as *cross-pollination*. The honeybee is probably responsible for over 90 percent of the apple pollination. Bumblebees and other wild bees may serve more effectively in pollination during windy or cold weather but there are too few of these insects.

The late R.H. Roberts of the University of Wisconsin and Cornell researchers, have found that the Delicious flower structure is such that the honeybee can poke his probosis between the filament bases and get nectar *without* crawling over the anthers and inadvertently transferring

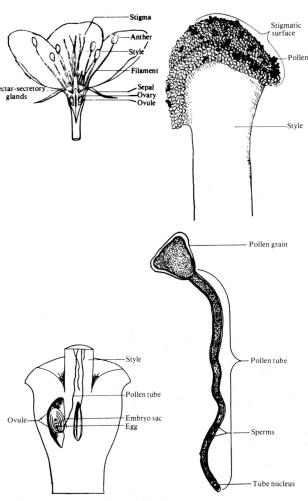

Figure 3. (Top left) Apple flower and parts. (Top right) Stigma with pollen grains. (Bottom right) Germinating pollen grain. (Bottom left) Base of female element showing lower part of style, the ovary, and an ovule, with pollen tubes growing down through style. (L.H. MacDaniels, Cornell University)

pollen to the stigmas. This could account for some of the poor set occurring on Delicious some springs.[2]

Pollen grains of the apple and most fruit plants resemble minute yellow dust particles. They are round or roughly triangular in shape with a diameter of 1/1000 of an inch. Each anther contains about 3500 pollen grains, and since there are 20 stamens, this would be 70,000 grains per flower. Apple pollen is sticky and adheres to the hairy body of the honeybee as it visits the showy flowers in search of nectar. The nectar glands are located near the base of the stamens, as shown in Figure 3. The number of pollen grains carried by a single bee could easily approximate 100,000. In visiting flower after flower, however, the bee rubs off pollen onto the stigmas and picks up additional pollen, bringing about self- and cross-pollination. Wind carries very little apple pollen. Honeybees fly but little during rains and heavy winds, or if the temperature is below 65° F. *Sunlight hours during blossoming when the temperature is above 70°F. and the air is fairly quiet are highly important.* A bee may visit 5000 blossoms on good days but works close to ground on colder days. Dandelions on the orchard floor should be controlled with herbicides or by growing a tight sod, as K31 fescue, to eliminate competition for bee attention.

The pollen grain germinates shortly after it comes in contact with the stigma (Figure 3), sending out a pollen tube. Germination and growth of this tube are faster when the temperature is above 70° F., but it probably is retarded at temperatures above 80°F. The pollen tube grows down the style until it reaches and penetrates the young ovule and finally finds its way to where the egg, or female organ, is located (embryo sac). During growth of the pollen tube, the two male germs (sperms) are formed in the pollen tube. These are discharged into the embryo sac, where one of them unites with the egg, and by this process, *fertilization* is accomplished. Fertilization, or the union of egg and sperm is quite similar, therefore, to that taking place in animals. When fertilization in the flower has taken place, there is an initial stimulation to the basal part of the flower tissues which prevents it from dropping.

Flowers of average vigor on an apple tree may not set fruit as readily as strong flowers due to the receptive period of stigmas being one to two days less; the longevity of the ovules being 2 to 3 days less and, thus, the effective pollination period being on the average about 3 days less. (Williams, 1965).

While eating an apple, it may be noted that there are five

<hr />

[2]Delicious has a problem with light fruit setting, particularly in North-Central USA. Spur strains bloom, set and bear annually better than standard strains of Delicious. Trend is toward spur plantings. An annual bearing pollinizer cultivar should be next to every Delicious row, even with full-dwarf trees. Provision for adequate bees, possibly biennial zinc sprays, boron sprays, annual pruning, non-caustic pesticide sprays, fruit thinning by chemicals, use of Alar, all should be carefully considered. See also Chapter VII.

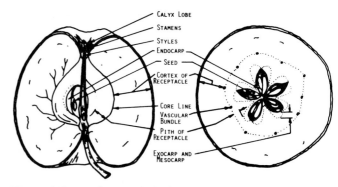

Figure 4. Parts of an apple fruit are indicated as they developed from the flower. See also Figure 3, upper left. Short-stem cultivars, as McIntosh, tend to drop from the tree near harvest more easily than long-stem cultivars, as Golden Delicious.

compartments or caprels near the core which contain two, one or no seeds (Figure 4). If pollination and fertilization have been good, the apple, therefore, may contain from a few to ten seeds, and such an apple will likely stick to the spur and mature. However, if pollination and fertilization have been inadequate due to poor weather conditions or other causes, only one to three seeds may develop. Seed development stimulates the apple tissue in the immediate vicinity of the seed. For example, if an apple contains three seeds on one side and none on the other, the tissues in the neighborhood of the seeds will grow normally, whereas the other side of the apple will develop slowly and the fruit subsequently will be lop-sided. (Figure 5). Also, an apple with only a few seeds is more likely to drop on the ground before maturing, especially if there is considerable competition between many unthinned fruits for water, soil nutrients, and carbohydrates.

Most apple varieties will not set fruit by self-pollination. Much of the difficulty experienced in obtaining a set of fruit in orchards is due to the fact that many importnat cultivars — Granny Smith, McIntosh, Delicious — will not form seeds nor set fruit when their blossoms are self-pollinated (Figure 6). Such varieties are known as *self-unfruitful*, and must have cross-pollination from another cultivar to set and hold their fruit. If a set of fruit results from self-pollination, the cultivar is said to be *self-fruitful*. Some apple cultivars are considered *partly* self-fruitful but none, except perhaps Yellow Transparent, has produced full commercial crops of fruit year after year by its own pollen.

There are cases, such as the Delicious cultivar, where pollen is viable or capable of germination, and the egg cells are normal, yet the variety will not set fruit after self-pollination. The variety, therefore, is said to be *self-incompatable*, as well as self-unfruitful. Some cultivars may be *cross-incompatible* where fruit does not set, as Cortland and Early McIntosh. Melrose and Delicious, which also are said to be *cross-unfruitful*.

 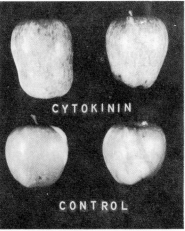

Figure 5. (Upper left) Note deformed apple due to poor pollination and no seeds on poorly developed side. Apple below has full compliment of ten seeds. (L.J. Edgerton. Cornell Univ.) (Right) A mixture of 1:1 gibberellins and cytokinins at 25-50 ppm can be used at the king-blossom-petal-fall stage to lengthen Delicious and increase fruit weight in warmer post-bloom climates. Promilan (A4A7 6-benzyladenine), a commercial preparation, can be used at about 125 ppm with similar results. (Right photo, courtesy Dr. G. Martin, Univ. of Calif., Davis).

Years ago, orchardists occasionally planted large blocks of single cultivars such as McIntosh for convenience in management. Difficulties immediately arose in obtaining commercial crops of fruit. This stimulated experimental work in pollination and fruit setting. Trees were placed in cloth cages (Figure 7) at blossom time, or individual branches or spurs were placed in cloth bags. In cross-pollination experiments, stamens of the enclosed flowers were removed before they shed pollen. Then by special technique, pollen from a different cultivar or the same cultivar was daubed with a camel-hair brush (hand-pollinated) on the pistils of the enclosed flowers to determine the percentage of fruit set. After several years of experimental work, the more common apple cultivars listed above were found to have *infertile* pollen and consequently are *ineffective* in self- or cross-pollination.

Thus, if any one of the above cultivars is used, the planting must consist of at least three cultivars. The two other cultivars must cross-fertilize each other in addition to the above variety. Pollen of commercial cultivars not listed above is usually effective in cross-pollination. Standard cultivars and their "bud sports" are generally unfruitful with each other. Seedlings are usually cross-fruitful with

TABLE 2. APPLE CULTIVARS WITH INFERTILE OR INEFFECTIVE POLLEN FOR SELF- OR CROSS-POLLINATION. (ADAPTED FROM GOURLEY & HOWLETT, 1941)°

Arkansas (Mammoth Black Twig)	Stark	Blenheim
Baldwin	Stayman	
	Winesap, Stamared	
	Scarlet Stamared	Boskoop
Canada Reinett		
Gravenstein, Red		
Gravenstein and Bank's	Summer Rambo	Bramley's
Hibernal	Tompkins King	Seedling
	Turlev	Jonagold
Paragon	Spigold	Jersey Red
Rhode Island Greening	Winesap	Mutsu

°All of these varieties have a triploid number of chromosomes which is closely correlated with infertile or ineffective pollen.

their parent varieties, except Rome Beauty and Gallia Beauty which are only partly cross-fruitful. Some varieties, like Jonathan, Delicious, Winter Banana, some crabapples and Golden Delicious produce unusually large quantities of viable pollen.

Some varieties are partly self-fruitful in large blocks, including Jonathan, Rome Beauty, Oldenburg, Wealthy, Yellow Transparent, Golden Delicious, Newtown, Grimes and York. Even with these varieties, however, cross-pollination generally should be provided. A Washington grower found a solid block of Golden Delicious to require less fruit thinning, a distinct advantage.

Suitable pollinators for various apple cultivars, based on tests at the National Fruit Trials (England), are *Cox* by Discovery, Gala, Gloster 69, Golden Delicious, Idared, Katja and Spartan; *Bramley* by Cox, Grenadier and Idared; *Mutsu* (Crispin) by Cox and Worcester Pearmain; *Discovery* and *Gala* by Cox; *Gloster 69* by Cox and Golden Delicious; *Idared* by Worcester Pearmain; *Jonagold* by Discovery, Jonathan and Spartan; *Spartan* by Cox and Golden Delicious; *Worcester Pearmain* by Gala, Golden Delicious and Spartan. *Golden Delicious* was only partially compatible with Gala and incompatible with Mutsu (Crispin).

Blooming period for different cultivars must overlap. For cross-pollination to take place, it is obviously important that the varieties bloom at approximately the same time. Length of blooming season varies from one week to slightly more than two weeks, depending upon the variety and weather conditions. Some varieties open their blossoms early in spring, such as Idared, Jerseymac, Julyred, Empire, Lodi, Paulared, Puritan, Tydeman, 20 oz., Jonamac, Vista Bella, Gravenstein, McIntosh, Melba, Milton, and Wagener. The late blooming varieties are Gallia Beauty, Northern Spy, Macoun, Northwestern Greening, Rome, Melrose, Quinte, York, G. Delicious, and E. McIntosh with Ralls and Ingram very late blooming. Most other commercial varieties are midseason

Figure 6. Some apple cultivars are self-unfruitful. The McIntosh on the left was cross-pollinated with insects and bore 23 bushels of apples. Insects were excluded from the tree on the right by cheescloth netting, with the result that it bore less than one-half bushel of apples. (The late A.J. Heinicke, Cornell University).

bloomers.

If the temperature is high during the blooming period, all varieties, excepting the late ones, may bloom very close together or almost simultaneously. In some years when a sudden hot spell at the start of blooming is followed by a protracted cold and rainy period, the time of blooming of varieties may be unduly long. In such seasons, varieties that come into full bloom rather early may be past the pollination stage before the others are ready to shed their pollen freely.

Use of Crabapples. Dwarfed crabapples in the tree row are being tested for only pollination use by Dr. R.D. Way, N.Y. Exp. Sta., Geneva, (14456). Several, including *M. sieboldii,* are showing promise of getting better fruit sets for a cultivar like Delicious.

Crassweller et al. in Ohio found the crabapple cultivars David, Simpson, 10-35 and Ellen Gerhart to match in bloom Delicious, Jonathan, Golden Delicious and Gallia Beauty; Donald Wyman, Indian Magic matched Jonathan, Golden Delicious and Delicious; E.H. Wilson, *M. robusta,* Erecta, Ormiston Roy, Sentinel, Turesi matched McIntosh. All pollen set fruit on Delicious.

In a hedgerow of trellised Delicious, e.g., a pollinizer crabapple can be planted midway between the 6th and 7th trees. Or, it can be grafted on a limb of the 7th tree.

Importance of bearing age. McIntosh on seedling stock comes into bearing at the age of 4 to 6 years, whereas Delicious and Spy tend to bear later at 6-12 yrs. Thus, McIntosh may flower before Delicious and Spy come into flowering and a third variety, as Cortland, is needed. See Chap. II for relative ages of varietal bearing. Delicious

may be induced to bear earlier by (a) bending limbs outward, (b) ringing, and/or (c) spraying with a growth inhibitor as Alar.

Consider alternate bearing habits. With improper fruit thinning, pruning and fertilization, some cultivars may tend to bear a large crop one year and a small or no crop the next. York, Lodi, Spy, Puritan, Transparent are examples. Obviously, there will be little or no source of good pollen in the "off" year from the alternate bearing variety. Under these conditions, a third variety should be employed. See Table 2, Chap. II, for alternate bearing cultivars.

Suggested Planting Plans. Generally, no tree should be farther than 2 rows from a pollinizer[3]. Growers prefer large blocks of a cultivar for easy management but R.L. Norton of Cornell in western New York suggests that wherever possible Delicious, which is *the* problem, should be next to its pollinizing cultivar on either side to get more seeds, bigger apples and yields, and shape uniformly. This plan pays in the long run. An exception is where the cultivar may be partly self-fruitful as Yorks, Golden Delicious, Rome, Empire and possibly Jonathan strains (not Jonagold). These cultivars may be planted in blocks of 6-8 rows with pollinizers on each flank. When Delicious is planted in double or triple rows with pollinizers on each flank, a precaution is to graft a limb on every 6th tree in the mid-block row with Winter Bananas or a selected crabapple solely for pollination. Other good pollinizers for

---

[3]If possible use a yellow cultivar(s) for top-working on a red cultivar, or vice versa. This enables pickers to keep the cultivars separate while harvesting.

```
Rome Beauty ........... R  R  R  R  R  R  R  R  R  R  R  R  R  R  R  R  R  R  R
Delicious   ........... D  D  D  D  D  D  D  D  D  D  D  D  D  D  D  D  D  D  D
Delicious   ........... D  D  D  D  D  D  D  D  D  D  D  D  D  D  D  D  D  D  D
Delicious   ........... D  D  D  D  D  D  D  D  D  D  D  D  D  D  D  D  D  D  D
Delicious   ........... D  D  D  D  D  D  D  D  D  D  D  D  D  D  D  D  D  D  D
Jonathan    ........... J  J  J  J  J  J  J  J  J  J  J  J  J  J  J  J  J  J  J
Delicious   ........... D  D  D  D  D  D  D  D  D  D  D  D  D  D  D  D  D  D  D
Delicious   ........... D  D  D  D  D  D  D  D  D  D  D  D  D  D  D  D  D  D  D
Delicious   ........... D  D  D  D  D  D  D  D  D  D  D  D  D  D  D  D  D  D  D
Delicious   ........... D  D  D  D  D  D  D  D  D  D  D  D  D  D  D  D  D  D  D
Rome Beauty ........... R  R  R  R  R  R  R  R  R  R  R  R  R  R  R  R  R
```

Figure 8. In this planting plan the Delicious cultivar is preferred in larger quantity, planted in 2-row blocks with good pollinizers on either side. Where 3 or 4-row blocks of Delicious are used, Richard Norton of the Cornell Extension Service suggests every 6th tree in a mid-row of a Delicious block may well have one limb grafted to Winter Banana, an excellent pollinizer for Delicious. Delicious needs the best pollinizing arrangement for large fruit and higher yields. In regions where Delicious sets lightly and irregularly, pollinizers on either side of a row is better.

Use of bees in the orchard. Due to the importance of honeybees in cross-pollination, most growers find it necessary to bring in bees a day or so in advance of the blooming period. The hives are scattered throughout the orchard so there is one strong colony for each one or two acres (Figure 10). One hive to five acres may be sufficient for young bearing trees. The grower sometimes owns his own bees, but attempts by growers to raise bees have usually been disappointing. It seems better for him to rent the bees from a beekeeper, due to the specialized nature of beekeeping. A medium strength colony contains 15,000 to 20,000 bees. Extra strong colonies (up to 50,000 bees or 8-9 lbs.) have been effective in pollinating over four acres of trees during good weather. During unfavorable weather, bees may travel only ½ to 2 standard trees from the hives. The most striking results from bringing bees into the orchard will be evident in a season with only a few hours of favorable weather during bloom. It is during these seasons that apples are usually scarce and bring the higher prices.

The orchardist should take care not to spray the trees with pesticides (phosphate types such as Sevin are particularly poisonous) while the bees are still working. Bees should not be left in the orchard throughout the year; aside from being in the way, they may bother the workmen.

Figure 7. Fruit breeders use the above technique to cross cultivars to get in one cultivar the combined good characters of the parents. The cloth cage at blossoming prevents insects, mainly honey bees, from bringing in unwanted pollen. Camel hair brushes are used by the breeders to daub pollen of the desired parent on the pistils of the caged cultivar.

Delicious are Rome, G. Delicious, Cortland, Empire and some of the crabapples tested by Dr. R.D. Way of Cornell. Suggestions also hold for dwarf trees.

If the grower desires to have the majority of his trees of one variety with as few of the pollinizing variety as possible, the planting plan shown in Figure 8 can be used. This has proven satisfactory, providing the blooming seasons overlap, the varieties come into bearing about the same age, they are cross-fruitful, and neither tends to bear biennially. Always consider any difficulties in spraying and harvesting of mixed varieties (Figure 9).

Where the pollen of one variety is of little or no value in cross-pollination, as with Stayman Winesap or Rhode Island Greening, it will be necessary to use a third cultivar with good pollen as Golden Delicious.

In low-chilling regions as the southern USA, the Anna and Dorsett Golden are being planted in small acreages of 5 to 10 acres. One is a red apple, the other yellow. They pollinate each other and are sold through roadside markets or pick-your-own.

```
Golden Delicious ........... GD GD GD GD GD GD GD GD GD GD GD
Golden Delicious ........... GD GD GD GD GD GD GD GD GD GD GD
Golden Delicious ........... GD GD GD GD GD GD GD GD GD GD GD
Golden Delicious ........... GD GD GD GD GD GD GD GD GD GD GD
Golden Delicious ........... GD GD GD GD GD GD GD GD GD GD GD
Golden Delicious ........... GD GD GD GD GD GD GD GD GD GD GD
Jonathan         ...........  J  J  J  J  J  J  J  J  J  J  J
Jonathan         ...........  J  J  J  J  J  J  J  J  J  J  J
Golden Delicious ........... GD GD GD GD GD GD GD GD GD GD GD
Golden Delicious ........... GD GD GD GD GD GD GD GD GD GD GD
Golden Delicious ........... GD GD GD GD GD GD GD GD GD GD GD
Golden Delicious ........... GD GD GD GD GD GD GD GD GD GD GD
Golden Delicious ........... GD GD GD GD GD GD GD GD GD GD GD
Golden Delicious ........... GD GD GD GD GD GD GD GD GD GD GD
```

Figure 9. Cultivars as Golden Delicious, York, Rome and possibly Jonathan that tend to be self-fruitful can be planted in blocks of 4 to 6 rows, possibly more, and get cross-pollination with a good pollinizer. When Golden Delicious is planted in solid blocks some Washington growers report less fruit thinning is necessary, but all factors must be favorable for pollination.

Figure 10. (Left) The honeybee is most important in pollen transfer. One strong hive per acre scattered through the orchard and mounted above the grass at blossoming helps get a good crop. Supply fresh water for bees near hives so they will not drink from spray-polluted puddles. Face hives toward most sun; give wind protection. (Right) Orchardists should contract with beekeepers early to get strong hives on time. (Left, Cornell University; right, Norman Sharp, Honeybees, Fishers, N.Y.)

Broadleaf weeds such as dandelion that compete with the apple bloom for the bee's attention can be controlled with a herbicide as 2, 4-D. A tight Ky-31 sod "squeezes out" dandelions.

The Japanese propagate and house a small fly, *Eristali cerealis* F., that will pollinate flowers under more adverse weather (temperature) than the honeybee. For information, contact The Director, Hort, Exp. Sta., Iitoyo, Kitakami, Iwate 024, Japan.

Top-working to provide pollinizers. Commercial growers today rarely make the mistake of planting solid blocks of a single cultivar. When this situation arises, it is possible to top-graft every third tree (standard) in every third row to a pollinizing variety (75-100 ft. apart). If the solid block consists of a variety with nonviable pollen, a tree next to each of the above-grafted trees can be top-worked to a third variety which is cross-fruitful with the other two.[3] Or, every third tree in every third row can be top-worked half to one variety and half to the other. These grafts will not bloom for three years. In the meantime, bring in bouquets of flowers in buckets or two-quart jars of water and hand the bouqets in the grafted trees. Bees should be provided in this case to insure maximum pollination. Grafts are pruned as little as possible to encourage early flowering.

Beehive inserts placed at the hive entrance and loaded with pollen from a pollenizer variety can be useful. However, improper handling of the pollen in the orchard quickly destroys the viability of pollen. It must be kept cool (thermos jug) and out of the sun until it is used in the insert. The insert pollen needs to be fed or renewed each one-half to one-hour period. Lycopodium powder (spores of club moss) is sometimes used to dilute the pollen. This practice is not recommended for pollen because it irritates the bees causing them to rub the pollen off their bodies before flying to the trees.

Too much cross-pollination. If all provisions have been made for good cross-pollination and the weather during the blooming period is favorable there may be excessive fruit set. At present, however, there is no method for obtaining a definite amount of cross-pollination and no more. It seems best to provide for a full commercial crop, then remove the overload by chemical and/or hand-thinning.

There may be sufficient wild insects in the neighborhood to provide adequate cross-pollination. Or, growers may remove the bees after one or two days of good weather.

Researchers and growers comparing the effects of chemical thinners on fruit set should be aware of control trees setting excessively, then dropping much of their crop, giving erroneous interpretation of the chemical effects on treated trees.

The effect of pollen on shape, size, and color of fruit (metaxenia). The shape and color of an apple are typical for the variety regardless of the source of pollen. It is true, however, that cross-pollinated fruits are often of better shape, size and color than those obtained from self-pollination. This is probably due to the cross-pollinated fruits having more seed, start growth sooner, and because of additional seed, they have more uniform shape, and better size and color at picking time. Pollen from a yellow variety, such as Golden Delicious, does not cause yellow streaks to appear on red apples, neither does the pollen of an oblong or flat apple change the shape to a round apple.

Factors affecting the set of fruit. *Nitrogen* is most frequently the limiting factor in orchards, and application to the soil and/or as a urea spray before bloom are usually effective in increasing the fruit set on mature bearing trees. *Pruning* the winter before an expected heavy crop is a common method of increasing the fruit set. Such a practice reduces the competition between the remaining flowers for carbohydrates, water, and nutrients. The practice of *ringing* is used only in stubborn cases where the tree produces flowers with little or no set of fruit. In this case, ringing must be done not later than full bloom to affect the set of the current blossoms.

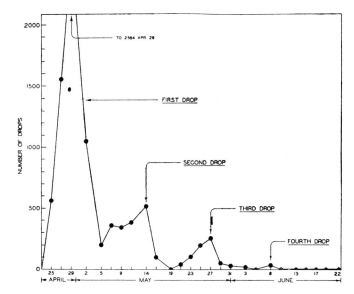

Figure 11. There are usually 4 waves of apple drops. The 1st and 2nd drops are generally lumped into the "1st drop", and the 3rd and 4th into "big 2nd drop" (June drop in northern hemisphere), because the apples are bigger, more noticeable. (The late A.E. Murneek, University of Missouri).

Temperature below 40° F. (4.4° C) at bloom not only inhibits bee activity, but hinders pollen germination. There is some germination at 40° to 50° F., but not until a temperature of 60° to 70° F. (15.5°-21.1° C) is pollen germination satisfactory. Optimum conditions for pollen germination and pollen tube growth are between 70° and 80° F., above which there is a decrease. Frosts just preceding or during blossoming may decrease the crop considerably. The farther open a blossom is when the frost occurs, the more susceptible it is to freezing. Fully opened apple blossoms may be killed at temperatures of 25° to 28° F. (-3.9 to -2.2° C). Delicious is quite susceptible, followed by Stayman Winesap, Arkansas, and Winesap. Although the first blossoms to open on these varieties may be killed the later blossoms set sufficient fruit to give full commercial crops. However, temperatures just above killing may limit fruit sizing. Late-blooming Rome and York often withstand frosts well as do frost-resistant blooms of Jonathan, Oldenburg, Grimes Golden and Wealthy, due partly to flowers opening on shoots after spur flowers.

The pistil, or female organ, is usually killed first by low temperatures. If the buds are unopened, freezing injury to the pistil can be detected by cutting the bud crosswise; dead pistils will be brown, live pistils green. Pollen is more resistant to frosts and can remain viable at several degrees below 32° F. If the temperature hovers at 29° F. or below only for a few hours, injury may not result. The longer the period of cold, the more likely the injury. Wind will aggravate damage at a given temperature.

Wind may affect the set of fruit by inhibiting bee activity, desiccating the stigmas, or excessively whipping the flowers and destroying their capacity to function. High *humidity* may prevent proper release of pollen. Low humidity may dry the stigmas to reduce pollen germination. *Rainfall* also inhibits bee flight and prevents release of pollen. Intermittent rainfall with periods of sunshine during the bloom period, however, ordinarily do not affect a commercial set adversely. Proper *nutrition* is important, particularly adequate nitrogen.

APPLE DROPS

Fruit growers are familar with the fact that though an apple tree may bloom profusely, only a relatively small percentage of the flowers will mature into fruit. Actually, only about one bloom in 20 is needed for a good commercial crop on a full-blossoming apple tree. Most of the blossoms fall soon after full bloom with smaller amounts dropping later. It is true that the various drops may be so great that the final yield is reduced seriously.

Two general drop periods are recognized (Figure 11), one defined as the "first drop" which begins shortly after petal fall and continues for two or three weeks. The "bigger second drop" (June drop, Figure 11) is more obvious to the fruit grower because the fruits have developed to a larger size. The "second" (3rd and 4th grouped) drop begins shortly after the first drop, continuing for two to four weeks. In some parts of the world, it may begin a bit earlier and be completed earlier, or begin later and be completed later.

The drops are remarkably uniform from year to year under varied weather conditions. The behavior has been regarded by some workers as an hereditary characteristic. The quantity of fruit that drops early or late varies with the cultivar. Some cultivars have a heavy drop shortly after bloom with a relatively light second drop. Examples of these are Stayman Winesap, Arkansas, Rhode Island Greening, Delicious, Tompkins King, and Winesap. With other varieties, the first drop is relatively light with the later drop heavier; these varieties include Baldwin, Grimes Golden, Wealthy, Yellow Transparent, Oldenburg, and Rome Beauty.

Information is still quite incomplete as to the cause of the various apple drops. It seems to be clear, however, that most of the flowers that drop soon after full bloom do so because of the lack of pollination, or as a result of self-fertilization. It is possible to reduce the early drop, if that be desirable, by providing the right cultivars for cross-pollination and by putting more bees into the orchards.

The "second" drop (3rd and 4th) consists of apples 1/2 to 1 inch in diameter. Because these apples stay under the tree longer and are more conspicuous, the apple grower frequently worries more about this drop than the more significant early drop. The cause of the comparatively late shedding of immature apples is probably due to competition among the fruits for food, water and nutrients. It is not certain if the supply of nutrients, principally nitrogen, carbohydrates, or some other indispensable substance becomes limiting first when the fruit load is excessive for the capacity of the particular tree. One relatively weak branch on a tree may release a large number of drops, whereas an adjoining more vigorous branch may shed only a few. Fruits which contain the fewest or weakest seeds are usually the first to drop. Although there does not seem to be any practical way of controlling the "bigger second" drop, it is probable that the maintenance of sufficient vigor and the development of healthy foliage will reduce its severity. Judicious fertilization with nitrogen and pruning also have a helpful influence.

Review Questions

1. Distinguish between pollination and fertilization.
2. What part of the flower produces the sperms; what part bears the egg?
3. What are the agents responsible for transfer of pollen from one plant to another; which is the more important?
4. List 2 commercial apple varieties which are good pollinizers and 2 which are poor pollinizers.
5. Diagram a plan for planting a poor pollinizing variety with good pollinizing varieties to secure effective cross-pollination. Use varieties commonly grown in your locality.
6. What would you do to an 8-year solid block of Delicious to secure good cross-pollination? Name the variety or varieties used and practices followed subsequently.
7. Can the shape of Delicious be lengthened in warmer climates? Explain.
8. List environmental and other factors which may affect adversely pollination and set of fruit.
9. Are the "bud sports" of standard varieties generally good pollinizers for their parent varieties? Explain.
10. What is an important factor causing lopsided fruits?
11. List two chemicals used as a spray that cause return bloom.

Suggested Collateral Readings

ALDWINCKLE, H.S. Flowering of Apple Seedlings 16-20 Months After Germination. HortSci. 10:124-126. 1975.

BATJER, L.P., M. Williams, G.C. Martin. Effects of alar on growth and fruiting of apple, pear, sweet cherry. Proc. ASHS 85:11-6. 1964.

CRASSWELLER, R.M. et al. Flowering crabapples for apple (Delicious) pollinizers. ASHS 105(3):475-77. 1980.

DAYTON, Daniel F. Overcoming self-incompatability in apple with killed compatible pollen. J. ASHS 99(2):190. March 1974.

ELLIS, M.D. et al. Honey bees for interpollination of plant germplasm collections. HortSci. 16(4) 488-91. August 1981.

FOGLE, H.W. Identification of tree fruit species by pollen ultrastructure. J. Amer. Soc. HortSci. 102(5):548-551. 1977.

FRANKHAUSER, R. and R. Schumacher, SADH at apple flowering time. Acta Hort. 34; Symp. England. 1974.

FREE, J. B. Honey bee efficiency in pollinating apple flowers. J. HortSci. 41:91-4. 1966.

FREE, John B. Insect pollination of crops. Academic Press; London, New York. 242 pp. 1970.

FREE, J.B., Y. Spencer-Booth. Honeybee foraging on dwarf apple trees. J. HortSci. 39:78-83. 1964.

GALSON, A.W. and P.J. Davies. Control mechanisms in plant development, Prentice-Hall, Englewood Cliffs, N.J. 184p. illus. 1970. HortSci. Vol. 6, No. 2, April 1971.

GREENE, D.W. and W.J. Lord. Scoring, limb-spreading, regulators on flowers and set, Delicious. ASHS 103:2. 208-10. 1978.

GREENHALGH, W.J. and L.J. Edgerton. Interaction of Alar and

Gibberellin on growth and flowering of the apple. ASHS 91:9-17. 1967.

GRIGGS, W.H., et al. Hand-collected and bee-collected pollen storage. Proc. ASHS 62,304. 1953.

GUTTRIDGE, C.G. GA inhibition on apple fruit bud formation. Nature 196: 4858. p. 1008. Dec. 8. 1962.

HARLEY, C.P., et al. Cause of Alternate bearing by apple trees. U.S. Dept. Agr. Tech. Bull. 792, 1942.

HARTMAN, F.O. and F.S. HOWLETT, NAA, fruit setting and apple development. Ohio Agr. Exp. Sta. Res. bull. 920 66pp. 1962.

HILLMAN, W.S. The physiology of flowering. Holt. Rinehart, Winston, New York City, London. 164pp. 1964.

HOCHBERG, R., et al. Girdling and 2,4-D effects on grapefruit sizes. HortSci. 12(3) 228. 1977.

INDISPENSABLE pollinators, The Rpt. (Mimeo) 9th Pollin. Conf., Univ. of Ark., Agr. Ext. Serv., Fayetteville. 1970.

IZHAR, S. et al. Pollen collector: Instrument for separation from air stream. HortSci. 10:426. 1975.

JAYCOX, E.R. Evaluating honey bee colonies for pollination. Univ. of Ill. Ag. Ext. Serv. Fruit Growing 20. Revised 1969. Pollen inserts for apple pollination. Ill. Ag., Fruit Growing 22. Making and using pollen inserts. Fruit Growing 23, 1969.

KOTOB, N.A. and W.W. Schwabe, Induction of parthenocarpic fruit in Cox's Orange apples. Jour. HortSic. 46:(1) 89-93. Jan. 1971.

KENDER, W.J. Ethephon-indiced flowering in apple seedlings. HortSci. 9:444-445. 1974.

LOONEY, NE.W., D.V. Fisher, J.E.W. Parsons. Effects of annual applications of Alar on apples. Proce. aSHS 91:18-30. 1967.

LOONEY, N.E. Growth regulators and fruit crops: Fundamental considerations. HortSci. Vol. 12(3) Juen 1977. pp. 211-24. 1977.

LORD, W.J., D.W. Greene, and R.A. Damon, Jr. Apple abscission and flower bud promotion by ethephon and SADH. J. Amer. Sco. HortSci. 100:259-261. 1975.

LU, C.S. and R.H. Roberts. Effect of temperature on the setting of Delicious apples. Proc. ASHS 59, 177, 1952. See reference also on Delicious flower structure, bees, etc.

MAGGS, D.H. Apple tree growth reduction due to fruiting. J. HortSci., 38s 2. p. 119-128. 1963.

MARTIN, G.C. et al. Changing apple shape with cytokinin and GA sprays. Calif. Agr. p. 14. April 1970.

MIZUTA, H.M. and C.A. JOHANSEN. Systemic insecticides and bees. Wa. Ag. Exp. Sta. T. Bul. 72. 1972.

McDANIELS, L.H. and A.J. Heinicke. Factors affecting apple fruit set. Cornell Bull. 407. 1930. Very good.

MODLIBOWSKA, I. Apple and pear pollen tube growth. J. Pom and H.S. 21, 57, 1945.

MURNEEK, A.E. The nature of shedding of immature apples. Mo. Agr. Exp. Sta. Res. Bull. 201. 1933.

NOEL, A.R.A. The girdled tree (a review). Bot. Gaz. 36:2. 162-195. 1970.

PESTICIDES and honey bees. U.S. Dept. of Agr. L-563. 7 pp. Revised 1981.

PRESTON, A.P. Apple bloom morphology and honeybee visits. E. Mall. Rest. Sta. Rpt. 64-7. 1948 (1949).

ROBERTS, R.H. and B.E. Struckmeyer. Notes on pollination of Delicious, Winesap and bees. ASHS 51: p. 54. 1948.

ROBINSON, W.S. Effect of apple cultivar on foraging behavior and pollen transfer by honeybees. J. Amer. Soc. HortSic. 104-(5):596-598. 1979.

ROBINSON, W.S. and R.D. Fell. Honeybee foraging behavior and 'Delicious' apple fruit set. HortSci. 16(3). 326-28. June 1981.

SIMONS, Roy K. Placental tissue and ovule development in 'Lodi' apple. J. ASHS 99(1):69. Jan. 1973.

SINGH. S. Behavior studies of honeybees in gathering nectar and pollen. Cornell Univ. Agr. exp. sta. Ithaca. N.Y. Mem. 288. April 1950.

STANGE, E.J., D.C. Ferree, and G.A. Cahoon. Effects of Postbloom. SADH, Urea, Dormant Zinc, and Zinc-Containing Fungicides on Fruit Set and Foliar Nutrient Content in 'Delicious' Apple. Ohio Agric. Res. and Dev. Cen. Res. Circular 239 pp. 13-15. July 1978.

STEMBRIDGE, G. and G. Morell. G.A. etc. on shape, set apple. J. ASHS 97:(4) 464-7. 1972.

STRYDOM, D.K. and G.E. Honeyborne. Increase in fruit set of

'Starking Delicious' apple with triadimefon. HortSic. 16(1):51, 1982.

SULLIVAN, D.T. and F.B. Widmoyer. Succinic acid, 2, 2-dimethylhydrazide (Alar) on bloom delay, fruit development, Delicious apples. HortSci. 5(2):91-92. 1970.

THOMPSON, A.H. and L.P. Batjer. Boron and pollen growth. Proce. ASHS. 56. 227, 1950.

TISSEYAT, B., E.B. Esan and T. Murashige. Somatic embryogenesis in Angiosperms. (Tissue culture). Horticultural Reviews. Avi. Pub. Co. 1:1-78. 1979.

TUKEY, H.B. and J.O. Young. Development of the apple flower and fruit. Bot. GAz. 104. 1. Abs. Proce. ASHS. 41. 104. 1942.

TUKEY, R.B. et al. Chemical aids to apple tree fruiting. Wash. E.M. 3517. Jan. 1972.

UNRATH, C.R. Commercial implications of gibberellin A4A7 plus benzyladenine for improving shape, yield of 'Delicious' apples. J. Amer. Soc. HortSci. 99:381-384. 1974.

VERHEIJ, I.E.W.M. Competition in apple, as influenced by Alar sprays, fruiting, pruning, tree spacing. Publ. 73.54 pp. Institut Voor Tuinbouwtechniek. Wageningen. Holland. 1972.

WAY, R.D. Pollination in apple planting. N.Y. Sp. (Cornell) Rpt. 2, 1971.

WEINBAUM, S.A. and R.K. Simons. Un ultrastructural evaluation of embroy/endosperm abortion and apple fruit abscission, post-bloom period. J. ASHS. 99:311-314. 1974.

WEINBAUM, S.A. and R.K. Simons. Seed number and fruit set in apple. Fruit Far. Jour. 30(3):82-4. 1976.

WILLIAMS, M.W. and E.A Stahly. Effect of cytokinins, gibberellins on shape of 'Delicious' apples. J. Amer. Soc. Hort. Sci. 94:17-19. 1969.

WILLIAMS, M.W. and D.S. Letham. Effect of gibberellins and cytokinins on development of parthenocarpic apples. HortSci. Vol. 4(3) 215-216. 1969.

WILLIAMS, R.R. Hand-pollination studies in fruit trees. Long Ashton Res. Sta. 79, 142-149. 1968: 23-28. 1969.

USA researcherx who have helped develop chemical fruit thinning over the years include E.C. Auchter, J.W. Roberts, West Virginia University; L.P. Batjer, C.P. Harley, USDA; M.B. Hoffman, L.P. Edgerton, Cornell University; and F.W. Southwick, D.W. Greene, University of Massachusetts. Above are (left) Max W. Williams, Washington State University (Wenatchee) and (right) Arthur H. Thompson, University of Maryland who in recent years have been leaders in this field on the West and East coasts, respectively.

CHAPTER VII

Thinning Apple Fruits and Alternate Bearing

Thinning is the removal of a part of the crop before it matures on the tree with the object of (a) increasing the marketability of the remaining fruit, and (b) reducing the alternate bearing tendency of the tree. Indeed, thinning may be grouped with pruning, irrigation and fertilization as among the important cultural practices which tend to induce and maintain tree vigor. Horticulturists, in general, consider it sound practice to provide for a full bloom by good orchard management, and then if conditions during bloom are particularly favorable for a heavy fruit set, it becomes necessary and advisable to chemical and/or hand thin the excessive crop at bloom or a few weeks after bloom. Chemical thinning of apples has been one of the most important developments in controlling biennial bearing of apples (Figure 1). The practice has gained widespread use in commercial orchards since 1949:

Fruiting is an exhaustive process to the tree, especially if the crop is heavy. Hence, the chief goal is to permit the tree to mature as large a crop as possible and yet conserve sufficient nutrients and carbohydrates for good shoot and spur growth, leaf development, and flower-bud formation for next year's crop. If the tree is permitted to mature an excessive crop, obviously it becomes devitalized to the point where it not only produces an inferior product, but it becomes increasingly susceptible to disease and low-temperature injury.

Thinning is practiced only on trees carrying a moderate to heavy crop of fruit. It accomplishes relatively more on mature trees making small annual growth, or on trees reduced in vigor with weak leaf surface than on young vigorous trees of the same cultivar. Response is better on light soils deficient in moisture than on heavy loams with adequate moisture. Trees growing in sod alone usually respond better to thinning than trees growing under mulch or some system of cultivation or chemical weed control.

After years of commercial experience in thinning apples, it has become increasingly apparent that thinning is necessary on all small-fruited cultivars which tend to retain an overload of fruit after the June drop. These cultivars include Yellow Transparent, Golden Delicious, Macoun, Early McIntosh and Wealthy. Although cultivars such as

Assisting in revision of this chapter were Max W. Williams, U.S.D.A., Wenatchee, Wash.; L. J. Edgerton (retired) and Warren C. Stiles, Cornell Univ., Ithaca, N.Y.; and Dr. Ronald Tukey, Wa. St. Univ., Pullman.

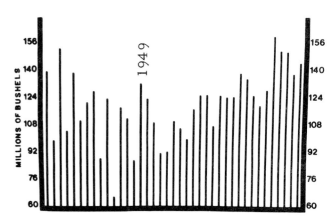

Figure 1. The use of chemical fruit thinning has reduced markedly the tendency toward biennial apple bearing over the United States. Note crop fluctuations before 1949 when chemical thinning generally started for U.S. commercial apple growers. (After M. W. Williams and L. J. Edgerton, USDA Bull. 289)

Jonathan, McIntosh and Stayman Winesap require relatively less thinning than the above cultivars, in some seasons after a particularly heavy set, thinning induces better "size-out" and quality of fruits on a tree. Delicious and its bud sports require more leaf surface per fruit than most varieties to attain high flavor and dessert quality; otherwise, the fruit may have a "starchy" flavor.

A thinning spray is said to be satisfactory when it removes enough fruit to assure an adequate return bloom the following year. Growers generally try to slightly overthin with chemicals in an attempt to avoid supplemental hand thinning later. Hand thinning, if needed after chemical thinning, can be done over a relatively long period without seriously affecting next year's crop or reducing the size and quality of the current fruit crop.

BENEFITS OF FRUIT THINNING

Reasons for thinning may be outlined as follows:
1. Increases annual yields of marketable fruit.
2. Improves uniformity of fruit size at harvest.
3. Improves color.
4. Improves eating quality.
5. Reduces limb breakage.
6. Promotes tree vigor and, where early chemical spray-thinning is practical, induces annual cropping.
7. Minimizes the handling and storage of low grade and

cull fruit.

8. Permits more thorough spraying of fruits during late-season applications.
9. Expedites all handling operations at harvest and reduces their respective costs.

Thinning increases fruit size. Probably the most pronounced effect of thinning is an increase in size of fruit, largely as a result of alloting more leaf surface for each fruit. Experimental evidence has shown that good size and quality can be obtained when fruits of most varieties are spaced to allow about 30 to 40 average size leaves in the vicinity of each fruit on standard-size trees. If 50 or more leave are left per fruit, there appears to be little additional increase in size and quality of the fruit. The usual commercial practice of spacing the fruits from six to eight inches apart on the branch allows about 30 average-size leaves per fruit for most cultivars.

With full-dwarf trees, it is interesting to note that about 10 leaves per fruit seem to be adequate, according to English researchers. More of the products of photosynthesis of the leaves apparently go into fruiting on dwarf trees. Also, more sunlight reaches the leaves, generally.

The late C. G. Brown (Ore. Cir. '76) showed the effect on size, grade, and cash returns of spacing Winesaps from three to four inches, six to seven inches, and nine to ten inches apart on 12-year trees in Oregon. Exact spacing, however, is not necessary since some cross-transfer of food within limbs allows bunched fruits to size well. Under conditions of this experiment, peak returns were obtained

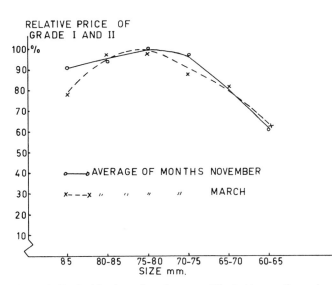

Figure 2. Fruit thinning of apples pays. The better auction prices brought by larger size fruits is shown for Golden Delicious in the market at Goes, The Netherlands. Fruits 75-80 mm are about 3-3¼ inches in diameter; 60-65 mm are about 2½ inches. U.S. chain stores are requesting medium size apples for bagging, over-raps, and children. (Courtesy S. J. Wertheim, Fruit Evp. St., Wilhelminadorp, The Netherlands).

by thinning the fruit a distance of six to seven inches on the branches. Gross cash returns were over twice as much for the thinned trees. Thinning a distance of nine to ten inches was no better than six to seven inches. See Dutch data, in Figure 2.

Thinning is not the only factor which influences size of fruit at harvest.

1. Some apple cultivars inherently produce small fruits and require more thinning as Macoun, Yellow Transparent, Wealthy and Yellow Newtown.

2. As the tree becomes older, the fruits tend to become smaller in size. This is because old trees set heavier crops than young trees, possibly because of the accumulation of a reproductive hormone in the older trees.

3. Fruit size may be markedly reduced under drought conditions, depending upon severity of the drought.

4. Fruits are usually larger when the trees have been adequately pruned the winter preceding a heavy crop.

5. Vigorous vegetative growth produces larger fruit than weak growth.

6. Foliage injury by caustic sprays and pests as mites during the growing season may result in smaller fruit. The relatively better size fruit obtained on heavily cropping trees today is likely due to the mild organic pesticides and to better fruit thinning practices.

Thinning increases fruit color. Fruit thinning tends to increase the amount and intensity of red overcolor and yellow undercolor of apples. C. G. Brown in Oregon Circular 76 showed that the more highly colored apples (Fancy and Extra Fancy) were obtained when the fruit was spaced six inches or more. This is important for apple cultivars such as Delicious which need considerable red color to fall in the higher grades. The general effect of thinning on color, however, is usually not as striking as its effect on size. Limb spreading helps to expose fruit to the sun for better coloring. Also, fruit on dwarfed trees receives better light and colors better than on large trees.

Thinning increases dessert quality. When a fruit is accompanied be adequate and efficient leaf surface and is well exposed to light, it is better supplied with carbohydrates and other materials which are needed for flavor and quality. The result is largely due to an increase in the sugar sucrose.

Thinning reduces limb breakage. A heavily loaded mature standard-sized McIntosh tree may carry almost a ton of fruit. Obviously, the leverage and strain of such a crop is tremendous and can be aggravated by high winds. The grower cannot afford to take chances on losing large sections of trees by overloading. Thinning not only reduces this danger, but helps to reduce the amount of propping. Dwarf trees have shorter limbs, less leverage and also may be staked, trellised or free standing. With proper training and annual pruning, propping may not be needed.

Thinning reduces disease and insect injured fruits.

Figure 3. High school boys and girls specially selected, are often used in hand thinning fruit. A foreman in charge of a group of 10 to 20 children checks the work, keeps time, and moves ladders for the girls. With full-dwarf trees on EM-26 or EM-IX this job is greatly simplified. In fact, it is becoming increasingly difficult to get labor to climb ladders.

Thinning offers an early opportunity to remove misshapen specimens and fruit injured by insects and diseases, all of which are bound to go into the cull class in the grading operation. These fruits not only rob the better fruits of nutrients, carbohydrates, and water, but are expensive to handle during the picking and grading season. Also, spread of insects and diseases can be checked greatly by removing injured fruits which may rub against healthy fruits. Clusters of 2 and 3 apples cannot be sprayed thoroughly.

Thinning reduces cost of handling the crop. Although there are no specific figures to demonstrate the reduction in handling costs as a result of thinning, it is obviously less expensive to handle a crop 95+ per cent in the upper grades with but few culls than one 75 per cent in the upper grades with 15 per cent culls. The cost of thinning is largely counteracted by the reduction in handling costs at harvest. Also, it is cheaper to pick or knock apples off to the ground at thinning time than to harvest, transport, store and grade out for ciders later.

Thinning affects yield. Experimental results of thinning on fruit yields are variable, but the majority of the experiments indicate that thinning by standard methods does

not, or if any, slightly reduces the yield. This is more or less to be expected since the practice is designed to decrease competition between fruits so that the remaining fruits will derive the benefit of increased water and food materials. The effect on yield depends upon the extent of reduction of the crop by thinning. With early-season chemical thinning it is quite probable that yields over a period of years are increased (Figure 1). One must be careful not to overthin and produce oversized fruits which are often inferior in eating and storage qualities, and may be difficult to market. It is important, however, to thin off the small fruit early (Figure 4).

Interrelation of pruning and nitrogen fertilizers. Pruning and thinning are interdependent. If a tree has been invigorated by pruning during the winter, there will be less need, if any, for fruit thinning the following season. On the other hand, if there has been light or no pruning during the previous season there may be a greater need for fruit thinning. It seems desirable not to try to eliminate thinning

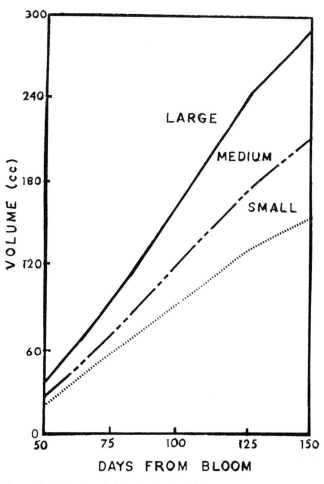

Figure 4. When hand thinning fruit, it is important to thin off the smaller fruit. Note that small apples are small at the start of the season and become even smaller, relatively, vs the large fruit as the season progresses to harvest. (From M. W. Williams and L. J. Edgerton, USDA Bull. 289)

92

by heavy pruning. On the contrary, pruning should be kept to a minimum consistent with its favorable effects, and the excess fruits removed by chemical and/or hand thinning.

It has been pointed out in the chapter on soil management that excessive application and poor timing of nitrogen fertilizers results in poor fruit color and condition. Hence, is it important to regulate carefully the nitrogen so that the color of the fruit is not affected adversely.

Alternate bearing. This is the tendency of a tree to bear heavily one year and lightly the next. York Imperial and Delicious tend to do this more than Rome Beauty, McIntosh and Jonathan. Chemical fruit thinning to reduce the drain of a heavy fruit set on a standard-size tree early in the season has done more than any other factor to correct "on-off" years of bearing. Other corrective practices are (a) annual pruning and the use of somewhat more pruning before the expected heavy-blossom season to reduce flowering points, (b) use of supplemental irrigation when needed, and (c) application of somewhat more fertilizer, particularly nitrogen, before the heavy-crop year to get large green leaves as early as possible to support the heavy crop. Supplemental urea sprays are effective in getting the nitrogen into apple leaves quickly and early in spite of adverse weather. One of the main problems now is for the researchers to devise a means of obtaining a good fruit set in spite of almost continuously bad weather during bloom. Growers in the humid areas who are using chemical thinning, the spur strains and other practices listed above generally are getting good return bloom each year, but with bad bloom weather the crop may be reduced greatly because of inadequate pollination by bees, with the grower helplessly standing by. Research is needed to try to overcome this problem.

CHEMICAL THINNING OF APPLES

Blossom or young-fruit thinning of apple and other deciduous tree fruits with chemical sprays has been a standard practice in commercial orchards of the world for many years. It is estimated that over 90% of the commercial apple growers in the world use some form of chemical fruit thinning. Among the leading researchers have been M. B. Hoffman and L. J. Edgerton, Cornell; Max W. Williams and the late L. P. Batjer and C. P. Harley, USDA; A. H. Thompson, Maryland; F. W. Southwick, Massachusetts; S. J. Wertheim, Holland; and many others. The following summary and recommendations are typical and based on the up-dated results available.

The principal value of chemical-thinning sprays is to improve size and finish of the fruit and to correct biennial bearing, or "on" and "off" years of heavy and light fruiting, thus making annual crops larger and more uniform. Also, spray-thinning costs less, reduces amount of hand thinning needed, and tends to reduce fire blight (bacterial) infection.

Although much has been learned about chemical sprays for thinning, much remains to be ascertained about the actual mechanics of their operation on living trees (see M. W. Williams, Hort. Rev. 1, 1979 for up-date). Their use is beset with complexities and hazards. Identical applications on the same trees in succeeding years may have very different results. Yet the use of these sprays is of such economic value that fruit growers have been willing to employ them despite the variability in results. Variation in results may be caused by timing of application, weather conditions, vigor of trees, concentration of spray material, cultivars treated, thoroughness of pollination, winter injury, frost damage, the chemicals used, and other factors listed in Table 1.

Chemical thinners add another to the arsenal of sprays already used by commercial orchardists to produce marketable fruits. Insecticides and fungicide sprays are

TABLE 1. CONDITIONS AFFECTING EASE OF FRUIT THINNING WITH CHEMICALS.
(AFTER M. W. WILLIAMS AND L. J. EDGERTON, USDA BULL. 289)

Trees are easy to thin when:	Trees are difficult to thin when:
1. Fruit spurs on the lower, shaded inside branches are low in vigor.	1. Fruit set on spurs in well-lighted areas of tree (tops and outer periphery).
2. Moisture or nitrogen supply is inadequate.	2. Trees are in good vigor with 12 to 18 inches of terminal growth with no mineral deficiencies.
3. Root systems are weakened by disease or physical damage.	3. Older trees in good vigor have a mature bearing habit.
4. Bloom is heavy, especially after previous heavy crops.	4. Light bloom or light fruit set occurs with the exception of young trees.
5. Young trees have many vigorous upright branches.	5. Trees have horizontal fruiting branches.
6. Thinners are applied to self-pollinated or poorly pollinated fruit.	6. Insects are active on cross-pollinated cultivars.
7. Fruit set is heavy on easily thinned cultivars, such as 'Delicious'.	7. Limbs and spurs have been slightly girdled following moderate winter injury.
8. The cultivars tend to have a naturally heavy June drop.	8. Biennial bearing trees are in the "off year."
9. Fruit sets in clusters rather than as singles.	9. Fruit set in singles rather than in clusters.
10. Bloom period is short and blossom-thinning sprays are used.	10. Cultivars such as 'Golden Delicious' and heavy setting spur types are to be thinned.
11. High temperature is accompanied by high humidity before or after spraying.	11. When ideal fruit growth occurs before and after time of thinning.
12. Blossoms and young leaves are injured by frost before or soon after spray application.	12. Low humidity causes rapid drying of the spray and decreased absorption occurs before and after spraying.
13. Foliage is conditioned for increased chemical absorption by prolonged cool periods.	13. Cool periods follow bloom, without any tree stress.
14. Rain occurs before or after spray application.	14. Endogenous ethylene production is low.
15. Prolonged cloudy periods reduce photosynthesis before or after application of chemicals.	15. Bloom is light and a high leaf-to-fruit ratio exists.

Figure 5. Chemical thinning in commercial apple orchards is a standard practice. Golden Delicious has responded particularly well in annual cropping of larger better quality fruit. Upper left photo shows a tree with light bloom that had been hand thinned the previous year; on the right is a neighboring tree that had been chemically thinned. Both carried about 17 bushels the previous year. Note the difference in follow-up bloom. Lower photos show unthinned Golden Delicious in New Jersey in mid-August on the left; chemically thinned on the right. With chemical thinning, apples are removed quicker and earlier, causing less drain on the tree of the excess apples. (Upper photos) Louis P. Edgerton, Cornell University.

used to control insects and fungus diseases, nutritional sprays sometimes are applied to the dormant tree or to the leaves to make better-nurtured trees, and sprays are used to keep fruit from dropping until the orchardist is ready to pick it. Some of the stop-drop sprays (NAA) are identical with some sprays used for chemical thinning. Thinning sprays are generally not recommended for us in combination with other spray materials that require uniform coverage; blossom-thinning sprays are best used selectively from tree to tree.

Spray-thinning research started in the depression years of the early 1930's, with the work of E. C. Auchter and J. W. Roberts. Growers wanted a spray that would entirely defruit apple trees of cultivars that would not pay their way. This forestalled the expense of spraying and harvesting a crop for which there was no market. After this initial venture in total crop removal, emphasis passed to finding spray materials that would correct biennial bearing in cultivars having that tendency. Early thinning was done with sodium dinitro cresylate (DNOC) and related dinitro compounds. These still are being used in some regions. Later, the hormone-type materials, particularly naphthaleneacetic acid (NAA), used originally in orchards to delay harvest drop, were found to be effective for thinning after the blossom stage and after the danger of frost had passed. Naphthaleneacetamide (NAD or NAAm) and carbaryl (Sevin) also are being used today as after-bloom sprays with the dinitros being used at bloom in

areas where frosts are a low risk.

Fruit trees do a partial job of thinning themselves. Usually not more than five to twenty per cent of the apple blossoms set fruit. Thinning may be required to reduce fruit set by a relatively small percentage on some cultivars. It is especially needed on cultivars that tend toward "snowball" blossoming and a biennial bearing. Growers have found chemical thinning profitable, lowering hand-thinning costs to 0 to 25 to 90 percent. Thus, even if the chemical spray does not do a complete thinning job, and some hand thinning is necessary, the saving in cost can be substantial.

FACTORS AFFECTING RESULTS
WITH THINNING SPRAYS

Hand thinning developed early in the apple-growing industry of the Northwest. Its purpose was to help produce a higher quality crop. However, hand thinning of fruit was, and is, one of the costliest operations in the production of fruit. Depression-born research using dinitro compounds to defruit unprofitable varieties and later work to reduce biennial bearing, indicated the feasibility of using chemical sprays for fruit thinning that could be applied with orchard equipment already in use.

Timing: Early experiments were directed toward obtaining information about timing and concentration of DNOC (dinitro or Elgetol) sprays. Experiments with

Figure 6. If the pistils are burned after a DNOC spray, the fruit will persist if the calyx leaves are distended (not folded down) and the fruitlet is beginning to size. Under these conditions there will be need for a postbloom spray. (From M. W. Williams and L. J. Edgerton, USDA Bull. 289)

DNOC on apples, which do the job by physical injury to blossoms (Figure 6) and physiological shock to the tree, have suggested that application be made in Washington when ther are 3 blooms/spur cluster open on the north side of the tree or at about full bloom (80% of blossoms are open on 3-to-4-year spurs, north side of tree). Not more than one spray should be used. Low temperatures and wet weather will increase effectiveness and can result in overthinning and more foliage damage. Growers usually have 3 to 4 days and can cover a sizeable acreage. Large acreage growers should start spraying as early as possible. DNOC is not adapted for use as a postbloom thinner. It can be used only in regions where postbloom frosts are not likely to occur. There has been some use of DNOC along the East coast but growers must be fairly well assured of frost-free weather.

Timing is rather critical when the hormone-like chemicals NAA and NAAmide are used on summer cultivars. These sprays should be applied on early cultivars preferably at the petal fall stage. If used much later than 10 days after bloom, stimulating effects manifested by premature ripening and fruit splitting are likely to occur. Sevin has

not been effective as a thinner for summer cultivars.

Important advantages of a postbloom thinning spray are (a) delaying the application to avoid the frost danger and (b) the opportunity to evaluate the degree of fruit set before applying treatments. Many timing studies on late cultivars have been conducted with NAA and NAAm. Unlike summer cultivars, the results generally indicate a wide latitude in time of application. At present most sprays including these chemicals are applied from 10 to 21 days after full bloom. Figure 7 stresses the importance of thinning as early as possible to improve next year's crop.

Sevin, used since 1960, also an insecticide, has as wide a range in timing as NAA and NAAm. L. P. Batjer and B. J. Thomson, working in Australia and Washington, effectively thinned several cultivars of apples when Sevin sprays were applied 5 to 30 days after full bloom. In general, results were consistent and uniform between 15 and 27 days after full bloom. Sprays applied earlier and later were somewhat more variable and in some instances failed to thin enough. How late in the season Sevin will cause thinning is likely to depend on the weather. During a cool postbloom period, "natural" fruit drop is delayed. When this occurs, the sprays are effective later in the season than if the weather is warmer.

Dr. L. D. Tukey (Penna.), using a plastic rule with different size holes, suggests that fruits should average 3/8 (easiest to thin) to 7/16 inch in diameter for chemical spray thinning of Delicious and Jonathan. Check fruit size each day per cultivar, using "king" or lateral fruit whichever sets first on sample trees.

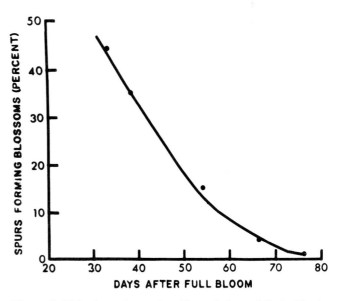

Figure 7. This chart shows the effect of time of fruit thinning after full bloom on formation of blossom buds for next year's crop. Fruit were thinned to one fruit per 70 leaves at points indicated by the black dots, 33 to 76 days after full bloom on the biennial-bearing Yellow Newtown in a good bearing year at Wenatchee, Washington. (After Harley et al. USDA Bull. 792)

Ethephon is being used on *bearing and non-bearing* trees to induce flower bud formation; with Alar its effectiveness is enhanced. Alar also controls growth and induces spur development. Avoid using either one on M.9 trees and moderately vigorous trees which may be stunted by over-blooming and setting. *Slow-to-bear* young trees or *light-blooming mature* trees can be helped by applying either or both. Alar is used 14-21 days after bloom and ethephon delayed until June drop begins, or 5-6 wks. after bloom to avoid over-thinning. Trees with a "snow-ball" bloom, as Golden Delicious, may require a thorough thinning plus use of Alar and ethephon to get good bloom the next year.

Concentration: Since the effective concentration of thinning sprays is related to weather conditions, tree vigor, cultivar, and possibly other factors, a "rule-of-thumb-" recommendation cannot be made. With NAA, reduction in set is greater with the stronger spray. However, with DNOC and Sevin (carbaryl) one may not find any difference between 2/3 and 1-1/3 pints per 100 gallons of DNOC, or one-half and 1 pound of 50% WP or equivalent of Sevin. It is well to be in contact with your local agency to keep abreast with any changes in recommendations being published annually.

Table 2 is an example of chemical fruit thinning recommendations for northeastern USA and Table 3 is typical of northwestern USA recommendations.

Cultivar: Each apple cultivar requires a different chemical fruit thinning program. Reaction of a cultivar varies with the climate and cultural conditions. Hence, a specific program has been developed for each cultivar at each production area, although, generally, they tend to be similar in a given rather large area. In general, chemical thinning can be used with greater safety and dependability with cultivars that tend to set heavy crops. With a moderately heavy bloom, production of a commercial crop usually requires 20 to 35 apples per 100 blossoming spurs, depending on the cultivar and conditions under which it is grown. It is generally necessary to remove fruit in excess of the amount desired if satisfactory fruit size and annual bearing habits are to be obtained.

Although there are some exceptions, cultivars that are generally classified as hard-to-thin set heavier than those considered easier-to-thin. The hard-to-thin cultivars are partially self-fruitful (set fruit with their own pollen) and tend to set heavily even under rather adverse weather conditions. Conversely, cultivars considered easy-to-thin are all self-unfruitful and may or may not set heavily.

In the fruit areas of Washington the partially self-fruitful cultivars, such as Golden Delicious, Yellow Newtown, and Rome Beauty, usually set 80 to 100 fruits per 100 blossoming spurs when carrying a heavy bloom. Thus, one can expect a fruit set on these cultivars of nearly three times the number considered desirable for a

TABLE 2. CONCENTRATIONS FOR CHEMICAL THINNING CERTAIN APPLE CULTIVARS IN NEW YORK. (WARREN C. STILES, CORNELL)

Variety	NAAm (ppm a)	NAA (ppm a)	Sevin 50 WP (lb./100 gal. b)	Combinations (ppm + lb./100 gal. b)
Jerseymac, Vista Bella	—	5-10	—	—
Lodi c	35-50	—	—	NAA 5-10 + Sevin 1-2
Transparent c	35-50	—	—	NAA 5-10 + Sevin 1-2
Quinte c	35-50	—	—	NAA 5-10 + Sevin 1-2
Early McIntosh c	35-50	—	—	NAA 5-10 + Sevin 1-2
Milton	35-50	5-10	—	NAA 2.5-5 + Sevin 1-2
Wealthy	—	15-20	—	NAA 5-10 + Sevin 1-2
Paulared	—	5-10	1-2	—
Tydeman	—	5-10	1-2	—
Jonamac	—	5-10	1-2	—
Jonathan	35-50	5-10	1-2	—
McIntosh	35-50	5-10	1-2	—
Spartan	—	10-15	—	NAA 5-7.5 + Sevin 1-2
Cortland	35-50	5-10	1-2	NAA 2.5-5 + Sevin 1-2
R. I. Greening	35-50	10-15	1-2	NAA 5-7.5 + Sevin 1-2
Macoun c	—	5-10	—	—
Empire	—	5-10	1-2	—
N. W. Greening	35-50	—	—	—
Delicious	—	5-10	1-2	—
Northern Spy	35-50	—	1-2	—
Idared	—	—	1-2	—
Golden Delicious	—	15-20	—	NAA 5-10 + Sevin 1-2
Yellow Newtown	—	15-20	—	—
Rome Beauty	—	10-15	1-2	NAA 5-7.5 + Sevin 1-2
Ben Davis	35-50	10-15	—	—

a Lower concentrations suggested for conditons favorable for thinning.

b When applied solely for thinning, use the 1-lb. rate. If insecticidal activity is also desired, use the 2-lb. rate.

c Petal fall applications only. NAAm at 25 to 50 ppm + Sevin 1-2 lb./100 gal. can be used instead of NAA-Sevin combination on these varieties if preferred. Applications on other cultivars should be made within 21 days after full bloom.

Many growers are using combination sprays successfully of Sevin and NAA or Sevin and NAAm on several varieties. For example, a mixture of Sevin 50WP at 1 pound per 100 gallons and NAA at 10 ppm or NAAm at 35 ppm has thinned Early McIntosh better than higher concentrations of either material alone. Combinations of Sevin and NAA also have been very effective on Golden Delicious, R.I. Greening, and Cortland. Timing and conditions for application of such mixtures should be similar to those suggested for NAA or NAAm along.

The use of Sevin as a thinner can precipitate pest outbreaks (e.g., woolly apple aphid, European red mite). The insecticide Vydate may act as a mild thinner if applied on apple trees in the 2-3-week postbloom period. Consider the need for thinning and the anticipated use of other chemical thinners before applying Vydate during this period.

satisfactory crop.

On the other hand, Delicious and Winesap may or may not set heavily, depending on the season and provisions for pollination. If these self-unfruitful cultivars are adequately pollinated, they usually set about 50 to 60 fruits per 100 blossoming spurs; this is only about twice the number of fruits required for a commercial crop. Therefore, because of the lighter setting tendencies of these cultivars, the margin of safety is less than with the partially self-fruitful cultivars mentioned. Consequently, there is more chance of overthinning.

BLOOM SPRAY — Spray to run-off. Based on 400 gallons per acre (for average size trees)

POST-BLOOM SPRAY — Spray to run-off. Based on 400 gallons per acre (for average size trees). Avoid killing bees on blooming cover croys.

Fruit Cultivars	Use any one of listed materials or combinations	Spray concentration (active ingredient)	Material per 100 gallons	Remarks and restrictions
Non-spur Delicious	1. Elgetol		2/3-1 pint	Apply when three blossoms per spur cluster are open on north side of tree. Both groups.
Golden Delicious Jonathan, Newtown Winesap, Spur-type Delicious	1. Elgetol		1-1½ pints	
Delicous	1. *Carbaryl			Apply carbaryl once, anytime from 10-25 days after full-bloom. Apply NAA 15-25 days after full-bloom. To increase thinning on spur-type Delicious, use a combination of carbaryl and NAA.
	Sevin 50% WP	150- 300 ppm	¼ -½ pound	
	Sevin XLR Savit 4F	150 -300 ppm	¼ -½ pint	
	2. NAA			
	NAA 200 (+ surfactant**)	2- 5 ppm	0.5-1.0 ounces	
	NAA 800 (+ surfactant**)	2- 5 ppm	0.12-0.3 ounces	
	NAA WP (+ surfactant**)	2 ppm	1½ ounces	
Delicious	1. Combination carbaryl + NAA			Combination spray for use where increased thinning is desired. Apply once, anytime 15-25 days after full-bloom.
	*Carbaryl			
	Sevin 50% WP	150- 300 ppm	¼ -½ pound	
	Sevin XLR Savit 4F	150- 300 ppm	¼ -½ pint	
	+ NAA			
	NAA 200	2- 5 ppm	0.5-1.0 ounces	
	NAA 800	2- 5 ppm	0.12-0.3 ounces	
	NAA WP	2 ppm	1½ ounces	
Golden Delicious	1. *Carbaryl			Apply carbaryl once at 10-25 days, Amide 7-14 days and NAA 15-25 days after full bloom. For greater thinning use a combination of carbaryl + Amide or + NAA 10-20 days after full-bloom but at lower rates. Amide + Alar gives greater return bloom. Amide plus ethephon gives greater thinning and return bloom.
	Sevin 50% WP	300- 450 ppm	½ -¾ pound	
	Sevin XLR Savit 4F	300- 450 ppm	½ -¾ pint	
	2. NAA			
	NAA 200			
	(+ surfactant**)	3- 5 ppm	0.7-1.0 ounces	
	NAA 800			
	(+ surfactant**)	3- 5 ppm	0.2-0.3 ounces	
	NAA WP	3- 5 ppm	2.2-3.5 ounces	
	(+ surfactant**)	17- 34 ppm	3-5 ounces	
	3. Amide (NAAm) (+ surfactant**)			
	4. Combination carbaryl +			
	NAA or + Amide (NAAm)			
	*Carbaryl			
	Sevin 50% WP	150- 300 ppm	¼ -½ pound	
	Sevin XLR, Savit 4F	150- 300 ppm	¼ -½ pint	
	+ NAA			
	NAA 200	3 ppm	0.7 ounces	
	NAA 800	3 ppm	0.2 ounces	
	NAA WP	3 ppm	2.2 ounces	
	or + Amide (NAAm)	17 ppm	3 ounces	
	5. Combination Amide (NAAm) + Alar			
	or + Ethephon			
	Amide (NAAm)	17- 34 ppm	3-5 ounces	
	+ Alar 85	1500-2000 ppm	1.5-2.0 pounds	
	or + Ethephon	300- 450 ppm	1.0-1.5 pints	
Winesap	1. *Carbaryl +			Apply carbaryl once, any time from 10-25 days after full bloom. Amide 7-14 days after full-bloom, NAA 15-25 days after full-bloom.
	Sevin 50% WP	450 ppm	¾ pound	
	Sevin XLR	450 ppm	¾ pint	
	Savit 4F	450 ppm	¾ pint	
	2. NAA			
	NAA 200 (+ surfactant**)	2- 5 ppm	0.5-1.0 ounces	
	NAA 800 (+ surfactant**)	2- 5 ppm	0.12-0.3 ounces	
	NAA WP (+ surfactant**)	2 ppm	1½ ounces	
	3. Amide (+ surfactant**)	17 ppm	2.7 ounces	
Jonathan Yellow Newtown Rome Beauty	1. *Carbaryl			Apply carbaryl once any time from 10-25 days after full-bloom, NAA 15-25 days after full-bloom. NAA is less effective on Jonathan and Rome Beauty.
	Sevin 50% WP	300- 600 ppm	½ -1 pound	
	Sevin XLR, Savit 4F	300- 600 ppm	½ -1 pint	
	2. NAA			
	NAA 200 (+ surfactant**)	3- 5 ppm	0.7-1.0 ounces	
	NAA 800 (+ surfactant**)	3- 5 ppm	0.2-0.3 ounces	
	NAA WP (+ surfactant**)	3 ppm	2.2 ounces	

Continued

97

Bartlett	1. Amide (+ surfactant**)	10-15 ppm	1.6-2.4 ounces	Apply 15-21 days after full-bloom. Amide
	2. NAA 200 (+ surfactant**)	10-15 ppm	2.4-3.6 ounces	may overthin varieties other than Bartlett.
				NAA may not adequately thin Bartlett
				some seasons. Not all formulations of NAA
				are registered for this use.

*Carbaryl (Sevin, Savit) is highly toxic to bees and predatory mites. See text.

**Use surfactant according to manufacturer's recommendations, but not more than 1 pint per 100 gallons of spray.

For easier and more accurate measurement of small amounts of liquids, dilute them first. For example, make a 10 to 1 dilution by putting 1 part in 9 parts water. From this solution, measure out and use 10 times the amount shown in the table.

Fruit set on most cultivars growing under eastern and midwestern conditions is lighter and generally more erratic. Success with thinning sprays is based on the assumption that fruit set will be in considerable excess of that necessary for a commercial crop of good size and quality. One of the major factors in overthinning is failure to set fruits. Certain cultivars as Delicious are more erratic in their setting tendencies than others. Aside from sprays other considerations, postbloom thinners rather than DNOC bloom sprays are best suited for such situations. Careful appraisal of fruit set is therefore vitally important in determining the need for, and the type of, thinning spray best adapted for a given situation.

In some instances, there may be little choice between the different chemicals, but in others a clear-cut preference is indicated. For example, Sevin has generally been the most satisfactory thinning spray on Delicious, Rome Beauty, and Jonathan in all sections of the country. It is also effective on other cultivars.

Under certain conditions NAA results in severe flagging and dwarfing of foliage. This condition most frequently occurs on summer cultivars. In order to partially avoid leaf injury, apply NAA as late as possible during the postbloom period. When this is done on early apples, premature ripening and splitting of the fruit are likely to occur. Thus, NAA is best suited for fall and winter

Figure 8. The branch of Red Delicious fruit on the left has not been thinned. In the center the fruit were sprayed with carbaryl (Sevin) 10 days after bloom. At the right, note the pygmy fruits resulting from spraying Red Delicious with NAAm 10 days after bloom. (After M. W. Williams and L. J. Edgerton, USDA Bull. 289)

cultivars, but it should be used on these cultivars only when Sevin or NAAm is not effective.

Under certain conditions young fruit suppressed in growth by NAAm does not absciss (Figure 8). It continues to develop, but final fruit size is greatly reduced with few or no seeds. Because of this condition, NAAm should not be used on the Red Delicious. This condition may also occur on other cultivars.

Weather: Weather before and after spraying affects the great variability that often results from thinning sprays. Environment can affect the rate of absorption and action of the spray material and the degree and nature of the fruit set.

One hazard with DNOC is rain following the sprays. Material deposited on the leaves may be rewetted. The resultant additional absorption sometimes seriously injures the foliage and excessively reduces the fruit set.

Factors affecting the absorption of NAA and NAAm sprays have received considerable attention. Unfavorable weather prior to and after spray application, such as cool temperatures, excessive humidity (Figure 9) or rainfall, or minimal sunshine, has resulted in heavier thinning with these chemicals.

Environmental factors affecting the action of chemical thinners, especially NAA are similar in many respects. The leaf is the primary organ in absorption of these chemicals. Absorption efficiency is affected in part by the physiological status of the plant and particularly by the cuticle, which is considered a major barrier to absorption. Factors such as humidity affect thickness, composition, and absorption rate through the leaf cuticle (Figure 9).

Sevin has been more consistent than other thinning chemicals. Experiments with Sevin and extensive observations indicate that weather has no consistent effect on the results obtained. This characteristic of Sevin is probably associated with the difference in mode of entry and site of action of the chemical.

Additives: Several investigators found that adding certain surfactants (wetting agents) to spray mixtures greatly enhanced foliar absorption of growth regulators. When Tween 20 (1 pint per 100 gallons) is added, NAA is suggested at half the usual rate.

This finding suggested that a surfactant possibly could be used with relatively low concentrations of NAA and NAAm and thereby less variability would result because of environment. However, the addition of a surfactant does not greatly reduce variability as might be expected from

Figure 9. Humidity before spraying with DNOC makes a difference in spreading of the spray over the leaf surface. Leaf on left had been in 100% humidity for a week before spraying while leaf on right had been in 30 to 50% humidity. Not beading on right. (From M. W. Williams and L. J. Edgerton, USDA Bull. 289)

controlled experiments. Nevertheless, the inclusion of an additive with hormone-type thinners has become a general practice in many apple-growing areas. The reduced amount of chemical used is a substantial saving in cost of NAAm sprays. A surfactant is desired that does not foam excessively when agitated in the spray tank.

Tree Vigor: Growth status of the tree affects results with thinning sprays. Over-thinning is less likely with these sprays when trees have normal vigor. Trees are more susceptible to the action of thinning sprays when suffering from the affects of inadequate light when closely planted and lightly pruned, from winter injury, "wet feet," low-nitrogen level, or any condition that may affect normal growth and the fruit-setting processes.

Trees suffering from the affects of any of these conditions may set less fruit. Furthermore, the set may be "weaker" and more easily thinned with spray chemicals. All chemical thinners reduce fruit set more on weak wood lacking in food reserve. Even with normal trees, thinning is heavier on the weak, shaded wood of the lower and inside branches of the tree.

Many observations indicate that when trees have cropped heavily previously, they are usually more easily thinned, even though they have a heavy bloom that sets normally. In such instances, a lower carbohydrate reserve may result in greater thinning by the chemical.

Young trees are more easily thinned than older ones with established bearing habits. Some cultivars, including Delicious (5 to 8 years old) that are just beginning to bear, may not set fruit in proportion to the amount of bloom. Even the fruit of cultivars that tend to set heavily on young trees is more easily thinned than on older trees. This response of young trees to thinning sprays is perhaps related to their faster vegetative growth and a consequent reduction in carbohydrates available to the young developing fruit in the early postbloom period. Young trees, particularly Golden Delicious, are frequently thinned safely with chemicals, but the spray concentration should be adjusted to approximately one-third to one-half that for older trees of the same variety.

Pollination, Bee Activity, Predators: Since successful spray thinning depends on heavy fruit set, weather during bloom is important in determining the adequacy of pollination may be poor when these cultivars are more heavy set of fruit and a good seed count which affects fruit size (Figure 10).

With favorable weather during bloom, self-unfruitful varieties such as Stayman, Winesap and Delicious may set heavily at least three tree spaces away from a pollination cultivar. Under cool, rainy, or windy conditions, pollination may be poor when these cultivars are more than one tree space from a pollinizer. It is more important to evaluate pollinating conditions carefully when using DNOC sprays. With postbloom thinners, however, one can evaluate the degree of fruit set before spraying.

Do not use Sevin at bloom to avoid killing bees, which are needed in pollination. Use with caution in a spray program encouraging mite predators. Predators are found mainly in the center of the tree; they can be bypassed by *not directing the spray* into the tree center and onto the trunks and lower limbs.

Amount of Bloom: Fruit growers often ask how much bloom is required before thinning sprays should be considered. To obtain this information, several tests were conducted in Washington with trees possessing only one-half as much bloom as other trees growing under the same condition. It was found that on trees with lighter bloom, fruit set per 100 blossoming spurs was substantially

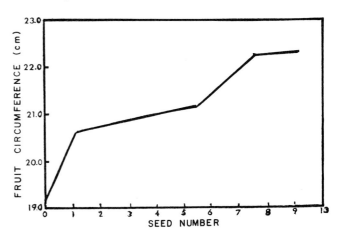

Figure 10. Note here that the number of seeds in Red Delicious at harvest have a marked influence on the size of the fruit. Hence, a grower should provide for good pollination by proper planting design and providing bees. (After M. W. Williams and L. J. Edgerton, USDA Bull. 289)

greater. Also, thinning sprays had less effect in reducing the amount of fruit set. Thus, sprayed trees varying from 50- to 95-percent bloom set about the same amount of fruit per linear unit.

Generally when bloom is light, fruit set is heavy and thinning from chemical sprays is reduced. Obviously, sprays should not be applied to a bloom or fruit set that is not heavy enough to require thinning. However, if an occasional tree with a light bloom is sprayed, there is little likelihood that appreciable thinning will result.

Number of Spray Applications: One application of a thinning spray on hard-to-thin cultivars usually does not thin enough. Also, it may be desirable to apply two sprays to other cultivars under conditions conducive to a heavy set. With a two-spray program there should be enough time between the two sprays for the effects of the first one to be evaluated before it becomes necessary to apply the second. In the Northwest it is common practice to apply a DNOC spray during the bloom period and follow 14 to 21 days later with a postbloom thinner if needed. Such procedure provides time to evaluate the effects of the first spray. The chemical used in the second spray is either Sevin or NAAm.

In humid regions, DNOC is erratic and rarely used. In these areas a 2-spray program may be used, applying NAA at petal fall and Sevin or NAA two weeks later. The 2-week interval is used to evaluate effectiveness of the first spray to decide if a second spray is needed. Leave a few un-treated trees to evaluate thinning effectiveness.

Precautions: The following summary precautions have been listed for New Jersey apple growers, which may be of general interest: (1) Chemical thin only when bloom is heavy and weather has been good for pollination. A heavy bloom is easier to thin than a medium to light bloom; (2) do not use if freezing temperatures occur during bloom or prior to time of application; (3) apply when temperature is between 70° to 75°F (21.1° and 24°C) if possible. Do not apply when temperature is below 60° or above 80°F (15.6° or 26.7°C; (4) direct dilute sprays at top half of tree. Wet thoroughly. Fruit and leaves must be covered with spray; (5) do not spray tree of low vigor; (6) young trees thin easier than mature trees; (7) thinning chemicals are at least one third more effective the year following a heavy crop.

Defruiting Trees. Defruiting young or dwarf trees (spot-applied to mainly the central leader while developing a desired framework), ornamental crabapples, and backyard apple trees often is desired. Application of ethephon (Ethrel) at 250-500 ppm at petal fall will defruit apple trees with no adverse effect on the foliage.

Inadvertent Fruit Thinning by Pesticides. Under some weather conditions some pesticides may also do a thinning job. Sevin, also used as a fruit thinner, and Cyprex may do this when applied near or shortly after bloom. Benlate, as

yet, has caused no concern. Follow directions carefully and confer with your specialist if a problem arises.

EASY AND DIFFICULT-TO-THIN CONDITIONS

When undecided on a fruit thinning program for a particular orchard block, two questions frequently arise: (a) "Will thinning be necessary?" and (b) "Will the fruit be easy or difficult to thin?" Below is a list of factors to consider.

Easy-to-thin conditions. (1) Fruit spurs on lower and inside branches that are shaded and less vigorous; (2) Trees with inadequate moisture or nitrogen supply; (3) Trees with weak root systems due to freeze damage, trunk girdling, too little or too much water in soil, insect damage, or herbicide injury; (4) Trees, limbs, or spurs in low vigor caused by first three factors; (5) Trees with heavy bloom, especially following previous heavy crops; (6) Young trees with many vigorous upright branches; (7) Self-pollinated and poorly-pollinated varieties; (8) Heavy fruit set on easily thinned varieties such as Red Delicious; (9) Varieties that tend to have a heavy "June drop;" (10) Fruit set in clusters rather than singles; (11) Short bloom periods with many flowers open and susceptible to blossom-thinning sprays; (12) High temperatures accompanied by high humidity before or after spraying that cause stress on foliage and fruits and increases chemical absorption; (13) Frost before or soon after spray application that injures blossoms and young leaves, thus increasing chemical absorption; (14) Prolonged cool periods before spraying that pre-condition the foliage for increased chemical absorption; (15) Prolonged cloudy periods before application of chemicals that reduce photosynthesis; (16) Tree spacing tight.

Difficult-to-thin conditions. (1) Trees in good vigor with 12 to 18 inches of terminal growth per year; (2) Light bloom or light fruit set after a heavy bloom; (3) Cross-pollinated varieties with adequate insect activity in or-chard; (4) Older trees with a mature bearing habit; (5) Fruit on spurs in well-lighted areas of tree (tops and outer periphery); (6) Horizontal fruiting branches; (7) Slight girdling of limbs and spurs following moderate winter injury; (8) Trees in biennial bearing habit with no crop in previous year; (9) Fruit set in singles rather than clusters; (10) Heavy setting varieties such as Golden Delicious; (11) Warm, sunny weather ideal for good growth prior to and after time of thinning; (12) Decreased chemical absorption resulting from low humidity before and after spraying that causes rapid drying of the spray; (13) Spur-type Delicious.

Review Questions

1. Define fruit thinning.
2. List 7 advantages of thinning fruit.
3. Discuss developments with the newer chemical fruit thinners.

4. What are the advantages of thinning blossoms with certain chemical sprays as compared with hand thinning fruit after the June drop? What are the disadvantages of these chemical sprays at blossoming?
5. How should thinning, nitrogen fertilization, and pruning be interrelated to attain the best size and quality of fruit?
6. Discuss briefly the reasons for so much variability in results with chemical hormone-type thinning sprays on apples.
7. List 5 conditions that make chemical thinning difficult and 5 conditions that facilitate chemical thinning.

Suggested Collateral Readings

Auchter, E. C. and J. W. Roberts. Spraying apples to prevent fruit set. ASHS 30:22-5. 1934.

Baird, L. A. and B. Webster. Anatomy, histochemistry of fruit abscission. Hort. Rev. Avi Publ. Co. 1:172-203. 1979.

Batjer, L. P. and H. D. Billingsley. Apple thinning with chemical sprays. Wash. Agr. Exp. Sta. Bull. 651. 24 pp. 1964. (Good bibliography included.)

Bukovac, M. J. et al. Conjunction of foliar absorbed NAA by selected fruit crops. Hort.Sci. 11(4):389-90. 1976.

Bukovac, M. J. Gibberellin - induced asymmetric apple fruits. Hort.Sci. 3:3. 1968.

Chemical thinning of apples. Exten. Folder F-177. Mich. State Coll. Ask for latest. Also, Univ. of Mass. Spec. Cir. No. 189 4 pp. Write your agricultural college or university for latest local recommendations.

Dennis, F. G. Jr. Factors affecting yield in Delicious. Hort. Rev. Avi Publ. Co. 1:395-422. 1979.

Donoho, C. W. Jr. NAA spray date and fruit size relation to thinning effectiveness. ASHS 92:55-62. 1968.

Donoho, C. W. Jr. Translocation and breakdown of $C^{14}NAA$ in apple. 16th Intern. Hort. Cong. Belgium. 1962.

Elfving, D. C. and C. G. Forshey. Effects of naphthaleneacetic acid on shoot growth of apple trees. J. Amer. Soc. Hort.Sci. 102(4): 418-423. 1977.

Fisher, D. V. Size thinning for apples. (For eliminating poorly seeded small apples). British Columbia Orchardist (July): 8-10. 1975. (Contact Summerland, B.C. Sta.)

Forshey, C. G. and C. C. Elfving. Fruit size and yield relationships in 'McIntosh' apples. J. Amer. Soc. Hort.Sci. 102(4):399-402. 1977.

Forshey, C. G. Interaction of Alar and fruit thinning sprays. N.Y. Food and Life Sci. (Geneva) Apr.-Sept. 1971. Also, Alar on vigorous McIntosh trees. Jr. ASHS 95:64-67. 1970.

Growth regulators in fruit production. A Symposium. Univ. of Minn. and Long Ashton Research Station, Bristol, England. Vol. I, II: 505, 85 pp. 1973. Request proceedings directly.

Herrera-Aguirre, E. and C. R. Unrath. Chemical Thinning Response of 'Delicous' Apple to Volume of Applied Water. Hort.Sci. 15(1):43-44. 1980.

Sakai, A. and Y. Nishiyama. Cryopreservation of winter vegetative buds of hardy fruit trees in liquid N. Hort.Sci. 13(3):225-7. 1978.

Schneider, G. W. Abscission mechanism studies with apple fruitlets. J. ASHS 103(4):45-8. 1978.

Tukey, R. B. and M. W. Williams, Editors. Tree fruit growth regulators and chemical thinning. Wash. State Univ., Coop. Exten. Pullman. 232 pp. $12.00). 1981.

Tukey, R. and M. Williams, Editors. Tree fruit growth regulators and chemical thinning. Wa. State Univ., Ext. Serv. 232 pp. Pullman, Wa. 99164. May 1981.

Young, E. and L. J. Edgerton. Effects of Ethephon and Gibberellic Acid on Thinning Peaches. Hort.Sci. 14(6):713-714. Dec. 1979.

Walsh, C. S. et al. Ethylene Evolution in apple following post-bloom thinning sprays. Hort.Sci. 14(6):704-706. Dec. 1979.

Williams, M. W. Chemical thinning of apples. Hort. Rev. Avi Publ. Co. 1:270-300. 1979.

Williams, M. W. and L. J. Edgerton. Chemical fruit thinning of apple and pear. U.S.D.A. Agr. Inform. Bull. 289. 22 pp. (Very good). 1981.

Williams, M. W. Retention of Fruit firmness and increase in vegetative growth and fruit set of apples with Aminoethoxyvinylglycine. Hort.Sci. 15(1):76-77. 1980.

Added References

Abbot, D. L. The effects of seed removal on the growth of apple fruitlets. Ann. Rept. Long Ashton Res. Sta. 1958:52-56. 1958.

Byers, R. E. 1978. Chemical thinning of spur 'Golden Delicious' and 'Starkrimson Delicious' with Sevin and Vydate. Hort.Sci. 13(1):59-61. Feb. 1978.

Ferree, D.C. and F.R. Hall. Growth regulators, pesticides on photosynthesis, transportation of apple trees. J. ASHS 103(1):61-64. 1978.

Gardner, V. R. et al. Fruit setting in Delicious Apple. Mich. Spec. Bull. 358. 45 pp. June 1949.

Harley, C. P., J. R. Magnes, M. P. Masure, L. A. Fletcher, and E. S. Degman. Investigations on the cause and control of biennial bearing of apple trees. U.S. Dept. of Agr. Tech. Bull. 792. March, 1942.

Leuty, S. J. SADH and response of McIntosh to fruit thinners. Hort.Sci. 9:193-195. 1974.

Longley, R. P. A study of the relationship between the amount of bloom and yield of apples. Reprinted Canadian Jour. Plant Sci. 40:52-57. January, 1960.

Luckwell, L. C. The auxins of the apple seed and their role in fruit development. Proc. VII Th. Int. Bot. Congr. Paris Sec. 11:377-379. 1954.

McKee, McKee, M. W. et al. Chemical fruit thinning and McIntosh repeat bloom. ASHS 88:25-32. 1966.

Nitsch, J. P. The physiology of fruit growth. Annl. Rev. Plant Phys. 4, 199. 1953.

Preston, A. P. Degree of thinning and apple yield, size and biennial bearing. J.H.S. 29, 269. 1954.

Robitaille, H. A., F. H. Emerson, and K. S. Yu. Thinning apples with ethylene-releasing chemicals. J. Amer. Soc. Hort.Sci. 102(5):595-598. 1977.

Schneider, G. W. Ethylene evolution and apple fruit thinning. J. Amer. Soc. Hort.Sci. 100:356-359. 1975.

Southwick, F. W., D. W. Green and W. J. Lord. Effect of SADH treatments on the response of 'McIntosh' apple trees to chemical thinner. Hort.Sci. 8(4):314. August 1973.

Stahly, E. A. and M. W. Williams. Effect of plant growth regulators on apple fruit and pedicel abscission. J. ASHS 97(6):724. 1972.

Tromp, J. Growth regulating substances, tree orientation and growth and flower bud formation in apple. J. Hort.Sci. 47:525-533. 1972.

Thompson, A. H. and B. L. Rogers. Chemical thinning of apple trees using concentrate spray. Jour. ASHS 94:1, 23-25. Jan. 1969.

Unrath, C.R. The commercial implications of gibberellin A4A7 plus benzyladenine for improving shape and yield of 'Delicious' apples. J. Amer. Soc. Hort. Sci. 99:381-384. 1974.

Wertheim, S. J. and M. L. Joosse. Chemical flower thinning with Ethrel-A on Winston. De Fruitteelt 64:410-411. (In Dutch.) 1974.

Wertheim, S. J. Chemical control of flower and fruit abscission in apple and pear. Acta Hort. 34:321-331. 1974.

Wertheim, S. J. Carbaryl: Chemical thinner for Golden Delicious. Profestation Voor De Fruitteelt, Wilhelminadorp. No. 9. August 1970.

World list of research workers in growth regulators in fruit production. 59 pp. I. H. Jonkers, Haagsteg 3, Posrbus, 30 Wageningen, Netherlands. 1971.

(See additional references in former book editions.)

101

Grafting and Budding Trees

Fruit growers should learn the technique of budding and grafting. Reasons for developing this art are:

1. The market demand for certain varieties may shift, leaving the grower with an orchard of fruit that cannot be sold at a reasonable profit. (Figure 1).

2. With dwarfing stocks being used increasingly, a knowledge and training in double-working, budding and grafting these trees is essential. (Figure 2).

3. The cultivars planted may not cross-pollinate properly. Other cultivars with effective pollen must be grafted on scattered trees.

4. Although trees may have been inspected in the nursery for trueness to name, it is not uncommon for jobbers and dealers to lose and jumble the labels on bundled trees.

5. The grower, himself, may make a mistake and order cultivars that later prove undesirable.

6. Small acreage growers may wish to propagate their own high-density trees. For big jobs, however, growers usually contract with a reputable nurseryman.

A knowledge of grafting technique may be needed also for repairing bark damage that may be caused by freezing

---

[1]In revising this Chapter, Ohio State University Bulletin 481 on ''Fruit Tree Propagation'' by Elden J. Stang, David C. Ferree and Fred O. Hartman was consulted and some sections adapted.

temperature, cultivating tools, canker diseases, or by mice and rabbits chewing away the bark.

DEFINITIONS[1]

The meaning of frequently used grafting terms should be understood at the outset:

Budding is a type of grafting. It consists of inserting a single leaf bud, the scion, with or without attached bark and wood piece, into the stock by specific techniques. T-budding, sometimes called shield budding, is done in the latter part of the growing season from late June into September. Chip budding may be done in the spring before growth starts or during the growing season when active growth temporarily ceases.

Budling is used to identify the plant resulting from the first year's growth after budding.

Budstick is current season's shoot growth from which single buds are removed for budding.

Callus is the mass of regenerating cells, called parenchyma cells developing from and around wounded tissue. The union between a rootstock and scion results from the interlocking of the cells from both parts. Likewise, roots usually arise first from the callus tissue at the basal ends of cuttings.

Figure 1. An undesirable apple cultivar has been converted to a Delicious bright-colored spur strain. Cropping started the 2nd and 3rd yrs. Union of cions and stocks (3) are pointed to at right by Ernest G. Christ of Rutgers University who did the grafting. The bark-graft was used.

Figure 2. With the world trend toward dwarf fruit trees, use of vegetatively, propagated clonal rootstocks is dominating the fruit tree nursery business. (Upper left) Removing soil and sawdust from around stool bed of E. Malling 9 rootstocks in preparation for cutting away the rooted shoots. (Upper right) Rooted layers of the stocks being removed for further use in propagating desired cultivars. (Lower left) Sorting rooted EM shoots into uniform size groups. Poorly rooted shoots will be made into hardwood cuttings for rooting. (Lower right) The lined-out rooted shoots ready for summer budding to Delicious and other cion cultivars. (Ohio Agr. Extension Serv., Columbus 43210)

Cambium Layer refers to a single layer of cells between the wood and bark tissues which surrounds all woody portions of a tree. This layer of cells, through cell division, produces two sets of cells that make up the growing tissues on both sides of it. On the outside, the new cells form phloem or bark. On the inner side, the wood or xylem tissues are formed. The cambium is thus the source of all growth in diameter of the woody stem. In propagating trees, the cambium of the scion must line up with the cambium of the stock as perfectly as possible if a good union is to result.

Clone (or clon) is a horticultural term denoting a specific cultivar propagated asexually or vegetatively. Rootstocks used in fruit tree propagation are called clonal rootstocks. (Figure 3).

Cuttings are sections of plant stems, leaves, buds or roots which root and grow after proper insertion in sand, soil, or other suitable media.

Cultivar is the preferred term to replace "variety", but both terms are being used interchangeably. Cultivar, used to designate horticultural varieties throughout the world, was adopted by the International Code of Nomenclature for Cultivated Plants in 1961.

Dormancy (seed) is a term referring to the failure of a seed to germinate even though ideal conditions exist. In such cases, pregermination treatment such as cold stratification is necessary to break dormancy. Dormant plants or buds are those not actively growing but can resume growth with favorable environmental conditions.

Grafting is a term referring to various techniques of inserting a section of stem with leaf buds (the scion) into the stock. Since dormant scions are used, grafting is done

Figure 3. Jonathan (12-yrs. old) dwarfed with 8-inch interstem of M.8 (arrow) on clonal Alnarp-2 rootstock. Both graft unions are above ground. The longer the interstem piece, the more the dwarfing. Growers, researchers and nurseymen are evaluating interstems for dwarfing to get a good root system (MM.111, MM.106, seedling) and a semi- to full-dwarfed tree. (R.F. Carlson, Mi. State Univ.)

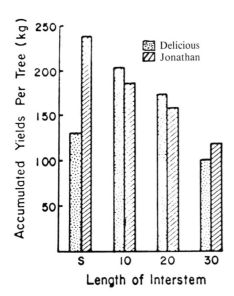

Figure 4. There is interest in interstem apple trees even though they cost more. They may be longer-lived and more productive. Trend involves, e.g., use of a MM. 111 rootstock with a 6-8 inch EM. 9 interstock and a Red Delicious cion top. Chart above shows accumulated Delicious and Jonathan yields of seedling rooted trees vs various length interstems of M. 8 in centimeters on Alnarp-2 roots. Six-yr. record.

The Stark Brothers Nursery and Orchards Company, Louisiana, Missouri, 63353, as a nursery, has pioneered in the interstem field of propagating compact fruit trees, with the objective of getting a more widely adapted and longer-lived root system than many clonal stocks provide. Robert L. Norton, Cornell Univ., has extensive tests. (Courtesy R.F. Carlson, Mich. State Univ.)

in early spring, usually before growth begins.

Interstem or **Interstock** refers to a section of trunk or the basic framework which is introduced between the rootstock and the scion cultivar. An interstem is chosen for specific vegetative characteristics or for the effect it may have upon tree size. Interstems may be used to develop desirable framework characteristics, winter hardiness or disease resistance, or to make possible the joining of two cultivars which are incompatible if grafted directly. Thus, such trees consist of three distinct parts: the rootstock, the interstem and the scion cultivar. (Figures 3 and 4.)

Mound Layering is a method of vegetative propagation. An individual plant may be layered, or plants may be lined out in rows for layering. First, the top of each plant is cut back. As shoots develop from the basal part of the stem, soil or other rooting medium is mounded (hilled) over the base of the shoots, without completely covering the new growth. Plant species and cultivars successfully layered form roots on the portion of the stem (shoot) below the soil surface. The rooted shoots are removed later and used as rootstocks for budding and grafting (See Chapter III.)

Rootstock is that part of a tree which becomes the root system of a grafted or budded tree.

Scion (or cion) denotes a short piece of twig or a bud with attached section of bark inserted into the stock.

Seedling refers to a plant grown from a seed.

Stock identifies a plant or plant root system to which a scion cultivar is grafted or budded.

Stool or **Stool Bed** designates a plant or group of plants of a specific clone or rootstock to be multiplied by mound layering.

Sucker or **Root Sucker** refers to shoot growth arising from the crown or roots of a tree, generally below the graft union or at just below the soil surface.

Top Working is the practice of changing the top of a tree from one cultivar to another through the use of budding or grafting methods.

Variety is the term that was used for many years to denote a cultivated variety of plant. It is being replaced by the term "cultivar" in horticultural literature (see cultivar).

Watersprout indicates a vigorously growing unbranched shoot of the current season. It generally grows vertically and may arise from a primary scaffold or smaller branch, often adjacent to a pruning wound.

SHOULD YOU GRAFT?

In the long run, is it cheaper to replace the tree or to perform the grafting operation? After surveying many top-worked bearing trees in Michigan, investigators found that there were as many failures or near failures as successes. The same is often true of trees completely or excessively girdled where numerous long cions will be needed. Usually, the younger and more vigorous the tree, the better will be the chance for successful recovery without seriously delaying the bearing life of the tree. Young trees of diameters less than two inches make excellent recovery if cut off below the girdled area and (a) cleft-grafted, or (b) allowed to send up a new trunk, provided it arises from wood of the named cultivar.

It usually takes from three to five years for a mature tree to recover to normal and expected production after a major grafting operation. (Figure 1). If a tree has been girdled for a full growing season or more, its chances are slim for satisfactory recovery after bridge-grafting. Certainly, trees which have been completely top-worked never catch up with the total lapsed production that a bearing tree would have given if its limbs had not been cut back for grafting. The question might be asked, "Will the new cultivar after five or so years give more net profit and satisfaction to the owner than could the old cultivar; and with girdled trees, is the injured tree worth the repair cost?" Although bridge-grafting is relatively time consuming, when balanced against the actual future value of a good tree, the cost is generally small. With girdled trees, it is always well to examine carefully the depth of injury to the bark. if the sapwood is not exposed, the cambium is probably still alive, and painting with water asphalt emulsion (roof paint with no creosote or similar ingredients), or mounding with soil will often suffice until the bark heals and thickens.

WHEN TO GRAFT

The best time for most grafting is when the buds are beginning to swell in the spring. Where you must split the wood before inserting the cion, as in cleft-grafting, this work should be done just before the bark begins to slip. If the bark is slipping readily, the wood may split along one line and the bark along another, making proper placement of the cion difficult. Cleft- and whip-grafting can be performed with dormant cion wood while the stock is dormant and as late as blossoming or later, but the latter is considered late for best results. Under Ohio conditions, the highest percentage of successful grafts were made experimentally in May, although grafts made in April, June, and July were almost as successful. Cions for the late grafting were kept dormant in cold storage until ready for use. Bridge-grafting can be done best after growth starts when the bark is slipping readily.

SELECTION AND STORAGE OF CION WOOD

Sometime during the dormant season, the grower should make a row by row inspection of his trees or record the location, cultivar, and amount of grafting needed. Thence, the necessary cion wood can be collected during the running operation. It is a wise practice to store cion wood each year for emergency jobs discovered after growth starts in spring.

Cion wood should consist of shoot growth made during the previous season. This can be distinguished by starting at the top of the branch and proceeding back to the first growth ring of bud scale scars which encircles the twig. This ring denotes the point where growth started the previous season; also, older wood back of it is of a different shade in color. The percentage success with cion wood older than one year is low. Good cion wood has the following qualifications: (a) growth of one to two feet during the previous season; (b) about as thick as a lead pencil (water sprouts are satisfactory, but tips should be rejected because of immaturity; water sprouts usually remain dormant longer in spring); (c) having large plump mature buds devoid of insect eggs and disease injury; (d) no discoloration of pith due to cold injury; and (e) absolutely dormant.

If a cion stick is divided into four parts, the center two parts are the best for grafting because the buds in this area are large and healthy and the wood is well supplied with stored food. The tip buds are often immature, winter injured, or may have flower buds while buds near the base of the cion are small and weak.

Proper storage of cion wood is extremely important. It must be kept cool and moist, but not wet. This can be done by wrapping the cions in cloth or heavy paper and burying them horizontally two feet deep in a well-drained spot, preferably on the north side of a building. Cion wood can be kept in common or cold storage in damp sawdust or peat moss, but it should be examined frequently and redampened if necessary. If cion wood dries or becomes too wet, its chances for growth are poor.

If during grafting more cion wood is needed, sometimes it is possible to obtain additional wood from dormant nursery trees in storage or from nearby nursery houses. Also, water sprouts in mature trees or shoots from young trees may be a source since they start growth several days after periphery wood. The farther the buds have pushed on prospective cion wood in the spring, the less likely such wood will succeed in a graft. Cion wood with swollen buds should be used only in a limited way in exceptional cases and then covered with asphalt emulsion and shaded with paper bags.

GRAFTING SUPPLIES AND EQUIPMENT

Equipment needed for orchard grafting is shown in Figure 5. Most of the tools can be purchased from the local hardware stores or nursery supply companies.[1] A rubber hammer can be used in place of a mallet. Rubber strips or plastic shields maintain an even pressure, expanding with growth of the stock and rotaway. A modified carpenter's apron is convenient for holding the equipment and cions while grafting.

Asphalt emulsion paint (roofing paint) is largely used today. It is applied cold by brush and stored at a temperature above 40°F. The ideal grafting paint should have the following qualifications: (a) exclude air and fungi and retain moisture in the wood; (b) is not toxic to tender tissue; (c) does not crack in cold weather; (d) does not melt in hot weather; (e) semipermanent; (f) is somewhat elastic to accommodate differences in growth rate of stock and cion; (g) has sufficient body during application to fill cracks; (h) relatively cheap; and (i) easy to handle. It is important that asphalt emulsion *not* contain creosote or similar materials toxic to plant tissues.

TOP-WORKING

As indicated earlier, the primary reason for top-working a tree is to change the cultivar. For the change to be suc-

---

[1]Companies include: A. M. Leonard and Son, Piqua, Ohio 45356; Bartlett Manufacturing Co., 3044 E. Grand Blvd., Detroit, Mich. 48202; Diston Div., H. K. Porter Co., 701 Grant St., Pittsburgh, Pa., 15219; Seymour Smith and Son, Inc, Oakville, Conn. 06799. Tyson Orchard Service, Flora Dale, Pa. 17307.

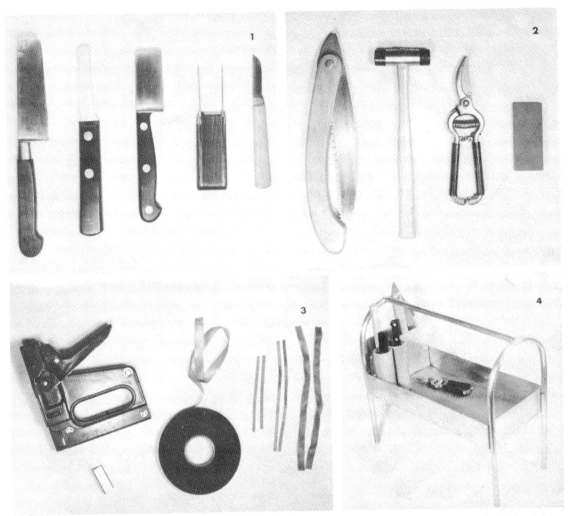

Figure 5. Grafting and budding tools. (1) l. to r. Side grafting knife; scion knife to prepare scions; wedge knife in cleft-grafting; patch bud knife (for nuts); budding knife. (2) Folding saw; plastic (or rubber) tip hammer; shears; carborundum sharpening stone (keep all tools razor sharp). (3) Stapler using 9/16 inch zinc-coated staples in bark grafting; plastic tape; rubber tie strips. (4) Aluminum carrying case or table. (Stribling's Nurseries, Inc. P.O. Box 793, Merced, Ca. 95340)

cessful, (a) the graft union between stock and cion must be sound, (b) big limbs must not be exposed to sunscald during the process, (c) the new cultivar must be compatible with the stock, and (d) the limbs to be grafted must be selected carefully.

Limbs selected properly for top-working on a mature apple tree can be (a) up to six to eight inches in diameter, (b) not shaded or exposed at right angles to sunlight, pointing upward at 45° angle or better rather than level or downward, and (c) located in a prominent position and well spaced around the tree (grafting insignificant limbs is a waste of labor and materials). The limbs should be grafted relatively low or back into the tree.

Top-working of trees older than 10 years has been done successfully, as shown in Figure 1. These trees were in good bearing within 2 to 4 years. A part of a block can be done each year over a three to five-year period to maintain sales income from the block.

Special care should be taken to avoid unduly exposing large limbs to sunscald which may lead to injury by flat-headed borers and subsequent entrance of wood-destroying fungi. Danger from sunscald can be reduced by lime-spraying the limbs or leaving water sprouts for shade until about the end of the second year. Fire blight sprays may be needed if the cion variety is susceptible. A lime mixture for painting limbs can be prepared as follows: 10 lbs. whiting lime (from paint stores; a carbonate form) or hydrated lime; 5 oz. soya bean flour (or caseine glue); 1 oz. salt; in 5 gallons of water. Exposed stubs and scaffolds usually escape sunscald when they run more or less parallel to the hottest rays of the sun between two and three o'clock in the afternoon.

If a novice, spread top-working over a two-year period. It is true, however, that experienced grafters can spot-graft in key positions the first year so that no additional grafting is necessary. Subsequent pruning in such a case should encourage the grafted limbs to assume the main framework of the tree, while the ungrafted limbs are pruned moderately heavy, dwarfed, and eventually removed.

Apple cultivars in general can be intergrafted successfully with each other, but it is wise to use cultivars of about equal inherent vigor. For example, a vigorous growing cultivar may be top-worked best on an equally vigorous cultivar, as McIntosh on Baldwin. The following cultivars and their strains are listed according to inherent vigor:

TABLE 1. APPLE CULTIVARS AND TREE VIGOR FOR GRAFTING COMPATIBILITY.

Vigorous Trees

Arkansas (Black Twig)	Fameuse	N.W. Greening	Smoothee
Baldwin	Gala	N. Spy	Spartan
Benoni	Granny Smith	McIntosh	Stark
Boskoop	Gravenstein	Maiden Blush	Spitzenburg
Bramley's	Hibernal	Mollie's Delicious	Twenty Ounce
Britemac	Hubbardston	Mutsu	Tompkins King
Cortland	Idared	Puritan	Winter Banana
Delicious	Landsberger Rette	R.I. Greening	Wolf River
Empire	Lodi	Red Astrachan	Y. Bellflower
			York Imperial

Medium Vigor

Antanovka	Franklin	James Grieve	Opalescent
Ben Davis	Fuji	Jonathan	Paulared
Chenango	Glockenapfel	Julyred	Ralls Roxbury Russet
Cox's Orange	Golden Delicious	King David	Stayman
Duchess	Goldparmane	Kidds Orange Red	Sturmer
Ein Shemer	Grimes	Macoun	Winesap
			Y. Newtown
			Y. Transparent

Relatively Small

Anna	Mother	Spur Strains
Beverly Hills	Ontario	Wagener
Dorsett Gordon	Rome Beauty	Wealthy
		Williams

Cleft-grafting. The cleft-graft is made by inserting a cion into the split stock, as shown in Figure 5 and 6. Limbs selected for cleft-grafting should have the following qualifications: (a) from one to two inches in diameter; limbs smaller than one inch in diameter should be wrapped firmly with string or tape for a few weeks to assure a strong union, (b) wood six inches below the cross cut must be straight-gained and free from large knots or scars, (c) accessible from the ground if possible, and (d) more or less upright; cions in horizontal stubs "take" poorly or grow upward at right angles, forming an undesirable scaffold limb.

The cut across the stock should be square, not sloping. Fine-tooth saws make a smoother cut and expose the cambium zone better. Short cions with two or three buds are less likely to be knocked out by birds or wind. Cions the size of a lead pencil with plump vigorous buds contain adequate food materials and water. Discard terminal portions of cion shoots because they may contain flower buds. Prepare the base of the cion with two sloping cuts,

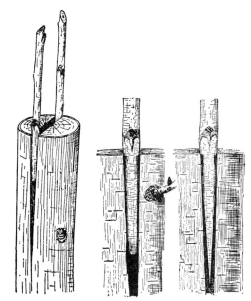

Figure 6. (Left) Here is a cleft-graft complete except for asphalt. Note position of the cion buds, number of buds, and the type of cuts. Split in stock was made with grafting chisel and then held open by a wedge on back of chisel. (Middle) The cion is correctly made and placed. Note the blunt end and close contact of cambiums of stock and cion. (Right) This shows the cion improperly cut; it should not be beveled to a point; cambium contact is poor and cions may rock with the wind. (Michigan Exp. Sta.)

starting at or slightly below the level of the lowest bud (Figure 6). The food stored around the bud is greater than between buds and, therefore, is thought to enhance union quickly enough to preserve the cion until internodal cion bark slowly unites. Do not bring the cion wedge to a point. The inside of the wedge should be thinner than the outside. This insures closer contact of the cambiums of the stock and cion. The top of the cion should be cut about one-quarter inch above a bud to reduce likelihood of the bud dying. Cion cuts should be straight and smooth with no wave. After a little experience, one stroke with a sharp knife makes the best bevel.

The stock stub is split across the center, using a chisel and a mallet. A four- to six-inch split is adequate. The split is held open by the wedge on the back of the chisel, or with a screwdriver. The two cions are inserted carefully, making sure that the cambium of the cion and the cambium of the stock come in close contact. One must bear in mind that the thickness of the bark is much greater on the stock than on the cion (Figure 7). Buds must be upright. Contact of the cambiums at the top of the stock is most important, and contact below should be as continuous as possible. Tilting the cion outward is dubious because the two cambiums may cross at a point where the cion bevel waves inward, preventing contact. The top of the cion bevels should be flush with the top of the stock. if the split in the stock is made too deep and the cions are held loosely, tie a

107

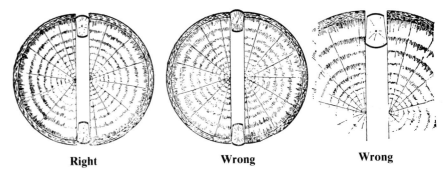

Figure 7. Reasons why some grafts fail. (Left) Cleft-graft properly made and properly set with cambiums of stock and cions in perfect contact. (Middle) This shows the failure of cambium contact between stock and cion; the cions are set out too far toward the outside of the stock. (Right) This shows the failure of cambium contact because of undue thickness of inner side of cion. (Michigan Exp. Sta.)

Right **Wrong** **Wrong**

strip of plastic tape, string-enforced, around the stock and leave it for about three months, after which it must be cut loose but not removed.

All cut surfaces should be sealed carefully with asphalt paint. Check each graft to be sure there are no pinholes left unsealed. Holes in the paint permit moisture to escape, resulting in drying of tissues and poor or no "take." Seal the split in the stock also with paint.

Over 90 per cent of the cions should take if the job has been done carefully. Common causes for failure in cleft-grafts are (a) failure to obtain proper cambial contact because of uneven bevel edges on the cion, (b) imperfect painting, (c) lack of dormancy in cion, (d) cion too thin and weak, and (e) fire blight infection.

The cleft-graft shown in Figure 8 shows an excellent "take" three months after grafting.

Bark or Veneer grafting. Bark-grafting can be understood by studying Figures 1, 9, and 10. Although cions may be more easily blown out by wind, it is preferred by most operators to the cleft-graft because it is not necessary to split the stub and it can be used on stubs too large for cleft-grafting. The job can be speeded up by making one lengthwise split in the bark, lifting it, slipping the beveled cion under, nailing and asphalting.

SUBSEQUENT CARE OF GRAFTS

Careful attention to the grafts for a few years afterward is important for two reasons: (a) the prevention of invasion by wood-rotting fungi, and (b) to encourage correct framework development of the new top. Where two or more cions have been set in a cleft- or a bark-graft, the one making the best shoot growth should be encouraged and pruned as little as possible. The others should be nipped back over a two-year period, beginning the second year. When the stock wound has healed over, the subordinated cions are removed. Presence of these subordinate cions is important in healing over the stump (Figure 9). If one cion should die, a nearby water sprout may be encouraged for awhile as the "subordinate cion".

Grafts should be checked periodically to repaint areas which have cracked and exposed the tissue. Asphalt, however, is pliable and is a big improvement over the old

waxing materials. Sunscald on a heavily cutback tree, as the one in Figure 1, is generally not a problem because sucker growth quickly appears covering these limbs. Periodic thinning and eventual removal of most suckers is a necessary followup job.

The Tongue-or Whip-graft. The tongue- or whip-graft is suited to top-working young trees in the orchard where the stock and cion are small and about the same diameter. It also is used for bench-grafting indoors in winter where the

Figure 8. A vigorous three-month growth of cions in a cleft-graft. Note temporary retention of nurse shoots close to the cions, and the excellent sealing of the union with wax. (U.S.D.A.)

108

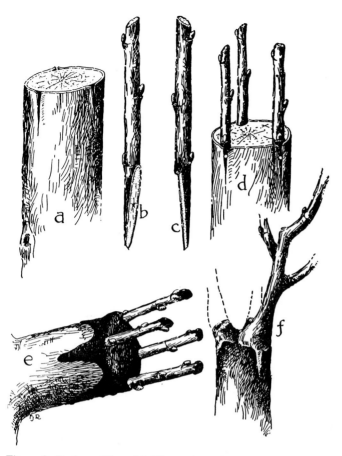

Figure 9. Bark grafting. (a) Slit stock ready for cion; if bark is thick, use 2 parallel slits width of cion. (b, c) Cion with straight bevel and shoulder bevel. (d, e) Cions nailed in place and asphalt painted. (f) Treatment one year later.

cion and/or interstock (double-worked) and clonal or seedling roots are grafted together, wrapped with string, stored in moist peat moss, and set in the field, as described

in Chapter III. The method of matching the stock and cion (with two to four plump buds) is shown in Figure 11. The uniformly sloping bevels are from one to one and one-half inches long. On both stock and cion, a slit is made halfway between the pith and the end or toe of the cut. The two are then slipped together as indicated. If the cion is smaller than the stock, union of the cambium should be provided on only one side. If the ends, or toes, of the stock and cions should hang over, these must be trimmed flush. In the orchard, the graft is then wrapped with rubber bands or nurserymen's tape. Exposed areas are covered with asphalt emulsion paint. Be sure to use *water* asphalt emulsion roofing-type paint that contains *no* harmful creosote. Whip-grafting can be done from the time before the bark slips to afterbloom, provided the cion wood is dormant.

Beginners may not be successful with this graft because of: (a) failure to make the sloping cut long enough, (b) uneven bevels arising from a dull knife or other causes, (c) improper placing of the slit, and (d) failure to press the tongues together deeply enough.

It requires about a month after growth starts for the union to take place, after which the rubber strips may rot loose or string should be cut to prevent ringing. At this time select the best shoot from the cion, remove the others, and begin to train the tree as described in the pruning Chapter IV.

Budding. Budding is a form of grafting in which a bud is used as the cion rather than a section of the stem. Budding is used mostly on trees in the nursery. It also can be used in the orchard on individual pencil-size sprouts or branches of young trees, but whip-grafting may put you a season ahead of budding. It can be used for top-working peaches, plums, and cherries in the field because gumming is not excessive and splitting of the wood is not necessary.

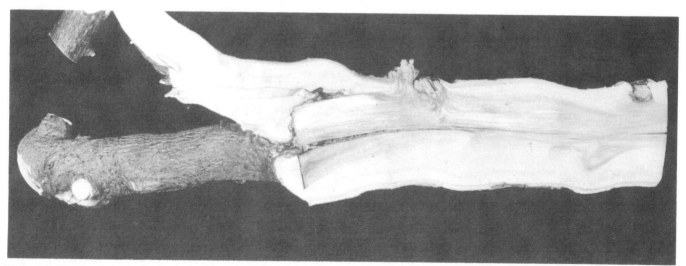

Figure 10. This is a longitudinal cut through a cleft graft (center) and bark graft (on side) after three seasons of growth. Bark grafts are satisfactory and are quicker and easier, particularly on large stocks. (Ernest G. Christ, Rutgers University).

Figure 11. In whip-grafting (upper) diagonal bevel cuts are made in both the cion and stock and each split down above the pith, then (middle) joined or "meshed" together with cambium layers in contact on at least one side and (bottom) taped or wrapped with rubber strips. (Stark Nurseries and Orchard Co., Louisiana, Mo.)

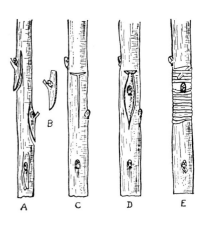

Figure 12. Budding. (A) prepared bud stick; (B) bud removed; (C) T-shaped incision in stock; (D) bud inserted; (E) bud tied with rubber strip. (R. F. Carlson, Mich. State Univ.)

Budding can be done in late summer or early fall. Buds are selected from the middle portion of vigorous current-season growth. These growths are called "bud sticks." The leaves are trimmed off, leaving three-fourths inch of the petiole or stem attached for a handle in manipulating the bud later (Figure 12, 13). The bud sticks are wrapped in moist burlap to prevent drying during the budding operations. Buds are more successful when inserted on the upper side and at the base of one-year wood where the bark is relatively thin. If the stock is one to three inches thick, as with peaches, a one-year side shoot is selected for budding, after which the stock is cut back the following spring just above the side shoot, and flush with it.

Using a special budding knife (Figure 5) a *"T-cut"* is made as described in Figure 12. The bud is removed from the bud stick by making a concave cut starting one inch

Figure 13. Fruit tree nurseymen hire their best labor for budding in summer for it is exacting to get a high percentage of "take". Left, a "T" slit is made i the seedling or clonal stock with a sharp budding knife, into which the bud from the desired cion is placed (Middle). Right, the bud is wrapped secure with a rubber strip or grafting tape. Top is removed above the bud the nest spring. To speed production in Europe, M.9 shoots in stoll bed are budded in summer, cut away and planted directly in the orchard next spring. (USDA)

110

CHIP-BUDDING

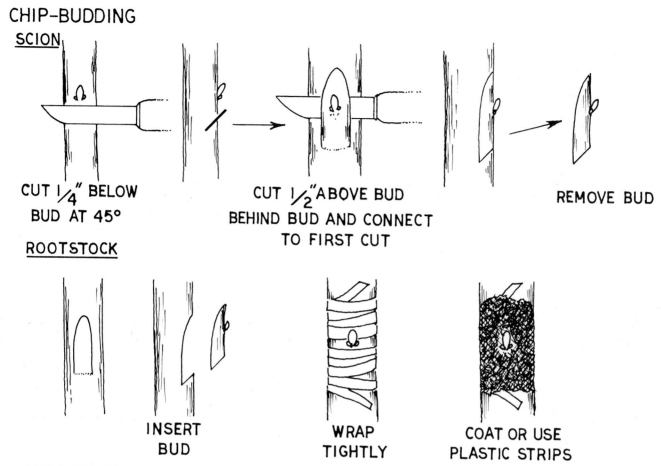

SCION

CUT ¼" BELOW
BUD AT 45°

CUT ½" ABOVE BUD
BEHIND BUD AND CONNECT
TO FIRST CUT

REMOVE BUD

ROOTSTOCK

INSERT
BUD

WRAP
TIGHTLY

COAT OR USE
PLASTIC STRIPS

Figure 14. Both "T-budding" and "chip budding" are forms of grafting. Chip budding is adapted to use in spring when the rootstock is dormant. Fully developed, dormant buds are essential for success in budding. (Ohio State University)

below the bud. A transverse cut is made about one-fourth inch above the bud to remove it. After the bud has been inserted *upright* into the opened cut, it is snugly wrapped with a rubber strip, taking care to leave the bud exposed. Ends of the rubber strips can be held in place by putting the free end back under the last turn. No asphalt emulsion paint is needed.

If the graft is successful, the bud should grow to the stock within two to three weeks, after which the rubber strip will begin to loosen, deteriorate, and drop. The graft was successful if the bud is plump; if shriveled, it will be necessary to rebud. The next spring before growth starts, the stock should be removed about one-half inch above the bud to force the bud into early growth. Shoots arising below the bud must be removed periodically.

Some operators prefer the *"chip" bud* system to the "T" bud. The chip bud is generally used on the smaller rootstocks or on limbs up to one inch in diameter for top-working. Figure 14 shows the technique. The stock is not cut back to the bud until union is complete and the bud begins to grow in spring, or if the chip budding is done in late summer or fall, the stock is cut back within about an inch of the bud the next spring as growth is beginning.

REPAIR-GRAFTING

Bark repair may be necessary on the trunk or base of the main limbs because of injury from mice, rabbits, winter freezing, cultivating tools, or disease cankers. Repairs must be done the spring after the injury occurred for best results. Large injuries, more than halfway girdling the tree and which have gone for more than one growing season may weaken the tree seriously and take it several years to recover, if such recovery is possible.

If the bark has been removed by rodents during the winter, especially on very young trees, an application of asphalt emulsion covering exposed areas should be made immediately to prevent excessive drying until a bridge-graft can be made.

Cions for repair work should be selected from hardy disease-resistant cultivars, such as Duchess, Fameuse, Northwestern Greening, Robusta 5, McIntosh, Hibernal, or Cortland. Less desirable cultivars are Baldwin, Delicious, Golden Delicious, Gravenstein, Grimes Golden, Northern Spy, Rhode Island Greening, Rome Beauty, Stayman Winesap, Winesap, and York Imperial.

Bridge-grafting. Bridge-grafting is used to bridge over a

111

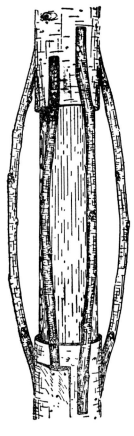

Figure 15. Bridge-graft showing three methods of setting cions. Cion set under flap at bottom is beveled on two sides. This method is timesaving on stocks with relatively thin bark. A bow in cions is important on young trees that sway with the wind. Cions are placed one to two inches apart around the trunk. (Michigan Agr. Exp. Sta.)

preparing the cion and nailing them in place is shown in Figure 15. The lower two- to three-inch bevel is prepared first, set in a slot or under a flap, and nailed. The upper bevel is then cut and placed against the stock and outlined with the knife, thence removing the bark slot. With young trees a small stick is placed between the center of the cion and the stock to give the cion a bow and prevent it from being pulled out as the tree sways with the wind. One must be careful to have all buds facing upward. Inverted cions will grow but the vigor and percentage "take" are lower. All exposed areas should be covered thoroughly with asphalt paint. The bridge-graft should be protected from future rodent injury by spray-repellent Thiram or wrap-around wire cloth (Figure 3). No protection is necessary if the bridge area is above the reach of mice and rabbits. Remove later any water sprouts arising on and near the cions.

The approach-graft. This is used on big standard-size trees. One or more nursery trees, from one to two years old, are planted at the base of the tree. Tops of the trees are inlay-grafted into the trunk as in bridge-grafting (Figure 16). This type of grafting is useful where the mature tree has received a bark or canker injury a few years previously, and grafting has been neglected. Many of the roots may have died and the limbs in line above the injury may have become weakened. Some growers have practiced approach-grafting on trees growing on shallow soil to increase the root system, but experimental data to confirm this practice are lacking. It is important to remove all suckers and side branches appearing on the seedling trees or the trunk of the mature tree until the young trees are well established.

bark area where the cambium is exposed or dead (Figure 15). On relatively young trees which have been completely girdled, the best procedure may be to cut them off at the girdle, causing shoots to arise above the nursery graft on the seedling root. If shoots arise only from the seedling root, it will be necessary to whip-graft or bud them to the desired cultivar, or, the stump may be cleft-grafted provided it is strong enough to hold the cion. Cleft-grafting these small stumps may be preferable to bridge-grafting.

Bridge-grafting should be performed when the bark is slipping readily, which is about the time buds are unfolding. Emergency bridge-grafting can be done in the summer, but careful selection of cion wood held over in storage is necessary.

The area to be bridged should be cleaned with a knife or a special bark scraper and painted with asphalt emulsion, preferably a day in advance of grafting to prevent the sapwood from drying and to facilitate the grafting job.

Cion wood for bridge-grafting can vary in size from that of a lead pencil to one-half inch in diameter, the larger and longer cions being used on larger wounds. The cion should be cut at least four inches longer than the area to be bridged. Long cions are easier to manipulate than short cions. If the area to be bridged is narrow, it may be better to inlay-graft the ends of the cion several inches above and below the injured area, using a long cion. The method of

Figure 16. (Left) A 6-year-old bridge-graft used for repairing fire blight damage on a mature apple tree. (Right) Inarching or approach-grafting may be used to repair pine mouse injury to roots, or to increase the root system under shallow soil conditions. Four seedling apple trees have been planted at the base of the tree and inlay-grafted into the trunk. Grafts are 4 years old. (Michigan Agricultural Experiment Station)

112

Contract Budding. Fruit growers frequently contract with a reputable nursery a year or so before planting to guarantee getting desired cultivars, stock, or interstocks for a specific planting date. This is good practice, particularly when desired cultivars on specific dwarfing stocks are scarce.

Tissue Culture. Other names used for this revolutionary technique are: tree cloning, micropropagation, embryo culture, test tube culture, and somatic embryogenesis. Tissue culture is the process of growing living tissues and cells in special, sterile, artificial culture media (in vitro). Auxin and Cytokinin growth regulators are used, sometimes in agar-based media, while others as thornless blackberry shoot tips start better in liquid to be transferred later to a gelatinous medium. The technique will enable nurserymen to produce thousands of trees, e.g., within a year or less. Other advantages are: (1) Speeds developing, testing and selection of superior new cultivars; (2) difficult-to-root rootstocks can be made readily available; (3) virus-free material can be propagated easily; (4) the plantlets are proving more vigorous and productive; (5) cost of nursery stock can be moderated; and (6) trees can be grown on their own roots faster than by traditional methods.

Interested nurserymen, others, have built their own facility in Gervais, Oregon, 97026, known as Micro Plant Nurseries, Inc., and are following the technique developed by Dr. Tsai-Ying Cheng, who has prepared the following tentative table:

TABLE 2. ROOTSTOCKS AND CULTIVARS PROPAGATED SUCCESSFULLY BY TISSUE CULTURE. (BY TSAI-YING CHENG, OREGON GRADUATE RESEARCH CENTER, BEAVERTON, ORE. 97075).

Plant	% Root Formation	Est. Ann. Plant Production
APPLE ROOTSTOCKS		
Antonovka KA 313	90	Millions
EMLA 7	70	
EMLA 9	60	
M 27	+ + +	
MAC 9	90	Millions
CHERRY ROOTSTOCKS		
Colt	+ + +	Millions
Mahaleb &		
Mazzard 14	90	Millions
PLUM ROOTSTOCKS		
Pixy	90	Millions
St. Julien X	90	Millions
APPLE CULTIVAR		
Stark Jumbo	60	

See Strawberry Chapter XXI for a tissue culture technique in commercial use. Promising tests are underway for pear, blueberry, grape, date, peach, nectarine and other commercially important fruits.

Suggested Collateral Readings

BEAKBANE, A.B. and E.C. THOMPSON. Anatomical studies of stems and roots of hardy fruit trees. IV. The root structure of some new clonal apple rootstocks budded with "Cox's Orange Pippin." Jour. Pom. and HortSci. 23:206-211. 1947.

BLAIR, D.S. Rootstocks and intermediate pieces. Sci. Agr. 19 (2), 85, 1938.

BREEN, P.J. Cyanogenic glycosides and graft incompatibility between peach and plum. J. Amer. Soc. HortSci. 99:412-415. 1974.

CHANG. W. Studies in incompatibility between stock and scion, with special reference to certain deciduous fruit trees. Jour. Pom. and HortSci. 15:267-325. 1937.

COLBY, H.L. Stock-scion chemistry and the fruiting relationships in apple trees. Pl. Physiol. 10:483-498. 1935.

CURTIS, O.F., JR., D.R. RODNEY. Ethylene injury to nursery trees in cold storage. Proc. ASHS 60, 104, 1952.

DOZIER, W.A. *et al.* Sprout control of apple nursery stock with NAA. HortSci. 11(4):392-2. 1976.

DURUZ, W.P. Grafting and budding contests. Ore. State College Ext. Bull. 530. 1939.

DUTCHER, R.D. and L.E. POWELL. Apple shoots from buds in *Vitro*. J. ASHS: 97-4, 511-14. 1972.

DWARF fruit trees. Agricultural Research Service, Hort. Crops Research Branch. U.S. Dept. Agr. Leaflet 407. 1975.

FERREE, D.C. 15 apple cultivars on MM106, M26. Fruit Var. J. 32:2. 40-2. 1978.

FUJII, T. and N. NITO. Studies on the compatibility of grafting of fruit trees. Callus fusion between rootstock and scion. J. Japanese Soc for HortSci. 41(1):1-10. 1972.

GARNER, R.J. The grafter's handbook, Faber and Faber, Ltd., 24 Russell Square, London. 260 pp. 1958.

GREEN, D.W. Cytokinin activity in the xylem sap and extracts of MM 106, HortSci. 10:73-74. 1975.

HARTMANN, H.P., D.J. HANSEN and F. LORETI. Propagation of apple rootstocks by hardwood cuttings. Calif. Ag. June 1965. Hartmann, H.T. and D.E. Kester. Plant propagation — principles and practices. 559 pp. Prentice-Hall, Inc. Englewood Cliffs, N.J. 1968.

HAUT, I.C. After ripening and germination of fruit-tree seed. Maryland Agr. Exp. Sta. Bull. 420. 1938.

HERRERO, J. Studies of compatible and incompatible graft combinations with special reference to hardy fruit trees. Jour. HortSci. 26:186-237. 1951.

HITCHCOCK, A.E. and P.W. ZIMMERMAN. Rooting leafy apple cuttings. Proc. ASHS 40, 292. 1942.

HUANG, S.C. and D.F. MILLIKAN. *In Vitro* micrografting of apple shoot tips. HortSci. 15(6):741-743. 1980.

HUTCHINSON, A. Dwarf Apple Trees on EMIX Rootstock: 30 year trial. Ann. Rpt. Hort. Res. Inst., Vineland, Ontario. 1970.

IBRAHIM, I.M. and M.N. DANA. Gibberellin-like activity in apple rootstocks. HortSci. 6(6): 541. Dec. 1971.

INTERNATIONAL Horticulture Congress Proceedings. See particularly 1962, '66, '70, '74 and subsequent proc. for dwarf trees, growth regulators, etc., and World Research in these areas Meeting (every 4 yrs.) in Hanover, W. Germany. 1982.

JANICK, J. Ethylene Effects on Apple Scions, HortSci. 10:70-72. 1975.

KOLESNIKOV, V.A. The root system of fruit plants. Mir Publishers, Moscow USSR, 269 pages. 1971.

LAGERSTADT, H.B. New device for hot-callusing graft unions. HortSci. 16(4). 529-30. Aug. 1981.

LAPINS, K. Cold hardiness of rootstocks and framebuilders for fruit trees. Canada Dept of Agr., Res., Summerland, B.C. SP-32, 36 pp. Oct. 1963.

LARSEN, F.E. Promotion of leaf abscission of deciduous tree fruit nursery stock with abscisic acid. HortSci. Vol. 4 (3) 216-216. 1969.

LARSEN, F.E. and G.D. LOWELL. Tree fruit nursery stock defoliation. HortSci. 12(6):580-2. 1977.

LASHEEN, A.M. and R.G. LOCKARD. Dwarfing stocks, stems on amino acid-protein in apple roots. J. ASHS 97:443-5. 1972.

LOCKHARD, R.G. Effects of rootstocks and length and type of interstock on growth of apple trees in sand culture. J. Amer. Soc. Hort. Sci 99:321-325. 1974.

LUCKWELL, L.C. Hormone production by the developing apple seed. J.H.S. 28, 14, 1953.

MANEY, T.J., H.H. PLAGGE and B.S. PICKETT. Stock and scion effects in top-worked apple trees. Proc. Amer. Soc. HortSci. 33:332-335. 1936.

McKENZE, D.W. Apple rootstock trails. Jonathan on E. Malling, Merton and Malling-Merton rootstocks. HortSci. 39:2. 69-77. Apr. 1964.

MOOSE, B. Graft-incompatability in fruit trees. Com. Bur. Hort. Planta. Crops Tech. Comm. 28. 36 pp. Bucks, England, 1962.

MOOSE, B. Bridge tissue in ring-grafted apple stems. J.H.S. 28, 41. 1953.

NELSON, S.H. and H.B. TUKEY. Temperature responses of apple rootstocks. J.H.S. 31, 55. 1956.

NORTON, R.L. Western N.Y. Coop. Ext. Spec. High-Density Apple Planting Using Clonal Rootstocks. N.Y. (Cornell) Agr. Exp. Sta., 1971 (Several spot reports) contact Co. Agr. Agts. Office, Rochester, N.Y. for latest rpts.

PARTRIDGE, N.L. and J.O. VEATCH. The relationship between soil profile and root development of fruit trees. Mich. Agr. Quar. Bull. Vol. XIV. 1932.

PRESTON, A.P. Apple rootstock studies: Malling-Merton rootstocks. Jour. HortSci. 30:25-33. 1955. Seek many valuable subsequent rpts., same journ.

PRESTON, A.P. Malling-Merton rootstocks. J.H.S. 30, 25. 1955.

PROEBSTING, E.L. Soil temperature and root distribution. Proc. ASHS 43. 1. 1943.

REHKUGLER, G.E., *et al.* Rupture strength of unions of apple cions with M.8, 9 and vigorous rootstocks. J. ASHS. 104(2):226-229. 1979.

ROACH, S.C. and G.E. DAVIES. Height of trunks that should be measured. Ann. Rpt. E. Mall. Res. Sa. 1953 ('54).

ROACH, W.A. Rootstocks and mineral nutrition. Ann. Rept. East Malling Res. Sta. for 1946, 88.

ROACH, W.A. and E.C. THOMPSON. Dye injection to study stock-scion incompatibility. J. Pom. and H.S. 23, 212. 1947.

ROBITAILLE, H.A. and R.F. CARLSON. Gibberellie and abscisic acid-like substances and the regulation of apple shoot extension. J. Amer. Hort. Sci. 101 (4):388-92. July 1976.

ROGERS, W.S. and M.S. PARRY. Effects of deep planting on anchorage and performance of apple trees. J. HortSci. 43, 103-6. 1968.

ROGERS, W.S. Growth and cropping of clonal-root apple trees on five

soils. J. Pom. and H.S. 22, 209. 1946.

ROOSJE, G.S. Experiences in handling high-density apple orchards. Res. Sta. for Fr. Growing. Wilhelminadorp, Netherlands. Write Dr. Roosje for publ. list. 1960's-70's.

SAX, K. Interstock effects in dwarfing fruit trees. Proc. ASHS 62: 201-204. 1953.

SAX, K. Stock and scion relationship in graft incompatibility. Proc. Amer. Soc. HortSci. 64: 156-158. 1954.

SAX, K. The control of tree growth by phloem blocks. Harvard Univ., Jour. Arnold Aboretum. 35: 251-259. 1954.

SCHNEIDER, G.W., *et al.* Growth contolling properties of apple stem callus, *in vitro*. J. ASHS 103(5):634-638. 1978.

SHARP, W.R., *et al.* Physiology of in vitro asexual embryogenesis. Hort. Rev. Avi Publ. Co. 2:268-310. 1980.

SHAW, J.K. Malling rootstocks and American apple trees. Proc. ASHS 48, 166, 171. 1946.

SMITH, P.F. Scion and rootstock on mineral composition of mandarin-type citrus leaves. J. Amer. Soc. Hort. Sci. 100:368-369. 1975.

SNYDER, J.C. and R.D. BARTRAM. Grafting fruit trees. Wash. St. Univ. PNW Bul. 0062. 18 p. 1982.

STANG, E.J., *et al.* Propagation fruit trees. Ohio St. Ext. Bull. 481. 29 pp. 1978.

SWINGLE, C.F. Regeneration and vegetative propagation. Bot. Rev. 18, 1. 1952.

THOMAS, L.A. Stock and scion invetigations. X. Influence of an intermediate stempiece upon the scion in apple trees. Jour. HortSci. 29: 150-152. 1954.

THOMPSON, E.C., *et al.* Reinvigoration by inarching. J.H.S. 29, 175. 1954.

THOMPSON, J.M. Technique of Budwood Grafting. Fruit Var. Jour. 29:58-61. 1975.

TISCORNIA, J.R. and F.E. LARSEN. Rootstocks for apple and pear — a literature review. Wash. Agr. Exp. Sta. Cir. 421. 45 pp. mimeo. July, 1963.

TUKEY, H.B. SR. Dwarfed fruit trees. MacMillan Co., N.Y. (Collier-MacMillan Ltd., London) 561 pp. 1964.

TUKEY, H.B. and K.D. BRASE. The dwarfing effect of an intermediate stem-piece of Malling IX. apple. Proc. Am. Soc. HortSci. 42: 357-364, 1943.

TUKEY, R.B., *et al.* Malling rootstocks during 12 years. Proc. ASHS 64, 146. 1954.

VARDAR, Y. Transport of plant hormones. 457 pp. North-Holland Publishing Co., Amsterdam, Wiley Interscience Div., John Wiley & Sons, Inc., New York 1968.

VISSER, T. The Effect of rootstocks on growth and flowering of apple seedlings. J. ASHS 98(1):26. 1973.

VYVYAN, M.C. Interrelation of scion and rootstock in fruit trees. Ann. Bot. 19: 401-423. 1955.

WALLNER, S.J. Apple fruit explant responses in vitro and textural characteristics of the derived tissue cultures. J. Amer. Soc. Hort. Sci. 102(6) 743-747. 1977.

WELCH, M.F. and G. NYLUND. Virus heat-treatment in apple clones. Can. J. Pl. Sci. 45: 443-454. 1965.

WESTWOOD, M.N., A.N. ROBERTS, and H.O. BJORNSTAD. Influence of in-row spacing on yield of 'Golden Delicious: and 'Starking Delicious' on M9 rootstock in hedgerows. J. ASHS 101(3): 309-11. 1976.

WHITE, R.G., *et al.* Antonovka framework and apple productivity. Can. Jr. pl. Sci. 45:455-460. 1965.

YADAVA, U.L. and D.F. DAYTON. The relation of endogenous abscisic acid to dwarfing capability of East Malling apple rootstocks. J. ASHS 97(6):701. 1972.

YERKES, G.E. and W.W. ALDRICH. Behavior of apple varieites on certain clonal stocks. Proc. ASHS 48, 227. 1946.

YOUNG, R.S. 1975. Observations of Apple Tree Growth on Malling 26. The Mountaineer Grower (April): 3-6.

ZEIGER, D.C. and H.B. TUKEY. An historical review of the Malling apple rootstocks in America. Mich. Agr. Exp. Sta. Cir. Bull. 226. 74 pp. 1960.

ZIMMERMAN, R.H. Length of the juvenile period in some apomictic crabapples. HortSci. 7(5): 490. 1972.

ZIMMERMAN, R.H. Phloroglucinol and rooting of apple cuttings. ASHS 106:5. 648-52. 1981.

CHAPTER IX

Freezing Injury to Fruit Trees

Probably the most important factor influencing the distribution of the fruit industry is minimum winter temperatures. They more or less mark the boundaries where certain fruits can be grown. In any fruit region, however, unusually low temperatures occur at times, causing widespread damage to fruit plants normally grown in that region. Also, some freezing injury occurs to nut and fruit trees in almost every region every winter. This is probably due to the fact that people tend to introduce economic fruits as widely as possible, often beyond the limits of their natural temperature tolerance.

At times, some people seem to think that the climate has changed and that more severe winters are being experienced. The available literature reveals that this is hardly true. Severe winters have been occurring periodically in the United States for at least the past 180 years at the ratio of about one severe winter in nine, but there appears to be no rhythm to their occurrence. Very cold winters may occur in succession for a few years, then none for several. Since 1900 "test winters" have occured in 1903-04, 1906-07, 1911-12, 1917-18, 1933-34, 1935-36, 1954-55, 1964-65, 1968-69, 1972-73, 1976-77 and 1981-82.

Winter injury is not confirmed to the colder or semimild areas alone. Greatest injury to deciduous fruits in mild climates may occur when rather warm spells in the winter are followed by moderately cold periods.

How plants survive freezing. Plants that survive freezing temperatures do so by tolerating ice in their tissues or by avoiding freezing through supercooling. Perennial species that survive freezing acclimate in response to environmental cues. Growth cessation is an absolutely necessary prerequisite to *cold acclimation* which normally occurs in two stages: the first stage (a) is photoperiodically induced. Leaves of plants are the photoperiodic receptors that initiate the acclimation. According to C.J. Weiser of Oregon State University, short days probably function as an early warning system in nature. As daylength decreases in autumn indogenous growth-inhibiting substances increase, growth ceases and acclimation begins. The second state of acclimation (b) is induced by low temperatures and frost. Hardiness increases slowly over a period of several weeks as temperatures decrease. Subfreezing temperatures

result in maximum hardiness. Many plants will acclimate sufficiently to survive -40°F in tender crops such as tomato, pepper, soybean and petunia without damage to tissues. Present evidence indicates the bacteria *Pseudomonas syringae* and *Erwinia herbicola* actually initiate or incite freezing and killing of tissues by serving as *ice nucleating* agents. The ice nucleating bacteria are ubiquitous in nature infecting a broad spectrum of host plants.

How freezing kills acclimated trees and plants. As temperatures drop below freezing, ice first forms outside of the cell in the extracellular spaces where crystals naturally form and grow. As temperatures continue to fall, more and more water is pulled from the cell through the cell membrane and cell wall to the extra cellular ice. This process is equivalent to a severe summer drought except that here the temperatures are so low that death occurs. In both freezing and drouth situations, water is removed from the cells.

How freezing kills. As yet, there appears to be no complete agreement among investigators as to how freezing kills. Different workers have presented different theories, each supported by rather extensive experiments. Ice masses have been observed both inside and outside the protoplasm while the tissue is frozen. Another explanation for cell death is an excessive strain upon the protoplasmic layer as a result of its rapid and perhaps uneven contraction when water moves out and freezes between the cell walls, or, between the walls of each cell and its protoplasm. Some plants or plant tissues are killed by a small amount of ice formation; others can withstand considerable ice formation before they are killed.

Wood which has been injured by freezing shows not only death of many of the cells in the sapwood, but also a clogging of some vessels with a black gum formation (Figure 1). After the severe freeze in 1933-34 in Maine, it was discovered that trees showing about a 50 per cent death or clogging of cells in the sapwood usually did not recover, whereas those showing only 20 per cent damage often recovered.

The amount of injury from freezing in dormant tissue is influenced by three factors: (a) The rate at which the temperature falls; (b) the duration of the low temperature, (c) temperature prior to the freeze, and (d) the rate of thawing. It appears rather certain that the more rapidly the

¹ Dr. David W. Buchanan, Fruit Crops Department, University of Florida, Gainesville, 32611, assisted with the revision of this Chapter.

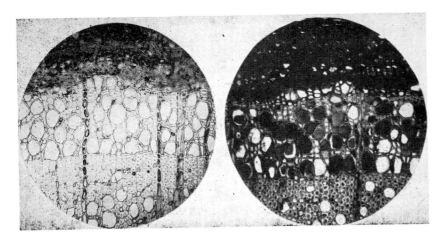

Figure 1. Sapwood from apple tree on the left is uninjured. That on the right was injured by the severe winter of 1933-34, and it shows characteristic clogging of the vessels. This injury is often termed "blackheart." (M.T. Hilborn, Maine Agr. Exp. Sta.)

temperature falls, the greater is the injury for the minimum temperature attained. Thus, injury under such conditions may be produced at a higher temperature than if the rate of fall had been gradual. Almost everyone can remember nights when the temperature dropped exceedingly fast to low levels. It is these nights which are likely to be the most damaging to plants, and which probably account for most of the severe injury to fruit trees. If rapid drops in temperature are accompanied by strong wind, the tissues are cooled faster, and the damage is accentuated.

Temperatures prior to a severe freeze also will determine the tissue acclimation or cold hardiness and will influence the damage.

The longer the cold period, the more the winter injury at a given temperature. According to the late G.E. Potter, the increased injury under these conditions may be due to death partly from desiccation as a result of cold drying winds; water movement in the tree is very slow at low temperatures.

Freezing injury is greater the faster the frozen tissue thaws. Often, but not always, after spring frosts when the leaves have been frozen, the shaded leaves and fruits are damaged less than those exposed to bright sunlight. In addition, apple fruits show less browning and breakdown if they thaw slowly at a temperature of about eight degrees above freezing than if thawed rapidly at a higher temperature.

Hardiness of tissues. The relative hardiness of tissues is different in winter and summer. When the tree is in active growing condition, the more active the cells, the more susceptible they are to cold temperatures, which means that the cambium layer and newly developed cells on either side are the first to be killed. This was clearly shown in an unusual cold wave occurring between November 11-15, 1940, in an area following roughly the Missouri River Basin, including Iowa, Missouri, Nebraska, and Kansas. The autumn had been unusually warm with sufficient moisture to keep the plants in active metabolism. The crop of pome fruits, in general, had been heavy and the trees were still in leaf when the storm struck. At Ames, Iowa on November 11, T.J. Maney reports the morning temperature was 51°F.; by noon, a 50-mile gale of wind developed, and by night, a temperature of 9°F. was recorded. Minimum temperatures on the four succeeding dates were 4°, -2°, -2°, and -2° F., (-15, -19, -19, - 19°C). Injury assumed all forms common to low-temperature midwinter damage, except root killing. The cambium was active; trees were killed outright. Few if any sprouts grew from live roots in spring due apparently to the maturing of a heavy crop and little carbohydrates stored.

Short day-lengths with (Ontario) or without (Florida) cold temperatures seem to enhance acclimation to cold hardiness.

When the tissues have become acclimated by the middle of winter, the cambium becomes the most resistant to freezing, followed in order by bark, sapwood, and pith. In fact, laboratory experiments have shown that acclimated cambinum during winter will not be injured by freezing at temperatures considerably lower than those occuring in orchards. In the roots, the cambium seems to be the most susceptible to cold followed by the bark, with mature sapwood and pith the most resistant.

Apparently, an accumulation of carbohydrates in the tissues is a most important factor contributing to maturity and hardiness. Trees which have carried a plentiful supply of healthy foliage during the growing season and which did not grow late in the fall, are usually the most resistant during "test winters." This is probably because abundant carbohydrates have been stored in the wood and bark tissues. This is borne out by the fact that cultivars of apples which mature their crops early, such as Wealthy, Duchess of Oldenburg, Hibernal, and Yellow Transparent, are generally more hardy than late-ripening cultivars (Haralson, an exception.) The late fall and winter varieties have the extra burden of ripening their crops and also storing sufficient carbohydrates that properly harden their tissues for winter.

Trees with weak or limited foliage are among the first to be injured. Weak foliage may be due to poor soil drainage, nutrient deficiency, drought, or damage from caustic

Figure 2. Late fall pruning can be hazardous. This central Ohio grower pruned the young trees at upper left in late fall, stopped for an urgent job and did not prune the row on the right til the following February. In the lower photograph he pruned this row on 7A rootstock also in the fall with serious freeze damage during the severe winter of 1978-79. Unpruned next row of trees showed no cold damage.

sprays, insects and diseases, or other causes. On the other hand, trees which have made excessive shoot growth and utilized most of their carbohydrates in growth tend to enter the winter poorly matured and are, therefore, readily susceptible to injury by cold temperatures. Thus, top-worked trees with many limbs recently removed may experience considerable injury during severe winters. Also, trees which have been cultivated late in the season, late fall pruned, and/or heavily fertilized do not acclimate sufficiently to withstand cold (Figure 2).

All of these facts, as stated previously, indicate that conditions must be favorable for an accumulation of carbohydrates in the tissues in order that they be properly matured and hardened for winter. It is probably safe to say that a well-matured tree of a tender variety is more hardy than an immature tree of a hardy cultivar. This, if true, may account for many apparent inconsistencies in field observations of winter injury among cultivars.

Any practice which tends to check the rate of tree growth in autumn, other than one which would cause premature loss of foliage, is likely to bring about better maturity and more hardiness. A vigorously growing cover crop planted in August or September is valuable from this standpoint by competing with the tree for moisture and nitrates. The various winter cover crops have been discussed in the chapter on "Soil Management for Apples."

Dormancy and rest period. The deciduous tree is said to be *dormant* when it is without leaves and there are no visible signs of growth activity. The *rest period* starts before dormancy and gradually intensifies so that by autumn the above-ground portions of the plant will not grow even though temperature, moisture, and other external factors are satisfactory for growth. The rest period is highly important to fruit plants because during this period they cannot be forced into growth by warm spells in the middle of winter. However, warm spells during rest can cause considerable loss of resistance to cold.

Fruit plants enter and come out of the rest period gradually. The earlier a plant enters the rest period in autumn, the sooner it may emerge the next year; conversely, the later it enters, the later it may emerge. This however, is dependent entirely on temperature. When temperatures are below 45°F, rest hours accumulate slowly. Researchers have demonstrated that rest-hour accumulation ceases at 0°F. Little difficulty is encountered with the apple by warm spells which force the buds to open early, exposing them to killing temperatures. The apple emerges from the rest period slowly and is much less responsive than other tree fruits to early warm spells. The greatest difficulty with apples is from lack of maturity in early winter. With peaches, the rest period is broken earlier than with apple and subsequent early warm periods may induce the buds to swell and open, only to be killed by freezes. With peaches in the milder regions, a program of cultivation and fertilization with nitrogen, combined with relatively heavy pruning is followed in order to induce the trees to grow late in the fall and thus enter the rest period later. Under these conditions, they usually come out of the rest period later and are likely to avoid late freezes. Such a practice in the colder regions, however, would be disastrous, inasmuch as warm spells in the middle of winter are not a problem, but early winter low temperatures may be destructive to the immature wood.

The rest period of different plants can be broken prematurely by drought or use of special chemicals, but with fruit trees it appears rather definite that subjection to low temperatures is the most important factor in breaking the rest. With many apple cultivars, a certain amount of cold temperature at about or below 45°F (Chap. III) is required. If the trees do not receive the necessary amount of chilling for the particular fruit and variety, they tend to come into leaf slowly and blossom irregularly.

Hormonal Balance. Abscisic acid (ABA) level in the tree

Figure 3. An injured and an uninjured Gravestein tree following winter of 1933-34 in Maine. The cambium in the tree on the left remained alive, but the sapwood apparently was unable to supply sufficient water to the top due to death of may cells and clogging by the black wound gum. This photo was taken in September, 1934; the tree died the following year.

tends to be high during the onset of rest, reaching a low level thereafter, while growth promoters as GA (gibberellins), cytokinins, respiration and auxins decrease. As spring opens, growth is fast after pollination particularly with Ga, cytokinins, ribonucleic acid and respiration increasing with the enzyme pool activity.

Hardiness of cultivars. After the severe winters of 1933-34 and 1935-36 in the northeastern U.S. to Maine, it was definitely decided that the following cultivars are hardy to cold: McIntosh, Fameuse, Cortland, Macoun, Hibernal, Virginia Crab, Charlamoff, Wealthy, Milton, Oldenburg, Melba, Lobo, Early McIntosh, Liveland Raspberry, and possibly Delicious. Crab apples, in general, are hardier than the standard commercial apple cultivars. In the 1968-69 Washington freeze of -22 to -35°F, Delicious showed mainly trunk damage, Golden Delicious crotch damage. Barlett pear was killed outright while D'Anjou showed dieback, crop reduction. Richared was more sensitive than other Delicious strains. Rootstocks were rated: *very hardy* — Charlamoff, *M. Robusta #5*, Beautiful Arcade (Quebec), *M. Baccata, M. Prunifolia, M. Sargentii, M. Zumi, M. Virginiana,* Hibernal, McIntosh; *hardy* — Transparent, Antonovka, Alnarp II, M 26, MM 111, 104, N. Spy, Grahams Seedling; *Sensitive* — Hawkeye Greening, commercial seedlings, MM 106, 109, M9. Baldwin roots/Hibernal scaffold, M-II.

Empire did not fare well in the Ontario freeze of 1981-82, a severe freeze.

TYPES OF WINTER INJURY

Wood and bark injury aboveground. There are several types of wood and bark injury which may be classified as follows: (a) blackheart, (b) crotch trunk, (c) crown and collar injury, (d) winter sunscald, (e) splitting of the trunk, and (f) the killing back of twigs and young branches.

Blackheart. This is one of the most common types of winter injury. The pith is usually killed and the heartwood is darkened (Figure 1) turning a shiny brown while the cambium and bark remain alive. Dark discoloration is partly due to the formation of a dark gum in the cells. With blackheart, the tree usually continues to grow and may form new sapwood and bark rather rapidly the following season, provided there is a sufficient amount of live sapwood, a good supply of stored food, and the early season weather is favorable to recovery. Blackheart is found in apples, peaches, plums, pears, and cherries alike following severe winters. It is often found in nursery trees, especially pears. It seems to be more weakening to young trees than to mature trees. It is highly recommended that nursery trees with blackheart be discarded.

If bearing trees affected with blackheart were in reasonably healthy condition before the injury, in most cases the live cambium will form a new layer of sapwood and bark rapidly, and the mature tree may recover and fruit satisfactorily for many subsequent years. The spring and early summer must be favorable to recovery and not excessively hot and dry. Limbs which are showing considerable blackheart tend to be brittle and may break with a moderate to moderately heavy crop. Wire bracing may be advisable on key limbs. Such wood is also quite susceptible to wood rotting fungi and areas exposed by pruning should be thoroughly covered with a good wound dressing, such as water asphalt emulsion or white latex paint.

Crotch injury. The bark, cambium, and sapwood in the crotches or forks may be killed when other portions of the tree are uninjured. This is said to be due largely to the fact that there is little foliage at the base of the scaffold limbs, especially on the inner and upper sides, and, as a result, these tissues mature last before going into the winter. The more upright the limb and the more narrow-angled the crotch, the greater the likelihood of injury in these areas. Injury may extend several feet up the limb from the crotch, particularly if a smaller limb has been removed during the summer in the region of the injury. If the injury is noticed a day after it occurred, the bark can be tacked in place and covered thoroughly with water asphalt emulsion to prevent drying and to encourage healing. Otherwise, little is gained by cutting away dead bark later and painting. Crotches showing considerable injury become weak and should be braced with wire and screw eyes (Chapter IV). Among the varieties which tend to show more of this injury are Grimes Golden, Northern Spy, Tompkins King, and Golden Delicious.

Crown or collar injury. These terms refer to a winter killing of the bark at or near the ground surface. It seems to be common with Grimes Golden, Tompkins King,

118

Gravenstein, Northern Spy, and Twenty Ounce. Grimes Golden often develops it shortly after coming into commercial production, and a large percentage of the trees may not live to be 20 years old before acquiring it. Portions of the bark may be killed on one side, or, the tree may be girdled. Some clonal stocks as EM IV, MM-106 may show it.

In Indiana, collar rot of Grimes Golden is said to be caused by a *Phytophthora* species of fungus found on peony. In an epidemic in 1933, from 43 to 60 per cent of the Grimes Golden trees in Indiana were partially or completely girdled. The disease may attack the crotches as well as the trunks. A 16-16-100 bordeaux mixture spray is recommended for susceptible varieties (including Rome Beauty), applied when buds are swelling in spring at the delayed dormant stage. Cankers should be cut out and painted with bordeaux paint, then bridge-grafted or inarched with young trees planted by the trunk. Varieties susceptible to crown injury are now commonly double-worked. A resistant interstock variety is inserted between the seedling root and the fruiting top, and the top-working is done above the crotches. Some growers mound their trunks (1 ft) over winter w/soil.

Winter sunscald. Sunscald on limbs may be caused in summer by excessive heat from direct sun rays. A similar injury may develop in winter on the southwest sides of tree trunks in the northern areas and the northwest sides in southern regions. Winter sunscald, shown in Figure 3, appears to be due to a rapid drop in temperature on cold, sunny, stills days in mid-winter. The direct rays of the sun strike the exposed side of the trunk in late afternoon, raising the temperature considerably above that of the air. After sunset, there is a sudden drop in air temperature and a slower drop in bark and wood temperature (0.1-0.3 °C/min.), resulting in this type of injury. Trees with low trunks where some shading from scaffold limbs occurs, are usually injured less than trees with high trunks. Exterior white latex paint sprayed on the exposed trunk sides is a good control measure for about two years.

Splitting of the trunk. Longitudinal splits in the trunk, often to the pith, may occur in extremely cold weather (Figure 3). If one happens to be in the orchard during such periods, an occasional trunk may be heard to "pop" as the trunk splits open. They are thought to be due to a higher water content near the center of the trunk and preponderance of tangential strain in the woody tissues when under ice pressure. The cracks usually draw together when the temperature rises, and the bark subsequently calluses over. Cracks are quite common on sweet cherry. In some cases, the bark may peel back, leaving a rather wide wound. If the bark is immediately tacked down with wide-headed roofing tacks, and thoroughly covered with asphalt paint, it may grow back, provided the cambium is alive and the tissues do not dry excessively. If healing does not

Figure 3a. Tree trunks sprayed with a good grade of exterior white latex paint on sun-exposed sides show much less temperature variation and cold damage. Trunks need repainting about every two years.

take place, the dead bark should be removed and the open wound painted with water asphalt emulsion, then bridge grafted as soon as possible.

Killing back of young branches and twigs. In a severe winter, this is common with many kinds of fruit trees, particularly if growth occurred late in the season and the twigs entered the winter poorly acclimated to cold. The injury occurs frequently on young vigorous trees and seems to be an inherent characteristic with certain tender varieties. The effect of such injury is similar to pruning back the tips, inasmuch as the live buds nearest the injured area grow vigorously and the ends of the branches assume a bushy appearance.

Injury to leaf and flower buds. The leaf and flower buds of the apple are generally more resistant to freezing injury than those of most other fruits. The vegetative or leaf buds are about as resistant as the combium in winter. There are a few cases where flower buds have survived better than leaf buds, but this is uncommon and occurs as a result of an early winter freeze. This is because flower buds harden sooner than vegetative buds. Later in the winter, however, the leaf buds develop more resistance to freezing than the flower buds. Flower buds of some varieties of apples will withstand -31° to -40°F. (-35 to -40°C). Buds may retain resistance after the rest period is over, provided growth activity is not induced by extended early warm periods. In large commercial fruit producing areas, winter injury to flower buds of apples is usually negligible. Uninjured flower buds may develop poorly on cold-injured spurs and substantial losses of crop may occur with cold damage at tight cluster bud, particularly on Delicious.

Buds of the apple require a certain amount of winter chilling in order to open normally in spring. Apple trees grown nearer the Equator than latitude 33° to 34° may fail

119

Figure 4. (Left) Splitting of the trunk may be associated with rapid drop in temperature to low levels. The crack usually closes with rise in temperature: the bark calluses may heal rapidly the following season. (Right) Bark and wood injury, known as sun-scald, on the sun-exposed side of a tree trunk is common in apple orchards. It is casued by rapid drop in temperature after sundown on very cold days.

to open properly, or, if they do open, blossoming is uneven and the trees remain weak and produce small crops. In regions where cold weather begins about the first of November, the average temperature must be lower than 48° F between the first of November and the first of February for proper opening of the buds in spring.

Killing of roots. Roots are not as hardy as parts of the tree above-ground. Roots of the apple may be killed at temperatures ranging from 10° to 25°F. (-12 to -4°C). Normality for roots is poor hardiness in autumn with an increase in hardiness during early and late winter reaching a maximum in late winter or early spring then declining rapidly after growth starts.

For several reasons, it is not necessary for the root to be as resistant to cold as the aboveground parts. The soil cools more slowly than the air and there is a certain amount of heat arising from the subsoil. For this reason, a very sudden drop in temperature after a warm winter day rarely kills roots. It is the long continued cold periods when the ground has adequate time to freeze that root injury may be prevalent. There may be some root killing every winter, and while this does not noticeably influence vegetative growth, it may have an effect on such a sensitive process as fruit setting.

A heavy blanket of snow, a heavy mulch, or a good cover crop during the winter tends to protect the roots. Root injury is usually greater on gravelly or open soils than on a good loam. The worse injury, however, may appear on heavy, poorly aerated, or poorly drained soils, partly because the roots are nearer the surface and also because they are not properly hardened due to the somewhat weakened condition of the tree. Mulching is being suggested in colder regions, particularly for shallow-rooted compact trees; bare soil with herbicidal usage and a cold winter with little snow could be disastrous.

In Minnesota, hardy seedling such as Dolgo and Columbia crab are used as understocks. They are much more hardy than seedlings of Delicious or Jonathan.

Interstems such as Hibernal and Clark's Dwarf are not being used nearly as much as previously. Since the seedling source is usually hardy, there is not as much necessity for scion rooting as formerly. Normally, it isnrecommended that in colder latitudes apple trees be obtained from a local nursery that uses a hardy understock.

Only in severe cases will the tops of affected trees show symptoms of root injury the first spring. Usually, by mid-summer the affected trees can be distinguished. Common symptoms are slow terminal growth, sparce, yellowed or dwarfed foliage, poor fruit set, dwarfed fruit, and the drying and discoloration of bark. If root damage is fatal, growth will continue until the top is depleted of moisture and stored nutrients when the tree will die. If root damage is not fatal, the weak growth will continue until enough roots are regenerated to maintain the tree, but this may take several years.

Treatment of winter-injured trees. If there is little or no injury to the cambium and leaf buds, a tree may survive moderately heavy wood and bark injury. When the leaf buds open and growth starts, the cambium will develop both new sapwood and bark tissues and gradually replace the injured areas. It is important, however, that the cambium cells be kept moist; otherwise, they may die. As pointed out earlier, the loose bark should be nailed in place as soon as possible, with wide-headed roofing nails and sealed with asphalt paint. Strips of bark, or the entire bark, may heal soon and help speed the recovery of the tree. The following late winter, obviously dead areas of bark can be removed and bridge-grafted, or if the damage is near the ground surface or under the ground, young trees can be planted near the trunk and inarched into it. However, if at the outset it is clear that the injury almost or completely girdles the tree, and the cambium has dried, it is wise to bridge-graft as soon as possible.

With trees which have received considerable sapwood injury after a severe winter, as evidenced by relatively weak growth in the spring, it is well to give them a moderately heavy application of nitrogen fertilizer in order to induce as much vegetative growth as possible and the formation of new layers of wood and bark by the cambium. Cultivation or use of herbicides under the trees will help to stimulate vegetative growth in orchards not being maintained in permanent sod-mulch culture. Pruning during the spring season immediately following winter injury is not recommended. Although pruning may seem to be a wise practice under such conditions, it has been pointed out previously that it has usually resulted in poor recovery. D'Anjou pears respond well to heavy stubbing back.

If an apple tree sets a heavy crop of fruit following winter injury, the drain on the tree of such a crop may inhibit or prevent recovery. Fruit setting can be prevented by timing a blossom-thinning spray so that all blossoms are removed. (See Chapter VII.) Hand removal of all fruits shortly after setting is also effective, but more expensive. The use of spray materials which are known to cause foliage damage under some weather conditions should be avoided on winter-injured trees.

Heaters on calm nights in mid-winter raise bud and wood temperatures but wind and/or snow nullify it. **Infrared** photography from satellites (Florida) and airplanes (Ontario) are being used to monitor ground temperatures, mainly for predicting freeze damage around bloom.

Review Questions

1. Distinguish between dormancy and rest period.
2. Give probable cause for death of plant tissue by freezing.
3. Discuss briefly the susceptibility of the cambium to freezing injury during the growing season and the winter period.
4. List 5 cultural practices which influence maturity of wood and explain briefly how each affects maturity.
5. Give 5 types of wood and bark injury found in the orchard.
6. Explain why it is not necessary for roots to be as resistant to cold as the top portions of the tree.
7. What cultural practices reduce freezing injury to roots?
8. List 4 hardy cultivars and 2 hardy rootstocks for apples.
9. What treatment is recommended for winter sunscald on the trunk?
10. What cultural treatment is recommended for fruit trees which show moderately heavy winter injury as evidenced by slow and small leaf development in spring?
11. Explain ice nucleating bacteria and their possible importance in orchard management.

Suggested Collateral Readings

BRADFORD, F.C. and H.A. CARDINELL. Eighty winters in Michigan orchards. Mich. Exp. Sta. Spec. Bull. 149. 1926.

BURRELL, A.B. and D. BOYNTON. Effects of nitrogen level on freezing injury to blossom buds of McIntosh apple. ASHS 46:32-4. 1945.

Cold Hardiness, Dormancy and Freeze Protection of Fruit Crops. A Symposium. Hort. Science (5):401-432. 1970.

CHANDLER, W.H. Cold resistance in horticultural plants: A review. Proc. Amer. Soc. Hort. Sci. 64:522-572. 1954.

CHANDLER, W.H., M.H. KIMBALL, G.L. PHILP, W.P. TUFTS, and G.P. WELDON. Chilling requirements for opening of buds on deciduous orchard trees and some other plants in California. Calif. Agr. Exp. Sta. Bull. 1937.

CHEN, P. and P.H. LI. Viability of apple blossom bkds after test freezing. HortScience 8(6):510. Dec. 1973.

COOLEY, D.R. and D.R. EVERT. Normalized electrical impedance and cold injury to 'Delicious' Apple stems. ASHS 104(4):561-3. 1979.

DENNIS, F.G., Jr. Dormany and Hardiness of fruit trees. HortSci. 12(5):444-445. 1977.

DORSEY, M.J. The low temperature hazard to set of fruit in the apple. Univ. of Ill. Bull. 473:147-170. 1940.

EGGERT, R. Cambium temperatures of peach and apple trees in winter. Proc. ASHS 45, 33. 1945.

EMMERT, F.H. and F.S. HOWLETT. Electrolytic determiniations of the resistance of fifty-five apple varieties to low temperature. Proc. Amer. Soc. Hort. Sci. 62:311-318. 1953.

EZ, A. et al. Breaking rest in deciduous fruits. Jr. ASHS 96:(4) July 1971.

HILBORN, M.T. and W.C. STILES. Low temperature injury to apple trees in Maine. Maine Tech. Bull. 64. 33pp. June 1973.

HOLUBOWICZ, T. and K. BOJAR. Frost tolerance of Belle de Boskoop apple wood. II. Reliability of methods used for frost injury. Fruit Sci. Rpts. Skierniewice, Poland. IV:(1) 9-17. 1977.

HOWELL, G.S. and C.J. WEISER. Fluctuations in the cold resistance of apple twigs during spring dehardening. J. Amer. Soc. Hort. Sci. 96 (2):190-92. 1971.

JOHNSON, D.D. et al. Regional analysis of injury to deciduous fruit trees by freeze of 1972, December. Wash. Agr. Res. Cent. Bull. 813, Pullman, 11 pp. 1975 July.

KELLEY, F.W. and R.L. McMUNN. Early winter cold damage to buds and wood. Proc. ASHS 40, 220. 1942.

KENNARD, W.C. Summer defoliation and winter injury to fruit trees. Proc. ASHS 53, 129. 1949.

KETCHIE, D.O. and C.H. BEEMAN. Cold acclimation in 'Red Delicious' apple trees under natural conditions during four winters. J. ASHS 98(3):257. 1973.

LAGERSTEDT, H.B. Tree trunk applicators for sunscald protection. HortSci. 13(5):533-4. 1978.

LEVITT, J. Frost, drought and heat resistance. Annl. Rev. Plant Phys. 2, 245. 1951. See also: The physical nature of the transpirational pull. Plant Phys. 31, 248. 1956.

LEVITT, J. Frost killing and hardiness of plants. Burgess Publ. Co., Minneapolis, Minn. 1941.

LI, P.H. Plant Cold Hardiness Research. HortSci. 13(3):222-224. 1978.

LUCAS, J.W. Subcooling and ice nucleation in lemons. Plant Physio. 29:245. 1954.

MEADER, E.M. and C.H. BLASBERG. Blossom hardiness of 45 apple varieties. Vermont Agr. Exp. Sta. (Publ. No. not known.). 1946.

MODLIBOWSKA, I. and C.P. FIELD. Tree injury by a cold winter. J. Pom. and H.S. 19, 197. 1942.

PAIVA, E. and H.A. ROBITAILLE. Breaking Bud Rest on detached Apple Shoots: Effects of Wounding and Ethylene. J. ASHS 103(1):101-4. 1978.

PAIVA, E. and H.A. ROBITAILLE. Breaking bud rest: gibberellic acid with chemicals. HortSci. 12(1):57-58. Feb. 1978.

PICKETT. B.S. and H.L. LANTZ. Survival of apple trees in 200 varieties after an early winter freeze. Proc. ASHS 40, 212. 1942.

POTTER, G.F. Tung research. Proc. ASHS 50, 443. 1947. Cold injury. 53, 114. 1949.

POTTER, G.W. Low temperature effects on woody plants. Proceedings of American Soc. for Hort. Sci. 36:185-195. 1938.

PROEBSTING, E.L., Jr. et. al. Supercooling apple buds in deciduous orchards. HortSci. 17(1):67. 1982.

PROEBSTING, E.L., Jr. and H.H. MILLS. A Synoptic Analysis of Peach and Cherry Flower Bud Hardiness. ASHS. 103(6):842-5. 1978.

PROEBSTING, E.L., Jr. and H.H. MILLS. Low-temperature resistance of flower buds. J. ASHS 103(2):192-198. 1978.

QUAMME, H.A., et. al. Relationship of Deep Supercooling and Dehydration Resistance to Freezing Injury in Dormant Tissues of 'Starkrimson Delicious' Apples and 'Siberian C' Peach. ASHS 107:(2) 299-304. 1982.

QUAMME, H., C. STUSHNOFF, and C.J. WEISER. The relationship of exotherms to cold injury in apple stem tissues. J. ASHS 97(5):608. 1972.

RAESE, J.T. Induction of cold hardiness in apple tree shoots with ethephon, NAA, and growth retardants. J. Amer. Soc. Hort. Sci. 102(6):789-792. 1977.

ROLLINS, H.A., Jr., F.S. HOWLETT, F.H. EMMERT. Factors affecting apple hardiness and measuring resistance to low-temperature injury. Ohio Res. Bull. 901, 77 pp. 1962.

SAKAI, A. Cold damage in young trees. Contr. of Inst. Low Temp. Sci. Sapporo, Japan. 1968.

SAKAI, A. Winter temperatures in trees. Physiologia Plant. 19:1966.

SAMISCH, R.M. et. al. A dormancy concept for peach. Proc. Int. Hort. Cong. III:1967.

SAMISCH, R.M. Dinitrocresol to shorten the rest period of apple trees. J. Pom. and H.S. 21, 164. 1945.

SAMISCH, R.M. Dormancy in woody plants. Annl. Rev. Plant Phys. 5, 183. 1954.

SCARTH, G.W. Cell physiological studies of frost resistance: a review. New Phylol. 43:1-12. 1944.

SEELEY, E.J. and L.E. POWELL, Jr. Abscisic acid changes in vegetative apple buds. ASHS 106(4):405-9. 1981.

SEELEY, E.J. and R. KAMMERECK. Carbon fluxes in apple trees: Use of a closed system to study the effect of a mild cold stress on 'Golden Delicious' J. Amer. Soc. Hort. Sci. 102(3):282-286. 1977.

SIMMONS, ROY K. Phloem tissue development in response to freeze injury to trunks of apple trees. J. Amer. Soc. Hort. Sci. 95(2):182-189. 1970.

SIMMONS, ROY K. Tissue response of young developing apple fruits to freeze injury. J. Amer. Soc. Hort. Sci. (94) (4):376-382. 1969.

STANG, J.G. and CECIL STUSHNOFF. Relative hardiness of apple cultivars. Fruit Varieties Journal 29(4)79-108. 1975.

STEINMETZ, F.H. and M.T. HILBORN. A histological evaluation of low temperature injury to apple trees. Maine Agr. Exp. Sta. Bull. 388. 1937.

TIMMIS, K.A. and L.H. FUCHIGAMI. Measuring dormancy: Rise and fall of square waves. HortSci. 16(2):200-2. 1981.

WESTWOOD, M.N. and H.O. BJORNSTAD. Winter rainfall reduces rest period of apple and pear. J. ASHS 103:(1) 142-4. 1978.

WESTWOOD, M.N. and H.O. BJORNSTAD. Winter injury and growth regulators, herbicides and rootstocks. ASHS 106(4):430-2. 1981.

WHITEMAN, T.M. Freezing points of fruits, vegetables and florist stocks. USDA Mktng. Res. Rpt. 196. Dec., 1957.

(See additional references in former book editions.)

LEADERS IN COLD RESEARCH OF FRUIT PLANTS. (From left) Dr. E.L. Proebsting, Jr., Washington State University, Pullman; Dr. Conrad (Bud) J. Weiser, Oregon State University, Corvallis; and Dr. Michael J. Burke, University of Florida, Gainesville. Among other researchers in this field over the years are: M.T. Hilborn, J. Levitt, David W. Buchanan, H. Quamme, Cecil Stushnoff, G.L. Rousselle, Peter Steponkus, Paul Li, I.I. Tumanov, Steven Lindow, A. Sakai, D.O. Ketchie, Alina Kacperska-Palacz and the late W.H. Chandler, George F. Potter and F.C. Bradford.

CHAPTER X

Harvesting, Packing and Processing Apples

One of the most important periods in the life of an apple is from the time it is picked until sold to the consumer. The grower cannot afford to become careless during this period in any of the fruit handling operations. Actually, it costs no more to handle fruit carefully than to permit an accumulation of bruises, stem punctures, and press marks. It is not an overstatement to say that, "Fruit must be handled like eggs," for almost every bump and bruise will be readily apparent sooner or later, certainly by the time the fruit reaches the display counter. The trade quickly recognizes quality unblemished fruit and will pay a premium for it.

PREPARING FOR HARVEST[1]

Estimating yields. With a little experience, growers will develop a "knack" for estimating crop yields several weeks before picking. This gives time to determine the amount of labor needed, picking equipment to provide, the amount and type of packages to purchase, grading and sizing equipment needed, and the amount of storage space to provide or engage from commercial storage houses.

Study the bearing habits of different cultivars. Some cultivars as Delicious (except in the Northwest), have a tendency to fool the estimator, and fall short of expectations. McIntosh and Rome Beauty usually do better than expected, because they bear heavily throughout the tops of the trees. Rome bears on both shoots and spurs; most cultivars bear largely on spurs.

The yield from an acre of mature trees varies with the age, cultivar, number of trees per acre, methods of management, and the region. According to the U.S. Census, the average yield for all orchards, large and small, well and not-so-well managed, has risen from about 1.0 bushel per standard tree in 1900 to 1.5 in 1925, 2.6 in 1940 and over 6 bu. for commercial trees, early 1980s. These figures only show that yields are rising but, certainly, few commercial growers can survive with these low yields.

Low-density commercial orchards should produce 15-20 bu/tree or 500 to 1000 boxes or more per acre (42 lbs./box) of packed fruit. Under high-density management on dwarfing stocks, yields may reach 1500 to 3000 packed boxes/A or more after 4 years. To these figures must be

added the lower-grade fruit going to by-products. The alert grower, however, seeks to reduce the amount of low-grade fruit and increase the quantity of quality stock. Better growers report less than 5 per cent culls almost every year; on the other hand, some growers report 15 percent or more culls.

A crop estimator who is new must be careful to base his estimate on average yields for many years, rather than on occasional bumper crop years. It is well for the grower to determine what the average yield is for his region and then through practices better than the average try to exceed this figure.

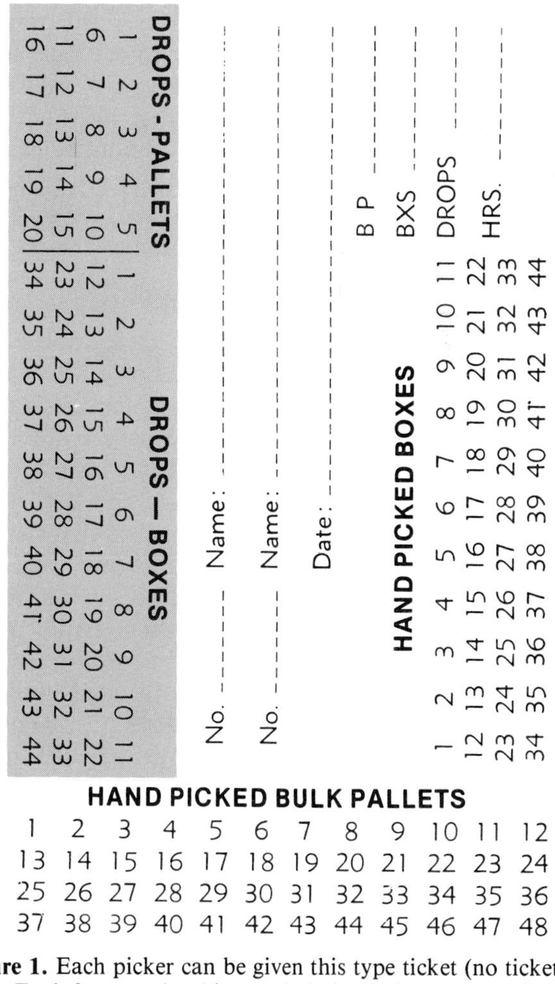

Figure 1. Each picker can be given this type ticket (no ticket, no pay). Each foreman has his punch design in large crews. Space is provided for totals, particularly total hours worked per day. (Courtesy W. Doe, Harvard, Mass.)

[1]William G. Doe, fruit grower and sales, Harvard, Mass., 01451, assisted in this chapter revision.

An estimate of the yield should be made at three periods during the year: (a) after the crop has set, (b) after the "June drop," and (c) about one month before harvest. Five random trees per acre should be inspected, being aware that heavier crops are likely to occur on outside rows, that a few trees may be carrying abnormally heavy loads, and that cultivars with a limited number of trees should not be given too much weight. These estimates should be recorded in a bound notebook so the grower later can compare them with the actual yield. If this is done year after year, he eventually can make estimates of considerable value.

Providing needed equipment. On a rainy "lax" day in midsummer, you can inventory all harvesting equipment in useable condition. Each picker should have an assigned picking receptacle (Figure 2) designed to handle the fruit with as little bruising as possible. It should be light in weight, easily manipulated if the picker is standing on a ladder, and provide the picker with free operation of both hands. For harvesting with ladder, the half-bushel metal- or canvas-sided picking bucket with canvas drop bottom causes the least injury to fruit. It is suspended from the shoulder, hanging in front or slightly to the side of the picker. The bucket is padded on the inside and around the top with felt; the rigid sides also protect the fruit. It is easily carried and emptied. Containers should be avoided with sharp edges that bruise or cut the fruit. True, any container may be satisfactory in the hands of a careful workman; any receptacle may be objectionable if used carelessly.

A ladder which is light, strong, and well balanced should be assigned to each picker who is held responsible for its care during the picking season. Choice of an easily handled sturdy ladder is important. The picker spends considerable time with a ladder and should have confidence in its strength. It pays to buy good ladders. Rung ladders flared at bottom and tapered at top are used for large trees. Ladders are set against the tree slightly tilted inward from the perpendicular, yet safe, putting most of the picker's weight on the ladder and ground, and not on the tree. It should be laid against a stable limb so it settles gently against it without dislodging apples.

There is a definite trend for growers to gradually lower big trees to a better working range of 10-12 ft., using an 8-10 ft. step ladder. It is claimed by many growers that "long ladders are the most costly orchard equipment," since harvest costs are more than double for tall trees vs. dwarfs.

Research shows a significant saving in growing semi-dwarf apple trees in hedgerows, and pruning the sides and tops with a special-built cutter bar with some hand pruning. Harvest is by shake-catch machinery or by building hydraulically operated worker stations on motor driven mobile masts. Such equipment obviously would be confined to more or less level land (Figures 3, 9).

Figure 2. Picking buckets of the Wells and Wade type are preferable to picking bags because they afford more protection against bruising and stem punctures. In emptying the picking bucket into the field boxes, the canvas flap should be lowered to the bottom of the box so that the apples will slip out gently. Boxes should be filled to slightly below the top so they can be stacked without bruising apples. (Wells and Wade, Box 1161, Wenatchee, WA. 98801; and General Box Co., 5451 Enterprise Rd., Toledo, OH 43612)

Fruit receptacles in the orchard. Although bulk-box handling of apples with tractor fork lifts is the practice in big orchards, there are still many orchard boxes used as field containers in the small orchards with or without pallets and fork lifts.

An orchard box, preferably with finger holes in the ends for lifting is a desirable container for field use. Extra wood strips can be nailed either in the tops or bottoms of the corners so that the boxes can be stacked with less likelihood of mashing the fruit below. Some growers use the final packing container as the "field box", in which case the new boxes are distributed through the orchard and the fruits drawn to the packing shed in them.

The bulk bin holds sixteen to twenty or more bushels. Processors like to use their own field containers so growers are more or less obligated to deal with them. Actually, the bulk box is a pallet too, since its floor is built to fit fork lifts. A hinged door at the base is convenient when apples for processing are poured into a truck, but where much of

124

Figure 3. This 6-yr. hedgerow of Cox's Orange apple trees on dwarfing rootstock has been trained by cutter-bar pruning for over-the-row shake-catch mechanical harvesting. (A.P. Preston, E. Mailing Research Station, Maidstone, England.)

this type handling is done, it is best to use hydraulic equipment that tips the boxes.

Harvest labor. Try to maintain a nucleus of capable and efficient workers, some of whom are hired throughout the year, to take the lead and set the pace in harvesting the crop. In established orchard regions, most workers have had some experience in harvesting. In addition, there is the influx of "floating" labor coming from distant areas to work throughout the harvest season. Contractors in the USA now provide labor from Puerto Rico, Jamaica, and Mexico, which, over the years, has proven satisfactory. Senior citizens coming from miles around in their trailers often can be used to advantage, working by piece at their own speed. An accumulated nucleus of local labor is highly desirable, using foreign help only in an emergency.

Workmen hired by the day tend to work somewhat slower and cause less injury to the trees and the fruit. It can be estimated roughly that workmen paid by the day will harvest from one-third to one-fourth less fruit as compared with those paid by box (100-150 + bxs./day. Figure 1). Some growers may contract their entire crop to a buyer who takes responsibility for the harvesting, packing, storage, and marketing operations.

Proper time for picking. Today, a large percentage of the crop is stored in refrigerated or controlled atmosphere storages before marketing. Apples may be kept in storage for a few weeks to several months. To maintain dessert quality, a long storage life, and bring high returns, it is highly important that they be picked at the *proper stage of maturity*. If picked prematurely, apples are likely to be small, poorly colored, sour, tough, starchy, off-flavor, and subject to functional diseases such as bitter pit and scald. On the other hand, overripe apples may develop water core while still on the tree, or, after picking, and they are likely to develop soft scald and internal breakdown (Figure 5). With overripe red cultivars, in some cases, the

color may become dark and dull and the skin greasy or oily. Overripe apples, especially with some cultivars, tend to be mealy and flat in flavor. With the advent of stop-drop hormone sprays, some growers have tended to be lax in getting the fruit off, or they leave it on the trees too long to try to increase color, resulting in over-ripe fruit that develops storage disorders.

In general, there is a period of about 5 to 20 days, depending upon cultivar and climatic and cultural conditions, during which the fruit can be picked with reasonable assurance that it will be free from storage disorders and develop good dessert quality (Figure 4). It is important to note that the fruit continues to increase in size as long as it remains on the tree. Thus, it is desirable to leave the fruit on the tree as long as dropping does not equal or exceed the total volume increase. It cannot be predicted, however, when excessive dropping is likely to occur and, therefore, picking must start while the fruit is still adhering well.

The following methods are used for determining the proper time to pick. It should be borne in mind, however, that none of these is entirely dependable under all conditions.

Time elapsed from full bloom to picking maturity. It has been found by an extensive survey among the leading commercial apple states that the number of days from full bloom to picking maturity is rather constant over a wide range of climatic and cultural conditions (Figure 6). According to Haller and Magness, this seems to constitute one of the most reliable indexes of the *earliest* maturity date of many apple cultivars. Delicious requires from 145 to 150 days from full bloom to reach picking maturity.

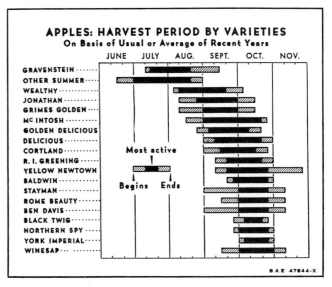

Figure 4. Above listed varieties are harvested approximately within the span indicated, although dates may vary in unusual seasons. Below the equator, June is December in Argentina and Tasmania and November is May. (U.S.D.A.)

125

Mean temperature seems to have relatively little effect on this time interval. However, relatively high temperatures just preceding harvest may result in rapid abscission. Heavy nitrogen fertilization may delay fruit color development and result in scald unless picking is postponed. On the other hand, fruit drop may be more pronounced from heavily fertilized trees than from those receiving medium or light fertilization. A light crop of fruit tends to mature somewhat earlier than a heavy crop. The extent to which these and other factors may retard or advance maturity has not been clearly established.

Full bloom is defined as that period when the first petals begin to fall. This period is established readily if the weather is warm during bloom. However, if the weather should turn cool after the king or center blossoms open, the period may be prolonged for a week or more and confuse the specific time of full bloom.

The days from full bloom to picking maturity for several popular commercial cultivars on which considerable information is available are shown in Figure 6. Apples may ripen during the early-maturity period (diagonal hatch) under conditions that would tend to hasten maturity, such as a light crop. Apples ripening during the late-maturity period (cross hatch), due perhaps to too much nitrogen, may become overmature and excessive dropping is a possibility. The period of optimum maturity, shown by the black area, is the number of days during which the apples can be picked for best handling and storage quality. The approximate time elapsed from full bloom to maturity of varieties other than those shown has been given in Chapter II.

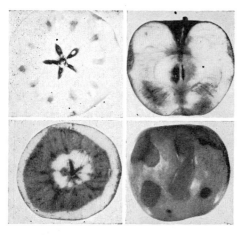

Figure 5. Common physiological diseases of apples which are apparently associated with over-maturity at picking time. (Top left) Water core, characterized by glassy or water-soaked appearance of flesh around the core or main vascular bundles. Such apples eventually may show internal breakdown. (Top right) Internal breakdown has general mealiness and brownish discoloration of the flesh. (Bottom left) Soggy breakdown. (Bottom right) soft scald makes the apples look as if they were rolled on a hot stove. (U.S.D.A.)

The results of R.M. Smock at Cornell University indicate that this method of determining fruit maturity does not always hold. For over ten years previous to 1945 at Ithaca, New York, a range of at least ten days was found from year to year for the period in which McIntosh should be picked. During the 1945 season, bloom occurred one month early and yet apples were picked within a few days of their usual picking date. In this case the number of days from full bloom to harvest was 154, whereas the average for McIntosh at Ithaca, New York is 127-130 days. Smock's studies have shown that ground color of McIntosh seems to be one of the better indexes for proper time to pick. From an interesting 9-yr. survey by D.G. Blanpied, Cornell University (Cornell Inform. Bull. 49, "Harvesting Fresh Market Apples in New York") a formula was developed with accompanying tables using days from full bloom and temperature, giving a 91% accuracy in predicting date of harvest of McIntosh in central New York.

Change in ground or flesh color. The ground or undercolor of an apple is a more reliable index of maturity than the red or overcolor. When most varieties of apples become mature, the ground color changes from a leaf green to a lighter shade and eventually to a yellowish color. With most varieties, the time to pick is when the first signs of yellowing begin to appear. However, with Jonathan, and Cortland, the fruit sometimes drops excessively before the color change takes place. This criterion of maturity cannot be used on red bud sports which become red all over before they are mature, leaving no uncovered ground color for observation. The usual result is that these red sports are picked before mature, resulting in the usual storage and flavor difficulties associated with immaturity. It has been found, however, that the red bud sports do not differ greatly in picking maturity from the parent varieties. Therefore, one could use the ground color of the parent variety as an indication if such parent varieties are in the orchard. A color comparison chart has been devised by the U.S. Department of Agriculture for use in determining picking maturity by change in ground color from green to yellow. These are available through the U.S. Plant Industry St., Beltsville, Md. With Golden Delicious and Delicious a change of flesh color from greenish white to yellowish white is a useful indicator. Green Goldens due to too much N are difficult to market at a price.

Ease of separation of fruit from the spur. When an apple is ready to pick, it can be separated from the spur without breaking the stem by lifting it with or without a slight rotating movement (Figure 10). There are popular varieties, however, such as McIntosh and Delicious, which may loosen and drop before maturity as a result of early frosts or other factors. On the other hand, there are certain varieties, as Jonathan and Stayman Winesap, which may retain their fruit until it is overmature. Thus, ease of

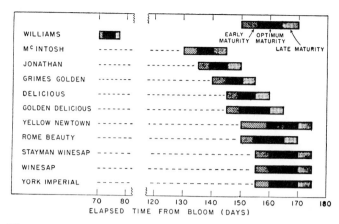

Figure 6. Days elapsing from bloom to maturity of fruit for 11 varieties of apples. The period of early maturity, as shown above, is when barely satisfactory maturity of the fruit normally occurs, but optimum maturity may advance to this period under conditions that would tend to hasten maturity. Similarly, the period of late maturity is when overmaturity of dropping may become imminent, but optimum maturity may extend into this period under conditions that retard maturity. (U.S.D.A.)

separation of fruit from the spur is not necessarily an indication of proper maturity, but it may indicate when picking is necessary to save the crop. If no sound fruit is dropping and the fruit can be picked only with considerable effort, the apples are still attached firmly to the tree. However, if a few sound apples are dropping and similar fruits can be separated rather easily from the tree it is definitely time to pick. One should not be misled by the dropping of wormy or otherwise injured fruits.

Harvest or "Stop-Drop" sprays, as described later, are being used by nearly all growers to make the apples "stick" to the tree longer. Naturally, with the use of these sprays, this index is of little value and, in fact, the fruit may tend to hang too long and become overmature, which is too often the case.

Firmness of flesh. Firmness of the flesh can be determined by removing a thin slice of the skin and flesh with a knife and using a special hand-operated pressure tester (Figure 9) which records the pounds pressure necessary for the plunger to penetrate the flesh (McCormick Co., 6111A Englewood Ave., Yakima, WA 98908). Used independently of other criteria, it is of value chiefly in determining when apples are too soft and ripe for storage, rather than when picking should begin. Publications listed at the end of this chapter should be consulted for further details as to the applications and limitations of the "mechanical thumb" or pressure tester.

Committee Decision. In Washington, e.g., a committee of growers, Federal and state workers and marketing representatives visit key orchards about harvest time to decide when fruit, mainly red sports of Delicious should be harvested. State regulatory men attempt by law to keep fruit from moving out of state before the initial harvesting

date is set. This helps to keep starchy apples from depressing market sales. Flesh firmness, sugar content (Figure 7), and general agreement among the committee based on experience are criteria used.

A simple reliable technique is needed whereby a grower can determine when an apple cultivar is ready to harvest. Accumulated seasonal heat units and temperature near harvest are among several approaches under investigation and refinement.

Picking maturity of different varieties. Considerable information has accumulated regarding the proper picking maturity for specific cultivars. As examples, and to point out the special problems involved, three leading cultivars will be discussed briefly. Detailed information on other cultivars commercially important can be obtained from a bulletin by Haller and Magness cited at the end of this chapter.

Delicious. Delicious develops very poor dessert quality if picked in an immature state. With the general practice of using the high-early-coloring cultivars, and the desire to get the better early prices, the tendency to pick Delicious immature has become a key problem. Thus, flesh color change from greenish white is one index.

Elapsed *time from full bloom to maturity,* as pointed our earlier, is probably the most reliable index for picking Delicious. Studies under widely varying climatic conditions from Washington to New York indicate that at least 145 days and preferably 150 days should elapse between full bloom and picking. In other words, harvest should begin at about 145 days and end between 155 and 160 days for satisfactory storage holding.

Delicious may become overmature under long season growing conditions. Under these conditions, the use of the *pressure tester* is advisable; apples should be picked before the pressure test drops below 15 or 16 pounds. Water core may develop if Delicious becomes overmature under long-growing season conditions. Another index is the fact that the *flesh turns yellowish* when in proper picking condition. Delicious stores well at 31° to 32° F. At higher temperatures, it may become mealy extremely fast; thus, it is not well suited to common storage and should be placed under refrigeration. Soluble solids should be 10.5-11.5% (Figure 7).

Delicious picked prematurely may develop scald, and in Washington, from 150 to 155 days is recommended from full bloom before picking to prevent scald development. When picking must start early, because the crop is large and packing and storage facilities are limited, the early picked apples should not be kept for storage but sold for immediate consumption. Several states are using the Maturity Committee's decision for Delicious harvest.

Promalin on Delicious. Warm clear days and cool nights a few weeks shortly after bloom tend to cause Delicious fruit to be long with prominent points at the calyx end, as under Washington conditions. If nights are quite warm a few weeks after bloom, the fruit tends to be flat with less prominent points. Promalin [(contains gibberellins A_4 and A_7 with cytokinin (6-benzyladenine)] improves "typyness" of Delicious where weather conditions a few weeks after bloom are unfavorable. Promalin must be used with caution if less than a full crop is expected since some thinning may result. The possibility of reduced crop must be balanced against the possibility of increased price for large fruit with more acceptable longer fruit with pronounced lobes. It is applied when first petals are falling from the king center blossoms at 1 pt./100 gals. at 100-200 gals./A. Up to 6x nozzelling can be used.

Stayman Winesap. Relatively late picking is desired with Stayman Winesap to get full color development and to avoid scald which develops from harvesting prematurely. Fruit left on the tree too long, however, may develop water core and storage breakdown, and in some seasons, dropping may be serious. Stayman requires at least 155 days from full bloom to earliest maturity, and 160 to 170 days for optimum maturity. For best storage, it should not be left on the tree until the pressure test is below 16 pounds. Fruit between 15 and 18 pounds have been found satisfactory for storage. The number of days from full bloom is probably the most reliable index of the time to start picking Stayman. This variety ripens quickly after it is picked and, therefore, should be placed immediately under refrigeration, particularly if picking has been delayed until the fruit firmness is on the low side.

McIntosh. McIntosh can be picked somewhat earlier than other fruits because it is almost immune to storage scald. However, the variety should be left on the tree long enough to develop high color and command a premium price; it is not susceptible to water core. The biggest difficulty with McIntosh is that it tends to drop even before prime picking maturity is reached (Figure 13). This tendency can be overcome by the application of "stop-drop" sprays shortly before harvesting, as described later. This is an important practice with McIntosh because the period elapsing from full bloom to proper picking maturity may be inconsistent. The minimum days from full bloom to picking maturity is 130; optimum maturity is generally reached between 135 and 140 days. Within these limits, picking may be determined by development of red overcolor and yellow undercolor and the firmness of the fruit which should not drop below 15 to 14 pounds pressure before picking (Figure 8). See previous comments under "Time elapsed from full bloom...".

Color Development in Apples. Factors that influence anthrocyanin (red pigment) development in apples are; (a) pruning to open the tree, (b) temperature, (c) nutrition, (d) moisture, (e) sunlight, (f) mite damage, (g) chemicals as Alar and Ethrel and (h) their genetic ability to become red. Weather conditions a few days or weeks before harvest, is

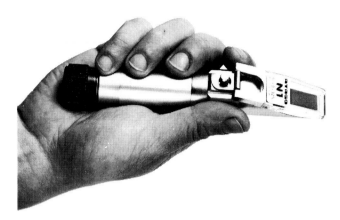

Figure 7. The pocket refractometer is useful at harvest to determine the percentage of soluble solids (sugar) in fruit. Standards are available with the instrument. (Atago N-1 Sugar Refract, Mutual Supply Co., Inc., 322 Harrison St., Oakland, CA 94607)

a predominating factor. Clear days with relatively cool nights are ideal for good fruit color. These conditions help overcome unfavorable nutrition, such as too much nitrogen available to the tree before harvest. A period of warm muggy and rainy weather one to three weeks before harvest can result in poor fruit color and condition. Drought for a few weeks before harvest will cause the fruit to be dull red, but the color will brighten almost overnight with a good rain. Pruning is the most important practice to admit light through the tree so apples will be red on all sides.

It seems unwise for a grower to cut drastically or omit nitrogen application the year following poor fruit color. A cut of not more than 25 percent in nitrogen from one year to the next should be about the limit. However, where natural fertility of the soil is good, we have seen a few New Jersey growers who kept their trees in good vigor and production by *annual pruning* with little or no nitrogen applied for several years, but yields must be watched carefully, using nitrogen again if yields begin to drop. Potassium applications may improve fruit color only when the nutrient is deficient in the soil. Iron deficiency may cause poor fruit color also.

There is a tendency among most growers to plant the red sports of standard varieties to try to insure acceptable fruit color every harvest season.

CONTROLLING FRUIT DROP WITH HARVEST SPRAYS

Since 1939, fruit growers have sprayed fruit trees with various chemicals before harvest to control fruit drop on varieties susceptible to dropping. Chemical sprays that retard fruit drop have reduced losses at harvest from 20 percent or more to only 5 percent and less. The chemicals in these sprays, known generally as "stop-drop" sprays, so

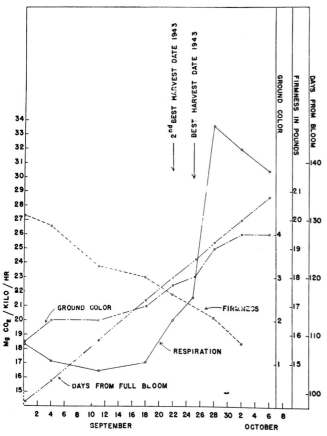

Figure 8. Maturity changes of McIntosh apples ripened on the tree in New York. The best picking date, based on ground color, firmness, and respiration rate, was found to be September 24 in this particular year.

tighten a tree's hold on its crop that the fruit is not likely to drop even when jolted by ladders or shaken by wind. Research is adding to the number of chemicals that can be used to stop fruit from dropping, and is also determining more specifically their effectiveness on particular cultivars, solution strengths, times of application, and such side effects as over-ripening and softening of fruit and damage to foliage and buds. Loosening of fruit on a tree is natural in the maturing process. As fruit nears maturity, a callous abscission (separation) layer forms where the fruit stem joins the spur, and from then on weakly-held fruit may fall.

Drop may be increased if trees are deficient in boron or magnesium, or if they have too little moisture. Trees fertilized heavily with nitrogen often drop more fruit than trees fertilized moderately.

All varieties are subject to drop, particularly the short-stem cultivars. Loss has been serious enough to lead growers of all commercial cultivars to adopt preharvest spraying, except in the case of early summer apples which can be picked before they are eating ripe. Protection against dropping by a preharvest spray may be gained at a relatively nominal cost. Before fruit-sticking sprays were

available, apple growers knew, and occasionally practiced, one drastic means of forestalling drop loss. This was to pick early despite market complaints. Still a bad practice.

NAA, 2,4,5-TP (Naphthalenaceatic acid and (2,4,5-trichlorophenoxyacetic acid) are two of the better stop-drop sprays with Alar. NAA was first used about 1939 by workers with the U.S. Dept. of Agriculture to retard fruit drop on apples. It can be used on all cultivars but in New York is suggested for McIntosh and earlier cultivars at the rate of 10-20 ppm with a lasting effect of 6-10 days. It becomes active within a few days of application. From the beginning, growers have valued NAA. It is the only chemical that can be applied by airplane spraying.

2,4,5-TP is used particularly on Delicious and later cultivars. The concentration should not exceed 5 ppm for Delicious under New York conditions; on other late-maturing cultivars it can be used at 10-20 ppm. Apply the spray before foliage is frosted or senescence develops from other causes. Apply at 70° or above if possible. At 5 or 10 ppm, control may last for 2 wks; at 20 ppm it should last for 3-4 wks. It is not suggested for McIntosh and earlier cultivars. Some uses of 2,4,5-TP have been cancelled or suspended; check with local authorities before using.

Figure 9. (Above) This is a pressure tester to determine by flesh firmness when the apple is ready to be picked, or its storage or sales status. (Below) Agricultural engineers in the USDA and state stations are cooperating with horticulturists in the development of machinery to harvest compact fruit trees with as little damage as possible. Soft paddles dislodge the fruit onto cushioned belts that carry it to the bin behind. Labor-saving and quick movement of the fruit to storage are the key objectives. (Courtesy Uniroyal, Naugatuck, Ct., and Penn. State Univ., University Park)

129

Alar 85 or SADH (Succinic acid 2,2 - dimethylhydrazide). This is an unusual chemical in pomology. It has many advantages, few drawbacks. It increases red color, reduces preharvest drop, may delay maturity, reduces cracking, water core, bitter pit, oiliness on Cortland, Cox's disease, and finger bruising; increases fruit firmness, increases green color on green cultivars, reduces fruit size slightly, and increases return bloom with the help, of course, of fruit thinners. It is used on most cultivars. On Golden Delicious it is used to increase firmness though it may delay yellow coloring. To control drop it is applied 60 days or more before anticipated harvest at 1000 ppm. For short period of drop control, use 750 ppm. If Alar has been used several years on Delicious, reduce concentration to 750 ppm. For McIntosh and earlier cultivars, at 1000 ppm drop control should last about 14-21 days; for later maturing cultivars it should last 2-4 wks.

Ethephon. This chemical has been used successfully on several apple cultivars to promote earlier coloring and maturity. It is available in 2 lb./liquid gal. and used at rates varying from 1/2 pt./100 gal. for fall cultivars to 1 ½ pts. for winter cultivars. Apply about 1 wk before anticipated harvest of late summer and fall cultivars and 2 to 2½ wks before harvest of later cultivars. A spray of Alar should be made 60-75 days before harvest to improve fruit firmness if ethephon is to be used. Also, a growth regulator as NAA at about 10 ppm must be applied with the ethephon to prevent excessive drop, where the ethephon is being used to improve maturity and color for hand-harvested fruit. For mechanical harvesting, ethephon can be used similarly without the NAA. If the temperature exceeds 75°F, watch fruit carefully for quick ripening and move for early consumption. Testing in various areas is continuing. This chemical is tricky and must be used with caution. It is well to check with your local fruit specialists for latest suggestions.

Climate considerations. Temperature will make some difference in results achieved with preharvest sprays. A relatively warm temperature, 70° F. or higher, at spraying time is an advantage, because the chemical will be absorbed more readily than when weather is cool. At warm temperatures the chemical will also take effect faster. Once a stop-drop chemical has become effective, temperature changes do not further alter its potency.

Considerable moisture from dew, fog, or rain is ordinarily an aid to the potency of the chemicals. Lack of moisture on the other hand, lowers their efficiency. Occasionally, the unexpected happens, as when McIntosh apple trees in Northeast orchards dropped fruit badly in 1955, when the growing season was rainy. Such situations are a reminder that, useful as the stop-drop chemicals are, their action is not understood completely.

Airplane spraying. Airplane spraying is ordinarily a custom arrangement with firms doing this work. The

Figure 10. To pick an apple, hold it as shown to left: lift to one side and up, giving a slight turn (center). Work with hands close together, making sure that the left hand does its share (right). (H.P. Gaston, Michigan Experiment Station)

method offers advantages of speed and convenience to growers who have a large fruit planting. For airplane spraying the only practical stop-drop chemical is NAA. Drift of 2,4,5-TP that might reach pears or other trees could damage foliage and fruit. Damage to the tops of apple trees also has been a problem with concentrate plane application of 2,4,5-TP.

HARVESTING THE FRUIT

Every hour is precious during the harvest season. Make detail plans well ahead. Stop-drop sprays and the development of mechanical aids and harvesters have helped to reduce "harvest tension," particularly in the medium-size and large orchards. The early developed mechanical apple harvesters have been clumsy to handle and expensive to buy and operate, but the size and the spacing of the large trees has necessitated this. As compact trees and hedgerow planting becomes widespread, it is likely that simplified and more efficient and lower-priced mechanical harvesters will be developed. Engineers and horticulturists are working together to perfect this equipment and cut labor to a minimum. But labor union resistance because of loss of jobs has caused some reduction in Federal funds to support the research in the early 1980s. The "shake and catch" harvesters (Figure 11) are doing an acceptable job for harvesting processing fruit with only about 15% of the fruit bruised or damaged which actually is but little more than found in hand harvesting. This harvester has two self-propelled frames, each with decelerator strips to break the fall of the fruit, and a floating boom limb shaker. Another type is the wrap-around, single-unit, inverted-umbrella, self-propelled machine with a Shock-Wave trunk shaker (see Chapter XIV). The Cornell oscillating tines rotated on circular drums is another idea for hedgerow plantings (Figure 11). Trend is to shape the tree to improved har-

Figure 11. These are two of the many ideas being tested and perfected for mechanically harvesting fruit. (Upper) Lincoln-Canopy trained apple trees in New Zealand with specialized shake-catch equipment (J.S. Dunn, Lincoln College, Centerbury). (Lower) The Cornell harvester has three frames inserted into the tree, two inflated after insertion with water at 2 lbs. pressure. Used on big trees, the total fresh marketable fruit based on physical damage was: McIntosh, 83.4; Delicious, 93.9; G. Delicious, 86.5; Idared, 95.6. (Cornell Agr. Eng. Dept., Ithaca, N.Y. 14850)

vester design rather than vice-versa (Chap. IV). See references and watch for developments in grower magazines.

Mechanical harvesters are very expensive. Until we have shifted more or less to compact trees, much of the world apple crop still must be harvested by hand. Key points to bear in mind are: (a) Take every precaution to reduce careless handling of fruit by pickers; (b) start with lower branches and move to the tree tops; (c) do not pull stems from the apples, or cut them with finger nails, or twist off spurs; (d) place fruit *carefully* in picking container, *don't drop it;* (e) set ladders so they fall in the tree if something slips; (f) drop adequate containers by the trees beforehand; (g) keep the picked fruit in the shade and take it to the packing shed and get it in storage as quickly as feasible to

minimize ripening; and (h) make every effort to start the picking and finish before dropping, overmaturing and wind-damage. With availability of CA storage, apples can be picked at peak maturity without the necessity of moving the crop for the early higher prices.

Pick-Your-Own can be used near population centers with considerable savings in harvesting, container, and handling, storage, marketing costs. Migrants may pick tops of big trees, PYO lower areas. See Chap. XXI.

Apples Orchard-to-Store Directly. Cornell found savings up to 50 percent in costs. Pickers are instructed not to pick undersized, misshapen, or damaged apples. This "orchard-run" fruit, tested at 16 supermarkets, increased sales 45% and brought good return sales. Fruit is picked in 1/4-bu. corrugated boxes, pallettized orchard to store, reducing handling from 16 to 6 times, and, hence, less damage to tender McIntosh.

CB 2-way radios, 40 mi. radius, are used for harvesting efficiency in the larger orchards (Gen. Electric Mobile Comm. Corp., POB 4917, Lynchburg, VA 24502).

THE PACKING HOUSE

Private or co-operative packing. Fruit may be (1) packed in the grower's own packing house, or (2) it may be hauled to a community or co-operative packing house.

(1) Many of the growers own their packing house and storage and can hire year-round help that works inside or outside in all kinds of weather. These grower-owned packing houses are more or less a necessity in orchards which are scattered, and the quantity of fruit harvested within a region hardly justifies a co-operative packing house.

(2) Community packing houses operated co-operatively or as a private enterprise, are used extensively in concentrated apple regions. The many advantages of a co-operative effort have been pointed out in Chapter III.

In community packing houses: (a) The grower delivers tree-run fruit; (b) he is given a receipt; (c) his fruit is graded, sized, packed out with low-grade fruit going to processing; (d) charges for handling, storage and packing

Figure 12. (Left) Tractor rear lift is used to line up bulk boxes for lumber type carrier. Sled carriers will reduce jolting. (Right) Fork lift (electric to avoid fumes) is used to stack bins in modern storages. (U.S.D.A.)

are deducted and returns to the grower are pro-rated through all or part of a season. Advances in cash to the grower can be made if needed.

On-the-farm packing facilities. There are several advantages of providing grading and packing service at the point or production: (1) Reduced per-bushel costs — wages, taxes, and overhead are usually lower in rural areas than in towns and cities, (2) makes it possible to prepare the size, grade and pack currently in demand, (3) makes it possible to use year-round farm help to advantage in the winter months, (4) keeps cull fruit off the fresh fruit market, (5) lowers transportation costs by disposing of cull fruit at nearby cider mills rather than in more distant markets, (6) makes retail sales easier and increases average net returns, (7) controls the all-important grading operation, (8) uses the packing house for several fruit crops and for other purposes during the off-season, (9) uses farm fruit storages to the best possible advantage, and (10) increases total net returns to the grower — the profit that otherwise goes to those who perform the packing service is added to that which he received from growing the fruit.

Grower-controlled community packing houses (growers sharing risks and profits), managed by professionals, and co-operative fruit exchanges also have most of the above advantages.

Cost of building and equipment. Cost of packing facilities vary on a box basis with the size of the plant. Building and equipment for handling 5,000 bushels for the season generally cost four times as much as facilities for handling 40,000 bushels, which in turn costs twice as much as a unit for handling 200,000 bushels.

In planning new structures, provide all of the space and capacity that can be used effectively. When amortized over a period of years (20 years is often used), the per box cost is relatively low. This means that it is usually more economical to provide facilities for anticipated needs than to build for the present and expand at a later time.

Location. Both the original and operating costs depend to some extent upon the packing house location. If operated with a fruit storage, it should adjoin or be close to this structure. The packing house should be in or close to the orchard so that fruit can be moved to it with a minimum of effort and expense. A more or less ideal location is near the center of the orchard and at a low level if the land is rolling or hilly (Figure 12). Ready access by trailer-truck may be essential.

Grading and packing equipment are operated by electric motors; good water is necessary for drinking, washing and cleaning purposes. This means that both water and 220-volt alternate current electricity should be readily available.

Packing house design. The efficiency with which grading and packing operations are performed depends, to a

Figure 13. (Top) Several ideas are under test for mechanically picking up drop apples. Apples must be washed and processed immediately. This machine operates with rubber fingers, picking up fruit without damaging it. (Courtesy U.S.D.A. at Mich. State Univ., E. Lansing.)

considerable extent, upon packing house design. Although no two houses are the same, there are several principles which you must consider before the packing house is built and equipped.

How is your fruit to be sold. Growers who plan to sell at retail should provide a readily accessible, conveniently arranged and attractive salesroom. Provide parking space for the peak number of cars (including those which belong to the help). If you expect to sell to truckers, provide a loading dock. Growers who plan to sell to jobbers or chainstore buyers should be prepared to pack and load the volume of fruit that these outlets will demand. The method of merchandising has a direct bearing on packing house design.

An attractive sign which will identify your packing house is a distinct asset. This is especially true if you plan to make retail or "trucker" sales.

Decide how the fruit is to be packed. Apples may be packed in open returnable boxes, baskets, cartons, cell, and tray packs and film bags.

Plan packing facilities around the packages that are or may be used. For example, the grower who plans to pack in poly bags or other consumer-size containers must provide enough space for the special equipment. Those who pack in cartons or cell-pack also must make room for the machines required as well as for storage of empty containers.

The layout in each case will be somewhat different and should receive careful attention. The wise grower will provide enough space to shift from one method of packing to another if circumstances and demand change.

Grading and handling equipment to be used. After choosing markets and packages, consider the number of boxes of fruit to be packed. The space required and the capacity of the equipment needed depends on the volume of fruit to be handled daily. If you are constructing a new packing house, it will pay to provide a structure that will accommodate standard equipment. Most concerns that make and sell grading equipment will supply the service of a qualified engineer upon request. Grading and packing equipment has been changing rapidly in recent years and, hence it is wise to seek help from established suppliers for the latest and most sufficient equipment. The engineer can help design a building that will accommodate standard grading, packing and handling units without installation or operation costs.

Will there be a connected refrigerated storage. Growers who do not have a refrigerated storage must provide facilities to complete their packing during or shortly after the harvest season. Most growers who pack more than 20,000 bushels should provide a refrigerated storage to extend their packing season over several months.

When the packing room is to be used with a refrigerator storage, it should be located in or near the storage building. When the seasonal volume is 10,000 bushels or more and the packing is done in a separate building, a lift truck to move the fruit quickly and easily is essential. The structures must be connected by suitable paved drives.

The requirements of growers who pack "out of storage" differ from those who pack at harvest time. The flow of both fruit and packages must be considered when the layout is planned.

Design for flexibility. All fruit packing operations should be flexible. The tonnage of any crop or combination of crops is likely to vary considerably from year to year. Average production in any orchard may vary as young orchards come into full bearing or old ones pass their prime. Day-to-day variations in volume during a single season are sure to occur. Thus, packing lines should operate effectively at a fraction of their capacity as well as at full load.

The facilities of any one plant can, for example, often be used to advantage to pack several different crops in succession if the shift from one to another can be accomplished quickly and economically. A shift from the use of boxes to fiberboard cartons or film bags, is often necessary. The line should be laid out in such a way that several grades of fruit and two or more types of packages can be assembled.

Layout and arrangement. From 2½ to 4 square feet of floorspace should be available for every box of fruit that will be packed in any one 10-hour day (Table 1).

If empty packages, supplies, and several grades of fruit are to move through a packing house in an orderly manner, two sides of the packing house floor should be readily accessible by truck. Suitable all-weather drives with ample room in which to make turns, and at least one dock of truck-bed height will be required.

When bulky packages, as fiberboard cartons or wooden boxes are used, provide ground floor storage space next to or near the packing room. This makes it possible to move the "empties" to the point where they are needed with a minimum of effort and confusion.

The layout should be arranged so that the fruit can be moved to the receiving belt of the grader line either directly from the orchard or from the storage space through the various steps in grading, packing, and shipping with the least effort and expense.

The grading and packing equipment should be laid out so that all the points at which fruit accumulates can be serviced by a fork-lift truck. The area in which ungraded fruit is received and stockpiled should be separate from that in which the packed fruit is loaded for shipment. Both these areas should be readily accessible to lift equipment.

All floor space to be used for storage, grading and packing operations should be at the ground level. This type of construction speeds the movement of fruit and materials in the building and nearby areas, particularly when fork-lift trucks are used.

Two layouts designed to fulfill somewhat different requirements are shown in Figure 14. In both instances the building was planned with the assumption that a highway lies to the east and runs north and south.

Floors. The packing house floor must be strong enough to support the weight of loaded trucks, fork-lift equipment, and stacked fruit. Floor must be level and smooth. A carefully trowelled, 4-or 5-inch concrete slab (reinforced with No. 9 wire at 6-inch intervals) poured over a sand or gravel base is recommended.

Walls and ceilings. The only requirements for walls and ceilings are that they keep the packing area dry and that they be durable and tight so that the area can be heated in cold weather if necessary. Tile, concrete, cinder block, metal, or wood construction are all suitable.

It is usually desirable to stack one unit load or box on another. A 12-foot ceiling usually is satisfactory, but some operators say 14 feet is better.

Doors and windows. The packing house should have at least one 12 by 12-foot overhead door at grade level, essential if you want to load and/or store trucks loaded with fruit during bad weather. Heavy equipment can be stored in the packing house during off-season.

Doors through which fruit is moved should be at least 5 x 8 ft. for lift trucks. Use door props for CA rooms while lowering the temperature to avoid a vacuum and collapsing of insulation or walls.

Windows increase construction costs, reduce the efficient use of wall space, and allow heat losses during cold weather. Regardless of the number of windows, sup-

Boxes Packed Per Season[1]	Capacity In Boxes Per Hour	Square Ft. Floor Space Needed[2]	Packing Equipment Generally Needed
5,000	25	1,000	12½-inch unit consisting of receiving belt, eliminator, brusher, sorting rolls, sizer, and two bins.
10,000 or 20,000 or 30,000 or	50	1,750	12½-inch unit consisting of receiving belt, eliminator, brusher, sorting rolls, two sizers, and three bins.
40,000	75	2,300	15½-inch unit consisting or receiving belt, eliminator, brusher, sorting rolls, two sizers, spacer belts, crossover belts, and a 20-foot return-flow belt.
50,000 or 75,000	100	3,000	19-inch unit consisting of receiving belt, eliminator, brusher, sorting rolls, two sizers, spacer belts, crossover belts, and a 20-foot return-flow belt.
100,000	150	4,000	22-inch unit consisting of receiving belt, eliminator, brusher, sorting rolls, three sizers, spacer belts, crossover belts, and a 30-foot return-flow belt.
150,000	200	5,000	24-inch unit consisting receiving belt, eliminator, brusher, sorting rolls, three sizers, spacer belts, crossover belts, and a 40-foot return-flow belt.
200,000[3]	250	6,500	31-inch unit consisting of receiving belt, elminator, brusher, sorting rolls, three sizers, spacer belts, crossover belts, and a 40-foot return-flow belt.

[1]Growers will pack about two-thirds of their production on the average.

[2]If automatic baggers and combination units accommodating more than one type fruit pack are used, it will increase costs.

[3]Equipment and techniques are changing. Contact a reputable supply representative for latest suggestions and figures. This table can give you only a rough idea and estimate in planning. See Figure 16 for large-scale modern packinghouse.

plemental light is needed in fall and winter. Thus, the fewer windows, the better.

Lighting. In most packing plants, more than half of the employees are either sorting fruit or doing other work that requires good light. Necessary light can be provided by fixtures, bulbs and operating costs are less. Because of the shape of fluorescent tubes and the quality of the light, many operators prefer them for packing house illumination.

When artificial lights are installed, the tubes or bulbs should be placed and shielded so that the light falls onto the work, and not directly into the eyes of the employees. A single fluorescent tube, because of its so-called "stroboscopic effect," is not a satisfactory source of light. Fixtures containing two or more tubes also will eliminate any unpleasant "flickering."

For the kind of work done at sorting belts and facing stations, lighting engineers recommend 100-foot candles of illumination on the working area. This probably can be obtained best by hanging fluorescent lighting fixtures directly above the work and within a few feet of it. Tubes that give either white or "cool white" light are recommended. For most other operations, 5- to 10-foot candles are considered adequate.

It is best to place the lighting fixtures near the ceiling in receiving and storage areas. Locating them in this way increases headroom, allows the light from a given source to illuminate the maximum amount of floor space, and reduces the total number of fixtures required.

Many power companies have equipment for measuring the intensity of light and employ men who are familiar with the use of these devices.

In many packing houses, the lighting conditions can be improved greatly by applying a coat of light-colored paint to the ceiling and inside walls.

Heating. Some form of artificial heat is necessary in fall and winter if the workers are to be comfortable enough to pack effectively. It is, however, undesirable (because of condensation and the possibility of shortening "shelf life" of the fruit) to raise the temperature of the fruit more than necessary. A temperature of about 55° to 60° F. in those areas where the workers stand is recommended.

A blower or radiant heater which directs heat toward the workers' feet is often desirable. In a few cases, the water warmed by passing through the condenser units of the storage refrigeration equipment is circulated through coils on which the workers stand. With an energy "squeeze", growers have directed heat from the compressor room into the packing area, sometimes accounting for 70% of the heat need.

Handling equipment. Most units of grading, packing, and handling equipment last for many years. Select them with care. Be sure to choose machines that are large enough to do the job. If the orchards involved are young, allow for increased volume.

Most growers who pack less than 10,000 bushels of fruit believe that they are not justified in investing in a fork-lift truck. They usually handle their fruit by means of power or roller conveyor, hand trucks and dollies. If this equipment is selected with care, it should enable the "small grower" to operate with reasonable efficiency.

Growers who produce more than 10,000 bushels of fruit find it to their advantage to invest in lift equipment. The machines eliminate much of the physical labor involved in handling operations. They also reduce bruising, spillage, and box breaking. They save time, help maintain quality, and have many other advantages. The suggested layouts presented here were designed so that a lift truck can be used to advantage.

The practice of handling apples in bulk boxes has become widespread. These containers are heavy and can be handled only by fork-lift equipment.

Grading and packing equipment. The function of grading and packing equipment is to provide a practical means of sorting out fruit of small size and poor quality, and of separating into size and color classifications the fruit that remains. The equipment should facilitate the filling and closing of market containers. It must have sufficient capacity to handle (with a minimum of labor) the volume to be packed; it must be constructed not to cause serious mechanical injury to the fruit.

All diverting surfaces must be well padded. Belts and rollers must not move at speeds of more than 30 feet per minute, and the pitch of sloping surfaces over which the fruit moves must not be excessive. Most manufacturers of grading equipment will, upon request, supply the services of a qualified engineer to help choose equipment that will fulfill volume and method requirements. Growers who are planning new lines or extensive changes in existing layouts should use these services. See Figures 15, 16.

Computerization. In the modern packing house line, apples, pears, and other fruits can be, e.g., 4-color sorted and each color sized in 12 sizes with all 48 distinctions recorded in a memory bank for immediate or future use, available on a moment's notice. Any size can be adjusted within one percent accuracy. Any size can be programmed out of any belt. The defects are only the hand-sorted fruit. Fruit can be programmed for immediate packing on tray pack lines or to flumes for refilling in bins for bulk storage, depending upon current market demand. The computer will "know" the weight and color of each fruit in every cup. When the fruit reaches the correct color and weight station, it is then lowered onto a transfer belt for packing or return to storage via water flumes. A microprocessor will provide total accounting. The grower knows what was in a particular lot right after the last apple passes the weight station. Data for hand-sorted defects and culls are also available. This brief summary indicates the type of data available in a modern computerized packing house.

A brief discussion of the basic units incorporated in a computerized grading/sizing packing line is shown later in

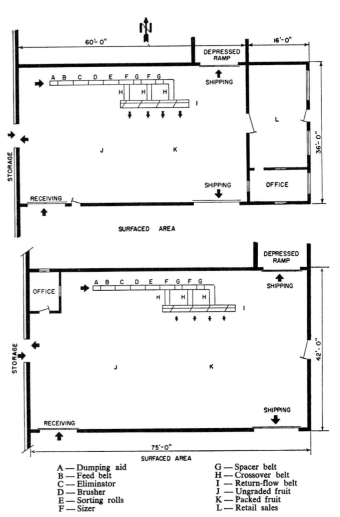

A — Dumping aid	G — Spacer belt
B — Feed belt	H — Crossover belt
C — Eliminator	I — Return-flow belt
D — Brusher	J — Ungraded fruit
E — Sorting rolls	K — Packed fruit
F — Sizer	L — Retail sales

Figure 14. (Upper) Packing house with capacity of 50 to 70 bu. per hr., or 23 to 30 thousand a season; (lower) 100 bu. per hr. or 50 to 75 thousand a season. Straight-line design with no turns (causing bottlenecks, bruises) is best. (Michigan State University).

Figures 16 and 17.

Dumping aids. Several mechanical dumping aids are available. These devices are relatively inexpensive, and tend to make the work easier and reduce the amount of injury to fruit. Growers who use bulk boxes require a mechanical dumper; fruit may be dumped directly on a rubber belt or into a flood tank, the latter reducing bruising to a minimum. Bulk-bin restacker units are available to restack four bins after dumping the fruit. Bin unstackers are available for stacked incoming fruit.

Feed belt. The feed belt moves the fruit from the head of the line to the eliminator section. A sloping feed table sometimes is used, but this equipment tends to cause bruising and is not recommended. Feed belts are relatively inexpensive; select one big enough to handle the peak volume to be packed.

Eliminator. This unit separates small fruit (less than two

135

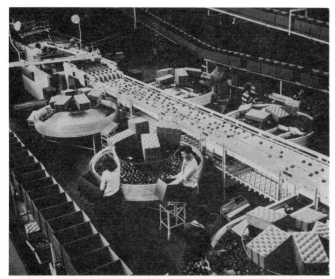

Figure 15. The fruit grading and sizing equipment shown above still is in use in many packing houses. (Above) A 6-belt weight sizer, conveying apples to revolving packing bins near Paw Paw, WV. Travelling in individual plastic cups, apples by weight are gently lowered into bins by counter-weight trip switch. (FMC, Jonesboro, AK 72401)

inches in diameter). When apples are graded, those which collect at this station usually go to the cider mill.

Brusher. Brushing removes dust, spray material, and foreign matter. It improves the appearance of pears and apples, usually sold from small operations. When buyers demand brushed fruit, this equipment is essential. Most brushers do not operate effectively on wet fruit. Growers who expect to brush damp fruit should select a unit designed to do this.

Electronic Color Sorter. The equipment is designed to increase speed and reduce labor costs in the selective grading of apples. Result is more accurate sorting into the pre-selected color classifications which will provide a

constant quality pack for best returns in the market place.

Sorting rolls. This equipment moves the fruit forward and turns it slowly over and over. This facilitates thorough inspection for workers who sort out inferior fruit. Sorting equipment should be big enough to accommodate the help required to sort orchard-run fruit containing a considerable percentage of culls when the line is at full capacity. Electronic machines can sort fruit by color, eliminate culls.

Sizing units. See discussion under "Sizing" to follow.

Packing belts and bins. After the fruit has been sorted and sized, it moves onto a moving packing belt or into a bin. From here, it passes into the packages in which it will move to market. The packing stations should be provided with cushioned aids that make it possible to transfer the fruit into the market containers with a minimum of bruising.

Return-flow belts. These machines are useful in moving fruit that has been graded and sized to the stations at which it will be packed. Such equipment is considered better than packing bins or one-way belts because the fruit moves at a relatively slow speed; when properly used, it prevents piling up and bruising. A two-way belt circulates the fruit continuously until it is shunted off the line into a package. This machine also makes it relatively easy to combine two or more size grades by merely removing one or more of the dividers which separate the grades.

Bagging machines. Growers who purchase bagging equipment may choose from several available machines. The choice will probably be influenced by the volume to be packed, the amount of space available, and the length of the season.

Automatic equipment for packing trays. Machines that will do this work are available. Operators who pack a considerable amount of fruit in containers should investigate the possibilities of installing automatic or semi-automatic equipment.

Miscellaneous equipment. Packing lines on which a considerable amount of fruit is to be packed often include other miscellaneous devices such as spacer belts, crossover belts and box turners. Most packing house operators are either familiar with the operation of these machines or can easily obtain installation and operational information from the agents who sell them. Automatic equipment is available to stamp the brand on each apple going through the line (Auvil Fruit Co., Inc., Orondo, Wa.).

Labor requirements. When an effectively and adequately equipped labor force is used to pick apples, the per-worker production rate depends on the packing methods used. The study of Gaston and Levin showed that when open-faced cartons or crates were "jumble-packed," per-worker production was about 10 bushels per hour. When containers were faced, a rate of about seven bushels per hour per worker was achieved. When apples were

TABLE 2. Relative Annual Costs of Operating On-The-Farm Packing Houses

After Gaston and Levin, 1957

(In the 1980's these cost figures would be about 3x higher)

Bushels Packed During Season	Total Annual Costs				Ann./Bu. Costs (Cents)			
	Over-head[1]	Main-tenance	Labor[3]	Total	Over-head	Main-tenance[2]	Labor[3]	Total[4]
5,000	$ 425.50	$ 84.00	$ 500.00	$ 1,009.50	8.5	1.7	.10	20.2
10,000	626.50	127.00	1,000.00	1,777.50	6.3	1.3	.10	17.6
20,000	626.50	127.00	2,000.00	2,777.50	3.1	.6	.10	13.7
30,000	626.50	127.00	3,000.00	3,777.50	2.1	.4	.10	12.5
40,000	819.00	162.00	4,000.00	4,981.00	2.0	.4	.10	12.4
50,000	1,057.50	210.00	5,000.00	6,267.50	2.1	.4	.10	12.5
75,000	1,057.50	210.00	7,500.00	8,767.50	1.4	.3	.10	11.7
100,000	1,530.00	290.00	10,000.00	11,820.00	1.5	.3	.10	11.8
150,000	1,860.00	355.00	15,000.00	17,215.00	1.2	.2	.10	11.4
200,000	2,267.50	440.00	20,000.00	22,707.50	1.1	.2	.10	11.3

[1]Overhead calculated on the basis of the building and equipment costs which appear in Table 1. Depreciation on buildings and equipment calculated at five and ten percent, respectively. Interest calculated at four percent; taxes and insurance at two percent each.
[2]Maintenance calculated at two percent on the basis of the first cost figures which appear in Table 1.
[3]Labor cost of jumble packing. To calculate labor costs of putting up face-and-fill pack, add 25 percent. To figure labor costs of bagging, add 50 percent.
[4]Total cost of jumble packing. To calculate costs of putting up face-and-fill packing, add 2½ cents. To figure costs of bagging, add 5 cents.

packed in film bags, the rate per hour per worker varied from four to six master containers, each holding about 40 pounds of fruit.

These figures can be used to calculate the amount of help required in any particular operation. For example, a grower who harvests 20,000 bushels of apples and wishes to pack 15,000 during a 30-day season must pack 500 bushels a day or 50 bushels per hour. If the fruit is to be jumble-packed, a crew of five would be required (50 bushels per hour divided by 10 bushels per hour per worker). If apples are to be put in faced containers, seven or eight workers would be needed. If the fruit will be put into three- to five-pound film bags, a crew of eight to twelve will be required. The per-worker figures represent the average production rates achieved by the commercial operations studied. The actual amount of help needed in a specific case will depend on the size of the operation and the efficiency with which it is performed.

Annual operating costs. The cost for operating a packing house will include labor, overhead, and maintenance. Packing house owners pay overhead and maintenance costs regardless of whether the facilities are used. Labor is the most important item in the cost of packing, and operators should make every effort to utilize labor to the best advantage. Table 2.

It is difficult to quote up-to-date cost figures in the packing house. It is suggested you request recent data from the departments of agricultural economics at Cornell University, or Michigan, Washington, or California state universities (see appendix for addresses).

Grades. Grade refers to the exterior quality of the apple. This includes color, condition as to firmness and soundness, and freedom from blemishes. The U.S. Department of Agriculture standards for apples provides for and defines the following grades: U.S. Extra Fancy, U.S. Fancy, U.S. No. 1, U.S. Commercial, United States Number 1 Early, United States Utility, United States Utility Early, Combination grades, United States Hail, and Unclassified. Some states recognize an extra fancy grade which is the highest degree of perfection in color, condition, and uniformity in shape. The only difference between U.S. Number 1 and U.S. Commercial is essentially color with somewhat more tolerance to blemishes in the latter grade.

Grade requirements of U.S. Fancy are given below only as an example. These are updated from time to time.

U.S. Fancy shall consist of apples of one variety which are mature but not overripe, carefully handpicked, cleaned, fairly well formed, free from decay, internal browning and breakdown, bitter pit, Jonathan spot, scald, freezing injury, broken skins and bruises (except those incident to proper handling and packing), and visible water core. The apples shall also be free from damage caused by russeting, sunburn, spray burn, limb rubs, hail, drought spots, scars, stem or calyx cracks, other diseases, insects, invisible water core after January 31st of the year following production, or damage by other means. Each variety of this grade shall have the amount of color specified. (Table 3).

The Federal grades have been adopted by many states and more detailed information on grade requirements can be secured either from Agricultural Marketing Service, U.S. Department of Agriculture, or from your local state department of agriculture. Many of the states have special grading and branding laws. It is highly important that the graders know the requirements for the grades which they are packing and that the grading be supervised by reliable foreman to see that the job is done correctly. In fact, special supervision is required at all phases of the grading, sizing, and packing to avoid bruising and price discount. See buyer demands, Ch. XII.

137

Sizing. Size refers to the transverse diameter of the apple at the point of its greatest circumference; size varies with the cultivar and growing conditions. *Any size of apple may fall into any grade, and vice versa.* A two and one-quarter-inch Jonathan and a three and one-half-inch McIntosh may be equally high in grade.

The variation within a given size must not be more than one-quarter inch in transverse diameter when the number of fruits as well as size are marked on the container. When the number of fruits in the container is not indicated, the minimum size of the fruit is all that is required, as for example "2¼-inch minimum." With uniform size and grade designations, the package looks much better, brings a higher return, and the buyer knows what to expect without opening and checking the package, provided the U.S. or state grades are mandatory and enforced where the fruit was packed. Unfortunately, there are a few fruit states where the sizes and grades are still not strictly enforced.

After the fruit has been sorted or graded, each grade is conveyed separately by belts to the sizing machinery. The sizing machine may be small or quite large, depending upon the amount of fruit to be handled daily. Large capacity power driven units may handle as much as 150 or more boxes per hour. Several batteries of these large units may be employed in co-operative packing houses. The smaller capacity machines may handle 45 or less boxes an hour for an individual grower. Most growers purchase or adapt their machines to handle two or three grades of several different sizes in each grade.

The sizing may be done mechanically *by weight* or *by size.* The sizing principle involves the use of a rubber or chain belt, or oscillating cups, perforated with the respective sizes through which the apples gently drop onto canvas aprons, and roll into padded bins. Another system is the use of revolving rubbed-tired wheels which are adjusted at different heights corresponding to the size of fruit they are designated to brush off the belt into the respective bins. These sizers have the advantage of sizing the largest fruit first, thus handling the best fruit the least.

Some sizing equipment does the job by weight. Each fruit rides in a small canvas or plastic tray along a track until it reaches a point where its weight slightly over-balances a spring-tension trigger, or a trigger which is counter balanced by a lead bead bag or another apple of the desired size. At this point the weight of the apple trips the trigger and it gently drops into a padded bin. The size of apples that the trigger will drop can be regulated by adjusting the spring tension, the amount of beads in the bag, or the size of the counter apple.

The collection unit in which the fruit accumulates before being packed may be either of the stationary or rotary type. Stationary bins have been used for many years for packing boxes and consumer packs and are still in use. The rotary bin is being used in packing houses for hand packing of boxes and cartons. The bins have a floating

TABLE 3. COLOR REQUIREMENTS FOR SPECIFIED U.S. GRADES OF APPLE VARIETIES, (SOME STATES OR COUNTRIES HAVE THEIR OWN STANDARDS.) CONTACT YOUR LOCAL DEPARTMENT OF AGRICULTURE FOR LATEST RULINGS.

Variety	U.S. Extra Fancy	U.S. Fancy	U.S. No. 1
	Percent	Percent	Percent
Solid red:			
Gano, Winesap, Other similar varieties[1], and Red Sport varieties[2]	66[12]	40	25
Stripend or partially red:			
Jonathan, Idared	66	33	25
McIntosh, Cortland, other similar varieties[3]	50	33	25
Baldwin, Ben Davis, Delicious, Northern Spy, Rome Beauty, Stayman, Turley, Wagener, Wealthy, York Imperial, and Other similar varieties[4]	50	25	15
Hubbardston, Stark, and Other varieties	50	15	10
Red June, Williams, Red Gravenstein, and similar varieties	50	15	([5])
Gravenstein, Duchess, and Other similar varieties[6]	25	10	([5])
Red checked or blushed:			
Maiden Blush, Twenty Ounce, Winter Banana, and Other similar varieties	([7])	([5])	([8])
Green varieties, and Yellow varieties	([9])	([9])	([9])
Golden Delicious	([10])	([10])	([11])

[1]Beacon, Esopus Spitzenburg, King David, Lowry.
[2]When Red Sport varieties are specified as such they shall meet the color requirements specified for red sport varieties.
[3]Haralson, Kendall, Macoun, Melba, Snow (Fameuse), Empire.
[4]Bonum, Early McIntosh, Limbertwig, Milton, Nero, Paragon, Melba.
[5]Tinge color.
[6]Duchess, Red Astrachan, Summer Rambo.
[7]Blush cheek.
[8]None.
[9]Characteristic ground color.
[10]Seventy-five percent characteristic color. Note: "Characteristic color" when the white around the lenticels predominates over the green color, creating a mottling effect on the surface of the apple, it shall be considered as the minimum characteristic color.
[11]33 percent characteristics color.
[12]66% red color is very lenient. Buyers now want full red color on U.S. Extra Fancy.

138

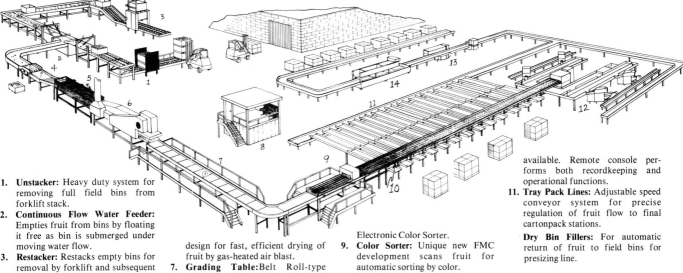

1. **Unstacker:** Heavy duty system for removing full field bins from forklift stack.
2. **Continuous Flow Water Feeder:** Empties fruit from bins by floating it free as bin is submerged under moving water flow.
3. **Restacker:** Restacks empty bins for removal by forklift and subsequent return to orchard.
4. **Small fruit Eliminator:** Eliminates undersized fruit from line.
5. **Washer/Waxer:** Designed to fit every requirement. May include unique traversing nozzle system for application of FMC Sta-FreshR Protective Coating.
6. **Dryer:** Unique new energy-saving design for fast, efficient drying of fruit by gas-heated air blast.
7. **Grading Table:** Belt Roll-type conveyor rotates fruit as it moves past inspection stations. Belt and cross roll conveyors operate at differential speed.
8. **Control Center:** Centralized controls for all automatic and computerized production and record keeping functions including Programmable Weight Sizer and Electronic Color Sorter.
9. **Color Sorter:** Unique new FMC development scans fruit for automatic sorting by color.

   Count/ Print System: Electronic counting and record-keeping system for use with mechanical weight sizers.
10. **Programmable Weight Sizer:** FMC combines computer technology with the industry's leading electro-mechanical design to provide the most advanced sizing system available. Remote console performs both recordkeeping and operational functions.
11. **Tray Pack Lines:** Adjustable speed conveyor system for precise regulation of fruit flow to final cartonpack stations.

    Dry Bin Fillers: For automatic return of fruit to field bins for presizing line.
12. **Bagging Systems:** A choice of automatic or semi-automatic systems to meet any need.
13. **Check Scale/ Counter/ Stamper:** Provides data for identification and control.
14. **Sealer:** Positive action prepares cartons for storage or shipping. Eliminates hand labor.

Figure 16. "The Systems Approach". This is a modern grading, sizing and packaging line for apples and pears. Dramatic advancements have been made over the early 1900s system of packing apples in barrels in the orchard. This line can be compacted in a rectangular packinghouse area. Water is used to handle fruit carefully in the dumping process and moving it to the grading and packing line. A special room is set aside for centralized controls for automatic and computerized production and record keeping, including the programmable weight sizer and electronic color sorter. (Courtesy R.A. Coffelt, FMC Corp., Box 448, Woodstock, VA 22664)

bottom which maintains the fruit at a specific level at all times and within easy reach of the packer. The bin rotates slowly and gives the packer opportunity to choose each apple; the rotating also facilities equal distribution of fruit in the bin. Figure 15.

Packing apples. Under ideal conditions, apples should be packed and stored or shipped immediately after picked. If the fruit is handled when more or less hard immediately after picking, there is less danger of bruising and of subsequent bluemold infection. The sooner apples are treated with a scald deterrent, the better. Another advantage of immediately sorting is that it gives an opportunity to sort out and immediately eliminate the culls which are not only a source of infection to the quality fruit, but may occupy valuable space in the packing shed or storage. Tendency is to pack fruit out of storage as sold.

Under practical conditions, it is desirable to keep some of the crop out of storage for a few days to a few weeks before it can be packed either for storage or for market. In northern areas this can be done with the cool autumn weather. With some cultivars susceptible to bitter pit, it seems advisable to delay packing for a month to six weeks to permit the disease to develop, and then eliminate affected fruit over the grading tables. If private storage space is available, most growers place the apples directly in storage, and pack them out in various containers as ordered. This practice is common today since most orchardists are growing high-grade fruit, but it is expensive for the orchardist with low-grade fruit, who pays for refrigerating a large quantity of culls which later will be discarded. He had best sort before storage.

The effect of delay in storage. Temperature has a profound effect on the ripening of apples. Softening of fruit proceeds about twice as fast at 70° F. as at 50° F., and at 50° it is almost twice as fast as at 40°, while at the latter temperature, it is fully twice as fast as at 32°. About 25 percent longer time is required for fruit to ripen at 30° than at 32°. Thus, it is clearly evident that the sooner fruit can be placed in storage and lowered to a temperature of 32° F., the longer it will keep in top-quality condition. Every effort within reasonable practical limits should be exercised to prevent the fruit from remaining in the orchard or in the packing shed longer than absolutely necessary.

Types of packages. Types of packages used for marketing apples have been everchanging. The wooden box has been replaced by corrugated tray-packed boxes for domestic distribution and export. Baskets of the one-half or one-bushel size are used only to a limited extent.

Several types of fiberboard containers are in use and may be packed similarly to a standard box. Most fiberboard boxes are designed to elminate bruising and flimsiness when packed. The tray-type separators, as shown in Figure 17, are used widely because of relative ease of packing and safety to fruit. Corrugated fiberboard is good insulating material, and consequently, it takes longer to cool the fruit, especially when sealed tightly. On the other hand it takes longer for cooled fruit to warm in these containers. Colored mesh bags have been replaced by "Poly" bags, mostly of three- to five-pound sizes (Figure 18).

In the choice of containers, there are several factors to consider. Some cultivars, such as McIntosh, are more tender than others and, therefore, demand a type of package which causes as little bruising as possible. In some seasons, the general crop is of higher quality than other seasons. Thus, it may justify a larger proportion of high quality containers. The grower should not be misled by the presence of a minor quantity of highly colored specimens in his crop. To pack these into the higher grades may so reduce the appearance of the remainder of the crop to make the project uneconomical.

When the general crop situation is short, the proportion of fruit packed in closed high-grade packages might be increased to an advantage. But when the crop is average or heavy, only the better fruit is likely to pay the attendant cost of the better packages. It is well for the grower to study the market preferences and make every effort to give the dealers and consumers the container and pack they want. It is too expensive and difficult to try to change the nature of the demand in order to suit the grower's own desires. Much of the fruit that is contended to be unsuitable for the better containers because of lack of uniformity, inferior color, and other reasons, is no longer profitable to grow for any purpose. The public has far passed the state where such fruit is acceptable to it, except in the form of by-products. Growers of this type of fruit must either change their practices or be forced out of business.

Packing in boxes. This operation has been replaced for the most part. For details, see former editions of this text.

Packing in consumer containers. For local trade, polyethylene bags (3-5 lbs.), shrink-poly trays of 4-6 apples, and small corrugated boxes or wire- or wooden-handle qt. or 2 qt. baskets are popular consumer packages. A small package of apples fits easily in the refrigerator and lasts until the next trip to the store. Corrugated containers and poly-wrapped cardboard trays are manufactured to accommodate a definite number and size of apples, packed uniformly. These small packages are packed out of storage and sold as needed throughout the winter or delivered to chain stores for their help to bag to please the trade.

Larger corrugated boxes containing about a bushel of fruit are usually jumble packed for near-by market outlets although some growers have used the tray pack system. If an orchardist is supplying apples to a nearby dealer

Figure 17. A programmable weight/sizer is at left, used where packing is by weight/count rather than physical measurement. Fruit is fed by molded singulator belts to individual cups. As the cup passes a scale with a setting corresponding to fruit weight, it is automatically dropped onto a soft belt to the packing table. (Right) This fruit is dropped from the weight/sizer onto cupped tray layers for the corrugated boxes to left bottom. Workers at upper right check fruit positioning and final quaility for uniformity. (Courtesy Hilltop Nursery, Hartford, MI)

regularly, these containers may be used over and over if the store is making sales by paper sack.

Waxing. Some cultivars produce more wax normally than others; brushing often is adequate on these to bring a gloss. With some packing houses, it is standard procedure to wax apples to reduce shrivelling, as with Golden Delicious, and it increases shelf life a few days vs. no waxing. There is little or no improved rot control. Apples are thoroughly washed with a special detergent, followed by a warm fresh water rinse, thoroughly heat dried before wax is applied. Customers are the ones to decide if they want to pay for extra glossiness. Waxing is done before the grading table. Careful checking is needed to avoid uneven "milky" streaks.

APPLE PROCESSING

Details of this phase of the apple business usually are covered in food technology. It should be noted, however, that the percentage of apple crops being processed has started leveling. About fifty percent of the United States apple crop goes into such products as sauce, juice and cider, frozen slices, powdered and concentrate apple juice (increasing sales), pies, baked, dried, frozen and canned products.

With the changing habits of the housewife toward less preparation of foods before meals, it is probable that a substantial amount of the crop will be processed in future years. About one-third of the processed apples are made into sauce, one-third into juice, cider and vinegar, about 9 percent frozen slices for bakery, and 5 percent dried.

Cultivars for processing. Studies at the University of Maryland have shown that for apples for slicing, York and Golden Delicious rank high in wholeness and firmness, the latter having particularly good color. Jonathan ranks next. Stayman, North Western Greening, and Rome Beauty are less desirable for this use. The latter cultivars, however, are good for baking. McIntosh and its relatives are generally down on the list with respect to quality for processing. Delicious is a good processor, but it has a good fresh market outlet.

A study was made by U.S.D.A. of the qualities of Delicious, Golden Delicious, Jonathan, Rome Beauty, Stayman, and Winesap with respect to applesauce and baking, as related to their raw qualities. Conclusions are: It is known that consumer preferences do exist for varying degrees of sweetness or tartness, firmness or softness of apples for eating raw. Nevertheless, from judges' ratings all apples in this study that were of good harvest quality were acceptable for eating raw before storage and after storage for as long as 5 months at 40° F. and for 6 months or more at 32°. In general, the same was true for apples used in making applesauce and baking. Delicious apples, though not commonly considered a cooking apple, made

acceptable sauce from apples freshly harvested or stored no more than 3 months. Jonathan and Stayman apples of higher acid content made smoother, thinner sauces than the other varieties. Jonathan and Rome Beauty made better baked apples. When of good harvest quality, Golden Delicious made acceptable baked apples. Delicious and Winesap baked apples had tough skins and hard flesh textures; hence, were less acceptable, as were Stayman baked apples because of soft and mushy texture.

Experience of H.F. Byrd, Inc., Winchester, Va., one of the largest apple growers and processors in the U.S., is that there is not a variety now grown that cannot be used to good advantage by the processors. Although certain varieties are best for certain products, *quality* and *proper stage of maturity* are more important. Some examples cited are: Golden Delicious is the best sauce variety, but if green or overly soft, it is not as good as other varieties. Stayman is the best juice apple, but sound, fully mature Delicious, Winesap, Jonathan, Grimes Golden, Rome and York are better for juice than a poor-quality Stayman. Most processors use a mixture of varieties in an effort to keep their apple products uniform in taste and texture throughout the year.

Apple butter. Processors can use any cultivar, but a high proportion of Ben Davis, rarely grown any more, gives a pleasing red color to the apple butter mix.

Apple juice. Sales of apple juice has been increasing, sauce declining. Again it is best to use a blend of cultivars. Byrd prefers 25% Golden and Red Delicious, 50% Jonathan, Winesap and Stayman, and 25% York and Black Twig. When one variety is used alone, Stayman or Winesap is preferred.

Apple sauce. A blend of at least four or five cultivars is suggested to maintain a uniform pack through the season. By using a number of varieties, processors can drop one that becomes scarce and add another without abrupt changes in flavor, color, texture or consistency of the sauce.

Apple slices. This may surprise some growers, but a number of cultivars now make just as good slices as York. Years ago, when canners started canning slices, York was the only cultivar that would stand up under the process. Buyers got into the habit of demanding Yorks for slicing. Processors have developed better methods, however, that permit them to make excellent slices from many varieties. Stayman is the favorite cultivar for slicing with the Byrd company and added that "eastern Red Delicious makes some of the best apple slices I have ever inspected." But a fully mature old York apple still is the best all-around cultivar for processing.

Apple varieties are listed in order of preference for processing:

First, old York; second, Golden Delicious; third, new Yorks; fourth, Stayman and fifth, Northwestern

Figure 18. (Left) Automatic bagger weighs fruit to set weight, fills and ties bags up to 18 bags./minute. One attendant can keep several machines in bags; a machine pays for itself in labor in about 1½ yrs. Preprinted twist-ties with cultivar names can be used, taking the place of preprinted bags of every size for every cultivar. (Right) Small hand-operated bagger with scales reading on right. (FMC, Woodstock, VA 22664)

Greening. After these, all cultivars are rated about the same. Three cultivars that may deserve slightly higher ranking are: Ben Davis, Gano and Lowry.

What processors want most is: *Clean, sound fruit that is fully mature.* This means getting apples at the stage when their flavor and sugar content are highest. Sugar content and flavor reach their peak at the same time in apples.

Large apples. Large apples are desired. For example, suppose a processor has 40 peeling units. If the apples are all 2¾ inches, he can handle 7,500 bushels in a nine-hour shift. Production will be about 10,200 cases of sauce. Now, if the processor has all 3-inch apples, he can handle 9,400 bushels in a nine-hour shift and production will be 13,000 cases. His fruit cost will be a saving of over 10% for the ¼-inch larger apples.

General Comments. At an apple processing conference held at the University of Maryland, College Park, a number of conclusions were drawn by processors, growers and government service workers which may be of interest. They are briefed as follows.

About 70% of the apple crop is processed in the Virginia area vs. 50% for the USA. Yield per tree in the U.S. has been increasing dramatically due to improved cultural practices and removal of marginal orchards. A big explosion has been and is occuring in the amount of Red

Delicious on the market. Golden Delicious is showing the biggest percentage increase because it is of value as a fresh and processing variety. Apple plantings seem to be governed more by current prices than probable future trends. Since it takes apple growers longer to shift out of the business than potato growers, they go through considerable misery while over-producing before the balance of production and marketing is adjusted. Processors are planting their own orchards to supply their business. There is a trend toward storing apples for processing in CA storages because it enables the processors to spread their peaks, minimize the labor problem, and cease building bigger plants to take care of peak operation. Growers in the northwest have a growing interest in processing whereas only limited interest was shown in the past. Freight rates show that there is an advantage for shipping of processed West Coast apples to the rest of the country as compared with shipping East Coast processed apples west.

It there is an overproduction of apples, growers can go to the U.S. government to get production-control laws similar to those in California. Future apple producing areas will be concentrated where climate, cost of production, processing and sales and distribution are the most favorable.

Figure 19. Selling apples in polyethylene bags has several advantages. Folding partition here can handle a number of cells in multiples of three. A 6-cell partition in 2 tiers is shown above, and, below, is a single 12-cell partition to protect the bagged apples. (Packing Corp. of Amer., Orrington Ave., Evanston, Il 60204)

Processors object to buying apples on a "junk" or "salvage" basis. Processing is becoming a paying proposition for both processor and grower and a quality product is needed. Michigan studies show that when there is a 10% price reduction in fresh apples or an apple product, there is a 5% increase in demand for fresh apples, a 44% increase in demand for applesauce, and a 23% increase in demand for apple juice.

Some apple growers want to produce for processors because they can "push" their trees to higher yields with more fertilizer, do less trimming, less spraying, do only limited chemical and hand thinning, undergo quick sales and movement of crop with little or no storage problem and lower labor costs generally. Growers estimate that they can save from 5 to 10% on growing costs when apples are produced for processors.

Cornell finds that apples can be harvested mechanically for processing in about as good condition as they can be picked. Some growers are permitting pickers to shake the trees and pick the fruit from the ground for immediate processing. With mechanical harvesting, one can do the work of 8 to 10 pickers. Damage to the apples is about 15% which is about the same as by hand picking. To use mechanical harvesting, a grower must be producing over 40,000 bushels. An automatic machine is needed to separate bruised apples by degree of bruising before processing. Bruised apples should be processed first, and

good apples possibly placed in CA storage. A bruise tends to grow in size with time — faster at a warm temperature; hence, bruised apples should be kept cool. A processor stated that with CA apples, a significantly better price per hundred pounds of processing fruit was obtained above the price for regular storage apples. CA storage has been found to reduce or arrest bitter pit development.

New York has a law that processors cannot accept fruit before a mutually acceptable price is reached. In western New York, 80% of the apples are produced for processing. The N content of McIntosh lvs is maintained at 1.7% for fresh fruit sales and 2.0% for processing fruit. Growers may double their yield by applying more N and maintaining the higher N content in the leaves. Cultivars processed are: Delicious, Golden Delicious, and Idared with Rhode Island Greening, McIntosh, Monroe, and Twenty Ounce of lesser importance. Cortland, Rome, Baldwin and Ben Davis also are processed. It is believed that McIntosh and Rhode Island Greening will continue for some time as processing cultivars.

Summer cultivars are generally not desired by processors. If breeders could produce an early cultivar adaptable to processing, growers could produce it more economically and it would help spread the processing season. An example of costs given by a Pennsylvania processor are: 35% direct cost of apples; 26% for containers; 16%, labor; 13%, sugar; 7%, overhead, 3%, cartons; and 0.6%, labels. Apple processors often complain of having no organized body of growers with whom to deal. It would be an advantage to both processors and growers to have a small talking body for each group to finalize deals.

Figure 20. Thick plastic "slip sheets" (under boxes) are widely used in some operations to replace pallets (take space, need repair, more expensive). Special attachment is needed on lift at right to clasp sheet, pull toward lift, then hydraulically push load off in storage or in truck.

143

Figure 21. Apples for processing are dumped into water tank, sorted, washed, peeled, cored and sliced, or squeezed, canned, heat-treated and packed in labelled cartons for storage or shipment. (Courtesy Tree Top Company, Yakima, WA.)

The citrus industry is using millions of dollars a year to promote fresh and processed citrus; processors and growers are on the same promotion team. California experience shows that it takes about four years to develop a product that will go well on the market. Cranberry promotion technique for juice should be used on apple juice to increase sales every month of the year, rather than having one tall peak of apple juice and cider sales at Hallowe'en. Ocean Spray Cranberry Company gives a bonus and helps finance advertising of poultry when cranberry sauce is included in the advertisement. Instruction from state agricultural extension services is needed to bring restaurant and bakery chefs up-to-date on how to bake good pies. This "gift" has been lost. Apple promotion booths should be set up at the annual National restaurant and dental meetings. Apple pie has decreased on menus due to an increase in tarts, which do not use as many apples as pies. A big volume of processed fruit goes to institutions and restaurants in No. 10 cans, and this outlet should be "nursed" and promoted more than in the past. U.S. Army personnel use more apples in fresh and processed form than the average civilian; a greater effort should be made to promote apple use by the U.S. Armed Services which is a big buyer. Consumption of canned peaches ranks first in the U.S. Army with applesauce second.

In California, there is Federal and State inspection of the fresh product before it is processed. This third party is needed for bargaining and protection.

The following cultivar characteristics are considered in apple processing: (a) Golden Delicious loses weight fast after harvest if not handled properly; (b) Spy has a tender skin as does Golden Delicious; (c) Stayman and McIntosh have a tough skin; (d) Rome and Idared are outstanding in storage life; (e) Rome and Monroe give high yield as peelers; (f) oblate or conical shaped varieties give less yield in processing; (g) Delicious has large seed pockets whereas Rhode Island Greening has small seed pockets; (h) York has a high ratio of processed product to initial volume of apples; (i) darkening of flesh near the core and coarseness of the fibrovascular bundles are undesirable characters; (j) McIntosh softens fast in a thermal-processing step, whereas York and Monroe are least affected; (k) Rhode Island Greening and Newtown Pippin score high in retention of juice while processing whereas McIntosh scores low; and (l) juice from McIntosh and Northern Spy changes color but little in storage, whereas juice from Red Delicious may brown. Apple juice is the biggest processed apple product in Canada with some interest in carbonated cider as in Europe and South Africa, both of which are marketing apple concentrate in the U.S.A. About 20% of the apple crop goes in apple juice, or 45% of the total processed apple crop. U.S.D.A. has developed a technique to identify adulterated juice that has been "watered down." An apple cider slush (ice crystals) is boosting sales in some areas.

Engineers and horticulturists at the West Virginia University, Morgantown, developed a technique for mechanically harvesting juice apples in the orchard, grinding the apples in the orchard, loading the slurry into a tank truck, hauling the slurry to the processing plant and unloading it into a tank, or directly into a juice line. Minutes later the slurry is pressed, strained, canned, pasteurized, labelled, boxed and ready to store or ship. Contact Steve Blizzard, Horticulture Department for details.

Cider. Cider, compared with apple juice, has no preservatives or sugar added and has not been heat-treated for canning. It is fresh squeezed and needs immediate refrigeration. Cider is selling the year round now with Florida a good market. Hot cider at ski resorts moves 2-1 to coffee. Stayman is a good base cultivar. For cider making, see U.S.D.A. Farmers' bull. 2125 (1971). (Day Equip. Corp., Goshen, Inc. 46526, sells equipment; also, Orchard Equip. Supply Co., Conway, Mass. 01341.)

Review Questions

1. Discuss the problems in estimating yields in orchard blocks.
2. What are the better techniques for deciding when a cultivar should be harvested? Analyze the problems involved.
3. What are the modern "stop drop" chemicals for holding apples on the tree at harvest? Discuss their merits and weaknesses. Their combined usage.
4. Discuss the importance of temperature during and after harvest up to storage.
5. Discuss modern packages for apples, merits of each.
6. What is meant by grade of apples? By size? Can different grades have different sizes or just one size, vice-versa? Give examples of grades, sizes, types of machinery for sizing.
7. List the factors important in designing a packing house.
8. Discuss mechanical harvesting, stage of development, efficiency, usage now and in the future.
9. Discuss the merits of popular apple cultivars for processing.
10. What factors are important in producing good color on red and yellow apple cultivars at harvest?

Suggested Collateral Readings

ABBOTT, J.A. et al. Acoustic vibration to detect quality of apple. ASHS 93. 725-738. 1968.

ABBOTT, J.A. et al. Effegi, Magnes-Taylor, and Instron fruit pressure testing devices for apples, peaches, and nectarines. ASHS 101(6):698-700. 1976.

AKEMINE, E.K. and T. Goo. Respiration and ethylene production during ontogeny of fruit. J. ASHS 98(5):378. July 1973.

ANDERSEN, E.T. Harvesting, storing and packing apples. Min. of Agr. and Food Bull. 44p. 1975.

ANDERSEN, E.T. and A. Hutchinson. High-density apple orchard studies in Ontario; Pluk-O-Trak harvesting aid. N.Y. Soc. Proc. 89-95. 1977.

APPLE profit pointers for Ethrel users. AmChem Products Co., Ambler, Pa. 19002.

BANGERTH, F., D.R. Dilley and D.H. Dewey. Effect of postharvest calcium treatment on internal breakdown and respiration of apple fruits. J. ASHS 97(5):679. 1972.

BATJER, L.P. and M.W. Williams. Effect of N-dimethylaminosuccinamic acid on watercore and harvest drop of apples. ASHS 88:76-79. 1966.

BETTS, Heather A. and W.J. Bramlage. Uptake of calcium by apples from postharvest dips. J. ASHS 102(6):785-788. 1977.

BIR, R.E., W.J. Bramlage, and J.R. Havis. Effects of freezing on mature apple fruit tissue. J. ASHS 98(2):215. March 1973.

BISHOP, C. and M. Klein. Photo-promotion of anthocyanin sythesis in harvest apples. HortSci. 10:126-127. 1975.

BLANPIED, G.D. Harvesting fresh market N.Y. apples. N.Y. (Geneva) Pl. Sci. Info. Bul. 49. 12 pp. (Good Bulletin).

BLANPIED, G.D. Apple ripening and light-dark cycles. J. ASHS 107:1 116-8, 1982.

BLANPIED, G.D. Predicting maturity dates for 'Delicious' apples in New York. HortSci. 14(6):710-711. Dec. 1979.

BLANPIED, G.D. et al. Ethephon to stimulate red color without hastening ripening on 'McIntosh'. J. ASHS 100:379-381. 1975.

BLANPIED, G.D. and V.A. Blak. Ethylene level and varietal flavor in 'Delicious' apples. HortSci. 11(6):596-7. 1976.

BORSBOOM, O. and H. Jonkers. Biblio. of growth regulators in fruit production. Sec. ISHS, le V.D. Boschst. 4, The Hague, Netherlands.

BREARLEY, N. and J.E. Breeze, Spectrophotometric measurements of skin colors of apples. J. Sci. Food and Agri.: 17pp. 62-64. Feb. 1966.

BRUN, C. et al. Optimum maturity for apple cultivars in Minn. Fruit Var. Journ. 35(3). 100-4. 1981.

CAREY, L.C. Containers in Common Use for Fresh Fruit and Vegetables. U.S.D.A. Farmers' Bulletin 2013. Request recent edition.

CARGO, C.A. and D.H. Dewey. Thiabendazole and Benomyl for the control of post-harvest decay of apples. HortSci. Vol. 5, No. 4, pp. 259. August 1970.

CREASY, L.L. Antitranspirant increases red color development in 'McIntosh'. HortSci. 11(3):251-2. 1976.

CUMMINGS, J.N. et al. Post-bloom Alar on Spigold. Fruit Var. Journ. 36:1 Jan. 1982.

DAVEY, Lance et al. Economic performance of mechanical tree fruit harvesters. Cornell Agr. Exp. Sta. June 1976.

DEWEY, D.H. (Ed) Hort Rpt. CA for storage, transport of perishable commodities. Proc. 2nd National CA. Res. Conf. at MSU. No. 28, 301 pp. July 1977. (Conferences are held at intervals; Wash. State Univ., 1981).

DOZIER, W.A., Jr., et al. Growth regulators on development of 'Delicious' apples. HortSci. 15(6):744. 1980.

DRAKE, S.R. et al. CA storage, processing on quality of 'Golden Delicious' sauce. J. ASHS. 104(1):68-70. 1979.

FARHOOMAND, M.B. et al. Ripening pattern of 'Delicious' apples and position on the tree. J. ASHS 102(6):771-774. 1977.

FMC Catalogues for fruit handling equipment. Contact the Lakeland, Florida or San Francisco, Calif. branches of food machinery and Chemical Corp. See July Amer. Fruit Grower.

FRIDLEY, R.B. Mechanical (fruit) harvesting. Wash. St. Hort. Ass'n. Proc. Dec. 1974. Contact author at Cal. Agr. Eng., Univ. of Cal., Davis. 95616.

GALLANDER, J.F. and D.W. Kretchman. Apple slice impregnation with fruit juices. HortSci. 11(4):395-7. 1976.

GREENE, D.W. and W.J. Lord. Light and spray coverage on red color of ethephon-treated 'McIntosh'. HortSci. 10:254-255. 1974.

GREENE, E.W., et al. Effects of low ethephon concentrations on quality of McIntosh apples. J. ASHS 90(3):239. May 1974.

GREIG, W.S. And L.L. Blakeslee. Potentials for apple juice processing in U.S. with implications for Washington. Coll. of Agr. Res. Ctr. Wa. St. U. Bull. 808. 49 p. 1974.

HAGEN, R.E., E.R. Elkins, and R.P. Farrow. Nutrient variations in canned fruits and vegetables. (Symposium Insert) HortSci. 14(3):251-6. (1979).

HALLER, M.H. and J.R. Magness. Picking maturity of apples. U.S.D.A. Cir. 711. 1944.

HAMMETT, L.K. el al. Soluable solids, acid content and days from full bloom of 'Golden Delicious' apple fruits. ASHS 102(4):429-431. 1977.

HARESNAPE, R.E. Canned deciduous fruit in Greece and Italy. FASUSDA M-304 Bull. 39. pp. 2. 1981.

HERTZ, L.B. Ethrel to stimulate coloring and ripening of apples. Fruit Var. 33(4):117. 1979.

HULME, A.C. Biochemistry of fruits and their products. Food Sci. Tech. Series of monographs. Vol. 1, 652 pp. Academic Press, N.Y., London, 1970. Vol. II 1971.

JAHN, O.L. and J.J. Graffney. Photoelectric color sorting of citrus fruits. Tach. bull. 1448. USDA, 56 pp. ilus. 1972.

JOHNSON, J.M. , A. Lopez and C.B. Wood. Relationship of apple grade and size to apple value in processing of apple slices. Food Technology 13: No. 7:385-390. Jul 1959.

KRAMER, A. and B.A. Twigg. Fundamentals of quality control of the food industry. Avi. Publ. Co., N.Y. City. 556 pages. 1966.

LABELLE, R.L. et al. The relationship of apple maturity to apple sauce quality. Food Technology 14:No. 9:463-468. Sept. 1960.

LAU, O. and N.E. Looney. Water dips increase CO_2-associated peel injury in 'Golden Delicious' apple. HortSci. 12(5):503-504. 1977.

LEUTY, S.J. Identification of maximum sensitivity of developing apple fruits to naphthalenaecetic acid. J. ASHS 98(3):247. 1973.

LIU, F.W. Interaction daminozide, harvest date, and ethylene in CA storage on 'McIntosh' quality. J. ASHS. 104(5):599-601. 1979.

LOMBARD, P.B. and R.R. Williams. The hard side of cider. HortSci. 9:420-424. 1974.

LOONEY, N.E. Ripening in 'McIntosh' I. Growth regulator effects on preharvest drop and fruit quality at four harvest dates. J. ASHS 100:330-332. 1975.

LOONEY, N.E. Control of Ripening in 'McIntosh' II. Effect of growth regulators and CO_2 on fruit ripening, storage behavior, shelf life. J. ASHS. 100:332-336. 1975.

LOPEZ, A. Some characterists of apple sauce canned in Virginia. Food Technology 16; No. 1:82, 85-86. Jan. 1962.

LOPEZ, A., C.B. Wood and J.M. Johnson. Trimming time and yield factors in processing of apple slices. Food Technology 13: No. 3:186-192. Mar. 1959.

MARINO, F. and D.W. Greene. GA and biennial bearing of McIntosh. ASHS Jrn. 106:5 593-6. 1981.

MARSHALL, H.N. New genetic sources of peonin; a new combination of anthocyanins in Rosa. J. ASHS 100:336-338. 1975.

MEADOR, D.B. Reducing russet on 'Golden Delicious' with silicon dioxide formulation foliage sprays. HortSci. 12(5):504-505. 1977.

MILLER, S.S. Preharvest antitranspirant sprays on size, quality 'Delicious' apples. J. ASHS 104(2):204-7. 1979.

MURPHY, E.F., C. Stiles and R.H. True. Effect of Succinic Acid-2, 2-dimethylhydrazide (SADH) on the sensory quality of 'McIntosh' apples. J. Amer. Soc. Hort. Sci. Vol. 96, No. 4,p. 472. 1971.

NATIONAL CANNERS ASSOCIATION. Monthly reports on canned stock of fruit. (Must be a member) 1133 20th St. NW. Wash. D.C. 20036.

NATURE, mechanisms and control of ripening. A Symposia. HortSci. 5(1):29-40. 1970.

OLSEN, K.L., H.A. Schomer and R.D. Bartram. Segregation of Golden Delicious apples for quality by light transmission. ASHS 91:821-828. 1967.

PETERSEN, D.L. and G.E. Monroe. Shaker-sequencing for tree crops. Trans. ASAE 17(4): 623-626. 1974.

POLLARD, J.E. SADH. ethephon and 2,4,5-T on color and storage quality of 'McIntosh' apples. J. ASHS. 99:341-343. 1974.

PRESTON, A.P. Relation of apple tree shape and fruit shape. Hort.Res. 17:9-13. 1977.

ROBERTS, B.L. and E.R. KRESTENSEN. Preharvest drop of 'Stayman' apples as influenced by SADH in dilute and concentrated form. HortScience 8(4):314. August 1973.

ROBITAILLE, H.A. and J. Janick. Ethylene production and bruise injury in apple J. ASHS 98(4):411. July 1973.

ROBITAILLE, H.A. and J. Janick and G.C. Haugh. SADH and apple bruise resistance. HortSci. 8(4):316. August 1973.

ROBINSON, J.R., C.W. Woodward and C.H. Hills. Making and preserving apple cider. U.S.D.A. Farmers' Bull. 2125. Seek up-date.

SCHNEIDER, G.W. Mechanism of fruit abscission in apple and peach. J. ASHS 102(2):179-81. 1977.

SCHOBINGER, U. and K. Darwoueska. Turbids in apple juice; effects on aroma. Zeit, fur obst-und Weinbau 108(82). Jan. 1973.

SCHOMER, H. et al. Effect of combinations of growth regulators on maturity and quality of "Tydeman's Red" apples. Hort. Sci. 6, Nov. 5, 1971.

SENSORY and Objective Evaluation of Horticutural Crops, Symposium. HortSci. 15(1):45-68. 1980.

SCOTT, K.J. and R.B.H. Wills. Postharvest application of calcium to control apple storage breakdown. HortSci. 10:75-76. 1975.

SFAKIOTAKIS, E.M. and D.R. Dilley. Induction of autocatalytic ethylene production in apple fruits by propylene in relation to maturity and oxygen. J. ASHS 98(5):504. Sept. 1973.

SHAW, G.W. Effects of harvest date and specific gravity on storage

behavior and raw and processed quality of 'Jonathan' apples. J. ASHS 99(1):63. Jan. 1973.

SHEAR, G.M. and C.R. Drake. Calcium in fruit with apple scab. Physiol Pl. Path. 1:313. 1971.

SLIP SHEETS - the pallet's successor? The Packer special sectn. Sept. 30. 1978.

SMITH, R.B. et al. Starch iodine test for determining stage of maturation in apples. Can. J. Plant Sci. 59:725-35. 1979.

SMOCK, R.M. and E.D. Markwardt. Harvesting and Packing Apples. Cornell Ext. Bull. 750. Revised Jan. Request recent edition.

SMOCK, R.M. and A.M. Neubert. Apples and Apple By-products. Interscience Publishers, Inc., New York, N.Y., 496 pp. 1950.

SMOCK, R.M. Freezing damage on attached and detached apple fruits. HortSci. 7(2):174. April 1972.

SOUTHWICK, F.W., I.E. Demoranville and J.J. Anderson. Influence of some growth regulating substances on pre-harvest drop, color and maturity of apples. Proc. Amer. Soc. Hort. Sci. 61:155-62. 1953.

SOUTHWICK, F.W., W.J. Lord, D.W. Greene, and L.G. Cromack. Residual effects of summer applications of succinic Acid, 2 2-Dimethylhydrazide on 'McIntosh' apple trees. J. ASHS 98(6):593. Nov. 1973.

SPANGLER, R.L. Standardization and Inspection of Fresh Fruits and Vegetables. U.S.D.A. Miscellaneous Publication 604. Request recent edition.

STADELBACKER, G.J. and K. Prasad. Postharvest decay control of apple by acetaldehyde vapor. J. ASHS. 99:364-368. 1974.

TAN, Soon Chye. Relations, interactions between pheylalanine ammonia-lyase inactivating system, and anthocyanin in Apples. J. ASHS. 104(5):581-6. 1979.

TUKEY, L.D. and J.J. Camba. Some mechanical properties of developing 'Delicious' and 'Golden Delicious' apple fruits as influenced by N-dimethylaminousuccinamic acid. J. A.S.G.S. 96:No. 2, March 1971.

UNRATH. C.R. Effects of preharvest applications of ethephon on maturity and quality of several apple cultivars. HortScience 7:(1). p.77. February 1972.

UNRATH. C.R. Interaction of irrigation, evaporative cooling and ethephon on fruit quality of 'Delicious' apples. HortSci. 8(4):318. August 1973.

U.S. STANDARDS (grade names) for farm products. USDA Agr. Hdb. 157. 35 pp. request recent edition.

VAN ARSDEL, W.B. Food dehydration. Volume I - Principles. Avi Publ. Co., N.Y. City. 196 pages. 1963.

WALSH, C.S. Endogenous ethylene and abscission of mature apple fruits. J. ASHS. 102(5):615-619. 1977.

WALTER, R.H. et al. Apple pomace is dairy feed. N.Y. (Geneva) Food and Life Sci. 8(1). 1975.

WALTER, T.E. Factors affecting fruit color in apples: a review of world literature. Rpt. E. Malling Res. Sta. for 1966 (1967). 7-82.

WATADA, A.E. et al. Apple sensory and headspace volatiles, soluble solids and titratable acids. ASHS 106(2) 130-2. March 1981.

WATT, B.K. and A.L. Merrill et al. Composition of foods, raw, processed, prepared. U.S.D.A. Handbook, 8. 190 pp. Request up-date.

WAY, R.D. et al. Growing. processing the Wayne Apple. N.Y. Food and Life Sci. Bull. 32.9 p. 1973.

WEBSTER, D.H., C.A. Eaves, and F.R. Forsyth. Stem-cavity browning of McIntosh apples. HortSci. Vol. 4(4):308. 1970.

WEISS, H.B. The History of Applejack, N.J. Agr. Soc., N.J. Dept. of Agr., Trenton, N.J. 08607.

WEST, D.A. et al. Labor management in apple picking. Wash. Agr. Exp. Sta. Cir. 533. 1971.

WILEY, R.C. and A.H. Thompson. Influence of variety, storage and maturity on the quality of canned apple slices. Proceedings. ASHS 75:61-84. 1960.

WILLIAMS, M.W., R.D. Bartram, and W.S. Carpenter. Carry-over effect of succinic acid, 2, 2-dimethylhydrazide on fruit shape of 'Delicious' apples. HortSci. 5:(4). August 1970.

YANG, S.F. Regulation of Ethylene Biosynthesis. HortSci. 15(3):238-243. 1980.

ZAHARA, M. and S.S. Johnson. Status of Harvest Mechanization of Fruits, Nuts, and Vegetables. HortSci. Vol. 14(5):578-582. 1979.

See additional references in former book editions.)

CHAPTER XI

Storing Apples

The price of apples during a normal storage season will gradually rise as the marketing season progresses. This normal seasonal price increase makes it desirable for the apple grower to devise a means of delaying his marketing to obtain the higher prices. To make the venture profitable, however, the cost of storage and any loss from decay of fruit during storage must be less than the increase in price return at the time of marketing. The venture is profitable as indicated by the increasing capacity of farm-refrigerated and CA (controlled atmosphere) storages.

Washington state probably has the best demonstration of the revolution occurring the past 20 years in increased production of Delicious and Golden Delicious and the extension of the marketing season by at least four months by the use of CA storages (Fig. 1), totalling a storage period of 11+ months. France also is in this class. Washington-grown apples dominate the market throughout the USA during the months of May, June and July and constitute a barrier to importation of apples from the southern hemisphere. Washington production will continue to increase to 1985 to 85 million boxes from 72 million boxes in 1980-81. This will necessitate even greater effort and ingenuity in improved storage techniques to get lasting condition and in moving these apples in the USA

and to foreign markets.

Reasons given by growers for owning their own regular and/or CA storages are: (1) Cost of storage on the farm is less than that of commercial storage, (2) the grower is better able to choose and satisfy his market, (3) the necessity of grading and packing at picking time is eliminated, (4) the apple storage can be used for holding strawberries, peaches, eggs, citrus and other products for rental or for better prices, (5) storage space is always available even in the heaviest crop years, (6) growers can receive the benefit of seasonal price advances, and (7) the benefits of quick cooling of apples from the orchard.

In the over-all picture, storages have three chief advantages whether owned by a commercial concern or by the grower himself: (1) To provide a means of holding apples in good condition for several months, thus permitting orderly distribution of the crop and preventing gluts on the market, (2) the orderly distribution of fruit tends to stabilize prices, and (3) a continuous supply of high-quality apples is available to the consuming public every month of the year. CA apples by the 1980s were competing with southeastern USA early apples, pressing an improvement in their market quality fall apples.

In concentrated apple growing regions such as in Washington State, the fruit is largely handled and stored in huge plants where the grower more or less loses contact with the fruit once it leaves his orchard.

Dr. William J. Bramlage, University of Massachusettes, Amherst 01003, assisted in this chapter revision.

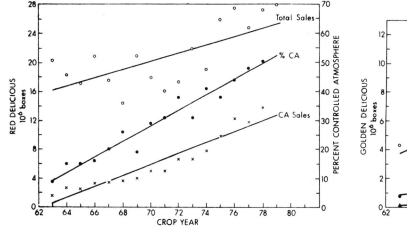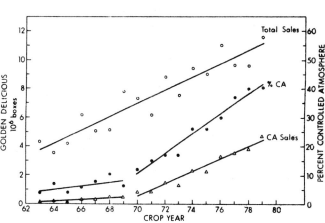

Figure 1. These two charts show the tremendous increase in sales of Washington-grown CA-stored Delicious and Golden Delicious apples since 1963. This trend is predicted to continue with the increased acreage and production in Washington, demanding more marketing pressure to move the fruit in the USA and to foreign markets. (Wenatchee Valley Traffic Association)

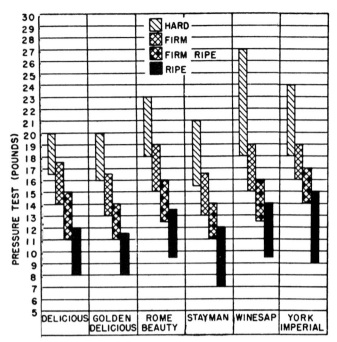

Figure 2. Chart shows a general range of fruit pressure tests, representing different stages of softening. Pressures of apple flesh can be obtained by using a Magness-Taylor pressure tester (see July Directory, American Fruit Grower). For maximum storage life, apples should be placed in storage at the "hard" stage. (U.S.D.A.)

THE FUNCTION OF STORAGES

Ripening takes place for the most part *before* harvest in the stone fruits, nuts, grapes, figs and berries whereas in the pear, apple, quince and persimmon ripening takes place largely *after* harvest. Ripening is described as the transformation of a physiologically mature fruit from an unfavorable state of color, firmness, flavor, aroma and texture to a more favorable stage for eating.

Harvested fruits are alive. They continue to carry on life processes which are essentially destructive. The basic object in storage is to keep these processes (ripening) at a minimum by lowering the temperature or by both lowering the temperature and modifying the atmospheric oxygen and carbon dioxide (CA storage).

The respiration rate of fruit (O_2 intake and CO_2 output) is doubled or trebled for each 18° F. (10°C) rise. Hence, an apple ripens two or three times as fast at 50°F. (10°C) as at 32°F. (0°C) and about two or three times as fast at 68°F. (20°C) as at 50°F. (10°C). For example, assume that apples are brought into the storage at 68°F. and are cooled to the "holding" temperature of 32°F. in one week. Assume the apples stay at 68°F. for 4 days, then the temperature is dropped to 50°F., held there for 3 days and then dropped to 32°F. The first 4 days at 68°F. are comparable to 28 days at holding temperature (32°F.), and the 3 days at 50°F. are comparable to 6 days at holding

temperature. In other words, the storage life of apples cooled under these conditions is shortened by thirty-four days. In actual practice, the conditions would not be so extreme because the "cool down" is gradual and starts immediately, and it is not expected that the apples would be at 68°F. (20°C) for 4 days. On the other hand, apples are often brought into storage at temperatures exceeding 68°F. *The importance of cooling the apples to holding temperature as rapidly as possible cannot be over emphasized (Fig. 2 and 3).* For this reason, refrigerating equipment is designed to cool the fruit in 24 hours. In actual practice the apples are not brought to storage temperature within this time, but actual practice has shown that this figure must be used to insure enough cooling capacity.

Respiration and other ripening processes must take place for the fruit to reach proper ripeness and eating condition. In ripening, the starch in mature firm fruit gradually changes to sugar; acids usually decrease; tannins and pectins change form; heat from respiration is given off, and the esters which are responsible for flavor and aroma of a variety, become more pronounced. As these chemical changes proceed, the fruit tends to soften and the ground color in apples changes from leafy green to yellowish shades. Eventually, the aroma and flavor develop fully, an optimum relationship is obtained between the amounts of sugar and acid, and the fruit softens to an ideal "eating stage." At this point, the fruit is said to be fully ripened with maximum quality (Fig. 4).

The generation of heat during the respiration and ripening processes is greater than is commonly realized and is a factor deserving important consideration in the design and operation of fruit cold-storage houses. The faster a fruit ripens the greater the quantity of heat generated. It is

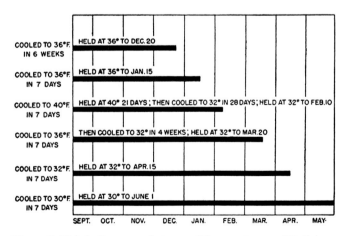

Figure 3. This is the normal storage life expectancy of Delicious apples when cooled at different rates and stored at different temperatures. For each week of exposure at 70 degrees F. before storage, deduct nine weeks of storage life at 32° F. for each week of delay at 53 degrees, deduct one month of storage life at 32 degrees. (U.S.D.A.)

148

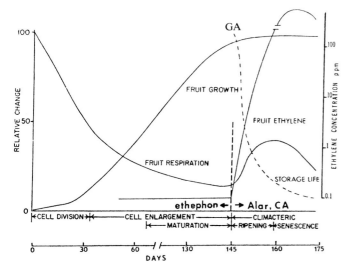

Figure 4. Growth and development of apple and pear fruits in relation to the effects of ethylene, ethephon, alar and controlled atmosphere storage on ripening and storage life. At the beginning of the climacteric, ABA (abscission) and ethylene are rising while GA (gibberellin) is decreasing. (David R. Dilley, Mich. State University, E. Lansing 48824.)

of interest that a Bartlett pear ripens faster than an apple at a given temperature, and, therefore, its greater heat of respiration results in large refrigeration demands, even when it is taken into storage at the same temperature as the apple.

As indicated earlier, the heat of respiration of fruit is collected and given off by machinery in the compressor room and some growers during the energy "squeeze" moved this heat into the packing house to reduce heating costs as much as 70%.

IMPORTANT STORAGE FACTORS

There are three key factors contributing to the longevity of apples in storage. These are *temperature, humidity,* and *composition* of the storage atmosphere. In operation of air-cooled storages the factor of *ventilation* is important.

Temperature. Ripening processes of fruit proceed slowly if the temperature is maintained at 30° to 32°F., which is considered most satisfactory for apple storage, except for some cultivars, as McIntosh, Jonathan and Yellow Newtown (brown core) which may develop soft scald or internal browning unless held at about 36°F.[1] These cultivars preferably should be kept in a separate room if available. The average freezing temperature for most fall and winter apples is abouit 28.5°F. with a maximum freezing temperature of 25.3°F.

---

[1]For relative lengths of storage season and susceptibility to storage scald for popular apple varieties, see Table 2, in Chapter II and Table 5, this Chapter.

CA storages may be run at a higher temperature during the holding period for certain cultivars, such as McIntosh; but when the storage is opened at marketing time, the temperature is usually brought down to 32°F. Consequently, CA storage design and capacity are based on this temperature of 32°F.

Humidity. Unless humidity is regulated in a storage, fruit will lose moisture and shrivel. The minimum relative humidity should be not lower than 85 percent. Relative humidities of 90 to 95 percent can be maintained without excessive fungus growth if the temperature is held at 32°F. The grower can determine relative humidity by using a sling psychrometer or a wet and dry bulb thermometer with accompanying conversion tables. These are available and inexpensive.

If the inside building surfaces or refrigeration equipment are substantially colder than the humid air of the storage room, condensation of moisture on the walls is likely to take place. This situation is common during the loading-in season when there is a 10°F. or more "split" between temperature of the return and discharge air from coils. Excessive condensation in a storage is undesirable because most of the moisture in the air during the storage holding months comes from the fruit; eventually, this situation will cause shriveling. Condensation of water on the walls and ceiling can be prevented during winter by adequate insulation in the walls to prevent the inner wall surface from becoming substantially colder than the air in the storage room.

Ventilation. Ventilation refers to the introduction of outdoor air into the storage room. Ventilation is necessary for air-cooled storages as a means of lowering temperature, as discussed later. However, ventilation for the benefit of the stored product itself is not essential. This is because in mechanically refrigerated storages of usual construction, carbon dioxide from respiration of the fruit does not build up to the point where it is toxic to the stored product, nor is oxygen reduced to the point where it is limiting in the respiratory process. However, oxygen may become so low in cold storages that some ventilation will be necessary for comfort of people working in them. Air circulation within a storage, as differentiated from ventilation, is important in moving air away from fruit and preventing the adjacent accumulation of ethylene gas and esters which, respectively, speed ripening and cause storage scald on susceptible cultivars. Do not store apples with potatoes, onions, cabbage, or nursery trees. The ethylene gas given off by the apples may damage these crops.

Fruit Condition. A most important factor in storage life of fruit is its condition. Proper firmness for the cultivar and maturity at time of storage are key. Only the best apples should be placed in CA storage for long holding. Cultural factors that govern condition such as nitrogen (Fig. 5) and calcium supply, pruning and use of certain

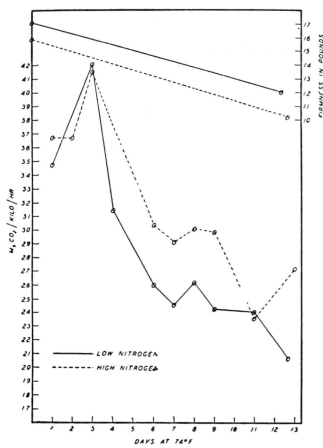

Figure 5. Respiration rate of apples is a good index of rate of ripening. Above chart shows that McIntosh from low-nitrogen trees respire more slowly and they are firmer than apples from high-nitrogen trees. (Cornell University).

chemicals as Alar, NAA and ethephon all can influence the condition of the fruit as it goes into storage.

TYPES OF STORAGES, OPERATION

There are essentially three types of storage buildings in use: (1) storages refrigerated with mechanical equipment, (2) refrigerated and controlled-atmosphere (CA) storages, and (3) air-cooled storages. A fourth approach, under experimentation, is a pressure-tight storage room where apples are held at only a fraction of atmospheric pressure. The air-cooled storages refrigerated with ice have for the most part disappeared in all except remote areas of the world.

MECHANICALLY REFRIGERATED STORAGES[1]

Estimating refrigeration load. *A word of caution is advisable. Salesmen for refrigeration equipment are*

---

[1]For latest information on *refrigerated farm storages,* request Cornell (Ithaca, N.Y.) Inform. Bull. 16, 33 pp, revised.

helpful in planning a storage and estimating needed equipment. The grower must be careful in quoting the rate of movement of fruit into the storage during the harvesting season. It is a common mistake for growers to underestimate this rate of movement; the grower must base his estimate upon the peak loading day. Salesmen are in competition and in order to underbid their competitors, inadequate refrigeration equipment is often sold and installed. It is, therefore, most essential that prospective owners of refrigerated storages know, or seek the advice of people who know, if the equipment in question has enough capacity to provide the desired conditions of both temperature and humidity under normal operation conditions for the storage.

Equipment that will handle the peak cooling load during harvest will be more than adequate for the rest of the storage season. The following quotes from Mich. Cir. 143 give the problems and methods involved for estimating the refrigeration load.

"The amount of refrigeration in British thermal units (B.t.u.) or tons of refrigeration (one ton of refrigeration is equivalent to a rate of heat removal of 288,000 B.t.u. per 24 hrs., or 200 B.t.u. per minute, in changing one ton of ice at 32° F. to water at 32° F. or 288,000 B.t.u.) required may be calculated rather accurately if the following information is available: (1) the area in square feet of the walls, ceiling, and floor; (2) the thermal transmission factors for the walls, ceiling, and floor or the detailed construction of each; (3) the average maximum difference between the outdoor and the storage room temperatures; (4) the maximum daily rate of loading of the product to be stored; (5) the maximum loading-in temperature of each kind of product and the length of time allowed to cool it to the desired holding temperature; and (6) the amount of heat that will be generated by workmen, motors, and lights in the storage room. In a more general way, one must calculate the amount of heat leakage through the walls, ceiling, and floor during the warmest period that the storage will be in operation, must calculate the cooling load for introduced goods, must calculate the heat generated by respiration of the stored goods, and must calculate or make an allowance for heat generated by workmen, motors and lights. Obviously, the calculation of the amount of refrigeration needed to accomplish a given job is rather complicated. Enough experience has been gained with farm storages so that it is possible to provide "rule of thumb" information as a guide to approximate refrigeration requirements.

"The amount of refrigeration required to take care of the daily heat leakage through walls, ceilings, and floors with *standard insulation* during the warmer portions of August and early September in Michigan for storages of 5,000, 10,000, 15,000, and 20,000 bushels capacity would approximate 0.9, 1.3, 1.9 and 2.2 tons, respectively, or from 0.11 to 0.15 ton per 1,000 bushels capacity. If the floor or ceiling insulation amounts to less than what is termed standard (standard recommendations given in this chapter), correspondingly greater refrigeration capacity would be needed to counteract heat leakage, and *if the floor is uninsulated, two to three times as much refrigeration would be needed to take care of heat leakage into the rooms.*

"The amount of refrigeration required to remove the field heat from products varies directly with the temperature range through which the fruit must be cooled and with the kind of product. Time or rate of cooling is immaterial if uniform quantities of product are loaded in daily. The same amount of refrigeration is required to do this cooling in one or two days as would be required to do the work in a week. To reduce the temperature of 1,000 bushels of peaches from 82° to 32° F. requires more than eight tons of refrigeration. The same quantity of apples maturing later when outdoor temperatures are lower, could be cooled from 72° to 32° F. with about six tons of refrigeration. The difference between the peaches and apples may be explained mostly by the ten-degree difference in initial temperatures and partly by the heavier weight of peaches.

"The heat generated by respiration of fruits must be taken into consideration (Table 1). Apples at 65° respire about eight times as rapidly as apples held at 32° F. This means that the former generate eight times as much heat as apples at 32° F. Therefore, if fruits are cooled slowly, they generate several times as much heat as do those that are cooled rapidly. The amount of refrigeration necessary to counteract heat generated while apples are cooling through a range of 40° F. in six days is at least one-third as much as the cooling load amounts to. If the cooling time is reduced to three days, only one-half as much refrigeration will be

TABLE 1. EVOLUTION OF HEAT BY APPLES
AT VARIOUS TEMPERATURES[1]

Temperature (F.)	Heat per ton in 24 hours
Degrees	*B.T.U.*
30 to 32	220 to 660
38 to 40	880 to 1,540
45 to 47	1,760 to 2,860
50 to 52	2,640 to 4,620
55 to 57	3,520 to 5,720
60 to 62	4,400 to 7,260
65 to 67	4,840 to 9,020
70 to 72	5,280 to 10,780
75 to 77	5,700 to 12,540
80 to 82	6,160 to 14,300
85 to 87	6,600 to 16,060

[1]These figures were taken from USDA Agr. Hdbk. 66, *The Commercial Storage of Fruits, Vegetables, and Florist and Nursery Stocks* by J. M. Lutz and R. E. Hardenburg.

needed to counteract heat of respiration. This means that the 1,000 bushels of apples referred to in the last paragraph would require an additional two tons and one ton of

refrigeration, respectively, for cooling during a six-day or a three-day period.

"Nearly one-fourth ton of refrigeration per day is required to neutralize the heat generated per horsepower by electric motors running continuously in the storage room. A workman generates about one-fourth as much heat in an hour as does a one horsepower motor, and nine electric lamps of 100 watts each would be the equivalent of another such motor.

"If the maximum daily rate of loading fall apples into a storage is 10 percent of its holding capacity (it should not be more than this, preferably), there should be about one ton of refrigeration capacity for each 1,000-bushel capacity of the storage. If the loading rate is 7 percent of the total capacity of the storage, one should be able to get good refrigeration with a machine that will deliver three-fourths ton for each 1,000-bushel capacity of the storage. These suggestions are approximations that take into consideration all the factors discussed in preceding paragraphs, but they must be regarded as rather rough measuring sticks for storages that are adequately insulated.

"Once the stored goods are cooled to a holding temperature of 32° F., little refrigeration is required to take care of heat leakage and the heat of respiration. One ton of refrigeration per day would probably be ample to maintain the temperature in a 10,000-bushel farm storage in late fall or early winter when outdoor temperatures are relatively low."

Refrigerants. A refrigerant is a liquid that evaporates or boils at low temperatures and relatively low pressures. When the liquid of refrigerant boils and changes to a gas in

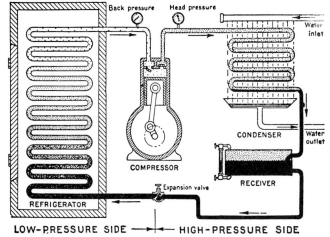

Figure 6. Essential parts of a compression refrigeration system. Refrigerant leaves compressor as a gas (dense stippled area) under pressure; gas is cooled and condensed to a liquid (solid-black area) in the condenser and thence stored in storage room, admitting liquid refrigerant to expansion coils in storage room; liquid refrigerant gradually changes to a gas and in the process absorbs heat from the storage room; gas then returns to compressor and operation is repeated. (U.S.D.A.)

the storage-room coils, it absorbs heat from the room and the stored product. The gas with the heat is then piped outside the storage room where it is compressed and passed through a condenser which absorbs and dissipates the heat, changing the gas back to a liquid for repeated use. The heat can be picked up and blown into the packing shed to reduce energy costs up to 70%.

Equipment needed for circulating and changing a refrigerant from a gas to a liquid is shown in Figure 6. The *compressor sucks* the refrigerant vapor from the evaporating coils, and compresses it. The vapor under pressure is then forced by the compressor into a set of coils known collectively as the *condenser* where cool air or water extracts the heat from the vapor and reconverts it to a liquid. The liquid is stored in a tank and released to the storage-room coils by an *expansion valve* which is opened and closed by a thermostatic switch. This process is done over and over in cooling and maintaining a cold storage-room temperature.

Refrigerants commonly used are Freon, ammonia, and methyl chloride. Freon is probably the most popular refrigerant in farm storages. It is odorless and nontoxic, but leaks are difficult to locate. Ammonia gas is toxic to fruit if it escapes in large quantities (Figure 7). Methyl chloride has the disadvantage of being poisonous to man in high concentrations. Cost of equipment and the refrigerant in the long run is about the same for the three refrigerants listed. Ammonia is widely used in Northwest CA rooms.

Compressors. A compressor is essentially a pump. It somewhat resembles a gasoline engine in that there is a crank shaft, connecting rods, pistons, and valves which require care similar to that needed by the parts in a gasoline engine. Compressors are either water-cooled or air-cooled. Those using Freon or methyl chloride are smaller, lighter, and are operated at faster speeds with less vibration as compared with the ammonia compressors. In buying compressors, company reputation is more im-portant than mechanical characteristics, since reliable companies will guarantee and repair their equipment.

The capacity of a compressor depends upon the number of cylinders, their diameter, the length of stroke, and the speed at which the compressor operates. Capacity is usually measured in tons of refrigeration per 24 hours, but this varies with temperature of refrigerant, cooling medium surrounding the condensing coils, and the speed of rotation. For example, a compressor using Freon will deliver 9.75 tons of refrigeration at a refrigerant gas temperature of 10° F., and 20.8 tons at a gas temperature of 30° F. At twice the operating speed, the machine will produce about twice as much refrigeration. The h.p. of a motor required to operate a compressor runs about 1.5 h.p. per ton of refrigeration for farm-size installations of from 2 to 20 tons capacity.

It is more economical to install two compressors than one of the same total capacity. The chief refrigeration load comes at harvest time. Considerably less refrigeration is needed once the products are cooled to the holding temperature. Thus, with two machines, one machine should be capable of producing about two-thirds of the total required refrigeration and the other producing the remaining one-third. Both machines will operate during the loading-in period, then the larger one can carry the load for a time, and eventually, the smaller one may provide the necessary refrigeration during the colder winter months. This arrangement is better and more economical than having one machine with a change of speed of operation according to load. The compressors are operated thermostatically on not more than a two-degree range in storage temperature.

Condensers. A condenser absorbs and dissipates the heat which the refrigerant picks up in the storage room. In one type, a pipe is placed within a pipe with cool water running in the inner pipe and the refrigerant running in the outer pipe. This type of arrangement is usually mounted on the wall in the compressor room. In another type of condenser, there is a series of coiling pipes within a large metal cylindrical shell. Water flows through the pipe and the refrigerant on the outside through the shell.

The evaporator condenser is commonly used where water is scarce. The coils carrying hot refrigerant gases are in a metal outside cabinet. Water is sprayed down over the coils while a fan blows air up through the coils, increasing evaporation and cooling. In winter only the fan is needed.

Expansion Coils. The coils in which the refrigerant evaporates or expands from liquid to gas may be either inside or outside the storage room. In what is known as the "brine system" the evaporating coils are usually outside of the storage room and immersed in a bath of saturated brine solution (calcium or sodium chloride). The brine is thus cooled and then circulated by pump into the storage room through coils. This method was used for cooling

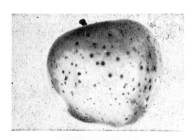

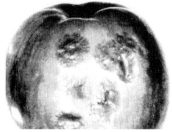

Figure 7. (Top) Injury from ammonia leakage from pipes in storage. (Below) CO_2 external injury in CA storage, occurring some seasons in spite of following recommendations. (Courtesy Ohio State and N.Y. Agr. Exp. Stas.)

some commercial storages, but rarely used in farm storages. The advantage is no danger of injuring the fruit by excessive gas leaks.

With the "direct expansion" cooling units, the refrigerant flows into coils in contact with the storage room air where it expands to a gas and absorbs heat; no brine solution is involved. In most designs the coils are concentrated into a small space and the air is moved rapidly through them by means of a high speed fan, as shown in Figure 8. This type of forced air circulation and refrigeration is widely used in farm storages. The warmer air enters the unit at the base, is sucked over the cooling coils, and blown out through the upper vents. The advantages of this system over numerous pipes along the walls or against the ceiling are (1) the air is moved rapidly throughout the room, avoiding "dead air" spaces, (2) the smaller amount of coil system can be defrosted easily at regular intervals, (3) considerably less space is occupied in the storage room by refrigeration equipment, (4) there is less trouble from storage diseases, such as brown core and internal breakdown, and (5) a uniform temperature is automatically maintained within a narrow range of 1° or 2° F.

Air Circulation. The fan in the blower should be large enough to move at least 100 cu. ft. per minute of air per ton of refrigeration. In other words, if the equipment is of five and one-half tons capacity, the fan should pass about 5,500 or more cu. ft. per minute.

Defrosting of blower units is necessary, up to several times daily, and less often during the storage season than during the loading period. Collection of frost on the coils not only reduces air circulation through the closely spaced coils, but also interferes with heat transmission into the pipes.[1] Defrosting can be accomplished by several methods: (1) passing hot refrigerant gas directly to and through the expansion or cooling coils; (2) shutting off the compressor and continuing to operate the fan when the storage temperature is 34° F. or higher; (3) drawing outside air over the coils by fan; (4) periodic spraying of water over the cooling coils, and (5) continuous spraying of brine water over the coils, or (6) electrical heaters.

Humidity Control. Moisture in the air must condense when the saturation or dew point (100 percent relative humidity) is reached for a given air temperature. Thus, when air at 34° F. with a relative humidity of 88 percent is cooled to 31° F. by coming into contact with refrigeration coils or wall surfaces, the saturation point of the atmosphere is reached; with further cooling, there is condensation of moisture on the walls or coils. Water so-collecting on the coils or walls and running out of the

Figure 8. (Top) Height of this storage ceiling accommodates 8 stacked apple bins. Note type of refrigeration system upper left. (Bottom) Looking up at unit coolers, pipes, and catwalk located overhead in the center of a large cold-storage room. Coils are defrosted by warm water from condenser, electrical heating element, or fresh water. (U.S.D.A.)

storage through drains must come indirectly from the stored apples or through the walls and ceiling, or from both sources. This moisture must be replaced, especially if it is coming from the fruit. With proper equipment operation, humidity can be maintained above 90% and prevent fruit shriveling.

So-called "high-humidity maintenance systems" are being used which utilize secondary refrigeration wherein water or anti-freeze solution is cooled and circulated through the room cooling unit. In CA storages this can be used as a CO_2 scrubber. The humidity loss is cut to 1% vs former 4%, or for 10,000 bu over 6 mos. CA storage this would be a loss of 100 vs 400 bu weight (42 lbs/box) in fruit water-loss.

STORAGE CONSTRUCTION

Walls. In the smaller refrigerated storages (Figure 10), a

---

[1] A blower unit is recommended capable of furnishing refrigeration at peak load with a 10° F. temperature difference (T.D.) between the refrigerant and the return air. The T.D. should drop to 2° F. after field heat is removed.

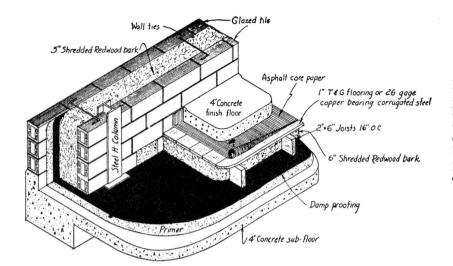

Figure 9. This diagram shows the junction of wall and floor of a refrigerated storage. Instead of lumber and shredded redwood bark between concrete slabs of floor, two to three inches of cork board, rock cork, or similar materials may be used. In place of the steel H-column, masonry pilasters may be built into and outward from the outer wall unit. (Michigan State University).

common type of construction is a four-inch glazed tile wood frame or masonry block wall and an inner wall of the same set three to six inches inside the first wall, with the space between the two walls containing fill-type insulation material (Figure 11). Regranulated cork, expanded mica, and shredded redwood bark fiber are filling materials that are commonly used. A vapor seal, if it seems advisable, is applied to the inner surface of the outer wall. A common construction of large commerical storages consists of a masonry wall of concrete, tile, steel frame, or brick at least

Figure 10. Farm apple storages. (Top) Fourteen thousand bushel refrigerated storage insulated with five inches of regranulated cork in the walls and floor and seven inches in the ceiling. Storage was first air-cooled with forced ventilation, then changed to forced-air circulation through melting ice, and finally equipped with mechanical refrigeration. (Bottom) A ten thousand bushel refrigerated storage with sales room in front. Note small entrance door for fruit at left and water-cooling system for refrigeration condenser at rear.

8 inches thick, a vapor barrier, and 4 inches of styrofoam. Insulation is set in asphalt adhesives or mortar. Or, a 2-3 inch spray-foam layer of polyurethane insulation-vapor-barrier may be used.

Doors. A *minimum number* of doors should be used. A 5 feet wide by 8 feet high door size is most desirable to accommodate lift trucks and pallets. Where only bushel containers are used, a considerable saving in refrigeration can be obtained if one or more doors about two feet square are provided, through which fruit can be moved on roller conveyors in and out of the storage (Figure 10). Hand operated or floor tripping mechanisms may be employed to open and close doors mechanically. An air door or air curtain may be used at one door to permit easy passage through an open door with a minimum rise in cold storage temperature (Figure 12).

Ceiling. About 20 to 25 percent more insulation should be provided in the ceilings than in side walls. Corkboard or other rigid type insulating materials can be applied below the joists as shown in Figure 10. Popular types of ceiling construction are either lath. (metal preferred) and cement plaster below the joists, copper-bearing sheet metal or redwood boards. The area between the joists is filled with dry-fill insulation, allowing it to rest on the rigid ceiling construction. If a loft floor is placed above the ceiling, a two- to three-inch air space should be left between the fill-type insulation and the floor in order to provide ventilation and drying to the insulation material. Insulation should be continuous at the joints of the ceiling walls. There should be no obstructions on the ceiling surface which will interfere with a clean sweep of cold air across the top of the stacked fruit. If beams are necessary, they should run parallel with the air flow.

Floor construction. Floors in air-cooled storages are seldom insulated. The usual procedure is to level the dirt floor, fill in with several inches of clay soil, pack well, and add two inches of pea-gravel. If a concrete floor is used in the air-cooled storage, it should be level in order to permit

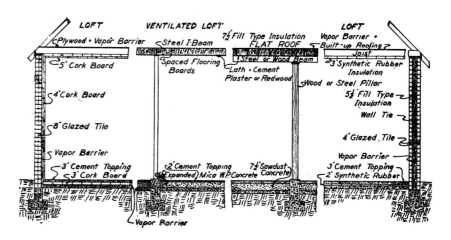

Figure 11. Several methods of construction are shown for refrigerated farm storages. Left section shows typical construction of walls, ceiling, and floor insulated with cork board. Other sections show various materials in sufficient amounts to provide same insulating values as corkboard. Ceiling construction should provide unobstructed air flow in storage room. The insulation of junctions of walls and floors, and walls and ceilings should be continuous. (Michigan State University).

water to stand to help raise the humidity.

Refrigerated storages must have insulated floors (Figure 9), because uninsulated floors may increase the refrigeration load by 30 percent. Methods of floor construction for commercial storage floors is to pour a concrete base three to four inches thick, apply an asphalt vapor barrier on top of the concrete, apply three inches of corkboard in asphalt, mop the top of the corkboard with asphalt, and then finish with three-inch cement topping for wearing surface. If other types of construction are preferred, an equivalent insulation should be provided. Floors should be designed to support 210 pounds per square foot for a ten-foot ceiling and 260 pounds per square foot for a twelve-foot ceiling, or greater support for higher stacking.

Insulation and Insulating Materials. Insulation is used in wall, ceiling, floor, or roof construction primarily to reduce the rate of heat transfer through the structure. The ability of a material to conduct heat through a unit thickness is called its *thermal conductivity;* the resistance of the material of unit thickness to the flow of heat is its *thermal resistivity.* The conductivity of a material is the reciprocal of its resistivity; that is, conductivity = $\frac{1}{\text{resistivity}}$.

In heat flow through a wall, the difference in temperature from one side to the other is the force that causes the heat to flow. The thermal resistivity of the insulation tends to retard the flow of heat, and the area of wall involved determines the total quantity of heat flowing through the wall.

The temperature inside the refrigerated storage is much lower than the outdoor temperature during loading time. Consequently, the temperature difference, or the force tending to move the heat, is relatively high. To keep the heat flow into the storage at a minimum, an insulation that has a high resistance to the flow of heat is used.

Many types of insulation materials are available. Some of them are commercial and some are native, as sawdust, shavings, and the like. To be of greatest value, the materials should have good insulating qualities, must be dry, and should be economical, relatively easy to put in place, odor free, and vermin proof.

Based on physical characteristics, insulating materials may be divided into four classes: (1) reflective, (2) rigid, (3) flexible, and (4) loose fill (Table 2).

Reflective insulation derives its name from the fact that it has a bright shiny surface that reflects radiant heat as aluminum sheets. For best results, a ¾-inch air space between this insulation and any other material, and between the layers of this type of insulation, is recommended. When reflective insulation is placed between studs, precautions must be taken to prevent air movement by convection between the layers. Air next to the layer on the warm side rises and that on the cold side falls thus setting up convection currents that take up heat on the warm side and give it up at the cold side. This increases the rate of heat transfer and reduces the effectiveness of the insulation. To prevent this air movement, horizontal wood strips should be placed about 30 inches apart between the layers.

Figure 12. In large cold storage rooms this type door can be left open while loading and unloading fruit. Above-door equipment creates an air curtain that holds cold air in storage room. (Top left, courtesy Mich. State Univ.; bottom left, W. Steuk, Venice, Ohio).

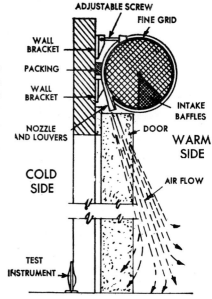

155

Rigid insulation is made up of rigid boards of insulating material that can be laid up against the sheathing. Rigid insulation has considerable structural strength, and some types are used as sheathing.

Styrofoam has largely been replaced by polyurethane which is within cost range and twice as effective (Table 2). However, polyurethane requires flame-proofing to be acceptable.

Flexible insulation is made up of blankets or bats of insulation material that can be laid up against sheathing between studs and joists. These blankets have no structural strength and depend upon the structure to support them.

Loose-fill insulation consists of loose or granular insulating material. This type of insulation has no structural strength and must be poured into a rigid container as the space between the inside and outside sheathing. Included in this class are native materials, such as sawdust and shavings.

TABLE 2. THERMAL INSULATION AND CONDUCTIVITY PRACTICAL VALUES FOR VARIOUS MATERIALS[1]

Material	Conductivity (k)[2]	Conductance (C)[3]	Thermal insulation Resistivity (1/k)[4] (per inch of thickness)	Thermal insulation Resistance (1/C)[5] (thickness listed)
Building materials				
Common woods (average) 1 inch thick	0.92	—	1.09	—
Common woods (average) 7/8 inch thick	—	1.05	—	0.95
Plywood, 3/8 inch thick	—	2.12	—	0.47
Stony masonry	12.50	—	0.08	—
Concrete (gravel aggregate)	12.50	—	0.08	—
Concrete (cinder aggregate)	4.90	—	0.22	—
Concrete (lightweight aggregate)	2.50	—	0.40	—
Concrete block, 8 inches thick	—	1.00	—	1.00
Concrete block, 12 inches thick	—	0.80	—	1.25
Cinder block, 8 inches thick	—	0.60	—	1.66
Cinder block, 12 inches thick	—	0.53	—	1.88
Plaster Board, Sheet Rock, Gypsum Board, 3/8 inch thick	—	3.73	—	0.27
Insulating materials				
Reflective				
Reflective sheets 5 thicknesses, spaced 3/4 and 3/4 inch between insulation and sheathing	—	0.077	—	13.02
Rigid				
Corkboard	0.30	—	3.33	—
Wood fibre board	0.312	—	3.21	—
Mineral wool board	0.321	—	3.12	—
Vegetable fibre board	0.346	—	2.85	—
Foamglass	0.40	—	2.50	—
Styrofoam	0.25	—	4.00	—
Urethane[6]	0.12	—	8.33	—
Blankets				
Mineral wool	0.27	—	3.70	—
Wool fibre (Insulite)	0.33	—	3.00	—
Cellulose fibre	0.27	—	3.70	—
Glass wool (Fiberglass)	0.27	—	3.70	—
Loose-fill				
Regranulated cork (3/16-inch particles)	0.31	—	—	—
Buckwheat hulls	0.36	—	2.78	—
Vermiculite	0.48	—	2.08	—
Shavings (ordinary dry)	0.41	—	2.44	—
Sawdust (ordinary dry)	0.41	—	2.44	—
Cinders (screened and fine material discarded)	1.25	—	0.80	—
Redwood Bark	0.26	—	3.90	—
Miscellaneous				
Air space (vertical, 3/4 inch or more, ordinary surfaces)	—	1.10	—	0.91
Surfaces (ordinary non-reflective wall) still air	—	1.65	—	0.61
15 mph wind velocity	—	6.00	—	0.17
Roofing materials				
Asphalt shingles	—	6.50	—	0.15
Built up roofing (3/8 inch)	—	3.53	—	0.28
Heavy roll roofing	—	6.50	—	0.15
Wood shingles	—	1.28	—	0.78

[1]These values are from various sources, such as United States Bureau of Standards and manufacturers specifications.
[2]*Conductivity* (k) is rate of heat transfer in B.T.U. per hour per degree difference in temperature (F.) per square foot of surface through 1 inch thickness of material.
[3]*Conductance* (C) is the rate of heat transfer in B.T.U. per hour per degree difference in temperature (F.) per square foot of surface through the thickness as manufactured and used.
[4]*Resistivity* (1/k), the reciprocal of k, is the insulating value of 1 inch of the material.
[5]*Resistance* (1/C), the reciprocal of C, is the insulating value of the thickness of the material as manufactured and used.
[6]Because of fire possibility, there is some shifting to fiberglass bats where 6 inches is equivalent to 4 inches cork. Or, cover urethane with 2 inches cement mortar or cover with the fire-barrier Zonolite-3300. And don't use storage as workshop. Polystyrene may be less expensive than Urethane.

To determine the particular insulation to use, the grower should choose the one that gives him the desired insulating value for the least expenditure for material and construction.

Materials of construction other than insulation also offer small resistance to the flow of heat. It should be included in determining the overall rate of heat flow.

There is additional resistance to heat flow from a solid surface to air in contact with it and from air to a solid surface. In storage-wall construction two of these surfaces need to be considered, one inside and one outside. The outside surface offers less resistance because the sweeping action of wind tends to increase the rate of heat transfer.

In some types of wall construction, air spaces are left. These air spaces resist the flow of heat mainly because of the resistance of the bounding surfaces. Under most normal conditions, the resistance of an air space increases with the thickness of the space up to ¾ inch. Beyond that, the increase is slight and is neglected. For this reason, the conductance of an air space is usually given for "¾ inch or more," and includes surface conductances.

Thermal insulating values, and conductivities and conductances of some of the materials more commonly used for refrigerated storage construction are given in Table 2.

Minimum insulation requirements. Through experience, minimum insulating values for floors, walls, and ceilings have been set for refrigerated apple storages in climates such as New York State. For walls, a minimum of 4 inches of corkboard or *its equivalent in insulating value* has been recommended. Where loose-filled types of insulation are used, a minimum of 6 inches is recommended. Although some of the loose-fill types have the same insulating value as corkboard, a greater thickness is recommended because plaster protruding from the joints in masonry walls reduces the effective thickness, and it is also difficult to pack these types of insulation to optimum density.

The thickness of insulation in the ceiling should be 25 percent greater than in the walls because roof and attic temperatures may run 30° F. higher than outdoor air temperatures in the summer and early Fall. A well ventilated loft may reduce this temperature difference to 10° F. A minimum of 5 inches of corkboard or from 7 to 8 inches of loose-fill type of insulation is recommended for the ceiling.

Up to 30 percent of the total heat leakage is through an uninsulated floor. For floor insulation, a minimum of 4 inches of corkboard or its equivalent is recommended.

Vapor Barriers. Keep insulation materials dry. Water is one of the best conductors of heat. Water vapor barriers in the walls, floors, and ceiling are essential. Movement of water vapor in most cases is from the outside to the inside; this is when the outside temperature is higher than the inside temperature. For storages to be operated at 32° F. throughout the year, it is recommended that a vapor barrier be applied between the outside supporting wall and the insulation. For storages operated at 32° F. from peach harvest until spring, no vapor barrier is needed if the outside supporting wall is well-laid face tile. Face tile itself is a good vapor barrier.

Since there is no perfect vapor barrier, use a material which reduces the vapor movement as much as possible. Building paper used as a barrier should be asphalt impregnated, coated and glossy surfaced, and should weigh at least 35 pounds a roll of 500 sq. ft. Rough-coated masonry walls should first be painted with two applications of cement plaster to give an even surface for the vapor barrier. Then the interior surfaces of the walls, ceilings, and floors are given a coat of asphalt paint to seal the surface, after which two layers of asphalt impregnated paper are cemented over the asphalt coated surfaces. No vapor proofing should be placed on the inside of the insulation material. If there is either natural or forced air ventilation in the loft, there is no need for a vapor barrier in the ceiling. Air-cooled storages with face-tile construction do not need a vapor barrier. Consult an engineer for latest vapor barrier improvements.

CONTROLLED ATMOSPHERE (CA) STORAGES

Kidd and West stimulated the initial controlled atmospheres work in England in the 1930's. It was developed commercially by Robert M. Smock, Cornell University, starting in the early 1940's. CA storages hold an important increasing tonnage of the apple crop stored over the world. Over 40 million bushels were CA stored in the U.S. in the early 1980s or over 40 percent of the stored apples. The advantages are: (1) storage life of apples can be prolonged beyond the normal life in regular cold storage, (2) some varieties subject to low temperature disorders, such as McIntosh, can be held for a long period at a temperature above 32°F., (3) fruit removed from storage keeps longer than fruit held an equal time in regular storage, (4) it is rodent proof, (5) a relative humidity can be maintained above 90 percent with little danger of mold growth, and (6) apples removed from CA storage have a better crisp "fresh apple" taste. CA apples have been bringing more money per box than regular stored apples, but this margin of difference may gradually lessen as more CA apples are available. CA storage costs were 40-60¢ more/bu than regular-stored apples in the early 1980s.

The essential features of CA storage are (see Fig. 13): (1) use of mechanical refrigeration to maintain temperatures of 30°F. or 36-38°F., depending on the cultivars stored; (2) the storage room is specially constructed *gas-tight;* (3) oxygen also is reduced and carbon dioxide is increased by the respiring apples; (4) excess carbon dioxide is removed by water scrubbing, or supplemented by caustic soda when necessary, or carbon dioxide is absorbed by dry (except in

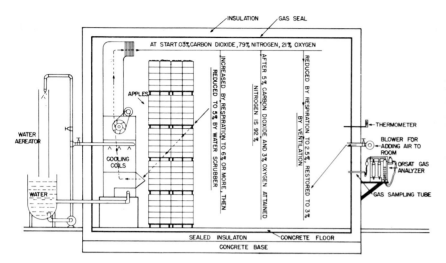

Figure 13. Vertical diagrammatic sketch of a conventional controlled-atmosphere (CA) storage room indicating how the atmosphere is controlled. With gas generators, the atmosphere machinery is outside the room flushing desired gas mixture into room. Latter system affords O_2 pull down from 20% to 3% in about 3 days vs 30 days by conventional system. (R.M. Smock, Cornell University).

"Low-O_2") hydrated lime or by a heat-regenerative material; and (5) oxygen level is usually held at about 3 percent and carbon dioxide about 2 to 5 percent, depending on the apple variety (Table 3). If oxygen is below 18% in a CA room, maintenace repairs must be made with a suitable air supply or oxygen mask. To load or unload fruit, the atmosphere must be flushed out to raise oxygen up to at least 18% and reduce carbon dioxide to a low level.

Fruit is inspected through a window and fruit sample may be taken by temporarily opening and reaching through a small porthole. Atmosphere samples are taken daily for carbon dioxide and oxygen analysis and the scrubbing of carbon dioxide, the increase in oxygen, or changes in generated atmospheres are made in accordance with the daily atmosphere tests. The cost of CA storage is higher than regular storage. Costs vary depending on type of CA, building and storing costs, length of storage, and other factors. Good condition CA stored fruit brings a premium price but may not continue to do so. When the controlled atmosphere is terminated in a room, the fruit remains under refrigeration until sold. The later the CA storage is opened, the sooner the CA fruit should be sold. Fruit from a late season CA opening should be sold within a few weeks. Some apples are held under CA conditions for processing but most CA fruit is intended for the fresh dessert market. CA storage has extended the normal storage season of many apple cultivars and has thus eased the marketing pressure through the harvest and storage season. With the advent of large CA storage holdings, (45 million bu in USA 1982), it is becoming increasingly difficult to market regular storage apples after the middle of the storage season.

CA storage operation has been simplified insofar as the grower is concerned by introduction of automatic equipment that maintains the desired gas mixture inside the storage room, flushes it through the room, and recirculates the desired O_2 and CO_2 levels.[1] The main advantages over regular CA are: (1) O_2 pull-down takes 3 to 5 days compared with 25 to 30 days for the former CA system.

A Holland gas generator (Oxydrain[1], will serve up to ½ million box storage) speeds O_2 pull-down 4 to 5 times faster by cracking ammonia at 2000°F. into hydrogen and nitrogen, then joining hydrogen with oxygen forming water. The nitrogen gas quickly displaces O_2 and CO_2 in the room which also gives better emergency hold-down with gas leaks.

Inflated apple warehouses, 25,000 bu, are in use at about half the normal cost. The E. I. DuPont Co., Wilmington, Delaware, 19899, has the information.

Prestorage Carbon Dioxide. Moisture introduced into the storage room by oxygen burners may cause carbon dioxide injury to the fruit. Hence, a pretreatment of 15 to 17% CO_2 for four or five days is used, room flushed with air, then the normal CA atmosphere is established with the oxygen burner, or, the excess CO_2 can be scrubbed from the atmosphere. This has been successful only on Golden Delicious in Australia, Virginia and Washington and even in Washington carbon dioxide injury has occurred on

TABLE 3. REQUIREMENTS FOR CONTROLLED ATMOSPHERE STORAGE OF APPLES

Variety	%CO_2	%O_2	Temperature °F
McIntosh	2—5	2—3	37—38
Delicious and	3—5*		
Golden Delicious	1.5—3*	2.5—3	30—32
Jonathan		3	32
Rome Beauty	2—3		
Stayman Winesap	5—8	3	30—32
Yellow Newtown		2—3	38—40

*See "Rapid CA" or "Low O₂ under Dr. Bramlage's remarks following.

[1]Pacific Columbia Co., POB 2921, Yakima, Wa. 98907; Doub Engineering, Bx 2080, Falls Church, Va. 22042.

[1]Designed by Pieter Noordzij of Wageningen, The Netherlands, consulting engineer for Food Industries Research and Engineering, Yakima, Wash.

Goldens from some blocks on which it is not used again.

Rapid CA. With this strategy the delay between harvest and establishment of the desired O_2 concentration is held to a minimum. The CA room is filled in 3 to 4 days and the O_2 reduced immediately with a catalytic oxygen burner or nitrogen gas flush. Results are the same as prestorage CO_2 treatment without the danger of CO_2 injury to Goldens. It is used on Delicious but not as dramatic results are obtained on McIntosh. The fruit must be cooled rapidly also, and if the equipment cannot do this, the fruit should be cooled first then restacked in the Rapid CA room.

"Zero" Initial Oxygen. This is a modification of Rapid CA and was used for Jonathan in Australia initially. There is minimum time between harvest (7-10 days) and the establishment of "nil" oxygen (less than 0.5%) with less than 1% CO_2 and 33 °F. core temperature. Five lbs. of lime per bin are placed in the airtight CA room. The O_2 is burned to 2% and then the apples in 4 days will further reduce the O_2 by respiration to 0.5%. After 10 days the atmosphere is brought to normal CA concentration. Strategy has increased storage life and reduced scald and internal breakdown.

Ultra-Low Oxygen. Strategy was developed in England for Cox's Orange Pippin in which three CA regimes are used: (1) 3% O_2 and 5% CO_2 for rooms opened until mid-February; (2) 2% O_2 with less than 1% CO_2 for rooms opened from mid-Feb. through March; and (3) Ultra-low O_2 (1.25% and less than 1% CO_2) for apples sold after April 1. In the latter regime, dangerously low O_2 is prevented by a computerized O_2 controller. They claim the flavor and firmness is better where they can hold the O_2 higher for the early sold apples.

In New York, growers have been slow to use very low O_2 because some seasons apples under their conditions may turn brown with bad "off-flavors" and must be dumped. Hence, they continue with 2.5%-3% O_2. It is believed that computerized O_2 controllers should be used as in England when very low O_2 is being maintained. They are expensive and perhaps for large scale operations only.

Ethylene Scrubbers. There is interest in these scrubbers to improve condition of McIntosh and Empire in New York and to reduce scald. There is some fear that scald inhibitors may be banned. Scrubbers tested are (1) heated catalyst, (2) ozone, and (3) K-permanganate. The problems so far have been high cost, high energy usage, and toxic waste disposal. The one initially used in Italy held the ethylene below 1 ppm for the season.

The above strategies are in the developmental stages and operators should use them only after considerable study and checking with authorities. For those planning CA, there likely will be a need for smaller CA rooms to permit a minimum delay between harvest and the establishment of the CA atmosphere. It is probable that fruit condition will be an even more important factor in the future market

place. Some losses may be encountered in adopting and learning these improved CA methods.

COMMENTS ON CA STORAGE CONSTRUCTION, OPERATION

Many commercial apple and pear storages constructed today are built for ultimate switching to CA storage, even though they may be used for regular storage initially. Also, some growers build a combination of regular storage for early movement of a portion of the crop and CA for later movement of the balance. The following comments by three experts may be of interest in designing, constructing and operating a modern CA storage.

Dr. W. J. Bramlage, University of Mass., Amherst, 01003 evaluated a trip to Washington state, making comparisons with eastern conditions. He notes that Washington in the early 1980s had a continuing and rapidly increasing CA capacity of over 30 million boxes. Their storage construction appears different in some respects than that in the East where humidity is higher as one factor. Perimeter storage walls are tilt-up concrete panels, poured at the construction site. Polystyrene insulation is set into the wet concrete before erection. The gas seal for the inside of the perimeter walls, which is a thin layer of sprayed urethane, is applied to the polystyrene after the panels are erected. Urethane in storage rooms is covered with a fire barrier (Zonolite-3300). Partition walls and ceiling are 3/8-to-1/2-inch plywood (waterproof glue) nailed to 2x6-inch wall studs or to ceiling joists, leaving 1/16-inch spaces on all sides. Seams between the plywood sheets are then filled and taped. Wall-wall, wall-ceiling, and wall-floor joists are flashed. The partition walls and ceiling are then spray-coated twice with an acrylic rubber coating. Ceilings and warm interior walls are insulated with fiberglass; walls common to two storage rooms are not insulated. The plywood-acrylic rubber gas seal is used for the partition walls and ceilings to cut costs. In regions where outside humidity is higher, the plywood-acrylic rubber-gas seal should be considered only for ceilings, and then only when attic spaces are well ventilated to keep the insulation dry.

Built-up roofs are installed and constructed with a slight pitch above aluminum, laminated-wood strusses, which may not be available in all areas. Although roofing felt between two concrete slabs is sometimes used to seal floors, a single concrete slab treated with a floor seal and hardener frequently is used. A metal-clad, sliding door is sealed with rubber gaskets between the door and jam or with duct tapes applied inside the room after the room has been filled. Most storage operators require a room pressure drop of 1 inch to no less than 0.75 inch water gauge in 1 hr. Most rooms in the East also can meet this test.

Most CA rooms are equipped with a Tectrol-Samifi or a COB oxygen burner. After the rapid O_2 pulldown, a CO_2 scrubbing is usually done with lime or a molecular sieve scrubber. The latter draws many kilowatts, which cost 1.1^c, which is low due to energy from the dammed Columbia River. Many operations still use an Orsat gas analyzer, but a few have Teledyne or Beckman O_2 analyzers. Most operators still rely on alcohol thermometers (Taylor 1106 or the more easily read Taylor 5499), which are placed at the CA door. At least one additional thermometer is placed adjacent to the windows located behind the evaporators. These windows also permit visual inspection of defrost. Rooms are quipped with breather bags to equalize pressure in the rooms. Pressure relief valves are used to release excessive pressure or vacuum in the rooms. Ammonia is a common refrigerant. All evaporators are dry coil and most are defrosted with water. Modulating back pressure valves on the evaporators are common when ammonia is the refrigerant. They automatically control the evaporator coil temperature according to the heat removal requirement in the room. Higher relative humidity can be maintained when these back-pressure control valves are used.

Four types of CA rooms for Delicious and Golden Delicious are in general use in the Northwest. (1) *Normal CA.* Rooms are filled in 7-10 days, oxygen is lowered to 2% (if possible) in 3 to 7 days with an O_2 burner. The room is maintained at 1.5 to 2.0% O_2 and below 1% CO_2. If the O_2 cannot be below 2%, the CO_2 is raised to 2%. This regimen is similar to the eastern CA storages except that they do not recommend O_2 concentrations below 2%. (2) *Rapid CA.* The room is filled and sealed in 3 days. Field heat removal requires 7 to 14 days. The O_2 is quickly burned to below 2% and held at about 1% (if possible) for 1 week. For the remainder of the season, the O_2 is held at 1.5% to 2% and the CO_2 below 1%. The short delay between harvest and the time when O_2 is below 2% results in a substantial increase in firmness. *For McIntosh, rapid cooling is more important than rapid O_2 pulldown.* Also, the 1% O_2 for 1 wk for eastern fruit could be risky. But this strategy is worth trial if apples are rapidly precooled in adjacent rooms and assembled in one room for CA. Also, the O_2 should be kept at 2 to 2.5% in the East. (3) *Low O_2 CA.* The room is filled as quickly as possible, but not so quickly that field heat removal takes more than 7 days. Immediately after filling, the room is sealed and the O_2 is reduced to below 2% with an O_2 burner. The O_2 is then held at 1.0 to 1.5% and the CO_2 below 1% for the entire season. Benefits from low O_2 CA seem to be similar to benefits from rapid CA. In the East, O_2 above 2% is recommended. Too many cases of low O_2 injury have occurred in the Northeast when lower O_2 concentrations were used experimentally and/or commercially (by accident). Low O_2 injury on Delicious can be tasted. (4) *High CO_2 pretreatment* (about 14% for 10 days) is rapidly being replaced by Rapid CA and Low O_2 CA because the latter two strategies yield the same flesh firmness advantage and will not cause CO_2 injury to the apples. With the exception of Washington and Virginia-grown Golden Delicious, high CO_2 pretreatments on other cultivars have not looked promising because injury has occurred when CO_2 was sufficiently high to increase flesh firmness.

Bin Spacing and Stacking Patterns. These should be given top priority. Yellow paint on the floor is used to assure at least 12 inches clearance from all walls and 4½ to 6 inches between rows of bins. To assure the fastest possible cooling and the most uniform temperature throughout the storage season, evaporators should be located to move the air quickly on a short route through the bins and back to the evaporators, i.e., the evaporators are located over the central aisles in large rooms and on the long wall in smaller rooms. In the large rooms the doors are located in the center of the short wall, but in small rooms (Figure 14) the doors are located at the edge of the short wall so bins can be stacked across the room, channeling the air quickly back to the evaporators. (See diagrams).

Comments by D. L. Hunter, P.E., Food Plant Engineering, Inc., Yakima, Wa. at a Symposium on CA Storage and Transport, Oregon State University, published by Ore. State Univ., Corvallis. 390 pp. (Priced), 1982. See the report (very good) for full details on this and

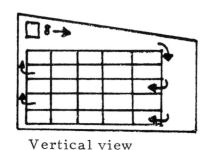

Vertical view

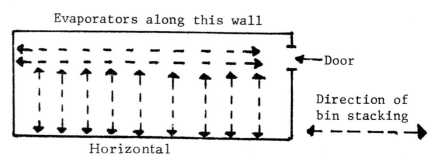

Figure 14 For small CA storage rooms with slant roof, evaporators are located (at upper left) to move air rapidly on a short route through the bins and back to the evaporator. Doors in the small rooms (right) are located at the edge of the short wall so bins can be stacked across the room, channeling the air quickly back to the evaporators. (W. J. Bramlage, Univ. of Mass.)

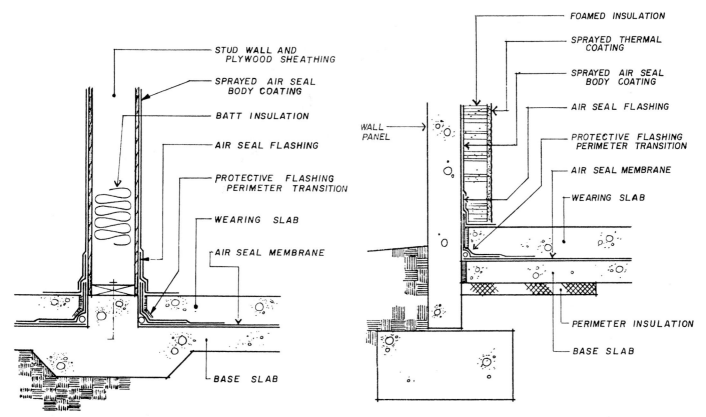

STUD WALL AND PLYWOOD SHEATHING
SPRAYED AIR SEAL BODY COATING
BATT INSULATION
AIR SEAL FLASHING
PROTECTIVE FLASHING PERIMETER TRANSITION
WEARING SLAB
AIR SEAL MEMBRANE
BASE SLAB

FOAMED INSULATION
SPRAYED THERMAL COATING
SPRAYED AIR SEAL BODY COATING
AIR SEAL FLASHING
PROTECTIVE FLASHING PERIMETER TRANSITION
AIR SEAL MEMBRANE
WEARING SLAB
WALL PANEL
PERIMETER INSULATION
BASE SLAB

Figure 15. All CA floors are concrete laid on grade. Where low O_2 is desired, some double-slab buildings have been constructed with roofing membrane in between. Most CAs have only one concrete slab as an air seal. (D. L. Hunter, Food Plant Engineering, Inc., Yakima, Wa.)

other CA related subjects.

CA storages are increasing rapidly in the USA. They are largely *tilt-up concrete* buildings, eliminating most of the poured pilasters by, instead, bracing the walls through the floor and roof system. The walls provide an excellent base for vapor barriers, insulation and seals. They also have a lower insurance rate and are not subject to dry rot in the walls, nor are they damaged easily. Walls shift out little if any vs metal use.

Concrete *floors* are laid on grade. While most CA storages have only one concrete floor as an air seal, some have a double slab with a built-up floor membrane between slabs where very low O_2 is needed (Figure 15).

Roofs on CA storages are either steel joists and steel deck or truss joists which look like steel long-span joists but have wood members for the top and bottom cord with pipe sections for interiors. The roof deck is steel where joists are used and plywood when truss joists are used. Truss joists and plywood deck are common in the Northwest, are lower cost but require an extra layer of sprinkler in the attic vs steel joists. In other areas of the country steel joists and deck are common although pre-stressed concrete roofs are being used. Single membrane roofing materials give greater reliability for leak-proof roofs, may cost a bit more but seem to provide a longer

lasting roof with less maintenance vs. built-up roofing with asphalt and felt.

Layout System. Most floor plans for CAs are laid out on the basis of the economy rather than on the amount of space a company has for the project. One of four plans in Figure 16 is common. Lower costs systems are built by Plan 4 but Plans 2 and 3 offer the best control and operating conditions. In Plan 4 there is little opportunity to view the fruit, the CA doors are exposed to weather and if you wish to expand space, there will be extra cost. But Plan 4 often is used to save initial cost. Study each system for any advantages from your standpoint; all will work.

Room Sizes. Size of the CA storage room will depend upon the varieties and amount of fruit to be stored, how fast the fruit is loaded in and how it will be marketed. Where CA rooms initially were around 5000 boxes in size, now they will contain 40,000, 80,000 and sometimes 100,000 boxes. In recent yrs. rooms 25,000 to 40,000 boxes are favored for the high quality fruit for long-term storage loaded in within about three days. The less partitions, doors and controls in a plant, the less the cost, hence the size of the room should be as large as practical. Most growers after carefully studying their situation will want to keep the option of holding the fruit the maximum period even though in some years they may sell early. "Rapid

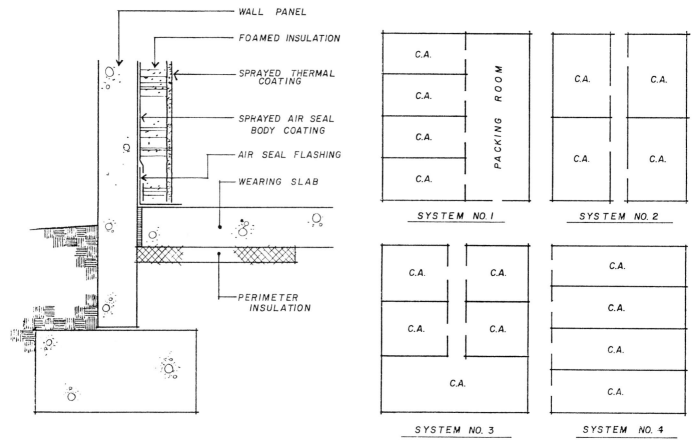

Figure 16. (Left) Most CAs have only one concrete floor as an air seal (Right). Most CA floor plans are based on one of the above. In Australia, some operators are subdividing CA rooms because with Rapid CA it reduces the effectiveness of the treatment if the room is later opened for an incoming cultivar.

CA'' seems to be practical and, thus reasonable size of the rooms chosen is in order.

Stacking Heights. Most rooms will accommodate 10 bins high for economy and these are safe. Small rooms and the use of bins greater than 30 inches high should accommodate 6 to 8 bins high.

Loading-in Rates. The usual rate of loading-in has been 7 to 8 days. Daily rate can be obtained by dividing the room capacity by number of days of loading. With "Rapid CA" operators want to complete loading-in within 3 days and bring the O_2 to less than 5% in another 3 days. This approach has brought good results and is being continued. Growers who have skimped on refrigeration capacity will have to load slower to attain proper temperature.

Air Seals. On concrete walls urethane with ½ inch fire retardant lightweight-concrete covering is common. Plywood walls are covered with a rubber-like material for sealing. Metal walls may leak and require annual maintenance. Rubber-treated walls may last 5 yrs. or more without after-season repairs or tightening except for damaged areas. High-density plywood may be relatively short-lived if there is high moisture exposure. The rubberlike material is sprayed or rolled on the walls. These

films are beneath insulation, acting as a vapor barrier and a high integrity air seal eliminatng dry rot. Polyurethane is satisfactory but needs fireproofing. This protective coating can be used with "Gaco" rubber on plywood walls.

Since the storage season is nearly all year, the urethane on plywood is preferred, or "Gaco" with an underhung insulated stud system of fiberglass rather than the usual system of blowing loose fill insulation over the top of the plywood ceiling. This results in too much moisture collecting; the plywood warps and the seal of air-tightness does not last. With modern CA, an exceptionally tight seal is needed for adequate control of O_2 for apples and pears. Now the requirement for low O_2 is 0.75 inch of water drop after one hr. pressure test, where formerly it was 0.25 inch. To get this, the 2-layer floor with built-up roofing material between is needed, as in Figure 15. Formerly standard CA construction may work with some tightening and special care.

Refrigeration. Ammonia is the common refrigerant in the Northwest. One large unit may be used in the room or several smaller air units. Multiple units have the advantage that if one goes bad, the others keep operating, whereas one unit "on the blink" can cause problems. Large single units require more H.P. to meet the needed air circulation, and the higher temperature difference across the cores causes slightly lower humidities. The large low-cost CA rooms, however, are using the large single units, even though there may be more weight loss in the fruit from loss of water in the fruit. It should be noted here that some storage contractors and owners are speculating in erecting CAs for lease for fruit they do not own or control. Hence, these buildings are built on a minimum budget, using refrigeration that can cause 1 to 2% loss in weight of the fruit during storage. Fruit is sold by weight and this loss of weight can represent a lot of money even though the difference is not easily noted. Red Delicious can be kept 7 months in a relatively low quality CA and the loss of weight is not detectable to the eye. But Golden Delicious and McIntosh may have shrinkage develop sooner.

Scrubbing The Air. Lime appears to be the best means of lowering the CO_2 in the CA storage. Fifty pound bags of lime have been placed on pallets in the CA room or a separate lime room, but these have tended to crust and the center lime in a bag is not fully utilized. A system is being developed in the Northwest to slowly feed the bulk lime from a truck in an enclosure as the air is pulled over it, permitting the lime to be used in bulk and more fully exposed to the passing air.

Donald H. Dewey Comments. The "Inside-Outside" method of construction of CA storages is common in Michigan and Ontario. Sprayed-in polyurethane and plywood sheeting are utilized in a post-frame wooden building to provide an air seal; this is in combination with good insulation adequately protected by a suitable interior thermobarrier. This is shown in Figure 17 where the polyurethane is applied to the outside of the interior plywood lining which has been nailed to the girt. Exterior sheeting is applied last; and ceiling is completed in a similar manner. Joints and nail marks are covered with self-adhering tape. The wide acceptance of this technique is due to simplicity of construction, economy, and dependability of tightness. Experience has shown them to last at least 5 yrs. with little deterioration and maintenance.

Summary Note. Materials and methods for building refrigerated and CA storages are changing constantly. Seek the help of a competent architect, builder, and refrigeration engineer. The above information should help you to discuss your project more intelligently with the contractors.

COSTS

Because of so many variables it is difficult to give clear-cut figures on costs of building and operating fruit storages. Rough figures, which will change with the current price level, can be obtained by phoning storage (fruit) specialists at the following universities: Washington (Pullman), Cornell (Ithaca, N.Y.), Massachusetts (Amherst), Michigan (E. Lansing), and Oregon (Corvallis). CA storage construction costs in Washington in the early 1980s were $3.75/bu. for 100,000 bu. and $3 for one million bu. capacity. Costs in the East were more nearly $5/bu. vs. the $3.75 figure. Costs increase with smaller capacities. Construction of cold storages should be somewhat less. See references offered as a basis for comparison.

SIZE OF STORAGE BUILDINGS

In calculating storage building capacities, about 2.5 to 2.8 cu. ft. of storage space is allowed for each bushel. The 2.8 cu. ft. ratio allows ample space for aisles and for proper stacking to facilitate good air circulation. Where palleted or bulk boxes are used, from 10 to 20 percent more fruit can be stored in a given area. Modern 25,000 box storages usually accomodate 6-8 bins stacked; those 100,000 boxes or larger may stack bins safely up to 10 high by fork-lift.

THE AIR-COOLED STORAGE

This type of storage, as stated previously, is cooled by judiciously admitting (night) air colder than storage-room air and emitting the warm air from the storage. The arrangement of air intakes and vents is shown in Figure 18. The cold air enters at several intakes in the lower right wall, and is drawn by fans through the fruit and exhausted

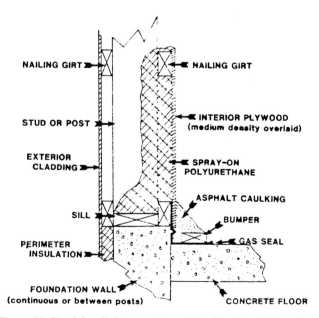

Figure 17. Partial wall-floor section of "Inside-Outside" method of construction of CA storage room initially used in Ontario and Michigan. (D. H. Dewey, Mi. State Univ., E. Lansing 48824, adapted from R. P. Stone).

163

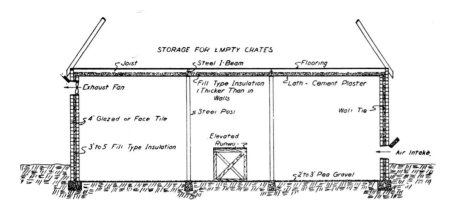

STORAGE FOR EMPTY CRATES
Joist — Steel I-Beam — Flooring
Exhaust Fan
Fill Type Insulation Thicker Than in Walls
Lath - Cement Plaster
4" Glazed or Face Tile
Steel Post
Wall Tie
3' to 5' Fill Type Insulation
Elevated Runway
Air Intake
2' to 3' Pea Gravel

Figure 18. Cross-section of an air-cooled storage showing insulated walls and ceiling and a pea-gravel floor. Cold outside air enters ducts at right, passes through stacks of stored fruit, and is exhausted by fans in upper-left ducts. These storages are still used in many European countries. (Michigan State University).

in the upper left wall. Well-insulated above-ground storages are usually better than storages built into a bank or surrounded by soil. The temperature of the earth runs between 50° and 60° F. which is considerably higher than the air temperature on many days during the storage season.

Ventilation may be by gravity or by forced air using power. The fans are located in the upper wall vents or the ceiling flues. With forced air ventilation, inlet openings at the base of the walls should be two and one-half to three feet square with doors hinged at the top; with gravity ventilation, the intake areas should be at least four square feet. These entrances must be covered with hardware cloth to keep out rodents.

Capacity of common storages varies from 2500 bushels to 12,500 bushels or more. Cost of construction is cheaper on a per bushel basis for the larger storages.

STORAGE TROUBLES

Aside from fungus rots, apples held for a number of months in storage are likely to develop one or more physiological disorders. Storage conditions may or may not be responsible for these troubles, but since they manifest themselves in storage they most commonly are referred to as storage troubles. Often the basic cause of these diseases is either inherent in the apples or is due to faulty nutrition, spray program, weather, or harvesting and handling before the fruit is placed in the storage room.

The diffuse browning of the skin of apples known as **apple scald** is perhaps the most widespread physiological disease of apples. York Imperial, Stayman, Rome Beauty, and Rhode Island Greening are particularly susceptible (Table 4). It also occurs on other cultivars, especially when harvested early in the season or with poor color development. Delayed regular storage and storage temperatures above 32° F. also favor its development. High nitrogen level in the orchard has been found to accentuate scald on some varieties, not on others; the picture is not clear. The disease seems to be worse following warm weather just before harvest.

TABLE 4. PHYSIOLOCIAL DISORDERS OF APPLE CULTIVARS

Cultivar	Water Core	Scald	Soft Scald	Bitter Pit	Miscellaneous
Arkansas	M	Se	N	Sl	
Baldwin	Sl	M	N	Se	
B. Davis	Sl	M	?	Sl	
Cortland	Sl	M	Sl	Sl	
Delicious	Se	Sl	N	Sl	Mealiness
Empire	N	Sl	N	N	
G. Delicious	Sl	Sl	Se	N	Shrivelling
Gravenstein	Sl	Sl	N	Se	
Grimes	M	Se	Se	M	Shrivelling
Idared	N	Sl	N	Sl	Jonathan Spot
Jonathan	M	Sl	Se	Sl	Jonathan Spot
Jerseymac	N	Sl	N	N	
N. Spy	Sl	Sl	N	Se	Spy spot; breakdown
McIntosh	N	Sl	N	Sl	Brown core
Mutsu	N	Se	N	Sl	
Oldenburg	Sl	Sl	N	N	
Paulared	N	?	N	N	
R. I. Greening	Sl	Se	N	Se	Mealiness
Rome B.	Sl	Se	M	Sl	
Stayman	M	Se	N	M	Crack; Internal
Spartan	Sl	Sl	N	N	breakdown
Transparent	M	N	N	N	
Wagener	Sl	Sl	Se	N	
Wealthy	Sl	M	M	Sl	
Winesap	M	M	N	N	
Winter Banana	Sl	Sl	Se	Sl	
Y. Newtown	Sl	M	N	Sl	Internal brown
Y. Imperial	Sl	Se	N	Se	Cork

N-none; Sl-slight; M-medium; Se-severe

Scald usually affects only the skin and therefore only the appearance of the apple, but may, in advanced stages, extend into the flesh. Fruit showing scald in storage is likely to have the trouble markedly increased within a few days after it is removed to room temperature.

Diphenylamine (DPA) and ethoxyquin (Stop-Scald) as a dip or spray or impregnated in paper wraps will markedly reduce apple scald in most years. Such treatments currently are the most effective and most widely used against scald. DPA under some conditions has been more effective than Stop-Scald, but in a critical scald year, both are less effective but far better than mineral oiled wraps. Under severe conditions, combinations of DPA and Stop-Scald may be more effective than either alone. The DPA dip method shortly after harvest affords good fruit

164

coverage and is generally somewhat more effective than wraps, although wraps sometime are as effective. DPA as dip or spray, 1000 ppm on York, Idared, Jonathan, Cortland; 2000 ppm on Delicious, Rome, Stayman and Arkansas. On latter varieties 1000 ppm may be satisfactory if fruit is late-picked or otherwise less likely to scald. Stop-Scald at 2700 ppm (3 pts./100 gals. 70% emulsion) is suggested. Coverage is better on warm fruit. Cost per bushel is small compared with possible scald losses. Good scald control can be obtained with 1.5-mg DPA oiled wraps.

Periodic measurements of the conc. of DPA in the drench tank can be made with Kit #121 by The Shield Brite Corp. "Drive through" spray application of DPA from mounted nozzles on and through bins 2-3 high on trucks are effective if movement is adequately slowed.

Preharvest tree sprays with 200 ppm DPA are questionable. CA Apples must be pretreated for scald. Tests indicate "Low-0$_2$ CA" will control scald or markedly reduce it.

Bitter pit, in its usual form, is characterized by sunken spots on the surface of the apple resembling small bruises (Figure 19). These spots are usually concentrated over the blossom end of the fruit and in the early stages have a water soaked appearance. Later they become deep red or light green and finally gray or black. When the apple is peeled or cut, areas of brown, spongy tissue appear in the flesh. The affected tissues are rarely bitter in taste as the name suggests. The spots are usually most numerous in the outer portions of the flesh just beneath the skin area, but frequently, may be found deep in the flesh. Bitter pit is a physiological disease associated with calcium deficiency in the fruit. See "Calcium Notes" at end of this chapter. It is most severe on apples picked immaturely; and on larger apples than on smaller ones. The severity of the disease increases in storage—new spots increasing in number and old ones enlarging. It does not spread from apple to apple. Baldwin, Rhode Island Greening, Stayman, Yellow Newtown, Delicious, and Gravenstein are among the most susceptible. Check for latest controls with calcium foliar sprays and post-harvest dips. See Chap. V and this chapter end.

Soft scald, which is distinctly different from ordinary scald, is characterized by blister-like or burned-appearing areas extending in irregular patterns over the fruit. The affected areas are usually brown in color, slightly sunken, and with definitely outlined edges. The flesh beneath such areas is often soft and discolored to a slight depth. Jonathan and Rome Beauty are the most susceptible varities, but soft scald may also occur on Cortland, Winter Banana, Golden Delicious, Northwestern Greening, and other varieties. The exact nature and cause of the trouble are unknown but Australian research indicates that it is increased by hexanol accumulation in the

fruit. It is associated with delay in moving fruit from orchard to cold storage, low-storage temperatures, and advanced maturity. Holding at 36° F, if the fruit is well matured or over-mature when harvested, is usually recommended, although the trouble appears to be reduced or prevented also by early harvest and immediate storage at 30° to 32° F. Gerhardt and Sainsbury report successful control of soft scald on Delicious apples by storing eight weeks at 34° F., then 30-32°. CA storage helps, as does a dip in DPA.

Again as with ordinary scald, Brooks and Harley were able to control soft scald commercially on Jonathan and soggy breakdown on Grimes Golden by subjecting the fruit for several days before storage to atmospheres containing 25 to 35% carbon dioxide.

Soggy breakdown is a disease very similar to soft scald in cause but manifests itself in a soft watery or soggy breakdown of the flesh, often without any external symptoms. The disease is most severe on Grimes Golden and Golden Delicious, and storage at 36° F is generally recommended to prevent its occurrence where prevalent.

Internal breakdown is a brown more or less discoloration of the flesh characterizing the end of normal storage life of apples. In advanced stages, the skin is also discolored, and the flesh becomes soft. Large apples are usually the first to show this condition. Over-maturity at time of harvesting, delayed cooling, high storage tem-

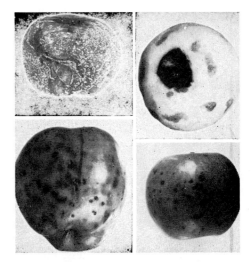

Figure 19. Blemishes and diseases appearing on apples during storage. (Top left) Bluemold rot, soft and watery, has a musty odor and frequently is covered with bluish masses of spores. Benomyl dip and cleanliness in storage room controls the rots. (Top right) A partly peeled apple showing how prominent so-called "slight bruises" appear, which emphasizes importance of careful handling at all times. (Bottom left) Bitter pit, a physiological disease, occurs as brownish spongy or corky spots or pits in the flesh just under the skin and usually is the most prevalent on blossom end of apple. (Bottom right) Jonathan spot is a superficial skin disease giving the apple a freckled appearance.

peratures and low brine calcium level can increase the disorder. It often follows water core and freezing. Calcium dip and CA storage can reduce it.

Jonathan spot is manifested as dark colored, superficial spots in the skin of the fruit and is most prevalent on the Jonathan variety (Figure 19). It is associated with over-maturity, delayed storage, high storage temperatures, and long holding. The colored side of the fruit is more susceptible than the uncolored. Controlled atmosphere storage controls the discolor. It also could be a calcium deficiency problem.

Shriveling is the visible evidence of excessive moisture loss from the fruit and is due primarly to too low humidity of the storage atmosphere. Fruit harvested in an immature condition loses moisture more readily than that which is allowed to become fully mature. Polybags reduce it.

Internal browning differs from internal breakdown in that the discoloration, which at first is confined to elongated areas radiating from the core in the upper half of the apple, appears while the flesh is still firm—usually by mid-storage. Later the entire flesh may become brown. The trouble is of most economic importance on Yellow Newtowns grown in the Pajaro Valley of California. The brown core condition, important in McIntosh apples in New York and New England, is similar if not identical. Unlike internal breakdown, these two disorders are induced by minimum storage temperatures. Little development occurs at 36° F and none at 40° F. Both McIntosh and Yellow Newtown respond well to modified atmosphere storage at these temperatures. Delaying the storage of susceptible cultivars for 5 to 10 days reduces the severity of the trouble but this delay at atmospheric temperature shortens the period during which the fruit can be held.

Water Core. This is usually associated with advanced maturity, hot days followed by cool nights, frosty conditions and high ratio of leaves to fruit. These translucent watery areas in the flesh develop only on the tree, may gradually disappear in storage. Degree of water core determines length of storage up to 5 months maximum.

Ethylene and Ripening. Dr. D. R. Dilley, Mi. State Univ., devised a technique for measuring ethylene gas in stored apples as they ripen. If gas is about 0.5 ppm or less, apples store longest; if 2.5 ppm or less, mid-term CA is suggested; if more than 0.5 ppm short-term storage is suggested.

Apple Rots. Decay of apples in cold storage is caused by fungus diseases. Most storage rot is caused by blue mold *(Penicillium expansum).* Low storage temperatures retard decay. Riper fruit decays more readily. Most rots develop where skin breaks have occurred. To minimize apple rot in storage a prestorage treatment of apples with Benlate (benomyl) effectively reduces decay. Good storage room sanitation and disinfection between storage seasons is desired.

Frozen apples in storage. Recommendations are (Mass. Agr. Exp. Sta.): (a) do not handle apples when frozen, (b) slow-thaw them to 40-45°F; (c) if saleable, sell soon. Experiments show: (a) any freezing softens apples; (b) freezing to 26-28°F is less harmful than to 22-24°F; and (c) unless apples were frozen to killing point, subsequent storage for a short time does not intensify the freezing injury. Golden Delicious may endure freeze damage better than Delicious, perhaps due to no water core, high sugar.

Mice, Rats. Methyl bromide fumigation is preferred. Contact Pomology, Cornell, Ithaca, N.Y. 14850 for latest control. CA is rodent proof.

More Information. See Cornell Bull. 440. Ithaca, N.Y. 14850.

COMMON TROUBLES IN REFRIGERATION OPERATION

Most troubles encountered in refrigeration operation can be eliminated by a periodic inspection during shut-down. When buying refrigeration equipment, always consider the local service facilities for that brand of equipment.

The more common operation troubles with remedies are listed below in Table 5. Where the remedy is obvious, this has been ommitted.

TABLE 5

SHORT CYCLING
(COMPRESSOR ON AND OFF FOR SHORT PERIODS)

Possible cause	Remedy
1. Too large a compressor	1. Smaller pulley on motor
2. Thermostat differential too close	2. Widen differential
3. Discharge valve leaking	3. Look for a leak, repair, recharge
4. Shortage of gas	4. Replace valve — use solenoid ahead of expansion valve
5. Leaky expansion valve	
6. Too much refrigerant	
7. Cycling on high pressure cut-out	5. Bleed
	6. Check water supply to condenser

UNIT OPERATES TOO LONG

Cause	Remedy
1. Shortage of refrigerant	1. Purge
2. Air in system	2. Clean points or replace control
3. Control contacts frozen	
4. Dirty condenser	3. Clean
5. Inefficient compressor	4. Service valves and pistons
6. Plugged expansion valve	5. Clean or replace
7. Heavily frosted coils	6. Defrost
8. Insufficient insulation in storage	
9. Unit of insufficient capacity	

HEAD PRESSURE TOO HIGH

Cause	Remedy
1. Too much refrigerant	1. Bleed
2. Air in line	2. Purge
3. Dirty condenser	3. Clean
4. Not enough water supply to condenser	

166

5. Water shut off to condenser

Cause	Remedy
1. Low oil level	1. Add oil
2. Defective belts	2. Replace
3. Loose pulley or fly wheel	3. Tighten
4. Worn bearings	4. Service
5. Mountings worked loose	5. Adjust oil level or
6. Liquid slugging[1]	refrigerant charge

Suction-line frosts

Cause	Remedy
1. Expansion value open too much	1. Adjust expansion valve

Cause	Remedy
1. Receiver shut-off practically closed or plugged	1. Open valve or clean

HOT LIQUID LINE

Cause
1. Shortage of refrigerant
2. Expansion valve open too much

Where ammonia has been used as a refrigerant, there have been a few explosions. From the evidence collected on the causes of one of the explosions, several conditions seem to have contributed:

Apparently, there was liquid refrigerant in the suction line which caused the compressor head to blow and to release the ammonia to the machinery room. Because there was not enough ventilation to clear the ammonia from the room, a combustible concentration built up and the mixture ignited and caused an explosion and considerable damage. The center of the explosion seemed to be at the switchboard, indicating that an automatic switch had arced.

From this experience, it is obvious that a pounding compressor should be shut off and checked. Adequate ventilation of the machinery room prevents the build-up of dangerous concentrations of ammonia if there are leaks. A master switch on the outside of the building permits all compressors to be shut off without personnel going into the danger area and where an arc will do no harm.

If trouble arises in the operation of any equipment, it is investment in safety to cease operation until the trouble is located and remedied. If the trouble cannot be found, an experienced service man should be called.

Calcium Notes: "Calcium Conference" was held by USDA, Beltsville, Md., late 1970s. Following summary notes may be of interest. Calcium shortage in the orchard may cause physiological problems later in storage.

1. Ca moves mostly in young wood under bark. Growing shoot tips have highest affinity for Ca, over and above the fruit. During a drought, shoot tips remove both water and Ca from developing fruit, favoring pit or cork.
2. Any cultural practice inducing more shoot growth may increase cork/pit problem, such as too much N, heavy winter pruning, heavy fruit thinning, light crop, big fruit and inherent cultivar vigor. Hormone TIBA seems to hamper Ca movement to fruit.
3. Application of $CaCl_2$ sprays, summer pruning and post-harvest Ca dips help to increase Ca in fruit. Late sprays are more effective than early sprays for pit control. Fruit dips with a surfactant, as 0.35% Keltral and 4% $CaCl_2$ can increase Ca from, e.g. 200 ppm to 400-

500ppm in fruit and forego or greatly reduce pit development in storage. J. S. Mason of Summerland, B.C. recommends a surfactant both in sprays and dips.
4. $CaCl_2$ may move down rapidly when applied to the soil but little or no Ca increase occurs in tree leaves the first season, according to Dr. Mason.
5. Heavy N applications to the soil decrease Ca uptake more than it decreases K or Mg.
6. Most Ca uptake is near the root tips. Suberization on older root sections reduces Ca absorption.
7. Small apples have higher Ca content. Fruit on trees with moderate to heavy crops show less cork and bitter pit, possibly due to the heavy crop holding back shoot growth.
8. A single rather concentrated spray of $CaCl_2$ (5%) about two weeks before harvest has given a 50% increase in fruit calcium (with some foliar burn). This may be adequate under British Columbia conditions.
9. Physiological disorders corrected other than pit and cork by calcium sprays are scald and internal breakdown. Firmness and storage life also are improved.
10. Between 1000 and 2000 ppm of Ca in the fruit is needed to get firmer fruit and hold firmness in storage.
11. Some cultivars as York, Baldwin, R.I. Greening and Spy are more susceptible to Ca disorders as pit. Less susceptible are Delicious, Golden Delicious, Rome and McIntosh.
12. Most of the Ca on the surface of a dipped apple goes into the outer flesh the first 2 wks. It takes 8-16 weeks to reach the inner flesh and core.
13. Storage humidity has a small effect on Ca movement into fruit. About 90% humidity is suggested for best penetration.
14. Vacuum forced infiltration of Ca helps speed movement into fruit. It has reduced bitter pit 20% and increased firmness about 2 lbs.
15. Withholding K over 10 yrs. to apple trees boosted Ca in leaves from 1.8 to 3.6%.
16. Pear cork spot will respond to $CaCl_2$ sprays and dips as the apple. With Old Home rootstock no pear cork spot developed in Washington State whereas Bartlett, *Calleryana* and Nelis seedling roots induced appreciable cork in fruit.
17. Over-tree irrigation reduces cork spot. It was suggested we try giving the Ca a different electrical charge than the leaf and fruit, perhaps causing Ca to move into the fruit better. This is being done with pesticide spray particles to make them stick to the tree better.

Review Questions

1. What are the benefits to the grower of storing his fruit in (a) refrigerated storage; (b) a CA storage, or (c) a combination of regular and CA storage?
2. What effect does lowering the temperature from 50° to 40° and 40° to 32° F. have upon the rate of ripening of apples?
3. How does humidity affect stored apples; what relative humidities are recommended?
4. What is the value of ventilation in (a) common, (b) refrigerated, and (c) CA storages?
5. How much space should be allowed for each bushel in calculating capacities for storage buildings?
6. List two popular insulation materials used in refrigerated storages and what respective thicknesses are recommended for side walls, floor, and ceiling.
7. What is vapor barrier, where it is located in a refrigerated storage and discuss the principles on which it functions.
8. What is meant by "high CO_2" pretreatment and "low O_2" storage of apples and on what physiological priciples are operating?
9. Describe generally how a controlled atmosphere storage is built and operated. List its advantages and disadvantages.
10. What factors must be known in estimating the refrigeration load for an apple storage?
11. List three refrigerants and give a disadvantage of each. Which ones are used in modern CA storages?
12. Trace the path of the refrigerant through the refrigeration system naming the important equipment involved.

---

[1]Other causes of slugging may be a leaky expansion or solenoid. It is difficult to get a solenoid tight after it has been used. If the condition persists, it may be necessary to install an accumulator or trap that collects the liquid and by-passes the compressor to the receiver. A large accumulation of liquid in the suction line may damage the compressor.

13. What are the advantages of using one large blower unit vs. several small wall or ceiling blowers in a refrigerated large storage?
14. Briefly describe the development of CA storage and discuss recent developments in construction and operation.
15. Describe three of the most important apple storage diseases in your area and suggest the better control measures.

Suggested Collateral Readings

ANDERSON, R.E. and J.A. ABBOTT. Apple Quality after Storage in Air, Delayed-CA or CA. HortScience 10:255-257. 1975.

ANDERSON, R.E. and R.W. PENNY. Quality of 'Stayman Winesap' apples stored in air, controlled atmospheres, or controlled atmospheres followed by storage in air. HortScience 8(6):507, Dec. 1973.

ANONYMOUS. Apples, pears, and grapes. AHRAE Guide and Data Book. Amer. Soc. Heating, Refrigerating and Air-Conditioning Engineers. (Request recent edition).

BANGERTH, Fritz. The effect of a substituted amino acid on ethylene biosynthesis, respiration, ripening and preharvest drop of apple fruits. J. ASHS. 103(3): 401-404 1978.

BLANPIED, G. D. and L. G. Samaan. Ethylene in McIntosh after harvest. J. ASHS 107:1. 91-3. 1982.

BLANDPIED, G.D. and A. Blak. Pressure tests, acid levels, sensory evaluations on overripeness in apples. HortSci. 12(1):73-4. 1977.

BLANPIED, G. D. Water loss and storage breakdown of 'McIntosh'. HortSci. 16(4) 525-6. Aug. 1981.

BLANPIED, G. D. World view of strategies for CA apples, N.Y. State HortSci. Newsletter 5-7. June 1982.

BRAMLAGE, W. J. Current developments in CA storage. Va. St. Hort. Soc. Proc. Jan. 1982.

BRAMLAGE, W.J. et al. Effects of Aminoethoxyvinylglycine on Internal Ethylene Concentrations and Storage of Apples. J. ASHS 105(6):847-851. 1980.

BUNEMAN, G. and H. HANSEN. Booklet, Storage of fruit, vegetables. For operators. (In German.) Verlag Eugen Ulmur, Stuttgart, Germany. 160 p. 1972.

BURT, S.W. et al. A wet-dry apple bin filler., USDA ARS W-40. August 1976.

COUEY, H. M. and M. W. WILLIAMS. Preharvest application of ethephon on scald and quality of stored 'Delicious' apples. HortSci. 8:56-7. 1973.

COUEY, H. M. and K. L. OLSEN. Prestorage CO₂ treatment for 'Golden Delicious'. Hort. Rpt. 28. Mi. State Univ., E. Lansing. 1977.

COUEY, H. M. and MAX WILLIAMS. The Wash. State apple revolution: production, storage, merchandising. HortSci. 17(1) 14-17. 1982.

DEWEY, D.H. and D.R. DILLEY. Managing and operating a controlled atmosphere storage for apples. Hort. Rep. 10. Mich. State Univ. Request recent edition.

EL-GOORANI, M.A. and N.F. SOMMER. Effect of modified atmospheres on post-harvest pathogens of fruits and vegetables. Hort. Rev. 3:412-461. Avi. Publ. Co., Westport, Ct. 1981.

FAUST, M. et al. Physiological disorders of apples. Bot. Rev. 35:(2). 169-194. 1969.

FIDLER, J. C. et al. Biology of apple and pear storage. Book, 235 pp. (Very good). Common. Agr. Bur. (Hort.) Slough SL2-3BN Eng. L5. 1973.

FINNEY, E.E., Jr. et al. Sonic resonance and apple texture. J. ASHS. 103(2):158-162. 1978.

FLOWERS, L. F. Hydrocooling, preservation of fresh fruits, vegetables. Palm Beach Refrig. Inc. 5520 Ga. Av., W. Palm Beach, Fl. 12p 33405.

GOUGH, R.E., V.G. SHUTAK, C.E. OLNEY and H. DAY. Effect of Butylated Hydroxytoluene (BHT) on apple scald. J. ASHS 98(1):14. 1973.

HALL, E. G. and K. J. SCOTT. Storage and marketing diseases of fruit. Supplement I-XXIV from CSIRO Food Res. Qtly. Australia. (Color) 52pp. priced. 1977.

HALLER, M.H. and L.P. BATJER. Storage quality of apples in relation to soil application of boron. Jour. Agr. Res. 73:243-253. 1946.

HAMMETT, L. K. Ethephon on Storage Quality of Starkrimson and Golden Delicious. HortSci. 11:57-59. 1976.

HARD, M. M. and A. R. HARD. Static and dynamic mearurer of fresh apple texture. J. Amer. Soc. HortSci. 101(4):361-7. 1976.

HARDENBURG, R. E. and R. E. ANDERSON. Keeping quality of apples treated with calcium chloride, etc. ASHS Jrn. 106:6. 776-9. Nov. 1981.

HRUSCHKA, H. W. Post harvest weight loss and shrivel in five fruits, five vegetables. Marketing Res. Rep. No. 1059. U.S.D.A. Feb. 1977.

HUNTER, D.L. Construction of CA storages (and transportation). In CA storage symposium at Ore. State Univ., Carvallis. 390 p. (Priced). 1982.

ISMAIL, M.A. and W.F. WARDOWSKI. Removal of Na O-phcnylphenate and other phenolic contaminants from packinghouse effluents. HortSci. 9:597-598. 1974.

KADER, A. A. and L. L. MORRIS. Modified Atmospheres. Horticultural reference list. CA 95616. 33 pp. Pomology Univ. of Ca., Davis. 1981.

LAU, O. L. and N. E. LOONEY. Factors Influencing CO₂-induced Peel Injury of 'Golden Delicious' Apples. J. ASHS. 103(6):836-838. 1978.

LAYER, J. W. Refrigerated farm storage. Cornell (N.Y.) Inform. Bull. 16. 30 pp. (Seek update).

LEE, G. and R. L. JACK. Eonomic Analysis of CA Apple Storage. W. Va. Univ. Agric. Exp. Sta. Bull. 634. 28 p. 1974.

LEE, J. J. L. and D. H. DEWEY. Calcium infiltration and temperature differentials and surfactants on 'Jonathan' fruits. ASHS 106(4). 488-90. 1981.

LIDSTER, P. D., W. W. PORRIT, B. DOWNING. Spartan breakdown synopsis. Orchardist. (b. C., Canada). 2 pp. August 1975.

LIDSTER, P. D. and S. W. PORRITT. Influence of maturity and delay of storge on fruit firmness and disorders in 'Spartan' apple. HortSci. 13(3):253-254. 1978.

LIDSTER, P. D. et al. McIntosh apples and low O₂ storage. ASHS 1062) 159-2. March 1981.

LIU, F. W. Effects of harvest date and ethylene concentration in controlled atmosphere storage on the quality of 'McIntosh' apples. J. ASHS 103(3):388-392. 1978.

LIU, F. W. Modification of apple quality by high temperature. J. ASHS 103(6):730-732. 1978.

LIU, F. W. Varietal maturity differences of apples in response to ethylene in CA Storage. J. Amer. Soc. HortSci. 102(1):93-5. 1977.

LOONEY, N. E. Calcium chloride and growth regulators to control storage breakdown of 'Spartan' apples. J. Amer. Soc. HortSci. 102(1):85-8. 1977.

LOONEY, N.E. et al. Factors influencing the level of succinic aidc-2, 2-dimethylhydrazide residues in apple fruits. J. ASHS 97(3):323. May 1972.

LOUGHEED, E.C. et al. Low-pressure storage, horticultural crops. HortSci. 13(1): pp. 21-27. 1978.

MASON, J. L. Calcium concentration, firmness of stored 'McIntosh' increased by calcium chloride solution plus thickener. HortSci. 11(5):504-5. 1976.

MASON, J. Spartan apple breakdown and calcium spray control. Contact Can. Exp. Sta. Summerland, B.C. 1972.

MINISTRY OF AGRICULTURE, FISHERIES and FOOD. Apple storage and nutrition. ASDA, Kent, England. 47 p. 1972.

OLSEN, K. L. and G. E. MARTIN. Influence of apple bloom date on maturity and storage quality of 'Starking Delicious' apples. J. Amer. Soc. HortSci. 105(2):183-186. 1980.

OLSEN, K. L. Rapid CA and low oxygen storage of apples. Proc. Wa. St. Hort. Ass'n. 121-5. 1980.

PATCHEN, G. O. Storage for apples and pears. USDA Mkt. Res. Rpt. 924, 51 pp. (Seek update). (Excellent bulletin).

PENTASTICO, Er. B. (Ed.) Postharvest physiology handling and utilization of tropical, subtropical fruits and vegetables. Avi. Publ. Co., Westport, Ct. (06880) 560 pp. 1975.

PIENIAZEK, S.A. Nature of the apple skin and rate of water loss. Plant Phys. 19, 529. 1944.

PIERSON, C. F. et al. Market diseases of apples, pears, and quinces. USDA Agr. Hdb. 376. 120 pp. (Seek update).

POLLARD, J. E. Pectinolytic enzyme activity and internal breakdown in

McIntosh. J. Amer. Soc. HortSci. 100:647-649. 1975.

PORRITT, S. W. and P. D. LIDSTER. The effect of pre-storage heating on ripening and senescence of apples during cold storage. J. ASHS. 103(5):584-587. 1978.

PRESTON, A.P. Summer pruning and N on growth, storage apples. Jour. Hort. Sci. 49:77-83. 1974.

RICHARDSON, D. G. and M. MEHERIUK. CA for storage and transit of perishable agricultural commodities. Symposium Ser. 1, Ore. State Unv., Corvallis. 390 p. 1982.

RYALL, A. L. and W. T. PENTZER. Handling, transportation of fruits and vegetables. Avi Publ. Co., Westport, Ct. (06880) Vol. I, II. 473. 545. 1972-4.

SALTVEIT, M. E., Jr., K. J. BRADFORD and D. R. DILLEY. Silver ion inhibits ethylene synthesis and action in ripening fruits. J. ASHS 103(4):472-475. 1978.

SCHOMER, H.A. and C.F. PIERSON. Waxing apples and pears. Wash. St. Hort. Assn. Proc. 198-200. 1967.

SCOTT, K. J. Vacuum infiltration of calcium chloride for reducing bitter pit, senescence of stored apples. HortSci. 12(1):71-2. 1977.

SMOCK, R. M. and A. M. NEUBERT. Apples and apple products. Interscience Publishers, Inc., New York. 486 pp. 1950. (Out-or-print).

SMOCK, R. M. Controlled atmosphere of fruits. Horticultural Reviews. Avi Publ. Co. 1:301-36. 1979.

SMOCK, R. M. and G. D. BLANPIED. Handbook for CA storage rooms. Cornell Dept. Pomology Mimeo. Bull. S-504. Request recent ed.

SMOCK, R. M. and G. D. BLANPIED. The storage of apples, (one of best). Cornell Ext. Bull. 440. (Seek update).

SMOCK, R.M. Chemicals for apple red color increase before and after harvest. ASHS 83:162-171. 1963.

SMOCK, R.M. The physiology of deciduous fruits in storage. Bot. Rev. 10, 560. 1944.

SMOCK, R.M. and D. BOYNTON. Nitrogen and keeping of McIntosh apples. Proc. ASHS 45, 77. 1944.

SMOCK, R.M. Maturity indices for McIntosh. Proc. ASHS 52, 176. 1948.

SMOCK, R.M. and G.D. BLANPIED. Some effects of temperature and rate of oxygen reduction on the quality of controlled atmosphere stored McIntosh apples. ASHS 83:135-138. 1963.

TUKEY, R.B. and TEAM. Should be contacted for latest harvest-storage work on Delicious and G. Delicious at Hort. Dept., Wash. State Univ., Pullman 99163.

TUGWELL, B. L. CA storage of apples and pears. Ext. Bull. 28.70. Dept. of Agri., South Australia. 30 p. 1970s.

U.S.D.A. Agr. Res. Service. A review of literature on harvesting, handling, storage and transportation of apples. U.S.D.A. ARS 51-4. 1965.

van den BERG, L. and C.P. LENTZ. High humidity of vegetables and fruits. HortSci. 13(5):565-569. 1978.

WALSH, C. S. The effect of delayed storage, slow cooling and polyethylene box liners on 'McIntosh' Breakdown. HortSci. 13(5):534-536. 1978.

WILCOX, J.C. and C.G. WOODBRIDGE. Some effects of excess boron on the storage quality of apples. Sci. Agr. 23, 332. 1943.

WILLIAMS, M.W. and H.D. BILLINGSLEY. Watercore development in apple fruits. J. ASHS 98:(2) 205. Mar. 1973.

WILLS, R. B. H. et al. Apple soft scald and antioxidants. ASHS Journ. 106:5. 569-71. 1981.

WILLS, R. B. H. Reduction of soft scald in apples with methyl linoleate. HortSci. 12(1):72-3. 1977.

WINDUS, N.D. and V.G. SHUTAK. Ethephon, diphenylamine, and daminozide on incidence of scald on 'Cortland' J. Amer. Soc. Hort. Sci. 102(6):715-718. 1977.

ZOCCA, A. and K. RYUGO. Changes in polyphenoloxidase activity and substrate levels in Golden Delicious, other cultivars. HortSci. 10:586-587. 1975.

Note: Most research and bulletins on apple storage have come from Cornell University, Michigan State University, U.S.D.A., England, British Columbia (Summerland), Australia, Wilhelminadorp (Netherlands), Univ. of California, Virginia Polytechnic Institute, and University of Massachusetts. Keep in contact with these institutions for the latest and future storage research. The International Apple Inst., P.O. Box 1137, 6707 Old Dominion Dr., McLean, Va. 22101, has a special letter on storage holdings and world apple situation (you must be a member to receive it).

(See additional references in Appendix and in former book editions.)

Much of the leadership in refrigerated and CA storage of deciduous fruits in recent decades is credited to Robert M. Smock (left), Cornell University and Donald H. Dewey (right) of Michigan State University. In fact, many researchers could be added to this list, including G.D. Blandpied and F.W. Liu of Cornell; H.M. Couey, M.H. Haller, G.O. Patchen, K.L. Olsen and R.E. Hardenburg of USDA; P.D. Lidster and W.W. Porritt of England; D.R. Dilley of Michigan State; W.J. Bramledge of Univ. of Mass and others.

CHAPTER XII

Marketing Fruit

INTRODUCTION[1]

The first and most important step in marketing is to *grow superior fruit*. With a high-quality and attractively packaged product, a grower's marketing problem is 90 percent solved. Michigan research clearly has shown that better growing, harvesting and handling methods are needed than now being used by many growers to get the fruit quality that brings satisfactory profits, particularly to growers who store under refrigerated controlled atmosphere (CA). In fact, there has been and is a marked expansion in "CA storage" of apples and pears over the world (the oxygen and carbon dioxide are controlled to extend storage life) which has altered our marketing system. For example, on December 1 in the USA, there may be 50 million bushels of apples in CA storage yet to be marketed over the next 7 + months. This is quite different than a few decades ago when last year's crop had to be moved out of regular refrigerated storage by early spring.

While the apple often is used in this chapter as an example, the principles apply for the most part to all fruits. You will find additional marketing discussion for specific fruits in the respective chapters.

METHODS OF SELLING

In any system of selling, it is highly desirable for a grower to follow his fruit through the marketing channels to the consumer sometime during the year so that he can observe what happens to the product and how it is received by the consumer.

Grower to retail buyer or consumer. The most simple and direct procedure in selling fruit is where the grower deals directly with local customers, retail grocers, pie companies, and similar outlets in nearby towns and cities. As an example, an Ohio grower sells practically his entire crop of 100,000 bushels to trade in Cleveland, Youngstown, and neighboring cities. Fruit is packed out of storage through the winter and delivered in large trucks traveling a set route once or twice a week. The men in charge of these trucks and fruit sales are especially selected and serve, in addition, as managers of the cultural program for 50-acre blocks of the orchard. The trucks rarely travel to cities farther than 100 miles.

[1]Fred W. Burrows, Executive Vice-President (retired), International Apple Institute, 6707 Old Dominion Dr., McLean, VA 22101, assisted in the revision of this chapter.

Selling to processors. About 40 to 46% of the U.S. apple crop (over 200 million + bxs.) goes to processors, and to juice (totals about 50% of processed products), dried apples, frozen and canned slices and baby foods. Many growers east of the Rockies grow some or all of their apples for the processor. The processor also takes packinghouse culls for juice and peeler products which is a significant tonnage, plus hail and hurricane damaged fruit for juice. (See end of Ch. 10.)

Co-operative operations are feasible wherever the industry is sufficiently concentrated.

The grower undoubtedly strengthens his position from a marketing standpoint by pooling his efforts with those of others engaged in the same business. There are many

Figure 1. This is a typical fruits and vegetables terminal market found in Boston, New York, Chicago, and, in this case, Los Angeles. There is a tremendous variety of items available for consolidation of mixed truck loads going out. Many large and small retailers have constructed their own shipping and receiving facilities off the market area where daily activity is frenetic long before sunup. (Courtesy Paul Bush and Linda Gallagher, The Packer, Shawnee Mission, KS 66201).

One of the largest terminals is the Hunt's Point Food Center on the East River, South Bronx, New York where fresh fruits, vegetables and other produce are brought in by truck, rail and ship for distribution to surrounding metropolitan areas and for some exporting. Air-conditioned space is set aside for auctions. Business is handled mainly by commission, by outright purchase and by joint account.

A large volume of fruit is purchased by chain stores directly from grower corporations and shippers and assembled at their distribution centers where orders are filled and trucked to local stores.

advantages in cooperative selling: (1) A standardized product can be offered; (2) the volume of produce handled is sufficiently large to attract the larger regular buyers; it is difficult for an individual grower to supply sufficient repeat orders for the big buyers unless he is a large grower; (3) an association can keep in close contact with market conditions through their specialists in the large buying and merchandising centers; (4) supplies and equipment can be purchased in wholesale lots at a considerable saving; and (5) an association can conduct advertising and publicity campaigns which are denied an individual grower. It is for the latter reason that the large apple organizations in the Northwest have been so successful in moving enormous quantities of their product. There are the disadvantages of the grower losing contact with the buyers and his right in some cases to gamble on a later market.

Growers in New Jersey and other apple areas of the Northeast, even though they are on the doorstep of the largest markets, also have found it to their advantage to join together in cooperatives to move their fruit systematically and at a price. Where there formerly were over a thousand buyers in this general area, the number has been reduced to less than a dozen. This is due to the dominating influence of large chain stores. Hence, local and regional growers are joining together to bargain with big chains and processors. Michigan Public Act No. 344 established a grower-marketing organization with exclusive control of an item if 51% of the growers pay the fee. These approaches have brought better returns to the growers.

The late Henry Miller, a grower in West Virginia has suggested for the independent grower, it is better to move a more or less even volume of fruit throughout the marketing season, and take lower prices than desired on some sales, rather than to hold large volumes for better prices later, and end up taking disastrous cuts. Mr. Miller pulled old apple varieties and after a planned program planted the cultivars shown in Table 1 to match more nearly the current demand at that time, and to space harvest dates to facilitate handling. Other growers could well follow suit to adjust to their marketing potential.

Roadside marketing. The happiest growers are often on well-traveled highways, moving a part or all their crop by roadside marketing. Peak sales are from mid-summer to late fall and early winter, but some roadside markets are maintained all months of the year. Most patrons are from the middle-upper income families who buy primarily to obtain fresh and better quality produce. Second-grade goods can be sold for canning and cooking if properly priced; low-grade or cull produce should not be offered. In an attractive friendly roadside market today, most customers will pay a higher price than in supermarkets for a high quality product, in spite of the grower's lower overhead and no delivery charges.

Figure 2. This fruit pie and bakery shop is fully equipped with modern ovens, mixers and refrigeration and is a part of a roadside market operation shown in Figure 3 in New Jersey. Wife of orchardist developed the shop. (C.W. Barclay, Jr., Eatontown, N.J.)

Saturdays, Sundays, and holidays are the best days between the hours of 2 and 5 P.M. Largest purchases are from motorists returning home. Motorists leaving the city usually buy only for consumption that day. A market located next to the in-coming lane of traffic to a city will often do twice the business of a market located near the out-going lane. The sales building should be neat, clean, orderly, but not necessarily expensively built. Adequate parking space on one or both sides of the road are of paramount importance. (Figure 3)

Many stands have cold storage space as part of the stand and some grade their fruit before the customers to emphasize the fact that the seller grows his own fruit. Attractive, concise, easily understood signs should be used for advertising the market; they should be placed at an angle to the road, legible at 150 feet or more, and far enough from the stand to give the driver ample opportunity to stop. Salespeople must be courteous, accommodating, and always attendant, making every effort to develop return sales. Growers' wives and children often operate the stand.

In several states a number of grower-operated roadside markets have teamed together. In New Jersey, e.g., they call themselves the "Jersey Certified Farm Markets, Inc., using an attractive symbol to indicate to consumers that they are of high standards, reputable, and seeking only

TABLE 1. REVAMP OF AN OLD ORCHARD TO ADJUST PERCENTAGE OF CERTAIN VARIETIES TO MARKET DEMAND AND TO SPACE HARVEST DATES TO FACILITATE HANDLING.
(AFTER THE LATE HENRY MILLER, WV)

VARIETY	PRODUCTION PERCENTAGE DESIRED IN PLAN	PERCENTAGE OF EACH VARIETY 3 YRS. LATER	APPROXIMATE HARVESTING DATES	USUAL PACKING & MARKETING DATES
Summer				
Lodi	5	4.788	July 1-15	July 1-20
*N.W. Greening	5	6.767	Jul. 25-Aug. 15	July 25-Sept. 1
McIntosh, Roger Strain	5	2.763	Aug. 15-Sept. 1	Aug. 15-Sept. 13
Early Fall				
Red Jonathan	5	5.342	Sept. 1-Oct. 1	Under present conditions, most of the fruit is picked, handled and stored tree-run and packed-out on orders throughout the marketing season.
Red Delicious including super strain	25	21.462	Sept. 15-Oct. 5	" "
Golden Delicious	5	5.262	Oct. 1-Oct. 5	" "
Late Fall				
Stayman Winesap	10	16.571	Oct. 10-Nov. 1	" "
Red York	15	17.661	Oct. 5-Nov. 1	" "
Winesap	5	2.841	Oct. 10-Nov. 1	" "
Red Rome	20	11.394	Oct. 10-Nov. 1	" "
Totals	100	94.851		

* Greening now being gradually replaced with Miller Red, harvested and marketed at same time. Percentage of Golden and Red Delicious production by compact trees is being increased, Winesap decreased.

high quality produce. This is a means of distinguishing themselves from the numerous grower or non-grower operated roadside markets of variable quality. Many state and provincial colleges of agriculture hold roadside market conferences (N.J. & Ohio). See references, write for proceedings.

Preventing Theft at Roadside Markets, PYO. In recent years shoplifting has become a problem. Suggestions for reducing theft are: (a) Maintain a good ratio between customers and clerks — particularly important on the busiest days; (b) locate the cash register so it is the last thing the customer sees on leaving; (c) provide clear plastic bags that clerks can see through; (d) do not use oversize bags; use the right size bag for the purchase; (e) interview future employees carefully, take time to check references for trustworthiness; (f) keep a family member in the market to discourage employee theft; (g) try to keep a mental inventory of what comes in and goes out; (h) see a laywer first if an employee is suspected. District attorneys may not prosecute in minor cases and, also, if you are wrong, a lawsuit for false arrest can result. The biggest problem in Pick-Your-Own is customers hiding fruit in the car. Separate the customers from their cars by providing a central parking place and locate the check-out-pay-center between the customers and cars (see Figure 4). Sometimes one picker will pick up another's harvest and pay for them. This creates problems. You can provide a carry-out service for customers with a central location where berries can be stored with a claim check.

Using marketing agencies. Although the small grower may move most of his crop at roadside market or direct to local retailers, the large grower must be prepared to move his crop in a standardized pack that can be sold on description and delivered on definite schedules to meet buyers needs.

Continuity of supply is essential to efficient marketing, as well as uniformity of pack and quality. Neither chain store buyers, purveyors who supply restaurants, steamship lines or individual retailers, nor exporters are interested any more in "one shot" deals. They all want to buy their supplies where they can come back and get more of exactly the same quality as needed. A cooperative association of growers with substantial volume and uniform control over quality and condition can service customers that would have no interest in dealing with a smaller supplier. The speculative buyers who go from one orchard to another looking for bargains in tree-run fruit, which they can peddle to retailers or repack themselves are no longer an important factor.

The following are marketing means and agencies available to the grower-packer or packer-shipper.

F.O.B. Sales Agents. As indicated earlier, these sales agents may operate at the market on an exclusive basis, or a grower-packer or packer-shipper may use several f.o.b. sales agents. Some cooperatives may act as sales agents and charge the standard commission.

Commission Houses. At one time the *commission merchant* in the terminal markets was a big factor in the marketing of apples consigned by growers. He put them on display in his store or on his sidewalk. He might sell one or two packages or several hundred to a customer. Now that chain stores are buying for shipment to their warehouses, there is less volume of buying in terminal markets.

Jobber. A *jobber* is a person or firm who specializes in supplying retailers, or others who require regular deliveries of relatively small quantities. One jobber may have a clientele of independent retail stores or delicatessens that depend on him. Those who supply restaurants, hotels and steamships are usually called "purveyors". They must have dependable quality and efficient deliveries.

Service Wholesaler. He is a jobber — an important factor in distribution of fruit in some areas, especially the Midwest and Southeast. He usually has a group of independent retailers or small chain supermarkets that depend upon him to purchase their supplies in volume lots and deliver to the stores, on a fixed margin. They are a purchasing agency for the retailers. Their service may also include assisting in making displays of fruit in the stores and helping in special promotions.

Broker. A *broker* is a selling agent who is a contact medium between seller and buyer. It is his job to offer what the shipper has to sell to a buyer who may need it and to know where to get supplies that buyers need. Brokers usually deal only in trucklots or carlots, but they will make up mixed loads with deliveries to several customers. When a sale is completed the broker issues a confirmation of sale, with a copy to the shipper and buyer. If both buyer and seller accept this, it becomes a legal contract. The brokerage fee is paid by the seller. In some markets there are buying brokers employed by buyers to inspect and purchase fruits and vegetables, whose fee is paid by the buyers.

Disposal by auction. The principal items sold at large fruit auctions are citrus, Northwest apples, California grapes, and Pacific Coast pears. The boxes of fruit are available for inspection on platforms or piers prior to and during the auction (Figure 5). The contents of each lot are listed on sheets available to all persons attending. Prospective buyers make hurried inspection and mark their lists to indicate on which items they will consider making bids. These lists are watched closely as the auction proceeds. There is a percentage commission charge. The main auctions for apples and pears are in New York City and Chicago. Auctions also are used extensively in Europe.

Pick-Your-Own. This method of selling for growers is on the increase for both large and small growers. Some growers sell only one item. Others plan and plant so that a series of fruits and vegetables will be available for several weeks or a few months. The neighboring population must be adequate and competition from other growers not excessive. The family and working staff must be able to handle people and like to do it. Some PYO operations may service one to two thousand people on a weekend. Growers are able to get 100% of the consumer's dollar — no costs

Figure 3. This has been one of the most successful roadside markets in the USA, located near Eatontown, New Jersey. Started as a husband-wife venture selling fruit and home-made pies, it developed into the enterprise above, serving over 4,000 customers on a weekend. It serves mainly upper-level income trade with top-grade fruit, cheeses, bakery goods (their own kitchen), spices, nuts and basic foods. An old orchard of Delicious apples surrounds the market which also is kept in top condition. There is adequate parking space, cold storage and food preparation rooms at back and on a well-travelled highway.

Figure 4. For Pick-Your-Own operation this flatbed has been made attractive for family ride to the fruit planting. Orchard workers man the tractors. Customers' cars are left in a nearby parking area. (Morris Fabian, Cook College, Rutgers University).

for picking, containers, storage, trucking, etc. Cash is paid, banked and ready for use immediately or left to draw interest. In Ohio, e.g., over 65% of their fruit is moved by PYO.

Other pointers to consider in a PYO operation follow. Harvests can be made on weekends when other labor is scarce. Some advertising (most use newspapers) is needed to get people started, names and addresses are taken and non-trouble makers are asked to return by postcard when season starts. Senior citizens come mostly early morning, wives and children during the day, families in the evenings. Some operators do not permit children under 12 in the field, or they must be accompanied by parents. Field supervisors are needed to control rows or trees assigned, how to harvest, other problems. Adequate parking space is needed nearby , about one acre for a 6-acre orchard; field used for hay or pasture rest of yr. Good neat ground cover needed in orchard; people do not like a jungle. Tall trees should be gradually pruned down to reach from the ground to reduce insurance problems, ladders, etc. Dwarf trees on trellis are ideal for PYO. Fruit over the tree should ripen rather evenly by using perhaps ethephon spray. People can be furnished containers, which most operators have found best, and haul them to the field on flat trailers (Figure 4). This reduces theft by hiding fruit in their cars. Check-out should be between the field and the parking lot. Arrange with bankers for weekend deposits. Check insurance policy. Most operators set their prices based on wholesale, neighbors' and supermarkets' prices. It is surprising what people will pay for *high quality attractive PYO fresh fruit* — almost as much as the supermarkets are charging. Some spend up to $1000 or more on advertising but most spend under $100-$200. Popular containers are qt tills, ½ bu bskt, 10-20 lb flats, miscellaneous paper and

poly bags. For most operators, from 10-20% of the farm income is from PYO. Small fruits (strawberries) are the most popular PYO operation, followed by tree fruits (apples, peaches), then vegetables (tomato, sweet corn, peas, peppers, beans, pumpkins, squash, and eggplant, in that order). Latter data from survey in New Jersey by Morris Fabian and John Hunter, Rutgers University. See references and suggestions for each fruit in subsequent chapters.

Vending machines. These automatic refrigerated machines are operated in schools, railroad stations, U.S. Armed Services camps, and areas of heavy traffic. They have proven successful for operators who may or may not devote full time to the venture. Only the best apples are used, giving a choice of three or four varieties. Money changers on the machines boost sales. Some horticulture and pomology clubs in universities buy one or more new or used machines and operate them in popular campus spots. Profits go for group tours and other activities.

SHIPPING POINT INSPECTION

In addition to a government inspection certificate on grade, pack, quality, and shipping condition at point of

Figure 5. (Above) This is an auction display at Hunt's Point Food Center (N.Y. Auction Corp., Bronx 10474), covering 154,000 sq. ft. and accommodating 40 rail cars at one time. There are four A/C auction rooms (below) with space for offices, coffee shop and parking for 300 cars of buyers. (Lower, courtesy Jeff Newton, The Packer)

174

origin, there also is provided by state or government officials an inspection certificate of the fruit upon arrival at destination. The certificates are accepted in the U.S. courts as *prima facie* evidence of the truth to the statements of quality, grade, pack and condition. This service encourages greater care on the part of shipping concerns and reduces the rejection of cars at destination because of trivial reasons when the market is oversupplied. Cost is relatively inexpensive. Further information can be obtained from the local state department of agriculture.

Several packing/storing operations in key producing areas use a full-time Federal or state inspector. But there are some in the East and Midwest USA who have little if any of their packs inspected. They operate with their own inspection and honesty. If a buyer should receive this fruit and has doubts, he calls for a terminal inspection and rejects it if not up to specifications. It is true, however, that some chains reject with or without inspection if the market is overloaded. The shipper usually accepts the "rejection" since he may lose a customer otherwise. It pays to ship *consistently* high-quality fruit attractively and well packed.

MARKET PREFERENCES

It is general knowledge among fruit growers that some cultivars, particularly Delicious and Golden Delicious, are in greater demand than others such as Rome Beauty. It is becoming an increasing problem to move summer apple cultivars since housewives in general are doing less home cooking and canning; also summer cultivar apples generally are "not the best" to eat out-of-hand. People turn to other kinds of fresh fruits in season or CA fruit.

Some cities are better markets for second-class fruit than others. Pittsburgh may be a good market for second-grade fruit, due probably to the large population of foreign workers in the mills, mines, and factories. Midwestern

Figure 6. Wenatchee, Washington apples are being loaded into a van for trucking or "piggy-back" rail to the Eastern USA. Most of the crop is trucked out; rail shipments account for about 20%. Shipment time is 4 to 7 days. (Courtesy Great Northern Railway).

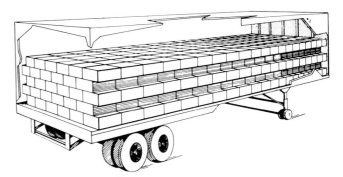

Figure 7. Fiberboard cartons of apples should be loaded to provide air channels (shaded areas) for efficient refrigeration. They also must be loaded solidly to prevent shifting. (USDA)

cities such as Kansas City, Fort Worth, and Omaha have often paid higher prices for a given pack and cultivar than large eastern cities, including Chicago. Each market and buyer has preferences: trays vs. bags, minimum size in bags as 2¼" or 2½", Fancy vs. Extra Fancy, price, or others. An eastern grower should consider freight rates, handling, and cartage charges before shipping fruit to midwestern markets. Unless there is a profit, there would be little reason, other than gluts on the eastern markets, to warrant sending fruit to the Midwest. None but the best fruit can be shipped these distances at a profit.

The U.S. Armed Services and the USDA School Lunch Program are among the biggest buyers of U.S. fruit and fruit products.

LOADING AND SHIPPING FRUIT[2]

The first requirement in shipping fruit successfully is to use rigid containers and pack them firmly. Containers must be stacked solidly against the car or trailer walls and against each other; ventilation should be provided in all parts of the car and throughout the stacked fruit. Packages which are defective in any way should not be loaded because the collapse of one such package may cause the entire load to shift, resulting in considerable damage to a large portion of the shipment. Railroads or trucking concerns will furnish directions for loading.

If the fruit has been outside over night, it should be loaded early in the morning while cool. If it has been in cold storage, so much the better. It may take several days to cool warm fruit in refrigerated cars or trucks. Fruit near the top and center of the car takes longer to cool. If the temperature of the fruit is 75° to 80° F. when loaded, it may take 12 hours for it to reach 45° F. in the bottom layer and six or seven days for fruit in the top layer to reach 50° F. Obviously, considerable ripening can occur in this time

[2]The metric system is being adopted around the World. Labelling in Canada is in French (Quebec) and English, metric only. Check your labelling w/Fruit and Vegetable Div., Agr. Dept., 930 Carling Ave., Ottawa, Ontario, Canada.

and shorten storage life. Rapid forced-air precooling of fruit (Chap. 14) in special rooms or freight cars is available.

Rail vs. Truck. Fruit shipments from the East and Midwest, USA are almost 100% by truck due to better rates and easier accessibility to markets (Figure 6). The same is almost true for Colorado, Idaho and Utah. Rail shipments out of Washington rarely exceed 20-22%. Shipment time in the East and Midwest rarely exceeds three days. Shipments from the Northwest to East are mostly 4-7 days. Unloading is on the day of arrival. Rates are changing and must be obtained from the companies.

Apples may be carried on unregulated trucks. It is more or less a personal bargaining arrangement between the trucker and the shipper. Trucks are invaluable for transporting fruit to and from wholesale markets in congested areas. The principal advantages of the motor truck are speedy service, less expense and less handling. The trucks are equipped with refrigerator service for the longer hauls. Some disadvantages have arisen with the use of motor trucks, but measures are being taken to correct them: (1) Inadequate terminal facilities for handling produce arriving by motor truck; (2) variation from one state to the next in motor-vehicle laws, (3) poor salesmanship and knowledge of market procedures on the part of the grower or truck driver, (4) lack of systematic control of movement of the trucks to the market, and (5) inadequate advance knowledge of market supplies by both the grower and terminal operators.

Maintenance of a "healthy" situation in *both* trucking and rail is highly desirable for switching at peak periods. Competition is desirable and, in fact, rail rates have been more economical and desirable at times.

IMPROVING THE SELLING AND ADVERTISING PROGRAMS

People normally eat about the same amount of fruit from one year to the next. If consumption of one fruit is increased by intelligent and persistent promotion, consumption of another fruit must suffer. The popularity of citrus is unquestionably due to extensive advertising programs to make the housewives conscious of the health values of citrus. The doctors have stressed pectin consumption in fruits and juices to reduce blood cholesterol and heart problems thus boosting fruit sales immeasurably.

Apple research in recent years has emphasized its health values to keep pace with citrus. A Michigan study has shown that students eating two apples a day had fewer tensions, headaches, emotional upsets, skin diseases, arthritic ailments, respiratory troubles, and missed less classes than those not eating apples by a 12 to 1 ratio. Dentists claim that an apple after a meal keeps the teeth and mouth cleaner.

Figure 8. Apples in polyethylene bags, whether summer, fall, or winter varieties, far outsell bulk display apples, although the two types of display are usually complimentary. (Cook College, Rutgers University)

Promotional organizations. In order for apple sales to keep pace with competitive fruits, it has been necessary for special organizations to devote more and more time and money to extensive advertising programs. Among the groups which have played a major and highly effective part in these programs are the *Washington State Apple Commission, Michigan Apple Committee, New York-New England Apple Institute, Western New York Apple Growers' Association, Virginia Apple Commission, Pennsylvania Apple Marketing Board, New Jersey Apple Industry Council, the International Apple Institute (IAI)* and the *National Apple Month, Inc.* The IAI Convention is in mid-November. The Washington State Apple Commission is among the most effective in having field representatives calling on chains, merchandisers and wholesale markets every week of the year over the USA.

Channels of promotion are advertising in leading national newspapers and magazines, outdoor posters, radio and TV spots, moving pictures, advertisements directed to the produce and retail grocery trade, direct messages to the trade by telegram and special bulletins, store display material sent to the trade upon request, apple books containing pertinent information of varietal and cooking uses, and "tie-in" advertising with other lines of items such as breakfast foods, cigarettes, and cooking recipes.

The *International Apple Institute* serves growers, exporters, importers, banks, ocean shipping companies and distributors. Frequent newsletters and an annual reference book are sent to paid members, covering crop estimates, storage holdings, market movements, export-import

Figure 9. Local and National queens help bring public attention to the merits of an important fruit crop. Rosemary Mood, daughter of a famous fruit growing family near Mullica Hill, New Jersey (Starking Delicious apple discovered in their orchard), served as a National Peach Queen. The National Peach Council sponsored her speaking and performing talents through National news media and at important meetings throughout the year.

situation, advertising and promotion, and practically all key developments and problems in apple production. IAI plays a key role in bargaining where needed. There are three departments: (a) marketing, (b) education and promotion and (c) legislative and government relations.

Many of the above organizations have special year-round representatives boosting the sales of apples in cooking schools, assisting in retailer education in setting up displays, and properly handling apples for the best sales possible. It is to the advantage of every grower to support one or more of these organizations. Some states, including Washington, Michigan, Calif. and N.J. have a tax per bu. (or 100 wt.) on apples processed or fresh sold. Revenue is used for promotion and production and marketing research. Eventually, there may develop a national or international apple and pear organization like Ocean Spray for cranberries or Welch for grapes which has its own brand advertising, research and development, processing facilities and its own sales contacts and/or retail outlets.

This could be owned privately or by participating growers who make their own rules and regulations, bargain for prices, and share in the total profits.

Boosting retail sales. Several pointers and suggestions are made for increasing sales at the retailer level:

1. There must be a co-ordinated program of advertising and selling efforts; high quality, well-packed fruits must be available in sufficient quantities to back the advertising program. If any one step in a promotional program breaks down, all efforts may collapse.

2. Most fruit sales in retail stores are made on Wednesday, Friday, and Saturday with Sunday being a big day if allowed. Afternoon sales are greater than morning.

3. The housewife still buys most of the food. Young people buy mainly Red and Golden Delicious, older people a wider variety. Apples are picked before bananas among high-income people, reverse for low-income. Apples are first for cooked desserts. Most people don't know brands, few know cultivars other than Delicious and Goldens.

4. Supermarkets move 75% of the total food sales. Concentrate your main efforts on these stores which are in a position to influence a greater proportion of the nation's housewives. Research has shown that three key factors affect fruit movement: (a) quality, (b) service, and (c) price.

5. There is no more potent advertising of apples than a beautiful display of apples particularly when a display is backed by aggressive, intelligent selling, and an adequate supply of high-quality fruit.

6. The better displays are artistic, clean, well-lighted, have an appealing color arrangement, have clearly readable cultivar, grade and price tags, and are well-stocked and full-looking at all times. Items closely associated with apples on menus should be included on the display when available. Apples sell better if displayed alone, not with citrus or bananas.

7. The medium to large apples of a variety may bring the quicker sales and better profit, although with the polyethylene bags it has been found possible to move large quantities of medium to small size apples. Small children can handle the smaller apples. Faced apples (red side out) may sell three times faster and bring gross profits four times as great as jumble arrangement. Good appearance of apples with no bruising is a tremendous factor in boosting sales. Quality and condition of apples are more important than price in sales of best grades in apples.

8. The grocer may figure an average shrinkage loss of about five percent. Although this figure will vary under different conditions, the grocer in pricing his fruit at the outset should figure on this handling loss to compensate for it.

9. The grocer should check his display frequently and sort out apples beginning to fade or show signs of deterioration. These should be sold immediately at

marked-down prices before the fruits are a complete loss.

10. If possible, clerks should receive special training in the proper handling and many uses of the different cultivars. Often this instruction can be obtained for sizable groups of clerks and store operators through the local state agricultural extension service or through special apple promotional organizations. Some of this information can be placed on "talking" price cards in self-service stores.

11. Small consumer packages or poly bags containing three to six pounds of apples are suggested, although the best size bag varies with different regions. These bags are especially convenient for rapid sales. The top layer of fruit should be clearly evident and open for inspection if in cartons. In poly bags, all apples should be seen clearly. Consumer packs prevent buyers from much fingering of apples and bruising them with their thumbs. With consumer packs, there is little or no leftover fruit of poor quality. Max Brunk of Cornell University has found that poly bags far outsale bulk display apples.

VARIETY	FLAVOR AND TEXTURE	EATING FRESH (SALADS TOO)	SAUCE	PIE	BAKED	WHEN AND WHERE SOLD
SUMMER-TIME	SOUR, TENDER	X	X	X		JULY-AUG.
JONATHAN	TART, TENDER	X	X	X	X	SEPT.-JAN.
GRIMES GOLDEN	SWEET MELLOW	X	X	X		SEPT.-DEC.
DELICIOUS	SWEET, RICH	X				SEPT.-APR.
McINTOSH	SPICY, TENDER	X	X	X	X	SEPT.-APR.
CORTLAND	MILD, TENDER	X	X	X	X	OCT.-JAN.
GOLDEN DELICIOUS	RICH, SEMI-FIRM	X	X	X	X	OCT.-APR.
STAYMAN	SPICY, SEMI-FIRM	X	X	X	X	NOV.-MAR.
NORTHERN SPY	TANGY TENDER	X	X	X	X	NOV.-MAR.
YORK	TART, FIRM	X	X	X	X	NOV.-MAR.
BALDWIN	MILD, FIRM	X	X	X	X	NOV.-APR.
ROME BEAUTY	BLAND, FIRM	X	X	X	X	NOV.-APR.
NEWTOWN-PIPPIN	TART, FIRM	X	X	X	X	NOV.-MAY.
WINESAP	SPICY, FIRM	X		X		DEC.-JUNE

Figure 10. Charts such as this are published and distributed as an aid to retailers and consumers in moving apple varieties in their proper season. Similar information on basis of local varieties could be stamped on corrugated boxes or printed on folders containing other pertinent information and dropped in each container or bag of purchased apples. (IAI, McLean, VA)

12. The chart shown in Figure 10, or a similar one bearing information on local cultivars helps both retailers and consumers in selling and buying wisely. They should be placed prominently near the display counters.

13. Health value of apples should be stressed in posters and in discussing apples with the housewife. Apples supply carbohydrates and minerals in the diet and have important therapeutic value. In institutions for the care of children in both Europe and America, remarkable relief of digestive troubles including diarrhea, dysentery, enteritis, and dyspepsia has been reported. Apple products are used for children to cleanse and detoxify intestines. Fresh fruit improves dental health and counters cholesterol buildup in the blood system (pectin is the key ingredient).

14. A small inexpensive folder provided either by the grocer, distributor, or retailer, is effective when placed in each package, giving details regarding uses for cultivars, a few cooking recipes, health value, and better methods for keeping apples in the home (Figure 10).

15. Provisions for cold storage of apples in the retail store are highly desirable. Otherwise, if possible, the retailer should buy from a jobber or seller every two or three days to keep a fresh supply coming.

16. Handled like eggs or butter, apples will go through the merchandising channels with little loss.

17. A survey in New Jersey showed that all-red apples are preferred by housewives 3 to 1 to red apples with some green showing. Women choosing the fruit with some green had the definite reason that these fruits were frequently of better quality, not over-ripe or mealy as the all-red apples sometimes are. This would indicate that about one-third of a display may have fruit showing some green.

18. One N.Y. grower pays the local supermarket $25 to $50/ad to use his name with apples being advertised in a local newspaper.

Why Buyers Don't Buy Your Apples. David Unger, Deciduous Fruit Buyer for Acme Markets, Philadelphia, Pa., has years of experience in dealing with growers and buying apples for his outlets. He looks for full-red apples with type and character, uniformly sized in adequate quantity from early fall to 7 or 8 months later. He wants them in proper proportions so, e.g., there are enough traypack 100s, teens and quarts as well as 2½-inch "baggers". He gets on the phone early a.m. first with the growers, then the grower representatives. It is mainly in the areas of grading and packing that he finds major fault. Every growers has a certain percentage of marginal fruit. How he handles the marginal fruit governs repeat sales. He must pack marginal fruit separately from the premium fruit and *be consistent*. It is *consistency* year after year that is key. The grower should try to establish high standards of performance for repeat business. Bigger is not better. A grower does not have to be big to prune, spray, thin an fertilize properly. Dave attends grower and marketing meetings regularly to get acquainted with the best growers with whom to deal. He often visits their operations to see for himself and get first call on the best fruit. He figures it pays off! There is no such thing as "instant quality" apples. It takes yearly, daily, hourly attention to develop a respectable end product. The grower who is so regimented, so inflexible and unwilling to change as times demand, will become a stumbling block to his own progress.

Marketing CA apples. In CA (controlled atmospheres) storage, refrigerated apples are held in a sealed room where the carbon dioxide and oxygen are regulated. The apples are of much higher quality when removed and have a "shelf-life" approximately twice as long as apples held in

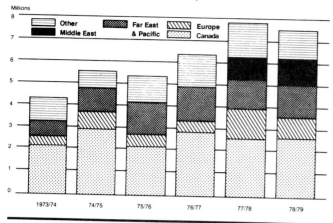

U.S. Exports of Fresh Apples (In cartons)

Millions

Other | Far East & Pacific | Europe
Middle East | | Canada

1973/74   74/75   75/76   76/77   77/78   78/79

Figure 11. This chart shows the trend in apple exports from the United States. Note the initiation of exports to the Middle East (Arab) countries which is becoming a key factor. Note also the general export growth to other countries. (USDA)

regular storage. Delicious, Golden Delicious, Jonathan and McIntosh, are the most common held. Other cultivars being held in CA storage include Rome, Newtown, York, Spy, Stayman, Cortland, Idared and others.

The amount of CA apples in the U.S. is on the increase, approaching 50 million bushels. CA storages are owned by the larger growers. About one fourth of the CA capacity consists of remodeled regular storage space; the balance is newly constructed. Chain stores now are demanding CA apples. Consumers apparently are not particularly concerned about the price as long as they can buy quality fruit at a "reasonable" price. Demand has been strongest for tray packs of 48- 56- 64- 72- 80- 88- 100- 113- 125- 138- 150- 163- and 175; and for cell packs of 80- 96- 100- 120- 140- 160- 200. CA apples ("they have arisen from a long sleep") are well-known to the public through TV, radio, newspaper and sales-tag advertising. With the tremendous increase (over 55% since the mid-70s) in CA apples, grocers are selling a big tonnage of apples in the February to August period due simply to a greater volume of good apples on which retailers can make a good profit. CA apples are competing with southeastern USA early apples, forcing growers to improve their market quality.

EXPORT-IMPORT

There are a lot of apples being exported and shipped around the world - some 2.5 million metric tons total or about 125 million boxes. Fruit production and processing in, e.g., Europe, Australia, New Zealand, Mexico, Canada, South Africa, Argentina and Chile have increased in recent years to the point where market disposal within the respective countries and the disruption of foreign markets by export has caused an international problem.

Holland has devised a plan to cut back on plantings. Australia *must* export due to its own limited population. Tasmania has reduced plantings. France has and can dominate the world market, a full Italian crop can supply all Europe; Japan is a big producer. Thus, some means of reducing world acreage must be taken or greater emphasis must be placed on local and international promotion.

Apples exported from the United States (7% of total crop), have become a *vital factor* in marketing the U.S. crop. Exports totalled close to 13 million bushels in the early 1980s of which 3.5 million bushels went to Taiwan alone. Without these exports, apples would bring a very low price some years in the USA. The amount exported varies with the size of the European, U.S. and Canadian crops; much of the Canadian exports are sent into the U.S. and to England. Although Canada and Mexico are fair export customers, for USA, most trade goes to Britain and possessions, West Europe, Mideast mainly oil countries, Far East, Phillippines, Hong Kong, Singapore, and countries south of USA. Germany and the Netherlands also serve as distributing centers for United States shipments to neighboring territories. Ports of export from the United States are Boston, New York, Philadelphia, Norfolk, Baltimore, Seattle, San Francisco, and Portland, Maine and Oregon. In Canada, Halifax is the chief port with Montreal, Quebec and St. Johns in the East, and Vancouver on the Pacific Coast, making shipments.

Fancy or better McIntosh and Newtowns in uniform cell cartons of 140, 160, and 200s are demanded in England and Scotland by *brand name*. Tray-pack Red Delicious, Red Romes and Golden Delicious, are popular, small sizes in Europe and large sizes, 88/100/113 in South America. Goldens must be clean, no russet or lenticel spots, greenish tinge for better keeping, and wrapped.

Season for U.S. export starts in August for South America and West Indies and continues until Argentine or other southern hemisphere apples fill their markets. Exports from Europe may start late August or early September depending upon competitive supplies, and continue till March or later. The United Kingdom no longer has license allottments to protect her growers. Southern hemisphere new-crop apples start coming in about March 1st.

Practically all apples exported now are sold at definite prices on definite specifications, f.o.b., port of shipment or C.I.F. port of destination. On an f.o.b. sale the foreign buyer pays for the fruit delivered on board the ship. On C.I.F. sales the exporter pays the ocean freight and collects by draft or "Letter of Credit" on delivered destination port basis. When a grower or shipper sells F.A.S. New York (free-along-side), or other port, he is obligated to deliver the apples onto the dock where the ship is loading but has no further responsibility. All apples sold for export must have government inspection at time of shipment and must meet at least U.S. No. 1 grade. They do not have to meet "standards of condition" unless the buyer so specifies in the contract. Exceptions to inspection may be made on lots of less than 100, where it may be difficult to get inspection.

Future expansion of export business only can be based upon dependable supplies of quality apples in good carrying condition and attractive packages that protect the fruit.

Apple Concentrate (70-72 brix) Imports. This has become big business. Some 60 + million gallons of single-strength-juice basis is being imported from Europe and the Argentine mainly which represents the equivalent of over 17 million bushels of raw apples. This concentrate competes, of course, with U.S. apples.

MARKETING CHANGES OVER 30 YEARS

Fred W. Burrows, retired from The National Apple Institute as Executive Vice-Pres., comments on 30 yrs. of marketing apples. "Thirty years ago there were a substantial number of firms in the distribution trade in the terminal markets that were essentially apple houses. To exist, these firms have had to take on a full line of merchandize. Direct buying from FOB retail sales agencies by chain stores has tripled at least. In other words distribution has changed radically. Also, consumer packages have greatly increased apple sales. Too, e.g., 1000 small growers have gone to 100 larger growers. This has resulted in more orderly distribution of apples. Too, there is a trend to more apple production, reaching over 200 million bushels in the next few yrs. The processor can take only so much and make a profit. Hence, more fruit must go to the fresh market and export — and it must be top quality. CA storage has helped spread the distribution over 10 months or so. We need more promotion like the citrus industry which spends three times as much as we do on apples..."

Review Questions

1. List and discuss briefly the various methods of selling fruit.
2. Briefly describe a well-operated roadside market for fruit, vegetables and other products.
3. What is the value of shipping point inspection?
4. What part does the motor truck vs. rail play in the transporting and marketing of fruit?
5. List 3 apple promotional organizations and state how they are aiding in disposal of apples and other deciduous fruits.
6. List 6 suggestions for increasing fruit sales in retail stores.
7. What can be done about theft in roadside markets?
8. How important are by-products in the utilization of apples? List the principal apple by-products.
9. Discuss the general apple export-import situation, varieties, packing and countries involved.
10. How has CA apples affected marketing?
11. Briefly discuss the PYO system of marketing fruits.

Suggested Collateral Readings

APPLE Marketing Game by Max Brunk, Cornell Univ.; Using gamemanship in apple marketing by Rod Sobczak; Grand master of apple marketing by Fred Burrows; other items on marketing in Amer. Fruit Grower. September 1982.

APPLE Exports At 41-Year High. Fruit South. Vol. 8, No. 2, March 1981.
ASHBY, B.H. Protecting perishable foods in transit. USDA Hdbk. 105. 142 pp. Rev. 1970.
BARITELLE, J.L. and D.W. Price. Long-Run Implications of Alternative Market Allocation Schemes for Wash. Apple Ind. Wash. Agr. Exp. Sta. Bull 785. 10 p. 1973.
BIRD, J.J. PYO fruits and vegetables. Tenn. Agr. Ext. Serv. Publ. 595. 16 p. Seek update.
BRAIN, K. and Robert L. Jack. A Least-Cost Model for Marketing Fresh Apples in the United States. WVU Agr. Exp. Sta. Bull. 619, 32 p. 1973. Fresh apple movement as related to residency. Bull. 626. 56 p. 1973. Interregional competition in apple movement. Bull. 6121. 72 p. 1973.
BREEDEN, R.G. Merits of Direct Marketing (grower viewpoint). The Mountain Grower (W. Va. Hort. Soc.) 15-23. June 1982.
COOP, F. A. Displaying produce at retail for optimum movement. United Fresh Fruit & Vegetable Assn. Yearbook. 1973. pp. 77-87.
DEWEY, D.H. and T.J. Schueneman. Quality and packout of storage apples — effects on cost and return. Mich. Res. Rpt. 147. 1972.
FABIAN, M.L. New Jersey roadside market conference proceedings (annual). Dept. Agr. Econ., Rutgers Univ., N. Bruns. 08903.
FARRELL, H. The Salinas Valley power struggle (Chavez vs growers). San Jose Mercury Newspaper, San Jose, Calif. July, 1971.
HUTCHINSON, T.Q., L.A. Hoffman, and R.L. Parlett. Improving the Export Distribution System for Fresh Fruits and Vegetables. USDA Mktg. Res. Rep. 1027. Wash., D.C. 75 p. 1974.
JACK, R.L. and K. Brian. Fresh Apple Utilization as related to Peoples' Age. WVU Agr. Exp. Sta. Bull. 627. 76 p. 1973. related to income, Bull. 625, 80 p.
LAWRENCE, Neil. Scandinavian Markets for Fresh and Processed Fruits and Vegetables. U.S.D.A. Foreign Agric. Service. FAS M-283. June 1978.
LIPTON, W.J. Compatability of small loads of fruit and vegetables. USDA-ARS 51-48. 4 pp. 1972.
MARKET DISEASES of Fruits and Vegetables. U.S.D.A. Misc. Publ. 498. 60 p. Color. Seek recent edition.
MATTUS, G.E., D.E. Kenyon and P.M. Aust. Rapidity of sale of apples in retail stores. HortScience 8(4):317. August 1973.
McGAHA. M.E. World competition in fresh apple sales, Pa. Fruit News, Apr. 1974.
MOYER, C., Buying guide for fresh fruits, vegetables, herbs, and nuts. Blue Goose, Inc. P.O. Box 46, Fullerton, CA. 92632. 1976.
O'ROURKE, A. Desmond. Factors Affecting Major Marketing Decisions for the Washington Apple Crop. Coll. of Agr. Res. Ctr. Wa. St. U. Bull. 793. 24 p. 1974.
PIERSON, C.F. et al. Market Diseases of apples, pears, quinces. USDA Hdbkm 376. 120 pp. (color photos). 1971.
PORTER, C.W. Successful Roadside Marketing. Pa. State University Spec. Cir. 70. 8 p. Seek update.
SHEPHERD, G.S. and Gene A. Futrell. Marketing farm products, Iowa State Univ. Press, Ames. 510pp. 1970.
SINCLAIR, G.E. Postwar record seen for U.S. Apple Exports. USDA Foreign Agriculture. 2 p. Nov. 1979.
SMITH, D.L. and D.J. Ricks. Applesauce price relationships. Mich. AER-210. 1972.
STRUBE, R.W. What a terminal market jobber has to face. United Fresh Fruit & Veg. Assn. 777 14th St., NW, Wash. D.C. 20005. p. 93-98. 1973.
THATCH, W. and D. Foss, New Jersey Agricultural Transportation Study. Rutgers Univ. (New Jersey), A.E. 362. 1976.
WAGLEY, H.O., Jr. Deciduous fruit canning in Australia. USDA, FAS M-240. 12pp. 1972.
A leading marketing agency in U.S. is the United Fresh Fruit and Vegetable Assn., 777 14th St., N.W., Wash., D.C. 20005. Only members receive periodic rpts., "The Packer" is a weekly newspaper full of marketing information from One Gateway Pl., Kansas City, Kansas. 66201. "International Fruit World" is published annually for the world marketing trade from Oscar Bauer Publications, Aeschengraben, 16, Basle, Switzerland, about sFr 45. 275 pp. color. Annual roadside marketing clinics are held at several state universities as Illinois, New York, Michigan, Ohio and New Jersey. Write for announcements and get on mailing lists.

CHAPTER XIII

Pear and Quince Culture

INTRODUCTION [1]

The earliest authentic record of pears in the United States is probably that of the Endicott pear tree planted near Salem, Massachusetts, about 1630. It was brought to America by the French and English colonists. Despite the early introduction and general popularity of pears, they have never become as widely grown as the apple in America. They rank fourth after the peach in the United States and third after apple in the world.

Expansion in pear growing since 1920 has been in the three Pacific Coast states where the conditions are favorable to economical and heavy production of high-quality fruit. This region and the Po Valley in Italy are the most intensive pear-growing areas in the world. Pear production in the eastern United States is of little commercial importance, except for a few regions around the Great Lakes. Production is largely limited to cannery outlets, local trade, and home orchards. In many ways, the pear is more desirable for home orchards than the apple because it grows and produces acceptable fruit with less attention. Also, pear trees such as Kieffer and Tyson are relatively long-lived. Once a Kieffer tree has become mature and well established, it may live and produce satisfactorily for 100 years or more.

Pear psylla, still a serious pest in the West, and fire blight were largely responsible for a marked drop in pear trees in eastern U.S., 1910 to 1930. Since 1930, this reduction in pear trees has been less marked.

Pear psylla has been shown to be a vector of an extremely potent and dangerous mycoplasma to pears known as "pear decline". Pear decline reached serious proportions in the Pacific Northwest during the 1950's and first appeared in California in 1959. Since then it has killed over a quarter of a million California pear trees, and the disease is still active, although its intensity has dwindled in recent years. There is no lasting cure; periodic treatments are effective (Fig. 6.) It had far reaching effect in the Pacific Coast pear industry, but with new plantings on better stocks the industry is returning.

Pear trees in the U.S. were close to 11 million in the 1970's of which about three million were nonbearing. The number of pear trees of all ages in the United States has decreased about one half since 1930. The decrease was about the same for both bearing and nonbearing trees.

In contrast with the above reduction in tree numbers, pear production has nearly tripled in the United States during the past 75 years, the increase having occurred largely in the Pacific Coast States. The 1980-2 three-year average production in the United States was 850,000 short tons. Leading states in tons were; California, 350,000; Washington, 248,300; Oregon, 185,500; New York, 18,000; and Michigan, 9,300. All other commercially important states produced together less than 20,000 short tons. Fresh sales have comprised less than 40 percent of the production; pears canned over 60 percent, dried and farm use about two percent.

Commercial pear production on the Pacific Coast is confined largely to nine districts. Progressing from Washington State south, these districts are the Wentachee and Yakima Valley areas in central Washington; the Hood River Valley in northcentral Oregon, and the Rogue River Valley around Medford in southern Oregon; in

Figure 1. Home gardeners can grow pear trees, other fruit trees in limited space on a trellis or against a wall receiving sun several hours a day. Pear cultivars on different rootstocks in different regions respond differently, as indicated on the wall here at the E. Malling Research Station, Kent, England. Local experiment stations can suggest desirable cultlivars, rootstocks.

[1]Dr. Robert L. Stebbins, Extension Horticultural Specialist, Oregon State University, Corvallis, James A. Beutel, Extension Pomologist, University of California, Davis, 95616, assisted in this chapter revision.

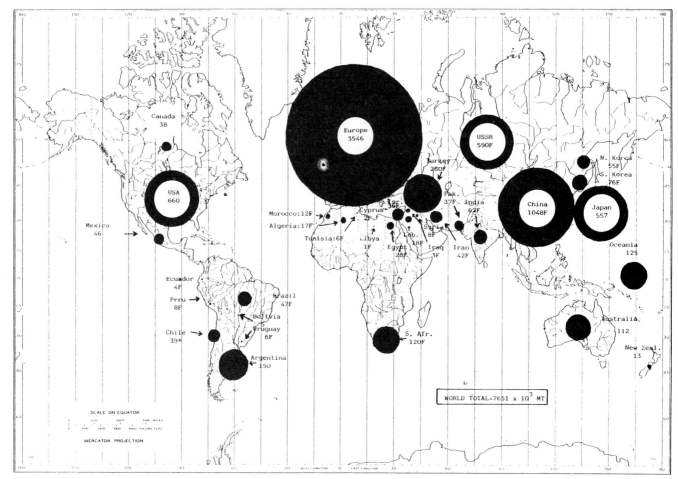

Figure 2. In the world production of pears, Italy ranks first with the USA second, and Spain and France a close third and fourth. (In metric tons 10³.) (From *The Pear* by T. van der Zwet and N.F. Childers, 1982, covering cultivars to marketing around the world).

California, the north coast area of Lake and Mendicino Counties, the Sacramento River district located southwest of Sacramento, the Sacramento Valley area around Marysville and Yuba City, the foothill district near Placerville, and the Santa Clara district south of San Francisco Bay.

Pear production around the world is confined largely to areas within the temperate zone. World production is *over 7 million metric tons* (Figure 2). The pear is popular in China, more so than the apple, and mainly of the Oriental types: *P. ussuriensus, P. bretschneideri, P. serotina* and some *P. pashia*. Most pears in Europe are eaten fresh, some are canned, and others pressed for cider known as "Perry." In the United States, more pears are eaten canned as halves or diced in fruit cocktail, than are eaten fresh. Argentina, Australia, South Africa, and New Zealand produce pears largely for dessert and cooking. Pear production in these southern hemisphere countries

For European research: Contact Centre de Recherches INRA 49, Angers, France; E. Malling Res. Sta., Kent, England; Research Sta. for Fruit, Wilhelminadorp, Netherlands; Instituto Coltivazioni Arboree, Univ. of Bologna, Italy.

has been increasing since 1930; from February to June, their exports are beginning to dominate many of the northern hemisphere markets. Most of their season is opposite that of the West Coast, but they do compete with late-stored winter pear cultivars like Anjou in the United States and United Kingdom.

CHOICE OF PEAR CULTIVARS

Pear cultivars have a great diversity in size, shape, texture, and flavor. Pear species vary from the small hard inedible fruits of the Oriental pear, *Pyrus calleryana Dec.,* to the fine-quality fruits of some varieties of the common European pear, *Pyrus communis L.* Also, there may be a considerable variation in fruit quality and shape within a cultivar from one region to the next. The Bartlett in Washington, for example, is longer and more narrow than in California, but it seems to attain higher quality where the summers are relatively hot than where they are cool.

All important pear varieties grown in the United States belong to the European species, except for a few hybrids

182

such as Kieffer, LeConte, and Garber which are crosses between the European and the Japanese pear, *Pyrus serotina Rehd*. Although there are more than 2500 minor cultivars and 100 major ones, commercial pear production is limited to a relatively few cultivars. Seven cultivars are commercially important on the West Coast. The Bartlett variety known as the "Williams" in Europe, New Zealand, Australia, and South Africa, usually accounts for about 80% percent of the U.S. commercial pear production. This is because the Bartlett fruit is well suited for canning, drying, and for fresh sales either locally or distant. The tree also is adapted widely to soil and climatic conditions. California has over 40,000 acres of which 95 percent is planted to Bartletts. Other cultivars in order are: Hardy[2], Comice, Winter Nelis, and Bosc. California, Rogue Red, and Sensation are among cultivars showing promise. Asian ("apple" or "salad") pears are being planted commercially.

In Washington the commercial cultivars are Bartlett and Anjou, with Bartlett representing 2/3 of all pears. Bartletts are canned and shipped fresh August through October, while Anjous are stored and shipped December through May.

In Oregon, Bartlett, Anjou, Bosc, Comice and Seckel are grown. At Hood River, Bartletts and Anjou are most important. In Medford high-quality Comice are sold in gift packages and Bosc develops a fine cinnamon russet.

The Kieffer cultivar is generally grown in the East. Although it is of inferior quality, it produces heavily, and the fruit is an attractive deep yellow. The tree is adapted widely to soil and climatic conditions and is hardier and more blight resistant than other cultivars grown in the East. Michigan and New York, the two most important commercial pear producing states in the East, and possibly Pennsylvania, are the only eastern states in which the Bartlett acreage generally exceeds that of Kieffer. Other commercial cultivars are Clapp, Maxine, Comice, Flemish Beauty, Bosc, Claireau, Seckel, Duchess, and Anjou. Magness has a problem in fruit set but is showing the most promise although with time for testings, other blight-resistant pears may gain commercial favor. Early Seckel is two weeks earlier than Seckel which it otherwise resembles. Gorham ripens two weeks after Bartlett, equal in blight susceptibility. Honeysweet is a blight-resistant Purdue introduction.

In the southern states, Kieffer, Bartlett, Garber, Baldwin are grown. The Tennessee Station has bred Morgan and Carrick, blight resistant. Very low chilling pears are needed in Florida, including Hood, Carnes, Orient, Pineapple, Kieffer, Baldwin, Ayers, Tenn and Flordahome. Hood serves as a pollinator for Flordahome.

---

[2]The "Beurre" and "Doyenne du" prefexes are rarely used by growers. Pear cultivars carrying these names are referred to as "Hardy," "Comice," or "Bosc."

Figure 3. Bartlett (or Williams) is the most planted pear. These trees are 3-years old, palmette trained, 4 ft. spacing, after pruning, on Quince A rootstock, producing 11 T/A the year of photo. Most fruit production in the Mediterranean area is by palmette trellis (J.A. Beutel, Univ. of Ca. 95616).

Gieser, Wildeman, Winterrietpeer are grown in Holland. In Italy, largest pear producing country in the world, the 6 leading cultivars are: Passe Crassane, Bartlett, Kaiser, Alexander, Abate Fetel, Coscia and Dr. Jules Guyot.

PEAR POLLINATION

Most cultivars of pears are self-unfruitful. Some cultivars (Bartlett, Comice, Hardy) under ideal conditions set huge crops of parthenocarpic (seedless) fruit. These ideal conditions for parthenocarpy are several days of warm weather (maximum temperatures of 70-85°F.) during bloom. When bloom occurs during cool, dry or wet weather with daytime maximums of 55-65°F., cross-pollination by bees and other insects is essential for adequate crops. In California a good correlation between parthenocarpic set of solid blocks of Bartletts and hours over 60°F. during a 10-day bloom period has been determined. If more than 80 hours over 60°F. occur during the 10-day bloom period, good to bumper crops are parthenocarpically set, but poor crops are set if there is less than 80 hours over 60°F. In Oregon, R.L. Stebbins notes that if there are 50 hrs. over 60°F., Bartlett will not set parthenocarpically; and if there are more than 150 hrs., an excellent crop sets, provided there is no frost damage. Most reports of better sets of Bartletts with cross-pollination are explainable based on this temperature relationship. In years of cool wet bloom periods (1965), cross-pollination by insects was most beneficial in many areas of California. However, when the temperature was

Figure 4. The spindlebush training system is frequently used for pears and apples in West Europe. Note the tree tops have been pruned to a weak side leader to discourage upward growth. A stock-cion combination, as an example, is Comice on Quince A rootstock. Windbreaks are common with dwarfed trees. (F.A. Roach, E. Malling Research Sta., Kent, England.)

too cold for bee activity (1967) in the Sacramento River district, cross-pollination could not take place and a crop failure occurred in orchards with and without pollinators. Hand pollination, although not economically practical, did provide fruit set under these conditions. Applications of pollen by airplane dusters or air blast sprayers have been of little or no value under these conditions. Small hand operated pollen dusters may (California) or may not (Oregon) be effective when temperatures are too low for bee flight.

For these reasons most California orchards are planted solid to Bartletts. As insurance against poor bloom conditions (cool weather which occurs about 10% of the time in the Sacramento Valley) some growers plant one pollinizer for every 16 Bartletts. Pollinizers used are Winter Nelis, which blooms ahead of Bartlett in California; Hardy, which blooms with Bartlett; Comice which blooms slightly ahead of Bartlett; and Bosc, which blooms with and after Bartlett. In California all pollinizers have less market demand than Bartlett fruit, so they are used on a limited basis in less than 25% of the orchards. In Washington, Bartletts are commonly used to pollinate Anjous and both have good market value in Washington.

Magness and Waite are pollen sterile and Bartlett and Seckel are incompatable for pollination. With these exceptions, other pear varieties will cross-pollinate each other. In the East and other areas where cool weather at bloom time necessitates cross-pollination, two or more cultivars should be planted. If both cultivars are equally valuable, solid rows of each variety should be used. If one variety is preferred, pollinzers may be scattered in every third or fourth row. Bartlett in California has shown earlier and more uniform stage of bloom on Old Home stock than on *P. betulaefolia* and *P. calleryana*.

Susceptibility to fire blight must be considered in selecting a pollinizing cultivar in pear orchards. Cultivars such as Bosc, Clapp Favorite, Flemish Beauty, and Gorham, which are relatively blight susceptible, may be of little value as pollinzers after a blight attack, necessitating the use of bouquets for several years until blooming returns. Experience has shown that where a minimum number of trees are required as pollinizers for a Bartlett planting, it might be well to use some trees of a blight resistant variety as Old Home, Magness, or of the lighter bearing Anjou variety. One tree in nine is the minimum number of a pollinizing variety that can be used. Solid pollenizer rows are better. The honeybee prefers flowers of other fruits to the pear's. Hence, supply an abundance of bees to insure a thorough cross-pollination.

Anjou fruit set is increased commercially the following year by applying 2, 4, 5-TP at 7.5 ppm dilute volume immediately after harvest. Bartlett set can be increased by using 2.5 ppm. same procedure, or by applying chlormequat or ccc (2-chloroethyl tri-methylammonium chloride) 1500 ppm 4 wks. AFB on young trees. NAA to reduce fruit drop also may increase set the following spring, as will a boron spray at bloom if B is a marginally deficient nutrient.

LOCATING THE PEAR ORCHARD

Pears require about 900 to 1000 hours of chilling below 45°F. (7.2°C) during winter to break their rest period. This is about the same amount of chilling as required for the average apple variety, except Bartlett which needs 1000-1100 hours under 45°F. In the southern United States and southern California, this is a factor to be considered. The uneven opening of flowers in spring due to insufficient winter chilling makes it difficult to time the sprays for codling moth, increases difficulty in controlling fire blight during bloom, and may interfere with cross-pollination in districts where it is needed.

Low-chilling pears (source: India) are being bred of fair quality for Florida, requiring 50 hrs. or less below 45°F. Hood and Flordahome require 100-150 hrs. chilling.

Most pear varieties, properly matured, will endure a winter temperature of -10°F (-23.3°C) without bad injury. Flemish Beauty, Anjou, Clapp Favorite are the most resistant to cold; Bartlett is the least. Pear buds and wood are less resistant to cold than those of the apple but more resistant than the peach. Pear planting is generally questionable in regions where temperatures may fall lower than -20°F. to -25°F.

TABLE 1. CRITICAL TEMPERATURES FOR BLOSSOM
BUD KILL OF PEAR* AT DIFFERENT STAGES
OF DEVELOPMENT (E.L. PROEBSTING, JR.)

	BUD DEVELOPMENT STAGE							
	Scales Separating	Blossom Buds Exposed	Tight Cluster	First White	Full White	First Bloom	Full Bloom	Post Bloom
Old Std. Temp.	18	23	24	28	29	29	29	30
Av. Temp. 10% Kill	15	20	24	25	26	27	28	28
Av. Temp. 90% Kill	0	6	15	19	22	23	24	24
Av. Date (Prosser, Wa.)	—	3/23	3/31	4/5	4/9	4/14	4/18	4/25

*For Bartlett. Anjou is similar in hardiness but may bloom earlier and, hence, may be more tender than Bartlett at the same date. Wash. State Univ., Prosser Station, Washington.

Although pear blossoms open earlier than apples and later than almonds, apricots, or peaches, spring frosts are a definte factor, and the selection of a frost-free site is important. Because of higher energy costs, overhead sprinklers and wind machines now are used in place of oil burners to protect against frosts in pear orchards. Frosts during bloom may hinder cross-pollination. Post-bloom frosts may kill pears and/or cause frost rings and spotting. The pear will withstand higher summer temperatures than the apple. Bartlett attains highest quality where summers are hot. Premature ripening is due to cool temperatures a month before harvest which may cause severe losses in some yrs. Core breakdown is due to overmaturity.

Water supply. Although pear trees are remarkably tolerant of drought or excessive moisture for relatively long periods, better and bigger crops can be obtained in most commercial pear regions in the West by irrigation during periods of low rainfall even though winter rainfall may be heavy. Portable sprinklers, flood irrigation and permanent set over-tree sprinklers are being used. Trickle irrigation is in limited use because of installation and operating costs but is very effective in establishing young orchards.

Soil. Pears will grow in a wider variety of soils and will probably do better on the heavier wet soils than almost any other fruit. However, the pear performs best on a soil that approaches the ideal fruit soil — deep, fertile, well-drained, easily worked, and not too heavy. In the West, freedom from all alkali in the soil is key, also freedom from salinity in irrigation water. Kieffer will tolerate the light droughty soils in western Michigan.

ORCHARD LAYOUT

Planting distances of 18-22 feet on the square in the U.S. were common before 1960. Most plantings since have been in hedgerows with distances ranging all the way from 8 x 12 to 14 x 24 feet (Figure 5). These plantings have all been on vigorous seedling rootstocks but training systems have varied. The trend is toward central-leader trees. Most Comice orchards and others in the Medford, Oregon area are planted on Provence BA-29 which gives some size control but trees on EM-A quince are smaller. Dense plantings of 200-300 trees per acre make more efficient use

Figure 5. Hedgerow Bartletts in Sacramento Valley, California, with permanent-set low irrigation, in-row herbicides, seedling rootstocks, 8 x 15 ft. spacing, 5 yrs. old, pruned and harvested from special-built scaffolds, and sprayed with 2-way vertical mast. (James A. Beutel, University of California, Davis.) (See Chapter XVIII).

185

Figure 6. Pear decline, probably due to a mycoplasma-like organism, vectored by the psylla insect, has responded to injection of 8 qts. after-harvest of oxytetracycline hydrochloride in 6-8 trunk holes under pressure (see references). Left, pear tree, untreated; right; treated fall 1970; photo 1971. More and better growth and fruit induced. Tests with 100s of growers in California, 1000s of trees, shows treatment feasible, economical on commercial scale. (Courtesy George Nylund, Cal. Agr. Exp. Sta., Davis 95616).

of land and result in higher early yield per acre. To avoid overcrowding and shading, special management procedures are necessary and considerable side hedging and topping are done. The 15 to 30-year old orchard, if properly maintained, regardless of tree spacing, will produce 15-25 tons per acre consistently.

In Europe, Quince A dwarfing stock under Comice, e.g., trained in hedgerows by spindlebush, may produce over 80 T/hectare. Planting distances are close: 4 to 8 feet apart in rows 10 feet apart. Interplanting old "decline" orchards, later pulling the old trees, is common practice on the West Coast, USA.

PROPAGATION AND ROOTSTOCKS

The most widely used understock for pears is the European or French pear (*Pyrus communis L.*). Relatively few trees have shown susceptibility to pear decline. Winter Nelis seedlings (Bartlett pollen) are now the preferred French-type rootstock in California. Old Home and Old Home X Farmingdale selections are resistant to decline, blight and suckering and are used as rooted cuttings for pear trees in some orchards, but Old Home is susceptible to *Pseudomonis syringae* and while vigorous may be unproductive. Seedlings of *P. calleryana* and *P. betulaefolia,* both resistant to decline, are used as rootstocks, especially in difficult soil conditions.

Pear decline. Pear decline, a disease which has over the past 35 years decimated millions of trees in the West Coast U.S., from British Columbia to central California is similar to, if not identical with, the Italian pear disease called *Moria.*

Pear decline, a mycoplasma (not virus, Japan, 1967), is spread by a pear insect, the pear psylla. Symptons may take two forms. A sudden and utter collapse of a perfectly healthy tree may occur within 60 days, or a year or more when the tree finally dies. The former is called *quick decline*, the latter is *slow decline*, but regardless of symptoms, tree death is indicated. Weakening and eventual death are due to blockage of the phloem vessels immediately above the graft union, which prevents the roots from obtaining nourishment. It is during this period of infection that a deterrent *brown line* forms encircling the tree in the cambial area immediately above the graft union. Periodic tetracycline injections subdue the disease (Figure 6.)

Pear cultivars grafted to Oriental rootstocks, such as *Pyrus serotina* and *P. ussuriensis,* are extremely susceptible to pear decline. At least 80% of the two million pear trees which have succumbed to pear decline in California were growing on these two Oriental rootstocks. However, not all Oriental rootstocks are susceptible. *P. calleryana* is highly resistant and *P. betulaefolia* is immune. The European rootstock *P. communis L.* is highly resistant. A botanical variety of this species *P. communis* var. *nivalis* has shown some slight susceptibility to pear decline. Pear decline does not apparently affect unbudded or ungrafted trees, for seedling trees of highly susceptible rootstocks (*P. serotina* and *P. ussuriensis*) have been innoculated with pear psylla which had previously fed on infected trees, with no evidence of decline. There has been some decline in orchards on quince stock.

Pydrin is proving effective against psylla. A predator

TABLE 2. Relative susceptibility of pear
rootstocks to damage from various causes
(M.N. Westwood, Ore. State Univ. Corvallis)

0 = not susceptible, 4 = very susceptible

	Pear decline	Fire blight	Freeze damage	Lime induced chlorosis	Pear root aphid	Nematodes
Bartlett seedling	1	4	0	1	4	3
Nelis seedling	1	4	0	1	4	3
French seedling	2	4	0	1	4	3
Bartlett, self-rooted	0	4	0	1	4	3
OH x F clones	0	0	0	1	2	3
P. calleryana seedling	2	0	3	3	0	0
P. betulaefolia seedling (OSU)	0	0	2	2	0	3
Provence Quince	0	3	4	4	0	0
Angers Quince (EM QA etc.)	0	3	4	4	0	0

*The OSU *P. betulaefolia* is the only source resistant to fire blight.

study is underway at Oregon State University for both psylla and codling moth control. Reason - Pydrin also controls mite predators and may cause increased costs in controlling mites. Growers with orchards grafted to Oriental rootstock cannot be certain how long their trees will escape infection. Countless observations and many experiments have shown that visible symptoms of pear decline appear to be triggered, or expressed under the following set of conditions: a) susceptible rootstock, such as *P. serotina* or *P. ussuriensis*; b) a population of "decline" infected pear psylla, and it need not be a high population; and c) conditions which will cause tree stress, in other words, excessive heat, drought, poor drainage, severe winter injury, or any combination of climatic and cultural factors which would tend to put the trees under a stress. Growers with orchards with Oriental rootstock can perhaps retard the advance of pear decline by spraying to reduce pear psylla, doubling the N, irrigating frequently, and pruning heavily, particularly in the cool foothill areas, and use of trunk injections (Figure 6). Contact Ore. State Univ., Corvallis and Univ. of Calif., Davis, for detailed characteristics of pear rootstocks and desirable stion combinations. See also Table 3.

Dwarf and semi-dwarf pear trees on quince stock (*Cydonia oblonga*) are being used for home planting and for high-density commercial plantings. The Angers and Provence quince clones are the most widely used. The EM A Angers is preferred in Europe; Comice, popular in USA, bears within 5 yrs. on Provence; 15 yrs. on French rootstocks. Most USA nurseries use Provence understock with EM A second choice. Africa (Stellenbosch Sta.) and Holland ('Adams') have promising dwarfing stocks. In Italy, Qunice A and B are popular with use of Provence increasing. Seedling stocks are used if the soil is poor, shallow or calcerous. In France, nurseries are going to BA 29 Provence with some Qunice A and B. Quince C is less vigorous than BA 29 and used for high density plantings.

M.N. Westwood of Oregon State University is introducing several promising new selected dwarfing clones.

Top-working. Top-working on fireblight resistant stocks is not done in recent years because of the availability of decline-resistant rootstocks and the ability to control blight by other means. For top-working techniques, see Chapter XVIII.

TRAINING AND PRUNING PEAR TREES

It is characteristic for most pear varieties to grow strictly upright, and not branch freely. Pears in general, and Bosc and Comice in particular, generally have very narrow crotches. In most tree fruits, narrow crotches tend to be weak and permit serious breakage when the tree is bearing heavy crops. But breakage of major scaffold limbs from the crotches of Bosc and Comice trees is rare. The wood seems to develop strength enough to prevent breakage of narrow crotches. But since narrow crotches are more susceptible to cold injury, they should be avoided if there is danger of freeze injury. *The trend toward central leader training in semi-dwarf apple orchards has carried-over into pears, without enough consideration of the differences between the two.* One clear drawback to the central leader pear tree is the tendency for fire blight to strike the leader, run straight down and kill half of the tree before it can be cut out. Central leader training is best for dwarf and semi-dwarf trees with a height of 10 or 11 feet. But most pear trees are not dwarf. They will eventually reach a height of 14 or 15 feet in most orchards even though a vigorous effort is made to control tree height.

It will be difficult to reach the top of such tall central-leader trees for picking or pruning. Finally, with Bartlett and Bosc it will be difficult to fill the zone from 8 to 14 feet

TABLE 3. Pear rootstock work in other
countries (M.N. Westwood, Ore. State
University Corvallis)

Researcher and Institute	Type of Work
1. A.F. de Wet and others, Fruit Technology Research Institute, Stellenbosch, South Africa	Two semidwarf stocks: B-13 (origin unknown) and B-27 (Kieffer x Forelle clone).
2. East Malling Research Station, United Kingdom	Two dwarf stocks: Quince A and EMLA Quince C.
3. J. Brossier and others, Tree Fruit Research Station, Angers, France	Tree dwarf stocks: Angers selections, Fontenay selections, and BAC-29 clone (Provence). Special calcium tolerant stocks: *P. amygdaliformis* seedlings.
4. Fruit Research Station, Skerniewice, Poland	Three dwarf hardy stocks: Quince clones S-1, S-2, S-3.
5. Research Stations in Russia, Moscow (Hdqtrs.)	Testing hardy Quince clones and seedlings.
6. H. Quamme and others, Harrow Research Station, Ontario, Canada	Testing dwarf *Pyrus* such as *P. fauriei* and *P. communis* hybrids for hardiness, blight resistance, and productivity.
7. H. Broadfoot, E.C. Whittaker and others, Gosford Research Station, New South Wales, Australia	Vigorous D6 low chilling clone of *P. calleryana* tested and released.

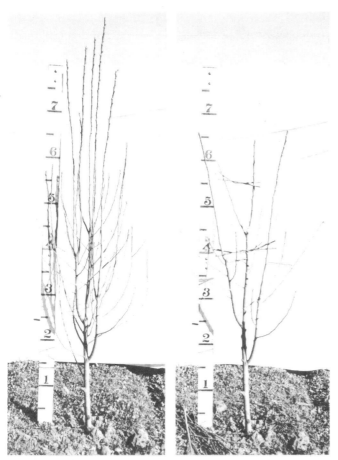

Figure 7. This is a suggested system for training pear in California. Pear trees tend to grow upright. Props are used to spread the main limbs early. Limbs are spaced around the tree and no limb has a strong lead. Dr. Stebbins of Oregon suggests leaving most of the "undergirder" limbs without heading to fill out the lower part of the tree later. (Univ. of Calif., Davis 95616).

with fruiting wood because of the strong tendency of Bartlett and Bosc limbs to bend downward under the weight of the fruit.

If the trees are 12 to 14 feet apart or more in the rows, there will be much waste space between the upper halves of the trees. Finally, the need to open apple trees to light for development of red color does not exist with pear trees. Overall tree shape does influence productive efficiency. Do not let the top of the tree overgrow and shade-out the lower limbs. The danger of this happening is greater with multiple-leader than with central leader trees.

The concept of an "open center" tree is not easily applied to pear because these varieties naturally have an upright, narrow carriage. Three or four upright leaders fairly close in the center tends to fit the tree's natural growth habit (Figure 7). Some orchards in southwestern France and South Africa are so designed and, carry crops of about 25 tons per acre with no significant breakage and usually without props, straps or wire. The trees are cone-

shaped or approaching cylindrical with the widest portion close to the ground. A 3-4 leader tree with a closed center is simple and not nearly as laborious as the central-leader system with spreading and limb tying.

The steps followed are as follows: Head the nursery whip at planting time to about 30 inches. Retain all the shoots that arise the first summer. At first dormant pruning, head the 3 or 4 topmost vigorous shoots to stiffen them and cause branching. Do not head the remaining shoots. These unheaded lower shoots could be called "undergirders" because they will undergird, or fill-out the lower part of the tree. If they are headed, they will grow upright parallel to the scaffold limbs and discourage branching on the scaffolds.

If they do not spread enough naturally, branching and early fruiting can be stimulated by mechanically spreading the undergirders and any other higher-side limbs that need it. If the tree is growing rapidly, head the leaders in early summer to stimulate branching. Otherwise, thin the leaders to a single upright shoot in the dormant season and head the shoot to about 2½ - 3 feet. Again, leave all side branches unheaded.

Rapidly-growing upright leaders on pear trees tend to branch only at the point of dormant heading and make two or three vigorous nearly parallel shoots from that point. But as the growing apex of the leader moves higher, its dominant influence over lower buds becomes diluted, and lateral shoots are formed. Repeat the procedure of thinning each leader to a single shoot and heading it each year until the tree has reached its final height.

On Comice do not prune any side limbs until they are at least 2 or 3 years old and loaded with flower buds. Then head into 2 or 3 year wood to a flower bud. This "stub pruning" isn't necessary with Bartlett and Bosc because they set fruit in abundance without it.

Limb spreading with wood or wire props to encourage early bearing is fast becoming a common practice in pears as well as in apples. The unspread limb tends to branch near its apex. Left unheaded, vigorous upright shoots of pear may not branch at all. Moderate spreading, to about 45 degrees from vertical, will reduce the vigor of the terminal shoots and increase the growth of shoots farther down the branch. A spreading to horizontal will greatly suppress growth of the apical shoot and will allow vigorous shoots to form all along the upper side of the limb. Spreading trees by tying to the next tree in the row, because one cannot control the limb angle very well, gives irregular and unpredictable results. It would be better to use various lengths of spreaders so that the limb angle can be controlled. Do not spread the main leaders in a 3 or 4- leadered pear tree unless you want a more open center. The side limbs on multiple-leadered trees tend to spread naturally under the influence of apical dominance, but sometimes additional spreading is desirable.

Figure 8. Comice and Anjou pears respond with increase in fruit set by heading into 2- or 3-yr. wood at "2" above a fruit bud. Note at "1" the heading cut, at "2" the scars where fruit were borne and at "3" the new shoots. Do not head the shoots of the past season. Leave them until they have set flower buds, then head to a bud. Remove completely all unwanted one-year shoots. (R.L. Stebbins, Oregon State University, Corvallis).

You are much more likely to train a tree successfully if you follow one training system from planting to maturity. Try to avoid changing training systems from year to year.

In recent years, a training system being favored is the hedgerow or wall system in which detail pruning is done from a multiple or 2-level moving platform, accommodating four or five workers. The platform also can be used in harvesting. These close-planted trees may or may not be on dwarfing stock since in arid regions growth can be controlled by judicious fertilization and irrigation. Also, the greater competition of tree roots for water and nutrients tends to keep the trees within bounds, particularly if they are fruited regularly and heavily.

Use of Alar in controlling growth and other characteristics in pear has shown little benefit.

Pruning mature trees. Start pruning by opening-out ladder bays. A fruit bud of the pear is similar to that of the apple, containing from five to seven flowers at the terminal of a leafy cluster base. Pear fruits are borne on spurs or terminally on longer shoots. Flower buds borne terminally on long shoots often bear fruit of inferior quality. Although well-lighted spur systems may live and produce for eight or ten years or more, the productivity of spur systems over four or five years old is usually reduced due to shading. Fruit buds borne on shoots usually blossom about ten days after the spur buds; thus, if spur buds have been destroyed by spring frosts, fruit buds on the shoots may give rise to the major portion of the crop. Therefore, on Bartletts where frost is likely, shoots left for fruit production should not be headed back because the fruit buds usually exist on the outer one-third of the shoot (See Figure 8 for Comice and Anjou). Otherwise, head back all shoots over about 18 inches in length where you wish more fruiting wood to develop. Direct all limbs in the upper third of the tree into an upright position, terminating in a single vertical headed shoot. This will allow the tree's internal hormone system, known as apical dominance, to control shoot development in the tree top. Head back or eliminate all old spur systems. Thin-out shoots, leaving enough to replace old spur systems with new fruiting wood. Head long shoots with flower spurs back to a flower

Figure 9. A standard-trained Bartlett pear, in California, 8 ft. spacing in a hedgerow, 4-yrs. old, on seedling rootstock, after pruning. Note vase-form, a few heading-back cuts, with mostly thinning out cuts. (James A. Beutel, University of California, Davis).

spur. Allow the lower branches to extend farther from the trunk and to assume a more horizontal or even drooping position than the upper branches. Remove or shorten one side of all limbs which are forked on the ends. Remove fruiting wood preferentially from the ends of branches so that the crop will be borne on heavier wood.

With mature trees, annual thinning out of new shoots and of an occasional older branch is to be recommended over heavy heading-back that may result in succulent growth susceptible to fire blight. Thinning-out tends to stimulate spur formation. In a bearing pear tree, new growth of about 18 to 30 inches each year is desirable. The type of pruning on bearing trees may vary considerably from one region to another. For example, the mature Bartlett pear in California is pruned more heavily by heading-back cuts in the Santa Clara Valley to maintain sufficient renewal wood and to prevent the production of large crops of small fruits. On the other hand, in the Sacramento Valley where vegetative growth is more vigorous, prune lightly by using mostly thinning-out cuts. Wood of the Bartlett pear in the Santa Clara Valley is distinctly softer and more brittle than in the Sacramento Valley.

When the Bartlett tree is mature and fully occupies its alloted space, there is apparently little effect of any reasonable system of pruning on the size of the crop and time of maturity. Based upon experience in California, this evidently is true regardless of the region. In other words, if adequate replacement wood is obtained without severe pruning, it makes no difference whether these results are obtained by thinning-out, heading-back, or by a combination of the two.

Figure 11. This shows the tremendous difference in fireblight resistance of some pear cultivars. At USDA grounds, Beltsville, Md., is the Dawn cultivar on the left and the DeVoe at right, trees almost dead from restrictions in growth by the bacteria.

Mature Comice and Anjou trees tend to set more fruit where a pruning cut is made adjacent to a fruit spur. Leave shoots of these varieties unheaded until they set flower buds, then head to a spur. Excessive pruning of Anjou increases the incidence of fruit corking, a disorder associated with low fruit calcium levels. Suckers are unwanted shoots, mostly located in the tree tops, which develop on horizontal wood. They are detrimental because pear psylla, scale and other insects hide among them where they are not easily reached by spraying. Avoid sucker development by avoiding horizontal limbs in the tree top. Direct the terminal of each major scaffold limb into a single vertical shoot and head it.

Kieffer trees in the East are often cut back to two-year-old wood every other year, or stubbed back each year, so as to remove about two thirds of last season's growth. This can be done with this variety because it is less subject to blight than Bartlett and most other European types. Also cutting back is a fruit-thinning process, and the Kieffer needs this since it is likely to set heavily, producing small fruits.

Fire Blight Control. Control blight by removing all traces of blight whenever noticed. Spraying will aid in maintaining a control. Thorough blight cutting requires a trained operator with good equipment, an abundant supply of sterilizing solution and the time to make several trips through the orchard. Combining the two jobs — pruning and blight cutting — is a poor practice.

There is marked difference in fireblight resistance among cultivars, affording a fertile ground for cross breeding (Figure 11).

If severe infection of the early bloom occurs, delay cutting until the extent of the infection can be determined. For late bloom infections, cut out as soon as noticed. During the spring and summer, cut at least 12-15 inches

Figure 10. There is a need for a structure from which hedgerow pear trees can be pruned and the trees harvested, as this homemade mobile platform with kick-boards to extend walkways into the trees.

beyond any visible discoloration. During the fall, immediately after harvest, inspect the orchard and remove all infections missed earlier. Cut 4-6 inches beyond discoloration which is enough at this time.

For a sterilizing solution, dissolve two tablets of mercuric chloride (7½ grains each) and two tablets of mercuric cyanide (7½ grains each) in one pint of water. Solution is very poisonous to man and animals. Use care. Use copious amounts of the solution on the tools and cuts. Sponge the tools with the solution after every cutting. It may be well to use rubber gloves to reduce skin absorption.

In the East and regions where fire blight is a problem, all water sprouts and spurs should be removed regularly from the trunk and lower portions of the main limbs to eliminate this source of infection. (See Chap. XVIII, also color section.)

Other precautions include: (1) avoid the type of pruning that encourages water sprouts, (2) spray with antibiotics, copperlime dust, or weak Bordeaux, as recommended by the local experiment station, and (3) keep growth moderate by judicious nitrogen application and management. Control deer. One grower uses a blow-torch in late winter, burning wood 6-8 inches above and below the fireblight canker until it "boils".

SOIL MANAGEMENT

Cultivation. The cultivation and cover crop system of soil management is commonly employed for pears even in the Medford area of Oregon where blight can be a problem. This is true in the heavy commercial areas of arid regions. Cultivation starts in the spring by turning under weeds or cover crop. Another cultivation may be necessary before the first irrigation. Frequency of cultivation is limited to 3 to 6 a year, depending largely upon the rate of weed growth. Strip-row chemical weed control under the trees, permanent sod in the middles and permanent-set irrigation is popular in the Hood River Valley of Oregon and parts of Washington.

Cover crops. Voluntary weeds may be used for winter cover if an even cover can be obtained. Otherwise, a winter crop such as yellow sweet clover, common vetch, and purple vetch may be used. Commonly used non-legume cover crops are the mustards and cereals such as rye, barley, and oats. Rosen rye is popular in Washington. These are generally planted in fall, early enough to give good cover before cold weather. For young trees, a non-leguminous cover crop seems to be preferable.

In humid areas, it seems advisable to cultivate the young pear trees early in the season or use strip-herbicide treatment in the rows. After the third year, the trees are placed in sod-strip-herbicide or sod-plus-mulch, both being the trend. Any subsequent cultivation, if practiced, should be on a very limited scale early in the spring. The grower should be cautious with practices which induce excessive and soft shoot growth.

Commercial fertilizers. Nitrogen is the main fertilizer showing response in pear orchards. Phosphorous has given increased yield response in New York, and magnesium deficiency is common along the Atlantic Seaboard and in recent volcanic soils of the West. Bosc is highly susceptible. Potassium shortage has appeared in many areas of arid California where 15-25 lbs. of potassium sulfate per tree or one ton/A is used to correct it (Figure 12). Muriate of potash tends to burn roots and kill limbs in arid areas. The need for supplemental P is rare and only a small percentage of the orchards in the Northwest will need K. To be effective in this area, the P and K should be applied in a narrow band or drilled into the root zone. Results with K are questionable in old orchards in heavy clay if drainage also is a problem. A 1-1-1 NPK mix such as 10-10-10 is used in humid regions.

In the use of manure or commercial nitrogen, fire blight is the chief consideration. Pear trees must be fertilized with extreme caution. Too much growth may result in loss of an

TABLE 4. PEAR LEAF STANDARDS FOR NITROGEN (R.L. STEBBINS, ORE. STATE UNIV.) (%)

Status	Bartlett		Anjou		Other	
	Hood River	State	Hood River	State	Hood River	State
Deficiency, below	1.9	1.9	1.8	1.5	1.8	1.7
Below normal	1.9-2.1	1.9-2.6	1.8-2.0	1.5-2.2	1.8-2.1	1.7-2.4
Normal	2.1-2.5	2.6-2.8	2.0-2.3	2.2-2.4	2.1-2.4	2.4-2.6
Above Normal	2.5-3.0	2.8-3.0	2.3-3.0	2.4-3.0	2.4-3.0	2.6-3.0
Excess, over	3.0	3.0	3.0	3.0	3.0	3.0

PEAR LEAF STANDARDS OTHER THAN N

	%				ppm				
	K	P	Ca	Mg	Mn	Fe	Cu	B	Zn
Deficiency, below	.4	0.10	.50	.18	20	40	1	25	10
Below normal	.7	0.13	.60	.24	25	50	2	30	15
Normal	3.0	0.60	2.5	1.0	200	400	50	75	80
Above, normal	4.0	0.65	3.0	2.0	450	500	100	100	300

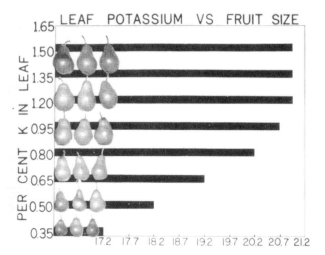

LEAF POTASSIUM VS FRUIT SIZE

PER CENT K IN LEAF

1.65
1.50
1.35
1.20
0.95
0.80
0.65
0.50
0.35

17.2 17.7 18.2 18.7 19.2 19.7 20.2 20.7 21.2

Figure 12. Potassium (K) shortage reduces fruit size, advances maturity, causes marginal burning and rolling of older leaves. Lower figures on chart refer to circumferences of fruit in cm. K deficiency may occur in sandy soils in humid regions. Deficiency also may occur in arid regions, "spotty" through the orchard, necessitating treatment of individual trees. (O. Lilleland, Univ. of Ca., Davis.)

entire orchard in a year or less due to blight.

Leaf analysis (by private labs or the local government experiment station) helps to diagnose a nutritional problem. In Oregon, the state specialists have established in Table 4 the standards for nitrogen and other minerals in the mid-terminal leaves in mid summer.

Where boron is deficient (Figure 13), use 30 lbs./A every third year of boric acid, early fall, to correct corky spot, skin and flesh cracking and leaf bronzing and rosette. On high pH soils of Washington, a fall spray of 3 lbs. borax/100 gals. is more efficient than soil applications, particularly against "blossom blast". With a sensitive alfalfa cover crop, use only 10 lbs./A of boric acid (Solubor or Boro-Spray). Be aware that the stink bug may also cause corky flesh areas. Iron, zinc, manganese and copper deficiencies can be a problem in some arid regions, magnesium in humid areas. (Figure 14).

Iron deficiency in calcareous soils is difficult to control, particularly where drainage is a problem. Multiple early spring applications of iron chelates will minimize the symptoms. Only improvement in soil drainage will provide long-term protection. Some leaf-yellow in pears may be due to sulphur deficiency, corrected with gypsum or S-containing compounds. Dolomite is the best long-lasting Magnesium source in humid areas; use sprays for short-term correction (18-24 lbs. Mg SO₄/A in 5-6 sprays).

FRUIT THINNING

Pears usually require little fruit thinning. Bartlett, Hardy and Bosc may set heavy crops of 3 to 5 fruits/spur

and need hand thinning to 1 to 2/spur. If the all-tree set is not heavy, however, these clusters should size well. With a heavy fruit set, thin 50-70 days after full bloom reducing fruits/cluster and excess clusters. Hardy prices have not justified thinning. Chemical thinning varies with region. See below.

In Washington, larger size fruits are required for canning and drying than for fresh fruit market. The growers usually secure this size by spot picking the larger fruit first. The remaining pears are permitted to hang on the tree for seven to ten additional days to attain adequate size. This increase in size may be 2.5 percent per day during this period. It is important, however, that Bartlett not be permitted to remain too long on the trees to attain the desired size, or losses from core breakdown will occur in cold storage or at the time of preparation for canning.

From 20 to 30 average-sized leaves per fruit are required for proper sizing of Bartlett and most pear varieties.

For Bartlett, Michigan suggests at petal fall, NAD 25 ppm low-vigor trees; 35 med-vigor; 45 for hi-vigor; New York suggests NAD 25 ppm 3-5 days AFB if heavy set

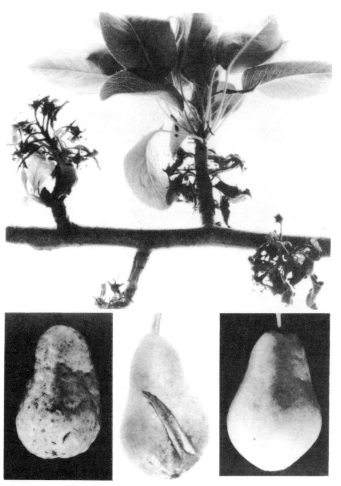

Figure 13. Boron deficiency in pear. "Blossom blast," is corrected by early fall boron spray. (Lower) Bartlett pitting at left; normal fruit, right; and split fruit at center. (U.S.D.A.).

192

Figure 14. Magnesium deficiency is seen frequently on pear in the humid regions and associated also with soils of recent volcanic origin in the Pacific Northwest, appearing a few weeks before harvest. Interveinal yellowing and browning are the symptoms along with early fruit drop. (C.B. Shear U.S.D.A.)

likely, or NAA 5-10 days AFB at 2 ppm for light set or up to 10-15 ppm when heavy set likely on Bosc. In Michigan 25 ppm may defruit Bosc. Later applications result in hanging pygmies. In Washington, NAD or NAA is applied 15-21 days AFB w/ wetting agent, but usage is not as common as with apples. Again, local advice suggested.

HARVESTING AND HANDLING PEARS

Pears are unlike most deciduous fruits in that they attain highest quality when harvested in a slightly "green" stage. At this stage, they must have developed sufficiently to reach highest quality when ripened off the tree, but not so mature as to impair quality of the ripened fruit. This is principally true for the Bartlett variety. Some varieties such as Anjou and Bosc, however, develop better eating quality by being permitted to become somewhat more mature before harvesting.

Progress has been made in mechanical harvesting of pears (Figure 15) but most of the crop is still harvested by hand due to several factors yet to be solved.

Picking maturity. It is rather difficult to select the proper time to pick pears. As the fruit develops and ripens to maturity, the most obvious stages include an increase in size, increases in sugar content, soluble solids, softness and odorous constituents, and a gradual change in ground color from green to yellowish-green followed by a greenish-yellow, and finally a full yellow. Size cannot be relied upon as an index for picking because fruits of different size may be of the same maturity. Fruit harvested when immature is subject to excessive water loss and subsequent shriveling.

The better criteria for determining maturity of pears are: color change, change of firmness of flesh, and change in soluble solids, all of which indicate a change in sugar content. Color charts may be used in California to note progressive ground color changes: No. 1 is green; No. 2 is light green; No. 3 yellowish-green and No. 4 yellow. Softness of flesh is determined with a firmness tester (July, Amer. Fruit Grower Source) as Magness Taylor or Effegi with a 5/16 inch plunger tip. Select 10 or more pears from a lot, remove a thin slice from each side of a pear and average the firmness. Firmness test limits for harvesting certain varieties of pears in Oregon are given in Table 5. These figures may vary somewhat in other states. The soluble solids are determined by using a refractometer on part of the juice obtained while making the firmness test. (McCormick also).

The ease with which the stem can be separated from the spur by an upward twist also is used as an index of maturity. Number of days between full bloom and maturity for pears is fairly consistent within a region, but may vary between regions. In Washington, the following intervals are suggested: Bartlett, 110 to 115 days, Bosc, 130 to 135; and Anjou, 145 to 150 days. Pears on heavily loaded trees usually mature somewhat slower than those on lightly loaded trees. Pears left on the tree too long show core breakdown later.

In California an improved picking maturity standard has been developed by Claypool *et al.*[1] Pears with higher soluble solids are mature at a higher firmness. This principle excludes weather and nutritional effect since these two indices operate in opposite ways. On Bartlett, there is no soluble solids requirements for pears having 19 pounds pressure or lower. If a pear has eleven percent soluble solids, it is mature at twenty-one and a half pounds. For each percent rise in soluble solids, one half pound increase in pressure is permitted up to twenty-three pounds for picking maturity. This system has been working satisfactorily for several years.

In picking pears, size of fruit is taken into consideration, in addition to the criteria mentioned above for picking maturity. Size is based on the largest cross diameter of the fruit and is determined by passing the fruit through a given diameter ring which each picker carries. After a little experience, the picker becomes proficient in estimating the size of fruit by eye, checking occasionally against the ring. On the West Coast, rather definite sizes are requested for given purposes based on the choice of the grower, the

[1]By correspondence.

TABLE 5. Harvest periods, firmness tests, and storage handling of pear cultivars. (R.L. Stebbins, Ore. State University)

Cultivar	Harvest Date Oregon	Firmness Tests[1] Pounds	Cultivar Picked with	Storage Life Months	Storage Required Before Ripening
Bartlett	mid-Aug.	23-18			
	early Sept.	20-17	—	3	none
Sensation	mid-Aug.	23-19	Bartlett	3	—
	early Sept.				
Anjou	late Aug.	17-13	(Hot climate)		
	late Sept.	15-13	—	7	1 month
	mid Sept.				
Red Anjou	early-mid Sept.	17-13	(Hot climate)		
		15-13	Anjou	7	1 month
Bosc	late Sept.	18-14	(Hot climate)		
		16-14	Comice	6	none
Comice	early Sept.	14-10	(Hot climate)		
	late Sept.	13-11	Bosc	5	1 month
Seckel	late Aug.	20-15	(Hot climate)		
	early Sept.	15-13	Anjou	4	none
Hardy	late Aug.-				
	early Sept.		Anjou	3	none
Forelle	late Sept.		Bosc, Comice	6	none
P. Barry	late Sept.		Anjou	7	4 months
	early Oct.				
Winter Nelis	Sept.-Oct.	15-13	Eldorado	8	none
Buerre Easter					2 months
Clapps Favorite	early Aug.	19-17	Early Bartlett	½	none
Starkrimson	early Aug.	19-17	Early Bartlett	½	none
Packhams	late Sept.	18-14	(Hot climate)		
		15-13	Bosc	7	none
Eldorado	late Sept.	18-14	(Hot climate)		
	early Oct.	15-13	Nelis	8	1 month
Rogue Red	late Sept.	15-12	Comice, Bosc	8	none
Red Angelo	late Sept.		Forelle	10	
Remier Red	early Sept.	13-11	Comice		none
Canal Red	early Sept.		Anjou		
California	mid Aug.	18-15	Bartlett	4	1 month (?)
	early Sept.				
Golden Doyenne	late Sept.		Bosc	5	

[1]Magness-Taylor tester, 5/16" plunger

buyer or shipper, or upon an agreement between growers and shipper. In general, Bartlett fruits which are less than two and three-eighths inches in diameter are too small for harvest and are left for sizing. Handle pears with care from the time they leave the tree until packed in the box. Abrasion of the skin and discoloration of the flesh can be reduced by lining the field boxes with a cushion such as cardboard.

Bulk Handling. There has been an almost complete shift in key areas to bulk handling with mechanical lifts, as described earlier for apples.

Hormone sprays to reduce pear drop. Pears, like apples, have a tendency to drop fruits before they can be picked. Bartletts are most likely to drop, with Bosc next. Other standard varieties may not drop seriously enough to require a preharvest spray.

Drop may be increased if the trees are deficient in boron, magnesium, or moisture, or if over-fertilized with nitrogen. The use of hormone sprays applied from ground or air, by pear growers has become a standard practice, using 10 ppm (25 grams/A) alphanaphthaleneacetic acid. The manufacturer's recommendations should be followed as to quantity of material and the use of a spreader. The spray is applied about five to ten days before harvest or when there is first evidence of drop of normal fruit. These hormone sprays do not slow down the ripening process; in fact, there is evidence to indicate that ripening is accelerated whether the fruit is on or off the tree. Pear fruits must be harvested *at the proper maturity* with little or no delay, stored as soon as possible, and the temperature of the fruit core reduced to 40°F. within 24 hours. and 32°F. within 48 hrs. On trees sprayed with preharvest sprays, there may be a number of overmature fruits which did not drop, making it necessary for the overmature fruit to be

Figure 15. Pears are among the most difficult to harvest mechanically. This is a decelerator-collector in position, hydraulically operated as devised by the University of California agricultural engineers. It appears to be substantially better than the shake-catch method for pears. (Courtesy R.B. Fridley, Univ. of Calif., Davis. 95616).

other than cool temperatures, such as an overdose of hormone, cannot be averted by application of Alar.

Accelerated harvest in cool seasons. Normally Bartletts in the Mid-Columbia district of Oregon drop about 1 pound in firmness (as measured by a tester) in 4 or 5 days. This means that Bartletts picked at a firmness of 19 to 17 lbs. should be harvested in a 10- to 12-day period for optimum quality. In seasons when prevailing temperatures are below normal before harvest, this optimum harvest period will be greatly reduced. In addition to a shorter harvest period, the fruit is more advanced physiologically and could be harvested at a slightly higher firmness test without a loss of quality.

Grading and sizing. In the packing house, the pears may be first run through a bath, and rinsed and dried in an air-blast before delivery to the sorting table. At the sorting table, the culls are eliminated, and the low-grade fruits are separated from the high-grade fruits. Each grade is sized into several sizes. The rotary bin and other modern types of machines, as described for apples in Chapter X, also are well adapted to pears. The machine must handle the pears with extreme care. Pears packed in boxes must be of uniform size. See "U.S. Standards for Summer and Fall Pears", and "Winter Pears" (obtainable from U.S.D.A. or your county agricultural agent) for grades, tolerances, sizes and packs. Unfortunately, there is no standard box for pears. They are shipped in boxes or half-boxes, but the dimensions of the boxes differ among shippers. Two examples: Full box - 19 x 11 3/4 x 9 inches; half-box - 18 3/4 x 5 5/8 x 5 1/8 inches, latter carrying 24 lbs. of fruit. Tight-filled cartons are popular because more of the packing can be mechanized (Figure 16).

Figure 16. Fiberboard boxes with poly liners perforated are being used for pear shipment, vibrated (above) for tight fill. Hartman wraps impregnated with mineral oil or ethoxyquin (scald control) are used when pears are individually wrapped. Wood boxes have given way to fiberboard.

sorted out either by the picker or by the packing crew. It cannot be over-emphasized that every effort should be made to harvest pears at the proper stage of maturity regardless of whether they have or have not been sprayed with hormone sprays. If you permit hormone-sprayed Bartletts, e.g., to hang 10 days after proper maturity, core-breakdown may occur. Alar 85 at 1000 ppm can reduce or prevent premature ripening if the spray can be applied 85-90 days after bloom or 18-24 days before anticipated harvest, with a night temp. below 50° F. on Bartlett (Wash.). Earlier or later applications are generally ineffective. Thorough coverage of the fruit with the Alar spray is important. The effectiveness of concentrate application has not been documented. Avoid spraying other pear varieties with Alar because of the possible effect on reduced fruit size. Premature ripening caused by factors

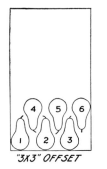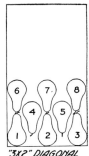

"3X3" OFFSET   "3X2" DIAGONAL

Figure 17. Two styles of pear packs commonly used. Stems in first row next to packer should point away from packer; stems of fruit in other rows point toward packer.

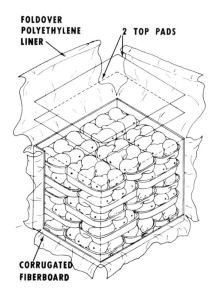

Figure 18. This shipping carton holding 5 or 6 layers (two sizes tested), of 25-30-6-pear trays was shipped successfully in carlot from west to east coast U.S., provided pears were NOT soft at start. Costs are a few cents more/lb. for pears than packaging in boxes.

Pear packing. Each packer handles only one size of pear from the rotating bins. The pear is picked up with the right hand, while the left is grabbing a sheet of wrapping paper. The pear is thrown into the left hand, stem up, with some force so that it rests between the thumb and forefingers. Corners of the paper are then folded over the calyx end of the pear, and the pear is turned up with the right hand while the left hand and fingers twist the paper around the stem of the fruit to form a point. The pear is then placed in the box with the left hand with folds down. The first row of fruit next to the packer is laid with the stems away from the packer, but for other rows the stems are all placed toward the packer The right hand reaches for another fruit while the left hand is placing a wrapped pear in the box. Wrapped pears stay in place better than unwrapped pears because, in addition they are provided with a cushion of paper which helps to restrict the spreading of rots. The two commonly used styles of packing pears are the "off-set" and the "diagonal." The "offset" or "3 x 3" pack is employed for sizes of pear that will give five or more fruits across the box, as shown in Figure 17. The "diagonal" pack, or "3 x 2" is used for larger pears. The pears should be arranged in the box so there is a 1½-to-3-inch graduated bulge at the topcenter of the box.

Packed boxes are marked with the total numbers of pears contained, the grade and the shipper's name and address. Boxes may contain the following number of fruits, depending upon their size; 70, 80, 90, 100, 110, 120, 135, 150, 165, 180, 195, 210, 228, and 245.

Pears in recent years are being packed in fiberboard cartons, volume-fill, followed by vibration to settle them. On arrival in Eastern markets, they are vibrated again. These have been in better condition on the retail counters than hand-packed pears, and there is a saving in cost.

In the early 1980s, almost all Oregon winter pears were being wrapped with the exception of a few Bosc (5%). Many packers are packing Bartletts without wrap and one is using some tight fill (shake fill) while another is hand packing some Bartlett pears and Bosc naked. Most winter pears are poly bagged but many Bartletts are being packed without poly bags, especially since it has increased in price. Where Bartletts are being tight-filled without poly or wrap, the containers are "curtain coated" (36 lbs. boxes) to

prevent scuffing as the pears shake down in the box.

Wood boxes are not being used because of cost. Most growers are trying to keep containers well below 50 lbs. and are moving closer to a 40 lb. net fruit package.

Polyethylene Bags. The most significant development in packing pears for shipment is in polybox liners to which pears have proven well adapted. They extend storage life from a six- to eight-week period or longer. After placing pears in the bag which lines the box and surrounds the fruit, air is withdrawn. An ordinary vacuum cleaner is rigged to do this. About 1½ gauge film is used and the bag must be air tight to provide a more or less "CO_2 gas-stored compartment." Since humidity builds to 100 percent in the bag, the fruit should be only the best and pretreated with a fungicide such as "Stop Mold" by Dow Chemical Company. When removed from cold storage for consumption the bags must be punched within 72 hours for proper ripening and flavor, taking seven to nine days. These poly-wrapped pears have a greater shelf life than other pear packs. Sometimes no air withdrawal from bags is done.

Precooling. The practice of precooling is recommended for the shipment of pears from the West to the East Coast. Methods of precooling are described in Chapter XIV. Precooling reduces ripening quickly. Mechanically refrigerated trucks and rail cars are being used.

STORAGE OF PEARS

Due to the fact that respiration and the breaking-down processes in the pear are more rapid than the apple, it is highly important that the temperature of pears after picking be reduced as quickly as possible using the most effective means of refrigeration. If there is a delay between harvest and storage, allowing the ripening processes to become accelerated, it becomes difficult to retain pears

Figure 19. Mechanical pear wrapping with polyethylene and carton filling in California has cut labor costs markedly. (The Blue Anchor, POB 15498, Sacramento 95813).

satisfactorily in storage. A storage temperature of 30° to 31° F. is recommended for the longest storage life of pears (Table 5). A temperature of 36 °F. reduces the storage life to one-third to one-half in the shorter-lived varieties, such as Bartlett, Comice, and Hardy. Pears at either temperature, however, tend to show more loss than apples under comparable conditions. Anjou will not ripen properly until they have been stored for at least 2 months. Comice and El Dorado require at least one month of storage before ripening. Bartlett, Bosc, Seckel, Packham and Forelle need no cold storage before ripening.

Although pears may be under-cooled in storage, their critical freezing temperature is about 27.7° F. This is only about two degrees below the minimum storage temperature recommended for retaining pears in best fresh condition. Anjou pears frozen for a week to 23° to 27° F. usually recover with little or no injury to the flesh, but if frozen for four to six weeks at these temperatures, the fruit becomes waterlogged under the skin and sometimes in the core region.

Ripening of pears in storage. With the fall and winter varieties, such as Hardy, Anjou, Comice, Bosc, Winter Nelis, Glou Morceau, and Easter Beurre', the highest quality is attained by storing and ripening under carefully controlled conditions of temperature and humidity. Because of the need of these rather definite conditions, an increasingly common practice is to store the fall and winter varieties in rooms at 30° to 31° F., removing them as the trade requires and ripening them in special rooms at temperatures between 60° and 70° F. with the humidity well controlled between 80 and 85 percent, before delivering to the retailer. This process insures maximum quality to the consumer. If pears are ripened about 70°F., they may not soften properly and remain slightly firm until decay or breakdown sets in. Also, they may be tough-textured and poorly flavored. These special ripening rooms have been established in the eastern terminal markets by the West Coast shippers.

It is important to have a knowledge of the limitations of each variety with respect to its storage life. For example, the Bosc is at its best from September 1 to December 15 in California and should never be held beyond the Christmas holidays. It must be held constantly at 30° to 31°F. and ripened at 60° to 70° F. Bosc will lose its ability to ripen if held for any length of time at temperatures between 34° and 35° F.

In Washington, Bosc and Clairgeau when stored at 30° to 31° F. can be utilized best from September 1 to January 15; Anjou, Conference, and Forelle, from October 1 to April 15; Comice from October 1 to February 1; and Winter Nelis and Easter Beurre are not ready until December 1 and may be kept until May.

Bartlett tends to have better more uniform color and texture for canning if stored immediately after picking for 15 to 30 days before being processed. Bartlett pears harvested at pressure tests of 18 to 15 pounds give a fairly good product when stored at 30° to 32° F. for as much as 60 days for canning. If they are retained in storage unduly long, however, core breakdown, rot, scald, softening, and browning of the tissues may result. This is particularly true if the pears are overmature when harvested, or if they are held at room temperature for three to six days after picking before they are stored. CA storage will lengthen storage life. See below.

The Kieffer pear has been shown to develop suprisingly good quality when harvested at 14 to 13 pounds pressure

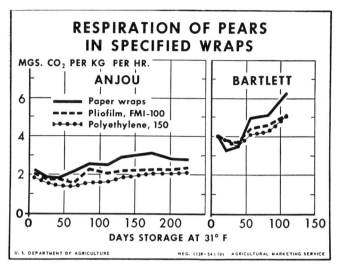

RESPIRATION OF PEARS IN SPECIFIED WRAPS

MGS. CO₂ PER KG PER HR.

ANJOU
— Paper wraps
--- Pliofilm, FMI-100
•••• Polyethylene, 150

BARTLETT

DAYS STORAGE AT 31° F

U. S. DEPARTMENT OF AGRICULTURE   NEG. 1139-54(10)   AGRICULTURAL MARKETING SERVICE

Figure 20. The process of respiration is an index of the rate of ripening of pears. Note from the chart that polyethylene bags reduce respiration more than paper wraps and pliofilm. Note also that Bartlett seems to have a higher respiration rate than Anjou. CA storage best controls ripening for extended marketing.

and stored for 90 days at 32° F., and then ripened at 60° F. Kieffer pears allowed to remain on the trees until overripe develop excessive grit cells, are apt to become dry and mealy, and soften too rapidly around the core. Pears removed from the tree can be ripened immediately at 60° to 65° F. in order to obtain full flavor and juiciness with splendid texture.

Although the pressure tester can be used effectively for determining harvest maturity of pears, it is not satisfactory for measuring the ripeness of pears during cold storage. Pears and apples should not be stored together.

Ripen pears with ethylene. Ethylene gas hastens pear ripening, except for the Kieffer variety which does not seem to be affected either by artifical treatment or by the natural emanation of ethylene gas from nearby ripening pears. The use of ethylene gas may be desirable and profitable in hastening the ripening of Bartlett pears for canning, which appear to be ripening unevenly. This has been demonstrated by placing containers of pears in a closed chamber and exposing them intermittently to concentrations of ethylene of from 1:1000 to 1:5000. At the end of each 24 hours, the ripening rooms are aerated for one hour, using a fan to exhaust the products of respiration. Treatments on four successive days are usually adequate. Where ripening of the fruit is uniform without ethylene treatment, use of this gas has no advantage. Ethylene can cause ripening of pears only if the gas is used a short time after harvest. If the pears have been in cold storage for several weeks, they show little or no response to ethylene gas. Effects of ethylene are most pronounced at temperatures of 65° to 70° with little or no effect at cold

storage temperatures. See Griggs et al. for tests with Ethrel.

CA Storage. The advantage of CA for winter pears is to provide a way to maintain fruit quality over a long period, thus extending the market season. Also, Anjou pears stored in a low O_2 atmosphere (2 to 2.5 percent) tend to be protected from scald. The benefits of using CA for winter pears was first shown by the development and commercial use of sealed polyethylene films as a packaging material. They created a lower oxygen and higher carbon dioxide concentration around the fruit. The seasonal occurrence of browncore in pears packed in sealed poly bags proved to be a serious problem and led to the use of perforated films. This practice prevented occurrence of the disorder, but the benefit of the modified atmosphere realized in sealed bags was no longer attained. Subsequent experimentation has shown that pears are highly susceptible to excessive CO_2. This is especially apparent following cool growing seasons and in full mature fruit. The safe concentrations of CO_2 for winter pears is below 1 percent. At this concentration, CO_2 has little beneficial effect and low levels of O_2 must be relied upon to provide the benefits of CA storage. Optimum and safe CA atmosphere for commercial use is 2 to 2.5 percent O_2 and 0.89 to 1 percent CO_2.

STORAGE TROUBLES

Although *core breakdown* is likely to be more serious in pear from some districts than others, it occurs widely. It is characterized by a breakdown of the tissues in the core area and may spread to the entire fruit. At first, the flesh is soft and watery. Later, it turns brown and the skin of the fruit becomes discolored. Affected fruit has a foul sickening odor and flavor. Core breakdown is definitely associated with harvesting in an overmature condition and with delayed cooling. Bartlett, Hardy, Bosc, and Comice are the important varieties that are especially susceptible.

Anjou scald is similar in appearance to apple scald and apparently is induced in part by the same factors; like apple scald it can be controlled by oiled wraps and CA.

The ordinary form of *pear scald,* however, is usually associated with core breakdown and apparently is due to prolonged holding in storage. It is not controlled by use of oiled wraps. The time when pear scald appears depends upon storage temperatures. Bartletts which may be free of scald even after 90 days at 30 or 31° F. are likely to show it in 70 to 80 days at 36° or in 30 to 35 days at 43°. Bartlett and Bosc are the most susceptible varieties.

Although pears may color at low storage temperatures, they do not always ripen. This is true of Bartlett, Bosc, Anjou and Comice; if held in storage too long, they lose their ripening capacity and will fail to ripen even after removal to suitable ripening temperatures.

Pears may occasionally suffer *freezing injury,* but in the

Bartlett variety at least, unless this is severe or prolonged, no subsequent damage seems to occur. A trouble of much more common occurrence is a wilting or shriveling of the fruit as a result of excessive moisture loss. A relative humidity of about 90 percent will hold the fruit in good marketable condition although an atmopshere approaching saturation is necessary to prevent moisture loss entirely.

Where fruit is carefully handled and graded before storage, fungus rots in pears are usually not serious. However, Anjou and Winter Nelis when stored for long periods may suffer serious loss from *gray mold* rot (*Botrytis sp.*). This trouble is also known as a cluster rot because a large number of affected fruits are frequently found in one position in the box surrounding the original infected pear. The fungus grows from one pear to another at cold storage temperatures. Infection may be reduced by good sanitation in the packing house, careful handling, and prompt cooling. The most effective control measure is the use of copper-treated wraps for packing to prevent the spread of the disease from infected pears to adjacent sound fruit.

Canning pears. Pears picked for canning usually have a lower pressure test than pears used for fresh fruit. They are permitted to attain a larger size on the tree and less pickings are necessary.

Canning factories specify the grade, range of sizes, and ratio of length to diameter of fruit, which they will accept. The ratio of length to diameter desired will vary from one district to another; a greater ratio is demanded for pears from Washington than for pears from California. Fruit is bought by the ton. A premium price is paid for fruit from certain production areas which the canners believe will produce a superior canned product. "U.S. Standards for Canning Pears" can be obtained from the U.S. Department of Agriculture, AMS, Washington, D.C. 20250.

Pears are placed in large ripening rooms of controlled temperatures and humidities upon arrival at the cannery. Fruit is sorted frequently in these rooms to process the individual fruits as they reach the proper stage of ripeness. If the cannery is overloaded when the fruit arrives, the pears are placed in cold storage at 30° to 32° F. and later removed to the ripening rooms at 60° to 70° F.

Drying pears. Only a small percentage of pears in North America are dried, but the drying industry offers a good outlet for the overripe pears. Some fruit is grown especially for drying and remains on the tree longer to attain maximum size. Pears are washed, halved, calyx and stems removed, dried, sulfured (gas) to good translucency, and sunned, covering a 2-4 week period.

Marketing. An increasing amount of pears likely will go into processing. The California Canning Pear Association and the Washington-Oregon Canning Pear Association, both grower organizations, have helped to stabilize prices

Figure 21. Boxed pears palleted and stacked on their sides in a commercial storage on the West Coast. Use of fork lift with pallets or "slip sheets" has facilitated greatly the handling of pears.

on both the canned and fresh market by carefully regulating the movement of pears into marketing channels. There is a trend among West Coast growers to operate their own processing plants.

A survey of housewives in Philadelphia and Chicago by U.S.D.A. showed that few mentioned pears as their favorite fruit, and only 22 percent stated they had bought pears the previous month. City and mid- to high-income people bought pears more than rural or low-income people. Pear buying, unlike apples, was likely to be unplanned. Attractive store displays are important. Contact Ore., Wash., Calif. Pear Bur., 601 Woodlark Bldg., Portland, Ore. 97203 for marketing help.

199

Store-Ripening of Bartletts. Ripening must be under controlled conditions. Requirements will depend upon fruit maturity, previous storage and desired speed of ripening. The following suggestions are made: (1) Ripen fresh Bartletts in original shipping containers. (2) Maintain a relative humidity of 90-95%. (3) Early-harvested Bartletts require more time to ripen than late-harvested fruit: Early - 7-10 days; mid - 5-7; late - 4-5 days. (4) Optimum ripening should occur between 64-72° F. (5) Best eating potential is at firmness of 3 lbs. or less. (6) If firmness has reached 8-10 lbs. cold temperatures (near 32 ° F.) will only slow ripening, not stop it. (7) Maximum uniformity of ripening can be attained by spreading out the containers and using a fan or blower. (8) Ripening is more uniform and rapid following a cold period of 32° for at least 2 wks. (9) Ripening of early to mid-season fruit which has had insufficient cold storage can be speeded by use of ethylene gas in a closed room, using about 100 ppm for 24 hrs. Late-season fruit with at least 2 wks. cold storage should ripen normally without use of ethylene.

QUINCE CULTURE

The quince has never attained more than minor importance among fruits. It is grown widely in the United States mostly in home gardens, though in a few states an occasional small commercial orchard can be found. In Argentina quince is important, production in thousands of tons annually.

Although the selling price of the fruit occasionally may be high, it does not necessarily follow that quince culture is correspondingly profitable. It is difficult to obtain good yields of high quality fruit because of the prevalence of diseases and insects, although the newer pesticides are making this more feasible. Also, the uses of the fruit are limited mostly to the making of jelly, marmalades, preserves, or for adding flavor to apples and pears when stewed or baked. Demands for the quince are strictly limited and, therefore, overstocking of the market could be easily accomplished.

The quince is a low spreading type tree which attains a height usually less than 15 feet. The quince differs from other deciduous fruit trees by blooming terminally early season on current-season growth; floral initiation takes place during the current season rather than the year before as in apple and pear. Cultivars begin to bear in three to four years and reach a maximum production at ten years, yielding about 1 bu. of fruit per tree. Cultivars are self-fruitful.

Cultivars. Pineapple is the most popular, followed by Orange, Van Deman, Champion, Rea, and Meech.

Propagation. Quince is budded on Angers quince as an understock. Angers stocks are propagated by mound layering or by cuttings. Most cultivars may also be multipled by cuttings, but some do not root readily.

Trees and planting. Two and three-year nursery trees are planted about 15 feet apart on the square, making 190 trees per acre. The trees can be trained by the open-center system as recommended for the peach, or the small tree can be cut at 10 to 12 inches above the ground and induced to form a bushlike tree.

Culture. The quince is highly susceptible to the fire blight disease and, therefore, every effort must be made to spray with streptomycin or copper at blossoming time. Probably the best management is to place the trees in sod after they have been strip-cultivated the first two or three years. Nitrogen should be applied very cautiously. Limited cultivation may be practiced in early spring if the trees are becoming obviously low in vigor. Strip chemical weed control and sod middles is a management program well adapted.

Pruning. Because of the habit of growth, comparatively little pruning is needed. Quince makes rather slow, crooked, angular growth. Dead branches and limbs which cross, crowd, or interfere should be removed. Pruning should largely consist of thinning-out cuts with occasional cutting-back of main limbs to stimulate moderate shoot growth upon which the fruits are borne.

Review Questions

1. Where are the commercial pear producing regions in the U.S.; the world?
2. What has been the general trend of tree population and pear production over the years. Comment on production by other countries, worldwide.
3. List pear cultivars grown in your general area, giving strong and weak characteristics of each.
4. Describe a planting for a pear orchard in your locality with Bartlett as the main variety. Adequate provision should be made for cross-pollination, if needed.
5. Compare the pear with the apple in climatic and soil requirements.
6. Discuss the rootstock situation for pears.
7. What rootstocks can be used as a preventive measure against fire blight?
8. Describe the methods for training and pruning a young pear tree (specify the cultivar) before it comes into bearing.
9. Discuss the pear decline problem and correction in the West Coast areas of United States.
10. How does the pruning system for a mature pear tree differ from that of a mature apple tree?
11. What system of soil management would you recommend for newly planted pear trees and for a mature orchard in your region?
12. When would you recommend commercial fertilizers or manure for a mature pear orchard? Why? Discuss potassium and boron shortage in pear orchards.
13. Compare fruit thinning of the pear with the apple.
14. What criteria are used for determining the best stage of maturity of picking pears?
15. Briefly discuss the use of hormones and other sprays for thinning fruits and for reducing pear drop at harvest time.
16. What temperatures appear to be the best for storing and ripening Bartlett pears?
17. What picking, storing, and ripening procedure has proven best for developing highest eating quality in Kieffer pears?
18. Discuss storage problems with pears. How about CA storage of pears?
19. Why has the quince never attained more than minor importance among fruits? In what country is the quince quite popular?

200

Suggested Collateral Readings

ALDWINKLE, H.S. and S.V. Beer. Fire blight and its control. Hort. Rev. Avi Publ. Co. 1:423-474. 1979.

APPLES, pears, grapes. storage guide. ASHRAE Guide and Data Book. Chap. 51:649-657, 1972. (Request recent annual edition).

BARNETT, W.W. et al. Integrated pest mgnet. of pears. Calif. Agr. 12-13. Feb. 1978.

BELL, R.L. et al. Inbreeding pears. ASHS 106:5. 584-89. 1981.

BEN-ARIE, R.L. Sonego. Changes in Pectic Substances in Ripening Pears. J. ASHS. 104(4):500-505. 1979.

BEN-ARIE, R. and S. Guelfat-Reich. Preharvest and postharvest applications of benzimidazoles for control of storage decay of pears. HortScience 8(3):181. June 1973.

BEARDEN, B.E., et al. Monitoring pear scab. Calif. Agric. 16. Apr. 1976.

BELL, R.L. and J. Janick. Heritability and combining ability for fire blight resistance in pear. J. ASHS 102(2):133-8. 1977.

BELL, R.L. and J. Janick. Fire blight resistance and fruit quality in pear. HortSci., 11(5):500-502. 1976.

BETHELL, R.S. et al. Copper-streptomycin sprays control pear blossom blast. Calif. Agric. 7-9. June 1977.

BEUTEL, J.A. et al. Research Review: Antibiotic injections control pear decline. Calif. Agri., 12-13. Aug. 1977.

BLAKE, R.C. and T. Van Der Zwet. The USDA Pear Breeding Program. Fruit Varieties Jour. 33(4):131-136. Oct. 1979.

BLANPIED, G.D. Core Breakdown for New York 'Bartlett'. J. ASHS 100:198-200. 1975.

BLANPIED, G.D. Pithy Brown Core in 'Bosc' Pears During CA Storage. J. ASHS. 100:81-84. 1975.

BOYNTON, D. and G.H. Oberly. Pear Nutrition. Chap. 13 in Fruit Nutrition — Temp. to Trop., Hort. Publ., 3906 NW 31 Pl., Gainseville, FL 32606.

CALLAN, N.W. and P.B. Lombard. Pollination effects on fruit and seed development in 'Comice' pear. J. ASHS 103(4):496-500. 1978.

CEPONIS, M.J. and J.E. Butterfield. Retail and consumer losses of western pears in New York City. HortSci. 9:447-448. 1974.

CHAPLIN, M.H. and M.N. Westwood. Nutritional status of 'Bartlett' pear on *Cydonia* and *Pyrus* rootstocks. ASHS. 105(1):60-63. Jan. 1980.

CHEN, P.M., and W.M. Mellenthin. Harvest Date on Ripening and Postharvest Life of 'd'Anjou' Pears. J. ASHS. 106(1):38-42. 1981.

CHEN, P.M. et al. Quality of low stored oxygen on Anjou pears. ASHS Journ. 106:6 695-8. Nov. 1981.

COLLINS, M.D. et al. Evaporative cooling for bloom delay on 'Bartlett', 'Bosc' pear. J. Amer. ASHS. 103(2):185-7; 187-9. 1978.

COMMERCIAL handling and storage of winter pears. Ore. State Univ., Corvallis, Spec. Rpt. 550, Oct. 1979.

COSTS. For up-to-date figures, contact Agr. Economics depts. at Wash., Calif., Oregon, Mich., and Cornell Universities.

COSTS of producing (a) Bartletts in Yakima Valley, EM-3779, 1973; (b) Anjous in Wenatchee Valley, EM-3553, 1972; and (c) Anjou packouts for 8 growers, EM-3773, Wash. Ag. Ext. Serv., Pullman. 1973.

COUEY, H.M. and T.R. Wright, Prestorage CO_2 treatment on the quality of 'Anjou' pears after regular or CA storage. HortSci. 12(3):244-5. 1977.

CROCKER, T.E. and C.P. Andrews. Pears for Florida. Fl. Fact Sheet-29. 4 pp. 1979.

DENNIS, F.G., Jr. et al. Hormones in pear seeds. II. Levels of abscisic acid, etc. on seed dormancy in *Pyrus* species. J. ASHS 103(3):314-317. 1978.

FALLAHI, E. and F.E. Larsen. Rootstock effects on quality of postharvest pears. HortSci. 16:5. 650-1. 1981.

FAUST, M. et al. Genetic transmission of bloomdate in pears. HortSci. 11:59-60. 1976.

FRENKEL, Chaim and M.E. Patterson. CO_2 on Ultrastructure of 'Bartlett'. HortSci. 9:338-340. 1974.

FRIDLUND, P.R. and S.R. Drake. Pear vein yellows virus on pear tree performance. J. ASHS 106(4):412-4. 1981.

GIL, G.F., G.C. Martin, and W.H. Griggs. Fruit-set and Development in the Pear: Diffusible Growth Substances from Seeded and Seedless Fruits. J. ASHS 98(1):51. 1973.

GUILLOU, R., W.H. Griggs and G. Geller. Weight sampling for size measurment of Bartlett pears for canning. Calif. Agr. April 1973.

GRIGGS, H. et al. Ethrel, cycloheximid on abscission, ripening of pears. HortSic. 5:(1). 1970.

GRIGGS, W.H. and B.T. Iwakiri. Asian pears in California, Calif. Agric. 7-12. Jan. 1977.

GRIGGS, W.H. and B.T. Iwakiri. 'California' — new fresh-market pear. Calif. Agr. 28:8-9. 1974.

GRIGGS, W.H. et al. Pear rootstocks recommended for new Bartlett plantings. Calif. 34: No. 10:20-24. Oct. 1980.

HANSEN, E. and W.M. Mellenthin. Commercial handling, storage, winter pears. Ore. Agr. Exp. Sta. spec. Rpt. 550. 12 p. 1979.

HARRIS, M.K. and R.C. Lamb. Resistance to the pear psylla in *Pyrus ussuriensis* L. J. ASHS 98(4):378. July 1973.

HARTMEN, H. Catalogue and evaluation of pear collection. Ore. Agr. Exp. Sta., Tech. Bull. 41. 1978.

INTERNATIONAL Society of Horticultural Science. Pear growing - a symposium. (65 participants; French and English) Fruit Res. Sta., Angers, France. 327 p. 1972. Others, 5-yr. intervals.

JANES, H.W. and C. Frenkel. Inhibition of ripening in pears by inhibitors of cyanide-resistant respiration and by silver. J. ASHS. 103(3):394-397. 1978.

JANES H.W. and C. Frenkel. Promotion of softening processes in pear by acetaldehyde independent of ethylene action. J. ASHS 103(3):397-400. 1978.

JANICK, Jules. 'Honeysweet' pear. HortSci. 12(4):357. 1977.

KAJIURA, I.K. Suzuki, and T. Yamazaki. Color Chart for Japanese Pear (*Pyrus serotina* var. *culta* Rehder). HortSci. 10:257-258. 1975.

KELSEY, M. P. and A. Johnson. Pear production costs. Mi. Agr. Ext. Bull. E-1115. 1979.

KOLBE, M.H. Pears in North Carolina. No. Car. Ag. Ext. Ser. Reprint. 1977.

LAMB, G. Highland - new winter pear. N.Y. Agr. Exp. Sta. (Geneva) in B.C. Orchardist. Nov. 1974.

LARSEN, F.E. Rootstock influence on 2, 4-D damage to 'Bartlett' and 'd' Anjou' pear trees. HortSci. 9:593-594. 1974.

LARSEN, F.E. and R. Fritts, Jr. Pear Scion/Root-stock influence on root suckering. HortSci. 16(2):169. 1981.

LITTLE, C.R., I.D. Peggie, and H.J. Taylor. CO_2 and maturity affecting pears in CA storage. Aust. J. of Exp. Agr. and An. Husb. 12:540-544. 1972.

LOMBARD, P.B. and M.N. Westwood. Six pear cultivars on clonal Old Home, double-rooted, and seedling rootstocks. J. ASHS. 101(3):214-6. 1976.

LOONEY, N.E. Interaction of harvest maturity, cold storage and two growth regulators on ripening of "Bartlett" pears. J. ASHS. 87:1. Jan. 1972. p. 81.

MADSEN, H.F. and M.M. Barnes. Pests of pear in California. Calif. Agr. Exp. Sta. Bull. 478. 40 pp. (Request latest edition.)

MARTIN, G.C. and C. Nishijima. Fruit set and persistance of 'Winter Nelis' following treatment with several gibberellins, cytex, abscissic acid, and GA^3, plus $CaCl_2$. HortSci. 13(3):255-6. 1978.

MARTIN, G.C. and C. Nishijima. Abscissic acid in pear seed, fruit and fruit exudate. J. ASHS 104(2):185-188. 1979.

MAXIE, E.C. et al. Rates of poststorage warming on ripening of 'Bartlett'. J. ASHS. 99:408-411. 1974.

McGREGOR, S.E. Pear pollination. In "Insect Pollination of Cultivated Crops". USDA Hdb. 496. 289-92. 1976.

McINTYRE, J.L. Fire blight protection with deoxyribonucleic acid from virulent and avirulent *Erwina Amylovora* Physio. Plant Path. 7:153-170. 1975.

MELDINGER, Scientific Reports of Agri., Univ. of Norway, As. Storage and ripening temps. on storage and shelf life of pears. Vol. 53 (NR.33). 1974.

MELLENTHIN. W.M. et al. Low O_2 on dessert quality , scald, and N metabolism of 'd'Anjou' in long-term storage. J. ASHS 105(4):522-527. 1980.

MELLENTHIN, W.M. and P.M. Chen. Ripening of 'd'Anjou' as influenced by simulated transit temperatures. J. ASHS. 106(1):35-38. 1981.

MELLENTHIN, W.M., C.Y. Wang and S.Y. Wang. Influence of temperature on pollen tube growth and initial fruit development in 'd'Anjou' pear. HortSci. 7(6):557. 1972.

MELLENTHIN, W.M. and C.Y. Wang. Friction, discoloration of 'Anjou' and fruit size, maturity, storage and polyphenoloxidase activities. Hort.Sci. 9:592-593. 1974.

NYLUND, George and W.J. Moller. Control of pear decline with tetracycline. Cal. Agr. Ext. AXT-446. 1974. Pl. Disease Retp. 57:8 634-7. Aug. 1973.

MILBOCKER, D.C. 'Aristocrat' pear. HortSci. 12(1):78-9. 1977.

OBERLY, G.H., et al. Pear culture. Pomology 13 Info. Bull. 126. (Ext. Pub. NY State Col. of Agr.) 1978.

PACIFIC Coast Pears. The goodfruit grower magazine carries annual up-dates on NW fruit. Aug. 15 was the pear issue, 1982. (1005 Tieton Dr., Yakima, Wa. 98902. $10.50/yrs).

PATCHEN, G.O. Apple and pear storage. USDA-ARS-Mkt. Res. Rpt. 924. 50 pp. 1971.

PROCEEDINGS. Third workshop on fire blight research. Apple and pear disease workers. Cornell Univ. N.Y. State Agri. Exp. Sta., Geneva. U.S.D.A. 1976.

QUAMME, H. Program at Harrow Res. Sta. to Develop Dwarfing Pear Rootstock. Fruit Var. Jour. 29:66-67. 1975.

RAESE, J., et al. Alfalfa greening of 'Anjou' pear. HortSci. 14(3):232-234. 1979.

RAESE, J. T. Max W. Williams and Harold Schomer. Yield and vigor of 'd'Anjou pears with early application of triazole and triazine herbicide. HortSci. 9(1):32. 1974.

RAMOS, D.E. et al. Mechanically hedging pear trees. Calif. Agr., Jan. 1975.

RAVETTO, D.J. An Unsolved (NAA?) Problem: Premature Pear Ripening. Fruit Grower. Canada (June):18B. 1975.

RIEDI, H. et al. Problems with pear psylla control. Calif. Agr. Oct. 1981.

RIEDI, H. and J.E. DeTar. Post-harvest codling moth infestation on pears - a potential threat for next year's crop. Calif. Agric. pp. 14-16. Nov. 1977.

RIEL, W.O. and J.A. Beutel. Pressure rig for injecting trees (for pear decline, iron deficiency, etc.) Calif. Agr. Dec. 1976.

ROACH, R.A. et al. Pears (in England). Ministry of Agr., Fisheries, Food. Bull. 208. HMSO-68p. net. 71 pp. (very good) Her Maj. Stat. Off. 1973.

ROGERS, B.L. et al. Boron and succinic acid, 2, 2-Dimethyl hydrazide (SADH) on fruitfulness and storage behavior of 'Magness' pears. Fruit Var. Jour. 30(3):74-7. 1976.

ROGERS, B.L. and A.H. Thompson. Effects of Post-Harvest Sprays of 2,4,5-T on fruitfulness of 'Magness' pears. Fruit Var. J. 32(4):85-89. 1978.

SCOTT, L.E. and A.H. Thompson. Presence of 'Viable' Seed in 'Magness' Pear. Fruit Var. Jour. 29:45. 1975.

SFAKIOTAKIS, E.M. and D.R. Dilley. Induction of Ethylene in 'Bosc' by Postharvest Cold Stress. HortSci. 9:336. 1974.

SHEN, T. Pears in China. HortSci. 15(1):11-17. 1980.

SOUTHWICK, L., et al. Identification of non-bearing pear trees. Ma. Agr. Exp. Sta. Bull. 421. 51 pp. 1944.

STAHLY, E.A. and M.W. Williams. Induction of earlier fruiting of 'Anjou' pear trees with growth regulators. HortSci. 11(5):502-4. 1976.

STEBBINS, R.Pear Collection Catalog. Fruit Var. J. 32(1):23. 1978.

THOMPSON, L.J.M., T. van der Zwet, and W.A. Oitto: Inheritance of grit content in fruits in Pyrus communis. J. ASHS 99(2):141. March 1974.

THOMSON, S., et al., Pesticide application can be reduced by forecasting the occurance of fireblight bacteria. Calif. Agri. 12-14. Oct. 1977.

TUKEY, H.B. Dwarfed fruit trees. Macmillan Publ. Co., New York City. See pear sections. 562 pp. 1964.

TUKEY, R.B. et al. Predicting harvest size of Bartlett pears. Wash. tree fruit production series E.M. 3403. June 1970.

WANG, C.Y. and E. Hansen. Differential response to ethylene in respiration and ripening of immature Anjou pears. J. ASHS 95(3):3140316. 1970.

WANG, C.Y. and M.W. Mellenthin. Different handling on methods of cooling rate and moisture loss of 'd'Anjou' pears stored in bins. HortSci. 11(4):397. 1976.

WANG, C. et al. Maturation of 'd'Anjou' pears in relation to chemical composition and reaction to ethylene. J. ASHS 97:1. January 1972. p. 9.

WANG, C.Y. and W.M. Mellenthin. Chlorogenic acid levels, ethylene production and respiration of 'd'Anjou' pears affected with cork spot. HortSci. 8(3):180. June 1973.

WANG, C.Y. and W.M. Mellenthin. Relationship of friction discoloration to phenolic compounds in 'd'Anjou' pears. HortSci. 8(4):321. August 1973.

WANG, C.Y. and W.M. Mellenthin. Temperatue and premature ripening, pear. J. ASHS:97-4. 1972.

WANG, C.Y. and W.M. Mellenthin. Short-Term High Co₂ Treatment on 'd'Anjou' Pear storage. J. ASHS. 100:492. 1975.

WANG, C.T. and J.T. Worthington. Nondestructive method for measuring ripeness and core breakdown in 'Bartlett'. J. ASHS. 104(5):629-631. 1979.

WATERWORTH, H.E., Scionwood of Pear available at U.S. Plant intro. Sta. Fruit Var. Journ. 35:(2) Apr. 1981.

WESTIGAND, P.H., M.N. Westwood, and P.B. Lombard. Host preference and resistance of Pyrus species to the pear Psylla, Psylla Pryricola Foerster. J. ASHS. 95:1. 34-36. Jan. 1970.

WESTWOOD, M.N. et al. 'Bartlett' pear on standard and Old Home x Farmingdale clonal rootstocks. J. ASHS 101:(2):161-4. 1976.

WESTWOOD, M.N. Inheritance of pear decline resistance. Fruit Var. Jour. 30(2):63-4. 1976.

WESTWOOD, M.N. and H.R. Cameron. Effects of vein yellows virus, growth: flowering and yield of 'Anjou' pear. J. ASHS. 99(5):425-6. 1974.

WESTWOOD, M.N. et al. Trunk and rootstock on decline, growth and performance of pear. J. ASHS. 96(2):146-50. 1971.

WESTWOOD, M.N. and H.O. Bjornstad. Fruit Set and Girdling, Early Cluster Thinning, Pruning of 'Anjou' and 'Comice'. HortSci. 9:342-344. 1974.

WESTWOOD, M.N. and H.R. Cameron. Vein Yellows and Virus on Growth. Flowering and Yield of Anjou. J. ASHS. 99:425-426. 1974.

WESTWOOD, M.N. et al. Long-term soil management test of pears in clay soil Ore. Tech. Bull. 82. 39 pp. 1964.

WESTWOOD, M.N., H.R. Cameron, P.B. Lombard and C.B. Cordy. Effects of trunk and rootstock on decline, growth and performance of pear. J. ASHS 96:2. March 1971.

WESTWOOD, M.N. Morphology of pollen, anthers of Pyrus. J. ASHS. 103(1):28-37. 1978.

WHITING, D.E., et al. B uptake by 'Bartlett' Trees. J. ASHS. 103(5):641-645. 1978.

WOODBRIDGE, C.G. Calcium level of pear tissue with cork and blackend. HortSci. Vol. 6, No. 5, 1971.

WOODBRIDGE, C.B. Effect of rootstocks and interstocks on nutrient levels in 'Bartlett' pear leaves, on tree growth, and on fruit. J. ASHS 98(2):200. March 1973.

VAN DER ZWET, T. and N.F. Childers (Edts.) The Pear - Cultivars to Marketing. 65 authors over world. 525 pp. Horticultural Publ., 3906 NW 31 Pl. Gainesville, FL 32606. 1982.

VAN DER ZWET, T. and H.L. Keil. Fireblight control a bacterial disease of Rosaceous plants. U.S.D.A. Agr. Hdb. 510 200 p. Mar. 1979.

VAN DER ZWET, T., W.A. Oitto, and R.C. Blake. Fire Blight Resistance in Pears. HortSci. 9:340-342. 1974.

VAN HEEK, L.A.G. and H.H. Allen. Mechanical havesting Tatura Trellis fruit (pear included) trees. J. ASHS 105(5) 695-9. 1980.

WILLIAMS, Max, et al. Pear Production. USDA Agr. Hdb. 526. 53 pp. 1978.

YOUNG, M.J. and M.N. Westwood. Wounding and Chilling on Rooting of Pear Cuttings. HortSci. 10:399-400. 1975.

(See previous editions for additional references)

CHAPTER XIV

Peach, Nectarine, Apricot, and Almond

PEACH CULTURE

The peach (*Prunus persica (L.) Batsch*) originated in China (near Sian) where it was grown as far back as 2000 B.C. Three wild species still are found there, namely, *P. davidiana* in the North which is used for a rootstock, *P. mira* on the Tebetan Plateau and *P. ferganensis* in the Sinkiang province both in West China. Some species near Harbin in North China grow in the open where winter temperatures may drop to -40°F; their eating quality is poor but their genes are valuable in breeding for cold resistance.

The peach gradually spread from China and is found commercially around the world between 24° and 45° latitude above and below the Equator. These limits may be extended somewhat by warm ocean currents, large deep lakes, or altitude. While the peach can be grown in most apple sections, it extends for the most part closer to the Equator because most cultivars are more tolerant of heat and require less cold to break the rest period.

Data in Table 1 give the approximate peach production by country. Leaders are USA, Italy, France, Japan, Spain, Greece and Argentina. While no data are available for China, production is moderate, particularly in the wide area around Peking. One variety, Tung-tao (The Winter Peach), is harvested very late and stores longer in regular storage than any known peach, up to 4 months. Peaches in the USSR are located in the southern regions.

Columbus and the Spaniards brought the peach to St. Augustine, Florida in their second or third visit where it spread rapidly from coast to coast in North America.

East of the Rockies, peach production has had many setbacks, largely as a result of planting on sites susceptible to spring frosts and winter freezes. Drought, insufficient winter cold and pests, have taken their tolls and caused shifts in the industry from one section to another. In spite of these setbacks, however, peaches are the "Queen" of fruits and rank second to the apple among deciduous tree fruits from the standpoint of production and value.

The upward trend in production in recent years is probably due to (a) better selection of sites and soils, (b) the introduction of somewhat hardier and better quality

James A. Beutel, Extension Pomologist, University of California, Davis, assisted in this chapter revision with Carl E. Gambrell, Clemson University, So. Car., Elgin Branch, 29045.

peaches, (c) increased marketing of the crop at the orchard or roadside stand, and (d) the use of hydrocooling, refrigerator trucks and rail cars to haul the perishable fruit quickly to adjacent or distant markets.

The first good crop of peaches can be obtained within 3 to 4 years after planting. Thus, the grower in many cases can benefit from the relatively higher market prices in good periods of economy. Peaches are sold within weeks after harvest.

TABLE 1. APPROXIMATE FRESH PEACH PRODUCTION (000'S METRIC TONS) FOR WORLD COUNTRIES. 1981-2.

1. Italy	1450	17. Australia	70
2. USA	1340	18. Romania	45
3. Spain	410	19. Canada	35
4. France	405	20. Peru	35
5. Greece	375	21. Uruguay	30
6. Japan	270	22. Korea (DPR)	30
7. Argentinia	250	23. Israel	25
8. Mexico	190	24. W. Germany	25
9. South Africa	185	25. N. Zealand	20
10. Turkey	170	26. Bolivia	20
11. Bulgaria	155	27. Lebanon	15
12. Brazil	140	28. Morocco	15
13. Hungary	135	29. Czechoslovakia	15
14. Yugoslavia	80	30. Pakistan	10
15. Chile	80	31. India	10
16. Korea (Rep.)	75	32. World	6000,

Countires producing about 10 thousand MT or less are: Egypt, Libya, Algeria, Madagascar, Tunisia, Paraguay, Venezuela, China, Cyprus, Iraq, Syria, Austria, Belgium and Germany (DR). Data from FAO (USDA) Production Yearbook.

Figure 1 shows approximate centers of tree location and the relative production of peaches by state. California is by far the leading state, accounting for about 65 percent of the total production. California peach production shows little variation from year to year, but production of the states east of the Rockies may vary considerably with weather conditions. Production figures in millions of lbs., 1980-82 averages are: California, 1259 clings, 442 freestone; South California, 318; Georgia 120; New Jersey 93; Pennsylvania, 83; Michigan, 38; Arkansas, 32; Virginia, 29; Washington, 26; North Carolina, 22; Colorado, 16. See Figure 1a.

The peach, like the apple, is getting more competition from other fruits and vegetables on the store shelves. The per capita fresh consumption has dropped from 13.2 pounds in 1947 to around 6.0 pounds in the early 1980s. About 9.0 lbs. per capita consumption are processed.

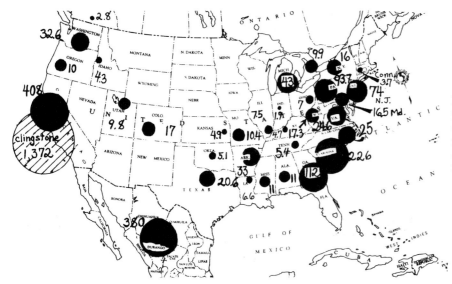

Figure 1. California is by far the leading state producing 60 to 70 percent of the total U.S. crop. Solid circles are located about where the industry is centered. Many trees are located around the Great Lakes where the deep water reduces temperature extremes. Cold dry winters limit peach growing in an area northwest of a line from Chicago to North Texas.

SELECTION OF PEACH CULTIVARS

Peach cultivars available today are far superior to those only a few years ago.

The cultivar list for peaches is probably changing more rapidly than for any other tree fruit. The rapid change is due to several factors: (a) The tree is relatively short-lived; (b) there is an urgent demand for improvement in hardiness and quality; (c) more good seedlings are obtained from peach crosses than with apples, pears, and most tree fruits; and (d) it takes relatively less time to develop, introduce and popularize a new peach.

Choice of peach cultivars for any one region is governed by three factors: (a) The type of market to be served, (b) distance to the market, and (c) adaptability to local soil and climatic conditions. If the orchard is located in regions of the country where the temperatures frequently fall to -12°F., or lower, hardy cultivars as Veteran, Redhaven, Reliance, Colora, Suncling and Summercrest are possibilities[1]. In areas where frosts are likely, it is considered good policy to set the more tender cultivars on the high ground and to locate the hardier cultivars on the slopes and lower elevations.

If the fruit will be sold at a roadside market, or by "pick-it-yourself," it is desirable to select a number of cultivars which will ripen over a period of several weeks to give a continuous supply to the store and U-Pickers. The breeders are attempting to develop a series of varieties ripening through the season that look alike to facilitate marketing.

If the fruit will be sold in large quantities to a cooperative fruit packing association, few cultivars are needed. Only those which are suitable for processing, or which have a wide reputation in the fresh fruit markets

should be grown in quantity. In the East, if the orchard is located a considerable distance from large fresh fruit markets, no doubt much of the crop will be sold locally, but in case it should be necessary to ship surplus quantities in the fresh state, a portion of the cultivars should consist of Redhaven or some well-known cultivars adapted to distant shipment.

Cultivars susceptible to diseases, insects and other pests is always a consideration. Breeders continually watch for seedling crosses resistant to the most troublesome problems which will vary with locality. Virus diseases, bacterial spot, brown rot, several canker (fungal and bacterial) diseases, oak-root rot are key diseases. Insects and other pests are mites, nematodes, Oriental fruit moth and plum curculio. Leaf chlorosis due to iron, zinc or manganese deficiency and spotty death of trees due to rootstock incompatability, rootrots, or virus may be problems in some regions (see references for details).

If the cultivar will be used for canning, as is true in California and certain other states, the fruit should be (a) of yellow flesh, (b) preferably a clingstone (although many freestones are being canned; they are a delicious dessert), (c) a small non-splitting pit, (d) firm, (e) of good symmetrical size, (f) no red color at the pit, and (g) slow flesh-browning. The cultivars should mature evenly, color well and stay firm on the tree for a single (mechanical) pick.

If the fruit is to be dried, it should be a freestone and particularly sweet in addition to the characters given above for canning. A cultivar that gives one pound of dried peaches from five pounds of fresh fruit is preferred over one which gives 1:7.

Home freezing of peaches has displaced home canning. Some good freezing cultivars are Redhaven, Triogem, Sunhigh, Washington, Jefferson, Madison, Halehaven, J.H. Hale, Elberta, Vedette, Veteran, Golden Jubliee, Fay

---

[1]See Ure, Edgerton in Literature cited.

TABLE 2. CHARACTERISTICS OF FRESH MARKET PEACH CULTIVARS IN NORTH AMERICA. LISTED IN ORDER OF RIPENING WITH NUMERICAL RATINGS ON QUALITY FROM 1 (POOR) TO 10. FOR OTHER WORLD AREAS, SELECT A USA CLIMATE SIMILAR TO YOURS, THEN SELECT CULTIVARS FROM THIS TABLE ACCORDINGLY. (CREDIT TO JERRY FRECON, FRUIT SPECIALIST, GLOUCESTER COUNTY, N.J. 08312)[1]

Ripening Season and Cultivar	Ripen'g Date in Days Before (-) or After (+) Elberta	Color of Flesh	Fruit Size	Stone Free-ness	Attrac-tive-ness	Flesh Firm-ness	Des-sert Qual-ity	Can-ning Qual-ity	Bac.-ter'l Spot Resist.	Chilling Require't	Zone of Adaptation U.S.
VERY EARLY											
Springtime	-61	White	3	3	7	3	6	3	6	650	Cal
Harbinger	-60	Yellow	5	3	8	4	6	3	8	—	Central, NE
Springgold	-58	Yellow	4	4	8	5	6	3	6	850	SE, Cal
Springcrest	-54	Yellow	5	4	8	6	7	3	6	650	Cal
Royal May	-51	Yellow	7	5	8	6	7	4	-	-	Cal
Earlired	-50	Yellow	6	5	8	6	7	4	7	850	E, SE
Desertgold	-50	Yellow	5	5	7	6	7	3	-	(350)	Cal
Early White Giant	-50	White	8	5	8	6	7	3	8	(high)	Central
Candor	-50	Yellow	6	5	7	6	7	4	8	950	SE, M
Early Coronet	-47	Yellow	7	5	8	6	7	4	-	650	SE, Cal
Cardinal	-46	Yellow	6	4	8	6	7	4	7	950	Se, E, NW
June Gold	-45	Yellow	6	5	7	6	5	3	5	650	SE, Cal
Early Redhaven	-45	Yellow	6	5	8	7	7	5	4	950	NW, NE
Stark Earliglo	-44	Yellow	6	5	8	7	7	5	5	950	Central, NE
Garnet Beauty	-44	Yellow	6	5	8	7	7	5	5	950	NW, E
Dixired	-42	Yellow	6	4	7	6	7	4	8	1000	Se, E, NW, SW
Maygold	-42	Yellow	6	4	7	6	7	4	6	650	SE
Merrill Gemfree	-40	Yellow	7	6	6	7	7	5	6	-	Cal
Sentinel	-39	Yellow	7	6	7	7	7	5	9	850	SE
Royalvee	-37	Yellow	7	6	7	6	7	5	7	950	NE, SE
EARLY											
Brighton	-35	Yellow	7	6	8	6	8	7	-	-	NE, M
Harbelle	-35	Yellow	7	7	8	7	8	7	7	-	E, Central
Coronet	-33	Yellow	7	7	9	8	9	7	6	750	SE, Cal
Babcock	-31	White	6	7	7	6	7	6	-	(low)	Cal
Redhaven	-30	Yellow	7	7	8	8	8	7	8	950	E, SE, NW, Central
Regina	-30	Yellow	8	7	7	8	8	7	6	850	Ca., NW
Harvester	-29	Yellow	7	8	9	8	6	7	7	750	SE & SC
Harken	-28	Yellow	9	7	8	7	8	7	9	-	Central, NE
Norman	-28	Yellow	8	8	7	7	8	7	8	-	SE
Harbrite	-27	Yellow	8	7	8	7	8	7	9	-	Central, NE
Raritan Rose	-27	White	8	8	8	6	9	7	9	950	E
Ranger	-25	Yellow	8	8	7	8	8	8	9	950	SE, E, NW, Central
Newhaven	-24	Yellow	8	8	9	7	9	7	7	-	NE, Central
Suwanee	-24	Yellow	8	8	8	8	8	-	5	650	SE
Redtop	-23	Yellow	8	8	8	8	8	8	6	850	Cal
Topaz	-23	Yellow	8	9	9	8	7	7	7	-	NE, SE, Central
Stark Early Loring	-23	Yellow	8	9	9	8	8	8	9	-	Ne, Central, SE
Velvet	-22	Yellow	8	7	7	7	7	7	5	750	NE, NW
Reliance	-22	Yellow	6	7	7	6	7	7	5	-	NE, Central, E
Envoy	-22	Yellow	8	7	8	8	7	7	6	-	NE, E, Central
Jim Wilson	-22	Yellow	8	9	8	8	8	8	9	-	SE
Stark Sunbright	-20	Yellow	9	8	9	8	8	7	6	-	Central, E
MIDSEASON											
Sunhigh	-17	Yellow	9	8	8	8	9	9	4	750	E
July Elberta (Burbank)	-16	Yellow	8	8	8	8	8	8	5	750	Colo., Cal, Central
Glohaven	-16	Yellow	8	8	8	9	8	8	7	850	Central
Redglobe	-14	Yellow	9	9	10	10	9	9	7	850	E, SE
Roza	-14	Yellow	9	8	8	8	9	8	4	-	NW
Earlihale	-13	Yellow	9	9	9	9	9	8	4	-	NW
Canadian Harmony	-12	Yellow	8	8	8	7	8	8	5	-	Central, NE
Loring	-11	Yellow	9	9	9	9	9	9	8	800	Centrla, E, SE
Winblo	-10	Yellow	8	8	8	8	8	8	8	-	SE
Baby Gold - 5	-10	Yellow	8	2		10	8	10	4	850	E, NE, Central
Redkist	-10	Yellow	8	9	8	8	9	8	8	-	NE, Central
Summergold	-10	Yellow	8	9	8	9	9	10	-	750	SE
Suncrest	-8	Yellow	9	9	9	10	9	9	4	850	Cal, NW
Cresthaven	-7	Yellow	9	8	8	8	9	6	-	850	Central
Madison	-7	Yellow	8	8	8	9	9	8	-	850	E
Stark Earlirio	-7	Yellow	9	9	9	9	7	8	6	-	West, NE, Central
Early Rio Oso Gem	-7	Yellow	9	9	9	9	7	8	5	-	West, NE, Central
Yakima Hale	-7	Yellow	9	8	9	8	8	8	-	-	NW
Merrill Fortyniner	-5	Yellow	8	8	8	8	8	8	5	-	Cal.
Sullivan Early Elb.	-5	Yellow	9	9	7	8	8	8	6	900	E, NW
Blake	-3	Yellow	9	9	10	8	8	7	6	750	SE, E, Colo
Early, Elberta (Gleason)	-3	Yellow	9	9	8	9	9	10	8	850	NW, E, Central
Baby Gold -7	-2	Yellow	9	2	5	10	8	10	5	850	E, NE, Central

205

Table 2. Con't.

Ripening Season and Cultivar	Ripen'g Date in Days Before (-) or After (+) Elberta	Color of Flesh	Fruit Size	Stone Free-ness	Attrac-tive-ness	Flesh Firm-ness	Des-sert Qual-ity	Can-ning Qual-ity	Bac-ter'l Spot Resist.	Chilling Require't	Zone of Adaptation U.S.
Redskin	-1	Yellow	9	9	9	9	8	8	9	750	E, SE, Central, Colo
Biscoe	-1	Yellow	8	9	8	8	8	9	9	750	SE, Central
Elberta	0	Yellow	9	9	7	8	9	9	7	900	NW, Colo
Dixiland	0	Yellow	9	9	9	9	9	7	8	750	SE, E
J.H. Hale	+ 1	Yellow	10	9	9	10	9	7	6	900	NW, Colo
Fay Elberta	+ 2	Yellow	9	9	8	9	9	10	-	750	Cal, NW
Jefferson	+ 2	Yellow	9	9	9	10	9	8	-	850	E
Jerseyglo	+ 3	Yellow	9	9	9	9	8	9	7	-	NE
Jerseyqueen	+ 3	Yellow	9	9	9	8	9	7	5	900	E
LATE											
Halberta Giant	+ 3	Yellow	10	9	9	10	9	7	6	900	Cal, Colo, NW
Belle of Georgia	+ 3	White	8	9	7	6	9	5	6	850	E, Central
Shippers Late Red	+ 3	Yellow	10	9	9	10	9	7	5	850	Cal, Central
Autumn Glo	+ 6	Yellow	9	9	8	9	7	8	5	-	NE
Fayette	+ 6	Yellow	9	9	10	9	9	8	6	850	Cal, NW
Tyler	+ 7	Yellow	8	9	8	8	8	7	-	950	E
Rio-Oso-Gem	+ 8	Yellow	10	9	8	10	9	8	5	900	E, NW, SE
Monroe	+ 12	Yellow	8	9	9	9	8	8	7	(high)	E
Stark Encore	+ 14	Yellow	8	9	10	9	7	9	9	-	
Emery	+ 14	Yellow	8	9	8	8	7	9	9	-	SE, NE
Kirkman Gem	+ 25	Yellow	9	9	8	9	9	7	7	(high)	Cal
Marsun	+ 26	Yellow	9	8	9	9	9	7	8	850	E

[1]California is introducing so many new cultivars that it is suggested you check the cultivars listed earlier in this Chapter and also contact for details the Peach Extension Specialist, Univ. of Calif., Davis 95616.

Elberta, and Rio-Oso-Gem (check your local experiment station).

The fresh fruit market prefers a yellow-flesh freestone peach, good annual producer, and relatively free from fuzz. It should spread the season or fill a vacant spot, be firm of good size and roundish, bright color, and if possible, a good shipper. In addition, it has distinct advantages if it can be canned, frozen or dried. Nectarines likely will be grown more widely in the future since the public is favoring this fuzzless peach at good prices.

Table 2 gives an evaluation of most of the peach and nectarine cultivars for commercial and home planting in the United States and Canada. We are growing and marketing over 120 peach cultivars in North America. Non-bearing trees comprise 20 to 30 percent of the total.

During mild winters in the warmer peach zones difficulty may be encountered with uneven and weak opening of flower and leaf buds of peach. Elberta fruit buds need

TABLE 3. PEACH AND NECTARINE CULTIVARS RECOMMENDED FOR TRIAL IN FLORIDA, SOUTHERN TEXAS, MEXICO AND SOUTHERN CALIFORNIA AND IN SIMILAR CLIMATES. (W.B. SHERMAN, UNIVERSITY OF FLORIDA, GAINESVILLE 32611)

Cultivar	Chilling needed (hrs.)	Days bloom to ripen	Flower	% Red color	Ground color	Fruit Shape[z]	Firm[z]	Size (g)	Taste[z]	Flesh Texture[z]	Browning[z]	Bacter-ial spot	Stone freeness	Flower[z] bud set
Flordabelle	150	105	showy	60	greenish	10	8	120	10	9	8	7	free	8
Maravilha H*	150	80	showy	80	yellow cream	9	8	70	8	8	7	6	semi-cling	8
Earligrande	200	75	non-showy	40	yellow	9	6	80	7	7	8	6	semi-cling	6
Flordaprince	150	80	showy	80	yellow	9	8	90	8	7	7	3	semi-cling	7
Flordagem H	250	85	showy	60	yellow	9	10	80	8	8	9	8	semi-cling	8
Sunred nect.	250	90	showy	100	yellow	9	7	70	10	8	8	8	semi-free	8
Desertgold H	300	75	non-showy	80	Br. yellow	5	8	70	8	8	9	7	semi-cling	9
Flordagold	325	90	showy	40	bright yellow	7	10	90	8	7	9	3	semi-cling	10
San Pedro H	325	80	showy	50	yellow	6	8	85	7	7	7	7	Semi-cling	7
Sunripe nect.	350	95	showy	70	dull	9	8	90	10	8	6	8	semi-free	8
Early Amber H	350	75	non-showy	40	dull yellow	8	7	80	6	8	6	9	semi-free	8
Flordaking	400	70	non-showy	50	greenish yellow	7	7	95	7	7	9	10	semi-cling	6
Sunlite nect.	450	85	showy	80	yellow	9	8	80	8	8	9	10	free	9
Rio Grande	450	105	showy	60	yellow	7	8	120	8	8	7	6	free	8
Sunfre nect.	500	85	showy	90	bright	9	8	90	8	8	9	9	semi-free	8

[z]ratings: 1 = lowest or poorest, 10 = highest or best ratings. *White flesh, others yellow flesh. H = Home garden use.

from 750 to 800 hours of temperature below 45° F. for proper breaking of the rest period. The leaf buds need around 1,000 hours below this temperature. If less cold than this is available, some trees may show considerable flowers with no leaves and uneven opening of both types of buds. Peaches developing after inadequate chilling will be smaller and production down. Table 3 gives the peach and nectarine cultivars for the warmer low-chilling regions (100-500 hrs. below 45° F.).

Aside from Elberta and a few others such as Redhaven and Rio-Oso-Gem, most peach cultivars are regional in their adaptation, performing well in one region or locality and poorly in another. Also, peach cultivar lists are changing continuously. It is wise for you to keep in touch with your local experiment station regarding the latest and best cultivars for the purpose desired.

Cultivars being grown and suggested for plantings across the U.S. and Canada are, in brief: *Canada: Fresh Market:* Candor, Garnet Beauty, Sunhaven, Redhaven, Harken, Harbrite, Vivid, Canadian Harmony, Loring, Cresthaven, Redskin. *Processing:* Babygold 5 and 7, Veecling. *Special purpose:* Earlired, Harbelle, Veeglow, Vanity, Madison. *Trial:* Brighton, Harglow, Biscoe (V68051, trial processing). *Nectarines (fresh market): Trial* - Harko, Hardired, Nectared 4 and 6 (trial, Mericrest). (R.E.C. Layne).

California: Major Canning — Loadel, Carson, mid-late July; Andross, Klamt, early August; Carolyn, late August; Halford, late August; Starn, early September; Wiser, Sullivan, Corona, mid September. *Canning freestones;* (almost thing of past), Fay Elberta; *Drying peaches* — Fay Elberta, Muir, Lovell. *Shipping fresh peaches* (start mid April ripening order to about mid September; major cultivars have asterisk*): May Crest, Springold, Springcrest*, Early Coronet, Regina, Redtop*, Flamecrest, Elegant Lady, Fortyniner, Fayette, Fay Elberta*, Angelus, Pacifica, Elberta, O'Henry*, Cal Red, Windsor, Parade, Summerset, Fairtime, Carnival, Autumn Gem (for * cultivars, total shipment is 800,000-1.2 milion packages/yr; for other total is 100,000 + packages) *Nectarines:* (start about mid May ripening in order to early September) Maybelle, Armking, Aurelio Grand, May Grand*, Early Sungrand*, Firebright, Spring Red, Independence, Moon Grand, Red Diamond, Flavortop*, Summer Grand, Sun Grand, Hi-Red, Niagara Grand, Frantasia*, Royal Grand, Red Grand, Red Free, Royal Giant, Late Le Grand, Flamekist*, Gold King, Regal Grand, Autumn Grand, Fairlane*, Richards Grand, September Grand (for * cultivars — one million packages shipped/yr; others total 100,000 + packages) (James A. Beutel).

Texas: (950 hrs.) Bicentennial, Sentinel, Ranger, Redglobe, Denman, Loring, Dixiland; (750 Hrs.) Bicentennial, Junegold, Sentinel, Harvester, Loring,

Milan, Redskin; (600 hrs.) Junegold, Sentinel, LaFeliciana; (300 hrs.) East Grande, Early Amber, Rio Grande, Flordaking. (T. Handwerker). *Colorado:* Elberta, J.H. Hale, Blake, Redhaven, (Flamecrest), Redglobe, Suncrest. (K. Yu). *South Louisiana:* Flordaking, Bicentennial, Junegold, Harvester, LaGold, LaFeliciana, Dixiland (J. Boudreax). *Missouri:* Redhaven, Topaz, Loring, Cresthaven, Rio-Oso-Gem, (Harvester and Biscoe - promising). (K. Hansen). *Midwest:* Redhaven, Reliance, Harbrite, Harken, Lori, Cresthaven, Redskin, Rio-Oso-Gem, Baby Gold series for processing. (K. Hansen). *Michigan:* Harbelle, Sunhaven, Redhaven, Newhaven, Harbrite, Glohaven, Kalhaven, Cresthaven, Redskin. Processing: Babygold 5, Ambergem, Suncling. *New York:* Collins, Brighton, Jerseyland, Redhaven, Triogem, Harmony, Glohaven, Madison, Cresthaven, Redskin. (G.Lamb). *New Jersey Area:* Harbelle, Garnet Beauty, Jerseyland, Redhaven, Harken, Harbrite, Topaz, Norman, Loring, Redkist, Biscoe, Cresthaven, Jerseyqueen, Jerseyglo, Rio-Oso-Gem, Encore, Emery. Nectarines: Mericrest, Flavortop, Fantasia, Red Gold, Late Gold (E. Christ). *Virginia, West Virginia:* Harbinger, Candor, Legacy, Garnet Beauty, Brighton, Harbelle, Redhaven, Pekin, Harken, Harbrite, Velvet, Norman, Harmony, Sunglo, Windblo, Loring, Cresthaven, Biscoe, Jerseyqueen, Tyler. (R. Byers). *North Carolina:* Candor, Redhaven, Norman, Windblo, Loring, Biscoe, Redskin, (D. Werner). *South Carolina:* Junegold (may split), Coronet, Redhaven, Harvester, Redglobe, Loring, Blake, Jefferson, Rio-Oso-Gem (Jere Brittain). *Georgia, South Carolina:* Camden, Springcrest, Flordaking, Sunbrite, Candor, Junegold, Surecrop, Redcap, Dixired, Flavor-

U.S. Peach Production and Prices

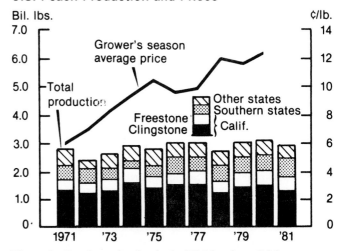

Figure 1a. Peach production in the USA has been fairly even over the past 10 yrs with between 60 and 70% of the crop coming from California. About 50% of the total crop is clings from California to be canned. Processing in the early 1980s was giving way to more demand for fresh fruit, not particularly shown here. Note rapid price increase with inflation. (USDA)

crest, Coronet, Redhaven, Harvester, Redglobe, Loring, Cresthaven, Blake, (Sunprince), Jefferson, Tyler, Monroe, Rio-Oso-Gem, O'Henry (Compromise 85% of all peaches shipped out of the two states.) White Flesh for roadside: Starlite, Raritan Rose, Nectar, Georgia Bell. (M.E. Ferree). *Florida;* See Table 3.

POLLINATION REQUIREMENTS

Practially all commercial peach cultivars are self-fertile. Only a few varieties are self-sterile, including J.H. Hale, Marsun, June Elberta, Halberta, Candoka, Chinese Cling, Alamar, and Giant. Only J.H. Hale has received wide planting, and it is giving way to better cultivars. If a self-sterile cultivar is used, it should be planted in double rows, alternating with two rows of a self-fertile cultivar. Bees in the orchard at blossoming provide greater assurance of cross-pollination during adverse weather.

ROOTSTOCKS FOR PEACH TREES

There is a definite rootstock problem with peaches in some commercial areas due to apparent transmitted viruses, incompatability between rootstock and cion with the ever-changing cultivar picture, lack of uniformity of seedling vigor and/or nematode susceptability. Scattered trees may gradually weaken and die. *Rootstock-hardiness, disease-resistance, compatability, and dwarfness research has become paramount.* Most rootstocks come from open-pollinated pits from canneries (Lovells, Halfords), wild trees, and from commercial cultivars such as Suncling, but these supplies have diminished. Almost all peach cultivars over the years have been budded on seedlings in the nursery row. However, rooting of peach and almond softwood cuttings and tissue culture is now successful and this should make it possible to select interspecific hybrids for hybrid vigor that provide uniform rootstocks free from and/or resistant to viruses, the several harmful nematode species, and to crown gall. These are the main rootstock problems today together with hardiness in the colder regions. Ontario workers believe a Siberian peach and their Harrow Blood may be the answer to hardiness and canker resistance and also give some dwarfing for dense planting of trees. The Bailey seedling rootstock from the midwest looks promising for hardiness, while the Lovell looks best in the southern states. Some experiment stations in the East have been maintaining Lovell trees to help supply nurserymen with adequate seed.

The West Virginia Experiment Station recommends that the grower visit the nursery and select his own trees and tag them, choosing the larger more vigorous trees. It is a 15-year investment and is worth this effort.

USDA research at Beltsville, Maryland has shown nematodes to transmit ring-spot virus of tomato to newly planted peach tree roots, causing trees to decline and die in

Figure 2. Deep soil fumigation with a nematacide before planting is effective in arresting nematodes and getting peach trees off to a good start. Liquid is pumped from tank on back of tractor through tubes behind the two soil breakers which are hydraulically operated. Nematodes may account for part of the replant problem in old peach growing regions. Furadan is cleared for nonbearing trees. (Courtesy Stuart Race, Rutgers University).

spotty areas. Soil fumigation (Figure 2) before planting is suggested in Mid-Atlantic states where this type decline is a problem.

In mild climates (Figure 3) as Israel and Mexico, inadequate chilling of a cultivar may occur. Dormancy can be broken by spraying not later than 4 weeks before expected bud opening with 2% thiourea and 0.2% Triton x-100 emulsifier, followed after drying by a "Winter wash" of medium heavy mineral oil UR-75 emulsified with 20% water containing 1.5% DNOC. A spray of 10% KNO_3 with the thiourea-Triton also has given good results. The mixtures are timed according to fruit species.

Tissue Culture. A new propagation technique is developing in which shoot tips of peach, other fruits (Chaps. 8, 21), are removed and grown under controlled conditions to get virus-free stock. Millions of rooted clonal stock can be obtained from one shoot within a year.

Dwarfing. There is no proven dwarfing stock for commercial peach, almond or apricot. For peach, St. Julien A stock gives intermediate vigor; common Mussel is

208

Figure 3. Peach cultivars differ in winter chilling requirements. For Elberta a duration of 750-800 hours below 45 degrees F. is required to induce opening of buds in the spring. (Left) Elberta tree shows symptoms of insufficient winter chilling. (Right) Ramona cultivar bore a good crop, indicating a lower winter-chilling requirement. (California Agr. Exp. Sta., Riverside).

a traditional stock for semidwarfness, and *P. besseyi* and *P. tomentosa* (the better) dwarfing in home plantings. Use only clonally propagated dwarfing stock. "Compact Redhaven" is a low spreading Redhaven but not well accepted by growers[1].

Genetic dwarfing genes are available from Mr. Fred Anderson's private breeding program, Merced, California (the Florey dwarf). Dr. Paul E. Hansche, University of California, Davis, (Figure 4) is using these genes in cross-breeding and has found the trees to produce 15-20 T/A the third growing season, spaced in densities of 1000-1500 trees/A. The mature trees are 5-6 ft. tall and will produce fruit averaging 2 3/4 to 3 inches diameter. Among the obvious cultural advantages are: no ladders, easier management, much less pruning, better use of water, space and light, better spray coverage, others. The projected net income after several yrs. is impressive. Improved fruit quality and spread of ripening are key objectives.

Nematode Problem. The Nemaguard (USDA) rootstock is quite resistant to the two more common root-knot nematodes and has replaced other stocks used previously where nematodes are a problem, but is sensitive to bacterial canker and, hence, where nematodes are not a problem, Lovell or Halford are preferred. Cancellation of DBCP postplant and similar systemic nematocides has caused some shift to Nemaguard and the Lovell which have some nematode resistance.

PLANTING, EARLY TRAINING

Planting recommendations in Chapter III also apply to the peach. Sites with good air drainage, good top soil, and not previously planted to peach are best. Do not plant in holes left by pulling old trees; plant in centers and run rows

Figure 4. Dr. Paul E. Hansche, Department of Genetics, University of California 95616, shows his planting of genetic dwarf peaches on Nemaguard rootstock at 1000 to 1500 trees per acre, yielding 15 to 22 tons per acre the third growing season.

up and down the slope (reduce frost damage) and/or north and south if possible (better light). Planting on the square about 18 to 24 feet (standard) with strip herbicides and some cultivation in the young tree rows, and sod middles with irrigation available when needed is being favored in both arid and humid regions. But there are a number of unique planting systems being studied as noted later. Peaches can be interplanted with apples provided the site is suitable for peaches and arsenic sprays will not be used (burns peach foliage). *Early* spring planting in northern areas and fall or late fall planting in milder climates is suggested. See Figure 5 for planting peaches on soils in Australia that drain slowly.

Trees planted on old apple tree sites may encounter arsenic accumulation in the soil which retards growth and production. Peaches after peaches has been a longtime world problem. Nematodes has been a likely factor but there may be other undetermined problems. Tractor drills, or better, a back hoe may be used to dig holes rapidly. Plow furrowing in loose sandy soils also is popular, using garden spades to set the trees.

Training at Planting, Standard Trees. Most peach trees are trained to the open-vase form. See Figures 6 and 7 for description. About 18 inches of trunk is needed for borer control and mechanical shaking. The side-leader method of starting trees which was initiated and now is widespread in Michigan is shown in Figure 8. Tree is planted with a wide-angled good limb 18-24'' high pointing into the

---

[1]Among researchers developing peach rootstocks are: Dr. J.N. Cummins, N.Y. Exp. Sta., Geneva; Dr. R.E.C. Layne, Canada Res. Sta., Harrow, Ont.; and Centre de Researches INRA de Bordeaux, France.

prevailing wind. Tree is cut back to this limb which, in turn, is cut back to 10-12 inches; all other limbs are removed. The first season select 3 wide-angled limbs from the side limb; remove others. Develop the tree from this framework. Michigan growers have found these trees to be strong and long-lived[1].

In some orchards of the milder peach growing sections, June-budded trees are set. Trees budded in the nursery in June and dug the same year for fall or winter-planting are usually only three to four feet in the height and may be more or less weakly branched. The side branches are frequently too low for framework use, and these are pruned flush to leave only a whip. Vigorous branches formed the first year in the orchard then are selected for the scaffold.[2] This can be done a few weeks after growth starts, removing unwanted framework limbs.

Subsequent Pruning. In training and pruning the standard peach tree from the second year to maturity, *prune as lightly as possible to attain the desired shape*. It is a common mistake of growers to prune young trees heavily either in an attempt to develop stocky trunks or because of a misunderstanding of the effect of such pruning on subsequent growth. Actually, heavy pruning results in smaller trunks, delays commercial bearing, and drastically decreases profits. Visit the trees once or twice during the early growing season to make scaffold correction cuts.

After the first season's growth, select the best three or

four *wide-angled* scaffolds which are well spaced around the tree. Most of these limbs will be the same ones which were selected immediately after planting. The branches should be spaced about six inches apart vertically around the trunk for the open-head tree and a little farther apart for the central-leader tree in a hedgerow (Figure 6). Remove all other branches arising on the trunk. Remove any strong upright-growing central shoots for the vase system, or, limbs that grow from one side of the tree across to the other side. The principal object is to train the tree to a symmetrical open-bowl tree, as shown in Figure 7.

The lateral scaffolds which have been selected should be headed back lightly only where growth has exceeded about 30 inches with little or no branching. If length growth of the scaffolds is less than 30 inches and heavily branched, several thinning-out cuts will need to be made along the scaffolds. Two or three strong secondary laterals are usually sufficient at this age, with none left closer than about 15 inches to the trunk. In this thinning-out operation, side branches on the scaffolds which grow toward the ground, toward the center of the tree, or straight to the sky are usually the first to be removed. Laterals on a scaffold limb which grow out and slightly up from the left and right are the most desirable.

In regions where Oriental fruit moth is a problem and sprays are not being used, the worms enter tips of growing shoots in early summer and stunt length growth, causing lateral branching. If excessive, the trees tend to become dense, necessitating many thinning-out cuts. With very dense vigorous young trees, some thinning-out during the summer may be helpful in speeding desirable framework.

---

[1]See Chap. IV for principles and methods of pruning.

[2]In California, the central-leader tree has been favored in hedgerow plantings. Short side limbs split less, have better young wood with less disease infection, according to J.A. Beutel, Univ. of Ca., Davis.

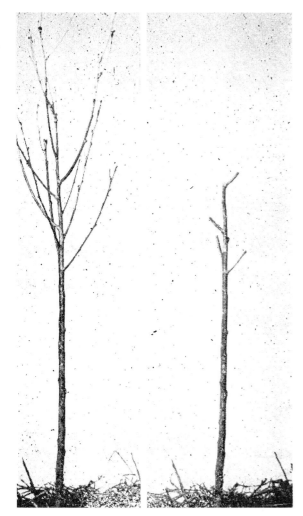

Figure 6. (Left) One-year peach tree after planting. (Right) Same tree after pruning. The tree was cut back to 30 inches. Four well-distributed side branches were left and cut back to short stubs to assist in developing an open-center head.

For hedgerow training, tree on right can be used to form central leader, except spaced two limbs are selected running fan-shaped with the row.

The tree should have its main framework well formed by the third year. Pruning then will consist largely of keeping the center of the tree open and spacing the lateral limbs and shoots on the main scaffold limbs. All short spurlike growth should be left which is not likely to become a competitive problem. These limbs contribute to fast development of the tree and are often the first to bear fruit. They should be maintained until the tree becomes large, at which time they may be removed because of reduced vigor as a result of overshading and competition.

During the third summer, some thinning-out pruning may help to keep the center of the tree open, admitting more light for better flower-bud formation. Flower buds of the peach are formed in late summer, later than on apple. Some fruit buds should form the second or third

summer for a light crop the following year. This is particularly true in milder climates where the growing season is longer and the trees develop faster. There is considerable experimental evidence from Ohio and other states to show that heavy pruning of peaches in the third, fourth, and fifth years greatly reduces the yield. The peach tree usually does not attain its full size until the fifth or sixth year. Hence, *light to moderate annual pruning attention* to attain strong desirable framework should be practiced so that the tree will attain its full size and production as soon as possible.

Special problems in starting the head. A large part of the top may die in recently planted trees due to winter injury the first year, or to an excessively dry period the first summer. A wayward shoot may appear near the base of the tree and grow ahead of the originally selected trunk and laterals. This vigorous shoot can be used to develop the new head provided it arises *above* the point where the

Figure 7. (Top) A 6-year old Elberta peach tree with strong framework. (Bottom) Same tree after pruning. Tips of all strong growing branches were cut back 12 to 24 inches to a side branch to keep the tree within a height and width spread of about 13 feet. The center was opened for light (medium-sized limb in center of tree will be removed in a few years). Lower limbs which tend to droop to the ground with fruit have been removed entirely or pruned to an upward-growing lateral. Dead twigs in center of tree were removed. Wood removed is shown near ladder. Some growers in Pennsylvania prune their trees low so all operations can be performed without ladders. (Ohio State University).

Figure 8. A newly planted peach tree, pruned to start its training by the side-leader method (bottom). One strong lateral branch is selected that is as nearly horizontal as possible. In planting, this branch should be pointed into the prevailing wind. Three shoots to be used as scaffold branches are allowed to develop the first season on this branch (top). Others should be removed. Many growers in Michigan use this system. (Courtesy Mich. State University).

seedling root was budded in the nursery. A new framework is developed from this vigorous shoot, and the old head is removed flush with the base of the vigorous growth.

SPECIAL TRAINING SYSTEMS

The California "Long" System. In the San Joaquin Valley where most of the California peaches are grown, the season is long, the soils deep and fertile, and adequate water is provided by irrigation. Thus, standard trees grow large and reach maximum size early. An essentially open-vase system of pruning is used in which three main scaffold limbs with strong crotches are selected (Figure 9). From five to seven secondary limbs are selected on the primary limbs. When bearing starts the third to fourth year, double bindertwine or small rope is used to encircle the main limbs to prevent the crop from spreading the tree. The next year No. 11 galvanized wire is used to encircle the outside secondary limbs about ¾ the distance up to hold the tree together and avoid breakage. Heavily cropping limbs are braced with 1x3 inch Oregon rough-sawn pine, placed so spraying can be done.

The advantages of this system are: (a) longer-lasting trees that have reduced breakage of important limbs; (b) greater bearing surface that helps account for the higher yields per acre; and (c) reduced over-all pruning on mature trees vs. the relatively heavier pruning in the standard open-center tree to keep the trees low, particularly on the better soils.

The first concern of growers using the open-center pruning is the height of these "Long" trees, necessitating the extra expense of reaching the top fruit. However, growers using the "Long system" claim it is worthwhile to go higher for the fruit if the yields per acre can be increased appreciably. This system of pruning probably would not work satisfactorily elsewhere, except in those areas where peach trees could reach maximum height with good soil and fertilization and with plenty of sunshine and adequate water. As compared with most California cultivars some cultivars grown elsewhere naturally have small thick and spreading type trees, which may be difficult to train by this system. Also, heavy summer rains in the East may soak the soil deep, causing heavily laden trees to sink down or topple. Early tree training and manipulation of the bracing wires may be too tedious and expensive for some growers, although the longer life of the tree should justify the effort.

Some California growers are "flat topping" their trees by cutter bar, and also evaluating summer pruned hedgerows. Check with your agricultural agent if this practice is being continued.

The Hedgerow System. Hedgerow training and pruning has been used for many years in the upper Mediterranean region with wire trellis up to about 12 ft. The hedgerow system without trellis has been researched and adopted by some U.S. growers, as shown in Figure 10.

The Street System. In Kentucky, the late Frank Street, a grower, has described a method of training peach trees

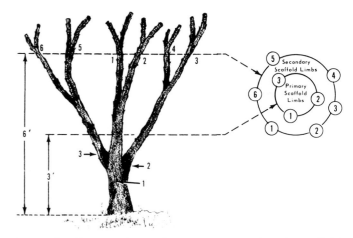

Figure 9. Diagram shows the arrangement of main scaffold system in trees trained by the California "Long" system. There are 3 primary limbs and about 6 secondary limbs, developed for mechanical harvesting of clings. (Calif. Agr. Exp. Sta., Davis 95616).

212

Figure 10. Attention is being directed toward hedgerow growing of peaches in the USA without trellis support, as used with trellis in the Mediterranean area of Europe. Tests have been conducted in Indiana and Georgia with trees 6, 9, and 12 ft. apart in rows 14 ft. apart giving yields about double those by standard 20 x 20 ft. spacing vs. the 9 x 14 planting. A number of growers have adopted the system. Contact Richard Hayden, Purdue, Lafayette, IN. 47907, or B.D. Horton, USDA, Byron, GA. 31008 for latest developments.

where only sharp-angle crotches are removed on the young tree until the tree reaches full size. The advantage is heavy bearing earlier. It should be noted, however, that the soil in this area is unusually good, and that the main cultivar, Elberta, tends to thin its limbs more than most cultivars and attains good fruit size even when cropped heavily. This training system may not work well on many leading cultivars and on light sandy soil.

Tatura Trellis System. This is one of the highest yielding systems, developed in Australia. Average yields in metric tons/hectare by year in Australia, New Zealand and South Africa since 1976 at tree densities of 1600 to 2000 trees/ha. are: 2nd yr. - 4; 3rd yr. - 26; 4th yr. - 45; and 5th yr. - 62. In the last 3 years all but 2, 6 and 7 T/ha. were canned, respectively. The V-shape system (Figure 11) is constructed with soldered together steel fence posts and galvanized wire anchored at the ends. Shoots inside and outisde the "V" are mowed by a special-built cutter bar. Hand labor is needed in winter to detail prune and guide and tie the "Y" leaders. Trees are propagated by soft-wood cuttings (Golden Queen on own roots) and planted about 1x6 m.

apart (1668 trees/ha.). For canning, the trees can be mechanically harvested with no more and usually less damage to the fruit compared with contracted hand harvesting. Trees start bearing in their second year in the above regions of the world and after four years of bearing may have an accumulated yield of 186 MT/ha. Improvements are being made yearly. Seek reprints from Irrigation Research Institute, Tatura, Victoria, Australia 3616; Dr. Steve Blizzard, W. Va. Univ., Morgantown 26506.

The Meadow Orchard. Developed in Israel (after Hudson on apple in England) and tested in Georgia and Florida, trees are planted about 1½ to 2½ ft. in the row and 7 to 9 feet between rows, totalling 3000 to 4000 trees per acre (Figure 12). Yields start the second year and soon reach two to three times annual yields of standard tree plantings. Trees are mowed off by cutter bar ½ to 2½ ft. above ground at harvest. Mechanical harvesters are used in Israel equipped with a cutter bar and a shaker chain belt to skake off the fruit, dropping it to a belt below for collection at rear. Trees are burned or chewed up and spread back on the field. Annual crops are obtained in long-growing-season regions, biennial crops in short-growing regions.

U.S. growers have hesitated to adopt the system for several reasons: (a) Land and labor have not become sufficiently critical; (b) management machinery must be redesigned; (c) where nematodes are critical in the warmer soils, trees must be budded on resistant stock which is expensive vs. soft-wood clonal cuttings; (d) cultivars must be used that are early-age heavy bud-setting as Redhaven and Flordagold, (e) system requires more expertise and care, and (f) they would rather not make such a drastic change in growing technique. U.S. researchers are not sold on shifting away from the standard system under present conditions. Interested growers can test the system with agricultural extensive service help on perhaps an acre or so.

PRUNING THE STANDARD
BEARING TREE

Bearing habit. Peach trees bear fruit laterally on wood that grew the previous year. Thus, the terminal and lateral shoots which have developed over the outer surface of the tree are the most important in fruit production. The best and most fruit is produced in the upper third of the tree. If the practice has been followed of leaving the center of the tree relatively open, as shown in Figure 7, a considerable number of new shoots and short growths or spurs will develop also near the center of the tree. The open-bowl type of head should be maintained, and the height and width of the tree also should be kept within easily managed bounds. About a 10 to 13-foot height and spread is acceptable but the soil, planting system, cultivar, climate and

Figure 11. Tatura Trellis Training System. (Upper left) Developed in Tatura, Victoria, Australia, this is Golden Trellis Queen cultivar in a commercial orchard. Trees propagated by soft-wood cuttings in right photo 1978, planted 1979, photo 1981, yielded 8.9 T/ha in 1981. (Lower left) Tatura commercial block from above, and (lower right) mechanical harvesting in 1981. (Courtesy, B. van den Ende, Irrigation, Tatura, Vic. 3616, Australia).

convenience for mechanical harvesting govern this.

Some growers in Pennsylvania and New Jersey train and maintain their trees so all operations can be performed from the ground. This is done by training limbs outward gradually by tipping back and strengthening the limbs.

Upright growing limbs are headed back and outward to hold them within a working range of 7-8 ft. height.

Fruit buds of the peach are plump and roundish; on the other hand the leaf or shoot buds are small, narrow, and pointed (Figure 13.) On the vigorous shoots, fruit buds at a

Figure 12. The peach Meadow Orchard idea comes from apple studies at Long Ashton Research Station, Bristol, England. Israeli researchers (I. Eres et al.) have perfected the system for their limited land and water situation. Above, test conducted in Georgia. Trees are being harvested. Note drip irrigation. U.S. growers are interested but slow in trying. (Photo courtesy G.A. Couvillon, Ga. Agr. Exp. Sta., Athens 30601)

given node may occur in numbers of one, two, or three, depending upon the cultivar and tree vigor. Where three buds are at a node, the usual arrangement is for the center bud to be a leaf bud while the two outer buds are fruit buds. On the shorter growths and spurs fruit buds are often borne singly beside a leaf bud. On very vigorous shoot growth of 30 inches or more, the lateral buds may consist almost entirely of leaf buds, particularly on the lower portion of such a shoot.

Well-grown bearing trees seldom fail to make enough fruit buds for a heavy crop of fruit the following year. Ordinarily, far too many fruit buds are produced and, hence, dormant pruning is helpful in thinning the crop as well as inducing proper renewal of fruiting wood throughout the tree. If a bearing peach tree 8 to 12 years of age is making from 12 to 16 inches of shoot growth on the majority of the outer branches, this is sufficient for maintaining good fruit production.

Bearing peach trees *must be pruned every year*. If regular annual pruning is not performed, the tendency is for the fruiting wood to develop farther and farther out and higher up. Eventually, a thick-topped leggy tree develops almost devoid of low-fruiting wood. To bring such a tree down to economical range and fruiting, it will be necessary to make some heavy heading-back cuts on the main limbs which may destroy a large part of the crop the first and second years following.

When and how severely to prune. In regions where winter killing of wood and buds is a factor, the presence or absence of freezing damage more or less governs the pruning procedure. If the temperature reached 10° F. below zero during the winter, at least some and perhaps all

fruit buds may be killed, depending upon the cultivar. In a mild climate, a temperature of -10° F. could be expected to cause more damage than in the North unless the trees had been hardened by cold weather sometime prior to this low temperature. The critical temperature for killing dormant peach wood in the colder peach growing areas is around 20° F. below zero, although there may be considerable variation in amount of injury, depending upon the cultivar and previous growth conditions. Winter injured wood can

Figure 13. (Left) A thick vigorous one-year twig of Elberta cut in two. (Right) A relatively thin twig cut in two sections. Note that the flower buds on the left shoot are larger and more numerous. Thick wood also is capable of producing more and larger leaves and fruit. Where three buds are located at a node, the center bud is usually a leaf bud. (New Jersey Agr. Exp. Sta.).

Figure 13a. Many plant diseases such as fire blight on apple and pear and bacterial canker on peach can be transferred from three to tree on pruning tools. Several peach trees in row above were infected with canker and died after pruning tools were used on a diseased tree. Where a serious disease as peach canker is prevalent, dip tools in strong disinfectant after each tree. (D.H. Peterson, USDA and Pennsylvania State University)

be identified by a browning of the inner sapwood to the pith. Fruit buds killed by low temperatures have dark brown centers (pistil is dead) when cross-sectioned. An estimate of the percentage damage can be obtained by sectioning 100 buds on each cultivar in different orchard exposures.

In northern areas in small size orchards, it is best to delay pruning until after danger of winter killing of buds and wood is passed. If there has been no winter injury to the fruit buds, a general over-all pruning then is recommended. If a portion of the buds has been killed, a relatively light pruning should be given because heavy pruning may reduce yield without improving quality. Under most conditions, however, the majority of the living buds will be found on wood in the top of the tree; pruning in this area, therefore, should be relatively light and so-governed to make the best of the prospects.

If practically all of the fruit buds appear to be killed in small orchards, delay pruning until blossoming time. If no blossoms appear, use this opportunity to thin out and moderately cut back to keep the tree within desirable height and spread. Special attention should be given also to proper branch distribution to space evenly the fruiting wood throughout the tree.

If the orchard is large, the grower must proceed with his pruning regardless of possible cold injury to cover his orchard completely before bud break. In mild regions tempered by the ocean or by a large body of water, it is usually safe to prune any time during the winter when most of the work is commonly done.

In regions where spring frosts are a greater risk than winter injury, the necessary thinning-out cuts can be made during the dormant season, but the amount of heading-back cuts can be deferred until after danger of frost injury is over. At this time, the degree of heading-back needed can be done with more certainty.

If the crop is lost entirely and the wood is injured severely, there may be temptation to "dehorn" the trees. "Dehorning" refers to large heading-back cuts four to six feet or more from the tips of the branches, leaving little more than stubs of the main branches. This practice was recommended back in the early 1900's, but experience has shown that these large cuts drastically reduce the crop for several years and may be fatal or severely weakening to the tree. The best treatment for severly winter-injured trees is not to prune, or to prune lightly after growth starts, in combination with an early and rather heavy spring application of a quickly available nitrogen fertilizer, such as nitrate of soda. This should be accompanied by cultivation, if possible, to restore growth conditions. After growth starts, the dead wood can be spotted and removed. If the trees recover, a moderate amount of pruning can be made the following spring to lower, thin out, and spread the top.

Replacing renewal cuts. As a tree reaches the height of about 9 feet, it is important to cut the main upward-growing branches back to outward laterals, as shown in Figure 7. The point at which this cut is made is known as the "renewal point" near which similar cuts will be made in future years. A renewal cut should be placed at the end of every main branch as soon as it reaches the desired height or width spread. The summer after this type of cut is made, one or more side shoots will appear below the cut. During the next winter pruning period, the more vigorous and outward-growing 2 or 3 laterals of these can be retained; the other laterals are removed, including the large side fruiting branch left the year before. Some growers make these first heading-back cuts on a tree when it has attained a height they can reach for lopper cuts from the ground level. Thus, in subsequent years it is possible for the workmen to make most of the renewal cuts without a stepladder. Also, with the bearing surface closer to the ground, the harvesting and thinning operations are facilitated.

Some thinning-out pruning is needed the following winter but the overall pruning is reduced appreciably.

In the northeastern USA, most large orchards are contract pruned for an agreed-price/tree. The men work fast with chain saws and pole pruners completely operating from the ground.

General recommendation. Peach pruning should be somewhat lighter during the first three or four years after the trees come into bearing. Later, a somewhat heavier heading-back type of pruning is desirable every third or fourth year to keep the bearing wood low. When the bloom has evidence of being heavy, the thinning-out pruning will assist considerably in reducing the need for thinning of the fruit later. However, this thinning-out pruning should not be excessive to the point of reducing yield.

Dormant pruning throughout the tree should be sufficient to admit several sun spots on the ground beneath the tree during the growing season. Thick annual terminal growth of 10 to 15 inches is desirable for maintaining good production and sizing of fruit. The pruning, fertilization, and soil management programs must be interrelated carefully to promote this type of terminal growth. Short slender shoot growth is generally unproductive and is characteristic of declining trees (Figure 13). On the other hand, trees which are overly vigorous and producing annual growth of over 30 inches are not only less productive but are difficult to manage in pruning. The accumulation of many dead twigs in the center and lower part of a tree is good evidence of too little pruning throughout the top center of the tree.

Pneumatic Platform Pruning. Costs can be reduced within the 10 to 15% range by use of power pruning tools, as described for the apple. Four persons work together, two on the ground pruning as high as they can reach and two on the platform with kickboards to walk into the trees

Figure 14. (Above) "Flat-Top" pruning by tractor cutter bar a month or so before harvest (below) has been adopted by many growers. There are several advantages. Little regrowth (done 1-15 Aug. in N.J.), reduced winter pruning, energy routed to fruit sizing and coloring and good flower-bud development for next year, others. Four-ft. canvas tied to cutter bar catches, drops cuttings between trees. (Upper, courtesy Ernest Christ, Rutgers University and (below) David Ferree, Ohio State University).

to reach the tops. In hilly orchards the platform is built to be tilted level. Workers favor this power equipment because it speeds, improves, and eases the job. In California, however, growers have almost quit using platforms as it is not adaptable to large crews and affords a saving of within the 10% range only.

"Flat-top" Mower Summer Pruning. Many peach orchards are being topped at about 7 to 11 ft. and some are side-hedged with cutter-bar equipment as shown in Figure 14. About 4 minutes per tree is required to mow the top and thin out in winter by loppers, as compared with 12 minutes for hand-lopping only. A canvas flap tied to and trailing the cutter bar helps collect and drop the prunings between trees.

"Flat-top" mowing about a month before harvest in tests at Rutgers University gave significant benefits: little regrowth is induced, fruit color and plump flower-bud set are enhanced with no effect on yield. Also, winter pruning is reduced to thinning-out cuts only. Growers may wish to study this pruning system on a row or two of each main cultivar. Where used under good light conditions in California, it is performed shortly after harvest.

Mice damage. Occasionally field mice will damage peach trunks, particularly during extended snow cover. Peach prunings left in the row middles may reduce damage to trunks if the snow comes in late winter. Mouse precautions taken for apple generally hold for peach.

SOIL MANAGEMENT

Young trees. Cultivation or chemical herbicides with irrigation (drip) should be used for young peach trees for at least the first two or three years after planting to obtain good survival, vigorous growth, and earlier commercial production. If the orchard is planted on the contour, either the entire middles or only narrow strips on either side of the trees can be kept bare during the spring and most of the summer. Middles of the rows may be sown at the outset to a semi-permanent cover as fescue. If the land is fertile and tree distances are such that intercrops of vegetables or small fruits can be grown, such a practice affords cash income until the peaches start bearing the third or fourth year.

Winter cover crops, if desired, are rye, rye grass, bromegrass, or wheat. Hairy vetch, Austrian peas, rye, oats, barley, or crimson clover are popular in the South. Where the winter cover crop is a grain, it is important that disking or mowing be done early the following spring, preferably when the growth is about knee high and before it has had opportunity to compete with the trees for water and nitrogen. Where spring frosts are a problem, land should be disced and packed by rain well before bloom to afford heat movement from soil upward on cold nights (Figure 15).

Figure 15. Four-year peach trees at Experiment, Georgia. Typical tree on (left) clean cultivated plot and (right) on adjoining sod plot. Sod is competitive for moisture; it should be kept a few feet from the tree trunk. Both trees were well fertilized with nitrogen. Strip-row chemical weed control with fescue sod middles and drip or portable irrigation is popular as a soil management system for peaches. Centers must be kept mowed, however, to reduce late-spring frost damage, slow drying of a thick sod, harboring of troublesome insects and diseases and interference with bee pollination, according to Dr. E.F. Savage, retired, Ga. Exp. Sta., Griffin.

Drip or trickle irrigation for both young and mature peach trees is in wide use by growers and experiment stations. Advantages are a saving in water where it is costly or limited and usually a lower cost in installation. The black plastic feed line with one or two emitters at each tree is laid down the rows, as described in Chapter XIX. Disadvantages of this type irrigation are: (a) it cannot be used to spray the trees with water for frost protection or to cool the trees during extremely hot periods. Care must be taken not to cut or harm the plastic lines with orchard equipment.

Bearing trees. If strip-in-row herbicides and/or cultivation is used in orchards, some type of cover cropping is suggested to maintain or increase organic matter in the soil, reduce erosion, and to reduce the possibility of winter injury. Shortly before or after bearing has started, however, it may be desirable to shift the soil management program from a cultivation cover-crop system to some form of sod management, depending upon the soil-type and rainfall conditions. It is generally agreed among horticulturists that cultivation should be reduced to a minimum; there is considerable evidence to show that excessive cultivation is eventually detrimental to the soil and to tree growth. What the minimum amount of cultivation should be cannot be stated definitely; it may vary from orchard to orchard depending upon the tendency of the soil to become compacted, the slope, and the moisture holding capacity. For example, an orchard on a fertile soil with high moisture retaining capacity could be managed to a good advantage under a system of semipermanent sod with annual row-herbicide treatment and the sod allowed to grow with one or two mowings in summer, using irrigation when needed. On the other hand, an orchard on a lighter and somewhat less fertile soil

probably could not be handled successfully by this method. Undoubtedly, under sandy soil conditions in a mild climate, it would require longer periods of cultivation to remove competition between the trees and the cover crop for moisture. Heavy clays may be entirely unsatisfactory because they present a drainage problem and are likely to be too wet at times and too dry at others (see Figure 5).

There is clear evidence from experiment stations in humid regions that peaches can be grown satisfactorily under sod mulch in the moderately heavy types of soil, provided a heavy mulch is maintained and two and three times the nitrogen (only) is applied as recommended under cultivation the first two years. Mulch, however, is becoming difficult to find at a reasonable price. The system is applicable on hilly sites and also in home gardens. R.G. Hill, Jr. of Ohio has shown under long-term test that good quality yields can be obtained in sod if ample nitrogen and water are supplied.

The size of the peach crop more or less governs the time of seeding a cover crop in late summer. If the trees are carrying a light or no crop, the cover can be sown earlier for the purpose of competing with the tree, reducing its growth, and thus reducing the likelihood of winter injury. On the other hand, if the trees are carrying a heavy crop of fruit and the weather is somewhat dry, the cover crop can be sown later to reduce competition for water with the maturing crop of peaches.

Rye grass and wheat have been popular winter cover crops in bearing orchards in the Northeast because they grow more slowly in spring and give the grower opportunity to mow or disk them down before they compete with the trees. Rye is a fast growing crop for which seed is cheap, available, and will germinate and take hold better

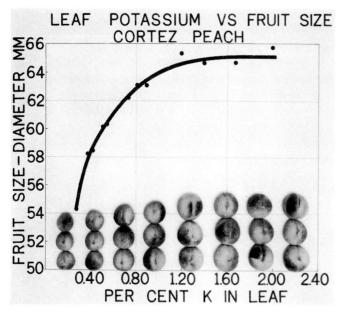

Figure 16. Maximum size of peach fruits and yield is reached at midseason potassium leaf levels of about 1.2%. (Courtesy Omund Lillilalnd, Univ. of Calif., Davis).

under adverse conditions.

Fertilization, with or without lime, at seeding time is practiced to obtain good covers. Most cover crops and especially legumes grow best in soils with a pH of about 6.0 to 6.5. Rye will grow on soils too acid for other cover crops. An application of 100 to 150 pounds per acre of a high-grade complete fertilizer is recommended on areas where the cover is sown, using a 5-10-5 for loamy soils of moderate fertility and a 10-10-10 with or without trace elements for sandy soils, or those of low fertility. Caution is needed against over-liming a peach orchard; damage to the trees can result.

In California, the following cover crops and seeding rates are used in cling orchards.

Variety	Amount of Seed (lbs/acre)
VETCHES	
Common	20 to 25
Purple	15 to 25
Hairy	15 to 25
MUSTARD	15 to 20
CEREALS	
Rye	30 to 40[1]
Barley	30 to 50

[1]The lesser amount may be used for early seeding.
See Calif. Leaflet 2455 for special fertilizer applications for peach.

Fertilization. Most peach growers rely on commercial fertilizers. Nitrogen is the element most often needed by peach trees; in some soils it may be the only element needed. In fact, for a given amount of nitrogen, more response is obtained in peach trees than almost any other fruit crop.

Application of nitrogen should be governed by cultivar and character of the shoot growth. If young peach trees are making approximately 18 inches of terminal growth and the foliage is of good color without fertilizer, they do not need fertilizer. The same can be said for bearing orchards if the annual shoot growth is 10 to 15 inches, the girth of the shoots is thick, and the yields good. If the growth exceeds this length for mature trees by several inches, it would be well to reduce the nitrogen for awhile. Careless use of nitrogen on peach trees has resulted in damage by over-stimulating the trees. *Each tree should be considered separately for its fertilizer needs.* Trees growing on the lower more fertile areas will require less fertilizer than those growing on somewhat eroded knolls.

It is difficult to recommend a definite amount of nitrogen-carrying fertilizer for a given orchard, or, for a given peach tree. When growth of the trees has been uniform, the problem is easier. However, tree growth in most orchards tends to be variable. Sulfate of ammonia, or ammonium nitrate is generally used at the rate of one-fourth or one-third pound of sulfate of ammonia per year of age of trees or its equivalent in actual nitrogen. Nitrate of potash or soda is used widely in some humid regions.

Figure 17. Potassium deficiency on peach is characterized by crinkling, marginal burning, and speckled dead spots between the main veins of the older leaves. (Rutgers University).

219

Figure 18. (Above) Magnesium deficiency developed under sandy loam conditions in North Carolina. When combined with low nitrogen, the leaf margins turn whitish green. (Below) Manganese deficiency usually develops under high pH soil conditions or on an over-limed orchard floor. Leaves have a herringbone appearance of light green between veins that are widely green. Three to 5 lbs. of manganese sulphate/100 gals. should correct it in 2 to 3 wks. (Upper: A.C. McClung, N.C. State Univ.; below: H. K. Bell, formerly Rutgers University).

When the trees have reached maturity after about 5 to 6 years, the application thereafter is 2 to 3 pounds per tree of ammonium nitrate or its nitrogen equivalent, depending upon annual shoot growth, amount of pruning, condition of the tree, and type and native fertility of soil. On the basis of pure nitrogen, this is about one-half to one-pound per mature tree. Cultivars with highly colored fruits such

as Jerseyland and Redhaven can use higher rates of nitrogen to get higher yields and still not hinder color commercially. If in doubt, apply at the lower rate.

Leaf analysis is used widely to govern fertilizer applications to peach, particularly where a nutrient problem in apparent. Following are average contents found in good yielding trees by standard laboratory procedure.

TABLE 4. AVERAGE MINERAL CONTENTS OF PEACH LEAVES ON GOOD YIELDING TREES.*

N	P	K	Mg	Ca	S	Fe	Mn	B	Zn	Cu	Mo
%	%	%	%	%	ppm	ppm	ppm	ppm	ppm	ppm	ppm
2.5	0.15	1.25	0.25	1.9	100	124	20	20	15	4.0	0.5
to	to	to	to	to	to	to	to	to	to	to	to
3.36	0.30	3.00	0.54	2.5	150	152	142	80	30	11.9	1.0

*Contents below minimum figures may result in deficiency; above the maximum, an excess.

There is evidence in humid and dry regions that potassium (Figures 16 and 17) may be a problem on young as well as old trees, particularly in the lighter soils. This is characterized by limited growth with curling leaves which show considerable tip and marginal burning. Phosphorus is most important to the cover crop but has been found a major deficiency in soils of Australia and New Zealand. Deficiency resembles zinc shortage. Other nutrients which may be deficient in peach orchards are zinc, manganese and boron in humid areas (Figures 18 and 19). In humid sandy soil areas where organic matter is low, the following nutrients in a ton of fertilizer can be used in a 5-10-10 mix at 1000 lbs./A: manganese, zinc, and iron as sulfates, 20 lbs. each; borax and copper sulfate, 10 lbs. each; ammonium or sodium molybate, one lb.; Mg oxide, 2% (Figure 20). Dr. Marshall Ritter on a Pennsylvania longterm NPK test found P applications gave increased yields after a few years of fruiting on a medium loam soil.

Irrigation. Peach trees respond well to readily available water throughout the growing season. Fruit which has fallen behind in size because of insufficient moisture during the growing season, even as early as two or four weeks after bloom, will never regain the size obtained on other trees receiving adequate moisture. But a peach fruit attains about 66% of its size in the last month on the tree. Peaches need about 36-acre inches of water a season, or about 10 gals./day/tree by drip to over 2X this by sprinkler irrigation. Irrigation is a regular practice in peach orchards where low or erratic annual rainfall makes it a necessity. Where water is plentiful, low in cost and the land level, furrow or flood irrigation can be used because initial installation is 25% the cost of portable sprinklers, although water application can be controlled better with sprinklers (frost control). Where water is scarce or expensive plastic pipe in-row "trickle" irrigation is used. (See Chapter XIX, also Figure 12).

Figure 19. (Upper left) Boron deficiency in British Columbia a month after leafing out in spring. Previous season the tree had good appearance. (Upper right) Iron deficiency showing network of fine green veins over yellow background, or in small leaf almost complete straw yellow. (Lower left) Boron deficiency developed in the green house, showing dying back of side shoots like Oriental fruit moth damage. (Lower right) Zinc deficiency, one of easiest to identify. Note wavy leaf margins with (or without) dirty whitish chlorosis with main veins greenish. LaRue et al., Univ. of Calif., find mycorrhizae (Cal. Agr., May '75) in peach roots assist in "foraging" for zinc. (Upper left, C.G. Woodbridge, formerly Summerland, B.C.; others, Hector R. Cibes, formerly Rutgers University). See also color section in Chapter 18.

221

Figure 20. Row of trees on the left received a complete fertilizer mix (see text) of major and trace elements. Row on right received only NPK. Response by peaches to trace elements often occurs on sandy low-organic matter soils as in the southeast USA humid region. (Courtesy Roy Ferree, retired, Clemson University, Clemson, S.C.)

Results of Feldstein and Childers on a deep medium loam soil near Doylestown, Pa., reported through Rutgers University, indicated that irrigation paid well five out of six years. In two of the years the fruit from nonirrigated trees was so small that over 75 percent was unsaleable, whereas fruit from irrigated trees was all saleable. B.L. Rogers in Maryland obtained an average of 29% larger fruit size for Sunhigh and 26% for Elberta over a seven-year irrigation test. Morris *et al.* in Arkansas in Figure 18 show interrelationship between irrigation, fruit thinning, pruning. Texas tests doubled crop value by irrigation.

The soil moisture content should not be depleted more than 85 centibars by a tensiometer to a 4 ft. depth. Excessive water may cause root and crown rots.

There is a close interrelationship between amount of pruning (and fruit thinning), irrigation and fruit sizing in a peach orchard, as shown by Dr. Justin R. Morris et al. in Figure 21. Amount of nitrogen used also is involved.

THINNING PEACH FRUITS

Fruit thinning is a standard practice on peach trees carrying a moderate to heavy crop. However, in spite of the many benefits from thinning demonstrated through long years of experience, fruit thinning is too often one of the most inefficiently conducted operations in peach growing. The late Stanley Johnston of Michigan gives the following reasons for growers slighting this job: (a) Failure to realize at thinning time how much the young fruits will expand in size before the harvesting season if they are given the proper opportunity; it is important to consider that it takes twice as many peaches of two-inch size as of two and one-half inch size to fill a bushel container; (b) failure to realize that it is better economy to pick the excess fruits after the June drop and throw them on the ground than to be compelled to pick them at regular harvesting season with the resultant extra handling costs and lower value of small peaches; (c) it is a monotonous job when

done only by hand and it is only natural to hurry through or to find excuses to do something else. Thinning crews must have constant and careful supervision for best results.

Hand and Mechanical Thinning. For this type thinning, start after the June drop (5-8 wks. after full bloom). Extent of the thinning task can be determined better at this time than earlier because peach trees generally retain practically all fruit to maturity which are attached to the tree after the June drop. Where certain insects are a problem, most of the injury is over by this time, and damaged peaches can be seen and removed in the thinning operation.

Early maturing cultivars are thinned first (Figure 22 and 23). Next, thin, the cultivars and the trees within a cultivar which are carrying the heaviest crop. To obtain the greatest benefit from thinning, the job should be completed as soon after the June drop as possible, although it has been shown that for many of the medium- to late-maturing cultivars,

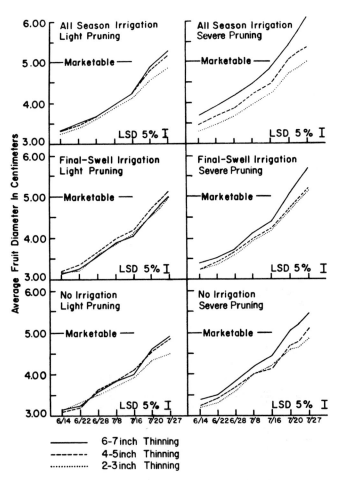

Figure 21. J.R. Morris et al. in Arkansas show in a three-year test that heavy pruning and/or fruit thinning may replace irrigation within limits, from the standpoint of fruit size. Actually, an attempt should be made to get maximum crop and fruit size with the proper irrigation (if needed), pruning and fruit thinning. This is a delicate situation to manipulate that comes with experience.

some benefit from thinning can be obtained as late as eight to ten weeks before picking. Fogle *et al.* of USDA states, "How many peaches should be removed from a tree by thinning depends chiefly on the size of the tree and its bearing capacity. If a tree cannot bear more than 1 or 2 bushels, only enough of the peaches that can develop to desirable size (those with a diameter of 2¼ to 2½ inches) should be left to meet this quantity. When a tree has a uniformity heavy set of fruit, it can be thinned to a fixed spacing, such as 6 to 8 inches along the twig. Usually, it is best to thin not according to a fixed spacing but according to leaf area, tree vigor, and bearing capacity. After a spring freeze, sometimes the only blossoms left alive are those at the bases of terminal shoots. When this happens, the fruits are not thinned although they touch each other, because the leaf area is sufficient for all.

Where labor costs are high, peach growers may choose to reduce the number of peaches that will be produced on their trees by pruning off a large number of shoots either before or at blossomtime. In localities where spring frosts occur, some detailed pruning may be postponed until blossomtime, when crop prospects are more certain.

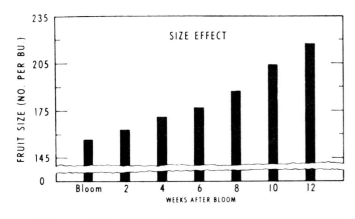

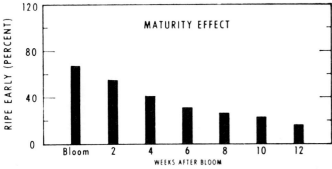

Figure 22. Graphs show effects of time of thinning Redhaven peaches (2-week intervals after bloom) on ultimate fruit size (above) and maturity time (below). Note that each successive thinning time caused smaller and later maturing peaches. Early thinning also increases leaf size and shoot growth. Among other early ripening cultivars that set heavily and so-benefit are Mayflower, Earlired, Cardinal, Coronet, Golden Jubliee and Triogem. (After Fogle et al., USDA).

In California, an attempt is made to grow fruits as nearly uniform in size as possible for canning. In thinning, a more or less definite number of peaches is left on a tree of given vigor and size. If 2½ inch peaches are desired from a 20 X 20 foot planting, it will be necessary to leave the following number of peaches per tree for a given yield; about 700 peaches per tree yields 10 tons/acree; 1,050 peaches yield 15 tons and 1,240 peaches give 18 tons. Based on a measurement at *Reference Date* (10 days after pit hardening, Figure 23) cling peach sizes can be predicted accurately so heavy thinning is necessary if peach diameter is 33 mm, moderate thinning if diameter is 36mm, and only touch-up if sizes exceed 38 mm at reference date.

The largest and best-colored peaches are produced on the more vigorous new wood. Thus, more peaches should be left on the outside and especially in the tops of the trees than on the inside and lower branches. Fruit in "hanger"[1] branches around the lower part of the tree should be thinned more heavily, perhaps picking all fruits from thin weak wood.

About 30-35 average size peach leaves are required to size a peach to marketable size. Generally, the smaller the natural size of the fruit for a cultivar at harvest, the more leaves and wider spacing of the fruit is needed.

Because of the high labor costs, considerable thinning has been done in recent years by rapid mechanical methods rather than by the older hand method. Some growers use poles 4 to 8 feet long or longer, with about 12 inches of hard rubber hose over one end. With such poles, the excess fruits are removed by tapping the branch or twig first at

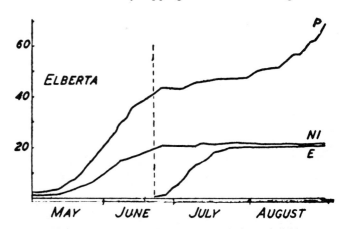

Figure 23. Growth curves of Elberta peach from full bloom to maturity for (P), pericarp or edible part; (NI), nucellus and integuments of pit; and (E), embryo in the pit. Note period of about five weeks after (dotted line) and during embryo development when the edible part, (P), shows little increase in volume size. Length of period from full bloom to dotted line is about the same for early, medium, and late cultivars, but period from dotted line to final increase in fruit size may vary from a week for an early cultivar (Greensboro) to six weeks for a late cultivar (Rio-Oso-Gem). Fogle and Faust (USDA) found most nectarine cultivars to have straight-line curves vs. the sigmoid curve of peach. (New York Agr. Exp. Sta. Geneva).

223

right angles and then lengthwise. Plastic baseball bats can be used. A teenager can do about 65 trees a day. Wire or brush brooms (dogwood or apple limbs one-inch at base) sometimes are used to thin peach blossoms, especially those of early ripening cultivars. A stream from a spray gun at 600 lbs. pressure can be run up and down the branch knocking off a percentage of the bloom. Blossom thinning, of course, is risky where frost damage is a factor.

Trunk shakers, custom or grower-owned, are an effective means of removing fruits on a large scale and are widely used Figure 25. The lower trunki is grasped by a cushioned arm, tightened, and the entire tree vibrated, shaking off the fruit in seconds. One disadvantage is possible removal of too many large fruit. Avoid over-thinning in the tree tops and do not rely on trunk shakers to do the complete job. First limb on a tree should be 15-18 inches above ground and the trunk must be trained straight with a stake, if necessary, the first two years. Motor-driven hand operated limb shakers, favored by some growers, have been used.

Chemical thinning. Many chemicals have been tested and discarded because of too much foliage and shoot damage, premature fruit softening along the suture, or due to necessity of applying at or too shortly after bloom in regions where post-bloom frosts may occur, further reducing set. In the arid mild climates or sections of the world where post-bloom frosts are a low-risk, and the

Figure 25. This type tree trunk shaker is being used to thin peaches, nectarines and other fruits and nuts, taking only seconds per tree. It also is used with a catching frame to harvest stone fruits. The trunk clasp, as constructed, causes little or no injury to the trunk. (Courtesy Orchard Machinery Corp., Yuba City, California, 95991).

chemical is not banned, Elgetol from 1 pt. (J.H. Hale) to 1½ pts. to 1 qt. (most cultivars) in 100 gals. of water is used with fair success, depending upon weather, tree vigor, intensity of bloom, and other factors. Spray is applied when 60-75 percent of the blossoms are open. Exact timing is important. Complete thinning is not recommended; excess fruits are knocked off manually with clubs.

Auxin (hormone) spray-thinning of peaches could be the best method for quick, easy, and economical peach thinning. Many auxins have been tested and discarded. No chemical as yet is fully satisfactory.

Carl E. Gambrell, Jr., Clemson University, South Carolina, after some 30 years of testing chemical thinners for peaches, suggests an ethylene releasing agent, CGA-15281 (2-chloroethyl-mythelbis (phenoxy) silane) which after 8 years of testing, appears to be an effective thinner of several cultivars. It has little or no effect on vegetative growth. Degree of thinning varies with the cultivar, stage of fruit development, temperature, concentration and application technique. Status of the chemicals for grower use had not been approved at this writing but acceptance by EPA appeared promising (developed by Woolfolk Chemical Works, Inc. PO Box 938, Ga. 31030).

With chemical thinning, advice of local specialists should be checked since materials and techniques are changing and the operation is risky.

FROST DAMAGE AND WINTER INJURY

In California the only injury from cold, which is not frequent, is due to spring frosts during bloom or after the fruit has set. Open blossoms are very tender, but small fruits are more tender, becoming increasingly so until one-half-inch in size. The seed is usually killed, causing the

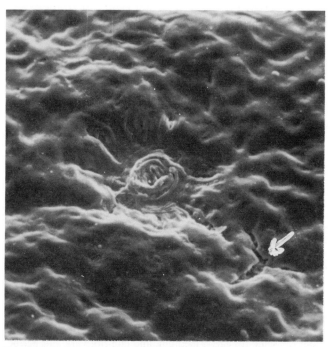

Figure 24. This is the highly magnified skin of a nectarine showing a stoma (pore, center) and a crack developing (arrow). Note the character of the skin surface. Moisture loss by leaves is controlled by the opening and closing of the stomata. (Courtesy H. Fogle and M. Faust, USDA).

fruit eventually to drop. Blossoms and fruit can be protected by orchard heating, but the grower must decide whether the increased returns brought by saving the crop over a period of years more than offset the cost of heating.

East of the Rocky Mountains, the most important factors influencing peach growing are spring frosts and winter injury in one form or another. Winter injury in its broadest aspects is experienced in peach regions above the Mason and Dixon Line. In South Carolina and neighboring states, the so-called "winter injury" is not so much due to low temperature as to cold March weather following a warm period in February which had induced growth activity. The results of winter injury in a region like Michigan and New York, however, are very clear-cut when a peach crop is lost or when the trees themselves virtually are killed by one extreme drop in temperature. Of almost equal importance to the trees in those regions are secondary effects of winter injury, including the resultant entrance of peach borers and the canker disease, which together may shorten the life of a tree.

The most common form of winter injury to peaches is the destruction of fruit buds. Leaf buds are usually not injured unless the twigs are killed. It is impossible to give a definite critical temperature for fruit buds of each cultivar. The danger point for Elberta during midwinter is usually between -10° and -12° F. and other cultivars are compared with it. Fruit buds of Elberta, Velvet, Washington and J.H. Hale are among the most tender in bud; Halehaven and Redhaven are medium hardy; whereas those of Rochester, Veteran, Cumberland, Reliance (good in home gardens), Jefferson and Erly-Red-Fre are among the more hardy to low temperature. A cultivar like Redhaven that produces many buds per foot of limb may come through cold weather when others that produce relatively few buds will not come through.

The farther the blossoms have opened, the more susceptible they are to cold; peaches in full bloom may be injured at about 25° F. (-3.9° C) whereas just before the petals open, they may survive 20° to 23 °F (Table 5).

TABLE 5. CRITICAL TEMPERATURES FOR PEACH BUDS (ELBERTA). E.L. PROEBSTING, JR., WASH. STATE UNIV., PROSSER.

Bud Development Stage*	1	2	3	4	5	6	7
Old Standard Temp.[1]	23	—	—	25	—	27	30
Ave. Temp. for 90% Kill[2]	1	5	9	15	21	24	25
Ave. Temp. for 10% Kill[2]	18	21	23	25	26	27	28
Average Date (Prosser)[3]	3/7	3/16	3/19	3/29	4/3	4/11	4/18

*Stage 1 is first swelling; 4 is first pink and 7 is postbloom.
[1]Critical temperatures as previously published in WSU EM 1616. All in °F.
[2]Average temperatures found by research at the WSU Research and Extension Center, Prosser, to result in 10% and 90% bud kill.
[3]Average date for this stage at the WSU Research and Extension Center, Prosser.

Winter injury is more a factor in weakening peach trees than most growers realize. Injury to roots due to extended periods of low temperature in colder areas may appear one or two years after the damage. Such injury tends to be greater in light sandy soils with no cover crop. Trees in weak condition are more susceptible to severe winters. Excessively vigorous trees are tender.

Following are comments for reducing loss from winter injury in Michigan, and, in whole or in part, are applicable to many other areas.

1. Do not plant commercial peach orchards in areas where the temperature frequently drops below -12°.

2. The peach site should have a moderately fertile well-drained soil with good elevation (except when near large deep bodies of water).

3. Select cultivars which are most hardy in fruit bud and wood.

4. Perform moderate to light pruning: avoid severe heavy pruning. Where canker is a problem, delay pruning until March. *Do not prune in fall with trees in leaf.* (Figure 26).

5. Apply fertilizers cautiously if the foliage has good color and the terminal growth is 12 to 18 inches. Peach trees making moderate growth live longer. White latex paint reduces trunk temperature spread. (See Chap. IX).

6. A recently cultivated loose soil or a cover crop under trees at bloom encourages frost damage (Figure 15).

7. At the last fall cultivation sow a cover crop covering the soil area to the trunks to give root protection. Herbicide usage may preclude this.

8. Pull soil up around trunk to form inverted cone a foot high in early fall, level in spring. Don't allow puddling around trunk in winter.

9. Thin the fruit of healthy bearing trees to conserve tree vitality.

10. Keep the foliage in a healthy condition.

TOP-WORKING AND BRIDGE-GRAFTING

It may be desirable to top-work peaches to change trees that did not come true to name, to change the cultivar, or, in an unusual case, when a pollinizer cultivar is needed. Peach cultivars are compatible with one another. Top-working is usually done on the younger trees which have an abundance of small pencil-size branches close to the center of the tree and fairly close to the ground. These branches may be top-worked by budding in late summer and cut back the following spring.

Rodents usually do not injure peaches except during extended periods of snow coverage. Methods and materials for bridge grafting are given in Chapter VIII.

HARVESTING PEACHES

Because the first fresh peaches on the market bring good prices, there is a tendency among growers to flood the

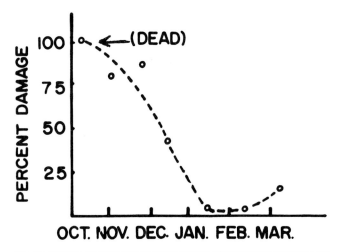

Figure 26. (Above) Fall pruning before winter cold can be disastrous to peach trees in areas where peach canker *(Pseudomonis syringae)* is a problem (W. Dowler and D. Peterson, So. Car.). (Below) This shows effect of pruning Dixigem trees in November foreground left and right, and pruning the following March in the background. Photograph taken in late April. Trees on left were on Yunnan rootstock and those on the right on Lovell roots (C.N. Clayton, No. Car.).

early market with immature peaches. Green, hard, starchy, shriveled peaches receive little or no demand, or, if bought, do not bring return sales and consequently the price often drops quickly. If the consumer were given his choice, he would prefer that the peach be removed from the tree at the peak of its color and quality. The grower, on the other hand, cannot afford to wait until the peach reaches this stage of ripeness. Such peaches bruise easily, lose condition rapidly, and may result in considerable loss during the handling operations. The grower knows that firmness is a primary factor in safety of handling; the degree of firmness at which the peach should be harvested depends upon the cultivar, size of the crop to be handled, availability of hydrocooling, and refrigeration for holding and in shipment, and distance to the market.

Probably the best time to harvest peaches is just as the ground color is beginning to change to yellow for yellow-flesh peaches or to white for white-flesh peaches. Also, just prior to maturity, there is a swelling of the flattened

side of a peach. It is usually necesary to pick the trees more than once during the harvesting season to attain the desired degree of ripeness. Some growers go over the trees "spot" picking two or three times, each time removing the fruits which are of first-grade color and of good size. Other growers may go over their trees five or ten times, removing only the largest, best-colored fruits and leaving the smaller ones to gain size and color.

South Carolina and New Jersey tests show *Alar* (N-dimethylamine succinamic acid) when applied as a post-bloom spray and near pit hardening will cause accelerated maturity up to 5 days, reducing pickings from 5 to 1 or 2, causing no adverse effects on under- or overcolor (may increase over-color), soluble solids, pH, titratable acidity and soluble solids - acid ratio of fruit. Reduced number of pickings favors mechanical harvesting of peaches. Evaluate cost vs. return. Follow label directions.

Where the fruit are to be shipped a long distance, the growers usually pick the fruit up to about a week before it would be ready to eat. This is under average weather conditions. If the weather has been cool and suddenly turns hot and muggy, ripening will be speeded up considerably. On the other hand, if weather has been hot and turns cool shortly before harvest, the ripening may be retarded.

The cultivar must be considered. Golden Jubilee for example, is of high quality but too soft and it is not well suited to shipment and should be sold locally. Redhaven is adapted to long shipment but must be picked promptly at a certain stage of maturity to avoid loss from dropping. With a little experience with different cultivars and different weather conditions, one can attain a fair degree of accuracy.

In commercial areas where peach orchards are located *relatively close* to the consumption centers, there is a trend toward picking the fruit at the *firm-ripe* stage, and using much greater care in packing and handling of the crop. Work at the Illinois Experiment Station has shown that if peaches are harvested when firm-ripe, which is around seven days later than many growers harvest peaches in Illinois and neighboring states, the size of the fruit, sugar content, and total yield can be increased considerably with little or no effect on keeping quality. Fruit picked firm-ripe and held in storage two weeks had good quality and better color and flavor than fruit picked somewhat immature. Such fruit sells easily with little waste. The results indicated that too early picking may result in sufficient loss of cash income to make the difference between operating the orchard at a profit or a loss in good seasons.

Peaches are highly perishable and require careful handling to prevent cuts and bruises. Pickers must be cautioned beforehand on carefully filling and emptying picking containers. Temperature is the most important factor affecting the ripening processes. Once peaches are removed from the tree they must be handled quickly and kept cool or as near to 32 °F. as possible until they reach the consumer's table. Trucks and trailers for transporting peaches in the orchard or to the market should be equipped to handle the fruit smoothly to reduce jolting to a minimum.

Mechanical Harvesting, Bulk Handling. Increasing labor problems and costs have stimulated the development of mechanical harvesting equipment on the West Coast for processing clings and in the east for freestones. Mechanical harvesters are expensive. One harvester unit with a 3-man crew can harvest in California the tonnage of peaches that could be picked in a 9-hour day by a 20 to 24-man crew with ladders. Lower limbs must be removed so fruit can fall directly and uninjured to the padded catching frame. Under these conditions mechanically harvested firm peaches show no more defects when canned within 24 hours of harvest than do hand-picked fruit. In one type, fruit is shaken off the tree with a trunk shaker, and all fruit is conveyed from the bottom of the catching frame conveyor belt to bulk bins of 1000-pound capacity. Usually sorting and sizing facilities are available on the frame, so only first-grade peaches reach the bin. All peaches are picked in a single pick. Those not wanted are dropped on the ground. See recent continuously moving over-the-row model being developed by USDA in Figure 26a.

A single unit harvester (Figure 27) developed by USDA, California and South Carolina agricultural engineers is used for clings and freestones. A trunk shaker is mounted under the catching frame which closes under the tree. Trees must be pruned so fruit can fall directly to the catching frame. Firm peaches are harvested with 14-16 pounds

Figure 26a. This is an over-the-row continuously moving peach harvester being developed by USDA at The Appalachian Fruit Research Center, Kearneysville, W. Va. by Donald L. Peterson et al. The equipment easily operates at three trees/minute and will do up to five trees/min. It is being developed for fresh fruit harvest mainly in the eastern U.S. The Station also is working on machines for the N.Z. "T" trellis apples and the Australian Tatura system.

pressure as measured by Taylor-Magness tester with 5/16 inch plunger, cling size desired usually is 2 3/8 minimum.

Development in these fields is fast and similar to that for the apple; any detailed discussion here soon may be obsolete. The reader is referred to the references and also to an up-to-date catalogue of a manufacturer (Orchard Machinery Corp., Yuba City, CA 95991).

Pick-your-own peaches. For peach orchards near population centers and where the manager enjoys dealing with many types of people, this system has worked with success. See Chapter X and its references for details; see also Index and Chap. XXI.

Yields. In California where trees are 15 feet high and 16-18 feet in diameter, production from 100 trees per acre averages 12-15 tons per acre for midseason freestones or canning clings. In the best orchards, some cultivars in certain years will produce 30 tons/acre, but 20-25 tons/acre of processing peaches is common for the better orchards. With the trees pruned lower in the humid east, yields are generally 400-800 bu/A depending upon many factors. This is 10-20 T/A.

Split Pits. Any treatment or environment that favors fruit growth during the initiation of pit hardening tends to increase split pits, namely (a) early excessive thinning of the fruit such as by frost with irrigation or rains following immediately, (b) girdling of tree limbs by wire, etc., (c) early maturing of some cultivars, (d) cultivars in which pit hardening is relatively late as Elberta, Dixon, and Phillips Cling, and (e) excessive use of nitrogen. Federal inspection on packing lines to check percentage splits ("dangerous" to children) has been resisted with success by the National Peach Council.

PACKAGING

There are three "types of grower labels" on peach cartons in the market: (1) Buyers know the label by reputation and buy without lifting the lid; (2) know the grower and may or may not lift the lid; and (3) lift the lid and evaluate carefully before buying, or just move on to the next display.

Selecting packages. In some areas, peaches are still sold in wood boxes of various sizes. One used is about 11½ X 18 inches and 3½ to six inches deep, in diagonal or offset rows, carefully sized 2 to 3 layers deep. One-half and one-bushel-baskets still can be found in limited use. Various size hampers or "peach baskets" are used for local trade, placing the fruit in poly bags inside the display baskets, pulling the bags of fruit out and tying for sale, retaining the display basket.

The trend for shipping peaches is toward corrugated and fiberboard cartons and boxes, as described in Figure 28. These are changing somewhat from year to year with perfection for specific needs. Tray packs are popular.

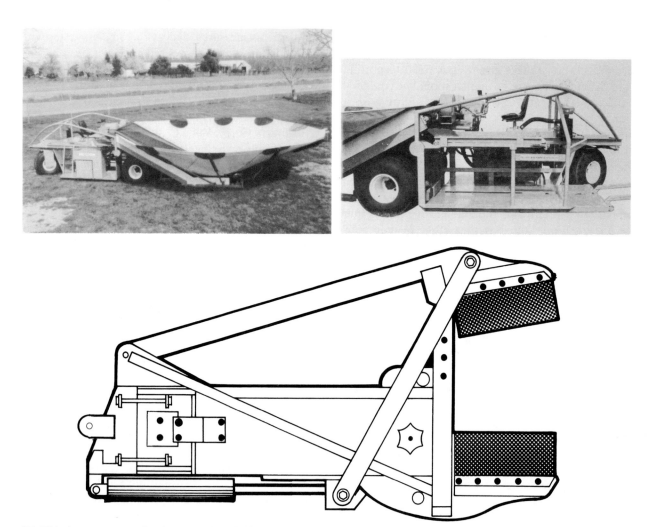

Figure 27. This is a compact, simple, rugged and efficient "Shock Wave" harvester in one unit, single operator. Fruit is collected on back side in dry or wet bin or by a fork-held bin. Inverted umbrella catching frame that folds back to approach a tree, can be extended 6 ft. for larger trees. Scissor-head (below) trunk clasp has a special built "pillow pad" to avoid trunk damage. (Orchard Machinery Corp., Yuba City, Ca. 95991.

Packing. Where peaches are raised in quantity, packing houses are essential. These houses are located in the orchards or near railroad switches to reduce hauling. A two-story frame house with the top floor for containers and other storage space is typical. The lower floor is used for packing and is usually open on at least three sides with a covered driveway. The fruit is delivered at one side and moved across the house during the packing operation, eventually going into refrigerated railroad cars or trucks at the opposite side or to cold storage rooms. The steps discussed and shown in Figure 29 cover the modern peach packing line. Some steps may be eliminated depending upon local needs.

Peaches are packed under the local government grades. Peach growers should follow carefully the Federal specifications where possible to stabilize the market and provide a uniform and dependable basis for doing business.

STORING PEACHES

Firm-ripe peaches that are not "overgrown" may be held in cold storage for two to four weeks at a storage temperatue of from 30° to 32° F and 85 percent humidity. If peaches are held too long in cold storage, the fruit tends to lose flavor and quality.

Time to remove peaches from storage is determined by the cultivar. J.H. Hale , if cooled promptly to 31 °F can be held 3 to 4 weeks.Elberta and Redhaven will hold 2 to 3 weeks. Tissues freeze at just below 30°F. Hence, it is risky to drop the temperature much below 31 °F.

If peaches are harvested at the shipping stage (Elberta testing 10-14 lbs. pressure with a 5/16-inch plunger with the Magness-Taylor tester on paired cheeks), they will become ripe in 2 to 4 days at 70-80°F. Ripening will proceed about as fast at 60° as at 70° or 80° and about half as fast at 50°. At 60° and above most peaches will ripen internal breakdown and loss of flavor, texture and appearance of peaches can be reduced and fruit quality maintained longer by (a) holding fruit in air at 65 to 68 °F a day or so before placing the peaches in cold storage, by (b) storing the fruit in CA at 1% O_2 and 5% CO_2, by (c) intermittent warming the fruit during cold storage in air, or by (d) an even better system of warming the fruit intermittently for 2 days in air at 65 to 68 °F during storage at 32 °F in CA, then ripening the fruit. Peaches and nectarines have held good quality up to *20 weeks* (see reference). Immature fruit so-treated had more acid than mature fruit. All fruit was stored at 11 to 14 lbs. firmness as soon after harvest as feasible. Fruit dipped in benomyl at warming had less rot, mainly brown rot (4% or less), and better internal appearance than fruit dipped only initially. Cultivar variability is a factor. Anderson notes problems that must be resolved before the latter technique can be used by industry but the importance of this research is apparent in hemispheric shipping and in marketing.

SHIPPING PEACHES[1]

In the U.S., e.g., Florida begins the shipment of peaches to northern markets in May, followed by Georgia, California, North Carolina, and Texas. The harvest season extends gradually northward until the peaches of Ohio, New York, and Michigan are marketed in September with a few late cultivars available in October. Breeders are trying to spread the ripening season both ways with high color and flavored cultivars.

The storage life of peaches may be increased several days by precooling to 30° to 32 °F. before shipment; also, quick precooling requires less refrigeration in the long run because there is less heat of respiration developing from the fruit. Precooling of a perishable fruit such as peaches can be done with special hydrocooling machinery (Figure 30), or by portable mechanical refrigeration equipment. The portable equipment on trucks is driven alongside refrigeration cars, attached, and by a special system of ducts in the door, air throughout the car is circulated rapidly over the refrigeration coils.

Mechanically refrigerated cars and trucks are in general use. They provide better control of transit temperatures than do ice refrigerated vehicles which have disappeared.

Hydrocooling has been used for many years by the larger peach growers who ship in quantity. Temperature of field fruit can be reduced by about 24° F. in the range 68-84° F. by passing it through an ice or mechanical refrigerator and flood type machine (Figure 30). Respiration and tissue breakdown are slowed markedly. A fungicide is used in the dip to help reduce disease

Figure 28. (Upper left) This corrugated master carton holds 8 four-lb. consumer packs of molded pulp, plastic trays or other consumer packs for shipment to terminal market or local retail outlet. (Right) This 38-lb. corrugated fiber-board container can be passed through the hydrocooler, retaining stacking strength and insulating qualities in transport. Other types of 38-lb. corrugated containers are available, with or without stitching, gluing, or taping needs, two compartments for stacking strength for packing after bulk hydrocooling. (Lower) Corrugated container holding 3 trays of 20 fancy peaches each for retail trade. Trays can be stacked 3 deep on sales counter for display and sale by the pound. (Courtesy Inland Container Corp., Indianapolis, IN. 46206.).

with good flavor, while if held at 50° for more than a week, the flavor may be poor. At 40° ripening is half as fast as at 50° and if held at 40 very long internal breakdown may occur. If held at 32 to 36°, ripening is almost stopped, but if held at 36 to 50° for 10 days or more, internal breakdown, off-flavor and mealiness will occur. If held at 31 to 32 °F. peaches will hold up longer than at 32° to 36°, and they can be ripened at room temperature without loosing flavor.

CA Storage, Intermittent Warming. Studies by R.E. Anderson, USDA, Beltsville, Md and associates show that

[1]Contact your local government marketing agency for labeling, packaging and shipping specifications.

229

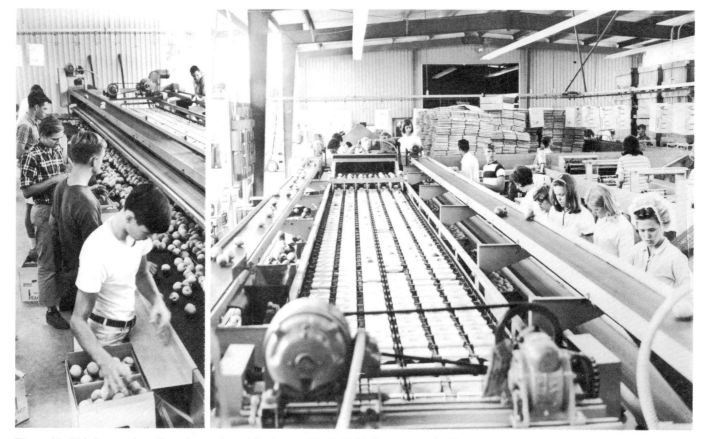

Figure 29. This is a modern Georgia peach packing house. The bulk-bin line starts outside the extreme right door, goes into far room by conveyors, eventually entering room shown here. From the field, bulk bins are placed in cold storage first, then the steps are: (a) hydrocooling; (b) submerged in hydrofeeder; (c) over trash eliminator; (d) hydrobrusher to remove fuzz; (e) over a one-size belt roll for presizing; (f) preliminary hand sorting as elevated to waxing machine (using special Johnson wax, Recine, Wis.) to help preserve freshness; (g) hand sorted on roller table, rejecting culls; (h) thence down the 6-lane weight sizer shown in this photo, equipped with 3 sizing and one eliminator sections; (i) right line is packing in consumer trays which are placed on belt at hand height and carried to overwrap machines at extreme right; (j) thence to rotating accumulation table where they are hand packed in corrugated master cartons for refrigerated shipment to northern markets. This equipment also handles apples, plums, and nectarines. An electronic peach sorter (reads color maturity) rapidly separates fruit when trunk shaking. (Contact FMC, Lakeland, Fla. for modern equipment and packing house plans.)

development. Benlate, botran and captan are effective against rots. Request U.S. Dept. of Agr. Inform. Bull. 293, U.S. Gov. Print, Off., Wash., D.C. to help check the efficiency of your hydrocooler.

CANNING AND DRYING

The peach canning industry in the early 1980s was in a slump as was much of the rest of the world economic situation. When contracts ran out, orchards often were pulled. It seemed that people were able to get adequate fresh products which they preferred. But these situations go in cycles. There seemed to be a tendency for some growers or corporations to get a ''corner'' on a new cultivar and specialize in growing and marketing it.

Over 90 percent of the canned peaches originate in California, pricipally the San Joaquin and Sacramento Valleys. The California fruit growers being far removed from large fresh fruit markets in the East, discovered early the merits of the clingstone peach for canning and increased this industry to a large scale. California produces practically all the dried peaches, except for a small amount from Washington. It also packs about half of the frozen peaches.

In California, the canning trade requests a fruit two and three-eighths inches or more in diameter for Grade 1; it must be firm, ripe, clean, and free from blemishes. Canners accept nothing but No. 1 fruit, except during periods of great demand. When canned, the fruit must be of a pleasing golden color, firm texture, and good quality.

Peaches for drying are picked when fully mature, though still reasonably firm. They are machine-cut about the suture with a knife, the pit removed, and the two halves laid on a clean tray with cut surfaces up. The full trays are treated with sulfur fumes for three to five hours, then

230

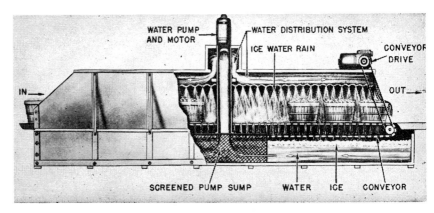

Figure 30. Diagram shows how a Stericooler or hydrocooler quick-cools peaches and sterilizes them with a fungicide in the bath to control brown rot. The same equipment can be used to quick-cool vegetables such as sweet corn. Chain stores and other large buyers of fresh peaches request hydrocooled fruit, having experienced its better hold-up on the market counters. Experience is available with a "hydrair cooler" that provides continuous flow of air through a water spray, giving faster cooling and a better appearing peach, reducing contamination by rots, other advantages (USDA tests, Ga. Ag. Exp. Sta., Athens, 30601).

exposed to the sun in the drying yard. Drying requires from two to six days until the fruit has a leathery texture. Total drying time varies, but 4 to 7 days is average. The fruit then is cleaned, sorted, and sweated in a storage building to equalize the moisture before delivery to the packer. The drying ratio varies from four to one for some cultivars and from eight to one with others. Average yield of dried peaches is about 2T/A for an 8:1 drying ratio. The market for dried peaches is upward after a decline for 30 years. In recent years many yellow canning peaches also have been dried. Common cultivars are Fay Elberta and Lovell; clings are not dried.

In the East, there are several advantages in growing peaches for the canning trade which tempts the grower to enter the business. The Babygold series of cling peaches from New Jersey is being grown increasingly and processed for baby food. Freestones also are being canned and sold increasingly. Processors want fruit of good size and quality.

MARKETING PEACHES

The greater majority of the peach crop, whether processed or sold fresh, is marketed through co-operative organizations and regular marketing channels as described in Chapter XII (Figure 31). However, there is a place for the independent grower/shipper who delivers a quality peach packed as the buyer desires it.

With the larger buyers (chain stores) becoming fewer (half dozen, e.g., on the East coast), the growers must group together to hold their price at a uniform and reasonable level rather than to remain independent and cut prices to each other's disadvantage. The ulitmate answer to this situation may be for all growers in a general area, perhaps as much as a third of the country, to join together in a cooperative selling agency. It has been the experience in the area of New Jersey that cooperative selling agencies, although handling over a million bushels each of apples and peaches, and serving a great purpose in the industry, may cut each other on price in critical seasons.

Peaches must be handled fast with little delay. Some co-operatives in the East sent their own representatives or agents to the larger wholesale markets during the harvesting and marketing season to check the peaches on arrival and assist in routing them through the wholesale or auction channels. Chain store buyers in the field have been buying directly from growers in the New York City-Philadelphia area; these buyers may practically "sit" on the doorstep of growers of fine peaches to get first option on their crops. Near population centers a vast amount of fresh peaches are sold through roadside stands owned by growers or former growers who have decided to devote full time to roadside marketing and buy from other growers or sources.

Retail sales. Because of the perishable nature of peaches, there is often much dissatisfaction among retail chain stores and merchants because of waste due to excessive bruising in handling and shipment, to rotting, and to immature green peaches.

There is considerable difference of opinion in the trade about the proper type of containers for shipping firm-ripe fruit. The Illinois and Michigan Experiment Station tests have shown that firm-ripe, well-colored properly treated and cooled peaches can be handled satisfactorily in shipment and retail stores with little or no bruising, and that they can be sold with much less difficulty at definitely higher prices than the general run of immature green peaches.

Tray-packs have become popular peach containers because they are easy to pack, display the fruit well and are not too expensive to construct (Figure 28). Prepackaging peaches in small consumer packs has made good progress. Six peaches in a pulp tray covered with shrink film is popular.[1]

At Clemson University, Dept. of Agr. Econ., Clemson, S.C. 29631, there is an Information Filter Center, coordianted by a Filter Center Staff, that gathers, condenses and distributes information sheets to buyers, brokers and

---

[1]Commercial peach growers should support the National Peach Council by being members and attending annual meetings. Main objective is to boost peach sales. Address: P.O. Box 1085, Martinseburg, W. Va. 25401.

Figure 31. This is a "buying room" at the New England Produce Center in Boston, Mass. Fruit is shipped largely by truck as far as the West coast. Buyers here are contacting the agent at the rear center desk, buying on the basis of displayed lots. Dozens of these rooms are provided at the Center. (Courtesy Tad Thompson and Linda Hineman, The Packer).

growers, enabling them to predict crops and evaluate current situations affecting peach marketing in the eastern markets.

COST OF GROWING PEACHES

There are many factors influencing the cost of peach production, but yield per acre is undoubtedly the most important single factor; the higher the yield, the lower the cost of production per unit container (Figure 32). This was clearly shown in California in a cling peach district comprising 653 acres. The orchards were divided into two groups — high and low producing. Net profit of the high-producing orchards was over sixteen times greater than for low-producing orchards.

The following practices were associated with high yields and good profits in Virginia orchards: frost-free sites, well-drained soils, suitable cultivars, fertilization to get 10-12 inches terminal growth yearly, adequate annual pruning, economical brush disposal with chopper or pusher, some cultivation with soil management to reduce erosion, adequate spray program, economical fruit thinning by pole method. Chemical thinning and/or use of mechanical tree shakers are further reducing these costs as will careful picking, grading and packing to deliver a high-quality product.

The value of a dollar has been changing but the following figures may be of interest. To establish a 40-acre orchard in Washington in 1980 (Wash. State Univ. Rpt. EM 4563, Pullman) with solid set irrigation cost was $12,300.61 per acre. However, with small crops the 3rd, 4th and 5th years, some revenue was obtained, based on 1-,

5- and 12-ton crops per acre, respectively. This resulted in a net establishment cost of $7,635.01/acre. Breakdown figures are available for each practice which gives relative costs irrespective of dollar value.

NECTARINES

Peaches and nectarines are similar in appearance of the trees, growth responses, bearing habits, and other general characteristics. The chief difference is that peaches have a fuzzy skin, nectarines are fuzzless and smooth. Also, nectarines are usually smaller in size, have greater aroma, are, in general, less melting in flesh, less suited for shipment to distant markets, more skin and flesh cracking, and because of lack of fuzz are more susceptible to curculio and thrip damage. Breeders in recent years, however, have improved nectarine fruit quality and size markedly. Nectarines can be grown in almost all regions where peaches are grown, but in humid areas, they are more susceptible to brown rot. With great improvement in fungicides and insecticides, brown rot, curculio, and thrip damage have been reduced to the point where nectarine growing is gaining in acreage. Many customers will chose fresh nectarines over fresh peaches, if quality is about the same. They are mistaken by customers for plums.

Origin of the nectarine is unknown, but its history goes back for 2000 years and merges into that of the peach. Genetically, the nectarine is an interesting phenomenon in horticulture. Peach trees may develop from nectarine seeds, and nectarine trees from peach seeds, or, peach trees may develop nectarines by bud sports and nectarine trees may develop peaches in similar manner.

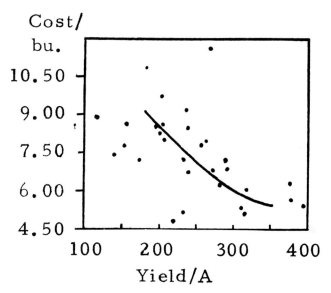

Figure 32. It is evident from this chart that as the production of peaches per acre goes up, the production costs per bushel go down. Data are from 30 New Jersey commercial peach orchards averaging 25 acres each.

232

California is the largest commercial producer of nectarines, particularly in the southern San Joaquin Valley where large quanitites of nectarines are shipped consisting mainly of the LeGrand series (May, Early Sun, Red, Late and Autumn Grand). Since Fred Anderson's (Modesto, Calif., private breeder) firm, yellow-flesh, commercial quality cultivars were introduced, the number of trees increased markedly in California where over 90% of the U.S. crop is grown in hot dry summers favorable to nectarine quality. Most nectarines are sold fresh and a few are canned and dried. Nectarine production is on the increase in many world peach areas. See California nectarine cultivars under "Peach Cultivars".

Rutgers University, New Jersey, has a number of large-fruited, good quality nectarine seedling crosses that look promising for the East, under the name Nectared, Nos. 1 to 9.

For recommendations on the culture of nectarines, the reader is referred to the previous discussion on peaches, since, in general, cultural practices are the same.

Harvesting and handling nectarines. Nectarines are shipped primarily for dessert purposes. Gower and the New Zealand seedlings are outstanding for home canning, but being tender, they tend to fall apart more than peach cultivars adapted to canning.

One and two-layer tray packs in wood or corrugated boxes are used for nectarines shipped fresh. Fruit sold locally is generally unpacked in varous size lug boxes.

APRICOTS

The apricot *(Prunus armeniaca L.)* probably came from western China while certain hardy strains known as Russian apricots came from Siberia. The apricot was brought to Rome about the time of Christ. Apricots were grown in Virginia as early as 1720. The commercial culture of this fruit is limited largely to the semi-arid-irrigated districts on the Pacific slope.

Based on the approximate available production data, the Soviet Union leads in apricot production, namely (000's metric tons) 450; Spain, 150; France, 110; USA, 100; Hungary, 100; Turkey, 80; and Italy, 70. Countries producing between 15-50,000 metric tons are Bulgaria, Romania, Yugoslavia, Czechoslovakia, No. and So. Africa, Argentina, Australia, Greece, Syria, Iran and Israel. China is a significant producer in the Liaoning, Shantung, and Hopei provinces but no production data are available. Natural forests of apricots can still be found near Lanchow in Kansu province.

U.S. production varies year to year with frost, mainly, approximately 100,000 ST for California, 2000 for Washington and 1500 for Utah.

The most important cultivars in California are Blenheim, Royal (the two cultivars are so similar they have lost separate identities) and Tilton; in Washington, the Large Early Montgamet and Wentachee Moorpark are grown; the Large Early Montgamet is the leading cultivar in Utah. Kernels of some cultivars of apricots such as the Early Montgamet are almost as pleasant in flavor as almond kernels. All apricot cultivars grown commercially in America are self-fruitful. New cultivars (Goldcot) from Michigan may encourage eastern plantings. There are a number of crosses between apricots and plums, called plumcots and cotplums.

The open flowers of the apricot are about as resistant to spring frosts as the peach, but they are more likely to be killed because they open earlier. For eastern conditions, Michigan's South Haven Nos. 6, 7, and 50 and the Curtis cultivar are the most promising. It appears that limited production may be possible for local fresh markets, where the best frost protection sites are used.

The total commercial crop of apricots tends to vary more in California from year to year than the peach crop, largely because of tendency of commercial cultivars to show biennial or triennial bearing. Frost and disease control can be problems. Squirrels are distructive in small plantings.

Rootstocks for commercial apricot plantings consist of peach, plum, and apricot seedling roots. Apricot roots seem to be better in sandy soils because of greater resistance to nematodes, athough there are now available some nematode-resistant peach stocks which are used. Myrobalan plum rootstocks are used frequently for apricot trees grown on the heavier more impervious soils. In Michigan, the Manchurian and South Haven No. 6 apricots were best. Peach roots (Lovell and Nemaguard) cause apricots to mature 3 days earlier than apricot roots.

Fruit thinning and pruning. Apricot fruits develop rapidly and ripen early in summer. Like the peach, the fruits have a period of retarded growth about the time the pit is hardening. The trees blossom and set fruit heavily, resulting in small size of harvest fruit. Some people believe fruit thinning does not increase the size of apricot fruits to the extent that it does for peach. Hence, pruning is used to reduce number of flower buds and fruit competition. Chemical blossom thinning with dinitro sprays can be used. Spray when blossoms are 90% open. Recommended concentration for apricots is 1½ to 2 pints of sodium dinitro ortho cresylate to 100 gallons of water for Blenheim and Tilton cultivars; 1 pint per 100 gallons for Wenatchee Moorpark. The risk of overthinning may be lessened by reducing the concentration or by delaying the spray application until full bloom or 1 to 2 days thereafter. Club thinned, the fruits are spaced 1½ - 2 inches apart. Chemicals on apricot have generally caused gumming and leaf drop. Trunk shakers are used in California.

While canning of apricots was in a depression in the early 1980s, drying of the fruit is showing a slight increase.

233

The apricot tree tends to develop large heavy branches, more so than the peach. Hence, the modified leader system of training, as described for apples, can be used, although the vase-form tree has proven satisfactory in most areas. Mature apricot trees are pruned somewhat less than peach trees, although more than the apple. The fruit is borne on short one-year spurs and also toward the tip of last year's shoot growth. After the branch containing these spurs has borne fruit for about three years, they tend to die and the object of the pruning is to induce new growth in these areas for subsequent fruit production. For young trees, pruning should be light and only sufficient for properly training the tree. For mature trees, it should be directed mainly at maintaining the proper height and width spread. Heavy pruning delays bearing and reduces yield. Mechanical topping of trees as for peach is used in California, with hand thinning of old wood inside the tree every third year to stimulate new wood.

Cultural systems for the apricot are similar to those for the peach, except that apricot trees require somewhat less nitrogen. There is also some evidence that they will grow and produce with a lower supply of potassium. Excess sodium and chloride in some California soils cause leaf scorch and low yields. Coastal California N suggestions are: 50 lbs./A. for Blenheims; Central Valley, 80 lbs.; and for Tiltons, 120 lbs. Too much N results in green shoulders and uneven ripening on Blenheims and Royals, delaying ripening on all cultivars. Heavy irrigation with contour basin checks has improved these orchards. Mechanized harvesting is used, but uneven maturity and problems in bin handling have limited its use.

The apricot in California is more sensitive to soil salinity than peach, almond, plum, apple or grape, in that order.

ALMONDS[1]

The almond (*Prunus amygdalus, Batch*) probably came from western Asia. Leading countries are Italy, Spain, Iran, Morocco, Portugal. Culture in North America is limited to California, mainly the San Joaquin Valley and Stanislaus County; acreage has jumped the past few decades to over 30 million trees. Production is over 225,000 tons some years. Yields may fall in some years. The California cultivars are from local seedlings of strains brought from southern Europe and northern Africa. The most extensively grown cultivar is the Nonpareil. Other cultivars are Mission, Merced, Ne Plus Ultra, Thompson and Peerless. There are several new cultivars being developed by USDA and the University of California but growers should be cautious in planting them extensively.

[1]A good reference is: "Almond Orchard Management" by W. Micke and D. Kester, University of California, Davis (Priced) No. 4092. 150 pp. Dec. 1978.

Climatic adaptions. Commercial almond growing in California and the Mediterranean area is limited to those areas with little or no frost hazard, due, to an early blossoming characteristic of the almond (See Table 6). The almond is also susceptible to injury by rains in spring and summer which increase blossom and fruit infection by brown and green rot organisms; rains in midwinter are apt to cause infection by a shot-hole disease, while foggy and rainy weather during the summer results in brown stains on the shells of the ripening nuts, lowering their market value.

TABLE 6. DAMAGE % LIKELY TO OCCUR TO SIX CULTIVARS OF ALMOND AT 3 DEVELOPMENTAL STAGES AT TEMPERATURES INDICATED (UNIV. OF CALIF., DAVIS)

Temp.	% Damage					
	Peerless			Ne Plus, IXL, Mission		
	SP*	FB*	SN*	SP	FB	SN
30°F						
29°			25			25
28°		25	50			50
27°		45	100			100
26°	25	75				
25°	50	100			25	
24°	75			60	50	
23°	100			80	75	
22°				100	100	
	Drake			Nonpareil		
30°						
29°			25			25
28°			50			50
27°			100			100
26°		25				
25°		50			20	
24°	25	75			40	
23°	50	100		10	60	
22°	75			20	75	

*SP = showing pink; FB = full bloom; SN = small nuts.

U.S. Almond Supply and Utilization

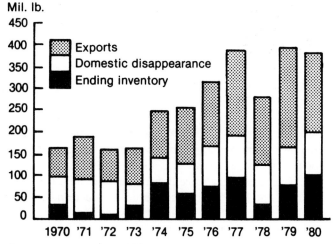

Season beginning July 1. 1980 preliminary.
Source: Almond Board of California.

Figure 33. Almond acreage and production have been increasing markedly in California, where most of U.S. almonds are grown. (USDA)

234

Pollination. Important almond cultivars in America are self-sterile; some are cross-incompatible. Pollination is almost entirely by the honey bees, and in view of the fact that almonds blossom early while the weather is likely to be too cool for good insect activity, it is necessary to interplant pollinizing cultivars closely. In some orchards, every tree is adjacent to a pollinizing cultivar, whereas in other orchards, blocks of one cultivar may be four rows wide if the rows are no farther apart than 25 feet. Differences in blossoming tend to be wide among some almond cultivars. Hence, the orchard should consist of more than two cultivars, preferably three or four. Nonpariel, Merced, Ne Plus Ultra, Mission are interplanted for cross-pollination. Other combinations are: (a) Peerless, Nonpareil, Mission; (b) Ne Plus Ultra, Peerless, Nonpariel; (c) Davey, Nonpareil, Mission; (d) Ne Plus Ultra, Nonpariel, Davey; (e) Merced, Nonpariel, Mission,. *Early bloomers* are: Jordanolo, Ne Plus Ultra, Peerless, Milow. *Late bloomers* are: Butte, Thompson, Mission, Mono, Yosemite, Ruby, Ripon, Planada. Other cultivars are largely midseason. Season and location have an effect.

Rootstocks. Almond trees grow best on almond roots. According to experienced growers, bitter almond stocks are slightly better than the sweet almond stocks. Almond trees on peach roots, mainly Lovell, although widely planted, have been shorter-lived in California, especially on soils high in lime and sodium. Marianna 2624 stock (plum) is compatible with some cultivars and tolerant of oak root fungus and nematodes. Nemaguard roots are used where nematodes are a problem. Selection of the right rootstock for a given set of soil conditions is very important.

Cultural requirements. Almond orchards produce best on the lighter sandy types of soils. Although the almond is more resistant to dry soils than most other orchard trees, it shows definite response to standard summer irrigation on all soils. The almond has a high nitrogen requirement similar to the peach. However, it will tolerate a lower available potassium content of the soil than prunes and apples and its zinc requirement seems to be a little lower than for most other fruits in California. Boron may be deficient in the sandy soils. The soil management program for the almond is similar to that of the peach in California. Chemical strip weed control and trickle, flood, sprinkler and furrow irrigation are used. Tree spacing has been 20-22 X 24-28 ft., depending on soil fertility; there are some hedgerow plantings 20 X 24 ft., running north-south.

With the fuel crisis, growers are using for frost contral under-tree sprinklers, getting a 4° F lift in temperature vs a 6° lift with overhead sprinkling. Water in ditches may give a 2° advantage.

The tax "bite" on almond orchards is the same regardless of the number of weak and missing trees. Every tree must be in top yielding condition or replaced immediately.

Pruning. Almond trees are pruned lightly, open-center: (1) to attain large bearing area, (2) there is no fruit sizing problem, (3) very little limb breakage from overcropping, and (4) no harvest problems. Most growers prune every second or third year only, because the benefits of pruning every year are usually not great enough to pay for the extra labor. Due to lighter pruning, almond trees tend to become large with long branches which may be very heavily loaded. For this reason, a modified-leader system of training often is used. Larger and fewer cuts are made on almond trees as compared with peaches. Cuts are made where the wood is three-quarters to one and one-half inches in diameter near a strong outward-growing lateral branch.

Yields and harvesting. Almond trees will bear some nuts the third or fourth year in the orchard, and by the eighth year will yield as much as 2000 pounds of nuts per acre. Yields of 3000 pounds or better per acre are occasionally reported but this is unusual. Fruit thinning is not practiced.

Harvesting starts when almonds in the shady portions of the tree show shriveling and cracking of the hulls. The usual sequence of events in the harvesting operation is to knock the almonds to the ground, usually with mechanical shakers or knockers; however, some growers are still using the rubber headed mallets. After several days of drying on the ground the almonds then are picked up with the hulls still attached. They are then run through the huller. Practically all of the shells remain intact. The nuts then are dried in almond dryers or dehydrators to the point where they can be broken without bending the kernel and then are delivered to the processing plants. At that point the almonds are either shelled if they are to be sold as kernels or bleached if they are to remain intact and sold as inshell almonds.

The land leveling preparation (Figure 34) which is needed to facilitate the use of pickup machines has resulted in some breakdown of the soil structure which impairs the infiltration of irrigation water and also causes a delay in harvesting, if there happens to be a few days of rain in the early fall when the crops are ready to be harvested. California workers have made considerable progress in solving this problem by adopting a non-tillage and strip weed control program. This seems to be an ideal soil management program.

A small portion of the crop in California is harvested in early June when the embryos first fill the seed coat. The green kernels are a delicacy with some people. Hulls of soft-shell almonds are mixed with alfalfa and barley for livestock feed.

Figure 34. In Oregon, this equipment is used to harvest nuts. Almonds in California are harvested similarly as the husks are splitting. Nuts are mechanically shaken from the tree on smoothed ground, windrowed and picked up with equipment shown in background. (Elwyn D. Obert, American Fruit Grower. Willoughby, Ohio).

Review Questions

1. Compare peach productions in California and in the eastern states.
2. Discuss the peach cultivar situation, in general, and under your local conditions.
3. Describe a good soil management program for young peach trees growing in a moderately fertile sandy loam soil.
4. Give a good soil management program for mature bearing peach trees growing in a moderately fertile medium-loam soil in your locality.
5. What system of training is employed for peach trees in your area? Compare with the training systems elsewhere.
6. Compare the merits and disadvantages of the following systems of training peach trees: Tatura, Meadow, hedgrow-trellis, hedgerow alone, "Long", Street. Are these systems used commercially and where?
7. What is meant by the "renewal system" of pruning bearing peach trees, and what is the purpose? Discuss mechanical "topping" of stone fruit trees.
8. Describe a fertilization program for a bearing peach orchard which is making 6 to 8 inches of thin terminal growth. The soil is moderate to low in fertility.
9. Prepare an orchard planting plan for a 10-acre peach orchard located on a 10 percent slope within a few miles of a large city. Disposal of the crop will be through a roadside market and trucking to neighboring markets.
10. When is the proper time for picking peaches for (1) local sale, (2) truck shipment to large cities within a distance of 200 miles, and (3) shipment by railway several hundred miles? Discuss hydrocooling.
11. Discuss the various aspects and techniques of (a) hand, (b) club, (c) shaker, and (d) chemical fruit thinning of the peach.
12. Discuss mechanical harvesting of cling and freestone peaches.
13. How long can peaches be stored; factors involved? Discuss CA storage.
14. What type of peach does the customer prefer to buy based on survey experiments? Explain. Discuss modern peach sizing, grading and packaging.
15. Discuss costs of peach production and point out how the best profits can be made.
16. Discuss important precautions against winter injury to peach fruit buds.
17. How does a nectarine differ from a peach? What is the future of the nectarine?
18. In what ways does the apricot and its management differ from the peach?
19. How does the almond and its management and requirements differ from the peach?

Suggested Collateral Readings

Peach and Nectarine

ABDALLA, D.A. and N.F. Childers. Calcium nutrition of peach and prune relative to growth, fruiting, and fruit quality. J. ASHS 98(5):517. Sept. 1973.

ALDRICH, J.H. et al. Nectarine and peach response to NAA sprout inhibition. Fruit Varieties Jour. 35(1). Jan. 1981.

ANDERSON, J.L. and S.D. Seeley. Bud hardiness of peach cultivars in Utah. Fruit Var. Jour. 31:(3) pp. 50-53. 1977.

ANDERSON, R.E. Long-term storage of peaches, nectarines intermittently warmed during CA storage. J. ASHS 107(2):214-16: 1982.

ANDERSON, R.E. et al. Peach CA storage w/intermittent warming. HortSci. 12(4):345-346. 1977.

ARNOLD, C.E. and J.H. Aldrich. Herbicide on peach seedling growth and weed control. HortSci. 15(3):293-94. 1980.

BAUER, L.L. Costs, returns on peaches in South Carolina. S.C. Agr. Exp. Sta. Bull. SB-617. Nov. 1978.

BAUER, L.L., *et al* Interregional competition in peach marketing. Fruit South, 8(2). Mar. 1981.

BAUMGARDNER, R.A. et al. Alar on peach. J. ASHS:97-4. 485-88. 1972.

BEN-ARIE, R. and S. Guelfat-Reich. Advancement of nectarine fruit ripening with daminozide and fenoprop. J. ASHS 104(1):14-17. 1979.

BENNETT, A.H., J.M. Wells. Hydraircooling for waxed peaches. J. ASHS 101(4):428-31. 1976.

BARMORE, C.R. and D.W. Buchanan. Effects of ethephon on peach maturity and storage in Fla. Proc. Fla. State Hort. Soc. 85:319-322. 1973.

BOWEN, H.H. and J.B. Storey. 'Milam' Peach. HortSci. 13(1):65. Feb. 1978.

BREEN, P.J. and T. Muraoka. Seasonal nutrient levels and peach/plum graft incompatibility. J. ASHS 100:339-342. Also, on carbohydrate changes. ASHS J. 100:253-259. 1975.

BREGGER, J.T. Peaches in Mexico. Fruit Var. Jour. 29:63. 1975.

BRITTAIN, J.A., et al. Peach cultivars for South Carolina. Fruit South. 166-170. July 1978.

BRITTAIN, J. et al. Peach tree short life management. Clemson, Univ., So. Car. Cir. 585. 18 pp. 1978.

BUCHANAN, D.W. et al. Cold acclimation of Florida peach and nectarine cultivars. HortSci. 11(4):398-400. 1976.

BUCHANAN, D.W. et al. Manipulation of bloom, ripening of peach, nectarine by sprinkling, shade. J. ASHS 102(4):466-70. 1977.

BYERS, Ross E. CGA-15281 and 17856 as peach thinners. ASHS 103(2):232-6. 1978.

CAIN, D.W. and R.L. Andersen. An efficient method of screening peaches. Fruit Var. Jour. 30-(3):80-1. 1976.

CAIN, D.W. and R.L. Andersen. Procedures for minimizing non-genetic wood hardiness variation in peach. J. ASHS. 101(6):668-671. 1976.

CAIN, D.W. and R.L. Andersen. Temperature and moisture on wood injury of cold-stressed 'Siberian C' and 'Redhaven'. HortSic. 14(4):518-519. Aug. 1979.

California Tree Fruit Agreement — Pear, plum, peach, nectarine (Acreage, production, etc.) 114 pp., annually (1983) P.O. Box 255383 Sacramento, Ca. 95865.

CARLSON, R.F. The performance of 'Suncling' peach on four peach seedling rootstocks. Fruit Var. Jour. 29:41-42. 1975.

CARTER, E., Jr. and M.M. Brock. Identification of peach cultivars through protein analysis. HortSci. 15(3):292-3. 1980.

CHALMERS, D.J. et al. Peach growth, productivity and water supply, tree density, summer pruning. ASHS 106:3:307-12. May 1981.

CHALMERS, D. et al. Productivity, mechanization of a Tatura Trellis orchard. HortSci. 13(5):517-21. 1978.

CHANDLER. W.A. and J.W. Daniell. Pruning time and *pseudomonas syringae* to short life of peach on old peach land. J. ASHS 11:(2):103. 1976.

CHAPLIN, C.E. and G.W. Schneider. Peach rootstock/scion hardiness effects. HortSci. 99(3):231. May 1974.

CHAPLIN, C.E., G.W. Schneider and D.C. Martin. Rootstock on peach tree survival on a poorly drained soil. HortSci. 9(1):28. 1974.

CHAPLIN, C.E. and G.W. Schneider. Resistance to the common peach tree borer (*Sanninoidea exitiosa Say*) in seedlings of 'Rutgers Red Leaf' peach. HortSci. 10:400. 1975.

CHILDERS, N.F. (Editor) Fruit Nutrition. Chap. on Peach Fertilization. Horticultural Publications, 3906 N.W. 31st Pl., Gainesville, Fla. 32606.

CHILDERS, N.F. (Editor) The Peach — varieties, culture, marketing and pest control. Summary Nat'l. Peach Conf., 3906 N.W. 31st Pl., Gainesville, Fla. 32606. Offset, color cover. 660 pp. Revised 1975. Over 140 authorities. (out-of-print to 1986)

COUVILLON, A. and A. Lloyd II. Summer defoliation effects on peach spring bud development. HortSci. 13(1):53-54. Feb. 1978.

COUVILLON, G.A. Obtaining small peach plants containing all bud types for "rest" and dormancy studies. HortSci. 10:78-79. 1975.

COUVILLON, G.A. and A. Erez. Rooting, survival, development of peach cultivars propagated from semi-hardwood cuttings. HortSci. 15(1):41-3. 1980.

CLAYPOOL, L.L. et al. Split-Pit of 'Dixon' Cling peaches in relation to cultural factors. J. ASHS. Vol. 97, No. 2. March 1972. P. 181.

CUMMINGS, G.A. Distribution of elements in peach tissues and influence of potassium and magnesium fertilization. J. ASHS 98(5). 474. Sept. 1973.

CUMMINGS G.A. and W.E. Ballinger, Influence of longtime nitrogen, pruning and irrigation treatments upon yield, growth and longevity of 'Elberta' and 'Redhaven' peach trees. HortSci. 7:(2). April 1972. p. 133.

DANIELL, J.W. Effect of time of pruning or non-pruning on fruit set and yield of peach growing on new or old peach sites. J. ASHS 100:490. 1975.

DANIELL, J.W. and W.A. Chandler. Iron on growth and bacterial canker of peach. HortSic. 11(4):402-3. 1976.

DANIELL, J.W. and R.E. Wilkinson. Effects of ethephon-induced ethylene on abscission of leaves and fruits of peaches. J. ASHS 97(5):682. 1972.

DEKAZOS, E.D. Aminoethoxyvinylglycine on peach. HortSic. 16(4) 520-22. Aug. 1981.

DOZIER, W.A. et al. Thinning 'Loring' peaches with CGA 15281. HortSci. 16(1):56-7. 1981.

DU TOIT, H.J. et al. Role of seed parts in peach seed dormancy and initial seedling growth. J. ASHS. 104(4):490-492. 1979.

EDGERTON, L.J. Cold hardiness, peach. Cornell Ext. Bul. 958. 1960.

EDWARDS. J.H. et al. Aluminum toxicity symptoms in peach. J. ASHS HortSci. 101(2):139-42. 1976.

EDWARDS, J.H. and B.D. Horton. Effect of NO_3: NH_4 ratios on peach seedlings. J. ASHS 107:1. 142-7. 1982.

EDWARDS, J.H. and B.D. Horton. Response of peach seedlings to calcium in nutrient solution. J. ASHS. 104(1):97-99. 1979.

EMERSON, F.H. and R.A. Hayden. High-density tree walls. HortSci. 10:550. 1975.

EREZ, A. Meadow Orchard for the Peach. Sci. Hort. 1-6. 1975.

EREZ, A., S. Lavee and R.M. Samish. Improved methods for breaking rest in the peach and other deciduous fruit species. J. ASHS Vol. 96, No. 4. July 1971. p. 519.

EREZ, A. Thiourea, a New Thinning Agent for Early-ripening Peaches and Nectarines. HortSic. 10:251-253. 1975.

EREZ, A. et al. The oxygen concentration on release of peach leaf buds from rest. HortSci. 15(1):3-41. 1980.

EREZ, A. et al. Cycle Length on Chilling Negation by high temperatures in dormant peach leaf buds. J. ASHS. 104(4):573-6. 1979.

EVERT, D.R. et al. Bacteria in peach roots preceeded phony peach. ASHS Jrn. 106(6). 780-2. Nov. 1981.

FELDSTEIN, J. and N.F. Childers. Effect of irrigation on fruit size and yield of peaches in Pennsylvania. Amer. Soc. Hort. Sci. 87:145-153. 1965.

FERREE, M.E. and P.F. Bertrand. Peach growers handbook. Co-op. Ext. Serv., Unov. of Ga., 30602. 1983. (Priced).

FOGLE, H.W. Evaluating combining ability in peach and nectarine. HortSci. 9:334-335. 1974.

FOGLE, H.W. Peach production. 90 pp. USDA Agr. Hndb. No. 463. 1974. (Good bulletin).

FOGLE, H.W. and M. Faust. Fruit cracking and growth in nectarines. J. ASHS 101(4):434-8. 1976.

FOGLE, H.W. and M. Faust. Ultrastructure of nectarine fruit surfaces. J. ASHS 100:74-77. 1975.

FOGLE, H.W. 'Cullinan' and 'Havis' peaches. HortSci. 13(3):305. 1978.

FORBUS, W.R. Handling peaches in pallet boxes. USDA-MRR. No. 875. pp. 1-18. April 1970.

FRECON, J. Stark[R] Encore peach. Fruit Var. Jour. 35.(2) April 1981.

FRECON, J. 'Stark Early Loring' — a midseason freestone peach. Fruit Var. Jour. Vol. (32)(3):57. 1978.

FREEMAN, M.W. and G.C. Martin. Mist, light, temperature during rest on peach bud break and abscisic acid. ASHS 106:3 333-6. May 1981.

FRIDLUND, P.R. Unusual mottle in some *Prunus besseyi x Prunus salicina* hybrids. Fruit Var. Jour. 35(2) April 1981.

FRIDLUND, P.R. Incompatibility between apricot and *Prunus tomentosa* seedlings. Fruit Var. Jour. 33(3):90. July 1979.

FUNT, R.C. and B.L. Goulart. Performance of peach cultivars on *Prunus tomentosa and Prunus besseyi* in Maryland. Fruit Var. Jour. 35(1). January 1981.

FUNT, R.C. et al. Redskin and Mar series peach cultivars: origin and description. Agr. Exp. Sta., U. of Md. MP-917. Aug. 1977.

GALLAHER, R.N., et al. Ca in healthy and decline peach tree tissues. HortSci. 10:134-137. 1975.

GAMBRELL, C.E. et al. Response of peaches to Alar as an aid in mechanical harvesting. HortSci. Vol. 92. No. 2. March 1972. p. 265.

GENGE, R.A. et al. Physical-biological properties of Babygold peaches as related to mechanical harvesting. Transactions of ASAE. 20(4):772-5. 1977.

GERDTS, M. et al. Growing shipping peaches, nectarines. California. Calif. Leafleat 2851. 31 pp. 1976.

GILREATH, P.R. and D.W. Buchanan. Overhead sprinkling during rest on nectarine bud opening. ASHS 106:3:321-24. May 1981.

GILREATH, R.P. and D.W. Buchanan. Low-chilling rest period model for nectarine. ASHS 106(4). 426-9. 1982.

GORSUCH, C.S. Borer pheromones: A potential alternative to trunk spraying. Fruit South. 8(2). Mar. 1981.

GUERRIERO, R.L., F. Vitagliano, C. Effetti di alcuni regolatori di alcuni regloatori di crescita sull'epoca di fioritura del pesco. Instituto di Coltivazioni Arboree Del''Universita di Pisa. Italy Pubblicazione n. 183. 1970.

GUR, A. and A. Blum. The Water Conductivity of Defective Graft Unions in Pome and Stone Fruits. J. Amer. Sc. Hort. Sci. 100:325-328. 1975.

HAIR, B.L. et al. Discoloration of processed peaches as influenced by SADH and Ethephon J. ASHS 11(2):105. 1976.

HALES, T.A., R.E. Moore and A.D. Dacus. Paint applications for reduction of radiational cooling. J. ASHS 98(5):426. Sept. 1973.

HARRISON, D.S. and D.W. Buchanan. Peach irrigation in Florida. Proc. Fla. State Hort. Society 85:313-316. 1973.

HARVEY, J.M., et al. Market diseases of stone fruit: cherries, peaches, nectarines, apricots and plum. USDA Handbook 414. 74pp. 1972.

HAWTHORNE, P.L. et al. 'Majestic' peach. HortSci. 15(3):320. 1980.

HESSE, C.O. Peach breeding. In advances of fruit breeding. J. Janick and J. Moore, Editors. 285-335. Purdue Univ. Press. W. Lafayette. Inc. 1975.

HESSE, C.O. Four new shipping freestone peaches for California. Calif. Agri. pp. 15. Aug. 1977.

HEWETSON, F.N. et al. Peach seedling weed control as part of a *Prunus* stem pitting control system. HortSci. 9:588-590. 1974.

HOOD, C. An electronic peach sorter. Peach Times 25(9). Sept. 1980.

HORTON, B.D. et al. Drip irrigation, soil fumigation on peach yields, growth. ASHS 106(4). 438-43. 1981.

JEN, J.J. et al. Amino acid composition of peach during maturation. HortSci. 10:129-130. 1975.

JEN, J. and W.H. Flurkey. Hydrophonbic chromatography of peach polyphenol oxidase. HortSci. 14(4):516-18. 1979.

JOHNSON, C.E. et al. 'Ouachita Gold' peach. HortSci. 16(3). 346-347. June 1981.

JOHNSTON, S. and R. Paul Larsen. Peach culture in Michigan. Mich. Agr. Ext. Bull. 509. (One of the best bulletins.) Request recent edition.

JOHNSON, P.W. et al. Population of *Pratylenchus penetrans*; effects on peach seedlings. ASHS. 103(2):169-172. 1978.

JONES, Jr. et al. Nutrient status of soils and trees for peach orchards. HortSci. 11(3):247-8. 1976.

KAMALI, A.R. and N.F. Childers. Growth and fruiting of peach in sand culture as affected by boron and a fritted form of trace elements. J. ASHS 95(5):652-656. 1970.

KAMINSKI, W. and R. Rom. A possible role of catalase in the rest of peach, *Prunus persica*, Sieb and Zucc, flower buds. J. ASHS 99(1):84. Jan. 1973.

KIRKPATRICK, H.C., et al. Aluminum on growth and composition of peach seedlings. HortSci. 10:132-134. 1975.

KOCHBA, J. and R.M. Samish. Effect of growth inhibitors on root-knot nematodes in peach roots. J. ASHS Vol. 92, No. 2. March 1972. P. 178.

KOCHBA, J. and R.M. Samish. Level of endogenus cytokinins and auxin in roots of nematode-resistant and susceptible peach rootstocks. J. ASHS Vol. 97, No. 1. Jan. 1972. p. 115.

KUITEMS, S. and E. Young. Effects of daminozide, ethephon, pruning, and seismomorphogenic factors on growth of Halford peach seedlings. HortSci. 15(5):582-3. 1980.

LAMBERT, D.H. et al. Stunting of peach following soil fumigation. J. ASHS 104(4):433-5. 1979.

LAVEE, S. and G.C. Martin, Ethephon in peach fruits. I. Penetration and persistence. J. ASHS 99(2):97. March 1974. III. Stability and persistence. 28-31. 1975.

LAYNE, R.E.C. Peach seedling rootstocks on perennial canker of peach. HortSci. 11(5):509-11. 1976.

LAYNE, R.E.C. and G.M. Ward. Rootstock and seasonal influences of carbohydrate levels and cold hardiness of 'Redhaven' peach. J. ASHS. 103(3):408-13. 1978.

LAYNE, R.E.C. et al. Irrigation and tree density on peach yields ASHS 106(2):151-6. Mar. 1981.

LEECE, D.R. et al. Nitrate reductase in leaves of *Prunus* Species. Plant Phys. 49:725-728. 1972.- P.M. Bag 10; Rudalmere, NSW 2116, Australia.

LEECE, D.R. and A.R. Gilmour. Seasonal changes in peach leaf composition. Aust. J. of Exp. Agr. and An. Hubs. 14:822-827. 1974.

LEECE, D.R. and B. Barkus. Diagnostic leaf analysis for fruit. 3. Nutritional status of peach orchards. Aust. J. of Exp. Agr. and An. Husb. 14:828-834. 1974.

LEMBRIGHT, H.W. Solutions to replanting peaches. Down to Earth 32(1):12-21. 1976.

LEUTY, S.J. et al. 'Veeglo' peach. HortSci. 16(3):347. June 1981.

LOONEY, N.E., W.B., McGlasson, and B.G. Coombe. Control of fruit ripening in peach. *Prunus persica:* Action of Alar and ethephon. Aust. J. Plant Physiol. 1:77-86. 1974.

LORD, W.J. and R.A. Damon, Jr. Mulch on residue accumulation and on injury to peach trees from dichlobenil. HortSic. 9:449-450. 1974.

LORETI, F. Nectarine production in Italy. HortSci. 12(5):441-444. 1977.

LORETI, F. Le Nectarine in Italia - Problemi e prospective della coltura. L'Italia Agricola III(5):1-32. 1974.

LORETI, F. and P. Fiorino. Monograph of nectarine varieties in Italy. Instituto Di Coltivazioni Arboree, Universita DePisa. Color illustrations of fruit, bloom, wood, descriptions, 340 pp. In Italina. 1973.

LLOYD II, D.A. and Gary A. Couvillon. Date of defoliation on flower and leaf bud development in peach. J. ASHS 99:514-417. 1974.

LUEPSCHEN, N.S. et al. Susceptibility of peach cultivars to *Cytospora* canker in Colorado. HortSci. 10:77-78. 1975.

LYONS, C.G., Jr., and K.S. Yoder. Poor anchorage of deeply planted peach trees. HortSci. 16(1):48-49. 1981.

McBEAN, D.M. Drying and processing tree fruits. Commonwealth Sci. and Indust. Res. Org., Australia. Div. of Food Res. Cir. 10. 20 p. 1976.

MARRIAGE, P.B., and H.A. Quamme. Weed control on winterhardiness of bark and wood of young peach trees. HortSci. 15(3):290-1. 1980.

MARTSOLF, J.D., C. M. Ritter, and A.H. Hatch. White latex paint on winter temperature of stone fruit tree trunks. J. ASHS 100:122-129. 1975.

MITCHELL, P.D. and J.D. F. Black. Response of replant peach trees to weedicide, irrigation, nitrogen and phosphorus. Austr. J. Exp. Agr. and An. Husb. 11:699-704. 1971.

MOORE, L.W. et al. Biological control of crown gall on fruit trees with K-84. Fruit South 3:28-34. 1979.

MORINI, S. et al. 3-CPA and Ethephon on growth and abscission of 'Cardinal' peach. J. ASHS. 101(6)640-642. 1976.

MORRIS, J.R. et al. Quality and postharvest behavior of once-over harvested clingstone peaches treated with daminozide. J. ASHS. 103(6):716-722. 1978.

NATIONAL Peach Council, monthly "Peach Time, U.S.A." This up-to-date report covers pertinent talks at annual meetings and current developments in the peach industry. Distributed to Council Members. P.O. Box 1085, Martinsburg, W. Va. 25401.

NESMITH, W.C. et al. Cultural practices affect cold hardiness and peach tree short life. J. ASHS 101(2):116-9. 1976.

OH, S. D. and R.F. Carlson. Extracts from peach, affects on growth of seedlings. J. ASHS. 101:54-7. 1976.

OLSEN, K.L. and H.A. Schomer. CA on quality and condition of stored nectarines. HortSci. 10:582-583. 1975.

ORMROD, D.P. and R.E.C. Lavne. Temperature and photoperiod effects on cold hardiness of peach scion - rootstock combinations. HortSci. 9:451-453. 1974.

PAULSON, A.T. et al. GA and ethephon on enzymatic browning of peaches. HortSci. 14(6):711-13. Dec. 1979.

PEACH packing equipment. FMC Corp. Woodstock, Va. 22664.

PEACH research, Institute National de la Recherche Agronomique. Mars 1974. Publications de la Staton de Recherches D'Arboriculture Fruitiere. Centre de Recheres de Bordeaux. Domaine de la Grande Ferrade, 33140 - Pont de la Maye, France.

PEST and disease control program for peaches and nectarines (issued each year) Calif. Agr. Exp. Sta. Bull. 20 pp. Check your local experiment station also.

PETROV, A.A. Reduction in growth of peach trees due to fruiting. C.R. Acad. Agric. G. Dimitrov (Bulgaria) 6:25-32. 1973.

PETROV, A. and P. Manolov. Effect of leaf fruit ratio on the translocation and distribution of ^{14}C assimilates in young peach trees. Proc. Res. Inst. of Pom., Skierniewice, Poland. Series E:111-117. 1973.

PETROV, A. Relationship between separate fruiting branches in peach nutrition. Compts 'Rendus De L'Academie Des Sci. Agri. en Bulgarie 3:131-136. 1970.

PHILLIPS, J.H.H. and G.M. Weaver. A high-density peach orchard. HortSci. 10:580-582. 1975.

PORPIGLIO, P.J. and J.A. Barden. Peach leaf drop with CGA-15281 and 17856, affected by temperature. J. ASHS 105(2):227-9. 1981.

PRINCE, V.E. and B.D. Horton. Influence of pruning at various dates on peach tree mortality. J. ASHS. 97(3):303. May 1972.

PRINCE, V.E. and W.R. Okie. 'Durbin' nectarine. HortSci. 16(3). 348. June 1981.

PROCTOR, J.T.A. and E.C.L. Lougheed. Effect of covering fruit during development. ASHS 11(2):108. 1976.

PROEBSTING, Jr. E.L. and Akira Sakai. T_{50} in peach flower buds with exotherm analysis. HortSci. 14(5):597-598. 1979.

QUAMME, H.A. Mechanism of Supercooling in Overwintering Peach Flower Buds. J. ASHS. 103(1):57-61. 1978.

REEDER, B.D. et al. Trickle Irrigation on Peaches. Fruit South. pp. 16-18. 1977.

REEDER, B.D. et al. Peach tree training and spacing. HortSci. 15(5):580-581. Oct. 1980.

REEDER, B.D. and H.H. Bowen. Nitrogen and bloom delay and abscisic acid, carbohydrates, and nitrogen in peach buds. J. ASHS. 103(6):745-59. 1978.

REEVES, J. and G. Cummings. The influence of some nutritional and management factors upon certain physical attributes of peach quality. J. ASHS. 95(3):338-341. 1970.

REID, J.T. and J.W. Daniell. A device for measuring the removal force of peaches. HortSci. 10:131-132. 1975.

REUTHER, W. *et al* Irrigating deciduous orchards. Calif. Leaflet 21212. 52 p. 1981.

RICHARDSON, E.A., S.D. Seeley, and D.R. Walker. Model for estimating the completion of rest of peach trees. HortSci. 9:331-332. 1974.

RICHARDSON, E.A. et al. Pheno-climatography of spring peach bud development. HortSci. 10:236-237. 1975.

ROBERTS, A.N. and M.N. Westwood. Rootstock studies with peach and *Prunus subcordata* Benth. Fruit Var. Journ. 35:(1) Jan. 1981.

ROBITAILLE, H.A. and K.S. Yu. Rapid multiplication of peach clones from sprouted nodal cuttings. HortSci. 15(5):579-80. Oct. 1980.

ROM, R.C. New philosophy for peach rootstocks. Fruit Var. Jour. 36(2):34-6. Apr. 1982.

ROGERS, E., G. Johnson and D. Johnson. Iron-induced manganese deficiency in 'Sungold' peach and its effects on fruit composition and quality. J. ASHS 99(3):242. May 1974.

ROGERS, E. Iron induced manganese deficiency in July Elberta peach trees. J. ASHS 98(1):19. 1973.

ROGERS, E. Mineral content of peach trees as affected by nitrogen source and rate. ASHS. 94(4):352-353. 1969. Effects of N source on peach. Colo. Tech. Bull. 116. 1972.

ROGERS, E. Iron-induced manganese deficiency in peach with manganese chelate. J. ASHS. 100:531. 1975.

ROGERS, E. Iron chlorosis and mineral content of peach trees as affected by iron chelates. J. ASHS 103(5):608-612. 1978.

ROSS, N. and A.D. RIZZI. Cling peach production. Univ. of Calif. Leaflet 2455. 1976.

ROWE, R.N. and P.B. Catlin. Differential sensitivity to waterlogging and cyanogensis by peach, apricot, and plum roots. J. ASHS 96:305-308. 1971.

SAVAGE, E.F. et al. Peach tree micro-climate and methods of modification. Res. Rull. 192: Ag. Exp. Sta. Univ. of Ga. Dec. 1976.

SENTER, S.D. Effects of SADH on flavor and select physicochemical properties of freestone peaches. HortSci. 9(1):30. 1974.

SHAYBANY, B. et al. 2-(3-Chlorophenoxy) propionic Acid and 2-(3-Chlorophenoxy) propionamide sprays on fruit size and maturity of peach. J. ASHS. 104(1):34-36. 1979.

SHAYBANY, B. et al. 3-CP for peach thinning. J. ASHS 104(1):34-6. 1979.

SHEARER, A.R. *Silver leaf* (Diseases of Tree Fruits, N.Z.) Gov. Print. Office, Wellington, N.Z. 1971.

SHERMAN, W.B., R.H. Sharpe and V.E. Prince. Two red leaf characters associated with early ripening peaches. HortSci. 7(5):502. 1972.

SHERMAN, W.B. and P.M. Lyrene. Bacterial spot susceptibility in low-chilling peaches. Fruit Var. Jour. 35:(2) Apr. 1981.

SIMS, E.T., Jr., C.E. Gambrell, Jr. and J.T. McClary, Jr. Alar on peach quality. J. ASHS. 96(4):527. July 1971.

SIMS, E.T., Jr. Post harvest effects on plant growth regulators, Alar and Ethrel, as an aid to the mechanical harvesting of peaches - a review. S. Car. Agr. Exp. Sta. Cir. 165. 1973.

SIMS, E.T., Jr., B.K. Webb. C.E. Hood, and C.E. Gambrell, Jr. Quality of fresh market peaches subjected to a mechanical harvesting and field handling: grading system. J. ASHS 98(3):253. 1973.

SIMS, E.T., Jr., C.E. Gambrell, Jr., and G.E. Stembridge. The influence of (2-Chloroethly) phosphonic acid on peach quality and maturation. J. ASHS 99(2):152. March 1974.

SPENCER, S. and G.A. Couvillon. Node position and bloom date, fruit size, and endosperm development of peach. J. ASHS 100:242-244. 1972.

STEMBRIDGE, G.E. and C.E. Gambrell. Jr. Measuring peach thinning and maturation responses. HortSci. 9(1):29. 1974.

STEMBRIDGE, G.E. and C.E. Grambrell, Jr. Peach fruit abscission as influenced by applied gibberellin and seed development. J. ASHS 97(6):708. 1972.

STEMBRIDGE, G.E. and J.W. Raff. J.W. Ethephon and peach fruit development. HortSci. 8(6):500. Dec. 1973.

STEMBRIDGE, G.E., J.W. Raff and N. Veinbrants. Seed development in peach and nectarine during induction of fruit abscission with ethephon. HortSci. 8(6):501. Dec. 1973.

STEMBRIDGE, G.E., J.W. Raff, and N. Veinbrants. Seed development in peach and nectarine during induction of fruit abscission with ethephon. HortSci. 8:501-502. 1973.

STIRLING, G.R. et al. Biological control of root-knot nematode on peach. Calif. Agr. Sept. 1979.

SUGERMAN, W. et al. Breeding peach rootstocks resistant to nematodes. HortSci. 16(4):523-4. Aug. 1981.

TAWFIK, M. et al. Effect of N, P, K on growth, yield, fruit quality of 'Mit Ghamr' peach. Agric. Res. Rev., Cairo 52, No. 3, 15-23. (Egypt). 1974.

TAYLOR, B.K. and L.G. Isbell. Superphosphate effects on newly planted peach trees. J. ASHS 46:3,251-261. July 1971.

TAYLOR, B.K. and B. van den Ende. Correlation between leaf nutrient status and tree crops. Aust. Jour. Exp. Agri. and An. Husb. 12:103-106. 1972.

TAYLOR, B.K. Response of young peach and apple trees to phosphorus. Aust. J. Agric. Res. 26:521-528. 1975.

THE FRUIT Situation. U.S. Dept. of Agr. — AMS Reports issued quarterly (priced). Washington, D.C. 20250. This covers important commercial deciduous fruits, including the peach.

TYSON, B.L. et al. Selecting optimum maturity distribution for mechanical harvesting of clingstones for processing. HortSci. 10:237-238. 1975.

UCHIYAMA, Yoshio. The effect of crotony-lidene-di-Urea fertilization on fruit growth, yield, quality, and chemical composition of white peach. J. ASHS 98(6):546. Nov. 1973.

UNITED States standards for peaches (1972), fresh peaches for freezing or pulping (1946), fresh freestone peaches for canning (1946), nectarines (1958), apricots (1958) U.S. Dept. of Agr. AMS, Washington 25, D.C. (Request recent edition).

URE, C.R. Frost injury to peach buds, western Colorado in recent years. Fruit Var. Jour. 27:3-5. Jan. 1973.

URE, C.R. Peach hardiness, Colo. Fruit Var. Jour. 27(1):3-5. 1973.

VAN HEEK, L.A.G. and H.H. Allen. Mechanical harvesting of Tatura Trellis fruit trees. J. ASHS 105(5):695-99. 1980.

VILEILA-MORALES, E.A. et al. Inherited short-fruit-development period in peach. ASHS 106(4):399-401. 1981.

WATADA, A.E. et al. Firmness of peaches measured nondestructively. J. ASHS. 101(4):404-406. 1976.

WATADA, A.E. et al. Sensory, compositional, and volatile attributes of CA stored peaches. J. ASHS 104(5):626-629. 1979.

WEAVER, D.J. et al. Elemental content of dormant peach trees and susceptibility short life. J. ASHS. 101(5):486-9. 1976.

WEHUNT, E.J. and J.M. Good. Nematodes on peach, in "The Peach". N.F. Childers (Ed.), Hort. Publ., 3906 N.W. 31st Pl., Gainesville, Fla. 32606. p. 377-387. 1975.

WEINBERGER, J.H. 'Fairlane' Nectarine. HortSci. 9:604. 1974.

WEINBERGER, H.J. Growing nectarines. Bull. No. 379, ARS, USDA, Hyattsville, Md. 22 p. 1975.

WELLS, J.M. and L.G. Revear. Hydrocooling peaches after waxing: fungicide residues, decay, moisture loss. J. ASHS. 11(2):107. 1976.

WERNER, R.A., L.F. Hough. C. Frenkel. Rehardening of peach fruits in cold storage. J. ASHS. 103(1):90-1. 1978.

WERNER, D.J. and J.R. Ballington. Peach flesh browning. Fruit Var. Journ. 36:1. 1982.

WERNER, D.J. and S. Chang. Stain-testing in viability of stored peach pollen. HortSci. 16(4):522-3. Aug. 1981.

WERNER, D.J. et al. 'Derby' peach. HortSci. 16(2):231. 1981.

WERNER, R.A. and C. Frenkel. Rapid changes in the firmness of peaches as influenced by temperature. HortSci. 13(4):470-471. 1978.

WERNER, D.J. and D.F. Ritchie. Peach cultivars (and breeding in N.C.) N.C. Sta. Bul. 464. 10 pp. 1982.

WOLAK, R.J. and G.A. Couvillon. Time of thiourea-KNO₃ application on rest and bud development in 'Loring' peach. HortSci. 11(4):400-402. 1976.

WOODBRIDGE, C.G. Split-pit in peach, nutrient levels. J. ASHS 103(2):278-280. 1978.

YADAVA, U.L. and S.L. Doud. Short life and replant problems of deciduous fruit trees. Hort. Rev. Avi. Publ. Co. 1:1-116. 1980.

YADAVA, U.L. and S.L. Doud. Rootstock on bark thickness of peach scions. HortSci. 13(5):538-9. 1978.

YADAVA, U.L. and S.L. Doud. Peach seedling rootstocks and orchard sites on cold hardiness survival of peach. J. ASHS 103(3):321-323. 1978.

YADAVA, U.L. et al. Different methods to assess cold hardiness of peach trees. J. ASHS. 103(3):318-321. 1978.

YOUNG, M.J., R.H. Sharpe. Annual top renewal of high-density nectarines, peaches. Fla. St. Hort. Soc. Proc. 58: 448-451. 1975.

YOUNG, E. Response of seedling rootstocks of peach to soil temperature. HortSci. 15(3):294-296. 1980.

YOUNG, E. and B. Olcott-Reid. Siberian-C rootstock delays bloom of peach. J. ASHS. 104(2):178-181. 1979.

YOUNG, M.J. and R.H. Sharpe. Growth and yield response of high density peaches and nectarines to annual topping. Fruit Var. J. 32(4):94-6. 1978.

YOUNG, M.J. And T.E. Crocker. Severe postharvest topping high density peaches, nectarines. HortSci. 17(2):220-2. 1982.

Apricot and Almond

ALMOND FACTS. Bi-monthly. Calif. Almond Growers Exchange, P.O. Box 1768, Sacramento, Ca. 95808. (Paid Membership).

ALMONDS. Pollen tube growth. Calif. Ag., July 1975; Production - Leaflet 2463, 20 pp. 1977.

ALMOND Industries of Italy and Spain. U.S. Dept. of Agr. Foreign Agr. Serv. FASM 228. May 1971.

BRADT, O.A. and E.T. Andersen. 'Viva-gold' Apricot. HortSci. 14(1):82. 1979. 'Velvaglo' Apricot. HortSci. 14(1):83. 1979.

BROWNE, L.T. Delay almond bloom w/ethephon. Calif. Agr. March 1978.

DEMETRIADES, S.D., et al. Boron deficiency in apricot in Greece. Ann. de L'Inst. Phytopath. Beniki. 10(2):226-228. 1971.

DRAKE, S.R., et al. Comparison of cultivar on drained weight and can corrosiion in processed apricots. J. ASHS. 103(1):49-51. 1978.

DRAKE, S.R., et. al. Comparison of 'Rival' and 'Tilton' for canning. HortSci. 12(1):75-6. 1977.

FACTEAU, T.J. and R.E. ROWE. Effect of fluoride and chloride on pollen in 'Tilton' apricot. J. ASHS. 102(1):95-96. 1977.

FERERES, Elias *et al.* Drip irrigation saves money in young almond orchards. Cal. Agr. Oct. 1982.

FISHER, D.V. Time of blossom bud induction in apricots. Proc. ASHS. 58, 19. 1951.

GERDTS, M. et al. Almond yield reduction. Calif. Agri. (March):14. 1975.

GRIGGS, W.H. and B.T. Iwakiri. Pollen tube growth in almond flowers. Calif. Agr. (June):4-6, 1975.

GUELFAT-REICH, S. and R. Ben-Arie. Maturation of ripening of 'Canino' apricots as affected by combined sprays of SADH and 2, 4,

5TP. J. ASHS 100:517. 1975.

HELLALI, R. et al. Morphology of noninfectious bud failure symptoms in vegetative buds of almond. J. ASHS. 103(4):459-64. 1978.

HELLALI, R. et al. Noninfectious bud-failure in almond. J. ASHS 101(5):494-497. 1976.

HENDRICKSON, A.H. and F.J. Veihmeyer. Use of water by almond trees. Proc. ASHS 65, 133, 1955.

INTRIERI, C. and K. Ryuko. Uptake, transport and metabolism of (2-chloroethyl) trimethylammonium chloride in almond seedlings. J. ASHS 99:349-352. 1974.

JOHNSTON, S. et al. Apricot growing in Michigan. Mich. Ag. Ext. Serv. Gul. 533, 9 pp, 1966.

KESTER, D. E., et al. Variability of bud failure in Nonpariel almonds. Calif. Agri. (March):10-12. 1975.

KESTER, D.E. and R.N. Asay. Variability in Noninfectious Bud-failure of 'Nonpariel' almond. II. Propagation source. J. ASHS 103(3):429-32. 1978.

KESTER, D.E. et al. Almond variety evaluation. Calif. Agr. 4-7. Oct. 1980.

KESTER, et al. Bud failure in almonds. Calif. Agr. 3/1975. Plus: Almond yield reduction (Gerdts et al.) Replacing bud failure trees (Browne et al) Bud-Failure-Free selection (Kester), same issue.

KESTER, D.E., et al. Chilling requirements for germination, blooming, leafing among seedling almonds. J. ASHS. 102(2):145-8. 1977.

KESTER, D.E. et al. Nut and kernal traits in almond. J. ASHS. 102(3):264-266. 1977.

KESTER, D.E. et al. Temperature sensitivity in clonally propagated almonds. HortSci. 11:55-57. 1976.

KOCHBA, J. and P. Speigel-Roy. Resistance to root-knot nematode in bitter almond progenies and almond x Okinawa peach hybrids. J. ASHS 7(5):503. 1972.

KOCHBA, J. and P. Spiegel-Roy. Nematode-resistant rootstock almonds; seed source. HortSci. 11(3):270. 1976.

LAYNE, R.E.C. 'Harcot Apricot. HortSic. 13(1):6 4-65. Feb. 1978

LAYNE, R.E.C. 'Harogem' apricot. HortSci. 14(6):758-9. Dec. 1979.

LAYNE, R.E.C. 'Hargrand' apricot. HortSci. 16(1):98-100.1981

LAYNE, R.E.C. 'Harlayne' apricot. HortSci. 16(1):97-98. 1981.

MAJERNIK, O. and I. Hricovsky. Water output and water deficit of leaves of apricot rootstocks of different taxons. Sbornik UVTI - Zahradnictvi. 1:91-99. 1974.

MAXIE, E.C. and F.G. Mitchell. Gas exchange in fruits of apricot and peach at elevated temperatures. HortSci. 9:336-338. 1974.

PONS Canals, D. Antonio y D.B. Simonet Salas. Plainficacion del cultivo del Almendro. 60pp. Jefatura AGronomica de Baleares. Palma de Mallorca. (Bolletin buena). 1970.

RAMMING, D.W. Apricot cultivar situation in North America. Fruit Var. Jour. 34(3):70-72. 1980.

RAMSAY, J. and G.C. Martin. Seasonal changes in growth promoters and inhibitors in buds of apricots. J. ASHS 95(5):569-570. 1970.

RYUGO, K. and J. Labavitch. Gums and mucilages in hulls of almonds. J. ASHS. 103(5):568-570. 1978.

SOMMER, N.F. et al. Chemical inactivation of heat-tolerant pectolytic enzymes in raw apricots which causes softening of canned product. J. ASHS 103(6):762-767. 1978.

SPIEGAL-ROY, P. and J. Kochba. 'Dagan' and 'Solo' almonds. HortSci. 11(3):271. 1976.

SUMMERS, F.M. Insect and mite pests of almonds. Calif. AG. Ext. SErv. Cir. 513, 16 pp. Up-date.

TOYAMA, T.K. Pollen receptivity period and its relation to fruit setting. Fruit Var. Jour. 34(1):2-4. Jan. 1980.

URIU, K., G.E. Martin, and R.M. Hagan. Radial trunk growth of almonds as affected by soil water and crop density. J. ASHS 95(2):166-169. 1970.

WANKIER, B.N., D.K. Salunkhe, and W.F. Campbell. Effects of controlled atmosphere storage on biochemical changes in apricot and peach fruit. J. ASHS. 95(5):604-609. 1970.

WEINBAUM, S.A. et. al. Increased stomatal resistance in two cultivars of almond sensitive to bud failure. HortSci. 15(5):583-585. 1980.

WEINBAUM, S.A. et al. Nitrogen increases yield without enhancing blossom receptivity in almond. HortSci. 15(1):78-79. 1980.

WEINBERGER, J.W. Growing apricots. USDA. Home & Garden Bull. 1971.

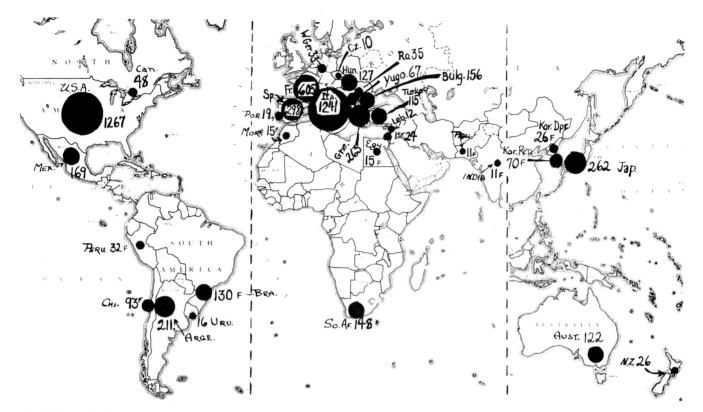

WORLD PEACH PRODUCTION. This segmented map of the world gives a quick evaluation of where and the relative tonnage of peaches produced by country. No data are available from the USSR and China. Certain other countries may produce peaches, but hardly in a commercial sense. Approximate figures represent 1000s of metric tons — one metric ton is 2204.6 lbs. "F" indicates data from FAO Production Yearbook, United Nations in Rome, Italy. An * indicates unofficial figures.

Peach breeders who have contributed to the greatly improved cultivars today include, l. to r.: the late Prof. Stanley Johnston, Michigan State University; Dr. L.F. Hough, retired, Rutgers Univeristy; Fred W. Anderson (private), California; and the late Grant Merrill (private) California. Also included are the late Prof. M.A. Blake, a pioneer at Rutgers University. Dr. John H. Weinberger, retired, USDA, California; Dr. C.D. Hesse, retired, University of California, Parlier; Dr. R.E.C. Layne, Canada Dept. of Agr., Harrow; and Prof. Ralph Sharpe, retired and Dr. Wayne B. Sherman, University of Florida (low-chilling peaches). Others who have made key contributions to the peach industry include the late Prof. A.M. Musser, Clemson University; Dr. E.F. Savage, retired, Ga. Exp. Sta., Griffin; Dr. Harold W. Fogle, retired, USDA, Md.; Dr. F.P. Cullinan, retired, USDA, Maryland; the late Dr. L.D. Davis, University of California; and Ernest G. Christ, retired, Rutgers University.

CHAPTER XV

Culture of Plums

Plums are adapted more widely in the U.S. and world than almost any other deciduous tree fruit. This is because there are many species and cultivars adapted to the many different climatic and soil conditions. Plums will thrive where winters are cold and the summers are hot, or where it is dry or the rainfall is heavy. For home use, they are suitable for most orchards throughout the temperate zone. But, commercially, their production is limited to definite areas typified by the West Coast of North America and southern Europe. Plums comprise over 50% of Romanian fruit while Yugoslavia leads the world.

In Europe, it is a question if plums rank first or second in importance among the deciduous tree fruits, whereas in the United States they are exceeded by apple, peach, and pear. In the eastern U.S., plums are grown largely for the local market, and with improved pesticides, there is a moderate increase in commercial plantings.

Below is the relative world plum production in *metric* tons.

Country	Production	Country	Production
Yugoslavia	690	France	65
USA	630	Japan	55
Romania	615	Germany (DR)	55
Germany (FR)	400	Czechoslovakia	55
Bulgaria	250	United Kingdom	40
Hungary	225	Switzerland	40
Italy	150	China	40
Turkey	130	Afghanistan	35
Poland	120	Australia	25
Mexico	85	Portugal	20
Austria	85	Greece	20
Spain	80	India	20
Argentina	70	Chile	15

Other countries producing plums and prunes are: Israel, Syria, Lebanon, Korea (Rep), So. Africa, Egypt, Canada, Albania, Tunisia and most other countries in Europe and those located near country listings above. Plums are of minor importance in the Far East.

U.S. production of plums and prunes by leading states in thousands of tons is approximately: California - 330 (150 dried prunes); Oregon - 30; Washington - 18; Michigan - 14; and Idaho - 8. Fruit largely for local markets is produced in Texas and states bordering the Great Lakes on the south and east. Per capita consumption of all plums and prunes has decreased appreciably since 1935 and the trend continues. Fresh consumption dropped from 2.5 lbs. to 2, processed from 5.5 to about 1.3 lbs.

Prunes are produced in greater quantities than plums.[1] Over three-fourths of the total U.S. crop is raised in California, mainly in the Sacramento Valley, central coastal valleys, and the San Joaquin Valley. In Idaho and Washington about 90% of the crop is sold fresh with the balance canned; in Oregon ⅓ is dried, ⅓ fresh and ⅓ canned with some frozen, but this varies widely from year to year. About 45,000 metric tons of U.S. prunes are exported.

Almost the entire commercial crop of plums is produced in California and Michigan. Michigan cans over half the crop with 300-900 tons frozen.

Plum trees in the U.S. have decreased from 35 million in 1925 to about 14 million in the 1980s, but production has been maintained at between 200,000 to 250,000 tons (56 lbs/bu.) due to improved practices and elimination of marginal trees.

Over 2000 cultivars of plums, referable to some 15

Figure 1. Distribution of bearing plum and prune trees in the United States. Commercial prune and plum growing is confined largely to the West Coast where over 85 per cent of the trees are located and about 93 per cent of the crop is produced. There has been a modest decrease in home and some commerical plantings in the East, largely localized in Texas, Michigan, and New York. Total U.S. trees have been around 14 million.

---

[1]A prune is a plum which because of higher sugar content can be dried whole without fermentation at the pit. Growers in California who ship their fruit to canneries are known as plum growers, while those producing drying varieties are known as prune growers. Commercially, the prune is largely dried, but it is also canned and sold fresh. Plums are sold fresh, canned, or split and dried with the pit removed.

species, have been grown in the United States. Few of these species and only a few of the cultivars are important commercially; namely, *Prunus domestica* (European plums), *Prunus salicina* (Japanese plums), and hybrids of the latter.

European type. This is the most important group of plums in the United States. The plum is characterized by a moderately vigorous tree with thick leaves which are glossy dark green above and pale green with considerable pubescence beneath; the leaf edges are coarsely notched or sawtoothed. The fruit is borne largely on spurs, is variable in size, color, and shape, and the stone either clings to or separates from the flesh. Due to the rather wide variation of color, shape, and flesh characteristics of the fruit, the European plums have been divided into the following subgroups:

(A) Prune group is usually distinguished from the other European plums because they can be successfully dried without removal of the pit. It includes such popular varieties as French, Sugar, Italian, German, Robe (de Sargeant) and all varieties of plums grown for drying.

(B) Reine Claude (Green Gage) group is characterized by more or less round fruit which has a very slight suture and of green, yellow, or slight red color. The flesh is sweet, tender, and juicy. Varieties include Reine Claude, Jefferson, and Washington which are important among canning varieties.

(C) Yellow Egg group is a comparatively small and relatively unimportant group which is desirable for canning only. Best known variety is Yellow Egg.

(D) Imperatrice group is a large group, including practically all of the blue plums. Chief fruit characteristics are blue, heavy bloom[2], medium-size, oval shape, firm flesh, and thick skin with only fair quality. Important varieties include Grand Duke, Diamond, Tragedy, and President.

(E) Lombard group is similar to the above group, except that the fruits are red in color instead of blue, probably of smaller size, and of somewhat lower quality. Varieties include Lombard, Bradshaw, and Pond.

Japanese type. Trees of the Japanese plums are early blooming and susceptible to frost. Many of the varieties are about as hardy to winter cold as the peach and can be grown under a wide range of conditions. Fruits of the Japanese varieties are quite variable but easily distinguished from other types of plums by their large size, oblate to heart - but rarely oblong - shape, and their bright yellow, red, or purplish-red color. Fruits are never blue. Flesh color is yellow, amber, or red in the so-called blood plums, juicy, and firm. The dessert quality ranges from fair to excellent, depending upon the variety. There is considerable variation in character of tree growth; some

varieties are spreading in habit while others grow upright. The bark is rough, even when young; peach-like as compared to the smooth gray bark of European plums. Leaves are medium-sized, sharp-pointed, and nearly free of pubescence. The Japanese sorts are distinguished also by their abundant flowers which are produced three in a bud on many-budded short or compact spurs and on one-year shoots.

The American plums are native to America, include several species used for fresh or culinary purposes, in breeding, or as a stock. A few of the more important are:

P. americana, Marsh. is native from Conn. to Montana, south to Fla., Tex., and Colo.; resistant to cold; varieties are Hawkeye, Wyant, DeSoto, Weaver, Terry.

P. hortulana, Bailey is thorny, bushy, more vigorous than the plum native farther south to Miss. Valley, less flavored, more resistant to brown rot, and makes good jellies and jams; varieties Golden Beauty, Wayland.

P. Munsoniana, Wight and Hedr., is resistant to spring frosts and fruit to brown rot; widely planted in lower Miss. Valley; variety Wild Goose.

P. Besseyi, Bailey, or "sand cherry," native Kansas to Manitoba, is used for hybridizing and as a dwarfing stock for stone fruits.

P. Maritima, Marsh. or "beach plum" grows well on beaches and sand dunes from Virginia to New Brunswick, Canada, and is used in jams and jellies commerically. Appears to be resistant to most diseases and pests except red mite.

P. subcordata, Benth., or Pacific plum is native and wild mostly in southwest Oregon and northwest California; is used in preserves and sauces, some eaten fresh.

Other plum types. In addition to the above species and types of plums, the following are worthy of mention because they: (a) are used as root stocks for commercial varieties, (b) have desirable characteristics for hybridizing, or (c) are often found in home orchards.

The *Myrobalan* or cherry plum (*Prunus cerasifera*) is used widely as a rootstock for European and Japanese plums. Seedlings are hardy, vigorous, and tolerant of wet soil. Fruit of the Myrobalan tree is small, round or oval, yellow or red in color, and with rather insipid flesh. A form with red foliage is called *Pissardi.* The chief value of the fruit is the seed from which the seedling rootstocks are grown. Some selected types, as Myro 29C, M-2624 and cross (probable) of *P cerasifera* and *P. monsoniana.,* are propagated from cuttings.

The *Simon* plum (*Prunus simoni*) has been used as a parent in the development of many so-called Japanese plums, e.g., Climax and Wickson.

Damson plums (*Prunus insititia*) are found occasionally in home orchards where the fruit is limited to culinary purposes because of its small size and sour or acid flavor.

---

[2]This refers to powdery film over skin, not to blossoming.

Trees resemble European plums but are smaller; they are hardy, productive, relatively free from diseases, require little care, and come nearly true from seed although varieties, as Frogmore and Shropshire, are known and are propagated by budding and grafting. St. Julien is a type whose seed is used for rootstocks.

CHOICE OF CULTIVARS

The geographical region and varieties of plums selected will depend upon the proposed market outlet. If a distant grower intends to ship a large portion of his crop on a fresh basis, it is important that he plant not more than six or eight cultivars of well-known shipping quality. Practically all miscellaneous sorts should be eliminated. The buying market is interested in obtaining large quantities of relatively few cultivars, and not limited amounts of a large number of cultivars. Many small shipments of from 10 to 20 boxes are undesirable and discriminated against by most big-scale buyers. In California, the early cultivars give greater promise of satisfactory returns than most mid-season or late sorts.

Cultivars for shipping in California are: May to September (100,000 packages or more): *Early* - Red Beaut. Beauty, Burmosa, Santa Rosa (1/5 of acreage) Tragedy; *Midseason* - Frair, Grand Rosa, July Santa Rosa, Mariposa, Duarte, Queen Rosa, Red Rosa, Simka, Wickson, Laroda, Eldorado, Nubiana; *Late* - Queen Ann, Late Santa Rosa, Elephant Heart, Kelsey, President, and Casselman. Many minor varieties are sold throughout the season. Blackamber is a Japanese type introduced to extend the Frair type season.

The following cultivars are used primarily for canning: Jefferson and Reine Claude (not commercial). The canning trade desires the large, firm, green or yellow plums. Large plums which are not smaller than 12 to a pound bring a premium as first-grade canning stock; plums not smaller than 20 to a pound are rated second class for canning. Cultivars for drying are grown mainly in the Interior Valleys and near the Pacific Coast.

In New Jersey, Brooks Italian prune, President and Stanley performed well over 15 other cultivars tested. Red Heart and Ozark Premier, in Japanese types gave fair to good performance.

The Pacific Northwest does not compete with California in the plum crop. A premium exists, however, for earliness of prunes in the Milton-Freewater area, Oregon; Yakima, Washington and Payette, Idaho, where growers plant early strains of the Italian prune such as Richard's Early Italian and Milton Early Italian. In general, California meets only limited competition from plums grown in other states. However, the early varieties meet considerable competition in the eastern markets with Georgia peaches, and the midseason and later varieties come into competition with California Bartlett pears and with shipping prunes from the Pacific Northwest.

For drying, the French Prune (Prune D'Agen) accounts for over 90 percent of the California acreage. Other important drying varieties are Imperial, Sugar, and Robe de Sergeant. Several French-type introductions are drawing interest: Germans Early French, Moyer, Victor Large French, Friedman French and 707 French, all *P. domestica*. Cultivars for drying are grown mainly near the Pacific Coast and in the Sacramento Valley.

If the plums are to be sold at the roadside market or at local stores, plant a number of cultivars that ripen over several months. In the East, the only varieties grown commercially and usually on a relatively small scale are Italian and Stanley prune. President and Brooks Italian do well in New Jersey.

Other varieties suggested by the New York Experiment Station for trial for roadside market and local trade are, in the order of ripening: Early Laxton, Beauty, Formosa, Santa Rosa, California Blue, Clyman, Oullins, Utility, Washington, Prinlew, Yakima, Reine Claude, Albion, and French or Shropshire Damsons. Varieties recommended for home and market in Texas are America, Compass Cherry[3], Gold, Munson, Omaha, and Opata. Popular varieties in Missouri are Munson, Red June, Gold, Wild Goose, Green Gage, Shropshire Damson, Lombard, Omaha, French Damson, President, German Prune, Italian Prune and Ozark Premier.

Lowest chilling plums is about 450 hrs below 45°F. Cultivars that are grown in latitude of North Florida and fruit best after fairly cold winters are: Early Bruce, Inca, Mariposa, Excellsior, Burbank, Methley and Ozark Premier. Plums in this area are grown on peach rootstock. Main problems are leaf scorch (bacteria) and short-life bacterial canker. Explorer is a fall-season Japanese plum for southeastern USA.

Contact your local governmental agency for local variety suggestions. Also, contact the Federal Plum Commodity Committee, 701 Fulton Ave., Sacramento, CA. 95825, for color folder of key varieties and annual reports.

POLLINATION

European plums. European varieties of plums fall into either one of two groups, self-fruitful or self-unfruitful (bees are needed). It has been shown that about 30 percent of the flowers will set fruit on self-fruitful varieties whether the flowers are cross- or self-pollinated; this is considered more than a sufficient set for a commercial crop. Flowers of the self-unfruitful cultivars, however, set

---

[3]Compass is a synonym. Leading Yugoslav variety is Pozegaca: blue, roundish, medium small, budwood obtainable from USDA, Glen Dale, Md. 20769.

Figure 2. Important plum growing counties in California are Fresno, Kern, Kings and Tulare with around 30,000 acres. Eldorado, Nevada and Placer have under 2000 acres. In the Sierra foothills area, above, the fruit ripens early, and there are good irrigation and transportation facilities. Trees are planted closer because soil is relatively shallow.

only about 1.5 percent; this is insufficient for a commercial crop, necessitating interplanting with pollinizing varieties.

Among the self-fruitful varieties are the following: Agen, Bavay, California Blue, Coates 1418, Czar, Drap D'Or, Early Mirabelle, French Damson, German Prune, Giant Goliathe, King of The Damsons, Monarch, Ontario, Mayer, Ouillins, Pershore, Purple Pershore, Sannoir, Shropshire Damson, Stanley, Sugar, Victoria, and Yellow Egg.

Among the *self-unfruitful* cultivars are: Altham, Allgrove's Superb, Anita, Arch Duke, Belgian Purple, Blue Rock, Bradshaw, Burton, Cambridge Gage, Clyman, Coe's Violet, Conquest, Crimson Drop, DeMonfort, Diamond, Esperen, Frogmore Damson, Golden Drop, Grand Duke, Hall, Hand, Italian Prune,[4] Imperial Epineuse, (French, Robe, Sugar, Burton are pollinators), Imperial Gage, Jefferson, Late Orange, Late Orleans, Miller Superb, McLaughin, pond, President, Quackenboss, Reine Claude, Rivers' Early, Rivers' Early Prolific, Sergeant, (French and Sugar are pollinators), Silver, Standard, Sultan, Tragedy, Transparent, and Washington (Figure 2).

Due to the fact that some of the above self-fruitful cultivars apparently have different strains in differnet regions, or the same strains respond differently under varied environments, *it is probably safer to interplant with at least one pollinizing variety.* Cultivars which tend to be variable include Italian Prune, Agen, Reine Claude, and German Prune, which may be self-fruitful in some regions. All varieties listed above in both groups, except for the Esperen, have good pollen for cross-pollination, if blooming seasons overlap sufficiently. Some combinations are cross-unfruitful because of close relationship. These include Golden Drop, Coe's Violet, and Allgrove's

Superb. Another cross-incompatible group is Cambridge Gage, Late Orange, and President.

The European plums in the East usually overlap sufficiently in blooming periods to provide adequate cross-pollination. In some localities, however, Italian Prune and Imperial Epineuse may bloom too late for adequate cross-pollination by such early-blooming varieties as Reine Claude, Lombard, or Grand Duke. In this case, another late-blooming or midseason-blooming variety should provide cross-pollination for the late-blooming varieties.

European cultivars grown in California, with the exception of Tragedy, fall into rather distinct groups with relation to season of blooming. *Midseason-blooming* cultivars are Agen, Clyman, Grand Duke, Diamond, Quackenboss, Jefferson, Standard, Suger (90% of crop), French, Robe, Burton, Imperial, and President. *Late-blooming* cultivars are California Blue, Hungarian, Pond, Giant, Italian Prune, Yellow Egg, and Washington. In normal seasons, those cultivars blooming after President are not cross-pollinated effectively by varieties of the early group. Tragedy, however, having a long blooming period, usually blooms along with several of the late-blooming Japanese varieties and extends into the blooming period of Grand Duke and Diamond.

Japanese plums. Most of the varieties in the Japanese group are self-unfruitful. These include Mariposa, Inca, Wickson, Eldorado, Queen Ann, Laroda, Formosa, Kelsey, Red Beaut (pollen sterile), Redheart, Duarte, Gaviota, Elephant Heart, Becky Smith, and Burbank.

Although Redroy, Red Rosa (Late Santa Rosa), Santa Rosa, Climax, Beauty, Nubiana, and Methley produce more fruits from self-pollination than other Japanese plums, they also should be interplanted with pollinizers unless their local self-fruitfulness is established.

Following varieties are not recommended for pollinizers because their pollen tends to be low in viability: Burmosa, Mariposa, Red Ace (Florida), Eldorado, Formosa,

---

[4]Italian prune is self-fruitful in the Pacific Northwest.

Gaviota, Red Beaut, and Kelsey. Shiro probably should be placed also in this classification. Varieties which are considered somewhat more dependable as pollinizers are Wickson, Laroda, Santa Rosa, Redheart, and Elephant Heart. Several cross-and inter-incompatible combinations are known. See Griggs and Hesse's Calif. Leaflet 163. Japanese plums bloom 3 to 4 weeks earlier than most European plums and are subject to frosts in northern latitudes where bee activity also may be restricted by cold weather at bloom. Morris (750 hrs chilling) is a promising Texas A. and M. introduction.

European and native plum varieties as cross-pollinizers. European plum varieties are not consistently effective in pollinizing Japanese plum varieties. Fair to good sets on Japanese varieties have been obtained by cross-pollination from Clyman, Ouillins, Reine Claude, Victoria, and Yellow Egg. Tragedy is fairly effective for cross-pollination of Japanese varieties, but the reciprocal relationship is unfruitful. American species of plums (see below) which possess viable pollen have been found to be most effective as pollinizers for Japanese varieties.

American species and hybrid plums. The following varieties of the American species are self-unfruitful: *Prunus Americana:* De Sota, Hawkeye, Rollingstone, Wyant Var. Mollis, and Wolfe; *Prunus hortulana:*

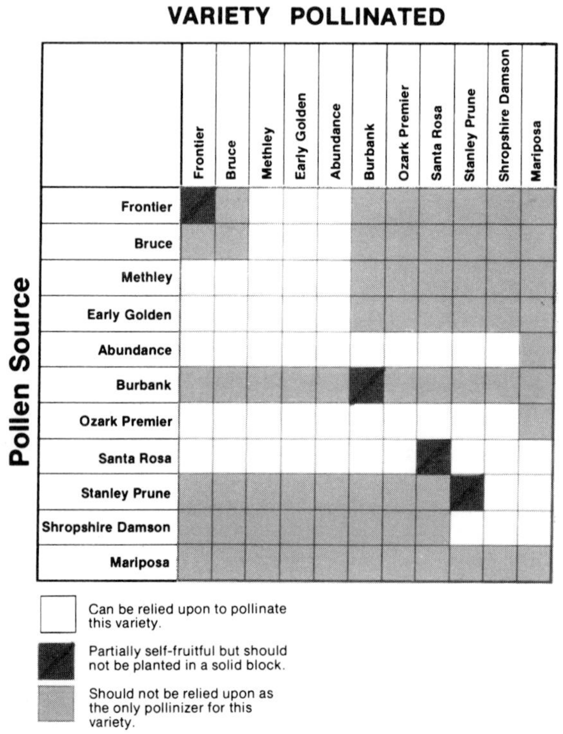

Wayland Var. mineri, Miner, and Surprise; *Prunus munsoniana:* Wild Goose and Newman; and *Prunus nigra:* Cheney. Some hybrids between American and Japanese species are self-unfruitful largely because of nonviable pollen; they include Red Wing, Monitor, Underwood, Elliott, La Crescent, Tonka, Radisson, and Fiebing; these varieties are obviously of no value as pollinizing varieties. The following varieties can be used for pollinizers, although they, too, contain considerable nonviable pollen: Assiniboin, Cheney, De Sota, Newman, Miner, Surprise, Rollingstone, Wyant, and Wolfe. The Surprise variety is the best single pollinizing variety for all the hybrids grown in the Mississippi Valley. Hybrids of the Sand Cherry (*Prunus besseyi*) produced by Hansen of North Dakota are also self-unfruitful, namely: Oka, Saca, Zumbra, and Compass. Compass can be used for a pollinizing variety. *P. subcordata* trees are self-unfruitful but the various selections of cultivars are inter-fruitful.

Planting plans for plums. For pollination purposes, as a whole, it is recommended in plum plantings that at least every third tree in every third row be planted to a pollinizing variety. Two to six rows of a variety alternated with one or two pollenizer rows is desirable when both are important commercially and to facilitate use of mechanical equipment. About one strong beehive/A through the orchard is needed for pollination. When cultivars produce little or no pollen, a pollinizer branch is grafted in every tree.

In California, trees planted 8x12 ft or 454 trees/A, cordon-trained, have yielded the 3rd, 4th, and 5th years approximately 2½-3, 5½-6, and 7½-16 tons/A, respectively. Yields of trees in standard orchards are 6-10 T/A. Labor/Ton was reduced markedly. Future plum orchards, like the pear, peach and apple, may be set in hedgerows. Most orchards, however, are planted on the square 18 x 22 ft., depending upon soil fertility and vigor of variety. Various types of hedgerow plantings with trees spaced 8 to 10 ft. in rows, 16 to 22 ft. apart, are under observation.

In Mississippi, some varieties require less winter chilling for good bloom and set. Suggested cultivars are: Methley, Santa Rosa, Bruce, America, and Starking Delicious (See Overcash).

Dr. M. Chaplin, Ore. State University, reports boron is critical at bloom time. If sprayed on, they have gotten up to 100% better fruit set where the tree has difficulty getting adequate B from the soil.

ROOTSTOCKS FOR PLUMS

Plum varieties do not come true from seed. They are propagated by budding on seedlings in the nursery similar to peach propagation. The plum is grown mostly on plum stocks (Myrobalan). It can be grown on seedlings of peach,

VARIETY POLLINATED

Figure 2a. This chart indicates which plum or prune cultivars recommended in some areas will set fruit alone or need cross-pollination for full crops. Honey bees are important in plum and prune pollination. (Courtesy Haley Nursery Co., Inc., Smithville, Tn. 37166.)

Figure 3. Preplant soil fumigation is good practice where old fruit land is being planted to plums. Trees above are on Myro 29C roots, three years old, in soil infested with *Pratylenchus vulnus* nematode. Trees at right are in soil fumigated with 1, 3 dichloropropene before planting; at left no fumigation. (Courtesy J.E. DeVay)

Japanese apricots and to some extent on almond. Seedlings are compatible with a variety of both Japanese and European plum varieties. See rootstocks Calif. Leaflet 158 for details.

Myrobalan stock also is tolerant to poor soil aeration and is adapted to a wide range of soils. In California, it is not so inclined to produce suckers from the roots, but in some of the areas it may sucker badly. It is hardy, long-lived, and deep-rooted, although not particularly vigorous. It also gives very satisfactory results on deep comparatively dry soils. The brown color of the roots usually distinguishes the Myrobalan seedlings from other stocks used for plums. In Western Europe the St. Julien stock frequently is used in addition to *P. domestica* and *P. cerasifera* clones (not stolon propagated because of a virus transmission). *P. cerasifera divaricata* is used in Poland. Myrobalan, Marianna and Buck plums are used in Australia. A commercially dwarfing stock is needed. The English ''Pixie'' rootstock shows promise.

In Canada, (Quebec), *P. americana* is a good stock planted deep to avoid sprouts.

In California, selected nematode resistant stocks of Myrobalan (Myro 29C) and Marianna 2624 (also resistant to oak-root fungus) plums propagated vegetatively are among preferred stocks. Preplant soil fumigation with halogenated hydrocarbons as EDB or methyl bromide is good practice against nematodes (Figure 3).

In New York, the Myrobalan seedlings may show ''chlorotic fleck,'' a leaf virus. These should be rogued. Stanley is particularly short-lived on ''fleck'' seedlings. Japanese-American hybrids should be grafted on American plum seedlings. The Western Sand Cherry (*P. besseyi)* is a dwarfing stock for European plums such as Stanley and Italian. Japanese varieties are very small on

this stock, making suitable home grounds trees.

Peach. In California, the nematode resistant stocks of peach (see Peach chapter) also have been gaining popularity as desirable stocks for plums.

About half the plum acreage is on peach except where soils are heavy, wet and oak-root fungus (*Armellaria melea*) exists. Possibly 50 per cent or more of the Italian prune trees in Idaho are on peach rootstocks.

Apricot. Before the advent of rootknot nematode resistant plum and peach stocks, plums were budded on apricots because of high immunity to nematodes. However, apricot stock is not generally recommended because of frequent unsatisfactory unions between stock and cion. Some growers, however, have reported success.

Almond. Few commercial varieties of plums are propagated on almond stock, although some varieties can be grafted successfully, others cannot. The almond as a rootstock is suited chiefly to deep, light soils.

TOP-WORKING

There is often considerable interest in top-working plum trees to change the cultivar or to provide cross-pollination. There is a wide variation in compatibility among cultivars of plums in top-working. Most Japanese cultivars can be top-worked successfully on European cultivars, but the reciprocal is not satisfactory. Do not top-work Italian prune on Damsons (latter carries dwarfing virus). See Calif. Cir. on plum rootstocks for additional information, or contact the Pomology Dept. Univ. of Ca., at Davis. Plums can be top-worked on peach, other stocks suggested above. Do not graft onto apricot or almond.

PRUNING PLUMS

Young trees. One-year European trees are sold as un-branched whips; the two-year and one-year Japanese trees are branched. Whips can be trained best by the ''deshooting system'' as described for the apple in Chapter IV.

Subsequent training and pruning of these trees is similar to the plan outlined for the apple in the case of the modified leader system, or for the peach (Chapter XIV) in case of the open-center system. The open-center system of training has been common for most species of plums. Choice of a training system, however, should be governed by growth habit of the variety; those varieties that have a spreading habit, such as Burbank and many Japanese varieties, are perhaps better adapted to the open-center training system, whereas those which grow upright, such as Stanley, Santa Rosa, and Wickson might be trained easier and better to the modified leader system. Generally, for Japanese varieties, 4 to 5 main scaffolds are developed plus a few more secondaries than on the peach in the open center system. Also, these trees produce many lateral

Figure 4. A plum tree being early trained in Italy to the palmette system (eventual tree wall) with canna poles, tape or string and an upper wire (arrows). These are high-density plantings on standard stocks, managed from the ground and from wheeled scaffolds. Courtesy Ernest G. Christ, Rutgers University.

shoots and water sprouts, necessitating much wood removal.

See Figure 4 for the palmette system. Hedgerows with central leader pryamid trees on St. Julien roots and summer hedged show promise for mechanically handled trees, as proposed by Dr. Tony Preston of England (see ref.).

With upright growing varieties special attention is necessary to cut the branches back to outward-growing branches to develop a more spreading tree. With the naturally spreading varieites, such as Burbank, cut back the branches which are growing straight out or downward to upward and outward growing branches. Most European varieties develop into well-shaped trees even if very little pruning is done (Figure 5). In general, plum trees require relatively little pruning while young.

Mature trees. The plum bears fruit laterally on one-year wood and on the vigorous spurs on older wood. It is important to encourage shoot growth of 10 to 24 inches on young trees and at least 10 inches on bearing trees. With trees making this much shoot growth, spur development also is encouraged and the productive capacity of the tree is increased considerably. Bearing P. *domestica* plum trees are pruned lighter than the peach or apricot.

If the fruit will be dried, trees are pruned less than if it will be sold on the fresh market. After the trees have borne many crops, terminal growth may tend to become short and spur growth weak unless moderate pruning, fertilization, and good soil management have been practiced. With these trees, a thorough thinning out of the small thickly spurred branches is necessary; lower limbs and tops of main limbs also should be thinned out and headed back to vigorous laterals. Larger and fewer cuts are made on some cultivars and the margin of profit is usually too

narrow to justify expensive practices on these varieties. Also, the branches tend to be brittle and break easily if allowed to become too long. About one-inch cuts are made back to laterals.

Prune the bearing trees annually to get good annual yields. Tree rejuvenation also can be done by thinning out thickly spurred branches.

Because of the tendency of many Japanese varieties to overbear, a heavier pruning is recommended on this group of plums than for most European varieties; amount of pruning is about the same as recommended for the peach. The Japanese varieties bear fruit laterally on one-year wood similar to the peach; they also bear laterally and heavily on spurs. Judicious pruning of these varieties will reduce materially the subsequent expense and need for hand thinning of the fruit. Japanese trees growing on the more shallow soils may require somewhat heavier cutting in order to reduce the size of the crop, but increase the individual size of the fruits. The varieties in California which tend to set a particularly heavy crop, and should be pruned somewhat heavier are Beauty, Nubiana and Wickson. Moderate pruning is required for Formosa, Queen Ann, Duarte, Gaviota, Eldorado, and Kelsey. On upright-growing varieties, it is important to thin the branches and the center top of the tree sufficiently to admit sunlight to the center and induce more vigorous spur growth and better coloring of the fruit in this area.

In pruning both the young and mature trees, it is important to prune as little as possible to attain the desired results. Heavy pruning in any case should be avoided.

Figure 5. A Stanley prune tree trained to the central leader system with central trunk larger than any lateral branch. The five or six strong lateral branches have wide-angled crotches and are well spaced. European plums tend to form good framework naturally.

Figure 6. The effect of thinning a heavy crop of Lombard plums on size of fruit in Michigan. (Bottom left) Twelve fruits from an unthinned tree. (Bottom right) Twelve fruits from a thinned tree. The effect of this thinning carried over to the following year in spite of crop failure the second year due to adverse weather. Note (top left) corresponding shoot from the tree which was unthinned the previous year, and (top right) shoot from the tree thinned the previous year.

THINNING THE FRUIT

Thinning for fresh market is a must. Good fruit size is paramount for good price. Hand thinning is delayed until after the so-called June drop. With plums, thinning not only increases the size and uniformity in color of fruit, but also reduces or prevents breakage of the tree, maintains good vigor (Figure 6), reduces insect injury, reduces spread of brown rot just prior to harvest, and decreases the labor required for handling the crop during and after harvest. Prunes are sold by count per pound. Although large fruits are worth more, all fruit is saleable.

At present, there are no chemical fruit thinners for prunes and plums. Summer lopping of over-cropped limbs can reduce limb breakage, but does little for fruit sizing and cropping. This crop is well adapted to mechanical trunk shaking. Clusters of fruit will be left on the tree, but average fruit size can be greatly enhanced. Note in the following table how fruit size and tonnage can be affected by mechanical shaking.

TABLE 2. TYPICAL RESULTS OBTAINED FROM MECHANICAL THINNING OF PRUNES. (AFTER L.B. FITCH, UNIV. OF CA. DAVIS 95616)

Orchard	Tons/A	Count/Lb	Dry Away
A None	3.4	100	3.26
(Mech. Thin)	2.7	78	3.04
B None	2.9	91	3.64
(Mech. Thin)	2.2	69	3.25
C None	5.7	104	3.64
(Mech. Thin)	4.5	87	3.26

Thus, if at least a third of the tree's fruit is removed, a 20 fruit/lb decrease can be had, resulting in an increase in fruit size and also a decrease in dry away. All trunk shakers appear to be satisfactory. Using heavier harvest weights on most shakers, only a light short shake seems satisfactory. Use a good shaker arm and clasp carefully to avoid bark damage.

Mechanical thinning should be done just before *full pit hardening* occurs. This can be determined by periodic sampling of pits. Heavily cropping trees will have 12,000+ fruit/tree. There will be some natural fruit dropping after the shaking and this must be taken into account. It may amount to 30 to 40 percent. With experience, the grower can judge the amount of fruit desired on a tree at harvest and leave on the tree at shaking enough to take care of the drop after shaking. Always bear in mind that annual dormant pruning also affects the amount of thinning needed.

In order to secure large uniform well-colored fruit, plums usually require a thinning of from one to three inches apart when mature, with the heavier thinning being recommended for the Japanese varieties. Burbank tends to set very heavy crops and requires relatively heavy thinning. Beauty probably demands the heaviest thinning of any. Santa Rosa and Climax tend to thin themselves as the fruit develops, and fruit thinning where necessary is usually light. In sections of the country where strong winds are likely to occur while the crop is maturing, the thinning need may be much lighter than otherwise.

SOIL MANAGEMENT

The same soil management systems as outlined for the young and bearing peach trees in the previous chapter will apply for the young and bearing plum trees. However,

Figure 7. Cultivated plum trees in New York on medium-heavy soil showed little or no response to applications of sodium nitrate. Trees in sod, however, which received 900, 900, and 1800 pounds per acre of sodium nitrate in successive years showed response to nitrogen but averaged only two-thirds as large as those on the cultivated plots. (Far left) cultivated; (middle left) cultivated with nitrate of soda; (middle right) timothy-rye sod with nitrate of soda; and (far right) timothy-rye sod without nitrogen fertilization. (Cornell University, Ithaca, N.Y.)

plum trees tend to perform somewhat better under sod or sod mulch than the peach. They withstand neglect and, thus, do well in home grounds. The future commercial management system likely will be herbicides in the row, sod middles of fescue, and irrigation when needed. Weeds around the trunks may prolong wetness and encourage trunk diseases.

Fertilization. Plum trees planted on the heavier types of soil, in general, do not show the response to fertilizer applications that most deciduous trees exhibit. Where cultivation or herbicides in the row are used, the need for nitrogen is reduced, as indicated in Figure 7. Plum trees growing in sod without nitrogen fertilization definitely are dwarfed as compared with those in sod receiving nitrogen. Plum trees will respond well to a system of sod-mulch plus additional mulch, although there may be increased difficulty from curculio with this system in eastern orchards.

Leaf analysis is being used to determine fertilizer needs, particularly where a nutritional problem exists. Approximate nutrient contents of leaves by standard analysis are: N, 1.80-2.10; P, 0.14-0.25; K, 1.50-2.50; Mg, 0.18; Ca, 2.00-4.00; S, 125-175 ppm; Mn, 53-93 ppm; B, 33-50 ppm; Zn, 25-50 ppm; Cu, 7-10 ppm; Fe, 50-100 ppm; Mo, 0.7-1.0 ppm. Ammonium sulfate, nitrate of soda (not in arid regions), ammonium nitrate, or potassium nitrate should give good response. In California the usual rate of application is from one to two pounds of ammonium sulfate for trees two to five years of age and from four to six pounds for bearing trees. The fertilizer is spread evenly over the ground surface under the branches and during the

dormant season. Trees in a sod system may require double or triple the N for cultivated or herbicide-treated plantings. A 10-10-10 mix frequently is used in humid areas, liming to pH 6.0-6.5.

Under arid conditions of California, suggestions are that the nitrate or urea form of nitrogen be applied in early fall and irrigated in for early use by bloom the next spring. If trees are weak, apply 2/3rds N supply in early fall and the balance the following spring before growth starts.

Boron deficiency in California causes dry hard pockets in the fruit flesh and may be corrected by a half-pound application of borax about every third year to a mature tree. Avoid areas where B is high in the soil and irrigation water. Be aware of excess chlorine, sodium.

The work of Abdalla and Childers has shown that very low calcium under controlled conditions reduces yield and increases culls but no cracking of fruit in Italian prune was noted. The effect of low calcium was less harmful to prune than to peach.

Copper deficiency in South Africa has been described to cause interveinal chlorosis or complete yellowing of young leaves and necrotic spotting between veins of old leaves. Soil applications of 1-2 pounds copper sulphate per tree may correct the trouble in one to two years. "Little leaf" or zinc deficiency is prevalent in some sections of the world and is corrected by dormant sprays of zinc sulphate (36 per cent) before the buds break in spring, using 10 to 18 pounds per 100 gallons, depending upon severity of deficiency. Annual applications may be necessary. Potassium and magnesium deficiencies have been reported

Figure 7a. While plum trees are more tolerant of wet soils than most fruit trees, shown here in California is a row on the left planted in soil that has been "ripped" to a 5 ft. depth before planting; on the right, neighboring row not "ripped". Growth is shown after a wet spring. Sub-soiling to 2-3 ft. often makes a noticeable difference in growth due to better aeration, water storage and root growth. (W.E. Wildman, Univ. of Calif., Davis)

both in humid and arid regions. Potassium shortage in arid areas (Figure 8) may necessitate heavy applications of 25-50 lbs/tree sulphate of potash every three years, plus heavy pruning and thinning to secure good growth.

Weed Control. None of the herbicides likely will control all the weeds but each is designed to control a group or singles. The herbicide program must be designed for each orchard depending upon soil type, tree age, and the type weeds at hand. Apply with extreme care not to overdose for a bad case of herbicide damage is difficult to correct. Herbicides being used are Dalapon, Casoron, Bueno 6, Devrinol, Solicam, Surflan, Goal, Paraquat, Treflan, Dinoseb and weed oil.

Irrigation. Irrigation is practiced only rarely in the East

or in several areas along the west coast of California. In the largest plum producing sections of the West, however, irrigation is a necessary practice. It may be done by furrows, portable pipe, or basin flooding. Application of water by the furrow system in California varies from a 24-hour application every 12 to 14 days in some sections to a 72-hour application only two or three times a season in other regions, depending upon soil type and topography. Sprinkler irrigation is in wide use in arid and humid regions; it serves also in frost control. But drip irrigation is being used increasingly for several reasons (Figure 9). Total water applied in the entire season varies from 15 to 36 acre inches. On the sloping Sierra foothills sprinklers with sod culture are used to cut erosion. A 5/32-9/64-inch nozzle is best on clay loams and a 1/8-7/64-inch nozzle on heavy clay loams to avoid compaction and get better penetration. Actually, strip-row herbicides sod middles is good management where heavy orchard machinery is used on level land. Irrigation costs in California for flood, hand-moved sprinkler, furrow and drip, respectfully, in the early 1980s were: investment per acre — $425, 510, 500, 800; overhead — $44,66,51,114; operating costs — $87, 122, 152, 85; and total costs: $131, 188, 203, and 200. Drip irrigation may use 1/2 ft. less water/per yr than flood or furrow irrigation. See U. Ca. Leaflet 2875.

The soil about the tree roots should be kept moist and this can be determined by using a soil auger at weekly intervals during periods of drought. Trees should never be allowed to show signs of foliar wilting before irrigating.

Fruit Cracking. End cracks on fruit are due to early tree moisture stress followed by an irrigation. Side cracks appear to be caused by direct sunlight on fruit and changes in moisture content within and on the skin (dew). These

Figure 8. Potassium deficiency is shown on Agen prune in the Sacramento Valley of California in the Northern Interior section. Note poor foliar development, scorching and dieback in the top. For review of plum nutrition (by Nels Benson et al.), see "Fruit Nutrition" book by Childers (Ed.) (Courtesy American Potash Institute, San Jose, Ca.)

Figure 9. Grower experience in California with drip irrigation on plums and prunes increased production of quality fruit, cut tractor costs by 80%, fewer weeds vs rill type (arid area), apply N through system, gain tax benefit for conversion to drip, can get quicker and better fruit sizing before harvest, and generally easier care. Installation must be properly planned, installed with dependable emitters and good filtration. (Blue Anchor, Sacramento, Ca.)

cracks could be due to a mineral supply problem such as boron or calcium but this has not been reported from research.

RESISTANCE TO FROST
WINTER'S INJURY

The average variety of European plum is about as resistant to cold as the Winesap or Baldwin apple. Lombard trees may be a little more resistant. Resistance to cold of flower buds varies considerably, with some less and others more resistant than apple flower buds.

Trees of the Japanese cultivars may vary in cold resistance from the Kelsey, which is less resistant than peach trees, to Burbank, Abundance, Ozark Premier and First which may be almost as resistant as European plums. Under good care, the flower buds of Japanese cultivars are about as resistant as European plums. However, if the trees are in poor condition, the buds may be more tender than peach buds. Most flowers of Japanese plums are somewhat more resistant to cold than apple flowers and the young fruits appear to be at least as resistant as apple fruits of the same age. However, with Japanese varieties, the flower buds tend to open much earlier than apple flowers and are, therefore, more likely to be killed by the late spring frosts.

After relatively warm winters in California, some varieties of European plums, such as President, may be very slow to begin growth and many flower buds may be abscissed. On the other hand, trees of some varieties, such as Tragedy, may not be delayed to any extent. Chilling requirements of the Japanese plums, except for Climax, are considerably less than that for most varieties of European plums. After warm winters when President shows considerable injury, trees of Japanese varieties also may be delayed in starting, but, except for Climax, not enough to prevent their making good growth and setting a fair crop of fruit.

Prunus nigra, the Candada plum, is one of the most hardy to winter cold of the deciduous fruits grown in North America.

DISEASES, INSECTS, PESTS

Diseases include: *Armillaria* and crown rot; *Phytophthora* crown and root rot; brownline (at graft); bacterial, *Cytospera* and *Ceratocystis* cankers; brown rot, russet scab, prune rust, post-harvest *Rhizopus, Aspergillus* and *Penicillum* diseases. Insects include: Mealy aphid, San Jose scale, mites, twig borer, bud moth, codling moth, leaf rollers, caterpillars, webworm, other wood borers; pin, ring, root lesion, and daggar nematodes. See Ramos for descriptions (color), controls.

HARVESTING

The stage of maturity at which plums should be picked depends upon how they are to be utilized. For local trade, roadside markets, and for canning, it is best to pick plums when they are well colored and firm-ripe. For jams and jellies the fruit should be fully ripe when picked. For long-distance shipping, plums must be hard and the early

TABLE 1. BUD KILL OF ITALIAN AND EARLY ITALIAN PRUNES AS RELATED TO TEMPERATURES AND BUDS (E.L. PROEBSTING, JR., WASH. STATE EXP. STA., PROSSER).

Bud Development Stage	First Swelling	Side White	Tip Green	Tight Cluster	First White	First Bloom	Full Bloom	Post Bloom
Old Standard Temp.	—	—	—	—	23	27	27	30
Ave. Temp. 10% Kill	14	17	20	24	26	27	28	28
Ave. Temp. 90% Kill	0	3	7	16	22	23	23	23
Averge Date (Prosser)	3/13	3/20	3/27	4/3	4/8	4/12	4/16	4/23

Obtain color bud development chart from Wash. State Exp. Sta., Prosser.

252

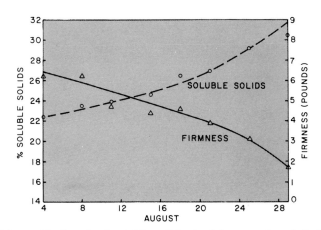

Figure 10. Trend of soluble solids (mainly sugars) and flesh firmness of 'French' prune during maturation. These data were taken on a tree moderately loaded with fruit. Fruit should be picked around 3-4 lbs firmness and no later than 2 lbs, depending upon intended use. (M.W. Miller, University of California, Davis)

varieties should be only partially colored. They should arrive at wholesale buyers or jobbers before fully ripe, and thence, at retailers' stands in good, firm-ripe attractive condition. Temperature at which the fruit is handled is the most important factor governing rate of ripening.

Most varieties of plums undergo rather marked changes in color within a period of about ten days to several weeks before becoming fully mature. Although these changes are gradual, they may be divided into several more or less distinct stages. With the Japanese varieties, the earliest stage occurs when the green of the stilar-tip changes to a lightish or yellowish green; this stage is often spoken of as "breaking." With most varieties, this yellowish green changes to a more decided yellow or straw yellow, after which the plums gradually assume their characteristic yellow or red. Commercially, the fruits are described as

"straw tip," "slight color," "red tip," "three-fourths red," etc. With the blue or purple varieties, the color changes proceed from green, to greenish-blue, or reddish-purple, followed by dark blue or purple.

Color changes are especially noticeable and, therefore, have been considered one of the main indices for maturity. As the color increases, there is normally a softening of the flesh. The firmness of the fruit when picked (Figure 10) is the best correlation with the way the fruit will hold up in transit. In California, a combination color-and-firmness-of-flesh standard has been suggested for a few of the leading plum varieties, as shown in Table 3.

The above table shows that plums can be picked somewhat more mature if they are to be shipped under precooled conditions. If the fruit will be shipped under standard refrigeration, it is best to place the more mature fruit at the base of the carrier where the temperature is 8° to 10° F cooler. The later maturing firm-fleshed European cultivars may be allowed to become more mature than the earlier more juicy thin-skinned cultivars. Canning factories usually specify that the fruit for canning must be firm-ripe and with maximum sugar content, standards required so specified.

Two to three pickings are usually needed. Fruit should be picked slightly firmer as season advances.

Ethephon at 50-100 ppm 4 and 6 wks before harvest on El Dorado and Queen Rosa hastened skin color and softening but not soluble solids or blush intensity. Post harvest ripening was similar for treated and untreated lots. J.T. Yeager, Univ. of Calif., reports that Alar at 2-4 lbs/A applied 2-4 wks before harvest (timing not critical) advanced harvest by 4-7 days. Thus, a part of the orchard could be sprayed to spread harvesting. He suggested beginning harvest at 5 lbs pressure with 2-3 lbs being ideal, and not letting the pressure fall below 2 lbs, depending upon the type sale anticipated.

TABLE 3. PICKING CONDITIONS FOR PLUMS (DOES NOT APPLY TO PRUNES), BASED UPON TEMPERATURES IN TRANSIT IN THE UPPER HALF OF REFRIGERATED CARRIERS (ADAPTED FROM ALLEN, UNIV. OF CA., DAVIS)

	WHEN SHIPPED STANDARD		WHEN PRECOOLED AND SHIPPED	
VARIETY	COLOR RANGE	FIRMNESS TEST[1] RANGE (POUNDS)	COLOR RANGE	FIRMNESS TEST[1] RANGE (POUNDS)
Beauty . .	Straw tip to trace pink tip	13— 9	Pink tip to ½ red	8— 6
Formosa	Straw tip to trace pink tip	13— 9	Pink tip to ½ red	8— 6
Climax . .	Straw tip to pink tip	18—13	¼ to ½ red	12— 8
Santa Rosa	Trace red to ½ light red	18—12	½ to full light red	12— 9
Burbank .	Straw tip to full straw slight red	20—14	Yellow to ¼ red	13— 8
Wickson .	Straw tip to yellow tip	15—12	½ to ⅔ yellow	11— 8
Duarte . .	⅓ to ¾ light red	15—11	Full light to medium red	10— 8
Diamond	Trace to ¾ light blue	10—15	Full light to medium blue	14—10
Giant . . .	¼ to ¾ light red	16—11	Full light red	10— 8
President	½ to full light blue	16—11	Full blue	10— 7

[1]The figures given in this column refer to the number of pounds pressure required to force the plunger point of a fruit firmness tester 7/16-inch in diameter into the flesh of the fruit 5/16-inch in depth. The pressure tester is described in U.S. Dept. of Agr. Circ. 627, "Fruit pressure testers and their practical applications" by M.H. Haller. 1941.

Figure 11. (Upper Left). Two parallel individually operated catching frames, one with a trunk shaker, are run along the tree row, "hitched," and the tree shaken as above in California's Sacramento Valley area. Prunes, largely French for drying, are conveyed to carrier behind (upper right). Bins carry the fruit to washer, grader, sugar testing, hot water dip, prickle-board, thence dried on trays in ovens at a temperature up to 615° F (lower right), or sun-dried for 3 to 5 days.

Yields. In Eastern orchards, a mature plum orchard may yield between three and five tons per acre or one to one and a half bushels to a tree. Prune trees yield somewhat more than plum trees, or two or three bushels per tree. Japanese varieties bear at from three to five years of age, while the Domestica varieties bear about two years later. Native American plums require a somewhat longer period to come into bearing.

The trees tend to come into bearing earlier on the Pacific coast and yield much larger crops. The average yield per acre in California runs six to 10 tons per acre. High density orchards may reach 16 or more tons.

Picking and handling methods. Special precautions should be taken to remove shipping plums with stems intact and to avoid breaking the skin. Due to the perishable nature of plums, they must be handled with extreme care. In filling the picking receptacle and sizing, grading, and packing, it is important to preserve as much of the bloom on the skin surface as possible. Keep the fruit in the shade of the trees immediately after picking. Handle the fruit from tree to storage with little or no delay. Plums may be transported from the orchard to the packing shed in either picking baskets or in pails, boxes or bins; the fruit has received less handling when picking baskets or pails are used.

Picking for distant shipment should be done early in the day and the fruit taken immediately to the packing shed, or, picking can be done in late afternoon and the fruit left in the orchard to cool overnight. If the plums are to be used in canning, they are handled mostly in lug boxes or bins with somewhat less care.

For prunes several weeks are required for harvest in the coastal areas of California, where fruit matures slowly with ripe fruit dropping while immature fruit is still on the tree. Objective in a dried prune is to obtain a glossy, dark reddish-black skin that is sweet, with an amber-colored flesh that is free of gas pockets (Fig. 10). Mechanical devices have been developed for harvesting prunes and plums (Fig. 11).

In interior valleys, harvest is a once-over operation, and begins about a week after sampling shows that chlorophyll has disappeared from the flesh and skin and under most conditions should permit completion of harvest before the flesh color has darkened seriously, exclusive of periods of heat above 100° F. (Claypool and Kilbuck).

Flesh firmness at 3 to 5 pounds may be an aid to color index as to when to start harvest, but the soluble solids is a better index. When the crop is of normal size or less, harvest may start when soluble solids attain 24 per cent. If the crop is heavy, soluble solids may not reach 20 per cent while the fruit is turgid, and thus the soluble solids index is of little value, according to Claypool and Kilbuck.

Where dehydrating, rather than sun-drying is used, the natural toughness of the skin, particularly in French prunes, is a problem. Investigations are under way to determine the cause of toughness and how to correct it.

About 2½ to 3 pounds of fresh prunes are required to give one pound of dried fruit; sugar content is probably the most important factor affecting the drying ratio. Machine-pitted dried prunes store better with improved quality.

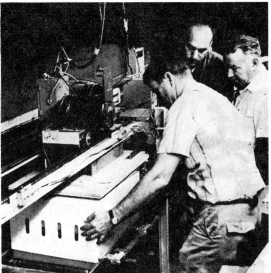

Figure 12. (Left). Partial view of Santa Rosa plums in a vibrated "tight-fill" fiberboard container as they arrived in New York City from California. Injury was equal to or less than hand or conventionally packed fruit. Note bloom intact. (Right) Fruit was settled into permanent position by vibrating machine as used for pears, before shipment. Most plums are mechanically packed.

PACKING[1]

Although some of the large growers in California individually pack their own fruit, there is a strong tendency toward community packing. Plum sizing is done mechanically by weight or by size (minimum dimension). The fruit is sorted into one or two grades by maturity, color, and blemishes according to the requirements of the U.S. Standards or the particular state standards. These qualifications usually are established by the growers themselves in order to protect and maintain a standard and quality of fruits from a given state or region. Some growers and packing concerns have been exceeding the minimum requirements of the standard law by issuing an extra fancy grade. Returns from this higher grade usually have been justified, especially during heavy crop years.

Containers. In the East, plums are often sold locally in Climax baskets of the two to twelve-quart size. One-half bushel tub baskets also are used. Small plums may be shipped in berry crates.

Plums shipped from California are packed in four-basket crates, fiber-board cartons, or peach boxes for larger sizes. The standard four-basket crates are from four to five inches deep with two or three layers, depending upon the size of the fruit; the count may range from 112 to 340 fruits per crate. This crate holds four three-quart till baskets and is 16 inches wide and 16 1/8 inches long. Each basket may be sold as a separate unit in the retail trade. Peach boxes as described in Chapter XIV also are used with the standard packs.

Fiberboard containers are the standard shipping container because they are less expensive, require less packing labor, and afford savings in loading and costs of rail shipments. One popular type is a two-piece full telescope box with roll ends which fold into place (Figure 11). Two-layer lugs and loose-fill cartons are popular.

Changes in packing equipment are needed for the random-fill fiber-board containers, machine vibrated and settled before shipment (Figure 12.) Costs are reduced appreciably. The "tight-fill" packs require careful grading, sizing, weighing, top padding, and lid fastening under some pressure. This packaging is increasing in popularity.

A cooling experiment by the California Experiment Station with 25-lb. fiberboard boxes of plums showed that the rate of cooling was speeded up by use of a 3 cu. ft. per minute cold air blast. The fiberboard boxes with open hand holes required about one-third longer to cool than the standard 4-basket crate or field lug; if poly liners were used in the fiberboard boxes, two and one-half times longer to cool was required. Fruit in the center of the box took the longest to cool.

Corrugated and fiberboard containers vary too much in size and content. Attempts are being made to meet the needs of handling for shipment, export and store movement with as few standardized containers as feasible for all fresh fruits (Fig. 13).

Each container is marked on the outside with the name and address of the orchard, the packer, the variety, net weight, and approximate number of fruits (within four of the true count in California) in the container or the subcontainer.

Transporting. In transporting plums from the packing house to the shipping point, place each box squarely on top of the box below. The boxes should be stacked firmly so that there will be no possibility of shifting. A light canvas over the top of the load will protect the fruit from sun and dust. Hauling by truck to local markets is done largely during the cool night hours.

---

[1]A bushel of plums weighs about 56 lbs. net. The August Herbort Machine Factory, Braunschweig, W. Germany, builds a plum pitter.

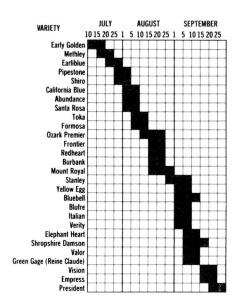
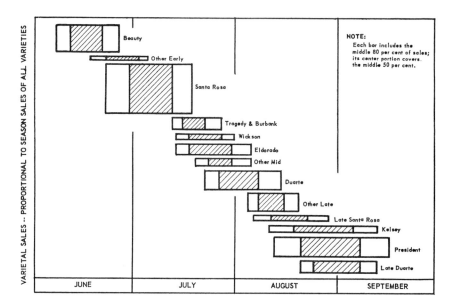

Figure 13. (Left) Average picking dates for plums in southwestern Michigan which should give a relative idea elsewhere (Hilltop Nursery, Hartford, Mi.). (Right) Varietal plum marketing periods on the New York market for California plums. Bar includes 80% of sales with cross-hatched area covering mid 50% of sales. Leading cultivars shipped in early 1980s were Santa Rosa, Casselman, Lorado, Red Beaut and Late Santa Rosa (Univ. of Calif., Davis).

STORAGE

Fruit of most varieties of Domestica plums can be held from two to four weeks at 30° F. during floods on the market. At higher temperatures of 37° to 50° F., which is usually the temperature range in a refrigerator car, plums will not keep so long. Fruit of certain varieties, such as Tragedy, Grand Duke, and President, will keep for nine weeks if they are harvested when full-grown and somewhat sweet, and held at a temperature of 30° to 32° F. If harvested greener, they may show various injuries at these temperatures; better flavor is obtained if plums are held at the higher temperatures of 37° to 50° F. Plums in storage and/or shipment may show jellying and/or internal browning which are slowed at 33°-34° F. Idaho research shows *internal browning* on the standard Italian prune to be reduced by fewer irrigations, avoiding any compression of the fruit, using sprays of GA (gibberellic acid), and with high N and high light intensity (latter controls skin color, as does storage temperatures — 33-38° F no increases; 43-49° F, increases).

Natural modification of storage atmosphere by use of sealed 1.5 ml poly box liners by USDA in California has provided a favorable environment for Nubiana plums at 32-34° F. The enclosed atmosphere of an average of 7.8% CO_2 and 11% O_2 reduced fruit decay, softening and loss of soluble solids up to 10 weeks. The longer the storage period, the greater the beneficial effects. Eldorado plums respond similarly but Santa Rosa was injured, indicating need for tests with each variety.

SHIPPING PLUMS

Most West Coast plums have been shipped to the East. With increased population on the West Coast, it appears that relatively more will be sold fresh on local markets early in the season before other fruits become plentiful.

Precooling of fruit to 40° F. before loading the rail car is highly desirable. By this system, it requires from 20 to 24 hrs. Fruit is precooled in a special room or cold storage before loaded in refrigerator cars. If precooling is to be most efficient, fruit temperatures in the center of the packages should be reduced to 40° F. or below.

Many refrigerator cars are equipped with blower fans under the floor-boards of the bunkers. These fans can be driven for precooling by motors attached outside the car, or they can be operated while the car is in motion by a friction wheel against the car wheel. Precooling is now generally used in California.

In California shipping plums must meet the requirements for U.S. No. 1 Grade to be eligible for inter- or intra-state shipment. In addition, a minimum size standard is applied to each variety, varying in accordance with the normal sizing ability of the variety. For example, an eight-pound sample of Santa Rosa plums must number no more than 69 fruits, which is roughly equivalent to a 4x5 standard four-basket crate pack.

MARKETING

Plums grown in the East are sold mostly to local markets

256

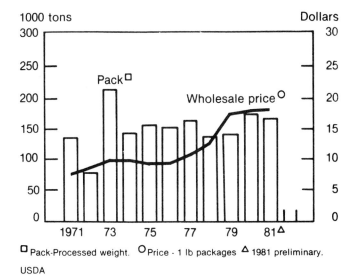

1000 tons   Dollars

☐ Pack-Processed weight.   ○ Price - 1 lb packages   △ 1981 preliminary.

USDA

Figure 14. Production and wholesale price of United States dried prunes.

or on roadside stands, for fresh consumption or for canning. Appearance of small baskets of fresh plums can be improved on the counter by mixing plum varieties of different color and/or by mixing plums with peaches, grapes, and perhaps other currently ripening fruits.

In the West, plums are sold through shipping agencies which deal with brokers, or which have their special representatives in the East. The fruit may be sold to an individual at a private sale, or it may go to public auction; this is usually determined by the sales manager of the shipping agency. Although plums are a perishable fruit, they are being shipped to all parts of the United States and some are being exported. West Europe may buy 80-90% of the California crop with Japan showing promise of taking increasing tonnage. Popular shipping plums have been Santa Rosa, Casselman, Lorado, Red Beaut and Late Santa Rosa.

Frozen prunes are a product with steady demand. Washington, Michigan and Oregon freeze several hundred tons a year. Both dried and fresh prune juices, nectars, and purees for babies are available, alone or combined with other fruit juices in punches, affording a broadening outlet for this fruit.

One of the major problems in normal times with marketing of plums is to move the large quantities of fruit from the West at prices satisfactory to the growers and shippers. This situation is being met by advertising campaigns put on by the marketing agencies, by improved packaging to get Mrs. Housewife's eye, and by sending special representatives to the Eastern markets to encourage and maintain good will. Efforts also are being made to distribute California plums, for example, to the smaller cities and towns throughout the United States. In this selling program, the grower himself must realize that small

fruits of miscellaneous varieties and of inferior quality will bring a price but not a profit. Informational signs on the sales counter help to move this less-known fruit, such as "Plump juicy Duarte plums — fine for school lunch, — cents/lb." (Fig. 14).

One of the cleverest and most effective advertising "breaks" on U.S. radio stations was on the value of the high iron content, and other health values of prunes, backed by the Federal Plum Commodity Committee of Sacramento, California. The California Fresh Plum Promotion Advisory Board, Belmont Ave., Fresno 93701, has had skilled merchandising agents travelling throughout the country during season, helping stores to use, display and promote plums. Streamers, banners and charts tell about each cultivar so buyers will shop by cultivar for repeat sales.

The California Prune Board (from 1952) promotes market research, advertising, better production techniques for better market quality.

Cost of Production. Costs of production are changing. Write to the university fruit extension services of Idaho, California, Oregon, Michigan or Washington, possibly Cornell for latest costs. Kelsey, (see reference) for 1979

Figure 15. Fiberboard boxes for shipment of plums have an indented pad in the bottom into which plums fit to help position the plums. Upper: The face tray has been removed to show orderly fill. Note cutdown sides which give the box a full appearance after shipment shakedown of plums. (USDA)

257

reported costs in Michigan for 10 acres of plums at: labor - $1129; Machinery - $584; Materials - $1488; total $3200.

Specifications for maturity standards, packaging and other shipping details can be obtained from the shipping agency or Federal or state marketing offices.

Review Questions

1. State briefly where plums are commercially grown in the United States, and for home consumption and local trade. List key world countries.
2. Name and differentiate briefly the different groups and subgroups of plums.
3. What is the difference between a plum and a prune?
4. List leading plum cultivars in your general area, stating to which group each cultivar belongs.
5. What governs the choice of cultivars of plums in California; in New York?
6. What is the most common rootstock for plum trees? What other stocks are used for plums in California? Why? Name a dwarfing stock?
7. Can European cultivars of plums be top-worked successfully on Japanese stocks? Why would such grafts be desired?
8. Differentiate between the pruning received by Japanese and European type plums.
9. Describe the precautions in training the Wickson cultivar.
10. At what time and at what distances are Japanese and European plum fruits thinned? Discuss fruit thinning by hand, by chemicals and by mechanical, trunk shaking.
11. What is a good system of soil management for young plum trees growing on a 10 per cent slope in medium heavy soil in your state?
12. Where and when is irrigation practical with plum trees?
13. At what stage of maturity should plums be harvested for long distance shipping, for roadside markets, for drying, and for canning?
14. Discuss mechanical harvesting — machinery, maturity desired, techniques.
15. What types of containers are popular for shipping plums? Discuss the merits of fiberboard containers: vibrating and cooling before shipment.
16. Discuss storage conditions required by plums, dependent upon cultivar and ultimate use. How about CA storage of plums?
17. Discuss briefly how plums are shipped from California to the eastern market?

Suggested Collateral Readings

ABDALLA, D. and N.F. CHILDERS. Effect of controlled Calcium levels on peach and prune. J. ASHS. 98(5):517-22. 1973.

ALDERMAN, W.H. and T.S. WEIR. Pollination studies with stone fruits. Univ. of Minn. Tech. Bull. 198. 16 pp. 1951.

ALDRICH, T.M., *et al.* Prune orchards — soil management, irrigation, fertilization. Univ. of Calif. Leaflet 21016. 18 pp. 1978.

BAILEY, JOHN S. The beach plum in Massachussetts. Mass. Agr. Exp. Sta. Bull. 422. 16 pp. 1944.

BARK-SPLIT — A virus disease of plums. Ann. Applied Bot. 45:No. 4. 573-579. December, 1957.

BENSON, N., R.C. LINDNER, and R.M. BULLOCK. Plum, prune and apricot nutrition. In Childers, N.F. Fruit Nutrition, Chap. XIV. Horticultural Publications, 3906 NW 31 Pl., Gainesville, Fla. 32606.

BOWEN, H.H. 'Morris' plum (Texas). HortSci. 14(6):760-761. Dec. 1979.

BRAINERD, K.E., *et al.* Anatomy, water stress of cultured 'Pixy' plum. HortSci. 16(2):173-175. 1981.

BREEN, P.J. and T. MURAOKA. Effect of indolebutyric acid on distribution of ^{14}C-photosynthate in softwood cuttings of 'Marianna 2542' plum. J. ASHS 98(5):436. Sept. 1973.

BRIERLEY, W.G. and J.S. McCARTNEY. Cold resistance of European plums. Proc. A.S.H.S. 55, 254. 1950.

CALIFORNIA AGRICULTURE. This montly resume of experimental research at the California Agricultural Experiment Stations frequently contains items on plums and prunes. The following subjects can be found in the respective months: Nematode resistance in plums, October, 1957; Mechanical fruit tree shaking. October, 1958; Time study of plum packing, May 1955; Quality of dried French prunes, August 1955; Improving prune dehydration, May 1952; Cooling fruit (plums and pears) in fiberboard, Feburary 1955; Prune harvest methods, costs, July 1955: Prune harvesting cost methods, July 1958; Boron requirements of prunes; August 1958; Fertilizer trials with plums. Febuary 1958: Factors in prune skin texture, November 1958; Quality of dried French prunes, August 1955; Parallel-flow prune dehydration, Aug. 1965; Fresh-pitted dried prunes, Apr. 1963. Controlling *Cytospera* in plum. Dec. 1974. G.M. Leavitt, *et al.* Ethephon hastens Jap. plum ripening. Cal. Ag. June 1977; J.J. Mehlschau, *et al.* Mechanical harvester for fresh mkt. plums. Cal. Ag. March 1977; Plum machine fruit thinning cost. April 1972. Correct Fe deficiency in plum by trunk injections. Mar-Apr. 1982; Soil Moisture on plum fruit size, Jan. 1975; Growth regulators and prune maturity, Dec. 1973; Japan plum market. Sept.-Oct. 1982.

CALLAN, N.W., *et al.* Fruit set 'Italian' prune following fall foliar, spring B sprays. J. ASHS. 103(2): 253-257. 1978.

CHAPLIN, M.H., *et al.* Fall-applied boron sprays on fruit set, yield of 'Italian' prune. J. ASHS. 97(5):500-501. 1977.

CHAPLIN, M.H., *et al.* Rootstock on leaf element content of 'Italian' prune. J. ASHS. 97(5):641-644. 1972.

CHAPLIN, M.H., M.N. WESTWOOD, and A.N. ROBERTS. Effects of rootstock on leaf element content of 'Italian' prune (Prunus domestica L.). J. ASHS 97(5): 641. 1972.

CLAYPOOL, L.L. *et al.* Physical and chemical changes in French prunes during maturiation in coastal valleys and the influence of harvesting procedures and storage on the quality of dried French prunes from coastal regions. Hilgardia 33:8, 311-348. 1962.

CLAYPOOL, L.L. and J. KILBUCK. The influence of maturity of Interior Valley French prunes on the yield and quality of the dried product. Proc. Amer. Soc. Hort. Sci. 68: 77-85. 1956.

COUEY, H.M. Modified atmosphere storage of Nubiana plums. Proceedings ASHS. Vol. 86, 1965. On Eldorado plums. ASHS 75:207-15, 1960.

DECKER, PHARES. Plums and rust (*Tranzschelia Pruni-Spinosae* (Pers.) Diet.) in Florida. Proc. Fla. State Hort. Soc. 89:254-255. 1976.

deGOEDE, C. Australian dried prune industry. USDA-FAS-M-97. 12 pp. 1960.

DOMOTO, P.A., and A.A. HERWITT. Ethephon increases endogenous auxins in seeds of *Prunus salicina* L. HortScience 8(6):503. Dec. 1973.

ELMORE, C.L., *et al.* Annual weed control in young prunes. HortSci. Vol. 5. No. 4. pp. 263. Aug. 1970.

EVANS, S., *et al.* Potassium Deficiency on Water Relations of French Prune. J. ASHS. 101(5):648-650, 1977.

EVEN-CHEN, Z. *et al.* High temperature on prune leaves. ASHS 106(2):216-19. Mar. 1981.

GRIGGS, W.H. and C.O. HESSE. Pollination requirements of Japanese plums. Calif. Leaflet 163.9 pp. 1963.

HANSCHE, P.E., C.O. HESSE, and V. BERES. Inheritance in *Prunus domestica* cv. Agen. J. ASHS. 100:522. 1975.

HANSEN, P. and K. RYUGO. Translocation and metabolism of carbohydrate fraction of ^{14}C-photosynthates in 'French' prune, J. ASHS 104(5):622-5. 1979.

HENDRICKSON, A.H. and F.J. VEIHMEYER. Irrigation experiments with prunes. Calif. Agr. Exp. Sta. Bull. 573. 1934.

HESSE, C.O. 'Durado', Fresh Market Plum. Calif. Agric. 12-13, Apr. 1976.

HUMMEL, R. Hardy No. Amer. *Prunus* cultivars. Fruit var. Jour. 31(3):62-68, 1977.

JANICK, J. (ED) Plum breeding by J.H. Weinberger. Advances in Fruit Breeding. 12 pp. Purdue Univ. Press, Lafayette, Ind. 1975.

KELSEY, M. and A. JOHNSON. Plum production costs in Michigan. Ext. Bull. F-1116. 1979.

KWONG, S.S. Nitrogen and potassium fertilization effects on yield, fruit quality, and leaf composition of 'Stanley' prunes. J. ASHS 98(1):72, 1973.

LaRUE, J.H. *et al.* Commercial plum growing in California. Univ. of Calif. leaflet 2458. 22 p. 1983.

LEE, F.A., *et al.* New York State dried prunes. N.Y. State Agr. Exp. Sta., Cornell Univ., Geneva. Cir. II, July 1968.

LEECE, D.R. and J.F. DIROU. Comparison of urea sprays containing hydrocarbon or silicone surfactants with soil-applied N and leaf N of prune trees. J. ASHS 104(5): 644-8. 1979.

LIN, C.F. and A.A. BOE. Effects of some endogenous and exogenous growth regulators on plum seed dormancy. J.ASHS. Vol. 97, No. 1, p. 41. Jan. 1972.

LYON, T.L., A.J. HEINICKE, and B.D. WILSON. The relation of soil moisture and nitrates to the effects of sod on plum and cherry trees. Cornell Univ. Agr. Exp. Sta. Mem. 91. 1925.

MARTIN, G.C., *et al.* Thinning French Prune with (2-chloroethyl) phosphonic acid. J. ASHS 100:90-93. 1975.

MARTIN, G.C. and R.C. CAMPBELL. Hormonal bioassay of French prune seed and pericarp. J. ASHS. 101(5):524-526, 1976.

NORTON, J.D. and K. S. RYMAL. 'AU-Producer' plum Alabama). HortSci. 13(4): 487-488. 1978. From Miss. Agn. Exp. Sta., Auburn: Homeside plum, cir. 218; Crimson and purple, Leaflet 85; plum leaf scald, Bull. 525. Bruce 12-4 plum, cir. 230.

NORTON, J.D. Bruce 12-4 plum breeding selection. HortSci. 11(5):523, 1976.

OVERCASH, J.P. Heat units required for plum varieties to bloom. Miss. Inf. Sheet 759. April 1962.

POSNETTE, A.F. and C.E. ELLENBERGER. The line-pattern virus disease of plums. Ann Applied Bot. *45:* No. 1, 74-80, March 1957.

PRESTON, A.P. and A. B. BEAKBANE. Pruning experiments with Victoria plum. J. Hort. Sci. 49:343-348. 1974.

PROEBSTING, E.L., Jr., *et al.* Very low irrigation rates on cherry and prune trees. ASHS 106:(2). 243-6. Mar. 1981.

PROEBSTING, E.L., Jr., and H. H. MILLS. Effects of 2-chloroethane phosphonic acid and its interaction with gibberellic acid on quality of 'Early Italian' prunes. J. ASHS 94(4):443-446. 1969.

RAMMING, D.W. Plum and prune cultivars, West Coast, America. Fruit Var. Jour. 35: (2) Apr. 1981.

RAMMING, D.W. and O. TANNER. 'Blackamber' plum. HortSci. 16(2):232. 1981.

RAMOS, D.E. Prune orchard management. (Very good-priced.) Univ. of Calif. Spec. Publ. 3269. 153 p. color. Aug. 1981.

REED, W. and G.C. MARTIN. Gibberellin A29 and Abscissic Acid in immature French prune, J. ASHS. 101(5):527-531. 1976.

ROBERTS, A.N. and L.A. HAMMERS. Pacific plum. Oregon Agr. Exp. Sta. Bull. 502. 1951.

RYUGO, K. and P.J. BREEN. Indoleacetic acid metabolism in cuttings of plum (*Prunus cerasifera x P. munsoniana cv.* Marianna 2624). J. ASHS 99(3):247. May 1974.

RYUGO, K., *et al.* Fruiting on carbohydrate and mineral composition of French prune. J. ASHS. 102(6):813-816. 1977.

SMITH, W.H. Some observations on ripening of plums by ethylene. J. Pom. and Hort. Sci. 21. 53, 1945.

SIMONS, R.K. Floral tube and style abscission in plum *(Prunus domestica* L. Cv. Stanley). J. ASHS 98(4):393. July 1973.

SOUTHWICK, L. and A.P. FRENCH. The identification of plum varieties from nonbearing trees. Mass. Agr. Exp. Sta. Bull 413. 1944.

SYMPOSIUM ON PLUMS in Yogoslavia. (Culture, economics, pests, storage processing). 303 pp. (summaries in English). Inst. for Fruit Growing. Cacak, Yugoslavia. 1968.

THOMPSON, J.M. Plum industry in S.E. USA. Fruit Vari. Jour. 35: (2) Apr. 1981.

THOMPSON, J.M. and V.E. PRINCE. Rotusto plum for S.E. USA. Fruit Var. Jr. 36:4. 112-3. 1982.

THOMPSON, M.M. and L.J. LIU. Pollination — alt. bearing, prune. J. ASHS:97-4. 489-91. 1972.

THOMPSON, M.M. and L.J. LIU. Temperature, fruit set, and embryo sac development in 'Italian' prune. J. ASHS 98(2):193. March 1973.

THERIOS, I.N. and S.A. WEINBAUM. Shading and defoliation of Myrobalan plum on nitrate uptake. HortSci. 14:(6) 715-716. Dec. 1979.

URIU, K., *et al.* K fertilization of prune trees under Drip Irrigation. J. ASHS 105:(4) 508-10. 1980.

U.S. STANDARDS for fresh plums and prunes. U.S. Dept. of Agr. AMS. 5 pp. Request recent addition.

VERNER. Leaf et al. Internal browning of fresh Italian prunes. Ida. Res. Bul. 56, 38 pp. 1962.

WEINBAUM, S.A., *et al.* Ethylene treatment of immature fruit of prune on the enzyme-mediated isolation of mesocarp cells and protoplasts. J. ASHS. 104:(2) 278-280. 1979.

WEINBAUM, S.A., *et al.* Seasonal variation in nitrate uptake efficiency and distribution of absorbed N in non-bearing prune trees. J. ASHS 103(4): 516-9. 1978.

WEINBAUM, S.A. Supplying nitrogen to prune trees with foliar nitrate. HortSci. 13(1):52-53. Feb. 1978.

WEINBAUM, S.A. and P.N. NEUMANN. Uptake of ^{15}N-NK0$_3$ by French Prune. J. ASHS. 102(5):602-604. 1977.

WEINBAUM, S.A., *et al.* Ethylene and pre-treatment fruit size on enlargement, auxin transport, and sink strength of French prune and 'Andross' peach. J. ASHS. 102(6)781-785. 1977.

WELLS, J.M. and M.J. BUKOVAC. Fruit thinning on size and quality of 'Stanley' plum. J. ASHS 103:(5) 612-16. 1978.

WESTWOOD, M.N., M.H. CHAPLIN, and A.N. ROBERTS. Effects of rootstock on growth, bloom, yield, maturity, and fruit quality of prune (*Prunus domestica* L.) J. ASHS 98(4):352. July 1973.

(See additional references in former book editions.)

Among the researchers who have contributed to the plum and prune industry over the years are, left to right: John H. Weinberger, retired, USDA, stone fruit breeder and rootstock studies, California; Claron O. Hesse, retired, University of California, stone fruit breeder; and David Ramos, plum specialist, University of California, Davis. Others include: The late Paul Shepard, Missouri State Fruit Experiment Station, Mountain Grove, breeder; the late Luther Burbank, breeder, California; David Ramming, breeder, USDA, Fresno, Calif.; the late U. P. Hedrick, N. Y. Agric. Exp. Station, Geneva; L. L. Claypool, retired, and S. A. Weinbaum, University of California, Davis.

CHAPTER XVI

Cherry Culture

Sweet and tart[1] cherries always have played a more or less important part in home fruit gardens, but it was not until the 1920's-30's and 1950's-60's that extensive U.S. commercial cherry plantings were made. The increased plantings were due to development of the canning and frozen-pack industries and to mechanized growing and handling. Cherries now are available to domestic and foreign consumers every day of the year instead of for only a four- to six-week period within a short distance of where they were grown. With the tendency of the housewife to do less canning and cooking of fresh fruits, commercial processing of cherries is continuing to grow; almost half the sweets and nearly all the tarts are processed.

Approximate cherry production figures for the world in thousands of *metric tons* are:

Soviet Union	470*	Poland	85*	Germany (DR)	40**
USA	275	Spain	75	Greece	30**
Germany (FR)	230	Czechoslovakia	65**	Japan	20
Italy	175	Rumania	65	Canada	15
France	110	Hungary	60*	Belgium-Lux.	15
Turkey	105	Bulgaria	60**	Australia	10
Yugoslavia***	100*	Portugal	45**	New Zealand	10

*Tart cherries predominate.
**Sweets predominate.
***Yugoslavia is competing with U.S. for the tart cherry market.

It is apparent that cherries are widely grown around the World and that the Soviet Union, United States, Germany (FR), Italy and France are leaders in cherry production. Except for the Far East where there is limited interest, cherries are grown commercially in Sweden, Netherlands, Australia, Japan, Norway, Denmark, Argentina, and New Zealand. From 1973-7 in California, there was a 10% reduction per year in cherry trees due to viruses, rootstocks, other causes.

U.S. cherry production has increased since 1890 from 90 to around 630 million pounds in the 1980s, while tree population generally has dropped from a peak of 15 million in 1935 to about 10 in recent years.

[1]"Tart" is preferred to "sour" in marketing channels, although the words still are used interchangeably among growers and professional workers.

Dr. Charles D. Kesner, Dist. Hort. Agt., Traverse City and George A. McManus, Jr., Traverse Co. Ext. Dir., Michigan State Univ. gave assistance in revision of this chapter.

Commercial cherries are grown principally above the Mason and Dixon line in the eastern U.S. This is mainly because cherry diseases and insects are difficult to control in the southern United States, and because the summer climate is too hot, except at higher altitudes. In the northern states, commercial cherry orchards are very much localized. Thus, most of the bearing trees in Wisconsin are in Door County; Oregon (after Albino virus problem) is up in production in the Williamette, Umpqua, and Walla Walla Valleys, and the Dalles. In Michigan, most of the cherry trees are grouped along the shores of Lake Michigan; in Utah, in the Great Salt Lake area, and in Colorado, along the Arkansas River Valley. In New York, cherry trees are largely confined to Wayne County and along the shores of Lake Ontario, while in Washington trees are in the Yakima and Wenatchee Valleys and below Seattle.

Although sweet and sour cherries are grown both in the East and West, sour cherries are largely grown east of the Rocky Mountains, whereas sweet cherries are concentrated in the West (Figure 1). The rank of states in production of all cultivars of cherries (1979-82 average, millions of pounds) and sweet and tart cultivars separately are as follows:

Area	All Varieties	Rank	Sweets	Rank	Tarts	Rank
Michigan	165.6	(1)	52.6	(4)	113.0	(1)
Washington	110.6	(2)	110.6	(1)	0.0	
Oregon	78.5	(3)	74.0	(2)	4.5	(6)
California	74.0	(4)	74.0	(3)	0.0	
New York	29.4	(5)	7.4	(6)	22.0	(2)
Utah	23.3	(6)	8.6	(5)	14.7	(3)
Penna.	7.8	(8)	1.2	(9)	6.6	(5)
Wisconsin	12.1	(7)	0.0		12.1	(4)
Mont.	3.3	(10)	3.3	(8)	0.0	
Idaho	6.1	(9)	6.1	(7)	0.0	
Colo.	6.7	(11)	0.0		1.7	
U.S. Total	512.4		337.8		174.6	

There has been a gradual increase in production of sweets with a modest decline of tarts in recent years.

Current problems for researchers in the San Joaquin County have been "tree decline", and death caused by *Phytophthora* crown and root rots, Western X (buckskin) disease, a stem pitting problem and rodent damage. By tissue culture technique, thousands of rootstocks are being tested in a short time for resistance to these problems.

U.S. Cherry Production

Thous. tons

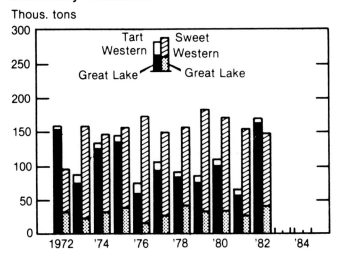

Figure 1. Most of the tart cherries in the United States are produced in the Great Lakes region. Most of the sweets are produced in the western states. Leading tart states are Michigan, New York and Wisconsin. Leading sweet cherry states are Washington, California, Oregon and Michigan. (USDA).

CHERRY CULTIVARS[1]

Most of the cultivated cherries grown today have been derived from two species; namely, the sour cherry (*Prunus cerasus*) from which both the light- and dark-colored sour cherries have developed, and the sweet cherry (*Prunus avium*) from which the sweet varieties and the Mazzard types have arisen. The Duke cherries, intermediate in type, are considered to be hybrids between the sweet and sour groups. Other species of cherries have not produced cultivars which are grown extensively on a commercial scale for their fruit. The Mahaleb cherry (*Prunus mahaleb*), native to Europe, is used as a rootstock upon which standard cultivars are budded. The Mazzard wild sweet cherry is also used for this purpose. A Chinese species (*Prunus tomentosa*) has been grown to some extent in the Upper Mississippi Valley and in the Canadian prairie provinces where winters are too adverse for common sweet and sour cultivars. Several of the Japanese species of cherries are grown widely for ornamental purposes in the United States (notably near the Washington Monument). The Bird cherry (wild sweet) is valued only for its wood. The Western wild cherry (*Prunus besseyi*) is used as a dwarfing stock for plum, prune and peach, but not for cherry.

Most of the important cherry cultivars grown in the United States are of European origin, coming from France, England, Holland, and Germany. Because of the fact that the cherry is inclined to reproduce comparatively true to type from seed, many similar seedlings have developed which hardly can be placed under the same cultivar heading. As a result, one speaks of a cherry as Morello-like, Napoleon-like, or Montmorency-like.

The cherry cultivar list has probably undergone less change than almost any other deciduous fruit. Northwest growers, due to uneasiness with winter injury and several virus problems, however, are testing the new sweet cherries Van, Sam, Ebony, Spaulding, Lamida, Chinook, Ranier, Corum, Macmar, and Compact Lambert (smaller than Lambert). California is testing the Mona, Larian, Jubilee, Berryessa, Bada; and New York, the Ulster and Hudson (very little cracking). Vista, Compact Sella and Vega are promising sweets from Canada. Michigan State University has had an active tart cherry breeding program for several years. Numbered selections are under test.[2]

There are at least 1,145 cherry cultivars (as described by Hedrick), which have been grown at one time or another in America. There are only a few, however, which can be grown commercially and which meet a ready market demand. Commercially important cultivars belong to either the sweet or tart group. Sweet cherries are used, about 40%, for fresh-fruit dessert, although increasing quantities are being brined and made into maraschino cherries. Tart cherries constitute much of the frozen pies and pie filling and canned cherries for use in restaurants, soda fountains, bakeries and in home for pies, ice cream, sauce, preserves, and other desserts. A few tarts also are being processed into maraschino cherries.

The sweet cultivars. Most of the sweet cherries belong either to the "Heart" or "Bigarreau" group. those cultivars belonging to the Heart group have a comparatively soft flesh and many of them are heart-shaped, although some cultivars are globose or oblate. Heart cherries may be divided further into dark-colored cultivars with reddish juice and light-colored cultivars with colorless juice. Among the light-colored Heart cultivars are Coe, Ida, Elton, and Governor Wood. Dark-colored cultivars are represented by Black Tartarian and Early Purple.

The Bigarreaus, most important commercially, are roundish in shape and of firm crisp flesh. Some, however, are heart-shaped. Black Bigarreaus are Windsor, Schmidt, Hedelfingen, Bing and Lambert, while light-types include Y. Spanish, Napoleon (Royal Ann), Emperor Francis, Ranier and Gold. The Heart group tends to be poor-keeping and shipping; some are excellent for home use and local market sales.

In the Northwest U.S., Lambert, Bing and Royal Ann are widely planted. Stella is favored in B.C. because of regular cropping, larger fruit than Lambert, cracks less than Lambert and Bing, but comparable to Van which is

---

[1]Request H. W. Fogle, et al. detail USDA handbooks on (a) tart and b) sweet cherries, Plant Industry Station, Beltsville, MD 20705.

[2]Michigan State University specialists are evaluating several Montmorency strains for bud hardiness, spur-type, lateness or earliness of bloom and ripening, fruit quality and virus tolerance.

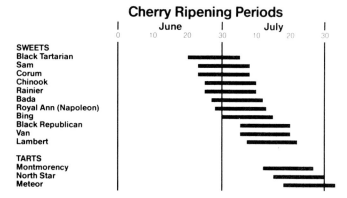

Cherry Ripening Periods

| | June | July |
| | 0 10 20 30 | 10 20 30 |

SWEETS
Black Tartarian
Sam
Corum
Chinook
Rainier
Bada
Royal Ann (Napoleon)
Bing
Black Republican
Van
Lambert

TARTS
Montmorency
North Star
Meteor

Figure 1a. Relative cherry ripening periods for Western Oregon which falls between the earliest and latest ripening areas in North America. (Courtesy Carlton Nursery Co., Parker, WA 98939). See also Figure 15.

used as a pollinizer. Also grown are Bada (pollenizer for Royal Ann), Black Republican (pollenizer), Ranier (may rain-crack), and Sam (Figure 1a).

In California, the Bing[1], Lambert, Republican, and Napoleon are the leading commercial cultivars of sweet cherries. In New York, the Black Tartarian, Schmidt, Napoleon and Windsor are grown commercially, while the Early Rivers, Victor (yellow flesh ripening before Napoleon), Emperor Francis, and Giant D'Hedellingen are recommended for trial. In Michigan, Schmidt, Napoleon, Emperor Frances and Hedelfingen are recommended, with Napoleon having the most acreage. In Ohio, Windsor has been the most dependable sweet cultivar. Lambert and Napoleon also are suggested. It is interesting to note that Bing tends to crack at maturity more than other sweet cherry varieties under Ohio and eastern conditions, whereas Bing is one of the more resistant cultivars to cracking in Idaho, followed by Black Tartarian, Napoleon, Lambert, and Republican.

Sweet cherry seedlings originating in America are Gov. Wood, Waterhouse (yellowish); Burbank, Chapman, Oregon, Bing, Lambert and Republican (dark-red shipping). Angela (Utah) may replace Bing or Lambert where X-disease causes serious damage.

Tart Cherries have only a few commercial cultivars and of these, the Montmorency is outstanding. It is used chiefly for canning and freezing. Early Richmond ripens a week to ten days earlier, but it yields less and the fruits are

slightly more acid and somewhat smaller in size than Montmorency. Early Richmond is planted mainly to extend the ripening season for local fresh market trade.

Meteor from Minnesota blooms and ripens one week after Montmorency. It is a spur-type semi-dwarf tree. Pit breakage in processing may be a problem. North Star is a dwarf home garden tart.

English Morello is a relatively small spreading tree which bears medium to small, dark red to almost black cherries that are tart and of good quality. English Morello matures relatively late and will hang on the tree for a long time after maturity without deteriorating. It requires thorough spraying because the foliage is highly susceptible to the leaf spot disease. English Morello has a limited demand on local markets and a very limited demand for commercial canning.

Duke Cherries have less important cultivars than the sweet or tart groups. Only three Duke cultivars are planted to any commercial extent in the United States; namely, May Duke, Royal Duke and Late Duke. Other cultivars grown occasionally in the East are Brassington and Reine Hortense.

General Cultivar Considerations. As pointed out previously, the cherry cultivars, like other fruit cultivars,

Figure 2. Both sweet and tart cherries grow poorly or die on heavy soils with poor drainage, particularly sweet cherries. (Top) Note missing Montmorency trees in low poorly drained area in center of orchard. (Bottom) Ten-year Montmorency trees dying in heavy poorly drained soil following an unusually wet spring in northern Ohio.

[1]Long-stem Bing is apparently resistant to buckskin virus and may prove of value in such virus-infected areas. Also, Mahaleb roots are resistant to buck skin virus. Injections of oxytetracycline in trunk holes, as with pear decline (Chap. XIII) is effective against this virus. Other viruses in the West are "twisted leaf," "albino," "little-cherry Western X complex," and "Lambert mottle," all of which are causing many sweet cherry trees to be removed.

The Agricultural Research Station, Vancouver, B.C., has devised a tissue-staining-ultra-violet technique for identifying "little cherry virus" on about 70 trees per week.

Figure 3. (Left) Montmorency leaves are shown with various types of necrotic ring spots and necrotic (dead) areas which have resulted in a first-year invasion of the ring spot virus. The Yellows virus usually follows ring spot in New York. (Right) Comparison of height of virus-free Royal Ann (A10) on the left and ring-spot virus-infected Royal Ann (A11) on the right. (Oregon State University).

are limited in commercial adaptability to rather definite areas. Disadvantages of the sweet cherry are the fact that although it is as hardy in wood as the peach, it does not recover as well from winter injury; it blossoms early in the srping, and hence, is more likely to be damaged by frost injury. The trees do not thrive on heavy or poorly drained soils. Likewise, the tart cherry is affected adversely by poor soil drainage (Figure 2).

The tart cherry tree is about as hardy as some apple varieties, but its flowers are tender to cold in the "water-bud" stage. In Michigan, although there has been a shift to better sites, one crop out of about three in the average commercial orchard is lost to spring frosts; in the one-third of the orchards on the best sites, crop loss from frost occurs less frequently than once in five years. The late V.R. Gardner states that "most growers, if asked to name their most serious problems or limiting factors, would mention frost injury to blossoms in the spring, yellow-leaf virus, and the difficulty in obtaining what they regard as a satisfactory price for their product." The yellow-leaf virus disease has become one of the most important limiting factors in tart cherry production in the East and Northwest (Figure 3). Cherries have a number of viruses. See

suggested Collateral Readings for descriptions and controls.

There has been increased effort in cherry breeding in the past two decades. The failure to develop new commercial cultivars of cherries, particularly the sweet cherry, may be due to the fact that cherries cannot be grown over such a wide area of the country as the peach and the plum, and to the failure of the seed to germinate and grow, especially with the sweet cultivars. Modest breeding programs are underway in New York, Michigan, Canada, California, Washington — USDA cooperating. The objectives are high-quality sweet cultivars that will prove more hardy in trees and blossom characters than many of those now available for planting. Even in the limited areas where sweet cherries will grow, there is definite need for firm-fleshed cultivars that do not crack and that will ripen over a long season. At present, there is no firm-fleshed early-ripening cultivar of the Bigarreau type. The Duke cultivars are excellent cherries, but there is a definite need for higher-producing cultivars.

POLLINATION

Sweet Cultivars. All sweet cherry cultivars appear to be self-unfruitful in that little or no fruit develop following self-pollination. All commercial cultivars of sweet cherries have viable pollen, but not all varietal combinations are fruitful. There are many cross-incompatible groups of sweet cherries. Cultivars within a group should not be planted together without a pollinizer. The cross-incompatible groups include: (1) Bing, Lambert, Napoleon, Emperor Francis, and Ohio Beauty; (2) Windsor and Abundance; (3) Black Tartarian, Black Eagle, Knight's Early Black, Bedford Prolific, and Early Rivers; (4) Centennial and Napoleon; (5) Advance and Rockport; (6) Elton, Governor Wood, and Stark's Gold; and (7) Early Purple and Rockport; (8) Black Tartarian,

Figure 4. Sweet cherry trees (right) in Ohio may be in full bloom ten days before the tart cherries (left) begin to bloom. Hence, tart cherry trees will not provide cross-pollination needed by sweet cherry trees. In Idaho, sweet cherries may bloom before tarts. (Ohio Agr. Exp. Sta.)

Early Rivers, V29023; (9) Sodus, Van, Venus, Windsor; (10) Bing, Emperor Francis, Lambert, Napoleon, Vernon; (11) Velvet, Victor, Gold, Merton Heart; (12) Hedelfingen, Vic (Heldelfingen is pollen-fertile with 14 other cultivars); (13) Hudson, Giant, Schmidt, Ursula; (14) Valera and (15) Seneca, Vega, Vista, V35033, V35038 (compatible with groups 8-14). Note: No. 8-14 from Publication 430, Fruit Varieties, Ontario Department of Agriculture and Food; (16) Konigskirsche and Heinrichs Riesen; (17) Royal Purple and Lambert, Ironside, Woodring Bing; (18) Schmidt and Orelund.

Sweet cherries must be interplanted for cross-pollination. Tarts cannot be used as pollinzers for sweet cherries since their blooming periods do not overlap in most regions (Figure 4). The Duke varieties are not reliable in cross-pollination with sweet cherries. Poor pollination in cool springs is the principal limiting factor in western Oregon.

In the East, blooming seasons of the commercially grown sweet cherry varieties usually overlap sufficiently to provide good crops. However, in the West, somewhat more care is needed in the selection of varieties on the basis of blooming dates. Early-blooming sweet cherries include Black Tartarian, Black Republican, Advance, Burbank, Chapman, Black Heart, and Early Purple. Napoleon, Rockport, Bing, Pontiac, Longstem Bing, and Lambert are considered late-blooming, and Deacon has been interplanted among these varieties in Washington and British Columbia as a pollinzer. The Black Republican and Black Tartarian usually overlap sufficiently in blooming period to pollinize most of the late-blooming sweet varieties. There may be a week spread in bloom between early and late blooming cultivars some seasons.

TABLE 1. DAYS FROM FULL BLOOM TO HARVEST FOR CHERRY CULTIVARS IN NEW YORK (AFTER H.B.)[1] TUKEY.

| VARIETY | No. SEASONS | LENGTH OF SEASONS | | | MAXIMUM DAY DIFFERENCES |
		SHORTEST	LONGEST	AVERAGE	
Sweets					
Bing	5	60	74	71	14
Black Tartarian	7	49	63	57	14
Gov. Wood	9	43	50	47	7
Knight	12	44	55	51	11
Lambert	7	61	72	69	11
Napoleon	6	67	74	68	7
Rockport	8	42	56	52	14
Schmidt	0	62	74	72	12
Windsor	6	65	76	75	11
Y. Spanish	6	60	70	67	10
Red (Sours)					
E. Richmond	17	47	57	50	10
E. Morello	29	60	74	70	14
Montmorency	14	54	64	62	10
Dukes					
Late Duke	5	60	72	66	12
May Duke	6	41	55	51	14

[1]Tukey, H.B. Proc. Amer. Soc. Hort. Sci. *40*: 133. 1942.

Tart cultivars. The common varieties of tart cherries;

namely E. Richmond, Montmorency, Northstar and Meteor are sufficiently self-fruitful to give commercial crops when planted in solid blocks, provided sufficient pollinizing insects are available.

Duke Cultivars. The Dukes are similar to the sweet cultivars in that cross-pollination is needed for commercial crops. With good cross-pollination, however, Duke cultivars in general are relatively low-producing, apparently due to the unbalanced constitution of the reproductive cells. The May Duke and Royal Duke are usually the most productive. The late-blooming sweet cultivars are used for cross-pollinating the early-blooming Duke cultivars, such as May Duke. Among the late-blooming sweet cultivars are Napoleon, Windsor, and Governor Wood. The Early Richmond and Montmorency tart cherries are effective as pollinizers for most late-blooming Duke cherries, Olivet being one exception.

Planting Plan. In both the East and the West, it is recommended that where cross-pollination is required, every third row be a pollinizing cultivar or that two rows of

Figure 5. A vigorous Montmorency tart cherry tree growing on a Mazzard rootstock in western Pennsylvania. Note difference in vigor of root and top. Where extremely cold temperatures are not likely to be a factor in the East, tart cherries on Mazzard stock are usually more vigorous, higher yielders, and longer lived than those on Mahaleb stock. In areas as Northwest Michigan, Mazzard roots are satisfactory where snow cover prevents soil freezing.

264

Figure 6. Efforts are underway to develop compact cherry trees. (Above) A compact Bing and Lambert high-producing sweet cherry orchard near Wapato, Washington with Montmorency trunks and Mazzard rootstocks. "Stub Pruning", as indicated, induces large-size fruit bringing premium prices (courtesy Paul Stark, Jr., Stark Nurseries, Louisiana, Mo.). (Low-left) Hedge-row planting of Bing sweet cherry high-budded on Mahaleb rootstocks in mid California gives insurance against "buck-skin" virus and also affords an easy-to-train early-bearing tree held to a desirable height (courtesy Kay Ryugo, Univ. of Calif., Davis). (Right) Radiation treatment with X-rays, gamma rays, and thermal neutrons induces dwarf mutant trees. Center two trees are compact Lamberts in seventh year, so-treated, as compared with standard Lamberts at side and rear (courtesy K.O. Lapins, Agr. Research Sta., Summerland, B.C., Canada).

F.E. Larsen, Wash. State Univ., Pullman has dwarfing rootstock and interstock tests with developing results that may be of interest.

the pollenizing cultivar be planted between every four rows of the cultivar needing pollination. This system facilitates mechanical harvesting.

Auxins. Experimental results from the East Malling Research Station in England indicate that GA_3 at 50 ppm or lower and 2,4,5-TP at 10 ppm at shuck split (cot-split) as an aquaeous spray has been effective in increasing set on Merton Glory and Van cherry. There was a consistent increase in yield with an occasional reduction in flower bud formation which did not appear to be important..

Ethephon at 1 pt./100 gals. in limited tests by Wash. State University, applied early September, has delayed bloom 3-5 days and increased hardiness $1°$-$3°F$.

ROOTSTOCKS FOR CHERRY TREES

Three rootstocks are used for cherry: Mazzard and Mahaleb seedling cherries and Stockton Morello softwood cuttings or suckers. Mazzard is a sweet cherry type with small black bitter fruits; it is native to Central and Southern Europe. Mazzard seed for rootstocks are obtained from Europe and from trees which have escaped cultivation in sections of the United States where the sweet cherry is grown. The Mahaleb cultivar is native in southwestern Europe and is probably more closely related

to the tart cherry types than to the sweet types. The tree tends to be thick, bushy-topped, spreading, and small in size. Seeds for rootstocks are obtained from trees in southern Europe. Seedlings from standard commercial cultivars of sweet cherries are used sometimes by nurserymen for rootstocks, but the trees are often less vigorous, less uniform, and less satisfactory than the true Mazzard. The tart and native "pin" or "bird" cherry seedlings are not considered satisfactory for rootstocks.

Mazzard is the main stock on the Pacific Coast for sweet cherries and to a considerable extent for other types. Trees are larger, root-knot nematode resistant, semi-resistant to oak-root fungus, gophers, mice, trunk borers, and out-produces trees on Mahaleb roots. Mazzard stock is preferred for both sweet and tart cultivars in eastern U.S. where winter temperatures are not extreme (Figure 5). Results obtained at the New York Agricultural Experiment Station have shown that the sweet, tart, and Duke cherries grown on Mazzard stock are larger, more vigorous, more productive, longer-lived, and show less mortality among young trees. In the East, however, it is clearly evident that the Mahaleb stock is hardier and more drought-resistant than the Mazzard, and in regions where droughts are common and extreme temperatures are likely to occur, the Mahaleb stock is recommended. In California the Morello stock is used for sweet cherries in soils likely to become wet, or as a semi-dwarfing stock. Satisfactory dwarfing stocks, clonal or genetic, are under study (Figure 9). Always specify *virus-free* stock.

The F-12-1 Oregon Mazzard is fairly resistant to bacterial canker where it is a problem. Van and Bing perform best on Mazzard in Washington. In Pennsylvania Napoleon survived best on Mahaleb. In Michigan, Mazzard is recommended for Hedelfingen.

In Utah, Mahaleb does better than Mazzard in porous gravelly soils, is more vigorous, hardy, earlier bearing, gives better yields.

'Vladimir' from California (Kay Ryugo) and 'Colt' from England are semi-dwarfing stocks being tested for cherries. Colt propagates easily and is compatable with both tarts and sweets. West Germany has some promising dwarfing stocks. Northstar and Meteor are genetic tart dwarfs.

In New York, nematodes may be a serious pest on cherry, reducing growth and production and increasing susceptibility to cold damage (Figure 7). Soil fumigants often are used before planting. State-inspected nursery stock *certified-free* of the common *viruses should be sought.*

RESISTANCE TO COLD

Sweet cherry trees in general are somewhat more resistant to cold than the average cultivar of Domestica plum. There is no *great* difference in cold resistance among cultivars grown extensively in the United States. Windsor, Governor Wood, and Yellow Spanish are more resistant than the average sweet cherry. Lyon has shown the most resistance, but it is a minor cultivar. Blossoms of the sweet cherry open somewhat earlier than the peach and are more likely to be killed by spring frosts. The amount of cold required by the sweet cherry for breaking the rest period is slightly more than for most peaches (1100-1300 hrs. below 45°F.; tarts - 1200).

TABLE 2. CRITICAL TEMPERATURES FOR SWEET CHERRY BLOSSOM BUDS*
(E.L. PROEBSTING, JR., WASH. STATE AGR. STA., PROSSER)

Bud Development Stage	1	2	3	4	5	6	7	8	9
Old Sandard Temp.[1]	23	23	25	28	28	29	29	29	30
Ave. Temp. for 10% Kill[2]	17	22	25	26	27	27	28	28	28
Ave. Temp. for 90% Kill[2]	5	9	14	17	21	24	25	25	25
Average Date (Prosser)[3]	3/5	3/13	3/23	3/27	4/1	4/4	4/8	4/13	4/21

* For Bing, Lambert and Rainier approximately 1 to 2 degrees hardier through Stage 6. Stage 8 is full bloom, Stage 9 is post bloom.
[1] Critical temperatures as previously published in WSU EM 1616.
[2] Average temperatures found by research at the WSU Irrig. Agr. Res. and Extension Center, Prosser, to result in 10% and 90% bud kill.
[3] Average date for this state at the WSU IAREC.

Many orchards have been heated to protect against frost damage. Smudge pots, wind machines, irrigation systems, and petroleum bricks have been used with varied degrees of success. Portable propane fueled systems have been used in the Northwest with the propane gas and irrigation water sharing the same main laterals. Fuel heating has become very expensive. Under and over-head irrigation is now used.

The tart cherry cultivars, except for the Russian cultivars, are about as resistant to cold as the medium-hardy cultivars of apple, such as the Northern Spy. Russian cultivars of tart cherries may be as resistant as the McIntosh apple and should be a good parent for hybridizing to extend the commercial tart cherry region northward.

If growth of the tart cherry trees has ceased relatively early in the growing season due to leaf spot disease, low nitrogen, or drought, the buds may be more tender to cold during the winter than the peach flower buds. In orchards under good management, however, much less trouble from winter killing of fruit buds is experienced. English Morello

Figure 7. Nematodes can limit growth and reduce yields of cherries. (Above) is a light sandy soil near Rochester, N.Y. Richmond L. Norton, left, of Cornell Extenion Service shows effect on tart cherries of (a) no treatment, (b) N only, (c) soil fumigation only and (d) N fertilizer with soil fumigation. Soil fumigation before planting, while expensive, should pay for itself on replant nematode-infested land. Nematodes tend to be more prevalent in the lighter sandy soils. Systemic nematocides should not be used on bearing trees.

has shown less bud killing due to cold than Montmorency or Early Richmond. In view of the fact that tart cherries ripen early in the season and that a short season is required for maturing the buds and wood, they can be grown at relatively high latitudes, provided large bodies of water are near (Norway, Sweden).

Late summer ethephon sprays may increase bud hardiness, delay bloom, dodge frosts, increase yields. (Proebsting, Jr. and Mills, Wash.)

PLANTING RECOMMENDATIONS

A good peach orchard site in an equally good cherry orchard site. Vigorous one-year nursery trees are desired for sweet cherries as well as for tarts and Dukes. In the milder climates, fall planting is suggested. In the colder climates *early* spring planting is recommended to avoid winter damage, except where snow may protect the tree into late winter. Root killing by winter cold and winter injury due to chemical or hand defoliation of nursery trees for early-fall digging can be problems in fall-planted trees in the colder climates.

Spring-planted cherry trees should be set as early as possible on fall-plowed ground. Delay in spring planting of

Figure 8. Cherry tree density and training research is underway at Michigan State University looking toward over-the-row mechanical harvesting and handling the trees. Trees are spaced 12-16 ft. between rows with trees 4-12 ft. in the row, using their new bud-hardy and better quality hybrids developed by their breeding program. The central-leader framework is used. (Courtesy R.F. Carlson, Mich. State Univ., E. Lansing, 48823).

cherry trees is probably responsible for the loss of more cherry trees the first season than all other factors put together. This may be due to the fact that cherry buds open relatively early and that evidently the cherry roots are a little slow in becoming established. This results in a greater demand for water by the tops than the roots can supply. Thence, the opening buds dry, the wood and bark shrivel, and the tree soon dies. This is one of the main reasons why fall planting is desirable in those sections where winter killing of the roots is not a factor.

Special care should be exercised in handling cherry trees during transit, storage and planting. Cherry buds are easily rubbed off being large and prominent.

Standard planting distances have been 15 x 15 ft. for Morellos, 20 x 20 for tarts and Dukes and 20 x 20 to 36 x 36 for sweets, depending on variety, vigor and soil. A shift to hedgerow planting is occurring to increase acre yields where mechanization of orchard operations will be used. See Mechanical Harvesting and Figure 8.

Where cherries are replanted on old fruit plantings, fumigation of the soil in fall when its temperature is 50-80 °F is suggested to get healthy vigorous trees.

PRUNING YOUNG CHERRY TREES

Tart Cherry. If the trees are one-year whips, they should be cut off 30+ inches above the ground. A selection of the scaffolds can be made that mid season or the following year. If the nursery trees are branched two-year-olds, about two or three well-spaced laterals should be selected around the leader, with the lowest limb 30-36 in. above ground (mechanized harvesting) on the southwest side of the tree or toward the prevailing winds (Figure 9). Heading-back cuts should be avoided on the branches left to form the head, because such practice has a definite stunting effect on sour cherries.

The tart cherry tree naturally has an open spreading growth habit. Commercial trees are trained to the open-center system. However, the general experience with open-center tart cherry trees has been too many weak rotting crotches. In recent years, there has been a definite trend toward the modified-leader system of training tart cherries, similar to that described for apple in Chapter IV. Although the modified-leader system of training trees requires somewhat more care and attention during the first four or five years in the orchard, it should add years to the life of the average tart cherry orchard.

Three or four scaffolds distributed over about three or four feet of the trunk above the lowest branch are desirable (Figure 9). The leader is then modified by cutting it to an outward-growing lateral. In tart cherries, it is particularly important to eliminate one branch originating parallel with another on the trunk. It is important, also, to avoid two scaffold limbs originating at the same height. If two scaffolds are permitted to develop close together on the same side or opposite to each other on the trunk, later development of the leader and branches above may be considerably subdued and choked. The moderately vigorous tart cherry tends to develop numerous lateral shoots on the scaffold limbs and leader, and one must take special care not to prune these too heavily. It is particularly important with young cherries to prune as little as possible to attain the desired scaffold arrangement. Heavy pruning may delay full bearing several years.

Sweet Cherries. Sweet cherry trees often come from the nursery as one-year whips which should be cut at a height of 30 to 48 inches from the ground, depending upon the vigor of the tree. The deshooting system of training one-year whips is often practiced with the sweet cherry as described for the apple in Chapter IV. If allowed to grow without training, the sweet cherry will usually develop into a central-leader which becomes too high for ecomanical production. It is important to prevent the leader and upper branches from being choked by opposite or closely placed scaffold limbs. Three or four lateral scaffolds with about 12 inches vertical distance between limbs, in addition to the leader which is modified to an outward-growing limb, will make a desirable framework for sweet cherry trees. The sweet cherry is susceptible to crotch splitting and, thus, it is especially important to eliminate at an early stage any scaffolds with narrow-angled crotches. TIBA and Alar sprays have shown promise in inducing more compact and wide-angled crotch trees from the nursery.

Wayward limbs. On young cherry trees, frequently one finds a limb which has started to outgrow the others, and, if left alone, may result in a one-sided unsymmetrical top. This limb can be subordinated by heading it back more or less severely. However, if this vigorous side limb has gained considerable dominance over the other limbs, it may be advisable to gradually prune away the weak limbs and permit the new growth to develop the tree.

PRUNING THE BEARING CHERRY TREE

Tart Cherry. Fruit buds of the tart cherry are produced laterally on one-year terminal growths and spurs (Figure 10). The terminal buds of shoots and spurs are leaf buds. If the terminal growth on sour cherries is less than about seven inches, nearly all lateral buds on such shoots will be flower buds. After fruiting, this wood becomes largely bare. On the other hand, when terminal shoots are more than about 7 in. in length, 1/4 in. thick, some of the lateral buds will be leaf buds from which spurs and lateral shoots develop. Trees with numerous spurs are very productive and the flowers open over several days, hence, some of them dodging a current frost.

Moderate pruning and good soil management are needed to encourage spur development. Dr. J.C. Cain of

Figure 9. A good start in the framework of a tart cherry tree beginning its second season in the orchard. Lowest limb should be about 30 inches from the ground where mechanical harvesting will be used. Central leader can be "chocked off" by two or more limbs arising at one point on the trunk.

the New York Station, Geneva, finds that 20 to 50 ppm of gibberelic acid 4 to 5 weeks after bloom (Mich. - 2 wks.) reduces fruit on one-year growth but encourages spur development and bloom throughout the tree the following year on wood best adapted to mechanical harvesting. GA also will negate some of the effect of yellows virus, but the economics is doubtful.

For Mechanical Harvesting. When trees that are designed for hand harvesting are to be harvested mechanically, they must be pruned a bit heavy the first year to change them from a system that encourages fruiting wood close to the ground to a system allowing trunk space for quick machine shaking and adjustment of the catching frame under the tree. Willowy limbs do not free the cherries well during shaking and must be removed. Bark damage results if the shaker arm rubs against one main limb while shaking another, hence, the main limbs *must* be freely accessible to shaker arms over a 30° arc while operating from one position. The shaker arm, some equipment has two arms (Figure 16), is attached to the catching frame, both of which are operated and moved by the same motor. Modern trunk shakers do not harm the bark and thus make the positioning of main lateral limbs less important.

268

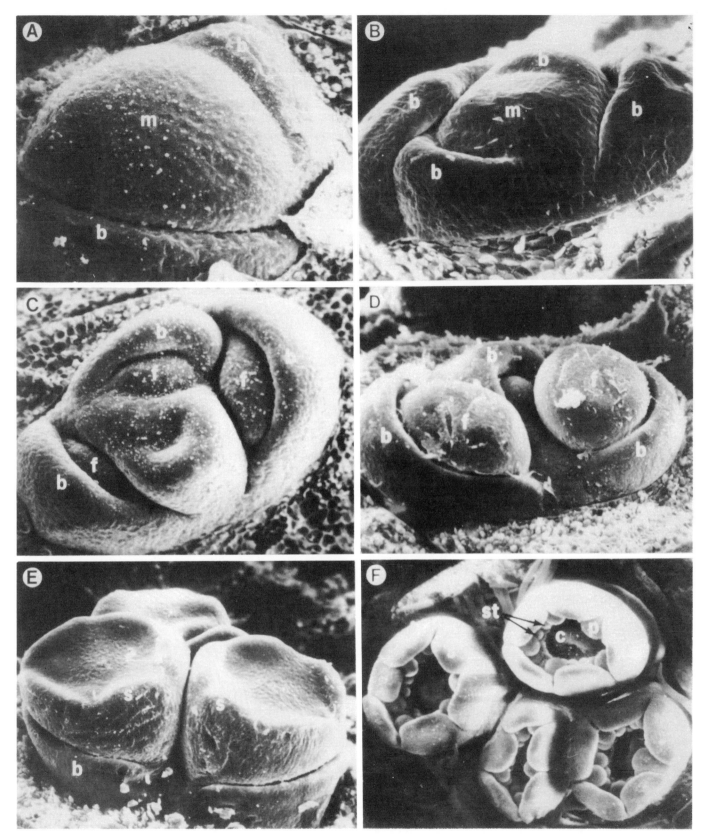

Figure 10. Scanning electronic microscopic photographs of the tips of 'Montmorency' cherry bud, showing changes during flower formation. (A) Change from vegetative to reproductive bud with rounded meristem (m) and two bract primordia ab (b), June 10, Michigan, 600x. (B) Flattened meristem (m) with 4 bract primordia, June 15, 400x. (C) Flower primordia (f) in 3 bracts and a 4th beginning to differentiate, June 30, 410x. (D) Flower primordia enlarged and rounded, July 10, 300x. (E) Sepal primordia (s) in pentagonal whorl, June 30, 300x. (F) All floral organs differentiated with stamens (st) and carpel (c). Sept. 29, 150x. (D.H. Diaz, H.P. Rasmussen, F.G. Dennis, Jr., Michigan State Univers. ASHS Jr. July 1981).

269

Subsequent pruning of the above trees is based for the most part on principles outlined below. Cutter bar mowing of trees, as for the peach, will keep trees within bounds and cut pruning costs and increase yields.

For Hand Harvesting. It is important to correct or eliminate any limbs with sharp crotch angles or those that crowd others, or grow across the center of the tree. Only sufficient pruning should be done to keep the tree from becoming dense and to thin out lightly through the top and sides for efficient light and spray penetration. Neglected dense trees result in considerable dying of spurs and limbs in the center and lower sections of the tree. Good air circulation through a tree is important in reducing the amount of brown rot developing shortly before and during harvest.

Sweet, Duke Cherry. Fruiting habit of sweet cherry is mainly on the tree's spur system. The trees grow more or less upright and the main limbs form much less lateral growth as compared with tart cherries. It is important to head-back the main upright limbs when they attain a height of about 15 to 18 feet to keep the tree within a 20-foot maximum height, or perferably lower for economical management. The main upright and spreading limbs should be cut back to strong laterals to keep the tree within bounds. Some Yakima growers tip back shoots to induce branching, better fruiting and hold the tree in bounds.

Sweet cherry trees tend to form long limbs with a whorl of side limbs located at long intervals on the central leader. Whorls of from three to five limbs should be reduced to two or three at the most the first dormant season after they have formed. It is difficult to correct such whorls if allowed to remain for two or three years. Big cuts at the whorl have a "ringing" or stunting effect. Make smooth flush cuts that heal quickly to avoid wood rotting fungi.

Duke varieties resemble the sweet cherry and are pruned similarly.

For mechanical harvesting, sweet cherries are shaped similar to tarts.

Girdling is not recommended generally but early season scoring with a knife may be acceptable to induce earlier bearing. Overgrowth breakage and gumming can be a problem.

Summer Hedgerow Pruning. With no proven dwarfing rootstock for cherries and the trend toward hedgerow planting, summer pruning has been shown by C.D. Kesner et al. of the Michigan State University to keep trees within bounds plus other benefits. Tart cherries are planted 18 x 14 ft. 172 T/A, trained to a central leader with 7-9 laterals, with the leader the last lateral limb. Summer pruning begins the third or fourth growing season about 45 days after full bloom. Trees are gradually shaped to an inverted wedge down the row. Harvesting starts about 60 days after full bloom and, hence, there are 15 days when growth is halted and carbohydrates and water are diverted into the fruit for better sizing. Summer pruning also has been shown by Kesner to induce, relatively, 103 vs. 25 ft. of terminal growth, flower buds 394 vs. 261, and spurs 67 vs. 48, favoring the summer pruning. Summer pruned limbs have been shown to have 26% more terminal growth, 51% more flower buds, and 40% more spurs.

Alar at 5 lbs./A 2 weeks after full bloom along with summer pruning has induced slightly easier removal of fruit by mechanical shaking and an increase in fruit size with an increase in yields of as much as 6.3 T/A with Alar vs. 3.3 T/A without Alar. Increase in size of fruit with Alar probably is due to fruit inside the tree sizing and maturing better. There also is an increase in firmness of the fruit.

Summer mowing always should be followed by dormant pruning to remove enough small limbs from the top center to allow 1/3 full-sun conditions in the center of the tree. This permits continued flower bud formation in the tree interior.

Limb Breakage. Stout plastic strapping is available from horticultural supply house to brace overloaded limbs near harvest. Limb breakage can be a problem in almost every orchard, particularly tart cherries. Windbreaks also reduce any wind damage periodically occurring near harvest.

SOIL MANAGEMENT

Cherry trees are almost as responsive to nitrogen and clean cultivation as the peach. Any early cultivation either should be done several weeks before blossoming or after the fruit has set. The soil surface should be rain-packed (not loose and preferably with no ground cover) at bloom time to permit radiation of ground heat to reduce frost damage, as described for peach. Actually, there has been a

TABLE 3. SUGGESTED MINERAL CONTENTS OF GOOD YIELDING CHERRY TREES.* NEW YORK

N	P*	K*	Mg*	Ca	S	Fe	Mn	B	Zn	Cu	Mo
Percent					ppm						
2.33	0.23	1.25	0.49	1.62	124	119	44	38	20	8	0.5
to	to	to	to	to	to	to	to	to	to	to	to
3.27	0.32	1.92	0.74	2.60	150	203	60	54	50	28	1.0
2.95**	0.25	1.67	0.68	2.09	—	203	150	50	—	57	—

* Values established in personal communications with J.C. Cain, N.Y. Agr. Exp. Sta., Geneva, for Montmorency.
** Values in this line are for Michigan from A.L. Kenworthy. Nutrient element balance in fruit tree leaves in Amer. Inst. Biol. Sci. Publ. No. 8. 1961.

Figure 11. (Left) Short annual growth (two to four inches) is associated with unproductive cherry trees; long shoot growth (seven to twelve inches) is associated with productive trees. Long 2-year growth at D has numerous fruiting spurs on lower 2-year wood; upper 1-year wood has mostly leaf buds which will form shoots and fruiting spurs in the following year. The three weak terminal growths of A, B and C are from 4 to 6 years old and have produced only 2- to 4-inch shoot growth each year. Note lack of spurs, due to practically all buds being fruit buds each year; such wood has low productive capacity. (Right) Terminal growths at A and B show flowering and leaf development on wood similar to C and D, respectively, in left photo. Note at C that fruit buds on 1-year wood have been killed by low temperature, whereas those on spurs were not injured. (New York Agricultural Experiment Station).

general commercial shift to sod with strip chemical weed control under the trees and "trickle" irrigation if needed. In some areas, Alta fescue (Ky. 31) or creeping red fescue is used for sod middles.

Mulching to 6-10 inches deep on a few backyard trees is a good practice and it may delay bloom a few days.

Cover crops that have been used in cherry orchards are millet, rye, oats, buckwheat, rye grass and Sudan grass.

A study of the effects of cultivation and nitrogen applications on young Montmorency trees is shown in Figure 12. These results are typical.

Leaf analysis by standard procedure may be used with the help of the local government experiment station to diagnose what appears to be a nutritional problem. While data for mineral content of good bearing cherry trees is scanty for some nutrients, the following contents are considered approximately normal for New York.

No attempt should be made to produce the above growth and fruiting conditions by pruning alone. In fact, pruning should play only a minor role, with most emphasis placed on soil management, particularly fertilization. In the East, there has been a trend toward use of an NPK fertilizer mix of a 1-2-2 or 1-1-1 ratio, especially on gravelly or sandy soils. Spotty reports of manganese, iron, and zinc shortages have been noted. Potassium now is generally used in humid regions on the lighter soils. This deficiency has been reported to be common in the north central U.S. cherry regions (Figure 13).

In the western arid sections, zinc, manganese (Figure 15), and iron shortages may be a problem; nitrogen is the only major nutrient used as a general rule, although occasional cases of P and K deficiencies are reported. Nu-Iron, an orgnanic iron product (Tennessee Corp., Atlanta), applied with standard pesticides in New York has increased the sugar content and quality of sour cherries; it is not certain if this is a nutritional effect of the iron or a safening of certain pesticides. Chelated iron on the soil (Geigy 138) is used in arid regions. See Chapter IV in Childers' *Fruit Nutrition* book for corrective measures for trace elements deficiencies. In Michigan, Mg is often deficient and is corrected by dolomitic lime to adjust soil pH if needed, plus syrup of epsom salts.

In general, young non-bearing trees of most sour cultivars should make an annual shoot growth of 12 to 24 inches, whereas young non-bearing sweet cultivars should make from 22 to 36 inches. Mature bearing sour and sweet cultivars should make a new shoot growth approaching eight inches each year to maintain high production. Failure to obtain this growth most often is due to lack of sufficient fertilizer (nitrogen mainly), although drought and certain types of winter injury may cause the same result. The uneven ripening of fruit more likely is due to inadequate leaf area to accommodate a heavy set than to too much nitrogen, as some growers surmise. Experimental evidence indicates that the more nitrogen added, up to the point where vegetative growth is excessive, the higher the yields and the more profitable the orchard. The rate of nitrogen applications for cherries is similar to that recommended

271

Figure 12. Montmorency tart cherry trees respond well to cultivation and nitrogen. The two left rows are under cultivation and the two right rows are in sod. The first and third row were fertilized the previous three years with 900, 900 and 1800 pounds per acre of nitrate of soda, respectively. The second and fourth rows received no fertilizer. On cultivated plots, nitrated trees were one-third larger than un-nitrated trees. On sod plots, fertilized trees were almost twice as large as unfertilized trees. Cherry trees on heavily nitrated sod plots were almost as large as unfertilized trees on cultivated plots. This is on a fairly fertile loam. In sandy soils response to N should be greater and to cultivation less. (Cornell University, Ithaca, N.Y.).

for peaches in Chapter XIV.

It should not be implied from this discussion that clean cultivation is being recommended unconditionally for mature cherry trees. There is a definite trend in Michigan, eastern states, and the west toward the use of sod, strip-row herbicides, and trickle or overhead irrigation if needed. Adequate water is important in arid regions; otherwise fruit size will be reduced on sweets with some twig dieback. This system is giving excellent results, provided sufficient nitrogen is applied; it has the main advantages of checking soil erosion, cutting costs, conserving soil structure and facilitating movement of mechanical harvest equipment.

The nitrogen requirement of sweet cherry trees is probably somewhat less than for the peach and tart cherry trees. On the West coast, tart cherry trees apparently can obtain sufficient potassium from soils in which apple trees and some cultivars of Domestica plums will show potassium deficiency. However, according to W.H. Chandler the sweet cherry trees, especially the old ones, are more apt to show zinc deficiency symptoms in semiarid districts of California than are other fruit trees, and it is more difficult to correct. Moderate liming of cherry orchards to maintain a pH of about 6.0 is suggested in humid areas, using high magnesium lime, principally for the cover crop. Avoid excessive liming; trace element deficiencies may be induced.

Irrigation is practiced only rarely for tart cherry trees in the East because the fruits mature early in the season before the soil is apt to become deficient in moisture.

However, if early dry periods occur, tart and sweet cherry fruits appear to be more sensitive to high transpiration and high daily water deficit than other deciduous fruits. This may be because the fruits are small and numerous and a higher percentage of the water within them can be removed by the leaves during hot dry periods of the day.

On the West Coast where sweet cherries are grown widely, irrigation is a regular practice is some orchards. Sweet and Duke cherries are quite sensitive to drought. Tarts are less sensitive but respond well to irrigation when needed. In the cool coastal areas of California, sweet cherries can be grown without irrigation in regions of about 15 inches of annual rainfall where other deciduous fruits ripening later in the season cannot be grown. Sweets are highly sensitive to deficient and excessive soil moisture. Trickle or daily flow irrigation at tree bases from perforated in-row plastic pipe is popular (see Chapter XIX).

Fruit thinning of tart cherry trees is not practiced because they ripen early in the season when soil moisture is usually adequate, and also because size of cherries is not as important as it is for larger fruits. Furthermore, V.R. Gardner has shown an apparent lack of correlation between size of fruit and size of crop on tart cherry trees. Chemical thinning of sweet cherries has not been perfected. Davenport et al. (Calif.) report an anti-transpirant spray (Mobileaf) at 2-3% applied 7-20 days before harvest will increase fruit size and yield on moderately heavily cropping trees plus other postharvest desired characters. No comment on fruit cracking. Tripling the N to "yellows" virus trees may increase yields by 20%.

Figure 13. Potassium deficiency in cherry is characterized by marginal scorching of leaves, moving from the lower to upper leaves on shoots. Scorch usually starts mid to late summer on older trees but may appear early on newly planted trees. Leaves are undersized when deficiency is severe, with limb dieback. (By Franklin A. Gilbert, University of Wisconsin).

Fruit Cracking. This is often a problem in arid regions, particularly with sweet cherries, varying with the cultivar. Susceptible cultivars are: Early Burlat, Early Purple, Schrecken, Chinook, Corum, Macmar, Knight's Early Black, Bing, Sue, Lambert and Black Republican. Firm sweet cultivars are more susceptible than soft ones. Losses can be reduced by harvesting as soon as maturity is reached, and if a rain occurs about this time, harvest as quickly as possible. Helicopters and airblast spray machines have been used to blow the water off the fruit after a rain. NAA spray 30 days before the harvest, Ca and Al sprays before harvest, and NAA followed by lime sprays before harvest all have been effective in reducing cracking (Westwood book, 1978). Any factor that advances maturity or causes a "hardening" of the fruit skin can aggravate cracking such as a drought, a nutrient shortage or a caustic spray. The best future approach probably is breeding to eliminate the character.

See Chapter V for chemical weed control.

HARVESTING CHERRIES

There is no standard degreee of maturity for picking the cherry. Flavor and over-all color as determined by sampling a few fruits of each variety, furnish the best guides for time to harvest. Cherries, like peaches, increase in size until ripe and should be left on the tree as long as feasible to attain the maximum poundage per tree. With firm-fleshed sweet cherries, there is some tendency among growers to harvest early to obtain better prices. This practice, however, results in less flavor and color and smaller size. Furthermore, cherries picked before fully mature will not ripen off the tree; if picked half ripe, they remain half ripe. Red tart cherries are harvested when they have obtained sufficient size and color for the canning market. However, it is usually determined by the ease of mechanical harvesting. Many tart cherry processors require less than 10 percent of the fruits to have stems attached (see Figure 15).

Investigations show that the final increase in fruit size may be 35 per cent from the time they can first be picked (although premature) until full maturity. Full mature cherries are less subject to shrinkage in volume when canned than those picked early. In fact, there is actually little reason for early picking of cherries for the cannery.

The period for picking cherries may be shortened by hot dry weather during ripening. The soft-fleshed juicy varieties tend to mature and deteriorate more rapidly than the firm-fleshed varieties which generally provide a longer period for picking and handling. Of the tart cherries, English Morello will hang on the trees longer without deterioration than Montmorency or Early Richmond. Brown rot, fruit deterioration can be prevented by using a fungicide prior to harvest and cooling rapidly after harvest.

Ethephon promotes fruit loosening for mechanical harvesting of sweets and tarts. Cultivar, concentration, time of applications, and climate before and after harvest are key. Suggestions in Michigan: 300 ppm for light sweets, 400 ppm for dark sweets; 200 ppm for tarts; applied 7-14 days before harvest; between 60° and 80° F. Do not use on stressed or low-vigor trees or those gumming. Consult label.

Alar is particularly valuable on tarts, advancing and concentrating maturity, increasing fruit firmness and color and promoting fruit loosening. For tarts, apply Alar-85 at 2-4 lbs./100 gal. 2 wks. AFB. One to 2 lbs./100 improves firmness without affecting maturity or other responses. For sweets, apply at 1-2 lbs./100 2 wks. AFB. Alar results in advanced maturity, more color, some reduction in fruit removal force. It is suggested for canning, fresh market sweets, but not for brining. Don't use on low-vigor trees; will advance maturity 5-7 days with no effect on quality.

Hand Harvesting. Where cherries are to be harvested by hand, either by grower-hired help or by pick-it-yourself customers, the grower must prepare well ahead to be supplied adequately with ladders, a weighing station, picking buckets, lugs, containers, and other equipment to get the crop off within 10-14 days. A high school teacher with his students may be contracted to do the job, releasing the grower for sales and other details. A picker in a commercial orchard may harvest 300-400 lbs. of tart cherries per day (highest on record, 1,357 lbs. of Napoleons). With mechanical harvesting taking over, commercial hand harvesting will become almost non-existent.

Mechanical Harvesting — Bulk Handling. Michigan State University, USDA and cooperating commercial companies and growers have led in the development of mechanical harvesting techniques starting in the 1950's-60's to cut harvest costs, simplify and speed the operation, and improve the product for processing where nearly all tarts now are utilized.

Tart Cherries. One type of equipment used to shake and catch tart cherries and get them to the processor quickly and in cooled condition is shown in Figure 16. Improvements in equipment are being made yearly. Average equipment can harvest 25 to 30 or more trees an hour. It is more efficient on: (1) well loaded trees (it takes as long to harvest a tree with 50 lbs. as 100 lbs., (b) on mowed or short ground cover, (c) on trees well pruned, and (d) on ground that is fairly level. In the early 1970's cost to harvest by machines was generally about 3.0 cents a pound and by hand picking about 5 cents. The money saved by machine harvesting 100,000 tons of tarts in Michigan, figuring amortization charges on equipment, was well over six million dollars. In the 1980s it could be 2 to 3 times this figure.

Michigan State University makes the following suggestions for machine harvesting cherries:

"**Prune** to reduce main limbs to 4, open lower part of the tree, eliminate willowy hanging branches, induce uniform ripening, reduce excessive tree spread. **Spray, fertilize,** (and heat during frosts if necessary) to induce heavy yields of firm, well colored, high grade fruit. **Level the ground** by cultivation tools and keep ground cover low during harvest. **Obtain machines early** with adequate spare parts. Check **water supply** and **containers. Discuss plans** thoroughly with processor field person to schedule arrival of cherries at plant. **Before harvest:** employ good responsible harvest crew, train them well, pad surfaces where cherries fall, arrange for plenty of ice, check fruit maturity and decide in what tree block to start harvesting, make a "shake-down run" to train crew and check equipment. **When harvest starts:** supervise closely, avoid undue haste, attach shaker arm claw to limb at right angle, shake in short bursts (½ - 3 sec.) at frequencies of 1000-2000/min. Allow fruit to clear collecting frame between bursts, obtain steady light flow of fruit, leave fruit on tree that does not free easily, stop shaker if leaves begin to fall, keep on tree that does not free easily, keep fabric tight on collecting surfaces, watch for oil leaks and keep any trace of oil away from fruit. **After picking:** avoid unnecessary handling, skim trash off tanks, keep water below 60°F with ice if needed, move fruit promptly to cannery on schedule. **Encourage processor at plant to:** hold fruit in cooled tanks until processing, handle fruit carefully avoiding drops, use well-designed water-filled flumes or well-adjusted conveyor belts, limit soak time (including orchard soak) to 10 hours, remove small and crushed cherries with eliminator, keep fruit one layer deep on eliminator, use mechanical destemmer for early-harvested fruit and provide a bypass for late-harvested fruit when stems are not a

problem, keep electric fruit sorters in proper adjustment, help growers avoid and solve any mutual problems, provide adequate fieldpersons, discourage late night-harvesting and on hot afternoons, and find a method to weigh-in fruit without draining the water away; latter procedure damages the fruit."

Sweet Cherries. Harvesting machines developed for tart

Figure 14. Zinc deficiency on sweet cherry (above) is characterized by whitish or dirty-white chlorosis between the main veins, rosetting of small narrow leaves, and dieback of limbs. Manganese deficient (lower) leaves have light-green areas near main veins with areas near main veins remaining a darker green. Zn and Mn deficiencies may be found in the same leaves. (Upper) Utah Agricultural Experiment Station; (Lower) Damon Boynton, Cornell University).

274

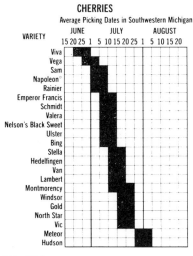

CHERRIES
Average Picking Dates in Southwestern Michigan

°Brining Maturity

Figure 15. At the left are the relative harvesting dates for several cherry cultivars grown in Michigan. (Hilltop Nursery, Hartford, MI 49057).

cherries are being used to harvest sweets, but more power is needed to shake effectively the larger trees, particularly on older trees. Special training, pruning, and other techniques on young sweet cherry trees no doubt will help adapt the trees better to machine harvesting.

Since sweets are not usually collected and transported in water, improved techniques are needed to fill the bins (46 x 46 x 24 inches deep filled to 16-20 inches) gently to avoid bruising. Dilute brine handling of cherries from orchard to processor improves quality.

Time to harvest is judged by pull or "feel." When fruit is ready to harvest, a sample of 15-20 fruit on a typical tree should detach "rather easily." Size and skin and flesh color and a "test shake" on one or two trees are also indices. Ethephon at 500 ppm cuts the stem "hold" on the tree. When sweets are harvested without Ethephon, there is more bruising, more cherries left on the tree, and less total size and weight of fruit, which generally is less desired by processors. Left on the tree too long, there is risk of fruit cracking, more brown rot, and the cherries becoming undersirably dark in color for the maraschino packers. Cherries brined for maraschinos immediately after harvest have significantly better processed quality than when there is a delay of 4 to 8 hours in brining.

Tension to pull cherries from the tree decreases from 450 to 300 grams pull for Schmidt over the two-week period before harvest. A simple device to take these measurements is available and known as a pull-force gauge. Cultivars being mechanically harvested in Michigan include Schmidt, Napoleon, Emperor, Hardy Giant, Black Tartarian, Hedelfingens, Gold and Windsor.

Volume Measurement. It became necessary with the advent of mechanical harvesting and bulk handling of cherries to find a new method for measuring the raw fruit before sale to processors and handlers.

Historically, cherries were sold by weight which was readily ascertained by determining the gross weight of a load of cherries, removing the fruit and determining a tare weight of containers and usually hauling equipment. However, in the case of mechanically harvested cherries in water (or brine) this became difficult and expensive. Thus, a method was devised whereby the fruit could be sold by volume.

A standardized container (pallet tank holding approximately 1000 lbs.) in terms of cubic feet per inch of depth plus a standardized calibrated gauge rod (dipstick) were devised. Subsequently a conversion factor "weight per cubic foot" of cheeries was determined.

In Michigan 47.45 lbs. per cubic foot is the conversion factor for red tart cherries. The conversion factor for sweet cherries in brine varies from 39-45 lbs. per cubic foot depending upon stems, maturity, etc. The average-agreed-upon conversion factor for sweet cherries in brine in Michigan is 42 lbs. per cubic foot.

Michigan weights and measures regulations permits the purchase of cherries by volume but do not permit the conversion of volume to weight. Thus, it is necessary for the industry to determine price by volume as well as by weight. The determination of price per cubic foot utilizes the pertinent conversion factor.

Pick-Your-Own. Where small orchards are located near cities, this method as described for peach and apple earlier, has worked satisfactorily for cherries.

Birds and Bear. Robins, starlings, and other birds may become a serious problem during harvest. They may damage more cherries than they eat. No remedy is 100% effective; try several. The insecticide, Mesurol, sprayed on trees up to 7 days before harvest repels the birds. Avitrol also works. Other practices to try for backyard trees are: (a) lobbing black thread back and forth over the tree; birds can't see it, touch it, are frightened; (b) placing pieces of glistening tin or heavy tin foil in the trees to dangle and shift with the wind; (c) using a scarecrow. If birds become a problem in large orchards, an automatic acetylene exploder or 2- or 3-inch firecrackers tied at intervals into a small rope "fuse" (obtainable on the market) should accommodate two to four acres of cherry orchard. Trapping of starlings in large special-built wire cages (U.S. Fish and Wild Life design) and cyaniding is permitted in most states. One company sells tapes of starling distress calls that frightens them away when played back on a loud speaker.

Ultra high frequency alarm systems are on the market that reportedly "jam" the birds audio system. Tests underway include (a) feeding birth control chemicals to birds which are unharmful to birds but eggs do not hatch, and (b) aerial spraying birds with detergent before a rain, destroying thousands. Automatic battery-driven alarms

Figure 16. Mechanical harvesting and handling of tart cherries has reduced costs markedly and improved quality. Increased tree plantings in leading cherry states has reuslted from this key advancement. (a) Self-propelled mobile catching frame has been moved into place and the attached two shaker-arms are positioned and ready to shake two of four main limbs. Equipment can harvest 25 to 40 trees an hour. (Mfg. by Friday Tractor Co., Hartford, Mich.). (b) Care is needed to keep an even but not excessive flow of cherries on conveyor; latter condition causes rolling, crushing and bruising of fruit, marring processed product. (c) Some growers use the trailer tank shown here for transporting cherries to the processor; others use the tanks (holding 1000 lbs. cherries shown in a & d) which are handled by fork lift. Water is held below 60°F

in tanks with ice to firm the cherries and reduce scald. (d) Cold water is circulated through the tanks for several hours at cooling station before transporting them to processor. Similar equipment is being used on sweet cherries except they are not handled in water. (Michigan State University, East Lansing).

are available.[1] A kite 100 ft. above ground with a hawk painted on the underside in Germany has frightened birds from 4-5 acres.

In Idaho and the Flathead River area of Montana, bear may cause heavy breakage of limbs while seeking sweet cherries in season. No fool-proof control has been devised.

DISEASES AND INSECTS

Most important fungus diseases of cherry east of the rockies are *leaf spot* of foliage and *brown rot* of fruit. *Powdery mildew* may be a problem in both the East and West. *Leaf spot* overwinters on fallen leaves which eject spores to the wind in spring, eventually germinating on new leaves and causing yellowish then brown spots in great numbers. *Leaf spot* is aggravated by damp weather. *Brown rot* is the number one problem in Eastern orchards, particularly where fruit has been injured by curculio or cracked by excessive rain or hail. Where infection is present, cracking can become a real problem in mechanically harvested tart orchards. Other fungus diseases include *black rot* and *leaf rust,* which are controlled by standard sprays for *leaf spot* and *brown rot.*

Virus yellows, frequently following *ring spot virus,* is a problem. Leaves show green and yellow mottling with waves of defoliation starting three to four weeks after petal fall. Trees infected for several years develop abnormally large leaves and few spurs and bear small crops of large fruit. The tree gradually deteriorates. The Balsgard Station in Sweden has a disease-resistance breeding program. Specify *virus free* trees from the nursery.

Insect pests include *black cherry aphis, plus curculio, leaf roller, fruit flies,* (cherry maggot), *Mineola moth, mites, scales, sawfly, lesser peach tree borer, American plum borer,* and *slugs.* The sweet cherry "pitting" problem (wrinkled sunken areas on fruit) is thought to be due to the sucking damage of the *green soldier beetle.* See chapter XVIII for controls. USDA Handbooks 451, 442 by Fogle et al. have details on insects, diseases.

CONTAINERS, GRADING, STORAGE

Containers. Cherries, particularly tart cherries, are packed in many types of containers, ranging from 16- and 24-quart crates of individual quart baskets to 4-quart climax baskets and various types of lugs. Most tart cherries for the fresh market are loose-packed with the stems on.

---

[1]Av-Alarm Corp., POB 2488, Santa Maria, CA 93454.

276

Figure 17. Hand-sorting cherries has been replaced by machine sorting (above), by electrically light-beam-scanning and kicking out defective fruit. Below, 10-ton tank trucks haul tart cherries in cold water from orchard to "receiving station" where cherries are assembled, weighted on automatic scales, cold-soaked, then flumed to tank trucks to go to processing plant. (Mich. State Univ., E. Lansing. 48823).

The most widely used containers for sweet cherries from the Pacific Coast continue to be the Calex Lug and the Campbell Lug, both standardized by California. The Campbell Lug, measuring 3 3/4 x 11 1/2 x 14 1/8 and containing 15-16 pounds net, is the most popular shipping package for fancy cherries. The fruit is packed in rows with the top layer, or two top layers, faced. The row count across the width of the container is marked on the package, also the cultivar and net weight. The Calex Lug, measuring 3 3/4 x 13 1/2 x 16 1/8 and containing approximately 18 pounds net, is extensively used for loose, bulk and bunch-faced packs. Bunch-faced cherries are arranged carefully to look much like the faced row-pack, and must be marked with the row size or minimum diameter in terms of inches.

There has been an increase in the marketing of fresh sweet cherries in transparent film bags and folding boxes or trays, either overwrapped or with film windows. The packages are shipped in master-containers. Fiberboard containers are the rule although some shippers use a slatted-type wooden box. There is no standard master-container. California cherries, if packed in other than master-containers, must be marked "Irregular Container." The film bags and over-wrapped trays usually

hold one pound or one-half pound. In Washington State, studies by U.S.D.A. showed that poly liners for the standard 15-pound lug reduced decay markedly and improved stem freshness and fruit brightness after simulated conditions of shipment and a two-day store treatment. (See Gerhardt *et al.*)

Grading. Cherries for fancy packs, canning, or freezing are graded from canvas trays or a moving belt (Figure 18). Fruits are removed which show evidence of insect damage such as curculio, fruit fly (maggot), brown rot, or cracking. Cherries showing wind bruising (brown discoloration of the skin) also are eliminated. All cherries that pass this inspection are put in Grade 1. Larger cherries may bring a premium. Sweet cherries for fresh trade frequently are sorted into several sizes after the blemished fruits have been removed. Highest prices usually are obtained for the largest fruits.

Storage. Cherries are not adapted to long storage, but may be held 10 to 14 days while the market is being cleared of an excess supply. They should be stored at a temperature of 31°-32° F. and 89-90% humidity to reduce wilting and brown rot. Sweet cherries can be held 31° F. for 25 days in 10% CO_2, then ripened for 2 days at 70°F. to fair quality with good appearance, comparable to sweets in sealed polyethylene liners. There is little benefit of CA over other storage of sweets but some growers are extending the marketing season by 42 days.

Prior to storage, research in Michigan indicates that a three-minute dip in hot water at 125° F. plus an appropriate fungicide such as Benlate eliminates brown rot and lessens other rots so that cherries may be stored satisfactorily in coolers for over three weeks.

Cherries to be shipped to distant markets should be precooled by hydrocooling or by pressure cooling to reduce field temperature from 80° to 40°F. in an hour, before shipping in refrigerated cars. Firm-fleshed sweet cherries may be shipped for a distance of a 1000 miles under conditions of non-refrigerated express. Soft-fleshed cherries hardly could be shipped successfully 200 miles. Some growers truck soft-fleshed cherries 100 to 300 miles over good roads, and firm-fleshed sweet cherries as much as 350 miles during the night and early morning hours to save cost of a refrigerator car and cartage at destination.

Freezing. Sweet and tart cherries can be frozen and held for a longer marketing season.

MARKETING

The largest percentage of both the sweet and tart cherries reach the consumer either directly or indirectly

Note: For up-to-date fruit container specifications, contact Agent-in-charge, 516 W. Jackson Blvd., Chicago, IL 60606. Great Lakes Fruit Grower News, POB 128, MI 49345 carries regular monthly news on cherries, other fruit crops in the midwest.

through the tin can or the frozen pack. The relative amount of sweet and tart cherries sold fresh, canned, frozen, or brined may vary somewhat from year to year (Table 5).

TABLE 5. UTILIZATION OF SWEET AND TART CHERRIES IN THE UNITED STATES (PERCENT).

	Fresh Market	Canned	Frozen	Brined	Juice
Tart	3	30	60	Negligible	7
Sweets	37	13	1	49	Negligible

Although the grower may not obtain a cannery or frozen-pack price he considers satisfactory, his crop is usually contracted before harvesting begins. The final problem of finding a consumer for the fruit rests mostly with the processor or re-manufacturer and not the producer.

Bargaining. Tart cherries in eastern U.S. are bargained to processors by American Agricultural Cooperative Marketing Association and its state affiliates. Similar organizations, such as the Flathead Lake Sweet Cherry Growers (cooperative) Association, and the Flathead Lake Cherry Growers, Inc., in Idaho, assist grower members in their marketing problems.

Promotion. The National Red Cherry Institute headquartered at East Lansing, Michigan and its state affiliates, the New York Cherry Growers Association, the Michigan Association of Cherry Producers, and Wisconsin Red Cherry Institute carries on National promotional activities to assist in selling processed tart cherries. February has been declared National assist Cherry month and many cherry promotion activities center around George Washington's birthday in remembrance of his chopping down a cherry tree. The National Cherry Festival is held in July each year at Traverse City, Michigan, the center of the nation's tart cherry industry. The industry wide promotion of sweet cherries is under the direction of the National Sweet Cherry Growers and Industries Foundation headquartered in Corvallis, Oregon. Many processors, pie bakers, maraschino manufacturers and other manufacturers of cherry products also carry on promotion programs aimed primarily at selling their own brand.

If fresh shipments are made to distant points, the cherry growers must follow trade channels similar to those described for apples in Chapter XII. Due to the perishable nature of cherries, the major portion is precooled and shipped by express. Sweet cherries washed and in poly bags move well in supermarkets.

There is less loss at the store level from bulk displays than from prepackaged sweet cherries. Parasitic and physiological diseases are more important than mechanical

Figure 18. (Above) Eliminator is separating small cannery Bings before the automatic sizer in Lodi, California. (Below) Automatic box fillers shut off at 18.25 lbs. This cherry packing-cooling facility accommodates 1000 packages/hr. (The Packer).

damage. USDA has color charts to identify by inspectors various types of damage to fruit.

In big centers of consumption such as Chicago and Detroit, a large amount of cherries are sold fresh-frozen as slush-pack. Restaurants use a sizeable percentage of these shipments in cherry pies and cobblers during the fresh cherry season. Some fresh cherries may be sold to hucksters who peddle the fruit for small sales. Roadside markets offer a good outlet for fresh cherries on well traveled highways. In fact, cherries come at a time when the roadside markets, restaurants, and retail stores are not well supplied with other fresh fruit. In order to cater to this type of trade, however, the medium to small cherry grower should plant a considerable number of varieties, beginning the season with an extra early variety, such as Vista or Valera and closing it with Hedelfingen, Vic or Van, or another equally late and equally good variety. Good roadside market trade will depend upon high-quality cherries packaged attractively.

Japan is a growing and important outlet for USA sweet cherries.

Housewife's needs. A Cornell University survey of 3,000 housewives in five scattered New York cities indicated about 75 percent of all cherries bought were used in pies. The balance was used in various desserts. Packs bought in order of preference were: canned, cherry pie filler, frozen cherry pies, and frozen cherries. Popular size pie tin for cooking was 8 to 9 inches in diameter and 1 1/4 inches deep. Available size tins were generally considered too small; 53 percent of the wives would like a larger size. Some objected to poor color of water packed cherries, the small amount of cherries in pie filler, and the small size of individual cherries. Convenience products such as frozen pies, frozen pastries, cherry cheesecakes, cherry shortcakes and "high" pies show increasing promise in cherry marketing.

Dried tart cherries ("chaisins") has a potential sales outlet in fruit bars, coffee cake, etc., and the advantages of a dried product in storing and handling.

Federal Order in Tart Cherries. The tart cherry industry of Eastern U.S. voted in 1972 to utilize provisions of the Federal Marketing Order legislation of 1937 permitting supply control. A board of six growers and six processors elected by their geographic constituency, administer provisions of this program in cooperation with the USDA to improve the marketing of tart cherries. The order in this industry was set up to correct the historical problem of widely fluctuating crops of tart cherries from one year to the next due to weather conditions. A portion of the crop is stored in years of heavy supply (thus removing it from the market) and subsequently re-entering the frozen stored cherries into the market in years of short supply. The order assists the industry in providing the market with a more stable supply of fruit than has historically been true, thus, over the long run increasing product and market development and ultimately consumption of the product.

COST OF GROWING CHERRIES[1]

The amount of profit that a grower can make from a cherry orchard will depend upon three factors: (a) yields, (b) production costs, and (c) current prices. Yields vary considerably from one area to another and from one orchard to another. Over a period of 30 years, the census yield per acre for Washington, Oregon, and California, was estimated to be 2200 pounds. In the eastern states, where most of the trees are of the tart cultivars, the average production is about 1200 pounds. These figures for both

the East and West include comparatively young-bearing trees as well as those in full-bearing, and likewise, those with poor care as well as the better orchards. Experienced growers will recognize these figures as being very low and not representative of good commercial orchards. Good commercial orchards in Michigan begin to bear at five to six years and reach 6000 to 10,000 pounds/A/year over a 10-year period, beginning with the 8th or 9th year at which time the orchard usually reaches full production. Trees continue at this production until about 20 to 22 years, after which they decline more or less rapidly as the case may be. There are authentic Montmorency yields in Michigan of 22,000 lbs./A These figures give some idea of what a Montmorency orchard can do when conditions are reasonably favorable with good cultural practices. Sweet cherries produce 1000 lbs./A at 8 to 9 years with an increase of from 7000 to 8000 when 14 yrs. old.

When the harvesting was accomplished by hand, the expected commercially productive life of tart cherry trees in New York was estimated at 30 to 40 yrs. and for sweet cherries, 50 to 60 yrs. However, mechanical harvesting has reduced this significantly. In Michigan these estimates are now as follows: Montmorency, 25 yrs.; sweet cherries, 30 yrs. The commercially productive life of a cherry tree may vary widely according to cultural practices, insects and diseases, regions, and other factors affecting tree vigor.

In Michigan, Montmorency is the big commercial tart variety. The English Morello has given satisfactory results in some regions, whereas in other regions it did not prove profitable. Early Richmond and Louis Phillipe were doubtful for extensive planting. Sweet cherries such as Windsor, Schmidt, Napoleon and like cultivars are the commercial sweet cherry cultivars. However, sweet cherries only do well in the north part of the state. Because of fruit cracking, the Lambert and Bing can be a liability.

The itemized man-hours per acre for growing and harvesting tart cherries in Michigan are given in Table 4. Picking (non-mechanized) required the most labor,

TABLE 4. AVERAGE HOURS OF MAN LABOR REQUIRED BY OPERATIONS IN 69 TART CHERRY ORCHARDS IN MICHIGAN, (ADAPTED FROM WRIGHT AND JOHNSTON)

Operation	Hours Per Acre
Growing	
Pruning and brush removal	17.3
Spreading fertilizer	2.1
Spraying	11.7
Cultivating	4.8
Other	3.7
Total	39.6
Harvesting*	
Picking (hand)	64.4
Total to grow and pick 1102-pound yield	104.0
Total to grow and pick 1937-pound yield	162.7

* Machine harvesting covers about 30 trees an hour, crew of four, taking 16 hrs./A. See Table 5.

---

[1]Recent growing costs can be obtained from the departments of agricultural economics in state universities where the tarts (Michigan) or sweets are largely grown (California, Washington, Oregon).

followed in order by pruning and brush removal, and spraying. With machine harvesting, costs can be reduced 75 to 80%.

Recent growing costs can be obtained from the departments of agricultural economics in state universities where the tarts (Michigan) or sweets are largely grown (California, Washington, Oregon). Cost of harvesting by hand per lb. is about 4 times as much as by machine. Or a crew of 4 can mechanically harvest, conservatively, about 30 trees/hour (Table 5) or an acre of trees in about 4 hours, totaling 16 man hours per acre as compared with 64.4 hours hand harvest. Hours devoted to cultivation also may be reduced where herbicides are used in the row and the middles are mowed.

TABLE 5. COMPARISON OF RESULTS IN MACHINE (SLOPING-SURFACE TYPE) HARVESTING TART AND SWEET CHERRIES IN MICHIGAN. MI. STATE UNIVERSITY, E. LANSING.

No. in crew	Kind of Cherry	Cultivar	Tree age	Trees per hour	lbs. per tree	lbs. per hour	% Fruit Removed	% Fruit Bruised
4	Sweet	Schmidt	11	30	79	2370	94	18
4	Tart	Mont-morency	16	36	83	2988	97	21

Cost of growing an acre of red tart cherries in New York (Cornell data) up to harvest showed a decline as the size of enterprise increased. The land charge was one-quarter to one-third the total cost. Farm labor accounted for about one-fifth of the total. Charge for power declined from 14 to 8 percent of the total cost of growing. This was in part due to the more efficient use of larger tractors. Sprays and dusts comprised a little less than one-fifth of the total growing costs and ranged from 14 percent of the budget in small enterprises to 21 percent for medium enterprises. The larger growers bought chemicals in larger quantities at reduced prices. Commercial fertilizer use rose as size of enterprise increased, reaching eventually 13 percent of the budget in large enterprises.

Prices received for cherries obviously fluctuate with supply and demand. Average prices paid per ton for tart cherries at the farm in the eastern states of Michigan, Wisconsin, Pennsylvania and New York, are close to the same, but the prices for sweet cherries per ton in the western states of Idaho, Oregon, Washington, Montana and California may be 50% higher than for sweets grown in Michigan and New York.

Higher prices may be obtained for early and particularly fancy products sold in small packages. However, the extra handling charges for the small packages usually absorb much of the difference so that in the end, the net profit obtained for a fancy packed product is not much more than that obtained for the product at the packing house or delivered to a cannery.

In order to make a profit, it is usually necessary for the yield of cherries to exceed 2500 to 3000 pounds per acre. Cherry orchards producing as little as 1200 pounds per acre are unquestionably a losing proposition, except perhaps during war periods when there is great need for food. Substantial profits can be realized from Montmorency orchards only where production costs per pound can be kept low by obtaining yields well over a general average of 50 pounds per tree.

In Michigan, V.R. Gardner stated: "Indeed, it may be questioned if the producer of any other kind of fruit has within his ability to obtain greater net profit than the cherry grower. This is far from stating the profits as certain. Probably as large a percentage of cherry growers fail to make expenses as is true with most fruits. Nevertheless, the possibility of a profitable industry exists where soil and climatic conditions are favorable for heavy and regular yields and where good marketing facilities are available; and this may become a certainty where cultural methods are employed that promote a vigorous growth and provide protection from injurious insects and diseases."

Review Questions

1. Discuss the leading world and U.S. commercial cherry producing areas.
2. Why has U.S. cherry production increased in some areas and decreased in others?
3. Discuss any changes in the tart and sweet cherry cultivar situation in recent years, giving reasons.
4. What is a Duke cherry?
5. List 2 important cultivars of tart, sweet, and Duke cherries.
6. What are the climatic and soil requirements of tart and sweet cherries?
7. What are the pollination requirements of the tart, sweet and Duke cherries?
8. Are tart cherry cultivars generally used for cross-pollination of sweet and Duke cherries? Why?
9. What rootstocks are frequently used for cherries? What are the respective merits? What is the situation on compact cherry trees?
10. What is the relative resistance to cold of commercial cultivars of sweet and tart cherries as compared with the peach?
11. What system of training the trees is suggested for sweet and tart cherries in your general area? Discuss training and pruning for mechanical harvesting.
12. With regard to other deciduous fruits, what is the relative amount of pruning recommended for the cherries?
13. What is the approximate length of shoot growth desired in young and mature tart cherry trees? Should the desired shoot growth be obtained by pruning, cultivation, nitrogen fertilizations, or irrigation as needed? Discuss.
14. Describe a good soil management system for young and mature cherry trees on a medium sandy-loam soil in your area.
15. Discuss fruit thinning of sweet and tart cherries.
16. When is the proper time to harvest: (a) tart cherries for canning, (b) sweet cherries for fancy pack? Discuss techniques, problems, advantages of mechanical harvesting and bulk handling for fresh and processing cherries.
17. List the growth regulator chemicals being usd before harvest; describe effects.
18. Under what conditions and how long should cherries be stored?
19. What is the approximate amount of tart and sweet cherries processed and sold fresh?
20. Discuss factors influencing net returns in cherry growth?
21. What is an approximate yield one may expect from a well-managed

orchard of tart, sweet, and Duke cherry trees in full bearing?
22. At about what year do tart cherries reach full production?
23. At what age under Michigan conditions do tart cherries begin to show a decline in production?

Suggested Collateral Readings

ACKLEY, W.B. and W.H. Krueger. Overhead irrigation water quality and the cracking of sweet cherries. HortSci. 15(3):289-290. 1980.

AEBIG, D.E. and D.H. Dewey, Ethephon improves marketability of 'Schmidt' sweet cherries picked without stems. HortSci. 9:448-449. 1974.

ANDERSON, R.L. Cherry situation in USA. (Good summary as of 1981 for all cherry states). Fruit Var. Journ. 35(3). 83-92. July 1981.

ANDERSON, P.D. and D.G. Richardson. Measuring fruit water as related to rain-cracking of sweet cherries. J. ASHS 107(3) 441-4. 1982.

ANSTEY, T.H. Full bloom prediction for apple, pear, cherry, peach and apricot based on air temperature. ASHS 88:57-66. 1966.

AXFORD, M.A. et al. Scion and rootstock on nutrients in leaves of scions and rootstocks of sweet cherry. HortSci. 10:234-235. 1975.

BASS, L.N. Cherry seed storage. (USDA, Ft. Collins, Colo.) Contact personally at USDA Seed Lab.

BOLEN, J.S. and B.F. Cargill. Mechanized harvest of tart cherries. Michigan Ext. Bull. E-660, Farm Sci. Ser. Cherry Harvest Mechanizations. (2) June, 1970.

BROOKS, R.M. and H.P. Olmo. Register of new fruit and nut varieties list 29. HortSci. 9:437-441. 1974.

BUKOVAC, M.J. et al. Effects of (2-Chloroethyl) phosphonic acid on development and abscission of maturing sweet cherry. J. ASHS. Vol. 96, No. 6., p. 777, Nov. 1971.

CHAPLIN, M.H. and A.L. Kenworthy. The influence of Alar ripening of 'Windsor' sweet cherry. J. ASHS 95 (5):536. 1970.

CHAPLIN, M.H. and M.N. Westwood. A method for estimating the yields of sweet cherry. HortScience 7(5):508. 1972.

CHILDERS, N. F. Fruit nutrition — Temperate to tropical. Cherry nutrition, Chap. VI, by M.N. Westwood and F.B. Wann. pp. 158-173 Hort. Publ., Univ. of Florida, Gainesville. 1966.

CLINE, R.A. and J.A. Archibald. Nutritional factors and low temperature injury in peach and tart cherry. Ontario Hort. Exp. Sta. Ann. Rpt. 1967.

CLINE, R.A. and O.A. Bradt. Soil drainage and compaction effects on growth, yield and leaf composition of cherries and peaches. Hort.

COUEY, H.M. et al. Ethephon and harvest method on quality of stemless sweet cherries for fresh market. HortSci., 9:587-588. 1974.

COUEY, H.M. and T.R. Wight. Bruising of Sweet Cherries, Temperature and Fruit Ripeness. HortSci. 9:587. 1974.

CUMMINS, J.N. Exotic rootstocks for cherries. Fruit Var. Journ. 33(3):74-84. 1979.

CUMMINS, J.N. Interspecific hybrids as rootstocks for cherries. Fruit Var. Journ. 33(3):85-89. July 1979.

CURWEN, D., F.J. Mcardle and C.M. Ritter. NPK effects on fruit firmness, pectic content of Montmorency cherry. ASHS 89:72-79. 1966.

DAVENPORT, D.C. et al. Crop load, growth, fruit size affected by antitranspirant. HortSci. 17(2):217-8. April 1982.

DAVENPORT, D.C. K. Uriu and R.M. Hagan. Antitranspirant film: curtailing intake of external water by cherry fruit to reduce cracking. HortScience 7(5):507. 1972.

DAVISON, R.M. et al. Changes in inhibitor (ABA) levels in tart cherry seed and pericarp. J. ASHS 101(5):519-523. 1976.

DIAZ, D.H. et al. Flower bud differentiation in sweet cherry. ASHS 106(4):513-5. 1981.

DRAKE, S.R., et al. Growth regulators on fresh and processed 'Rainer' cherries. J. ASHS 103(2):162-164. 1978.

FACTEAU, T.J. Sweet cherry, hydrogen flouride fumigation and N levels. J. ASHS. 103(1):115-119. 1978.

FACTEAU, T.J. and K.E. Rowe. Factors associated with surface pitting of sweet cherry. J. ASHS. 104(5):706-710. 1979.

FRECON, J. Starkrimson, Cherry (Zaiger 16-200). Fruit Var. Journ. 34(1):18-20. Jan. 1980.

FRENCH, A.P. Plant characters of cherry varieties. Mass. Agr. Exp. Sta. Bull. 401.1943.

GARLEY, B. Ah-oon-ye-ya-pa, The Sand Cherry: Its origin, improvement and nomenclature. Fruit Var. Journ. 34(1):13-17. Jan. 1980.

GERHARDT, F. et al. Sealed liners for packaging cherries. USDA-AMS-21. 8p. Sept. 1956.

GREAT LAKES FRUIT GROWER News. POB 128. Sparta, Mi. 49345 carries regular monthly news on cherries.

HARRINGTON, W.O., et al. Ethyl oleate sprays to reduce cracking of sweet cherries. Hortsci. 13(3):279-280. 1978.

HEDRICK, U.P. Cherries of New York. N.Y. Agr. Exp. Sta. Geneva. (out-of-print). 1925.

HOPPING, M.E., Young, and M.J. Bukovac. Endogenous plant growth substances in developing fruit of *Prunus cerasus* L. VI. Cytokinins in relation to initial fruit development. J. ASHS. 104(1):47-52. 1979.

HOWELL, G.S. and S.S. Stackhouse. The effect of defoliation time on acclimation and dehardening in tart cherry. (*Prunus cerasus* L.) J. ASHS 98(2):132. March 1973.

JANICK, J. Advances in Fruit Breeding. Chap. on cherries by H.W. Fogle. 19 pp. Purdue Univ. Press, Lafayette, IN 47907. 1975.

KENWORTHY, A.L. Effect of sods, mulches, fertilizers on production, soluble solids, leaf and soil analysis of cherry. Mich. Tech. Bull. 243, 39pp. June 1954.

KESNER, C.D. et al. Mechanical summer tipping of cherry trees Fruit Var. J. *322.* 26-8. 1978.

LANE, W.D. Compact sweet cherries. Fruit Var. J. *32*:2. 37-9. 1978.

LARSEN, F.E. Sweet cherry dwarfing rootstocks. Good Fruit Grower (Canada). Feb. 1, 1972.

LARSEN, F.E. and M.E. Patterson. Interstock/rootstock effect on Bing cherry fruit quality. Fruit Var. Journ. Vol. 35, No. 1, Jan. 1981.

LIDSTER, P.D. et al. A texture measurement technique for sweet cherries. HortSci. 13(5):536-538. 1978.

LIDSTER, P.D. et al. Texture modification of 'Van' sweet cherries by postharvest calcium treatments. J. ASHS 103(4):527-530. 1978.

LIDSTER, P.D. et al. Preharvest and postharvest calcium treatment on fruit calcium and susceptibility of 'Van' cherry to impact damage. J. ASHS. 104(6):790-793. 1979.

LIDSTER, P.D. Emulsifiable coatings on sweet cherry fruit. ASHS 106(4). 478-80. 1981.

LYON, T.L., A.J. Heinicke and B.D. Wilson. The relation of soil moisture and nitrates to the effects of sod on plum and cherry trees. Cornell Agr. Exp. Sta. Memoir 91 (New York). 1925.

MARSHALL, R.E. Cherries and cherry products. Interscience Publishing, Inc., N.Y. 283 pp. 1954.

MICKE, W.C. et al. Pruning methods for bearing sweet cherry trees. Calif. Ag. May, 1968.

MICKE, W.C. and W.R. Schreader. Rootstocks for sweet cherry. Calif. Fruit Var. J. *32*:3. 29-30. 1978.

MIELEKE E.A. and F.G. Dennis, Jrs. Hormonal control of flower bud dormancy in sour cherry (*Prunus cerasus* L.). III. Effects of leaves, defoliation and temperature on levels of abscisic acid in flower primodia. J. ASHS 103(4):446-449. 1978.

MIRCETICH, S.M. Root and crown rot of cherry trees. Calif. Agric. Aug. 1976.

MITCHELL, F.G., et al. Injuries cuasing deterioration of sweet cherries. Calif. Agr. Apr. 1980.

MODLIBOWSKA, I. and M.F. Wickenden. GA3 and 2,4,5-TP on cherry fruit set. J. Hort. Sci. 57(7):413-22. 1982.

OOSTEN, H.J. van. Studies on dwarfing rootstocks for sweet cherry. De Fruitteelt 64:231-233. 1974 (In Dutch).

O'ROURKE, A.O. et al. Sweet cherry consumers. Wash. State Univ. Cir. 577. 11/74; Competition in fresh sweet cherries. Wash. Bull. 803; Marketing Northwest sweet cherries. Wash. Bull. 800. 10/74.

PEST Control of cherries. Contact your local government experiment station or agricultural extension agent for up-to-date recommendations.

POLLACK, R.L. et al. Studies on cherry scald. Part I and Part II. Food Technology *12*: No. 2 pp. 102-105, 106-108. 1958.

POOVAIAH, B.W., H.P. Rasmussen, and M.J. Bukovac. Histochemical localization of enzymes in the abscission zones of maturing sour and sweet cherry fruit. J. ASHS 98(1):16. 1973.

PORRITT, S.W. and J.L. Mason. CA storage of sweet cherries. ASHS

87:128-130. 1965.

PORRITT, S.W. et al. Storage surface pitting of sweet cherries. Canadian Jour. of Pl. Sci. 51:(5) p. 409-414. Sept. 1971.

PROCESSING of cherries. Contact food technology departments at Oregon State Univ., Corvallis; N.Y. Agr. Exp. Sta., Geneva; Hort. Res. Instit. of Ontario, Vineland, Canada; Mich. Sta. Univ., E. Lansing.

PROEBSTING, E.L. and H.H. Mills. Bloom delay and frost survival in ethephon-treated sweet cherry. HortScience 8(1):46. 1973.

PROEBSTING, E.L. and H.H. Mills. A comparison of hardiness responses in fruit buds of 'Bing' cherry and 'Elberta' peach. J. ASHS 97(6): 802. 1972.

PROEBSTING, E.L. Jr. G.H. Carter, and H.H. Mills. Quality improvement in canned 'Rainier' cherries. J. ASHS 98(4):334. 1973. July.

PROEBSTING, E.L., Jr. and H.H. Mills. Daminoxide on growth, maturity, quality, yield of sweet cherries. ASHS 101(2):175-9. 1976.

PROEBSTING, E.L. Jr. and H.H. Mills. Ethephon increases cold hardiness of sweet cherry. J. ASHS 101:31-33. 1976.

PROEBSTING, E.H. and H.H. Mills. Season and crop load effects on Bing cherry maturity. ASHS 106(2) 144-3. March 1981.

RYUGO, Kay. Alar effects on red color in sweet cherry. ASHS 88: 160-166. 1966.

RYUGO, K. and W. Micke. Vladimir, a promising dwarfing rootstock or sweet cherry. HortSci. 10:585. 1975.

SAWADA, E. Studies on the cracking of cherries. Agr. and Hort., Vol. 6 No. 6, pp.3-30. 1931 (in Japanese with English summary).

SEELIG, R.A. Sweet cherries (Botany to sales). Fruit and Vegetable Facts and Pointers. 1019 19th St., N.W., Wash., D.C. 20036. 16p. 1974.

SHERMAN, W.B. 1977. Cherry breeding in Florida. Fruit Var. Jour. 31:(3)60-61. 1977.

SMITH, R.B. and F.I. Cook. Weight-to-volume relationship of cherries suspended in water. Hort. Res. Inst., Vineland, Ontario 1970 rpt.

STEBBINS, et al. Sweet cherries on clonal understocks. Fruit Var. J. 32:2. 31-7. 1978.

STEWART, W.L. and D.M. Baumgartner. English sparrow and startling control. Washington EM-3772 mimeo folder 13pp. June 1973.

SURANYI, D. Self-fertility and self-fertility in Prunus by stamen-number-pistil-length ratio. HortSci. 11(4):406-7. 1976.

TEHRANI, G. Effects on "Montmorency" cherry of four successive years application of succinic acid 2, 2-dimethylhydrazide (SADH). J. ASHS 98(5):468-. Sept. 1973.

TVERGYAK, P.J. and D.G. Richardson, Diurnal changes of leaf and fruit water potentials of sweet cherries during harvest period. HortSci. 14(4):520-521. Aug. 1979.

URIU, K. et al. Preharvest antitranspirant spray on cherries. Calif. Agr. Oct. 1975.

U.S. Standards for sweet cherries and for sweet cherries for export, for sulphur brining, U.S. Dept. of Agr. AMS. Washington, D.C. Request latest report.

WADE, G.L. and D.H. Dewey. Control of internal browning of Schmidt sweet cherries by handling in water. 10:583-584. 1975.

WADLEY, B.N. 'Angela', and X-Disease Resistant Sweet Cherry. Fruit Var. Jour. 29:70. 1975.

WAY, Roger D. Cherry varieties in New York State. N.Y. Food and Life Sci. Bull. 37.6 p. 1974.

WESTWOOD, M.N. Mahaleb X Mazzard hybrid cherry stocks. Fruit Va. J. 32:2.39. 1978.

WESTWOOD, M.N. Temperature Zone Pomology. W.H. Freeman. Co., San Fransisco. 428 pp. 1978.

WHITTENBERGER. R.T. et al. Electric sorting machines for tart cherries. USDA-ARS 73-45 (2116) Oct. 1964.

WILDE, M.H. and L.J. Edgerton. Histology of ethephon injury on 'Montmorency' cherry branches. HortSci. 10:79-81. 1975.

WITTENBACH, V.A. and M.J. Bukovac. Cherry fruit abscission: Peroxidase activity in the abscission zone in relation to separation. J. ASHS 100:387-391. 1975.

WITTENBACH, V.A. and M.J .Bukovac. Cherry fruit abscission: A role for ethylene in mechanically induced abscission. J. ASHS 100:302-307. 1975.

WITTENBACH, V.A. and M.J. Bukovac. Cherry fruit abscission: Effect of growth substances, metabolic inhibitors and environmental factors. J. ASHS 98(4):348. July 1973.

YU, K.S. and R.F. Carlson. Gas liquid chromatography determinations of phenolic acids and coumarins in Mazzard and Mahaleb cherry seedlings. HortSci. 10:401-403. 1975.

ZAGAYA, S.W. Effect of termination temperatures on development of seedlings from immature embryos. Bull. Acad. Polon. Sci. CL. V. 9:591-592. 1963.

(See additional references in former book editions.)

Tart Cherry research has been centered largely in Michigan. Among the leading researchers has been, l. to r.: the late Dr. Harold B. Tukey, Sr., the late Professor V. R. Gardner and Dr. M. John Bukovac, all of Michigan State University, East Lansing. Other key contributors have been Dr. C. D. Kesner and Dr. R. E. Marshall, Mich. State University; Dr. U. P. Hedrick, N.Y. Agr. Exp. Sta., Geneva; and Dr. E. L. Proebsting, Jr., Wash. State Univ., Prosser.

CHAPTER XVII

Edible Nuts, Minor Tree Crops

EDIBLE NUTS

The important edible nuts produced in the United States are pecan, English walnut, filbert and almond. The almond, because of its close relationship to the peach, was discussed in Chapter XIV. Combined, the total commercial production of nuts, including the almond, macadamia and pistachio, places the nut crop among the ten most important evergreen and deciduous fruit crops in the United States.

In addition to the commercially grown nuts listed above, there are several kinds of nuts in North America found growing for the most part in the wild and in home yards which are harvested largely for home use. These include the black walnut, the hickories, butternut, and the chestnut. The American chestnut was commercially important until the famous blight eliminated nearly all the trees as they grew in their natural habitat, particularly through the Appalachian Mountain range to Alabama.

In the USA the total commercial nut production is about 670,000 tons. Of this total about (in 1000s) 210 are pecans, 210 walnuts (Ca.), 200 almonds (Ca.), 27 pistachio (Ca.), 27 macadamia (Haw.), and 14.5 filberts (Wa, Ore.). Total nut production is gradually increasing. Pecans and

almonds have been increasing but show the most fluctuations year to year. Macadamia and pistachio nuts have been showing gradual increases.

Almonds, filberts and walnuts are factors in other countries, principally those in and bordering the Mediterranean; pecans are produced mainly in the U.S., Australia and Mexico but plantings are increasing in southern Brazil and South Africa.

In the World nut picture approximate production in 1000s of metric tons after 1980 is: *Walnuts:* USA 190; France 25; Italy 15; India 15; Iran 3; *Filberts:* Turkey 295; Italy 85; Spain 25; USA 12; *Almonds:* USA 120; Spain 50; Italy 15; Iran 8; Portugal 3; Morocco 3.

It is interesting to note that the commercially important nut trees in the United States are of the catkin-bearing type. This is exemplified best in Figure 2, showing the long staminate catkins of the pecan with the inconspicuous pistillate flowers being born separately at the tip (and sometimes laterally) on the shoot. Several catkins originate from one compound bud at the upper node of last years growth; there also is a vegetative growing point in this bud, but it soon will abscise unless the branch has been pruned back above the bud before growth starts. Flower buds undoubtedly are formed by the end of a growing season for the crop the next year, since a heavy crop of nuts one year is likely to reduce both the staminate and pistillate flowers appearing the next spring. When the staminate and pistillate flowers are borne separately on the same plant, it is said to be monoecious.

The pecan, walnut and hickories belong to the family *Juglandaceae;* the filbert, hazelnut or cobnut belong to the family *Corylaceae,* the chestnut to *Fagaceae.* The botanical name of the commercially important English or Persian walnut is *Juglans regia,* L.; of the pecan, *Carya illinoensis,* Koch. *(Carya pecan,* Engl. and Graebn.), and of the filbert, *Corylus avellana (maxima),* L.

CARYA SPECIES[1]

The pecan is the most important of about twenty species of *Carya* found in an area from eastern North America to

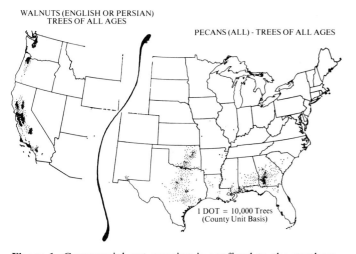

WALNUTS (ENGLISH OR PERSIAN) TREES OF ALL AGES

PECANS (ALL) - TREES OF ALL AGES

1 DOT = 10,000 Trees
(County Unit Basis)

Figure 1. Commercial nut growing is confined to the southern states where the pecan predominates, and to California and Oregon where the English walnut is grown. Filberts are largely confined to Oregon and Washington on a commercial basis. These nuts, however, can be grown in other areas but hardly in a commercial sense. U.S. Bureau of Census.

[1]Dr. J.P. Overcash and Dr. Timothy E. Crocker, Mississipps and Florida Stations, respectively, gave suggestions on the pecan section. If you are a pecan grower, you should subscribe to PECAN SOUTH, The Pecan News Magazine, 1800 Peachtree Rd., NW, Suite 516, Atlanta, Ga. 30309.

Figure 2. Nature of growth and blossoming habits of hickories and walnuts are illustrated by the pecan. A Twig showing staminate flowers (a) borne axillary on growth of the past season and (b) pistillate flowers borne terminally on growth of the current season. B. Section of the catkin showing three staminate flowers of the many that form on each catkin (usually two 3-stalked catkins in each bud — three buds per node). C Enlarged staminate flower containing several anthers (a): b, sepal. D. Single pistillate flower with rough stigma at a. U.S.D.A.

Mexico (Figure 1). Belonging to this group also are pignuts (*Carya blabra,* Sweet; *C. ovalis,* Sarg., the small pignut) and the shellbark (*C. laciniosa,* Loud.) and shagbark (*C. ovata,* Koch.) hickories. Except for the pecan, all of these nuts are classified as hickory nuts which have shells that are harder and more roughened than pecan, and are shorter and rather flattened instead of being roundish like the pecan. All species have a four-lobed husk that develops from an involucre and when mature, dries, splits apart and pulls away from the nut.

Nearly all hickory trees are seedlings from the wild which generally have a long tap root, making them difficult to transplant. Young trees grow and come into bearing slowly. While there are several named cultivars of hickory, it is essential to select those for a given region which have come from the wild in that region. This is because southern selected seedlings are not likely to mature their nuts in the shorter growing season and reduced summer heat found in the colder areas.

There are hybrids between the pecan and the hickory known as hicans. The nuts are longer than hickory nuts but the shell tends to be thick and rough like the hickory nut; they have gained but little interest in competition with the pecan.

Commercial production of pecans from native seedlings, and from improved grafted cultivars each total around 100,000 tons, but both fluctuate widely from year to year. The commercially important pecan producing states and their approximate total production (in millions of lbs.) are: Georgia, 33; Texas, 23; Alabama, 11; Louisiana, 10; Oklahoma, 8; New Mexico, 7; Mississippi, 4; Florida, 2.5; Arkansas, 1.5; South Carolina, 1.3; and North Carolina, 1.2.

In the western arid regions, the native[1] pecan trees are found along streams, whereas in humid areas they are found in well-drained deep soils, also along streams, and occurring in clumps and over considerable areas from Mexico to as far north as southern Ia., Ill., Ind., W. Tenn. and Ky. USA imports about 1200 mT/yr, largely from Mexico and Australia; and exports about 1500 mT, mainly Canada and W. Europe.

Cultivars. The pecan is one of the few tree nuts that has such extensive native distribution in North America. Cultivars now grown were selected from natives for their superior qualities. Controlled USDA breeding in several southern states also has introduced Barton, Comanche, Choctaw, Wichita, Sioux, Apache, Mohawk, Cherokee and others. The Oklahoma station introduced several small-nut cultivars with excellent shell-out and unusually fine kernel qualities. Many of the earlier commercial selections were made from the wild in Florida in the mid 1800's by John Hunt of Bagdad, Florida, others by E.E. Risien, Texas.

Cultivars which have originated from natives in the drier western area of the pecan growing section are not adapted to the eastern growing pecan sections because they are more susceptible to scab. With the advent of good scab control chemicals such as dodine, maneb, or polyram, scab control is not the problem it was.

Native so-called "paper-shell" strains selected in the southern part of United States are not well suited to northern sections because they have a longer required growing season of from 205 to 215 days in New Mexico, for example, although some cultivars are said to require an even longer growing season to fill their shells with kernels. Pecans selected from the wild in Northern areas generally have a smaller nut with a thicker shell, but they will mature and fill the shell in 180 to 200 days. Pecans are quite tolerant of heat, producing satisfactorily in the 110° to 120° F. temperatures, but best around 80° with warm days and nights. There are no pecan cultivars that will mature their nuts in the relatively short growing season from about New Jersey, North to New York and Canada, although the trees will flower and develop attractive foliage that can be used for shade.

Since the introduction of named pecan cultivars, more

---

[1]"Wild" and "Native" seedlings are used interchangeably; "Native" preferred.

TABLE 1. QUALITIES OF PECAN CULTIVARS GROWN IN THE SOUTHERN UNITED STATES.

Cultivars	Nuts Per Lb.	Kernel %	Oil in Kernel	Kernel Quality	Ease of Cracking	Filling of Kernel %	Scab Resistance	Where Grown Mainly	Productivity	Harvest Season	Flower type
Barton	89	53	78	E	F	E	R	O, N, T	VG	M	Good Overlap
Caspiana	68	49	73	E	—	E	M	L	G	—	PA
Curtis¹	102	54	69	E	G	VG	VR	Fl	VG	La	PA
Dependable	52	42	71	E	—	E	M	L, G, A	M	—	PA
Desirable	52	46	70	E	G	G	R	A, Fl, C, N, L, G, T	VG	M-La	PA
Elliott¹	78	43	68	G	F	G	R	A, Fl, G, N, L	VG	M	PG
Farley	57	47	71	E	G	VG	R	C, Ga, A	VG	M	PA
Flotcher	64	47	65	M	—	M	F	Mi	M	—	—
Lewis	51	46	69	VG	—	G	M	Mi	VG	—	—
Mahan	40	40	66	P	G	P	S	N, L, C, Mi, T	M	M	PG
Monarch	65	27	53	P	—	P	S	Mi	P	—	—
Moneymaker	58	43	70	F	F	F	S	L, Mi, Fl	E	Ea	PG
Moore¹	84	44	67	VG	F	M	VR	L, Mi	E	Ea	PA
Odom	53	45	57	P	—	P	S	Mi	P	—	PG
Sabine	45	49	77	E	—	E	—	L	G	—	—
Schley	80	55	72	E	G	VG	VS	A, O, Mi, C, Ga	F	M	PG
Stevens	90	44	62	E	—	E	S	Mi	M	—	—
Stuart	56	45	72	E	—	E	VR	Fl, Ga, A, Mi, L, T	VG	—	—
Success	65	48	66	G	F	M	R	A, Mi, C, Ga	G	M	PA
Squirrel	62	47	72	E	—	VG	S	O, K, N, T	E	Ea	PA
Tesche	70	45	68	M	—	P	R	Mi	VG	—	—
Van Deman	67	39	73	G	—	G	S	Mi	M	—	—
Wichita	53	60	78	E	G	E	M	Ga, T	M	M-La	PA
Western Schley	66	47	71	E	—	E	S	O, N, T	E	Ea-M	PA
Seedlings	75-200	30-52	50-72	E	—	VG	Varies	All over	P	Vary	Varies

Symbols: A-Alabama; C-Carolinas; E-Excellent; Ea-Early; F-Fair; Fl-Florida; G-good; Ga-Georgia; K-Kansas; L-Louisiana; La-Late; M-Medium; Mi-Mississippi; N-New Mexico; O-Oklahoma; P-Poor; R-Resistant; S-Susceptible; T-Texas; V-Very

¹These nuts give good seedling understocks.

Northern area cultivars include: Illinois, Buice, Giles, plus Squirrel, Mahan, Farley, Elliott, seedlings.

PA - Cultivar in which the pollen is mature most years before the stigma is receptive, known as protandrous.

PG - The stigma is receptive most years before the pollen is mature, known as protogynous. PA and PG cultivars should be intermixed for good fruit set.

Note: Suggest you contact your local experiment station for latest recommendations.

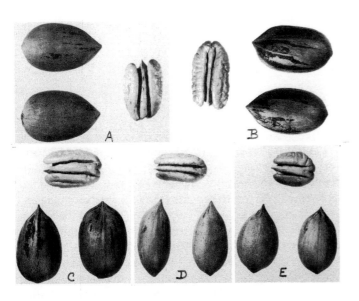

Figure 3. Among the more popular cultivars, showing shell and kernel characteristics are left to right: A. Desirable, B. Stuart, C. Cape Fear, D. Curtis and E. Elliott. Wichita and Moneymaker are among those that could be added. Productiveness and percentage kernel crack-out are key characters. (Courtesy James B. Aitken, Clemson Sandhill Sta., Columbia, S.C. 29202.)

than 200 seedlings have been advertised and sold. Only a few meet the standards of a good commercial variety, namely: (a) come into bearing early, (b) be a prolific and annual producer, (c) has nuts of large size that crack easily with plump straw-colored kernels of good flavor and quality (Figure 3), (d) high percentage kernel for total weight (Table 1), and (e) be resistant to diseases or at least sufficiently so that it can be sprayed economically. The shape of the nut for a given variety and the superficial markings on the shell are characteristics for that variety and can be used in identifying it.

Most cultivars under good management require four to seven years to begin bearing and seven to 12 years to produce commercial crops but these periods are being shortened by irrigation and better management. The trade that likes unshelled pecans will favor the larger thin-shelled varieties with high quality kernels. However, much of the pecan crop, 65 to 70%, is now going to the shelling plants. Thus, prolific cultivars that produce small to medium-sized nuts of good quality are in demand by shellers. Low-quality nuts, sold on percent kernel whether large or small, generally bring low prices and are hard to move in heavy production years. Planters should choose probably not more than three to four of the best varieties for their respective area.

Pecan cultivars change rather slowly. Those being planted by states are: *Florida* - Desirable and Stuart are first choice with Elliott, Curtis and Moneymaker popular, but Curtis is small and has a "fleck" problem. *New Mexico* - W. Schley, Clark, Barton, Mahan, Desirable, Squirrel, plus USDA new introductions. *Texas* - Barton, Desirable, Sioux, Apache, Choctaw, Wichita, W. Schley, E. Schley, SanSaba, Ideal, Stuart, Burkett, Mahan, Squirrel, Texan, Riverside, and Evans. *Oklahoma* - Squirrel, Barton, W. Schley, Mahan. *Mississippi* - Stuart, Stevens, Monarch, Odom, Lewis, Tesche Pabst, Van Deman, Moneymaker, Frotcher, Success, Moore, Schley, Mahan. *Louisiana* - Stuart, Sabine, Caspiana, Magenta, Dependable, Elliott, Jennings, Desirable, Moore, Schley, Mahan, Moneymaker. *Carolinas* - Stuart, Farley, Mahan, Schley, Hastings, Dependable. *Georgia* - and *Alabama* - (scab is the problem) Stuart, Desirable, Elliott, Farley, Success, Schley, Hastings, Dependable. *Kansas* - Illinois, Buice, Squirrel, Giles.

In the northern regions, probably the best known cutlivars which grow from Missouri to Kentucky are Busseron, Indiana, Butterick, Green River, Kentucky, Posey, Major and Niblack. The southern cultivars can be grown as far north as southern Missouri. Since the pecan is relatively late to leaf out and flower in the spring it is seldom injured in commercial growing areas by late spring frosts. The wood also becomes dormant well before freezing weather in the fall.

New cultivars showing commercial interest are 'Kiowa' (Mahan x Odom) in the southwest and 'Cape Fear' in Georgia and Alabama and Sumner and Woodward in Georgia. Check locally for up-to-date cultivar trends.

Soils and sites. The natural habitat for the pecan seems to be along the deep fertile soils next to streams, particularly in arid regions where possibly the lowest cost production is possible. Profitable pecan orchards also are being grown on high-priced irrigated land. Pecans will thrive on either high or low ground provided it is deep, well drained, and moisture is adequate; trees may survive and fruit for over a hundred years if the soil meets these requirements. Pecan trees will grow and fruit satisfactorily on the sandy to sandy loam soils of Florida to the heavier types in other areas. The sandy type soils require more fertilizer attention as pointed out later.

Size of the tree, tree tops, and spread of the roots at different ages is shown in Table 2 from Georgia. It is apparent that mature pecan trees should have a four- to six-foot or better rooting depth.

Propagation. The stronger growing pecan seedlings (Curtis, Elliott, Moore) are used for stocks. Seedlings from cultivars which are known to be resistant to scab are used in the humid areas. Seedlings are lined out in the nursery

and grown for two or three years. The roots grow about twice as fast as the tops. Trees are budded in mid-summer, 2nd or 3rd year, using the patch bud as shown later for the Persian walnut. The tongue-graft can be used on small seedlings in humid areas (Chapter VIII). When the bud is fitted into place on the stock, it is held tightly in place by rubber or plastic strips, and can be coated with an air-tight material (water asphalt emulsion) to keep the patch from drying until it grows to the stock.

The bud-wood is collected in winter and stored at 32° F. in cold storage in moist peat moss. Cions are removed from storage about a week before they are to be used and held at a temperature of 80° to 85° F. in moist peat moss. The higher temperature facilitates peeling of the bark. If all bud sticks are not used they can be stored again at 32° F. for use during the next two- to three-week period.

The inlay graft is used in dry regions (Chapter VIII) on one- to two-inch stubs, differing from apple by covering 4-6 inches of the stock stub after grafting with aluminum foil, then pulling a poly bag over the cion and securing it at the base of the cion and 4-6 inches below with poly tape to reflect heat and keep good humidity. Tip of cion is coated with orange shellac. See Texas planting and grafting pamphlets.

TABLE 2. HEIGHT AND SPREAD OF BRANCHES IN RELATION TO DEPTH AND SPREAD OF ROOTS OF TREES OF DIFFERENT AGES (GA. EXP. STA. BULL. 176).

Age of Trees (years)	Height of Tree (feet)	Spread of Branches (feet)	Depth of Roots (feet)	Spread of Roots (feet)
1	1	0	1-3	1-2
2	2-3	1-2	2-4	3-4
3	4-5	2-3	3-5	6-8
4	5-6	3-4	4-5	15-20
6	6-8	3-6	4-6	20-30
10	15-20	25-35	4-6	40-60
20	35-45	55-60	4-6	80-120
25	45-55	70-80	4-6	100-150

Planting. Permanent tree spacing is generally 50 to 60 feet or more on the square, depending upon moisture supply and soil fertility. Trees sometimes are planted as close as 25 x 50 feet to provide space for intercropping and after a number of years every other tree in the row is removed, leaving about 13 trees to the acre. High-density plantings (Figure 4) are under test of 72 (17½x35 ft.) to 193 (15x15) trees per acre, with the trees pruned and hedged to keep them within limits. A search is underway for dwarfing stocks. The W.R. Poage Pecan Field Station (USDA) at Brownwood, Texas is testing Womack Simple-leaved, Bauer Simple-leaved, Mercer Dwarf, L.E. Scott Dwarf, and the Taylor Simple-leaved pecan. Tree training is not as exacting, offering several intriguing advantages. Compact trees should be watched as more experience is

Figure 4. High-density plantings of pecan are under test and observation by growers and researchers. Enough room is left between rows to accomodate the machinery. Every other tree in the row later may be removed or "fanned" up before removing. Trees on the left have been "A" topped and will be hedged later. Dwarfing stocks which are available and are being tested will help to bring the trees down to better working conditions. Summer tipping is being used only on young trees to induce better branching. (USDA)

gained. Machine mowing of sides and tops is under test. It is suggested that the *Pecan South Magazine** be checked often for this and other key research developments.

Since the pecan has a long tap root (Figure 5), dig a hole about 3 feet deep using, if available, a tractor back hoe. Growth the first year may start late and be slow.

Nursery trees may have rootstocks 3-5 yrs old budded to cultivar tops of 1-2 yrs, 3-10 ft high, ¾ to 2" dia. 6" above bud. Transplant trees soon after dug in nursery to avoid roots drying, remove about half the top, mulch and/or water as needed, paint trunk with white latex paint over 5-7 yrs, or whitewash with lime to avoid sunburning, and rub off buds as shown in Figure 10 to get wide-angle strong branches. First branch should be 5-6' off ground to provide for mechanical trunk shaking. Prune sparingly to develop early foliage.

CULTURAL MANAGEMENT

Young trees. Strip chemical weed control or strip cultivation should be practiced next to the trees. If an organic mulch such as sawdust, pine needles, wood shavings, or hay is available, this applied to a depth of six or more inches keeps the soil about the roots cooler and moist. Additional nitrogen may be needed at first to assist in the decomposition of the mulch and prevent nitrogen deficiency in the tree.

Pecan trees are slow to "take hold" generally after

*Publications South, Inc., 741 Piedmont Ave., Atlanta, Ga. 30308.

planting but with drip irrigation they will respond to fertilizer the first year.

In the arid West only nitrogen and zinc are used. One-half to one pound of urea, ammonium nitrate, or an equivalent nitrogen fertilizer is applied for each year of age of the tree, broadcasting it in a zone from one to six feet from the trunk and working it in with a disc or rotovator. A zinc foliar spray (Figure 6) is used at 2 pounds of 36% zinc sulfate in 100 gals (use 2 lbs. hydrated lime in humid areas) as needed to eliminate "rosette." In humid areas, a

Figure 5. The pecan has a long tap root as shown at left. The tree with many lateral roots is best. The hole should be deep and roomy enough to accomodate the roots after some trimming of broken and weak roots. At right is shown a high graft union between the seedling stock and the cultivar top. (N. Mex. State University, Las Cruces)

287

10-10-10 can be ringed under the tree at ½ to 2 lbs. for each year of tree age in early spring. ZN-EDTA (12%) sprays also are effective. The compound NZN applied at mfgr's recommendation is effective (Allied Chem. Co.). Consult your government specialist.

When pecan trees were widely spaced, the practice was to grow intercrops, and some are still grown, such as cotton, corn, small fruits, truck crops, pears or Satsuma oranges, but in recent years, trees are planted closer and there is an effort to give first management to the trees to get them in production as early as possible.

Bearing trees. Strip-row chemical weed control with microjet or drip irrigation under the branch spread year round is a trend, which also facilitates nut pick-up at harvest.

In case of pecans alone, a few growers may use a summer legume of lupine, or crimson, giant bur, white or Hubam clover and fertilize with 300-500 lbs. of an 0-10-12 or 0-14-14. Winter legumes may be used as crotolaria, beggar weed and hairy indigo. The legume may or may not be disced down (Figure 7) in spring with the native cover taking over during summer. Basic fertilizer applied to pecan usually includes NP and K. The 1-1-1 ratio or 10-10-10 at 1000-1500 lbs/A, split 2/3 rds February and 1/3rd June if soil is sandy, is common, with additional N where needed.

By standard leaf analysis, Table 3 gives mineral contents suggested for "normal" producing pecan trees.

Nitrogen deficiency is the most common for pecan in all commercial growing sections. Symptoms first appear as a light green color in the leaves followed by a yellowish even green, then a greenish yellow and finally a uniform yellow as the deficiency becomes acute. Here again small reddish brown dead spots will develop between the veins giving the

TABLE 3. SUGGESTED MINERAL CONTENT OF PECAN LEAVES FOR TREES IN GOOD PRODUCTION. (C. OWEN PLANK AND W.S. LETZSCH, AGRONOMY DEPT., UNIV. OF GA., ATHENS 30601)

		Percent						Parts per million			
N	P	K	Mg	Ca	S	Mn	Fe	Al*	Cu	B	Zn
2.5	0.12	0.75	0.3	0.70	0.20	100	50	2000	6	15	50
to	to	to	to	to	to	to	to	to	to	to	to
3.0	0.30	2.50	0.6	1.75	0.50	800	300	less	30	50	100

*If aluminum is higher, it indicates low pH or poor soil aeration.

leaves a russet appearance. The leaves drop earlier as the deficiency increases. From year to year the leaves become smaller in size, shoot growth progressively shorter, with some shoots dying. For young trees use about ¼ to ⅓ lb actual N per inch trunk diameter. For mature trees, the rate of actual N per acre is 120 to 150 lbs., for trees alone. Where sod is involved, additional nitrogen will be needed to feed both the trees and sod.

Phosphorus deficiency is noted in South Carolina as a delay in opening of the spring foliage. Old leaves later in the season will change to a dull green and then to a yellowish green with some parts of the leaves losing green color. Small areas die and turn brown and the leaves take on a bronzed appearance. Under acute conditions shoot growth is short and slender. Tip and marginal burning of the leaves is apparent with subsequent drop of the leaves while many of the younger leaves will be unaffected. Where complete NPK mixes are being used, phosphorous should not be a problem.

Potassium deficiency rarely occurs in pecan to the point where marginal and tip burning and upward rolling of the leaflets occur on older leaves; but yields may be reduced. From 25 to 50 lbs. of K_2O or 40-80 lbs. of 60% muriate of

Figure 7. (Above) Early deep cultivation, erosion, and soil compaction by heavy machinery limits rain penetration and root development in the upper soil layer which is the more fertile, yet here is tight and poorly aerated. (Below) Note compaction (1.72 g/cc) and loss of soil (base of trunk) before a sod-strip-herbicide program was initiated 8 yrs. later. Lower trench was cut 10 inches closer to the trunk. Note also that most (85%) of the roots of a mature pecan tree are within the upper foot of soil. Use of a rotovator-type equipment to 2-3 inches depth may help this situation. (Courtesy A.C. Trouse, Jr. USDA, Auburn, Al 36830.)

potash should provide the needs on an acre.

Pecan trees were among the first on which *zinc* deficiency, or leaf "rosette", was discovered and corrected (Figure 6). The pecan ranks with sweet cherry, Japanese plum, and the apple as being among the most apt to show zinc deficiency. Soils in the arid regions of the West have a high fixing power for zinc, making it necessary to use larger quantities for correction of deficiency. In arid regions, rosette is most economically controlled with 2-3 lbs 78% ZnEDTA wettable powder/100 gals. when the

leaves are 1/8 grown and before pollen shedding. NZN at mfger's recommendation is effective.

Spray applications of zinc are used more or less in all pecan areas and while quick response is obtained, the effect is not as lasting nor as uniform as soil applications where effective. In New Mexico, 2 lbs. of a 36% $ZnSO_4$ in 100 gals. is used, but no leaf burn resulted in experiments where 6-8 lbs. were used. Applications are made starting after pollination at 4- to 6-week intervals as needed, and continuing each year until full correction. In humid areas, as Florida, 2 lbs. to 100 gals. of water with 2 lbs. hydrated lime are used, or where copper Bordeaux is being used as a fungicide, 4 lbs. of $ZnSO_4$ is added to the mix. Young foliage responds best. In South Carolina, rule of thumb for soil zinc application is ½ to 1 lb. for each year of tree age, or 1 to 2 lbs. of $ZnSO_4$ per inch of trunk diameter. Application in late February or early March is recommended for the soils in Georgia.

In Florida where soils are on the acid side 2½ lbs. of zinc sulphate per tree, spread evenly under the branches is usually sufficient on sandy soils. Sandy loams and heavier textured soils may require 5 to 10 lbs. of zinc sulphate per tree to accomplish the same result. For young trees 2 to 4 ounces should be sufficient. Once the deficiency is corrected additional zinc applications should not be more often than once in five to ten years since high zinc levels are quite toxic to plants. Periodic leaf analysis is suggested.

Manganese, boron, calcium, and magnesium levels should be watched particularly in sandy type soils of humid areas. In the Southeast, yields have been increased by USDA worker, J.H. Hunter at Albany, Georgia, by maintaining the pH of the soil around 6.0 with the application of lime, perferably dolomite (contains a higher percentage of magnesium as well as calcium). Pecan growers generally have avoided the use of lime because of fear of aggravating zinc deficiency. However, this worker and others in Florida have found that yields can be increased by double or more by holding the soil pH at a slightly acid level by lime applications.

When leaf *manganese* in pecan is less than 100 parts per million, "mouse-ear" or little leaf may be observed particularly in door yard plantings in Florida. Manganese levels in pecan leaves should be rather high, or from 150-500 parts per million. Manganese deficiency may be particularly noticeable in marl soils. A broadcast of 2 to 10 lbs. of manganese sulphate with 15 lbs. of ammonium sulphate or 5 lbs. sulphur per tree to lower the pH should be adequate to correct the deficiency in such soils, depending upon tree size.

Normal content of *boron* seems to range from 10 to 90 parts per million in pecan leaves and while no deficiency symptoms have been reported in the Florida area, they do recommend that boron be included in the pecan fertilizer for the cover crop using 10 to 15 lbs. of borax per ton of

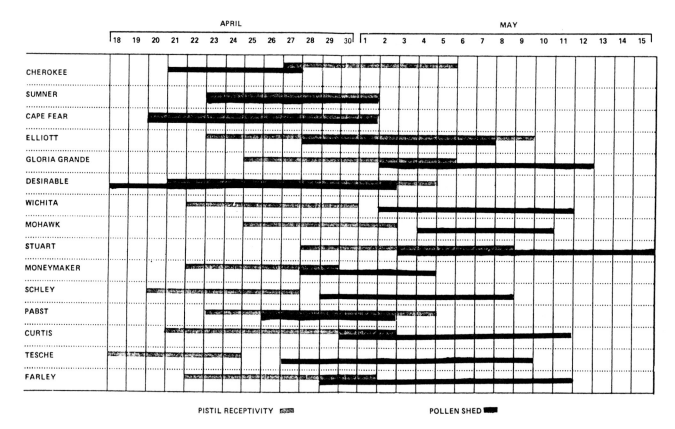

APRIL | MAY

PISTIL RECEPTIVITY   POLLEN SHED ▬

Figure 8. With pecan cultivars, the female stigma may be receptive before (a protogynous cultivar) the male pollen is shed. In other cultivars, the male pollen is shed before (a protandrous cultivar) the female stigma is receptive. Thus, two or more cultivars should be planted in groups of rows of 7-10 of each cultivar to insure cross-pollination (better ylds) and to facilitate mechanical harvesting. (Courtesy R.E. Worley, Coastal Plain Exp. Sta., Tifton, Ga. Three-yr. average.)

fertilizer.

Boron deficiency in South Carolina is characterized by small water-soaked spots appearing on normal leaves which later turn a purplish reddish brown. Younger leaves may become misshapen, and smaller in size as the deficiency becomes acute. Later, ends of the shoots together with buds will die.

Sulphur deficiency also has been reported in South Carolina resulting in loss of color of the young leaves. Loss of green occurs first on the sides of the mid-rib of the leaves extending toward the margins with green spots surrounded by yellow developing as the deficiency advances. This is followed by small reddish necrotic spots, marginal burning and loss of leaves. Later, the new and very small yellow leaves will appear. This deficiency is found only in unattended trees, since fertilizers and spray materials used in good orchard management contain sulphur.

Pollination, fruit set, alternate bearing. Mature bearing pecan trees will normally produce large quantities of pollen which is shed when the humidity is below 85%. Pollen may be carried 3,000 ft. by wind. The flowers are wind pollinated. However, since the male and female flowers do not mature at the same time, known as dichogamy, the trees often are not adequately self-pollinated. Some cultivars will shed most of their pollen before their pistillate flowers are receptive, and in others the situation is the reverse. A given variety may be dichogamous one year and not the next. Where the orchard consists of many trees of one variety, there probably is sufficient overlapping in pollen shedding and receptiveness of the pistils between the individual trees to get normal crop setting. However, where only a few trees are planted it may be advisable to select a combination of cultivars which will provide pollen from early until late in the flowering season as shown in Figure 8.

Romberg and Smith at the USDA Field Station near Austin, Texas found that where cross-pollination between cultivars was accomplished, this resulted in more nuts per cluster at harvest than where self-pollination occurred; also, the nuts from cross-pollination were generally larger in size and contained heavier kernels. It, therefore, seems advisable to interplant two or more cultivars in commercial orchards, alternating groups of 7 to 10 rows of each cultivar to facilitate machine harvesting and pick-up.

In New Mexico alternate bearing of light and heavy

Figure 9. This shows the bearing habit of the pecan with nuts terminal on current season growth and "shoot" (big) and catkin (small) buds below (2 mos. before harvest) ready for next yrs. growth and fruiting. Note the husks on the nuts which will split away at maturity.

crops seems to be more of a problem than in the eastern areas where the pecan nut casebearer is a factor in thinning the fruit. Harper and Enzie were unable to correct alternate bearing by thinning the nuts experimentally on three common cultivars. Random branches in accessible areas of the trees were thinned to one, two and three nuts per cluster. There was a local increase in size of kernel due to thinning. In pruning trials preceding the heavy crop year where the main branches were cut back into second year wood, some improvement in the "off" year was obtained. Early-season chemical thinning of pecan, as with apple may be more effective in securing annual production, but the technique has not been perfected.

As with the apple, there are about three waves of dropping of flowers and young nuts. The first drop consists of pistillate flowers at about pollination time due sometimes to imperfect development of the apical flower and the one next to it. This may be associated with a heavy crop the preceding year or to unfavorable soil or weather conditions. The second drop of nuts takes place due to eggs not being fertilized; this may be due to insufficient pollen or rains at pollen shedding and can be helped by interplanting different cultivars. The third drop will occur later and into the fall in Georgia. This occurs particularly on trees that are heavily loaded with nuts and may be caused by embryo abortion in some nuts. Water or nutrient deficiencies also may be factors as well as insect and disease injury.

It is rather surprising in the pecan that fertilization of the egg does not take place until five to seven weeks after pollination; in fact, the embryo is not readily apparent until 9 weeks or more after pollination.

The hard shell of the pecan is essentially the ovary wall and the hull or husk develops from the involucre. The kernel or embryo starts rapid enlargement about 12 weeks after pollination and continues for six to eight weeks. This period of rapid growth does not occur until the shell is almost full size and the seed coat or integument has reached the size and form of the mature kernel. The endosperm which is largely the edible portion and is inside the seed coat is essentially a storage area for the embryo to draw upon when it starts to grow into a seedling tree.

The shells may not be filled with kernels if, during the period of their rapid growth, nutrient and water deficiencies occur or the leaves become unhealthy for one reason or another, there is an excessive crop, or there is insufficient summer heat or too short a growing season. These same factors may result in small nuts if they occur early in the development period of the nut. Too close planting of trees without proper pruning may cause poor filling of nuts.

When the nut matures, the husk begins to dry and will split four ways starting at the apex (Figure 9). This ac-

Figure 10. Wide-angle strong crotches are important in pecan trees. (a) At node on young tree are shown 3 buds: Primary (top), secondary (mid), and tertiary (bottom) buds. Mop off the primary bud permitting either the secondary or tertiary bud to develop which will form a wide-angle crotch as shown at "C"; this tree has 3 seasons of bud-pinching practice. In "B", note how the primary bud has "taken off", forming a sharp-angle crotch. At "D" is shown the result of permitting the primary bud to develop. (G.D. Madden, H.J. Amling, Auburn Univ., Ala. 36830.)

291

Figure 11. Pecan harvesting. (A) A level sodded grove floor is needed for efficient pickup of nuts shaken from trees by modern trunk and limb shakers. Peaches sometimes are interplanted with pecans for first few years. (B,C) Large equipment (for 100A up) to pick up nuts windrowed by brush at E. Leaves, twigs blown off in model at B and dropped off the chain at model in C (nuts fall through chain). Rotary mower can be used to chew up twigs, leaves from top of windrow before nuts at ground level picked up. Small equipment that encircles trees at G for 10-20A +. Herbicide applicator, homemade, at D for weed control strip under trees in A. At F is the complete line of equipment for harvesting, left to right: sweeper, pick-up and cleaner, and hopper. N. F. Childers' photos from Georgia, Florida.

292

celerates the drying of the shell and the kernel, which is desirable. If the growing season retards the proper drying and opening of the husk, the embryo may germinate within the nut and start growth before it falls which indicates of course that the nut, like many other seeds, is capable of germinating without a rest period.

Pruning. The pecan tree naturally forms a relatively strong framework (Figure 10). Limbs are well-spaced with wide-angled strong crotches, generally speaking. An effort is being made by some growers to control tree size by pruning and use of dwarfing spray chemicals to keep them in workable range as is done with apple. Lowest limb at tree maturity should be at 5-7 feet. When weak, broken, or dead branches are removed, the technique described in Chapter IV should be followed. Due to their size, actually it is difficult to prune pecans regularly as with apple or peach. Texas research shows that Alar and heading-back pruning on 18-year trees will maintain a smaller regular bearing pecan tree, permitting initial hedgerow or closer planting of trees.

Pest control. In the arid sections of New Mexico leaf diseases are not a problem, but two aphids, the black pecan and the black-margined aphids, must be controlled to keep the foiliage normal and active.

In most other pecan areas there are a number of pests. Scab is the problem disease of the nut and foliage. Other pests attacking the nuts include pecan weevil, hickory shuck worm, stink bugs and pecan nut casebearer. Other foliage pests are webworm, walnut caterpillar, aphids, and several minor diseases. The twig girdler, trunk borer, crown gall, sun scald, and winter injury may be minor wood problems. Birds (crows/bluejays on papershells), are busy early morning and late afternoon; are controlled by starting a week before with earliest birds, using "cracker shells", exploders, Av-alarms, poison baits (permission), guns, etc. Mammals as rats, racoons, deer, squirrel (worst) are controlled by habitat management, barriers, trapping, poisons, shooting (Ga. Bull. 609). Rats and mice during storage are controlled by poison, trapping, and rodent-proof room construction. Shading by heavy growth of Spanish moss is controlled by a regular spray program of 6-2-100 Bordeaux.

Helicopters, fixed-wing airplanes and air-blast sprayers are widely used in pesticide applications. Southern experiment stations and USDA have up-to-date spray recommendations and pest descriptions.

Harvesting, Marketing. In commercial groves the ground under the trees is prepared early by shallow disking or rotovating, levelling, packing the soil and sowing and mowing a sod cover with an herbicide strip down the tree row (Figure 11). Harvesting starts when the hulls have split apart. Most of the pecan crop today is jarred, shaken or bamboo-poled from the trees. Limb or trunk shakers for walnut or plum trees are used. Or, a homemade

arrangement can be used where a padded cable is attached to the limbs by hand and jerked by an eccentric and piston on a tractor. Nuts are caught on large sheets under the tree, or they are windrowed (Figure 11), then sucked or swept up by special machinery that blows off the leaves and debris and drops the nuts in a bin to be taken to the packing house.

Pecans are marketed through auctions, private sales, and co-op associations. Some are sold directly to consumers in 5, 10, 25, 50 and 100 lb. packages and bags. Growers generally deliver the nuts orchard-run to distributors who do the cleaning, size-grading, conditioning, cracking, shelling (90% of nuts), size-screening, drying (to 4.5% moisture), inspection, color-grading, storage (32°F), and packaging (Figure 19). But in heavy crop years it may pay growers to do the latter jobs themselves prior to marketing. About 10% of the production goes to distributors as whole nuts to be moved before Thanksgiving and Christmas. These nuts are cleaned, bleached, then processed to restore color before sold.

U.S. and state (where established) standards are followed in sizing and quality grading. Some sizing equipment will separate nuts into large, medium and small; larger equipment separates nuts into six sizes from 10/16 in. to 15/16 in. at 1/16 in. increments. Grades are U.S. No. 1, U.S. Commercial, and Unclassified. U.S. No. 1, as an example, calls for the following: Ninety percent of nuts uniform in color, fairly well shaped, and free of external defects such as stains, adhering hulls, split and broken shells, loose hulls and other foreign material. Up to 10 percent may be off-quality in external appearance, but only 3 percent may show serious damage caused by stains, adhering hulls, and other factors. Eighty-five percent of kernels by count must be free from internal defects that affect quality such as moisture, rancidity, worm injury, shriveling, discoloration, and other factors. Of the 15 percent permitted below U.S. 1 requirements, only 6 percent may have serious damage. Quality scores tend to favor Texas pecans.

Around 9 percent of the pecan crop goes to the shellers, who sell them as half and piece kernels for baking, confections, ice cream, and other products. Pecan shelling equipment is highly mechanized (see similar walnut equipment, Figure 19), consisting of sizers, crackers, cleaners, hand-picking belts, and driers. Driers bring the kernels to constant weight by reducing moisture to 4.5%.

U.S. Grades for shelled pecans are: U.S. 1 halves; U.S. 1 halves and pieces; U.S. Commercial halves; U.S. No. 1 pieces; U.S. commercial pieces; unclassified. Details can be obtained from your state Sec'y of Agriculture.

An increasing proportion of the crop is being stored at about 32° F.; short storage periods of two to three months at 37° to 40° F. and 85% humidity is satisfactory for early deliveries. At 32° F. nuts should store for about a year; at 5° F. they will hold and not become dark and rancid in two years. If kernels are allowed to dry below about 4.5% moisture, the normal percentage for cured kernels, rancidity and brittleness will develop. Above this moisture, undesirable texture and blue mold will develop. Kernel flavor is retained better if stored in sealed cans, glass jars, or moisture-proof bags. The nitrogen and vacuum packs in glass containers in Florida were satisfactory at 32° F. but none would keep kernels fresh for more than two to four weeks at room temperature in summer months; under cool room temperature or in air-conditioned stores rancidity should not develop for several weeks after removal from cold storage. Pecans have wide usage in candies, ice cream, cakes, pies, salads and general cooking. Per capita consumption has been between 0.35 to 0.40 lb over many yrs.

Pecan kernels are high in energy (fat) and fairly high in vitamins B_1 and B_2. From waste pieces of kernels, about 75 percent of the oil can be recovered by heating to 200° F. and pressing with 12 tons psi. Pecan oil as a liquid or emulsified is a good cooking fat and salad oil and it has good keeping qualities. Crushed pecan shells can be mixed equally with builders' sand to form a good rooting medium for greenwood cuttings.

WALNUTS[1]

The genus *Juglans* includes all walnuts. The only commercially important walnut is the English or Persian, *J. regia,* L., which is grown for the most part in California and eastern Oregon (Figure 13), although it is found growing in the East as far north as Niagara Falls, N.Y.. The 3-year average for 1980-82 was: California 210,000 tons; and Oregon less than 1,000 tons. Crop size fluctuates considerably from year to year. In one year for California, for example, production was 226,000 tons (all-time high) while a previous year was 145,000. About 35 to 40% of the crop is sold in-shells and the balance shelled. Price has been over $1000/T with a total U.S. value of over $225 million dollars. About 2.5 percent of the crop has been exported; the percentage is increasing. Per capita consumption of walnuts has increased from 0.3 to 0.5 lb since 1960.

Europe no longer dominates the walnut industry of the western hemisphere, as was the case a few decades ago. USA is producing (in 1000 mT) about 200 vs France, 30; India, 15; Italy, 15; Turkey, 10; and Iran, 3. USA exports about 45, France and China (PR), 10 each; India, 9;

[1]Dr. George C. Martin, Pomology Department, University of California, Davis, and Lonnie C. Kendricks, Jr. Agricultural Agent and Walnut Specialist, University of California Extension Service, Merced, Ca., assisted in revision of the walnut section.

The up-to-date Proceedings (periodic) of the Walnut Short Course (priced) Nov. 1982, is obtainable mid-1983 from Univ. of Calif., Agric. Sciences Publications, Berkeley 94720.

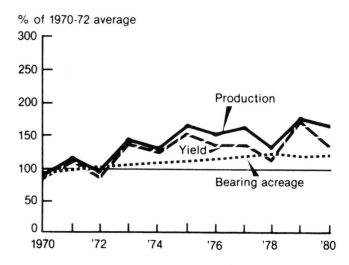

Figure 13. California accounts for most of the walnut production in the United States. Since 1970, the acreage, production (210,000T) and yield per acre has been increasing. Oregon accounts for less than 1000 tons. A peak production was reached in 1981 with 226,000 tons in California. (USDA)

Turkey, 3; Italy, 4; Iran, 2.

Walnut production in California has moved from southern counties to north of the Techachipi mountains of the central coast and San Joaquin and Sacramento Valleys where production and quality are better. Trend of total bearing acreage, yld/A and production of walnuts are shown in Figure 13. Increased production/A is due mainly to better cultivars and management in recent yrs.

There are many kinds of walnuts, other than the Persian walnut, growing both in the wild and in dooryards in the United Sates. The eastern American black walnut, *J. nigra.* L. is by far the most important in this group. The kernels are among the richest in flavor but the large hulls are difficult to separate from the nuts and the shells are thick and hard to crack without getting a black pungent powder mixed with the kernels. The trees are difficult to propagate and transplant and come into bearing slowly. Better cultivars selected from the wild and available from nurserymen are Thomas, Ohio, Stabler, and Rohwer. Possibly the biggest *J. nigra* tree is in Geisenheim, Germany — 150 ft. in height and spread.

Roots of the eastern black walnut are thought to create a toxic substance, possibly juglone, which stunts growth of apple, tomato, potato, blackberry, alfalfa, the heaths and some wild species of plants when their roots come in contact with or grow near the walnut roots.

The butternut, *J. cinerea,* L., which is the most cold resistant species, is native from Arkansas and Georgia to New Brunswick, Canada. The tree is slow growing and has richly flavored nuts but the shells are thick and the kernels slim and small. Cultivars selected from the wild and propagated in a limited way by nurserymen include Van der Poppen, Kenworthy, Sherwood, Thill, Love, and Irvine.

J. ailantifolia, Carr., the Japanese walnut, produces smooth-shelled nuts for the most part although there are some strains that bear rough-shelled nuts, suggesting hybridity. The heartnut (*J. ailantifolia,* var. *cordiformis,* Rehd.) is closely related and bears heart-shaped nuts. These species are fairly hardy in the Northeast but may show tree damage in severe winters and occasional crop loss.

Walnut species hydridize readily. Some hybrids make acceptable rootstocks for the Persian walnut.

The Persian Walnut

Climatic Limitations. The main climatic limitations for Persian walnuts in the western U.S. are: (a) spring and fall frosts, (b) extreme summer heat, and (c) insufficient winter chilling.

Sites should be avoided where spring frosts below 30° F. are likely to occur. Catkins, new growth, and young fruits may be injured. Early fall frosts are likely to injure young shoots causing them to fail to leaf out the next spring. Winter temperatures in the West rarely injure dormant walnut trees. The cultivars Mayette and Franquette have endured winters without severe injury when the minimum temperature fell to 0° F. which explains why these varieties are occasionally seen growing in dooryards in the Eastern United States.

In the Northeast, cultivars of Carpathian origin, introduced from Poland, are hardy, particularly the variety, Broadview. Other grafted cultivars available from nurserymen in this area are Schafer, Little Page, McKinster, Metcalf, Colby, and Jacobs[1].

If temperatures above 100° F. are accompanied by low humidity, sunburning of the exposed walnuts is likely to occur. If sunburn occurs early in the season the nuts may become "blanks" (no kernels), but if it occurs later the kernels may be partly shriveled, dark in color, or they stick to the shell and stain it, classifying it as a cull.

In the warm coastal areas of southern California some walnut cultivars do not receive adequate chilling, causing them to leaf out and bloom late. Nuts will be small and the crop greatly reduced. The soft-shell types of the Santa Barbara group are better suited to the southern areas of California whereas the French cultivars such as Franquette and Mayette which require more chilling are better adapted to central and northern California and Oregon.

Soils. The ideal walnut soil is a well-drained silt loam at least five to six feet deep containing abundant organic matter, free from a high or fluctuating water table, and free from alkali. Soils not well suited to walnut orchards

are those which are coarse and sandy, heavy adobe, and clay underlain with adobe.

Most of the high-water tables in arid regions of California carry some alkali. If the water table is within nine to ten feet of the surface, deep-rooted trees are likely to be injured by the salts even though there seems to be a substantial layer of good soil above the water table. Some orchards are being grown with success on land with a high-water table but the injury is reduced by more rainfall, a well-drained soil, and irrigation water relatively free from salts. Orchards that have been damaged by alkali water table have been improved to some degree by installation of drains. Walnut trees are among the most sensitive to alkali.

Only a small amount of boron in irrigation water will cause leaf scorch and occasional severe defoliation with a reduction in yield and quality. It is well to seek competent advice and run tests for the site and irrigation water before planting.

Winter irrigation will be needed in those areas where the rainfall (a) is insufficient to produce a winter cover crop and (b) to penetrate the soil to a depth of six feet.

Cultivars. Walnuts grown in southern California largely originated from nuts (probably from Chile) planted by Joseph Sexton near Santa Barbara in 1867. While nuts of some of the seedlings had hard shells, it is the so-called Santa Barbara soft-shell types that now comprise the industry. Nearly all commercial varieties except Payne and Eureka are descendants of this original planting; they include Placentia, Pride of Ventura, Neff, Prolific, Wasson, Ehrhardt and Chase.

Key characters desired in a walnut cultivar are good annual yields of high-quality nuts which have a strong well-sealed shell that withstands handling, packing and shipping without cracking. Proportion of kernel to total weight of nut should be 50% or greater in crack-out.

Promising cultivars released by the University of California, and which have been accepted fairly well, in order of ripening starting 5 days after Payne: *Serr* (San Joaquin-Sacramento Valleys, hotter areas; excellent quality, good producer, vigorous, needs pollinizer, sunburn resistant); *Chico* (Sacramento Valley; a good pollinizer for Payne, Vina, Ashley); *Vina* (Vina-Red Bluff area; heavy quality producer, blight resistant, susceptible to sunburn); *Amigo* (same as Chico; a good pollinizer); and *Tehama* (Tehama county.)

USDA and Oregon State University introduced the Hartley, Spurgeon, Adams UC 49-46, Adams No. 10, Chambers No. 9 and Webster No. 2 for limited commercial testing.

Hartley is the leading cultivar in California. Nuts are large, shells bleach well, kernels reasonably light colored, good flavor, blooms before Franquette, small pin hole in end of nuts (entering moisture discolors kernels in Oregon), and a lateral bearing habit that increases

[1]A list of nut tree nurseryman is in the Appendix.

295

production. Seasons, plus other problems, are not wholly favorable to this cultivar in Oregon.

Placentia. This variety is grown in Southern California. Trees grow rapidly, are precocious yielders annually but the nuts blight badly in some areas, and may spring open at the apex if dried too rapidly. Nuts do have a desirable size, a smooth shell that is usually oval, thin and strong, with a smooth, plump, light-colored kernel. It is considered the standard of quality and appearance. The kernel attains best quality in California. *Eureka* trees grow vigorously, come into bearing late, bloom late and escape spring frosts, ripen three weeks later than Placentia, nuts long and parallel with sides rounding to square ends, mold a problem and kernels may show "shrivel tip", particularly in inland districts, losing favor in some areas due to inadequate yielding. *Franquette,* was second in California and the leader in Oregon, blooms four weeks later than Payne and after Eureka escaping spring frosts, is slow to reach bearing; nut elongated, pointed, moderately rough; shell well-sealed, very well filled with light-colored kernels; has been recommended for central and northern California and Oregon. Trees vary considerably. While tree population has been high in California, old trees in some regions are being interplanted with Hartley to eventually take over. *Mayette* trees are large, spreading, starting growth about two weeks before Franquette. Kernels are relatively small in proportion to shell size, good color; tree holds catkins late and may be used for pollinizer for Franquette; grown in central and northern California and Oregon. There are several strains of Mayette: Triple X strain has a heavy shell and is well sealed, not bearing consistently large crops; San Jose is poorly sealed, requires packing in cartons, and has a round hard-shelled nut; Triple X has a long-type well-sealed nut which gives high yields in some districts. *Payne* was discovered by G.P. Payne near Campbell, California; it is grown in most walnut areas. Trees bear early, heavily, and make slow growth when young due to heavy cropping; nuts are exposed prominently on outside of trees and subject to sunburning; shell of medium thickness, pitted, well sealed; kernel of full good quality. Payne or Payne types (10 released from Calif. breeding program) are the most prominent cutlivars in the recent California plantings. Payne is highly blight susceptible. *Ashley* is like Payne, comes into bearing slightly faster, with a bit higher kernel yld that is lighter in color. Codling moth is the major threat.

Approximate younger-tree rank of cultvars in California are: Serr, Hartley, Ashley, Payne, Vina, Franquette, Trinta, Eureka.

Oregon is testing Manregian (Manchuria) seedling in search of a better cultivar. Cultivars for testing in the Northeast are Clinton, Gratiot, Greenhaven and Somers.

Pollination. Walnut flowers are similar to the pecan.

Use two or three cultivars at least to get adequate pollination.

Rootstocks. The best rootstock for the Persian walnut has been J. *hindsii,* the northern California black walnut. It makes a good graft union, shows some resistance to oak root fungus (*Armillaria*), is apparently resistant to the common rootknot nematode (*Heterodera marioni,* Cornu) and the nematode, *Cacopaurus pestis,* but may be injured by the Meadow nematode *(Pratylenchus pratensis,* De Man). It is susceptible to crown rot. Care must be exercised by the nurseryman to be sure to get the northern California black walnut since it can be confused with the southern California black walnut (J. *californica,* S. Wats.); they are found growing together. Manregian seedings are used as stocks in Oregon.

Hybrid rootstocks known as Paradox, a cross between the Persian and any of the black walnuts, and Royal hybrid, a cross between Eastern black walnut and either of the California black walnuts, are being used only in a limited way. Paradox is used only where added vigor of the hybrid is of special importance. Royal hybrid is limited by the difficulty encountered in producing the hybrid seed stock.

Persian walnut seedlings are being used for stocks in southern California; they are vigorous, but are susceptible to oak root fungus and alkali soil; they make a smooth graft union free from constriction; are more resistant to

Figure 14. Technique for patch-budding nut trees is shown on the left; a bud tied in place is shown above. On the right, a shield bud is shown before and after (above) placement. (Cornell University)

296

crown rot and root rot; more subject to injury by the common root lesion nematode than northern California black walnut; and they are objectionable to nurserymen because of slow initial growth.

Unfortunately, all stocks are susceptible to root-lesion nematode, and all but Persian are susceptible to Blackline, a real problem in the Santa Clara region and creeping into other areas (Figure 17).

Propagation. Walnut trees are propagated in the nursery by grafting in southern California and by budding in northern California. High budding on the black walnut trunk gives a short section of black walnut trunk and decreases sunburn and entrance of oak root fungus where these are problems.

A year after planting when the trunk is one inch or more in diameter at ground level, soil is hoed away from the tree crown to two or three inches and the scion is grafted into the stock just below ground level. The scion is tied, asphalt coated, and the soil hoed back to cover the scion to a depth of one to two inches. Grafted trees are grown another year in the nursery, trained to a leader with no laterals and tied to stakes 1 x 2 inches by 8 feet.

Patch budding in late summer (Figure 14) can be used on fast-grown one-year trees. Preripen the bud by removing the leaf blade (not petiole) 10 days before removing the bud. Plastic or rubber bands may be used to tie the bud firmly in place on the stock. Grafting by anyone of several methods is more successful in Oregon than budding.

Starting Young Orchards. Old orchards that have been the most productive are planted 50 to 70 feet apart for permanent trees. Trend, however, is toward high-density plantings 30 x 30 ft. and 35 to 40 ft. apart which with high-budded lateral buds (Hartley), proper pruning, irrigation, and nitrogen control will prove satisfactory and high-yielding per acre. Payne type cultivars are smaller and planted 20-35 ft. apart. Trees are planted in late winter allowing adequate depth of 18 to 30 inches for the tap root; width of the hole should be sufficient to accommodate lateral roots of 6 to 8 inches length. An early bearing Payne-type filler tree in the center of the square often is used.

In the northern walnut areas of the west coast, some growers plant black walnut trees, then top-work them in the orchard. Considerable skill and consistent follow-up care are needed. One-year black walnut trees may be planted in the orchard, the preferred way, or the seed may be planted. When seeds are planted, two to four nuts are set at each location, leaving the most vigorous one for grafting. Trees should be top-worked when they are young to avoid the need for propping and tying on the older trees. A single graft on the young trunk is easiest although individual budding may be done on several main limbs. Patch budding is most common and is done when the bark slips well in midsummer although early spring may be satisfactory.

Grafting usually is done in spring after growth starts; use the side graft (See Chapter VIII) on small branches or the bark cleft or kerf grafts for stubs 3'' to 5'' in diameter. Usual care of the grafts as described in Chapter VIII is suggested.

Because of the *blackline* disease (line forms at xylem of scion and stock, Figure 17), Oregon growers do not use the black walnut as a stock.

Training Young Trees. Nursery trees are headed five to six feet above the ground at planting and protected from sunburn by whitewashing or special tree wraps or protectors. Buds and growth are rubbed off the lower section of the tree as growth starts. Where sunburn is a problem in hot interior districts, trees may be cut back to 5 to 7 buds above the rootstock union (about 18''). The most vigorous upright branch is selected after one year of growth, removing the others, but leaving one or two small lower branches on the southwest side to protect the tree from sunburn. The tree is trained to either a vase-shape with a high head or the central or modified leader (Chapter IV). The main advantage of the central-leader type tree is that there is greater strength of the framework. Laterals are spaced about two feet apart vertically and spirally around the tree. Vase-shaped trees, which have most of their branches developing within a limited area, tend to be weaker and are subject to more breakage. In a vase-shaped tree there should not be more than three or four main branches. Eureka and Franquette can be trained to the central leader easier than Placentia, Payne and Mayette,

Figure 15. Homemade knives on the left are used for shield- or patch-budding nut trees. Tool on right is used for patch-budding and is obtainable from nursery supply houses.

which tend to be spreading and are somewhat better adapted to the vase form. The first main framework branch should be four to six feet from the ground. Secondary laterals on the main limbs tend to become horizontal eventually and should not arise closer than eight feet from the ground, except where the tree is naturally small such as Payne, or where there are strong prevailing winds.

Whether the grower selects the central leader, the modified leader, or the vase shape for his trees, the framework of the tree should be selected so that the branches are spaced as far apart as practicable, both vertically and horizontally. Excess branches should be removed at winter pruning during the first few years, but in interior districts a few small low branches on the southwest side of the trunk should be stubbed back and left for shade until the top is fully developed.

Soil Management. Cultivation insofar as a deep-rooted walnut tree is concerned is of relatively little importance. It is practiced mainly to disc in cover crops and organic matter, to keep down summer weed growth, to permit better penetration of irrigation and rain water, to smooth the soil for harvesting, and to prepare a good seed bed for cover crops. Sub-soiling is not recommended in walnut orchards nor should the soil be worked when wet or excessively dry.

Strip-row herbicide applications under the limb spread in the fall before rains is being used in walnut orchards to control mainly annual weeds. Consult local government service for up-to-date recommendations.

Common cover crops and pounds per acre to plant are: (a) melilotus clover — 20 lbs.; (b) purple vetch — 40 lbs.; and (c) mustard — 5 to 10 lbs. Slow-growing legume crops such as vetch and melilotus clover should be planted immediately after harvesting. Fast-growing crops such as mustard and rape may be planted later. They grow very rapidly and will produce a heavy tonnage of organic matter in 90 to 100 days. An application of nitrogen may be needed with the latter crops. Cover cropping in the drier sections may necessitate one winter irrigation to replace that used by the cover crop.

Irrigation. Walnuts need adequate moisture most during the five to six weeks immediately following bloom. No amount of midsummer or late irrigation will compensate for a deficiency during this period. With inadequate moisture after bloom, nuts at harvest will be small and of poor quality due to lack of plumpness of the kernels, reducing yields.

Since walnuts are deep-rooted, the grower must use a soil tube or auger to sample the soil at depths up to six feet. Most observations indicate that soil moisture control to a depth of nine feet in walnut orchards is sufficient to maintain proper vigor and production. About 80% of the moisture used by the tree to a depth of nine feet comes from the upper six feet. In heavier soils most of this water comes from the upper three feet, whereas in lighter soils, withdrawal is about equal in the 0-3 and 3-6 feet depths.

In the interior valley soil may dry during the harvest period necessitating an irrigation after harvest to mature the wood properly and avoid killing-back from winter frosts. If rainfall during the winter does not wet the soil to a depth of six feet, a late winter irrigation will be necessary to make up for the deficiency and provide adequate moisture for the tree when they leaf out and bloom. The nuts make nearly all of their volume increase in size within the first six weeks of their growth, after which the shells begin to harden.

Methods of applying water include flooding, furrow, low-head sprinklers, and drip or microjet. The latter systems meet the need on a daily basis. Choice will depend upon water availability, operation costs, soil texture, land slope and frost hazard.

Intercrops. With the trend toward high-density plantings and a greater effort to initiate high early production, intercropping with vegetables, etc., has become rare.

Fertilization. Soils in the arid walnut regions of the West have a larger natural supply of nitrogen than soils in humid areas. Frequently the amount of nitrogen available in these soils will maintain good growth of walnut trees for many years. Legume cover crops also will supply a small amount of nitrogen. When nitrogen begins to become deficient, however, the foliage will be smaller and lighter overall green, sparse, with some twig dieback and a reduction in yield.

A nitrogen test in Oregon showed that 6 lbs. actual N/mature tree increased yeilds 14-25 lbs./tree, and increased size of nut and the percentage kernel and filling, covering by several times the cost of the ammonium nitrate. Kernel weight from N-treated trees was increased 5 times as much as the shell weight.

California volcanic soils are deficient in P. Control may be difficult.

Zinc deficiency or "little-leaf" occurs in the interior districts and for some obscure reason is particularly troublesome on spots where corrals were formerly located, regardless of soil type. When severe (below 15 ppm), there is no normal foliage; leaves are small, yellow, twisted and showing chlorosis between the main veins with dieback of the shoot tips. Where less severe there will be good shoot growth only in spring but yellowing and curling of leaves will appear in midsummer. Treatment consists of foliar sprays of zinc sulfate (1 lb/100-36%) or chelate (2 lbs. Zn EDTA/100) 2-3 times at 2-3 wk. intervals after the foliage is about ¾ full size in spring. One treatment lasts for several years. NZN at Mfgrs. recommendation is effective.

Soil treatment can be used where the fixing power of the soil is not high such as in very sandy soils. Zinc sulphate is placed in a trench about four to six inches deep and about two feet from the trunk, using 5 to 10 lbs. for trees two to eight inches in diameter and up to as high as 30-50 lbs. for larger trees. Apply in early winter. Spray treatments of zinc have not been entirely satisfactory on walnuts, except for the chelates.

Mn deficiency may be found in the central and south-coastal areas of California. Herringbone leaflet chlorosis and scorch are typical. Apply 5 lb. MnSO$_4$/100 gal when leaves are almost fully expanded.

Cu deficiency may be found in the areas of Mn deficiency in California. Shriveled kernels, die-back, yellowing and dropping of tip leaves are typical. Bordeaux foliar sprays (10-10-100) at end of pollination to only deficient trees is a corrective.

Boron deficiency (below 20 ppm) or die-back is occasionally a problem in Oregon, resulting in brown-spotting of the tip leaflet between the veins; elongated leafless shoots or shoots with misshapen leaves; and nuts not setting well, dropping off when the size of peas. Boron toxicity (above 300 ppm) also may occur where the irrigation water is high in boron, or excess borax has been

used. Symptoms are more or less similar to deficiency symptoms. Sodium above 0.1% and chlorine above 0.3% are toxic.

Boron deficiency is corrected by applying to the soil in late winter about three lbs. of borax or equivalent for a 12- to 14-year tree or four to six lbs. for an 18- to 24-year tree. The borax is broadcast under the tree. Correction may last for about three years.

Suggested mineral contents of leaves of "normal" producing walnut trees follow:

% D.W.						PPM					
N	P	K	Mg	Ca	S	Mn	B	Zn	Cu	Fe*	Mo*
2.5	0.12	1.2	0.3	1.25	170	30	35	20	4	75	0.7
to	to	to	to	to	to	to	to	to	to	to	to
3.25	0.3	3.0	1.0	2.5	400	350	300	200	20	155	1.0

*No data available in literature; values are approximate amounts found in other woody fruit and nut plants.

Pruning Bearing Trees. Walnut trees are generally *under-pruned,* probably due to their size. Good yields are

Figure 16. On the left is a double boom of circular saws for hedging close-planted hedgerows of nut trees in California. Yield and nut quality were little affected with other apparent advantages. (D.E. Ramos, Univ. of Ca., Davis. 95616).

299

Figure 17. (Upper) Walnut blackline virus may attack a few trees to over 80% in the graft-union zone. Center, is shown damage done by the costly midsummer walnut aphid. Below left is bacterial blight which can reduce ylds 50-80%. (Upper, courtesy John Mircetich and Univ. of Ca., Davis.)

associated with good vigor in mature walnut groves. In interior districts from 8 to 12 inches of shoot growth is

desired in the top-most shoots, whereas in coastal districts, 4 to 6 inches is a desirable minimum. Trees with less vigor may be due to a deficiency of nitrogen or another of the nutrient elements listed above, or inadequate irrigation, or an accumulation of injurious salts, or scale insects. Detail pruning throughout the periphery of the tree may give beneficial results on weak trees. Neglect in pruning results in lower yields and gradual loss of trees.

In general, there are two types of pruning on walnut trees. One is the removal of the lower limbs to facilitate cultural practices. In the other, the trees are thinned throughout the tops to admit more light to the center and to develop more fruiting wood in this section. As trees become older, the tendency is for the periphery to be the only bearing area with the center of the tree more or less shaded out. Some kind of mechanical lift is needed to get pruners into needed areas of the trees.

Walnut Insects and Diseases. Major insects are the codling moth, walnut aphid (Figure 17), walnut husk fly and the red spider; there are a number of minor pests. Among the key diseases are walnut blight, blackline, melaxuma (canker), crown gall, crown rot and winter injury or dieback. Consult references for details and seek the latest spray schedules from local government services.

Harvesting and Marketing Walnuts. *Factors effecting Crop Quality.* Walnuts will drop naturally over about a two-month period. Trees are shaken by mechanical trunk and limb shakers before the nuts drop naturally to obtain the highest quality (Figure 18). Number and vigor of shakings depend upon the climatic conditions and cultivar. It varies from two to four times. In cooler areas the nuts mature more slowly and over a longer period of time. Cracking of the hull and maturity of the kernel occurs about the same time in cool areas and because of this three to four light shakings are usually desirable. In hot interior areas, however, kernel maturity usually precedes hull cracking; earlier and more vigorous shakings bring better quality in these areas.

The nuts should be gathered, hulled and dried immediately after shaking to avoid damage from rain and/or fog, increasing the percentage of culls.

Husks on some nuts adhere tightly and are called "sticktights"; kernels in these nuts are likely to be inferior to nuts where the husks fall away clean. "Sticktights" are likely to be greater during seasons of high temperatures and sunburning. Droughts during the latter part of the growing season, aphids, red spiders or any factor causing leaves to drop prematurely will result in a higher percentage of "sticktights" and inferior nuts.

Commercial grades are set according to the percentage of edible kernels, light-colored kernels, and shell appearance. Use of mechanical shakers and harvesters to pick up the nuts from the ground have aided considerably in reducing the number of moldy nuts and culls resulting

300

Figure 18. (A) English walnut trees are shaken by limb and trunk shakers ("Shock-Wave" type widely used). Nuts fall on previously smoothed or mowed ground, are brushed into windrows (B) or directly swept from the floor (C), dehulled, cleaned, destained and stored in bins for processing (Courtesy Diamond Walnut Growers, Inc., and Ramacher Mfg. Co.)

from slower harvesting techniques. This mechanical equipment also reduces labor costs. Mechanical harvesting has been more effective in the interior sections where the nuts ripen over a shorter period and where more vigorous

shaking is required. Mechanical shakers also do a better job of removing the nuts from the trees. They are particularly effective with Payne, Eureka, Mayette, and Franquette. The ground must be smoothed before harvest (Figure 18).

Hulling. Careful judgment is needed to shake the trees at the proper time so that most of the hulls will be ready to fall away from the nuts naturally. If shaking is done too early there will be a high percentage of hulls sticking to the nuts. Hulling is done by hand or by machine. Machine hulling is quicker and more economical and removes the hull before the shell cracks open. Oregon tree shaking starts when 75% of the hulls split.

Use of Ethylene Gas. Once the kernel is mature the biggest obstacle to rapid harvesting is the large amount of green "sticktights" that fall at the first shaking. In some interior sections the kernel will mature two to three weeks ahead of hull loosening. While water-sweating can be used to assist in removing the hull it is not always satisfactory. Use of ethylene gas is more rapid and effective. But it has been used successfully only in the warm interior districts of southern California, mostly on Placentia and Eureka. In coastal districts it may cause darkening of the green veins on kernels. To be effective the kernels must be mature. The green nuts are separated out and placed in an airtight bin equipped with forced draft ventilation. The gas is injected at the rate of one cubic foot of ethylene to a thousand cubic feet of air with the temperature ranging between 70° and 80°F. The bin is ventilated with fresh air every twelve hours for twenty minutes to one and a half hours, regassing after each ventilation. Treatment is continued until 96 to 98 percent of the hulls are removed, requiring 24 to 72 hours.

Ethephon. The chemical, 2-chloroethylphosphonic acid (ethephon), is used to eliminate many of the steps outlined above in the harvesting and hulling of walnuts. It is expensive and must be handled with some testing at first for experience. When the packing tissue[1] turns brown on key varieties, ethephon foliar sprays at 500-1,000 ppm (4 pts/100 gal) is applied 27-10 days before normal harvest. The sprays cause dehiscence of hulls and enable complete nut removal from trees with a single mechanical shake as much as 3 wks. earlier than normal. Walnuts are hullable and the quality generally superior to controls. Treated nuts require less drying time. Cost reduction is obvious. The practice is widely used among California walnut growers to regulate harvesting block by block with a reduced crew, starting earlier and spreading the total job over more days.

Washing. Nuts are washed after the hulling to remove juice of the crushed hulls which otherwise will stain the

---

[1]Packing tissue is the white, pithy material that fills all the space between the lobes of the cotyledons and between the cotyledons and the shell of an immature nut. In the mature, dry walnut the remains of the packing tissue form the major septums and the thin layer that lines the shell.

shell and make bleaching difficult or impossible. Sunburned or blighted hulls will retain their stain. Large, cylindrical drums are used with coarse wire netting to wash the nuts. The nuts are revolved in this cylinder under a stream of water for two to three minutes.

Dehydration. After hulling and washing the nuts must be dried immediately to remove excess moisture from the kernels and shells, (a) bringing the nut to a stable weight, (b) preventing molding and darkening of kernels and splitting of shells, (c) reducing labor and (d) speeding walnuts to the consumer. Walnuts have a critical temperature of 110° F. Higher temperatures will cause rancid kernels to develop within a few weeks.

Packing and Selling. After curing, the nuts are delivered to a local packing house as shown in Figure 19. This plant[2] processes about 75 percent of the California crop.

On reaching the packing house the nuts are passed under a vacuum hood which removes the "blanks" or improperly filled nuts. Nuts with full kernels pass on to an endless belt where they are hand-culled to remove those which are obviously imperfect. The nuts then pass through a revolving drum containing a bleach solution of sodium hypochlorite for two to three minutes. The bleach is harmless to humans and the kernels; it removes dirt and stains leaving them uniformly bright and clean. The nuts then pass to a belt where workers pick out those with imperfections revealed by the bleaching, such as wormy, sunburned or moldy nuts. The nuts are then sized mechanically into three standard grades: large, medium and baby. Since the larger size nuts bring the higher prices it is obvious that the best cultural practices should be used to get the bigger nuts. Each size grade of nut is run through a large thoroughly ventilated bin where the moisture is removed which was absorbed in the bleaching process. From the drying bins the nuts pass on to another culling belt before they are individually labeled for this particular brand, then packed mechanically into one- to two-pound cellophane bags or larger cartons. Over 80 percent of the in-shell walnuts are marketed in cellophane bags, the rest in bulk cartons.

Many of the walnuts picked out as culls have good kernels and are cracked along with others by machine. The kernels in the factory shown in Figure 19 are separated electronically on a color basis and sold as shelled walnuts which comprise about 40 percent of the crop. Surveys indicate a declining willingness of customers to crack nuts; they are preferring high-quality meats ready to use.

Kernels are sold in 4- and 8-ounce vacuum cans. In vacuum canning, machines do the filling, weighing, pulling of the vacuum and sealing. In recent years, research has developed a tasteless chemical substitute, an antioxidant,

Figure 19. (Upper left) Headquarters of Diamond Walnut Growers, Inc. at Stockton, California, covers 14 acres of a 50 acre site showing cold storage tower and receiving bins at right: offices and cafeteria are at left with mechanized handling of walnuts in main plant in center of picture. This is one of the most efficient and best organized plants handling fruits or nuts in the country. This highly automated plant will process 50,000 to 75,000 tons of nuts each year or approximately 75% of walnuts produced in the U.S. 98% of U.S. production is in California. (Upper right) New products are developed and tested. (Lower left) Closeup of electronic kernel sorting machine which accepts walnut kernels of specified color and rejects others. (Midbottom) Forty electronic color sorting machines handle 90,000 pounds of nut meats per eight hour shift. (Lower right) Constant check on kernel quality is maintained in the standards laboratory. (Courtesy Diamond Walnut Growers, Inc., Box 1727, Stockton, California, 95201.)

for the "pellicle" or skin of the nut that prolongs it by reducing the moisture to 3.2 to 3.7 percent.

Kernels not used in consumer packages are packed in cartons for commercial use in ice creams, cookies, cakes, and the like. Inedible kernels and shells are processed into various by-products, such as oil for paints, walnut meal (shells and meat particles) for poultry and cattle, and a good percentage of shells, of course, are burned in the plant's furnaces for fuel.

Walnut kernels contain a high proportion of unsaturated fatty acids to the saturated types. In one cup of kernels, aside from oil, water, and other minerals in the ash, there are the following: 15% protein, 15.6% carbohydrates, 30 International Units of Vitamin A, 480 micrograms of thiamin (B group), 130 micrograms of riboflavin (B group), 1.2 mg of niacin (B group), 380 mg. of phosphorus, 2.1 mg. of iron, and 83 mg. of calcium.

---

[2]A brochure is available, giving details of history, organization and operation. It is the largest walnut packing house in the world. Write Diamond Walnut Growers, Inc., Stockton, California. 95201.

Most of the walnut crop is packed and sold by the Walnut Growers' Association which is a noncapital, nonprofit, cooperative and composed of local associations in all walnut districts. In California the Board of Directors of the Central Association is composed of one representative from each local association. Association members receive the market price of the particular grades of their delivery, less the cost of packing and marketing. Those growers who are not association members sell their crops to commercial packers.

FILBERTS[1]

The commercial filbert industry is centered primarily in Oregon and Washington. The U.S. crop has increased markedly since the 1920's when it totalled around 50 tons. The 1980-82 average for Oregon was over 14,000 tons and 300 tons for Washington. Total U.S. production is only a fraction of that for almond, pecan and Persian walnut.

In the world picture, Turkey produces about 295,000 mT of filberts although the crop may fluctuate considerably; Italy about 90,000 mT and Spain 30,000 mT. The United States exports over 3000 mT. World and U.S. production trend is upward.

Filberts also are found in the Northeast where people may grow a few trees on odd bits of fertile ground around farm and home buildings. Filberts also can be grown as a tall hedge, but hedges are not likely to bear as heavily as single-trunk trees. In the area of Geneva, New York, winter injury of shoots and catkins is likely to be severe and occur frequently enough to reduce yields below a profitable level. The objectives of the Oregon State University filbert breeding program are hardier cultivars of better kernel quality, thinner shell, mite resistance and earlier in maturity.

The hazel tree goes far back into history. Garden culture of this tree seemed to have begun in Italy where six cultivars were grown as far back as 1671. Many cultivars were known in England in 1912. Kentish Cob (known also as DuChilly) was from a seedling grown about 1830. Hazelnuts or filberts *(C. colurna* L.) are grown extensively in northern Turkey.

Botany. The filbert (sometimes called cobnut[2]) and native hazelnuts belong to the genus *Corylus* (family, *Corylaceae)* which includes a number of species, but only one, the European filbert *(C. avellana)* is cultivated extensively for its nuts. The cultivars of this species are numerous and are the basis for the rapidly expanding filbert industry in Oregon and Washington. Cultivars of

this species also are cultivated extensively in southern and central Europe. Two species of *Corylus* are indigenous in eastern North America, namely: *C. cornuta,* the horn or beaked hazel, and *C. americana,* the American hazel. Both of these species grow as low shrubs, sucker freely and are common along fence rows and in wasteland. While *C. cornuta* is of little value for its nuts, it is the more hardy of the two. *C. americana* is the more promising; a few cultivars such as Winkler and Rush have been selected from the wild by those who are interested in the improvement of native nuts. But the best cultivars are inferior to the European filbert. Because of their hardiness and fruitfulness, however, they are useful in breeding.

The Turkish tree hazel *(C. colurna)* is of interest only as an ornamental large tree reaching a height of sixty feet or more and having a rough, corky, rather picturesque bark with handsome foliage. Since the tree does not sucker, grows rapidly, and is very late coming into bearing, the species is being tested in the Northwest as a rootstock for commercial cultivars.

Cultivars. There are some 220 cultivars of filberts tested in the United States and of these there are perhaps only a dozen of commercial interest. In Oregon the main cultivar is Barcelona with Davianna as a pollinizer; Brixnut is of limited planting. In Washington, companions for Barcelona are DuChilly, Royal, Ennis, Butler, others or it is planted alone. Best New York cultivars suggested by the New York Exp. Station are Cosford and Medium Long.

Pollination. The filbert is monoecious. Staminate and pistillate flowers are born separately on the same plant (See Figure 20). The pistillate flowers are born in small scaly buds with the stigmas being visible during the flowering season only. They are reddish, threadlike, and appear in very small short bundles. The pistillate flowers usually appear a few days before the catkins begin shedding pollen. Nearly all cultivars are self-unfruitful, which means that in commercial plantings there should be two or more cultivars interplanted. Filberts are wind-pollinated, not needing bees in the orchard. The same pistil may be receptive for over a period of several weeks. After pollination, the pollen tube grows to the stigma base, enters a resting stage of four to five months, when the pollen tube resumes growth and the eggs are fertilized. The filbert shell is the ovary wall and the kernel is largely embryo. It takes a few months after pollination for the nut to show development after which the shell sizes rapidly and then the embryo develops.

In California, filberts fruit at high elevations up to 2000 feet but they also have been reported to fruit at the low elevation at Davis, California. Flowers when fully open will endure considerable frost with no injury as noted when the temperature dropped to 16° F. during the pollinating season at Geneva, New York. If high winds accompany this temperature, however, the staminate flowers are

[1]Robert L. Stebbins, Extension Horticulturist, Oregon State University, Corvallis, assisted in the filbert section revision.

[2]Cobnuts often are described as short round nuts that are not entirely covered by the husk or involucre; the filbert is entirely covered (Figure 20).

Figure 20. (Upper left) Filbert flowers: (1) Catkin or staminate flower, (2) pistillate flowers at shoot tip, with tiny flower parts protruding from bud tips, and (3) a winter-killed catkin, above. (Right) types of husks on filberts: (top) cluster, Italian Red; top row, left to right, Barcelona, Kentish Cob, and Nottingham; lower row, White Aveline, *C. americana,* and *C. Cormuta.* (Lower left) Filbert cultivars showing shapes and sizes: (1) Cosford, (2) Medium long, (3) Italian Red, (4) Barcelona, (5) Kentish Cob, (6) Red Lambert, (7) Noce Lunghe, (8) Neue Riesennuss, (9) Red Aveline, (10) Purple Aveline, (11) White Aveline, (12) Bixby, (13) Rush, (14) Winkler, (15) *C. Cornuta* and (16) *C. Colurna.* (N.Y. Exp. Sta., Geneva)

destroyed. Considerable freeze damage occurred in Oregon with a drop to -6° and -15° F.

Climatic Requirements. Chilling requirement for such cultivars as DuChilly and Cosford is about the same as for most apple cultivars. With inadequate chilling, however, filbert flowers will open together better than apple or peach. When filberts are not located near large bodies of water or near similar site protection, the pistils frequently are killed in many parts of the United States and Canada because of opening too early.

Site, Soils, and Planting. It is possible to plant filberts on frosty locations not suitable for other fruits, although, of course, it is safer to plant at higher locations. In Oregon they are grown in the foothill and river bottoms, whereas in the East, they should be grown near large bodies of water that will delay opening of the flowers. Northern slopes are preferred. In the East a search should be made for native filberts to destory them since they harbor the Eastern filbert blight which will quickly spread to the European species.

It is best to plant filberts on soils considered good for apple or peach avoiding the light sands and very heavy clays, although the filbert is more tolerant of heavy clays than the pecan or walnut. The filbert is not tolerant of excessive soil moisture, however, and may prove uneconomical on such soils.

Since filberts do not have a tap root they are much easier to transplant than other nuts; they more nearly resemble the apple in this respect. Most propagation is by tip-layering from stool beds. It is one orchard tree in which the top and root of a tree are of the same variety. Growers can obtain these trees by heaping soil around the trunks of orchard trees where suckers have formed. After the suckers have developed roots the soil is removed, the tree is cut away and transplanted. Suckers otherwise are controlled by a herbicide.

With an expanding industry, however, a faster means of propagating trees has been developed by Dr. H.B. Lagerstedt of Oregon State University. Nursery stools of Davianna after 5-6 years will develop 10 + whips 5-6 ft. long. Whips are bent to side and centers covered with soil with 2 ft. of tip sticking out. Cions of Ennis (new, limited

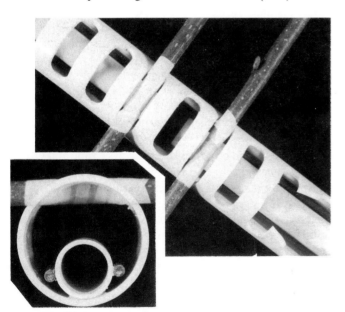

Figure 21. This is part of a system for propagation of filbert trees (will work on other fruits) devised by H.B. Lagerstedt, Oregon State University. Two electric cables in the sectioned polyvinyl tubing provide heat of 75° to 80° F to whip grafts for quick callusing in the field. Water equalizer is in the inner tube. Base is whip of Davianna stool and cion is Ennis, a cultivar in demand. Foam pad strip is held in place on the grafts by a 2x4. See text. (USDA)

wood, in demand) is whip-grafted on the tip of the whips, then "hot-callused" as shown in Figure 21. When the Ennis cion has grown 2 ft., the bottom is strangled with a wire, causing rooting. Cion then is removed and planted to start a new stool bed. A large number of rooted starts can be produced much faster than by the old method. The extra cost is compensated by fast production of saleable trees by nurserymen.

Except when grown in hedgerows or as bushes the tree (preferred) should be set in the orchard 15-20 feet apart. A cultivation herbicide program is used with drip irrigation.

Fertilization, Pruning. The fertilizer and pruning program for filberts is about the same as that used for peach in a particular area. Diligent removal of suckers at the base of the trunk as promptly as they appear is necessary. The filbert bears its fruit laterally and terminally on wood of the previous season's growth and pruning after the tree has come into bearing should be such as to stimulate a moderate amount of new growth each year, as in the case of the peach. Some thinning out of the tree is necessary to admit light to the center and prevent the tree from bearing only on its periphery. Pruning, however, is not as severe as with the peach. Where frost is likely to be a factor as in New York, pruning is delayed until near the close of the blossoming period. Oregon tests show 6 pounds KCl per mature tree every third year increased yields and quality of nuts, provided the soil or leaf test shows a deficincy. NPK on cover crops should supply PK needs on valley floorland. A mature tree requires about 1.5-2.0 pounds N with fractions thereof for smaller trees, applied well before growth starts. Soil pH should be slightly acid.

The mineral content of "normal" filbert leaves should be about as follows:

percent						ppm					
N	P	K	Ca	Mg S¹		Fe	Mn	B	Zn	Cu Mo¹	Cl
2.3	0.10	0.9	0.6	0.2 100		236	100	20	23	8 0.7	0.06
+	to	+	to	+ to		to	to	to	to	to to	to
	0.22		1.4	150		500	600	50	50	11 1.0	0.36

Data suggested by Michael Chaplin and H.B. Lagerstedt, Oregon State University, Corvallis.
¹No data available; figures are based on reasonable amounts found in other fruit and nut trees.

Pests. Bud mite, leafroller, mealy bug, aphids and bacterial (Oregon) and fungal (New York) blights are problems. Main pest in Oregon is filbert-worm.

Yields. Filberts reach maximum production between fifteen and twenty-five years of age. Yields in some years may reach 3000 or more pounds per acre. In New York 5 to 10 lbs per tree may be expected.

Harvesting and Marketing. Filberts are permitted to drop to the ground before harvesting. Most of the time the shells are well sealed and may lie on the ground half of the winter without serious damage. Usually there is a once-over harvest after all nuts are down. "Blanks" can be a problem, the cause unknown, with no kernel, may account for up to 25%. Ethephon spray (1000 ppm) when nuts change from green to brown and abscission has begun, speeds senescense and is a commercial harvest aid. Mechanized harvesting, cracking and processing of nuts, and bagging or canning is much the same as for other nuts.

After drying, filberts are stored but should not be held in a dry room for long periods because they tend to lose flavor; however, they will regain the flavor if held in a humid atmosphere. If Barcelona nuts are held at 80 percent humidity, they will contain between 12 and 15 percent water, which is about the desired amount. Filberts will absorb and release water readily to the atmosphere causing the weight and volume of the nuts to vary with humidity in the storeroom.

Standard grades have been established by the U.S. Department of Agriculture. The first and second grade in general must consist of unshelled filberts which are clean, dry, bright, uniform in color and shape, sound and free from damage caused by insects, mildew or other means, and not rancid or badly discolored. Cracking tests of the nut should show at least 90 percent plump kernels. Separate size specifications are set up for the round-type nuts such as Barcelona, and for the long-type as Davianna. The marketing of filberts has become more orderly in the past few years. The crop is attractive to growers because it can be produced with the minimum of labor and brings a fairly high income per acre. It has a relatively low risk of crop failure. There is a good demand for trees. The filbert has a more or less untapped potential market as a consumer product because of a distinct flavor and the fact that its oils are polyunsaturated.

CHESTNUTS

The chestnut belongs to *Fagaceae,* the same family as the beech and oak. *Castanea dentata,* Borkh., the American Sweet Chestnut, is native to the United States east of the Mississippi River and particularly from the northeast south through the Appalachian Mountain range. Nuts of this species were prized because they were richer and sweeter in flavor than other species. Trees were stately, good timber, but destroyed by a still-active fungus blight on young seedlings.

Chestnut exports in mT from Italy are about 18,000; Portugal 6500; Spain, 5000; France 2000. USA imports 4000 mT.

Note: The Filbert Control Board of growers and handlers regulate through USDA the disposal of filberts from Oregon and Washington. The Oregon Filbert Commission is a research (new uses) and promotion body. Some consideration has been given to California Almond Growers Exchange regarding the possibility of their processing and marketing Northwest filberts through their advanced machinery and marketing organization, cutting costs.

The Oriental species, *C. mollissima.* Bl. is not only highly resistant to chestnut blight but some trees are known to produce nuts of good flavor. Nanking is the most widely planted. Trees of this species should be valuable in breeding to obtain blight resistant varieties of possible commercial importance. *C. crenata,* Sieb, and Zucc., the Japanese chestnut also is highly resistant to blight, bears earlier, is a smaller tree, and has larger nuts which also may be valuable in breeding for blight resistance.

C. sativa, Mill., known as the Spanish or European chestnut, is cultivated to some extent in southern Europe and has been widely planted in homeyards in America. Its nuts are not the best quality but they do comprise an important food supply in southern Europe.

The Golden Chinquapin, *C. chrysophyllum,* (Douglas) A. DC, grows native in Nevada, California and Oregon and is not attacked by the blight fungus under its natural conditions but it has been killed when subjected to the fungus under greenhouse tests. The American Chinquapin, *C. pumila,* Mill., is relatively resistant to chestnut blight and the fruit is sweet but hybrids with other chestnut species have shown little promise.

The Oriental species of chestnuts can be grown in the northeastern United States but they must be located in protected areas. They are more susceptible to cold than *C. dentata;* the American chestnut. *C. mollissima* trees have more resistance to cold than most peach tress.

The pistillate flowers are born at the shoot tips and the staminate flowers at the mid or basal portion of the previous season's growth. Three chestnuts are borne in a hull or burr which has numerous spines. At maturity the burr splits open releasing the nuts.

The Connecticut Station (New Haven) has introduced nine (C1-C9) blight resistant hybrids for home-yard plantings, scions of which are available for the asking (see Jaynes and Graves). USDA has introduced the two Chinese orchard blight resistant cultivars Crane and Orrin.

Most chestnut trees will set fruit without cross-pollination but there is an indication that cross-pollination is desirable to get better yields. There is evidence that the pollen from large-fruited chestnut cultivars may cause nuts to be larger on a tree than when flowers are fertilized with pollen from a small-fruited variety. Good native soil fertility and fertilization with particularly N, spread in a ring at the outside branch drip, will induce better and larger nuts. For good results the site should be well-drained on sandy loam on a moderate slope. Chestnuts are harvested from the ground at 1-2 day intervals over about two weeks. They can be mechanically harvested but removal of burrs is a problem. Mold in storage can be reduced by hot water bath (125° F for one hour) and stored for about two months. They can be held for a year if dried to 10% moisture.

months. They can be held for a year if dried to 10% moisture.

THE FIG

The common fig, *Ficus carica*, L., belongs to the same family as the mulberry, *Moraceae*, which includes many tropical fruits and ornamental species. Fruits of this family are composed of small achenes or drupes attached to a fleshy axis which form an aggregate fruit known as a syncarp. Although the fig and mulberry are of the same family they cannot be hybridized, nor can the rootstocks of one be used for the other.

The fig has been grown since prehistoric times in the Mediterranean Basin. It is mentioned in the Bible and eulogized by the well-known Greek writers, Homer and Plato. At one time the fruit was so highly prized in Greece that by law its export was forbidden. In several southern European countries today the fig is thrown at newlyweds much the same as rice in America.

Mission fathers of Spain brought the fig to California in the mid eighteenth century. Fig trees now are grown mainly in California, although many trees are found in the region south of a line extending roughly from Norfolk, Virginia; through Raleigh, North Carolina; Columbia, South Carolina; Augusta, Georgia; Tuscaloosa, Alabama; Shreveport, Louisiana; and Austin, Texas. North of the cotton belt figs may give satisfactory results where the growing season between killing frosts is 190 days or more and a temperature as low as 5° F. is not experienced every winter. The bearing wood can be killed by a considerably higher temperature than 5° F if the winter weather is not sufficiently cold to maintain the trees completely dormant.

Backyards. Occasional fig trees in backyards are seen as far north as New Jersey but they must be planted in protected areas, on a southern slope with good air drainage, or at the side of a building, wall or hedge. Young trees can be protected by banking the trunks with soil to a height of 18'', or by bending them to the ground, pegging and covering them with a foot of soil. Tops of larger trees can be drawn together and tied, then wrapped in heavy paper or sacking, or covered with pine boughs or corn stalks. A removable frame sometimes is placed around the trees and filled with straw or leaves and then a waterproof cover placed over the tree to shed the rain and snow. Where winters are severe the figs can be grown in tubs and stored over winter in a cool cellar.

Commercial fig orchards generally have been unsuccessful in the more humid parts of the southeastern states, but a small home planting will supply family needs and any surplus sold. Figs must ripen on the tree and for this reason they are too soft and short-lived to ship well except with special precautions. The fruit can be eaten fresh, canned, preserved and dried. It is easily digested,

palatable and a helpful sweetener. Figs are popular in cakes, candies and salads.

Based on a recent Census there were over a million fig trees in the USA with about one fifth nonbearing. California had approximately (in 1000s of trees) 950; Texas 55; Mississippi 18; Georgia 17; Alabama 14; Louisiana 12; Florida 4; North Carolina 4; and South Carolina 3. Total average production of figs in California from 1980-82 was about 40,000 tons of which about 95% were processed and the balance sold fresh.

Botany. Both the fig and the mulberry fruit develop from an entire inflorescence of many flowers, the tissue of which is merged with tissue of the flowering axis or peduncle. Flowers of the mulberry, however, are attached on the outside of the peduncle while flowers of the fig are located on the inside of the peduncle. The inflorescence axis of the fig and the mulberry often is termed the receptabcle. Actually, each flower in the entire inflorescence has its own receptacle attached to the axis. The fruit is called a syconium.

Another way to view the fig botanically is as a fleshy hollow receptacle bearing flowers on the interior surface. At the apex of all fig fruits is an ostiolum (eye or mouth) which is usually more or less closed by scales. Within certain receptacles of most if not all species of *Ficus* there are various species of insects whose larvae develop from eggs to adults inside the individual flowers. When the fig wasp (*Blastophaga psenes)* abandons the fruit through the ostiolum, it is dusted with pollen if the staminate flowers near the mouth are mature. This pollen is carried to other figs into which the insects enter to lay eggs, and pollination then is accomplished unwittingly.

Types of figs. There are four general horticultural types: (a) The largely inedible caprifig has flowers with short-styled pistils while the (b) Smyrna, (c) White San Pedro, and (d) the common types have flowers with long-styled pistils, making it practically impossible for the fig wasp to lay eggs among them.

The *caprifig* is the primitive type of fig indigenous to southwest Asia. It is quite probable that the three types of edible figs grown in the United States have evolved from the caprifig. The short-styled flowers of this fig produce pollen and are adapted to egg laying by the fig wasp. The receptacles of the three successive crops during a season harbor the larvae, pupae, and temporarily the adults of the insect. Caprifigs, with few exceptions (Croisic and Cordelia) are not eaten by man because of very poor quality.

The edible figs listed below do not produce pollen.

The *Smyrna* type figs will mature only after their long-styled flowers have been pollinated and the seeds develop. Without such stimulus, most of the immature figs of both the first or *breba* crop and the main crops will shrivel and drop when about an inch in diameter; a few brebas may develop without this stimulus. Presence of the fertile seeds, however, is necessary to develop quality.

Pollination of the Smyrna fig is accomplished by the fig wasp which carries the pollen from the June crop of caprifigs to the Smyrna figs. This process is called *caprification*. Man actually modifies the normal life history of the fig wasp by placing mature June-crop caprifigs in perforated bags in trees in the Smyrna figs instead of other caprifigs. The female which generally loses her wings as she pushes her way between the scales of the eye in the end of the fig, crawls over the long-styled flowers in a *vain* attempt to deposit her eggs, and pollination thus is inadvertently accomplished.

The *common type* figs are parthenocarpic. They do not require caprification to mature their fruits. Cultivars of this type include the important Mission, Adriatic, Kadota, Celeste, and Brown Turkey. Probably all common figs could produce fertile seeds if the flowers were caprified.

The *White San Pedro* type fig is actually a combination of characters of the common type and the Smyrna-type figs. Figs of the first (breba) crop on the San Pedro type trees are parthenocarpic (without seeds) whereas figs of the second crop are non-parthenocarpic and like those of the Smyrna type, fail to set and mature unless their flowers are pollinated and fecundated (fertilized). King is a cultivar introduced into California. San Pedro type figs are of relatively poor quality.

Cultivars. There are six commercial cultivars grown in California all of which originated in the Old World. In the order of importance they are: Adriatic, Calimyrna (California Smyrna or Lob Injir), Kadota, Mission, Turkey (San Pedro, Brown Turkey, or known as Brunswick in the southern states) and Brunswick. In the Gulf and southeastern states cultivars grown for the most part are Brown, Turkey, Brunswick (Magnolia in Texas) and Celeste.

The *Adriatic* variety is the principal drying fig in California although its product is not of the highest quality. The *Calimyrna* is identical with the principal drying fig of Smyrna. It is of the highest quality for fresh consumption locally, for distant shipping, and for drying. The *Kadota* (Dottato of Italy) has been planted mainly for fresh-fruit canning in California and Texas although large tonnages are being dried. The *Mission* is an excellent fig both grown in the Coachella Valley of California and in the vicinity of Los Angeles. It is a heavy producer of large figs for the fresh fruit market. It is worthless as a dried fig and is quite susceptible to souring in the San Joaquin Valley where it cannot be grown successfully. The *Brunswick* (Magnolia) fig has been grown for many years in England and is characterized by narrowly lobed leaves, particularly in the foliage of sucker wood. It is grown in Texas as a canning and preserving fig under the name Magnolia. Texas figs have been largely canned in glass whereas California figs are canned in tins. The *Celeste*

variety, eaten fresh, is best suited to the Gulf States because the ostiolum (eye) is tight, making it difficult for insects to enter and cause souring or other troubles. Celeste has good flavor.

A seedling fig called *Conadria,* developed from a 30-year fig breeding program in California, is showing promise both for fresh and dried fruit markets. See references by Condit for detailed descriptions of these and other varieties.

Climatic Requirements. The fig is a deciduous sub-tropical tree (Figure 22) which loses its leaves for only a short period in the climate of California. It is native of the arid semi-desert regions of the Old World where successful culture is limited more by low temperatures of winter than by high heat of summer. In California there are three seasons when serious frost damage may occur to young trees: the fall seasons during October and November while the foliage is still green, the dormant winter period, and the season of early spring when the new growth is appearing. In California dormant fig trees can be expected to withstand winter temperatures of 15° F. without injury but usually suffer at temperatures lower than this.

Figs for drying are produced best in regions which have long sunny days and relatively low humidity. Figs for preserving and canning are being produced in regions where summer showers occur and there is a fairly high humidity. Vigor of the fig tree can be controlled by cultural methods, particularly irrigation, so that they can withstand extremes of heat without serious injury to fruit quality. Windy weather and rains during the caprification season may interfere with normal flight of the fig wasps. Gentle breezes during the drying season, however, are desired since they favor the proper maturing of the fruit.

Soils. Deep clay loam soils are best for fig culture but during the first few years vigorous tree growth may occur on these soils at the expense of fruitfulness. Trees can be grown successfully on sandy soils but they are likely to become unprofitable because of nematodes. Some of the best Adriatic orchards are found on a very heavy, sticky clay soil at Merced, California, where there is a hard pan about 28'' beneath the surface.

Propagation. The only method of propagation used, because it is so successful, is rooted woody cuttings. In California, cuttings are made during the pruning season in January and February. Bundles of the cuttings are placed butt end up in a well-drained trench and covered with several inches of sandy soil, well packed. They are set in the nursery in early spring and the soil kept moist to maintain steady even growth.

Culture. Establishment of fig orchards in California and the southern states is much the same as for peach or other deciduous fruits.

Unlike the peach tree which bears its fruit on wood of the previous season's growth, the fig normally bears two

308

Figure 22. Figs. can be trained almost to the desires of the gardener - dwarf, espalier, or commercially, the Kadota above which is common in the California fig districts, is trained to the open-center, then cutting the inner branches short, leaving the outer ones longer. All are headed at the same height from the ground. (Univ. of Calif., Davis)

crops each year — the first crop appearing on wood of the previous season, and the second crop on new wood of the current season's growth. Since the fruiting habits of different fig cultivars vary, they are pruned differently. For example, the Mission tree is notably unproductive under a system of very heavy pruning or stubbing back of the branches, while trees of the Turkey and Kadota usually produce best under such pruning treatment (Figure 22).

The young Adriatic tree is pruned very little except to remove the lower spreading branches and a certin amount of thinning out of the interior branches when they become too thick. Mature trees are pruned annually or biennially throughout the top to induce new vigorous wood and to prevent the accumulation of dense growth of short weak twigs. The Mission fig forms a tall many-branched tree requiring little pruning except for an occasional thinning out and removal of interfering branches. Calimyrna trees produce long upright branches without laterals on current season's wood. These branches are inclinded to become top heavy with the weight of fruit and leaves and the pruning problem therefore is to produce stocky branches which are capable of standing upright under future heavy crops. Either heavy winter pruning or light summer

pruning may be used to shorten the intervals between laterals in such trees. In the bearing Calimyrna trees an occasional thinning out and heading back of the top is needed to stimulate a succession of new vigorous wood on the main framework branches. Annual or biennial pruning of the top will help to prevent early decline of the tree and encourage production of fruit-bearing wood.

Since the Kadota fig is grown primarily for fresh fruit, the trees are trained low to facilitate economical harvesting. A low, nearly flat top tree is produced by pruning the inside branches shorter than the outside branches. The amount of wood left and the extent of the cutting depends upon the vigor of the tree. Harvesting in the tree center is facilitated by a pruned opening in one side.

Irrigation of fig orchards is necessary in California except where there is a relatively high water table.

Winter cover crops and spring and summer clean culture has been the practice. As with other fruits, strip-row herbicides under the trees, sod or no-sod middles with sprinkler and microjet irrigation are used.

N fertilizer is applied in the San Joaquin Valley only to trees with poor color. Too much N causes frost susceptibility, fruit splitting and souring.

Maxie and Crane, California, found fruit growth stimulation from 2, 4, 5-T sprays to be due to ethylene production. They suggest ethylene as a regulator to speed growth period III, and quicker maturation of fruits.

In the process of caprification, perforated paper bags containing the caprifigs are attached to the trees requiring pollination by the fig wasps. Calimyrna figs are receptive to pollen when about 3/4-inch in diameter and remain receptive over a period of several days. The fig wasp carries with the pollen the spores of injurious fruit diseases as well. Therefore, the number of caprifigs and wasps distributed to Calimyrna trees should be reduced to a minimum to insure a reasonable crop of edible fruit. It is generally considered better to obtain a light crop of clean figs by caprification, rather than a heavy crop inclined to rot on account of greater fungus infection. About one caprifig is needed for each 18 square feet of bearing tree surface as experiments have demonstrated in the Fresno area. Four distributions of caprifigs are needed over a period of about 15 days.

Because caprification is expensive and the wasps may induce souring of the fruit, ways have been sought to develop fruits without caprification, such as use of growth regulator sprays to induce parthenocarpic fruit setting. Many substances have been tried by California workers (see references) but none has been commercially acceptable.

Harvesting. While fig trees may bear as early as the fourth season in the orchard, commercial bearing starts at about seven years of age. Calimyrna trees will produce from 1.25 to 1.5 tons of dried figs per acre while the

Mission and Adriatic orchards will produce 2 to 2.5 tons per acre. Kadota trees are heavier producers than other varieties except the Turkey. Trees three to four years of age will produce a few hundred pounds of fresh fruits per acre while those from five to seven years of age will produce from 1.0 to 2.5 tons per acre; older orchards will produce from 5 to 7 tons of fresh figs.

Harvesting of figs is one of the most tedious of all fruits. Fruit of some varieties will not drop until overripe and rather dried and because of this it holds to the tree tightly when harvested for fresh fruit or canning. Use of an ethephon spray 250-500 ppm one to two wks before harvest aids the uniform ripening and release of figs. Pickers wear cotton gloves to protect them from the exuding latex which may irritate the skin. Since the figs are rather soft at harvest they must be handled very carefully for they crack easily and are not protected by a waxy skin like apples.

Fresh figs are usually available from June to October as follows: June, 9%; July, 9%; August, 35%; September, 28%; October, 19%. The average per capita consumption of fresh figs is less than 0.05 pound. More than 87% of the fig crop is sold dried. Texas production goes almost entirely into canned figs and preserves.

Fresh figs from California are shipped in one-layer boxes in which cardboard fillers are used to provide a separate cell for each fruit. The number of cells varies with the size of the fruit but the boxes are uniform in depth. Weight is 5 pounds net per flat. Shallow baskets have a top dimension of approximately 8 sq. inches and a bottom dimension of 6¾'' and a depth of 1¼''. The baskets are packed with a single layer of fruit and shipped four to a crate.

Figs are highly perishable because they must be fully ripe to be of good quality. A ripe fig is soft and varies in color from greenish yellow to purplish or almost black according to the variety. Over-ripeness is detectable by a sour odor which is due to fermentation of the juice. Bruised or mechanically injured fruit should not be packed. It breaks down rapidly in shipment and marketing. There are no U.S. Standard grades.

For commercial storage, figs should be held at 31°-32° F. and a relative humidity of 85 to 90 percent. Under these conditions, however, they cannot be expected to keep satisfactorily for more than about ten days. The reserve stocks in retail stores should be kept cold and if possible the stock on display should be refrigerated. Figs on display counters should be watched carefully because any decay will spread rapidly from one fruit to another.

In a pound of figs there are 357 calories; 6.4 gms protein; 1.8 gms fat; 89 gms carbohydrates; 245 mgs calcium; 145 mgs phosphorus; 2.7 mgs iron: Vitamin A, 360 International units; thiamin .25 mg.; riboflavin .23 mg.; niacin 2.5 mgs; and ascorbic acid, 7 mgs. Figs have a definite laxative effect due probably to fiber and bulk of seeds together with some specific solvent in the juice. They also have an high excess alkalinity of ash.

Fruits of varieties other than Calimyrna can be frozen in syrup at 0° F. and are about as good eating as fresh fruits but they are highly perishable upon thawing.

The canning trade prefers fruit without crunchy seeds such as the Kadota of California and the Brunswick (Magnolia) in Texas. A variety is desired that does not become too soft at maturity and that holds its yellow color on canning. Canned figs are necessarily higher in price than canned peaches and apricots because they are more expensive to grow, harvest and process.

Drying. Fruit for drying is permitted to hang on the tree until it drops. It loses some water while still on the tree just before dropping and also on the ground before it is gathered. Methods of drying vary with the cultivar and district in California. The light colored figs such as the Kadota and Calimyrna are picked up frequently and dried on trays in the sun. Adriatic and Kadota figs are sulphured lightly to hold the bright color while Calimyrna figs when carefully handled will dry naturally to a straw color. Mission figs in some districts are placed in half-full sacks and left open in a sunny place to dry. About 3 lbs of fresh figs are required to make one lb of dried.

Pests and Diseases. Pests and diseases are the root knot nematode, the Mediterranean fig scale, fig mites, Pacific red spider and a leaf mosaic disease to which the Mission variety is especially susceptible. Pests and diseases affecting the fruit include birds such as the house finch, characteristic splitting of immature fig fruits of certain varieties such as Calimyrna, souring due to yeasts and bacteria, smut or mold on dried Adriatic and Calimyrna figs, and endosepsis or internal rot due to a fungus carried by the fig wasp. Contact your local extension service or experiment station for a pest control calendar.

California Fig Institute was organized by fig growers to: (a) Promote the dried fig industry; (b) nutritional research and education; (c) production research; and (d) trade and tariff negotiations. It is non-profit and cannot own fig orchards. One hundred percent of the (dried) fig growers belong. Headquarters is P.O. B. 709, Fresno, Ca. 93712, same as Calif. Dried Fig Advisory Board which is a policing group providing inspection and enforcement of raw and finished product. The Board has five each producer and processor members and one public member. Active advertising and publication of recipe booklets is a part of the promotional program.

PERSIMMONS

The Orinetal or Japanese persimmon. *(Diospyros Kaki, L.)* is the only commercially important persimmon in the United States. It is probably native to China for it was

310

introduced into Japan from China. In Japan it ranks next to apple in importance and is considered their national fruit. The Oriental persimmon first was introduced into the United States by Commodore Perry's expedition which opened world commerce to Japan in 1852. It later was introduced as grafted trees of better cultivars by the U.S. Dept. of Agr. in 1870.

Almost all of the crop comes from California where the average production is between 1500 and 2000 tons. Size of the crop may fluctuate considerably year to year. Other states reporting Oriental persimmons and their approximate tonnage are: Texas, 40; Florida, 15; Hawaii, 11; Louisiana, 3; Mississippi, 3; Alabama, 2; and Missouri, 1. The following states produce less than a ton: Arizona, Georgia, Indiana, Kansas, Oklahoma, Pennsylvania, South Carolina and Utah. The census shows about 50,000 trees in United States. Trend has been downward. Yield per tree varies between 30 and 50 pounds but on well-managed trees production should be appreciably better. The trees have a low chilling requirement.

There are several problems in the southern states which have limited the persimmon commercially. Some of the problems apply also to California. These include a lack of concentration of plantings with no organization for handling and vigorously advertising the fruit. This, in turn, has been largely responsible for erractic returns to shippers. Shipments to the markets have been sporadic with no effort to maintain a steady supply or demand in any one market; hence, prices have fluctuated widely. Fancy prices obviously cannot be expected from a fruit that has no U.S. standard grades and is generally unknown to the public. While there is a limited but loyal public buying persimmons there are those who have tried the fruit for the first time and found it hard, astringent and puckery. This is due to lack of accompanying instructions. This, of course, could be overcome by proper advertising. Also, the growers have planted small acreages of numerous cultivars some of which were not suited for marketing because of lack of good size or dark-color flesh. Poor fruiting or heavy dropping of the young fruits due to inadequate cultural knowledge has resulted in poor returns to the grower. If the above difficulties could be overcome, and it seems possible, a satisfactory and growing demand for this fruit undoubtedly could be developed.

Not all the Oriental persimmons are astrigent when firm. Cultivars which have dark-colored flesh are usually sweet and non-astringent, and may be eaten before they become soft. Cultivars that have a light-colored flesh, which are preferred by the public, tend to be astringent until they soften, with one exception, the Fuyu cultivar. Astringency is due to tannin, the same substance found in tea. Frost is not necessary as an aid in reducing the tannin and in softening and ripening the persimmon. With time, the tannin will disappear and the fruit ripen and sweeten

naturally. The fruit will ripen as well off the tree as on the tree. The Japanese have a special method of removing the pucker by placing the fruit in casks that have been used for sake, Japanese beer. Depending upon weather, they remove the fruit from the casks when it loses its astringency in five to fifteen days. In this country the persimmons are allowed to sweeten naturally at room temperature, although they can be held in firm condition for periods of two to three months at 30°-32° F. and 85% to 90% relative humidity. Average freezing point of the flesh is 28.2° F.

Cultivars. The leading commercial cultivar in California is Hachiya, mainly because of its large handsome fruit. It is usually seedless in Calfornia but may contain one or more seeds when grown in Florida. Hachiya, as shown in Figure 23 is oblong-conic, apex rounded, terminating in a black point; skin glossy, deep orange-red; flesh deep yellow, astringent until soft, rich and sweet when ripe. Fuyu is the most important nonastringent cultivar in California; reddish flesh, sweet and mellow, does not attain the size of Hachiya and is flattened.

The Tanenashi is the leading variety in the southern states. The fruit is medium to large (Figure 23), broadly conical with a somewhat pointed apex; skin a light bright orange changing to light red when ripe; flesh yellow, nearly always seedless, astringent until ripe and with a pasty texture. Other minor cultivars are: Zengi, Taber No. 23, Okame, Jumbu, Triumph, Hyakume, Yemon, Tamopan, Costata, Eureka, Tsuru and Ormond.

The Oriental persimmon tree may reach a height of 40 feet, is a beautiful tree in the home landscape, will survive winters where grown, and has but few insect and disease enemies. The chilling requirement is only slight, with the buds opening with but little delay even after the warmest winters in southern California. Trees are grown in all parts of California and Florida and as far north as Missouri, southern Indiana and Virginia.

Flowering and Pollination. Buds on last year's wood contain indeterminate shoots, some of which will have flowers in the axils of the leaves. Basal flowers on the shoots may have been formed as early as July of the previous summer, whereas flowers near the tips of the shoots may have been formed in late winter or early spring of the year growth starts. These later flowers are not as vigorous as the early flowers, but they may set fruit. Staminate flowers are about a third of the size of the pistillate flowers (Figure 24).

Three kinds of flowers may be borne on Oriental persimmon trees: (a) perfect flowers having both stamens and pistil, (b) pistillate flowers having a pistil and no stamens, and (c) staminate flowers having stamens but no pistil. In the early classification of Oriental persimmons difficulty was encountered because one or more of these types of flowers was being borne on any one tree.

Figure 23. (Left upper) Fruit of the Hachiya persimmon (2 to 4 inches diameter) which leads in California and is grown to a limited extent in Florida. (Left lower) Young tree of Tanenachi cultivar in Florida; some trees may reach 40 ft. (Right) Cluster of Tenanachi persimmon in Florida. (Fla. Agr. Exten. Service of IFAS, Gainesville)

Some commercial cultivars as Tanenashi, Hachiya, and Tamopan are parthenocarpic, setting fruit without seeds and pollination. In other cultivars the fruits are usually seedy and pollination is necessary for setting fruit. With the latter cultivars interplant a cultivar like Gailey (ratio 1:8) which is most frequently used because of its profusion of staminate flowers. It should be noted that the native American persimmon, *D. viriginiana* will not cross with the Oriental and thus cannot be used as a source of pollen.

Pollination problems are not as important in California as in Florida. This, no doubt, is due partly to the fact that three of the main cultivars, Hachiya, Tanenashi and Tamopan, will bear fruit without pollination.

Propagation and Rootstocks. Seedlings of the native American persimmon, *D. virginiana,* have been found best in California and are used almost exclusively in the southern United States as a rootstock for *D. kaki.* This rootstock, however, is difficult to transplant due to a long large tap root and the trees tend to be short-lived (10 years) and dwarfed. Trees, however, come into bearing early, two to three years after grafting. Seedlings with crown gall, to which persimmon is highly susceptible, must be discarded.

Nearly all propagation is done by grafting the scion on the seedling root, using the whip-graft for small-diameter stocks and the cleft- or inlay-graft on large stocks. It is better to replant with young stock rather than topwork old trees.

General Culture. The Oriental persimmon performs best on *well-drained* lighter soils which have a good subsoil containing some clay. Trees are transplanted during the winter months at distances of 15' x 15' to 20' x 20'. The same cultivartion and cover cropping system can be used as for the peach. In California the amount of nitrogen used is about the same as for the peach to obtain shoots about a foot long. Excessive N, however, will cause a high percentage of young fruits to drop. In Florida, an N-P-K fertilizer is suggested of a 1-2-1 ratio, using about one pound of fertilizer per year of age of the tree; some difficulty with zinc deficiency is encountered and this is corrected by applying two ounces of zinc sulphate for each

312

Figure 24. The small Japanese persimmon flower on the left is staminate; the larger ones on the right are pistillate. Perfect flowers having both stamens and pistils sometimes are borne. A tree may have only one or more of these types of flowers. Fla. Agr. Exp. Sta., IFAS, Gainesville.

year of age of the tree under the leaf spread. In California, only N is used at ½ to 5 lbs./tree, young to mature. Shoot growth should not exceed one foot a season.

Since the wood of the Oriental persimmon tends to be brittle and breaks easily with a load of fruit, the trees should be trained as nearly as possible to the modified leader system (Chapter IV). When the trees begin to occupy their full allotted space, head them back annually as with the peach to keep them within width and height bounds. They can be grown as espaliers or in tubs by heavy pruning.

On some cultivars young fruits may drop heavily early in the season. To some extent this is an advantage in sizing up the remaining fruits at harvest, for the large fruits draw a premium. If dropping becomes excessive, however, scoring or girdling of the trunks in late May or early June (Chapter VI) in southern California will help reduce the drop; also a reduction in nitrogen supply should help. Hand thinning of the fruit would be difficult since it adheres tightly to the calyx and stem making the job tedious and expensive.

Persimmons are resistant to drouth, but repsond well to irrigation.

Fruit Handling. Fruits are harvested when they have attained a yellow to reddish color but are still firm. They are clipped from the tree with shears leaving the calyx attached to the fruit together with a short stem. Great care is needed to avoid bruising. Fruits are wrapped individually in paper and packed in a single-layer crate. A polystyrene box with 2 polyvinyl trays is popular.

Since the general public is uninformed on how to ripen the fruit before it is eaten, the wraps on each fruit should carry instructions on how to avoid astringency. Instruction such as follows could be used: "Persimmons soften at room temperature. Ripe persimmons are delicious. Flesh is sweet and jellylike. Chill, and eat out of hand or in a bowl with cream."

Marketing. Most of the persimmons are eaten from Halloween to Christmas to New Year's. Fruits shipped should be well-shaped, plump, smooth, highly colored, with unbroken skin and with stem cap attached. An ideal way to display persimmons on a sales counter is in a single layer nested in wrapping paper to prevent bruising. Persimmons are delicate; it is essential to minimize handling as much as possible.

In a pound of seedless Oriental persimmons there are: 344 calories; 3.5 protein; 1.8 fat; 88 carbohydrates; in gms., 26 of calcium; 114 of phosphorus; 1.3 of iron; 0.22 of thiamine; 0.2 of riboflavin; 28 of ascorbic acid and 11,900 International units of Vitamin A.

American Persimmons. *D. virginiana,* L. is a native from Texas to Florida and north to latitude 38° which runs through southern Missouri; some cultivars may grow as far North as 40°. The trees grow wild over the countryside, spreading like a weed in pastures, but there is a fungus, *Cephalosporium diospyri,* which may kill many wild persimmons in large areas.

The fruits when ripe are 1 to 1½ inches in diameter, full of seeds, sweet and rather pasty. They are very astringent before ripe and do not lose this until they are too soft for marketing. The tree has no commercial importance but it is liked by many people in the areas where it grows.

The bell-shaped staminate and pistillate flowers are almost always on separate trees. The staminate trees not having to bear a crop are usually somewhat more upright and vigorous in appearance than the pistillate trees. Some varieties have been picked from the wild and named, including Early Golden, Ruby and Miller. Pollination is by insects and it has been noted that pistillate trees may be pollinated from staminate trees several hundred feet away. Parthenocarpic (seedless) fruits are occasionally set on some cultivars as Early Golden and Ruby. John Rick cultivar shows promise in the midwest.

THE KIWI (Chinese Gooseberry)

The Kiwi *(Actinidia chinensis),* from China, is popular in New Zealand, a deciduous vine, grown on a trellis, fruit size of hen egg, brownish rough hairy skin, flesh light green, with light-colored rays and many seeds (tiny soft) radiating from the center. Eaten out-of-hand, it resembles grape flesh, delicate flavor, used in salads and a variety of culinary preparations (Mary Beutel, Calif., 1974). Acreage in California has risen fast in a few years. Good early profits were made. Marketing is fairly advanced. About 10,000 tons were produced in 1982; trend is upward.

Kiwi is confined to sub-tropical climate due to young growth being susceptible to frost but requires about 200

313

TABLE 4. COST AND RETURNS SUMMARY FOR FULL-BEARING KIWIFRUIT. 5 ACRES KIWIFRUIT. PART OF 40 ACRES OF VINES AND ORCHARD NO FROST PROTECTION. FOGGER-MISTER IRRIGATION SYSTEM. TULARE, FRESNO AND KINGS COUNTIES. J.H. LARUE ET AL. UNIV. OF CALIF. 1981.

	Unit	Price or Cost/Unit	Quantity	Value Or Cost Per Acre	Your Cost
1. Gross Receipts from Production:					
Kiwifruit	Flat	9.500	1942.000	18449.00	
Total Receipts:				18449.00	
2. Variable Costs:					
Preharvest:					
Pre-Emerge Herb.	Acre	30.000	1.000	30.00	
Weed Control	Acre	30.000	1.000	30.00	
Pest Control	Acre	20.000	1.000	20.00	
Nitrogen	Lbs.	0.350	100.000	35.00	
Dormant Prune	Hour	5.000	80.500	402.50	
Brush Shredding	Acre	10.000	1.000	10.00	
Prune-Tie-Sucker	Hour	5.000	11.500	57.50	
P-T-S Materials	Acre	10.000	1.000	10.00	
Misc. Labor	Hour	5.000	5.004	25.02	
Tractor (Fuel-Lube-Repairs)	Acre			3.41	
Equipment (Fuel-Lube-Repairs)	Acre			96.03	
Buildings (Fuel-Lube-Repairs)	Acre			7.83	
Irrigation (Power-Lube-Rep)	Acin	4.105	30.700	126.04	
Machinery Labor	Hour	5.650	18.811	106.28	
Irrigation Labor	Hour	5.650	6.300	35.60	
Interest on operating cap.	Dol.	0.14000	552.045	75.82	
Total Preharvest Costs:				1071.02	
Preharvest Cost Per Flat				0.5515	
Harvest (November):					
Pick	Flat	0.250	1942.00	485.50	
Pack	Flat	2.250	1942.00	4369.50	
Hauling	Flat	0.050	1942.00	97.10	
Storage-3 mos.	Flat	0.750	1942.00	1456.50	
Selling Charges	Flat	0.950	1942.00	1844.90	
Total Harvest Costs:				8253.50	
Harvest Cost Per Flat				4.2500	
Total Variable Costs:				9324.52	
Variable Cost Per Flat				4.8015	
3. Income Above Variable Costs:				9124.48	
Income Per Flat				4.6985	
4. Overhead:					
Personal Property Taxes:				9.10	
Real Property Taxes:				50.00	
Misc. Office & Bookkeeping (2.50% of Total Variable Costs)				233.11	
Total Overhead:				292.21	
Overhead Cost Per Flat				0.1505	
Total Cash Costs:				9616.73	
Total Cash Cost Per Flat				4.9520	
5. Income Above All Cash Costs:				8832.27	
Income Per Flat				4.5480	
6. Ownership Costs:					
Depreciation:					
Machinery & Equipment	Acre			40.01	
Irrigation System	Acre			132.18	
Buildings	Acre			298.90	
Trees, Vines or Stand	Acre			355.77	
Total Depreciation:				826.87	
Capital & Interest:					
Machinery & Equipment		0.14000	250.895	35.13	
Irrigation System		0.14000	730.417	102.26	
Buildings		0.10670	1812.131	193.35	
Trees, Vines or Stand		0.10670	10673.000	569.40	
Land		0.10670	5500.000	586.85	
Total Interest Charge:				1486.99	
Total Fixed Costs:				2313.86	
Fixed Cost Per Flat				1.1915	
7. Total of Above Costs:				11930.59	
Total Cost Per Flat				6.1435	
8. Net Returns:				6518.41	
Net Returns Per Flat				3.3565	

For Sacramento Valley Kiwi costs, see mimeo tables by Bill Olson et al. University of California (c/o J. A. Beutel, Pomology), Davis 95616. 1982.

hrs. chilling below 45° F. Deep friable sandy loam is best but will grow on wide variety of soils if drainage is good; very susceptible to nematodes. See production costs, Table 4.

ELDERBERRIES

The elder or elderberry (*Sambucus sp.,* family *Caprifoliaceae)* grows wild in the temperate and subtropical zones, and also has limited cultivation as bushes en masse or hedgerows for the large clusters of berries. Principle products are jellies, jams, pies and wine. There has been increased interest in recent yrs with some breeding at the New York and Nova Scotia experiment stations with a few superior named selections (Figure 25): York and Adams from New York and Scotia, Nova, Kent and Victoria from Canada. The plant spreads by stolons and can be propagated by hard-, greenwood or root-cuttings. Plants grow rapidly and should flower and fruit the second year. It produces best on good fruit growing well-drained soils but it has been seen in a vigorous orchard (3-4 ft trunks) in Austria on a gravelly hilltop rather infertile

Figure 25. There is growing interest in the elderberry which grows in the wild over the temperate and subtropical zones and with some cultivated plantings. Dr. C.M. Ritter of Pennsylvania State University is shown here with a harvest of named selections to be used in jellies, jams, pies and wine. (Pa. State Univ.)

drouthy soil, but fertilized. Trees were about the size of a peach tree planted on the square or by rectangle in mowed sod. Flowering is in early midsummer and fruiting in the fall. Bushes can be attractive en masse in a large landscape. The large-fruited cultivars can be mechanically harvested. The better handling methods and mechanical separation of the seeds have helped overcome processing limitations. Superior elderberry jams are now available through the year on many U.S. markets. Farmers and urban people also are making their own wine from the wild or cultivated berries. See references.

MACADAMIA

The macadamia or Queensland nut (Australia), *Macadamia integrifolia,* does well in the upland areas of Hawaii where most of the commercial crop is grown for the USA. Trees may reach 30 ft., slow in growth and bearing, need nearly frost-free sites, as resistant to cold as lemons, needing an average daily temperature of 60° F., similar to orange, some everbearing, others seasonal. Wailua and Ikaika are cultivars used in Hawaii; Keauhou, Kakea and Ikaika are grown in California. These are smooth-shelled. *M. tetraphylla,* is rough-shell, namely Burdick and Elimbah (from Australia). Nuts are 60-70% oil, very high in flavor, expensive on the market, shell is thick, hard, round, inch in diameter, cracks with difficulty. Seedlings are used for rootstocks; grafting is by side-wedge a month after ringing the cionwood for fall grafting. Rooted cuttings can be used. Trees are somewhat drouth resistant but do better with adequate water, need 3 + ft. rooting depth, transplanted from tar-paper pots 25-5 ft apart in hedgerows or on the square. Apply fertilizer several times a year modestly using about as much as for avacado or citrus. Iron deficiency is corrected by chelated iron. Avoid narrow-angled crotches that may split with heavy ylds. Central leader seems best. Pests include gophers (must be controlled), root-rot fungus, cankers, thrips, tobacco budworm larvae, orangeworms, scale, husk borers and moths. Herbicides are used for a clean-harvest floor. Nuts are caught in "hammocks" or swept from ground once a week to prevent mold, avoid rats. Additional details are available from University of California and Hawaii. U.S. production, mainly Hawaii, has been around 100,000 mT, and expanding.

POMEGRANATE

The shiny-leaved ornamental pomegranate, *Punica granatum L.,* has showy carnation-like flowers lasting for several weeks. The 3 to 5-inch diameter fruits are showy red in fall with a leathery rind, numerous seeds surrounded by a soft astringent juicy flesh that children enjoy picking apart. Tree is "tough", sturdy, 6-10 ft. tall, or can be trained as a bush. Performs best in hot desert-like valleys and has very low chilling needs. The Wonderful cultivar is suggested. Propagated from hardwood cuttings or it can be top-worked by grafting or budding. Performs on a wide range of soils, even those somewhat saline. Weak trees respond to fertilizer, mainly N, but often do not need fertilizer. Three to four shoots are selected and trained to a multi-trunk tree, removing other sprouts annually. Remove any dead wood and thin out from time to time. Harvest at full color (may split otherwise), do not tear skin (rots quickly) and store in cool dry place up to three months. Tree is remarkably free from pests, needs little attention.

PISTACHIO

The pistachio, *Pistachio vera L.,* is best grown in hot interior valleys and desert climates, reaches the size of big peach tree very slowly, large divided greyish leaves, pink-blushed nuts in clusters, with yld less than almost any other nut tree. The deciduous species is as resistant to cold as the almond but has a longer chilling requirement, is drouth resistant. Cultivars are Red Aleppo and Trabonella with Peters or USDA 23 as pollinators. Male and female flowers are on separate trees, or a male limb can be grafted on a female tree but must be pruned to keep in check. Pollen is windborne, bees not needed. *P. chinensis, P. atlantica* or *P. terebinthus* seedlings make good root-stocks, not *P. vera*. Tree is tolerant of poor soil, can be an ornamental but climate must be correct for fruiting. Tree is trained low to a vase shape with little future pruning. Harvest when shell is loose, remove covering and boil nuts in salt solution for a few minutes, then dry. No pesticide spraying is needed. Production in 1000's of metric tons in the early 1980s was Iran, 30; Turkey, 15; USA, 10; Syria, 6; Greece, 2.5; and Italy, 2. Trend in USA is up.

Collateral Readings

CHESTNUT
ACKERMAN, W.L. Budding the epicotyls of sprouted chestnut seeds. HortSci. 15(2):186-187. 1980.
CHESTNUTS resistant to blight. USDA Farmers Bull. 2068. 21 pp. 1954.
HARRIS, H. *et al.* 'AU-Cropper', 'AU-Leader', and 'AU-Homestead' Chinese Chestnuts. HortSci. 15(5):665-666. 1980.
JANICK, J. and J.N. MOORE (Eds). Advances in fruit breeding. Chestnut. By R. A. Jaynes. 490-504. Purdue Univ. Press, Lafayette, Ind. 1975.
REED, C.A. Chinese chestnut. Proc. ASHS 49, 139, 1947.

ELDERBERRY
DARROW, G.M. Minor Temperate Fruits in Advances in Fruit Breeding. Purdue Univ. Press., W. Lafayette, In. 1975. (This book also has discussions on Saskatoon berry, pawpaw, cranberry bush, wild fig, mountain ash, Cornelian berry bush, honeysuckle, and barberry.)
MAZZA, G. Separation and processing effects on aromatic components of Saskatoon Berries (*Amelanchier alnifolia* Nutt.) HortSci. 15(6): 754-755, 1980.
OURECKY, D.K. Minor fruits in New York State, N.Y. St. Coll. of Agr. and Life Sci. Inform. Bull. II. 12 p. 1974.
RITTER, C.M. and G.W. MCKEE. The Elderberry. Pa. Agr. Exp. Sta. Bul. 709. 1964.
WAY, R.D. Elderberry growing in New York State. N.Y. St. Coll. of Agr. and Life Sci. Ext. Bull. 1177. 4 p. 1972.

FIG
BEUTEL, J.A. Home fig growing. Calif. Agr. Ext. Serv. Publ. AXT-123. Seek update.
CALIFORNIA AGRICULTURE. This monthly publication from the University of California, Berkeley, contains progress reports on fig research from time to time. Subjects covered include: Promising new seedling fig. June, 1956; Biological control of fig scale. August, 1954; Phomopsis canker of fig. November, 1949; Parathion tested on fig pests. September, 1949.
CONDIT, I.J. Fig culture in California. Calif. Agr. Ext. Ser. Cir. 77. 67 pages. Request recent edition.
CONDIT, I.J. The Fig, A book. Chronica Botanica Company, Waltham, Mass. 222 pages. 1947.
CONDIT, I.J. Fig varieties: a monograph. Hilgardia 23: 11. 323-538. February, 1955.
CONDIT, I.J. and J. ENDERUD. A bibliography of the fig. Hilgardia 25: 1-663. July, 1956.
CRANE, J.C., N. MAREI and M.M. NELSON. Growth and maturation of fig fruits stimulated by 2-chloroethylphosphonic acid. J. ASHS 95(3):367-370. 1970.
DAVIS, C.S. *et al.* Pest and disease control program for figs (published frequently) Calif. Ag. Exp. Sta. Leaflet, 70. Ask for recent edition.
ETHEPHON to speed fig harvest. Blue Anchor, p. 34. July/August, 1977.
GERDTS. M. and G. OBENAUF. Ethephon speeds maturity on figs. Calif. Agri. May, 1972.
KOLBE, M.H. Fig culture in North Carolina. No. Car. State Univ., Raleigh, No. Carolina. Reprint. 4 p. 1978.
KREZDORN, A.H. and G.W. ADRIANCE. Fig growing in the south. USDA Ag. Handbook. 196, 26 pp. 1961 (popularized version. "Growing figs in the south for home use," Home and Garden Bull. 87. USDA. 11 pp., 1962.)
LENDEGREN, J.E. *et al.* Nematode "controls" carpenterworm in fig. Ca. Agr. Jan-Feb. 1981.
MAREI, NASR and J.C. CRANE. Ethylene effects on fig. Plant Physiol. Vol. 48. September 1971.
NAUER, E.M. and S.B. BOSWELL. NAA on shoots of top-worked fig trees. HortSci. 12(3):250-251. 1977.
PUECH. A.A. *et al.* Plastid pigments in skin of 'Mission' fig fruits. J. ASHS. 101(4): 392-4. 1976.
PUECH, A.A. and J.C. CRANE. Translocation of ethephon in fig (*Ficus carica L.)* Shoots. J. ASHS. 100: 443-446. 1975.
SISSION, R.F. The wasp that plays cupid to a fig. National Geographic. 138 (5): 690-697. Nov. 1970.

FILBERT
JONES, S.C. *et al.* Filbert insect pest control. Ore. Ag. Ext. Circ. 728. (Seek latest).
KWONG, F.Y. and H.B. LAGERSTEDT. Ethephon in filbert. HortSci. 11(3): 264-5. 1976.
LAGERSTEDT, H.B. Filbert. Rep. from 61st Ann. Report. Northern Nut Growers Association. Inc. 61-67. 1970.
LAGERSTEDT, H.B. Filbert grafting. Proc. Ore. Hort. Soc. 62:60-63. 1971.
LAGERSTEDT, H.B. Acceleration of Filbert Nut Drop by ethephon. J. ASHS. 97(6): 738-740. 1972.
LAGERSTEDT, H.B. Survey of Freeze Injury on Nut Crops. Ore. St. Hort. Soc. 1972.
LAGERSTEDT, H.B. 1973. Filbert training to tree and bush forms. HortSci. 8(5):390-391. 1973.
LAGERSTEDT, H.B. and M.M. THOMPSON. Evaluations of New Filbert Selections. Proc. Nut Growers Soc. Ore. Wash. 59:21-25; 47-53. 1974.

LAGERSTEDT, H.B. Rooted filbert plants from scions in one year. Rep. from 67th Annual Report of the No. Nut Growers Assoc. 56-60. 1976.

LAGERSTEDT, H.B. Blanks in the filbert and possible causes. Economic Botany. Vol. 31:(2) 153-159. 1977.

LAGERSTEDT, H.B. Spacing, training, culture of filbert. Ore. Wash. Nut Growers Proc. 7 pp. 1976.

LAGERSTEDT, H.B. 'Ennis' and 'Butler' Filberts HortSci. 15(6): 833-835, 1980. Also in Fruit Var. Jr. 35(3). July 1981.

MACDANIELS, L.H. Nut growing in the Northeast. Cornell Information Bull. 71. p. 20. 1981. (Priced).

MAURER, K.J. Die hazel (Corylus) aus der Sicht der literature and eigener untersuchungen and im lichte der welternahrungslage sowie des umweltschultzes, (Geisenheim/Rheingau, Germany), a review of the hazel nut literature to 1973 with bibleo Sonderdruk aus, No. 12, December 1973.

OURECKY, D.K. and J.E. REICH. Numerical scoring system for filberts. HortSci. 9(1): 18. 1974.

PIERCE, J.D. Filbert production and propagation. Amer. Fruit Grower 6-7. August 1982.

REICH, J.E. and H.B. LAGERSTEDT. Paraquat. Dinoseb and 2,4-D on filbert suckers. J. ASHS. 96(5): 554-556. 1971.

SCHREIBER, W.K. Nut inudstry in Mediterranean basin. Proc. Nut Grower's Soc. Oreg., Wash. 33, 101, 108. 1947.

STRONG, W.J. Nut culture in Canada (filberts, butternuts, etc.) Ontario Dept. of Agr. Bull. 494. 25 pp. 1952.

THOMPSON, M. Pollen incompatibility in filbert. Proc. Nut Grower's Soc. Ore. and Wash. 56:73-79. 1971.

THOMPSON, M. Inheritance of Big-Bud Mite Susceptibility in filberts. J. ASHS. 102(1): 39-42. 1977.

THOMPSON, M.M. Inheritance of Nut Traits in Filbert (Corylus Avellana L.) Euphytica 26(1977) 465-474. 1977.

THOMPSON, M.M. et al. Evaluation system for filberts (Corylus avellana L). HortSci. 13(5): 514-517. 1978.

SALESSES, G. Cytological study of filbert. Genus C. Avellana. Ann. Amelior. Plantes 23:59-66. Station d-Arboriculture fruitiere, Centre de Recherches de Bordeaux, I.N.R.A., France. (Contract the Station for additional fruit breeding reprints.)

For up-to-date papers on commercial filberts (and E. walnuts) refer to Nut Growers Soc. Proc. (Ann.) of Ore., Wash. and B.C. c/o Dept. of Hort., Ore. St. Univ., Corvallis, for copies. (Priced)

KIWI

BEUTEL, M. Recipes for Kiwifruit lovers. Univ. of Calif. Pomology Dept., Davis. 1975.

FLETCHER, W.A. Growing Chinese Gooseberries. N. Z. Dept. of Agr. Bull. 349. Wellington. New Zealand. 1971.

MINISTRY OF AGRICULTURE and Fisheries. Proceedings of Kiwifruit Seminar. Tauranga. N. Z. 1974.

PRATT, H.J. and M.S. REID. Chinese Gooseberry (Kiwi): Seasonal patterns in fruit growth and maturation, ripening, respiration and the role of ethylene. J. Sci. Fd. Agric. 25:747-757. (Reprint). 1974.

SCHROEDER, C.A. and W.A. FLETCHER. The Chinese Gooseberry (Actinidia chinenesis) in New Zealand. Econ. Bot. 21:81-92 (Reprint). 1967.

MACADAMIA

COOIL, B.J. et al. Phosphorus effects on growth, yield, leaf composition of Macadamia nut. Hawaii Ag. Exp. Sta. Tech. Bull. 66, 71 pp. Dec. 1966.

HAMILTON, R. Growing Macadamia nuts in Hawaii. Several Hawaiian publ., since 1960s. Contact Mr. Hamilton at Univ. of Hawaii, Honolulu, 96822.

ITO, P.J. and R.A. HAMILTON. Quality and yield of 'Keauhou' macadamia nuts from mixed and pure block plantings. HortSci. 15(3):307. 1980.

LABANAUSKAS, C.K. and M.F. HANDY. The effects of iron and manganese deficiencies on accumulation of nonprotein and protein amino acids in macadamia leaves. J. ASHS 95(2):218-222. 1970.

OOKA, H. Macadamia nut production in Hawaii. Fruit Var. Journ. 30(4): 110-115. 1976.

SALEEB, W.F., D.M. YERMANOS, C.K. HUSZAR, W.B. STOREY, and C.K. LABANAUSKAS. The oil and protein in nuts of Macadamia tetraphylla. L. Johnson. Macadamia intergrifolia Maiden and Betche, and their hybrids. J. ASHS 98(5):453. 1973.

SHIGEURA, G.T., J.LEE and J.A. SILVA. The role of honey bees in macadamia nut production in Hawaii. J. ASHS. 95(5): 544-546. 1970.

PECAN

AITKEN, J.B. Chemical defoliation of young, budded pecan trees. HortScience 8(1):50. 1973.

AITKEN, J.B. Pecan herbicides: now and future. And Ga. Herbicide trials (J.W. Daniell) Pecan South. Apr. 1975.

AITKEN, J.B. and R. FERREE. Growing pecans in South Carolina. Clemson Univ. Cir. 482. 22 pp. Seek update.

AITKEN, J.B. Perennial grass control in young pecan orchards. Pecan South. 4:(3). 113-115. Apr. 1977.

ALLISON, J.R. Costs and returns from pecan groves. Pecan South. Nov. 1974.

AMLING, H.J. and K.A. AMLING. Onset, intensity, and dissipation of rest in several pecan cultivars. J. ASHS 105(4) 536-540. 1980.

AMLING, H.J. and W.H. DOZIER. Alternate bearing in pecans. Proc. S.E. Pecan Growers Assoc. 62:37-39. 1969.

AMLING, H. J. and K. A. AMLING. Differentiation of pecan and pistillate flowers and cold requirements for initiation. JASHS. 108:(2) 195-8. 1983.

ARNOLD, C.E. Terbacil. Diuron and Paraquat in pecan orchards. IFAS. Agr. Res. Center. Monticello, Fla. 1977.

ARNOLD, C.E. and F.P. LAWRENCE. Pecan production in Flordia. Fla. Ext. Cir. 280-13. 31 pp. 1980.

ARNOLD, C.E. and C.P. ANDREWS. Pecan cultivar review — southeast. Fruit Var. Jour. 35 (2) Apr. 1981.

ATOR, D.W. et al. Pecan production, Louisiana, economic aspects. DEA Res. Rpt. 555. 75 pp. 1979.

BANIN, A., J. NAVROT, and Y. RON. Tree implanted zinc-bentonite paste as a source of slow-release zinc for 'Delmas' pecan. HortSci. 15(2): 182-184. 1980.

BOETHEL, D.J. and J.E. EZELL. Pecan phylloxera; life history. Pecan South 4(2):52-60. 1977.

BRISON, F.R. Pecan Culture. Capital Printing, Austin, Texas. 292 p. 1974.

CAMPBELL, C. and G.C. MARTIN. Moisture in walnut seeds by near-infrared spectrophotometry. HortSci. 11(5): 494-6. 1976.

CARPENTER, T.L. and W.W. NEEL. Survey of resistance of pecan varieties to insects and mites. Pecan South 7(3): 10-22. 1980.

CARPENTER, T.L. and W.W. NEEL. Comparison of aerial vs speed sprayer application of insecticides for control of yellow aphids on pecans. Pecan South Vol. 7(2):6-9. March 1980.

CHAPLIN, M.H. Estimates of tree size, bearing surface and yield of tree fruits and nuts. Ann. Rept. Ore. Hort. Soc. 64:94-98. 1973.

CHAPLIN, M.H. and A.R. DIXON. Development of standard ranges for leaf nitrogen in the filbert. J. Amer. Soc. Hort. Sci. 104(5): 710-712. 1979.

CONDRA. D. Rate of return on investment in pecans, El Paso Valley. Pecan South. 4(2):62-22. 1977.

CREWS, C.E., et al. Carboxylase activity and seasonal changes in CO_2 assimilation rates in three cultivars of pecan. J. ASHS 105(6): 798-801. 1980.

CROCKER, T.F. Pecan production in Georgia. Ga. Ext. Bull. 609. 31 pp. 1982.

DANIELL, J.W. Scheduling drip irrigation using pan evaporation for pecans. Pecan South 3(4) 19-23, June 1981.

DANIELL, J.W. Effective use of sinbar in pecan orchards for weed control. Pecan South 7(4): 6-8. 1980.

DAVIS, J.T. and D. SPARKS. Assimilation of carbon-14 by pistillate inflorescences and fruits of 'Stuart' pecan. HortSci. 11(3):262-3. 1976.

DAVIS, J.T. and D. SPARKS. Assimilation and translocation of carbon-14 in shoots of fruiting pecan trees. J. ASHS. 99: 468-480. 1974.

EPPERSON, J.E. and J.R. ALLISON. Price futures for the United States pecan industry. HortSci. 15(4): 475-478. 1980.

EPPERSON, J.E. and J.R. ALLISON. Importance of rising energy costs on pecan production costs in Georgia vs. Arizona. HortSci. Vol. 14(6): 716-718. Dec. 1979.

GALLAHER, R.N. and J.B. JONES, JR. Total, extractable, and oxalate calcium. Other elements in normal and mouse-ear pecan tree tissues. J. ASHS. 101(6): 692-969. 1976.

GAMMON, N. JR. Mechanical harvesting of pecans vs. soils. Pecan South 3(5):482-3. 1976.

GAST, R.T. and J.P. OVERCASH. Pecan rootstocks and scion cultivars produced by commercial nurseries in the southern United States. Pecan South 7(2) 14-18. March 1980.

GEMOETS, E.E. et al. Cycles in U.S. pecan production 1919-1974. Identified by power spectral analysis. J. ASHS 101(5): 550-553. 1976.

GOING, W.D. The pecan in Rhodesia. Hortus Rhodesia 11;7-10. 1969.

HEATON, E.K. et al. Handling, storage, processing and utilization of pecans. Ga. Res. Bull. 197. 77 pp. 1977.

HEDGER, G.H., et al. Computer prediction and control of the pecan weevil. Pecan South. 198-208. 5(5) Sept. 1978.

JANICK, J. and J.N. MOORE. Breeding temperate nuts. In Advances in fruit breeding. (walnuts, filberts, pecans, almonds, chestnuts, hickories) Purdue Univ. Press, Lafayette, Ind. 385-505. 1975.

JAYNES, R.A. Editor, Northern Nut Growing. Northern Nut Growers Ass'n., 300+ pp. (Very good book), Univ. of Conn., Storrs. 1969.

JOHNSON, J.L. Economics of establishing young pecan orchards. Pecan South. Nov. 1975.

JONES, R.W. A simple-leaved pecan. HortSci. 12(6): 583-4. 1977.

KAYS, S.J. and D.M. WILSON. Pecan Kernel Color. Pecan South. 3(5):471-3. 1976.

KAYS, S.J. and D.M. WILSON. Pecan kernel color and color stability during storage. ASHS 103(1): 137-141. 1978.

KAYS, S. Changes in the internal environment of the nut during shuck split. Pecan South. pp. 68-70. Mar. 1978.

KOLBE, M.H. Growing pecans in North Carolina. The No. Carolina Ag. Ext. Serv. Reprint. 1979.

LAICHE, A.J., JR. Effects of root pruning and seed size on nursery grown pecan trees. Pecan South 7(4): 10-16. June 1980.

LAW, J.M., et al. A high density spacing... An alternative for pecan growers. Pecan South Vol 7(2): 36-41. March 1980.

LOCKWOOD, D.W. and D. SPARKS. 14C in tops and roots of pecan in spring following assimilation of 14CO₂ previous growing season. J. ASHS 103(1): 38-45: 45-9. 1978.

LOCKWOOD, D.W. and D. SPARKS. Translocation of stored carbohydrates from tops and roots of pecan during the spring flush. Pecan South 7(4): 22-29. 1980.

MACDANIELS, L.H. Nut Growing in the Northeast. Cornell Information Bull. 71. 20 pp. 1981. Priced.

MCMEANS, J.L. and H.M. MALSTROM. Pecan ylds and quantity, quality nutmeat oil. HortSci. 17:1. 69. 1982.

MADDEN, G.D. 'Tejas' Pecan. HortSci. 8(6): 515. Dec. 1973.

MADDEN, G.D. and E.J. BROWN. 'Kiowa' pecan. HortSci. 11(5):522. 1976.

MADDEN, G.D. and H. TISDALE. Chilling, stratification on nut germination of northern and southern pecan cultivars. HortSci. 10:259-260. 1975.

MADDEN, G.D. and E.J. BROWN. Budbreak, blossom dates, nut maturity and length of growing season of the major pecan varieties grown in the West. Pecan South 2:96-97. 1975.

MALSTROM, H.L. and G. MADDEN. New variety performance in the Southeast. Pecan South 2:100-101. 1975.

MALSTORM, H.L. and J.L. MCMEANS. Yield, nut quality of pecan varieties. SW-USA Pecan South. Vol. 3(5) 486-90. 1976.

MARTIN, G.C., et al. Effect of calcium in offsetting defoliation induced by ethephon in pecan. J. ASHS 105(1): 34-37. Jan. 1980.

MATTA, F.B. and J.B. STOREY. Container, BA, GA₃ on growth of seedling pecans. HortSci. 16:5. 652-3. 1981.

MATTA, F.B. et al. Air Temperature on 'Western Schley' pistillate flower development. Pecan South 4(2): 80-82. 1977.

MEKAKO, H.U. and H.Y. NAKASONE. Floral Development and Compatibility Studies of Carica Species. J. ASHS. 100:145-148. 1975.

MEKAKO, H.U. and H.Y. NAKASONE. Sex inheritance in some Carica species. J. ASHS. 102(1): 42-5. 1977.

NATIONAL PECAN CONFERENCE. Dallas, Texas, 1970. (Tex. Pecan Growers' Assn., College Station). Covers research, marketing, mech. harvesting, Cheyenne var., taxes, rootstocks, etc. Published 1972.

NORTON, J.A., et al. Effects of herbicides on roots and pecan nut quality. Weed Sci. 18:520-22. 1970.

O'BARR, R.D. Pecan nutrition — an overlooked factor. Pecan South. 512-519. Nov. 1976.

OSBURN, M.R., et al. Insects, diseases and control on pecan. USDA Ag. Handbook 240. 55 pp. Sept. 1966 (very good bulletin).

OVERCASH, J.P. and W.W. KILBY. Pruning and training on yields young pecan trees. Proc. S. E. Pecan Growers Assoc. 66:63-71. 1973.

OVERCASH, J.P. and R.C. SLOAN, JR. Pecan nursery trees in containers. Pecan South. Jan. 1982.

PAYNE, J.A., et al. Aerial infra-red photography to locate pecan orchards. Pecan Quarterly. Vol. 6(1). February 1972.

PAYNE, J. A., et al. Insect pests and diseases of pecan. USDA, New Orleans, La. 1979.

PECAN NURSERY DIRECTORY. (Fla. to Tex.) Pecan South. Published annually.

PECAN SOUTH (Journ.) Jan. 1976 has good articles on nutrient deficiencies, marketing, income tax mgmt., cultural, etc.

PLANK, C.O. and W.S. LETZSCH. Monitoring nutrient status of pecan trees. SE Pecan Growers Assn. 75th Proceedings, Sec.-Tres. Starkville, Miss. 125-30. 1982.

POWELL, J.V. Competition in Marketing Domestic Tree Nuts. Pecan South 2:198. 1975.

PROCEEDINGS S.E. Pecan Grower's Assn. Ann. Publ. 270 pp., Mrs. Chesley Hines, Starkville, MS. Exec-Sec'y-Tres. Members receive rpts. (Priced)

PROEBSTING, E.L. and E.F. SERR. Edible nuts. Chapter in Fruit Nutrition. Horticultural Publications, N. Childers, Ed. 3906 NW 31 Pl., Gainesville, Fl. 32606. (Priced).

PULS, E.E., et al. "Tip-pruning" pecans. Am. Fruit. Gr. Dec. 1975.

REED, C.A. and J. DAVIDSON. Improved nut trees of North America and how to grow them. The Devin-Adair Co. New York City. 404 pp. 1954.

REFRIGERATION units buy time for pecans. Pecan South 7(3): 30-33. 1980.

SCHROEDER, H.W. and J.B. STOREY. Aflatoxin in Stuart pecans as affected by shell integrity. HortSci. 11:53-54. 1976.

SENTER, S.C. Carotenoids of pecan nutmeats. HortSci. 10:592. 1975.

SHEPARD, M. and R.L. HOLLOWAY. Seasonal trend of pecan weevil. Pecan South. Vol. 3(5):464-467. 1976.

SHERMAN, W.B. and T.E. CROCKER. Polycotyledons in pecans. Pecan South 7(3): 29. 1980.

SHUHART, D.V. and C.E. BRACK. Return bloom and fruit set of pecan after leaf and fruit removal. HortSci. 7:131-132. 1972.

SMITH, M.W. and J.B. STOREY. Washing procedures on loss of certain elements from pecan leaflets. HortSci. 11:50-52. 1976.

SMITH, M.W. and H.J. CHIU. Seasonal changes in rooting of juvenile and adult pecan cuttings. HortSci. 15(5): 594-595. 1980.

SMITH, M.W., et al. Two methods of foliar application of zinc and adjuvant solutions on leaflet zinc conc. in pecan trees. HortSci. 14(6): 718-719. Dec. 1979.

SMITH, M.W., et al. Zinc, sulfur in pecan as affected by application of sulfur and zinc to calcareous soils. HortSci. 15(1): 77-78. 1980.

SMITH, M.W., and J. STOREY. Zinc concentration of pecan leaflets and yield as influenced by zinc source and adjuvants. J. ASHS 104(4):474-477. 1979.

SPARKS, D. Bud break in pecan following boron toxicity. HortSci. 11(5):494. 1976.

SPArKS, D. Sub-freezing temperatures on bud break of pecan. HortSci. 11(4):415-6. 1976.

SPARKS, D. Pecan zinc nutrition. Pecan South 3:304-309. 1976.

SPARKS, D. Nutrition on dieback of germinating 'Curtis' pecan seedlings. HortSci. 12(5): 496-497. 1977.

SPARKS, D. Fruiting on scorch, premature defoliation and nutrient status of "Chickasaw" pecan leaves. J. ASHS. 102(5): 669-673. 1977.

SPARKS, D. Method of grove establishment and elemental conce. of pecan leaves. HortSci. 12(1): 69-71. 1977.

SPARKS, D. and J.A. PAYNE. Freeze injury of non-juvenile trunks in pecan. HortSci. 12(5): 497-798. 1977.

SPARKS, D. Nutrient removal in nut harvest. Pecan South. Nov. 1975.

SPARKS, D. and H. BAKER. Growth and nutrient response of pecan seedlings to N levels in sand culture. J. ASHS. 100:392-399. 1975.

SPARKS, D. Alternate fruit bearing — A Review. Pecan South 2:44. 1975.

SPARKS, D. and C.E. BRACK. Return bloom and fruit set of pecan from leaf and fruit removal. HortSci. 7:(2) April 1972. p. 131.

SPARKS, D. Nutrient conc. of pecan leaves associated with deficiency and normal growth. HortSci. 13(3): 256-257. 1978.

SPRAY CALENDAR. California Agr. Ext. Serv. Leaflet 80. Request lastest edition.

STUCKEY'S and PECANS. At the Top. Pecan South 3:324-327. 1976.

SULLIVAN, D.T. and E. HERRERA. Winter injury to pecans. Pecan South 3(4):11-14. June 1981.

TAYLOR, G.G. and R.E. ODOM. Some biochemical compounds associated with rooting of pecan stem cuttings. J. ASHS. 95(2): 146-150. 1970.

TAYLOR, R.M. Influence of gibberellic acid on early patch budding of pecan seedlings. J. ASHS 97(5): 677. 1972.

THOMPSON, T. E. et. al. Comparison of four methods of pecan orchard establishment. HortSci. 17:(6). 972-3. 1982.

TREE NUTS. World Production and Trade. Issued by USDA-FAS. Wash., D.C. 20250. Trends and statistics, annually.

VAN LAM, H. Cu requirement for pecans. Pecan South. pp. 90-91. 1978. (Mar.)

VAN STADEN, J. et al. Temperature on pecan seed germination. HortSci. 11(3): 261-2. 1976.

WAGNER, A.B., JR. Maintaining peak quality in pecans. Pecan South 4(2):60-62. 1977.

WELLS, J.M. and J.A. PAYNE. Aflatoxin contamination in Southeastern pecans. Proc. Fla. State Hort. Soc. 89:256-257. 1976.

WETZSTEIN, H. Y. and D. SPARKS. Anatomical and age-related scab resistance and susceptibility in pecan leaves. JASHS. 108:(2)210-218. 1983.

WHITE, JR. et al. Legumes and nitrogen supply in pecan orchards. Pecan South 8(4) 24-31. June 1981.

WHITE, A. W., Jr. Lime & fertilizer placement to total pecan growth. HortSci. 17(3):380-381. 1982.

WILLIAMS, F.W., M.G. LAPLANTE, and E.K. HEATON. Evaluation of quality of pecans in retail markets. J. ASHS 98(5): 460. 1973.

WOODROOF, J.G. Tree nuts — production, processing, products. Avi Publ. Co., Westport, Ct. 731 pp. 1979.

WOOD, B. W. Changes in indoleacetic acid, abscisic acid, gibberellins, and cytokinins during budbreak in pecan. JASHS. 108(2):333-8. 1983.

WOOD, B. W. Ethephon thinning pecan. HortSci. 18:(1)53-54. 1983.

WOOD, B.W. and J.L. MCMEANS. Carbohydrates fatty acids in pecan fruit. J. ASHS 107:1. 47-50. 1982.

WORLEY, R.E. et al. Growth, yield, nutritional correlation pecan. J. ASHS: 97-4, 514-21. 1972.

WORLEY, R.E. and R.L. CARTER. Effect of four management systems on parameters associated with growth and yield of pecan. J. ASHS 98(6):541. Nov. 1973.

WORLEY, R.E. Effect of N.P.K. and lime on yield, nut quality, tree growth and leaf analysis of pecan (Carya illinoensis W.) J. ASHS 99(1):49. 1973.

WORLEY, R.E. Pecan nutlet set and carbohydrate level of various tissues in the spring as affected by fungicide sprays. J. ASHS 98(1):68. 1973.

WORLEY, R.E. et al.Pressure trunk Zn injection promising for pecan, other trees. HortSci. 11(6): 590-1. 1976.

WORLEY, R.E., S.A. HARMAN, and R.L. CARTER. Effect of repeated N.P.K. and lime applications on soil pH, P. and K. under old and young pecan trees. J. ASHS 99(1):57. 1973.

WORLEY, R.E. et al. Magnesium sources and rates on correction of acute Mg deficiency of pecan. J. ASHS. 100:487. 1975.

WORLEY, R.E. Drip irrigation on pecan. J. ASHS 107:1 30-4. 1982.

WORLEY, R.E. Fall defoliation date and seasonal carbohydrate conc. in pecan wood tissue. J. ASHS 104(2): 195-199. 1979.

WORLEY, R.E. Pecan yield, quality, nutlet set, and spring growth as a response to time of fall defoliation. J. ASHS 104(2): 192-194. 1979.

WORLEY, R.E. Performance of Davis pecan at the Ga. Coastal Plain Exp. Sta. Pecan South 7(3): 34-36. 1980.

WORLEY, R.E. and R.H. LITTRELL. Ineffectiveness of foliar application and pressure trunk injection of Mg-N for correction of Mg deficiency of pecan. HortSci. 15(2): 181-182. 1980.

WORLEY, R. E. and WOODWARD, O. J. 'Woodward' pecan. HortSci. 17(3):415-416. 1982.

YOUNG, W.A., et al. 'Melrose' Pecan. HortSci. 15(3): 321. 1980.

Note: State agricultural stations in Southern U.S. have bulletins on local pecan growing recommendations. Contact them for publications.

POMEGRANATE

LA RUE, J.H. Growing pomegranates in California. Univ. of Cal;if. Leaflet 2459. 8 p. 1980.

PERSIMMON

BEN-AIRE, R. and S. GUELFAT-REICH. CO_2 treatment on stored persimmon fruits. Jour. ASHS. 101(2): 179-81. 1976.

CAMP, A.F. and H. MOWRY. The cultivated persimmon in Florida. Fla. Agr. Ext. Service Bulletin 124. Revised 1945.

CHARNEY, P.F. and R.A. SEELIG. Persimmons in Fruit and Vege. Facts and Pointers, U.S. Fr. and Veg. Ass'n., Wash., D.C. 7 p. 1967.

FRUITS AND TREE NUTS, bloom, harvesting and mkting dates, etc., by states. USDA Hdbk. 186. July 1960.

GOULD, H.P. The Oriental persimmon. U.S. Dept. of Agr. Leaflet 194; 1-8 May, 1940.

HODGSON, R.W. Girdling to reduce fruit drop in the Hachiya persimmon. Proc. Amer. Soc. Hort. Sci. 36: 405-409, 1939.

HODGSON, R.W. Floral situation, sex condition and parthenocarpy in the Oriental persimmon. Proc. Amer. Soc. Hort. Sci. 37: 250-252. 1940.

HODGSON, R.W. Rootstocks for the Oriental persimmon. Proc. Amer. Hort. Sci. 37: 338-339. 1940.

KADIURA, M. The physiological dropping of fruits in the Japanese persimmon. National Hort. Exp. Sta. Res. Bull. 19. 1944 (in Japanese with English summary).

MCDANIEL, J.C. American persimmon. An emerging horticultural crop. Fruit Var. Jour. 27:16-18. Jan. 1973.

OVERHOLSER, E.L. Ripening and removal of astringency in Japanese persimmons. Proc. Amer. Soc. Hort. Sci.: 256-266. 1927.

PRESTON, W.H., JR. and E. GRIFFITH. Use of apples to remove astringency from Persimmon fruits. Northern nut Growers Assn., Inc. 53rd Annual Report-1962. pp. 29-34.

PRESTON, W.H., JR. and E. GRIFFITH. Current status of Oriental persimmon in temperate eastern United States. Northern Nut Growers Assoc. 57th Ann. Rpt. 112-123. 1966.

RIZZI, A.D. The Oriental persimmon in California. Calif. Ag. Ext. Serv. Publ. AXT-87, 8 pp. 1964.

PISTACHIO

CRANE, J. and I. M. AL-SHALAN. Physical and chemical changes associated with growth of the pistachio nut. J. ASHS 99(1):87. Jan. 1973.

CRANE, J.C., I.M. AL-SHALAN and R.M. CARLSON. Abscission of pistachio inflorescence buds as affected by leaf area and number of nuts. J. ASHS 98(6): 591. Nov. 1973.

CRANE, J.C. Abortion and parthenocrapy in blank pistachio nuts as affected by rootstock. J. ASHS. 100:267-270. 1975. Mech. Harv. Cal. Agr. Nov. 1975.

CRANE, J.C. and I. AL-SHALAN. C and N in pistachio on shoot extension, yield. J. Amer. Soc. HortSci. ASHS. 102(4): 396-399. 1977.

CRANE, J.C. Quality of pistachio nuts as affected by time of harvest. J. ASHS 103(3): 332-333. 1978.

CRANE, J. C. and IWAKIRI, B. T. Shell dehiscence in Pistachio. HortSci. 17: (5) 797-8. 1982.

MARANTO, J. et al. Pistachio orchard costs, S. San Joaquin Valley, Calif. Univ. of Calif. Spec. Publ. 3087. 6 p. 1981.

MARANTO, J. and J.C. CRANE. Pistachio Production. Univ. of Calif. Leaflet 2279. 18 p. 1982.

PORLINGIS, I.C. Flower bud abscission in pistachio (Pistacia vera L.) as related to fruit development and other factors. J. ASHS 99(2): 121. March 1974.

TORABI, M. Ethephon on ripening, splitting of pistachio nuts. HortSci. 15(4): 521. Aug. 1980.

WALNUT

ALDRICH, T.M., et al. Walnuts — Modified leader trees. Calif. Leaflet 2471. 12 pp. Aug. 1975.

BLACK WALNUT as a crop. USDA Gen. Tech. Rpt. No. 4. So. Ill., Univ., Carbondale. 4 pp. 1973.

BLACK WALNUT for home use. USDA Leaflet 525, 9 pp. 1974.

BROOKS, M.G. Black walnut trees, effects on vegetation. W. Vir. Agri. Exp. Sta. Bull. 347. 31 pp. 1951.

BROOKS, R.M., and H.P. OLMO. Register of new fruit and nut varieites. 2nd Ed. Univ. of Calif. Press, Berkeley. 708 pp. 1972.

BROWNE, L.T. *et al.* Walnut rootstocks compared. Calif. Agric. 14-15. July 1977.

CALIFORNIA AGRICULTURE. This popularized monthly report from the University of California contains up-to-date research on English walnuts. A sample of these are as follows: B Vitamin in Walnuts, Nov., 1954; Blackline in Walnut, March, 1959; Walnut Aphid Investigations, March, 1959; Vitamins in Walnut meats, August, 1959, Filbertworm Injury to Walnuts, September, 1957; Migrating Aphids on Walnuts, June, 1953; Walnut Aphid Investigations, July, 1954; Walnut Branch Wilt, October, 1955; The Walnut Husk Fly, May, 1956; Navel Orangeworm, June, 1956; Frost Damage to Walnut Kernels, June, 1956; Root — Lesion Nematode on Walnuts, May 1958; Frosted Scale on Walnuts, April, 1956; Fumigation of Walnuts, July, 1952; Mites on Walnuts, February, 1951; Timing of spray treatments for codling Moth, March, 1950; Walnut Aphid Studies in 1955, March, 1956; Control of Walnut Blight, March, 1956; Spider Mite on Walnuts, Nov., 1957 and July, 1956; and Filbertworm Injury to Walnuts, January, 1956. Pre-emergence herbicides for weed control in walnuts, 1967. (Spraying with zinc, April 1970); Ethephon/walnut drying, June 1976; Walnut aphid, June, 1982; Irrigation and bark canker, May-June, 1982; Blackline - a graft virus, Nov.-Dec. 1981; Bacterial blight, Sept.-Oct., 1981.

CLARK, F.B. Black walnuts for timber. USDA Forest Serv. Leaflet 487, 10 pp. 1976.

GAGNAIRE, J., and C. VALLIER. Variations in leaf K of grafted walnut trees, *Juglans Regia/Juglans Nigra,* grown under natural conditions (in French). C.R. Ocd. Agr. France. 54(2): 81-86. 1968.

HANSCHE, P.E., V. BERES, and H.I. FORDE. Estimates of quantitative genetic properties of walnut and their implications for cultivar improvement. J. ASHS. 97(2): 279, March 1972.

HOROSCHAK, T. Walnut industries of the Mediterranean Basin. USDA. For Agr. Serv. FAS M-245. April 1972.

INTEGRATED PEST MANAGEMENT for walnuts in California (cultural practices included) Univ. of Ca., Div. of Agr. Sciences. Publ. 3270. Color Illus. 97 pp. (priced) 1982.

KADO, C.O., *et al.* Susceptibility of walnut cultivars to deep bark canker. J. ASHS. 102(6): 698-702. 1977.

KUHLMAN, F.W. Cost of producing filberts and walnuts in Oregon. Ore. Agri. Exp. Sta. Cir. of Inform. 499. Request recent data at Corvallis.

LEE, K.C., and R.W. CAMPBELL. Nature and occurrence of juglone in *Juglans nigra* L. HortSci. 4(4):297-298. 1969.

LIN, J. *et al.* Pistillate flowering and fruiting in English Walnuts. J. ASHS. 102(6):702-705. 1977.

MARTIN, G. *et al.* The movement and fate of 2-chloroethyl phosphonic acid in walnut. J. ASHS. 97 (1): 51. Jan. 1972.

MARTIN, G.C. *et al.* Effect of delays between harvesting and drying on kernel quality of walnuts. J. ASHS. 100:55-57. 1975.

MARTIN, G.C. and H.I. FORDE. Incidence of Blackline in Walnut on Various Rootstocks. J. ASHS. 100:246-249. 1975.

MARTIN, G.C. *et al.* Effect of drastic reduction of water input on mature walnut trees. HortSci. 15(2): 157-158. 1980.

MARTIN, G.C. *et al.* Chemical "pruning" of walnut trees. Calif. Arg. 34 (10): 16-17. Oct. 1980.

MAURER, K.J. Grafting compatability in walnut. Baumschulpraxis 6:164-170. (In German.) 1974.

MILLER, P.W., C.E. SCHUSTER and R.E. STEPHENSON. Diseases of the walnuts in the Pacific Northwest and their control. Ore. Agric. Exp. Station Bull. 435 44 pp. Seek update.

OLSON, W.H. Walnut variety susceptibility to codling moth. Calif. Agri. p. 15. Oct. 1977.

OLSON, W.H. *et al.* Lower ethephon rates effective in walnut harvest. Calif. Agr. p. 6-7. July 1977.

PERRY, E.J. and A.D. RIZZI. Whitewash sprays against walnut sunburn. Calif. Agr. April 1970.

RAMOS, D.E. and G.S. SIBBETT. Mechanized hedging close-planted walnuts. Calif. Agric. 10. Jan. 1975.

RAMOS, D.E. *et al.* Water stress affects size and quality of walnuts. Calif. Agric. pp. 5-7. Oct. 1978.

REED, A.D. Walnut production Costs. Calif. Leaflet 2744. Seek update.

RITTER, C.M. *et al.* Black walnut variety trials — 1950-1977. Fruit Var. Journ. 33(4): 126-130. Oct. 1979.

RODRIGUEZ, R. Roots from walnut cotyledons. HortSci. 17(2):195-196. 1982.

RYUGO, K. and D.E. RAMOS. Effects of defoliation and pruning on flower-bud initiation and differentiation in 'Chico' walnut HortSci. 14(1): 52-54. 1979.

SEIDEL, K.W. and K.A. BRINKMAN. Black walnuts on strip-mine land, Kansas. USDA (Forest) Tech. Paper 187. 1962.

SERR, E.F. *et al.* Nutrient deficiencies (G4564L) VL; Training young trees, AXT-86; Combined old and new plantings, Leaf. 143; Suitable varieties, Leaf. 144; Rootstocks, AXT-120. All walnut. Calif. Ag. Exp. Sta., Davis. 1966; '67; '62; '62; '65, resp. Seek updates.

SIBBETT, G.S. *et al.* Effects of prolonged drying and harvest delay following ethephon on walnut kernel quality. Cal. Agr. 12-13. June 1978.

SIBBETT, G.S. and M. BAILEY. Sunburn protection for newly-grafted Payne walnuts. Calif. Agri. (April): p. 18. 1975.

THOMPSON, B. Black walnuts for profit. 285 pp. Walnut Press, 4431 Nol. 85th St., Scottsdale, Ariz. 85251. 1976.

WALNUTS, ENGLISH. (University of Calif., Davis): Costs-Leaflet 2744. 1977; Production-Leaflet 2984, 1977; Varieties - AXT-360; 1972: Nutrient deficiencies - 1961; Pollination habits leaflet 2753, 1972; Training young trees - Leaflet 2471, 1975.

320

CHAPTER XVIII

Control of Insects and Diseases

Because of favorable soil and climatic conditions, fruits are grown year after year in the same regions. Hence, there is a tendency for insects and diseases to build up in these regions and for certain species to develop increasing resistance to spray chemicals used against them. Examples of this buildup of resistance to spray chemicals are the mites, apple scab, codling moth, and, in the West, pear psylla. While the introduction of DDT in the early 1940's brought remarkable control of the worst apple pest, codling moth, it killed predators, particularly those of mites, and left the mites little affected. Mites are now one of the main problems.

As a result of initial entomological research in Nova Scotia, most tree fruit research stations now are developing spray programs that control serious pests but also encourage predators of these pests, in an attempt to reduce the cost and amount of spraying needed (Figure 1). There are chemicals on the market that more or less meet this requirement. Another approach is the release of millions of male codling moths sexually sterilized by radioactive chemicals. And some pesticides are being injected into tree trunks with successful scab control, experimentally. Synthetic female sex attractants (pheromones, or lures) are being used to trap males and disclose population trends. Computers are being used with previous years' data to predict probable insect and disease problems.

All these programs fall under so-called "Integrated Pest Management (IPM)," where the grower or a private consultant conducts a monitoring program, noting pest developments in the fruit planting, then recommending a spray program to control the pests *only as needed* rather than the old style of spraying at *regular* intervals regardless. Together with monitoring, the predators of key pests are encouraged by the special designed spray schedules. This is an entirely new approach to pest control vs. 20 to 50 yrs. ago.

The Mediterranean fruit fly (Medfly) is an example of a scare created in the United States on occasion (1980-1982) when it was accidentally brought in from the tropics. The larvae feed on a wide variety of fruits (damage resembles apple maggot) and vegetables, rendering them unfit for

Figure 1. A striking example of the effect of releasing a spider mite predator, *Metaseiulus occidentalis,* on plum trees at right. Note damage to trees on left by the uninhibited Pacific and two-spotted mites. The road barrier in the center helped confine the predator mites. This predator strain is resistant to Sevin and to permethrin. (Courtesy Marjorie A. Hoy, University of California, Davis)

consumption. Hence, expensive government effort must be amassed each time to eliminate the fly or a similar pest by spraying, fumigating and introducing sterile males. The fly can be very destructive because of its ability to multiply and spread rapidly.

Nematodes (microscopic root worms) have been more of a problem with fruit crops over the years than fully appreciated, particularly in light-textured warm soils.

To fight pests intelligently and economically, and to adjust the program to changing conditions, the fruit grower must have a thorough knowledge of equipment, and modern methods of applying them. In this regard, there has been a gradual shift from high-volume (dilute) to low-volume (concentrate) spraying, with the many obvious advantages. The technique of low-volume spraying came to North America from Europe and South Africa in the early 1960's. High-volume spraying, however, is still needed and used for certain orchard requirements. Changes also have been rapid over the years in spray materials but this has slowed somewhat in recent years due

Arthur Retan, Entomologist, Wash. State Univ., Pullman 99163. C. M. Custer, Product Specialist, FMC, Jonesboro, Arkansas 72401 and William (Bill) Doe, fruit grower, Pres. Doe Ag. Sales, Inc., Harvard, Mass. 01451 made many suggestions for revision of this chapter.

Figure 2. Types of fruit insects: (a) Plum curculio on peach, (b) tent caterpillar on apple, (c) rosy apple aphids on opening apple bud, (d) spring cankerworm on apple, (e) cherry leaf beetle on cherry, (f) black cherry aphis causing leaf curling on sweet cherry, and (g) pear slug on pear. Biting insects are represented at a, b, d, e, and g. Sucking insects are shown in c and f. See also color section.

to a Federal requirement for thorough evaluation of a chemical before it is released for general use. Also, we are getting increasing government pressure from EPA, FDA, OSHA, and other sources to use safe chemicals and techniques to not pollute our food, land and streams.

Although there are many key practices in successful fruit growing, pest control probably is the most important cultural practice. Between 25 and 50 per cent of the total cost of commercial production of fruits is devoted to insect and disease control. Without this expenditure, the trees would be short-lived and the fruit almost worthless. In previous chapters, it has been emphasized that the general public is critical of the fruit it buys. Buyers are no longer dependent on a few sources of supply and if the product is inferior, they turn to citrus, vegetables or to other sources.

Spraying may be defined as the application of chemicals in liquid form to fruit plants as a preventative and combative measure against attacks by insects and diseases. Dusting is the application of chemicals in the form of dust for the same purposes. Although the grower may use other measures in combating insects and diseases, he still (1983 +) relies mainly upon spraying.

Some pests make a more or less regular appearance year after year and occur in sufficient quantities to require standard control measures. Other pests may be destructive only under certain conditions or when a new chemical is ineffective or kills the predator.

Insects and diseases can be divided into groups, based on their distinct characters and the type of injury caused.

Types of insects. Insects may be grouped on the basis of their mouth parts, namely, (1) chewing, (2) sucking (and rasping in case of thrips), and (3) lapping (flies).

The chewing insects possess hard mouth parts (mandables) with which they bite off parts of the plant (Figure 2). Examples are the worm stage of the codling moth which feeds largely on the fruit, and the tent caterpillar which feeds on the leaves. Other examples are the red banded leaf roller that causes damage mainly to apple fruits, the grape flea beetle which is destructive to grape leaves, and the plum curculio which attacks stone and pome fruits.

Sucking insects have tubelike mouth parts they insert through the epidermis and tissues of the leaves, fruits and stems (Figure 2). The juices of the plant are thus withdrawn and digested. Examples of sucking insects are the aphids (plant lice), scales, true bugs as tarnish plant bugs, and the leafhoppers. The red mite and two-spotted mite have sucking and rasping mouth parts that cause fruit and leaves to lose color and become bronzed.

The third group of insects possess lapping mouth parts with which they lap up liquids from the outer surfaces of the plant. Common fruit insects of this type are the cherry fruit fly, the medfly and the adult fly of the apple maggot.

An insect may pass through several stages during its development (known as metamorphosis); as for example, egg, larva, pupa, and adult (Figure 3). An insect of this kind may have different types of mouth parts while passing through different stages. For example, in the larva stage, the cherry fruit fly has piercing-sucking mouthparts, whereas the adult fly has relatively harmless lapping mouth parts. The same is true for the apple maggot and medfly. The aphid has sucking mouth parts from the time it is a small nymph to a full-grown adult.

Figure 3. Four stages in the life cycle of the codling moth, a major apple insect, are shown. Eggs are laid on the leaf by adult moth; small larvae crawl to fruits, enter, gain full size; leave fruit, crawl down trunk or drop to ground, spin a cocoon; pupate; emerge as a moth; and start the life cycle again.

Types of diseases. A fruit disease may be caused by a fungus, bacteria, mycoplasma or virus (Figure 4), or it may be due to a physiological disorder.

Most fruit diseases controlled by sprays or dusts are caused by *fungi* which are lower plant forms lacking chlorophyll or green coloring matter found in higher plants. They are usually microscopic in size, although when vigorously present, they may be apparent to the naked eye. Examples are scab lesions on apple leaves and fruit, blue mold on apples in storage, and brown rot on peaches, plums, and cherries (see color section). Propagation of fungus diseases is by microscopic spores that may be transported by wind, light air currents, rain, insects, or other agents. Moist surroundings are favorable for spore germination and fungus development under most conditions. In the spraying program, it is desirable to cover the fruit and foliage with spray or dust materials before rainy periods occur to prevent or inhibit spore germination and fungus growth.

The *bacterial* diseases of fruits are difficult to control by spraying and usually are combatted by other means. Best example of bacterial disease of fruit trees is fire blight of

Figure 4. Typical fungus, bacterial, and virus diseases of fruits: (a) Peach leaf curl (fungus) (b) crown gall on raspberry (bacterial,) (c) brown rot on plum (fungus), and (d) red suture virus on peach. (a and d, Michigan State College; (c) Botany Dept., Purdue University; (b) New York Agr. Exp. Sta.) See color section.

apple, pear, and quince. Bacterial spot on peach, particularly hybirds from the J.H. Hale parent, is a very difficult bacterial disease to control. The usual control of bacterial diseases requires carefully timed sprays, which frequently are not completely effective, along with roguing and pruning out of infected areas. Plant resistance breeding also can be a help.

Virus diseases are caused by ultra microscopic organisms which cannot be controlled directly by spraying. An insect or nematode vector, if involved, must be controlled. Plants affected often are removed from the planting and destroyed by burning. Probably the best approach to combatting these diseases is by cross-breeding for development of resistant cultivars. Examples of virus diseases are yellows and leaf pucker on peach, rubberwood and russet ring on apple, streak disease of brambles, and yellows disease of the strawberry.

Virus diseases have been of commercial importance mainly on raspberry, strawberry, cherry, and peach. But in recent years they are being identified on most fruits, where their importance may be greater than heretofore thought. A number of virus diseases of apple have been noted in the United States; a total of 15%, in fact, have been described in the world, mostly in Europe. A blueberry stunt virus has caused some concern. Pears and grapes have their share.

More research attention now is being directed toward these problems.

Mycoplasma diseases are caused by micro-organisms that do not have cell walls and can pass through filters that will trap bacteria. They can live on organic cultures and are life-like vs viruses which are not. Tetracycline trunk injections have been used to inhibit or kill them as in case of pear decline (see Chap.13).

There are many *physiological* diseases which may be due to unbalanced nutrition, adverse weather conditions, poor stock/cion relationship, or other factors. Common examples are scald, internal breakdown and bitter pit of apple fruits, black-end of pear fruits, cork in apple fruits, Jonathan spot in apple and "little leaf" of many fruit trees caused by zinc deficiency.

ROLE OF EXPERIMENT STATIONS AND OTHER AGENCIES

The governmental experiment stations play a vital role in the testing and search for new spray chemicals and better methods of applying them. The large spray machinery and spray chemical companies likewise play an indispensable role. In fact, their field representatives along with hired consultants are effective in advising and helping growers, while experiment station and extension workers are devoting more time to research and unbiased published material, and to coordination of grower meetings. It is only through the co-operation between these agencies, fruit journals, growers and private research groups that outstanding progress has been made in the past and will be made in the future. From 1945 to the early 1970's the fruit industry probably underwent its greatest transformation in methods and machinery for insect and disease control that has occured in human history.

To keep well informed on rapidly changing pest control, it is essential that the grower attend fruit meetings, subscribe to progressive fruit journals, and contact representatives of commercial companies as a safeguard and insurance in his orcharding program. The state and provincial experiment stations are particularly valuable because of their unbiased recommendations based upon sound research.

The agricultural extension service or similar service groups provide punctual and rapid communication to the growers on *when* and *what* to apply in the insect and disease control program. Under typical conditions, the Cooperative Extension Service distributes spray informa-

tion to the growers through these channels: (a) by newsletters, (b) by radio broadcast, (c) by TV, and (d) by computers where established. Spray schedules are distributed to the growers before the spray season starts. The schedule contains information on concentration of sprays, approximately when they should be applied, and the insects and diseases they are designed to control. The grower orders the necessary spray materials well in advance and overhauls his spray equipment to place it in good working condition. When the spray season begins, the growers are informed by radio broadcast, by advanced newsletters, and in spray meetings, by calling coded phone numbers, by their consultant, or by computer where established, exactly when (within hours) they should spray. Time of spraying is governed mainly by occurrence of rains, prevailing temperature conditions, and other factors which influence germination of disease spores and the emergence of codling moths and other pests.

The above information on "when to spray" is obtained through the co-operation of several key growers and fieldpersons in the area. During critical periods, growers and fieldpersons regularly send samples of leaves or blossoms to the plant pathologists of the state extension

TABLE 1. This insecticide control and cost guide is a sample of information issued to western New York apple growers by Richard L. Norton, Cornell Extension Agent, POB 150, Albion, N.Y. 14411. (1982). Data also are available for fungicides, herbicides and nematicides.

Material and Rate Per 100 Gallons	P.C.[1]	Rosy Apple Aphid	Green Aphid	WALH[2]	RBLR[3]	Codling Moth	Apple Maggot	OBLR[4]	STLM[5]	Cost/100 Gallons* %
carbaryl (Sevin 50% WP) 2 lbs.	Good	Poor	Poor	Good	Poor	Good	Good	Poor	Poor	146
demeton (Systox 6E) ¼ pt.	Not effective	Poor-Good	Good	Fair	Not effective	Not effective	Not effective	Not effective	Poor	83
Diazinon 50%, 1 lb.	Fair	Poor	Poor	Poor	Not effective	Good	Good	Not effective	(?)	155
dimethoate (Cygon EC) 1 pt.	Fair	Good	Good	Good	Not effective	Good	Good	Not effective	Poor	160
endosulfan (Thiodan 50 W), 1 lb.	Not effective	Good	Good	Good	Poor	Not effective	Not effective	Poor	Good	156
ethion 8E, ½ pt.	Fair	Good	Good	(?)	(?)	(?)	(?)	(?)	Poor	90
Guthion 50% WP, ½ lb.	Good	Poor	Poor	Poor	Good	Good	Good	Poor	Poor	100
Imidan 50% WP 1-1½ lbs.	Good	Poor	Poor	Poor	Good	Good	Good	Poor	Poor	90-135
malathion 25% WP 2 lbs.	Fair	Fair	Fair	Poor	Fair	Fair	Fair	Poor	Poor	89
methomyl (Lannate L or Nudrin) 8E, 1-2 pts.	Fair	Good	Good	Good	Good	Good	Fair	Good	Good	143-286
parathion 15% WP 2 lbs.	Fair	Poor	Poor	Poor	Good	Good	Fair	Poor	Poor	60-76
PennCap-M 2 EC 1-2 pts.	Good	Fair	Poor	Poor	Good	Good	Good	Good	Poor	110-152
phosalone (Zolone 3 EC) 1-1½ pts.	Good	Good	Good	Poor	Good	Good	Good	Poor	Poor	165
Phosdrin 4 EC, ½ pt.	(?)	Good	Good	Poor	Good	Poor		Good	Poor	61
Phosphamidon 8 EC ¼ pt.	(?)	Good	Good	Poor	Poor	Poor	Poor	Poor	Poor	69
Vydate 2L 1 pt.	Not effective	Good	Fair	Fair	Not effective	Not effective	Not effective	Not effective	Fair	189

[1]/P.C. = Plum Curculio
[2]/WALH = White Apple Leafhopper
[3]/RBLR = Red-Banded Leaf Roller
[4]/OBLR = Oblique-Banded Leaf Roller
[5]/STLM = Spotted-Tentiform Leaf Miner
*Costs obviously will vary from year to year. Cost of Guthion ($2.88/100 gal.) is 100%; others are on a relative basis.

service, who examine them microscopically to ascertain the rate of development of, e.g., scab spores. Cooperating growers also maintain codling moth bait traps and report to the extension service the number of emerging codling moths plus any other important data. With this information and weather forecasts, the extension service prepares radio broadcasts for specific fruit growing areas. In the USA these data are phoned or sent via computer to the county agricultural agents who broadcast them over local radio stations at a regular time. This information has been available to all growers free of charge.

In recent years, private field consultants are servicing by contract a number of growers in a region, monitoring the insect and disease problems, suggesting when and what to spray, together with other needed grower information. Consultants frequently are former fruit extension staff who also may cooperate with the governmental extension agents in getting the information directly to the growers.

INTEGRATED PEST MANAGEMENT (IPM) MONITORING INSECTS
(Mich. Ext. Bull. E-154)

Integrated pest management (IPM) is a means of using all suitable controls and techniques in a manner that maintains pest population at levels below those causing economic injury. In IPM, numerous tactics, tools and techniques are used in crop protection. For most pests there are population levels that can be tolerated without significant loss. IPM does not seek to wipe out pests. There are several reasons for not overkilling pests: (1) moderate levels of some pests help to maintain populations of natural enemies (Figure 1,9,10); (2) overkill of pests leads to more rapid selection of pest strains resistant to pesticides; (3) excessive use of pesticides can cause environmental problems beyond the area of application; and (4) since pesticides are poisons, conservative use is important to maintain a suitable human environment. A most important thing to keep in mind is that pest complexes, cultural practices and weather vary from season to season. IPM strategies also must change.

Biological monitoring is keeping track of harmful organisms and their buildup. More specifically, it refers to checking orchards for the presence of pest species and following their development through time so that control decisions can be made. For most fruit pests, the methods of monitoring, and stages to watch for, are mentioned in the discussion of each insect.

With increased costs of insecticides, miticides, labor and fuel, insect control is one aspect of a grower's production program which can be altered to maximize profits. Through biological monitoring, the pests present are identified and control programs designed specifically for them.

By following the development of a pest through the season, the most vulnerable stage can be attacked very precisely. Biological monitoring of insects doesn't always mean reduced control costs, but this is certainly one of its goals. You may need as many, or more sprays as in the past—but you spray only if the pest is present in numbers thought a threat to the crop.

All insects are "cold blooded" organisms and their seasonal development is tied primarily to the fluctuations of temperature. Likewise, temperature patterns vary from year-to-year, making it impossible to associate the presence of a pest with a particular date or even a stage in the development of the fruit tree. By following the development of a pest through season, the vulnerable stage may be precisely determined and appropriate controls applied. This requires extra effort on the part of the grower, scout, or professional fieldman. Following are the techniques and tools used for biological monitoring of tree fruit insect pests.

Regular Inspections. Inspection of overwintering sites or sites where a pest is likely to be found during the growing season is perhaps an underrated monitoring method. This may require more effort and may not be as specialized or sensitive as other monitoring techniques, but is especially useful in detecting the presence of small, relatively immobile pests such as asphids, scales, mites, pear psylla nymphs, etc. Inspections are the only practical means of detecting the presence of some pests, such as climbing cutworms, before they cause damage. By simply marking sites where pests are located and returning at regular intervals, stage changes can be observed to aid in the timing of control applications.

Figure 5. This pheromone trap, using a female synthetic sex hormone to attract the targeted male insect, is visited for daily count for timing a control spray application. Photo taken at the Research Station and University of Natal, Pietermaritzburg, South Africa.

Leaf Sampling-Brushing. Another monitoring technique used specifically to detect the presence and relative numbers of mite pests is leaf sampling and brushing. A sample of leaves, usually 50 to 100, are picked from trees throughout an orchard. The leaves are then passed through a mite-brushing machine where mites on the surface of leaves are brushed off and counted.

Pheromone Trap. The other type of monitoring trap is the pheromone trap or sex lure (Figure 5). Pheromones are synthetic, chemical substances, which imitate the natural hormones for sex attraction in the female of an insect species. Plastic wicks or capsules with minute quantities of these attractants lure the males of the insect involved. The interior of these specially-designed traps is pre-coated with adhesive. Since each insect species generally has its own sex hormone, only a pure culture of the specific insect monitored is collected. This feature makes insect detection and identification easier.

Pheromone traps offer new dimensions in near-perfect orchard detection, emergence timing and monitoring of red-banded leafroller, codling moth, fruit tree leafroller, tufted apple bud moth, and Oriental fruit moth (Figure 12). These traps may be used for no other purpose than to determine insect presence or absence in an orchard. They may lead to an eventual systems-approach to assessing insect populations, emergence trends, and economic damage thresholds. They eliminate much of the previous guess-work in spray timing for many of the more troublesome fruit insects.

Pheromone traps have been successfully used in experimental orchards programmed to integrated mite control and new pest management concepts. The mites are brushed off the leaf onto a sticky plate. The mites on a predetermined area of the plate are counted and the average number of mites per leaf calculated. This technique is not only useful in detecting pest mites but also reveals the presence of predator mites and is an important tool in integrated mite control.

Bait-Lure Trap. There are currently two trapping techniques used to monitor the presence and seasonal activity of fruit insect pests. (a) The bait-lure trap is designed to monitor fruit flies, and (b) pheromone traps are designed to attract moth species which are fruit pests. The bait-lure attracts adult fruit flies (cherry fruit flies, apple maggot, or blueberry maggot) through a combination of their attractive color and the color and the odor given off by the bait (usually a mixture of protein hydrolasate and ammonium acetate). The flies are trapped in a sticky substance coating the trap. By inspecting them at regular intervals, their presence and relative activity, or abundance, can be judged. The attractive powers of these traps are known, and if fly populations are low (as in most commercial orchards) the ability of the trap to attract and therefore detect individuals, is questionable. However, traps placed in aban-

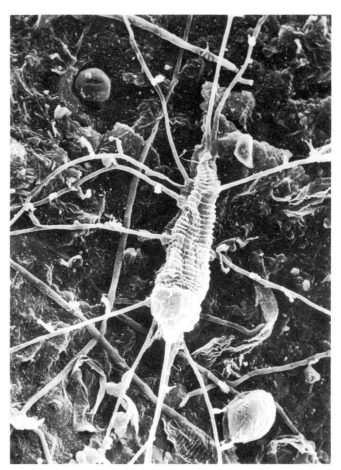

Figure 6. Some diseases will control insect and mite pests. This electron microscope photograph shows a rust mite being attacked and shrivelled by a fungus, *Hirsutella* sp. (Clayton McCoy, IFAS-LA-REC, Florida).

doned orchards, or commercial orchards with annual problems are useful for this purpose. Bait-lure traps are supplemented re-inforcements and not replacements for other commonly used insect monitoring procedures. They can help you better know your insects; which ones are present, and when "to" or "not to" fight them.

Light Traps. Traps that use various types of lights including black light may be useful in capturing insects that are not easily caught by other traps. They may be battery-operated or serviced by plug-in cords. They must be strategically placed in the orchard and can be used only to determine the presence of certain insect pests.

SPRAY MATERIALS

Spray chemicals may be classified according to use into several control groups, among the more important: (a) *fungicides*—to control fungus diseases; (b) *bactericides*—bacterial diseases; (c) *insecticides*—insects; (d) *miticides*—mites (e) *nematicides*—nematodes; (f) *her-*

bicides—weeds; (g) *repellants*—birds, animal pests; (h) *fumigants*—several types of pests, but used as special treatments such as injections into the soil or treatment of stored products; (i) *ovacides*—eggs; (j) *growth regulators*—to control growth, earliness or lateness of bloom and other tree developments; and (k) *accessory materials*—(adjuvants) used as correctives, stickers, spreaders, activators, flocculators, emulsifiers.

A chemical may be effective against one pest but ineffective against another, and it may be useless against diseases. On the other hand, there are some chemicals that control both insects and diseases. The grower must know the merits and weaknesses of the various materials, and in addition, their relative costs. New chemicals are being placed on the market every year and, again, the grower must decide if he should discard the old material and adopt the new. He must base his decision as much as possible upon known facts and not upon opinions, then proceed with judgment with as little risk as possible.

MATERIAL FOR DISEASE AND INSECT CONTROL
(Read all container labels carefully before using)

There are two general types on *insecticides*: (a) stomach poisons, and (b) contact insecticides. Most insecticides for fruits are of the contact type, although some may act as both a contact and stomach poison. Acid lead arsenate, being used less in recent years, and phydrin are examples of a stomach poison; the phosphates may act as either.

Insects that obtain food by biting and chewing or by lapping may be controlled by stomach poisons. Insects that obtain food by sucking sap from the plant tissues are controlled by contact insecticides which kill by suffocating, burning, or paralyzing them. Contact insecticides also will control many chewing and lapping insects and, thus, comprise most of the insecticides used today.

Some poisons used against insects and mites are *systemic* which means that they are absorbed directly into the plant and translocated to all parts. these chemicals are highly effective against pests such as aphids, mites and nematodes. Obviously, the material may be absorbed into the fruit, creating a hazard to human consumption and this is monitored by the Environmental Protection Agency (EPA) and by the Food and Drug Administration (FDA) before permission for its use is given.

The following is a discussion of the kinds of insecticides, miticides, and fungicides available on the market, plus other key information, based on a discussion provided by specialists at Michigan State, Washington State, Pennsylvania State, Cornell and Rutgers Universities. To this list new materials are being added yearly. The best place to keep up-to-date on pesticides is at your local spray meetings conducted by government service representatives and fieldpersons.

FUNGICIDES

Approved chemicals are being added and withdrawn yearly. Keep abreast. See also color insert in this chapter.

Benomyl *(methyl 1-(butylcarbamoyl)-2-benzimidazol carbamate)* is registered for the control of scab on apples, and powdery mildew, sooty blotch, flyspeck, and postharvest fruit rots caused by Botrytis (gray mold), *Penicillium* (blue mold or soft rot), and *Gloesporium* (Bull's-eye rot) on apples and pears. It is formulated as a 50% wettable powder under the trade name Benlate. On both apples and pears it is used at 4 to 6 oz. per 100 gal. of water and on apples it may also be used at 2 to 3 oz. plus 1 qt. of non-phytotoxic superior type spray oil (60 to 70 sec. viscosity) per 100 gal. of water, or in combination with several other fungicides. For control of postharvest fruit rots on apples and pears, it may be used (without oil) as a preharvest spray at 6 oz. or as a postharvest dip or spray at 8 oz.

On stone fruits, it is used on peaches, nectarines, apricots, cherries, prunes, and plums for the control of brown rot, powdery mildew, peach scab, and cherry leaf spot. It is not effective for control of peach leaf curl. Benomyl is particularly effective for the control of brown rot. Sprays may be started at early bloom and continued as necessary through harvest. Benomyl may also be used as a postharvest dip or spray. It will not control fruit rots caused by *Rhizopus* sp. or *Alternaria* sp.

The widespread development of benomyl resistant pathogens of tree fruits has made this fungicide ineffective in many orchards. If used, it should always be combined with Captan. The combination will give at least some degree of control should benomyl-resistant strains be present.

Bordeaux mixture is a combination of soluable copper sulfate (bluestone), hydrated lime, and water. It is used for the control of fire blight on apples and pears (Figure 7), for peach leaf curl on peaches, and for brown rot blossom blight on sweet cherries. In a 2-6-100 Bordeaux, for example, the first figure of the formula is copper sulfate in pounds, the second figure is spray lime in pounds, and the third figure is water in gallons. Homemade Bordeaux is superior to prepared dry mixes.

Bordeaux has many compatibility problems. Before combining with other pesticides, check the compatibility chart and read the label on the can carefully.

Captan *(N-trichloromethylthio-4-cyclohexene-1, 2-dicarboximide)* is used for control of apple scab, brown rot, and cherry leaf spot. It is also fairly effective against several minor diseases including: black rot, Botrytis blossom-end rot, Brooks fruit rot, Botryosphaeria rot, bitter rot, sooty blotch, and fly speck. It will not control apple rust, powdery mildew or fire blight. Recommendations are based on a 50% wettable powder formulation. Several dust formulations and an 80% wettable powder formula-

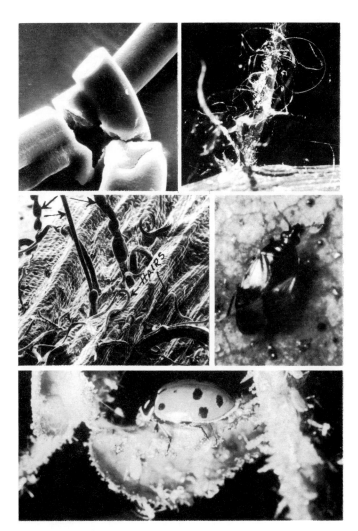

Figure 7. FIRE BLIGHT, PREDATORS. (Upper left) Smooth broken strands of fire blight *(V. inequalis)* magnified 780x. (Upper right) Aerial ooze-like strands produced by fire-blight infected pear or apple tissue; contain the troublesome bacteria in a matrix, magnified by scanning electron microscope. (Mid left) Aerial strands, smooth and beaded, (arrows) of fire blight on Bartlett pear, among leaf hairs. (Mid right) Pirate bug (anthocorid) feeding on a 2-spotted mite. (Below) Famous lady bird beetle feeding on an aphid; they also feed on mites when populations heavy. (Blight photos, H. L. Keil & T. van der Zwet, USDA; predator photos, Uniroyal Co., Conn.)

tion are available and should be used at equivalent rates.

For early season scab control, Captan is used at 2 lb./100 gal. of dilute spray. Though primarily a protectant fungicide, it will eradicate scab if used within 18 hours after the beginning of an infection period at average temperatures above 50° F. It should be applied at relatively short intervals during critical scab periods, when growth is rapid, or when rains are frequent.

Captan is associated with good finish on russet-susceptible apple varieties like Golden Delicious. On Red Delicious, it has caused a leaf spotting when used at full strength early in the season, especially when used in combination with sulfur. On other varieties, it may be combined with sulfur or with dinocap for powdery mildew control. It is incompatible with oil and should not be used in combination with oil or near oil applications.

On stone fruit crops, Captan is used for early season control of brown rot on apricots and for combined control of brown rot and cherry leaf spot on sweet cherries starting at petal fall. On prunes, plums, and peaches, it is used for control of brown rot on the maturing fruit.

Dichlone *(2, 3-dichloro-1, 4-naphthoquinine)* is sold as a 50% active wettable powder under the trade name Phygon. For scab control, it should be used at the ¼ lb. rate with a protectant fungicide and should be used only from budbreak through the first-cover period. It is used mainly for the control of brown rot blossom blight on peaches, plums, prunes, tart cherries and sweet cherries. For this purpose, it is applied during the bloom period at the ½ lb. rate.

Difolatan *(Cis-n[1,1,2,-tetrachlorolthyl]thio]-4-cyclohexene-1,2-dicarboximide)* is cleared for use on machine harvest tart cherries only to control brown rot and cherry leaf spot. It is formulated as a flowable solution containing 4 lb. of Difolatan per gallon. On apples, Difolatan is registered as a single application at green tip for apple scab.

In tests, Difolatan has consistently provided good leaf spot control in seasonal schedules when used at 6 pt./acre. Control with 3 pt./acre has been good in light to moderate leaf spot years where proper timing and thorough spray coverage were practiced.

Human skin sensitization has occured in some instances where Difolatan was used. Only a small percentage of the population is sensitive. A few farm workers have developed a reaction to the product after exposure to residues of Difolatan on the twigs, leaves and fruit. People who may come in contact with it must be warned of the possibility of this allergic reaction.

Dikar is a coordinated product of zinc ion and manganese ethylene bisdithiocarbamate, dinitro(1-methyl heptyl)phenylcrotonate and certain other dinitro phenols and derivatives. These are the active ingredients of Dithane M-45 and Karathane. Dikar has provided combined control of powdery mildew and apple scab on mildew susceptible varieties when used routinely. For best mildew control, the addition of a spreader-sticker is suggested.

European red mite suppression has been obtained when applied on a seasonal schedule and where superior oil was used before bloom. Best results have been obtained when used at the 2-lb. rate. Dikar is incompatible with oil. Good fruit finish has been obtained with Dikar. However, workers in some states have reported moderate fruit russet on McIntosh and Cortland where used at high spray concentrations.

Dinocap *(Karathane) (dinitro capryl phenyl crotonate)* is a

329

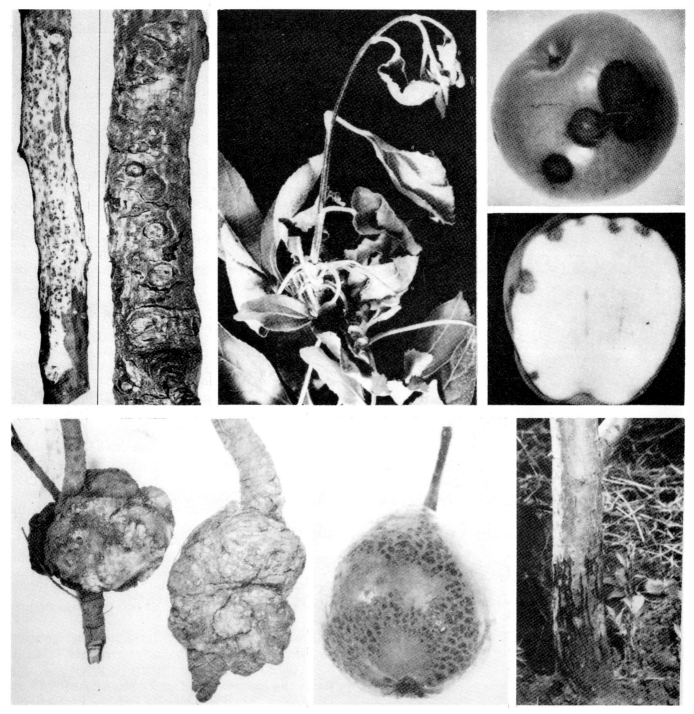

Figure 8. POME DISEASES. (Upper left) Apple bark measles (necrosis) due to excess Mn or deficient B or both (A. B. Groves, Va. Ag. Exp. Sta). (Upper center) Fireblight bacterial disease on apple. (Upper right) Bitter rot, fungus, mid USA. (Mid right) Bitter pit Ca deficiency. (Lower left) Bacterial crown gall on nursery stock. (Lower center) Pear scab, a fungus. (Lower right) Collar rot on apple, a fungus, although on MM. 106 it could be cold damage. (From N. E. Reg. Ext. Bull. 16 or Univ. of Ill. Ext. Serv. Cir. 909. 4/65).

25% active wettable powder sold under the trade name *Karathene*. It is used primarily at the ½ lb. rate for the control of powdery mildew on susceptible apple varieties. A liquid formulation is also available. It is often used in the summer when high temperatures make the use of sulfur questionable on some varieties. This material may be combined with other fungicides used for scab control but should not be used with oil or liquid insecticides having an organic solvent (kerosene or xylene) base.

Dodine *(n-dodeclyguanidine acetate)* is an excellent

fungicide for apple scab and cherry leaf spot control. It is sold under the trade name Cyprex and is formulated as a 65% active wettable powder. Dust formulations are also available. Dodine is primarily used as a protectant against apple scab, but also has eradicant properites. During critical periods for spore discharge and for longer back action, it is used at ½ lb. per 100 gal. of water.

As a protectant, it is used at ¼ to ⅜ lb. and has given good scab control at these rates with proper timing and coverage. The lower rate is used primarily during the cover sprays. This material is particularly effective in reducing secondary spread of scab where it has been applied at regular intervals. It will reduce the production of spores in established lesions and also reduce spore germination.

Dodine is commonly used with oil, but a physical incompatibility may occur when a hard water source is used. Furthermore, lime should not be used with Dodine since it reduces its effectiveness.

Dodine has given good cherry leaf spot (Figure 7) control on tart cherries at ¼ to ⅜ lb. under light to moderate conditions. Under severe conditions ½ lb. will be necessary. A post-harvest spray is a must for late season control. It is also used on sweet cherries where brown rot is not a problem.

Ferbam *(ferric dimethyl dithiocarbamate)* is formulated as a 76% wettable powder. It is used as a protectant for control of apple scab, pear scab, cedar-apple rust, peach leaf curl, and brown rot. Rates of use vary from 1½ to 2 lb. It is used in combination with wettable sulfur on plums, prunes, and sweet cherries for control of leaf spot. Ferbam can also be used as a lead arsenate safener at ½ to ¾ lb. where lime cannot be used for this purpose. In some cases, yellow apple varieties have produced inferior finish when this material was used.

Fixed Coppers are neutral, insoluble forms of copper compounds which usually require the addition of spray lime as a safener. Fixed coppers are sold under many trade names and differ in their metallic copper content. Recommendations of fixed coppers therefore are given in amount of actual copper to be used.

The main use for these compounds is on tart cherries for the control of leaf spot. For this purpose, they are used at the rate of 0.75 lb. of actual copper plus 3 lb. of hydrated lime starting at second cover.

Lime-Sulfur is used primarily as an eradicant in the silver tip to pre-pink period of bud development for the control of scab. It is available as a liquid and is used at the 2 gal. rate. Dry forms are also available. Lime-Sulfur is also used to some extent as a dormant spray on peach for peach leaf curl, on prunes and plums for black knot, and as a bloom spray on each of these crops for brown rot blossom blight. Although the use of lime sulfur was once quite prevalent, it has generallly been replaced by less phytotoxic or milder fungicides. It will partially control mites.

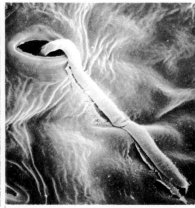

Figure 9. With development of scanning electron microscope, it is possible to see the structure and "modus operandi" of living organisms. Left, are ascospores (eggs) of fire blight bacteria, *Venturia inequalis,* on surface of apple leaf, magnified 1500x. Right, is germinated spore of cherry leaf spot fungus, *Coccomyces hiemalis,* with infection hypha entering a stomate (pore) on cherry leaf. (Courtesy Alan Jones, Michigan State Univ., E. Lansing. 48823.)

Streptomycin is a bactericide for use against fire blight on apples and pears. It is very effective against the blossom blight phase of this disease if sprays are well timed and thorough. Best results are obtained if sprays are applied when maximum temperatures above 65° F. exist or are likely, and are accompanied by precipitation or following rainy days. Apply the first spray before or within 24 hours after favorable conditions. Apply a second spray if favorable conditions reappear, or if blossoms are opening rapidly and favorable conditions persist, 1 to 2 days after previous spray. Repeat applications if warm, wet conditions prevail.

Recently, post-bloom sprays of Streptomycin have been approved on pears up to 30 days before harvest, on apples up to 50 days before harvest. Although sprays for the control of shoot blight need further study, the following is suggested for those who may wish to try this new procedure. In orchards with a history of severe fire blight, but where overwintering cankers have been removed and a well timed blossom blight program has been followed, use Streptomycin at 100 ppm. Follow a 7-day protective schedule starting at petal fall or 5 to 7 days after the last in-bloom spray. During periods of wet, humid weather, shorten intervals to 5 to 7 days. Continue program until terminal growth stops.

Sulfur is available as a wettable powder and as a paste. Because of their convenience, the wettable sulfur formulations are generally used. Recommendations are based on a 95% wettable sulfur formulation. Formulations containing less sulfur should be used at higher rates. Once used extensively as a protectant for scab, it has generally been replaced by organic materials of the protective-eradicant type.

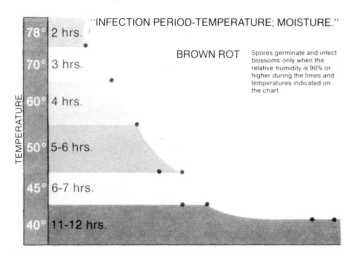

"INFECTION PERIOD-TEMPERATURE; MOISTURE."

78°	2 hrs.
70°	3 hrs.
60°	4 hrs.
50°	5-6 hrs.
45°	6-7 hrs.
40°	11-12 hrs.

TEMPERATURE

BROWN ROT — Spores germinate and infect blossoms only when the relative humidity is 90% or higher during the times and temperatures indicated on the chart.

Figure 10. The importance of *temperature and humidity* is emphasized above for the main disease of stone fruits — brown rot *(Monilinia laxa)*. The effect of these two factors holds true for most insects and diseases. (E. I. DuPont Co., Wilmington, Dela.)

Sulfur is effective against powdery mildew and is used at the 2 lb. rate with scab fungicides for the control of this disease on susceptible apple varieties. When sulfur is used at reduced rates in a mildew suppression program, applications should be initiated at silver-tip and continued until cessation of terminal growth. Omit sulfur in applications where superior oil is used.

Sulfur is used on all stone fruits, except apricots, to control brown rot. It is especially important in the bloom and early cover sprays on peaches to control not only brown rot, but also peach scab and powdery mildew.

SMALL FRUITS

Benomyl (Benlate) is registered for use in blueberries, grapes, strawberries, and raspberries. In blueberries, it is registered for control of mummy berry disease. It gives excellent control of blossom infection (which causes the berries to mummify). However, Benlate will not control the shoot blight phase of the disease. In grapes, Benlate gives excellent control of black rot and powdery mildew. It gives fair control of dead arm disease, but is totally ineffective on downy mildew. In strawberries, Benlate gives excellent control of grey mold, stem-end rot, leaf blight and leaf spot. It will not control leather rot, however. The addition of captan will control leather rot. In raspberries, Benlate is registered for control of *Botrytis* sp. and *Penicillium* sp. fruit rots and powdery mildew. Field research data indicate that Benlate will also give very good control of spur blight and anthracnose.

Bordeaux is used for control of spur blight in red raspberries. Bordeaux is an effective fungicide, but is somewhat injurious to tender foliage.

Captan is used in blueberries in combination with Ferbam for effective control of the blossom infection stage of mummy berry disease. It gives only fair to poor control of the shoot blight phase of the disease. In grapes, captan gives excellent control of dead arm disease and downy mildew. It also gives fair control of black rot disease, but gives no control of powdey mildew. In strawberries, it gives fair control of fruit rots and leaf diseases. In raspberries, captan gives good control of anthracnose.

Ferbam, used in combination with captan in blueberries, gives fair to poor control of the shoot blight phase of mummy berry disease and good control of the blossom infection phase (which gives rise to mummified fruit). In grapes, ferbam is one of the best fungicides for black rot control. However, it gives very little control of downy mildew or dead arm disease and no control of powdery mildew. In raspberries, ferbam gives fair control of anthracnose.

Folpet *(Phaltan) (n-trichloromethylthiophthalimide)* is formulated as a 50% WP. It is closely related to captan and is used effectively against black rot and dead-arm in grapes. It is also effective against grape powdery mildew and downy mildew.

Funginex *(Triforine, Saprol—N, N'-[1,4-piperazine-diyl-bis-(2,2,2-trichloroethylidene)]-bis-[formamide]).*

Funginex is a new systemic fungicide for the control of mummyberry disease. This fungicide comes as a 20% emulsifiable concentrate (E.C.).

Funginex should be applied by conventional ground equipment when possible. However, it does give excellent control of mummyberry disease of blueberry when applied by airplane in 5 to 10 gallons of water per acre.

The only full use label currently available is for control of mummyberry disease of blueberries.

Karathane gives good control of powdery mildew on grapes, especially in Concord, Niagara and other American varieties.

Mancozeb *(Dithane M-45 and Manzate 200)* is maneb *(manganese ethylenebisdithiocarbamate)* in combination with a zinc ion coordination product as a safener. It is an 80% wettable powder. In grapes, mancozeb gives excellent control of dead arm disease and downy mildew and good control of black rot. This product does not control powdery mildew.

Wettable sulfur gives fair to good control of powdery mildew in French hybrid and *vinifera* (European) varieties. Sulfur injures many American varieties and some French hybrid varieties. Sulfur can cause injury to tolerant varieties if the temperature is 85°F., or above, during spraying or shortly after spraying is finished.

Zinc-maneb *(Manzate E or Dithane M-22 Special).* This is an 80% wettable powder of Maneb plus zinc as a safener. It is used for the control of the same diseases in grapes as listed under Mancozeb.

332

INSECTICIDES
(see also Table 1)

Ambush (see permethrin)

BAAM (Amitraz) is a formamidine insecticide-acaricide. It effectively controls psylla, rust mite and blister mites on pears and European red mite, two spotted mite and rust mites on most other fruit crops. It has proven to be excellent in controlling summer populations of pear psylla. It has demonstrated activity on both egg and mobile forms of mites and has a good vapor and systemic activity.

Carzol is a non-phosphate miticide-insecticide registered for use either pre-bloom or post-bloom on apples and pears to control the European red or two-spotted mite and the white apple leafhopper. It is most effective for controlling immature and adult forms of European red and two-spotted mites, but does prevent the hatching of mite eggs present at time of spraying. It is efficient against organophosphate resistant mites and also controls those resistant to other types of pesticides.

Formulated as a completely water-soluble powder, containing 92% formetanate hydrochloride, it dissolves rapidly in water to leave an invisible crop residue. Correct dosage rates and thorough tree coverage are important, since Carzol primarily kills the active stages of mites. Repeat applications should be made as needed or whenever mite infestations appear. No more than 4 lb. per acre can be applied in any one crop season and no closer than 7 days before harvest. If practicing integrated mite control, do not use after June 1 as Carzol is highly toxic to predatory mites.

The product is not stable in alkaline water. Its spray mixture must be freshly prepared just before application. It is compatible with many orchard spray materials, moderately toxic to honeybees and comparatively non-toxic to fish, birds, man and animals.

Figure 11. In the controlling of any pest, it is wise to take extreme precautions to time the early sprays properly. Once a disease or insect becomes established it is difficult to control for that season. Early scab, curculio, and mite control are as important as early codling moth control. (Purdue University, LaFayette, Indiana).

Chloropropylate, trade-named *Acaralate,* is a miticide for control of European red mite and two-spotted mite on apples and pears. As an emulsifiable concentrate, it kills young and adult forms of these mites. It is useful in pre-bloom preventive sprays or whenever mite infestations first appear. Pre-bloom applications are made as close to egg hatch as possible for best results. Correctly applied, they give residual control until mid-summer. It is highly toxic to predatory mites, and if attempting integrated mite control it should not be used post-bloom.

Post-bloom spraying must be repeated as often as necssary to control mite populations. Two applications spaced 7 to 10 days apart are required for maximum performance. Since only the active stages of mites are killed, it is essential that correct dosage is used and thorough coverage of trees obtained. Dilute or concentrate sprays must reach all parts of the tree, especially the underside of leaves. **Do not mix Acaralate with spray oils due to possible plant injury.** Virtually non-toxic to warm blooded animals, it is also safe to bees and other beneficial insects.

Cythion ULV is a formulation of 95% technical material of malathion. Its only uses are for Ultra Low Volume applications by air to control cherry fruit fly and blueberry maggot.

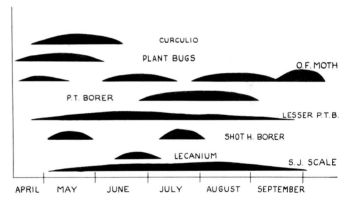

Figure 12. This chart shows when certain peach pests are most active under New Jersey conditions, and at what periods control is most important. Relative emergence periods should be about the same under conditions of other regions where these pests are present.

Demeton, better known as *Systox,* is formulated as a 6 lb./gal. E.C. and a 2 lb./gal. E.C. The Systox 6 E.C. mixes with Cyprex. Systox 2 E.C. does not mix with Cyprex. It is a contact and systemic phosphate formulated as an emulsifiable concentrate. It is generally utilized for systemic control of sucking insects such as aphids, leafhoppers and mites. Its major use has been on apples and pears, either pre-bloom or early post-bloom, for clean-up of aphids. As a systemic, Systox quickly penetrates plant tissues and is translocated throughout the plant. This

333

distinctive feature makes it less harmful to beneficial insects. Like parathion or certain other phosphates, this chemical is highly toxic to man and safety precautions must be given due attention.

Diazinon ranks intermediate between parathion and malathion in toxicity to humans. It is active against a variety of fruit pests, offering residual activity of 11 to 14 days and has clearance for use on apples, pears, cherries, peaches, plums, prunes, strawberries, grapes and brambles. The principal uses of diazinon involve a 50% wettable powder formulation for control of cherry fruit fly on sweet and tart cherries, summer insect complex on apples after First Cover and insects troublesome to strawberries in mid-season. Drenching crown treatments of emulsifiable concentrate will kill the overwintering stage of raspberry crown borers when they are a problem. Diazinon is proving to be a selectively useful insecticide in integrated control programs, since it is relatively non-toxic to important predatory mites.

Dimethoate is marketed as *Cygon* and *De-Fend* for control of a wide range of insects on bearing apples and pears. Sold as a 2.67 lb./gal. emulsifiable concentrate or 25% wettable powder, its systemic properties have specific value in aphid control. It is effective for white apple leafhopper at twice the rate of application required for aphids and when applied for aphids provides excellent control of tarnished plant bug. Compared to many insecticides, it is practically without compatiblity problems. While toxic to bees, the product is one of the least poisonous of the organic phosphates to humans and animals.

Ethion has use on apples in combination with oils to control overwintering stages of mites, aphids and scale. Oil plus Ethion have given better control of San Jose scale than oil alone. However, the addition of a phosphate insecticide does not improve the miticide effectiveness of oil. Several formulations of Ethion-oil are available or the Ethion can be purchased separately and added to the oil prior to application. Ethion should not be sprayed after bloom on apple varieties maturing before McIntosh, since severe leaf injury and subsequent fruit drop are likely to occur.

Fenvalerate (Pydrin 2.4 E.C.) is a member of the new class of insecticides known as synthetic pyrethroids. Fenvalerate is a stomach and contact poison with low mammalian toxicity and very high insecticidal activity. It exhibits a long residual activity of about 21 days. It is also more effective in cool temperatures that are prevalent during its recommended use period. It is registered as a pre-bloom spray on pears. When applied at white bud stage, it gives outstanding control of green fruitworm and pear psylla. To avoid potential resistance, growers should limit its use to the pre-bloom period, even if ultimately registered for post-bloom application.

Guthion has been the most widely used insecticide in Michigan orchards since DDT and related chlorinated hydrocarbons began phasing out. Available as a 50% wettable powder or 2 lb./gal. spray concentrate, it has provided good broad spectrum control of many primary fruit pests with a residual action of 10 to 14 days. The spray concentrate is not cleared for apples and pears. There have been no phytotoxicity or residue problems when the compound is used properly and in accordance with label directions.

To avoid prohibitive residues, no more than 8 applications of Guthion on deciduous fruit, nor 3 to 4 applications on grapes, strawberries and blueberries are permissible in a season. While Guthion is similar to parathion in toxicity to humans, it is of low toxicity to predaceous orchard mites. Make use of the safety measures reserved for organophosphate insecticides when handling this material.

Imidan is a phosphate chemical with a low toxicity to mammals comparable to Sevin. It is formulated as a 50% wettable powder for pre-bloom and post-bloom application on apples, pears, peaches, cherries, plums, prunes, grapes and apricots. It provides good broad-spectrum control of many fruit pests.

Imidan has been outstanding in performance on apple maggot. The material can be a boon in attacking maggot outbreaks close to harvest. It also suppresses European red mite and two-spotted mite when used in a seasonal program, without significant interference to species of predatory mites important to integrated pest control. Imidan represents a biodegradable pesticide which in a short time interval dissipates into non-toxic residues harmless to man, wildlife and other living forms.

Kelthane, used as a specific miticide, has performed well against the nymphs and adults of red mite, two-spotted mite and rust mites during the past several years. For best results, apply Kelthane when the average temperature is predicted to be above 70° F. for 5 to 7 days. Repeat applications 7 to 10 days apart are often necessary and advisable. Its toxicity ranks comparatively high in safeness to man and wildlife. It is highly toxic to predatory mites and should be used prior to June 1 if practicing integrated mite control.

Lannate (see Methomyl).

Lorsban is an organophosphorous insecticide used on peaches. Applied as trunk sprays by handgun, it effectively controls peach tree borers. Applications before newly hatched borers enter the trees made in early June and aimed at the lower scaffolds will also control lesser peach borer.

Malathion is a mild phosphate that controls an unusual variety of fruit and pecan insects and is especially useful against several species of aphids. However, its residual effectiveness seldom exceeds 2 to 3 days. Thus, it can often be employed to best advantage in late season sprays. Its use is particulary indicated where a high degree of safety to man and animals becomes desirable. Obtainable as

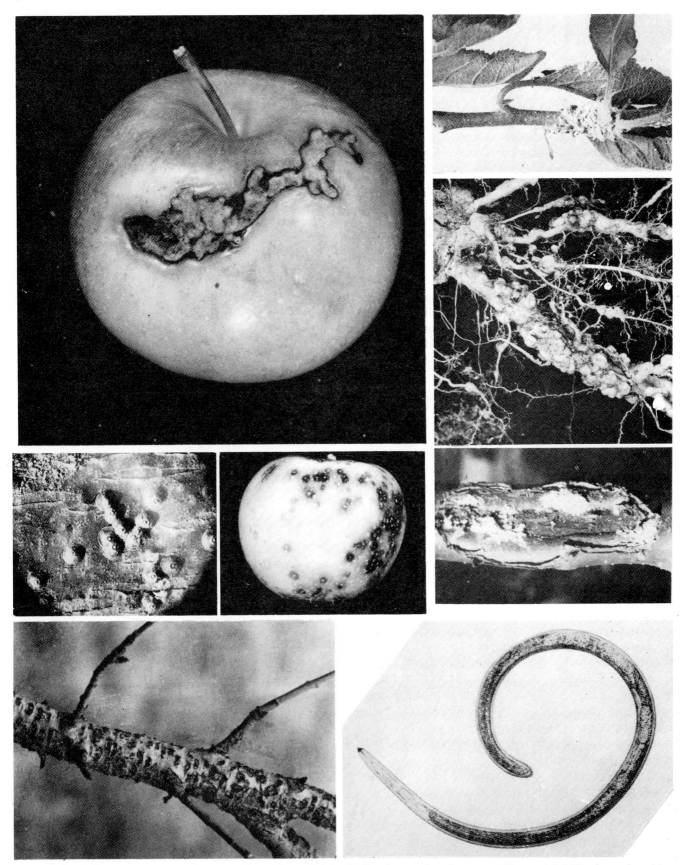

Figure 13. INSECTS, NEMATODE. (Upper left) Red Banded Leafroller damage late in season. (Upper right) Wooly apple aphis on shoot, above, on roots and root response, mid, and on wounded trunk area, lower. (Mid left) San Jose scale closeup at left and on apple to right; red spots show early before harvest around scale under which is sucking insect. (Lower left) Damage on peach limb bark due to egg-laying of Buffalo Tree Hopper. (Lower right) One of many species of nematodes (150x) that feed on roots of woody trees, stunting them. (From Ohio Res. Bull. 930. 1963; lower right, R. I. Ag. Exp. Sta. Bull. 360. 1961). See color section.

emulsifiable concentrate, wettable powder or dust, Malathion is presently used in Michigan for certain insect pests attacking brambles, currants and blueberries. Unlike many chemicals, it is generally compatible with every insecticide and fungicide in common usage.

Mesurol is a broad spectrum carbamate insecticide that at high rates is an effective bird repellant. It repels grackles, robins, starlings, and cedar waxwings from the treated crop area, and minimizes fruit loss due to bird damage. It is registered on cherries and blueberries and effectively controls cherry fruit fly and blueberry maggot. It is highly toxic to bees and predators. Its use is limited to two applications of the high rate and three applications of the lower rate per season.

Methomyl (Lannate or Nudrin) is registered for use on apple only as a 90% soluble powder and 1.8 lb./gal. E.C. Methomyl is primarily effective as a contact insecticide, though some systemic activity is also evident. Methomyl residues remain effective for about 5 days. Correct timing is a must.

Methomyl is effective in controllng green fruitworm, certain leafroller and leafminer pests which are difficult to control with other broad spectrum compounds. At the same time, it provides control of indirect pests such as aphids. For these reasons, Methomyl may be important where its combination with other broad spectrum insecticides would provide optimum control of a pest complex neither alone would adequately control.

Toxicity of Methomyl, while less than parathion, still requires the safety precautions necessary for such highly toxic compounds. Methomyl is extremely toxic to fish and bees, so avoid use when bees are active and keep out of any body of water. CAUTION: Outbreaks of wooly apple aphid may result from a season-long (multiple applications) of Methomyl.

Methoxychlor has moderate residual activity and, although a relative of DDT, exhibits very low toxicity to humans and other warm-blooded animals. It will restrain such major fruit invaders as plum curculio, codling moth, apple maggot and cherry fruit fly, but is generally inferior to alternative chemicals for these purposes. Also sold under the trade name *Marlate,* its only suggested use is in dust form as an optional material on blueberry insects. It is rarely plant phytotoxic.

Morestan—This miticide is formulated as a 25% wettable powder. It is registered for pre-bloom use on apple and pear for control of mites and their eggs. It should not be applied after the first bloom. Its residual activity makes this miticide particularly useful in controlling mites during seasons when weather conditions prevent the application of oils. Morestan is not highly toxic to humans but is toxic to fish and should not be used in any manner where water would be contaminated. Morestan in only slightly toxic to predaceous mites but should not be used after bloom.

WARNING: do not mix with or follow oil applications.
Nudrin (see Methomyl).

Omite is closely related to Aramite in chemical structure and gives good control of mites. It is effective against the mite strains resistant to phosphate and chlorinated hydrocarbon miticides, and is cleared for use on apples, peaches, pears, plums and prunes. Omite is not a systemic, therefore complete coverage of upper and lower leaf surfaces and fruit is important for maximum results. Likewise, it is not a pre-bloom miticide, since performance is best when temperatures are 70° F. or higher. Mites hit by the spray stop feeding and die within 48 to 78 hours. Initial kill is slow, often 3 to 5 days, but is compensated for by long residual action. This material is not an ovicide, and is mainly effective against young and adult mite stages. It has minimal effect on beneficial insects, is reportedly less harmful to predator mites and data indicate it to be relatively non-toxic to man and animals. For best perfor-

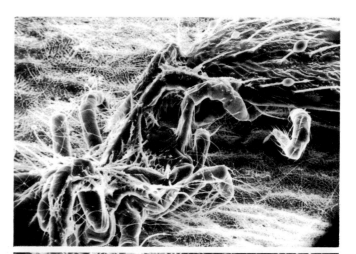

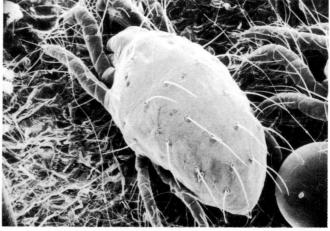

Figure 14. ORCHARD MITES. By scanning electron-microscope you see a predator mite (upper right) feeding on a red mite on an apple leaf, removing its life juices, deflating it. Below is one of the most troublesome orchard pests, difficult-to-control — the red mite feeding (rasping and sucking) on the underside of an apple leaf. (Uniroyal Co., Naugatuck, Ct.). See color section.

1—SILVER TIP 2—GREEN TIP 3—HALF-INCH GREEN

4—TIGHT CLUSTER 5—FIRST PINK 6—FULL PINK

7—FIRST BLOOM 8—FULL BLOOM 9—POST BLOOM

Apple flower bud development. These are the stages in bud and bloom development in apple in the spring. Spray applications are timed according to these stages. Also, given below are the critical temperatures for frost damage at the various bud-blossom stages. (Courtesy of Seth Berkerman, Editor, Wash. State Univ., Pullman, for color separates and to P.J. Chapman, N.Y. Agr. Exp. Sta. for 1-6; Curtis Strausz, grower, Yakima County 7-8, and Harlan Mills, Wash. State Univ. for 9).

CRITICAL TEMPERATURES FOR BLOSSOM BUDS*

Bud Development Stage	1	2	3	4	5	6	7	8	9
Old Standard Temp.[1]	16	16	22	27	27	28	28	29	29
Ave. Temp. for 10% Kill[2]	15	18	23	27	28	28	28	28	28
Ave. Temp. for 90% Kill[2]	2	10	15	21	24	25	25	25	25
Average Date (Prosser)[3]	—	3/20	3/27	4/3	4/8	4/11	4/18	4/25	—

* For Red Delicious. Golden Delicious and Winesap approximately 1 degree hardier; Rome Beauty, 2 degrees hardier; except after petal fall, when all varieties are equally tender.

[1] Critical temperatures as previously published.

[2] Average temperatures found by research at the WSU Research and Extension Center, Prosser, to result in 10% and 90% bud kill.

[3] Average date for this stage at the WSU Research and Extension Center.

Data from Wash. Ext. Bull. 0913 by J.K. Ballard, E.L. Proebsting, Jr. and R.B. Tukey.

ROASY APPLE APHID *(Dysaphis plan-taginea)* Overwintering eggs, spring hatch, nymph sucking damage on leaves, fruit.

CODLING MOTH *Lasperyresia pomonella.* Spring adults, eggs, feeding larva, damage.

Note: For details on insects, mites and diseases of fruit, request respective identification sheets in color from N.Y. Agr. Exp. Sta., Geneva 14456, USA. whom we acknowledge here for use of the color separates.

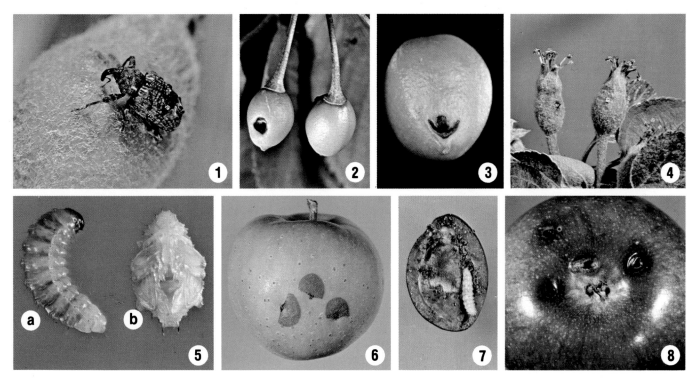

PLUM CURCULIO *(Conotrachelus nenuphar)*. Adult, bite into which egg deposited, larva, healed sting, plum feeding, larva exit from fruit.

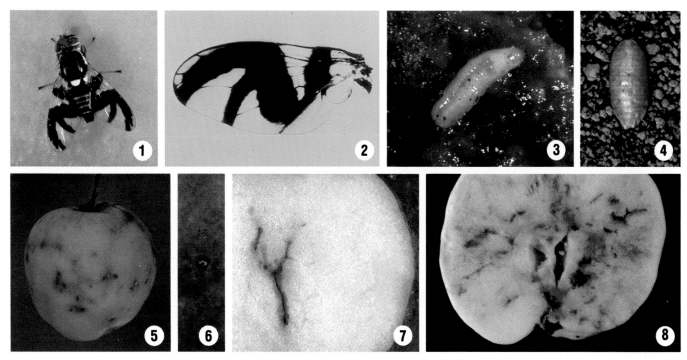

APPLE MAGGOT *(Rhagoletis pomonella)*. Adult fly emerges from soil early summer, eggs, maggot in apple, pupa, "railroad worm" travelling through flesh, browning, other damage appearing at harvest.

WHITE APPLE LEAFHOPPER *(Typhlocyba pomaria)* Adult, egg, sucking nymphs, leaf damage, honeydew hard-to-remove spots on fruit.

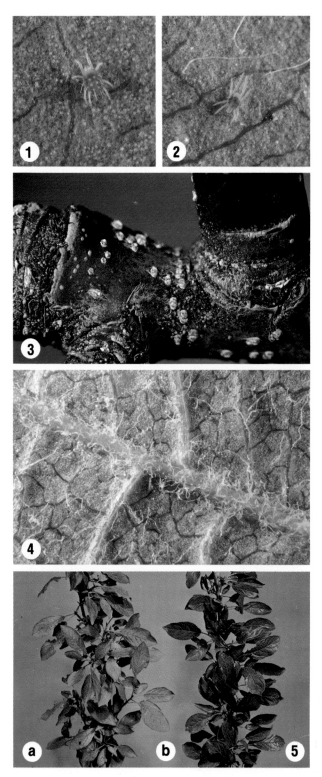

EUROPEAN RED MITE *(Panonychus ulmi)* Female and male adults, overwintering eggs, underleaf webs, mites, leaf-feeding damage reduces food manufacture, fruit coloring in fall.

OBLIQUEBANDED LEAFROLLER. (Choristoneura rosaceana) Spring adults, egg masses, early larvae leaf-feed and damaged fruit as indicated in fall, second brood leaf feeding and some fruit damage in fall, pupae in folded leaves.

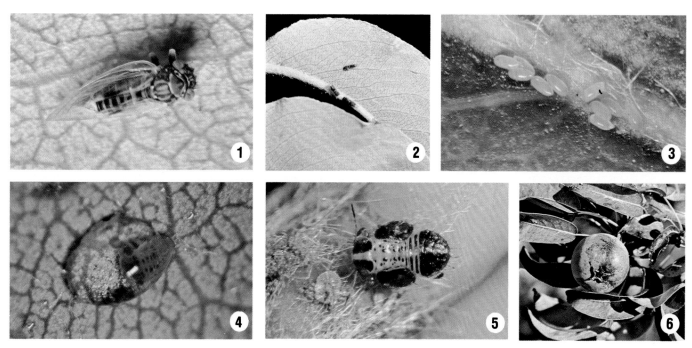

PEAR PSYLLA *(Psylla pyricola).* Overwintering adult, eggs deposited in row often before bud burst, later on leaves, feeding nymph with honey dew drop on top, later hardshell nymph, causing "psylla scortch" on leaves, skin russeting damage on fruit, with sooty blotch developing on honey dew.

GREEN FRUITWORM *(Orthosia hibisci)* Night-flying adults lay eggs at green-tip stage, larvae feed on leaves, fruit, causing damage at harvest.

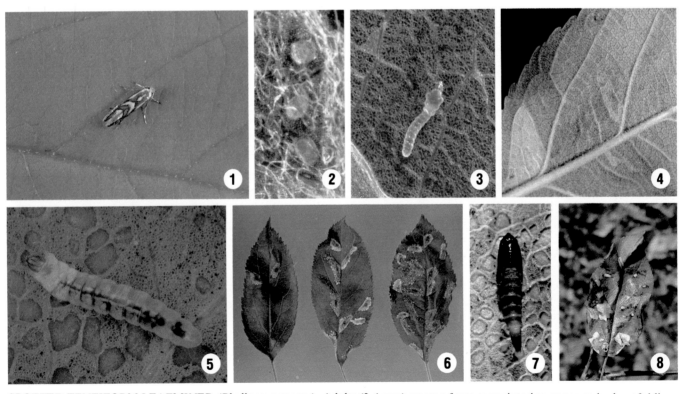

SPOTTED TENTIFORM LEAFMINER *(Phyllonorycter* sp.). Adults (2-4 mm) emerge from overwintering pupae as buds unfolding, eggs laid on leaves, larvae feed between upper lower epidermis but blistering seen from underside and susceptible to spray injury.

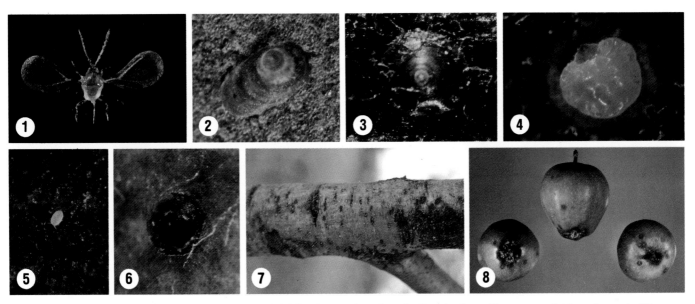

SAN JOSE SCALE *(Quadraspidioutus perniciosus)*. Male, 1 mm winged, seeks female about bloom, eggs laid, under scale (3), seen beneath scale (4) crawlers produced by female (5) suck sap, secretes white cap, then blackened scale covering, bark infestations weaken tree (7), and scales on fruit induce red, purple coloring spots.

PEACHTREE BORER *(Synanthedon exitiosa)*. Wasp-like male (1) and female emerge mid summer, eggs laid in bark near or at ground level, larvae hatch, feed near cambium reaching full size and degree of damage in spring, ringing, destroying trees (7). Pupa at 4.

BROWN ROT, STONE FRUITS *(Monilinia sp.)* Spores overwinter in mummies, infect blossoms spring, twigs, then fruit about harvest. Important.

APPLE SCAB *(Venturia inequalis)* Spores overwinter in dead leaves on ground, ejected spring, early summer, wind-rain dispersed, produce scabby areas on leaves, small and mature fruits.

FIRE BLIGHT *(Erwinia amylovora)*. Overwintering bacteria in cankers (1) oozes with spring warming, rain splashed, infect kill blossoming points, twigs (4) and ooze from fruit.

POWDERY MILDEW *(Podosphaera leucotricha)*. Fungal strands overwinter in infected buds, become active in spring, infecting blossoms, twigs, young leaves, shoots with powdery white covering, white spotting on leaves and weblike russeting on fruit.

D. Iron deficiency on the shoot tips of the apple.

H. Copper deficiency. Dieback is often associated with rough bark.

C. Iron deficiency. Left to right — severe to none.

G. Boron deficiency. Left to right — severe to none. Spur and near shoot tip leaves are the ones that usually show the small-leaf leathery big-vein symptoms.

B. Molybdenum deficiency on the tree. (Due to chloride accumulation.)

F. Magnesium deficiency on the tree. Older leaves have fallen down, leaves show deficiency symptoms near fruit, due to migration of magnesium into fruit from leaves.

A. Molybdenum deficiency of shoot tip leaves. Left to right — most severe to none.

E. Phosphorous deficiency.

NUTRIENT DEFICIENCY SYMPTOMS IN APPLE (All nutrient deficiency color separates courtesy Miklos Faust, USDA and Avi Publishing Co., Westport, Ct.)

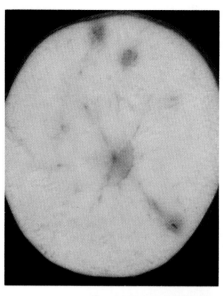

L. Cork spot, mild.

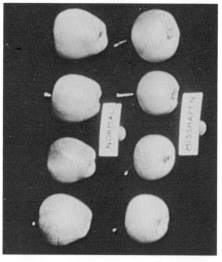

P. Round fruit uncharacteristic of Delicious cultivar is often caused by low boron in the Northwest USA. However, warm nights early in the season in the eastern United States and New Zealand also can produce such fruit.

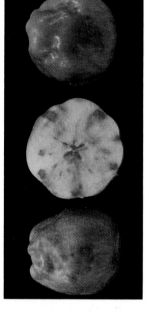

K. Cork spot, severe, a disorder prevented by high calcium in the fruit but not caused by calcium deficiency.

O. Skin cracking occurring on low boron tree and preventable by boron treatment.

J. Calcium deficiency on the tree.

N. Sulfur deficiency on the tree at left.

I. Calcium deficiency on the tree. It is visible only on young rapid growth of the tree.

M. Crinkle, severe, a disorder prevented by high calcium in the fruit but occurs on fruit exposed to the sun.

NUTRIENT DEFICIENCY SYMPTOMS OF APPLE (Original apple color slides A, B, C, D, F, G, H, I, N, P, Q, R, S, T, V, X, by N.F. Childers and associates.)

Q. Copper deficiency on peach. Left to right — severe to none. Note mottled chlorosis.

R. Zinc deficiency on peach in sand culture.

S. Iron deficiency on the peach tree in California.

T. Boron deficiency on peach tree in sand culture. Dieback of side shoots.

U. Sulfur deficiency on peach in Washington.

V. Nitrogen deficiency on peach. Left to right — severe to none.

W. Magnesium deficiency on peach tree.

X. Potassium deficiency on peach. Left to right — severe to none.

mance in cleaning up summer mite populations, make two applications 7 to 10 days apart.

Parathion is extremely toxic to man and animals. Along with a complete understanding of the label, adequate safety precauions include rubber gloves, suitable protective clothing and an approved face mask. It has been widely used since 1949 for control of many fruit pests. No injury from this material has been observed on peaches, plums and cherries. Apples, and occasionally pears, have been injured when parathion was used in excess of suggested dosages. For pecan, effective against leaf casebearer, aphids, mites.

Penncap-M is a newly formulated version of methyl parathion. The methyl parathion is encapsulated (packed in small microcapsules) which significantly reduces the toxicity hazard to humans and other non-target organisms while extending the residual activity of the material. Formulated as a flowable containing 22% methyl parathion, the microcapsules are suspended in water. The methyl parathion slowly diffuses from the capsules over time providing residual control.

Penncap-M is registered for use on cherry, nectarine, plum, prune, peach, pear, apple and grape for control of key pests such as codling moth, oriental fruit moth, plum curculio, leafrollers and grape leafhopper. Penncap M is similar to Parathion in toxicity to predacious mites and should be used prior to June 10 or following the predator-prey interaction if practicing integrated mite control. WARNING: Cautiously mix with emulsifiable concentrates, organic solvents and some surfactants because they may damage the microcapsules. Because of the size of microcapsules, don't use screens or nozzles finer than 50 mesh.

Penncap-M is toxic to certain species of birds, wildlife and fish. Use with care around bodies of water. WARNING: **Penncap-M has been implicated in a number of bee poisonings.** This material and others may be collected from flowers by adult bees when foraging for pollen. It is then taken back to the hive where it is fed to the brood resulting in hive mortality. Penncap-M should not be used in orchards with bloom present, where cover crops are in bloom or where adjacent orchards or foliage are in bloom. These precautions will reduce the potential for bee poisoning and permit use of this effective insecticide.

Permethrin (Ambush or Pounce) is a member of the class of insecticides known as the synthetic pyrethroids. These compounds exhibit low mammalian toxicity while having very high insecticidal activity. They act as stomach and contact poisons. A section 18 is pending for its use to control climbing cutworms on grapes. Check with the extension agent in your area to see if this emergency exemption has been approved for grapes.

Phosphamidon offers limited usefulness in the battle between man and insects for the fruit crops. Its chief asset lies in its ability to control aphids and mites as both a contact and systematic poison. Therefore, as an 8 lb./gal. emulsifiable concentrate, it favorably joins Systox and Dimethoate as an optional choice on apples pre-bloom and early post-bloom for disposal of aphid populations. Phosphamidon warrants the same precautions granted any cholinesterase-inhibiting chemical and it is highly toxic to mite predators.

Plictran, formulated as a 50% wettable powder, is a non-phosphate miticide with outstanding activity on destructive plant-feeding mites—those both susceptible and resistant to other miticides. It is registered for post-bloom use on apples, plums, peaches, nectarines and pears to control the mobile forms of European red, two-spotted and rust mites.

No more than 4 sprays can be applied between petal fall and harvest to apples nor more than 3 on pears. Since Plictran kills the active stages of mites, coverage of foliage must be thorough and complete to include uniform wetting of upper and lower leaf surfaces. The product mixes readily in water to form a suspension that can be applied with any conventional spray equipment. It is usable alone or compatible in tank-mix combinations with those insecticides and fungicides generally employed in orchard spray schedules. No phytotoxicity or adverse effects on fruit finish have been reported. Plictran is a preference miticide for "integrated-control" programs since it is not harmful to beneficial insects or predatory mites. Used as recommended, it presents no unusual health, contamination or environmental problems. It is non-toxic to honey bees, on-

Figure 15. Adult cicada shortly after shedding nymphal skin. When wings and body are dry, the insect will turn darker. This is a troublesome pest which damages orchard and nursery trees by laying eggs in the bark. Nymphs suck sap from roots, weaken trees particularly year before emergence. Do not prune young trees winter before scheduled emergence. (Union Carbide Chemicals Co., New York City).

337

ly somewhat hazardous to birds and fish, moderately toxic to wildlife and of low toxicity to man.

Pounce (see Permethrin).

Pydrin (see Fenvalerate).

Sevin is formulated as a 50 WP and 80 WP. Carbaryl by common name, it finds its place somewhere in the spray program for almost every fruit crop. Its residual effectiveness varies from 10 to 14 days, depending on the insects to control. In most cases, it can be applied within a day or closer to harvest without fear of excessive residues. Sevin is not a miticide, may encourage aphid buildups and is inclined to be **seriously toxic to bees.** It is compatible with most pesticides and gives good control of certain pests resistant to other frequently used insecticides. Sevin offers a high degree of safety to animals and plants. There is the added advantage of its low toxicity to man and fish, lessening the hazards from spray drift that are associated with many pesticide chemicals. In as much as Sevin is a **recognized fruit thinning agent,** its use is avoided until at least 30 days after full bloom on McIntosh, Jonathan, Northern Spy and Delicious apple varieties. Effective against pecan weevil and shuckworms.

Superior Oil—"Superior oil" has been recommended as one of the preventive European red mite control programs. Based on research information from Michigan we feel the 70-sec. viscosity oil is not a dormant-type oil. It is lighter and more volatile than the original "superior oil" which was used as a dormant spray. The principal advantage of the lighter 70-sec. oil is the reduced possibility of plant injury. It is safer because it is more volatile, resulting in less persistence on the tree. It remains on the tree long enough to kill the mites but not so long as to interfere with vital plant processes or oil-incompatible pesticides which may be applied later.

Because of this safety factor, the 70-sec. oil can be applied between Green-Tip and Pre-Pink stages of tree development. European red mite eggs are most susceptible to control by oil when they are about to hatch. Under Michigan conditions, the period of egg hatch starts about the time the trees are in the Pre-Pink to Pink stage. Thus, the closer the application to Pre-Pink, the greater the kill of mite eggs. Oil applied earlier than Green-Tip is not as effective as later applications. The addition of a phosphate insecticide does not increase the miticidal value of oil.

Preventive European red mite control programs are designed to control the mites at an early stage in their development to prevent any build-up through the season. Supplemental measures are usually required in mid- to late-season. Eradicative mite control programs, on the other hand, attempt to control mites after they have increased sufficiently in numbers to damage the crop. The eradicative programs have been expensive and not very successful in controlling established mite populations. Oil applications have no value in controlling the two-spotted mite.

Table 2. The *Minimum* specifications for the 70-sec. viscosity "superior oil".

TABLE 2. THE MINIMUM SPECIFICATIONS FOR THE 70-SEC. VISCOSITY "SUPERIOR OIL".

Properties[a]	Orchard Spray Oil
Viscosity at 100° F.[1]	
Saybolt Universal Seconds	66-90
Gravity[2] API (minimum)	33
Unsulfonated Residue[3] (%)	92
Pour Point[4], °F. (maximum)	20
Distillation, °F.	
10 mm Hg at 50% point[5]	438 ‡ 25
10%-90% (maximum)	150
or	
760 mm Hg at 50% point[6]	675 ‡25
10%-90% range (maximum)	120

[a] The following ASTM methods are to be used:
[1] D445-61 and D446-53; [2] D287-55; [3] D483-61T;
[4] D97-57; [5] D1160-61; [6] D447-59T.

Thiodan, a distant relative to most conventional chlorinated hydrocarbons, has been an effective insecticide available for peach tree borers. Both the lesser borer and true peach borer are controlled by this product. Thiodan is suggested for growers who have severe borer problems on peaches, plums and cherries. A period of 21 to 30 days between last application and harvest, depending on the crop treated, must elapse if the fruit is to be within safe residue tolerances. Post-harvest sprays of Thiodan reduce late season infestations and there are no restrictions for post-harvest use of the product. It has further use on pears, in a comparable manner to Perthane, for control of pear psylla.

Numerous failures of Thiodan in controlling pear psylla have been reported. Recent research results indicate that this material is ineffective in controlling certain psylla populations that have apparently developed resistance to it.

Thiodan has excellent insecticidal effectiveness against aphids, white apple leafhopper, tarnished plant bug, rust mites, green fruitworm and leafminer adults. Plant bug control for peaches and strawberries would be difficult, if not impossible, without Thiodan. A 50% wettable powder and 3 lb./gal. emulsifiable concentrate are available for any of the described uses, with no more than two applications after petal fall and during the fruiting season. Of moderate toxicity, Thiodan requires the same caution granted any chlorinated product similar to it.

Trithion is an effective multipurpose organophosphate insecticide-acaricide registered on many fruit crops. It effectively controls pests on apples, apricots, tart and sweet cherries, grapes, nectarines, peaches, pears, plums, prunes and strawberries. It controls aphids, mites, scales and overwintering aphid and mite eggs.

Vendex is formulated as a 50% wettable powder, non-phosphate miticide with very good activity against a wide range of plant-feeding mites. It is registered for use on apples and pears to control European red, two-spotted, and rust mites. Apply no more than 4 times/season, and no more than 3 times between petal fall and harvest. Do not apply within 14 days of harvest. This product mixes readily with water to form a suspension that can be applied with any conventional spray equipment. It is usable alone or in tank-mix combinations with those insecticides and fungicides generally employed in orchard sprays. No phytotoxicity or adverse affects on fruit finish have been reported. Apply when mites appear. Vendex is a preferred miticide for integrated mite control and has the same good attributes as Plictran. It is of low toxicity to predaceous mites and can be utilized to adjust predator-prey ratios. Used as recommended it presents no unusual health, contamination or environmental problems. It is toxic to fish and should be kept out of ponds and streams. It is nontoxic to honey-bees and of low toxicity to humans.

Vydate L is a systemic and contact carbamate insecticide-acaricide-nematicide. It is currently labeled as a nematicide and miticide on non-bearing trees, and as an insecticide-miticide on bearing apple trees. It gives excellent control of aphids, leafhoppers, mites and leafminer larvae; however, it is highly toxic to bees and predators. WARNING: Do not apply within 30 days after bloom at a rate greater than ½ pt./100 gal. or fruit thinning may occur. Outbreaks of wooly apple aphid may occur from season-long program of vydate.

Zolone is a non-systemic phosphate insecticide-miticide. Presently registered for use on apples, pears, grapes, pecans and the stone fruits, it controls most major fruit pests and suppresses or controls many minor pests. Marketed as an emulsifiable concentrate containing 3 lb. of active ingredient per gallon, and a 25% wettable powder, it can be applied to within 14 days of harvest on the crops indicated. Somewhat weak in its Michigan performances on plum curculio, Zolone is recommended in cover spray applications following First Cover if not practicing integrated mite control since it is highly toxic to mite predators.

Zolone is compatible with most fruit fungicides, some insecticides, offers residual properties averaging 7 to 14 days and has crop residue tolerances of 10 ppm. While somewhat hazardous to fish, Zolone is only moderately toxic to honeybees, comparable with diazinon in having an average mammalian toxicity and much less harmful than DDT to quail, ducks, pheasants and other birdlife. It does not persist and accumulate, but rapidly metabolizes to non-contaminants in soils.

Synthetic Pyrethroids—Reasearch is continuing on the efficiency of these newly developed insecticides against tree and small fruit pests. Pyrethrums are botanical insecticides derived from the chrysanthemum plant. Their insecticidal activity has been known for centuries but their residual activity was short due to rapid breakdown in the environment lending only limited applicability to modern agriculture. Recently, chemists have synthesized the toxic portion of the pyrethroid molecule and stabilized it against rapid breakdown. The result has been an increased residual activity of pyrethrum, providing in some cases outstanding insect control. Two of these materials, Pydrin and Ambush, have been discussed above.

APPLE SCAB CONTROL

Note: Details of apple scab control are given here as an example of the problems involved in controlling a key orchard pest. You can obtain details on other pests and their

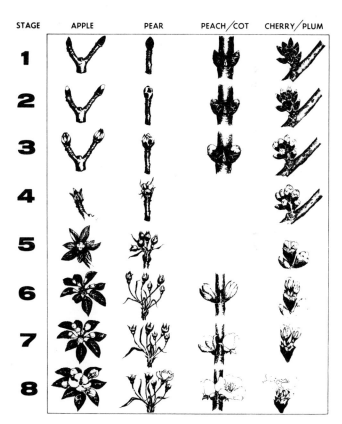

Figure 16. TIMING SPRAY APPLICATIONS. Spray applications to fruit trees are timed according to the opening of the leaf and flower buds in spring. Secure from your local county agricultural agent (usually the county seat, courthouse or postoffice) or governmental experiment station, a suggested spray program of currently recommended chemicals. Time your sprays according to the suggested opening of the flower buds and clusters, as indicated above. Openings by number above are approximately these designated stages for apple only: (1) Dormant; (2 - 3) silver tip to delayed dormant: (4) green tip: (5 - 7) tight cluster to pink: (8) early bloom. See color section. Buds and flower development also are shown for pear, peach, apricot and cherry/plum. (Wash. Agr. Ext. Bull. 419. Request new edition annually).

control in Michigan bulletin E-154 issued annually, or similar bulletins from other major fruit states. (Cornell, Penn. State Universities, Wash. State, and Univ. of Calif, e.g.).

The key to effective apple scab control is to *prohibit the establishment of the fungus during the primary scab infection periods.* If scab is not controlled at this time, a grower is forced to spray longer into the summer. Four general approaches to primary scab control are described.

1. Protectant spray program—Protectant sprays are applied before infection occurs. They set up a chemical barrier between the susceptible plant tissue and the germinating spore. The scab fungicides listed in this chapter may be used as protectants, although some act in other ways as well.

During primary infection, protectants are usually applied on a set schedule. The frequency of application depends on the ability of the compounds to resist weathering action of rainfall and the rate of new growth during this time. Generally, compounds such as ferbam, glyodin, and sulfur that only protect are applied more frequently than compounds that can act in other ways as well.

2. Eradicant spray program (back-action sprays)—Eradicant sprays "burn out" the fungus within certain periods of time after infection begins. Eradicants should be used at their full recommended rate, because at lower rates, their ability to eradicate is reduced or lost. The number of hours a compound remains effective after the beginning of an infection period is given in Table 3.

TABLE 3. EFFECT OF FUNGICIDES ON ERADICATION OF APPLE SCAB

Fungicide	Rate/100 gal. dilute	Eradication from beginning of infection period*
captan 50% WP	2 lb.	18 to 24 hr.
dichlone 50% WP	½ lb.	36 to 48 hr.
dichlone 50% WP	¼ lb.	30 to 36 hr.
dodine 65%	½ lb.	30 to 36 hr.
lime sulfur	2 gal.	60 to 72 hr.
polyram 80% WP	2 lb.	18 to 24 hr.
ferbam 76% WP	2 lb.	None
sulfur 95% WP	5 lb.	None

*Growers should use beginning of rain as the start of infection, based on average temperature of 50 to 60° F. At average temperatures lower than 50° F., use higher eradicative time figures.

Timing of eradicant schedules for primary apple scab is based on wetting and prevailing air temperatures (see Table 4). Eradicants are applied after the length of wetting is sufficient for infection to occur. For example, at an average temperature of 58° F., primary infection will occur 10 hours after the start of the rain. After 22 hours of wetting, the degree of infection will be severe. Because the eradicant action for most fungicides is limited to a few

hours or days after infection, they must be applied soon after conditions for infection are satisfied. If a protectant fungicide is not applied before or within 9 hours after the beginning of the rain, chemicals with eradicative properties must be used.

TABLE 4. APPROXIMATE NUMBER OF HOURS OF WETTING REQUIRED FOR PRIMARY APPLE SCAB INFECTION AT DIFFERENT AIR TEMPERATURES*

Temperature Average	DEGREE OF INFECTION		
	Light	Moderate	Heavy
°F	hrs.[a]	hrs.	hrs.
78	13	17	26
77	11	14	21
76	9½	12	19
63 to 75	9	12	18
63	9	12	19
61	9	13	20
60	9½	13	20
59	10	13	21
58	10	14	21
57	10	14	22
56	11	15	22
55	11	16	24
54	11½	16	24
53	12	17	25
52	12	18	26
51	13	18	27
50	14	19	29
49	14½	20	30
48	15	20	30
47	17	23	35
46	19	25	38
45	20	27	41
44	22	30	45
43	25	34	51
42	30	40	60
33 to 41[b]	—	—	—

3. Protectant-eradicant schedules—Most fungicides used for apple scab control are active as protectants and as eradicants. When applied at the eradicant rate, they control infections that may have occurred a few hours or days previously and also protect exposed tissues for several days after the time of application. These compounds are usually applied on a 5- to 10-day interval, depending on the weather and tree growth.

4. Single application techniques—A single spray is applied at the green tip stage of bud development and through retention and redistribution protects new growth for several weeks. The only fungicide registered for use in this manner is Difolaten. It is used on apples at 3 gal. or at 5 gal./acre as a single spray applied at the green tip stage of bud development. In this program, start using other suitable fungicides in a regular program at pink when the low rate is used or no later than early petal fall when the high rate is used. Apply Difolatan under good drying conditions to avoid excessive loss of deposit from rain or undried deposits. Thorough spray coverage, especially in the top half of the tree, is essential for uniform redistribution and control.

Difolatan is not effective against powdery mildew. On mildew-susceptible cultivars, use the 3 gal./acre rate and initiate a strong powdery mildew control program in early pink.

SCAB CONTROL FUNGICIDES

The usual apple scab control fungicides are listed below for the general area of Michigan. Timing and selection of a particular fungicide depends on the type of program the grower wishes to use in his orchard. Protectant fungicides should be applied more frequently than protectant-eradicant fungicides provided full rates are maintained for fungicides with eradicant properties. Timing of eradicants is based on rainfall and infection periods.

Primary scab usually starts at silver tip and is completed about 4 weeks after petal fall. However, maturation and discharge of ascospores may vary considerably from season to season and important deviations in timing will be announced by the District Horticultural Agents.

If primary scab is well controlled, the rates used during summer are reduced and the sprays are applied on a 10- to 14-day interval, or less frequently than during the primary period. If primary scab is not controlled, fungicide rates and intervals should not be reduced until scab lesions are inactivated.

Additional Comments on Scab Fungicides: Lime sulfur is used at the silver tip to pre-pink stage of bud development. Do not use sulfur compounds, diclone (Phygon), captan, Dikar, or dinocap (Karathane) with oil, or near oil applications.

When primary infection is light, the standard program at high rates and with good timing is usually sufficient to prevent secondary spread. However, where infection is more severe, the following approaches are suggested for suppressing lesion development and sporulation and for protecting emerging tissues.

Use dodine 65% WP at 12 oz./100 gal. and apply 2 applications one week apart. The first application should be applied as soon as possible after infection occurred or, if necessary, as soon as possible after lesions appear. In orchards where both dodine and benomyl resistance are suspect, use captan 50% WP at 2 lb./100 gal.

Breeding for Resistance. Purdue, Illinios and Rutgers University have cooperated in a breeding program to develop apple cultivars resistant to the scab fungus. This was done by crossing high quality desirable cultivars with small-fruited scab-resistant crabapples, as the Siberian crab. Two of the hybrids being planted by mainly home gardeners are Prima and Priscilla.

TABLE 5. RESISTANCE OF 62 APPLE CULTIVARS TO IMPORTANT DISEASES. (CORNELL ANN. PEST CONTROL BULL.)

Cultivar	Resistance rating			
	Apple scab	Cedar apple rust	Fire blight	Powdery mildew
Baldwin	3	1	3	4
Barry	3	2	4	—
Beacon	3	3	3	—
Ben Davis	3	3	4	3
Britemac	3	2	2	3
Burgundy	3	3	4	—
Carroll	3	2	2	—
Cortland	4	3	3	4
Delicious	3	1	2	2
Early McIntosh	3	2	2	—
Empire	4	2	2	3
Gloster	3	3	2	—
Golden Delicious	3	4	3	3
Granny Smith	3	2	4	4
Gravenstein	3	2	3	3
Holly	3	1	3	—
Idared	3	3	4	3
Jamba	3	3	2	—
Jerseymac	4	1	3	—
Jonagold	4	3	4	3
Jonamac	3	2	3	3
Jonathan	3	4	4	4
Julyred	4	3	3	3
Liberty	1	1	2	2
Lodi	3	4	4	2
Macfree	1	3	2	—
Macoun	4	2	3	3
McIntosh	4	1	3	3
Milton	3	1	3	3
Mollies Delicious	3	1	3	—
Monroe	3	3	3	3
Mutsu	4	3	4	4
NY 58553-1	1	2	3	2
Niagara	4	2	4	2
Northern Spy	3	3	2	3
Nova Easygro	1	1	2	3
Paulared	3	2	3	3
Prima	1	4	2	2
Priscilla	1	1	2	3
Puritan	3	2	3	3
Quinte	3	3	3	3
Raritan	3	3	4	—
Rhode Island Greening	3	3	4	3
Rome Beauty	4	4	4	3
Scotia	3	2	3	—
Sir Prize	1	3	4	2
Spartan	3	2	3	2
Spigold	4	4	4	3
Spijon	3	3	3	3
Stark Bounty	3	3	2	—
Stark Splendor	3	3	2	—
Starkspur Earliblaze	3	2	3	—
Stayman	4	3	2	3
Summerred	3	4	3	3
Twenty Ounce	3	4	4	3
Tydeman	3	1	3	2
Viking	3	2	2	—
Wayne	3	3	3	3
Wealthy	3	3	3	3
Wellington	3	2	2	3
Williams	3	2	2	—
York Imperial	3	4	4	3

Key to resistance rating

1 = very resistant. No control needed. (Very few cultivars in this category for any disease.)

2 = resistant. Control only needed under high disease pressure.

3 = susceptible. Control usually needed where disease is prevalent.

4 = very susceptible. Control always needed where disease is prevalent. These cultivars should receive first priority when control is called for.

341

ORDERING SPRAY MATERIALS

Spray materials should be ordered several months in advance of the spray season. However, every year is different and only the minimal spray needs should be purchased far in advance unless a spray dealer is willing to take back unused materials. Careful monitoring of the orchard may indicate the need for fewer sprays of less chemicals than originally estimated. You should join the mailing list for spray schedules and other spray information from the local county agricultural agent, farm advisor or other sources (See table 1). The first consideration in ordering is to determine as nearly as possible the spray schedule to be followed, especially during the early part of the season. The up-dated state schedule will suggest the number of sprays to be applied, the materials to be used, and the dilutions. Considerably more spray material will be required for the afterbloom than for the prebloom applications. The gallonage in Table 6 are for dilute sprays of 300 or more gallons per acre only. Growers using concentrate sprays are applying 20-100 gpa on various sizes of trees. Young trees require very small amounts of spray but care must be taken not to overspray these trees at concentrate rates.

TIME AND AMOUNTS OF SPRAY APPLICATIONS

Most insects and diseases tend to build up as the growing season advances. It is, therefore, particularly important that the correct materials be applied thoroughly at the proper time early in the season to reduce as much as possible the early generations of insects and diseases. The progenies of a single overwintering codling moth, if uncontrolled, can destroy about 140 bushels of apples (Figure 11) in one season. To control codling moth effectively, it is often good judgment early in the season to apply "top off" sprays between the regular cover sprays to cover adequately tops of big trees and keep the rapidly expanding surface of the young apples fairly well covered with spray material (Figure 17). The surface area of young apples may double every seven days early in the season. Where wild trees, abandoned orchards or other pest sources exist nearby, it is often wise to apply border treatments to reduce the threat of continuing buildups. Use of pheromone and other traps can be helpful in monitoring and timing border sprays.

Most fungus diseases thrive best in the presence of moisture from continued rains. During such periods, the spores readily germinate and the organism becomes established on the host, provided temperature is satisfactory (Figure 10). With most fungicides used today, it is important to have the spray materials on the foliage and fruit prior to the rainy period to prevent the spores from germinating. If in case of apple scab, the disease has made considerable headway, it may be advisable to use a "back-action" spray lime-sulfur, dichlone or polyram to "burn-out" the established fungus. The use of heavy fixed copper and Bordeaux sprays have reduced the incidence of bacterial diseases such as fire blight, walnut blight and bacterial blast in some areas of the U.S.

SPRAYER CALIBRATION

Accurate calibration of orchard spray equipment is important for efficient use of pesticides. The selection of the right chemical and its time of application are equally important. Tree spraying requires a sprayer with adequate capacity to distribute the spray evenly throughout the trees. Individual sprayers are designed to operate most efficiently at certain gallonages per acre, and the best spray coverage and deposit are obtained within the manufacturer's recommended range.

DILUTE AND CONCENTRATE SPRAYING

The amount of dilute spray required to cover trees adequately varies with the size of trees. Unless adjustments are made in the rate of delivery and spray pattern required by the differences in tree size, difficulties such as inadequate pest control or excessive application of material will result. Approximate dilute gallonages required in different orchard situations are indicated in Table 6.

The amount of pesticide required to treat an acre of large trees is considerably greater than the amount re-

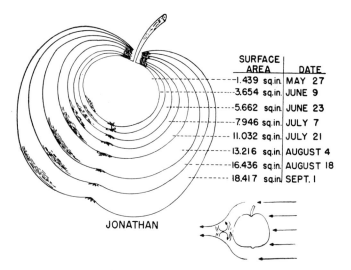

SURFACE AREA	DATE
1.439 sq.in.	MAY 27
3.654 sq.in.	JUNE 9
5.662 sq.in.	JUNE 23
7.946 sq.in.	JULY 7
11.032 sq.in.	JULY 21
13.216 sq.in.	AUGUST 4
16.436 sq.in.	AUGUST 18
18.417 sq.in.	SEPT. 1

JONATHAN

Figure 17. Jonathan apples will double their surface every two weeks to a month during early development. Hence, there is need to keep the fruit surface reasonably well covered for protection. At lower right is an apple with *fine spray droplets* directed at it. Note swirling and coverage on the far left side of the apple. *Large droplets may shoot on by and give poor coverage on the far side.*

quired on an acre of trees planted at a higher density. Proper application requires that adjustments be made to compensate for these differences.

Concentrate spraying must be considered in terms of reducing the gallons of water per acre for the row-spacing and tree-size combination being sprayed. As the gallonage of water is reduced, errors become more critical. Concentrate sprays eliminate run-off. Sprays applied at 3 X or higher concentrate levels result in a 20 to 25% increase in deposit, thus allowing a similar reduction in rate of pesiticide application without a reduction in pesticide deposit. From a practical viewpoint, the acceptable concentrate level depends on several factors including the pest being controlled, density of foliage, weather conditions, and material being applied. Dilute sprays are generally more effective and are preferred for applying growth regulators, nutrient sprays, fungicides for mildew control, acaracides, and insecticides for control of pests such as scales and woolly aphid. In most other instances concentrate sprays in the range of 6 X to 8 X usually provide satisfactory results. Additional savings in cost of application above this level of concentration are minimal, and frequency of poor spray performance increases, according to W.C. Stiles of Cornell.

CALIBRATING A CONVENTIONAL AIRBLAST SPRAYER

The gallons of spray desired per acre and the time required to spray an acre determine the rate of output for which the sprayer must be nozzled. Since volume of spray needed per acre varies with tree size, the most-common row-spacing for the tree size to be sprayed should be used in calibrating the sprayer. The *gallons of dilute spray* required for various row-spacing and tree-size combinations are indicated in Table 6. *Gallons of concentrate spray* re-

quired is determined by dividing dilute gallonage by the concentration desired. The *rate of output* by the sprayer is calculated by dividing the gallons of concentrate spray by time required to spray 1 acre, Table 7.

TABLE 7. APPROXIMATE TIME REQUIRED TO SPRAY 1 ACRE OF ORCHARD (TWO-SIDED-SPRAYER OPERATION)

Distance between rows	Linear feet of row/acre*	Travel speed (mph)***				
		1	1½	2	2½	3
feet	feet	minutes/acre**				
40	1089	12.4	8.2	6.2	5.0	4.1
30	1452	16.5	11.0	8.2	6.6	5.5
25	1742	19.8	12.4	9.9	7.9	6.6
22	1980	22.5	15.0	11.2	9.0	7.5
20	2178	24.8	16.5	12.4	9.9	8.3
18	2420	27.5	18.3	13.8	11.0	9.2
16	2722	30.9	20.6	15.5	12.4	10.3
14	3112	35.4	23.6	17.7	14.1	11.8
12	3630	41.2	27.5	20.6	16.5	13.8

*Linear feet of row = 43,560 ÷ distance between rows.
**Minutes per acre = linear feet of row/acre ÷ speed in feet/minute.
***Speed in feet/minute = mph x 88.

Example:

Rows 30 feet apart, trees 20 feet wide X 15 feet high.
A 4 X concentrate application will be made at a speed of 2½ mph.
1. Table 6 indicates 300 gal dilute spray per acre.
2. 300 (gal) ÷ 4(X) = 75 gal of 4 X concentrate per acre.
3. Table 7 indicates 6.6 minutes to spray 1 acre of 30 foot rows at speed of 2½ mph.
4. Total sprayer output for 2-sided operation = 75 (gal/a) ÷ 6.6 (min/a) = 11.36 gal/min.
5. Output required per side = 11.36 ÷ 2 = 5.68 gal/min.

Consult owner's manual or manufacturer's guide to determine the combination of pressure, whirl plates, and nozzle discs that will provide the required output per minute. Select combinations that will provide ⅔ of the total output in the upper ⅓ of the effective airblast and the remaining ⅓ of the output in the lower ⅔ of the airblast.

Nozzle both sides of the sprayer manifold to provide the same pattern. Mount a presure guage on the manifold and set pressure *at the manifold while all nozzles are spraying.* Adjust nozzles and air vanes to obtain the desired spray pattern. Check speed by determining the time required to travel a measured distance. Finally, fill the sprayer with water needed to refill the tank, and determine whether the spray rate per acre obtained was the same as calculated.

Whirl plates and nozzles discs are subject to wear, which results in increased output with time. When the amount of spray applied to the same orchard has increases by 10% or more, all nozzle components should be checked for

TABLE 6. GALLONAGE OF DILUTE SPRAY PER ACRE REQUIRED TO PROVIDE EQUIVALENT COVERAGE FOR MATURE TREES OF DIFFERENT SIZES AND SPACINGS (CORNELL BULL, 7826).

Distance between rows	Tree width	Tree height	Maximum tree volume/acre*	Minimum dilute spray ±
ft	ft	ft	(1000) cu ft	gal/acre
40	28	20	610	425
40	28	16	488	350
30	20	15	436	300
25	16	12	348	250
22	14	10	272	200
20	12	10	261	185
18	10	10	242	175
16	8	8	174	125
14	6	8	149	105
12	6	6	131	90

*Maximum tree volume/acre = tree width x tree height x linear feet of row per acre. Linear feet of row/acre = 43,560 ÷ distance between rows.
± Minimum dilute gal/acre = approx. 0.7 gal/1000 cu ft of tree volume.

damage and replaced if necessary.

Adjustments in spray rate per acre for differences in row-spacing X tree-size combinations can be made by changing nozzles, opening or closing nozzles, changing speed, and (or)changing tank-mix concentration. Sprayers equipped with flip-over nozzle bodies can be calibrated either for 2 concentrations for the same row-spacing X tree size combination *or* for the same concentration for 2 diffenent row-spacing X tree-size combinations. In some cases, particularly in smaller trees, alternate-row spraying provides further flexibility in matching sprayer output to desired rates of spray application.

FEDERAL REGULATIONS, RESIDUE TOLERANCES

Certain small amounts (residues) of pesticides may remain legally on harvested fruit. This legal residue is known as tolerance. The grower alone is responsible for producing legally marketable fruit. By following three rules, the grower can be reasonably sure his harvested fruit will be "within the limits of the law"': (1.) Do not increase dosage rates above those currently recommended. (2.) Do not use materials on crops not listed in current schedules for fruit. (3.) Do not use materials closer to harvest than is indicated by the latest recommendations.

Materials used in the dormant, pre-bloom, and post-harvest periods ordinarily do not present a residue problem on harvested fruits. Federal and state pesticide regulations change frequently. *Growers are advised to check with county agents or pest control consultants for the latest information before applying any chemical.* Growers should not apply any pesticide if the intended use is not on the label. The same or similar products produced by different manufacturers may not have the same uses on the label.

Pesticide Reentry Standards. The Environmental Protection Agency (EPA) has established regulations to protect workers entering fields treated with pesticides. Unprotected workers must not be permitted in fields treated with the following pesticides until the indicated number of hours has passed:

48 Hours
ethyl parathion
methyl parathion (the Penncap M form requires only that the spray be allowed to dry before workers enter treated areas)

demeton (Systox)	Meta-Systox-R*
azodrin*	bidrin*
carbophenothion (Trithion)	endrin

24 Hours

azinphosmethyl (Guthion)	EPN
phosalone (Zolone)	ethion

*Not for use on tree fruits.

With pesticides other than those listed above, unprotected workers must not be permitted in treated fields until sprays have dried or dusts have settled.

If label directions are more restrictive than the standards, the label directions take precedence. For example, the endrin label says to keep all persons and pets out of sprayed orchards for 30 days.

Workers may enter treated fields before the end of the reentry period if protective clothing is worn. Protective clothing includes a hat or other suitable head covering, a long-sleeved shirt and long-legged trousers or a coverall type of garment (all of closely woven fabric covering the body, arms, and legs), and shoes and socks.

Warnings must be given to workers who are expected to work in treated fields. Warnings may be given orally, or by signs at the usual entrances to the field, or by signs on bulletin boards where workers usually assemble. It is the responsibility of the owner or lessee of the treated field to see that workers comply with the standards.

With any pesticide, unprotected persons must not be allowed in areas being treated, and workers, other than those involved in the application, must not be exposed to drift.

Pesticide Residues on Fruit. Residues of pesticides are permitted on harvested crops only when they do not exceed tolerances established by the Envrionmental Protection Agency (Table 8).

Growers are also advised to check with their buyers, processors, or packers before applying chemicals. In some cases, buyers and processors will not accept fruit treated with certain materials, even though these materials are approved for use by federal and state agencies.

To avoid illegal residues, it is imperative that directions be followed carefully with respect to rates of application number of applications and harvest. Drift must be avoided, especially where other crops are adjacent to or interplanted with the crop being treated. Pesticide residues that are permitted on one crop may be illegal when present on another.

Do not feed cull fruit or the by-products of fruit processing, such as apple and pear pomace, to live stock unless it is certain there is no residue problem. The use of many of the pesticides recommended today may prohibit the use of cull fruit as feed for livestock.

Pesticide Residues on Cover Crops. Even though pesticides are applied to orchard trees, some of the spray or dust will settle on the cover crop. Since normal spray programs frequently involve pesticides which are not permitted on animal feeds, it is essential that cover crops not be grazed or fed to any livestock.

Volatile and Drift-Susceptible Herbicides. Check with your Federal or State Department of Agriculture on spray orders for the area where the herbicides are to be used.

Restricted Use Pesticides. *State regulations* restrict the use of a number of pesticides to certified applicators or to persons under the direct supervision of certified applicators. State restricted-use pesticides which are likely to be used in orchards include the following: Endrin — 2.5 per cent and above: Parathion and methyl parathion — 1.1 per cent and above: Phosdrin; Systox (demeton): 2.4-D — all formulations in containers of 1 gallon or larger to be used in some states. *Federal regulations* will also restrict the use of a number of pesticides to certified applicators. The restricted use designation appears (or will appear) on the product label.

Licensing (Certification). Those who sell, distribute, apply, or advise on the use of pesticides may need to be licensed by the state department of agriculture in one or more of the following categories. All licenses must be renewed annually. *Commercial applicator:* Any person applying pesticides for hire to the lands of another. *Pesticide Dealer and Dealer Manager:* Any person who sells pesticides. Dealer outlets must also employ a pesticide Dealer Manager. *Pest Control Consultant:* Any person who offers recommendations, technical advice, or aid in the use of pesticides, except those packaged only for home and garden use. *Private Pesticide Applicator:* Any person who applies restricted-use pesticides on the lands of another on a trade-work basis without obtaining a commercial applicator's license.

Pesticide User Permits. A user permit serves as a temporary certification which allows growers who are not licensed to buy and use restricted-use pesticides. These permits may be issued by licensed pesticide dealers at the time of sale.

State Laws and Regulations. Complete state laws and regulations can be obtained from your Pesticide Branch of the state department of agriculture.

Horticultural Pest and Disease Boards. Washington counties have interestingly established Horticultural Pest and Disease Boards to control and prevent the spread of horticultural pests and diseases. At the present time, such boards are located in all of the major fruit-growing counties of Washington. Purpose of the boards is to prevent spread from neglected or abandoned orchards. Pests most often listed as persistent are San Jose scale, codling moth, cherry fruit fly, and pear psylla. Others may be selected in a few areas. The boards have the authority to require owners of neglected fruit trees to effectively control these pests. Other fruit growing areas may wish to consider this approach.

Tank Mixes. Tank mixes of two or more pesticides and applications of one pesticide immediately or shortly following the application of another have been put into three categories by EPA: 1. The use is indicated on the label of one or more EPA-registered products. 2. The use is covered by state registration. 3. The use has been tested and recommended by Agricultural Experiment Stations, State Departments of Agriculture, or is a common agricultural practice.

Applications recommended on EPA-approved labels (category 1) are legal.

State registrations (category 2) remain valid until replaced by EPA registrations.

Other uses (category 3) will be permitted if dosages do not exceed label instructions for any product in the mix used singly for the same pests on the same crop and if labels do not explicitly instruct against such a mixture.

EPA has not reviewed the effectiveness or the human or environmental hazards of combinations of products in categories 2 and 3. The user applies these mixutres at his own risk with respect to effects on crops and equipment, applicator safety, environmental effects, and pre-harvest tolerance intervals. If a particular mixture causes adverse effects, the EPA will on a case-by-case basis, rule that it is not permitted.

HEALTH HAZARDS
(Suggestions from Washington State Ext. Bull 419 U.S.)

Each year there are a number of poisonings, and in some years deaths, attributable to the use of organic phosphorus insecticides. This should make every grower pay attention to the health hazards involved.

Research indicates that all pesticides, even the most hazardous, can be used with safety provided that recommended safety precautions are followed. The accompanying Table 9 shows the relative hazard to spraymen of the various pesticides.

Safe use of compounds in the "Most Dangerous" category requires full attention to all recommended precautions. Materials in the less hazardous categories may be used safely with correspondingly less protective clothing and equipment.

The more toxic materials easily enter the body through contact with the skin as well as through breathing. Ingestion of any of these compounds may be fatal. Repeated exposures may, even without symptoms, increase susceptibility to poisoning.

Take These Precautions: 1. If you plan to apply any of the more dangerous pesticides, make sure your physician knows the types of compounds you are using. If you anticipate using the more toxic organic phosphorus materials, he may suggest that you have a pre-seasonal blood test to determine your normal cholinesterase activity level. He then will be in a better position to deal with a sudden illness. If he should provide you with a supply of atropine tablets for organic phosphorus poisoning, do *not* take them before definite symptoms occur. If you ever take atropine tablets, call your physician as soon afterward as possible. Any person who is ill enough to receive a single

TABLE 9. RELATIVE HAZARD OF AGRICULTURAL CHEMICALS TO APPLICATORS. (WASH. STATE UNIV. EB-0419)

Most Dangerous[1]	Less Dangerous		Least Dangerous	
Demeton (OP)	Amitraz (M)	Alar (M)	Epson Salts (M)	Orthorix (M)
Lannate (C)	Azinphosmethyl (OP)	Amide (M)	Ethephon (M)	Oryzalin (N)
Methomyl (C)	Baam (M)	Bordeaux Mixture (M)	Ethrel (M)	Perthane (CO)
Nudrin (C)	Cygon (OP)	Boron (Borax) (M)	Ferbam (D)	Plictran (M)
Paraquat (M)	Defend (OP)	Boro-spray (M)	Gardona (OP)	Princep (M)
Parathion (OP)	Diazinon (OP)	Calcium (Chloride or	Gibberellic Acid (M)	Ramik (M)
Strychnine (M)	Dimethodate (OP)	Nitrate) (M)	Glyphosate (M)	Roundup (M)
Systox (OP)	Endosulfan (CO)	Captan (M)	Hinder (M)	Rozol (M)
	Ethion (OP)	Carbaryl (C)	Iron Chelate (M)	Sevin (C)
Dangerous	Guthion (OP)	Casoron (M)	Karathane (N)	Silvex (CO)
Carzol (C)	Imidan (OP)	Coposil (M)	Karmex (M)	Simazine (M)
DNOSBP (N)	Mesurol (C)	Copper (Sprays and	Kelthane (CO)	Sinbar (M)
Elgetol (N)	Penncap-M (OP)	Salts (M)	lime (M)	Sodium Polysulfide (M)
Endrin (CO)	Phosalone (OP)	Cyprex (M)	lime-sulfur (M)	Solubar (M)
Methyl Parathion (OP)	Pydrin (M)	Cython (OP)	Magnesium Salts (M)	Streptomycin (M)
Supracide (OP)	Rebelate (OP)	2, 4-D (CO)	Magnetic 6 (M)	Sulfur (M)
Zinc Phosphide (M)	Thiodan (CO)	Devrinol (M)	Malathion (OP)	Surflan (N)
	Thiram (D)	Dichlobenil (M)	Maneb (D)	Terbacil (M)
	Toxaphene (CO)	Diclone (M)	Manzate 200 D)	2,4,5-TP (C0)
	Zolone (OP)	Dikar (D + N)	Morestan (M)	Terramycin (M)
		Diphacinon (M)	NAA (Naphthalene	Urea (M)
		Dithane M45 (D)	Acetic Acid) (M)	Vendex (M)
		Diuron (M)	Napropamide (M)	Zinc Chelate (M)
		Dodine (M)	Oil (M)	Zinc Sulfate (M)
			Omite (M)	Zineb (D)
				Ziram (D)

[1] The classification into hazard groups is both approximate and relative. These estimates are based on use experience as well as on studies with experimental animals.
[2] The chemical class to which the pesticide belongs is designated as follows: C, carbamate; CO, chlorinated organic; D, dithiocarbamate M, miscellaneous; N, nitro; and OP, organophosphorus.

dose of atropine should be kept under medical observation for 24 hours, because atropine may produce only temporary relief of symptoms in what may prove to be a serious case of poisoning. Keep atropine tablets away from children. An antidote for treating organic phosphorus poisoning, 2-PAM, has been developed. This antidote should be available at the U.S Public Health Service Toxicolgy Laboratories and at hospitals and clinics serving major agricultural areas.

2. Wear protective clothing, preferably water repellent, while spraying hazardous materials as toxic pesticides can be absorbed into the body through the skin. Change and launder clothing and bathe daily.

3. Wear a respirator mask when loading or mixing wettable powders or when applying dusts. *The respirator should be approved for the material in question by your federal government services.* An approved respirator should be worn whenever the more volatile of the toxic compounds are being used. The filters and pads should be changed at regular intervals.

4. Empty liquid pesticide containers should be made as safe as possible before disposal. Rinse thoroughly three times with water. Pour the rinse water into the spray tank for application with the spray. Glass jars should be broken and metal containers crushed or punched with holes to make them unusable before disposal. Containers and waste pesticides must be buried in a sanitary landfill approved for this purpose. Combustible containers may be burned if burning is specifically indicated on the container

and is not prohibited by air pollution regulations. Stay out of the smoke. Never measure or leave mixtures of pesticdes in beverage bottles or in labeled cans or boxes which have contained food. Each year tragic, preventable poisonings occur when children play with "empty" pesticide containers or obtain food containers filled with pesticide. Never leave concentrate materials unattended.

5. Keep your pesticide storage room locked (empty cans too).

6. Do not smoke, chew tobacco, or eat while spraying or while your hands are contaminated, especially with concentrate materials.

7. Mix insecticides according to directions and apply at the recommended rate.

8. Experience shows that poisoning occurs most often in hot weather. Spray with the more toxic materials during cooler periods insofar as possible. Spray when necessary with milder materials during periods of high temperature.

9. Fruit thinners and other people have been poisoned by working in orchards treated with parathion less than 72 hours earlier. Therefore, it is advisable to wait longer than 72 hours before beginning work in treated orchards.

10. Bury spilled insecticide and wash the contaminated area with soap and lots of water. The breakdown of these insecticides can be speeded up by using a weak lye solution.

11. Cover crops should not be fed livestock.

12. Do not feed insecticide-contaminated apple or pear pomace to livestock.

13. There have been a number of cases of irritation of

skin, eyes, and respiratory tract from the use of some pesticides. These cases have occurred to sprayers from direct contact with the material and to thinners and pickers whose only exposure was to residues on fruit. There have also been a number of cases of skin irritation as a result of contact with Morestan.

Watch for these Symptoms: The initial symptoms of organic phosphorus poisoning are giddiness, headache, nausea, vomiting, excessive sweating, and tightness of the chest. These are followed by or accompanied by blurring of vision, diarrhea, excessive salivation, watering of the eyes, twitching of muscles, especially in the eyelids, and mental confusion. One of the most characteristic signs is constriction of the pupils, but this may be preceded by dilation. Late signs are fluid in the chest, convulsions, coma, loss of urinary or bowel control, and respiratory failure.

The symptoms of poisoning by the chlorinated organic compounds , such as dieldrin and endrin, are primarily due to their effect on the nervous system and include hyperexcitability, tremors, and convulsions. General symptoms are malaise, headache, fatigue, and possible lack of appetite and weight loss.

What To Do For Poisoning: 1. In severe cases of organic phosphorus poisoning, breathing may stop. In such a situation *artificial respiration is the most important first aid until breathing has resumed.*

2. Get the patient to a hospital or physician as soon as possible. Give artificial respiration on the way if the patient turns blue or stops breathing. If you know which pesticide may be involved, *take along a label for the doctor's information.* If the label cannot be removed easily, take along entire pesticide container.

3. Never try to give anything by mouth to an unconscious patient.

4. If the insecticide has been swallowed but the patient has not vomited, induce vomiting by giving a tablespoonful of salt dissolved in one-half glass of warm water.

5. Where excessive amounts of the insecticide, especially in concentrate form, have come into contact with the skin, immediately remove all clothing and bathe the patient with generous amounts of soap and water, rinsing thoroughly.

6. If the eyes have been contaminated with spray, especially with insecticide concentrate, wash them immediately with flowing water.

7. Make the patient lie down and keep him warm.

Skin Penetration. Oral cavity is not the only place pesticides can be absorbed into the system. Most pesticides can penetrate the skin. Illness and death can occur. Percentage absorption of the following is an indication:

	Parathion	Malathion	Sevin
Forearm	9	7	74
Abdomen	18	9	—
Palm	12	6	—
Scalp	32	—	—
Forehead	37	23	—
Scrotum	100	—	—

Note high absorption in the head and scrotum of parathion, and how easily Sevin enters the body. Importance of protective clothing is stressed.

BEE PROTECTION

Bees are necessary for the pollination of fruit trees. Orchardists must make a sincere effort to protect them. The following precautions will help insure adequate pollination. Please note that bee hives are difficult to contract when honey prices are good. Contract for bees well ahead of bloom.

TABLE 10. TOXICITY OF INSECTICIDES TO BEES

Hazardous at any time on blooming crops	Not hazardous if applied in late evening except during high temperatures	Not hazardous if applied in evening or early morning except during high temperatures	Not hazardous to bees at any time on blooming crops
Azinphosmethyl (Guthion)	Malathion EC	Dieldrin G	BAAM
Carzol	Pydrin	Dylox	Karathane
Chlordane		Elgetol (1½ pint per	Kelthane
Cygon		100 gal. or less)	Lime-sulfate
Diazinon		Endrin	Mitac
Dieldrin		Ethion	Morestan
DNOSBP		Methoxychlor	Oil Sprays
Imidan		Perthane	(superior type)
Lindane and BHC		Systox	Omite
Malathion ULV		TEPP*	Ovex
Methyl parathion		Thiodan	Plictran
Parathion		Tiovel	Sulfar
Penncap-M		Trithion	Vendex
Phosdrin		Zolone	
Phosphamidon			
Sevin			
Supracide			

*Do not apply near honey bee colonies because of fumigation hazards.

347

1. Do not place bees in an orchard until 10 to 20 per cent of the blossoms are open. This will help prevent the bees from working other flowers in the area.

2. *Never apply* insecticidal sprays or dusts when any blossoms are open or when drift of the material may get on open blossoms in adjoining orchards or interplants. *If misused, Penncap-M is particularly hazardous to bees through pollen contamination and should never be sprayed on either fruit blooms or cover crop blooms.* Check specific regulations for your area for details.

3. Mow or beat down orchard cover crops before applying sprays hazardous to bees—especially Penncap-M and Sevin. Treatment with 2,4-D is the best way to remove dandelion blooms. This is especially important in relation to the first cover spray in apples, which is applied during a critical foraging period when bees will fly several miles to obtain pollen and nectar from even a few blooms of dandelion, mustard, etc. Grass sod cover crops should be encouraged to prevent bee losses.

4. Except for the insecticide Sevin, which is also used to thin apples, none of the other growth regulators, herbicides, fungicides, or nutrients is known to be hazardous to bees. Sevin is highly toxic to bees (Table 10). Therefore, do not apply when bees are still working in or near the orchard on late bloom or late-blooming varieties, cover crop, or weeds. To reduce bee hazard, delay use of Sevin as a thinner until at least 10 days past full bloom.

5. Ask beekeepers to remove bees from your district before starting your spray program. The orchardist must know who owns the bees in his orchard and where the bee man can be contacted. Beekeepers should establish a holding yard at least 4 miles from orchards to be sprayed.

6. Beekeepers should register their bees with the county agent and should *never* place unmarked colonies next to orchards.

COMPATABILITY OF SPRAYS

Every year several organizations including the experiment stations and the American Fruit Grower magazine publish up-to-date compatability charts to show which combinations of chemicals, new and old, are (a) compatible (no injury resulting on fruit or foliage), (b) incompatible, or (c) should be tried with caution on a limited scale (Figure 18).

SPRAY SCHEDULES

Spray chemicals and ways of using them are changing every year. The commercial manufacturers are performing an excellent service in developing new and better pesticides. Experiment stations also are an important link in testing the chemicals and reporting results in unbiased reports. In the USA, the Pure Food and Drug Administration (Federal) demands that all new chemicals must be "cleared" by their standards (Miller Bill). Other countries may have similar standards.

Detailed spray schedules for each fruit are not given here since they are changing annually with new chemicals and problems. It is suggested you mail a card to or phone your county agricultural agent for the latest schedule for the fruits you have. If you live outside the USA the state bulletins are available to you by writing; there may be a small fee. Inquire first. State experiment station addresses are in the Appendix.

In some fruit regions, spray schedules are devised for special needs, rather than suggest a general program for all conditions. For example, Virginia suggests separate spray programs to reduce cost wherever possible, for (a) orchards where the chlorinated hydrocarbons are still effective and pest resistance is not an important problem, (b) maximum protection, (c) for varieties grown for processing (principally York Imperial); and (d) for non-bearing blocks (York alternate bears in spite of all precautions in some orchards).

In nearly all apple areas, it has been found necessary to use different materials on different cultivars to get maximum finish on fruit of particularly sensitive cultivars such as Golden Delicious, Jonathon, and Grimes Golden.

PROGRAM FOR YOUNG NONBEARING FRUIT TREES

Dormant trees showing scale on the bark and eggs of aphids or red mite near young buds should receive a dormant spray. A dormant spray for peaches for leaf curl and a summer borer trunk spray are needed. Young apple trees need late bloom and first cover scab sprays in scab trees, plus a green aphis spray if they are heavy. A spray for canker or measuring worms may be needed at pink and calyx-cup periods. Tree hoppers (particularly from an alfalfa field) may slit young bark to lay eggs, damaging growth. Sprays, mowing the cover or cultivation are controls. Young cherry trees need a leaf spot and slug spray, rarely a dormant spray.

Check young peach trees early fall and early spring for white grub borers in bark near soil surface and in upper trunk framework. Remove with wire or knife or use Penncap M, parathion or Thiodan sprays or as locally recommended.

Special precautions are necessary among all young fruit trees in years when the periodical cicada (17-year locust in the North, 13 years in the South) is due to appear. Specific dates and years they will appear can be secured from the entomologist at the local agricultural experiment station. Control is especially needed for young trees located near

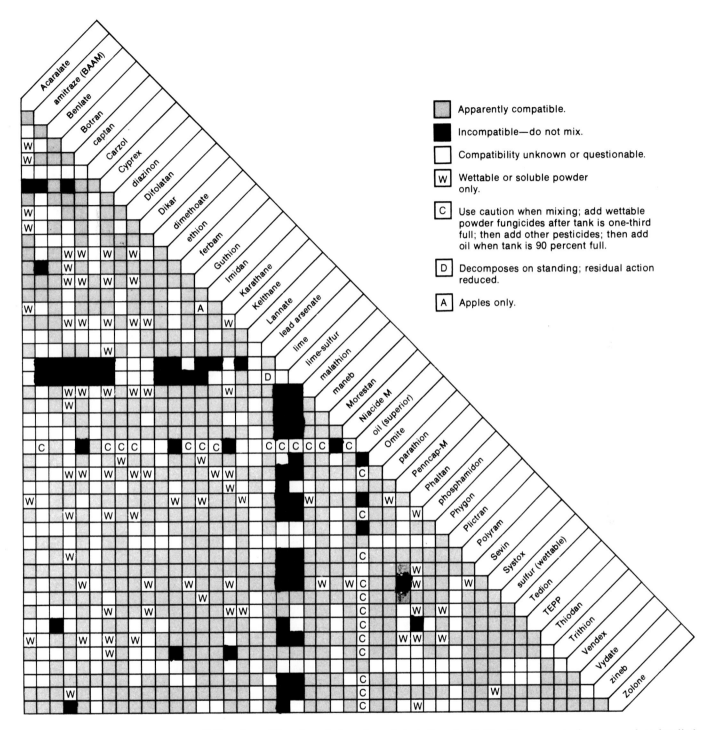

Figure 18. Tree fruit spray compatibility chart. The chart is based on data believed reliable. No warranty is expressed or implied regarding the accuracy of this information. The chart does not imply registration nor recommendations on specific tree fruits. For details, consult the container label. (Rutgers University, New Brunswick, N.J.).

old apple trees or woodlands which have maintained a heavy brood of cicadas in previous years. The insecticide Sevin has controlled the cicada satisfactorily. It has a relatively long residual effect. See adult cicada in Figure 19.

In midsummer, colonies of caterpillars, such as the red-humped apple caterpillar, yellow-necked datana, and fall webworm, may defoliate certain limbs or the entire tops of small trees. European corn borer may attack and break over the leader limb. A prompt spray with guthion or *Bacillus thuringiensis* should suffice, using low-volume spraying that dries quickly.

While any of the pesticides listed for insect and disease control on bearing trees may be used on non-bearing trees, some products are restricted to non-bearing trees only.

Bayleton 50 wp, a fungicide for the control of powdery mildew, is resticted to use on non-bearing trees only. This fungicide should be applied dilute to drip at 2 oz./100 gal. of spray. No more than 16 oz. of the product should be applied per acre per year and no trees should be treated that will bear fruit within the following 12 months. A special-local-needs registration has been granted for the use of Bayelton in Washington (Section 24 (c), FIFRA) and possibly other states.

Phosphamidon may be used only on non-bearing apple trees. This material is effective for the control of apple aphid and white apple leafhooper.

SPRAY AND WEATHER INJURY

Spray and weather injury to leaves and fruit are confused frequently. It may be necessary to examine neighboring unsprayed trees before the relative amount of spray injury can be determined on sprayed trees. Spray injury develops when improper materials have been employed (Figure 20) or when the correct materials have been applied in the wrong way, or when certain weather conditions tend to increase spray injury. Weather injury results from exposure of the fruit to extremes of temperature or moisture. Apple cultivars vary greatly in susceptibility to spray injury and diseases as shown in Table 10.

Trees low in vigor are frequently injured more by spray and weather conditions than moderately vigorous trees. Also, foliage which has been injured by insects, diseases, wind whipping, or hail is more susceptible to spray injury than healthy foliage.

Russeting and weather injury. Low temperature and frost during the blossoming period and early part of the

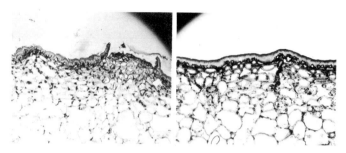

Figure 20. The cuticle or skin on the left apple has been dissolved or broken by adverse external factors; the one on the right is unharmed. Caustic spray materials can cause such damage, russeting the apple and causing it to lose water and shrivel quickly in storage. USDA.

growing season may cause varying amounts and kinds of russet injury to fruits (Figure 20). This injury usually takes the form of a belt of russet around the apple. Weather injury to the leaves is characterized by dwarfing, crimping, and when severely injured, blisters may develop on the under surfaces. Such leaves may turn yellow and drop prematurely. During extremely hot days in mid-summer, exposed fruit may show sunburning on one cheek. A discoloration of the skin is evident and in extreme cases blistering, cracking of the skin and sunken corky areas. Very hot weather may also cause a bronzing of the red color and a whitening of the green color of the fruit. Stayman cracking is worse where russeting is present.

Golden Delicious, Delicious and Jonathon are easily russeted by spray chemicals and freezing air temperatures (32° F. or lower) which occur frequently in northern areas after Pre-Pink. Following comments are from Washington State University Bulletin O-419 for their conditions. Other state bulletins may have additional local comments.

Faulty spray equipment, poor mixing and agitation, highly concentrated materials, or extremes of weather

TABLE 10A. DEGREES OF SUSCEPTIBILITY OF APPLE VARIETIES TO DISEASES AND SPRAY INJURY.

Variety	Scab	Bitter Rot	Blotch	Brooks Spot	Fire Blight	Cedar Rust	Bordeaux Russet	Lime-Sulfur Russet
Baldwin	Moderate	Moderate	Slight	Slight	Slight	Slight	Very	Very
Ben Davis	Very	Very	Moderate	Slight	Slight	Slight	Very	Very
Cortland	Very	Very	Very	Slight	Very	Moderate	Slight	Slight
Delicious[1]	Very	Moderate	Slight	Moderate	Slight	Moderate	Slight	Moderate
Duchess	Moderate	Slight	Very	Slight	Slight	Slight	Slight	Slight
Empire	Very	Moderate	Slight	Moderate	Slight	Moderate	Slight	Moderate
Golden Delicious	Slight	Very	Moderate	Very	Slight	Slight	Very	Very
Grimes	Slight	Very	Slight	Very	Very	Slight	Very	Very
Jonathan	Slight	Very	Slight	Very	Very	Moderate	Very	Moderate
McIntosh	Very	Very	Very	Slight	Slight	Slight	Slight	Moderate
N. Spy	Very	Moderate	Slight	Slight	Slight	Slight	Slight	Slight
R. I. Greening	Moderate	Very	Slight	Slight	Very	Slight	Moderate	Moderate
Rome	Very	Moderate	Moderate	Moderate	Moderate	Very	Slight	Slight
Stayman	Moderate	Moderate	Slight	Moderate	Slight	Slight	Moderate	Moderate
Wealthy	Moderate	Slight	Slight	Slight	Very	Moderate	Slight	Slight
Winter Banana	Very	Very	Slight	Slight	Slight	Moderate	Moderate	Moderate
Yellow Transparent	Moderate	Slight	Slight	Slight	Very	Slight	Slight	Slight

[1]Cultivars like Delicious, Rome, Stayman, etc., include the red sports of those varieties.

during or following spraying may lead to fruit or foliage injury. The risk of spray injury is greater when drought stress or extremely dry, cold, or hot weather exists.

Russeting of Golden Delicious or Jonathon is most often caused by cool, rainy, or humid weather in the early growing season. Russeting may be increased by pesticides or nutritional sprays if they are applied when such conditions occur or if sprays are applied at night. *Emulsifiable materials, in foliage applications, are more likely to cause injury than wettable powders.*

The following is a list of some of the common pesticides and the injury observed following their use. *Alar*—Application to pear following summer sprays of oil or fixed copper can injure foliage and fruit. *BAAM*—Emulsifiable concentrates may cause fruit injury if applied when cool, moist, or poor drying conditions exist or when night temperatures are below the dew point. *Calcium chloride, calcium nitrate*—Can russet pear fruit and cause leaf burn. *Captan*—Avoid applying during the pre-pink to petal-fall period because of danger of reduced fruit set. May cause injury to leaves and fruit when applied within 7 to 10 days after the application of oil, particularly following a frost or during slow drying conditions. *Cyprex*—May injure Golden Delicious apples when applied under slow drying conditions. *Demeton (Systox)*—The 2 pounds per gallon EC formulation has caused injury to pears and Golden Delicious apples when used in excess of ½ pint per 100 gallons of water. *Dikar*—It is not labeled for pears and may cause russeting. Dimethoate (Cygon, De-Fund)—May cause damage to apple foliage. Do not use or allow to drift on stone fruits. *Imidan*—Causes injury to cherry foliage. *Karathane*—May cause foliage burn and defoliation of apples, particularly if any extreme condition occurs during or following its use. Do not apply during periods of slow drying or extreme heat. Avoid overspraying or settling out of the chemical due to delays in spraying or poor agitation. *Do not apply if oil has been applied to the foliage* and do not apply oil within 21 days after an application of this material. *Lime-Sulfur*—May cause injury when followed by hot weather. Do not use on apricots. Drift from postharvest applications on pears may cause defoliation of adjoining apple blocks. This problem is most severe where Winesaps are adjacent to pears. *Malathion*—Emulsifiable concentrates have caused foliage injury to cherries. Technical grade malathion (Cythion) is used in ULV application, and foliage injury can result without proper nozzles. The Beecomist spinning dispenser must be used with a 20-micron sleeve to avoid damage. *Mesurol*—May cause leaf spotting and marginal burn under some conditions. *Mitac*—See BAAM.

Oil—The following conditions may cause injury: application in cool, damp, extremely dry, or windy weather; broken emulsions; applications of oil or oil-lime sulfur at the pre-pink stage; summer applications preceding or

following many organic insecticides or fungicides; and faulty application, including poor agitation and mixing. *Omite*—May cause foliage or fruit injury on apples during hot weather. May cause severe injury to pears. Do not apply Omite if oil has been applied to the foliage and do not apply oil if Omite has been applied to the foliage. *Parathion*—Causes fruit and foliage injury to McIntosh apples and under certain conditions has caused russeting of Golden Delicious. EC formulations damage Tydeman and Spartan varieties. *Perthane*—Emulsifiable concentrate formulations may cause russeting or spotting of pear fruits. *Phosphamidon*—Registered only for non-bearing apple trees. Applications on bearing trees are illegal and may cause injury. Has injured apple fruit and foliage during prolonged cool weather. May also damage foliage when trees are under moisture stress. Do not use or allow to drift on stone fruits, pears, or bearing apple trees. *Plictran*—Do not apply oil to foliage sprayed with Plictran. Do not spray Plictran on foliage within 28 days after oil has been applied. *Sevin*—If applied as a first cover spray may cause marginal foliage burning of Bartletts and usually causes fruit thinning of apples. *Suflur and Sulfur Compounds*—Sulfur should not be applied when temperatures are expected to exceed 90° F. within 24 hours of application. Do not use on apricots. Treat Delicious apples and Anjou pears only during prebloom. *Systox*—See Demeton. *Trithion*—Has caused injury to the fruit and foliage of apples when used as a cover spray. *2,4,5-TP*—Can cause injury and even the death of apple and pear shoots when applied as a concentrate. Can cause severe injury to prune trees when combined with surfactants, urea, pesticides, or nitrogen leaf sprays. *Urea*—May injure stone fruits, apples, and pears. Use only formulations with less than 2 per cent biuret. *X-77*—Can result in fruit russet on apples and pears, particularly during cool weather or slow drying conditons. *Zinc Sulfate*—Can russet apple and pear fruit and will defoliate apricots as a post-harvest spray.

Mechanical injury. Mechanical injury to the foliage and fruit results from improper use of spray equipment or guns. Injury consists of russeted fruit, dwarfed or torn leaves, and in some cases a lack of finish and quality of the fruit. Mechanical injury is caused by *(a)* poor breakup of the liquid at the nozzle *(b)* coarse particles in the spray materials, *(c)* drenching of the foliage, and operating airblast equipment too close to the trees.

Importance of lime in preventing spray injury. The main purpose of lime in summer sprays, when and where recommended, is to prevent spray injury. It also may serve as a guide to the spray operator to see where the foliage is covered thoroughly with spray materials. Freshly manufactured hydrated lime is preferred which is free from grits and is so finely divided that 99 per cent of the particles will pass through a 325-mesh sieve; all particles should pass through a 300-mesh sieve. Lime kept over 90 days in the spray shed should be added to the soil and not used for spraying purposes. A supply of specially hydrated spray lime obtained in the spring should be satisfactory throughout the season. Lime contains the nutrient calcium which is being found as a spray to control physiological diseases not previously understood, as apple bitter pit.

Effect of sprays on color, quality, and yield. Continuing research with new pesticides needs to be done by state and federal research workers on the effect of spray chemicals on blossom bud formation, set, yield and quality of fruit, since pronounced effects are found by some materials.

Garman and coworkers in Connecticut reported typical results. They drew the following conclusions: *(a)* No significant effect of the insecticides on sugars could be detected for the pesticides they tested but there was a slight trend toward increased sugars from the non-arsenicals. Some fungicides increased sugars strongly. *(b)* Total acidity appeared to be depressed slightly by arsenicals. This was more apparent from analyses of the pressed juice than of the whole apple, and was more apparent in one year than another. Some fungicides also effect acids strongly; for example, a complete schedule of *Phygon*-lead arsenate reduced acid content. Others such as lead arsenate-*Captan* gave no indication of depression; in fact, a slight increase was noted for *Captan*. *(c)* No differences could be detected in ascorbic acid content due to treatments. *(d)* Minerals were depressed by arsenical sprays. Other elements in the spray mix have not been demonstrated to have any effect. Depression of boron in particular appeared to be important from a number of standpoints. *(e)* Both insecticides and fungicides may affect the physical appearance on the apple as by russeting (arsenates, sulfur), sun scald (sulfurs), color reduction (any black spray too late in the season), and bleaching (sulfurs). Some combinations reduced yield (parathion-sulfur, lead arsenate-sulfur); others had little effect (lead arsenate-thiram, parathion-thiram) while others containing nitrogen (fermate) may increase it. *(f)* Lead arsenate has consistently affected flavor unfavorably in Baldwin and Gravenstein, but not so much in McIntosh. Very significant preferences for thiram-sprayed fruit when compared with sulfur (in combination with both lead arsenate and parathion) developed over the three-year period and were relatively consistent from year to year. *(g)* Flavor tests require careful operation and are sometimes difficult to evaluate. Complete examination of fruit, processed and unprocessed, refrigerated and fresh, is indicated. Examination for off-flavors as well as general preferences should be considered.

Air pollution damage. Damage to foliage from air pollution has been known for over 200 years. The problem became more apparent after World War II with increased and widespread industrial development and a great increase in automotive equipment on highways. Early pollution damage was believed to be limited to that caused by

sulfur dioxide, ethylene and illuminating gas. With new war industries, heretofore unknown, other pollutants were discovered, including chlorine, hydrogen flouride, ozone mixtures, titanium, and others. Some states are passing laws to enforce filtering of pollutants on smoke stacks and exhaust pipes.

Damage usually becomes apparent during seasons when the air becomes heavy, foggy and quiet, as in autumn. Heavily industrialized areas such as Los Angeles, New Jersey, and sections of the Northwest have registered complaints. Injury involves leaf speckling, marginal and interveinal scorch, premature yellowing and leaf drop, silvering, and chlorosis. Tender leaves of vegetables are affected first. There is resemblence to magnesium deficiency in some cases.

Fruit Growers must be fully cognizant of any pollutants they may be contributing to the environment in view of the public's awareness of this topic. Every effort should be made to develop a good image for the farmer.

HISTORY OF ORCHARD SPRAYING

Since the 1880's when early efforts were being made to control insects and diseases, spraying equipment has

Figure 21. This is John Bean, the man who started the present well-known spray (and fire engine) company. He is holding the sprayer he invented in 1883 and started manufacturing in 1884. (Now a division of Food Machinery Co. (FMC), Jonesboro, Arkansas).

shown tremendous improvements, particularly since the early 1940's. The late H.G. Ingerson, former official of the John Bean Division of Food Machinery Company (Jonesboro, Ark.) has covered this interesting progress in a brief history cited below.

Back in the period of commercial orchard hand spraying from 1884 (Figure 21) to 1890's, the regular spray crew included two men who alternated at pumping and holding the 10- to 14-foot long spray "rod." The spray material was usually discharged through one or two nozzles at the end of this long rod. At the end of a long hard day's work, only 1 acre of mature apple orchard had been sprayed.

Today, two men *riding* comfortably, one on a tractor and one on a supply truck, and operating "push buttons" or valves, can protect 70 plus acres of mature apple orchard or more in 10 hours.

From hand pumps, the evolution of spraying methods and equipment took a step forward when, at the turn of the century, gasoline engines were adapted to farm use. Power sprayers were shown and demonstrated in the early 1900's.

The period from 1910 to 1920 was one of rapid expansion of orchard acreage. Large individual and company-owned orchards were coming into bearing. The labor shortage of World War I called for the development of larger, faster sprayers. Pumps of 12 to 15 gallons per minute became regular equipment, with tank sizes to 300 gallons. Gasoline engines had been improved, made lighter in weight, and 6- to 10-hp sizes were available for these larger pump sizes. Using the larger of these sprayers, a two- or three-man crew protected 10 to 15 acres of mature orchard per day.

One of the most important contributions to labor saving came in 1916 with the invention of the *adjustable type spray gun* which made it possible to change the spray pattern quickly and to secure effective spray coverage at greater distances.

Even with improved spray guns, it was difficult under some wind conditions to spray the tops of large fruit trees with the sprayman on the ground. It logically developed that spray "towers" or platforms were mounted on the sprayers. These devices were usually homemade.

In the period from 1920 to 1935, pump capacities were increased to 45 gpm and tank sizes to 600 gallons. In the early 1920's crawler tractors were beginning to be used for hauling orchard sprayers, and by the late 20's wheel tractors were coming into this service.

The next step was the replacement of the sprayer engine with tractor power take-off drive under favorable operating conditions. As larger-capacity, heavy-duty pumps were available and larger tractors put into orchard use, this combination of tractor with power take-off driven sprayer became almost universal.

In the period from 1920 to 1935, with larger-capacity

pumps available and suited to pressures of 500 to 600 pounds, stationary sprayers found a place in orchards too steep or too closely planted to permit the use of portable equipment. In some of these piped orchard installations the most distant hose connection was more than a mile from the sprayer, and high pressure was required at the pump to overcome loss of pressure in the long pipe lines. (These systems have almost passed out of existence by the 1980's.)

While steel sprayer frames, axles, and wheels had been regular construction for some years, wooden spray tanks were still regular equipment until 1935. The first line of all-steel portable sprayers was offered in 1935, and within a few years steel had largely replaced all wood in sprayer construction.

With 35 gpm pump capacity and 500-gallon tank size, and a two-man spray crew, it became regular procedure to protect 20 to 30 acres of mature apple orchard in a day's work.

The period from 1935 to 1945, including the labor shortage of World War II, showed the need for still larger labor saving devices in orchard spraying. By 1947 rapid conversion began from hand directed spray guns to semi-automatic and then to entirely automatic spray devices, known as spray masts or booms.

The use of air as the carrier for spray chemicals was practiced in a limited way for many years. This was done as dusting, mist-dusting, mist-spraying, and various other combinations of application methods.

All the methods and equipment used until 1937 were dependent on relatively low volumes of air, in the range of 3000 to 8000 cubic feet per minute, usually at relatively high velocities of 100 to 150 mph at the air outlet. This combination of low volume air with high velocity had limited carrying power or penetration, and, accordingly, its use was limited to the few hours in the day or night when there was little or no wind.

Fortunately for the orchard industry, a grove caretaker in Florida, with several thousand acres of groves to be sprayed several times a season, started on a new approach to air spraying equipment. This was the use of a large volume (30,000 cfm or more) at medium velocity (90 to 100 mph). From this start in 1937 has come the almost complete changeover from hydraulic to air spraying, with a reduction of labor costs.

In reviewing the evolution of high pressure or hydraulic spraying, experienced spraymen know that as pump and nozzle capacity is increased the rate of travel of the sprayer and the "rate of work" is increased. For this reason, the grower with large acreage selects the hydraulic sprayer with large pump capacity, while the medium-acreage grower can protect his smaller acreage in the same limited time with less pump and nozzle capacity.

This same principle applies to air spraying. Air sprayers

of different air capacities are available for different acreage requirements, including air attachments for hydraulic sprayers.

After the principle of modern air spraying was proven, several so-called "air attachments" were developed for use on high pressure sprayers. These attachments served to convert a medium to large capacity high pressure sprayer into a one-man air-type sprayer. The first of these air attachments was lacking in air volume and was suited only to spraying of small trees. As larger units with more air capacity were developed and put into service, they helped to bridge the changeover from hydraulic to the present type complete air sprayer.

The completely automatic Speed Sprayer was introduced in the period from 1937 to 1945 during the acute labor shortage of World War II—first into the citrus groves of Florida, then into the apple and peach orchards of the East and Central states, and by mid-1940's into the orchards and groves of California and the Pacific Northwest. This development was the most revolutionary in spraying methods and equipment since the introduction of power sprayers.

The Speed Sprayer (generally termed "air-blast" sprayer) was unique in that it used a *large volume of medium velocity* air to carry the finely atomized spray liquid into and through the trees. The spray pattern was quickly adjustable to size and shape of trees and adequate to completely spray one side of each of two rows of trees as the sprayer was hauled between the rows at speeds to 3 mph.

While the Speed Sprayer was being developed and refined, research workers at federal and state experiment stations and in laboratories of spray chemical manufacturers were mixing and testing spray solutions in more concentrated forms than the regular "dilute" solutions used up to that time.

Sprayer manufacturers worked closely with all researchers to design and adapt sprayers to the most practical and economical application of these concentrated solutions.

Attention was then focused on the design of the air and liquid discharge sections of large volume air sprayers for greatest efficiency and economy.

After several seasons of field use with concentrations of from 2x to 10x regular dilute-strength material, the concentrations generally recommended by research and extension departments were 3x to 4x the original dilute strength. Both theory and commercial practice showed that at these concentrations, complete coverage and practical rate of travel could be combined. At higher concentrations, it was usually necessary to reduce the rate of travel to a point where maximum acreage could not be sprayed in a day.

Use of these air sprayers with air volume in excess of 50,000 cfm has made it possible for one tractor-sprayer operator to protect from 60 to 70 acres of mature apple orchard in a 10-hour day with spray material hauled to the sprayer by a supply unit, usually motor-truck mounted.

The change from hydraulic to modern air spraying with concentrate materials represents the greatest saving in orchard costs of almost any change in orchard practices during the history of the fruit industry.

The transition of large air volume sprayers has also brought several other important advantages to the commercial grower. He now is able to cover his entire acreage within the short period when insects and diseases are most effectively controlled. One large air volume sprayer usually replaces two to three hydraulic sprayers, which in turn reduces the number of tractors required and the number of year-around employees.

During the 1950's and early 1960's there was a trend toward air sprayers of still greater air volume which in turn allowed more rapid spraying with further reductions in labor costs. However, in the late 1960's and continuing into the early 1980's the trend has shifted to smaller units, smaller droplets, less volume spray per ground area and use of higher concentrations.

The newer plantings are generally on dwarf or semi-dwarfing rootstocks with smaller trees and many more trees per acre. Large pruning machines, hedgers, and toppers have been utilized to materially reduce the size of older trees and to maintain the smaller size trees. Picking labor has refused to pick tops of tall trees, or insist on higher wages making large tall trees uneconomical. Irrigation has made possible higher density plantings in many areas, too. All of these changes in cultural practices have lessened the need for larger air sprayers.

Another trend has been to use tractor power take-off (PTO) machines because of the availability of larger tractors with "live" PTO units if the grower has enough other needs for a large tractor.

In many areas the air-blast sprayers now spray 2 complete rows of trees with one pass. They drive in *every other row* of trees, alternating each spray, with satisfactory results because of smaller trees and a saving in time and labor. Also, where local water supplies permit, sprayer operators are obtaining their own water, dispensing with the portable supply units. With large wheel tractors with appropriate road gears they can make trips to water lines much faster. (Latter few updated paragraphs by a FMC representative.)

SPRAY MACHINERY AND EQUIPMENT

There are three fundamental requirements for good spray equipment: (1) obtain a complete spray coverage of the tree or plant; (2) apply the spray materials during the most effective period, and (3) obtain good coverage at the lowest cost possible. There is no set method of application and no one piece of equipment which will assure these

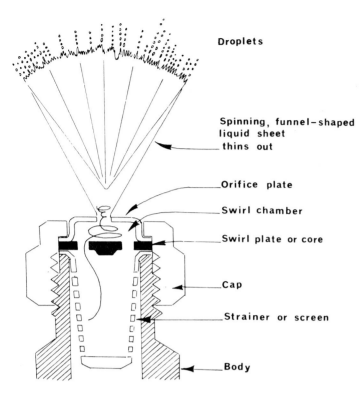

Droplets

Spinning, funnel-shaped
liquid sheet
thins out

Orifice plate

Swirl chamber

Swirl plate or core

Cap

Strainer or screen

Body

Figure 22. Cross-section of a hollow-cone nozzle (R. W. Fisher, Canada Ministry of Agriculture, Ontario).

results for all growers. A satisfactory method and piece of equipment for one set of conditions may be entirely unsatisfactory for another. To make a wise choice of equipment to suit conditions, the buyer must have a fundamental knowledge of different types of spray equipment, their advantages and limitations and know how to operate them for best insect and disease control.

BASIC MECHANICS OF SPRAYERS

Spray atomization. Sprays are formed by pumping liquid through nozzles or by shearing it with high-speed air. The droplet size varies with the pressure on the liquid, the shape of the swirl plate, the orifice size, the velocity and direction of the "carrier" airstream, and the velocity of the shearing airstream with air-shear nozzles. The following information comes from Publ. 373, Ministry of Agriculture and Food, Ontario, Canada (R.W. Fisher, et al.):

Hydraulic Pressure with Fan and Cone Nozzles. When a liquid flows through a swirl plate, the sloping holes in the plate spin the liquid rapidly as it enters the swirl chamber (Figure 22). When the spinning liquid emerges from the orifice, it forms a funnel-shaped sheet, which thins out as it widens. Instability and air resistance cause the thin sheet to break into pieces which then round up into droplets. Any interference with the smooth swirling action and uniformity of the liquid sheet, caused by worn or dirty swirl plates and orifice discs, produces an irregular droplet

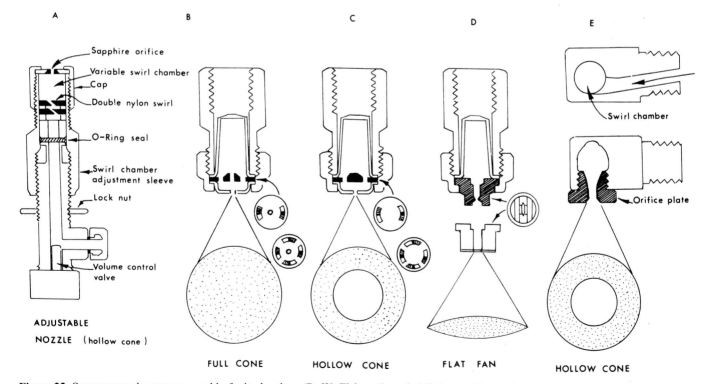

Figure 23. Sprayer nozzle patterns used in fruit plantings (R. W. Fisher, Canada Ministry of Agriculture, Ontario).

355

spectrum. Shape of swirl plate, size of disc, depth of swirl chamber, and pressure all determine the width of spray angle and the pattern (Figure 23, a, b, c, e)

A round hole makes a cylindrical stream that breaks into large droplets after traveling a long distance. A round hole plus a one-, two-, or four-hole swirl plate (Figure 23,c) or with a swirl chamber instead of a swirl plate (Figure 23, e) produces a hollow-cone spray. A center hole in the swirl plate (Figure 23, b) fills the cone and gives greater drive. In a spray gun (Figure 28) and in adjustable nozzles (Figure 23, a) the swirl plate position is adjustable, and the swirl chamber between swirl and disc can be shallow or deep. A deep swirl chamber makes a narrow spray; the shallow chamber gives a wide spray with finer droplets. Higher pressure increases output and decreases droplet size. Large discs increase output and spray width. Larger swirl open-

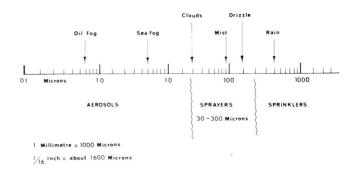

Figure 25. Diameters of some common spray droplets (R. W. Fisher, Canada Ministry of Agriculture, Ontario).

ings increase output but decrease spray width.

A lens-shaped hole (with no swirl plate) makes a flat fan spray with elliptical shape (Figure 23, d). An oval hole makes a flat fan rectangular pattern. These are fan-type nozzles.

Air-Shear Atomization. When hydraulic nozzles are placed in a sprayer airstream, additional shearing or breakup occurs, with the amount depending on the direction of the nozzles. Spraying into the airstream, makes the finest droplets; at 90° to the airstream, intermediate breakup; and along with the airstream, least breakup and largest droplets.

Some nozzles, however, use only high-speed air (no swirls or discs) to shear the liquid. Several examples are shown in Figure 24 with the air speeds required to break up the liquid.

Droplet Size—Characteristics, Collection and Measurement. Figure 25 illustrates the size ranges of some common droplets.

All orchard sprayers produce a range of droplet sizes, varying in diameter depending on gallons per minute output, nozzle sizes, pressure, and airstream velocity. Low volume sprays of 5 to 20 gallons per acre, with fine nozzles, may produce a droplet range from 5 to 300 microns; medium volumes of 50 to 75 gallons per acre, a droplet range from 5 to 500 microns; and high volumes with coarse nozzles a droplet range of 20 to 1000 microns. Air-shear sprayers which perform best at low volumes (Figure 24) are sometimes used to apply high-volume dormant sprays. However, at these volumes atomization is poor and droplet size is very large.

Large droplets are wasteful. A gallon of spray per acre in 400-micron droplets deposits 22 droplets per square inch (3.4 per square centimetre). When the diameter is halved to 200 microns, the number deposited is eight times as great, i.e. 176 per square inch. A gallon per acre in 40 micron droplets will produce 1,000 times as many droplets per square inch as a gallon in 400 micron droplets (Figure 26).

Large droplets in a spray pattern easily strike a leaf or fruit. Small droplets, however, follow the airstream around rigid targets and therefore require a high velocity

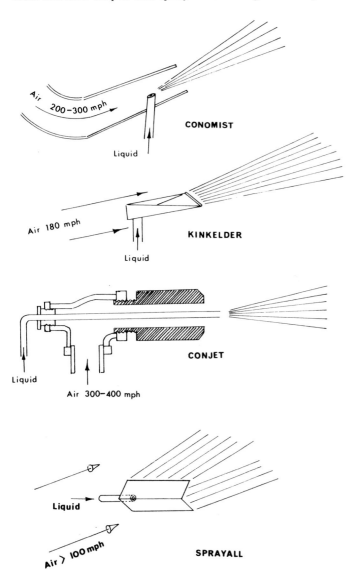

Figure 24. Air-shear nozzles (R. W. Fisher, Canada Min. of Agr., Ontario).

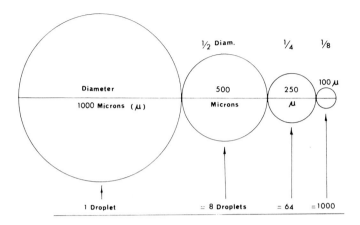

Figure 26. Relationship of size and number of droplets in spray pattern (R. W. Fisher, Canada Min. of Agr., Ontario).

to force them to travel in a straight line. Small droplets are effective at close range where air velocity is high, but in treetops where velocity is low, only a small number stick to the target.

In a sprayer survey, samples of droplets were trapped on specially treated glass slides. The size and number were recorded with an analyzing computer and the information used to establish a Mass Median Diameter (MMD). The MMD of a spray pattern is the diameter at which half the *volume* of a spray liquid is in smaller droplets and half in larger droplets. A coarse spray has a larger MMD than does a fine spray. Of the sprayers examined during the sprayer survey, only one produced a MMD below 250 microns. A badly worn nozzle gives an irregular spray with a large MMD. Figure 27 shows how a fine spray may produce 64 percent more droplets than an irregular spray, from the same volume of liquid.

Effect of Evaporation of Droplet Size and Deposit. Evaporation of droplets between sprayer and target is important in spray coverage. On a hot summer afternoon (27°C) 15 to 50 percent of water is lost in the 30-foot travel to a treetop. The loss from large droplets is not serious, but

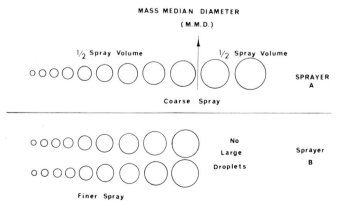

Figure 27. Comparison of droplet number and size for coarse and fine sprays (R. W. Fisher, Canada Min. of Agr., Ontario).

fine droplets may become so small that they will not stick to the foliage, and in even a light breeze of less than 5 mph, 5- to 10-micron droplets will not come down in the orchard at all. It is therefore important, especially for low volumes per acre, to spray when the humidity is high and evaporation low (Table 11). On hot dry days, the deposits in treetops might be reduced to one third due to reduction in droplet size.

TABLE 11. PERCENT EVAPORATION OF WATER FROM FINE AND COARSE SPRAYS IN DRY AND HUMID WEATHER ON A HOT SUMMER DAY (27°C).

Relative humidity	Droplet size	Distance from blower (ft.)				
		4	12	20	28	36
		Percent evaporation				
Low	250 microns	4	5	9	15	28
	125 microns	13	23	35	51	75
High	250 microns	2	2	2.5	3	5
	125 microns	3	6	10	12	

Effect of Pressure on Droplet Size. Increased pump pressure in standard swirl-type nozzles decreases the droplet size. However, to cut the diameter in half requires an increase in pressure of four times; e.g. to change droplet diameter from 400 to 200 microns, pressure must be increased from 100 to 400 psi. With air-shear nozzles, on the other hand, an increase in pressure provides more liquid to be sheared and droplet size is larger.

Nozzle Abrasion and its Effect on Spray Pattern, Output, and Droplet Size. Nozzle discs and swirl plates wear according to the abrasiveness of the spray fluid, the pump pressure, and the hardness of the material used for the nozzle components.

Soluble pesticides cause little wear by abrasion, but may cause chemical corrosion and loss of metal if nozzles are not washed after use. Wettable powders are abrasive, as well as corrosive, and cause increased wear as the concentration of the spray is increased and as pressure is increased.

Wear of disc and swirl openings distorts the spray pattern so that an excessive number of coarse and very fine droplets are produced. Also, the output increases very rapidly and can be of serious proportions when applying concentrated sprays. An increase in orifice diameter from 4/64 to 5/64 inch gives a 21 percent increase in output (Table 12). Also, wear on the inner edges of the disc hole increases output even though the diameter at the center is unchanged.

Therefore, it is important to use discs that resist this wear and remain sharp on the edges. Brass is the softest metal and must be examined for wear at short intervals. It is not suitable for concentrate spray nozzles, for dilute sprays at high pressure, or for wettable powder suspensions. Hardened stainless steel is the harder metal in

TABLE 12. INCREASE IN OUTPUT WITH SPRAYING SYSTEMS ORIFICES WHEN ABRASION INCREASES THE DIAMETER TO THE NEXT SIZE (AT 80 PSI AND WITH A NO. 25 SWIRL PLATE).

Disc size	Output (gal./min.)	Diameter (inch)	% increase
#3	.22	3/64	
#4	.33	4/64	50
#5	.40	5/64	21
#6	.52	6/64	30
#7	.61	7/64	17

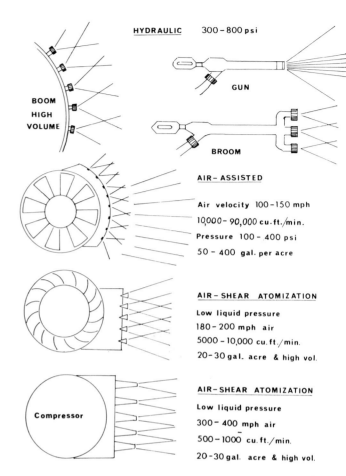

Figure 28. Types of spray atomization (R. W. Fisher, Canada Min. of Agr., Ontario).

nozzles and will last much longer than brass. It too is not suitable for *high* concentrate or high pressure.

Tungsten carbide and ceramic discs and swirls, and sapphire orifices are suitable for high-concentrate and high pressure sprayers. However, with Spraying Systems tungsten-carbide nozzles, the shape of orifice plate must be such that the swirl chamber wall is totally enclosed with tungsten-carbide. Brass disc holders and nylon spacer rings will not withstand abrasion for long.

With concentrated spray mixtures and high pressure it is very important to have a close pressure balance above and below the swirl plate. For example, use of a No. 23 swirl and a No. 6 disc causes a low pressure in the swirl chamber. The swirl then wears very quickly in the center of the top side and in the openings. Use of a No. 45 swirl and a No. 3 disc causes a higher pressure in the swirl chamber and wears the disc and the underside of the swirl plate. Any wear distorts the smooth-sheet discharge.

Sprayers with low liquid pressure and straight outlet tubes or other air-shear-type nozzles do not have wear problems when applying high-concentrate sprays. Conomist, Kiekens, Conjet, and Kinkelder sprayers, therefore, require less regular examination for abrasion, but nozzles should be checked for alignment in the air-stream.

How Sprays are Projected to the Target. Hydraulic Pressure. Spraying without an airstream to help carry the droplets to the target requires high pressure on the liquid (Figure 28). Where a gun is used, a pressure of 300 to 400 psi is adequate for trees about 12 to 15 feet high because the swirl chamber can be lengthened to give a narrow spray angle for closeup work. However, if a broom with fixed-angle nozzles is used, the pressure must be 500 to 800 psi. In addition, the swirl plate holes must be larger to give higher output with a narrow spray angle in order to get enough driving force for high targets. Higher pressure gives better breakup and smaller droplets. Where nozzles are enclosed in a hood and a strong driving force is not necessary (for vineyards and hedgerow plantings), smaller nozzles with wider angle patterns give fine droplets that fill the leaf canopy, and deposit well on all surfaces. In some *vinifera* grapes, full cone sprays are necessary for penetration of very dense foliage.

In small trees and grape rows where nozzle-to-target distance is short, low-volume hydraulic spraying within a

hood using 40 gallons per acre works effectively with little drift. Hooded air sprayers may effectively use 20 gallons per acre.

Airstream Assistance. Two schools of thought exist about what is an ideal airstream. One states that enough air volume must be used to replace all the air in the tree with spray-filled air from the sprayer. The other says that a small volume with high starting velocity fills the tree with droplets by driving a thin band of turbulent air into the canopy, or a wedge of compressed air that expands quickly, loses velocity, and deposits its load of droplets. Regardless of which idea is considered, the air is used to transport the spray droplets from the sprayer to the tree. The sprayer evaluation survey has shown that both systems give good coverage throughout the tree when used under ideal conditions.

Airstreams lose velocity very rapidly after they leave the sprayer, regardless of air volume or starting velocity. The weight of water in the airstream is very important and larger volumes give more droplets of a size that will hit the foliage at the treetops. As the air volume increases from 800 to 60,000 cubic feet per minute, the water in the airstream makes up less and less of the total weight of airstream and increasing evaporation reduces droplet size.

In Table 13 measurements have been recorded with simple wind meters on airstreams from 4 sprayers of different size, in a stationary position, and moving at 1 to 5 mph between trees and inside of an apple tree with a dense canopy.

TABLE 13. MAXIMUM VELOCITIES (MPH) OF AIRSTREAMS AT VARIOUS DISTANCES FROM THE SPRAYER BLOWER OUTLET (AVERAGE OF 4 SPRAYERS).

No. of ft. from sprayer	0	5	10	15	20	25	30
Sprayer stationary	141	46	27	17	12	9	7
Moving at							
1-1¾ mph			40	21	13	11	
2-2½ mph			40	21	10	7	
3-5 mph			27	17	5	3	

	Velocities within the tree		
Moving at	Inside the canopy	Centre bottom	Tree top
1 mph	8	12	3
2 mph	8	8	4
3 mph	5	11	0

When the sprayer is moving, the velocities are reduced rapidly as driving speed increases. Table 13 shows that at 20 feet from the sprayer, an original air blast of 141 mph reduced to 12 mph, and when the tractor moved at 3 to 5 mph in the orchard, the air blast is further reduced to 3 mph. It is obvious that better penetration can be achieved by driving slower.

Types of pumps. All spray pumps are essentially similar in basic principles with the exception of pumps used with knapsack sprayers of the compressed air and diaphragm type. Knapsack sprayers of the compressed-air type con-

tain a simple air-displacement pump inside a small cylindrical tank (Figure 29). The tank is filled about three-quarters full of spray, the lid replaced, and the air within the tank compressed with the hand pump to a pressure of 50 to 75 pounds per square inch. When the spray nozzle is opened, the air pressure forces the liquid through the nozzle. The chief disadvantage of the compressed-air knapsack sprayer is the fact that the spray pressure will decrease as the liquid level decreases and the air expands. While these sprayers are handy for home garden use and for a limited scale in weed control in orchards, they are not suitable where a uniform spraying pressure is desired.

The knapsack sprayers which have contant pressure pumps are of two types, plunger and diaphragm, both of which are of the positive-displacement type (Figure 29). These pumps are fitted with a small air-cushion chamber within the tank to maintain uniform pressure. With this type sprayer, it is not necessary for the tank to withstand any pressure because the pump may be mounted either on the inside or the outside of the tank. The tank serves only as a reservoir of spray solution for the pump. The equipment is mounted on the sprayman's back and he must pump slowly but continously while spraying. The pump maintains a more or less uniform pressure of from 50 to 75 pounds per square inch. Knapsack sprayers are suitable for low-growing crops and weed control.

The type of pump used in hydraulic power sprayers is of the displacement single-acting reciprocating type, examples of which are shown in Figure 30. They are available in a wide range of sizes and capacities with working pressures up to 1000 pounds per square inch or higher (Table 14). The capacity of these pumps depends upon: (a) the number of cylinders; (b) diameter of each

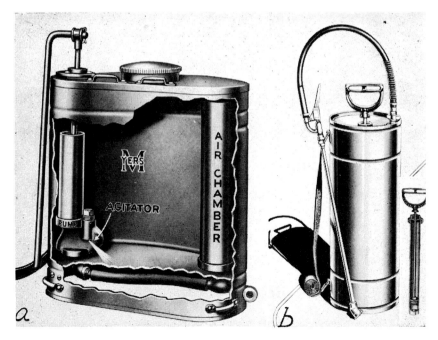

Figure 29. The knapsack sprayer (diaphragm-type) is carried on the back of the operator with straps over the shoulders. The operator pumps continuously and an air chamber provides an even flow of solution from the nozzle. (b) The compressed-air knapsack sprayer holds from two and one-half to four gallons. The tank is filled three-quarters full of solution and the air compressed to 50 to 75 pounds. It is necessary to stop spraying and pump at intervals in order to keep up pressure. Cross-cut of pump unit is shown at lower right. See Fig. 49 for motor-driven knapsack mist blowers. (F.E. Myers and Bros. Co., Ashland, Ohio).

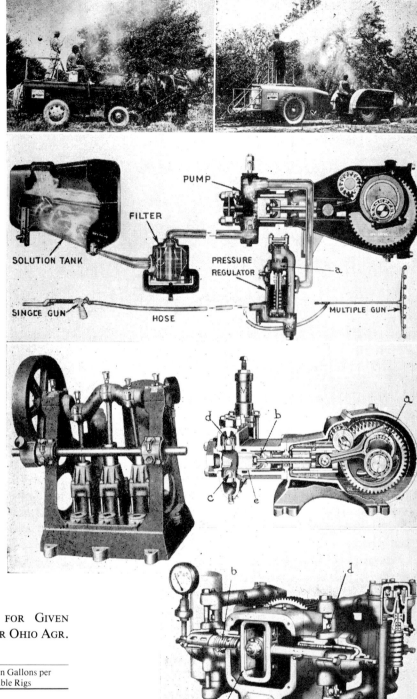

Figure 30. (Top) High-pressure pumps used in the early 1940's. Gun and multiple nozzle broom spraying by hand is still used in small plantings and some foregin countries. (Top right) Power take-off sprayer attached to tractor. (Middle) Channels through which spray solution flows from solution tank through the filter, the pump, the pressure regulator, and out through a single nozzle gun (left) or multiple nozzle broom gun (right). When nozzles are shut off, spray solution by-passes from pressure regulator back to tank (return pipe at "a" to tank not shown). (Middle left) A 3-cylinder vertical-type spray pump, showing crank shaft and connecting rods. Inlet and outlet ball valves are housed on either side of base of each cylinder. (Middle right) Horizontal-type pump with eccentric drive shown at "a". connecting-rod drive and removable rubber-fabric plunger-cap packing at "b", porcelain cylinder walls at "e", inlet valve at "c", and outlet valve at "d". (Bottom) Spray pump using Scotch-yoke drive at "a", to which horizontal opposing plungers are attached. In operation, yoke moves back and forth. At "b" the stationary outside-type packing for cylinders is shown. Spray inlet-ball valve is shown at "c" and outlet valve at "d". (Top three) FMC, Jonesboro, Arkansas. (Middle left) The Hardie Div. Lockwood Corporation, Gering, Neb. (Middle) F.E. Myers and Brothers Co., Ashland, Ohio. (Bottom) Friend Mfg. Co. Gasport, N.Y.

TABLE 14. SIZE OF PUMP TO PURCHASE FOR GIVEN QUANTITIES OF SPRAY PER APPLICATION (AFTER OHIO AGR. EXP. STA. BULL. 655). DILUTE SPRAYING

Spray Material Required for One Application	Pump Size Required in Gallons per Minute on Portable Rigs
Less than 500 gallons	Hand pumps
500 to 3000 gallons	Power pumps rated up to 10 gallons
3000 to 6000 gallons	Power pumps rated at 12–15 gallons
6000 to 10,000 gallons	Power pumps rated at 15-22 gallons
Above 10,000 gallons	Power pumps rated at 35 gallons or more according to need or air-blast sprayers

cylinder; (c) length of stroke; (d) number of strokes of plunger per unit of time; and (e) the volumetric efficiency of pump.[1] All spray rig manufacturers rate pumps accor-

ding to their maximum capacity in gallons per minute at a given pressure. With very little leakage past the valves or plunger packings, the volumetric efficiency of reciprocating-type pumps on sprayers should be 90 percent or more. Then there are the centrifical pumps under lower pressure that move larger volumes of liquid with good

[1]This is defined as the actual volume of spray discharged divided by the plunger displacement.

agitation and used in low-volume sprayers.

Valves. In small hand sprayers and dusters, the "poppet" air valve is common. It usually consists of a leather flap held in place over the hole by a small spring. Under pressure the spring gives and the valve opens, allowing air to pass one way, but not the other. In the simplest type of poppet valve on dusters, no spring is used. The flap is attached at the side of the hole, allowing the air current to pass one way.

The modern power sprayers have shifted for the most part from hardened stainless steel ball-type valves in the pressure regulator to the seating plunger-tip valves in the pressure regulator shown in Figure 31. This modern regulator is more simplified in construction and operation. The balls in ball-type valves where used (Figure 30), the plunger tips, and the valve seats are all corrosion resistant. No gaskets are used with the modern valve seat assembly which eliminates a source of leakage formerly troublesome.

Plungers. There are two types of plunger-displacement mechanisms in use in high-pressure rigs: (a) A plunger with an exanding cup fitted to the end of the plunger; thus, the cup moves with the plunger, as shown in Figure 30; and (b) a plunger which operates through a stationary packing which acts as the cylinder wall for the displacement chamber (Figure 30). Neither of these two systems is free from wear by abrasive chemicals manipulated under high pressure. On the pressure stroke, the plunger cups which are constructed of molded rubber and fabric, expand against the cylinder walls. This seals and prevents leakage past the cup. Although most cylinder walls are coated with acid-resistant porcelain, there eventually is some abrasion and wear of the cylinder walls. When this occurs even the plunger packing will not prevent leakage entirely.

Plungers which operate through packing in the walls of the cylinders are made of stainless steel, inasmuch as abrasion and erosion of the plunger must be avoided as much as possible to prevent leakage. The packing should be adjusted so that there is a very slight leakage which indicates that the packing is not so tight as to cause scoring of the plunger.

The reciprocating motion of plungers in high-pressure spray pumps can be obtained by several different mechanisms, the most common of which are (a) crank shaft and connecting rods, (b) eccentric and connecting rods, and (c) the Scotch-yoke assembly (Figure 30). The Scotch-yoke assembly has two opposing plungers, operating from one reciprocating mechanism; sprayers using this system must be either two or four cylinders. The other two systems usually involve three cylinders. It is immaterial whether the cylinders are vertical or horizontal.

The working parts of a high-pressure pump are enclosed to provide for self-oiling systems and to afford protection from dust. In purchasing this type rig, it is important to consider the ease with which the pump can be taken apart and repaired.

The pressure regulator. Perfection of the pressure regulator by the Bean Spray Pump Company in 1914 was one of the biggest advances in spray machinery. In power systems, some type of automatic by-pass is needed to divert spray solution back to the tank when the spray nozzles are shut off suddenly but the pump continues to operate. In other words, the pressure regulator serves as a safety device. It also has two other functions: (a) to maintain a uniform pressure at the spray nozzles; and (b) to permit the pump to operate at a greatly reduced load when no material is being discharged through the nozzles.

The construction of a modern widely used type pressure regulator is shown in Figure 31. When pressure builds up against the hydraulic cup, over and above the tension on the spring as determined by the pressure adjusting nut, the spring gives, lifting the seated plunger tip and allowing solution to flow back to the supply tank.

In the older type pressure regulators two stainless steel ball valves were used as diagramed in Figure 30, middle and bottom photos. When in these types, the pressure of the liquid exceeds the resistance offered by the compression spring, the spring gives and lifts a rod which in turn lifts a ball valve and permits excess liquid to by-pass under the ball and through a pipe back to the supply tank. A check valve (Figure 30) is employed between the diaphragm or plunger and the pump discharge line to assist the pressure regulator in acting as an unloading device as well as a pressure release valve. The release-valve ball and check-valve ball must fit perfectly in their seats in order that they function sensitively. If the check valve were removed from the system, the pressure regulator would then function merely as a release valve.

A spray machine is functioning properly when a little liquid is by-passing through the pressure regulator and going back to the supply tank while the spraying is in progress. If no liquid is by-passing back to the spray tank,

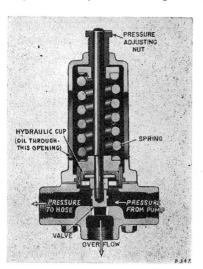

Figure 31. Modern pressure regulator for power sprayers with a rubber fabric diaphragm-type regulator; when solution pressure on diaphragm exceeds pressure desired, spring raises the valve stem which allows solution to by-pass back to spray tank. (FMC, Jonesboro, Arkansas).

361

the discharge of the spray guns is probably too great for the capacity of the spray pump, provided the pressure regulator is properly adjusted and the valves are not leaking.

Agitators. Some kind of agitation is needed in all spray tanks in order to provide a more or less uniform concentration of spray solution from the time the tank is full until empty. Agitation for hand sprayers and small power sprayers may be obtained by: (a) swishing of the solution as the operator moves, (b) small by-pass spirt of solution from pump chamber back into supply tank (Figure 29), or (c) simple paddles connected to the pump handle which swish the solution as the pump handle operates.

Agitation is usually provided in power-sprayer tanks by two or more paddles mounted on a lengthwise shaft in the tank, as shown in Figure 30. The paddles may be of the propeller or flat type. To obtain the same degree of mixing, propeller-type paddles require a greater speed of rotation than square-end flat paddles. However, for certain spray mixtures, the square-end agitators tend to whip an excess of air into the liquid when the tank is almost empty; this causes the pump to operate less efficiently toward the end of the tank supply.

The agitator shaft may be driven either by chain and sprocket, V-belt, or by gears on the spray pump. The agitator shafts are usually mounted so that the paddles sweep within one-half inch of the bottom of the tank. Some spray solutions require greater agitation than others. For example, oil sprays and especially tank-mix oil sprays require considerable agitation. On the other hand, some spray mixtures in which the suspended materials tend to separate, such as lead arsenate, oil and detergent, will require a reduced amount of agitation. It is important that obstructions, such as pipes, braces, and filler screens be reduced to a minimum because they tend to produce quiet spots and lower the efficinecy of agitation. Some larger power sprayers provide agitation by jets of spray solution which are pumped under pressure out of a pipe located near the bottom of the supply tank.

For the same amount of agitation, the circular-bottom type of solution tanks require more agitator-shaft speed and horsepower (80 and 50 per cent, respectively) than the semiflat bottom tanks.

Spray tanks. Large tank capacity can be damaging to the soil, particularly in wet orchards or those without a permanent or semi-permanent sod culture. Concentrate or semi-concentrate rates with smaller tanks are better particularly in young and high density orchards. Stainless steel is the best tank material. Fiberglass and other plastics are also good but may be more easily damaged.

Single or double plastic coating on the inside of the bigger tanks is available for protection against rust and corrosion. Flat-bottom tanks may have a slanted bottom for complete drainage at the lower side. Some steel tanks have

been known to last through more than twenty years of service.

SMALL HAND AND POWER SPRAYERS

These sprayers for fruits may be either: (a) knapsack or (b) wheelbarrow, estate or greenhouse sprayers. The knapsack sprayer has been discussed under "Type of Pumps."

Figure 32. There are several types of small estate or greenhouse sprayers on the market. This one (Peerless) is a 3-wheel type pulled by hand (some motor-driven), gasoline motor driven pump (some equipped with electric motor), with 5 gpm capacity and 50-gallon corrosion-resistant tank. a heavy-duty model is available and also 2-wheel or skid models. (Courtesy H. D. Hudson Manufacture Co., Chicago, Ill.)

Estate or greenhouse sprayer consists of a spray tank of 5- to about 50- gallon capacity, mounted on 1 or 4 wheels (Figure 32). The pump may be operated by hand or by a gasoline or electric motor. The advantages are: (a) the operator carries only a part of the load while moving the sprayer, (b) the tank is readily cleaned, (c) has efficient agitation, (d) *pressure* is fair and even, and (e) it is useful for spraying one or two fruit trees and a few grapevines and bush fruits. The sprayer has the disadvantage of accommodating only one or two acres of low plants. It is useful around the home grounds or greenhouse.

The pump is the cylinder-plunger type. When equipped with an air chamber, a continuous even supply of spray solution is provided. Steel or rubber-tired wheels are available.

LARGE PORTABLE POWER SPRAYERS

Rigs with auxiliary engines. This type of power sprayer is a complete unit with tank, pump and auxiliary engine, all mounted on a chassis and pulled by a tractor (Figure 30). With this type of equipment, the capacity and pressure of the pump are independent of ground conditions or of the type of power used for transportation. The tank,

Figure 33. Several types of air-carrier sprayers still in use by orchardists. (Upper photos) These machines are available in four sizes: (1) 95,000 CFM total air volume 5 100-120 MPH, 232 HP engine, 100 GPM pump 5 100 PSI; (2) 67,000 CFM total air 5 95 MPH, 188 engine, 100 GPM pump 5 100 PSI; (3) 52,000 CFM 5 100 MPH, 100 HP Engine, 100 GPM pump 5 75 PSI; and (4) 35,000 CFM 5 100 MPH, 70 HP engine, 25 GPM pump 5 400 PSI. The larger machines have 500 gal. tanks; smaller ones, 300-400 gal. tanks. (Mid-photos) On the left is a 500-gal. tank tender loading water through a strainer while attendant dumps in spray material. At right is shown the type of clothes and "breather" mask spraymen should use when applying highly toxic materials as parathion. (Lower photos) At left is a multiple-row nozzle air-blast sprayer applying both sides, mist concentrate and (at right) a PTO, 300-500 gal. tank inside fiberglass coated 20 gpm pump, 400 psi, 29-inch fan. (FMC, Jonesboro, Arkansas).

pump, and auxiliary engine may be mounted on a motor truck. This arrangement is preferred by operators of custom sprayers who may travel a considerable distance from one small orchard or homegrounds to another making spraying their business part of the year.

Auxiliary engines of power outfits should be capable of operating the spray pump at maximum output without being loaded to more than 75 per cent of their rated horsepower. The engine should be provided with a governor to regulate its speed according to the pump load. Water-cooled engines are employed on all sprayers except some of the smaller portable outfits. Some engines are cooled not by radiators and fans, but by pipe coils installed in the spray tank. This method is satisfactory provided the

sprayer is not operated for long periods with one tank of spray material, in which case the spray solution may be injured by the heat absorbed from the coils. There is also the additional disadvantage of the pipe coils reducing the effectiveness of agitation in the spray tank. The chief advantage of this cooling system is the fact that the pump and engine can be completely enclosed under a hood which protects them from dust and spray materials.

Speed, air-carrier, or air-blast sprayers. This type of spraying (Figure 33-42) has largely displaced other types in commercial fruit growing in North America and is gaining favor in foreign countries. It is well adapted to concentrate as well as dilute spraying. The advantages over high-pressure spraying are: (a) saves 70% labor, (b) saves

Figure 34. A modern air-drive sprayer that runs air through efficiently to reduce energy usage and distributes it evenly over the trees despite adverse wind conditions. Nozzles and internal and external deflectors are adjustable. Nozzles have ceramic whirl plates and discs that give long term uniform size droplets and will flip over to give concentrate or dilute spraying. Strainers are used throughout to prevent clogging with easy cleaning. Pumps are of advanced styling with almost a 100 yrs. experience in designing. Tanks are non-corrosive of stainless steel or fiberglass. Power is available for small or large trees. (Courtesy FMC, Jonesboro, Arkansas 72401).

30-50% time and (c) saves 20% material.

The principle is based on the use of a pump of varying sizes and styles which pumps the pesticide to a series of nozzles on a fixed boom which is located near a large fan that blows the spray mixture into the trees. The actual fans, manifolds and nozzles vary considerably from one type sprayer to another. John Bean (FMC) bases theirs on low pressure centrifugal pumps and depends on considerable air volume, often over 50,000 cubic feet per minute. Other manufacturers may use higher pressure or smaller fan outlets which produce harder air with less air volume, 10-30,000 cfm.

The large sprayers can spray out large volumes of water per hour (1,500-2,000 gph) but many of the smaller air-carrier machines cover as much or more acreage by applying more concentrated rates of water to chemical.

Air-carrier spraying has shown outstanding performance with peaches. The double head which throws from left to right, as shown in Figure 34, is preferred for low-growing trees. The equipment also can be adjusted for ground spraying for mouse control (Figure 36).

Accurate control of the air stream is provided through a

Figure 35. This PTO (power-take-off from tractor) air-drive sprayer is capable of low-gallonage applications, light-weight, with non-corrosive construction. Parts are readily available which is important when considering foreign makes vs domestic. This is a 200 gal. tank machine built for vineyards and dwarf trees but will handle trees up to 18 ft. (Friend Mfg. Co., Gasport, N.Y. 14067).

Figure 36. This air-blast sprayer can be adjusted for orchard floor coverage for mouse control. Field representatives of such spray equipment can advise on size of nozzle disks, ground speed, angle of nozzles and other adjustment. (FMC, Jonesboro, Arkansas).

system of fins or guide vanes (Figure 34). These fins can be adjusted easily and quickly from a panel to direct the air stream higher or lower, according to the shape and height of the tree and the wind condition. The amount of spray material being discharged can be regulated inasmuch as there are several nozzle pipes on each side of the delivery head. Each nozzle pipe supplies a varied number of nozzles depending upon their location in the air stream. Certain nozzle pipes are equipped with petcocks which may be turned on or off as needed. A master control gate valve is provided for instantly feeding or cutting off the material to all nozzles. Provision also is made for adjusting the number of nozzles to avoid waste of material and drenching of foliage and fruit when traveling at slow speeds. The speed usually ranges between one to four miles per hour. A computer or "slip stick" is available for adjusting the factors that govern efficiency of spraying (Figure 37). A remote control box is mounted on the tractor, providing the ignition-starter switch, engine throttle and controls for the two spray-control valves, plus engine and engine air-cleaner gauges.

The space occupied by an apple tree with a 35-foot limb spread and 20 feet high is 24,500 cubic feet. If the sprayer is moving past the tree at a rate of two miles per hour, it passes a 35-foot tree in about 12 seconds, in which time over 25,000 cu. ft. of air is discharged.[1]

Based on spraying capacity, a single unit should be able to service from 60 to 70 acres of average bearing apple trees and about double this acreage of peaches and cherries. Some growers who have only 50 to 75 acres of orchard are using air-blast sprayers because they reduce the spray

job to a minor operation and, thus, give more free time for attention to other tasks on a diversified farm. These growers apparently charge the extra initial expense of the sprayer to over-all operations, rather than to the orchard alone.

Every effort and adjustment should be made to avoid two possible disadvantages of the air-blast sprayers: (a) in the foliage sprays the top-centers of tall trees may not be sprayed thoroughly even though the spray mist may be blown high above the top, and (b) in the dormant or delayed dormant sprays the twigs and branches may not wet on all sides because each side of the tree is sprayed from a fixed position.

Power-Take-Off (PTO) Rigs. These rigs are popular where the tractor not only pulls the rig but also provides the power for the spray pump (Figure 35). The PTO connection between the tractor and sprayer has been perfected and with the current use of tractors with adequate power, the combination works well. These are increasingly popular in high density plantings where smaller tractors and sprayers can be used. A comparison of PTO and engine-driven rigs is below:

PTO	Engine-Drive
1) lower initial cost	higher initial cost
2) lower operating & maintenance	higher operating & maintaining
3) requires higher tractor H.P.	less H.P. requirement
4) less flexibility	more flexibility
5) greatly affected by terrain	not as affected by terrain
6) less soil compaction	more soil compaction
7) can operate on moist ground	limited to relatively dry ground
8) smaller, more maneuverable	larger, less maneuverable
9) more affected by wind	less affected by wind
10) generally concentrate only	dilute capabilities

Figure 37. A computer or "slip stick" has been designed to assist growers in coordinating the proper speed of machine, gallons per tree or per acre, tree spacing, and trees per acre receiving concentrate or dilute spraying. (FMC, Jonesboro, Arkansas).

---

[1]Request "Orchard and Field Crop Spray Computer" (plastic disc cards) for determining tree spacing, MPM, No. trees, time, gpt, gpm, swath width, etc. F. E. Myers, Co., Ashland, Ohio 44805.

Figure 38. Spray equipment used in Europe. (a) 24-meter wide spray boom for dwarf fruit trees, nursery row trees, or trees in beds; (b) mist blower elevated for spraying experimental trees in beds. (Courtesy E. W. M. Vorhey. Instituut Voor Tuinbouwtechniek, Wageningen, The Netherlands). Note: Fruit Machinery Co., Mercersburg, Penna., 17236, handles Holland-built sprayers in the U.S.A.; (c) Nozzle direction and cone width can be varied for row-crop strawberry spraying; and (d) mist blower for standard size trees.

Transport trucks and wheel equipment. The power take-off rigs are usually mounted on a two-wheel trailer-type chassis (Figures 30,35). With this arrangement, the tractor wheels assume a part of the load of the sprayer, and this additional weight increases traction of the tandem wheels. Double wheels, large airplane rubber tires (Figure 36), tandem wheels, or crawler-type tracks may be used. The chief advantages are that they distribute the load better on the soil surface and facilitate moving of the equipment over ridges and moist, rough ground. Crawler tracks are best used when ground conditions are frequently soft or muddy.

As stated previously, motor trucks often are used to carry sprayers where the soil terrain permits. Commercial sprayer operators sometimes use this system because sprayers can be transported between orchard units separated from each other by miles. Also, if water trucks are not used in the orchard, high-speed larger tractors can save considerable time in returning sprayers to the water supply tank for refilling.

Pneumatic rubber tires are used exclusively for spraying equipment because: (a) They increase the life of the sprayer if much traveling is required on hard-surfaced or gravel roads; (b) draft is less on loose or sandy soils; (c) on wet soils, the large-diameter tractor-type tires clean themselves and do not ball up with mud as do steel wheels; and (d) the equipment can be pulled at higher speeds either for refilling or highway transportation. The small-diameter truck or bus tires are not satisfactory under muddy orchard conditions because they tend to slide along rather than roll. In case of motor-truck outfits, the oversize balloon tires are a distinct advantage because: (a) They do not break down irrigation furrows; (b) they have better traction; and (c) they cause less packing of the soil.

The chief disadvantage of pneumatic rubber tires is the initial cost of depreciation. Some farmers have avoided the higher initial cost by purchasing used truck, airplane or bus tires which are satisfactory if muddy conditions are not a problem. Pneumatic tires installed new should last as long as tractor tires, or about seven years or longer.

Wall Sprayers and Spray Towers. A wall sprayer as shown in Figure 41 is available for hedgerow or wall-

366

Figure 39. (Left) This air sprayer has twin 36-in. fans, delivering 70,000 cfm air volume with gasoline or diesel engine. (Right) Air sprayer with one 36-inch fan, delivering 30,000 cfm air volume, PTO, corrosion-proof GlasStran parts. Designed for orchard crops. Left machine can be used on the tall pecan trees. (F. E. Myers & Bros. Co., Ashland, Ohio).

trained and mowed trees, and for vineyards. Air-blast carries the spray into the walls left and right. Or, the tops and sides of trellissed grapes can be covered. A home-made high-pressure double boom is shown in Figure 40 for hedgerow pears in California.

For tall trees as walnuts, spraying to 15 to 30 feet high may be necessary. Telescoping hydraulic towers have been used in California. With these units, the operator in the "crow's nests" can control his height by opening or closing a hydraulic valve. Some "crow's nests" have a "catwalk" which permits the spray operator to stand almost over the top center of the tree. The extremely tall "catwalk" towers which can accommodate two men and which are used for spraying walnut trees from a height of 30 feet, are mounted on special trailers with wheel treads considerably wider than used for most sprayers to give stability. Pecan and walnut trees, however, are being trained lower and older trees are mowed mechanically to lower them, so that standard sprayers with improved chemicals can handle them adequately.

SPRAY MIXING PLANTS AND REFILLING EQUIPMENT

Low-volume concentrate spraying has reduced the need for water in orchards considerably. However, there are some growers using for one reason or another a substantial supply of water in spraying commercial orchards. Considerable time may be wasted in returning to the water tower for refilling unless a modern PTO high-speed tractor combination is being utilized to refill. Timeliness of application is a prime factor in effective spraying and therefore, the time required for refilling should be reduced to an absolute minimum. The usual refilling time is about 20 minutes, but this may be reduced to three to five minutes by operating a special portable water-supply tender truck in conjunction with the spray rig. Refilling time also can be reduced by locating water tanks throughout the orchard. A common recommendation is one tank of sufficient size to accommodate each 20-acre block of the orchard. These tanks which are about 3000-gallon capacity (Figure 42) may be supplied by gravity or pressure pumping from a larger master tank, which in turn is filled by pumping from a spring or similar water supply. Discarded railroad oil tanks often are used for these water supply tanks. They are mounted on about eight-foot concrete or brick pillars. Some growers use a one-half inch layer of oil on the water surface in these tanks to prevent corrosion of the walls as the water rises and falls. It is important, however, never to drain completely a supply tank into the sprayer tank to avoid oil contamination.

The size of the storage tank needed for an orchard or a block of trees will depend upon the supply of water and upon the amount of water needed for one spray period. If the supply of water is small, a pump of small capacity should be used, and the tank should be large. If the pump must operate 24 hours a day, the tank should hold nearly one day's supply of water. If the supply is so small that the pump cannot deliver enough water in 24 hours, then the storage tank should have a capacity sufficient for two or

Figure 40. Several types of sprayers on the market. (Left) High pressure air-carrier sprayer for hedgerows and compact trees, small orchards, bush fruits, and up to 10x concentrate spraying: 20 gpm pump, 400 psi, 300 gal tank, 21'' axial fan, narrow overall width of 53½''; 1420 lbs. total. (Right) Spray mast, home-made by pear grower in Sacramento Bay area for both sides spraying of hedgerow-trained pears 16 ft. high, planted 12 x 14 ft. (left FMC, Jonesboro, Arkansas:) (Right N. F. Childers).

Figure 41. (Upper Left) Sprayer built for hedgerow or wall applications used in B.C., Canada. Also can be used in vineyards, built by Okanagan Turbomist Co., Summerland, B.C. (Courtesy A.H. Retan, Entomologist, Wash. State Univ., Pullman); (Upper right) Friend Mfg. Co., Gasport, N.Y. machine used in tall, dwarf and semi-dwarf trees and vineyards. The Air Kadet AKII is a 200 gal. PTO for dwarf trees; (Lower left) helicoper being used for cranberries and weed control, concentrate application (Bell Aircraft Corp., Buffalo, N.Y.), and (Lower right) an air-blast sprayer equipped for single-gun spraying for jobs as borer control on peach trunks. (Hardie Div., Lockwood Corp., Gary, Inc.)

more days of spraying.

The following problems are typical for calculating the size of tank, based upon water supply and water needed.

Example 1. What size tank should be installed to supply 9000 gallons of water for one spray if the water supply furnishes only 1½ gallons of water per minute?

A water supply of 1½ gallons per minute, if pumped for 24 hours, delivers 1½ gallons × 60 minutes × 24 hours, or 2160 gallons per day. For three days the pump will deliver 2160 × 3, or 6480 gallons. Since 9000 gallons are needed for one spray and the pump delivers only 6480 gallons in three days, the storage tank at a minimum should hold the

difference, 9000 − 6480, or 2520 gallons. In this case the pump is supplying less than is needed or used and a surplus must be stored. The storage tank should hold twice the amount needed, or approximately 5000 gallons.

Example 2. What size storage tank should be used to supply 9000 gallons of water for one spray if the water supply is three gallons per minute?

Three gallons × 60 minutes × 24 hours = 4320 gallons per day. In this case the pump is supplying in 24 hours a sufficient amount of water for one day's spraying, but one must have a reservoir to hold the water pumped during the night, or as a minimum one half of 4320, or approximately

Figure 42. Centrally located in orchard blocks, large water storage tanks can be used to fill rapidly the sprayer tank. Used oil storage tanks or railroad tank cars can be mounted on concrete piers. A layer of oil on top of the water reduces rusting of tank. With high-geared tractors, and concentrate PTO sprayers for compact trees, the tender to carry spray solution to sprayers in the orchard can be eliminated. (FMC, Jonesboro, Ark.).

2000 gallons. A 3000-gallon storage space should be provided.

Example 3. When the water supply is large so that a large-capacity pump can be used, the elevated storage tank

Figure 43. The home-made hooded boom, used on grapes and caneberries back in the 1940s, is in use again. It traps such insects as the leafhoppers and gets good coverage in spite of wind. It can be used on compact trees. Design and construction is in Wa. State Univ. Ext. Bull. 0638, Pullman 99164. Used with a hydraulic pressure sprayer, it can be designed to fit your conditions. (Courtesy Carl H. Shanks, Jr., Wa. State Univ. Sta., Vancouver 99665).

may be comparatively small. If a pump is used, the capacity of which is equal to the rate used for spraying, the elevated storage tank need be only twice the size of the sprayer tank and the pump may be run only during the daytime. For example, suppose that 9000 gallons are needed for one spray and that the water supply furnishes five gallons per minute. Five gallons x 60 minutes x 10 hours = 3000 gallons per day. Since this is equal to the amount needed, storage space is actually needed only for one spray tank, or 500 gallons. An 800- or 1000-gallon storage tank should be used. Of course, a larger tank may be used but it is not needed except in case of a breakdown of the water pump.

Spray out a tank immediately; chemicals left standing (while lunching) may alter effectiveness. Alkaline water source may have same effect (check pH). Insecticides usually react more than fungicides.

As stated previously, one of the methods of refilling a portable spray tank is to use a portable tender tank which is pulled alongside the sprayer and emptied into the spray tank. Transfer of spray mix may be done by a low-pressure rapid operating pump which is driven by a special one-cylinder motor or by a power take-off from the truck motor.

STATIONARY SPRAY PLANTS

The stationary spray system consists of a permanently and approximately centralized pumping and mixing plant and a connected piping system in the orchard through which the spray solution is forced. The pipelines are equipped with hydrants to which the rubber spray-hose lines are attached. A sprayperson thus can spray a block of several trees from a single hydrant. Stationary spray systems are used in steep orchards where portable equipment cannot travel. However, there are so few of the stationary systems now in use, except in some foreign countries, that the reader is referred to the 1949 edition of this text and to references for such details as layout, plans of buildings, and operation. Growers now are planting orchards on level or rolling land with good air and soil drainage that is better adapted to labor-saving modern machinery, such as air-blast sprayers and mechanical pruning and harvesting equipment.

AIRPLANE AND HELICOPTER SPRAYING

Air spraying is frequently employed in emergencies at seasons when ground conditions are too wet for operation of ground machines (Figure 44). The atomizing devices are located under each wing. A rolling cloud of atomized liquid is dispersed while the plane flies as close to the crop as possible at a speed of 90 to 115 miles per hour. The chief

Figure 44. Airplane spraying and dusting for pests and diseases is on the increase, particularly in fruit regions where land is relatively level and weather is more or less reliably good as in desert areas, although plane and helicopter pest control is now seen frequently in the humid East. Helicopter and biplane spray and dust application can be made when ground travel is too soggy in the spring as frequently happens in the Northeast U. S. and Quebec, Canada. Biplanes are better than monoplanes. Scale should be controlled by ground spraying, or, half the oil can be applied by air, half from the ground. (Michael Szkolnik, New York Agr. Exp. Sta., Geneva).

disadvantage of air spraying is that weather conditions must be more nearly perfect than for ground rigs. Furthermore, airplane spraying is limited to commercial operators, since most farmers do not own and operate their own plane. The helicopter also is well adapted for the job.

There now is considerable orchard spraying by air in Washington state. The early pear psylla sprays are applied by air in a number of orchards due to water shortages early in the season. Many late season sprays also are applied by air due to the extreme difficulty of the ground sprayer in attempting to wiggle between tree props, low-hanging limbs and bins throughout the orchard. Washington is using a number of "beecomist" ultra-low-volume (ULV) applicators for orchard spraying, using both fixed wing and helicopter aircraft.

The following materials have given satisfacotry results in New York at the rates recommended for low-volume sprays: Captan 50 or 80WP, dodine 65WP, dichlone

50WP, Dikar, Dithane M-45, Manzate D, and Polyram. All materials tested by aircraft failed to control apple powdery mildew. These include the fungicides mentioned as well as the mildewcides, sulfur and Karathane, applied with each scab spray throughout the spring and early summer.

It is suggested that application in conventional orchards be made to 1 row at a time, near treetop level. Higher flights may result in poor control. Most of the aerial application in New York State has been by fixed wing with an effective swath width of about 40 feet. Poorer control of scab has occurred where application was made to more than 1 row at a time, particularly in instances where the normal swath coverage of the aircraft was exceeded.

WEED SPRAYERS

Chemical weed control is a well established practice in orchards. Two types of herbicides are generally used, preemergence and postemergence. A preemergence herbicide is applied and controls weeds before they emerge from the ground. A postemergence herbicide is applied to the foliage of plants that are already established. A postemergence herbicide may be selective or non-selective. An example of selective herbicide is 2, 4-D, which kills broadleaf weeds, such as dandelion and dock, while leaving the grass unharmed. An example of non-selective herbicide is paraquat. Care must be taken to keep all herbicides off the foliage of tree and fruit. Shift herbicides for difficult-to-control weeds. Degradation of herbicides under trees is diagrammed in Figure 45.

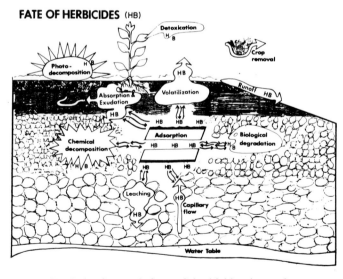

Figure 45. Behavior and fate of herbicides in environment. Degradation processes are characterized by splitting of herbicide (HB) molecule. (T.J. Monaco, No. Car. State Univ., Raleigh 27607).

370

Figure 46. Equipment for orchard and small fruits weed and ground cover control in the U. S. and Europe. (a) Hoods for herbicide strip-application between strawberry rows; cloth flaps at rear of hoods drop down to confine mist. (b, e, d) Boom weed sprayers with pump, motor and tank mounted on tractor rear. Operator can shut off spray between young trees, giving square control area around tree. (d) Young Delicious on EM VII in western Pennsylvania under a comparison of mulching and chemical weed control around trees. (e) Orchard rotary mower with adjustable working width for narrow-row plantings of dwarf plantings in Holland. (Courtesy (a, c, e, and f) E. W. M. Vorhery, Institute voor Tuinbouwtechniek, Wageningen. The Netherlands: (b) Bill Young, FMC, Jonesboro, Ark. and (d) Rutgers University).

371

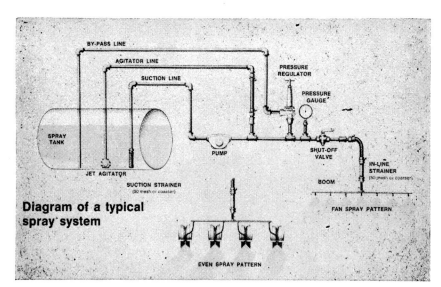

Figure 47. This diagram shows the essential parts of a weed sprayer for row crops and strip-row applications, in case a grower wishes to build his own sprayer. A solenoid shut-off valve, triggered by hand at the tractor seat, can be installed for "spot" application on either side of young trees. Cornell Idea Sheet 65 (Agr. Eng. Dept., Ithaca N. Y. 14850) will help you design applicator. (Courtesy Geigy Agricultural Chemicals, Ardsley, N. Y.).

The equipment needed for applying herbicides as sprays consists of a pump, a supply tank, and a boom having a series of nozzles which emit either a flat fan-type spray or a cone spray, all mounted on some type of chassis for transportation (Figures 46,47). Synthetic rubber parts must be installed in sprayers using oil.

On the market are sponge-roller equipment that rolls on a wide swath of herbicide lightly but heavily enough to do the job. For some low crops, the advantage is no drift, applying exactly on the designated area.

Tractor tracks or large diameter pneumatic tractor tires may be necessary for the weed sprayer to prevent bogging down during muddy weather in the spring. A track-layer chassis is more satisfactory for tanks containing more than 400 gallons.

The triplex reciprocating orchard spray pump can be used for weed sprayer. However, a high pressure orchard spray pump is not necessary, inasmuch as only 75 pounds per square inch pressure is needed. Rotary pumps may be satisfactory for nonabrasive materials, but they may wear rapidly if abrasive materials are used. They can be run from the fan belt of automobile trucks or pickup trucks. The tank with boom also may be mounted on the truck.

Special acid-resistant centrifugal pumps are available on the market for applying dilute sulfuric acid sprays.[1] Cost of these sprayers may be high due to special construction materials. The ordinary cast iron pumps are satisfactory for noncorrosive liquids. A single-stage centrifugal pump is satisfactory, provided its speed is between 2400 and 3600 r.p.m. in order to develop sufficient pressure. About three-fourths to one gallon of spray material will be required per

minute per foot of boom used. The length and design of the boom will need to be governed by the crop sprayed.

The better booms have been constructed of one and one-quarter-inch extra heavy pipe. The pipe should be brass for acid sprays and of black iron for noncorrosive sprays. Booms often consist of three sections: one section extending out from each side of the sprayer and one middle section mounted either in the rear or the front of the machine. The sections which extend to the side of the rig must be supported both vertically and horizontally in order to prevent whipping, and they must be arranged so that they can be folded forward while passing through a gate or a narrow pass. The mounting of the boom should be made adjustable for height. Under trees, it may be necessary to spray within a few inches of the ground.

Nozzles which give a flat fan-shape spray are available on the market. They may be attached to the boom by means of quarter-inch short nipples tapped into the one and one-quarter-inch main pipe. Nozzles that deliver spray at an included angle of 60° should be spaced one foot apart; 80°, 18 inches apart; 90°, two feet apart. The wide spacing of nozzles is more desirable because the cost is then smaller and larger orifices in the disks tend to reduce the danger of clogging. Figure 48 should be of assistance in selection of nozzles for a given boom and of different field speeds for various quantities of spray materials per acre. Figures in this chart are based on a nozzle spacing of one foot. For 18-inch spacing, multiply the discharge per nozzle by 1.5; for two-foot spacing, multiply by 2.0.

It is important to calibrate the boom before taking it into the field. This can be done by placing a trough or small containers under the nozzles and calculating the total discharge per minute. Discharge can be varied somewhat by adjusting the pressure. Nozzle disks of several sizes are available.

Under some conditions, growers are switching from her-

[1]Manufacturers and distributors of sprayers for weed killing include: FMC, Jonesboro, Arkansas; Friend Mfg. Co., Gasport, N. Y.; 14067; F. E. Myers & Bros. Co., Ashland, Ohio, 44805; Skibbie Mfg. Co., Sodus, Michigan 49126; California Heater Co., 1511 W. Second St., Pomona, Calif., 91766. To construct your own weed sprayer, contact your county extension agent or your local agricultural experiment station (see Fig. 47).

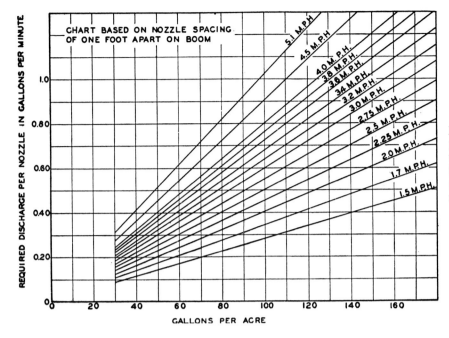

CHART BASED ON NOZZLE SPACING OF ONE FOOT APART ON BOOM

Figure 48. A chart showing required discharge per nozzle in a boom to give quantity per acre at various field speeds. If nozzles are spaced 18 inches apart on the boom, multiply the indicated discharge per nozzle by 1.5; if spacing is 2 feet, multiply by 20. (FMC, Jonesboro, Arkansas.).

bicides to speciality mowers and shallow rotovators, due to increasing costs, the need for some soil stirring and unknown accumulative effects of herbicides (Figure 45).

DUSTING MACHINERY AND EQUIPMENT

Commercial orchard dusting and even small garden dusters have gradually given way to spraying. The changeover has been due to drift problems and to EPA and state regulations for commercial operators. The small liquid hand bombs have displaced the small dusters for garden use. If reader would like to review dusting machinery and techniques as used before the 1970s, discussions can be found in previous editions of this book.

Figure 49. This mist blower is used in the U. S. and Europe in the smaller plantings, greenhouses, etc. Several models are available. Specifications for one model are: 5 H.P. engine: fuel, 1 qt/hr; weight, 25 lbs; horizontal spray to 35 ft. vertical to 25 ft; spray tank, 3 gals: fuel tank, 3½ pts. The Junior 410 model is on the left. (Courtesy Solo Industries, Inc., 5100 Chestnut Ave., Newport News, Va., 23605.)

APPLICATION OF PESTICIDES

Applying spray. The most important factor in efficient spraying is the sprayman himself. He must start each application on time, finish on time, and use the equipment and methods skillfully so that every tree is sprayed thoroughly inside and out, top to bottom, with finely-broken spray fog or mist applied in such a way as to give safe uniform coverage. There is no substitute for a skillful, alert thorough-working spraymen.

It is relatively easy to do a good spray job on small trees, but as the trees reach 12-15 feet, the tops and especially the top centers become increasingly difficult to cover thoroughly. Scabby, wormy, scaley or mite affected fruit at the end of the season often tell the story of poor spraying in this section of the trees.

Most spraying failure can be attributed to too much speed and "skimpy coverage." After what appears to be a thorough spray application, the top of the tree often carries one-third less chemicals than the bottom. The top third, or "pest nest," must receive special attention (Figure 50). As shown in Figure 17, apples may double their surface area a week or two soon after fruit set. Some cultivars increase rapidly in size early in the season, such as Delicious, Rome, and Rhode Island Greening and may need somewhat more frequent coverage than cultivars that grow more slowly at this period.

Timely, speedy applications, based on monitoring, are needed in early season scab sprays to cover the upper surfaces of the expanding leaves and blossoms. It is especially important to cover all sides of the apples for controlling such pests as codling moth, bitter rot, Brook's fruit spot and blotch.

373

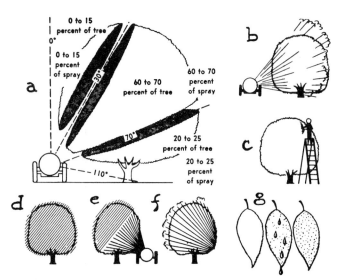

Large trees with bushy interiors and branches hanging to the ground cannot be covered by any practical method of spraying. It is highly important that the pruning program be co-ordinated with the spray program to lower tops of tall trees, eliminate underhanging branches, thin out dense areas and open spray channels (Figure 51) to permit thorough penetration of sprays. This is especially important where blast sprays are used which apply spray while moving.

A good method for the grower or students to study spray coverage is to use sensitized paper on poles in different parts of typical trees. This method can also be used to check on the efficiency of different types of spray equipment.

Although a better job can be done by spraying with the wind, many difficulties may be encountered when growers insist on spraying with the wind (Figure 52). Often the orchard is not completely sprayed within the necessary time interval for best pest control. With some sprayers, it may be possible to develop a technique of spraying at an angle into the wind and securing adequate coverage without wasting material.

Northwest growers generally are urged NOT to spray during windy periods. They are urged instead to put lights on the equipment and spray during the night when calmer weather hopefully will prevail.

Figure 50. In order to spray a tree effectively the nozzles and nozzle sizes on an air-blast sprayer should be located about as shown at "a" on the upper left; slight variations in this pattern will be needed to conform with individual orchard conditions. At "d" is a tree with the contained air all quiet. At "e" the air sprayer is moving too fast; this is about as far as the mist may carry. At "f", nozzle sizes, distribution of nozzles and sprayer speed are about right for thorough penetration of the entire tree; good penetration is shown at "b" also. At "c" it is well to check a few trees in tops and on all sides to be sure coverage is adequate. At "g" the right leaf is sprayed correctly; the middle leaf is over-sprayed and dripping, wasting material, time and money. (FMC, Jonesboro, Arkansas).

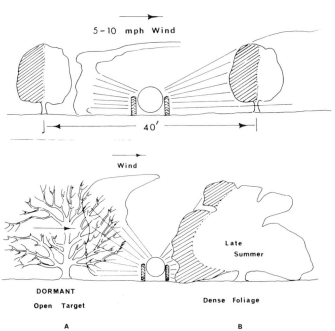

Figure 52. Wind can cause spray problems. Note at upper left that only half the tree was sprayed due to wind for small standard trees on wide spacing. Note at A below the wind has stopped the spray before it gets half way through the tree. On the right at B, the dense outer canopy catches most of the spray and leaves the tree interior poorly covered. Often it is better to put lights on the equipment and spray after dark with little or no wind. (R. W. Fisher et al., Res. Sta., Vineland, Ontario).

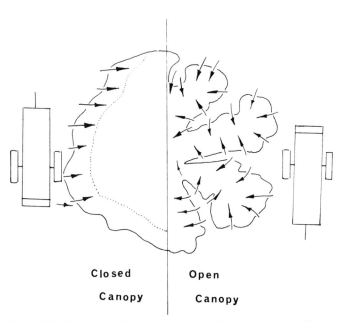

Figure 51. Top view of tree canopy showing spray penetration, poorly at left; well distributed at right. For best penetration, channels should be opened in the tree by pruning, which also admits more light for better quality and coloring of the fruit. (R. W. Fisher et al., Res. Sta., Vineland, Ontario).

374

Suggestions for air-blast spraying. Since air-blast spraying essentially uses air to give spray-mist coverage, it is important, according to the manufacturers, for air in a tree to be replaced completely with spray-carrying air from the machine. Another opinion is that a small volume of air with a high starting velocity fills the tree with droplets by driving a thin band of turbulent air into the canopy, or a wedge of compressed air that expands quickly, loses velocity, and deposits its load of droplets. Regardless of which idea is used, air is used to transport the spray droplets from the sprayer to the tree. Surveys have shown that both systems give good coverage throughout the tree when used under ideal conditions. Airstreams lose velocity very rapidly after they leave the sprayer, regardless of air volume or starting velocity. The weight of water in the airstream is very important and larger volumes give more droplets of a size that will hit the foliage at the treetops. As the air volume increases from 800 to 60,000 cfm, the water in the airstream makes up less and less of the total weight of the airstream with increasing evaporation reducing droplet size.

If a sprayer is moved past the tree too fast, the tree will NOT be filled with spray mist; conversely, if the sprayer moves too slowly, the trees are over-soaked, they drip, and expensive material is wasted (Figure 50).

The air pattern achieved by a machine forms the spray pattern and determines the sprayer performance. In order to control 30,000 to 60,000 cu. ft. of air per minute at 100 miles per hour, it is essential to gain control of the air while it is still in the machine. Every engineering feat must be employed to guide the air through the sprayer smoothly. Turbulent, uncontrolled air wastes fuel and increases engine wear because the air "fights" to leave the sprayer. Whirling and rolling air currents after leaving the sprayer are without control and may miss parts of the tree; also, such air does not travel as far as straight-flowing air.

For good movement of air through a large air-blast sprayer, the air should enter a more or less bell-shaped opening, but all manufacturers are not in agreement, and there are different configurations. The fan should push the air in as straight a line as possible, thus keeping control while it packs and accelerates the air. The U.S. Air Force uses the axial fans and flow principle in its jet engines because it moves the most air for its size.

Any sharp entrance corner in the sprayer is likely to start loss of control of the air, and also reduces the amount of air entering the blower. A centrifugal type fan is probably not the best type because it whorls the air off the blade tips, starting a boiling action like that in a clothes washing machine.

An air-straightening tunnel is used in some sprayer types after the fan to gain control of the air and prevent it from leaping, twirling and fighting itself. As the air is discharged, it is turned by curved metal. Air hurled against a flat

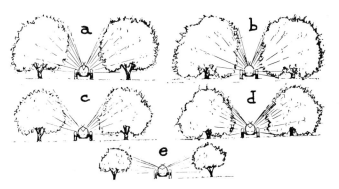

Figure 53. Diagrams show how an air-carrier sprayer is adjusted for different sizes and pruned trees. At "a" with 25-ft. tall high pruned lower limbs, top nozzle petcocks are open, external vanes raised, internal upper deflectors raised, internal lower diverters raised slightly, bottom nozzle petcocks closed (see also Figure 34). At "b", for 25-ft. tall trees with unpruned lower branches, top nozzles are open, external vanes raised, internal upper deflectors raised, internal diverters lowered, bottom nozzle petcocks open. At "c" and "d" for 15- to 20- ft. trees, the 4 top petcocks are closed; at "c" the external vanes are partially lowered, internal upper deflectors partially lowered, internal lower diverters raised slightly, and bottom nozzle petcocks closed; while at "d" the external vanes are raised slightly, internal upper deflectors raised about 45°, internal diverters about horizontal, and bottom nozzle petcocks open. At "e" for dwarf, young, or low-growing trees, the top nozzle petcocks are closed, external vanes aimed at tree tops, internal upper deflectors lowered, internal lower diverters about horizontal, with bottom nozzle petcocks closed. (FMC, Jonesboro, Arkansas).

surface, sharp corner, or against another air stream before leaving a sprayer is splintered and may go out of control.

The larger the droplet size the more the cfm of air needed to carry the droplets to the target. High volumes of air over 50,000 cfm with air velocities over 100-120 cfm are likely to cause damage to fruit and tree. The smaller the droplets the less cfm required of air needed to deliver the droplets; thus, air velocities up to 220 cfm can be used without damage. Velocity of air without large air volume does little or no physical damage.

The largest portion of the spray material should reach the "10 o'clock to 2 o'clock" shoulders of the spray pattern (Figures 53 and 54). Up to 70% of the tree's bulk is in these shoulders. With this sharp spray pattern, the sprayer does not work as hard in reaching all parts of the tree, thus saving gas, oil, and wear and tear.

Alternate Middle Spraying is particularly adapted to cover sprays on high-density apple plantings, but can be used on all tree fruits. This method gives good control of codling moth and apple aphis if sprays are well timed and spray equipment is operating properly. The first cover spray is applied at every other middle; the second spray is applied at alternate middles to provide complete coverage after two applications. Spray all borders at each application to lessen chances of pest entry from outside sources.

The spray strength used is the same as recommended for conventional sprays. As a result, when alternate middles are sprayed only half the normal rate is applied per acre, giving a 50 per cent saving in spray material and a 50 per cent reduction in application time. In addition, there is an increased survival of beneficial species.

Sometimes it is desirable to spray alternate middles, but spray more often than on a normal schedule. In blocks with overtree sprinklers, a normal schedule may leave gaps because of the removal of deposits during irrigation. three alternate middle sprays (½ sprays) at 14-day intervals will provide better coverage over time than two whole sprays at 21-day intervals. The alternate middle sprays will still save money and time.

More frequent alternate middle sprays also may be desirable when pest numbers (particularly codling moth) are very high.

Alternate middle sprays are not recommended for orchards where pests that require complete coverage for control (San Jose scale, mites, pear psylla, etc.) are present. This spray method may not be satisfactory in orchards where trees are large and coverage is difficult.

Electrostatic Spraying. This system of applying spray chemicals is not new and is being used by a few growers. It may increase in popularity. As the spray liquid is broken into droplets by vacuum jet nozzles, each particle is negatively charged by a special plate. This is an induced charge. Little or no extra power or fuel is needed. The charged particles are driven by high velocity air blast toward the tree which draws an equal and opposite charge from the earth, strongly attracting the spray. Thus, the spray is literally pulled toward surfaces of the tree or vine and thoroughly covers them. Advantages are: A more even spray covering, better chemical adherence, less drifting, no dripping and less wastage, with a better coating on the underside of the leaves as well as the tops. Good coverage has been gotten at 7 mph, at faster speeds than normal.

SELECTING AN AIRBLAST SPRAYER

For the experienced grower, selecting a new sprayer should not be any hardship because of his knowledge of his former machine's shortcomings, but for a new grower the choice is not as easy. The sprayer must have the capacity to spray the largest trees in the orchard or the projected size for the next 10 years. Though the current trend is toward size-controlled trees, the established plantings of mature standard trees in most orchards prescribe that the sprayer have the capacity to spray the largest trees and the versatility to spray small trees. It must be kept in mind, however, that high trees may be sprayed with smaller machines travelling more slowly or when the wind is low.

The determining factor is the ability of the sprayer to maintain uniform spray coverage on the large trees during

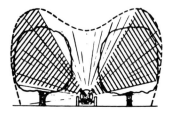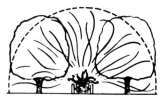

Figure 54. Spray pattern for large standard trees on the left is giving good efficient coverage; note the shoulder areas where volume and velocity are needed. Spray pattern on the right is not fitting the need. Bottom ⅓ of air is poorly directed. Because the shoulder area is not reinforced with air from the lower portion of the sprayer, part of the tree is not sprayed thoroughly, and some parts are over-sprayed. (FMC, Jonesboro, Arkansas).

the entire season. With the changing shape of the tree and the increasing density of the foliage, the spray coverage normally declines as the growing season progresses. Hence, the best time to assess sprayers is in late summer.

As a general rule on sprayer efficiency, it is possible for any sprayer to do a satisfactory job of application if properly matched to tree size, spacing, and pruning, land condition and acreage, and regional weather conditions. The time required to spray an orchard is an important consideration in sprayer selection, particularly when threat of crop loss occurs. This happens more frequently with disease than with insects because of the rapidity with which a disease can spread.

The diseases of most stone-fruit trees are controlled with protective fungicides, but even with these crops time may be of the essence when sprays are required before a rain. For apples, the timing of treatment is most important if disease infection has occurred; eradicant fungicides must be applied within a specified period to inactivate the fungus. Some orchardists overcome this problem by spraying a portion of the orchard when a rainfall is predicted. Others depend on aircraft applications where such service is available. See previous discussion on sprayer calibration to determine the size of sprayer for your need.

Further savings in time and therefore in sprayer size and cost may be obtained by (1) shortening of the travel route, (2) installation of a rapid-fill overhead water source, (3) use of a nurse tank, and (4) use of additional operators. No significant time saving is realized by spraying more than 5 to 6 acres per tank.

The sprayer must be able to combat the prevailing winds. For various reasons, certain orchards have more winds than others and this is an important consideration in sprayer selection. In general, the high horse-power airblasts are able to combat wind better than low-volume airblast sprayers (Figure 55). However, some operators successfully use low-volume sprayers by spraying at night or after the wind has dropped. Because wind affects spray coverage, particularly on large trees or small trees widely spaced, the following characteristics should be noted:

1. The combination of air velocity and air volume should be sufficient to cause air turbulence in the upper center part of the tree. (Air-shear sprayers have higher velocities to atomize the spray.)

2. Guide vanes must be adjustable to direct the airflow.

3. Models with moveable air outlets should be adjustable to direct both airstreams to one side to counteract wind, even though driving time is doubled. It may be necessary to drive closer to the windward row with all sprayers.

The sprayer should be easy to repair and maintain. Machine breakdown is common and has led to lack of control in some orchards. For this reason, sprayer parts and qualified mechanics should be readliy available. Keep in mind that time is limited after infection has occurred and actual spraying time may be very short for some of the critical sprays.

The sprayer should be suitable for other jobs. While the majority of growers use the sprayer only on fruit trees, others use it for additional crops. Be sure to try the optional attachments for each model to see if they are suitable.

While the above information will help a grower select a suitable sprayer, surveys have shown that other factors are very important, such as orchard site, soil type, underdrainage, pruning practices, availability of reliable help, rates of materials needed, and timing of applications.

COMMENTS ON LOW-VOLUME CONCENTRATE SPRAYING[1]

Author's Note. The following comments from a field consultant, formerly a grower and college graduate in engineering, may help clarify some points on LV spraying.

The word, "Concentrate," has been used freely in describing "low-volume" (LV) application of pesticides. Actually, it is referring to the fact that much greater concentrations of chemical are being mixed in the spray tank with the accompanying need of caution in the handling of these solutions. It becomes increasingly important (a) to respect the different chemicals, (b) to read the label on the chemical package and never to exceed the manufacturer's recommended dosage, (c) to clean the spray system carefully following usage, (d) to be aware of where the flushed drainage is going, and at all times (e) to treat the concentrate solution in the tank with respect. However, the application is truly a Low-Volume or "LV" delivery system and this is the terminology used today. It is

[1]Prepared with the advisement of Mr. William G. Doe, President, Doe Ag. Sales, Harvard, Massachusetts 01451, and Dr. A. H. Retan, Entomologist, Wash. State Univ., Pullman 99164.

Figure 55. This sprayer has the capacity and power to reach the taller trees as pecans and walnuts as a concentrate or dilute mix. It delivers spray at 100 gpm/200 psi. (FMC style 757CP,957CP, Jonesboro, Ark. 72401).

low volume because greatly reduced volumes of spray are used per acre to get the same disease and insect control. Where we have been saying 300 to 500 gallons per acre (gpa) to obtain control in commercial apple orchards on a dilute basis or lx concentration (with reductions of 100 to 150 gals/A in peaches and other smaller growing plants) and 100 to 150 gallons per acre at 3x and 4x with speed-sprayers at semi-dilute, we now are suddenly talking 15 to 25 gallons/A LV depending on tree size and density of planting. It is easy to understand why low-volume is more descriptive of the technique and implies many of the advantages of this method such as: (a) less water required per acre, (b) less weight in size and weight of equipment as there is less need to have so large a sprayer tank, (c) less chemical required per acre, as run-off or drip is practically eliminated, (d) less fuel per acre to operate, (e) less maintenance and running costs, (f) less labor required, (g) less time required per acre which gives greater flexibility in selecting the best time of application, and (h) reduction of chances of spray injury. This is due to the small particles

TABLE 15. RATES TO APPLY CONCENTRATES BASED ON GALLONS OF DILUTED SPRAY NORMALLY USED (AFTER LA PLANTE)

	Dilute materials		Concentrate material		
Concentration of materials (times)	1X	2X	4X	6X	8X
Rates of application	1	1/2	1/5	1/8	1/10
Gallons to tree	5	2 1/2	1	5/8	1/2
	10	5	2	1 1/4	1
	15	7 1/2	3	1 7/8	1 1/2
	20	10	4	2 1/2	2
	25	12 1/2	5	3 1/8	2 1/2

377

Figure 56. In the Okanagan Valley of British Columbia the orchardists are demanding relatively lightweight inexpensive but efficient mist sprayers that are easily maneuvered through their low acreage mostly hilly orchards, where formerly stationary spray equipment was used. (Upper left) McIntosh sprayed with a surfactant. Right apple, no surfactant. (Upper right) Very small power take-off rig, 100 Imp. gal. steel tank, spraying 2 acres at a filling, and costing much less than a turbo-mist sprayer with an auxiliary engine. (Mid photos) Left machine is a low-volume PTO mist blower, sprays two sides, of European design (The Fruit Machinery Co., Mercersburg, Pa., dealer). Right machine is a 50-gpm Victair low-volume sprayer, PTO, 2-sides (or all nozzles adjustable to one-side spray), 150 mph air velocity, steel tank, diaphragm pump 100-400 psi, 4A filling, squirrel cage blower, made in British Columbia. (Lower photo) Left machine is a one-side concentrate sprayer applying 50 gals. per acre. Right photo shows a spray-frame used in assessing orchard sprayers to eliminate inefficient types. Targets are distributed on the rack; dyed water is sprayed at them under different wind and weather conditions. (James Marshall, Summerland, B. C.; (middle left) E. W. M. Vorhey, Wageningen, The Netherlands).

drying faster and the chemical liquid does not float to the margins of leaves and tips of fruit accumulating to the point where it causes burning.

What Size LV Unit? As in the case of air-blast sprayer and for that matter all spraying equipment, proper sizing of units to the job at hand is equally important with LV sprayers. Early attempts to design these sprayers did not consider the importance of the relationship between droplet size, air velocity and air volume. While these factors may vary some with size of tree to be sprayed, it is generally agreed that a droplet size of 50 to 75 microns is desirable, with air velocity of 180 to 210 miles per hour, coupled with a volume air movement of 20,000 to 30,000 cubic feet per minute. This uniformly small droplet is accomplished by using (a) venturi type nozzle where the

chemical is actually sucked from a metering manifold by vacuum and then sheared off by the high-air velocity along a shear edge. Because of this action, a simple centrifugal volume pump is all that is needed to supply both the pressure needed to maintain chemical solution at the metering manifold and to give good hydraulic agitation. (b) The Beko ultra-low volume mist nozzle developed by Dr. A.J. Howitt of Michigan State University is a well designed nozzle for making uniformly tiny droplets. This principle uses two counter revolving fine-meshed cones to shear off the small droplets. It obviously is more sophisticated with related service and maintenance problems. The third method (c) is to increase pressure to 400 or even 600 pounds per square inch on conventional airblast (speedsprayers) type sprayers and reduce the

378

TABLE 16. RELATIVE GALLON-PER-MINUTE CAPACITY OF DISC-TYPE HOLLOW-CONE NOZZLES AT DIFFERENT PRESSURES. NOZZLES WITH TUNGSTEN CARBIDE ORIFICES AND CORES ARE RECOMMENDED, AS IS 100-120 PSI.

Nozzle orifice no.	Core no.	PSI (lbs./square inch) and GPM (gal.-min.) nozzle cap.*									
		70	80	90	100	110	120	130	140	150	200
2	24				.20						
	25	.21	.22	.24	.25	.26	.27	.27	.28	.29	.34
3	24				.22						
	25	.25	.26	.28	.29	.30	.31	.32	.33	.35	.40
4	24				.32						
	25	.38	.40	.42	.45	.47	.49	.51	.53	.54	.62
5	24				.42						
	25	.45	.48	.51	.54	.56	.58	.60	.62	.65	.75
6	24				.50						
	25	.58	.62	.66	.70	.73	.76	.79	.82	.85	.97
7	24				.57						
	25	.68	.73	.77	.81	.84	.88	.91	.95	.98	1.18
8	24				.70						
	25	.82	.89	.93	.97	1.02	1.06	1.11	1.15	1.19	1.36

*Pressures less than 80 psi may not give satisfactory control, and those above 200 psi may cause additional nozzle wear and undesirable fogging of spray.

orifice size in the disc nozzle. This is satisfactory for making droplets of around 100 microns, VMD[1], but does increase the operational problems of plugged nozzles and variance of calibration from week to week due to wear of the nozzle orifices. Tungsten carbide (TC) and ceramic nozzles reduce the wear factor, but the problem remains along with the plugging. Also, as the VMD increases (working toward larger droplets), so should the gallons applied per acre increase to insure good coverage.

Fighting Wind. Many critics of LV sprayers contend they cannot fight adverse winds and that there may be control problems in the tops (pest nest) of big trees. This is hardly true. To contend with winds the sprayer must be adjusted and operated properly or spraying done at night or early morning. Kenetic energy (energy resulting from motion) is that used to project spray droplets and is determined by mass of the droplet times the velocity squared. Consequently, with the appreciably higher air velocity there is adequate energy to propel the smaller droplets of LV

[1]VMD is the "Volume Median Diameter" referring to the micron size of the spray droplets. VMD is the micron size of droplets at the point where two collecting containers are equally full from a sampling of a spray pattern, the one (a) being filled with the largest droplets working toward the smallest droplets and the other (b) starting with the smallest and working toward the largest.

TABLE 17. CHARACTERISTICS OF CONCENTRATE MACHINES

Type of sprayer	Power source	Initial cost	Operating cost	Tractor H.P. rqmt.	Tank	Air volume cu. ft./min.	Effect of wind	Weight lb.	Speed A/day
Dilute-conv. to conc.	Engine	High	High	—	Mild steel or stainless	20,000 to 50,000	Low	3,000 to 4,000	Mod
Conc.-conventional equipment	Engine	Variable	Medium	—	Mild steel	20,000 to 40,000	Mod	1,500 to 3,000	High
	PTO	Low	Low	40-50	Stainless steel optional	20,000 to 40,000	Mod	1,500 to 2,000	Mod-High
Conc.-conc. equip.	Engine	Variable	Low to medium	—	Usually stainless steel	8,500 to 30,000	Variable	1,400 to 4,000	High
	PTO	Low	Low	35-40	or optional galvanized iron	8,500 to 17,000	High	1,200 to 1,600	Mod-High
Conc.-air shear	PTO	Low	Low	35-50	Mild steel galvanized or stainless steel		High	1,500 to 1,750	

Figure 57. (Left) A 3-point PTO hitch mounted air sprayer, two sizes, requiring 25 and 35 HP, developing respective volume and velocity. Shown is the 35HP unit, 100 gal tank, stainless stell, 10 gpm at 500 psi, weighing 800 lbs. (Right) Dual (2-disk) nozzles head for quick switching form one pre-set application rate (e.g., dilute) to another rate (concentrate) by rotating nozzle head 180 degrees. (FMC, Jonesboro, Ar. 72401).

sprayers. However, with reduced volume of air the spray pattern is more easily bent. This, while a factor, becomes of lesser importance because with air velocities of about 200 mph and droplets of 50 microns, the axial air flow of the spray pattern bending and travelling down wind accomplishes adequate coverage. Care must be taken to be extra cautious on the outside rows of a tree block operating against the wind. Also, by directing the spray heads properly the bending of the pattern can be reduced or even eliminated. Growers who own LV sprayers ofter will tell you that they can operate their LV units under more adverse conditions than their previous type sprayers. Also, with less time required for spraying with LV and with greater efficiency, a grower can be more selective in his timing and often wait until severe adverse weather conditions have passed before applying his spray program. Annual pruning of trees is of utmost importance in getting good spray coverage with any type of equipment.

LV and Intergration (IPM). Another aspect of LV spraying which is becoming of increasing importance is the way in which it complements integrated pest management spray programs. By monitoring his orchard a grower can get in quickly to apply only those sprays really necessary. Of greater importance, however, is the reduction in spray run-off which allows reduced applications of chemical per acre (up to 25%). The run-off usually contains excessive chemicals due to the floating action of material still in suspension explained earlier. This drips to the ground where most predators live and will decrease populations, reduce their effectiveness, and induce other problems. With a sprayer designed for LV application making a droplet size of 50 to 60 microns, it should be possible to strike a branch immediately after application and observe little or no drip. This generally cannot be done with LV sprayers converted from orchard air-blast sprayers, using disc-type nozzles. The reason is the inability to make small enough droplets.

Evaporation of a droplet before it hits the target is another common misconception. This of course is related to humidity, surface area, air velocity, etc. Suffice to say, owners of LV sprayers do not complain about this. As a matter of fact, there are a few growers who have shifted to LV spraying who are considering returning to dilute or 3 to 4x application methods.

Advantages of LV. A review of advantages of LV spraying over conventional spraying follows:

1. Reduced chances of spray burn or damage due to more rapid and uniform drying.

380

2. Savings in chemicals due to the elimination of run-off and buildup of chemical on the low edge of leaves or lowerside of fruit.

3. Appreciably less water used per acre, being reduced from 300 to 500 gals/A dilute to 15 to 25 gals/A.

4. Reduced fuel consumption—as many LV sprayers are lighter and often use PTO power.

5. Lighter equipment due to a small tank carrying less spray solution, lighter less expensive centrifugal pump and often no second engine.. This reduces soil compaction and rutting of the orchard floor.

6. Initial capitalization is generally less for LV sprayers of equal ability.

7. Maintenance and operation costs are lower.

8. Labor costs are reduced.

9. Worker morale is generally improved.

10. More efficient equipment allows for better timing and selection of optimum spraying conditions.

11. Quality of fruit is as good or better than other spray methods and visible residue is reduced or eliminated.

Mixing of Chemicals. In the early days of LV spraying it was thought that many chemicals especially fruit thinning sprays, growth regulators, nitrate and other nutritional sprays should not be applied as LV sprays. Today, all sprays used commonly in air-blast sprayers can work equally well in LV's. Manufacturers' recommendations found on every chemical package should be read and followed. When shifting from what has been conventional spraying to low volume, it is strongly advised that you contact and work with your county extension agent, or farm advisor, or pest management consultant, chemical company fieldperson, and your sprayer manufacturer representative or sales technician. They should be aware of your change and help you make the changeover.

In mixing chemicals most manufacturers of LV equipment will ask that you forget "x" or so many units of chemical per 100 gallons and think of units of chemical per acre or row length. Practically all chemical bags as well as extension service spray guides offer both rates of chemical per acre, and rates of chemical per 100 gallons of solution. In the case of chemical per acre you determine how many gallons of spray to be applied per acre and into each of these gallon units in the tank mix the proper amount of chemical. For example: if you have a 200-gallon tank and decide to apply 20 gallons per acre you obviously would spray 10 acres per tank and would mix in your tank ten times the dosage-acreage rate as given on the chemical bag or from your spray guide. It is easy to see how simple this system becomes after all the confusion and misunderstandings that have been experienced in other systems. Twenty gallons per acre is a dosage rate where many LV sprayer sales technicians recommend starting for standard trees. If trees are all high density plantings, are well pruned, or are peach trees, this rate will be reduced. However, it is a safe and realistic starting point.

Metering. The one other important concern is metering. There are three variables which must be related: (a) gallons per acre; (b) forward speed and (c) row spacing or swath width. This is done with a simple formula which works for all sprayers. Gallons per acre can be determined either alone or with the aid of your extension service fruit specialist or sprayer salesman. Your ability to make uniformly small droplets determines the degree to which you can safely reduce your gallons per acre. For your forward speed you must evaluate the size, density, and row spacing of your trees. If your particle size is between 50 to 75 microns, you should be able to operate at about the same speed as with an orchard air-blast sprayer; that is, between 2 and 4 mph. However, the best check is to operate the size LV sprayer you may purchase under your own conditions using only water. Your forward speed should be such that your spray pattern visibly reaches ¾ of the way through the tree row as you move forward. If the

Figure 57a. This is a power-take-off (PTO 3P-50) Pony Kinkelder sprayer used in the high-density apple tree tests in Ohio by Hall and Ferree.

TABLE 18. NUMBER OF TREES PASSED AT DIFFERENT DRIVING SPEEDS

| MPH | Feet per minute | Different spacings (feet) | | | | | | |
| | | 20 | 25 | 30 | 33 | 35 | 40 | 45 |
		Number of trees passed per minute						
1	88	4.4	3.5	2.9	2.7	2.5	2.2	2.0
1½	132	6.6	5.3	4.4	4.0	3.8	3.3	2.9
2	176	8.8	7.0	5.9	5.3	5.0	4.4	3.9
2½	220	11.0	8.8	7.3	6.7	6.3	5.5	4.9
3	264	13.2	10.6	8.8	8.0	7.5	6.6	5.9

Figure 58. This PTO UULV hydraulic mist blower attachment has been developed with the design and assistance of the research staff of the Long Ashton Research Station, Bristol, England. It accommodates low fruit trees, vines, or plants on stakes, trellis or free-standing, applying 2 qts, 4 qts or up to about 20 gpa. The English researchers, for example, have found that they can apply with this equipment 1/10th the ethrel used by U.S. workers and get the same effects on apple, which is an appreciable saving in cost of material alone. The equipment uses somewhat larger holes in the 4 nozzles mounted on the slowly rotating circular rack with a 21,000 cu ft/min air blast. (Courtesy Norman G. Morgan, Long Ashton Research Station, Bristol, England: The Kent Engine Co. and Drake and Fletcher (spray equipment), Maidstone, England.)

particles are too small to see, watch for leaf movement which will also tell you how far you have reached. Should your spray pattern penetrate completely through the tree and out the other side then your forward speed is too slow. Conversely, if your pattern reaches only half way, then you are driving too fast. Tractor speed should be confirmed or checked, which is easily done. A speed of 88 ft. per minute equals 1 mph. Thus, operate the LV sprayer under spraying load, (fulltank of water and PTO engaged and running at recommended PTO rpm if it is a PTO powered unit) and measure the distance in feet travelled in one minute either with tape or by counting known tree spacings and divide by 88 ft. which will give you your forward speed. This should be done for several of the tractor's lower gears so that you know the speeds available to you. *Row spacing* is the distance between rows in feet and not the tree spacing in a row. When these 3 variables are determined, turn to the formula:

$$\frac{\text{Gals/A x Speed x Row Spacing x 60}}{500} = \text{gals/hr.}$$

(Note: multiplying by 60 gives rates/hour and 500 is a constant).

The result is gallons-per-hour that a sprayer (regardless of type of delivery or brand name) must deliver in order to meet the three variables. Most of the LV sprayers are calibrated in gallons-per-hour, so the metering valve is set on the required gallon rate.

F.R. Hall and D.C. Ferree, Ohio Agricultural Experiment Station, tested low-volume spraying and pest control on high-density apples over two seasons (see reference) and made the following conclusions. "Low volume applications of pesticides will control insects and diseases of apples if correctly applied. Timing and rate are especially important with apple scab. When trees are mechanically pruned and are not followed with hand pruning, control of certain pests such as mites and apple scab may be expected to be more difficult, particularly where low volume units are used. Decreased ground speed of LV sprayers (2-2.5 mph) is needed for adequate penetration into such trees. Degree of difficulty in control of certain fruit pests will vary considerably with mainly weather from year to year.

General conclusion. Low Volume spraying has been accepted as an effective method of applying all pesticides by commercial fruit growers throughout North America and the world. But equally good crops of fruit are being grown with dilute or 3x to 4x speedspraying. The cost-squeeze in recent years has caused many commercial growers to study seriously the LV concept.

NEMATODE CONTROL FOR FRUIT CROPS

Plant parasitic nematodes cause extensive injury to fruit crops. Research has shown that many fruit crops respond to soil fumigation with nematicides. It is important to purchase high quality nursery stock produced on nematode-free, fumigated or nematicide-treated soil. Fumigation of soil prior to planting trees or vines on old fruit sites is essential to produce vigorous and healthy orchards or vineyards (Figure 59). Likewise, strawberries to be planted in soil infested with root-knot or root-lesion nematodes will respond to soil fumigation practices. Dagger nematodes are capable of transmitting viruses to several fruit crops including blueberries, grapes and raspberries. They are responsible for the union necrosis problem with MM106 on apples.

Proper soil preparation prior to nematicide application is essential for maximum effectiveness. Plow the soil to a depth of at least 12 inches and remove old roots that are turned up. Fall treatment and spring planting is the usual practice. The fumigant is injected into the soil to a depth of 8-10 inches with shank applicators 8-12 inches apart. Roll the soil or cultipack after treatment. Fumigant is applied in bands 6-8 ft wide centered on the row. While nematodes will invade the area again, by that time the roots will have grown deeper into the soil than the operational level of the nematodes. By the time the tree bears, the fumigant will have dissipated from the soil and tree.

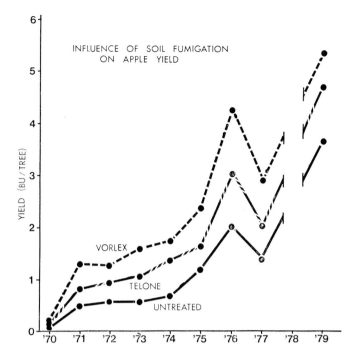

Figure 59. *Preplant* soil fumigation may affect yields of compact apple trees, particularly in the lighter soil types in New York. Nematodes are a factor but there could be other adjustments needed in the soil and the tree. (Richard L. Norton, POB 150, Albion, N. Y. 14411).

The soil should be in excellent tilth and soil moisture should approach that desirable for seeding. Dry soil allows too rapid escape of fumigants. Dispersion of fumigants in excessively wet soil is poor. At soil temperatures below 45° F., soil fumigants do not volatilize and spread properly. Above 80° F., the materials escape too rapidly from the soil. Some of the better nematicides are being banned. The Dept. of Entomology, Mich, State Univ. E. Lansing has up-to-date information in Ag. Ext. Bulls. E-800, E-801.

FRUIT VIRUSES

According to A.F. Posnette et al., East Malling Research Station in Kent, England, virus diseases have such diverse effects on fruit trees that the economic loss they cause is difficult to estimate. The few that affect only fruit, such as stony pit of pear (Figure 60), can be assessed merely by taking into account the number of infected trees and the proportion of fruit rendered unsaleable. Most virus diseases affect the growth and productivity of the tree, however, and some (e.g. proliferation) also reduce fruit size and color. By impeding the growth rate, some viruses considerably delay the production of economic quantities of fruit by young trees, but once the trees have attained their allotted space, viruses that reduce their growth may have no appreciable effect on yield per acre (on M.9 stocks).

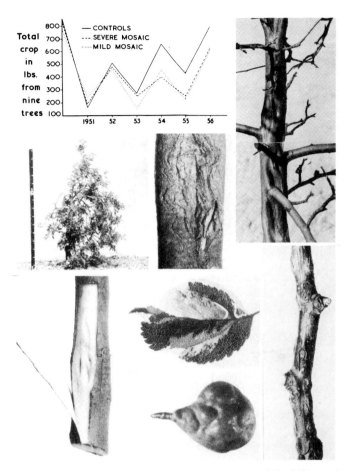

Figure 60. VIRUSES — APPLE, PEAR. (Upper left) Effects of mosaic virus on young Cox Orange apple yield by tree age. (Upper right) Apple "Flat Limb". (Mid left) "Apple Rubbery Wood" and at right, wood damaged area. (Lower left) Apple "Stem Pitting", found also on peach. (Lower center) Sectorial chimaera on apple resembling virus but is genetical. (Lower center) "Stony Pit" of pear; flesh has corky stony areas. (Lower right) Pear "Blister Canker" resembles bark measles. (For details, see excellent loose-leaf book by A. F. Posnette, E. Malling Res. Sta., Maidstone, Kent, England. Tech. Comm. 30, 141pp. 1963).

"Viruses that cause overt systems (diseases) generally produce measurable effects on the crop (Table 20), but some viruses occur in apple and pear trees, e.g., which appear normal, and nothing is yet known about the effect, if any, of these latent, infections (Figure 61). By analogy with similar conditions in other crops, we may guess that latent infection is harmful rather than beneficial to the tree, but this may not always prove to be true from the grower's point of view. The grower's aim is to produce maximum crops of optimum quality as early in the life of the tree as possible, and, if this can be achieved more economically from small trees, he is usually prepared to plant the trees closer together to increase yield per unit area of land.

"In attempting to estimate the economic effects of virus

383

TABLE 20. EFFECTS OF SOME VIRUS DISEASES ON SENSITIVE APPLE AND PEAR CULTIVARS

Disease	Observed influence on			
	extension growth (%)	tree girth (%)	fruit yield (%)	fruit quality
Apple				
Mosaic	-50	-20	-30	reduced size
Rubbery wood..	-50	-20	-25	no effect
Star crack	-25	-20	-90	blemished
Rough skin	no effect	no effect	? no effect	blemished
Chat fruit	+ 17	no effect	-30	reduced size and colour
Pear				
Stony pit	no effect	no effect	? no effect	proportion inedible
Vein yellow	-40	-15	not known	no effect

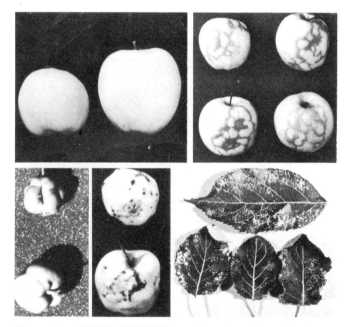

Figure 61. APPLE VIRUSES have been for a long time in orchards but only in the past few decades have researchers begun to "pin down" the various kinds, their symptoms, and the damage they do to yields and quality. Stone fruit viruses and those on brambles and strawberries were pin-pointed first as to their damage, but only in relatively recent times have the symptoms and damage been noted in the pome fruits because the pomes apparently can carry viruses with less *apparent* damage to the yield and quality of the crop. (Upper left) "Flat Apple" the normally cone-shaped apple at right is flattish at left with flared calyx end. Golden and Red Delicious often affected. Trees smaller, scaly bark, thick narrow leaves. (Upper right) "Russet Ring." Not prominent on Red Delicious and Rome but on Goldens. Varies yr to yr apparently with temperature conditions. (Lower left) "Green Crinkle." Resembles aphid damage, tree decline, found in Golden Delicious and Winesap. (Mid-lower) "Star Crack." Fruit show "star" cracks at russet areas, trees in severe decline, poor fruit shape. (Lower right) "Mosaic." Yellowish and white leaf spotting and along veins; Golden Delicious and Jonathan may show it. (See Wash. Ext. Leaflet 770 SC).

diseases of fruit trees, one must consider four facts of prime importance. First, each fruit tree consists of two different cultivars or species, the rootstock and scion. Secondly, cultivars differ markedly in their reaction to infection by a single virus. Thirdly, viruses occur in a range of strains, often varying from virulent to those causing no symptoms. Fourthly, viruses may "interact", i.e. one virus may greatly influence the effect of another in the same plant; the influence may be synergistic and increase the severity of symptoms or antagonistic and protective.

"These four facts influence the result of virus infection in a particular tree to the extent that no prediction can be made with any certainty unless the identity of the scion variety and rootstock, the strain of the virus with which one is concerned and the extent of latent infection with other viruses are known. Usually only the first of these factors is known.

"Climate also undoubtedly influences the effect of these virus diseases. Pear mosaic, for example, may increase the susceptibility of trees to frost damage. At the other extreme it is known that several viruses can be inactivated in apple and pear plants maintained at 37° C. for 2 or 3 weeks, and the "masking" of symptoms during periods of active plant growth. Diseases such as apple mosaic, chat fruit and rough skin are less severe in warm, sunny summers than in cool, wet ones, and might be expected to cause greater losses in countries where summer temperatures are low than in those with a Mediterranean climate. In England apple mosaic reduced by 30 percent the number of fruit on trees of Cox's Orange Pippin and Allington Pippin on M.IX rootstocks, but in countries where fruit setting is excessive and the final crop determined by thinning, the effect of apple mosaic may prove to be negligible.

"Effects in nurseries. In stone fruit trees, virus infection has been found to influence the survival of scions, particularly of bud-grafts in the nursery. Nurserymen may offset this effect by retaining the smaller trees for a second year's growth in the nursery, but this obviously increases cost of production.

Certain viruses cause losses in nursery propagation by inducing a type of incompatibility. The vegetatively propagated rootstocks in general use, such as Quince A and the Malling and Malling-Merton apple clones, are tolerant of viruses commonly latent in scion varieties of apple and pear; indeed several of the M. and MM. clones are themselves infected with one or more of these viruses.

"Latent infection. In attempts so far made to estimate the effects of these virus diseases in field experiments, inoculated trees have been compared with "healthy" controls. Although the latter are now known to carry latent virus infections, these experiments are a true reflection of orchard conditions, for practically all commercial apple and pear trees have this "background infection". Until trees of commercial varieties free from latent virus infection have been procured, as is now being done by *heat treatment,* and their performance compared with that of our present "healthy" trees, the effect of this latent infection will not be known. Preliminary results obtained at Long Ashton Research Station indicate that less nitrogen fertilizer may be required for virus-free-trees. At East Malling, virus-free scions derived from the original Bramley's Seedling grew 10 per cent taller in the nursery row than scions carrying a latent infection with chlorotic leaf spot and *Malus platycarpa* scaly bark viruses.

"**Spread.** Most viruses spread only slowly, if at all, in orchards and they usually originate in the nursery by propagation from previously infected trees. Certain nematodes in cropped land may carry, e.g. tomato ring spot virus and infest roots of newly planted peaches.

"**Future trends.** The economic importance of virus diseases. . .has increased, and will probably continue to do so, as the standard of fruit production improves. As cultural methods and means of controlling fungal diseases and insect pests improve, virus diseases become not only relatively but actually more important factors to overcome in the efficient production of fruit crops. It cannot be over-emphasized, however, that fruit trees are almost as permanent as factories; while methods of production can quickly be changed, trees and buildings take years to produce and faults in construction may prove irreparable. Viruses "built into" fruit trees during propagation, being little affected by pruning regimes, soil management methods or spray schedules, will remain to plague the grower until he decides to pull down the factory and rebuild with better materials."

Always specify virus-free stock where possible.

For pome viruses refer to Comm. Agr. Bur. "Virus Diseases of Apples and Pears". A.F. Posnette, Ed. 141 pp. E. Mall. Res. Sta., Kent, England. Tech. Comm. No 30. For Stone fruit viruses, refer to USDA Handbook 10. U.S. Gov'n Printing Office, Wash., D.C. 275 pp. Recent Edition.

COST OF CONVENTIONAL CONCENTRATE SPRAYING

The cost of any type of orchard spraying is influenced by a number of factors such as length of rows, capacity of sprayer tanks, and rate of travel in spraying. Whether the amount of spray chemicals per tree or per acre can be reduced safely below what previously has been considered to be necessary, depends upon several factors such as disease and insect carry over, size of trees, pruning, use of monitoring and IPM, and how evenly the particular applicator distributes the spray throughout the entire tree.

Cost comparisons of spraying data are difficult to find. John Linde, Jr., a former Pennsylvania grower, over several years compared spray application with an air-blast sprayer at 3x and a high concentrate sprayer at 33x. With 90 acres of apples and 68 of peaches, his data showed 19% less cost per acre per application for 33x vs. 3x for apples and 41% less for peaches. This can amount to considerable saving in a year of spraying. He also found less fruit russeting with 33x spraying. Control of current pests was satisfactory on apple trees no higher than 18 ft. or farther apart than 35 ft. Wind was not a problem on peaches but could be on large apple trees. Operators on 33x machines were well protected from drift.

W.H.A. Wilde, University of Guelph, Guelph, Ontario, Canada, compared the cost of LV, MVS, (medium-volume spraying) and HVS (high-volume spraying). His data represented 8 to 14 growers in each class and accounts for all costs entailed. The total cost of medium-volume spraying was the most. High-volume spraying was next at 11% less, and the low-volume spraying cost the least at 25% less than MVS.

Table 19 gives comparison cost data for tractors and or-

TABLE 19. TRACTOR AND ORCHARD SPRAYER COST PER HOUR AND PER ACRE FOR SEVERAL GROWERS IN OHIO. (R.C. FUNT, FRUIT GROWER SPRAY EQUIPMENT COST - 1981. OHIO STATE UNIVERSITY, DEPARTMENT OF HORTICULTURE, COLUMBUS.)

Growers	Tractor						Sprayer						Total Cost Per	
	Year	Size	Initial Price	Hours/ Year	Cost/ Hr.		Year	Size	Initial Price	Hours/ Yr.	Cost/ Hr.		Hr.[1]	Acre[2]
22	1975	70 D	12,000	500	$ 8.21		1975	100 hp	$18,000	50	$69.41		$83.12	$320.01
14	1977	50 G	7,500	300	9.19		1979	125 hp	13,000	100	34.93		49.62	173.67
23	1979	60 D	10,000	700	6.09		1968	140 hp	6,900	230	19.25		30.84	123.36
24	1975	50 D	9,000	500	6.02		1976	140 hp	11,000	200	23.51		35.03	122.60
2	1979	45 D	9,600	250	8.90		1979	100 PTO	4,200	120	6.01		20.41	102.05
5	1980	60 D	16,000	450	12.74		1967	300 PTO	4,000	50	2.37		20.61	58.74
7	1976	70 D	12,000	200	13.88		1976	300 PTO	5,600	50	18.97		38.35	81.30
10	1973	60 D	11,000	600	6.69		1972	250 PTO	5,000	400	3.13		15.32	39.82
12	1977	70 D	11,000	500	7.91		1979	300 PTO	7,600	260	5.08		18.49	53.62

[1] Includes labor at $5.50/hr., gasoline at $1.30, diesel fuel at $1.20, straight line depreciation for 10 years use, interest at 10% before 1980 and 14% interest for 1980 or later.
[2] Each grower had different tree size and spacing which required different travel speed and hours per acre. All growers assumed to have 15 applications for 1981 season. All growers rated at two side delivery. Multiply by 2 for one side delivery.

chard sprayers in Ohio for 1981 which may be of some assistance to growers in calculating costs.

Custom spraying. In some fruit regions, we may find many small orchards or vineyards, each of which hardly justifies good power spraying equipment. As a result, pest control with too-small or poorly kept equipment is unsatisfactory. A truck-mounted or tractor-pulled sprayer owned by a custom sprayman can service many such orchards or vineyards, and in most cases the results are a definite improvement in market quality of the fruit. Custom spraymen know how to spray properly and are familiar with selection of proper materials. Low-volume spraying is well adapted to custom spraying.

CONTROL MEASURES OTHER THAN SPRAYING AND DUSTING

Natural control measures. A common important means by which insects and diseases are controlled are natural factors which operate without the assistance of people. These include inherent resistance of the species, or immunity; environmental conditions, as unfavorable temperatures, moisture and light; and the natural plant and animal enemies of horticultural pests, included under the subject, "Biological Control." As indicated earlier, the releasing of male sterilized codling moths, e.g., and the use of synthetic sex attractants to reduce and monitor populations and the feeding of birth control chemicals to bird and animal pests are in use.

Different cultivars of the same fruit exhibit different degrees of resistance toward insect and disease pests. The exact cause or causes of resistance and immunities are not known but certainly some of them are hereditary. Different degrees of resistance will be exhibited by the same kind of plant at different seasons of the year, and by different parts of the same plants in different stages of growth and development. Natural factors which may contribute to the immunity of a plant to attacks by plant and animal pests are thickness of the cuticle and cell wall, the size and abundance of stomata and lenticels, the presence or abundance of hairs and other physical structures on the plant, and numerous other factors may contribute to resistance. Growth and germination of fungi may be inhibited on some plants because of their chemical composition. Likewise, such a plant may be repellant or even toxic to insect pests and be a barrier to the development of bacterial and virus diseases. It is generally true that a moderately vigorous plant is more resistant to insect and disease attacks than a weak one. The most progress in developing resistance in plants to animal and plant pests is through cross breeding and selection of mutations.

Sooner or later, almost all insects and diseases have natural enemies which prey upon them so that a natural system of checks and balances exist. Shortly after cottony-cushion scale was introduced into the United States, it became a serious pest in orchards until its natural enemy, the lady bird beetle, was introduced, after which the scale pest was reduced to one of minor importance in fruit orchards. Entomologists are on continual look-out for predatory insects which can be propagated and disseminated for the purpose of reducing major insect pests of fruit crops. The pomologist, as well as the entomologist, encourage the perpetuation and multiplication of birds, fungi, bacteria, and insects that aid in keeping the plant and animal pests of fruit plants under control. Researchers also are attempting to find pesticides that control the major pests but cause little or no harm to their predators, thus reducing need for expensive materials and cutting spray costs. Ryania is one such pesticide.

Other control measures. There are several physical methods of controlling insect pests and diseases, namely, (a) destroying or burying the diseased plant or portion of a plant, (b) mechanical guards, (c) soil cultivation, (d) sanitation, (e) crop rotation, (f) official nursery inspection of propagation material, (g) sterilization of pruning tools and the pruning wounds where disease portions have been removed and (h) the releasing of males sterilized by radioactive colbalt to cut certain insect populations.

Many pests of orchard crops overwinter in plant refuse, such as dropped leaves and fruits, weeds and other plants about the trees and along fence rows. These harboring areas should be cleaned up and burned each dormant season, which also lessen the danger of mice and rabbits. Disposal of cull fruits by burying or similar means is highly important in controlling insects and diseases. Also, sanitation around the packing shed is important to prevent spring emergence of codling moths harbored over winter in old boxes, crates, and packing rooms. Old boxes should be placed in a tightly closed room and fumigated to kill adhering cocoons. Some insects and diseases, such as the Oriental fruit moth of peaches, the grape berry moth and brown rot of stone fruits, are partly controlled by spring disking. Wire guards around the base of trunks of trees are helpful in reducing mouse and rabbit injury.

About the only effective control available for some pests and diseases in roguing and destroying affected plants. Examples are crown gall of nursery stock, mosaic diseases of brambles and peaches and cedar rust of apples. The cedar tree, the so-called alternate host, is rogued.

Official nursery inspection service is highly effective in reducing the dissemination of diseases and insects from nurseries.

Defruiting Trees in Dooryards. Two lbs Sevin/100 gals, or fraction thereof as needed, applied at blossom petal fall should remove most of the undesired fruit. Sevin, however, aggrevates red mite damage in a dry hot season.

CARE OF MACHINERY, EQUIPMENT

Frequent and thorough lubrication of all working parts of spray machinery is highly important during the operating season. At the end of each day of use, thoroughly rinse the tank, and pump clean water through the system. Open the nozzles until the water is discharged. Where using a hose, do not drag it on the ground except when spraying. When going for a refill, either disconnect the hose from the rig or coil it upon hangers at the rear or sides of the machine. Do not permit kinks to form in the hose.

At the end of the spray season, it is highly important to do a thorough job of rinsing the machine with clean water, then drain the pump, the engine, and the tank. In order to prevent rusting of the pump during the winter, pump used lubrication oil through it. Store hose in a cool dark place. Drain it completely and coil it over an elevated barrel or stretch it out on a bench or shelf. Do not suspend it on nails or similar objects which cause it to kink and crack.

The spray machine should be gotten out ahead of time in the spring and gone over completely, thoroughly cleaned, and "tuned up" ready for use. The following suggestions are given by technicians of the Jonesboro, Arkansas Food Machinery Company, for trouble-shooting, adjustment, overhauling, and care of air-blast sprayers. While the suggestions do not apply to all makes of equipment, they are a guide. With low-volume sprayers the suggestions are even more important.

PROBLEMS, DO'S AND DON'TS[1]

Pressure Losses

1. If no spray solution comes from the nozzles, make certain that:

    a) There is liquid in the tank.
    b) All valves are in their proper positions.
       (The by-pass valve is not open)
    c) The water level is above the level of the pump.
    d) Air is not trapped in the suction line of the pump.
    e) The packing is well lubricated and not dried out.
    g) Drive belts are not slipping.
    h) Cover on suction strainer is sealed.

2. If insufficient spray solution comes from the nozzles, make certain that:

    a) All valves are in proper position.
       (The by-pass valve is closed.)

    b) Nozzles are not clogged.
    c) Main strainer is not clogged.
    d) Pipe and hose lines are not clogged.

3. If the pressure drops rapidly upon opening the valves, it's generally an indication that the impeller vanes on the centrifugal pump are plugged. The pump must be disassembled and the impeller cleaned to correct this trouble. Indications similar to this can also be caused from a collapsing suction line between the strainer and pump.

Care of the Sprayer Tank. The spray tank, if steel, is treated on the interior with a rust inhibitor type finish.

(a) *Flush Daily.* To avoid plugging of the spray nozzles it is important to prevent scale buildup on the inside of tank and piping system.

   Immediately after each day of operation, if spray other than oil has been used, run sufficient clean water through to flush the tank, pump, and piping system. After cleaning the tank, flush with straight spray oil.

(b) *Interior.* At the end of the spraying season the tank interior should be cleaned thoroughly.

   When working inside the tank, it is suggested that a sack or mat be used on which to stand to prevent damage to the protective coating. Also, a respirator and gloves should be used.

   Use a fiber brush when washing the interior surfaces.

   Coat with oil or grease if the sprayer is to be idle more than one week.

(c) *Exterior.* Many spray materials are very corrosive and damage paint and metal surfaces. When spraying with other than oil spray, it is suggested that the entire outside of the sprayer be cleaned and coated with oil after each day's spraying. Regular lubricating oil, reduced with kerosene or tractor fuel can easily be sprayed with an air pressure chassis sprayer, or even an insect hand sprayer.

   A coating of oil on the sprayer will prevent the corrosive material from adhering to the sprayer, protect it from the corrosive action and also make the entire sprayer easier to clean.

(d) *Agitator.* The mechanical agitator provides sufficient mixing for either dilute or concentrate spray materials. Four paddles are employed which are mounted on a 1-3/16″ diameter shaft carried in packed and lubricated bearings at each end of the tank.

   When mixing extremely heavy solids it may become necessary to advance engine throttle a little to speed agitation; also open the by-pass valve for additional pump agitation.

---

[1]Each spray machine manufacturing company can provide a complete instruction manual for the proper care of your respective equipment.

Tighten the packing nut on the front agitator bearing as necessary to prevent leakage. When the packing nut has been turned all the way in, unscrew and insert an additional packing ring.

If leaking persists, disassemble packing nut agitator shaft, and remove packing. Clean and inspect the shaft and replace if worn sufficiently; replace old packing with new, being sure to stagger ends, and to coat rings with grease when installing.

Drain to prevent freezing. Open all valves in the piping system. In addition, remove plugs (or open petcocks) and drain at the following points:

1. Radiator (at bottom on radiator)
2. Engine Block (both sides)
3. Strainer Assembly (remove cover)
4. Pump and Piping
5. Spray Tank
6. Spray Manifold and Hose Lines
7. Remove the fitting on the line "to Pressure Gauge" to drain the water from the pressure gauge line.

Preparing gas engine for storage. A manual of instructions is available for diesel engines.

The operator will avoid serious repairs and will be money ahead by rust proofing engines that are to stand idle.

Most engines are stored in places where they are subject to temperature changes. As the temperature falls and rises, condensation coats the engine's inner surfaces with moisture. The resulting water plus metal results in rust.

The following materials will be needed:
1) Engine rust preventive oil. Suggested brands are Texas Oil Company (their #651 and 652), Sinclair Refining Company (their #10-Rust-O-Lene), or equivalent.
2) Rust Inhibitor for the cooling system.
3) Masking tape.

The following procedure is recommended:
1) Drain lubricating oil from the engine. Then add 2½ quarts of the rust preventive lubricant.
2) Drain the cooling system. Add good grade "Rust Resistor" and fill with clean water.
3) Run the engine at idle speeds for 3 or 4 minutes. This will do several things:

   (a) The rust resistor in the cooling system will coat the radiator and the inside of the engine.
   (b) The rust proofing oil will be distributed throughout the system and on the cylinder walls. Avoid overheating. (If it is not possible to run the engine on its own power, turn it over with the starter several times.)

4) Remove the top of the carburetor air cleaner elbow. Run the engine at approximately 100 RPM. Pour about ½ pint of engine rust preventive oil through the carburetor air intake. This should choke the engine. If not, shut off the ignition as soon as the ½ pint has been drawn into the system. Smoke coming from the exhaust will indicate when this has been done. (If it is not possible to run the engine under its own power, pour the ½ pint rust preventive into the carburetor air intake while the engine is being turned over with the starter.)

5) Drain the rust proofing oil from the crankcase. This oil may be re-used until five cycles are completed. Replace the drain plug.

6) Remove the spark plugs. Pour into each cylinder through the spark plug hole, one (1) ounce of engine rust preventive oil (the same as listed on previous page). Turn the engine over 4 or 5 revolutions with the starter. Replace the spark plugs.

7) Drain the cooling system by opening the radiator drain. *Caution:* Remember to open the drain in the side of the water jacket on the cylinder block (starter side.)

8) Drain the excess gasoline from (1) the carburetor, (2) the fuel pump, and (3) the gasoline tank. Gasoline standing over periods of time tends to "gum."

9) After the above steps have been completed, seal all vents which permit air to enter the idle engine.

   1. Carburetor air intake.
   2. Oil filter pipe.
   3. Oil vent pipe at manifold side of the engine.
   4. Manifold exhaust opening.
      A good seal can be made with masking tape or adhesive.

10) Place a warning tag on the engine to serve as a reminder that the oil and coolant have been drained; and that the engine should be properly serviced before using.

Accurate scales and measuring cans should be available. It is a wise investment to have a good stock of repair parts for the engines, pumps and rig frames before the season begins. Although some manufacturers attempt to give air-express service on repair parts from the factory, as much as a day or two may be lost in securing these parts during a critical period. In most fruit growing areas, there are sales outlets of the major spray machine companies; these distributors carry a full stock of parts which can be gotten in hours. However, it is wise for growers to carry a stock of key parts such as agitator paddles, gaskets, connecting rods, spare belts, disks and vortex plates for nozzles, gaskets for nozzles, hose clamps, connections and washers, extra nozzles, spark plugs, stove bolts, suction strainer for hose, valve balls, seats, springs, repair tools and possibly other items suggested by the field representative. If several outfits are working in an orchard, it may be well to have in reserve an extra engine and pump, both in good working condition with all connections. The spray machine parts should be pigeon-holed by classification and those subject to corrosion should be protected by a heavy coating of oil or grease.

Review Questions

1. List the types of insects (based on mouth parts), with examples, as found in fruit plantings.
2. What groups of diseases, with examples, are found in orchards and small fruit plantings?
3. Give the types of insecticides used for controlling the insects listed under question 1, with examples.
4. Explain "insect pheromones."
5. Discuss integrated control and monitoring of insects.
6. List one each apple cultivar highly susceptible to scab, to spray injury, and to adverse weather injury?
7. Discuss spray atomization or breakup and how it is accomplished in modern orchard spray machines.
8. Where can alternate-row spraying be used? Advantages?
9. What are the purposes of the pressure regulator and describe briefly how it works?
10. Give the parts of a disk nozzle and state briefly the purpose of each.
11. What effect does varying the depth of the eddy-chamber have on the type of spray cone?
12. What effect does an increase in pump pressure have on size of spray droplets and angle of spray cone?
13. Give advantages and any disadvantages of the types of spray tank agitators available.
14. How do you account for the popularity of the air-blast orchard sprayer?
15. Describe the air-blast sprayers and their principles of operation.
16. What type concentrate sprayers are on your market today? Advantages, disadvantages of each.
17. Why have stationary spray systems more or less disappeared?
18. Discuss PTO concentrate sprayers? Advantages, disadvantages.
19. In case of pesticide poisoning, what would you do for the spray operator?
20. Give pertinent recommendations for effective spraying of mature apple trees with a modern air-blast sprayer.
21. How would you avoid bee poisoning during blooms?
22. Describe how the spray service of the state agricultural extension service, a contracted field consultant and the spray machine fieldperson may cooperate to assist the fruit grower in using the correct materials at the critical time.
23. Describe techniques for night spraying and when is such spraying advisable?
24. From cost figures from your local supply house, calculate the cost of materials for a season of spraying a 100-acre peach or apple orchard, following the spray schedule of your local extension service. Calculate also the man-labor costs, gasoline, grease, oil, depreciation on equipment and other costs if such data are available to you. (Your local air-blast orchard sprayer representative can give you basic data, or consult with a local commercial grower.)
25. What do we mean by "back action" or an "eradicant" in a scab fungicide?
26. What is meant by a cover spray?
27. Discuss methods other than spraying to control diseases and pests, advantages and disadvangates.
28. Discuss low and high concentrate spraying, advantages and disadvantages.
29. Discuss advantages and disadvantages of aerial spraying.

Suggested Collateral Readings[1]
GENERAL

ANDERSON, H.W. Diseases of fruit crops. McGraw-Hill Book Co., Inc., New York City. 501 pp. 1956.

ASQUITH, DEAN and F.H. LEWIS. Mite control by helicopter in Pennsylvania. Pa. Fruit News, 4 p. March 1965.
AVERY, D.J. and J.B. BRIGGS. Damage to leaves caused by fruit tree red spider mite. J. Hort. Sci. 43:463-473. 1968.
AYERS, J.C., JR. and J.A. BARDEN. Photosynthesis, Respiration of Apple as Affected by Pesticides. J. ASHS. 100:24-28. 1975.
Backyard Fruits—Disease and Insect Control. Write your state experiment station. Following stations are known to have good editions: Ohio, New York, Michigan, Missouri, and Indiana.
BARNES, M.M., and H.F. MADSEN. Insect and mite pests of apple in California. Calif. Ext. Cir. 502, 31 pp. Request latest edition.
BEER, S.V. and S.H. ALDWINCKLE. Fireblight in New York. New York's Food and Life Sciences, Geneva, 16-19. 1974.
BELL AIRCRAFT CORP. The utility helicopter. Request descriptive literature. Bell Aircraft Corp., Buffalo 5, N.Y.
BETHELL, R.S. et al. Sex pheromone traps to reduce orchard sprays. Calif. Agric. May 1972.
BYERS, R.E., et al. Less russeting of 'Golden Delicious' with 2,4,5-TP, other compounds. HortSci, 18(1)63-65. 1983.
CARTER, M.V. and T.V. PRICE. Biological control of *Eutypa armeniacae*. II. Studies of the interaction between *E. armeniacae* and *Fusarium lateritium,* and their relative sensitivities to benzimidazole chemicals. Aust. J. Agric. Res. 25:105-19. 1974.
CHILD, R.D. Bullfinch damage to pear buds. Long Ash. Hort. Res. Sta., England. Report 110. 1967.
DAYTON, D.F. et al. Scab-resistant apples. Hort. Sci. 12 (5):434-436. 1977.
DONOHO, C.W. et al. Cicada and soil pH effects on apple-tree decline. HortSci. II: 4. 149-150. 1967.
DRILLEAU J.R. and L. DECOURTYE. Selecting Pome Fruits Resistance to Fireblight (In French). Ann Amelior. Plantes. 23 (2). 115-125. 1973.
FARM CHEMICALS HANDBOOK. Annual. Meister Publ. Co., Willoughby, Ohio 44094. About 475 pp. Priced. 1983.
FERREE, D.C. et al. Spray adjuvants and multiple applications of benomyl and oil on photosynthesis of apple leaves. HortSci. 11(4):391-2, 1976.
FRUIT DISEASES. Following agricultural experiment stations have good general bulletins or specific circulars by disease or by fruit crop. New York (Cornell), Michigan, Ohio, California and Illinois. Ann. Update.
GARMAN, P., L.G. KIERSTEAD, W.T. MALTHIS. Quality of apples as affected by sprays. Conn. Agr. Exp. Sta. Bull. 576. 46 pp. 1953.
GOONEWARDENE, H.F. and E.B. WILLIAMS. Resistance to European red mite. *Panonychus ulmi* (Koch), in apple. J. ASHS 101(5):532-537. 1976.
GROVES, A.B. Weather injuries to fruits and fruit trees. Va. Poly. Inst. Bull. 390. 39 pp. 1946.
HALL, F.R. and D.C. FERREE. LV spraying and pest control (high-density plantings). Ohio Research Bull. 220. 19-22. July 1976.
HATCH, A.H. Nutrition and Fungicides on Russeting of 'Goldspur' Apple. J. ASHS. 100:52-55, 1975.
LAGERSTEDT, H.B. Tree trunk spray boom. HortSci. 6(5). 1971.
MADSEN, et al. Male Coding Moth removal from orchards by sex pheromone traps. J. of Econ. Entom. 69:(5)597-98. 1976.

---

[1] Catalogs and operation manuals from spray equipment companies are valuable for study and comparison of the various types of equipment on the market. Companies include: FMC, Jonesboro, Arkansas; Dobbins Manufacturing Co., North St. Paul, Minn.; Friend Manufacturing Co., Gasport, N.Y.; H.D. Hudson Manufacturing Co., Chicago, Ill.; Messinger Manufacturing Co., Tatamy, Pa.; The F.E. Myers and Bros. Co., Ashland, Ohio; Root Manufacturing Co., Cleveland, Ohio; Tecnoma, P.O.B. 195, 51-Epernay-France; KWH Whirlwind Holland NV. Wadenoyen-Netherlands P.O.B. 47. See also the July issues of the American Fruit Grower Magazine, Willoughby, Ohio, for up-to-date indexes of spray materials and machinery manufacturers.

Spray and cultural fruit bulletins are updated and published annually (priced), e.g., by the state universities in Washington, Michigan, New York (Cornell), Pennsylvania and Rutgers (New Jersey). They are helpful in keeping up-to-date.

METCALF, C.L. and W.P. FLINT. Distructive and useful insects—their habits and control. McGraw-Hill Book Co., Inc., New York City. Fourth edition. 1962. Request latest edition.

METCALF, R.L. and W.H. LUCKMAN. Introduction to Insect Pest Management. John Wiley Publishing Co., New York. 587 pp. 1975

MILLIKAN, D.F. and R. DZIECIOL. Biochemical alterations associated with grafting of healthy and virus-infected apple buds on Spy 227 rootstock. J. ASHS 98(2):160. March 1973.

MOLLER, WILLIAM J., MILTON N. SCHROTH. Biological control growth of crown gall. Cal. Agr. p. 8-9. Aug. 1976.

Pesticide Manual. Lists world pesticides, use, etc. British Crop Prot. Council. Clack's Farm. Boreley, Droitwich, Worcester, England, updated regularly.

PAYNE, J.A. et al. Aerial photography with infra red film to locate pecan pests and diseases. Pecan Quarterly. Nov. 1971.

Pollutant impact on horticulture and man. HortSci. 5(4):23554. 1970.

POSNETTE, A.F. and R. CROPLEY. Indicator plants for latent virus infection in apple. J. Hort. Sci. 36:168-173. July 1961.

POWELL, D.B. JANSON and E.G. SHARVELLE. Diseases of apples and pears in the midwest. North Central Reg. Publ. 16. Ill. Ext. Serv. Cir. 909, 26 pp. April 1965.

Principles of Plant and animal pest control. Div. of Bio & Agr. Nat. Res. Council. 6 vols. 2101 Constitution Ave., Washington, D.C. 20418. 1971.

SCHREIBER, L.R. and W.K. HOCK. Benomyl and Thiabendazole on Growth of Several Plant Species. J. ASHS. 100:390-313, 1975.

SIROIS, et al. Fungicide effects on photosynthesis of entire apple tree. Me. Agr. Exp. Sta. Bull. 629, 18 pp. Dec. 1964.

SPOTTS, R.A. et al. Pesticide trunk injection for apple disease and insect control. Ohio Research Bull. 220. 25-7. July 1976.

Spray schedules for fruit. All state experiment stations will provide local published recommendtions on request. Among the more complete and detail recommendations are those of *Michigan, Ohio, California, Washington, New York, Virginia* and *Illinois*. Priced.

STIER, E.F. et al. Flavor of fresh, canned and frozen foods as influenced by herbicides, fertilizers, fungicides and insecticides. N.J. Agr. Evp. Sta. Bull 808. 34 pp. 1964.

TAYLOR, O.C. and A.E. MITCHELL. Soluble solids, total solids, sugar content and weight of the fruit of the sour cherry. (*Prunus cerasus*) as affected by pesticide chemicals and time of harvest. Proc. Amer. Soc. Hort. Sci. 68:124-130. 1956.

VRIE, M. VAN DE. Orchard mites. Bull. of Res. Sta. for Fruit Growing, Wilhelminadorp (Goes), The Netherlands. (Dutch, English summary.) 68 p. 1973.

WAVE, H.E. and W.C. STILES. Influence of superior oil sprays on growth and bark necrosis of 'Delicious' apple trees. HortSci. 7:(2) April 1972. p. 171.

WALTER, T.E. Russeting and cracking in apples: a review of world literature. Rep. E. Malling Res. Sta. for 1966 (83-95 pp). 1967.

ZWICK, R.W. et al. Effects of mite population density on 'Newtown' and 'Golden Delicious' apple tree performance. ASHS 101(2):123-5. Mar. 1976.

SOIL NEMATODES

GOOD, J.M. and A.L. TAYLOR. Plant-parasitic nematodes—chemical control. USDA Agr. Handbook, 286, 28 pp. 1965.

HEDDEN, O.K. et al. Equipment for applying soil pesticides. USDA Agr. Handbook 297, 36 pp. 1966.

WEED CONTROL

FISCHER, B. and A. LANGE. Herbicide residues—banding vs. broad—casting. Calif. Agric. May. 1972.

PUTNAM, A.R. Chemical Weed Control for horticultural crops. Mich. Agr. Ext. Bull. 433. Seek update.

ROBINSON, D.E. and W.J. LORD. Response of "McIntosh" apple trees to soil incorporated Simazine. J. ASHS 95(2):195-198. 1970.

ROM, ROY C. et al. Glyphosate Toxicity to Apple Trees, HortSci. 9:594-595. 1974.

Sources of up-to-date weed control information for fruits: Univ. of California, Davis (most fruits); Washington St. Univ., Prosser (most fruits; cranberry at Long Beach, Wash.); Michigan St. Univ., E. Lansing (most fruits); Indiana (Purdue), Lafayette, small fruits; Univ. of Wisconsin, Sturgeon Bay (cherry); Ohio Agr. Exp. St., Wooster (small fruits); Kansas St. Univ., Manhattan (most small and tree fruits); Pennsylvania St. Univ., University Park (most fruits); N.Y. Agr. Exp. Sta., Geneva (most fruits). Weed Control Manual and Herbicide Guide, Meister Publ. Co., 37841 Euclid Ave., Willoughby, Ohio 44094. Annual.

VIRUS DISEASES

CATON, DONALD. Dwarf fruit and tree decline, a virus disease of apple. Mich. Quart Bull. 42.4. 722-727. May 1960.

"Flat-limb" virus in apple. Aust. Journ. of Agr. Res. 15:4, 548-59. July 1964.

FRIDLUND, P.R. Temperature and viruses of *Prunes, Malus, Pyrus.* Wash. Agr. Exp. Sta. Bull. 726. 1970.

GILMER, R.M., K.D. BRASE and K.G. PARKER. Control of virus diseases of stone fruit nursery trees in New York, N.Y. Agr. Sta. Bull. 779, 53 pp. 1957.

McCRUM, R.C. et al. Apple virus diseases—illustrated review. Agr. Exp. Stations of Maine (Bull. 595) and New Hampshire (Tech. Bull. 101) 63 pp. June 1960.

MINK, G.I. and J.R. SHAY. Latent viruses in apple. Purdue Agr. Exp. Sta. Res. Bull. 756, 23 pp. 1962.

POSNETTE, A.F. Virus diseases of apples and pears. Commonwealth Bureau of Hort. and Plantation Crops, E. Malling, Kent. Eng. Tech. Communication 30, 141 pp. Seek update.

SCURFIELD, G. and D.E. BLAND. The anatomy and chemistry of "rubbery" wood in apple var. Lord Lambourne. J. HortSci. 38:297-306. 1963.

SEIDL, V. and V. KOMARKOVA. Contribution to the Test for Latent A p p l e
Viruses by means of Indicators. 'Spy 227' and 'R 12740-7A.' Ochr. rostl. 7:195-202. 1971.

SMITH, KENNETH M.A. Textbook of plant virus diseases. Acad. Press. NY. 648 pp. Jan. 1973.

THOMAS, H. EARL. Virus diseases of apples. Hilgardia 31:435-456. Nov. 1961.

Viruses in fruit crops. Symposium insert. HortSci. 12(5):463-490. 1977.

Viruses of horticultural plants. Proc. XVII International Horticultural Congress Vol. III: 79-102. Univ. of Md., College Park, 1966.

APPLICATIONS

Aerial applications of agricultural chemicals. USDA Agr. Handbook 287, 48 pp. Seek update.

CARLTON, JAMES B. Electrostatic charging of sprays by airplane coverage, Farm Chem. 131:8. pp. 40-42. 1968.

HAINES R.G. Controlling fruit insects by aircraft application. Mich. Qtrly. Bull. 41:2, 410-420. Nov. Seek update.

AIR POLLUTION

BRADY, NYLE C. Agriculture and the quality of environment (a book on air pollution). Amer. Assoc. for Adv. Sci. Publ. No. 85. Wash. D.C. 460 pp. 1965.

STERN, A.C. (Ed.) Air pollution and its effects. Vol. 1. Analysis, monitoring and surveying. Vol. II. 694, 684 pp. resp. (Environ. Sci. and Monograph Ser.) Academic Press. New York and London, 1968.

WILSON, B.R. Ed. Environmental problems—pesticides, thermal pollution and environmental synergisms. J.B. Lippincott Co., Phila.-Toronto, 183 pp. 1968.

(See additional references in former book editions.)

CHAPTER XIX

Frost and Drouth Control

To make a comfortable living, a grower must try every way possible to insure a full fruit crop every year. Periodic frost (freeze) and/or drouth damage in fruit growing regions have been something with which many growers in the past have been willing to take a gamble. The money loss, however, can be heavy when a frost or drouth does occur and when the grower is not prepared for them. Today, most growers are taking steps to minimize as much as possible the money loss from these acts of nature.

This chapter reviews frost and irrigation problems in the business of fruit growing and their suggested solution. Elsewhere in the book (see the index) you will find brief discussions pertinent to the crop in question. Sources of information also are listed at the end of the chapter for a more thorough study of a specific problem.

FROST CONTROL[1]

Due to the OPEC fuel oil crisis in the 1970s, there has been increasing acceptance of *energy and cost saving* techniques for frost control. In the USA, overtree wind machines were scarce until the late 1970s when 1000s of them were installed over the country with over 2000 alone in Washington. Wind machines can be used effectively alone or in combination with fuel burning pots properly placed in the blocks, depending upon the severity of the frost. Overtree and undertree irrigation systems also are being used to control frost where adequate water is available and the soil and trees can handle it. Some 26,000 acres of citrus in one Florida county alone were equipped with undertree sprinkling systems in the early 1980s to replace fuel heat. In fact, Florida growers use fuel heat only to save the trees. Also, more attention is being given to the selection of orchard sites less subject to killing frosts.

Factors Influencing Frost (Freeze) Damage. The *advective freeze* occurs when an arctic cold mass moves in frequently dry and accompanied by winds. Orchard heating, of course, is made more difficult by cold arctic air

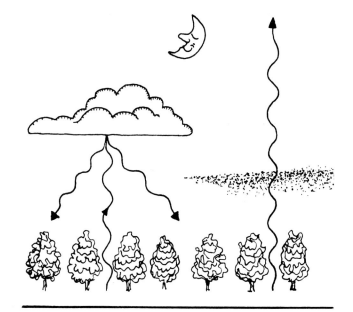

Figure 1. Energy radiated from the ground at night is in the form of long-length waves. Long waves are absorbed and radiated back by clouds, but pass right through smoke. Energy radiated from the sun during the day is in the form of short-length waves. Short waves pass through natural clouds, but do not pass through smoke.

[1]David W. Buchanan, J. David Martsolf and Fred S. Davies, University of Florida and Steven Blizzard, Tara Auxt and Mary E. Curtis, West Virginia University made suggestions for revision of the frost-control chapter. Some of the information is from Extension Bull. 634 (1981) by J. K. Ballard (Yakima) and E. L. Proebsting, Jr. (Prosser), Washington State University, to whom appreciation is expressed for use of the material and the photographs and diagrams.

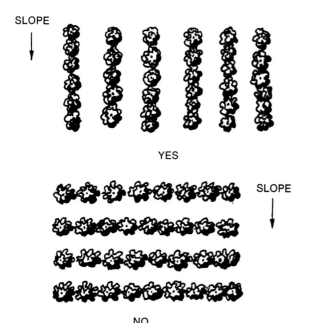

SLOPE

YES

SLOPE

NO

Figure 2. Hedgerow planted trees should run downward on a slope for best air drainage. This can be done on modestly rolling land without a soil erosion problem by using strip-chemical-weed control in the rows and permanent sod between rows. Natural draws should be kept open for air drainage by removing trees and brush.

Figure 3. (Above) Electronic digital thermometers are accurate with an easy-to-read quick response. They can be carried through the orchard. (Below) Electronic frost alarms are available for monitoring temperatures with accurate gauges. Circuitry is failproof with standby battery to trigger the alarm at temperatures as low as 25°F (-3.9°C). The electronic thermometers can be used as remote sensors placed on high poles to determine inversions. (Right) A sling psychrometer can be used to determine dew points. Instructions and a table accompany the instrument. (Wash. State Univ.)

which may last for several days when day temperatures seldom exceed 50°F. Most *orchard* heating equipment becomes less protective with advective freezes. *A radiation frost* occurs on cloudless relatively quiet nights. Ground heat radiates to the sky (Figure 1). Air near the soil level is cooled and the heavy cold air will drift to low spots in the orchard (Figure 2). At a peak, heat loss from the ground on cold clear nights may reach 900,000 BTU/A. About sundown, input of heat is equal to output. Humidity and clouds will vary the heat loss from the ground during the night but a peak is reached in heat loss just before sunrise. Many nights may have both radiation and advective factors operating.

Critical Temperature. This is defined as the temperature on a properly exposed orchard thermometer (Figure 3) at which the buds, flowers, or fruits (Figure 4) will endure 30 minutes or less without injury. Under the tree-fruit discussion in this book, temperatures are given at which a 10 or 90% kill of flower buds may occur at different stages of development. Many factors, however, may alter the ability of flower buds to remain alive at the various stages and temperatures, such as wind, humidity, cultivar, tree vigor, rate of thawing of tissue that has been frozen, and cool-temperature conditioning of tissue before the freeze, and other factors.

Inversions, ceilings. An inversion occurs when a layer of warm air floats over cold air near ground level. In daytime the ground absorbs heat from the sun; air near ground level is warm then becomes cooler as you go up. On a cool clear quiet night, however, some 50-800 ft. above ground the air is warmer than at ground level, hence, an inversion. The magnitude of this inversion varies from night to night, being strong or weak. Effectiveness of overtree wind machines and orchard heaters, of course, varies with the magnitude of the inversion. A *ceiling* is reached when the

Figure 4. Red Delicious on left shows pinched calyx end due to frost damage early in its development.

hot air from orchard heaters reaches the warm air layer above. Following warm days the night ceiling is low and less heat is needed. A high ceiling usually follows cold days and more heat is required to do the job. With an influx of cold arctic air and with wind or no wind, the ceiling tends to be very high, complicating orchard protection.

Wind. Night winds more than 4 mph during an inversion tend to mix the warm and cold air and the temperature drop is slow, or, if the wind is strong the orchard temperature may actually rise. During advective freezes winds have no warming effect due to cold air continually moving in.

Clouds and Smoke. The diagram in Figure 1 describes how clouds and smoke influence orchard heating.

Dewpoint is the temperature at which moisture begins to condense from the air mass. The more water vapor in the air, the higher the dewpoint temperature. As water vapor condenses and changes back to liquid water it releases latent stored heat. Thus, when the dewpoint is above the critical temperature (freezing of tissue) of the crop, the fruit grower benefits by a slower temperature drop due to latent heat being released from water vapor as it condenses to dew or frost. If the dewpoint is several degrees below the critical temperature of the crop, the temperature drop is faster. Orchard dewpoints in arid regions that are higher than 30°F are considered high; less than 20°F are low Dewpoints below 0°F are rare. Dewpoints in the lowei ranges indicate dry air and difficult heating conditions. Thus, the temperature drops fast at the lower dewpoints, making it difficult or impossible to heat even with 40 heaters/A. Temperature may drop as much as 10°F. in 15 minutes.

Weather Monitoring Equipment, Frost Alarms. It is disturbing to sleep through a frost. Advance weather forecasts help avoid this. Most fruit growing areas of the

United States now have highly tailored frost warning services. As an example, the Federal-State Frost Warning Service of Florida has serviced the citrus industry for over 40 years. County agricultural agents will contact the National Weather Service forecaster before and during frosts and communicate to growers frost protection methodology. This program also is available in the Yakima Valley of Washington. The Florida system is using the GOES satellite infrared imagery to display a color-coded thermal map of the State on a microcomputer-driven color-TV screen (Figure 5). This is done through NASA support. These thermal maps are disseminated from an automated (by computer) data acquisition and processing system called The Satellite Frost Forecasting System operated by the National Weather Service and developed

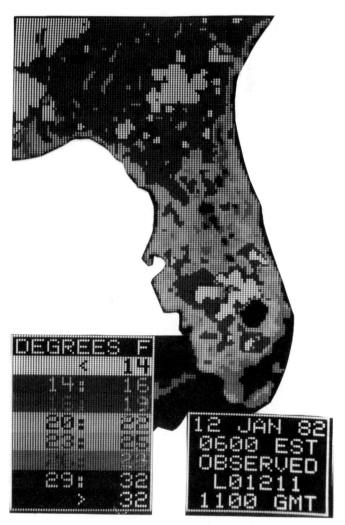

Figure 5. This is a TV screen (in color) picture of Florida taken from a satellite at the Fruit Crops Department, University of Florida, Gainesville, the night of January 12, 1982. The eight colors from white to black (shades of black to white here) are available to county agricultural agents in the respective areas at short intervals for crop protection procedures. (J. David Martsolf, Univ. of Fl., Gainesville)

by the University of Florida. These machines pass the "raw" materials from which these maps are made to other microcomputers over the State so that fairly elaborate networks of weather information at short intervals can be passed on to growers.

The temperature-sensitive unit (Figure 3) should be located in a low area of the fruit planting with the buzzer in the grower's home. Electronic alarms (more accurate, faster response) in the early 1980's cost from $90 to $250 (Figure 3). Thermostat units in the orchard should be a *standard thermometer shelter,* protected from dust, sprays, insects, etc., which may interfere with the bimetal points. Just before the frost season, have them checked for accuracy and electrical circuitry. Use two double-check thermometers and place the sensor in an ice-water slush for checking accuracy at 32°F, after stirring.

One type thermometer suggested where thermometers are used, is a straight-tube alcohol type registering minimum with an etched scale on the tube, called a "standard orchard thermometer." At least two thermometers are needed, one in the coldest location and another nearby outside the heated area to indicate when to stop temperature modifying equipment. Orchard size and topography govern the numbers of thermometers needed. They *must* be placed in *standard thermometer shelters* and after the frost season stored upright with bulb down in a cool place. National Weather Service stations will test thermometers for accuracy. You should always watch for alcohol separation in the column, shaking the thermometer, bulb down to eliminate the separation, or place the bulb in a pan of water, slowly heating the water until the separations come together, then reduce the water temperature slowly.

Hand-held Digital. Shown in Figure 3, these are accurate and quick, battery operated, lighted at night for easy reading and can be carried throughout the orchard for checking cold spots. Cost is around $200.

Sling psychrometers. Since dewpoints are not stable during the night, some weather stations, on request, will broadcast hourly readings of dewpoints. Where this is not available, a sling psychrometer can be used (Figure 3), which has two thermometers, the bulb of one having muslin (kept clean and renewed often) over it dipped in water. The thermometers are twirled by holding the handle; the difference between the readings on the wet and dry bulb thermometers (conversion to dewpoint) can be read from a chart that comes with the equipment, or, can be obtained from the Weather Bureau. U.S. Weather Service Bull. 235, obtainable from the U.S. Supt. of Documents, Washington, D.C., has this and other usable information. Dewpoint readings below 32°F are a bit complicated and directions are given.

Heating Fuels and Equipment. U.S. Growers have had to store or dispose of much of their heating equipment

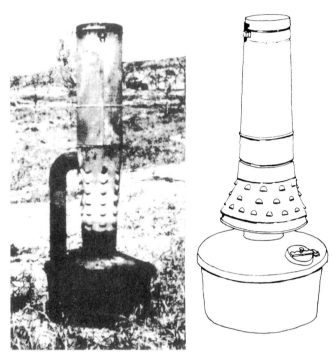

Figure 6. (Left) The return stack oil heater is the "queen" of individual heaters. (Right) The large cone heater emits slightly more radiant heat than the return stack but requires cleaning and burns more oil. Where oil is used, these are the main heaters.

because of oil prices. A few California growers still use heaters but most have gone to water in one form or another. In Mexico, however, as long as the price of oil stays within reason, oil heating will be used (Figure 6). Any heating system should have the capacity to lift the temperature at least 7°F; 40 heaters/A will be required, depending upon site. Grower experience on a site determines this. It is a proven fact that many small fires are more effective than a few large ones. High-density hedgerows may require more heaters than standard trees. Heat should be directed horizontally toward the trees; radiant heat from heaters varies from 20-70% of the total heat output. Hence, the upright stack design tends to direct the heat toward the trees.

The two types of orchard *heaters* most popular are given below; see Figure 6:

Return Stack. This is the best of individual type heaters, burning 0.3-0.6 gal/hr, not exceeding the smoke ordinance, radiant heat is ⅓ the total output, using plastic covers when under-tree sprinklers are used.

Large cone. Advantages are: slightly more radiant heat than the return stack; lower profile making its handling in and out of the orchard easier; resists taking in sprinkling water. It does soot up faster, necessitating cleaning, and burns 0.7 gal of oil/hr.

Pressurized Oil Systems. With the oil squeeze, these systems are not on the market and are not in use in orchards.

Propane Gas Heaters. Liquid propane (L.P.) used in the Northwest can be expensive (heat unit basis) and may have delivery and handling problems. It was popular among growers in the early 1970s, which indicates advantages over other orchard fuels. If costs should come within reason, one should be acquainted with its characteristics. It turns from a liquid to a gas at -44°F. Rate of vaporization of gas, which passes into the orchard plastic pipe system, depends upon the size of storage tank, outside air temperature, and total demand of the heaters. If the system calls for more vapor than the tank can supply the liquid cools and slows its vaporization. Also, as the L.P. level in the tank drops, vaporization slows (tank must not be filled over 82% of its capacity for safety reasons). Hence, some growers provide extra large tanks to circumvent these problems, in addition to having an adequate fuel supply on hand and obtaining it at reduced rates or, special vaporization equipment is used to heat the L.P. either by hot water or indirect fire to increase vaporization. Since L.P. gas is heavier than air, it will flow along the ground from a leak to a low area in the orchard or near the tank and is *highly explosive.*

About 500 gals of L.P. is required/A as a safe minimum for two nights of firing. A 30,000 gal tank has merits for protecting an orchard of 60 acres or more. Combustion chambers are available on the market or the grower can make his own from various pipes, pails, or U.S. Army shell casings.

With L.P., the grower can operate the system on "pilot light" standby in anticipation of a frost, then increase flame as needed. This prevents overheating and saves fuel in comparison with a system using oil or solid fuel.

Heating Procedures. If you are using fuel heat, light orchard borders first on windward or upslope side, then light every other heater or row, and with L.P., light all heaters as a "pilot" standby. Patrol the orchard and be careful not to overheat at first causing a cold-air influx particularly along the borders.

Five problems common to growers in the Northwest and suggested solutions are described below by Alan Jones, National Weather Service, Wenatchee, Washington.

1. The critical temperature is reached. You've made your first lighting of heaters. Occasional light puffs of wind are noticeable and you observe a sudden temperature rise. This may be delayed air drainage. If erratic, it probably won't last, particularly if it is still several hours before sunrise. You may reduce heat, but patrol the thermometers or cold spots regularly. Winds occuring several hours before sunrise can quit again. Your thermometer readings are your guideline for turning the heat up or down.

2. The critical temperature is reached. The temperature control equipment is started and the temperature suddenly rises. This time you observe a cloud drifting over. Leave your equipment as is, unless a solid cloud bank is moving in.

3. The sun has risen after a long, arduous night of firing. Check your outside thermometer readings before turning the equipment off. It takes time for the natural temperature rise to take over, particularly if the low level air is smoky. If you have a normal cold air drainage into the orchard, you may observe a sudden drop in temperature after sunrise.

4. The frost alarm rings. You prepare to start your equipment but the thermometers all read 3 to 5 degrees above the critical temperature. The sky is clear and winds have subsided. The forecaster predicted a low dewpoint of 15°F. with a high ceiling. This means a fast temperature drop. With cold air masses over the district, temperature drops of 9 degrees in 15 minutes have been observed. With an abnormally low dewpoint, you will have trouble holding the temperature above critical. It is better in this case to start the equipment a little early.

5. An advective freeze is upon you. You have done everything right and still the temperature falls. This tells you your temperature control is inadequate for future severe situations. For the time being, keep the equipment operating. You will get some damage but not as much as if you give up and turn the equipment off.

Wind Machines. With high fuel prices most Washington growers have gone to wind machines with or without pot heaters spaced around the block borders. Price of oil in Mexico is lower and some growers are still using heat with the return stack and jumbo heaters.

When there is an inversion of warm air above and cold air near the ground, downward tilted wind machines are effective in mixing the warm air among the trees. Actually, wind machines provided with heating devices have proved less effective than those without. Added heat makes the air more bouyant, causing it to rise. If the upper warm layer is out of reach of the machine, no benefit is gained by turning it on.

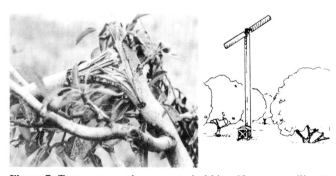

Figure 7. Trees may need support to hold ice, if not on trellis. At right is a wind machine with motor at base for easy maintenance. Propellers are flat-bladed, efficient. L.P. gas or diesel oil may be used to avoid gasoline theft. (Ballard and Proebsting, Wa. Bull. 634)

Wind drift direction must be determined prior to the installation of a wind machine. This drift is generally less than 3 mph and usually occurs from the same general direction each night. It is not always from the same direction as the daytime winds. This must be determined under cloudless conditions after sunset. Wind drift causes the shape of the protected area to be eggshaped with the greater area downdrift from the machine. Knowing the direction of the nocturnal drift will allow for a more accurate placement of the wind machine and afford the greatest amount of frost protection. Placement is generally more to the updrift side.

A 50 ft. pole with instant reading electronic thermometers at 5, 30, and 50 ft. will help determine whether to use the machine. It is difficult to predict the usefullness of a wind machine. If the site consistently has a 3°F to 8°F warmer inversion at the 30 to 100 ft. layer, a wind machine may be useful (Figures 7, 7a). One machine can handle from 6-20 acres, but this depends on the site, size of machine and nearness to other wind machines. Two machines tend to enhance their single effectiveness and protect a few more acres.

Wind machines have maintenance problems to keep them in running condition such as vandalism of parts and fuel, rodents chewing on belts and hoses and difficulty starting in cold weather. Once in place, they are relatively economical. Used and electric machines in the early 1980s cost 6 to 10 thousand dollars to set in place. New gasoline ones cost $13,000 to $15,000 with possible tax benefits of 10%.

Unfortunately, the deciduous fruit areas of California lack temperature inversion and, hence, wind machines are not used, except in citrus where there are inversions.

Helicopters. The helicopter is becoming more attractive to growers with multiple frost pockets in their orchards (Figure 7a). This method of protection is similar to the wind machine in that the helicopter blends the higher warm layers of air with lower cold air. A big advantage of the helicopter over the wind machine is its mobility. Cost for renting helicopters is from $200 to $500 per hour depending on their size. Care should be taken to reserve aircraft in advance and have the pilot pretest the site to

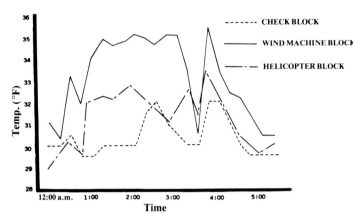

Figure 7a. In an experimental orchard, Kearneysville, West Virginia, Mary E. Curtis and Steven H. Blizzard tested the helicopter and a wind machine on a common site when there was an inversion of 3°F above 50 ft. If the inversion were less than 3°, no benefit was derived at ground-10 ft. level. Temperatures reached 19°F. Machines were started at 1° above the critical temperature. As noted, the wind machine was more effective than the helicopter under their conditions. (Univ. of W. Va.)

avoid last minute delays. Actual area of protection will depend on size of aircraft and size of frost pockets to be protected. The aircraft should fly approximately 10-12 mph at 40 ft. from the ground level. It is important that an area not be left unprotected for more than six minutes.

Sprinkling. *Overtree.* This technique of frost portection has been world tested (Figure 8), is convenient, clean, and operating (energy) costs are lower than other methods (Table 1) but there are risks. With the energy crisis, many fruit growers are switching to overtree sprinkling for irrigation, which also can serve for heat suppression, insect and mite suppression, and application of chemicals as well as frost control and bloom delay (for bloom delay see also Wash. EM-4113 bull.).

In California, water is most important for frost protection in grapes, Kiwis, and almonds where sprinklers over vine or under tree (almonds) are used. Overhead sprinklers give 6-7°F protection with 0.10 to 0.15 inch precipitation per hour or 50-60 gal/minute/acre. Overtree sprinklers are sometimes used in apple and pear orchards. Most grapes in Napa and Mendocino (north coast) use

TABLE 1. PER-ACRE OWNING AND OPERATING COSTS OF VARIOUS FROST PROTECTION
SYSTEMS (10 ACRE BLOCK, 1970s' WASH. EXT. BULL. 634, 1981)*

| | 35 Heaters Per Acre | | | 28 Oil Pots | |
	Stack Heaters	Oil Pressure Heaters	L.P. Gas	With One Wind Machine	Overtree Sprinkling
Capital Investment Per Acre	$756.14	$737.26	$1,016.69	$1,085.11	$817.68
Operating Costs Per Acre	243.25	225.10	195.46	76.08	19.95
Labor (Total Season)	22.50	17.00	17.00	17.50	9.50
Equipment (Total Season)	11.00	3.35	1.25	5.87	1.85
Fuel (Total Season Gallons)	(700)	(682)	(455)	(90 oil + 32 gas)	
Fuel (Total Season Cost)	210,000	204.75	169.71	42.21	8.60
Investment Overhead Per Hour	3.24	3.03	3.65	3.04	.92
Total Annual Costs Per Acre	$ 12.80	$ 11.67	$ 11.16	$ 5.96	$ 1.45

*Inflation will change these figures but a relative idea can be gained.

Figure 8. Overhead sprinklers also are useful in protecting flower buds from frost damage where water is not at a premium. Sprinkling is started at 32° to 33°F and continued til ice starts to melt on buds after dawn. (Courtesy Don Heinicke, grower and consultant, Ione, Washington 99139)

overhead sprinklers for frost protection. Kiwi growers use mostly overhead sprinklers. Many growers run water in furrows during light frosts and get 1-2°F protection.

With continuous water application, the tree tissue temperature remains at or above 31.5°F, even though a layer of ice is forming. If water application stops, the ice and plant tissue become colder than the air because of the cooling effect of evaporating water. Ice is a poor insulator. Evaporating water absorbs 7½x as much heat as the same water freezing to ice gives off.

Water application must continue until ice begins to thaw (at dawn). The big problem is excessive weight of the ice which may break limbs. Hedgerow dwarf trees, (particularly those on trellis), have the advantage of taking this weight over standard-size trees. An exposed thermometer *in* the sprinkling area is needed (Figure 9).

The minimum water application rate to carry protection down to 20°F is 0.15 to 0.20 inch/hr, depending upon the average dewpoint and wind speed. Experience has shown that at a low dewpoint with wind, water can be applied at 0.15 inch/hr and protect blossoms to 20°F. This is the minimum at which all economically justified heating systems begin to fail. In the Northwest U.S., such conditions occur only about once in 10 years at around bloom time. The 0.2 inch/hr could be used on the upwind side of the planting where more evaporation cooling occurs. A rate of 0.15 requires 67.3 gal/A/minute or 4,038 gal/A/hr accumulating 1½ inches in a 10-hr run. Water supply should be adequate for several successive (at least 3) 1-hr night runs. If irrigation water has not been turned into the canals, special wells or holding ponds may be good in-

surance. Water in ditches or ponds may give a 2°F protection.

Table 2 below was developed by Pennsylvania State University researchers for eastern humid conditions to give sprinkler application rates based on wind speeds.

TABLE 2. SPRINKLER PRECIPITATION RATES FOR ADEQUATE PROTECTION FROM FROST OF A TWO CENTIMETER WIDE LEAF (IN INCHES PER HOUR).*

Temperature °F	Wind speed in miles per hour					
	.5	3.0	6.0	12.0	20.0	30.0
26.0	.01	.03	.04	.05	.06	.08
24.0	.04	.08	.11	.15	.19	.23
22.0	.06	.13	.18	.25	.32	.39
20.0	.08	.18	.25	.34	.44	.53
18.0	.10	.23	.31	.44	.56	.68
15.0	.14	.30	.41	.57	.73	.89
12.0	.17	.37	.50	.70	.90	1.09
10.0	.19	.41	.57	.79	1.01	1.23

*From Perry, K. B. Sprinkler Irrigation Models in Frost Protection. Ph.D. Thesis, Penn. State Univ., Univ. Park. 104 pp. 1979.

Equipment. An *even* distribution of water over the tree is important. The system must be large enough to sprinkle the entire planting; hence, large mainlines, pump and motor will be needed vs. use for irrigation block-rotation. Engineering specialists must be consulted. Sprinkler heads must rotate at least once a minute, and two is better. Design of sprinkler heads must not permit ice buildup around the activator spring. Pump must be capable of operating far below freezing. Breakdowns for only a few minutes may result in loss of crop.

Sprinkler Spacing. A 40 x 40 ft. spacing is better than wider spacing. Full protection and overlap must be

Figure 9. A wire trellis will give support for compact fruit trees with icicle weight from an overhead sprinkling system for frost control. Insert shows clear ice (not milky) from water applied at about 0.2+ inch/hr on apple flower buds. Low microjet sprinklers mounted on the low wire for irrigation also may give some frost protection. (Courtesy J. David Martsolf, Penn State Univ. and University of Florida).

provided around the borders. In general, the maximum spacing between sprinklers should not exceed 50% of the wetted diameter.

Operation. Start sprinkling when the temperature reaches 33°F on the protected thermometer in the coldest spot of the planting. This is the margin of safety against water freezing in the system. Cease sprinkling when the temperature reaches 33°F after dawn.

Precautions. Central leader trees will support more ice than open-vase ones. Spur, twig, limb breakage and bending of branches is greatest the first season of sprinkling. Roping or some form of branch support may be needed on obviously weak main limbs. Water should be well filtered to be free of sand, silt and debris. Due to a muddy condition in the orchard at frost sprinkling time, it

Figure 10. Sprinkling, misting and shading fruit plants at various stages of growth and flower bud development are of interest. (Upper) The Ohio Agr. Exp. Sta., Wooster, after J. LaMar Anderson et al.'s initial finding in Utah, have shown the effect of intermittent misting G. Delicious on M. 9, background, after rest period is completed when temperature rose above 45°F; foreground, no misting. Bloom was retarded over 2 wks. but misted trees showed some fireblight and excess water symptoms. (Lower left) Sprinkling apple trees on hot days gave Unrath et al. of N. C. State Univ. better fruit color, sizing. (Lower right) Plastic mesh covering is being tested in several areas for hail protection (Mexico, Austria, Italy), reduced frost risk, wind damage, as photographed by Paul Stark Jr., Stark Nursery of Louisiana, Missouri, 63353.

may be well to arrange to apply sprays by plane or helicopter. Also, excessive water application may leach N, B and other readily soluble key nutrient elements from the rooting area.

Undertree Sprinkling. Low intermittent high-volume microjet sprinklers may have a place in frost control of compact trees. The Florida citrus growers in one county alone (Polk) on over 30,000 acres were using this system in the early 1980s. They could use high amounts of water (0.3-0.5 in/hr,) which is readily available (one sprinkler/tree) on their well drained sandy soils. They were getting about a 6°F protection to 3 ft. above ground and 4° up to 6 ft. with little protection from 6 ft. up. In arid regions as Washington where water is limited and soil cannot take large volumes of water, this approach may not work.

If the dewpoint is high before sprinkling, adequate frost protection is possible in large blocks, but if it is low and more than 3°F is needed for protection, serious damage can occur. California research advises against undertree sprinkling where dewpoints are below freezing. If above freezing, *no* evaporative cooling will occur and if all water is being frozen, a considerable amount of heat is being released as the water turns to ice. Part of this heat will go into the ground and part into the air. Transfer of heat to fruit buds is by both radiation and conventional transfer. Further study is underway in Washington.

Electric Trellis Cable. This frost control approach has been discussed by Michigan growers but no tests have been made due to budget problems. Trellis support wires, possibly two, would be electric cable (available), actuated by an automatic thermostat when the temperature fell below a critical level either in mid-winter or during a spring frost. Engineers note that radiant heat should reach out to about three feet or more on either side. Electricity likely would be needed on but a few nights a year. Cost could be within reason. One problem, the same as for gas, the orchard would need four million BTUs an acre when a city would most need the energy. Farmers are last on the list to receive elecric energy under these conditions.

Artificial Fogs. Fogs have been tested in Florida and California with little practical significance.

Misting, shading. Cold-water misting of dormant fruit trees is a simple (no pollution) approach to holding back flower bud opening to avoid frost damage (Figures 10, 11). The idea was conceived and demonstrated by J. LaMar Anderson, Arlo Richardson, et al. of Utah State University, Logan (84321). They have designed a mathematical model (Figure 12) to count the accumulated chill units (one hour below about 45°F = one chill unit) an apple tree, e.g., has had during the winter dormant period. An apple tree requires about 1200 chill units (Chap. 3) to break its rest. "Rest period" is that period during dormancy when the tree will not grow in spite of favorable

Figure 11. A Rome Beauty orchard in Utah is shown in bloom except for a center group of trees (arrow) that had been held back from blooming by intermittent misting cold water on the buds during warm periods a few weeks before bloom. This can be a safeguard against late frost damage. (J. LaMar Anderson, Utah State University, Logan 84321)

environmental conditions, mainly temperature. When the rest period is completed Anderson et al. start intermittent misting with an overhead sprinkler system (special nozzles) when the temperature is above about 45°F, misting for 2 minutes, off 4 minutes. They have held back apple bloom for 17 days. Elden Stang et al. of the Ohio Agr. Res. and Devel. Center, Wooster (44691) confirmed the results with Delicious on M.9 rootstocks (Figure 10), but induced more fireblight in a blight season with some signs of excess soil water damage in a medium loam soil. Some reduced bloom the next year also was noted.

Some researchers are cautious in recommending this approach to frost control but if the overhead system is installed for irrigation, it also can be used for misting to delay bloom in consultation, of course, with local specialists. In addition to irrigation, the system also can be used for cooling the trees a few weeks before harvest to retain or induce better fruit coloring and sizing (Figure 10). The advantage of cooling the trees and fruit before harvest during a particularly hot season has been demonstrated by C. Richard Unrath of No. Car. State University, Fletcher (28732).

David W. Buchanan et al. of University of Florida, Gainesville (32611), have held back peach bloom by 11 days by misting. Texas researchers of Texas A. and M. University, College Station (77843), have held back bloom of a commercial crop of peaches for about two weeks by misting and obtained one-third of a crop vs. no crop on controls.

Bacterial Ice Nucleation. This approach is in the experimental stages but shows promise. Most plants cannot tolerate ice formation within their tissues, disrupting the cells and causing frost damage. Certain species of bacteria, *Pseudomonas syringae, P. fluorescens* and *Erwinia herbicola,* can act as non-aqueous catalysts for ice formation at temperatures only slightly below freezing. These bacteria are present on leaves of healthy plants naturally in

tremendous numbers (100 million per gram) in the field. If these bacteria are inhibited or neutralized, plant tissues may be under-cooled without ice formation to 20°F. Three present approaches are being tested for controlling the bacteria: (1) Use of bactericides as Streptomycin or oxytetrocycline at least 10 days before an expected frost; (2) use of antagonistic bacteria which are competitive with ice-nucleation bacteria, so-dominating them they become inactive, relatively ineffective and (3) use of bacterial ice nucleation inhibitors such as extremes of pH surroundng the bacteria, various heavy metals in sprays including copper and zinc, certain cationic detergents and several other conditions. The heavy metals, e.g., also can serve as pesticides and/or a source of needed trace elements as zinc. Researchers contributing to these studies are: S. E. Lindow et al, University of California, Davis, and David W. Buchanan et al, University of Florida, Gainesville.

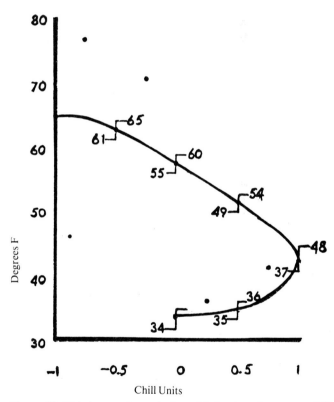

Figure 12. This is a mathematical model developed to count chill units for fruit trees. Note that the tree is gaining units as the curve goes to the right to about 45°F, above which the curve turns to the left and the tree starts losing chill units. A certain number of chill units may be gained up to a warm period when the temperature goes above 45°F (some say 43°F) at which time the tree will lose units that it had gained. One "chill unit" gained is one hour of chilling below about 45°F. An apple tree needs about 1200 chilling units to break its rest period, after which intermittent misting can be started to hold back flower bud opening. (Courtesy Arlo Richardson, Utah State University, Logan, 84321).

DROUTH — IRRIGATION

Most deciduous fruits are grown between 25° and 55° latitude both north and south of the equator. Annual precipitation (mainly rain and snow) varies from less than 5 in/yr, as in certain regions of North Africa and Southwestern United States, to more than 100 inches. Where precipitation is generally less than 20 in/yr, irrigation is necessary, and in regions of 20 to 30 inches some supplementary water application is needed most years. Where 30 to 50 inches occur, fruit trees usually can survive periodic drouths but growers may lose money once every 4 to 6 years due to small apples, poorer quality, and reduced yields. The trees may be damaged in an extended drouth so that recovery, if at all, is slow and subsequent monetary loss occurs. Today, many tree fruit growers, particularly those with the shallow-rooted dwarf trees as well as the berry growers are providing some means of water application to protect the crops. The irrigation equipment, if of the jet or sprinkler type, also can be used for frost control, cooling the plants in hot weather for better fruit quality and for application of herbicides (late winter) and fertilizer as is being done in some Northwestern U.S. orchards.

During the winter months when trees are without leaves, they use very little water. Much of the winter precipitation is stored in the soil if it is deep and has a moderate supply of clay particles that retain moisture well. Soil depth, its water holding capacity, and the evaporating power of the air will determine the need for irrigation where the yearly average of precipitation may be more or less adequate but where its distribution is erratic.

Root Distribution, Water Absorption. Roots of deciduous fruit and nut trees will be extensive in deep well-drained soil which is free of an impervious layer or a high-water table. Depth of rooting in California may be 16 feet for apricots, 12 feet for walnut and 6 feet for peach and plum. Apple roots have been found 30 to 35 feet deep in the uniform wind-blown loess soil of Nebraska. In New York in a well-drained uniform brown soil, cherry and peach roots will extend to 5 ft, and apple and prune to 6 ft. If there is a mottled grey poorly-drained layer, however, apple, peach or cherry roots will not penetrate it but prune roots have been found to do this which may account for prunes and plums performing better under such conditions where other fruits except possibly pear perform poorly.

Roots have been found to extend laterally 2 to 3 times the branch spread in sandy soil and 1.5 times in loam or clay soils. Where roots are deep and extend well laterally and the soil holds a good supply of winter precipitation, there will be less need for or frequency of irrigation (Figure 13.) Where rooting is shallow the tree is likely to become water-deficient, even during short periods of rainfall deficiency. *Hence, it must be emphasized that the need for*

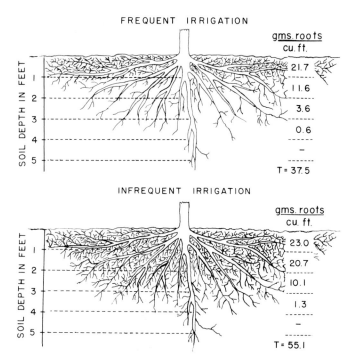

Figure 13. Fruit trees tend to develop a deeper and heavier root system if water is supplied by irrigation only as needed. Too much water can be as detrimental as too little. Note difference above in amount of roots in various depths with frequent and infrequent irrigation. (Courtesy of Garth A. Cahoon, while at Univ. of Calif., Riverside)

irrigation and its frequency will be greater for the growth-controlling rootstocks of high-density trees than for the standard low-density orchards.

The number of the small so-called feeder roots of a tree become fewer with increasing distance from the trunk both vertically and laterally. Maximum density of these roots is in the upper 3 ft. of soil beneath the branch spread and, in fact, 80 to 90% may be found in the upper foot with an established program of mulching.

Water absorption from the soil by roots increases as the leaf surface of the tree increases in spring and most of the water comes from the upper soil layer which is warmer and has greater feeder-root penetration.

If a portion of the root system is in a soil mass at the wilting percentage (% water in a soil when a plant such as sunflower wilts), water uptake by the roots in that area is reduced and under high transpiration (water-vapor loss by leaves) conditions, a water deficit will occur in the tree, depending upon the percentage of the root system involved.

Water status within a tree changes from day to day and hour to hour, while soil water changes slowly. Tree usage of water and transpiration increase with increased air temperature mainly and also with increased air movement and sunlight intensity and lowered relative humidity. A water deficit may occur in a tree when transpiration is quite high, even though soil water is adequate. For example, with adequate soil moisture the water in apple leaves may decrease 6 to 7% from early morning to noon on a warm clear day while bark water will decrease 3%. Maximum water deficit in the leaf usually occurs around 2 p.m. on a clear day and the reverse about 2 a.m. Soluble solids are highest at about 3 p.m. and lowest at 6 a.m. Water accumulates in the tree overnight.

Stomatal Activity and Leaf Processes. Stomata are the pores in the epidermis (skin) of a leaf (see cross-leaf diagram, Chap. IV) through which carbon dioxide, oxygen and water vapor pass in the processes of photosynthesis (food manufacture), respiration (energy and heat release) and transpiration (water-vapor loss). Water, and soluble solids content, pH, light and other factors govern the opening and closing of these pores. In peach, prune and apricot, which is typical of most fruit trees, their maximum degree of opening occurs between 9 a.m. and noon after which they begin to close. Stomata are open less wide and a shorter time on trees (a) in a dry soil vs those in a moist soil and (b) on trees during a high temperature and low relative humidity vs those on a cool humid day. When dryness is acute, stomata may not open at all and thus help to conserve water in the tree.

When stomata are less active or closed due to dryness, both photosynthesis and transpiration are reduced as much as 40% before the leaves show wilting, and over 90% at wilting. Food and energy loss by respiration increase during drouth conditions.

In a soil with inadequate water, the bark of a fruit tree may show 10-15% more sugar and 25% less starch than in a tree with adequate water. Effects of auxin sprays such as 2, 4, 5-T may be enhanced by irrigation when needed, resulting, e.g., in larger apricot fruit that mature sooner than fruits not so-treated.

Vegetative Growth and Water. Water deficiency is associated with reduced shoot length and leaf size, particularly with an early season drouth. If, however, there is adequate stored soil moisture early in the season, shoot growth may be equally good in non-irrigated orchards due to shoot growth being completed within about six weeks after growth begins. Trunk diameter of fruit and nut trees, however, likely will be reduced by a mid- or late-summer drouth. In fact, trunk growth measurements with very sensitive equipment are a more exact indicator of hourly and day and night water fluctuations in a tree than fruit growth measurements.

Observations indicate that roots will not grow into dry soil at the wilting percentage; in fact they grow very slowly in soil just above the WP.

Fruiting. During a dry or moderately dry season researchers agree that the number of fruit buds initiated on apple and pear, e.g., will be increased appreciably, thus giving a good bloom the following spring. The biennial bearing habit on apple, however, can be reduced by regular application of water when needed in adequate but not excessive amounts.

Little or no data are available on the effect of irrigation on fruit set. Little water is used during winter months; hence, adequate water usually is available shortly after growth starts at fruit setting time. Irrigation the previous season when needed, however, helps to develop strong flower buds that are more likely to set than weak buds that develop during a drouth. It is doubtful under orchard conditions if an early season dry period will affect the usual so-called "June drop" of small fruit one to two months after bloom.

Fruit growth, as measured by its circumference increase has been used as a sensitive and practical measurement of water stress in the tree. The different fruits and nuts may respond differently to water stress, depending upon the time the stress occurs; this is because they have different patterns of growth. If water is ample, the fruit growth rate of apples and pears is almost uniform to maturity. In the lighter sandy soils of California, apple and pear growth may be unaffected as long as the soil water is above the wilting percentage. In medium to heavy loams, however, in the New England area of the U.S., the number of 3-inch apples has been shown to decrease when the available soil water drops below 25% of the field capacity (amount of water it will hold against field capacity) of the soil.

Seasonal growth of stone fruits follows a double sigmoid curve (see chart in Ch. XIV) when there is little or no fruit swelling during pit hardening, after which growth may be rapid to maturity. Once a fruit falls behind in growth due to drouth, it never will attain the ultimate size of fruit receiving ample water.

In peach about two-thirds of the final fruit volume is attained the last 30 days on the tree and, hence, ample water supply is critical during this period. In cherry about 80% of the "final swell" occurs during the last 25 days. Plums, prunes, and apricots show similar double-sigmoid growth curves.

With nuts there is no "final swell" period. Ultimate size is reached about mid-summer, when the kernel begins to fill and mature. Full size of almonds is reached in about 50 days after bloom in Calfornia. Kernel development occurs mainly during the latter 2 months on the tree. Early soil water stress affects the size of the nut whereas late stress can affect kernel development. this also holds true with pecan and walnut.

Fruit cracking may be due to rapid increase in fruit size, due to rapid absorption of water through the roots or the skin. Cherry cracking is associated with rapid absorption of water through the skin from rain or irrigation. In apple, grape, and pecan, cracking may occur when water is supplied by rain or by irrigation following a rather extended dry period. Irrigated and nonirrigated fig trees may show no difference in cracking.

Plum fruits may show end or side cracking. Cracks on the side of the fruit may develop at the beginning of the "final-swell" regardless of irrigation practices, whereas end cracks may occur any time during fruit development with water application after a dry period, except at the end of the "final-swell" period. A dry spell and/or a nutrient shortage or caustic sprays seem to cause hardening of the skin which becomes tight and "brittle", cracking when water subsequently is applied.

A preharvest drop of peaches may occur on trees that have been under water stress and then irrigated near harvest. Apple drop just before harvest and poor fruit coloring are common on trees suffering from drouth, at which time effectiveness of "stop-drop" sprays such as NAA is reduced. Preharvest drop of hazel nuts has been reduced or stopped by regular application of water where needed. Pecan leaves will drop before fruit drop. Cool water spray on trees will delay apple harvest up to 2 wks.

Yield, Quality. Any tree subjected to WP conditions can be expected to have a reduced *yield* and poorer quality of fruits or nuts. An ample water supply is more important with a heavy crop than a light one. Quality of canned cling peaches may be tough and leathery, and fresh peaches dry and bitter when grown under dry soil conditions. Pears may be hard and green after the ripening period, prunes sunburned, and nut kernels poorly filled during a drouth.

Irrigated apple, peach, and plum fruits tend to be lower in soluble solids (sugar) and higher in water; apples are less firm and acidic but juicier; and apples and peaches may show more storage problems. However, when soil water is maintained above its wilting point, soluble solids are likely to be higher and water less in fruit than when water is held at a high level. Over-irrigation can be quite harmful (Figure 13).

S. R. Drake, Prosser, Wash., has shown that trickle irrigated Golden Delicious were higher in yellow color, soluble solids, more mature and lower in moisture and acidity than Golden Delicious from sprinkle-irrigated plots. Apple sauce was superior from trickle plots in consistency and less "weep." The sprinkle irrigated apples were better for apple juice and canned or frozen slices due to higher water content. Sprinkled apples were better for long storage. Drip irrigation induced a broader tree, more flower bud set on one-year wood, more fruit sunburn, fewer aphids, more total bud set, but no fruit color difference.

Drouth, Defoliation and Winter Injury. Trees under water stress tend to drop leaves early and if a rain occurs or water is applied late in the season, growth may start, some bloom appear and, hence, the June drop reduced the following year.

The dry cold air of winter may dessicate tree tissues resulting in winter injury or freezing if the tree enters dormancy under dry soil conditions. An irrigation in arid country is suggested to alleviate this situation, while under humid conditions an irrigation at this time has been found to enhance winter injury. Trees in soil with about $\frac{1}{3}$ available water have shown less frost damage during bloom than trees in soil held at a higher moisture level. E.L. Proebsting, Jr., Prosser, Wash., during a crucial water shortage found that dehorning peach trees saved the trees vs. no dehorning.

Drouth, Diseases and Insects. Figs and walnuts are subject to sunburn under drouth conditions which may invite the branch-wilt fungus. Increasing soil moisture is associated with increased fire blight on pear. The apricot gummosis fungus has shown little relation to level of soil moisture, as some workers had suspected.

Mites will increase rapidly under dry conditions and over-tree irrigation is one way of reducing them. Such irrigation, however, may increase crown rot of apple, scatter the fire blight infection from higher to lower parts of a tree and favor fruit rot and twig infections particularly on stone fruits. Under-tree irrigation will solve some of these problems.

Drouth and Nutrient Supply. Any problems associated with a marginal or deficient supply of a nutrient such as boron usually is aggravated by a drying soil; less water is available as a carrier of the nutrient from the soil particles into the tree roots. Excess irrigation or an over water supply, however, may decrease the percentage of a nutrient in the tree tissue.

When a nutrient such as nitrogen, boron, magnesium or potassium is highly soluble in water, excess rains or irrigation can leach the nutrient downward below the rooting zone and result in a deficieny of the elements in the tree.

After a series of dry years in California, leaf scorch on apricot occurred due to excess absorption of sodium from the soil. It took double the usual water application to leach out the sodium and reduce the injury.

Irrigation water high in boron, bicarbonate and calcium may result in chlorosis and toxicity to the tree. In irrigated orchards, incipient leaf chlorosis (yellowing) sometimes can be reduced by merely reducing the frequency of irrigations.

IRRIGATION METHODS

The main methods of applying water to orchards are (a) basin or flood, (b) furrow rill, (c) sprinkler and (d) trickle (drip or microjet).

The *basin* or *flood* system is economical and used when the land is fairly level and the flood basins are level and of acceptable area. Small dikes are built with special equipment along contour lines and the area within dikes flooded with several acre-inches of water. The soil must be able to hold or store from 4 to 8 acre-inches of water. Caution is needed for this type irrigation where root diseases are a problem as with crown rot on MM106 apple rootstocks.

In the *furrow type,* the water runs between the trees in furrows or rills spaced usually about 3-4 ft. apart; closer in sandy soils. There must be a gentle slope of the furrows. Tree rows remain dry. If slope is too great, water accumulates at the end of furrows; if the soil is too sandy or there is too little slope, too much water sinks in near the source and over-irrigates some trees. Even distribution of the water over the entire orchard is the goal and initial engineering assistance is needed.

Sprinkler irrigation has been increasing rapidly over the years with the light-weight, portable aluminum pipe (being less used) or over- and under-ground (18-24'') iron or plastic pipe, and with small sprinkler heads becoming available. Under-tree or over-tree sprinkler application of water has the advantages of (a) more uniform and complete coverage of an orchard block, (b) applicable to rolling land and/or sandy or gravelly soils and (c) is adapted in humid regions having only periodic drouths during a growing season. Portable pipe is usually placed under the trees, with one or two daily moves to new spots, allowing cultivation, harvesting, etc., in one direction. Permanent over-tree sprinkler equipment (just high enough to clear trees) is in use in the arid Northwest; growers are using it for frost control, application of herbicides (dormant season), fertilizers, and for cooling the trees in particularly hot weather. Main disadvantages are (a) higher initial cost, (b) the need for pumping equipment and the over-tree type may increase some disease problems, but it will reduce mites. Growers in humid areas are studying similar uses under their conditions. Application rates vary from 1/10'' to 25/100 inch/hr depending upon crop and soil with pressure of 40 and 70 psi. Nozzle spacings are about 50% of the diameter coverage along the line and about 70% of the coverage diameter between lines.

Several sprinkler manufacturers now supply automatic equipment for the permanent-set system where the controllers automatically turn the sprinklers off and on at predetermined periods, as well as change from a long sprinkling period to a short cooling period which is determined by a pre-set thermostat. The thermostat will turn the sprinklers on for short periods ranging from 2½ minutes to 5 minutes in frost control or longer and up to 30 to 60 minutes off in a continuous cycle until the thermostat is "satisfied" at the pre-set thermostat setting. The sprinkling cycle, again then is returned automatically by the controller and proceeds through the cycle to allow the full irrigation. The equipment will, also, turn sprinklers on for frost control by a thermostat pre-set. The thermostat also can automatically turn the sprinklers off at the

predetermined setting of the thermostat; however, it is suggested that the system should be turned off after the orchard is inspected to make sure that most of the ice has melted or is melting rapidly. If frost protection is desired, 50 to 60 gallons per minute per acre should be applied continuously during the frost period. The sprinklers should be turned on before the freezing period is reached — generally, to be safe, at temperatures from 34° degrees to 38°F., depending upon the dewpoint. The lower the dewpoint, the earlier the sprinklers should be turned on and left running continuously until the ice is melted or rapidly melting.

For compact trees, the undertree microjets are being evaluated for frost control, giving 4-6°F or more protection to 6 ft, depending upon several factors.

Trickle or Drip Irrigation is showing improved profits in both arid and humid regions (Figure 14). "Drip" (Israel) or "Daily Flow" (Australia), which originated in South Africa, are two other names given to the more popular U.S. name, "Trickle Irrigation." This type irrigation refers to the best use of a limited or expensive supply of water to *prevent moisture stress* (rather than correct it) and also to give an optimum supply of water to the tops in at least a portion of the root system area. Water is supplied near the tree or plant base through perforated plastic hose

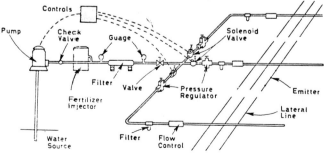

Figure 14. The essential parts of a trickle irrigation system are indicated. Fertilizer injection also is shown.

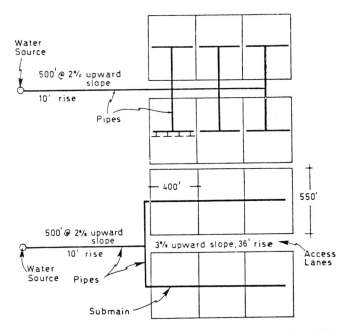

Figure 15. Charts show pipelines and plot layouts for trickle irrigation system above, and overhead system below, planned for strawberries, blueberries, raspberries, apples, peaches or grapes (NRAES 4 Bull., Cornell Univ.)

or a series of emitters which meter water evenly under about 15 psi delivering 1 to 2 gals/hr (GPH) to hold the soil in one or two spots under a tree at or near its *field capacity* (amount of water it will hold against gravity).

Relative cost comparisons of sprinkler and trickle systems are given in Table 1 and 2.

This approach has proven workable since moisture to the top of a plant or tree tends to equalize throughout the plant. Only different organs such as leaves, fruit and growing points respond differently when moisture stress occurs. For example, W. H. Chandler in Missouri back in 1914 showed that the osmotic situation in a leaf had a stronger drawing power for water than in the fruit and, thus, during a dry period water was withdrawn from the fruit by the leaves until the fruit shrivelled. About one-

fourth of the root system if supplied with adequate water can prevent moisture stress throughout the tree.

An efficient trickle irrigation system should provide equal water delivery from each emitter. Hence, friction loss as water moves down the plastic pipes, amount of head pressure, varied elevations in the planting and any other factor affecting flow of water must be considered in designing the entire system.

In a model system tested in several orchards by A. L. Kenworthy of Michigan State University, he used the Australian system of microtube emitters at the tree because they were easy to install, available and economical. A ¾-in. solenoid valve and time clock were installed to activate the system for a predetermined time each day. From the valve, a 2-in. black plastic main line, usually buried, was run to about the highest level point in the orchard. A 100-mesh in-line screen and pressure regulator were installed, beyond which the 2 in. line was continued as a header to which the ½ inch above ground plastic in-row lateral lines were attached as indicated in Figures 15, 16. Ends of the ½ in. lines were closed by folding back and holding them secure with clamps. The microtube outlet inside diameter (ID) was 0.036 in. or about the size of a thin-lead mechanical pencil. Length of the microtube was adjusted to get the desired delivery rate at a given pressure. Microtubes inserted in a hole in the ½ in. line made by (provided) hand equipment and held in place by friction.

Rate of Water Application. From 1-2% of the orchard floor area is irrigated for newly planted orchards and 10-50% for mature orchards. Hence, conventional means of measuring soil moisture cannot be used as an index of when to irrigate. Experience in Israel and Australia indicate that evaporation rate of water from a free-water surface is the best index. The mid-summer month of July in Michigan showed the greatest 20-yr evaporation average of 0.243 in/day or 6598 gals/A (1 A-inch = 27,154 gals). For June it was 6408 and for August, 5620 gal/A/day.

Based on these figures Kenworthy draws the following calculations: (1) Assuming the mature trees occupy 50% of the orchard floor and that we need to replace 75% of the evaporation from a free water surface, the

TABLE 1. COMPARISON OF INITIAL AND ANNUAL COSTS FOR SPRINKLER AND TRICKLE IRRIGATION, MARYLAND. (R.C. FUNT ET AL., MD. MP-950. JULY 1980)

Crop	Initial Cost/Acre		Ann. Cost/Acre[a]		Ann. Cost/Plant, Tree	
	Sprinkler[b]	Trickle[c]	Sprinkler	Trickle	Sprinkler	Trickle
Apples						
A. 6x14	$1,187	$ 824	$159	$101	$0.31	$0.19
B. 10x18	1,187	665	159	97	0.66	0.35
C. 14x22	1,187	1,235	159	171	0.89	1.12
Peaches	1,187	500	159	73	1.59	0.72
Grapes	1,187	557	159	83	0.29	0.15
Raspberries	1,187	459	159	70	0.09	0.04
Blueberries	1,187	468	159	71	0.22	0.10
Strawberries	1,187	1,222	159	363	0.02	0.06

[a]Annual cost for both systems, includes fuel, straight line, depreciation, interest on average investment, repairs and insurance. Costs need to be adjusted for inflation. The figures do give a relative comparison.
[b]Complete sprinkler system itital cost, does not include fuel.
[c]Complete installation cost of trickle system for each crop plus prorated cost of shared components (pump, filter and main pipe).

404

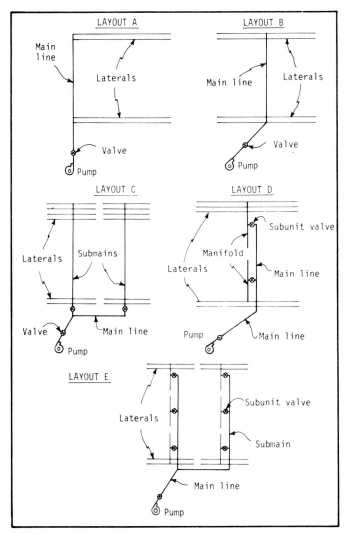

Figure 16. Here are several types of pipe layouts in a trickle irrigation system, depending upon local needs. (Cornell North Reg. Agr. Eng. Serv. Bul. 4. 1980, "Trickle Irrigation in the Northeast U.S.")

following can be calculated for July:
        6598 divided by 2 = 3299
        3299 multiplied by 0.75 = 2474 gal per day
Thus, in July, the irrigation should supply 2474 gal per day (103 gph or 1.7 gallons per minute (gpm) per acre with average rainfall.

For convenience, a need for 2400 gal per acre per day or 100 gph per acre can be assumed. This would require a continuous flow of 1 gph per tree for 100 trees per acre; if 200 trees per acre — 0.5 gph per tree. (3) To allow time for soil moisture equalization or drainage, a program of no more than 12 hr irrigation, rather than continuous flow, would be desirable. Thus, in a mature orchard with 100 trees per acre, a flow rate of 2 gph per tree for 12 hr daily would be required.

The time interval for irrigation should vary with tree age or size and number of emitters per acre. Using 100 trees per acre with one emitter per tree as a base, the time interval for irrigation should be scaled down to perhaps 1 hr daily in newly planted orchards.

This suggests daily irrigation for 1 hr for each year of tree age up to 12 hr. If lesser amounts are required because of above normal rainfall, the calculated amount of irrigation should be in ratio to tree age; 1 for newly planted orchards and 12 for mature orchards.

Acreage and Well Capacity. From the above figures it is evident that a low-capacity well or small reservoir for trickle irrigation will be needed for a given acreage vs. sprinkler, floor, or other irrigating systems. A 10-gpm well should provide 14,400 gal/day. If friction loss in the pipes does not reduce water flow this would irrigate 6.7 acres (14,400 ÷ 2400).

A well can be used to full capacity by applying water to a given area on a 12-hr/day basis, then shifting to another block the next day.

Elevation Changes. Water pressure in a line obviously will change with elevation in the orchard. This factor is critical with the low-pressure system in trickle irrigation. A change of elevation of 2.3 ft will cause a gain or loss in pressure of 1 lb. For example, if the friction loss in a given pipe at a given flow is 1 lb/100 ft of pipe, a 2.3 ft drop in elevation will equalize this loss.

As the rate of flow of water increases through a pipe, there is more turbulence and the friction loss increases with each successive increase in flow. These figures may be supplied by sales people to assist in laying out a trickle system.

Microtubes per Acre and Tree. In trickle irrigation the rate of movement of water laterally in the soil from an emitter or microtube is important. Particle size in the soil governs this (Figure 17), being slower in coarse (sandy) particle size vs. small size (silt, clay). If free water is present, lateral movement is greater. Water application must exceed penetration. This combined with duration of flow, results in one microtube wetting a relatively large soil mass, or at least 25% of the root system of a tree.

Tests have shown that in most orchard soils a flow of 2 gph water for 6-12 hrs can wet a soil mass of 12-20 ft diameter, not wetting the upper 6-12 in.so well but mostly at the 12-36 in.depth. The wetting pattern in silt loam soils is balloon-shaped with an elongated shape for sandy soils. With a sub-clay layer, the balloon is flattened at the base.

With 100 trees/A, there would be 100 emitters; or with 200 trees, 200 emitters and flow rate would be cut in half.

For dwarf trees, one microtube/2 trees may be adequate. For example, a 10 lb pressure giving a 2 gph flow would require a microtube 11.2 inches long; for a 1.5 gph flow an 18.4-inch microtube is needed; and at 1.0 gph the microtube should be 35.2 inches long.

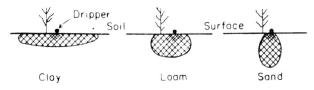

Figure 17. Water distribution patterns under drip irrigation applied in equal quantities at the same rate as affected by soil texture. Note that the lateral spread in the case of the clay soil is due to surface ponding. (Calif. Leaflet 21259)

405

How Much Water to Apply. Since rate of evaporation varies so much from one area to another, the grower should keep an evaporation record in his own orchard. This helps you to make the most efficient use of water. The following inexpensive technique should help you to make reasonably accurate measurements.

(a) Obtain a rigid plastic or metal container having a minimum diameter of 10 in. and a minimum depth of 12 in. The container should not taper appreciably from top to bottom. (A 30-lb can as used for frozen cherries is close to these dimensions.)

(b) Install the container in the open. Elevate or enclose the container to prevent use by animals.

(c) Fill the container with water to within 2 in. of the top and record the depth with a ruler. (If daily measurements are made, a hole may be drilled 2 in. below the top and used as an overflow.)

(d) Measure the water depth again at a set time each day (or week) and adjust the water level to the original depth.

(e) Calculate *net water loss* on a weekly basis by subtracting inches of rainfall from inches of evaporation. This *net water loss* indicates the amount of water to be applied the following week.

(f) The amount of irrigation for the following week can be calculated as follows.

a) Following the assumed need to replace 75% of the evaporation on 50% of the area, we find that each 1 in. of net water loss requires 10,183 gal of water per acre for the next week or 1,455 gal per acre per day.

Dividing 1,455 by the number of emitters per acre will provide gallons per day per emitter. Dividing gallons per day per emitter by the gph delivery will provide hours of daily irrigation. With 100 microtubes or emitters per acre and delivery at 2 gph this would be:

$1,455 \div 100 = 14.55$ gal per emitter per day

$14.55 \div 2 = 7.28$ hr irrigation each day

g) If there is no net water loss or if less than 1 hr irrigation each day is required, the irrigation system can be turned off for the week.

Observations from Israel indicate that trickle irrigation permits use of water having a higher salt content than can be used in sprinkler or furrow irrigation. Accumulated salt is leached to the edge of the wetted soil mass and trickle irrigation takes the highest salt concentration away from the tree or plant. Furrow irrigation results in an opposite action.

Few wells and lakes used as a water source for orchard operations have water of high salt content. Also, of the system installed in 1971, only one well resulted in plugging of the 100-mesh screen. On all others no deposit was seen on the 100-mesh screen.

TABLE 2. RELATIVE WATER ENERGY, LABOR, AND TOTAL COST COMPARISION OF OVERHEAD AND TRICKLE IRRIGATION. (FUNT, R.C. ET AL. MD. MP950. 1980)

Item	Total 45 acres[1] Overhead	Trickle	Trick. vs. Overhd. %
Water/year	16.9 mil. gal.	7.6 mil. gal.	54%
Energy cost 1 yr.	$1,291.00	$343.00	74%
Labor (hours)[2] 1 yr.	25	25	0%
Initial Cost	$53,400.00	$26,701.00	50% less

[1] For 6 different fruit crops consisting of 7.5 acres each.
[2] Labor is for operation, not for maintenance.
Overhead was 2 self-propelled 150 gpm sprinklers covering 320 ft. dia.

When to Start Irrigation. June, July and August in the northern temperate climate are the high evaporation months, but May and September can be dry months for fruit plants in some years. With adequate winter rains the soil usually is well supplied with moisture in the rooting zone. Start taking water-loss data (described above) as growth begins in spring. When water-loss accumulates to about 3 inches, irrigation can start particularly for sandy soils. A silt loam soil with good depth has greater water-holding capacity and, hence, irrigation may be started at a somewhat later date.

Water Quality and Source. Water from a well, pond, river or other sources may be used, but it should be reasonably free of solid particles that will plug the system. Water from sources other than a well should be screened by a 100-mesh filter before the pump. Place the suction pipe in a gravel or sand bed, or build a box 3 ft. on a side and cover it with fine nylon cloth to keep out algae, moss, and other particles.

Somewhat higher salt content in the water can be used for trickle irrigation vs. sprinkler floor or furrow irrigation. Trickle irrigation moves the highest soil salt content away from the tree. Furrow irrigation does the opposite. Few wells and lakes have high salt content. Well water ordinarily does not plug the filter with particles.

Plugged Microtubes or Filters. Some types of emitters under the trees are adjustable and are self-flushing. However, a 100-mesh filter, recommended regardless, will screen particles and prevent plugging. Mount emitter through a hole in a stake to keep it from sucking soil during pipe drainage. In Florida, plugging by iron-sulfur-bacteria materials is a problem and can be corrected (see Ford). Consider extra-expense items at installation to reduce clogging. There is an Italian system (Irrisor) claimed to be free of clogging by using (a) orifices no less than 5 mm width and (b) emitting water intermittently at high velocity and pressure (Intertec Corp., POB 2247, Lynchburg, Va. 24501).

Fertilizer Application Through Irrigation. A suitable injection pump which operates on hydraulic pressure or on an electric circuit can be used to inject fertilizer solution into the main line after the water pump. In arid regions this approach of fertilizer supply to plants is essential since rainfall is not adequate to wash soil-surface-applied fertilizer into the rooting zone. Nitrogen and to some degree potassium can be added directly to the water to maintain plant nutrient levels throughout the season. With trickle, the fertilizer is placed near the roots, with little or no leaching and in some soils up to 50% less fertilizer is needed. Chelated liquid trace nutrients can be injected vs. solid types but cost may be a problem. Some difficulties have been encountered with application of non-chelated trace nutrients: Phosphorus can be injected but must be acidified to keep it from becoming insoluble with calcium.

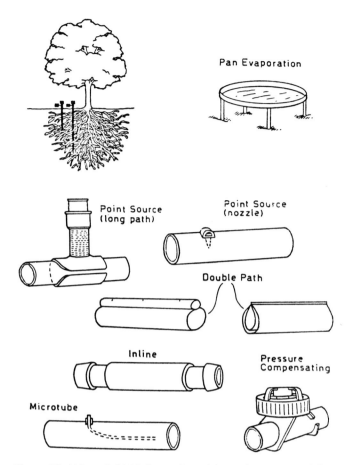

Figure 18. (Above left) Moisture detecting tensiometers sunk into ground at two depths in root zone. Relative water supply in soil is indicated on an attached meter. (Upper right) Another method for detecting moisture need for irrigation is the evaporation pan. When 0.5 inch has evaporated, apply about 0.4 inch water. (Lower) Trickle emitters give uniform discharge of 0.5 to 2.0 gph. each designed for different purposes. Usually, the Point-source is for tree crops. Line-source for close crops as strawberries, a pressure-regulating type if topography is uneven. Pressure drop across the emitter must be great enough to counteract minor pressure differences caused by topography and friction loss and yet the orifice must be large enough to prevent clogging. (NRAES 4. Cornell 1980).

Market mixes are avaiable.

Miscellaneous Suggestions. The *80-lb. black plastic pipe* is more than adequate for most trickle systems and does not need to meet drinking-water standards. Do not mix grades of plastic pipe; avoid light-weight thin-walled grades (Figure 18).

Black plastic pipe can be manipulated best when warm; it stiffens and shrinks when cold. Hence, it is wise to slowly flush cold water through the system as the microtubes are cut to proper length and holes in the ½ in. laterals are punched for the microtube insertion. Also, insert the microtubes on the header (water-source) side of the tree so it will not be pulled closer to the trunk if the header line shrinks in cooler weather.

Clamps in initial installations have been provided at all couplings. The friction fit of coupling should hold after it has been subjected to maximum cold contraction. Clamps are desirable on sections of the main line but may not be necessary on the laterals or header.

T-Connectors. T-connectors where the ½ in. line enters the main line may not be necessary. Drill a hole in the header line 1/16 in. smaller than the outside diameter of the lateral (OD 0.742 for ½ in. pipe; or 0.944 for ¾ in. pipe). This friction fit can withstand about 50 lbs pressure. Use a slant cut on the end of the ½ in. lateral for insertion.

Winter Effects. It is doubtful if low temperature will harm the black plastic pipe, but traffic and rodents may harm the small ½ in. laterals.

Windmills for Power. R. N. Clark and A. D. Schneider of Texas Agr. Exp. Sta. have developed an experimental windpowered machine to cut 40 percent the electrical energy usage of a conventional irrigation pump. Recent model wind machines can generate 10 to 200 kilowatts and overcome wind variability. Equipment was constructed from commercially available materials and installed in an existing irrigation well.

Planning Installations. The layout for a trickle irrigation installation will vary so much from orchard to orchard that it is difficult to give general cut-and-dried instructions. A system to cover 5 to 10 acres for each pressure regulator and header line is known to be easier to manage, at least based on present experience. This is particularly true if microtubes are used. Where the slopes are appreciable, smaller blocks may be needed.

For a larger acreage, a 3- to 4-in. main line may be used to deliver water to the orchard and a 2-in. header line may be used for each block. Thus, each block to be covered

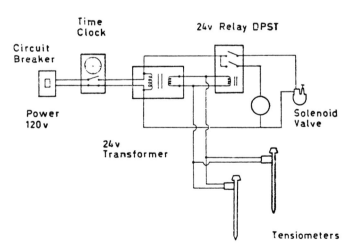

Figure 19. Wiring for automatic irrigation control (mixed voltages). Tensiometers (Fig. 18) measure moisture in one field block. Time clock with multiple switches or several time clocks may be set so each block in a field is irrigated in sequence. Tensiometers and relays then are wired to control water for each block (NRAES 4. Cornell Univ. 1980).

407

would have a 2-in. header line and pressure regulator. If water is limited for irrigation of the entire block at once, a manual or automatic means will be needed to change water flow from one block to another (Figure 19).

In case the number of rows in each block exceed the capacity of the pressure regular for each header, the main line can be run down the center of the orchard with header lines taken off both sides (Figures 15, 16).

Drip Irrigation and Salt Movement. In arid regions, salt movement to the soil surface can be a problem. The system must be engineered to deliver the needed amount of water but no faster than the soil can accept it. Pulse (off/on) irrigation may be necessary to prevent ponding and runoff, by automation (Figure 17). Properly engineered, soil water remains high, aeration adequate, with salt relatively low in the wetted zone.

Illustrations and Installation of Systems. The several diagrams used in this Chapter should help you design your particular system. Some of the diagrams were taken from "Trickle Irrigation in The Eastern United States", NRAES No. 4, Riley-Robb, Cornell, Ithaca, N.Y. 14850, Feb. 1980. For detailed assistance in installing a trickle system on variable blocks, seek assistance from the local agricultural extension service and from commercial salesmen.

THE IRRIGATION PROGRAM[1]

Water Usage. Amount of water needed by trees obviously will vary with their size, density of planting and evaporating power of the air. Large trees require 7 to 9 acre-inches/mo in mid-summer in arid regions. Water need in spring and fall is less. Large trees require about 40 total acre-inches a year under arid conditions.

In warm humid areas about 4- to 5-acre inches in mid-summer are needed for low-density apple trees; peaches need somewhat less. In the cooler climates as in Canada and Northern Europe, less water is needed.

Irrigation Timing. Factors governing the timing of irrigations are: (a) amount of water available, (b) rooting depth, (c) rate of use by trees, (c) evaporating power of the air, (e) seasonal stage of fruit and tree development, (f) the water quality, and other "interfering" orchard operations.

Tests with sensitive instruments such as soil tensiometers, trunk dendrometers, and soil gypsum blocks have shown that trees should be supplied with supplemental water when the soil moisture reaches 50% of the available water (water in the soil between its field capacity and WP).

When trunk dendrometers are used on apple, water is applied when the rate of trunk expansion falls below 80%

of that of the frequently irrigated trees (see Verner). For peach, 20 fruits are tagged on a few frequently watered trees and compared in growth rate every 3 days with 20 tagged fruits in the rest of the orchard, as follows: apply water during pit hardening when 80% of the fruits stop growing, and when in "final swell" 50% of the fruits stop growing, and in the last 4 weeks before harvest when 50% of the fruits show less than 0.1 cm increase/day.

Rate of evaporation of water from an open pan (receives rain also) can be used against established equations to determine need for water vs average precipitation for a particular month or accumulative for the season.

Questions

1. Describe and differentiate between (a) a radiation frost (freeze) and (b) an advective freeze.
2. Discuss weather-monitoring equipment for the orchard and how it is installed and operated.
3. List and compare (a) orchard heating equipment and (b) fuels for heating.
4. Define, "critical temperature" in an orchard.
5. Discuss air movement through plantings of fruit trees planted (a) on the square, (b) in hedgerows, (c) across an incline, (d) rows up-and-down the incline and (e) when near wooded areas.
6. With an energy crisis, discuss the merits of wind machines, helicopters, sprinkling, flooding and running water through the ditches.
7. Describe over-tree irrigation vs. under-tree systems and how effective they are, relative costs, general usefulness, and principles and operation.
8. Discuss "Trickle Irrigation," materials used and how it is installed and operated. What are its chief advantages, disadvantages?
9. Discuss effects of water deficiency on (a) fruit bud formation, (b) fruit set, (c) fruit drop and (d) fruit growth of apple, peach and nuts.
10. Discuss water deficiency on fruit (a) splitting, (b) yield, (c) size and (d) quality.
11. Discuss the relationship between irrigation and insects, diseases and nutrient supply to fruit trees.

Suggested Collateral Readings
Frosts and Freeze Prevention

ALFARO, J.F. et al. Preventative freeze protection by preseason sprinkling to delay bud opening. Trans. ASAE 17(6). 1025-8. 1974.

ANDERSON, J. LaMar et al. Evaporative cooling on temperature and development of apple buds. J. ASHS 100 (3) 229-231. 1975.

ASHCROFT, Gaylen et al. Determining chill unit and growing degree hour requirements for deciduous fruit trees. HortSci. 12(4):347-348. 1977.

BARFIELD, B.J. and J.F. GERBER. Aerial modification of plant environment. Am. Soc. Agr. Eng. 538 pp. St. Joseph, Mi. 49085. 1979.

BREWER, R.F. Soil applied water and frost protection. Calif. Citrog. 48:283-4. 1977.

BREWER, R.F. Trends in frost protection in California. Proc. Int. Soc. Citriculture Vol. 1. 196-9. 1977.

BRAINERD, K.E. and L.H. FUCHIGAMI. Adjustment of apple plants to low relative humidity. ASHS 106(4). 515-18. 1981.

BUCHANAN, D.W. et. al. Citrus tree cold protection with high and low water rates by under-tree microjet sprinklers. Fla. State Hort Soc. Proc., 1982. Publ. 1983.

CORDY, C.B. Pear frost protection with sprinklers. Ore. Spec. Rpt. 196. 11 pp. Mimeo. 1965.

CRASSWELLER, R.M., D.C. FERREE and E.G. STANG. Over-tree

---

[1]For a rather complete discussion on "Drip Irrigation Management", request Leaflet 21259 from Div. of Agr. Sciences, University of California, Davis 95616. 39 pp. 1981, also, "Irrigating Deciduous Orchards", Leaflet 21212, 55 pp. 1981..

misting for bloom delay on pollination, fruit set, and nutrient elements in 'Golden Delicious' apple tree. J. ASHS. 106(1):53-56. 1981.

FUNT, R.C. Sprinkler vs. trickle irrigation of six fruit crops, Maryland. Md. MP-950. 15 p. 1980.

GERGELY, I. et al. Polyethylene glycol induced water stress effects on apple seedlings. J. ASHS 105(6):854-857. 1980.

GUBBELS, G.H. Frost protection of crops by sprinkler irrigation. Can. J. Plant Sci. 49:715-718. 1969.

HAGEN, R. M. et al. Irrigation of Agricultural Lands. Am. Soc. Agron., Madison, Wis. 1180 p. (Fruits Included) 1967.

HUOVILA, S. and A. VALMARI. Artificial ventilation for prevention of radiation frost. Geophysics, Helsingfors. 8:303-312. 1966.

KETHCHIE, D.O. and C. MURREN. Use of cryoprotectants on apple and pear trees. J. ASHS 101:57-59. 1976.

LASKO, A.N. Season changes in apple stomatal response to Leaf Water. J. ASHS. 104(1):58-60. 1979.

LI, P. H. and A. Sakai. Plant cold hardiness and freezing stress. Vol. (I) II 695 p. Academic Press, New York. 1982.

McCARTHY, C.D. Minimum temperatures: hedgerows versus open-planted-citrus. Calif. Citrograph, 53:438: 453-454. 1968.

OKE, T.R. Temperature profile near ground on calm clear nights. Quart. J. Roy. Meteorol. Soc. 96:15-29.

OPITZ, K.W. et al. Protecting citrus from cold losses. Calif. Leaflet 2372. 19pp. 1979.

SMOCK, R.M. Facts and fancies on freezing damage to apples. Proc. N.Y. State Hort. Sco., 1970. 115:199-203.

PARSONS, L.R. et al. Low-volume microjets under-tree irrigation for frost control, citrus. Fl. State Hort. Soc. Proc. 94:55-9. 1981.

REEDER, B.D. Trickle irrigation on peach tree. HortSci. 14(1):36-37. 1979.

ROBERTSON, J.S. and E.J. STANG. Economics of over-tree misting for bloom delay in apples and peaches. J. ASHS 103(2):242-245. 1978.

PERRY, K.B. et al. Radiant output from orchard heaters. J. ASHS 102(2):105-109. 1977.

SMAJSTRLA, A.G. and D.S. HARRISON. Seek mimeo irrigation frost progress reports from IFAS, Univ. of Fl., Gainesville 32611.

SODERBERS, M.E. Advance frost warning procedures. W. Mich. U.S. Dept. Commerce/Environ. Sci. Serv. Admin. Tech. Memo. WBTM-CR-28. 1969.

SOLOMAN, K. and M. KODAMA. Tricle Irrigation answers. Rain Bird Spkles Mfg. Corp. Glendora, Ca. 91740.

STABY, G.L. et al. Plant microclimate and stress symposium insert. Leaf petiole epinasty in ponsettias. HortSci. 15(5):615-634. 1980.

STANG, E.J. and M.L. PALMER. Sprinkling trellis trees for frost control. Amer. Fruit Grower. 5 pp. Apr. 1978.

STANG,E.J. et al. Overtree misting for bloom delay in 'Golden Delicious' apple. J. ASHS 103(1):82-7. 1978.

TAN, C.S. and R.E.C. LAYNE. A simplified evapotranspiration model for predicting irrigation requirements of peach. HortSci. 16(2):172-173. 1981.

Trickle irrigation in Eastern U.S. NE Reg. Agr. Eng. Serv. Riley Robb, Cornell Univ. 23 pp. 1980.

Frost and the prevention of frost damage. USDC, National Oceanic and Atmospheric Admin. 35 pp. Revised 1972.

YOUNG, F. Frost and prevention of frost. USDA Farmers Bul. 1588. April 1929.

UNRATH, C. R. and R.E. SNEED. Use of overtree irrigation for crop cooling and frost and freeze protection on apples. Fruit South. 150-152. July 1978.

VALLI, V.J. Natural gas heating to prevent spring freeze damage. Agr. Meteorol. 7(6):481-486. 1970.

VAN DEN BRINK, C. et al. Growing degree days in Mich. Mich. Res. Rpt. 131, 48 pp. 1971.

IRRIGATION

ALDRICH, W.W. Irrigation studies on Anjou pear. Oregon State Hort. Soc. 25th Annu. Rep. p. 30-35. 1933.

ASSAF, R., B. BRAVDO and I. LEVIN. Effects of irrigation according to water deficit in two different soil layers on the yield and growth of apple trees. J. HortSci. 49:53-64. 1974.

BALLINGER, W.E. et al. Irrigation, nitrogen and pruning interrelationships of peach in North Carolina. ASHS Proc. 83:248-258. 1963.

BLACK, J. and D. FERGUS. "Daily Flow" Irrigation for fruit trees and row crops. Leaflet H191, Department of Agriculture, Victoria. 23 pp. 1971. (Australia).

California Agriculture - Special water issue (Drip Irrigation included) 47 pp. May 1977.

CRANE, J.C. and K. URIU. Irrigation, 2, 3, 5-T on apricot fruits. ASHS Proc. 86:88-94. 1965.

DAVIS, L.D. Split-pits in peach. ASHS 39:183-189. 1941.

DEGMAN, E.S. et al. Soil moisture and apple fruit bud formation. ASHS 29:199-201. 1932.

DRAKE, S.R. et al. Trickle vs. sprinkle irrigation on 'Golden Delicious' fruit quality. ASHS Journ. 106:3. 255-258. May 1981.

Drip Irrigation Management. Calif. Leaflet 21259. 39 pp. 1981.

FORD, H. and D.P.H. TUCKER. Blockage of drip irrigation filters and emitters by iron-sulfur-bacterial products. HortSci. 10:62-64. 1975.

FORD, H.W. Controlling slimes of sulfur bacteria in drip irrigation systems. ASHS 11 (2): 133. 1976.

FORSHEY, C.G. Irrigating New York orchards. N.Y. State Hort Soc. Proc. 103rd Annu. Mtg. 90-93. 1958.

FRITTON, D.D. and J.D. MARTSOLF. Reducing energy loss under an orchard heater. HortSci. 15(6):747-748. 1980.

FRITTON, D.D. and J.D. MARTSOLF. Soil management and frost protection. HortSci. 16(3):295-6. June 1981.

FRITTON, D.D. and J.D. MARTSOFF. Solar energy, soil mgmt. and frost protection. HortSci. 16(3):295-6. 1981.

Frost protection symposium. Fl. St. Hort. Soc. Proc. 94:39-74. 1981.

GOODE. J.E. and K.J. HYRYCZ. Soil moisture and apple tree response. J. ASHS 39:254-76. 1964.

HEINICKE, A.J. and N.R. CHILDERS. Water deficiency on photosynthesis and transpiration of apple leaves. ASHS 33:155-159. 1935.

HENDRICKSON, A.H. and co-workers. Prunes and water relations. Hilgardia 1:479-524. 1926; Water relations and clingstone peaches. ASHS 24:240-244. 1927; Dry soil on root extension. Plant Physiol. 6:567-576. 1931; Irrigation of pears on clay adobe soil. ASHS Proc. 34:224-226. 1937; Factors affecting rate of pear growth. ASHS 39:1-7. 1941; Irrigation effects on French prunes. ASHS. Proc. 46:187-190. 1945; Nitrogen, irrigation on walnut tree growth. Plant, Psysiol. 25:567-72. 1950a; Irrigation of apricots. ASHS Proc. 55:1-10. 1950b; Water use, rooting depth of almond trees. ASHS 133-8; 133-8. 1955a.

HEWETT, E.W. and K. YOUNG. Modification of fruit bud temperatures by elevated tissue water level. HortSci. 13(3):247-249. 1978.

LARSON, K.L. and J.D. EASTIN. Drouth injury and resistance in crops. Soil Sci. Soc. of Amer., Madison, Wis. 88 pp. 1971.

LEVIN, I., R. ASSAT and B. BRAVDO. Effect of irrigation treatments for apple trees on water uptake from different soil layers. J. ASHS 97:521-526. 1972.

LEVIN, I., B. BRAVDO and R. ASSAF. Relation between apple root distribution and soil water extraction in different irrigation regimes. Ecological studies. Analysis and synthesis 4:351-359. 1973.

MAGNESS, J.R. et al. Apple irrigation in eastern U.S. orchards. ASHS Proc. 29:246-252. 1935.

MARTIN, L.W. et al. Drip irrigation research in Oregon (blackberries, pear). Spec. Rpt. 412. 28 pp. Apr. 1974.

MARTSOFF, J.D. and J.F. GERBER. Florida satellite frost forecasting. Fl. State Hort. Soc. Proc. 94:39-43. 1981.

MEYER, J.L. and MARSH A.W. Permanent sprinklers for deciduous orchards and grapes. Calif. Leaflet 2435. 10 pp. 1977.

MORRIS, J.R. et al. Interactive effects of irrigation, pruning and thinning on peach. ASHS. Proc. 80:177-189. 1962.

PARKER, J. Drough resistance in woody plants. Bot. Rev. 22-4: Apr. 52 pp. 1956.

PONDER, H.G. and A.L. KENWORTHY. Hydraulic displacement of tank fertilizer solution(s) into a trickle irrigation system. HortSci. 10:261-262. 1975.

PROEBSTING, E.L. Fruit tree rooting in California. ASHS Proc. 43:1-4. 1943.

PROEBSTING, E.L. et al. Altered fruiting and growth characteristics of 'Delicious' apple associated with irrigation method. HortSci.

12(4):349-50. 1977.

RAESE, J.T. Over-tree misting apple trees in fall for cold resistance. HortSci. 16:5. 649-50. 1981.

RAWLINS, S.L. Bubbler ''drip'' system. Amer. Fruit Grower p. 18. Aug. 1976.

ROSS, D.S. et al. Trickle irrigation - an introduction. NRAES No. 4, 28 p. Riley-Robb, Cornell Univ. Ithaca, N.Y. 1980.

SCHNEIDER, G.W. and N.F. CHILDERS. Soil moilsture on apple photosynthesis, respiration and transpiration. Plant Physiol. 16:565-583. 1941.

TAERUM, R. Soil moisture, climate, stomatal behavior, growth of apple. ASHS 85:20-32. 1964.

URIU, K. Post-Harvest soil moisture, subsequent apricot yield. ASHS Proc. 84:93-97. 1964.

UNRATH, C. R. and R. E. SNEED. Evaporative Cooling of 'Delicious' apples — The economic feasibility of reducing environmental heat stress. J. ASHS 99:372-375. 1974.

VEIHMEYER, F.J. and A.H. HENDRICKSON. Soil moisture, root distribution in orchards. Plant Physiol. 13:169-177. 1948; Basic soil concepts, soil moisture, and irrigation. Wash. State Hort. Assn. Proc. 45:25-41. 1949; Soil moisture and fruit tree, vine responses. ASHS Proc. 55:11-15. 1950; Soil moisture and plant growth. Ann. Rev. Plant Physiol. 1:285-304. 1950b; Soil moisture effects on fruit trees. Int. Hort. Congr. Rep. 13th, London 1:306-319. 1952.

VERNER, L. and E.C. BLODGETT. Cracking of sweet cherries. Idaho Agr. Exp. Sta. Bull. 184, 15 p. 1931.

VERNER, L. et al. Trunk growth guide to orchard irrigation. Idaho Agr. Exp. Sta. Res. Bull. 52, 32 p. 1962.

WELLER, S.C. Pinoleve-base antitranspirant on 'Golden Delicious' apple trees and fruit. J. ASHS 103(1):17-19. 1978.

WELLES, J.M. et al. An orchard foliage temperature model. J. ASHS Sci. 104(5):602-610. 1979.

WESTIGARD, P.H., ULO KIIGEMAGI, and P.B. LOMBARD. Reduction of pesticide deposits on pear following over-tree irrigation. HortSci. 9(1):34. 1974.

WILCOX, D. and F. S. DAVIS. High-volume under-tree sprinklers on air and citrus leaf temperatures. Fl. State Hort. Sci. Proc. 94:59-63. 1981.

ZIONI, E. Cultivation, irrigation on hazel nut preharvest drop. (Ital. with Eng. and French summaries). Frutticoltura 25:363-7. 1963.

(See additional references in former book editions.)

Leading researchers in fruit tree irrigation and frost control, respectively, include, (left) Dr. John R. Magness, retired, USDA, Beltsville, Md., and (right) Dr. J. David Martsolf, University of Florida, Gainesville. Among others in irrigation studies are the late Dr. A. H. Hendrickson, the late Dr. F. J. Viehmeyer and Dr. K. Uriu, University of California, Davis; those in frost control studies include Dr. J. LaMar Anderson, University of Utah, Logan; Dr. David W. Buchanan, University of Florida, Gainesville; Dr. E. L. Proebsting, Jr. and James K. Ballard (retired), Washington State University, Prosser; Robert Brewer, University of California, Riverside; and V.J. Valli and Steven Blizzard, West Virginia University, Morgantown.

CHAPTER XX

Grape Growing

INTRODUCTION[1]

Grapes are popular in home gardens the world over. Commercially, they are the world's biggest and most widespread deciduous fruit crop (Chap. I, Table 1). In USA, the industry (Figure 1) is in three general regions based on the type of grape grown: (a) regions with European-type grapes *(Vitis vinifera),* including mainly California, and the southwestern USA; (b) regions with native American cultivars *(V. labrusca* and its hybrids with *V. vinifera),* located mainly east of the Rocky Mountains and north of the Gulf states plus the Northwest and Northern California with limited commercial acreage; and (c) regions with Muscadine *(V. rotundifolia),* and hybrid bunch grapes (with *V. labrusca),* including the South Atlantic and Gulf states. Grapes also are grown in the tropics.

About one acre in every 125 cultivated acres in the world is in grapes and one person in every 100 works in some phase of the grape and products business. There are about 25,000,000 acres of grapes in the world.

In the United States, the *V. viniferas* (largely California) comprise about 92 per cent of the grapes produced. This grape is exemplified by Thompson Seedless and Flame Tokay commonly seen on the fresh fruit markets in the East. Most *vinifera* grapes are characterized by a relatively thick skin that adheres to a firm pulp which is sweet throughout. Most *viniferas* require a mild climate, such as found in California and Arizona. Certain cultivars as Thompson Seedless can be used for raisins, wine and the table. Others are used mainly for wine and/or table. A U.S. boom planting of grapes for wine occurred in the 1970's due to an appreciable increase in U.S. and world wine consumption, but this was levelling by the early 1980s.

The native American or Fox type grape *(V. labrusca),* which is grown principally in the Great Lakes region of the

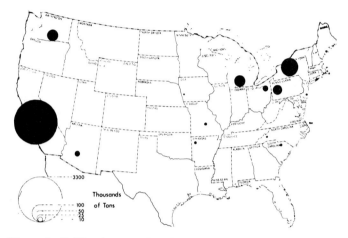

Figure 1. California procudes 90 to 95 percent of the grapes in the United States, consisting almost entirely of the European-type grape *(Vitus vinifera).* The American-type grape or its hybrids with American and *Viniferas* are grown mainly in the central and northeastern states, while the Muscadine *(V. rotundifolia)* is grown in the Gulf and South Atlantic states, New York, Washington, Michigan, Pennsylvania, Ohio, Arizona and Arkansas rank in order after California. Grapes from eastern areas are mainly consumed fresh or made into juice. In California, grapes used for raisins are grown around Fresno, wine grapes come mainly from San Francisco Bay area, and table grapes come from vineyards in the Sacramento and San Joaquin valleys and from the southern section of the state.

United States and Canada, and in Washington, is the second-most important grape, commercially. Concord is the leading and typical variety. It has a relatively thin skin that is sweet underneath and adheres loosely to the pulp; the pulp is soft and relatively acid near the seeds. The American grapes require a temperate climate such as found near the Great Lakes.

In the Northeast USA there is growing interest in the French-American hybrid grapes mainly for wines. Most have been introduced since World War II. The French hybrids include new cultivars or interspecific hybrids obtained by crossing the European types with native American species, mainly *V. rupestris* and *V. lincecuni.* The French breeders often have incorporated their names in the cultivars as Seibel 9549 and Vidal 256. The U.S. research stations and growers are evaluating these cultivars. Wine is the main use but some have potential for processing and table use. They lack the "foxiness" flavor of the American types and the wine has a more neutral,

[1]Dr. Garth A. Cahoon, Ohio Agr. Res. and Devel. Center, Wooster, gave assistance in updating this Chapter (Eastern USA). Others who have assisted are: Dr. Ronald B. Tukey, Wash. State Univ., Pullman, and Dr. Nelson Shaulis, N.Y. Agr. Exp. Sta., Geneva.

Grape schools are held annually. Contact the Pomology Dept., Ohio Agr. Exp. Sta., Wooster 44691, or Penn State Univ., Univ. Park, 16802, or your local gov'n. agr. exp. sta. for meeting dates.

Contact N.Y. Agr. Exp. Sta., Geneva 14456, for the Finger Lakes Grape Growers meeting, February, annually.

subtle and refined flavor. Under favorable growing conditions the yields and vigor are good. They ripen over a longer growing season which extends the marketing period for a roadside stand or the home. In the Great Lakes region hardiness is needed and special care must be taken not to let the vines weaken themselves to cold damage and low yields by overbearing. Disease, phylloxera and virus resistant rootstocks are needed. Commercial plantings should consist only of cultivars specified by the processor who will buy the crop.

The European *(Vitis vinifera)* cultivars grown in the more temperate northwestern and eastern U.S. climate vs. the California type climate tend to be less hardy in these areas. Their production can be more erratic and smaller in New York, for example, in comparison with native cultivars. They require the best sites, are more subject to fungus diseases, and require the best vineyard management. They should be grown on phylloxera-resistant rootstocks. If the season is relatively short as in New York, only the earlier ripening sorts should be grown. In the Northeast USA the white cultivars have produced higher quality wines than the red cultivars.

The *muscadine* grapes *(V. rotundifolia)* are grown mainly in the southeastern section of the United States. They are relatively long lived, vigorous in vine, seldom seriously affected by diseases and insects, bunches relatively small with thick-skinned berries having a musky odor, large seeds, may ripen unevenly and shatter when the bunches are ripe. Breeding programs in Georgia, North Carolina, Mississippi and Florida have made big strides in improving quality and general usefulness. The fruit is adapted to home use, wine, and culinary purposes, but not for distant shipment as a dessert grape. Florida breeder,

John A. Mortensen, is breeding for seedless bunch grapes, hybrids between the Muscadine and Concord types.

California has over 655,000 acres in grapes. One grower, e.g., has over 10,000 acres, visiting his blocks by helicopter. The relative importance of California in grapes is shown in Figures 1 and 2. In the early 1980's, the approximate annual grape production in short tons by the five leading states was: California 5,100,000; New York 164,000; Washington 145,000; Pennsylvania 57,000; Michigan 53,500; and Ohio 10,900. About 40% of the *vinifera* grapes grown in California are raisin cultivars with the other portion divided 48% wine, and 12% table cultivars. Wine consumption in the U.S. is over 2 gals per capita and continuing to rise. Wine imports are approaching 25% of the total consumption of over 500

TABLE 1. WORLD GRAPE PRODUCTION, METRIC TONS, BY COUNTRY, EARLY 1980s. (FAO PRODUCTION YEARBOOK, UNITED NATIONS, VOL. 35-6, ROME, ITALY).

Country[1]			Production
	MT		MT
Italy	22,800	Germany (FR)	880
France	10,300	Hungary	860
Spain	6,500	Australia	760
USSR	6,500	Brazil	600
USA	4,500	Mexico	480
Turkey	3,500	Afghanistan	460
Argentina	3,100	Austria	370
Greece	1,600	Japan	340
Romania	1,500	Syria	330
Portugal	1,400	Czechoslovakia	225
Yugoslavia	1,400	Morocco	210
South Africa	1,100	Total world	66,000
Iran	985	Wine	35,000
Chili	960	Raisins	8,800

[1]Other countries producing grapes in approximate order from 200,000 to 50,000 MT annually are: Cyprus, India, China, Tunisia, Lebanon, Uruguay, Switzerland, Israel, Canada, Korea (Rep), Albania, Yemen (Ar), Saudia Arabia and Peru.

U.S. Grape Production

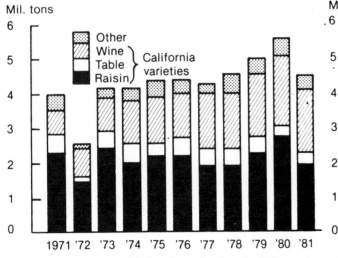

U.S. Grapes: Utilization

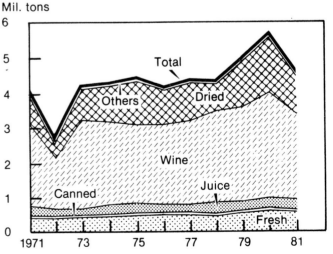

Figure 2. While grape production showed a drop in 1981, acreage of young vines was increasing. Bearing acreage in California is approaching 600,000 with non-bearing about 115,000 acres. Wine cultivars account for 350,000 acres, raisin 285,000 and table grapes about 65,000 acres. Both production and wholesale price of wine had been increasing. (USDA)

million gals. About 11 million gals are exported. U.S. table wines account for 83% of the total, dessert wines 13% and others 4%.

About 55% of the world grape production goes into wine and about 15% into raisins. The balance is grown mainly for table grapes, juice and other products. The *vinifera* grape predominates. Approximate world grape production by country is given in Table 1.

AMERICAN BUNCH GRAPES AND HYBRIDS

Vineyard Location

The three main factors that govern where these grapes can be grown are (1) climate, (2) site, and (3) soil.

Climate. American bunch grapes are likely not to succeed e.g. (1) in the West and Southwest where rainfall or irrigation water is quite limited, (2) where winters are severe, (3) growing seasons are very short, and (4) where temperatures and humidity are very high, encouraging diseases. The major commercial areas are located where the growing season is 150-180 days, the relative humidity is low and soil moisture does not become critically deficient. Grape varieties have rather exact requirements with respect to total and mean temperatures of the growing season. Also, the number of days required for proper maturity of the wood and fruit varies with the cultivar. As an average, American-type grapes will mature in about 165 frost-free days provided summer heat is adequate; *labrusca-vinifera* hybrids require a longer period and *viniferas* require at least 175 days. Largest production is located along the shores of the Great Lakes because of the tempering effect of the large bodies of water and the lengthening of the growing season. These areas are especially adapted to such long-season cultivars as Catawba. Concord requires fewer days than Catawba for maturity and will generally succeed in areas where the average length of the growing season is

Figure 4. Vineyards of *Vitus vinifera* grapes can be seen in southern Europe (Germany, France) with rows up and down the slope for better sun penetration and air drainage and where land is precious (FAS USDA)

about 170 days; it is of doubtful success in regions of 157 days and generally unsuccessful at 145 days. Note special adjustment of climate in Israel in Figure 3.

Site. Commercial plantings of grapes should be confined to favorable sites in established areas. In the East, there are many small vineyards outside the commercial regions supplying grapes for local markets and for home use. Special attention should be given to selection of a frost-free site and the use of adapted cultivars. The vineyard should be somewhat above the surrounding country. The ground may be almost level provided there is opportunity for cold air to drain on one or two sides. Air drainage through and away from the vineyard not only reduces the danger from late-spring and early-fall frosts, but also is highly important in the control of many diseases of grapes. In the southern extensions of the industry, the tempering effect of large bodies of water is not such an important factor, but air drainage is of primary consideration. Southern slopes in the northern hemisphere may get more

Figure 3. In the climate of Israel, grapes largely of *vinifera* blood are advanced to harvest about three weeks by using metal hoops covered by plastic mesh to lift temperature, protect from frost. Lower half of plastic is removed before bloom. (Courtesy S. Lavee, Volcani Center, Hebrew University, Bet-Dagan.)

413

direct sunlight, and if in low-rainfall areas, the rows, as in Europe where land is precious, may run up and down the slope for better sun penetration and air drainage (Figure 4).

In New York, the site for commercial use is *excellent* if winter temperatures do not reach -5° F more than 3 times in 10 yrs. or reach -10° but once in 10 yrs. with long term minimum temperature not lower than -10° F. This should be suitable for all commercial cultivars. The site is *poor* if winter temperatures reach -10° 5 times or more in 10 yrs. or -15° 3 or more times in 10 yrs. Situations between these extremes are commercially suitable mainly for the medium or greater hardiness cultivars. Cold-tender cultivars may be damaged at least once in 10 yrs. A site may be good for a winter hardy cultivar like Concord but unsuitable for White Riesling which is cold tender. See Table 2.

Soil. The best vineyards in the East are growing on moderately fertile, well-drained, sandy, or gravelly loam soil (four to six feet rooting area) which contains a good supply of organic matter. Grapes will grow on a wide variety of soils both in the East and West, including the heavy clays provided they contain plenty of organic matter and are *well drained* with at least 30-40 inch rooting depth. In general, the lighter sandy type of soils promote earlier

TABLE 2. GRAPE CULTIVARS (ADAPTED FROM OHIO BULL. 509 AND N.Y. (CORNELL) MISCELLANEOUS BULL. 111).

Cultivar	Color[1]	Climatic Adaptation[2]	Approx. Season	Approx. Days from Bloom to Harvest	Principle Use[3]	Remarks
				American		
Himrod (seedless)	W	2-3	V. early	75	T-H	High dessert quality — medium to low productivity, susceptible to black rot.
Canadice (seedless)	(R)	2-3	V. early	75	T-H	Flavor similar to Delaware, good clusters, productive. Responds to GA.
Seneca	W	4	Early	80	T	European characteristics predominate.
Van Buren	B	1	Early	80	T-W	Vigorous, hardy, Concord type.
Schuyler	B	3	Early	80	T	European characteristics predominate.
Buffalo	B	2	E. mid.	85	T-J-H	Excellent quality, distinctive flavor, Concord type.
Price	B	2	E. mid.	85	T-J-H	Excellent quality, distinctive flavor, productive.
New York Muscat	B	2-3	E. mid.	90	T-W-H	Muscat flavor, sweet, pleasing.
Fredonia	B	1-2	Midseason	95	T-J	Concord type, vigorous, hardy.
Alden	B	2-3	Midseason	100	T-W-H	Large berries, non-slipskin, very productive.
Bath	B	1	Midseason	105	T-H	Productive, hardy, Concord type.
Steuben	B	2	Midseason	105	T-W	Concord type, vigorous, good for wine.
Delaware	R	2	Midseason	100	W	Excellent for wine, high sugar, good keeping quality. Requires best soils.
Niagara	W	2	Late Midseason	110	W-T	Excellent for wine, standard white grape grown with Concord. Moderately susceptible to diseases.
Remaily (seedless)	W	2-3	Late Midseason	110	T-H	Good size and texture, nonslipskin, new.
Concord	B	1	Late	115	J-W-T	Standard of quality for juice, jam and jelly. Susceptible to Eutypa disease.
Cayuga White	W	1-2	Late	115	W-H	Good new wine cultivar for Ohio, hardy, productive.
Century	B	4	Late	115	T-H	Excellent quality dessert grape.
Sheridan	B	2	Late	120	T-H	Needs long season, Concord type.
Catawba	R	1	Late	120	W-J	Principal wine grape. Disease susceptible.
				French Hybrids		
Foch (Kuhlman 188-2)	B	2	Early	80	W	Extremely vigorous, small, tight clusters.
Aurore (Seibel 5279)	W	2	Early	80	W	Small tender berries, low vigor, susceptible to black rot.
Seyval Blanc (Seyval Villard 5276)	W	2	Early Midseason	95	W	Excellent white wine grape. Susceptible to black rot and mildew, med. vigor.
Baco Noir (Baco #)	B	2	Early Midseason	110	W	Extremely vigorous, productive, small berries, small clusters.
Chancellor (Seibel 7053)	B	2	Early Midseason	100	W	Very productive, good vigor, moderate hardiness.
Dechaunac (Seibel 9549)	B	2	Midseason	105	W	One of the best red wine grapes. Good vigor, hardy, desirable growth habit.
Vidal Blanc (Vidal 256)	W	2	Late Midseason	110	W-T	Excellent vigor, productive, hardy, good wine grape.
				European		
White Riesling	W	4	Late	115	W	One of most hardy vinifera types. Famous wine grape of Germany.
Chardonnay	W	4	Late	115	W	Second in hardiness to W. Riesling. Outstanding white grape of France.
Cabernet Sauvigono	B	4	Late	115	W	Less hardy than Riesling. Demands the best sites. Outstanding red wine grape of France.
Pinot noir	B	4	Late	115	W	Will grow only in very best sites in Ohio. Of questionable adaptability. The wine grape of Bordeaux, France.

[1]Fruit color: W = white; B = black or blue; R = red.
[2]Adaptability rating: 1 = good; 4 = poor.
[3]T = table or dessert quality: W = wine; J = juice; H = good for home plantings.

ripening and higher sugar in the grapes than do heavy soils. If soil maps are available, study them with help of the local fruit specialist.

CULTIVARS

The American bunch grapes are complex hybrids from native species and the European *V. vinifera.* Cultivars adapted to the northern and central areas of the U.S. are mainly from *V. labrusca,* the fox grape so-named because of the Concord type "foxy" flavor and aroma. Cultivars from *V. riparia,* the frost grape, are extremely cold hardy for northern areas with small berries that ripen early. Most cultivars in the South were derived from species of *V. rupestris, V. champini, V. lincecumii* and *V. bourquiniana.* Fruit is medium size, ripens late and the vines may lack winter hardiness. Cultivars adapted to the Gulf Coast were derived from *V. Simpsonii* and relatives.

Cultivars with a high percentage of *V. vinifera* have better quality fruit for table and wine but are more susceptible to diseases and insects. The American-French hybrids developed over the past 90 yrs. in France (with *V. vinifera)* blood) are subject to foliage diseases and the phylloxera root louse but are high producing and fine for wine. Acreage of these cultivars in comparison with Concord is still less than 5%. Thus, choice of a cultivar with *vinifera* blood is a compromise between fruit quality and the ease of culture of the American species.

Characters of the American-French hybrids and European cultivars that are being grown in the eastern U.S., mainly the northeast, are in Table 2.

American-type grapes which are generally recommended for commercial plantings in the Great Lakes regions are in the order of ripening: Niagara (white), Delaware (red), Concord (blue), and Catawba (red).

Niagara has large compact bunches of high quality yellow-green berries. The vigorous vines are adapted to a wide variety of soils. Since white grapes are limited in market demand, they should be planted in amounts to suit local requirements. Two disadvantages of Niagara are tenderness to winter cold and the fruit and leaves are somewhat more susceptible to fungus diseases than those of Concord. *Delaware* is midseason (being less planted), hardy, one of the highest-quality table grapes, ships and stores well, and makes good wine. Bunches, berries, and vines are relatively small. Delaware is a slow-growing grape which should be planted closer than most varieties (6-7 ft. in row) and requires good soil management and fertilization with relatively close pruning. *Concord* is the standard blue grape in the East. It succeeds under a wide variety of soil and climatic conditions. The vine is vigorous, hardy, highly productive, and resistant to downy mildew and phylloxera galling. Fruit may ripen evenly, stands reasonable shipment and storage, and is highly

prized for juice, jelly, and table use. It is used in blending dry table wines and there is a growing market in frozen concentrates. Probably over 70 per cent of the cultivars grown in the Great Lakes region consist of Concord, but fewer are being planted. *Catawba* requires a longer growing season than Concord. Berries and bunches are of medium size, ship well, and can be stored until almost midwinter under proper conditions; the vines are fairly productive and hardy, medium in vigor, (good in North Carolina, Ohio, poor in NE Ohio), and less susceptible to fungus diseases than *viniferas* and French hybrids.

In New York there are limited commercial acres of the following cultivars which indicates growing interest in them. *American cultivars:* Cayuga white, Duchess, Elvira, Ives, Moore's Diamond, Vincent. *French-American* cultivars: Aurore, Baco Noir (Baco 1), Cascade, Chancellor (Seibel 7053). Chelois (Seibel 10878), De Chaunac, Marchal Foch, (Kuhlmann 188-2), Rougeon (Seibel 5898), Seyval (Seyve-Villare 5-276), Vidal 256, Vignoles (Ravat 51). *V. vinifera* cultivars: Chardonnay, White Riesling, Gewurziraminen, Pinot Noir, Cabernet Sauvignon. *Dessert* cultivars for table use: The seedless cultivars are much preferred by the public, namely, Interlaken, Himrod, Lakemont, and Romulus. Others are Canadice, Seneca, Buffalo, N.Y. Muscat, Steuben and Yates. Many of these cultivars are grown throughout the Northeast and can be checked with your local state experiment station or extension service which also have publications with cultivar description details.

In the Northwest, Concord comprises 90% of all commercial grapes, some Diamond; Delaware is being grown for wine; wine cultivars (10% of acreage) are Riesling, Chardonnay, Chenin Blanc, Semillion, Cabernet Sauvignon, Pinot Noir, Gamay Beaujolais and Perlette; for home use Concord, Seneca, Campbell Early, Diamond and Delaware with some *V. viniferas.* (Wash. Ext. Cir. 391). See also Wash. Ext. Serv. EB-635.

Bunch grapes in Florida resistant to Pierce's disease, a common problem, are Stover, (fresh, wine, dooryard), Lake Emerald (wine) and Blue Lake (juice, jelly, dooryard).

PROPAGATION

Since grapes will not grow true from seeds, they must be propagated by cuttings, layering or grafting. Most big growers buy their plants from nurserymen ready to set to the field. But occasionally a grower or a home gardener may want to propagate a few plants of a cultivar for testing or for which available plants are limited.

By Cuttings. Most grape propagation is by cuttings selected from well-matured pencil-size canes with 3-4 buds, 8-12 inches long, cut as shown in Figure 5. Tie uniform lengths in bundles of 25, bury slanting and base down in an

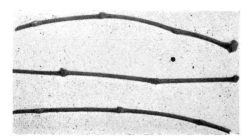

Figure 5. Grape cuttings for propagating new vines in the nursery. (Top) Mallet-type cutting is frequently used, consisting of current season cane with small section of 2-year wood at base. (Middle) Type of moderately grown well matured cane most commonly used. (Bottom) Cuts on this cane are improperly made.

outside well-drained trench and cover with 3 inches of soil and a 6-10 inch layer of straw to protect against severe cold. Work the nursery bed to a depth of 8-12 inches, using a well-drained sandy loam soil with fair organic matter as the preferred site. After frost danger, set the cuttings 6 inches apart in rows 3 ft. apart as in Figure 7. Firmly pack the soil leaving only the top bud exposed. The cuttings can be set through black plastic or a herbicide can be used to control weeds. Irrigation (drip) and a regular spray program are needed to keep the foliage healthy and develop strong root systems. Dig rooted cuttings in the fall, grade to size, bury in well-drained and packed soil or store under moist conditions at 34° F. Plant in place in *early* spring.

By Layering. This method can be used to replace a dead vine or open space in the grape row, or it can be used to develop a few new plants of a desired cultivar. Use a current shoot that lies on the ground about mid season. Bury a foot or so near the tip to a depth of 6-8 inches, leaving a few inches of the tip exposed. Mark with a stake to dodge in cultivation. The buried portion will take root during the balance of the growing season. The rooted plant can be separated from the mother plant the next spring and planted elsewhere, or it can be left in place, cut from the mother plant, the tip cut back to 2-3 buds.

By Top-working. Grafting of an established vineyard over to another cultivar has been difficult and not very successful in the past. Converting vines by field grafting has been tested by over 15 growers in New York State with about an 85% success, considered good. Obtain a copy of "Converting mature vineyards to other varieties" by K. H. Kimball, N.Y.S. Agr. Exp. Sta., Geneva 14456, Spec. Rpt. 22. It is wise to conduct limited trials in your vineyard before attempting large-scale grafting (Figure 6). *Vinifera* (European) cultivars and the American and French hybrids usually perform better on rootstocks resistant to root parasites. Phylloxera (root louse) and nematode resistant stocks are Couderc 3309 and 3306, Clinton and Baco No. 1. These rootstocks are propagated by cuttings, then

grafted over to desired cultivars. Grafted plants can be purchased from the nurseries ready to plant in place.

Most American cultivars are on their own roots. Own-rooted Concord usually performs satisfactorily on new sites. But on old sites they perform best when grafted on resistant roots. Clinton, Catawba and Baco No. 1 also may do well on their own roots on new sites. But Delaware, Ives and *viniferas* always should be on grafted stocks, which are available.

Tissue Culture. Thousands of grapes can be produced from a single tissue culture in half the time it takes by cuttings. Dr. W.R. Krul, USDA, Beltsville, Md. 20705, by adjusting a nutrient solution in test tubes, has induced undifferentiated callus cells to form embryos which can be cultured into mature vines, true-to-form with disease resistance, other desired characteristics. Technique is developing rapidly. See Chapters VIII and XXI.

PLANTING THE VINEYARD

Nursery Stock. One-year No. 1 plants, certified free from viruses and root parasites with good roots, are best (Figure 8a); 2-yr. plants are questionable. Commercial growers buy nursery-grown plants, preferably nearby. *Plant early spring,* or, if early arrival, break the bundles, spread in a furrow on north side of building, cover most of tops with soil and place burlap on top.

Nematodes. These parasites are a leading yield reducer around the world, particularly in light sandy soils, warm climates. Current controls are: crop rotation, fallowing, and fumigation on lighter soils with registered

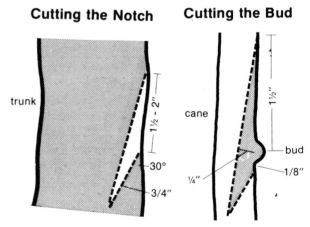

Figure 6. Chip-budding (C. J. Alley, Univ. of Ca., Davis) is being used in California and New York to convert vineyards to other cultivars. Trunks up to 3½ inches diameter are used a foot above ground late summer. Notch and bud are shown above. Scion wood is soaked in water before using, cambium layers must touch, wrap entirely with 1-inch tape, underlapping ends, and make careful slit over bud with sharp knife. Use string to support shoot next spring. Dip tools in disinfectant after each graft.

Figure 7. Grape cuttings in an Ohio nursery in July will be sold as 1-year plants the next spring. Mulch prevents heaving in cold climates; cuttings are set directly to nursery in fall or spring in mild climates.

nematocides, *preplant*. Use nema-free stock, sanitary tools. Nema-resistant stocks are of definite value (Figure 8). Use of foliar and soil applied systemics which travel throughout the plant are questionable during fruiting as they could harm human health.

Preparing, Planting. Start a year before planting, level the ground, install drainage tile if needed, grow a high-fertility crop as corn or use herbicides to control thistle, quackgrass or dock, using chemicals not usable after planting. On sloping land use paraquat over row area, fall plow and spring rototill, leave centers in sod. Or, on level land, fall plow with cover crop of rye/bluegrass, apply animal manure if reasonable cost in fall 10-12T/A or 75 lb./100 sq. ft. Lime to about pH 6.5 in fall. Cahoon (Ohio) suggests Surflan herbicide the first year for weed control and Devrinol after the first year. Or use black plastic strips over row, paraquat either side of poly, spade-cut holes for plants, stake first year, set trellis second yr. Or, plow out furrow and set plants in it. Modern USA vineyard has sod middles with strip-row herbicide use, drip irrigation as needed. Fall-set Concord vines have done well in the upper northeast U.S., but it is not advisable on fine-textured imperfectly drained soils that may heave the young vines. Plow a 4-6 inch mound of soil to the base of the vines after setting for cold protection.

Planting distances vary with cultivars and type of soil. Vigorous cultivars such as Niagara and Concord, on good soils should have the rows spaced about nine feet apart with the plants seven to nine feet apart in the row. Less vigorous cultivars as Catawba and Delaware may be set seven to eight feet apart in the row. For number of plants needed/A, divide 43.560 by width plants in row x width of rows.

Rows spaced nine feet apart are desirable to facilitate spraying, other machinery and for convenient hauling at harvest. In large commercial vineyards, provide cross alleyways every 300-400 ft. to facilitate machinery.

On rolling or somewhat level ground, rows arranged in the north/south direction are preferred, except for the Geneva Double Curtain training system where yields have not been improved. Contouring can be done with the help of local soil conservationists but it may create problems in machine handling of the crop, spraying in a wind, trellising and maintaining it and other problems.

Before setting the plants, prune the roots only enough to cut away broken portions and ragged ends, as shown in Figure 6. Place and arrange roots well in the hole, firming the soil around and over them. The top is cut back to two buds on the best single cane after planting.

SOIL MANAGEMENT

Where erosion is likely not to be a problem, shallow cultivation and a winter cover crop as rye, rye grass, winter wheat, or oats or buckwheat (will winter-kill before spring) can be used, but rye particularly must be knocked down before it competes with the vines in the spring. Rototilling type cultivation is preferred where possible to avoid cutting

Figure 8. Own-rooted Concord vines at New York Agr. Exp. Substation, Fredonia, are short plants; on either side are Concord taller vines grafted on resistant Coudere 3309; both planted in May on a replant site, photographed in early November. Own-rooted Concords perform safisfactorily on non-replant sites. Resistance is to root parasites or unfavorable soil conditions. In California a nematocide to 22- to 36-inch depth is used preplant for nematodes.

417

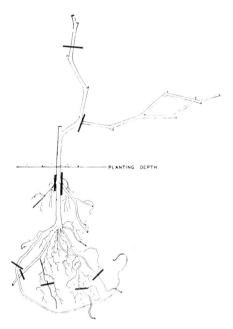

Figure 8a. Before planting a rooted grape cutting the tops and roots are pruned as indicated by black marks. The planting depth is shown.

Figure 10. Chemcial weed control is the best and most economical weed control under trellis wires in a commercial vineyard. Diuron kept the plots here nearly free of weeds all year (foreground). Vetch cover in row middles had been mowed recently. Swiss find a cover crop in row middles reduced shoot die-back problem 50%. (Courtesy J. H. Dawson, W. J. Clore, V. F. Burns, Wash. State Univ., Prosser.)

the roots with discing which can do more harm to the vines than weeds. A management system in common use is permanent mowed sod middles (K-31; bahia in the South) with a narrow strip cultivation either side of trunks (once in spring after bloom) and herbicides with or without irrigation (Figure 9). Drip irrigation under many eastern conditions has been shown to be a good investment for higher yields, better fruit quality and for better "take" of newly set vines.

Chemical weed control. Chemical weed control under the grapevines is widely used (Figure 10). Grapes are highly sensitive and almost permanently stunted or killed by 2, 4-D and 2, 4, 5-T; they should not be used in fields anywhere near grapes to avoid drift or used in spray equipment in

Figure 9. A trend in soil management in vineyards is mowed sod middles in Ohio with strip cultivation/weed control by approved herbicides in the vine row, with or without irrigation. Garth A. Cahoon of the Ohio Agr. Exp. Sta. Devel Ctr., Wooster, is suggesting the "Single Curtain No-Tie" training system for economical management.

vineyards. MCP, TCA (sodium-trichloroacetate) are detrimental or fatal to grapes. Surflan herbicide can be used the first year of a planting and Devrinol or Surflan can be used starting with the second year. Contact local authorities for approved herbicides which change rather frequently. Roundup (glyphosate) can be used on grapes; also paraquat, simazine and diuron (Karmex).

Liming. Rye and rye grass cover crops will grow in a relatively acid soil. It usually is not necessary to add lime, unless the pH is below 5.5, magnesium deficiency is apparent in the leaves, or it may benefit the cover crop. Dolomite is used to correct Mg deficiency at one ton/A. to lift the pH one unit. Avoid too much lime. It can induce Mn and other trace element deficiencies.

Manure. Strawy manure is probably the best general all-around feritlizer for grapes. Applied during the winter or late fall at the rate of 10 to 12 tons per acre, manure may increase yield by 30 percent, but it has become too limited for large scale use. Also, commercial growers can control nutrition better with well-timed quick-acting chemical fertilizers. As indicated earlier, rotted manure or strawy manure works well in backyard plantings.

Commercial fertilizers. Grapes in general have not responded as readily to nitrogen fertilizer applications as other fruit crops, except perhaps on exhausted soils. This may be due in part to the heavy annual pruning given the grapevine. However, when growth becomes unsatisfactory to support the proper number of buds per vine after pruning, nitrogen fertilizer applications are usually beneficial. Nitrogen shows the most immediate and

Figure 11. A drilled wheat cover crop photographed in September in northern Ohio. Modern herbicidal treatment will keep soil bare under vines. (U.S.D.A.)

greatest effect on vines on sandy and gravelly soils. On the heavier soils, it may require two or three years before a response is indicated from nitrogen. Applications can be made in late fall or early spring. For vines of moderate vigor, use 150 lbs. ammonium nitrate or equivalent per acre or 500 lbs. 10-10-10 mix, broadcast with a PTO spreader. On the basis of a single vine, this would be about 0.3 pound of ammonium nitrate, or the equivalent in nitrogen in another source for vines of moderate vigor. For weak vines, about one-half pound per vine is suggested.

A 6-ton grape crop per acre removes about 120 lbs./A of N, P, K, Mg, Ca, S, Fe, Mn, B, Zn, Cu and Mo. Nutrient deficiencies in humid areas that have been noted in vineyards are N, K, Mn, Mg, Fe and B. Ca and certain trace elements may become deficient under special conditions or in sandy low-organic matter soils. In arid regions, N, Zn, K, B, Mn and Fe may be found, rarely Cu. Deficiencies vary from area to area, farm to farm and within the same farm area.

When deficiencies become moderate to acute, they can be recognized in the leaves, fruit and growth characters. Marginal deficiencies occur, however, and are not apparent except in reduced yield and quality. The modern approach is to have the grape leaf petioles ("leaf stems") chemically analyzed for their levels of essential nutrient elements. Equipment to do this is expensive and, hence, a state experiment station well equipped will service several area states at a cost of about $10+/sample — N.Y., Pa., Ohio, Me., Fla., Mich., Colo., Calif., Ore. to name a few. Standards have been established for "normal" levels of each element for satisfactory vigor and yield of good quality.

Briefly, visual symptoms of deficiencies frequently found in grapes are: *Nitrogen* deficiency causes low vigor and yield, light green foliage, small leaves. If 60-90% of

the trellis is covered with dark green foliage for 8 ft. spaced vines and 3 lbs. of prunings are removed, N may not be needed. *Other factors* causing light green foliage are drouth, sun scald, leafhoppers, mildew, dead arm, winter injury, certain herbicides and others. Low *potassium* appears as a marginal and interveinal scorch on mid-shoot leaves and as black leaf, low vigor and yield, small berries and delayed maturity (Figure 12). Band 300 lbs. KCL or 360 lbs. K_2SO_4/A. *Magnesium* shortage may occur on low pH soils, affecting the older leaves. Light green to whitish

Figure 12. (Upper) Marginal scorch of older grape leaves due to potassium deficiency. (Lower) Magnesium deficiency whitish yellowing between main veins of older grape leaves. (Upper) A. F. Wilhelm, Freiburg, Germany. (Lower) Dr. Memetriades, Benaki Phytopath. Inst., Greece.

Figure 13. Zinc deficiency on grape causes straggly bunches with small berries (above, control on left), and a whitish chlorosis and general stunting of the leaves. The leaves also tend to be twisted, distorted and some having wavy margins. (Cal. Agr. Ext. Serv., Fresno.)

areas occur between the main veins as shown in Figure 12 on older leaves. About a ton of dolomite/A should help and/or 16 lbs./100 gals. of $MgSO_4$ (epsom salts) at 200 gals./A in 2 post-bloom sprays. Low *manganese* may appear on high-lime or pH (7.0+) soils as interveinal light greening on more exposed leaves. One-half to 1 lb. Mn-

SO_4/vine banded under the trellis, or 5 lbs./100 gal. spray should correct it. Low *iron* appears as a yellowish-whitening of the younger leaves, frequently on high lime or pH (7.0) soil or poorly drained "cold" soils. Ammonium sulfate as the N source is suggested in N.Y. Iron chelate at manufacturer's recommendations to the soil is suggested in some areas. Low *boron* results in deformed leafing-out in spring, split shoots, shot berries (small), or no fruit at all. Be careful not to over-apply B. About 10 lbs. borax or equivalent per acre every other year is suggested in So. Carolina. Sprays of 1-2 lbs. borax or equivalent/100 gals. once or twice may be needed in soils of high pH. Low *zinc* is common in arid regions and may be found in humid areas, particularly in sandy soils (Figure 13). Paint pruning wounds during pruning with 1 lb. Zn SO_4/gal. water, or spray with Zn chelate at mfg. recommendation. See Dr. J.A. Cook's grape chapter in Childers' *Fruit Nutrition* book.

Plant Regulators. *Gibberellin (3)* at 1000 ppm 11 days after bloom has increased set and reduced early berry drop on Concord (see Himrod, Figure 14). On Delaware only, bunches (not foliage) can be dipped in 100 ppm gibberellin 10 days before full bloom and again 10 days after to induce seedlessness, bigger berries, and advance maturity 2-3 weeks. A GA spray before bloom and one at bloom on Thompson Seedless gives a looser bunch, berries dry faster, less trouble w/diseases and no need for turning the bunches at harvest in trays. *Alar* (SADH) at 500 ppm just before full bloom is widely used to increase yield on selected cultivars (Federal label, check local updated regulations): Concord (Table 3), Niagara, Himrod (Figure 14), Aurora, Chancellor, and De Chunac. *Cycocel* has increased set on Thompson Seedless in New York. Where natural berry color development is poor, *ethephon* applied to berries and foliage at 15% berry color at 100-300 ppm will increase anthocyanin pigment in the berries and advance maturity.

TABLE 3. TWO-YEAR STUDY OF ALAR ON CONCORD GRAPES*. WA. STATE UNIV., PROSSER (M. AHMEDULLAH).

Bloom-time Alar treatment at 1 lb. per acre		Double Curtain		Single Curtain	
		Yield T/A	Sugar °B	Yield T/A	Sugar °B
Alar	1.0	17.5	15.1	14.6	15.2
Untreated	0	15.1	15.9	13.6	16.1

*The figures represent the means for 1979-80 and 1980-81 data.

THE TRELLIS

Plants can be staked the first season after planting, and the strongest shoot for each vine trained to the stake. Or, an alternate is to install the posts and one top wire to which the trunk-to-be shoots are tied. The trellis should be in place at the beginning of the second season. While the

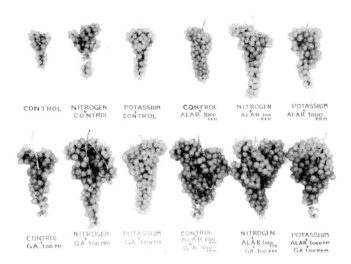

CONTROL NITROGEN CONTROL POTASSIUM CONTROL CONTROL ALAR 1000 NITROGEN + ALAR 1000 PPM POTASSIUM ALAR 1000 PPM

CONTROL GA 100 PPM NITROGEN + GA 100 PPM POTASSIUM + GA 100 PPM CONTROL ALAR 1000 PPM G A 100 PPM NITROGEN + ALAR 1000 PPM GA 100 PPM POTASSIUM + ALAR 1000 PPM GA 100 PPM

Figure 14. Himrod grape bunches and berry size are shown above in Ohio as influenced by: Control (no Treatment); ammonium nitrate, ½ lb./vine; potassium sulphate, 1½ lbs./vine; Alar, 1000 ppm first bloom and GA (Pro-Gibb) 100 ppm, shatter stage. Ethephon sprays can be used to get better more uniform coloring and maturity of grapes with less sourness. (Courtesy Garth A. Cahoon, Ohio ARDC, Wooster.)

trellis is an important expense item (about one-fourth establishing cost), it pays to establish a strong durable support system at the start.

Posts. Posts should be set from 24 to 30 feet apart with three vines between posts. Exact distance will depend upon whether the planting distance between the vines in the row is eight, nine, or ten feet. Posts to last 20 yrs. should consist of durable wood, such as white oak, locust, or cedar, preservative impregnated to prolong life (creosote, chromated copper arsenate (need permit), or pentachlorophenol). Metal posts cost more than wood but they are more durable, free from frost heaving, drive down and handle better and look neater. An occasional metal post among wood or concrete posts will help ground lightening. End wood posts should be heavier and longer than line posts with a top diameter of five to eight inches, and a length of about 10 feet to permit setting up to four feet in soil, as shown in Figure 15. Reinforced concrete sometimes is used for end posts. Line posts can be somewhat lighter, or at least three inches in top diameter and about eight feet long to permit driving two feet in the ground where a Kniffin type system of training is used. Pointed wood posts (heave less) can be driven into the ground with a maul (12-14 lb.) from a truck bed, or pressed down with a tractor lift in moist soil, or use a PTO tractor pounder.

End posts will require sturdy bracing. A satisfactory bracing system can be employed where a 4x4 inch brace is run from near the top of the end post obliquely toward the ground and fitted against a short post set about eight feet

back in the row from the end post. A second method of bracing is to carry a heavy brace wire from the top of the endpost to a large rock or old car wheel ("dead-man") buried a few feet in the ground beyond the end post. Objection to this bracing method is that the brace wire is frequently caught by cultivating tools. A third method is shown in Figure 15, in which a second post is set six to eight feet back in the row from the end post. An end-post brace for Geneva double-curtain training system is shown

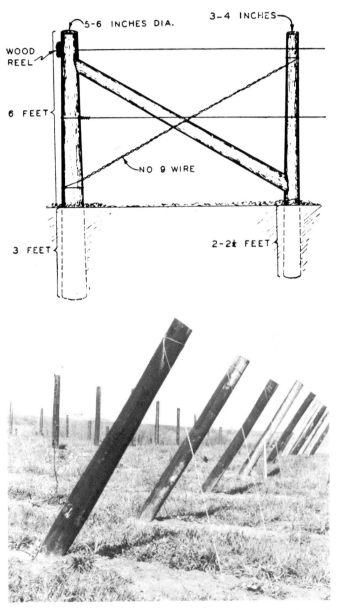

Figure 15. Trellis end posts are particularly strong when braced as shown. Life of posts is increased by soaking lower ends in copper salts or a wood preservative before setting. Wood reel may be used with ratchet for tightening wire. Experience has shown that end posts hold better if 10 ft. in length, sunk 4 ft. in the ground instead of 3 ft. as shown here. Similar trellises can be built for full-dwarf trees. In Italy, only the top wire may be installed to hold, "slender-spindle" trees.

421

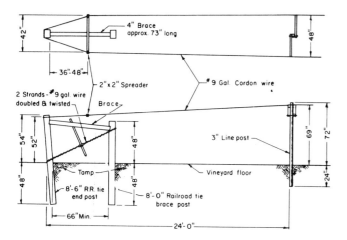

Figure 16. Suggested end-post and brace construction for Geneva Double-Curtain trellis system. Keep the cordon wire and brace sufficiently high. Construction success depends on the deep setting of the wide surface railroad ties. (Courtesy Nelson Shaulis, N.Y. Agr. Exp. Sta., Geneva). Metal arms for GDC system sold by Wolverine Metal Stamping Co., St. Joseph, Mi. 49085.

in Figure 16. If mechanical harvesters will be used, leave at least 20 ft. at row ends for turning.

Wires. If a Kniffin system of training is used (Figure 20), a two or three-wire trellis is satisfactory with the upper wire consisting preferably of the heavier No. 9 gauge and the lower wire of No. 10 or 11 gauge. Plastic wires tend to shrink and expand, are not strong enough or well suited to vineyards and may be cut while pruning. The amount of wire needed can be calculated from data below:

Gauge of Wire		Feet per Pound	
	9		17.05
	10		20.57
	11		25.82

For the umbrella or Kniffin system, the upper wire is located six feet from the ground. French hybrids with short internodes tie better to 3 wires.

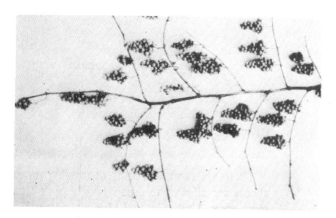

Figure 17. A defoliated fruiting Catawba cane showing location of best clusters and where most fruit is produced. On the average, the fifth, sixth, and seventh buds from the base of main cane develop most productive shoots. (Ohio State University.)

Long staples are used for securing the wires to line posts or holes are electrically drilled before or after setting through which the wire is threaded. The wire should be loose in the staples, so that it can be tightened at the end posts. Wires are more secure if placed on the windward side of the posts, or on the upper side in hillside vineyards. Iron wires contract during cold weather and should be loosened in the fall to prevent undue strain on the end posts. In spring after pruning is completed and before the canes are tied, the posts should be driven down where necessary and the wires tightened, using vises or a wire stretcher. Each wire should be fastened securely to the end posts (Figure 15).

Another method for tightening wires is to cut the wire midway between end posts and use a wire stretcher, then splice the wire after it is drawn taut, or use a wire clamp into which the end wires are inserted and held tightly[1].

Construction details for the Geneva Double Curtain trellis are shown in Figure 16.

PRUNING (General Concepts)

Growth and Fruiting Habits. Grape clusters are borne laterally near the base of leafy shoots which arise from buds on one-year wood or canes as shown in Figure 17. Shoots which arise from wood older than one year are generally unproductive.

For good grape production, it is important that the vines be pruned annually so that an adequate amount of one-year wood conveniently placed is available from year to year near the trunk of the vine. Average yield from a Concord vine grown under good conditions is about 15 pounds. A bunch of Concord grapes may weigh 0.15 to 0.25 lb. About 100 bunches are needed to produce the 15 lbs. of fruit. If each fruit bearing shoot produces from one to three bunches, the vine after pruning should produce 15

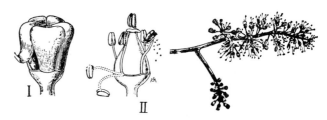

Figure 18. (Above) At "I", cap of the flower bud loosens at the base and "pops" off. At "II" is shown the pistil in the center with two types of stamens around it. Some cultivars as Brighton have depressed stamens, others have upright stamens. At right is a flower cluster, appearing at a shoot node early in the season. (U.P. Hedrick, Systematic Pomology, Macmillan, 1925).

---

[1]Commercial trellis materials and pruning equipment are available from Amberg Bros. Nursery, Rt. #2, Box 269, Stanley, N.Y. 14561; A. M. Leonard and Son, Piqua, Ohio 45356 and Corona, P.O. Box 1388, Corona, Ca. 91720.

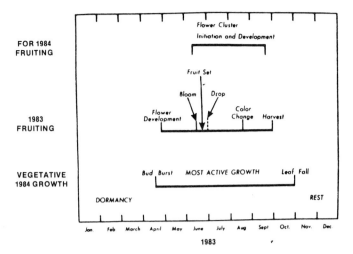

Figure 19. Chart shows the calendar of grapevine development for the Concord cultivar in New York, USA. The various stages of growth are given by month, and also for flowering and fruiting from the periods of rest and dormancy. (N. Shaulis and C. Pratt, N.Y. Agr. Exp. Sta., Geneva 14456).

lbs. easily from 50 buds. Relatively heavy annual pruning is necessary because a vine before pruning contains an excessive number of buds. Heavy pruning also is necessary to prevent an undesirable amount of old wood accumulating and to select a proper number and length of desirable fruiting canes from year to year.

Parts of Vine Defined. (See Figure 20). *Trunk:* The main unbranched stem of the vine. *Arm:* Short branch of old wood extending from the trunk. *Old wood:* Parts of the vine older than one year. *Shoot:* Leafy growth developing from a bud, which may support blossoms (Figure 18), and later, fruit. During the growing season such growths are called shoots; after the leaves have dropped, they are called canes. *Canes:* The dormant shoots which have become woody and which carry buds or eyes.

Lateral: Side branch of a shoot or cane. *Spur or renewal spur:* A cane which has been cut back to a short stub carrying one or two buds and placed to develop a shoot to be used as a fruiting cane the following year (Figure 20). *Node:* The joint on a shoot or cane where leaves, tendrils or flower buds (Figure 18) are located. *Internode:* The portion of the shoot or cane between the nodes. *Eye:* The compound bud at each node on the cane. *Primary bud:* Largest bud at a node. *Secondary bud:* Smallest bud at a node, which can produce a 50% crop if primary bud is frost-killed. On French hybrids, they may produce 70-100% crop. Such a shoot is less productive than from a primary bud. *Sucker:* A shoot which arises from below the ground. *Water sprout:* A shoot that arises along the trunk

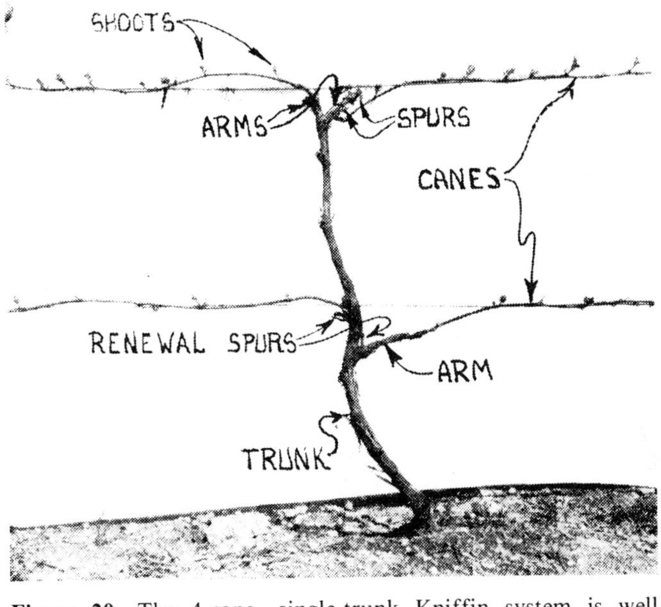

Figure 20. The 4-cane, single-trunk Kniffin system is well adapted to vigorous varieties of grape such as Concord and Niagara. The vine is pruned to 4 canes, totalling 40 to 50 buds. A renewal spur with two buds is left near the base of each cane to develop fruiting wood for next year's crop.

Figure 21. In grapes, as in all fruit growing enterprises, there is a continuing effort to reduce labor costs. Power pruning is shown in a *Vinifera* vineyard in California. A tractor-powered pneumatic system, self guided by furrow, is shown at top; smaller unit is below. In addition to the pneumatic shear, below, there is a power saw tool to remove large "fruited-out" trunks. For limited acreage, the hand shears or short wood-handle loppers are useful. In many large acreages, mechanical pruning is being used as shown later. (Courtesy A. N. Kasimatis, Univ. of Ca., Davis and, below, Miller-Robinson Co., Los Angeles, Ca.)

or arm. See Figure 19 for calendar-year development of the Concord cultivar in New York.

Season For Pruning. In the northern latitudes, the best time to prune is after danger from heavy freezes and until the buds begin to swell. Canes will "bleed" sap from cut ends if pruned after the sap starts to run and while the buds are swelling. Bleeding may annoy workers but it is not serious. Pruning should be completed as early as possible. Vines should never be left without annual pruning. Pruning is inadvisable during the growing season, since grapes do not require direct sunlight to develop color. Summer tying of shoots is needed with the upright training systems such as the Fan, Chautauqua and Keuka High which accounts for the gradual disappearance or conversion of these systems to the drooping cane systems described below.

PRUNING YOUNG VINES

There are several systems of training and pruning grapes, but the trend is toward those where shoots are allowed to droop as the Single Curtain ("No-Tie", Figure 22), Hudson River Umbrella (Figure 23) and the Munson system (see Muscadines). These systems have proven to be

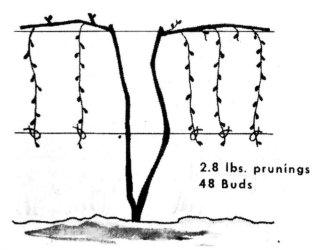

Figure 23. This is the Hundson River Umbrella system for pruning grapes (developed in N.Y.). The arms or cordons at left and right are at least 2 ft. long. Note the 2-bud spurs for renewal canes the next year. Fruiting canes this year are tied to lower wire. Prunings removed this year totalled 2.8 lbs. leaving 48 buds to develop fruiting shoots this year. (N. Shaulis, N.Y. Agr. Exp. Sta., Geneva 14456).

cost-saving for most cultivars. Trend is toward development of double trunks in case one is lost.

First year. Immediately after planting, remove all but the strongest cane and cut it back to two buds (Figure 6). As shoots become woody in early summer, special attention should be given to pruning the young vines to develop one or two vigorous shoots to become the trunk(s). Each vine can be trained to a five-foot stake, about 2x2 inch size, or tied to a top trellis wire, to aid in developing a straight trunk.

Second year. Assuming that the trellis is ready at the beginning of the second year, remove all side branches and tie to the lower wire, and with an extension string anchor the tip to the top wire. If a cane reaches above the top wire, cut it three inches above the wire. If the trellis is not ready at the beginning of the second year, it is best to stake the canes if they have not already been staked to develop and maintain straight trunks. If at the beginning of the second year, the cane growth is weak or less than three feet, cut off all but the best single cane and cut this back to two buds as recommended after planting.

Third year. A vigorous vine at the beginning of the third year can carry about 25 buds after pruning. Choose your training system first (Figures 20, 22, 23), then select the best cane(s) (number depends on vigor) and prune away the rest, leaving one renewal spur with two buds near the base of each selected fruiting cane as shown in Figures 20 to 23. The two canes at a wire level, one trained to the right and the other to the left, can be spiraled around the wire and tied loosely to it. These canes the following year become the cut-back arms or cordons (Figure 20, 22) from which fruiting canes are selected in later years.

Figure 22. This is the "Single Curtain" or little or "No Tie" training system developed by Garth Cahoon of Ohio Agr. Exp. Sta., Wooster 44691, for lower vigor cultivars. Maintenance costs are relatively low. It is adapted to mechanical pruning. The trunks, arms, renewal spurs (one to two nodes) and the fruiting canes (4 to 6 nodes) left after pruning can be seen. Note the triple wire. Initial shoot for trunk is trained to top wires by stout string. Note mowed sod middles with herbicide-treated strip in vine row. In-row drip irrigation often is initially installed for good uniform growth and yield. (Courtesy Garth A. Cahoon).

424

PRUNING MATURE VINES[1]

Purpose of pruning old vines annually is to maintain the trunk and arms or cordons so that the minimum amount of old wood supports the desirable type, length, number, and distribution of canes. The renewal spurs are provided near the base of each fruiting cane to give a source of desirable new canes for fruiting the following year.

Long-Cane Systems (Kniffins). The canes selected for fruiting should be stocky and carrying plump vigorous buds (Figure 20). Concord canes and other cultivars of similar vigor should measure ¼ inch in diameter between the fifth and sixth nodes from the base of the cane. Canes with eight to ten buds after pruning are the most desirable length. These canes should arise as near the trunk of the vine as possible and renewal spurs should be provided near the base of each cane, as shown in Figure 20 for the *Four-Cane Kniffin* system. Remove all surplus wood, leaving only fruiting canes and spurs. Then tie ends of fruiting canes to the trellis with jute twine, light wire, or hand staplers[1], using a loose tie. Plastic chains, twine, rubber tubing or metal wires can be used to tie trunks and cordons to wires. The *Six-Cane Kniffin* system can be used with three wires for vigorous cultivars (Figure 27).

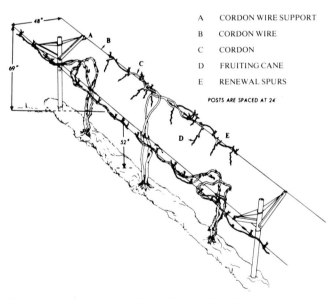

A	CORDON WIRE SUPPORT
B	CORDON WIRE
C	CORDON
D	FRUITING CANE
E	RENEWAL SPURS

POSTS ARE SPACED AT 24'

Figure 24. Basic design of the Geneva Double Curtain training system for grapes is shown. While considerable acreage of this system is under cultivation for vigorous cultivars, the Single Curtain system developed by Garth Cahoon in Ohio for moderate vigor cultivars is receiving attention for reduction in initial costs and operation (Figure 22) vs. the cane-tying in the Hudson River Umbrella system (Figure 23). (Diagram courtesy Nelson Shaulis, N. Y. Agr. Exp. Sta., Geneva 14456).

---

[1]Commercial trellis materials and pruning equipment are available from Amberg Bros. Nursery, Rt. #2, Box 269, Stanley, N.Y. 14561; A. M. Leonard and Son, Piqua, Ohio 45356 and Corona, P.O. Box 1388, Corona, Ca. 91720.

Each vine provides a different problem. In every vineyard, one will find weak and strong vines. Pruning must be adapted to the age, vigor, and to the individual canes on the vine. Vigorous Concord vines in well-managed vineyards may carry 40 or more buds after pruning, whereas with weaker-growing vines and cultivars, half this number of buds may result in better fruiting. With *Long-Cane* pruning systems, usually the fifth, sixth, and seventh buds, counting from the base of the vigorous cane (Figure 17), will develop the most productive shoots, and such canes pruned to eight and ten buds are desirable for fruiting.

Short-Cane Pruning systems. The Geneva Double Curtain (Figure 24), Single-Curtain (Figure 22) and Hudson River Umbrella (Figure 27) with the 5 + bud canes are fruitful on the 1-5 buds and even the 1-2 bud spurs due to good wood maturity and sun exposure.

Single Curtain System. This system is similar to the Geneva Double Curtain system, except that it is developed on a standard two or three-wire trellis and has only a single curtain of foliage (Figure 22).

The trunk is attached to the top trellis wire and is approximately 6 feet in height. Two horizontal cordons are developed along the top wires and extend 4 feet in each direction. If the vineyard is converted from one of the Kniffin training systems, 1-year-old canes are positioned along the top wire to develop into cordons in future years. Extra canes also may need to be retained during this transition year to maintain the balanced pruning concept.

Cordons are secured to the top wire by loose plastic ties or similar material. One advantage of the Single Curtain system compared to the Kniffin systems is a reduction in tying time.

Five-bud canes are selected from the cordon, plus 5-6 single bud renewal spurs. Shoots are later positioned downward for maximum exposure to sunlight during the growing season and also to facilitate the pruning operation.

This system is suitable for low to moderate vigor vineyards. For high vigor vineyards, the Geneva Double Curtain system is recommended because it allows essentially twice the amount of surface area per vine as the Single Curtain system (8 feet per cordon as compared to 4 feet). Modifications of this system are known by other names. The Hudson River Umbrella System, for example, utilizes long canes (8-12 buds instead of 5 buds).

Hudson River Umbrella. This system is a modification of the old Umbrella Kniffin in which the arms, at least 2 ft. long, rest along the top wire (Figure 23). From these arms or cordons, the spurs arise and the canes which grow or can be bent downward are tied to the bottom wire in a 2- or 3- wire system. This system is productive and suggested for a cultivar like Concord. Pruning is fast and easy at head-height. It costs less to maintain.

The Geneva Double-Curtain (GDC) System. This training system (Figure 24) was developed by Nelson Shaulis of the New York Agricultural Experiment Station, Geneva, for grape cultivars with vine growth like Concord, Niagara, Catawba and Delaware, used primarily for processing. It is adapted to mechanical harvesting. The GDC system has been adopted widely over the world for a wide range of the more vigorous cultivars. Yields may be increased 50 per cent for vigorous vines and soluble solids may be increased significantly by about one per cent due apparently to better light exposure.

Conversion from a Kniffin to a GDC system has shown a modest labor cost for the vines and trellis, plus cost of growing the crop the first year. Trellising and tying materials cost are additional, more for metal trellis arms than wooden forms. There is a cost for new and/or

Figure 25. The Geneva Double Curtain training system being used for vinifera grapes in California (above) and for Concord bunch grapes in New York (below). System provides for more growth, better light exposure, higher yield and quality. (Above, courtesy H. E. Burger, Agr. Eng., Univ. of Ca., Davis and below, Richard Hazel, grower, New York).

replacement posts; this varies considerably with the condition of the existing trellising system and the individual operator. Much of this conversion the first year must be considered a capital investment for subsequent years. Experience has shown that cultural operations, such as weed control, insect and disease control, cultivation, and hand harvesting, cost about the same for GDC as for other training systems. With the GDC system, more fertilizer may be needed in humid climates, particularly for nitrogen and potassium. Cultivars grafted on resistant stock is important with this system to get the vigor needed.

Trellis construction has the important feature of T-top or cordon wires (Figure 24). One vine is trained for about 16 feet along one of these wires, 8 ft. to the left and 8 ft. to the right, while an adjacent vine in the same row is trained 16 feet along the parallel wire. Trellis space per vine is about doubled over other training systems. Two trunks per vine is suggested; five-bud spurs and one-bud renewal spurs should be maintained on each cordon or arm. Each year, the shoots from these spurs are positioned by hand so that they grow vertically downward to form a curtain of foliage suspended from each cordon wire, hence, a double curtain of foliage is the final effect from each row of grapes with good light exposure.

Increase in net returns per acre should offset the additional cost of building the trellis and positioning the shoots each year. For details, consult the references by Nelson Shaulis *et al.*

Other training systems. The *Munson* system is suited to home vineyards where there are several cultivars in the planting, and other crops grown underneath. The trellis resembles a T-type telephone pole arrangement with two or three wires on the cross bar on which the vines are trained (see Muscadines). The system can be used for the more vigorous cultivars, regardless of type of grape, but it is particularly adapted to the muscadines.

The *arbor* system for grapes frequently is used in the home landscape. Placement of trunks, canes, and spurs is similar to that for the Kniffin system, except more wood is left to provide shade at the sacrifice of some fruiting (Figure 26).

Balanced pruning. N.L. Partridge of the Michigan Experiment Station, and N.J. Shaulis of the New York Experiment Station, Geneva, have suggested the balanced pruning system for grapes by which the number of buds left on a vine after pruning is kept proportionate to the vigor of the vine (Figure 27.) This is done by weighing all the one-year wood pruned from the vine. Shaulis found the weight of this wood to vary per acre from one to four pounds or more. For vigorous varieties more than one pound of wood is removed because of their inherent vigor, and at least 40 fruiting buds are left on the vine. Ten buds then should be left for each extra pound of wood removed. For example, if three pounds total is removed from a

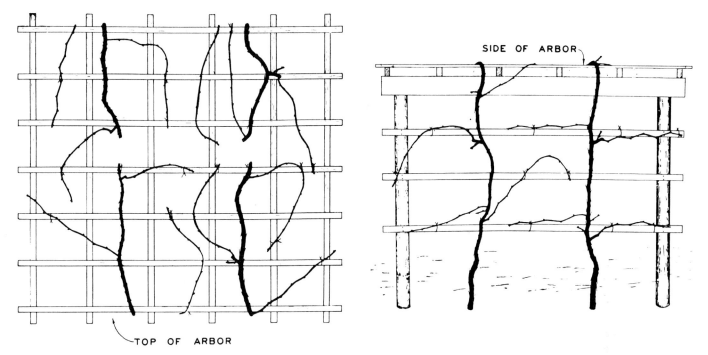

Figure 26. On backyard arbors, more fruiting canes are left than for trellis pruning because shade as well as fruit are desired. A modification of the Single-Trunk-Kniffin plan (Figure 20) of training can be used. The diagram shows vines after pruning. A cordon system with the canes pruned back to 2-bud spurs over the arbor could be used, leaving 1-bud spurs for replacement fruiting wood for next year (see Muscadines).

vigorous cultivar, then 40 plus 10, plus 10 buds, or 60 buds in all, are left on the vine. For practical purposes, it is suggested that the grower estimate the weight of one-year wood on the vine, prune the vine, and weigh the one-year wood removed. This can be repeated on ten or more vines until the pruner comes to know the appearance of one, two, three, or four pounds of wood on a vine. Then he can again estimate, prune, and weigh several vines until he becomes adept at estimating wood weight. By this balanced pruning, Shaulis has been able to lift the yields per acre by double or more, as compared with leaving approximately the same number of buds on every vine in a vineyard, regardless of its individual vigor.

For Concord, 30 buds are left for the initial pound of one-year prunings, plus ten buds for each additional pound of one-year prunings. For American hybrids, use a 30 + 10 ratio; for French hybrids use a 20 + 10 or a 20 + 5 ratio.

Mechanical Pruning. Advancements have been made in adapting machinery to mechanically prune grapes with follow-up hand pruning. Done manually, grape pruning takes 24-30 man hours to prune an acre. Quality manual pruning is becoming increasingly difficult to find; women have been doing most of it in the New York region. Pruning is done between November and March in the Northeast. Weather can be trying some winters. Figures 31 and 32 show equipment used and principles involved. Research has been done at Michigan State University and

by Cornell University in the Fredonia district. The equipment[1] is perfected to the point where year after year pruning can be done with consistent production of sound grapes for mechanical harvesting. Comparative figures of manhours it takes to manually and mechanically prune grapes are given in Table 4.

There is a better saving of labor in mechanical pruning if shoots have been positioned. Shoot positioning will increase yields by a half ton per acre,[2] and the follow-up hand pruning to get the proper number of buds per vine is reduced. This follow-up pruning can be done from the ground or from a special tractor-mounted seat with power shears on the same pass with the mechanical pruner.

Crop Control, Summer Pruning. C. W. Haeseler, Penn. State Univ., Northeast, suggests "crop control" other than balanced pruning, particularly for the French-American cultivars that tend to be over-productive. He suggests removing all flower clusters on vines one and two yrs. old. On vigorous vines one cluster per vine may be left the second year, and two clusters on three-yr. vines if vigorous. On low-organic matter soils, Foch may need little thinning of clusters, e.g. cluster thinning is done up

---

[1]Contact Bill Moffett, Eastern Grape Grower and Winery News, POB 329, Watkins Glen, N.Y. 14891 for equipment sources. Chisholm-Ryder Co., Niagara, N.Y. 14305.

[2]Mechanical shoot positioners, tractor attached, are available, replacing 15-18 workers a day. Slawson and Mead, King Rd., Forestville, N.Y. 14062.

TABLE. 4. HAND VS. MECHANICAL PRUNING GRAPES - HUDSON RIVER UMBRELLA AND GENEVA DOUBLE CURTAIN. JAMES MERRITT, GROWER, CHAUTAUQUA-ERIE GRAPE AREA, NEW YORK.

Pruning System	Hours Per Acre		
	Equipment Operator	Hand Pruning	Total Labor
Single Top Wire Cordon (HRU)			
No shoot positioning, Hand Pruned	—	17.6	17.6
Shoot positioned, Hand Pruned	—	11.7	11.7
No Shoot positioning, Machine Pruned, Hand Follow-up	20.0	8.3	10.4
Shoot Positioning, Machine Pruned, Hand Follow-up	2.2	4.5	6.6
Geneva Double Curtain (GDC)			
Shoot Positioned, Hand Pruned	—	10.5	10.5
Shoot Positioned, Machine Pruned, Hand Follow-up	3.3	5.4	8.6

Published in Eastern Grape Grower and Winery News, April 1979.

to one week before bloom if fruit setting is a primary factor; if not, it can be done up to 10-14 days after peak bloom to: (a) reduce crop size when needed, (b) improve fruit quality, (c) enhance bud and wood maturity, and (d) improve fruit set.

Removal of suckers (from below ground) and water sprouts (off the trunk) should be done early in the season to divert energy where better needed. Subsequent trips through the vineyard may be needed as growths develop.

Examples of number of clusters to leave per node in "crop control" are given in Table 5.

PRUNING NEGLECTED VINES

If mature vines have been neglected for a year or more, they become rangy with too much old wood. The best fruiting wood will be found some distance from the base of the vine. Select four to six reasonably desirable canes for fruiting as near to the central trunk of the vine as possible. Remove also any additional old wood coming from near the base of the vine or the main trunk, which will not be needed in fruiting in subsequent years. After two or three

TABLE 5. NUMBER OF FRUIT CLUSTERS LEFT PER NODE FOR CERTAIN WINE AND TABLE GRAPES. (AFTER C. W. HAESELER, PA. STATE UNIV., NORTHEAST)

Cultivar Desired	Max. No. buds/vine					
	yld./ vine (lbs.)	35	40	45	50	55	60
Foch	18	3	3	2	2	2	2
Seyval	25	2	1	-	-	-	-
Delaware	18	3	3	3	2	2	2
DeChaunac	25	2	2	2	1	-	-
Cayuga White	25	2	1	-	-	-	-

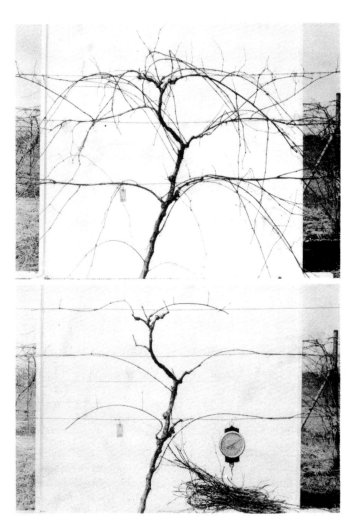

Figure 27. This is "balanced pruning" on a six-cane Kniffin trained Concord Vine (before pruning, above). The vine was pruned by the "30 plus 10" formula (leave 30 buds for first pound of one year wood removed plus 10 buds for each additional pound of such wood removed. Removed from this relatively vigorous vine were 3.4 lbs. of one-year wood, leaving 54 buds to produce the new crop. (Ohio Agricultural Experiment Station, Wooster).

years of renewal pruning and selecting fruiting canes closer and closer to the main trunk, neglected vines can be brought back within bounds to a fairly manageable pattern.

Sometimes it is possible to select a sucker arising from the base of the trunk for training straight to the upper wire to be used as a future central trunk for the new vine, eventually removing the old trunk.

CONTROLLING INSECTS AND DISEASE

Insect and disease problems vary in different vineyards. It is impossible to recommend a spray schedule for grapes that will have a general application. For a given vineyard, it seems desirable to study the quality of the crop

Figure 28. The grape leaf on the left has been fed upon by a large population of leafhoppers; the one on the right was taken from a vine sprayed properly. A nymph and adult grape leafhopper are shown at lower right; normal length of adult is about 1/8 inch. (Top) George W. Still, U.S.D.A. Grape Insect Laboratory, Sandusky, Ohio.

previously produced and the type of insect or disease injury, if any, which was present. If one or more insects or diseases persist year after year, sprays designed to correct these troubles must be used. Application of spray to both the upper and lower surfaces of the leaves, properly timed, with the proper materials is highly important. You can get up-to-date schedules from your county agricultural agent or from the agricultural mailing room, your state university.

The following is a brief description of the common diseases and insects in eastern grape-growing regions. *Grape-berry moth:* Small brown worms that develop in the fruit, causing it to color prematurely. Infested berries later crack open or shrivel and drop from the bunch. *Grapevine flea beetle;* Small, steel-blue jumping beetles that eat the opening buds in spring and destroy the new canes and fruit. The dark brown larvae feed on upper surface of the leaves in early summer. *Grape root worm:* Small grayish-brown beetles which eat chain-like marks in the upper surface of the leaves in early summer. Larvae feed on grape roots. *Rose chafer:* Long-legged, yellowish-brown beetles about one-half inch long; they eat blossom buds, newly-set fruit, and foliage, and are limited principally to sandy areas of vineyards. *Climbing cutworms:* Brown cut worms that hide on the ground near canes by day and feed at night on the opening buds in early spring. *Leafhoppers:* Very small elongate pale green insects marked with yellow and red, which jump from the leaves when disturbed. They suck sap from underside of leaves, causing speckled or rusty appearance of upper surface of leaves (Figure 28). *Black rot:* The fruit rots, then blackens, shrivels, and is covered with tiny black pimples. Leaves show brown spots having gray centers with black pimples (Figure 29). *Downy*

mildew: Leaves have indefinite yellowish areas above, with white downy patches beneath. Young shoots are covered with white downy mildew. Fruit has poor size, color, and flavor while some berries cease development and show gray mold on the surface. If almost mature, they shrivel, dry completely, and turn brown. *Powdery mildew* is similar but whitish mainly on the upper leaf surface.

Eutypa (dead arm) is spreading in the East, caused by the fungus *Eutypa armeniacae,* weakens or eventually kills one or more sides of the vine. In early summer the leaves are yellowish, stunted, crimpled and curled on one or more canes. Cut and burn canes in *early season* well back of injured areas (disinfect pruning tools). Apply Benlate 50W (1/5 lb./gal.) to the prune wounds day of the cut. Contact the Ohio Station, Wooster, 44691 for latest treatment.

Lightning in grapes may wipe out an entire row. Partially injured plants may show a distinct marginal necrosis on the leaves. Plastic wires is one solution. *Hail* may destroy an entire crop, but the vines usually recover within a year or so.

The microscopic *bud mite* may cause serious crop loss in Western States. Symptoms are short basal internodes, scarification of bark, flattened canes, dead terminal buds, zigzag shoots, and absence of fruit. There is no known effective control.

Netting will cover backyard vines for bird control (Conwed, Corp., 29th Av. SE, Minn., Minn. 55414). Mesurol spray will repel birds.

Spray machinery. Modern spray chemicals and machinery (Chap. XVIII) have simplified and increased

Figure 29. Black rot fungus is one of the worst diseases of *Labrusca* grapes. It appears on leaves during rainy periods in early summer. Spots are small, translucent in center, browning toward the outside with concentric rings, pinhead black pimples and a blackline margin encircling the spot. Berries infected with black rot shrivel into hard black mummies covered with numerous tiny pimples. Most mummies shell and fall to the ground.

Figure 30. This low-volume (LV) equipment was built for grapes and hedgerow fruit plantings for fast efficient coverage with less gallonage per acre. The fan is located horizontally rather than vertically which gives more twisting of the foliage and better coverage on both upper and lower leaf surfaces. (FMC, Jonesboro, Arkansas).

control of grape pests and diseases (Figure 36). Most, if not all, vines should be sprayed for insects and diseases even before vines come into bearing. As the vineyard becomes older, diseases and insects tend to increase. Stapling brown No. 2 bags around bunches when berries are beginning to touch is done in home gardens to protect against second generation berry moth worms and birds.

Airplane application. Aerial spray applications are on the increase with improved planes, sprays, fertilizers herbicides, and additives to reduce drift (175 million crop acres/yr. USA alone). Time and labor are saved plus quick coverage of large acreages.

FROST CONTROL, IRRIGATION

If a late-spring frost severely injures new grape growth, remove all new growth ("stripping"). Grape buds are compound and this will force the secondary bud to develop, giving a partial crop. If shoot growth is long and terminal tips and leaves are frosted, it is probably safer not to strip. These vines should produce a partial crop. The French-American hybrids may produce a full crop on secondary non-count buds.

The microjet system for irrigation and frost control should be studied for economy and effectiveness. Citrus growers report up to 4°F protection to six feet with microjets. The overhead sprinkler system has proven effective and trellised grapes can take the weight of the ice. Cost of sprinkler vs. trickle, according to R. C. Funt,

formerly of Univ. of Md., is about twice as much to install and operate for grapes[1].

HARVESTING AND MARKETING GRAPES

Stage of maturity. It is a common mistake to pick grapes too early. Unlike most fruits, there is practically no increase in color and sugar in grapes after they have been removed from the vines. Sour, poorly colored grapes on the market discourage subsequent sales.

The time for picking grapes depends upon the particular way in which they will be used. For jelly making, the fruit should be picked somewhat early to obtain light clear jelly free from crystals. For table use, grapes are picked when color and flavor are at the peak and before berries begin to shatter from the bunch, which varies with the cultivar. For juice, the grapes should be allowed to hang until full maturity is attained. Full maturity of grapes for wine or juice is judged by the soluble solids/sugar ratio, using a hand refractometer or Balling hydrometer (see Winkler et

Figure 31. This is (above) Jim Merritt's mechanical pruning equipment in the Chautauqua-Erie region of New York. Cutter bars are shown mounted at left. Below, is the vineyard before (right) and after (left) pruning. (Courtesy J. William Moffett, Eastern Grape Grower and Winery News, Watkins Glen, N.Y.)

Figure 32. Mechanical grape pruning machinery is perfected to reduce labor by 3 to 6 fold. Above equipment is designed for Concord in New York, consisting of a triangular arrangement of 3 reciprocating cutter bars which establish the length and position of canes for the GDC, Single Curtain and HRU systems for machine pruning in subsequent years. The cordon-riding-spiked-wheel-guide in lower photo and cane-thinning with pedestal-mounted-circular saw is in upper photograph. Left insert shows crimped wire support and first acceptable cane to leave for fruiting with 2 to 3 buds, others are cut at "A" manually. (Courtesy N.J. Shaulis and J.G. Pollock, Cornell Univ., 14850.)

al. 1974). Indications often used to judge maturity other than by taste are browning and slight shrivelling of the stem, ease of separation of the berries, browning of the seeds, freeness of the seeds from the pulp, and a reddening or browning of the wood. Grapes have more natural resistance to storage rots if picked as soon as fully mature and before they are wet by rain.

Containers. Containers should be ordered well in advance of the picking season. The number and type needed obviously will depend upon the amount and quality of the yields. Yields vary tremendously with variety and growing conditions. Concords may vary from one to eight tons or more per acre. An average commercial yield in the better northern Ohio vineyards is about two and one-half tons with some growers obtaining yields up to six tons per acre. Profit is doubtful with yields under two tons. Weak-growing cultivars such as Delaware and Catawba average one to two tons per acre, occasionally reaching four.

The climax baskets of the two-, four-, and twelve-quart sizes are popular for use with the bunch grapes. The wooden baskets with the wire handles or the cardboard baskets with single or double-weight walls and a wooden handle have been used in the Great Lakes regions. Cardboard containers are light, somewhat more economical, and better suited to advertising copy on the sides. The two- and four-quart containers are used for table grapes, whereas the twelve-quart basket and the bushel or half-bushel basket are employed for juice or wine purposes. The shallow-depth bulk boxes or wheel trailers are being used with or without mechanical harvesters to collect and carry grapes to the winery or juice plants.

Hand Picking and Packing. Grapes for table use should be handled carefully from the time they are picked until sold. Preserve the powdery bloom on the berries as much as possible. Handle the bunches by the stems and do not pull them from the vines. Remove bunches with special shears or a sharp knife. The better bunches on a vine are picked first and packed as Fancy or Number 1 grapes,[1]

Figure 33. A light portable stand for hand harvest is convenient for filling baskets along the trellis. It should be about waist high to discourage pickers from dropping bunches into containers.

---

[1]For all government grade specifications on Eastern and Western grapes, contact the Agricultural Marketing Service, U.S. Dept. of Agr., Washington, D.C., 20250. These include U.S. Standards for (a) Table Grapes, (b) Sawdust Pack Grapes, (c) American Bunch Grapes (Eastern) for Processing and Freezing, (d) Juice Grapes and (e) American (Eastern) Bunch Grapes.

Figure 34. (Upper) "Slapper Type" mechanical grape harvester, knocking off grape berries to belt below, thence up and over parallel row to 3½ T self-dumping hydraulic vineyard trailer, then to end of row to discharge into 8-12 T bulk-tank truck, which is (lower photo) discharged at processing plant. Five to 15% of grape clusters must be "busted" by special chain-mesh equipment at plant, also removing any trash. This Chisholm-Ryder machine is adjustable also to harvest grapes trained to the Geneva Double Curtain system. (Michigan State University, E. Lansing).

whereas the imperfect bunches are picked later and packed as Number 2 grapes. The poorer small bunches may be placed in a separate container for juice. In packing the basket, it is placed on the picking stand (Figure 30) in a slanting position and the corner nearest the picker is filled first with the stems pointing downward. The picker then

proceeds to fill the basket from bottom to top until the farthest corner is filled last. The baskets are carefully packed to about an inch above the rim, after which they are placed in the shade of the vine until taken to the shelter house, which should be as soon as possible. Allow the grapes to settle from four to six hours before basket tops are applied. Many baskets are sold, however, without tops.

For the higher grade packages, the small, poorly colored, diseased, or insect-infested berries can be removed at picking and packing time, provided the current price will justify the extra labor. Cloudy dry days are best for picking. Decay is likely to occur if grapes are picked wet.

Mechanical Harvesting. To reduce harvesting labor costs, mechanical harvester machines have been perfected primarily for processing grapes for wine, juice, and other products (Figure 34). The Geneva-Double-Curtain and Single Curtain training systems are well adapted to mechanical harvesting.

Grapes should be processed as soon after harvesting as possible to avoid deterioration and self-crushing in the large collection trailers. Most USA juice-wine vineyards (over 95%) are mechanically harvested. See also mechanical harvesting under vinifera grapes. Labor union entrance into the grape and other agricultural enterprises and lack of labor has stimulated increased grower and engineer efforts to replace much of the migrant and other labor with automated equipment, particularly in harvesting. (See note below).

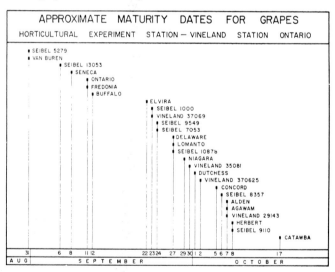

Figure 35. This chart gives the ripening order of grape cultivars, from left to right, grown in Ontario, Canada. This same ripening order for cultivars such as Seibels, Delaware, Niagara, Concord and Catawba should more or less hold in other regions where these cultivars are grown. (O. A. Bradt, Hort. Exp. Sta., Vineyard St., Ontario.)

Note: Grape harvester research is being headed by Dr. Marshall, USDA, and Galen Brown at Mich. State Univ. E. Lansing, 48823; R. B. Fridley, U. of Ca., Davis. 95616.

432

U.S. Grapes: Utilization

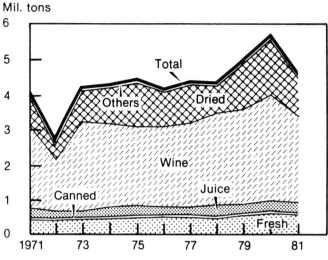

Mil. tons

U.S. Wine

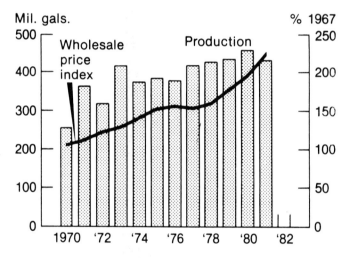

Mil. gals.   % 1967

Figure 36. There is increasing interest in wine, particularly in California but also in the East. California acreage is over 700,000 with 1/6th non-bearing. Wine acreage accounts for 49 percent of the total. Increased plantings of the French-American cultivars in the East reflects this interest. Table grapes acreage has been declining. (USDA)

Marketing. Grapes should be taken to market on the day they are picked, or not later than the next day. The less they are handled from picking until they reach the consumer, the better. If a roadside stand is available near the main highway, a portion of the crop can be sold through this channel (Figure 37.) Container costs can be saved by removing the grapes from the cartons and placing them in paper or poly bags for the customer. Some stores may return the containers for repeat use but they may stretch with age.

It may boost sales to mix red, white, and blue grapes together with apples, peaches, pears and other fruits in a 2-qt. family container. The average housewife is canning and

preserving less grapes than heretofore, reducing fresh sales of grapes and diverting more to processing. Wine offers increasingly large outlets for grapes (Figure 36).

National Grape Co-operative is an increasing farmer-owned business with over 2000 members growing Concord and Niagara grapes in seven areas of the United States — New York, Pennsylvania, Ohio, Michigan, Arkansas, Missouri and Washington. Welch Foods is the Co-operative's marketing subsidiary with over 1500 employees processing and marketing a variety of grape and non-grape products in the United States and some 60 other nations. Welch Foods processing facilities are located in the nation's principal Concord grape growing regions: Westfield and Brocton, New York; North East, Pennsylvania; Lawton, Michigan; Springdale, Arkansas; Grandview and Kennewick, Washington. Together, National Grape and Welch Foods form the world's largest and leading Concord grape growing, processing and marketing enterprise. The purpose of the organization is to provide a ready and secure market for members' Concord and Niagara grapes; to return to members a fair price for their produce and to provide consumers with readily available, high-quality products at reasonable prices.

Storing grapes. Eastern-type grapes cannot be stored successfully for more than about one or two months (Table 6) without special treatment. Controlled atmosphere (CA) storage shows promise of more than doubling this period. During a season when there is a heavy supply of grapes, it may be desirable to store a portion of the crop for later marketing. Grapes should be stored immediately after picking, using only the Fancy or No. 1 grapes which are in sound condition. They preferably should be placed in cold storage at 31° to 32° F. with a humidity of 80 to 85 per

Figure 37. An exciting display of northern Ohio Concord and Niagara grapes in a Cleveland supermarket. The two quart cartons with wooden handles are attractive; polyethylene wraps will preserve freshness and add attraction. Baskets with mixed fruits — apples, pears, peaches along with grapes, may sell well. (Dick Meister, American Fruit Grower magazine.)

cent. Stack the containers with frequent aisles running both vertically and laterally to provide free air circulation. To reduce mold development it is a common practice to spray the storage room and picking boxes with a solution of two pounds copper sulfate with 50 gallons of water several days before picking starts.

TABLE 6. STORAGE LIFE OF LABRUSCA BUNCH-TYPE GRAPES IN WEEKS.

Concord	4-7	Catawba	5-8
Niagara	3-6	Worden	3-5
Delaware	4-7	Moore	3-6

Better keeping varieties are Delaware, Diamond, Concord, Catawba, and Sheridan. The red grapes are usually somewhat better keepers then the black, white or blue cultivars. Eastern cultivars are not fumigated with sulfur dioxide, as western cultivars, because of their susceptibility to damage. Recent studies, however, by Haeseler and Yeager of Penn. State Univ. show promise in holding the cultivars Suffolk Red, Festivee (not seedless), Himrod, Lakemont and Candice in plastic packages with and without SO_2 packets (emitting 4-7 ppm) obtained from Quality Packaging, Inc., Antioch, Ca. 94509. One pkt. was used per 9 Kg of grapes. The SO_2 had little effect on quality at 1-2 °C storage up to 90 days. All stored well up to 39 days, but the SO_2 controlled mold and decay to 90 days, with some shrivelling of stems but not fragile, except for Himrod and Lakemont at low temperatures. A box of treated Lakemont was displayed aside Thompson Seedless; the latter outsold the former only because the berries were smaller and consumers were not acquainted with the Lakemont. After trying Lakemont all acknowledged approval and chose it after the price had been dropped 10-20¢/lb. Researchers were of the opinion one-third of the Thompson Seedless market could be captured by these seedless cultivars in the East.

SOUTHERN MUSCADINE AND BUNCH GRAPES

Muscadine and bunch grapes in the southern warmer climate are limited to areas where the temperature rarely goes lower than 10°F and almost never reaches 0°F. A number of large muscadine and bunch type vineyards have developed for wine which is the largest single outlet. Other uses are in preserves, jellies, jams and blending in fruit juice with some fresh sales. Canned grapes are used in pies. Most muscadine cultivars belong to *Vitis rotundifolia; two other species are V. munsoniana and V. Popenei.* Upper boundry of growing area in the U.S. extends from eastern North Carolina to southeast Missouri (excluding most of Tennessee) to central Oklahoma and south to Houston, Texas.

Grape breeders in North Carolina, Georgia, Mississippi,

Arkansas and Florida have been introducing improved muscadines and there are now commercial cultivars of the bunch type, using Concord, e.g., to get the desired characters. Pierce's disease has been the key limiting factor with bunch grapes but the newer introduced cultivars have been surviving satisfactorily.

Sites and Soils. Air and water drainage is important (Figure 38). Muscadines have the advantage of leafing out rather late and are not so subject to frost. They must have good sunlight. Vines perform best in sandy loams high in organic matter and in fertile red clays but rooting must be to a depth of two ft. and better to 4-6 ft. Barren clays and wet soils are unsatisfactory.

Cultivars. Commercial muscadine cultivars have either pistillate (female) or perfect flowers (self fertile). The latter cultivars can pollinate themselves as well as female cultivars. In the planting plan, pollinating cultivars should be within about 25 ft. of pistillate cultivars to get good production. In a single female cultivar row, use a pollinizer every third plant, or every third plant in a row in every third row, or three rows of a female cultivar to one row of a pollinizer for mechanical harvesting. Pollen type will not affect color, flavor or size of fruit.

Table 7 gives some characteristics of muscadine cultivars in North Carolina. Table 8 gives suggested cultivars and uses for northern Florida. This table includes the bunch grapes introduced and tested for resistance to Pierce's disease. Mississippi State with USDA (at Meridian) have introduced bunch-type cultivars. MidSouth, Miss Blue, Miss Blanc, Regale and Doreen muscadines. These newer cultivars have been fully tested in the southeast and are promising. Arkansas is suggesting Higgins (female), Dearing (female), Roanoke (self-fertile), Magnolia (SF), Hunt (F), Creek (SF), Bountiful (SF), Chief (SF) and Cowart (SF). Cultivars are changing in all areas with introduction of improved cultivars; contact your local institution or county agricultural agent for detail cultivar descriptions and records.

The new bunch grape from Florida is 'Conquistador', a purple quality fresh grape, good for wine, dooryard, and processing. (Fla. Cir. S-300, 1983).

Propagation. Layering is the common practice; it is generally more successful than by cuttings. A 25 per cent or less "take" with Muscadine cuttings is due to a very hard wood that does not callus or root freely. It may prove more satisfactory to purchase vines from the nursery, requesting two-year plants rooted by layering. Concord and Delaware, *labrusca* grapes, can be grown successfully in the south on Dog Ridge stocks *(V. Champini)* but new bunch-type cultivars are proving better.

Planting Distances. For muscadines, distance between rows may vary from 10 to 14 ft. with a compromise for efficient land utilization and adequate space for machinery operation. Spacing in the row is 20 ft., giving 180

Figure 38. This is a muscadine planting in Mississippi, trained to the Geneva Double curtain system. Note the rolling land with good air drainage. Muscadines tested in Mississippi show the following yield in T/A: Regale, 10.1; Magnolia, 8.9; Noble, 8.8; Higgins, 8.6; Carlos, 8.4; Roanoke, 7.0; Creek, 7.3 and Scuppernong, 5.6. New bunch grapes are Miss Blanc, MissBlue and MidSouth. (L. Hancock for Mississippi State Univ.)

TABLE 7. SOME CHARACTERISTICS OF MUSCADINE[1] CULTIVARS IN NORTH CAROLINA.

Variety	Color	Vigor[2]	Quality[2]	Berry size	Yield per vine	Maturity[3]	Sugar as total soluble solids
				Grams	Pounds	Harvest date	Percent
Creek . . . . Dark		10	6	3.9	61	Oct. 5	17.3
Dearing[4] . . . . Light		8	7	3.4	57	Sept. 27	19.2
Dulcet . . . . Dark		9	8	3.6	44	Sept. 17	17.3
Higgins . . . . Light		7	6	9.5	52	Oct. 1	16.0
Hunt . . . . Dark		9	8	5.8	70	Sept. 17	17.1
Magoon[4] . . . . Dark		8	7	4.1	64	Oct. 3	17.9
Scuppernong. . . . . Light		7	8	5.4	43	Sept. 23	16.8
Topsail . . . . Light		10	10	5.9	46	Oct. 1	21.8
Yuga . . . . do		8	7	4.1	64	Oct. 3	17.9

[1]Except for Higgins, ratings and figures for all cultivars are averages in a 5-year test conducted at Raleigh, N.C. Higgins was tested 2 years. Vines were 4 years old at beginning of test. Contact N. C. St. Univ., Raleigh 27607 for additional and latest cultivars.

[2]Rating: 2, very poor; 4, poor; 6, good; 8, very good; 10, excellent. A rating of 6 is low as would be suitable for general planting.

[3]Average date of maximum maturity at Raleigh; date would be about 2 weeks earlier in Georgia and Mississippi. Most cultivars have some ripe fruit 10 days before given maximum maturity dates.

[4]Perfect flowered. Other cultivars are pistillate, and require perfect-flower pollinizers.

TABLE 8. GRAPE CULTIVARS FOR NORTH FLORIDA. (J. A. MORTENSEN, UNIV. OF FL., LEESBURG).

MUSCADINES		
Albermarle (D) (2)	Jumbo (F) (3)	Welder (W) (4)
Cowart (D) (2)	Noble (W, Ju, Je) (2)	Dixiland (T) (4)
Dixie (F, W, D) (4)	Regale (W) (2)	Dixired (T) (4)
Doreen (W) (1)	Southland (F, D) (2)	**BUNCH GRAPES**
Fry (F) (1)	Summit (F) (1)	Blue Lake (Ju, Je, D)
	Triumph (F, D) (4)	Conquistador (F,W,T, Ds, Ju, Je) (2)
		Lake Emerald (W)
		Stover (F, W, D)

Symbols: F = fresh; W = wine; Ju = juice; Je = jelly; D = dooryard; T = trial.
(1) = Bronze female; (2) = Black, self-fertile; (3) = Black, female; (4) = Bronze, self-fertile.

plants/A. On lighter less fertile soils, as in Florida, spacing may be 15-18 ft. in the row. Where dooryard shade is needed, the arbor or overhead system of planting is used and planting distance may be 15x15 ft.

With bunch type grapes, planting distances are about 10 ft. in the row and 11-12 ft. between rows. Rows should run north and south, with about 45 plants/row and length of rows about 450 ft., allowing room for turning at ends.

Trellises. A 1-(top wire only, Figure 39), 2- or 3-wire vertical trellis can be used or the Geneva Double Curtain system, which is relatively expensive; the grower should be sure of his processing market beforehand. These systems are adaptable for both muscadine and bunch grapes. The Munson "T" with two top wires at 5 ft. also can be used (Figure 39.) See previous discussion for trellis and arbor or overhead construction.

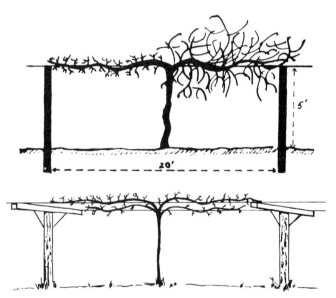

Figure 39. (Top) A one-wire trellis showing trunk, arms or cordons to left and right, before (right) and after (left) pruning. The one- to two-bud spurs left after pruning are shown. Vines and posts are 20 ft. apart for the muscadines. (Below) This is a more vigorous muscadine cultivar trained by the Munson system showing the double wires on "T" posts, with two arms and spurs after pruning to the left and two arms to the right. Arms should about touch for neighboring vines. (Justin R. Morris, Univ. of Ark.)

Training and Pruning. The first year set a 5.5 ft. stake next to each plant and tie the stake to the top wire of the trellis. As shoots appear from the recently set plant, select the more vigorous shoot and secure it to the stake with string. Remove all other shoots. The selected shoot becomes the trunk. Remove side shoots and sprouts as they appear during the first season, except to leave a shoot to follow out each wire to the right and to the left. Cut the tip of the trunk shoot as it reaches the top wire so that a shoot will grow each way along the top wire.

Permanent arms or cordons are established along the wires whether on vertical cross arm or GDC wires (Figures 39, 40). Pruning on the 2-wire system takes less time, is preferred commercially. The 3-wire often is used for the dooryard.

On mature muscadine vines, remove tendrils and branches not to be used for spurs and fruiting arms. Prune away branches less than 3/16 inch in diameter. Leave spurs with 2-3 buds, depending upon vigor. Remove many of the spurs near the trunk top to prevent bushiness which interferes with harvest. Replace arms no longer vigorous. Mid winter is the best time to prune and toward spring while the vines are dormant. Late dormant season "bleeding" at cuts is not harmful to the vines.

The 2-wire 4-Cane Kniffin system discussed earlier or the Munson "T" system shown in Figure 39 can be used for bunch grapes in the South. Note the short arms with spurs and the canes for each wire to the left and right. The "Balanced" pruning is used removing more wood for the more vigorous vines. Twenty-two lbs. were removed in this case.

Fertilization. In the lighter less fertile soils of Florida recommendations for muscadines are for a soil pH adjusted to about 6.0 with dolomite in acid soils, 5 lbs./100 sq. ft. The first yr. apply ¼ lb. of a 1-1-1 fertilizer, 20-30% N from natural sources in bands with the row a ft. from the plant after growth starts. Repeat in May, June, early September. The second yr. use 2/3rds lb. in late March, May and immediately after harvest. Rates subsequently can be increased up to 4-6 lbs. total/plant/year, split.

In the medium loams of Arkansas for muscadines, adjust the pH to 6.0; the first yr. apply 3-4 ft. away from plant, not under the trellis (encourages weeds) ½ lb./vine 1-1-1 mix before growth and side-dress ¼ lb. sodium nitrate mid June. The second yr. use 1 lb. of mix and ½ lb. of nitrate broadcast 5 ft. from plant. The 3rd yr. broadcast except for 18-inch width under trellis, 2 lbs. mix per vine. In succeeding yrs. use 2-4 lbs./vine depending upon vigor, before growth starts in spring. Root growth by this time will cover the entire area. Desired growth/yr. is 30-36 inches; apply more or less fertilizer to get this growth.

Bunch grapes have less vigor and hence will need less fertilizer, using essentially the procedure above. Use of trace elements in the mix may be beneficial on low-organic

Figure 40. (Upper left) MidSouth muscadine grape, end of 4th yr., on a 3-ft. 2-wire cross arm, 5 ft. 9-inch post, before pruning; (Upper right) Same vine after pruning in March by long-cane balanced formula, removing 11 lbs. total, leaving 40 buds for first lb. removed, then leaving 10 buds for each additional lb. of wood removed, totalling 140 buds. (Lower left) Volume of wood removed. (Lower right) Muscadine in 7th yr. leaf, yielding up to 150 lbs. grapes/vine. (Courtesy J. P. Overcash and C. P. Hegwood, Mississippi State Univ., 39762-5519).

matter sandy soils (see Chap. V).

Irrigation. In light sandy soils, irrigation is a must to get regular quality production. It sould be installed by planting time. The drip and microjet systems are being used mainly because of economy and efficiency. Irrigation is particularly important with young vines. There seems to be a trend toward the microjet system even though more pressure and water are needed vs. the drip. Overall the advantages are: (1) Dry or liquid fertilizer can be applied successfully; (2) wets a larger area; (3) does not wet foliage and encourage diseases; (4) can be operated at night with low evaporation; (5) twice a wk. is satisfactory during dry

Figure 41. This home-made catching frame can be hung on the wires and each arm jerked to loosen berries, or 10x20 ft. burlap or canvas sheets under the vines on either side can be used to catch the berries. Motor-driven machines with hand-held rubber-finger shakers and catching frame are on the market for limited acreage. Over-the-row mechanical harvesters are used for large commercial acreages. (Univ. of Ark.).

periods; (6) less energy and water than sprinklers but more than drip; (7) can see and unclog or replace clogged jets easily; and (8) *can be used during spring frosts* to raise the temperature 4-6°F to 6 ft. height.

Weed Control, Birds, Animals. Shallow cultivation the first year is suggested no deeper than 3 inches. Chemical weed control under the vines with a turf strip in the middle of the rows for traffic is suggested beginning the second season. See previous discussion this Chapter and contact local specialists for latest herbicide recommendations.

On dooryard plants, netting, chicken wire, scare devices (larger planting) may be used to help control birds. Mesurol spray used by label is a repellent. Rats, racoons and rabbits can be controlled by traps or extermination.

Harvesting and handling. The average muscadine cultivar receiving good care should give 25 to 30 bushels of grapes per acre from four-year vines, 50 to 75 bushels from five-year vines, and 100 to 150 bushels from vines in full bearing. This is about three to six tons per acre. Cultivars such as Scuppernong yield less than Noble and Regale. Grapes for the winery or culinary purposes are harvested

as noted in Figure 41. Grapes for table use, including those that shatter from the cluster as well as those that remain attached to the cluster, are harvested carefully by hand and placed on the market in two- and four-quart climax baskets and strawberry crates.

Store at 40°F to prolong berry life; CA storage extends quality further.

Bunch grapes ripening earlier than muscadines can be handled much the same as in the Northeast. Pick-Your-Own system of harvesting is becoming popular for both muscadines and bunch grapes. See FS-7 Circular, University of Florida, Gainesville, 32611 for home preservation of Florida grapes.

Problems, Needs of Muscadine Industry. L. F. Flora, Ga. Exp. Sta., Experiment 30212 has listed the needs of the muscadine industry: (1) Production areas are too small and scattered for efficient processing industry; (2) low inefficient production in old vineyards increases costs, destroys competition; (3) too much labor needed to harvest muscadines; (4) uneven ripening a problem; (5) open wet stem scars a problem; (6) nurserymen should reduce cultivars sold to only the best; (7) season is short, shelflife short, discouraging acceptance by markets; (8) they are not competitive in price with other grapes due to high labor costs; (9) no promotion and a lack of familiarity by customers; (10) need for better quality seedless cultivars, and (11) a lack of coordination of cooperative effort to stabilize and increase markets. Research and extra effort is needed to overcome these problems.

GROWING VINIFERA GRAPES[1]

Vinifera grapes comprise most of the world grape production. About 72% of all grapes are produced in Europe, 13% in North and South America, 6% in Africa, 7% in Middle East, and 2% in Australia.

In the U.S., *viniferas* are grown primarily in the semiarid warm-temperate and subtropical regions of California, Arizona, and lower Texas along the Rio Grande River. Some are grown in the Northeast U.S. The vines require a hot dry summer and a cool wet winter (rain may be replaced or supplemented by irrigation). A favorable mean daily winter temperature is between 35° and 50°F., gradually rising to between 70° and 85°F. in summer. An average yearly rainfall of 20 to 25 inches is usually sufficient if well distributed during the autumn, winter, and spring.

Cultivars. Importance of *vinifera* cultivars in the USA is exemplified by the over 700,000 acres of these grapes in

---

[1]Best detailed book on grapes, especially *viniferas,* is Winkler et al. General Viticulture. Univ. of Calif. Press, Berkeley, Los Angeles, London. Revised 1974.

James A. Cook, University of California, Davis, has helped revise this section.

California. Approximate rank of the 20 leading cultivars follows: Thompson Seedless (RT)[1]; Carignane (rW); Zinfandel (rW); Cabernet Sauvignon (rW); French Colombard (wW); Emperor (T); Barbera (rW); Grenache (rW); Chenin Blanc (wW); Flame Tokay (T); Ruby Cabernet (rW); Muscat of Alexandria (rW); Petite Sirah (rW); Rubired (rW); Chardonnay (rW); Pinot Noir (rW); White Riesling (wW); Ribier (T); Alicante Bouschet (rW) (shipped east for wine-making); and Mission (rW). Cabernet Sauvignon (claret of France) is a high-quality dinner wine. To emphasize, Thompson Seedless can be used for raisins, wine and table and constitutes about 38% of the State's grape acreage.

Wine cultivars in California, accounting for over 95% of the U.S. *viniferas,* constitute over 51% of the total raisin cultivars over 39% and table types about 10%. Wine cultivars have tripled in acreage over the past 15 yrs. They are used only for wine. Some table grapes also now are used for wine as Flame Tokay and White Malaga. Flame Tokay due to fall rains in the northerly table grape region, cannot compete now with the newer red cultivars in the San Joaquin Valley, Cardinal and Queen. It is inferior in storage to the Emporer, hence now used for wine and brandy. The red Emperor also can withstand periodic sulfur dioxide fumigation and long storage periods, as also can the white Almeria and Calmeria which are harvested in the favorable season September and October and marketed from cold storage to March. There is need for seedless cultivars with these qualities.

Most table grapes of the near future will be seedless, a marked increase in demand, which concerns the European and Asian countries. Perlette seedless is early maturing in May, commanding premium prices (Table 9).

Thompson Seedless has taken over the raisin cultivar Muscat of Alexandria which now is used for wine. Black Corinth or Zante currant is steady with use in cakes and cookies. Fiesta has not been well accepted, nor Canner.

The wine grape boom started in 1970 but is levelling. Plantings of French Colombard and Chenin Blanc supply the demand for moderately priced white wines. Premium cultivars Chardonnay and Sauvignon Blanc also shared in the increased acreage. Machine harvest has aided the Cabernet-Sauvignon in increased acreage to overcome labor problems with other cultivars. GA use is universal to increase berry size of seedless grapes. Thompson Seedless is well adapted to mechanical harvesting but the long-cane pruning will delay an easy solution to mechanical pruning. Wine cultivars adapted to mechanical handling are needed.

The two color publications from University of California, 4009 and 4069, priced, on Wine Grape Varieties for San Joaquin Valley and North Coast Counties, California, respectively, are good references.

Washington state has three publications on cultivar adaptability for different regions of the state, soils, and climates: Cir. 382; WSU XC 524, and WSU EB 635. The American types are very hardy and grown widely. Moderately hardy European *vinifera* types for medium fertile sandy loam soils in the warmer climates are, as an example; Chardonney (white), Chenin Blanc (white), French Colombard (white), Helena (white), Melon (white), White Riesling, Barbera (blue), Cabernet Sauvignon (blue), Chauche Noir (blue), Gamay Beaujolais (blue) Limberger (blue), Royalty (blue), Mennier (blue), Rubird (blue), Zinfandel (blue), Chauche Gris (red).

Propagation. Rooted cuttings of the desired fruiting cultivars can be used only in soils not infested with the phylloxera insect or nematodes. In soils infested with these pests, cuttings of resistant rootstocks must be grafted to the desired fruiting cultivar either before (whip-graft) or after rooting (by whip-, cleft-, or groove-grafting or chip budding). Soil fumigants can be applied by flooding to established plantings for controlling most (ectoparasitic) nematodes. Use virus-free rootstocks resistant to phylloxera and nematodes, particularly on replant sites and on deep coarse sandy low-fertility drouthy soils. The University of California and USDA have developed indexed vines of 34 table and raisin cultivars, 50 wine and 14 rootstock cultivars (available through Calif. Dept. of Agr. Nursery Serv., Sacramento; Harmony and Freedom rootstocks are gaining prominence) which have earlier and larger production, uniform vigorous vines and fruit with full color and maturity. Certified heat-treated "virus-free" stock should be used. (See Alley for improved field-budding technique).

Planting distances. One hundred square feet or more are required per vine in fertile soils and hot climates where vines grow large. For cooler climates, less fertile soils or for smaller growing cultivars, about 80 square feet or even less may suffice. Trellised vigorous raisin cultivars are planted 8 by 12 feet. With modern machinery, rows mostly are 12 ft. apart with avenues of 18 to 20 feet at intervals of 300 to 600 feet, or equivalent to the length of the irrigation furrows.

Vine supports. Cultivars trained to the vase-form are supported by stakes four to six feet long. The stakes are removed after six to ten years when the vines become self-supporting. Stakes can be set rapidly and without injury to roots if grapes have been planted, by using a water jet from a special spray machine gun (Calif. Leaflet 2860, 1976). For a simple two-wire trellis (Figure 42), a substantial six-foot stake or post at each vine is sufficient with two No. 11 or No. 12 smooth galvanized fencing wires stretched along the row at 34 and 46 inches from the ground. For vigorous cultivars, such as Thompson Seedless, a "wide top" trellis is often constructed by tying a cross-arm (two by two inches by three feet) to the top of each alternate stake and bracing the lower end to hold the cross-arm at an angle of

---

[1]R-raisin; T-table; r-red; W-wine; w-white.

TABLE 9. MAJOR CULTIVARS OF CALIFORNIA TABLE GRAPES (BLUE-ANCHOR, NOV.-DEC. 1977). CALIFORNIA TABLE GRAPE PRODUCTION IS OVER 500,000 TONS, OR ABOUT 10% OF THE TOTAL OF 5.4 MILLION TONS. (USDA).

Storage of some cultivars makes possible their availability for longer periods than indicated on the chart.

Cultivar	May	June	July	August	September	October	November	December	January	February	March
PERLETTE (seedless): The "Little Pearl" comes in large, compact clusters with crisp green berries and a mild, pleasing taste.	X	X	X								
BLACK BEAUTY (seedless): This juicy grape is the earliest black variety on the market, and has medium to large berries.	X	X									
CARDINAL: The large, mild tasting Cardinal grapes have lustrous, dark red berries with a grayish bloom.*		X	X	X							
EXOTIC: This beautiful black grape has crisp flesh with a subtle flavor and grows in long, full clusters.		X	X								
THOMPSON (seedless): Thompsons are light green and medium to large in size with a sweet, sprightly taste.				X	X	X	X				
RED MALAGA: This sweet red grape has round to oval shaped berries and large conical clusters.				X	X						
RIBIER: Sometimes called the "King of the Blacks," Ribiers come in medium large clusters with mild tasting berries.			X	X	X	X	X	X	X	X	
QUEEN: A mild tasting red grape variety that features large berries arranged in full clusters.					X	X					
LADY FINGER: Lady Fingers are refreshing light green grapes with slender, elongated berries. They have a mild flavor and long, loose clusters.					X	X	X				
ITALIA: A variety featuring large golden berries with a whitish bloom* and a distinctive, mild flavor.					X	X	X				
TOKAY: This is a handsome, red grape that grows in very large clusters with a subtle taste and large berries.					X	X	X				
EMPEROR: The Emperor has large, cherry flavored red berries and is a popular Thanksgiving and Christmas variety.						X	X	X	X	X	X
ALMERIA: Almerias are characterized by large, oval shaped, frosty green berries with firm flesh and mild flavor.						X	X	X	X	X	
CALMERIA: This table grape variety has an elongated light green berry that's also mild in flavor.						X	X	X	X	X	

Figure 42. Training and pruning systems being used for vinifera grapes in California, other regions. (Top left) This is a head-pruned vine used for cultivars that bear well on spurs, including most wine, some raisin and table grapes as Tokay. (Upper right) A mature horizontal bi-lateral cordon-pruned vine, used for table types and widely used for spur-pruned wine cultivars. (Lower) A long-cane pruned vinifera for raisin and wine cultivars on a 2-wire trellis. In large plantings, some of these systems have been transformed to the duplex or double-curtain system for higher production and sugar content and for mechanical harvesting (see Figure 44).

about 30° from the horizontal. Three wires are used on the cross-arms and one just beneath on the stake. Advantages of this system are more fruiting wood, clusters better exposed to light and air, better distribution of wood and bunches, and cultural and mechanical harvesting operations are facilitated. The Duplex system of training is shown in Figure 44 which facilitates mechanical harvesting and increases yields and also soluble solids (by about one percent) with earlier maturity. Machines also are available that will harvest vines trained on vertical trellises. Conversion of old vines to the Duplex system is shown in Figure 44 and described in detail in a California bulletin AXT-274. Table grapes are still harvested by hand. Figure 43 shows a training system for the home grounds.

Pruning. Principles of pruning are similar to those for the Eastern grape. Three popular systems of training and pruning are shown in Figures 42 and 43, each adapted to growth and fruiting habits of certain cultivars. Head pruning is almost always used for wine grapes that bear well with short spur pruning, also for the Flame Today table grape and the Muscat raisin grape. Cane pruning is

universally used for *vinifera* cultivars that do not have fruitful buds near the base of the canes, such as Thompson Seedless, and also for such small-clustered wine-grape cultivars as Sauvignon Blanc, Pinot Noir and Chardonnay. Cordon pruning is used for practically all of the seeded table grapes except Tokay and some White Malaga. Pruning is done annually during the dormant season. Pneumatic power pruning has reduced labor by at least 30% and also fatigue. Labor can be reduced further by trimming off canes of spur-pruned cultivars by tractor mowing far ahead of subsequent detail pruning. Tests with more sophisticated mechanical pruners with hand follow-up have been variable with the cultivar and age of the vine (see Venne, 1980). More research is underway. Suggestion for pruning a home-grown vineyard is in Figure 43.

Fruit Thinning. Three types of fruit thinning are used on *vinifera* grapes; namely, flower-cluster thinning, cluster thinning, and berry thinning. Each type of thinning results in a reduction in the number of flowers or fruits and better growth and development of those which are left. The method of thinning used depends upon the type of fruit produced by a vineyard of a given cultivar. *Flower-cluster thinning* is used on cultivars which develop loose straggly clusters, such as Muscat of Alexandria. The vines should be pruned with long spurs or fruit canes and some flowers removed as soon as possible after the clusters appear. *Cluster thinning,* or the removal of entire clusters soon after berries are set, is the most widely used. Enough wood

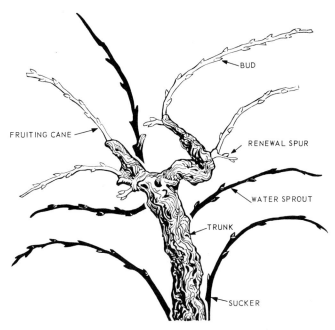

Figure 43. The system above is suggested for pruning the home vinifera vineyard. The blackened growth is removed, leaving the renewal spurs (3) and fruiting canes (4), for this vigor vine which is average. More fruiting wood is left for the more vigorous cultivars and on the better soils. (Univ. of Calif.)

441

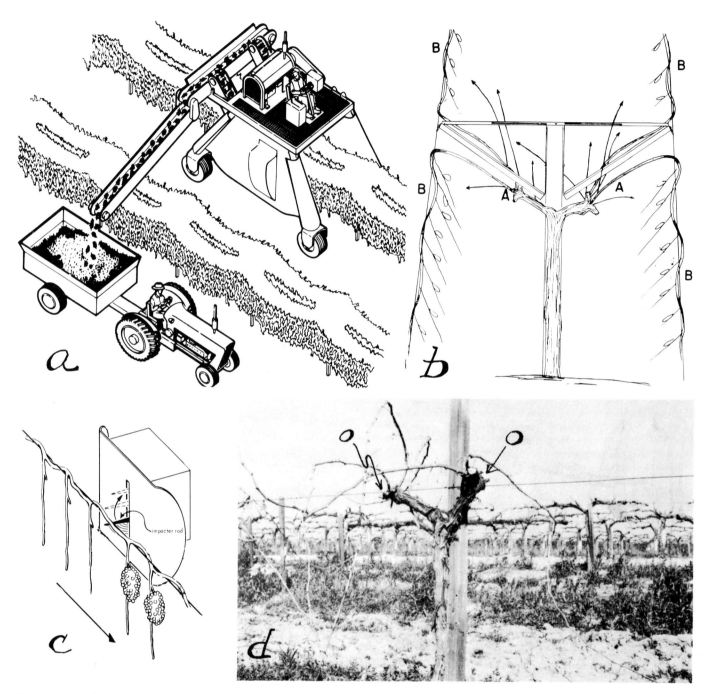

Figure 44. Vinifera grapes for processing are mechanically harvested to cut labor costs and get grapes to the processor rapidly. (a) Shows essential principles of mechanical harvesting equipment; improvements are being made annually. The "slapper" type machine knocks the grapes off of standard trellises into moving belts and escalators, thence to trailer alongside. The "impactor" type harvester (c) is designed to shake bunches apart and onto a belt (gondola training system). The "Duplex" or Geneva Double-Curtain training system shown in "b to d" is adapted to the impactor-type harvester. In "b", "A" shows replacement zone to furnish fruiting canes; the selected shoots remaining after spring deshooting and deflorating are indicated with arrows. "B" shows fruit-bearing zone on wires, the pendant shoots with flower clusters arising from fruiting canes. The "d" photo shows a cordon-pruned Palomino variety vine, 8 years, after conversion to the "duplex" system, showing shortening of side trunks at "o" and the canes saved to be wrapped on wires after assembly in "b" is in place. At "c" is the strong "needle" of the impactor-type harvester that extends out in the mid-wire section and shakes off bunches onto moving belt. (University of California, Davis.)

442

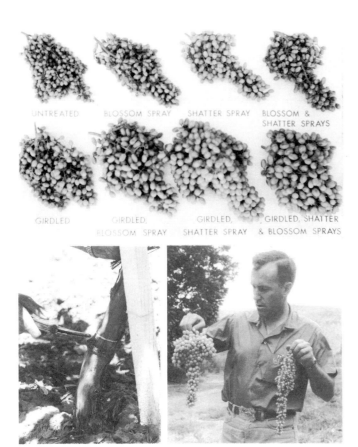

Figure 45. (Upper) Thompson seedless grapes in Utah showing effects of spraying with gibberlic acid (GA³) and girdling of vines. Largest bunches and berries (lower right) were obtained by thinning clusters to 12/vine and spraying with GA³ on June 13 at 20 ppm (blossom) and on June 23 at 40 ppm (shatter stage), plus girdling the trunk on June 23. Grapes were harvested August 24. (Lower left) a special knife to remove strip of bark. A girdle made previous year below has heeled over. (Lower right) Treated bunch on left is compared with untreated at right. Treatment is used on Zante currants and Black Corinth in California. (Courtesy J. LaMar Anderson, Utah State University, Logan.)

is left at pruning time each year to produce a crop in so-called poor years, but if a good year later is in prospect, the overload is then removed by cluster thinning which results in large regular crops almost every year. *Berry thinning* is practiced by cutting off the end of the main stem and several branches of the cluster, or by cutting off enough of the main stem to leave only the desired number of berries. It is limited to cultivars which set very compact or very large clusters. Berry thinning is practiced as soon as the berries have set.

Girdling. The removal of a 3/16-inch strip of bark from around the main trunk at blooming time increases the set of seedless berries (Figure 45). Girdling improves the yield of Black Corinth which normally sets straggly small clusters of mostly tiny seedless berries. Girdling is practiced on Thompson Seedless vines for increasing berry size of table grapes; it is performed as soon as possible after

berries have set.

Gibberellins. This group of growth regulators, which occurs naturally in grapes and other plants, can be sprayed on certain cultivars at specific times to enlarge berries and loosen clusters (Figure 45). With girdling, use of GA, (gibberellic acid, or commercial Gibrel) has become standard practice on Thompson Seedless, the leading variety. Spraying before bloom has reduced bunch rot in some wine varieties; spraying in bloom has loosened bunches of Thompson Seedless and has replaced girdling in production of Zante currants. Use of kinins, Ethrel, morphactins, 4-CPA, Alar, dormant sprays of 2, 4-D, and other growth regulators has given interesting results in quality improvement, fruit set, delay in bud opening, and berry release for mechanical harvesting. Ethephon (Ethrel by Union Carbide) has been approved for use as a spray on Tokay table grapes for increase in color, applied when 5 to 15% of the berries show color at a rate of 200-300 ppm. On Thompson Seedless for advancement of maturity for raisins, response was negative; pinkishness developed in the berries. There was no benefit on black cultivars. Softening and loss of acidity may occur, so the rate of application must be carefully adjusted to minimize these factors. Up-to-date use of these and other chemicals should be checked with local authorities.

Fertilizer. Nitrogen is usually the main nutrient to which these grapes respond in California. Response to potash is rare. Recent marked response to phosphorus has been reported. Ten to twenty tons per acre of manure or winery pomace, if available at reasonable cost, are good fertilizers. Zinc deficiency may be a problem in some areas. Treatment consists of painting the pruning wounds at pruning with a solution of one pound of zinc sulfate in one gallon of water. Timing and amount of N in vinifera vineyards is important, based on a number of factors. In *young vineyards,* on a sandy loam to loamy soil which have been in cotton, orchards or alfalfa and N has been used, the vines may not need N for a few to several yrs. If in doubt, use about 20 lbs./A actual N. On loamy soils, use, 25-30 lbs., and on coarse sandy soils use 40-50 lbs., split into 2 applications of 20-25 lbs., one early spring and the second in early July.

In *mature vineyards,* use 0-40 lbs. actual N in deep, fine sandy loams with high vigor cultivars. Higher rates can be used where more foliage is desirable, as for Thompson Seedless on a big trellis for late market. With Emperor cultivar, be careful not to over-fertilize and delay color. Note that repeated applications of 60 lbs./A/yr. can build into excess nitrogen, which means no N for several yrs.

Sometimes crabgrass and/or watergrass is allowed to grow in late spring through summer, mowed as needed and disced in the fall. Additional N may be needed, mainly for the grass. This is a common practice with table and wine grapes. It also has the advantage of the cover using N later in the season and helping to "harden" off the vines and improve fruit quality.

Permanent grass sods are not suggested in California because they compete with the vines early in the season and may demand more than 60 lbs. N/A. Acid topsoils may result from long term use of ammonium, urea and nitrate forms of N, except for calcium nitrate.

Do not use an all ammonium fertilizer after bloom, if needed; they take too long to change over to nitrate for the vine's use. Irrigation will carry the nitrate to the roots immediately (ammonium and calcium nitrate). Urea is slow acting. Apply in the furrow about 3 ft. from the trunks to be carried down by irrigation on the sandy soils. On heavier soils, it can be broadcast. Ammonia volitilization will occur for the ammonia and urea fertilizers if left on the soil too long without discing. or washing in. Or, the fertilizer can be drilled to a depty of 2 inches. Some spot applications may be necessary where the soil obviously is not "strong".

Legume cover crops of sub-clover, rose clover, melilotus may add 20-25 lbs. N and improve soil tilth, particularly in soils easily leached.

Commercial growers may want a copy of "Grape Nutrition" bulletin special for the San Joaquin Valley, Univ. of Ca., Berkeley 94720, priced, including photographs of deficiencies, other problems.

Weed Control.[1] With strip-row chemcial weed control, little in-row cultivation is being practiced in *vinifera* vineyards. Annual weeds are no problem but perennials such as Johnson and Bermuda grasses must be controlled by *timely* applications (see your specialist for latest recommendations). Cover-crop row middles in Switzerland is reducing a shoot die-back in old vineyards by at least 50%. Roots of the cover crop may be bringing needed nutrients up from lower levels in the soil.

Irrigation, Frost Control. Irrigation is practiced in California chiefly in the interior valleys, and there are undoubtedly many vineyards in the south and north coast regions which would benefit from it. The entire rooting area ·should be wetted by each irrigation checking penetration with a probe. Some soils hold less than 1 inch of water/ft. depth, others 2+ inches. Application can be by basin, checks, furrows, sprinklers, drip or microjet (on rough contour). Microjets have been shown to attain a 4-6°F advantage to about 6 ft. The solid-set overhead sprinklers do not require extensive labor to operate, are clean and quiet in operation, do not use large amounts of fossil fuels and also can be used for irrigation, pest and disease control, heat suppression, vine establishment, and spring and fall frost control. They do require a substantial water supply and are relatively expensive to install. See Chapter XIX.

Experimental "off-on" automatic misting of field *viniferas* in California has been found experimentally to reduce irrigation water needed and cool the grapes, lifting yield and quality.

Harvesting. *Table grapes.* Most California table grapes are marketed 2,000 miles or more from the vineyards. Transportation is by refrigerated trucks, rail cars or by air; time for rail shipping is 7 to 11 days, trucks 3-4 days, and only hours by air. Proper time of harvesting is judged by the sugar content, using a hydrometer (saccharimeter) with accompanying instructions. By experience, the picker judges maturity roughly by: (a) color and condition of the cluster stem; when top of cluster stem is brown and woody or when framework stems of cluster are light or straw yellow, (b) taste of the berries (used only at intervals due to a dulling of the taste), and (c) the characteristic change in color of berries of different cultivars which is recognized only with experience. It is usually necessary to go over a vine three or more times to harvest most of the table grapes at the proper stage. *Wine grapes.* The picking time for wine grapes varies with the kind of wine to be made. Grapes are picked earlier for dry wines than for sweet wines. Grapes for dry wines are picked when the sugar content tests 18° to 23° Balling, while grapes for sweet wines are harvested at 24° Balling or more. For ordinary wine, the entire crop is harvested at a single picking which is the usual practice in California. Several pickings are made for very fine wine. Grapes are mechanically harvested (Figure 44) and taken to the processing plant and crushed as soon as possible. Grapes for raisins are picked at 23° Balling or more. The degree of maturity at which raisin grapes are picked is a compromise between leaving the grapes as long as possible for better quality and heavier yield and yet to avoid the possibility of early fall rains which may interfere with sun drying. If the grapes are to be dehydrated in special ovens, weather conditions are a minor factor in picking, but the grapes must be removed before early rains cause deterioration on the vine.

Mechanical harvesting of grapes in California has levelled to about 25% of the wine grapes. There are problems with wine quality and machine damage to the vines as well as varying situations with prices and labor. It is economical only on large acreages, generally above 250 acres. If hand labor costs increase appreciably, machine harvesting may have the competitive edge. Owners of harvesters are generally satisfied because of increased control over operations and freedom from labor problems. Other problems cited are vine and stake damage and with juicing.

In mechanical harvesting, a breeding program is needed to develop cultivars with bunches that "fall apart" easily

---

[1] For weed control commercial literature, contact E. I. Du Pont, Wilmington, Dela., and Geigy Agr. Chem., Saw Mill River Rd., Ardsley, N.Y. 10502. Meister Publishing Co., Willoughby, Oh. 44094, publishes annually an up-to-date softback on "Farm Chemicals", 350-400 pages, with full descriptions and use, restrictions. Priced.

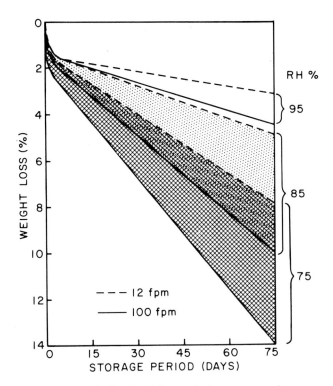

Figure 46. The relative humidity and air movement in a grape storage room have a pronounced effect on weight loss in the grapes. The faster the movement of air and the lower the humidity, the greater the weight loss. (K. E. Nelson, Viticulture, Univ. of Calif., Davis 95616).

on shaking and with berry scars (where pedicel is attached to berry) that do not break open readily.

Insect and disease resistance of *V. rotundifolia* has been transferred to the *V. vinifera* good fruit quality and vine fertility by backcrossing hybrid *V. rotundifolia* x *V. vinifera* to *vinifera* in California.

Temperature and storage conditions. Recommended storage temperatures for *vinifera* (California type) grapes are 30° to 31°F. Although temperatures as low as 28°F have not been injurious to well-matured fruit of some cultivars; other cultivars of low sugar content have been damaged by exposure to 29°F. A humidity of 87 to 92% at temeratures of 30° to 31°F is recommended.

TABLE 10. STORAGE LIFE OF VINIFERA TABLE GRAPES.

Emperor, Ohanez, Alphonse Lavallee (Ribier)	3-5 months
Malaga, Castiza (Red Malaga), Cornichon	2-3 months
Sultanina (Thompson Seedless)	1-2½ months
Flame Tokay, Alexandria (Muscat)	1-1½ months

Some storage plants in California have precooling rooms where grapes are cooled to 36° to 40°F in 20 to 24 hours before they are placed in storage. In most plants all of the cooling is done in the storage rooms, but only a few have sufficient air movement to cool the fruit as quickly as desired. Experience has indicated that about 4,000 to 6,000

cfm per car or truck load of fruit is needed in rooms used for precooling. A load of about 1000 lugs occupies a space 2000 cu. ft. After the fruit has been precooled, the air velocity should be reduced to that which will maintain uniform temperature throughout the room and distribute the SO_2 evenly.

In the storage of grapes there is little need for ventilation except to provide for exhausting sulfur dioxide-laden air following fumigations, as will be described later. Accumulation of carbon dioxide would not be objectionable and may benefit the grapes. Grapes do not give off appreciable amounts of ethylene or other substances that accelerate ripening as do apples and pears.

The normal change that takes place in grapes in storage involves chiefly loss of water (Figure 46). The most noticeable effect of this is drying and browning of stems and pedicels and shriveling of the fruit. Grapes become slightly sweeter during storage due to concentration of sugar by loss of moisture, but the total amount of sugar present slowly diminishes as does the acid content.

Since the turgidity of grapes increases as the temperature is lowered, they may split in storage. With prolonged holding, moisture loss eventually causes the fruit to lose its turgidity and to soften. During storage the pedicel attachment becomes weakened, probably as a result of changes in pectic substances; consequently shattering (loss of berries from the stem) is sometimes a problem on susceptible cultivars as Thompson Seedless. The color of red or blue cultivars gradually becomes darker in storage. White cultivars, such as Ohanez, Thompson Seedless, and Malaga, may turn brown. This browning becomes worse with longer storage and cannot be prevented by storing at 36°F instead of 31°F. Browning of white cultivars also is sometimes associated with over-maturity, and fruit from one vineyard may be affected more severely than that from another.

Fumigation. Grapes are usually stored in rooms by themselves, for if they are to be held more than a few weeks they should be fumigated for mold control with sulfur dioxide, which is injurious to other storage commodities.

The normal storage life of the principal cultivars of California table grapes at 30° to 31°F is shown in Table 3. Under exceptional conditions sound fruit will keep longer than indicated; for example, Emperor grapes have been held in good condition for seven months, and Sultanina for four months.

The storage life of grapes is affected in large degree by the attention given to selecting and preparing the fruit. Grapes should be picked at the best maturity for storage, especially Thompson Seedless and Ohanez. Stems and pedicels should be well developed and the fruit should be firm and mature. Soft and "weak" fruit should not be stored. The display lug is a satisfactory package for storage

Figure 47. Grading and packing room for California table grapes on the left (a) shows lugs on pallets, delivered to girls on right (b) who improve bunches with shears and pack in boxes carried by belt to refrigeration. (Blue Anchor).

since it can be cooled and fumitaged easily. Sawdust packages cannot be fumigated effectively, so it is necessary to fumigate the grapes before they are packed. South African packs of wrapped bunches in excelsior have proved to be good storage packages. Precooling to 40° to 45°F is advised for grapes that are to be in transit a day or two before reaching storage. (See USDA Agr. Handbook 159 on storage problems of grapes.)

Diseases and pests. These include eutypa, powdery mildew, black measles, black knot, Pierce's disease, little-leaf, Phylloxera, nematode, grape leafhopper, cutworms, red spider, grape leaf roller, rabbits, and gophers. Ozone is a by-product in exhaust fumes causing brown stipple on young or mature leaves in fall in southern California; laws making muffler filters mandatory have helped.

Researchers are integrating the effects of natural control agents, chemical use, and cultural practices in an attempt to cut costs of pest control in California. Contact local government services for control charts.

Costs. Contact your county agricultural agent or Dept. of Agr. Economics, Univ. of Ca., Davis 95616 or Wash. State Univ., Pullman 99163 for up-to-date costs.

Marketing. Fresh *vinifera* grapes are sold in conventional wood boxes (Figure 47), shipped 100s to 1000s of miles under refrigeration. Better handling is obtained when containers are vibrated before shipment to avoid a loose-pack. Aside from the standard box, one to 3 lb. colored plastic boxes are attractive containers on the counter. Exports of table grapes have been increasing.

There has been a dramatic increase in the U.S. demand for seedless bunch grapes. The cultivars 'Superior' and 'Flame Seedless' have been added to the favorites, 'Thompson' Seedless', 'Perlette' and 'Beauty Seedless', making up over 92% of the grapes from the Coachella Valley. Seedless grapes constitute over 55% of the total grapes shipped from California.

Customers will pay a premium price if the grapes are of good eating quality and seedless. California seedless are competing well with the expensive Chilean seedless. August-September sales have increased even though the grapes are competing with other established in-season fruits and vegetables. In the early 1980s, the per capita consumption of all grapes was 4 lbs. With U.S. grapes available the year round and with imports, it is probable that the per capita consumption will grow to 18-20 lbs., as for other major fresh fruits and bananas. The booklet, "Harvesting and Handling California Table Grapes for Market", priced, Publ. 4095, 65 p. 1979 (color) is very good.

446

Review Questions

1. Indicate the approximate regions where the European-, American- and Muscadine- type grapes are grown in the United States.
2. What is the relative commercial importance of the above three types of grapes in the United States?
3. What are the five leading states in grape production? How do you account for the heavy production in these states? What world countries lead in grapes?
4. What is the chief method for propagating the native American-type grapes?
5. Discuss leading *V. Labrusca* cultivars if grown in your area.
6. Briefly describe a soil management system for a (a) young and (b) mature vineyard in your locality, including recommendations for cultivation, cover crops, and manures or commercial fertilizers.
7. Diagram the Geneva Double-Curtain method of training grapes. Advantages? Disadvantages?
8. Diagram, label, and briefly describe the 4-can Kniffin system of training and pruning a mature Concord vine. What is "balanced" pruning?
9. How does pruning grapes on arbors differ from that described in the previous question?
10. How do you judge picking maturity for table grapes in your area?
11. What type of spray equipment is most effective in insect and disease control in commercial vineyards?
12. Discuss *current* aspects of mechanical harvesting of grapes. Limitations?
13. Essentially, how do Muscadine grapes differ from the native American-type in berry and cluster, vigor, training systems and use?
14. For the *Vinifera* grape in California, e.g., discuss the modern concepts of 4 of the following topics: cultivars, rootstocks, harvesting techniques, GA use to improve marketability, SO$_2$-treatment of harvested grapes, training systems for vines, pruning mature vines, drying for raisins, scoring or girdling the vines, storage requirements, and market situation.

Collateral Literature

AMERICAN GRAPES, HYBRIDS

ABDALLA, D. A. and H. J. Sefick, N, P, and K effects on yield, chemical composition, juice quality of Concord in South Carolina. ASHS 87:253-258, 1965.

American and French Hybrid grape varieties. A guide. 28p. Foster Nur. Co., Fredonia, N.Y. 14063. Priced. 1970s.

AHMEDULLAH, M. Grape Growing and Cultivar Review of Pacific Northwest. Fruit Jour. 34(3):61.55. 1980.

ANDERSON, K. A. et al. Phenological development of different *Vitis* cultivars. Fruit Var. Jour. 34(1):5-7. Jan. 1980.

AUGER, Jaime G. et al. Pierce's disease of grapevines: A bacterial etiology. Science 184:1375. 1974.

BALLINGER, W. E. et al. Anthrocyanins and wine color quality from 39 black grapes, *Vitis rotundifolia*. J. ASHS 99:338-341. 1974.

BERTRAND, D. E. and R. J. Weaver. Effect of K gibberellate on "Black Corinth" grapes. J. ASHS 97(5):659. 1972.

BRADT, O. A. and A. Hutchinson. Grape rootstock studies. Vineland Ont. Ann. Rpt. 28-44. 1970.

BRADT, O. A. 'Ventura' Grape. HortSci. 10:430-431. 1975. Festive and Veeblanc Grape. HortSci. 13(3):304. 1978.

BRUSKY-ODNEAL, M. Grape winter-bud injury, 1981-2. Fr. Var. Jr. 17:2. 1983.

BURR, T. J. et al. Grape pest control, N.Y. Cornell Co-op Ext. Cir. 050. 7p. 1981.

CAHOON, C. et al. Ohio's Re-emerging grape wine industry. HortSci. 7:(3)229-31. 1972.

CAHOON, Garth A. Grape production in four No. Central States and Kentucky. Fruit. Var. Jour. 34(3):54-59. 1980.

CAHOON, G. and R. Hill. Grape growing. Ohio Ext. Bull. 509 24pp. Request update.

CAHOON, G. Daminozide on Concords. J. ASHS 102:(2)218-22. 1977.

CAHOON, Garth et al. Fertilizing fruit crops (grapes). Ohio Ag. Ext. Bull. 458. 20 p. Request Update.

CAWTHON, D. L. and J. R. Morris. Yield, quality of Concord as affected by pruning, etc. J. ASHS. 102(6):760-767. 1977.

CLORE, W. J. and R. D. Fay. Effect of preharvest applications of Ethrel on Concord grapes. HortSci. 5(1):21-23. Feb. 1970.

CLORE, W. J. and R. B. Tukey. Training grapes in Washington. Wa. Ext. Bull. 637. 12 p. 1978.

COOK, James A. Grape nutrition. Chap. in Fruit Nutrition Book, edited by N. F. Childers. 777-812. Hort. Publ. 3906 N. W. 31st Pl. Gainesville, Fla. 32606. ($25). 1966.

COOMBE, B. G. Set and development of the grape berry. Acta. Hort. 34. Smyp. on Growth Regulators. 261-269. 1974.

CROWTHER, R. F. and O. A. Bradt. Evaluation of grape cultivars for production of wine. Hort. Res. Inst. Ontario (Vineland). 1970 rpt.

DAILEY, R. T. et al. Costs, mechanical grape harvesters. Wash. Cir. 540. July, 1971.

DENBY, L. G. and D. F. Wood. Soverign Rose grape. HortSci. 12(5):513. 1977.

DETHIER, B. E. and N. Shaulis. Cold hazard in N.Y. vineyards. Cornell Ext. Bull. 1127. 1964.

DOW, A. I. and M. Ahmedullah. Grape fertilization. Wash. Ext. Bull. 0874. 4 p. 1981.

ELFVING, D. C. Trickle irrigation (Review). Hort. Rev. 4:1-48. 1982.

Ethephon for color, maturity in table grapes. Blue Anchor. p 12. Dec. 1982.

FISHER, D. V. et al. Location of fruit on grapevines in relation to cluster size and chemical composition. J. ASHS. 96:(6). P. 741. 1971.

FISHER, K. H. Ontario cluster-thinning de Chaunac French hybrid. J. ASHS 102(2)162-165. 1977.

FISHER, K. H. Grapes in Ontario. Hort. Res. Inst. of Ont. Vineland Sta. Ontario. Publ. 487. Request update.

FUNT, R. C. Grape culture economics. Contact Ohio State Univ. Columbus 43210 for update.

GALLANDER J. F. and A. C. Peng. Wine-making for the amateur. Ohio Agr. Ext. Serv. Bull. 549. 16 pp. 1972.

GOOD, D. L. et al. Grape economics in N. Y. Finger Lakes area. Cornell mimeo. AE-EXT. 75-18 and 14. Request updates.

Grape-Wine Shortcourses in Ohio. Proceedings: Culture, Pests, Mimeo Annual. Ohio Agri. Res. and Dev. Ctr., Wooster. (Ask for latest proceedings). Dr. Garth Cahoon, Editor.

Grape varieties for eastern Washington. Wash. Ext. Cir. 394. Pullman, Washington. 1975.

Grapes. Their characteristics and suitability for production in Washington. Wash. Co-op Ext. Serv. EB-635. Jan. 1972.

GUTTADAURO, G. J. History references of American grapes, wines, raisins. (Mimeo) Agr. History Center, Univ. of Calif., Davis. July 1976.

HAESELER, C. W. Grape cultivar Chelois as grown in Penna. Fruit Var. J. 32(1):1720. 1978.

HAESELER, Carl W. SADH On Concord in Pennsylvania. HortSci. 11(3):265-7. 1976.

HAESELER, C. W. and L. Yeager. Storage, Mkting. N. E. grapes. Pa. State Hort. Ass'n. Proc. 65-71. 1981.82.

HARTMAN, H. T. and D. E. Kester. Plant propagation - principles and practices (grape rootstocks and grafting). Prentice-Hall, Inc., Englewood Cliffs, N. J. 07632. 700 pp. 1975.

HARVEY, J. M. and W. T. Pentzer. Market diseases of grapes, small fruits. USDA-AMS Agr. Hdbk. 189, 45 pp. Recent edition.

HIRABAYASHI T. et al. *In vitro* differentiation of shoots from anther callus in *Vitis*. HortSci. 11(5):511-12. 1976.

IWAGAKI, HAYAO and SHUNJI ISHIKAWA. Suffolk Red seedless grape in Japan. J. of Tokyo Noko Univ. Fuchu-shi, Tokyo, Japan. P. 66-70. 1974.

IWASAKI, K. and J. Weaver. Chilling, calcium cyanamide, budscale removal on bud-break, rooting inhibitor content of buds of Zinfandel. J. ASHS. 102(5):584-587. 1977.

JANICK, J. Fruiting grapes in pot culture. HortSci. 18:(1) 56-7. 1983.

JOHNSON, Hugh. World Atlas of Wine. Simon and Schuster, New York. 1971.

JOHNMOORE, J. N. et al. Mechanical harvesting of wine grapes. USDA-ERS-Ag-Econ. Rpt. 385. 28 pp. 1977.

JOHNSON, D. E. and G. S. Howell. Cultivar and critical temperature on primary grape buds. ASHS. Journ. 106:5. 545-9. 1981.

KENDER, W. J. and N. J. Shaulis. Management practices and oxidant injury in Concord. J. ASHS. 101(2):129-132. 1976.

KENNEDY, J. M. et al. Weed control in Concord grapes in Arkansas. J. ASHS 105(5):710-712. 1979.

KIMBALL, K. H. Converting mature vineyards to other varieties. N. Y State Agri. Exp. Sta. Spec. Rpt. 22. 19 pp. 1976.

KIRPES, D. J. Costs for Concord and wine vineyards. Wa. Ext. Bulls. 873, 875. 1981.

LANGE, A. et al. Special type weed control in grapes. Weeds Today. Feb.-March 23-29, 1977.

LIDER, L. A. and Nelson Shaulis. Resistant rootstocks for New York vineyards. N. Y. Food and Life Science Bull. 45. 1974.

McGREW, J. R. Growing American bunch grapes. U.S.D.A. Farmers' Bull. 2123, Wash. D.C. 26 p. 1977.

McGREW, J. R. AND G. W. Still. Grape diseases and insects, E. USA. Farmers' Bull. 1893. 35 pp. 1979.

MOORE, J. N. Cytokinin-induced sex conversion in male clones of *Vitis* species. J. ASHS 95(4):387-393. 1970.

MOORE, J. N. and E. Brown. Venue grape. HortSci. 12(6):585. 1977.

MOORE, J. N. Grape Cultivar Situation in Ark. Mo., Okla., and Texas. Fruit. Var. Journ. 34(3):59-60. 1980.

MORRIS, J. R. et al. Temperature and SO₂ addition on quality and postharvest behavior of mechanically-harvested juice grapes in Arkansas. J. ASHS. 104(2):166-169. 1979.

MORRIS, J. R. and D. L. Cawthon. Ethephon on Concord grape quality. ASHS 106:(3)293-5. May 1981.

MORRIS, J. R. and D. L. Cawthon. Concord grape yield, quality juice, soil depth and in-row vine spacing. ASHS 106:(3)318-20. May, 1981.

MORRIS, J. R. and D. L. Cawthon. Trunk-shoot control on Concord grape with NAA. HortSci. 16(3). 321-22. June, 1981.

MULLINS, C. A. et al. Performance of certain grape cultivars in Tennessee: I. French Hybrid type; II. American type. Fruit Var. Journ. 35(3). 62-99. July, 1981. Winter temperature stress on grapes. Fr. Var. Jr. 37:2. 1983.

OMURA, M. and T. Akihama. p -Fluorophenylalanine on genetics of grape. HortSci. 16:5. 653-4. 1981.

OONO, Toshio. Seedless Delaware grapes by GA treatment. Japan Agri. Res. Quart. 7. 7:35-37. (Reprint) 1973.

OVERCASH, J. P. et al. 'Miss Blanc' bunch grape. Miss. Bul. 909, 6p. 1982; 'Midsouth' and 'MissBlue' bunch grapes. Miss. Res. Rpt. 18. 1981.

PAUL, N. H. French-Amer. hybrid grape names. Finger Lakes Wine Growers Assn. Naples, N. Y. August, 1970.

PEREZ, J. R. and W. M. Kliewer. Nitrate reduction in leaves of grapes, fruit trees. J. ASHS. 103(2):246-250. 1978.

POLLOCK, J. G. et al. Mechanical pruning American grape hybrids. ASAE. Trans. 20:(5)817-21. 1977.

POOL, Robert M. and Lloyd E. Powell. Cytokinins on *in vitro* Shoot Development of Concord Grape. J. ASHS. 100:200-202. 1975.

POOL, R. M. et al. Remaily Seedless grape. HortSci. 16(2):232-233. 1981.

POOL, R. M. Grape cultivars - northeast region. Fruit. Var. Journ. 34(3):50-54. 1980.

POOL, R. M. Mediquat chloride on Concord. J. ASHS 107:(3)376-80. 1982.

PRATT, Charlotte. Reproductive system of Concord and two sports. (*Vitis labrusca* Bailey) J. ASHS 98(5):489. Sept. 1973.

Processing grapes. For up-to-date information on *V. labrusca* types, contact the agricultural experiment stations of New York, Geneva; Ohio, Wooster; Georgia, Griffin: Canada, Vineland, Ontario: Washington, Puyallup. For vinifera type, contact Univ. of Cal., Davis.

PROEBSTING, E. L., Jr. and V. P. Brummund. Yield and maturity of Concord grapes following spring frost. HortSci. 13(5):541-543. 1978.

REISCH, B. et al. 'Horizon' grape. HortSci. 18:(1) 108-9. 1983.

RIPLEY, Brian D. et al. Residues of Dikar and ethylenethiourea in grapes and commercial grape products. J. Agric. Food Chem. 1978.

ROBSON, M. G. et al. Small fruits manual. Rutgers Ext. Bul. 432. 48 pp. 1981.

SHAULIS, N. Cultural practices for N. Y. vineyards. Cornell Ext. Bul.

805. 39p. Request update.

SINGH, I. S. and B. S. Chundawat. Effect of ethephon on ripening of 'Delight' grapes. HortSci. 13(3):251. 1978.

SMIT, C. J. B. and G. A. Couvillon. Modified Munson and 4-Arm Kniffin training on changes in pectic substances of Concord grapes. J. ASHS. 96(5). P. 547. 1971.

SNOBAR, B., B. Cargill, J. Levin, D. Marshall. Grape harvester recovery and losses. Am. J. Eno. Vitic. 24:(1), 10-13. 1973.

SORENSON, K. A. Grape Insects. N. C. Ag. Ext. Serv. Folder 315. 1975.

SPAYD, S. E. and J. R. Morris. Irrigation, pruning severity and yield, quality of Concord. J. ASHS. 103(2):211-216. 1978.

STERN, V. M. et al. Control of grapeleaf skeltonizer. Calif. Agri. May. 1980.

STEVENSON, D. W. 'Diamond' grapes and irrigation frequency with and without cover crop. HortSci. 10:82-84. 1975.

STOVER, L. H. Growing Florida bunch grapes. 513 S. Fla. Av., Tampa 33602. 10 pp. 1980.

SWENSON, E. et al. 'Edelweiss' and 'Swenson Red' grapes. HortSci. 15(1):100. 1980.

TUKEY, L. D. Relation of temperature and Alar on berry set in the Concord grape. HortSci. 5(6):481. Dec. 1970.

TUKEY, R. B. and W. J. Clore. Grape varieties for Wash. Wash. Co-op. Ext. Serv. EB-635. Jan. 1972.

WALLINDER, C. J. et al. Glyphosate exposure to 'Concord.' HortSci. 18:(1) 57-9. 1983.

WIEBE, John. Canopy widening and shoot tip removal on grape. J. ASHS. 100:349-351. 1975.

YOKOYAMA, V. Y. Effect of thrips scars on Tanle grape quality. J. ASHS. 104(2):243-245. 1979.

NOTE: An Eastern bi-monthly grape and wine publication is "Eastern Grape Grower and Winery News". 46 p. Bx. 329, Watkins Glen, N.Y. 14891. Price.

VINIFERAS

ALLEY, C. J. Improved field budding of grapes. Ca. Agr. (Feb.). 1975

BURLINGAME, B. B. et al. Frost protection costs, north coast vineyards. Calif. Agr. Ext. Serv. Cir. 267. 10p. 1971.

California Agriculture is a monthly publication from Univ. of Calif., Davis, containing poplular articles on agricultural research, including grapes. The articles following are examples. Loosening Thompson seedless bunches with bloom GA sprays. Nov. 1965; grape berry thinning with GA, Nov. 1966; GA timing for table grapes, Mar. 1966; irrigating Tokays, Apr. 1961; B deficiency in vineyards, Mar. 1961; grape leafhoppers - spray resistance, July 1961; grape container testing, July 1962; improving grape pruning labor, Mar. 1963; vineyard salinity, May 1963; kinins effects, Sept. 1963; grape leafhopper parasite, Apr. 1965; bark-grafting grapes, Mar. 1965; soil management effects on vineyard irrigation, June 1968; Storage conditions, planting time on rooting Thompson Seedless cuttings, Dec. 1970. Spider mite situation in So. Joaquin on Thompson Seedless, Nov. 1971; T-bud grape grafting, July 1977. Feb. 1975. Eutypa, Jan.-Feb. 1981; March-Apr. 1982; mite predator resistance to sulfur, May-June, 1981. Viticulture and enology, 100 Anniv. Issue, 40p July, 1980; Biological grape leafhopper control. May-June 1983.

CHRISTIANSEN, L. P. et al. Grape nutrition and fertilization in San Joaquin Valley, Univ. of Calif. Public. 4087. 40p color. 1978.

COOK, J. A. et al. Phosphorus deficiency in California vineyards. Calif. Agr. 37:(5,6). 16-18. 1983.

DAVIS, M. J. et al. Casual bacterium in Pierce's disease of grapes. Science 199:(4324) 75-7. Jan. 1978.

FRANCOIS, L. E. and R. A. Clark. Accumulation of sodium and chloride in leaves of sprinkler-irrigated grapes. J. ASHS. 104:(1)11-13. 1979.

Gallo Winery, Their Cup Runneth Over. (Gallo Story) Forbes Magazine, 5th Ave. N.Y.C. 10011. 7pp. Oct. 1975.

HARMON, F. N. and J. H. Weinberger. Chip-bud propagation of *vinifera* on root stocks. USDA Leaflet 513, 8pp. July 1962.

HENDRICKSON, A. H. and F. J. Veihmeyer. Irrigation experiments with grapes. Calif. Agr. Exp. Sta. Bull 728. 31pp 1951.

HEWITT, W. B. Rots of grape bunches. Calif. Bul. 868. 50p. 1974.

HOY, Marjorie A. and A. Standow. Resistance to sulfur in a vineyard spider mite predator. Calif. Agri. May-June, 1981.

JOHNSON, S. S. Mechanical harvesting wine grapes. Calif. Ag. Econ. Rpt. 385. 30pp. 1977.

KASIMATIS, A. N. et al. Wine grape varieties in San Joaquin Valley. Univ. of Calif. Publ. (priced) 4009. 31p. Color. 1980.

KASIMATIS, A. N. et al. Wine grape varieties in No. Coast Ca. Univ. of Ca. Publ. 4069. 30p. Color. 1981.

KASIMATIS, A. N. et al. Growth, yield of 'Thompson Seedless' by trellising. Calif. Agric. 14-5. May, 1976.

KASIMATIS, A. N. et al. California offset-press leaflets as follows: grape rootstock varieties, AXT-47; standard wine varieties, AXT-59; Thompson Seedless for table use, AXT-61; Thompson Seedless for raisins and wine, AXT-60; non-irrigated, head-pruned varieties, AXT-158/; non-irrigated, head-pruned wine varieties, AXT-157*; irrigated, cane-pruned premium and wine varieties, AXT-156*; and 226*; standard wine varieties, AXT-55*; Emperor grapes, AXT-54*; drying fruits at home, HXT-80; producing quality raisins, AXT-235; vineyard irrigation, AXT-199; *These are cost-of-production pamphlets.

KLIEWER, W. M. Effects of N on growth and composition of fruits from Thompson Seedless grapevines. J. ASHS. 96:(6). P.816. Nov. 1971.

KLIEWER, W. M. et al. Effects of controlled temperature and carbohydrate levels of Thompson Seedless grapevines. J. ASHS. 97:(2). P.185. March, 1972.

LIDER, L. A. et al. Pruning severity and rootstock on yield of two-grafted, cane-pruned wine grape cultivars. J. ASHS. 98(1):8.1973.

LIDER, L. A. Nematode-resistant grape stocks. Hilgardia 30:4. 123-139. July, 1960. Ca. Leaflet 114. 1959; Ca. Leaflet 101. 1958.

LOOMIS, N. H. and J. H. Weinberger. Inheritance studies of seedlessness in grapes. J. ASHS. 104(2):181-184. 1979.

McKENRY, W. B. et al. Vineyard management and nematodes. Calif. Agric. pp6-7, Oct. 1977.

MEHR, S. Raisin industry of Iran. USDA-SASM-114. 37pp. Apr. 1961.

MEHR, Stanley. Competition in world raisin market. USDA-FAS-136. 71pp. June, 1962.

Mexican Growers and table grapes. Blue Anchor. July/August. pp28-33. 1977.

MOLLER, M. J. and A. N. Kasimatis. A Dying-Arm Disease of Grapes. Cal. Agr. (Feb.):10-11. 1975.

MOSESIAN, R. M. and K. E. Nelson. Girdling and GA effects on Thompson Seedless. Amer. Jour. of Eno. and Vitic. 19:1, 37-46. 1968.

NELSON, J. M. and G. C. Sharples. Chlormequat, SADH. cytokinin on fruit set of "Cardinal" Grape. HortSci. 9:598-600. 1974.

NELSON, K. E. Harvesting, handling Calif. table grapes for market (very good). Univ. of Calif. Publ. (priced). 67pp. 1979.

OLMO, H. P. et al. Training and trellising grape vines for mechanical harvest. Calif. Agr. Ext. Serv. AXT-274. 16pp. 1968.

OLMO, H. P. Grape variety acreage in Arizona, California. Fruit. Var. Journ. 34(3):65-69. 1980.

OVERCASH, J. P. et al. 'Regale' and 'Doreen' muscadines for Southeast, Miss. Res. Rpts. 14,8. 1981, 1982, resp.

PEACOCK, W. et al. Testing ethephon-treated table grapes for berry firmness. Cal. Agric. 8. April 1978.

PEACOCK, W. L. 1977. Chlormequat doubles yield of Malvasia Bianca Grapes. Calif. Agric. pp9-10. June, 1977.

PHATAK, S, C. et al. Ethephon on muscadines. HortSci 15:(3) 267-8. 1980.

POOL, Robert M. and Robert J. Weaver. Internal browning of Thompson Seedless grapes. J. ASHS. 95(5):631-634. 1970.

RASKI, D. J. et al. Grape fan-leaf virus-nematode control by soil fumigation. Calif. Agr. Apr. 1971. Grape nematodes. Calif. Cir. 533. 1965.

SAUVIGNON, Cabernet, et al. Temperature on Ontogeny of berries. *Vitis vinifera*. J. ASHS. 99:390-394. 1974.

SEELIG, R. A. (Editor) Grapes (inclusive review). Fruit and Vegetables Facts and Pointers. 28, pp777. 14th St. N. W. Wash., D.C. 20005.

STAFFORD, E.M. and R.I. Doutt. Grapes insects, North Carolina Cir. 566. 1974.

SPIEGEL-ROY, R. A. et al. 'Shani' and 'Sivan' grapes. HortSci. 16(6)791-2. 1981.

STUDER, H. E. and H. P. Olmo. Coiled wire training of grapes. ASAE 21 (3):402-6. 1978.

THOMPSON, V. (a) Calif. heat-treated grape plants. (b) Subirrigation saves water, increases yield, inhibits weeds in Calif. Goodgrape Grower (B.C. Canada). April 15, 1971.

VENNE, R. V. (Editor). Viticulure and enology. Calif. Agr. (100th Anniversary Issue). 34:(7)40 p. 1980.

WEAVER, J. and M. Pool. Berry response of 'Thompson Seedless' and 'Perlette' grapes to GA. J. ASHS. 96(2). March, 1971.

WEAVER, R. J. and A. N. Kasimatis. Trellis height with and without crossarms on yield of Thompson Seedless grapes. J. ASHS. 100:252-253. 1975.

WEAVER, R. J. Grape growing. John Wiley & Sons. New York. 371pp. 1976.

WEINBERGER, John H. and Frank N. Harmon. Flame Seedless Grape. HortSci. 9:602. 1974.

WEINBERGER, J. H. and N. H. Loomis. Fiesta Grape. HortSci. 9:603. 1974.

WEAVER, R. J. and O. J. Leonard. 2, 4-D dormant effects on pruned, non-pruned Tokay. Hilgardia 37:18. 661-675. Jan. 1976.

WEAVER, R. and R. M. Pool. Effect of (2-Chloroethyl) phosphonic acid. (Ethephon) on Maturation of *Vitis vinifera*. J. ASHS. 96:(6). Nov. 1971. p725.

WEAVER, R. J. and R. M. Pool. Thinning 'Tokay' and 'Zinfandel' grapes by bloom sprays and Gibberellin. J. ASHS. 96:(6). Nov. 1971. p. 820.

WINKLER, A. J. et al. General Viticulture. Univ. of Calif. Press. Berkeley. 710pp. 1974.

Zinc Correction in vineyards. The Blue Anchor p23. July/August, 1977.

MUSCADINES

BAGBY, John. Muscadine grapes. Alabama. Ala. Agr. Ext. Serv. Circ. P-25, 11pp. Request update.

BALLINGER, W. E. et al. Light-sorting Muscadine Grapes for Ripeness. J. ASHS. 103(5):629-634. 1978.

BRIGHTWELL, W. T. and M. E. Austin. Plant spacing on yield of Muscadine grape. J. ASHS. 100:374. 1975.

BROOKS, J. F. Muscadine grape production guide. N. C. Ag. Ext. Serv. Cir. 535. 30p. 1975.

CLARK, J. R. Catch frames for harvesting Muscadine. Miss Inf. Sheet 1306. 4p. 1981.

CLAYTON, C. N. Diseases of Muscadine and bunch grapes in N. Car. N. C. Agr. Exp. Sta. Bul. 451. 37pp. 1975.

CROCKER, T. D. Muscadines in Florida, Univ. of Fla. Fruit Crops Fact Sheet 16. 4p. 1980.

FLORA, L. F. Identifying problems and needs of the Muscadine Industry. Fruit South. 120-123. May, 1978.

GOODE, D. K. et al. Rooting Muscadine cuttings. HortSci. 17(4). 644. 1982.

Grapes in Florida. A Symposium. 22pp. IFAS, Gainesville, 32611. 1981-82.

GURSKY, D. M. and R. P. Bates. Home preservation of Fla. grapes. Univ. of Fla. Fact Sheet 7, 4p. 1979.

HALL, F. Planting, care of hybrid Muscadines. Proc. Fla. State. HortSci. 89:253-254. 1976.

HOPKINS, D. L. et al. Tolerance to Pierce's disease and rickettsia-like bacterium in muscadines. J. ASHS. 99:436-439. 1974.

LANE, R. P. Yield of Muscadines and Cane Pruning. J. ASHS. 102(4):379-380. 1977.

LANE, R. P. and J. W. Daniell. Effect of several herbicide systems on weed control and yield of muscadine grapes. HortSci. 8(1):32. 1973.

LANIER, M. R. and J. R. Morris. Evaluation of density separation for defining fruit maturities and maturation rates of once-over-harvested muscadine grapes. J. ASHS. 104(2):249-252. 1979.

MORRIS, J. R. Muscadines in Arkansas. Ark. Ext. Leaflet 488. 1971.

LANE, R. P. 'Triumph' Muscadine Grape. HortSci. 15(3):322. 1980.

LANE, R. P. and L. F. Flora. Effect of ethephon on ripening of 'Cowart' muscadine grapes. HortSci. 14(6):727-729. Dec. 1979.

MORTENSEN, J. A. Dog Ridge, a superior grade rootstock for Florida. Proc. Fla. State Hort. Soc. 85:275-279. 1973.

MORTENSEN, J. A. et al. Resistance to Pierce's Disease in *Vitis*. J. ASHS. 102(6):695-697. 1977.

MORTENSEN, J. A. Liberty Grape. HortSci. 12(5):511. 1977. 'Conquistador' grape. Fla. Cir. S-300. 1983.

MORTENSEN, J. A. Resistance segregation to black rot in selfed grape seedlings. Fruit. Var. Jour. 31(3). pp59-60. July 1977.

MORTENSEN, J. A. Irrigation systems for grapes. E. Grape Grower, Winery News. Apr. May. 1982.

Muscadine grapes for southern U.S. USDA Farmers Bull. 2157. 16pp. Request recent edition.

NELSON, K. E. Packaging and handling trials on export grapes. Blue Anchor. 47(4):9, Dec. 1970.

NESBITT, W. B. and H. J. Kirk. Plot size and number of replications on efficiency of muscadine grape cultivar trials. J. ASHS. 97(5):639. 1972.

NESBITT, W. B. and V. H. Underwood. Dixie Grape. HortSci. 11(5):520-1. 1976.

WOODROOF, J. G., S. R. Cecil and W. E. DuPree. Processing Muscadine grapes. Ga. Agr. Extp. Sta. Bull. N. S. 17. 35pp. Recent update.

WINE

AMERINE, M. A. and A. J. Windler. California wine grapes: composition and quality of their musts and wine. Calif. Agr. Exp. Sta. Bull. 794. 83pp. 1963.

AMERINE, M. A., H. W. Berg and W. V. Cruess. The technology of wine making. The Avi. Publ. Co. Inc., Westport, Conn. 799pp. 1967.

AMERINE, M. A. and V. L. Singleton. Wine. An introduction for Americans. Univ. of Calif. Press, Berkeley. 357pp. 1965.

THOMPSON, Bob. California Wine Country. A Sunset Travel Book. 96pp. Color, priced. 1971. Lane Books, Menlo Park, Ca.

VAN BUREN, J. P. et al. Bitterness in Apple and Grape Wines. HortSci. 14(1):42-43. 1979.

NOTE: The Amer. Soc. of Enologists meets annually, publishes proceedings. Contact Dept. of Enology, Univ. of Calif., Davis, for changing meeting places and address of secretary.

AMONG THE LEADERS IN GRAPE RESEARCH are (above) J. W. Winkler, retired, University of California, Davis; Garth A. Cahoon, Ohio Research and Development Center, Wooster; and (below) the late U.P. Hedrick and Nelson Shaulis, retired, New York Agricultural Experiment Station, Geneva. Other key contributors include W. J. Clore and Ronald B. Tukey, Washington Agricultural Experiment Station, Wenatchee and Pullman, resp.; James A. Cook, H. P. Olmo, A. N. Kasimatis and R. J. Weaver, University of California, Davis; J. N. Moore and J. R. Morris, University of Arkansas, Fayetteville; R. M. Pool, Cornell and N.Y. Agr. Exp. Sta., Geneva; and John A. Mortensen (low chilling grapes), University of Florida, Leesburg.

CHAPTER XXI

Strawberry Growing

The strawberry is among the first of the fresh fruits on the market in spring. It is in great demand locally in all regions in which it is grown. Due to its wide adaptation to climate and soils, the strawberry (hybrid between *Fragaria virginiana* Duch. x *F. chiloensis* (L) Duch.) is available fresh from the tropics to the subarctic (Alaska) the year round. Air-freight has spread the fresh strawberry to almost any world market every month of the year. World production of strawberries by countries is given in Table 1.

From the concentrated areas of U. S. production in Figure 1, considerable quantities of strawberries are shipped to distant markets. In the eastern United States, the first commercial berries are harvested in Florida near

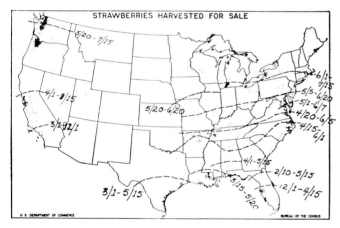

Figure 1. Strawberries are grown commercially from tropical Puerto Rico, subtropical Florida and Texas to Minnesota, Maine, Canada and Alaska. Concentrated areas of commercial production are shown in such states as Florida, Louisiana, Arkansas, Missouri, Tennessee, Illinois, New Jersey, California, Washington, and Oregon. Lines and dates show the approximate shipping season for each commercial section. Shipments start about December 1 in Florida and continue to July 15 in New York, Michigan, and Washington. California harvests strawberries most of the year. Black dots indicate where commercial crop is produced, each dot represents 10,000 lbs. of fruit.

[1]Richard C. Funt, Ohio State University, Columbus, 43210 and Donald H. Scott, retired, USDA, assisted in this Chapter revision. Former assistance has come from George M. Darrow of USDA and John P. Tompkins of Cornell Extension Service, Ithaca, New York.

[1]THE STRAWBERRY by N. F. Childers and world authorities is an indepth discussion of cultivars to marketing. 600 pp. Hort. Publ. 3906 NW 31 Pl., Gainesville, Fla. 32606. $21.90 domestic; $25.00 foreign.

TABLE 1. APPROXIMATE WORLD PRODUCTION OF STRAWBERRIES IN 000s OF METRIC TONS. 1970s VS. EARLY 1980s.[1]

Country	1770s	1980s	Country	1970s	1980s
USA	224	314	Germany (DR)	—	34
Italy	74	205	Romania	—	32
Japan	115	198	Turkey	—	23
Poland	100	177	Netherlands	32	22
Mexico	110	88	Belgium	25	21
France	57	82	Hungary	21	17
USSR	—	81	Czechoslovakia	15	17
Spain	8	80	Norway	10	17
Korea (Rep)	—	74	Greece	5	10
United Kingdom	50	53			
Yugoslavia	56	44	World	897	1726
Germany (FR)	49	36			

[1]There is little interest in the Far East in strawberries where only fruits with peels are preferred for sanitary reasons. We have no data from South America, Africa or South Africa although appreciable production occurs in the Provinces of Transvaal, Natal, and Cape of Good Hope, and particularly near the large cities of Cape Town and Johannesburg. Strawberries are grown widely in South America in small plantings near large cities.

Homestead, December 1, and as the season progresses northward, strawberries are shipped from Louisiana, North Carolina, Arkansas, Tennessee, Missouri, Kentucky, Maryland, and New Jersey. Among the last strawberries to ripen are those in the regions of the Upper New England States, New York, Wisconsin, Washington and Canada. Strawberries are harvested in California almost every month of the year.

Strawberry growing is probably more equally distributed among southern and northern states, USA, than any other important fruit. Table 2 gives data for the commercially important states.

Due to restrictive labor problems in the United States, strawberry production in both Mexico and Canada increased markedly in the 1960's, then leveled. Most of these crops go to processing and have had an effect on the U. S. strawberry production and market. Fresh berries from the U. S. now are being air-freighted to foreign markets and harvesting machines are minimizing peak labor needs in large plantings contracted for processing. In many states over 90% of the berries now are being harvested by public Pick-Your-Own to help solve the labor problem and to bring better net profit to growers.

See in Chapter 22 a comparison of relative labor, costs/A/yr and rate of return for strawberries vs other fruits.

TABLE 2. FRESH MARKET AND PROCESSING STRAWBERRIES: ACRES PLANTED, HARVESTED AND YIELD PER ACRE. 1978-82. USDA.

State	Acres	Harvested* 1000 Cwt	Yield Cwt/A
California	11,000	5,115	465
Oregon	5,300	463	89
Washington	2,900	174	60
Florida	2,500	475	190
Michigan	2,400	124	54
Wisconsin	1,800	57	38
Ohio	1,500	105	70
New York	1,500	87	62
Louisiana	700	39	60
New Jersey	650	27	42
Arkansas	400	26	64
Total 11 states	31,500	6,315	
Total US	34,000	6,790	

*Of the harvested berries above, the amount processed in four states was: California - 1609; Oregon - 420; Washington - 128; Michigan - 39. New York processed a small amount.

California is by far the leading state in strawberry production from an acreage and volume standpoint. The state accounts for about 75% of the production on 32% of the acreage.

LOCATING THE PLANTATION

Factors of first importance in locating a commercial strawberry plantation are: (a) accessibility of markets — wholesale, auction, roadside or Pick-Your-Own, (b) transportation facilities, (c) adequate labor supply, (d) community interest, and (e) climate. If strawberries are to be grown for the general market, it is best to select a site among other growers. Benefits are: (a) easier to get experienced pickers, (b) cooperative buying of supplies, and (c) combined shipments at less expense. Possibility of a pick-your-own enterprise should be explored. Nearness to urban centers is key in pick-your-own.

Before producing strawberries on a large scale, the grower should have reasonable assurance that there will be an adequate supply of labor, especially during the harvesting season. Under nonirrigation conditions, it requires the time of one person for each four or five acres up to harvest, whereas under irrigation it requires one for each acre. From five to ten pickers per acre are needed during harvest. Failure to secure labor during picking may result in severe losses.

Important factors in selecting the site are water and air drainage, slope, exposure of the land, and character of the soil. Because the strawberry grows close to the ground, the blossoms may be killed by spring frosts in years when fruit trees are unharmed. For this reason, it is particularly important to have good air drainage in frost regions.

The strawberry may require some cultivation and, consequently, sites with a slight slope are better than those with a steep slope. If steep slopes are used, contour plantings should be made with or without terraces to conserve soil and moisture; in fact, contour planting is

considered good practice on sites with only a slight slope. Southern exposures absorb more sun heat and the berries may ripen several days earlier than those growing on a northern slope in the same locality. A succession of ripening can be obtained by placing berries on both the northern and southern slopes and using a ripening succession of cultivars.

The strawberry can be grown on almost any type of soil, from poor sand to heavy clay, provided it is well supplied with moisture and organic matter and is well drained. Berries ripen somewhat earlier on sandy soil than on clay soils, other conditions being similar. There is a definite

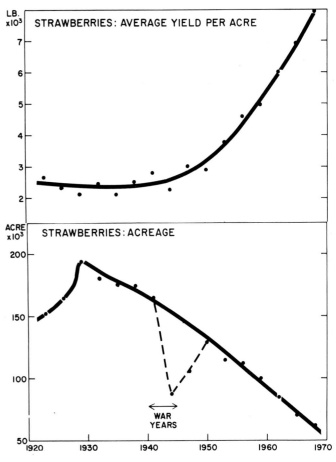

Figure 2. This chart shows rather dramatically two key trends in the strawberry business during a critical period of the industry. Note above the marked increase in yield/A of strawberries and the accompanying drop in acreage in the USA from the 1920s. This more or less continuing trend is typical of the strawberry regions throughout the world. Rise in yield/A is due mainly to the relatively "virus-free" plants, the breeding programs for better yielding and quality, and general improvement in cultural practices. The strawberry is an intensive crop, requiring considerable hand and "back-breaking" labor which accounts in part for the drop in acreage. Horticulturists and engineers, however, are developing automated equipment and techniques to reduce this labor as much as possible. (Courtesy Cecil H. Wadleigh, USDA, Beltsville, Maryland 20705)

452

varietal adaptation to soils, some growing better on heavy soils and others growing better on light soils. There is less difference, however, within a variety when grown on different soils, if the soils are high in humus. In the drier areas, it is well to avoid alkali soils; strawberries are sensitive to this condition.

CHOOSING CULTIVARS[1]

The strawberry cultivar picture has been changing rapidly in almost every key area, even within a 10-year period. In the next 10 to 20 years this pace may slow somewhat with virus-nematode-free stock and cultivar(s) relatively more resistant to problem diseases. However, the many breeders in this field are ever busy; there is room for improvements. See Tables 3 and 4 for current cultivars.

The cultivar(s) selected will depend upon the climate, soil, and the purpose for which the crop is grown. Experience of the growers in a given locality is one of the best guides in selecting profitable cultivar(s). Some cultivars bear firm berries well adapted to long-distance shipping. Others bear large attractive berries of excellent quality but too soft for shipment and thus suitable only for local trade or home use. Many federal and local experiment stations in the U. S. and abroad have breeding programs where special varieties are developed for each region. Importance of varieties may change rather rapidly. For example, Northwest variety dropped from second to sixteenth place in five years. For a detailed description of varieties and the regions in which they are best adapted, see Scott et al. Also, contact the local state college or experiment station (see appendix for addresses). Table 4 gives important varietal characteristics, some of which may change with more experience.

In the home garden, it is desirable to have varieties of excellent dessert quality which ripen in succession over a long season. For market gardeners who sell the berries

Table 3. Strawberry Cultivars Adapted to Eight Regions of the USA and Neighboring areas of Mexico and Canada, (D. H. Scott, R. C. Funt, Consultants, 1983)

	Area	Cultivars	For Trial
1.	Southeast and Gulf States	Douglas, Sequoia, Florida Belle, Tangi, Tioga, Tufts	Dover
2.	East Central Coast	Raritan, Surecrop, Red Chief, Albritton, Atlas, Cepallo, Allstar, Sunrise, Pocohontas, Earliglow	Earliglo, Prelude, Sentinel, Rosanne, Tribute, Sumner
3.	Northeastern	Guardian, Raritan, Midway, Catskill, Surecrop, Sparkle, Redcoat	Allstar, Honeoye
4.	North Central	Earliglow, Redcoat, Redchief, Delite, Guardian, Midway, Cardinal, Honeoye, Raritan, Stoplight, Robinson, Sparkle, Badgerbelle	Gilberts Badgerglo, Scott
5.	South Central	Sunrise, Pocohontas, Tennessee Beauty, Delite	Cardinal, Arking
6.	Plains and Rocky Mtn. States	Trumpeter, Sparkle	Ft. Laramie (everbearer)
7.	Northwestern States	Hood, Totem, Shuksan, Olympus	Linn, Benton
8.	California, Southwest	Pajaro, Tufts, Heidi, Douglas, Aiko	Selma, Vista, Hecker, Brighton

Note: See 1969 Modern Fruit Science edition for situation 1946-65; for 1970-75, see 1976; for 1977-78 see 1978 edition, p. 718.

closeby, or for berries to be frozen, the majority of the berries may consist of a variety not especially adapted to shipping. However, when local markets become overloaded, it may be wise to have one or two later ripening varieties adapted to shipping or to freezing, for berries cannot be stored fresh more than about ten days.

When strawberries are raised for the general market, it is important to include only two or three varieties, since buyers prefer to obtain full truckloads of one variety, rather than loads of mixed varieties which may differ in shipping quality and may have different flavors, colors, and shapes. In large shipping regions, not over three varieties are grown. In regions where spring frosts are a factor, it may be wise to raise more than one variety so that if blossoms of one variety are killed, those of a later blooming sort may escape. For Pick-Your-Own, some growers use only one cultivar to avoid a number of problems in handling the public.

In a typical strawberry breeding program (Figure 6), the objectives in the late 1970's, as examples of the market needs, were: (a) Develop a series of varieties earlier than Midland and later than Jerseybelle that generally look alike to the customer (this eliminates the need of trying to sell the customers on each type of berry as the ripening season progresses), (b) develop a large productive berry for mechanical harvesting and processing that peak ripens heavily with easy removal of green calyx, (c) a low chilling requirement to break rest is important in mild climates, (d)

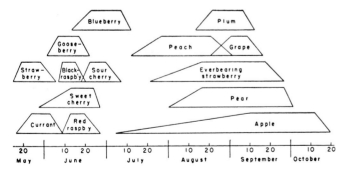

Figure 3. The strawberry is the first fresh fruit on the local market in most states east of the Rockies. If grown and marketed attractively it finds a ready sale. These ripening dates for important fruits are for the general area of Virginia, but the relative order of ripening should more or less hold elsewhere. (Virginia Polytechnic Institute and State University, Blacksburg)

453

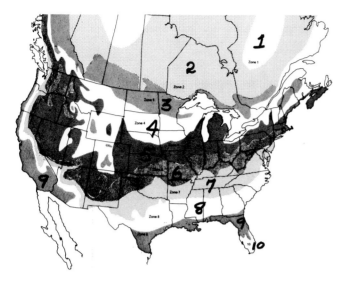

Figure 4. ZONES WHERE STRAWBERRY CULTIVARS PERFORM BETTER.
Strawberry cultivars are "particular" about where they are grown. They may perform well in one region or zone but not so well in another. Various zones are indicated in the map above. Here are a few examples of cultivars suited to certain zones; Zone 3: Micmac, Bounty; zones 4-8: Robinson, Surecrop, Ft. Laramie, Quinalt; zones 5 to 8: Sunrise, Sparkle, Delite; zones 5-7: Guardian, Raritan, Catskill, Redchief, Marlate, Vesper; zones 6-8: Pocahontas, Tennessee Beauty; zones 8-9: Dover, Pasaro, Douglas; zone 10: Tufts.
It is well to check with your county agricultural agent, your university extension specialist or a local nurseryman to learn the latest on strawberry cultivars performing best in your area. New cultivars come on the market faster than for peach or apple. It takes about 10 years from time of cross in breeding to introduction of a new cultivar. (Chart courtesy Bountiful Ridge Nursery, Princess Anne, Maryland 21853)

develop firm high quality cultivars, superior to one now available, resistant to wet seasons and that hold up well in shipping and on the sales counter, (e) breed firmer and better quality everbearing cultivars resistant to key diseases and pests such as red stele, verticillium wilt, leaf scorch, powdery mildew, viruses, red mite, bacterial blight and other key and local pests. The several races of the red stele fungus make the problem difficult. A cultivar may be resistant to some races, not others.

PROPAGATION

Strawberries are propagated commercially by runner plants. Dividing the crowns of older plants is too tedious and expensive for cultivars that produce runner plants readily. Plants raised from seed are undesirable because strawberry seedlings are too variable. For this reason, old strawberry beds may have many untrue-to-name seedlings undesirable for propagation. Meristem propagation (tissue culture) shows considerable promise (described later).

Where virus and nematodes are present, and this is likely to be true in most commercial areas, the growth and production of plants may be reduced by half or more. Strawberry plants that are substantially free from disease-causing viruses (at present there is no practical way of knowing that a plant is free of all viruses) are available from most nurseries the world over. In addition, the plants from most nurseries have been raised in fumigated soils to get commercial control of nematodes (Figure 7). Growers who plant virus-free, nematode-free stock and keep it clean protect themselves from two common causes of serious strawberry losses. Viruses weaken plants and cut runner formation, as well as reduce yields. Nematodes, tiny eel-like worms, feed on the roots.

Most plants now are cold-storage spring-set or summer-set (Calif.) and are purchased from reputable nurserymen who sell certified virus-nematode-free stock. This is propagaged as foundation stock in screen houses to prevent aphis-spread of viruses, or is grown in isolated fields (a mile from wild or cultivated strawberries) with aphis controlled, or propagated by tissue culture. Growers should locate new plantings as far away from older

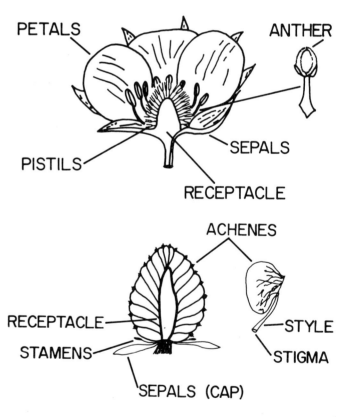

Figure 5. Parts of the strawberry flower are above. Parts of the "fruit" are below. We eat the receptacle consisting of the medulla (center) and the cortex (outer) with the achenes (seed-like structures) attached to the outside, which actually are the true fruits (carpels with ovules inside). (M.N. Dana, Univ. of Wis., Madison)

454

TABLE 4. CHARACTERISTICS OF LEADING STRAWBERRY CULTIVARS WHEN GROWN IN FAVORABLE AREAS. USDA FARMERS' BUL. 1043 UP-DATED BY D. H. SCOTT, 1983.

Variety	Plant disease resistance					Fruit characteristics					
	Leaf spot	Leaf scorch	Red stele	Verticillium wilt	Virus tolerance	Ripening season: days after Midland	Size	Flesh firmness	Skin firmness	Dessert quality	Processing quality for freezing
Aiko[1]	Intermediate	Unknown	Susceptible	Susceptible	Tolerant	10	Medium-large	Firm	Firm	Fair	Unknown
Albritton	Resistant	Very resistant	Susceptible	Susceptible	Susceptible	12	Large	Very firm	Firm	Excellent	Good
Apollo	Resistant	Very resistant	Susceptible	Intermediate	Unknown	7	Large	Very firm	Firm	Good	Good
Aptos*	Unknown	Unknown	Susceptible	Partial Resistant	Tolerant	5	Medium	Medium	Firm	Good	Unknown
Atlas	Resistant	Very resistant	Susceptible	Intermediate	Unknown	3	Very large	Firm	Firm	Good	Poor
Badgerbelle	Resistant	Susceptible	Susceptible	Unknown	Unknown	14	Large	Soft	Soft	Fair	Fair
Badgerglo	Unknown	Susceptible	Susceptible	Susceptible	Unknown	14	Large	Medium	Medium	Good	Unknown
Benton	Unknown	Unknown	Resistant	Unknown	Tolerant	16	Large	Soft	Tender	Very good	Good
Blakemore	Susceptible	Very susceptible	Susceptible	Resistant	Tolerant	3	Small	Firm	Tender	Fair	Good
Brighton*	Unknown	Unknown	Suscetible	Resistant	Tolerant	5	Large	Soft	Medium	Fair	Unknown
Canoga	Unknown	Unknown	Susceptible	Resistant	Unknown	10	Large	Very firm	Firm	Fair	Unknown
Cardinal	Resistant	Resistant	Susceptible	Susceptible	Unknown	7	Large	Firm	Firm	Fair	Good
Catskill	Susceptible	Resistant	Suceptible	Very resistant	Very susceptibl	7	Very large	Soft	Soft	Good	Fair to good
Cyclone	Resistant	Unknown	Susceptible	Unknown	Tolerant	3	Large	Soft	Soft	Very good	Good
Darrow	Intermediate	Intermediate	Resistant	Intermediate	Unknown	3	Large	Firm	Firm	Good	Very good
Delite	Resistant	Resistant	Resistant	Resistant	Unknown	12	Large	Medium-soft	Firm	Fair	Unknown
Douglas	Unknown	Resistant	Susceptible	Susceptible	Tolerant	3	Very large	Medium	Firm	Very good	Unknown
Dover	Unknown	Resistant	Susceptible	Resistant	Unknown	3	Large	Medium	Firm	Good	Unknown
Earlibelle	Very resistant	Very resistant	Susceptible	Susceptible	Tolerant	3	Large	Very firm	Very firm	Good	Very good
Earliglow	Resistant	Resistant	Resistant	Resistant	Unknown	3	Medium-large	Firm	Firm	Very good	Very good
EarliMiss	Resistant	Resistant	Susceptible	Unknown	Unknown	5	Medium-large	Medium	Medium	Good	Unknown
Fairfax	Resistant	Resistant	Susceptible	Unknown	Susceptible	7	Medium	Firm	Soft	Excellent	Fair
Fletcher	Resistant	Very resistant	Susceptible	Susceptible	Unknown	7	Medium	Medium	Soft	Very good	Good
Florida Belle	Unknown	Unknown	Susceptible	Unknown	Unknown	5	Large	Medium	Tender	Good	Unknown
Florida Ninety	Very susceptible	Very susceptible	Susceptible	Susceptible	Unknown	5	Very large	Soft	Soft	Very good	Fair
Fort Laramie	Intermediate	Intermediate	Susceptible	Unknown	Unknown	7	Medium	Medium	Medium	Good	Unknown
Gem	Susceptible	Resistant	Susceptible	Unknown	Unknown	7	Small	Soft	Soft	Fair	Fair
Guardian	Resistant	Resistant	Resistant	Very resistant	Unknown	7	Very large	Firm	Firm	Good	Fair
Headliner	Resistant	Unknown	Susceptible	Unknown	Unknown	7	Large	Medium	Medium	Good	Good
Hecker*	Unknown	Unknown	Susceptible	Resistant	Tolerant	5	Medium	Medium	Medium	Good	Unknown
Heidi[1]	Unknown	Unknown	Susceptible	Unknown	Tolerant	7	Large	Firm	Firm	Good	Unknown
Holiday	Resistant	Resistant	Susceptible	Intermediate	Unknown	5	Large	Very firm	Very firm	Good	Good
Honeoye	Resistant	Resistant	Susceptible	Resistant	Unknown	5	Large	Firm	Firm	Good	Good
Hood	Resistant	Resistant	Resistant	Resistant	Susceptible	10	Large	Medium	Medium	Very good	Good
Jerseybelle	Very susceptible	Susceptible	Susceptible	Susceptible	Susceptible	14	Very large	Soft	Firm	Fair	Poor
Linn	Unknown	Unknown	Resistant	Unknown	Intermediate	17	Large	Very firm	Very firm	Fair	Good
Marlate	Resistant	Resistant	Susceptible	Susceptible	Unknown	14	Medium-large	Firm	Firm	Good	Unknown
Micmac	Unknown	Resistant	Susceptible	Resistant	Unknown	7	Large	Soft	Medium	Fair	Unknown
Midland	Resistant	Resistant	Susceptible	Susceptible	Susceptible*	0	Large	Firm	Soft	Excellent	Very good
Midway	Very susceptible	Susceptible	Resistant	Intermediate	Unknown	10	Large	Firm	Firm	Good	Very good

455

Northwest	Resistant	Unknown	Susceptible	Intermediate	Tolerant	14	Medium	Medium	Medium	Good	Very good
Ogallala*	Unknown	Unknown	Susceptible	Unknown	Unknown	7	Medium	Soft	Soft	Good	Good
Olympus	Unknown	Unknown	Resistant	Unknown	Tolerant	14	Medium	Medium	Soft	Good	Very good
Ozark Beauty*	Resistant	Resistant	Susceptible	Susceptible	Unknown	14	Medium	Medium	Medium	Very good	Good
Pajaro	Unknown	Resistant	Susceptible	Susceptible	Tolerant	7	Large	Very firm	Firm	Good	Good
Pocohontas	Resistant	Intermediate	Susceptible	Susceptible	Unknown	7	Large	Medium	Medium	Good	Very good
Prelude	Resistant	Resistant	Susceptible	P. Resistant	Unknown	3	Large	Firm	Firm	Excellent	Unknown
Puget Beauty*	Resistant	Resistant	Susceptible	Unknown	Susceptible	7	Large	Medium	Soft	Very good	Good
Quinault*	Resistant	Resistant	Resistant	Unknown	Susceptible	7	Medium	Soft	Soft	Good	Fair
Rainier	Unknown	Unknown	Resistant	Resistant	Tolerant	16	Large	Medium	Medium	Very good	Excellent
Raritan	Susceptible	Susceptible	Susceptible	Susceptible	Unknown	7	Large	Firm	Medium	Fair	Fair
Redchief	Resistant	Resistant	Resistant	Intermediate	Unknown	7	Large	Firm	Firm	Good	Very good
Redcoat	Resistant	Unknown	Susceptible	Susceptible	Unknown	7	Medium	Medium	Medium	Fair	Unknown
Redcoat	Unknown	Unknown	Susceptible	Unknown	Unknown	10	Medium-large	Medium	Medium	Good	Unknown
Redglow	Susceptible	Intermediate	Resistant	Susceptible	Unknown	3	Large	Firm	Firm	Good	Very good
Redstar	Susceptible	Resistant	Susceptible	Intermediate	Tolerant	18	Large	Firm	Firm	Good	Good
Robinson	Intermediate	Susceptible	Susceptible	Resistant	Tolerant	10	Large	Soft	Soft	Fair	Poor
Rosanne	Resistant	Resistant	Susceptible	P. Resistant	Unknown	12	Large	Very firm	Very firm	Very good	Unknown
Sequoia	Unknown	Unknown	Susceptible	Susceptible	Tolerant	0	Very large	Soft	Soft	Very good	Unknown
Sentinel	Resistant	Resistant	Susceptible	Susceptible	Unknown	12	Large	Firm	Firm	Very good	Unknown
Shuksan	Unknown	Unknown	Resistant	Resistant	Tolerant	16	Large	Medium	Medium	Good	Excellent
Sparkle	Susceptible	Intermediate	Resistant	Susceptible	Susceptible	12	Small	Soft	Soft	Very good	Very good
Sunrise	Very susceptible	Resistant	Resistant	Resistant	Unknown	0	Large	Firm	Firm	Good	Fair
Sumner	Resistant	Resistant	Susceptible	Susceptible	Unknown	5	Large	Very firm	Very firm	Good	Unknown
Surecrop	Resistant	Resistant	Resistant	Very resistant	Tolerant	5	Large	Firm	Medium	Good	Good
Tangi	Resistant	Resistant	Susceptible	Unknown	Unknown	5	Medium	Medium	Medium	Good	Unknown
Tenn. Beauty	Resistant	Resistant	Susceptible	Unknown	Tolerant	12	Small	Firm	Firm	Good	Good
Tioga	Susceptible	Unknown	Susceptible	Susceptible	Tolerant	10	Very large	Firm	Firm	Good	Good
Titan	Resistant	Resistant	Susceptible	Susceptible	Unknown	3	Large	Firm	Firm	Good	Good
Toro[1]	Unknown	Unknown	Susceptible	Susceptible	Tolerant	7	Large	Medium	Medium	Fair	Unknown
Totem	Unknown	Unknown	Resistant	Unknown	Tolerant	14	Large	Medium	Medium	Good	Good
Trumpeter	Very susceptible	Unknown	Susceptible	Unknown	Tolerant	10	Medium	Soft	Soft	Good	Very good
Tufts[1]	Intermediate	Unknown	Susceptible	Susceptible	Tolerant	7	Large	Firm	Firm	Good	Unknown
Veestar	Resistant	Susceptible	Susceptible	Resistant	Unknown	3	Medium	Soft	Soft	Very good	Good
Vista	Unknown	Unknown	Susceptible	Susceptible	Tolerant	5	Large	Firm	Medium	Good	Unknown

[1]Patented. *Everbearers.

Note: Following are cultivars too new to be listed in the table: Arking, Tribute, Tristar, Scott, Kent, Gilbert, Scarlet, Selva, Soquel, Tustin. Five to six yrs. are needed of testing by growers and extension personnel before nurserymen will or will not propagate these extensively.

plantings as feasible. If aphid-free stock is set, it may not pay most growers to dust. However, where aphids are abundant, as on the Pacific Coast, some control measure is needed. Dust twice or more in early spring and twice or more in the fall. Check with the local agricultural extension agent for details.

In milder climates, because of nematodes and the need of plants for a cold rest period to produce runners, growers obtain a limited number of plants each year from cool climate nurseries. Plants are set in winter about three feet apart in rows four feet apart, and serve as mother plants for propagation. Some growers obtain all plants each year from northern nurseries and are convinced they obtain better results than by using their home-propagated stock. In southern California, plants for setting to the field are obtained from northern California nurseries because some dormant period is needed for vigorous growth later.

Pot-grown plants are popular in home gardens. The pots

Figure 6. Strawberry breeders, mainly in the USA, Canada and Europe, have contributed to an improved and changing cultivar picture (see Table 3). George Darrow and Donald Scott, USDA, have led able USA and Canadian breeders. Here shown is the crossing of one variety with another by daubing pollen onto the emasculated flower's stigma with a camel hair brush. (USDA)

are sunk in the ground near the parent plants and the first runners to appear are rooted in them. Good results can be obtained by this method because there is little or no shock in transplanting the strawberries to new beds.

Tissue Culture Propagation. One of the big recent advancements in propagation of strawberries and other fruit plants is by tissue culture. Apple rootstocks are being propagated at a ratio of 60,000 plants from a single shoot tip in eight months (Jones et al. Propagation *in vitro* of M. 26 rootstocks. J. Hort. Sci. 52:235-8. 1977). Under favorable conditions one strawberry meristem (Figure 8)

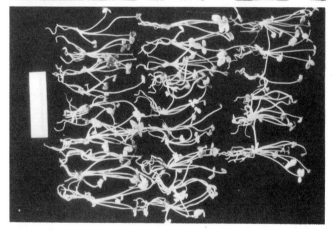

Figure 8. Millions of strawberry plants can be propagated in a year from the tip (meristem) of a runner. (Top) Plants propagated from a single runner tip in a jar of nutrient agar. under antiseptic conditions and transfer (middle). Below are plants ready for greenhouse flats, thence to the field. (Courtesy D. H. Scott and R. M. Zimmerman, USDA)

Figure 7. This is a screenhouse (Washington) for the propagation of virus-free strawberry plants grown in fumigated nematode-free soil to be distributed to growers and nurserymen. The plants are protected from sucking insects that spread the virus from wild and other plants. Typical of other states, this project is sponsored by Washington State University, Mt. Vernon area.

can be multiplied to yield more than 10 million plants in a 12-month period (See Boxus, Nishi).

Essentially, the method involves the use of small pieces of excised meristematic tissue from the growing points of plants that are cultured under sterile conditions in test tubes containing special nutrient media.

The methods are precise. Different nutrient formulae are used for different crops. The formula used for multiplication usually has a different ratio of auxins to cytokinins than that used for rooting the explants (the small unrooted plants in the culture tubes). The culture tubes or jars are placed in growth chambers or rooms where the temperature is held at 25°C under electric lights. Flourescent tubes are used that provide from 1,000 to 4,000 lux of light. Usually 1,000 to 1,500 lux are sufficient.

Advantages of the method are the rapid multiplication of plants, small space required for multiplication (75-150 explants in a one-qt. glass jar), freedom from diseases, insects and nematodes and year-round propagation of plants.

The main disadvantages are the initial expense of a special laboratory and equipment, autoclave to sterilize cultures, balances for precise weighing of nutrients, a still for distillation of water, micropore filter, laminar flow cabinet for transfer of cultures, dissecting microscope, dispensing machine for culture media, growth cabinet, growth room, and greenhouse mist system and cost of supplies. (Prepared in consultation with Dr. D. H. Scott, retired, USDA, Beltsville, Md. 20705.)

SOIL PREPARATION

Formerly it was advisable to cultivate for one to two years, previous to planting strawberries to free the land of white grubs and quack grass or similar persistent weeds. Fall fumigation is now used commercially about once in five years; controls white grubs, wireworms, ants that

Figure 9. Nematodes and soil diseases can be a serious problem in some areas for strawberries, particularly in warm sandy soils, although medium loams here in California will give a response to fumigation in growth, flowering and marked increases in yield, as shown at right vs. no prefumigation on left. (Stephen Wilhelm, Univ. of Calif., Berkeley 94720)

harbor root aphis, and many other pests. Sod land can be plowed, harrowed, and planted at once. If the soil is nematode infested (Figure 9), and this is true of most old strawberry land, fumigation with such chemicals as dichloropene, ethyl dibromide, or dibromochloropropane at the manufacturer's recommendation, is usually advisable before planting. Nematodes can stunt plants and reduce yields appreciably. See McGrew under "Pests".

Lime supplies calcium and magnesium, and also ties up toxic aluminum. In a humid region if the pH is 4.5 to 5.3, apply 1 to 2 tons of dolomite per acre to raise the pH from 5.5 to 6.5. It is best to lime a year ahead of planting. In arid areas avoid soil above pH 7.5, sites with more than 10% slope and requiring excessive leveling.

Strawberries should not follow peas, tomatoes, white potatoes, and beets, because of possible injury from diseases common to both crops, nor should they follow corn, due to humid climates with no soil fumigation in (a) plow in autumn and sow rye and: vetch or crimson clover; (b) plow in the spring and raise cultivated vegetables other than those listed above; (c) plow again in autumn and sow rye and vetch. Plow under the cover crop the following spring and plant strawberries.

If it is the practice to grow strawberries on the same land for two or more years, the humus content of the soil should be increased before setting each new planting. This can be done best by applying eight to ten tons of manure to the crop preceeding strawberries. If no manure is available, two green manure crops preceeding the strawberries, both turned under, may be advisable on soils of low humus content.

Before planting strawberries, the land should be pulverized thoroughly and in most cases, leveled. Where ridges are needed on level, somewhat poorly drained areas, they can be made by throwing two or more plow furrows together and leveling the top with a drag plank. In California, special mechanical equipment is described in their bulletins (Leaflet 2959, 15 pp) for building and leveling the ridges shown in Figure 20.

Strawberries more nearly resemble vegetables in their need for phosphorus. Make a soil test and apply accordingly, making any other adjustments suggested.

ESTABLISHING THE PLANTATION

Planting Time. Fruit buds are initiated the fall of the first season. With spring planting, use only healthy vigorous plants. The larger the plants at the end of the first growing season, the larger the succeeding crop of berries.

In temperate humid climates, most planting is done in spring. If the weather is undesirable, plants can be held in storage in poly bags at 31° to 32° F. until conditions are favorable. Cold-storage plants usually grow as well as freshly dug field plants.

Planting in late summer may be done near large cities in a region like New York City and a crop harvested the next year. With this practice, the soil must be rich and irrigation should be available. Large plants with good root systems are set as close as four to six inches apart, in rows three feet apart, using the double-row hill system.

In the Northwest irrigated sections, plants are set from Feb. to June, but April-May is preferred. In all California, most cultivars can be summer-planted (twin rows) with cold-storage plants. Timing is from July 1-15 in Central Valleys. Fall planting can be done in mid-Sept. for some cultivars in So. Calif. If planted too early for a cultivar, plants lack vigor and yield and quality are low. If planted too late, yield is low but fruit size and quality are good. If planted very late, runners develop in March, and crops are light. In Santa Maria and So. Calif., plants from high-elevation nurseries can be set in winter (single rows). If grown above 3000 ft. with the early chilling, winter planting is good, using clear poly-mulch on beds after planting. Spring planting is not suggested in California (See Calif. Leaflet 2959). Mid-fall is a satisfactory planting time in regions like Florida. In a region like mid-Louisiana, plants produce well when set in November, or, as late as December 20. In southwestern Texas, plants can be set in early fall and a crop harvested the next spring.

There are physiological responses of the strawberry that may help explain why the plants do better when planted at two different seasons, summer or fall, in areas around the world with climates similar to California. Strawberry cultivars have both sexual and asexual development stages. Fruit buds are initiated during the short-day season (winter) if temperatures are sufficiently high (above 50 °F) to encourage plant growth. Runner formation takes place during long days and warm temperatures of late spring and summer.

If the chilling requirement is satisfied during the winter, a normal growth cycle occurs: leaves and flowers develop

Figure 11. In Florida, raised 2-row hill system is used with black plastic (1-1 ½ mil), covering top and sides of bed, held down by soil on the sides. Fumigant and fertilizer are applied before the plastic. Wait 2 weeks before planting certified disease-free plants. Overhead irrigation is important to protect newly set plants from frost. (Sal J. Locascio, Univ. of Fl., Gainesville 32611)

in spring and runners are produced in summer. In California in the central and southern regions, winters are rarely cold enough to completely satisfy the chilling requirements. When incomplete winter chilling is followed by cool summer temperatures, as in the California coastal region, high production and a prolonged fruiting season will result.

Each cultivar has an optimum chilling need for best performance. Weak growth and small soft fruit with short shelf life may result from insufficient winter chilling. Excessive chilling causes poor fruit production and excessive runners. Choice of planting time, system, and site, therefore are important decisions in commercial strawberry production.

Training systems. Three training systems are in general use; (a) the hill, (b) the spaced row, and (c) the matted-row system.

In the *hill* system, as commonly used in California (Figure 10), Louisiana and Florida (Figure 11), on cultivars developing few runners, as Douglas and Tioga, all runners are removed from the mother plant. Individual plants become quite large and bear more than those in the matted-row system, described later. Plants are set 8 to 14 inches (commonly 10 to 12 inches) apart in twin rows 8 to 12 inches apart; 38-44 in. between twin rows. With this system a small garden tractor or a field tractor can be used for tillage, greatly reducing expense of hand labor. In the home garden where hand labor is used, the rows can be spaced closer, or 24 inches apart (Figure 12). In some cases, triple rows are set. However, these are only modifications of the hill system with the plants set the same distance apart in the row in each case.

The *spaced-row* system also is used for cultivars which are moderate to weak in sending out runners and

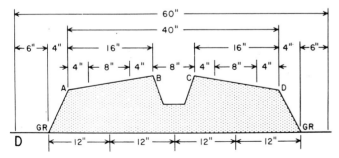

Figure 10. Victor Voth 60-inch bed width modified furrow for 4-row strawberry planting, shaped with (a) bed-shaper equipment, (b) 4-row planting groover opening furrows for plants, (c) and a rolling cone press with top press cylinder for closing and reshaping beds with midbed furrow after planting, designed for drip irrigation with 53,630 plants/A.

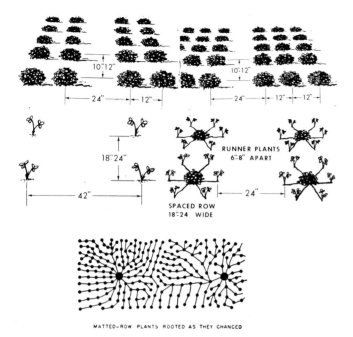

Figure 12. (Upper left) Double-row hill system; (upper right) triple-row hill system; (below) spaced-row system, initial planting and at right the plants filling in by runners and daughter plants, giving eventually a solid row. With the hill system the beds can be level or raised, the latter being a trend. Black plastic (in East) or clear plastic (West) can be used to control weeds and conserve moisture. Drip or overhead irrigation can be installed. See Figures 10, 11 for raised bed system used in California and Florida. (Bottom) The matted row system of training strawberries on level beds can be used for machine harvesting for processing. Runners take root by chance.

producing daughter plants. In this system, the daughter plants are spaced at definite distances by covering selected runner tips which become plants, until the desired number of daughter plants is obtained for each mother plant (Figure 12). Later-formed runners are either removed as they appear or all surplus runners are removed at one time, using special tools described later.

With the *matted-row system,* the plants are set 18 to 42 inches apart in single rows three to four and one-half feet apart (Figure 12). All, or a large part, of the runners that form during the first summer are allowed to take root and produce daughter plants between the mother plants. A mat of plants up to twenty-four inches in width is kept narrow by a rolling tractor-drawn disc that cuts off outside runners. Harvesting is easier with the matted-row system if the rows are narrow, or not wider than two feet. Some growers maintain the width of matted rows at about 12 inches. Twin matted-rows sometimes are allowed to form, 6 to 24 inches apart, then a wide alley is left and two other rows, 6 to 24 inches apart are formed. The two rows may be formed by permitting a 24- to 30- inch wide mat to

---

¹Request up-date Leaflet 2959, Univ. of Calif., Co-op. Exten. Serv., Berkeley, on "Strawberry production in California," 15 pp.

form, then plow up the center 12 inches of the row. For mechanical harvesting, level matted rows are formed with 4-ft. centers (Figure 28).

See Figures 13, 14 for a planting system used by some Eastern and Northwest growers with special-built planting and maintenance equipment.

Midland or similar varieties which do not form runners readily should not be set farther apart than 18 inches in the matted-row system. Dunlap, Blakemore, Surecrop and Catskill will form runners quite readily, and may be set at

Figure 13. Richard McConnell, Mt. Vernon, Oh., explains 6" single-row raised beds, 38" centers, Earliglow planted May 1 to fruit next year. (Mid) Runners in above bed sucked up, mowed off every 10 days, variable time with cultivar. (Lower) Fruited bed in August with tops mowed off, rejuvenated each yr. for about 4 yrs.

Figure 14. This equipment was designed by Richard McConnell of Mt. Vernon, Ohio to (above) lay the plastic on double rows, (2nd down) shape the raised single-row beds, (3rd down) suck up and cut off the runners, (bottom) and rototill, chew up straw, old plants, retain shape of beds for renewing planting after 3-4 yrs. cropping. (Win Cowgill, Rutgers University, New Jersey)

greater distances apart. Where there is danger of some loss from white grubs or severe drought, planting distance in the rows should not exceed 18 inches for all varieties. On steep slopes, rows should be at least four feet apart. Plants of a given variety should be set farther apart on fertile land than on land low in fertility.

Although the matted-row system of growing strawberries is probably the simplest and least expensive to handle, production records of high-quality fruit have not equaled those where the plants are spaced by hand. In fact, as strawberry production becomes more and more intensive in a section, the growers are forced to adopt some method of spacing the plants. Of course, spaced rows cost more and any net return increase must be evaluated. Considered, too, is the fact that more plants may survive in matted rows if white grubs and a severe drouth or winter is encountered.

Some cultivars give better yields in the hill and spaced rows than in the matted-row system, whereas others perform best in matted rows. Tioga is usually grown in hills, whereas Surecrop and Trumpeter are grown almost entirely in matted rows. The latter two cultivars form so many runners, in fact that it is too expensive to attempt to space them properly.

Pyramid and Barrel Planting Systems for Home Yard Planting. These systems are used in back-yard strawberry plantings where land is limited. A 25-or 50-gallon wooden barrel can be used. Holes are bored in the side of the barrel as shown in Figure 16. The barrel is filled gradually with

Figure 15. The Dutch are experienced in forcing strawberries. Polytunnels used from Scotland to Italy are located on a level site, well-drained soil, protected from high winds, propane heaters used, fertilized before planting, drip irrigation and early blossom and runner removal. Advantages are advancement of season for better prices, better quality berries. Technique not explored in USA apparently because of less expensive winter production in southern U.S. and Mexico. (D.H. Scott, retired, USDA)

461

fertile top soil as plants are inserted through the holes with the roots spread and covered with soil. The top of the barrel is left open for rain water or irrigation as needed. Runners are removed.

In the pyramid system (Figure 16) which can be square or round, wood frames are made by nailing one by six to ten-inch planks together end to end. Or, circular, strips of sheet metal can be used. For example, the first frame may be six feet square, the next about five feet square, then four, three, two, and one, consecutively. The bigger frame is laid on the ground first and filled with fertile soil, the five-foot frame is placed and filled with soil, and so on, until the pyramid is formed. The strawberry plants are set about a foot apart on the steps. All runners are removed periodically. Note irrigation arrangement, Figure 16.

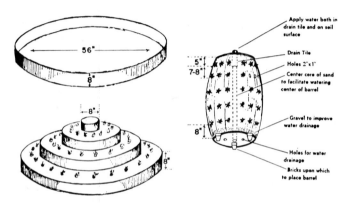

Figure 16. For home gardens the strawberry pyramid, round or square with 2x10 planks (left) or barrel (right) are space-saving convenient methods of growing berries for the table. A hose or water pipe with sprinkler nozzle can be run up through the center of the pyramid for easy watering.

Marking rows. On level ground, a plank or pipe to which chains are attached at points corresponding to the planting distance can be dragged across the field. Plants set in straight lines and in rows spaced evenly are much easier to cultivate and maintain than irregular rows. Plants set in check rows can be cultivated both ways until the runners begin to grow freely. No marking of rows will be necessary if the plants are grown on ridges or raised beds. Rows should run the long way of the field for convenience and economy in cultivation. On sloping land, they should run on the contour.

The planting distance is governed, as pointed out previously, by the system of planting used, the plant-making habit of the variety, the slope, the soil, the climatic conditions, the danger from white grubs, and the cost of labor. To determine the number of plants needed per acre, multiply the two widths in feet and divide into 43,560 (sq.ft. in acre). Plant density may vary from less than 20,000 plants per acre in California on 2-row beds to over

53,000 on wide beds. Double bed rows are suggested for summer planting and 4-row beds for winter plantings. Double row beds in California vary from 40-52 inches, center to center, with perhaps 48 inches the more efficient. Four-row beds in winter may vary from 60-64 inches (Figure 10).

Strawberry plants are too expensive under present conditions to replant. Do a good job and get a 100% "take" the first planting. Request up-date Leaflet 2959, Univ. of Calif., Co-op. Exten. Serv., Berkeley, on "Strawberry production in California," 15 pp.

Care of plants on arrival. Plants at the nursery are packaged in bunches of 25 and packed in different size slatted crates, or bare-root in boxes with poly liners. If, on arrival, the plants cannot be set immediately, place them in a refrigerator or cold storage. Or, they can be healed-in on the shady side of a building (Figure 17). Roots on good plants should be fresh and slightly yellowish in color, or somewhat dark if grown on muck soil. Old and undesirable plants can be distinguished by their black and dead roots. Plants coming from the nursery should be protected from the sun and wind by covering them with a piece of wet burlap or other wet material. Bare-rooted plants in poly bags can be stored at 31-32° F. CA storage at 12% CO_2, 6% O_2 and 32° F will hold plants in better condition if facilities are available.

Setting the plants. The plant in Figure 18 has a healthy vigorous root system, is trimmed properly, and all but one good leaf has been removed. It is ready for planting. Two things are important in setting strawberry plants: (a) Set each plant so that the crown is even with the surface of the soil after it has been packed about the roots (see dash mark in Figure 18); and (b) firm the soil well around and over the root system. Plants may be set either by hand with a dibble, spade, or punch (Figure 18), or with a planting machine used for large-scale setting of vegetable plants (Figure 19).

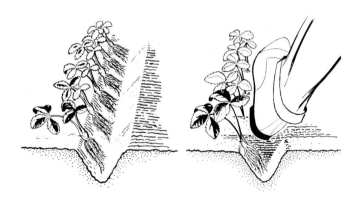

Figure 17. Plants can be held temporarily by heeling them in on a shady, well drained side of a building. Place them in a trench as at left with crowns at ground level and tamp the soil about the roots. (USDA)

TABLE 5. STRAWBERRY PLANTS REQUIRED AT DIFFERENT SPACINGS

Distance (ft.)	Plants to the Acre	Distance (ft.)	Plants to the Acre	Distance (ft.)	Plants to the Acre
	Number		Number		Number
3 by 0.5	29,040			4 by 0.5	21,780
3 by 1	14,520	3½ by 1½	8,296	4 by 1	10,890
3 by 1½	9,680	3½ by 2	6,223	4 by 1½	7,260
3 by 2	7,260	3½ by 2½	4,980	4 by 2	5,445
3½ by 1	12,446	3½ by 3	4,148	4 by 2½	4,356

To obtain number of plants/A, multiply the two widths in ft. and divide into 43,560 (sq. ft. per A).

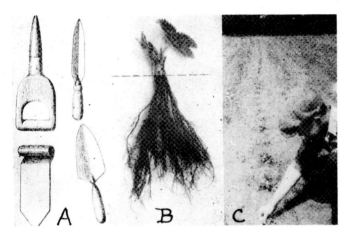

Figure 18. At "A" are several types of dibbles and trowels for hand-planting. At "B" is the proper planting depth, at crown level, and at "C" the blossoms are removed early to help develop a vigorous plant. (USDA)

One person working alone may set around 5,000 plants a day. If he has a helper who carries the plants in a bucket of water and hands them to him, his capacity is increased by three or four thousand in a ten-hour day. A short-handled hoe or dibble in one hand is convenient to open the hole for planting.

With a planting machine, about 25,000 plants can be planted in an 8-hour day if using a 2-row planter, setting at 18 to 24 inches apart; 29,000 may be set at 5 to 6-inch spacing per day per acre. One person operates the tractor while the two others are seated at the rear of the planting machine close to the ground where they can drop plants alternately as the machine opens and closes the furrow and applies soluble fertilizer starter solution from a large barrel (Figure 19). In machine setting, plants must be relatively uniform in size, roots straight, trimmed, and arranged in one direction in the plant holders. One person is needed to follow the machine to tamp the soil about the roots, straighten misplaced plants and to plant the gaps. Good results have been obtained with these machines, but a more careful job usually can be done by hand.

COMPANION CROPS

Under intensive cultivation and in home gardens where the greatest possible returns per unit of ground is desired, vegetables are sometimes grown between the strawberry rows during the first season. Most vegetables can be used and the extra cultivation and fertilization given them also will benefit the strawberries. Quick-maturing plants such as lettuce and radishes, can be grown between the rows. Onion sets are sometimes grown in the rows. The vegetables should be removed before the strawberry plants begin to send out runners. Companion crops, such as beans and cabbage, may be set about six inches to one side of the berry rows in the southern regions where the growing season is longer. This system is not adapted to the north because the season is not long enough to mature the vegetables and also allow the strawberry plants to develop sufficiently to bear a full crop the following year. With companion crops, such as cabbage and beans, the strawberry rows are often set four or four and one-half feet apart with the vegetables placed in the center of the cultivated area. In northern districts with a shorter growing season, the mat of strawberry plants must be more narrow than in southern regions when this system of management is used. Avoid potato, tomato, eggplant, pepper *(Verticillium* wilt problem).

Strawberries can be used as an intercrop between dwarf or young tree rows (Figure 20), and these should not be left longer than two or three years. Adequate space should be left on either side of trees to disk or use herbicides. Straw

Figure 19. A two- or three-row tractor-drawn vegetable planter can be used to set strawberry plants rapidly, dropping starter solution in each hole. (Hollander Transplanter Co., Holland, Mi. 49423)

Figure 20. In the large commercial strawberry operations in California, the soil (A) is fumigated with a combination of methyl bromide/chloropicrin under polyethylene tarp, sealing any accidental holes afterward; (B) grooving Voth type built-up beds with special equipment ready for planting at "C"; at "D". polyethylene (clear) is stretched over the bed, held down with wire loops or soil at edges; drip irrigation lines are underneath the poly. Machine here is punching holes through which plants grow. At "E" a 2-row raised bed is being planted; beginning harvest at "F"; and grading berries at "G". Puree at "H" is filling plastic crocks for ice creams, etc. (Photos courtesy Paul Bush and Tim Linden, The Packer, Kansas City, Ks. 66201)

464

decomposition may reduce N to trees, thus a need for extra N. Spray programs must be integrated.

CULTURE DURING FIRST MONTHS

Removing flowers. Flower stems should be removed as they appear on the plants the first months after setting (Figure 18). Otherwise, the flowers will create a drain on the vitality of the plants, reducing the number and size of daughter plants and the subsequent crop of berries. The removal of flower stems from cultivars which naturally produce a small number of daughter plants will increase greatly the number of runners and plants set.

Thinning and spacing plants. With the hill system of culture, the runners should be cut as soon as they appear, using a sharp hoe or a circular cutter blade (made from blade of crosscut saw) about eight or ten inches in diameter and equipped with an upright handle. Also, considerable hand labor can be saved by equipping the cultivator with two rolling disk cutters attached just far enough apart to cut runners along the outside borders of the rows. This cutter cannot be used, however, in stony land or where there is straw mixed with the soil.

With the spaced-row system of culture (Figure 12), the runners are moved into place and the tips covered with soil as they begin to enlarge. The work must be done by hand. The first daughter plant is placed in the row between the mother plants. The next ones are placed the length of the runner out from the original row on either side. This makes three rows of plants and either all runners thereafter may be removed or additional runners may be rooted until a wide bed has been formed with plants spaced six to twelve inches apart, or as desired. Thereafter, all other runners should be cut. With this system, the plant-spacing and weed-hoeing jobs both can be done at the same time.

A machine is available (Figure 14) that lifts the runners up by suction and cuts them off.[1] It cannot be used on pebbly soil.

With the matted-row system, surplus plants should be removed from the outsides of the rows during late summer or autumn, using a cultivator equipped with a special disk, described above, and by hand hoeing in the row. Some growers run a spike-toothed harrow down the middle of the row in late summer or autumn with the teeth slanting backward so that only the weaker, poorly rooted plants are dislodged. The harrow must be tried carefully first, however, to make sure it is not loosening too many plants. Another practice is to run a bull-tongue plow with a four- or five-inch-wide point down the center of the row, tearing up the center plants and dividing the matted row into two parts.

Cultivation. The strawberry field must be kept clean

---

[1]S. S. Simons Machine Works, Cornwells Hghts., Penna. 19020.

during the first season by cultivation, herbicides and/or plastic to control weeds and conserve moisture. Work the soil toward the plants in cultivating. Most soil must be kept around the crowns continuously, but not covering them. Cultivator teeth should be shortened so as to stir only the upper one or two inches of soil. Cultivation should be continued until the first hard frost or until the straw mulch is applied in regions where it is used. Weeds should not be allowed to start growing in the fall; otherwise, they will give severe competition early the next spring. A field free of weeds the first season will have few if any developing prior to harvest the next season. If weeds are present during the months when the fruits are sizing, they interfere with honeybee movement and proper pollination of the blossoms, causing many "nubbins" to develop. Only a moderate amount of weeds has been known to reduce yield by 1200 quarts per acre.

Plastic film. Black or green plastic film (Florida, Louisiana, France; clear plastic, California) is used as a mulch for the hill system to control weeds and conserve moisture, but some scalding of berries may occur on hot days. Berries are kept clean, and rots and mold are reduced. Bloom may be speeded up, exposing them to early frost, where frost is a problem.

The film is machine-laid over newly set plants and held in place by soil laid on the edges (Figure 14). Plants are pulled through slits cut in the film with a knife. Runners must be removed with knives, shears or mechanical cutters (sucks up runners; cuts with rotary blades). Cost of the film has been within reason in the early 1980's. In Florida, black poly mulch saved the industry in the early 1960's where pine needles were used as mulch rather ineffectively. With the poly, yields were lifted from 245 flats/A to 1583 flats. Advantages of the poly mulch were: much reduced weed growth, less fertilizer leaching, better soil temperature, better soil moisture retention, and more effective soil fumigation under the mulch.

Weed Control. Hand weeding and machine cultivation of strawberries are expensive. Annual weeds from seed are the main problem; they may "take over" during rainy periods making cultivation difficult or impossible. Common problems are chickweed, henbit, lambsquarters, vetch, nettle, purslane, shepherds-purse, annual bluegrass, and certain perennials such as morning glory and nutgrass. The perennials may need separate treatment. Nutgrass has no completely and economically effective chemical or manual control.

Pre-plant *soil fumigation* for nematodes, when needed, often also gives fair to good control of weeds.

Herbicides are used in strawberry growing to control weeds. In Chapter 18, application equipment and techniques are given, but chemicals cleared for use are changing. Contact your local governmental extension service for latest recommendations.

Growth, Flowering Regulators. Any chemical that advances and/or concentrates the peak ripening date, improves firmness, color and/or quality and increases yield or saves labor is always viewed with interest. Potassium gibberellate, Alar, Ethrel, and maleic hydrazide have been checked for strawberries, and while there are some benefits in their use, they have not been labeled by EPA for use and their clear-cut value in a commercial program has not materialized.

FERTILIZERS

Before the strawberry plants are set, much can be done to insure high production by placing the soil in the best possible state of fertility. As pointed out earlier, high organic matter content in addition to the fertilizer elements is of paramount importance.

When strawberries follow cultivated crops, they ordinarily do not show response to fertilizers other than nitrogen due to an adequacy left from fertilization of the previous crops. If the strawberry leaves are dark green and the foliage abundant, no fertilizer should be applied unless trial plots for the particular soil have shown their value. The kind, amount, and time of applying fertilizers vary in different regions with the kind of soil, amount of rainfall, market and transportation conditions, varieties, and other factors.

Soils in most states vary greatly in fertility. With the help of your agricultural agent, test your soil to find the specific fertilizer needs. Strawberries need adequate nitrogen and water early the first year to build runners and strong crowns and develop fruit buds in the fall for next year's crop. Recommendations in Michigan are typical. If soil fertility and organic matter are low, a green manuring program is suggested for one to two years before planting. Otherwise use a 1-4-4 or 1-4-2 fertilizer, depending upon soil test. If growth is weak, apply a 1-1-1 fertilizer four weeks after setting plants, using 30 to 35 lbs. actual N per acre. Repeat in three to four weeks if growth is still weak.

Strawberries in the North Carolina region respond well to nitrogen application because the soils tend to be lower in available nitrogen than those to the north. There are some areas, however, farther north along the coast where strawberries respond well to the equivalent of 60 pounds per acre of actual nitrogen in organic or inorganic form, applied about August 15 in Maryland and around September 1 in New Jersey and Virginia. If nitrogen is added where not needed, it tends to cause a vigorous top growth with a decrease in yield and shipping quality of berries. Strawberries on acid soils definitely respond better to nitrate of soda than to ammonium sulfate. This is particularly true in the Atlantic Coast states, whereas in the Central states more of the soils are near the neutral point and response is better to ammonium sulfate.

In the spring of the fruiting year, an application of nitrogen on fertile soils will either show little or no response or may produce excess foliage and reduce the crop. On poor soils, however, nitrogen application in early spring may be worthwile, using a quickly available form.

Nitrate of soda shows the best response when applied during the latter part of August. Stable manure may be used in place of, or, in addition to nitrate of soda. If free from weed seed, stable manure can be applied as a strawy mulch to protect the plants from heaving during severe winter weather. The nitrogen, humus, and other elements in manure tend to stimulate leaf growth the following year which aids in supporting a large crop of berries.

The addition of phosphoric acid in the Mississippi Valley region, ranging from 100 to 800 pounds per acre of superphosphate has increased yields greatly. The amount needed for a specific soil can be determined best by soil test or small trial plots. In the East and Northwest the importance of phosphorus has been demonstrated. In fact, the strawberry is more like vegetables in its phosphorus requirement than woody fruit plants. A 1-2 ratio of N-P is in common use in the East. See B. R. Boyce and D. L. Matlock's review of strawberry nutrition literature in Childers' *Fruit Nutrition* book.

On most soils, potash shows little or no response. Application ranges from 50 to 300 lbs. per acre of muriate of potash, depending upon response obtained in local test plots. In some areas of western Washington boron is applied *broadcast* at the rate of two lbs. of actual boron per acre. In California, N is usually the only nutrient needed. In the NW USA, others as P, K, S, B (Figure 21) and Mg sometimes are needed. Apply N in spring of fruiting year only when plants are weak.

Soils vary tremendously in fertilizer needs, not only from one region to the next, but from one field to the neighboring field. Thus, it is sound practice for a large grower to maintain small test plots and seek local advice.

Figure 21. Strawberries can be grown for a cash crop between young fruit trees and nut trees, here in a filbert orchard in Oregon. Portable irrigation is in use for water supply and frost control. (W. A. Sheets, Ore. Ext. Serv., Hillsboro)

Time to apply. Fertilizers may be applied: (a) At time of planting, (b) during the first summer (most common in eastern USA) and (c) just before blossoming in the fruiting seasons. Growers make only application (a) in some regions, whereas in others (a) and (c) are made, or all three.

Potash and phosphoric acid, if needed, may be applied prior to the setting of the plants, but nitrogen should be applied at the critical periods listed above. Potash and phosphorus may be broadcast or drilled where the plant rows will be located. Later application of these materials and nitrogen either may be scattered on the plants or drilled along the side of the rows. When applied to the plants by hand, which is the common practice, the plants should be dry and later brushed or dragged over to remove the fertilizer from the leaves and prevent foliage burning. If the plantation is being renewed for a second or third fruiting, fertilizer should be applied at the time of renewal in midsummer.

Nitrogen is the principal nutrient needed by strawberies in California. For winter plantings, slow-release fertilizer placed under the plants in the planting slot and covered with about 1 inch of soil as part of the planting operation, work best. For summer planting, all nutrients, including nitrogen, can be top-placed or sidedressed in bands in the beds, preferably after planting. Nutrients other than nitrogen are not mobile in the soil, and repeated applications may cause salty areas in the beds which are damaging to plant growth and survival.

Starter solutions. On plant-setting machines, use a starter solution instead of water only. Apply about one cup per plant of a completely soluble 13-26-13 at the rate of 3 lbs. in 50 gallons of water. If a 5-10-5 is used, 8 lbs. in 50 gals. is needed, mostly on sandy low-organic matter soils.

Leaf Analysis. Modern diagnosis of fertilizer needs of agricultural crops is by leaf and soil analysis in commercial or government laboratories. Table 4a give leaf analysis data based on research on strawberries to date.

Lime. Lime not only reduces the acidity, but serves as a source of calcium. If dolomitic lime is used, magnesium also is added to the soil. Strawberries grow well on soils

having a pH of 5.7 to 6.5. However, if the organic matter content is high, they will grow satisfactorily at a wider pH range of 5.0 to 7.0. Lime applied at the rate of 1000 to 2000 pounds per acre on acid soil tends to tie up free aluminum which is particularly toxic to strawberry plants; it also makes calcium and magnesium readily available, and induces better tilth of the soil. The lime should be applied a year or two in advance of planting strawberries. Lime is usually beneficial on the acid soils of the Atlantic Coast states, but not commonly needed in the Mississippi Valley and the Pacific Coast states. A word of caution should be made against overliming. Too much lime may induce manganese and other trace element deficiencies. Manganese deficiency can be corrected by spraying the plants with manganese sulfate, 3 lbs./100 gallons, or placing it in the irrigation water at 15 lbs. per acre.

IRRIGATION

Irrigation must be available for good strawberry production, even in humid regions where short drouths will reduce yields and damage the relatively shallow-rooted plants. Commercial growers are now judiciously irrigating during harvest to get better fruit size and quality. A good source of water must be assured that does not go dry in the severist of drouths. Trickle or drip irrigation, where it can be used best, is growing in popularity. Sprinkler types, however, are valuable in areas where there may be heat (above 85°F) stress and need for frost control (to 20°F), using 50-60 gpm water.

Trickle or Drip Irrigation. First big installations were made in California and Florida. Reports in California show 15-20% increase in yields of better berries, 30% saving in water and energy, less disruption of picking schedules, better water supply during winter season, less rotting of berries hanging in water, the heavier soils can be used, and possibility of irrigating during harvest without muddy isles. See Chap. XIX for details and contact local sales outlets for latest improved installations. Initial installation cost may be about half the permanent or semi-permanent set systems but the latter have added assets in certain regions.

"Solid-set" System. In frost-prone areas, sprinkler systems are preferred. A system of this type, e.g., uses 2-inch portable aluminum laterals off an adequate size main with a take-off elbow and drop pipe, allowing you to dig a trench about 4 inches deep across the headland to bury the first piece of pipe. Hence, the system need not be disturbed while managing the planting. Laterals can be placed on top of the strawberry row without using riser pipes. The low sprinkler heads do not interfere with cultivation, spraying booms, etc. When renovation is necessary, all rows can be renovated except where the pipes lay. Then without lifting a pipe, it can be moved over one row while the rows are

TABLE 4a. APPROXIMATE RANGE OF LEAF CONTENT
OF NUTRIENTS IN STRAWBERRY PLANTS FRUITING
SATISFACTORILY (RUTGERS UNIVERSITY).

N	P	K	Mg	Ca	Mn	B	Zn	Cu	Fe
%	%	%	%	%	ppm	ppm	ppm	ppm	ppm
2.35	0.178	1.10	0.28	1.25	129	111	58	6.2	70
to	to	to	to	to	to	to	to	to	to
2.93	0.238	1.70	0.34	1.48	170	170	73	7.0	80

Note: More data are needed from first-year and fruiting-year field plants to refine these data. Variety differences also can be a factor. Strawberries are sensitive to B excess; figures from literature above seem high, but this plant may tend to accumulate B. No data are available for Mo and S; Mg, Ca, Zn, Cu and Fe data are from Webb and Hollas, 1966.

renovated. Vegetation may tangle the sprinkler arms and this is prevented by placing a tablespoon of herbicide at each sprinkler, eliminating a few sq. ft. of berry production/A. Lines are blown with an air compressor at end of season. Cost figures indicate that the solid-set system pays in northern areas of USA over a 10-15 yr. or more life period.

Surface irrigation. Furrow irrigation can be used only where the soil, or particularly the subsoil, is heavy, and where the slopes are uniform and gentle. Victor Voth in California used a 60-inch bed (U. S. standard 40-inch) with one irrigation furrow serving 2 adjacent beds, reducing space used by irrigation furrows and increasing production with other advantages. Irrigation furrows 200 to 250 feet long are used.

Portable Pipe and Hose. On sandy soils, irregular or level (Figure 21) land, the portable aluminum pipe system can be used. Eyelet plastic hose can be used for home gardens.

The portable aluminum pipe system can be shifted readily to sweet corn, potatoes, peaches, and other crops. It also can be set up quickly for frost and heat-stress control. A 4-inch main line with 3-inch laterals is set up with rotation sprinkler heads mounted at 40-ft intervals, using about 1,100 ft. of laterals/A.

COLD PROTECTION

Strawberry leaves harden with cooler temperatures in early fall and often can withstand a temperature of 15°F. without injury in late fall or early winter. If the temperature falls to 0°F. or below during winter with no blanket of snow, they may be damaged severely. Also, alternate freezing and thawing of the soil, especially heavier soils, will heave the plants out of the ground, causing severe damage by the next growing season. Mulch is effective in minimizing this injury. Mulching has the advantages of smothering weeds, keeping the berries clean, and conserving moisture. In the South and West where winter cold protection in unnecessary, mulching with pine needles, straw, etc. has been replaced with plastic mulch.

Mulching with marsh hay, grain straw, sawdust or pine needles and ferns is recommended on the dates shown in Figure 23 for the respective regions. Marsh or salt hay and pine needles are free from weed seed which makes them particularly desirable. In the upper Mississippi Valley, about six tons of straw per acre should provide sufficient protection. In the rest of the country where mulch is needed, two to two and one-half tons per acre are sufficient. The straw should be as free from weed seed as possible. If straw is scarce, Sudan grass can be raised for mulching material; but it should be cut before becoming coarse. Oats may be sown thickly in the alleys at the rate of one and one-half to two bushels per acre. Oats kill in early

Figure 22. Boron deficient strawberry leaves are distorted, small and berries are misshapen on left, nubbins with few "seeds". (F. A. Gilbert, formerly Rutgers University). "Hunger In Strawberries" describes other nutrient deficiencies in color by F. D. Johanson, 40 pp., 2703 5th St., Everett, Wa. 98201 (priced).

winter and furnish mulch. Use only *spring* oats.

Straw distributing machines[1], as used in highway grass seeding, are available for quick spreading on large acreages.

When growth starts in spring, surplus mulch should be pulled from the tops of the plants to the alleyways. A light covering of straw can be left on the plants for some insurance but mulch may delay ripening by a few days to a week, depending upon the thickness of the mulch.

Frosts will destroy the earliest and most valuable blossoms and berries (Figure 24). While mulching is effective in frost control, if left on too late in spring it delays the crop. Infra-red heating units are expensive as are smudge pots. In Michigan and New Jersey most of the strawberry acreage is protected by overhead irrigation (Figure 25). Special "fogging" frost nozzles are used at 70 lbs. plus pressure. Start fogging when temperature near plants in low areas is 34°F. Continue fogging as long as ice forms. On-off cycling of nozzles saves water and is ef-

[1]Reinco, P.O.B. 584, Plainfield, N.J. 07061.

468

Figure 23. Map showing areas in which cold injury to strawberry plants may be expected often enough to make mulching pay. Growers in each area should be ready to put on the mulch by the first date listed and should have applied the mulch by the latter date. Mulch is being less used in many areas due to cost and often unavailable. Spring sprinkler irrigation is used for frost control and where winter cold damage is not a problem. (USDA)

fective. Other systems are too expensive.

If an unseasonable spring frost is expected, it may be advisable to pull the straw back over the plants. It may be the difference of crop or no crop where irrigation is not available.

If the region is particularly susceptible to frost injury, everbearing cultivars can be used, and if the first crop of blossoms is killed, another set of flowers will appear. Also, the use of late-blooming cultivars should be considered in frost-susceptible regions.

RENEWING THE PLANTATION

It is seldom profitable to renew plants in hills; may be too costly. With the matted row system, however, the cost

of renovation is usually less than the cost of setting and caring for a new planting.

The number of crops harvested from a strawberry field varies in different sections of the country from only one crop to two, three, or even more crops before the plantation is plowed under. The number of crops that can be harvested depends upon the cultivar, the amount of weeds in the field, infestation of insects and diseases, character of the soil, and the cost of renewing an old plantation as compared with the cost of setting a new one.

With better weed control methods, virus-nematode-free stock, and better resistance to diseases, it now may be possible to fruit the planting two or three or more years without the planting "running out."

If the field is heavily infested with weeds as white clover, purslane, chick weed, or crab grass, it may be advisable to harvest only one crop and plow up the field. White clover is difficult to eradicate once started; it is usually easier to start a new plantation than attempt to combat it.

If humus content of the soil is low, only one crop may be profitable. With such soils, it is best to turn under green manure crops or apply stable manure before setting the strawberries so that the plantation will be profitable for more than one year.

If intensive cultivation is practiced, the planting probably should be kept for at least three crops, and sometimes for five or six crops, or as long as it gives profitable returns.

If the planting is to be renewed, the field should be mowed immediately after harvest close to the crowns but not injuring them. If renovation is delayed, do not mow the field. Broadcast a fertilizer supplying about 50 lbs./A of N. Narrow the rows to 8-10 inches with a plow or rotovator, chewing up the old foliage, crowns and any light straw (Figure 14). A strip of plants can be left on the side of the old row or down the center. With a hoe, thin the

Figure 24. At the right are two blossoms killed by frost near Aurora, Oregon, vs. two at bottom left unharmed. Light mulch cover and/or sprinkling are used in an attempt to avoid this damage. (Oregon State University)

Figure 25. Ice-coated strawberry leaves and flowers during a cold-night sprinkling. Most plant tissue freezes at about 28°F. Liquid water freezes at about 32°F and gives off heat of fusion as it freezes, keeping the plant from freezing as long as water is applied and the plant is wet. (Robert Hill, Ohio Agr. Exp. Sta., Wooster)

remaining plants to 6 to 8 inches apart. Or, a spike tooth harrow can be dragged across the rows once or twice and down the rows once. Irrigate after fertilizing if needed. Try to get as healthy and vigorous plants as possible by the end of the season by good weed control and watering.

After the harvest, established weeds may be pulled or destroyed with a herbicide. Where the stand of plants is thick, some plant thinning with a hoe is helpful. Should the plants need stimulation, an NPK application is suggested. In late fall the mulch should be replenished for winter protection. The second crop of berries from undisturbed plantings handled in this way usually are significantly larger than from similar plantings receiving a renewal treatment that involves narrowing the rows by cultivation.

HARVESTING

Hand-Pick for Market. Pointers in hand-harvesting for the market are: pick soft-fleshed cultivars before fully ripe; leave firm-fruited cultivars (Raritan) until nearly ripe;

cultivars as Midland can be harvested over 4 wks or more, but Jerseybelle has a short season; pick some cultivars every day, others every 2-3 days; ripening is faster in hot weather; do not leave any ripe or rotted berries in the field; pinch off each berry with very little stem attached; morning-picked berries keep better; berry life is cut in half for each 15 °F rise in temperature; pay pickers by piece and give a bonus to those who remain to the end; 2 pickers/A are needed for small yields or 8-10 for peak picking in high-yielding fields; plastic or straw mulch helps keep the pickers and berries clean. A field yielding 216 24-qt crates or 375 12-lb flats can be covered by 4 pickers working every day (Figure 26). See big operation in California in Figure 27.

Pick-Your-Own method of harvesting strawberries has become a substantial way of moving strawberries. The average customer returns about 5 times a season, picks 20 qts or 30 lbs, travels 20-22 miles, and frequently makes it a family recreation experience. A small acreage (3) with high local demand may cause traffic jams and problems and,

Figure 26. Pick when berries are red or at least pink all over; use both hands; pinch off stems; do not squeeze; hold 3-4 berries per hand; pick directly in pints or quarts or grade/pack later; comb back leaves; and pick over-ripes and place them in special container to reduce rot spread. (Courtesy Her Majesty's Statistical Office, London, England.) Ref. Bk 95 from her Majesty is a 108 p. bul. (priced) on strawberries. A grower-book on "Protected Strawberry Production", 49 Doughty, London WC1N 2LP 40 p. is available. Fruit Station, Wilhelminadorp, Netherlands has a thick strawberry bulletin, in Dutch.

Figure 27. In California, strawberries are harvested directly in 12-pt. labelled corrugated flats for shipment East. Note the special raised beds with two double rows on wide beds covered with clear plastic. California Leaflet 2959 is (Strawberry Production in California) available at Div. of Agr., Univ. of Calif., Berkeley 94720. (Photos courtesy Bill Uyeki, The Packer)

hence, a Wisconsin grower increased gradually his acreage to 90 and accommodated about 1500 people on a June Saturday and 1000 on July 4th. He used 12 field supervisors (college students, local teachers), eight scales and 2 cash registers at check-out. He sells by the lb, not by volume and includes the cost of corrugated standard containers (to discourage customers bringing all types of containers).

Narrow rows (24") with roomy aisles (15") works well, assigning customers to aisles, not rows, telling them they can pick all within reach, then setting a long white stake in the aisles where they stop picking, indicating where next picker starts. Best advertising is satisfied customers, but some radio and newspaper usage is needed to get an operation started. A standard reply to phone inquiries is taped to the phone or an automatic taped reply to phone calls (rented from phone company) can be used. A name and address file is built up and postcards are sent to previous customers just before harvest starts.

Customers like *big berry* cultivars. Small berries from a last-harvest-early-variety may cause dissension over big berries ripening from a later cultivar. Hence, some growers have no late cultivars for this reason. Key essentials are: weed-free attractive field, friendly supervision, highly productive quality berries, irrigation and frost control, liability insurance, and plenty of customers (see references).

To break even on PYO operations, the grower must produce about three tons of berries per acre. In the early 1980s, tonnage and profits were about as follows: 4 - $1400; 5 - $2500; 6 - $3800; 7 - $5000; and 8 - $6200, according to R. C. Funt of Ohio State University.

Machine Harvesting. Labor problems and the need for good net financial returns have encouraged research in machine harvesting of strawberries. Figure 28 shows a design at the University of Arkansas. This machine combs out larger riper berries in a "once-over" swipe; fruit is processed. Future research objectives are (a) to continue to improve design of equipment for more careful handling and selection of berries with a satisfactory mechanical grading technique, (b) new varieties through breeding with concentrated peak ripening and easily accessible and firm berries, and (c) development of plant growing techniques adapted to machine harvesting. With these and possibly other improvements, a better product for processing can be obtained and a good percentage of the harvested fruit may be acceptable to the fresh market.

Crates and carriers. A 12-pint flat or non-returnable fiberboard box often is used to market directly or ship berries (Figure 29). Berries shipped by air freight are precooled in special rooms and taken to the plane in refrigerated trucks. Altitude of the plane keeps the cargo at about 40°F. Berries are picked directly into the veener pint

Figure 28. Mechanical strawberry harvesters have been used for several years for processing berries. This University of Arkansas machine is used on two matted level rows of berries with 4-ft. centers, operating on a pneumatic-stripping once-over principle. (Courtesy Justin R. Morris, University of Arkansas, Fayetteville, 72701)

Figure 29. A 12-pint moisture proof pack for strawberries, other berries, that folds together quickly and, lower photo, an 8-quart two-piece shipper display tray pack. Both wood and meshed plastic containers are used. (Packaging Corporation of America, 1603 Orrington Ave., Evanston, 60204)

boxes, arranged in 12-pint master fiberboard containers in which they will be shipped and retailed. The present rapid growth of air transportation with further reduced rates makes it possible to harvest ripe berries one day and ship them into distant markets that day or the next day (Figure 30).

Strawberries shipped to distant markets by air frequently come in half-pint containers, twelve to a fiberboard flat. The U.S. customer often will pay about as much for a half-pint of berries as for a pint or quart very early in the season.

Cold storage. Strawberries can be held in storage a maximum of about ten days, even though the temperature is held at 32 °F. After this period, the fruit begins to lose its fresh bright color, shows some shriveling and deteriorates in flavor. At temperatures of 40° or above, loss from gray mold rot, rhizopus rot, and leather rot may become serious. Commercial CA (Tectrol) storage in California shows that strawberries can be held 2 to 7 days with virtually no deterioration (Figure 31).

Frozen pack. Certain varieties of strawberries freeze as well or better than almost any other fruit. About half of the total commercial strawberry crop of the United States or about 100 thousand tons, is frozen either for manufactured products or for dessert use (Figure 20). Varieties with high flavor and bright red color such as Hood, are desired for ice cream trade. Midland, Midway, Hood, Honeoye, Pocahantas, Redchief and Tennessee Beauty are good processing varieties.

Yields. Factors which influence yield are the general vigor of the plantation, freedom from virus and nematodes, the variety, the season including possible losses from frost injury at blossoming time, and distribution of rainfall or use of supplemental irrigation. Many of the better growers produce 5000 to 6000 quarts per acre regularly with occasional higher yields reaching 8000 to 11,000, particularly when grown under irrigation. The net profit from 3200 quarts per acre is doubtful in the northeastern states, whereas in other regions with cheaper labor costs, a small profit may be realized. Twenty T/A the first year and 25 to 30 T the second year are obtained in California where berries are harvested most months a year.

In any strawberry operation, yield per acre is most important in determining production costs per crate and profit to the grower. Every effort must be made to get top yields of quality fruit. This is where the profit lies. Production costs such as spraying, planting, mulching, weed control, etc. do not vary greatly regardless of the yield obtained. Fields can be cropped for more than one year and up to 4 yrs on a location, depending upon vigor of the planting.

In Table 6 are estimates from Mark G. Robson, Rutgers University, New Jersey, for costs of establishment of an acre of strawberries, costs of growing, and costs of har-

TABLE 6. ESTIMATED PRODUCTION COSTS/A/YR. FOR STRAWBERRIES IN NEW JERSEY. (MARK G. ROBSON, RUTGERS UNIVERSITY, NEW BRUNSWICK, N.J. 08903. (1981).

Establishment Costs	$
Plants (5000)	350
Fumigation	380
Labor	80
Machinery	40
Total	$850

Growing Costs/Yr./A	$
Labor	400
Machinery	180
Fertilizer, lime	150
Pesticides & Herbicides	350
Irrigation	120
Mulching	250
Land cost	75
Total	$1625

Harvest costs/A/Yr.	$
Picking, handling at 25¢/qt.	$1750
Qt. boxes at 5¢	350
Crates at $1.40/crate (500 16 qt. crates)	613
Total	$2713

Notes: Irrigation was 6-acre inches per irrigation @ $20/acre inch. Mulching was 2 T/A @ $125/T. Average yld. was 7000-8000 qts./A. Establishment costs should be distributed over 3-4 yrs. Pick-Your-Own harvesting will alter harvesting costs.

vesting by pickers. PYO would lower the harvesting costs and increase the returns for the grower. The establishment costs must be distributed over 3-4 yrs of a planting.

In Table 7, data are given for the Maritime provinces in Canada for PYO operations at three levels of yielding. When picking was done by hired labor, the cost of harvesting and marketing at the 7500 qt/A level was: first yr — $3360; second yr — the same; and for a 3-yr ave. — $2240.

TABLE 7. PYO COSTS PER ACRE FOR STRAWBERRIES AT THREE YIELDING LEVELS, MARITIME PROVINCES, CANADA (W.L. HANLON AND A. HAMILTON, AGRIC. CANADA (BASED ON CANADIAN DOLLAR)*. EARLY 1980s.

Yield Levels	Harvest Yrs. First	Harvest Yrs. Second	Av./Yr. 3 Yrs.
5,000 Quart Yield			
Growing Costs	1704.48	1148.50	1607.81
Harvest & Marketing	463.00	463.00	308.67
Management (3¢/quart)	150.00	150.00	100.00
Total Costs	2317.48	1761.50	2016.48
7,500 Quart Yield			
Growing Costs	1704.48	1148.50	1607.81
Harvesting & Marketing Costs	639.00	639.00	426.00
Management (3¢/quart)	225.00	225.00	150.00
Total Costs	2563.48	2012.50	2183.81
10,000 Quart Yield			
Growing Costs	1704.48	1148.50	1607.81
Harvest & Marketing Costs	826.00	826.00	550.67
Management (3¢/quart)	300.00	300.00	200.00
Total Costs	2830.48	2274.50	2358.48

*Total establishment costs for each level of production first year was $1970.44. Figures based on 100A farm with 10A of strawberries. Any inflation must be figured for subsequent years.

Figure 30. Shipment of strawberries, other fruits, fresh vegetables is made by jet to get them e.g. from California to New York market next day or to foreign markets. Pallett of strawberries is sealed in plastic impregnated with CA gas to control rot. No damage to berries if loaded with mixed wet vegetables. (Calif. Strawberry Advisory Bd.)

TABLE 8. ESTIMATED OPERATING AND OWNERSHIP COSTS PER ACRE FOR STRAWBERRY PRODUCTION, WEST CENTRAL FLORIDA, 1981. (J.W. PREVATT, UNIV. OF FL., BRANDENTON 33508).

Item	Month	Unit	Quantity	Price/Unit of Material	Price/ Gross Acre
I. Operating Costs					
Pre-harvest					
Dolomite	May	Ton	0.33	$ 23.00	$ 7.59
Disk	May	Acre	2.00	9.89	19.78
Plant	June	Acre	1.00	2.90	2.90
Sorghum Seed	June	Pound	50.00	0.55	27.50
Rotovate	Sept.	Acre	2.00	9.89	19.78
Lay of rows	Sept.	Acre	1.00	5.80	5.80
Press beds	Sept.	Acre	1.00	5.80	5.80
Fertilizer	Sept.	Acre	1.00	5.80	5.80
6-8-8	Sept.	Ton	1.50	143.80	215.70
Fumigate	Sept.	Acre	1.00	11.60	11.60
Fumigant (MC-33)	Sept.	Pound	175.00	0.96	168.00
Plastic (44 inch)	Sept.	Thou. feet	11.00	19.50	214.50
Labor	Sept.	Hour	4.00	3.50	14.00
Set plants					
Transplants	Oct.	Thousand	23.00	35.00	805.00
Labor	Oct.	Hour	40.00	3.50	140.00
Cultivate	Nov.-May	Acre	3.00	6.81	17.43
Spray	Oct.-Apr.	Acre	36.00	3.59	129.24
Captan (36 appl.)		Pound	216.00	1.59	343.44
Banlate (16 appl.)		Pound	16.00	11.15	178.40
Dibrom (6 appl.)		Gallon	1.25	29.50	36.88
Plictran (6 appl.)		Pound	12.00	15.75	189.00
Phosdrin (12 appl.)		Gallon	1.50	18.85	28.28
Remove plastic (labor)	May	Hour	8.00	3.50	28.00
Irrigation (elec.)	Oct.-Apr.	Acre	1.00	65.00	65.00
Interest	May-Apr.	Dollar	2,679.42	0.12	321.53
					3,000.95
Harvest				$/Flat	
Picking labor	Dec.-Apr.			$1.15	
Labor benefits				0.15	
Containers				0.60	
Packing shed labor				0.10	
Supervision				0.10	
Transport				0.10	
Total					$2.20
Marketing				$/Flat	
Marketing charge[1]	Jan.-Apr.				$0.50
					$0.50
II. Ownership Costs/A[2]					$1,247.00

[1]Marketing charge is based on handling cost per flat which was approximately 10% of the market price.
[2]Ownership costs include depreciation, insurance, repairs, taxes and interest on land and equipment for strawberry production.

Figure 31. The 12-pint cardboard container has been popular for a picking, shipping and display container for several years. They are moved in bulk by skids or slip sheets with electric lifts. Stacks are covered with polyethylene bag for Tectrol Modified Atmosphere use in distant shipping. (Paul Bush, Tim Linden, The Packer)

In the early 1980s, U. Seyman, Farm Advisor of Santa Clara County, California, gave cost and return data for 2 of 2 years, yielding 3500 crates/A or about $1/crate. Total harvest cost was $7352/A or $2.10/crate. Income above all cash costs was $3950/A or $1.13/crate. Contact Dept. of Agric. Economics, Univ. of Calif., Davis 95616 for latest figures and breakdown item by item.

In a Pick-Your-Own operation, which accounts for over 90% of the strawberry operations in some states, P. J. Kirschling and G. H. Sullivan, Purdue University, Indiana 47907, state that profits start at about 6000 lbs/A and reach substantial returns at 16,000 lbs/A (Purdue Sta. Bul. 232, 46 p.)

Table 8 gives the estimated operating and ownership costs per acre for strawberry production by techniques in Florida, courtesy J. W. Prevatt, Univ. of Fl., Bradenton 33508.

DISEASES

With strawberries it is possible to rotate the ground frequently and consequently, diseases and insects are not likely to become as serious a problem as where the fruit crop occupies the ground for many years. The diseases below (see Figures 32, 33) are among the most common. For more specific control measures, you are referred to your local agricultural experiment station and to a special USDA bulletin by McGrew.

Leaf spot (Mycosphaerella fragaria) is in almost all regions where strawberries are grown, pratically in some Gulf-state regions. Varieites vary in susceptibility; Earlibelle is resistant. Benomyl, captan, ferbam are suggested which also control *Botrytis,* a fruit rot. *Leaf scorch (Diplocarpon earliana),* dark purplish spots one-quarter inch across, can be reduced with dithane or copper mixes. *Leaf blight (Dendrophoma obscurans)* is characterized by large red to brown spots surrounded by purplish margins; it occurs largely on old fruited plants, not young ones. Remedies are not warranted. *Crinkle,* a virus disease, is commonly found in Pacific Coast states, occasionally in the East. Leaves may be distorted, wrinkled, lighter shade of green, petioles short with leaves lying flat on the ground, giving the plants a dwarfed appearance. Use certified virus-free stock on isolated fields away from crops harboring aphids (the vectors), and dust or spray for aphids. *Yellows (Xanthosis),* a virus transmitted by strawberry aphis, is prevalent from Puget Sound to

Figure 32. Strawberry diseases include (top left) leaf spot; (top right) leaf scorch; (middle left) noninfectious leaf varigation or June Yellows; (middle right) spring dwarf caused by a nematode; (bottom left) summer dwarf caused by a nematode; (bottom middle) black-seed disease caused by strawberry leaf spot fungus; and (bottom right) strawberry leaf blight. (USDA)

TABLE 9. SAMPLE STRAWBERRY INSECT AND DISEASE CONTROL (OHIO AGRICULTURAL EXTENSION SERVICE AND EXPERIEMENT STATION, COLUMBUS AND WOOSTER.) FOR LOCAL RECOMMENDATIONS, CONTACT YOUR COUNTY AGRICULTURAL AGENT, STATE UNIVERSITY OR LOCAL GOVERNMENTAL SERVICE.

Pests	Symptoms of Injury	Control
STRAWBERRY LEAF ROLLER	Leaflets folded and webbed together with a small green larva feeding within.	Spray with Guthion ½ lb 50% Wet. Powd./100 gals. Not within 5 days of harvest.
ROOT WORMS (Strawberry leaf beetle)	Small beetles at night eat numerous holes in leaves. Larvae feed on roots.	Plow down infested beds in mid-summer to kill larvae. Rotate beds with new plantings at some distance from old ones. Use methoxychlor on beetles if many.
CROWN BORER	Crown of plants hollowed out by white legless grubs about 1/5 inch in length.	Same as for root worms
SPITTLEBUGS	White frothy masses ½ inch or more in diameter covering small greenish yellow insects on stems and leaves.	Guthion as above can be used when masses first appear.
TARNISHED PLANT BUG	Brassy-brown bugs feed on buds before bloom and deform fruits causing 'button berries', seedy tips.	Use Guthion on plants, mulch, area as above just before blossoms open.
WHITE GRUBS	Large fleshy white grubs that attack roots of new plants.	Don't plant in newly plowed sod or where grubs are abundant. Under present regulations, nothing can be done after planting with chemicals.
TWO-SPOTTED SPIDER MITE CYCLAMEN MITE	Leaves, blossoms, curl, distorted, lose color. Silken webs may occur on lower leaf surface.	Spray with Kelthane 2 lbs. 35% WP or 2 qts. 18.5% EC/100 gals up to 2 days of harvest (100-300 gals/A, thorough coverage, depending on size of plants).
SLUGS	Burrow into ripening fruits leaving slimy trails.	Apply a commercial metaldehyde bait according to directions on the container.
(1) LEAF SPOT (2) LEAF BLIGHT (3) SCORCH	(1) Leaves show purplish spots, with gray centers. (2) Reddish purple, almost circular, sometimes elliptical spots on leaflets. If spots occur on a prominent vein, fan-shaped injured areas extend to margin of leaflet. No gray or white centers are evident. When infection is on calyz, stemend rot of berries may occur. (3) Large, irregular-shaped purplish spots without light centers. Badly infected leaves often curl and 'burn.' Infection may also occur on leaf petioles, fruit pledicels, and on the sepals of the calyx.	Cultivars differ greatly in susceptibility to the leaf diseases. When feasible select varieties which are least susceptible. Where control is necessary, spray new plantings at 10-day intervals with 2 lbs. per 100 gallons of either ferbam or captan. Spray second year plantings after harvest with same materials. Repeat at 2-week intervals if necessary. One lb Benlate/A can be used similarly.
FRUIT ROT	Decay of blossoms on green and ripening fruits, and harvested berries. Most damaging in wet seasons.	Spray or dust plantings thoroughly every 5 to 7 days from start of blossoming until first fruit picking. Apply 3 lbs. of actual captan, or thiram per acre.
RED STELE ROOT ROT	Plants wilt and die, usually just preceding or during harvest. Roots of plants decay and show red cores. Roots devoid of fibrous, lateral rootlets, giving the roots a 'rat-tailed' appearance.	Set only disease-free plants on well-drained, porous, fertile soil which is uncontaminated by red stele fungus. Rotate crops with at least four years between strawberry crops. Use red stele resistant cultivars whenever feasible, especially if trouble with red stele disease has been experienced. Sparkle, Midway, Guardian, Red Chief, and Surecrop are suggested.
VIRUS DISEASES Transmitted by Aphids	Reduced runner formation and decreased vigor and yields of plantings. No conspicuous symptoms. Aphids can spread the viruses.	Set only virus-free 'registered' plants. Virus-free stock of most cultivars is now available. If planting is from virus-free stock and will be used for plant production, spray with Malathion (25% WP) 2½ lbs/100 gals. every 14 days. Make first application when growth starts in spring and continue until frost in fall. Do not apply during harvest.

Note: Cultivars resistant to, e.g., stele, verticillium, mildew, leaf scorch and leaf spot are available in some areas and should be used. R. C. Funt's Fruit Handbook is useful in strawberry and all fruit growing, Ohio State University, 2 in thick. 1983.

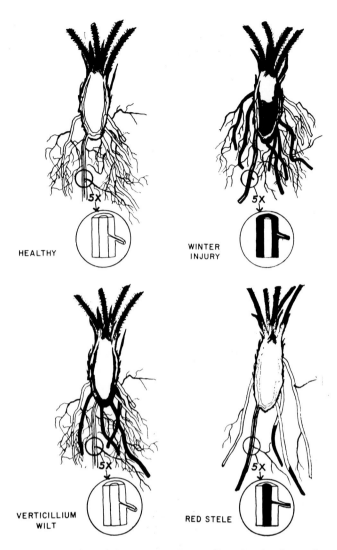

Figure 33. Winter injury, *Verticillium* wilt and red stele are three key diseases of strawberries, all resulting in death of the plants. Identification of each is diagrammed. (USDA)

Figure 34. A key purpose of the California Strawberry Advisory Board is to supply "Good Ideas" each year to marketing outlets. These are used in TV ads and in new display material. Different ways of serving California strawberries are promoted. Board address is P.O. Bx 269, Watsonville, California 95076. (Bill Uyeki, The Packer, Shawnee Mission, Kansas 66201)

southern California and is frequently present in the East. Affected plants are dwarfed and somewhat yellow, occurring in strips in a row. Leaves may be cupped with less point at the tips, and showing dull green centers with yellow edges. See control for crinkle virus. *June yellows* is due to an hereditary factor. Leaves show mottling and streaking with yellow and green. The markings differ with the variety and season. Blakemore, and Dixiland are susceptible. Species of *nematodes* are responsible for a summer dwarf (Figure 32) appearing during high summer temperatures, and for a spring dwarf appearing early in the season. Control is by rigid state inspection of nursery plants and soil fumigation. *Red Stele* root disease is caused by a fungus occuring largely in the northeastern states, resulting in stunting and dwarfing in spring and wilting and dying leaves (Figure 33). Fungus invades central cylinder (stele) of root, causing it to turn dark red with

outer part of root appearing healthy. Disease is aggravated by cold wet soils. Resistant cultivars are Darrow, Delite, Earliglow, Totem, Hood, Linn, Shuksan, Surecrop, Redchief, Guardian, Sunrise, Midway, Redglow, Scott, Allstar, Tristar, Tribute, Arking, Sparkle usually. Nursery inspection is the recommended control. *Blackseed fungus (Mycosphaerella fragariae)* causes black spots around one or a few seeds on a fruit, marring appearance. Use spray schedule for leaf spot. Verticillium Wilt *(V. alboatrum)* causes wilt in midsummer with outermost leaves dying. New leaves are stunted and plant lies flat (Figure 33); Guardian, Siletz, Catskill, Surecrop are highly resistant. Soil fumigation with 2 to 1 proportion of methyl bromide/chloropicrin under poly tarpaulin (machine laid) is used in the West and East. Crop rotation also is suggested in the East. Strawberries should not be planted on soil where potato, pepper, eggplant or other crops showing the disease have been planted recently. Use clean stock. *Anthracnose* is serious in southeastern USA; benomyl gives fair control. *Mottle virus* is frequently present in eastern and western USA plants which are weakened with less runner production.

INSECTS

White grubs (Phyllophaga or *Lachmosterna)* may cause

476

considerable trouble by girdling crowns and feeding on roots (Figure 35). *Leaf roller (Arcylis competana fragariae)* larvae roll the leves after feeding for a short time in the spring and continue to feed from within the enclosed chamber; serious losses sometimes occur. *Strawberry weevil (Anthonomus signatus)* lays eggs in flower buds, and then girdles the stem. Larvae feed in buds, destroying them. Injury may become serious in some regions. The *Cyclamen Mite (Tarsonemus pellidus)* occurs widely in the northern states and in California and Canada, causing dwarfing and/or loss of entire crop. Nursery planting stock treated for mites is available. New plantings should be made some distance from old infested fields. The *Spittle bug (Phalaenus leucophthalmus)* is frequently found. Two-spotted red mites can be a real problem, difficult to control (See Figure 35).

The accompanying spray schedule for strawberries for Ohio gives information on materials and techniques for controlling the common pests in that area. Each state can supply specific recommendations through the county agricultural agent.

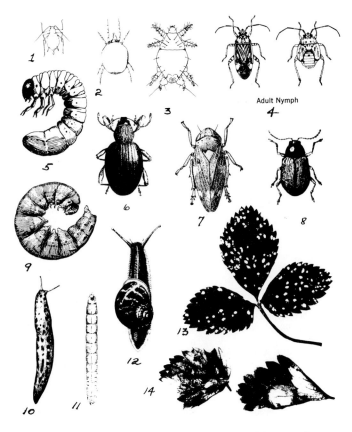

Figure 35. Strawberry insects, pests. (1) aphid; (2) mite; (3) cyclamen mite; (4) lygus bugs (tarnished plant bugs); (5) white grub; root weevil adult; (7) spittle bug (surrounded by foam); (8) rootworm adult; (9) cutworm; (10) slug; (11) wireworm; (12) snail; (13) rootworm adult feeding; (14) leafroller worm. See USDA Farmers Bull. 2184 for detailed descriptions and accompanying Table 9.

EVERBEARING STRAWBERRIES

Everbearing varieties of strawberry bear fruit at the usual time followed by a period of little or no production until late summer when another crop is harvested throughout the fall if growing conditions are favorable. Everbearers, principally Ozark Beauty, Gem, Quinault, others (Table 3), are valuable in valleys of western states where spring frosts may kill blossoms of standard varieties. They are used in the home garden in sections of the United States north of North New Jersey and in the higher Appalachian range. The present varieties are not adapted to the South. Everbearing strawberries are not considered profitable for the general market, although Dr. Wesley P. Judkins both in Ohio and Virginia (2000 feet altitude) has obtained good yields and profits from everbearers.

Best berries are obtained in the fall following the spring planting and many fields are kept only for one season. Deblossoming should be discontinued about the first part of July to obtain a fall crop the first year. If the bed is kept a second season, the fruit is borne at the normal time, followed by a rest period and then by further bearing, but the fruit may be small both in size and yield. Everbearing varieties need a very fertile soil and adequate soil moisture in order to develop berry size and satisfactory yields. They may be planted by the matted-row or hill system, depending upon the runner-forming habit of the variety. The culture, otherwise, is similar to that recommended for standard varieties.

Review Questions

1. Discuss the leading commerical strawberry production areas in the United States and foreign areas and indicate trends in outlets and shipping.
2. Why is it possible to grow strawberries under so widely differing soil and climatic conditions?
3. Describe a desirable location and site for a commerical strawberry enterprise in your region.
4. What factors are paramount in selecting a strawberry cultivar for local market? For distant market?
5. Discuss precautions needed in getting good planting stock in strawberries.
6. Describe preparations necessary for growing strawberries on land which has been in sod.
7. Why is early planting of strawberries in the upper eastern states so important?
8. Describe briefly, by diagram if necessary, how the hill system of training strawberries differs from the spaced-row and matted-row systems.
9. What is the proper depth for setting strawberry plants?
10. Describe a desirable cultivation and fertilization program for strawberries during the first season in your locality. Discuss value and use of herbicides.
11. Of what value is lime in strawberry culture?
12. In almost all regions where strawberries are grown, irrigation is frequently the deciding factor in successful strawberry production. Why is this true?

13. In mulching strawberries in your region, if practiced, what materials can be used, when are they applied, and why?
14. How would you handle a pick-your-own operation?
15. What instructions would you give your picking crew to reduce damage to the fruits as much as possible?
16. Discuss the key aspects of mechanical harvesting.
17. List an important insect and disease of strawberries in your region and modern control.
18. Under what conditions should a strawberry plantation be renewed?
19. Give briefly the steps for renewing a plantation trained to the matted-row system; the system used in California
20. Discuss the strawberry virus and nematode situation, their possible effect on yields, and how to control them.
21. Discuss strawberry containers, storage and key marketing problems.
22. Discuss meristem (tissue) culture propagation of strawberry, its advantages, disadvantages and future.

Suggested Collateral Readings

ALBREGTS, E. E. and C. M. Howard. Influence of defoliation at transplanting on strawberry growth and fruiting response. Hort-Science 7(6):569. 1972.

ALBREGTS, E. E. and C. M. Howard Polyethylene mulch color and frames on strawberry yield. Proc. Fla. State Hort. Soc. 118-120. 1973.

ALBREGTS, E. E. and C. M. Howard. Composition of Strawberry Fruit. J. ASHS 103(3):293-296. 1978.

ALBREGTS, E. E. and C. M. Howard. Strawberry transplant stress. HortScience 17(4):651. 1982.

ALBREGTS, E. E. and C. W. Howard. Poultry manure on strawberries. J. ASHS 106:3:295-8. May 1981.

ANDERSON, William. The strawberry — a world bibliography — 1966. Scarecrow Press, Inc. P.O. Box 656, Metuchen, N. J. 08840. 731 pp. 1969.

Anonymous. Soft fruit-growing — strawberries. Ministry of Agriculture. Fisheries, and Food Bull. 95. 50 pp. Her Majesty's Stationary Office, London, Request update.

ABBOTT, A. J. et al. Relation of achene number to berry weight in strawberry. J. HortSci. 46(3):215-222. July 1970.

ASHTON, F. M. et al. Strawberry weed control, California. Univ. of Cal. Leaflet 2926. 4 p. 1980.

BAKER, A. S. and W. P. Mortensen, Mg, trace elements in Washington loamy sand. Wash. Agr. Exp. Sta Bull. 776. 6/1973.

BARRITT, B. H. Single harvest yields of strawberries in relation to cultivar and time of harvest J. ASHS 99(1):6. Jan. 1973.

BARRITT, B. H. Strawberry parent clones with easy calyx removal. J. ASHS, 101(5):590-591. 1976.

BARRITT, B. H. Breeding Strawberries for Fruit Firmness. J. Amer. Soc. Hort Sci. 104(5):663-665. 1979.

BARRITT, Bruce H. and C. H. Shanks, Jr. Breeding strawberries resistant to two-spotted mites. HortSci. 16(3). 323-4. June 1981.

BARRITT, B. H. and H. A. Daubeny. Inheritance of virus tolerance in strawberry. J. ASHS 107:(2):278-282. 1982.

BARRITT, B. H., et al. Early Flowering in day-neutral strawberries. J. ASHS 107:(5):733-6. 1982.

BIAIN DE ELIZALDE, M. and M. R. Guitman. Propagation in ever-bearing strawberry with morphactin, GA₃, and BA. J. ASHS. 104(2):162-164. 1979.

BLAIR, D. S. et al. Strawberry culture in eastern Canada. Canada Dept. of Agr. (Ottawa) Pub. 1005 19 pp. Request latest.

BLATT, C. R. P and B interaction on growth of strawberries. HortSci. 11(6):597-9. 1976.

BLOMMERS, J. Glasshouse strawberries. Res. Sta. for Fruit Growing, Wilhelminadorp, Nether. Publ. 2. 64 p. 1974. Strawberries in open. 48 pp. 1973. (In Dutch)

BOE, A. A., et al. 'Cataldo' everbearing strawberry. HortSci. 13(3):303. 1978.

BOXUS, P. H. Production of strawberry plants by *in vitro* micro-propagation. J. HortSci. 49:209-10. 1974.

BOXUS, P. H. et al. Large scale production of strawberry plants from tissue culture. In applied and Fundamental Aspects of Plant Cell, Tissue and Organ Culture by J. Reinert (Ed.) at al. Verlag Co., Berlin, Heidelberg, New York City. 1977.

BOYCE, B.R. and D.L. MATLOCK. Strawberry Nutrition in Fruit Nutrition. Ed. by N.F. Childers. Horticultural Publications, 3906 NW 31 Pl., Gainesville, Fla. 32606. 518-548. 1966.

BOYCE, B. R. and R. P. Marini. Cold acclimation of everbearing strawberry blossoms. HortSci. 13(5):543-544. 1978.

BREEN, P. J. and L. W. Martin. N effects on three cultivars of strawberry. ASHS J. 106:3:266-272. May 1981.

BROWN, G. R. and J. N. Moore. Inheritance of Strawberry Fruit Detachment. J. ASHA. 100:569. 1975.

California Agriculture, published by Univ. of Calif., Davis, has monthly items regarding strawberries. Examples are: Effects of Alar and top removal on yield of Fresno strawberries at three digging dates, Feb. 1968; Sequoia and Tioga, new California strawberry varieties, May 1968, April 1964 respectively; preplant fertilizers on winter planted strawberries, Oct. 1963; water penetration in strawberries aided by seeding grain in furrows, Apr. 1966: control of strawberry powdery mildew, Feb. 1967; Strawberry irrigation systems. 7/73. Ramularia leafspot. 6/74. Botrytis rot control. 2/74. Tarp thickness, dosage, fumigation strawberries. 12/73.

California Strawberry Advisory Board (under State Dir. of Agr., P. O. Box 269, Watsonville, Calif. 95076) issues frequent newsletter advice to growers, others, from planting to marketing. (Priced)

CAMPBELL, Roy E. and E. A. Taylor. Strawberry insects—how to control them. USDA Farmers' Bull. 2184, 20 pp. Update

CHILDERS, Norman F. Fruit Nutrition, Chapter 13. Strawberry nutrition by Bertie R. Boyce and D. L. Matlock. pp 518-548. Horticultural Publication. 3906 NW 31 Pl., Gainesville, Fla. 32606.

CHILDERS, N. F., Ed. The Strawberry. Proc. 1980 Nat. Strawb. Confer., St. Louis, Mo. 600 pp. $21.90; Foreign $25.00. 3906NW31PL., Gainesville, Fl. 32606. 1981.

CHOMA, M. E. et al. Fruiting effects on strawberry photosynthesis, respiration. HortSci. 17(2):212-213. 1982.

CHOMA, M.E. and Himelrick, D. G. Ethephon on day-neutral and everbearing strawberry. HortSci. 17:(5):773-4. 1982.

CLEMENT, S. L. et al. Black cutworm pheromone trapping in strawberries. Calif. Agr. 18-21. July 1982.

CONVERSE, R. H. and L. W. Martin. Strawberry cultivars compared for virus content, runner and fruit production. J. ASHS 99(2):163. March 1974.

COURTER, J. W. ED. Annual Illinois Strawberry Schools Proc. Univ. of Ill., Simpson. 62985. (Very good Update Info.) Priced proceedings.

COURTER, J. W., and C. M. Sabota. Data Collection by Customer Harvest of Small Fruits. HortSci. 16(1):59-60, 1981.

CRANDALL, P. C. and J. E. Middleton. Scheduling Irrigation of Strawberries from Pan Evaporation. Wa St. Univ. Cir. 581. 15 p. 1975.

DARROW, G. M. The strawberry: history, breeding, physiology, 447 pp. Holt, Rinehart and Winston. New York, Chicago. San Francisco. USA. 1966.

DARROW G. M., J. R. McGrew, and D. H. Scott. Reducing virus and nematode damage to strawberry plants. U. S. Dept. of Agr. Leaflet 414.8 pp. Update.

DAUBENY, Hugh. The Strawberry in Canada. In the strawberry book. 600 pp. 1981. 3906NW. 31 Pl., Gainesville, Fla. 32606. ($22.00).

DAUBENY, A. and H. S. Pepin. Strawberry clones for fruit rot resistance. J. ASHS. 102(4):431-435. 1977.

DAUBENY, H. A. et al. Performance of cold-stored stawberry cultivars in Pacific Northwest. HortSci. 1(2):101. 1976.

DAUBENY, H. A. British Columbia red raspberry, strawberry breeding. Fruit. Var. J. 32(1):2-5. 1978.

DODGE, J. C. et al. Growing strawberries in Washington. Wash. Agr. Ext. Serv. Bull. 246. 19 pp. Request recent edition.

DRAPER, A. D. et al. 'Tribute', 'Tristar' everbearer strawberries. HortSci. 16(6). 794. Dec. 1981.

EAVES, C. A. and J. S. Leefe. Ca sprays on strawberry firmness. Canadian J. Pl. Sci. 42:746-7. 1962.

FISHER, E. G. and Ray Sheldrake. Growing strawberries for home use. Cornell Exten. Bull. 943. Request recent edition.

FRANK, J. Ray, et al. Sorting strawberries by size. HortSci. 13(3):276-277. 1978.

FUNT, R. C. Growing strawberries in your garden. Univ. of Md. Fact. Sheet 223. 1976.

GALLANDER, J. F. Amino acids and strawberry time of harvest. HortSci (1):48-49. 1979.

GALLETTA, G. J. The 'Scott' strawberry. HortSci. 15:(4):541-2. Aug. 1980.

GALLETTA, G. and A. D. Draper, 'Allstar' Strawberry. HortSci. 16(6). 792-3. 1981.

GALLETTA, G. et al. USDA Strawberry breeding program. HortSci. 16(6) 743-6. Dec. 1981.

Genetic Engineering. Calif. Agr. Special Issue 36 p. August 1982.

GINDER, G. and H. Hoecker. Management of pick-your-own marketing operations. Dela. Coop. Extg. Serv., Newark, pp. 66. Request update.

HANLON, W. L. and A. Hamilton. Production costs of strawberries in Atlantic provinces, Canada. 50 p. A81-800. May 1981.

HARVEY, J. N., et al. Air transport of Calif. strawberries by modified atmospheres. USDA Mkt. Res. Rpt. 920. 10 pp. 1971.

HARVEY, J. M. et al. Truck shipments of strawberries from California; temp., CO₂, effects. USDA AAT-W-12. July 1980. Also, Plant Disease Rptr. 57:1. Jan. 1973.

HERTZ, L. B. Sudangrass straw, poly mulches on 'Trumpeter' strawberry. HortSci. 14(3):236-8. June 1979.

HILL, R. G., Jr. Growing strawberries in Ohio. Ohio Coop. Ext. Serv. Bull. 436. 16 pp. 1975.

HOLLAND, A. H. et al. Strawberry production in southern California. Calif. Agr. Ext. Serv. AXT-50, 16 pp. Request recent edition.

HOWARD, C. M. and E. E. Albregts. The 'Dover' strawberry. HortSci. 15:(4):540. Aug. 1980.

HUFFAKER, C. B. and C. E. Kenneth. Experimental studies on predation: predation and cyclamen-mite population on strawberries in California. Hilgardia 26: 4 pp. 191-222. October, 1956.

HUGHES, et al. Mycorrhizal influence on strawberries. J. ASHS. 103(2):179-181. 1978.

HULL, Jerome, Jr. Commerical strawberry culture in Michigan, Mich. Ext. Bull. E-682. Update.

IBRAHIM, A. M. F. et al. Chromosome behavior in strawberry during meiosis. J. ASHS 106(4):522-26. 1981.

JANICK, J. and J. Moore (Eds) Adv. in Fruit Breeding. Purdue Univ. Press, Lafayette, Ind. Strawberries, by D. Scott and F. Lawrence. p. 71-98. 1975.

JOHANSON, Frank D. Nutrient deficiencies of strawberries. Bull. in color. 40 p. 1980. 5th St., Everett, Wa. 98201.

JOHN, Matt K. et al. Sampling Time on Composition of Strawberry Leaves, Petioles. J. ASHA. 100:513. 1975.

KARTHA, K. K. et. al. Cryopreservation of Strawberry Meristems and Mass Propagation. J. ASHS 105(4):481-484. 1980.

KEEFER, R. F. et al. Strawberry yields, soil fumigation, nitrogen. HortSct. 13(1). 51-52. 1978.

KIDDER, E. H. and J. R. Davis. Frost protection with sprinkler irrigation. Mich. Ext. Bull. 327. Request update.

KRAUSS, R. E. Canoga and Honeoye strawberries. Fruit Var. Jour. 34(1):21. Jan. 1980.

LAWRENCE, F. J. et al. 'Linn' Strawberry. HortSci. 13(4):489-90. 1978.

LITTLE, C. R. et al. Storage treatment of strawberry runners for summer planting, Aust. J. of Exp. Agr. and An. Husb. 14: 118-121. 1974.

LOCASCIO, S. J. and J. M. Myers Trickle irrigation and fertilization of strawberries. Florida State Hort Soc. 58. 185-189. 1975.

LOCASIO, S. J. et al. Sprinkler irrigation of strawberries for freeze protection. Fla. St. Hort. Soc. Proc. 208-11. For Nov. 1967

LOCKHART, C. L. and C. A. Eaves. CA storage of strawberry plants. Can. J. of Pl. Sci. 46:151-154. 1966.

MAAS, J. L. Red stele of strawberry: Soil pH, pathogen, and cultivar interactions. HortSci. 11(3):258-60. 1976.

MAAS, J. L. Resistance to fruit rot in strawberries and red raspberries: review. Hort-Sci. 13(4):423-6. 1978.

MAAS, J. L. and W. L. Smith, Jr. 'Earliglow' resistance to Botrytis fruit rot. HortSci. 13(3):275-6. 1978.

MARINI, R. P. and B. R. Boyce. Low temperature during dormancy on 'Catskill' strawberry. J. ASHS. 104(2):159-62. 1979.

MARTIN, L. and J. R. Morris. Strawberry Mechanization. Ore. Sta. Bul. 645. 250 p. 1980.

MARTIN, L. W. and P. J. PELOFSKI. Comparison 5 strawberry cultivars for hand, machine harvesting. Fruit Var. Journ. 37:(2). 37-41. 1983.

MC CALLEY, N. F. and N. C. Welch. Furadan controls root weevil on strawberries. Cal Agr. 16-17. June 1978.

MCGREW, J. R. Strawberry diseases, USDA Farmers' Bull. 2140. 27 pp. Recent edition.

MELVILLE, A. H. et al. Seed germination, vigor in inbred strawberry selections. Hort Sci. 15:(6)749-50.

MELVILLE, A. H., et al. Transmission of red stele resistance by inbred strawberry selections. J. ASHA 105 (4): 608-10. 1980.

MILLER, P. W. and R. O. Belkengren. Elimination of certain virus complexes from strawberries by excision and culturing of apical meristems. Pl. Disease Reporter 47:4. 298-300. 1963.

MINCHINTON, I. R. et al. Poultry Manure Phytotoxicity. J. Sci. Rd. Agric. 24: 1437-1448. 1973.

MITCHELL, F. G. and G. Mayer. Basket design on holding strawberries. Calif. Agr. 32(5):17-18. 1978.

MONTELARO, Joseph, et al. Growing Louisiana strawberries. La. Agr. Ext. Serv. 1096, 21 pp. Request recent edition.

MOORE, J. N. Insect pollination of strawberries. J. ASHS 94(4):362-364. 1969

MOORE, J. N. and H. L. Bowden. Date of planting effects on strawberries. J. Am. Soc. Hort. Sci. 91:231-235. 1968.

MOORE, J. N. et al. Strawberry Clones for Once-over Mechanical Harvest. HortSci. 10: 407-8. Force to detach berries. HortSci. 10: 405-6. 1975.

MORRIS, J. R., et al. A mechanized system for production, harvesting and handling of strawberries. HortSci. 13(4): 413-22. 1978.

MORRIS, J. R., et al. Acetaldehyde on quality of mechanically harvested strawberries for processing. J. ASHS. 104(2):262-4. 1979.

MORRIS, J. R. and D. L. Cawthon. Post-harvest Quality of Machine-harvested strawberries. J. ASHS 104 (1):138-41. 1979.

MULLIN, R. H. and D. E. Schlegel. Cold-storage maintenance of strawberry meristem plantlets. HortSci. 11(2): 100. 1976.

MULLINS, C. A. et al. Performance of New Strawberry Cultivars in Tennessee. Fruit Var. Jour. 35:1. Jan. 1981.

NIJSSE, L. Strawberry growing in narrow plastic tunnels. Klein-fruitteeltadviezen 1: 2-4. Varieties. Kleinfr, 2:5-7. (In Dutch). 1974.

North American Strawberry Growers Association changes hdqtrs. recently John Tompkins, Pomology, Cornell Univ., Ithaca, N.Y. 14850.

NISHI, Sadas and Katruji Oshawa. Mass Production method of virus-free strawberry plants through meristem callus. Japanese Ann. Res. Quarterly 7:3 189-94. 1973.

NYE, William P. and J. LaMar Anderson. Insect pollinators on strawberry: effect on yield, quality. J. ASHS 99(1): 40. Jan. 1973.

OEHLER, Nellie, Home freezing fruits, vegetables. Wash. Ext. Bull. 658. 4/1975.

OURECKY, D. K. Berries in New York, N.Y. Food and Life Sci. Bull. Geneva. 39. 6 p. 1974.

OURECKY, D. K. and J. E. Reich, Frost tolerance in strawberry cultivars. HortSci. 11(4):413-14. 1976.

OURECKY, D. K. Small fruit breeding program; New York. Frt. Var. J. 32: 3. 50-57. 1978.

PARKER, B. L. and R. P. Marini. Strawberry deformities Vt. Bull. 683. 13 p. 1978.

Pest, disease control-strawberries. Calif. Agr. Exp. Sta.& Exp. Serv. Bull. 12 pp. Jan. Update.

PELOFSKE, P. J. and L. W. Martin. Effects of mechanical harvest on strawberry renovation. HortSci. 17(2):211-212. 1982.

PORTER, F. M. and W. H. Tietjen. Containers for strawberry shipment HortSci. 8(4):307. August 1973.

POE, S. L. Chemicals for the control of spider mites on strawberries. Proc. Fla. State Hort. Soc. 121-123. 1973.

RENQUIST, A. R., et al. Poly mulch, summer irrigation on fruiting of 'Olympus' strawberry. J. ASHS 107:(3) 373-6. 369-372. 1982.

ROBSON, M. G., and L. A. Miller. Small Fruit Production Manual. N. J. Coop. Ext. Ser. Bull. 432, April 1981.

ROSATI, P. et al. Anther culture of strawberry. HortSci. 10:119-20.

1975.

ROSATI, P. and D. H. Scott. Comparison of strawberry cultivars, Po Valley, Italy. Fruit Var. Jour. 29:50-54. 1975.

SCHAEFERS, G. A. Deformed strawberries by tarnished plant bug. Farm Res. (N.Y. Ag. Exp. Sta., Geneva) June-Aug. 1963.

SCHAEFERS, George A. Lorsban for strawberry "Bud" weevil in Strawberries. Down to Earth. 35:1. 1-3. Fall 1978.

SCOTT D. H. Forcing strawberries (in USA): unexplored. Amer. Fruit Grower. 2 p. May 1975.

SCOTT D. H. Preservation of small fruits germplasm. Fruit Varieties 28:83-85. 1974.

SCOTT D. H. et al. Screening strawberries for resistance to phytophthora. Plant Dis. Rep. 59 (3):207. 1975.

SCOTT D. H. Strawberries in S. E. USA. USDA Farmer's Bull. 2246. 33pp. 1977.

SCOTT D. H. and F. J. Lawrence. Strawberry breeding, in Advances in Fruit Breeding. by J. Janick and J. N. Moore, Editors. Purdue Univ. Press. W. Lafayette, Ind. 71-97. 1975.

SCOTT D. H. et al. Strawberry varieties in the U. S. USDA Farmer's Bull. 1043. 16 pp. Request update.

SCOTT, D. H. and A. D. Draper. Reaction of strawberry seedings inoculated with race composites of Phytophthora fragariae Hickman. J. ASHS. 101(4):355-358. 1976.

SCOTT, D. H. Mass Screening of Young Strawberry Seedlings for Resistance to Phytophthora fragaria Hickman. HortSci. 11(3):257-8. 1976.

SEELIG, R. A. Strawberries (botany to harvest, shipping, nutritive value retailing) 24 pp. ($1.90) United Fresh Fr. and Vege. Ass'n. 1019 19th St. NW. Wash., D.C. 20036. 2/1975.

SETH, J. N. and S. D. Lal. New varieties of Strawberry for U. P. Hills (India). Fruit Var. Jour. 34(1):11-13. Jan. 1980.

SHOEMAKER, J. S. Small fruit culture. Avi Publ. Co., Westport, Conn. 339 pp. 1975.

SISTRUNK, W. A., et al. Treatments for color stability of frozen machine-harvested strawberries, J. ASHS 107:(4) 693-7. 1982.

SISTRUNK, W. A. and J. R. Morris. Storage stability of mechanically-harvested strawberry products. J. ASHS. 103(5):616-20. 1978.

SPAYD, S. E., et al. Peroxidase Polyphenol Oxidase on Puree of Machine-harvested Strawberries. The Strawberry 600 p. Hort. Publ., Gainesville, Fl. N. F. Childers, Ed. 1981.

SPAYD, S. E. and J. R. Morris. Immature strawberry fruit and holding on puree quality. ASHS 106(2) 211-16. March 1981.

SPRAY schedules for strawberries: Contact your local, federal provincial or state agricultural extension service or experiment station for up-to-date spray schedules. See also Chapter XVIII.

SOMMER, N. F. et al. Reduction of postharvest losses of strawberry fruits from gray mold. J. ASHS 98(3):285. 1973.

STOLTZ, L. P., et al. Mineral nutrition of strawberry plants in relation to mite injury. J. ASHS 95(5):601-603. 1970.

Strawberries, Bull. 95, Her Majesty's Stationery Office, London, Engl 84 p. Update

Strawberries in California. Write to Victor Voth. Pomology, Univ. of Calif., Davis, 95616 for latest Bulls., since they are producing 75% of the U. S. crop at high, low elevations, winter and summer. 1983.

TAFOZOLI, E. and B. Shaybany. N. deblossoming, growth regulators on the 'Gem' everbearing strawberry. J. ASHS 103 (3):372-4. 1978.

TOMPKINS, J. P. and D. K. Ourecky. Growing strawberries in New York State. Cornell Info. Bull. 15. 14 pp. Request recent edition. Ourecky. D. K. Varieties — berries, N. Y. Bull. 39. March 1974.

ULRICH, Al. et al. Guide to strawberry nutrient deficiencies (color-very good) Univ. of Ca., Berkeley 94720. 60 p. Priced. 1980.

VOTH, Victor. Strawberry irrigation systems. Calif. Agric. Sept. 1973. Seek update.

VOTH, Victor. et al. Bed system, bed height, clear polyethylene mulch, effects on yield, soil salt and temperature in California strawberries. J. Am. Soc. Hort. Sci. 91:242-248. 1968.

WAISTER, P. D. Yield of 'Olympus' strawberry. Fruit Var. Jour. 33(4):136-43. 1979.

WAITHAKA, K. et al. Growth substances and growth of strawberry stolons and leaves. J. ASHS 103 (4):480-482: 103:(5)627-28. 1978.

WALL, G. B. et al. Pick-your-own marketing (very good). Univ. of Fla. IFAS cir. 481. 34 p. 1980.

WAY, D. W. Further observations on the field performance of heat-treated strawberry clones. Journ. Hort. Sci. 40:No. 2., 167-174. Apr. 1965.

WEBB, R. A. and D. G. Hollas. The effect of iron supply on strawberry, var. Royal Sovereign. J. Hort. Sci. 41:179-188. 1966.

Weeds, Insects, Disease Control in Washington. 18 p. Issued annually. 1982.

WELCH, N. C. et al. Control of strawberry fruit rot caused by Botrytis. California Agriculture 1974. (February).

WELCH, N. C. et al. N. stabilization with nitrapyrin for strawberries. Calif. Agr. 12-13. Sept. 1979.

WELCH, N. C. and James Quick. Fertilizing summer planted strawberries, Calif. Central Coast Ca. Agr. Sept.-Oct. 1981.

WELCH, N. C. et al. Strawberry production in California. Calif. Leaflet 2959. 14 pp. 1982.

WETHERELL, D. F. Introduction to in vitro propagation. Avery Publ. Group, Inc., 87 pp. Wayne, N. J. 07470. 1981.

WILHELM, Stephen. Diseases of strawberry — a guide for the commercial grower. The Strawberry by N. Childers, Ed. Horticultural Public., 3906 NW 31 Pl., Gainesville, Fla. 32606. 1981.

WORTHINGTON, John T. Successful response of cold-stored strawberry plants dug in the fall. J. ASHS 95(3):262-266. 1970.

NOTE: Poland ranks high in world strawberry production. For European trends, varieties and culture, contact the Director, Institute for Pomology Research, Skierniewice, Poland.

NOTE: The formulations, chemicals and recommendations for weed control in strawberries are changing year to year. Contact your weed specialist at your local university or experiment station or your county agricultural agent for latest recommendations for your area.

(See additional references in former book editions.)

CHAPTER XXII

Bush Fruits

INTRODUCTION

Included among the bush berry fruits of commercial importance are the brambles, (caneberries), gooseberry, currant, and blueberry. The blueberry has shown a marked increase in popularity in recent years, but it, like the cranberry, is of commercial importance only in a few areas of the world. The cranberry also is discussed briefly in this chapter, but actually, it is too prostrate to be considered a bush fruit in the strict sense of the term.

THE BRAMBLES[1]

The brambles are perennial plants that have a biennial growth and fruiting habit. Included are raspberry (red, black, yellow, white, purple), blackberry, trailing dewberry and their hybrids and mutations. The brambles differ somewhat in climatic requirements. Where one succeeds, the other may produce poorly or not at all. Thus, more than half of the raspberry acreage in the United States, according to the U. S. Census, is confined to four northern states; namely Michigan, 8,010 acres; Oregon, 2100; Washington, 2800; and New York, 2213 (see Figure 1). Raspberry acreage in the South is limited to the high cool elevations, although there is a tropical black raspberry *(Rubus albescens),* grown in south Florida, cultivars Mysore, Ceylon and Hill. The Loganberry, probably a red-fruited sport of the wild blackberry, is confined more or less to the Pacific Coast where over two-thirds of the acreage (450) is in the Willamette Valley of Oregon. Loganberries are canned, frozen, used fresh, crushed into juice and wine, whereas the red and black raspberries are used fresh in jams, ice creams and jellies or frozen for pies. The flavor and aroma of raspberries can hardly be equalled by any fruit.

The general decline of commercial brambles, particularly in the USA, has been due largely to poor nursery stock, viruses, child labor laws and increased hand-labor costs. A general upturn in production is likely with use of

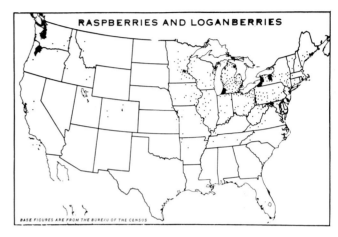

Figure 1. Raspberries thrive better in the upper-cool states. Michigan, Oregon, Washington and New York lead. Loganberries are grown in the West, principally the Willamette Valley of Oregon. The lower Fraser River Valley, British Columbia, is important in red raspberries as is the cool coast area south of San Francisco, California. Black dots indicate commercial areas. (USDA)

herbicides, "virus-free" stock, improved cultivars[2] (Table 2) and mechanical and pick-your-own harvesting.

Table 1 may be of interest to the prospective small fruits grower to evaluate the various fruit crops with respect to his own conditions. Raspberries and the thorned blackberry apparently have some advantages.

World raspberry production by leading countries in 100's of metric tons is approximately as follows: U.S., 325; Germany (all), 225; U.K. (Scotland), 165; Yugoslavia, 160; Hungary, 125; Poland, 110; Canada, 85; Netherlands, 50; France, 45; Norway, 25; and Australia, 15. Poland is expanding plantings.

The *red raspberry (Rubus idaeas)* produces fruit on leafy shoots of erect one-yr. slender canes. It is progagated by suckers which arise from the roots of the parent canes. Typical red cultivars are Latham, Newburgh, Taylor, Cuthbert and Willamette with Southland, Canby, Liberty and Hertiage (Figure 3) gaining in popularity and withstanding many difficult winters. Reveille (PYO-soft), Citadel and Sentry are cultivars released from the

[1]Thanks to Dr. Richard C. Funt of Ohio State University, Columbus, 43210, for this revision and W. Arden Sheets, Wash. Co. Ext. Agt., Hillsboro, Ore., Dr. Robert G. Hill, Jr., Ohio Agr. Res. and Devel. Center, Wooster, 44691, and Dr. D. K. Ourecky, formerly N.Y. Agr. Exp. Sta., Geneva, 14456, who have helped revise the brambles in former editions of this book.

[2]Raspberry breeders are developing aphid (the virus vector) resistant cultivars and also resistance or tolerance to spur blight, fruit rots, other problems.

TABLE 1. ESTIMATED PER-ACRE COSTS, YIELDS, PRICES AND REQUIREMENTS OF LABOR AND CUSTOMERS FOR SMALL FRUITS IN SOUTHERN ILLINOIS IN 1982. (UNIVERSITY OF ILLINOIS, SIMPSON 62985).

Fruit	Establishment[a]		Annual production requirements[b]		Yield	PYO prices	Gross sales	PYO sales to harvest
	Time	Total cost	Labor	Cost				
	years	dollars	hours	dollars	pounds	dollars per pound	dollars	number
Strawberry	1¼	$2,056	74	$1,253	8,000	$.50	$4,000	400
Black raspberry	2	1,843	110	819	2,700	.80	2,160	180
Red raspberry	1-2	1,081	40[c]	569	4,000	.80	3,200	300
Blackberry								
Thorned	2	999	38	520	4,900	.80	3,920	300
Thornless	2	2,556	92	844	9,000	.80	7,200	450
Blueberry	4	2,718	124	1,017	6,000	.75	4,500	450
Grape	3	2,857	63	697	8,000	.33	2,646	800 table 80 wine

[a]Includes plants, materials, labor, equipment, and fixed costs to first commercial harvest. This cost is spread over several seasons.
[b]Includes all production costs and fixed costs, except harvest and land costs.
[c]Low labor requirement for fall crop system.

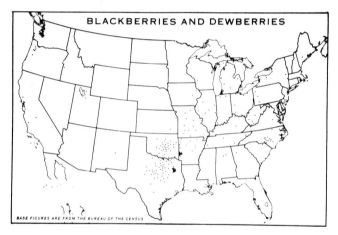

Figure 2. Blackberries are grown in a warmer climate than raspberries. Leading states are Oregon and Texas. Leading areas for the dewberry or trailing blackberry are Berrien County, Michigan; Hudson River Valley, New York; and North Carolina. They are mostly erect in the southern U.S. Black dots indicate commercial areas. (USDA)

University of Maryland and have done well in Wisconsin, New York, Ohio and Pennsylvania.

There are yellow and white fruited raspberries. Golden Queen is a yellow cultivar; Gold West, from the Washington State Station, is better for the Northwest. Amber is a large conic berry. Malling Orion and Admiral are under test in England.

The *black raspberry, (Rubus occidentalis)* often called "blackcap," bears black and somewhat more seedy and aromatic fruit than the red raspberry. Canes of the black raspberry, as contrasted with the red, become arched in late summer and take root at tips. These rooted tips can be cut away from the parent plant and used for propagation material. "Blackcaps" in general are not as hardy as some red cultivars and are grown where temperatures do not drop below -15 to -18°F. Cultivars such as Early Logan, Logan, Bristol, Allen, Jewel and Dundee are popular while

Figure 3. Growers, backyard gardeners, Northeastern USA, may wish to grow fall bearing red raspberries that bear a crop on the tips of current season's growth and another crop the following summer on lower portion of canes. Heritage cultivar (New York), shown here is widely adapted from Illinois to Maine, has erect canes, fruit medium size, firm, good quality. Bears fall crop on upper ¼ to ⅓ of canes, ripening 3 wks. earlier than the September everbearer. Commercially for PYO, grow fall crop only, sickle-bar mow within 3 inches of ground after frost; canes erect, don't need support, fruits will not melt or crumble, yields high. Big acreages are being planted for pick-your-own fall-crop management only (Courtesy Donald K. Ourecky, formerly N.Y. State Agr. Exp. Sta., Geneva, 14456).

Cumberland, Huron, Pearl and Black Hawk are less popular. Lowden black raspberry has shown promising resistance against orange rust disease.

Everbearers or fall bearing red raspberries, as Heritage, Fallred and Scepter bear a summer and fall crop. Only Heritage produces 85% or more of its crop on current season canes. Fall bearing cultivars make fruiting possible where winter temperatures may injure or kill summer-type fruiting cultivars. Mulching and/or irrigation is needed through the months of July and August to allow optimal fruit numbers and size. Fall crop raspberries can be either PYO or wholesale because cooler days and night temperatures aid in firm berries which reduces spoilage (Figure 3). However, fall bearing cultivars require a larger number of pesticide applications. There are no commercially good everbearing black raspberries.

Purple-fruited raspberries (Rubus eubatus) are hybrid crosses of red and black raspberries. They are generally more vigorous and productive than the parents, but resemble the blacks in habit and propagation. The cultivars Clyde, Marion, Sodus and Amethyst are less popular than the new Brandywine. Royalty is a 1982 release which is hardy and resistant to raspberry aphid and fruitworm.

The *blackberry (Rubus allegheniensis)* differs from the black raspberry in that the black raspberry fruit separates from the receptacle at harvest. The harvested blackberry contains the receptacle and both the berry and receptacle are eaten.

Blackberries, both erect and trailing types (*R. allegheniensis* and *R. canadensis,* respectively), can withstand more heat and dryness, less cold than raspberries (Figure 2). The upright cultivars can tolerate -18° to -20° F. However, cold driving winds can cause tip burn and lower yields. In Arkansas, J. N. Moore has crossed Brazos w/Darrow to obtain adapted cultivars as Cherokee, Comanchee and Cheyenne which have done well also in central Ohio at -17°. United States rank in blackberries is Oregon, Texas, Washington and Michigan. For Boysen, Logan and Young berries, the rank of states is: Oregon, California, and Arkansas. A limited acreage of blackberries is found on a line from Maine to Missouri. Commercial dewberry sections are Berrien County, Michigan; the Hudson River Valley of New York; North Carolina and northeastern Texas. Brison, Rosborough and Nomek are new Texas cultivars.

The *erect blackberries* grow wild in many areas of the U.S. Improved cultivars have firmer, better keeping fruit with earlier ripening seasons. Raven, Ranger (Md.), Cheyenne, Comanche, Cherokee (Ark.) and Darrow are erect types and are hardier than the trailing (thornless) types. However, the thornless ones can produce nearly three times the yield of erects when grown under the proper environment.

The *trailing blackberry (referred to as running or ground blackberry or dewberry;* northern is *R. flagellaris;*

TABLE 2. SUGGESTED RASPBERRY AND BLACKBERRY CULTIVARS BY REGIONS.

New England North Central	Mid Atlantic Mid West	Northwest
Red Raspberries		
Latham	Latham	Canby
Newburgh	Newburgh	Fairview
Hilton	Hilton	Newburgh
Canby	Canby	Willamette
Citadel	Reveille	Puyallup
Reveille	Heritage	Summer
Heritage	Southland	Washington
Taylor	Taylor	eeker
Milton	Fallred	
Black Raspberries		
Allen	New Logan	Plum Farmer
Bristol	Bristol	Munger
Dundee	Jewel	
Huron	Allen	
Purple Raspberries		
Amethyst	Brandywine	
Brandywine		
Sodus		
Blackberry - Erect		
Eldorado	Raven	
Darrow	Ranger	
Hedrick	Cheyenne	
Alfred	Darrow	
Blackberry - Trailing		
	Thornfree[1]	Thornless Evergreen
	Smoothstem	Young
	Black Satin	Boysen
	Dirksen	Aurora
	Hull	Chehalem
		Marion

1. Not cold hardy below -10°F.
2. Floridagrand (Florida); Mayes (Texas) are specific trailing types for their area.

southern is *R. trivialis)* has a semi-erect to prostrate growth habit. Semi-erect hybrid cultivars as the Aurora, Chahalem, Marion and Thornless Evergreen blackberry cultivars are grown in mild climates of the northwest coast (Table 2). Young and Boysen lead in the West and South. The thornless blackberry cultivars grown east of the Mississippi River are Smoothstem, Thornfree, Black Satin, Dirksen and Hull. These cultivars all lack the cold hardiness of erect types and cannot be grown without winter protection when temperatures during any part of the winter approach -10°F. Thornfree and Smoothstem are not as hardy or as productive as Dirksen, Black Satin or Hull. Hull and Dirksen have been the most productive and highest quality in southern Ohio.

Bramble culture in the United States is limited to rather definite regions due to sensitiveness to extremes of heat, cold, and excess or deficiencies of moisture. You should determine from the accompanying Figures (Table 1), the foregoing discussion, and your neighbor's experience, which of the brambles is most likely to succeed and be profitable in your locality. Most commercial growers rarely plant more than 10 to 50 acres, usually less than 20. Fresh sales are more or less limited to local towns and cities, but in Oregon 50-100 acres are machine harvested

Figure 4. (Top left) Bundle of 27 Taylor red raspberries as shipped from nursery. These should be heeled in, as shown at top right if they are not to be planted immediately. (Bottom left) All three are good nursery plants. Note difference between Taylor red raspberry, left, Columbian purple raspberry, center, and Cumberland black raspberry, right. The right plant has been propagated by a cane tip being covered by soil and taking root (tip layerage). (Bottom right) Raspberry plants should be fertilized with ammonium sulfate or a complete fertilizer about one month after planting, using two medium-sized handfuls per plant and distributed as shown. (Bottom right) Ohio Agr. Exp. Sta.; (Others) U.S.D.A.

with up to 95% preserved by frozen-pack and canning. Since the fruit is soft and highly perishable, the crop must be either disposed of quickly in the fresh state or preserved. If to be processed, an early contract should be made with the processor. Many growers are planting brambles specifically for the pick-your-own trade.

Selecting the site and soil. Good air drainage is important in reducing danger from spring frosts, winter injury, and diseases in regions where troublesome. A northern slope is not necessary but preferred, because the brambles naturally respond well to cool areas somewhat protected from the hot sun. Areas subjected to drifting snow, winds, are undesireable due to breakage of the canes, although some snow cover will help to protect the canes from winter injury. Brambles will grow on a wide range of soils from coarse sand to medium loams, provided they are *well drained* to a depth of at least three

feet, preferably deeper. It has been shown that the leaves of brambles lose moisture more rapidly than those of most fruit plants, and, *thus, provision for adequate soil moisture throughout the season is one of the most important factors in successful bramble culture (Figure 5).* The incorporation of organic matter to help retain moisture, as recommended for the strawberry in the previous chapter, is most important. In general, the red, black, and purple raspberries and the erect blackberry perform best on medium loams, while the trailing blackberry will tolerate heavier soils. Select *Verticillium* free soils (don't follow tomato, potato, eggplant, pepper or previous brambles). Isolate the black raspberry from the red raspberry because insects will transmit virus from one to the other. Erect blackberry, thornless blackberry and purple raspberry can be planted near black raspberry when virus-free plants and a good insecticide program is used.

Figure 5. This is a first-year planting of brambles in Oregon, Willamette Valley north of Corvallis, solid set irrigation usable also for frost control, rows 10 ft apart with plants 5 ft apart in the row and a 2-wire vertical trellis. (W. Arden Sheets, Ore. State Univ. Ext. Serv., Hillsboro, Ore. 97123)

Remove wild brambles or use herbicides to control them at least 1,000 feet away from planting.

The best and safest source of planting stock is from a reliable nursery which sells registered stock. *Registered stock* (or virus-free stock) is propagated from virus-free material and is labeled as such from an inspector or state department of agriculture. Certified plants are inspected to be free of disease. Stock obtained from old plantations or neighboring growers should be selected with extreme care to avoid mosaic, anthracnose, etc.

A new method of rapidly propagating raspberries from tissue culture (see Chap. XXI) has been developed. Not all species are easily propagated by this method.

As pointed out earlier, the red raspberry produces new plants from the roots of the parent plant; 1-yr. plants (avoid older ones) are dug and bundled for shipment by the nurserymen, as shown in Figure 4. Black raspberries and purple raspberries are propagated from tips of canes which have bent over and taken root. If many plants are desired for propagation, canes at the "rat tail" stage of tips, before they touch ground, are inserted 2+ inches deep vertically behind a spade, soil pressed with foot, usually in early fall. Late summer stem cuttings can be rooted in mist bed.

Blackberries can be propagated from shoots from the roots as in the case of the red raspberry, using one-year plants. They are also propagated by root cuttings. In the fall, moderate to large roots of the blackberry are dug by nurserymen and cut into pieces two to four inches long. They are stored over winter in moist but not wet sand or sawdust in a cool place not subject to freezing. In the spring these roots are laid four to eight inches apart in furrows three to four inches deep and covered with friable soil. Under good cultivation and care the first season, the plants should be ready for sale and transplanting the following spring. Root cuttings can be made in the spring, but the percentage take is often considerably less. The plants also develop more slowly.

The *trailing blackberry* is propagated by tip layering or by stem cuttings similar to black and purple raspberries.

When ordering from the nursery, specify No. 1 grade state-inspected stock with vigorous root systems. Some cultivars of raspberry have been heat-treated by USDA and other specialists, as with strawberry, to free them of the troublesome viruses. Virus-free raspberry cultivars should be specified where available and a program of planting and dusting followed to keep them free of vectors. The availability of virus-free stock[1] may serve as a stimulus to the raspberry industry bringing back this crop in areas where it has been failing because of unprofitable yields and relatively poor quality. If the plants cannot be set to the field immediately on arrival, they should be heeled-in, as shown in Figure 4, or stored at 32 °F in plastic bags.

Field Preparation and Planting. Field preparation as well as ordering plants should be done one to two years prior to planting. Control weeds by planting grain crops such as corn followed by wheat or rye. If perennial weeds as morning glory, thistle, quackgrass, nutsedge or poison ivy persist, use Roundup or similar herbicide on non-crop land in September or October. Fumigation with 67% methyl bromide and 23% chloropicrin can be very beneficial in controlling soil pathogens and nematodes. Fumigation is best accomplished in September after thorough plowing or rototilling to make the most use of fumigants but before soil temperatures are low and moisture is high.

Take a soil sample and have it tested for major and trace elements plus organic matter. Apply the recommended amounts of calcium, magnesium, phosphorus and potassium in the fall prior to spring planting. The pH of the soil should be 5.8 to 6.4, 80 to 100 pounds available phosphorus, 180 to 230 pounds magnesium and 280 to 320 pounds potassium per acre. Increase the organic matter to 2 to 3% by animal manures (8 to 10 tons per acre) or green (plant) manures as rye.

Spring planting is preferred so that roots can make better contact with the soil. In regions where winters are warm, fall planting may be successful when roots and stems are protected by mounding soil around them. Order 5 to 10% more plants of black or purple raspberries or blackberries than needed due to normal plant mortality.

[1]Most nurseries handling brambles have "virus-free" stock available. The New York Fruit Testing Association, Geneva, N.Y. 14456, was a pioneer in offering this stock for sale. Registered stock is fieldgrown, 4-yr. maximum, from screenhouse.

[1]In Oceania area, a good research small fruits station is at Levin, New Zealand. Write for reprints.

Red raspberries will fill in the row if only a few plants do not grow. Set the plants the same depth as they grew in the nursery.

Bramble cultivars will vary with the region, depending upon cane hardiness, productiveness, soil and climatic conditions and the way in which the fruit is utilized. Aside from adequate continuous moisture to the roots, *selection of the proper cultivar for the local conditions is of utmost importance for success*. It is suggested that you be in contact with your local governmental agricultural service (county agricultural agent, experiment station or university) to consult on the best up-to-date locally tested cultivars. Table 2 gives suggested cultivars by region. (See USDA Info. Bul 155 for raspberries, 97 for blackberries; Bull. 2165, N.Y. Exp. Sta. for descriptions).

Brambles have the possibility of transforming from a completely too-expensive-to-grow crop to one that is almost completely machine handled. This is a key objective. Bramble crops actually are in high demand by the public who will pay surprisingly good prices if available and of good quality.

Care should be taken in selecting *blackberries* to obtain varieties that are sufficiently hardy in the northern states. Eldorado answers this requirement best if stock true-to-name can be obtained. The acreage of cultivated blackberries has declined in recent years because it is difficult to get plants of true cultivars. Unknowingly, nurseries have sold virus-infected plants that produced little fruit, or they have sold wild plants as known cultivars.

For small farms specializing in PYO brambles, cultivars can be selected to provide production for most of the summer season. This attracts repeat sales from satisfied customers. Here is a suggested planting with approximate ripening dates in the Mid-Atlantic region: Reveille — red raspberry June 15-20; Southland — red raspberry June 20-25; Latham — red raspberry June 25-30; Jewel — black raspberry June 25 to July 4; Bristol — black raspberry June 28 to July 8; Brandywine — purple raspberry July 8 to July 15; Cheyenne — erect blackberry July 20 to Aug. 1; Dirksen — thornless blackberry July 20 to Aug. 5; and Heritage — red raspberry Aug. 20 to Sept. 20.

Planting plans. The distance between rows depends on the type of tractor and equipment the grower may own. For the small farmer or home gardener a small 12 to 20 horse power tractor less than 50'' in width for a 9 to 10 foot row width will be satisfactory. Special motor driven hydraulic sprayers with 25 to 100 gallon tanks can apply pesticides. This row distance is best where the slope of the land does not exceed 5 to 7%.

Growers who have larger equipment in the 35 to 40

horsepower range and between 50 and 64'' wide, need 12 feet between rows. Special trellis systems are required in some types to control plants to allow equipment to move down the row.

The main planting systems are the *hill, hedgerow* and *linear*. The *hill* system can be used in home gardens, cultivating both ways. Dewberries are frequently grown in hills, as with any of the brambles. The total yield is reduced as compared with the hedgerow system, but the fruits are large and usually of higher quality and are more easily harvested. A source of low-price stakes should be available. The hill system is suggested only on level or gently sloping land where erosion will not be a factor. The *hedgerow* system consists of a continuous row of canes covering a strip of ground about one to two feet wide at the base. It is adapted to the blackberry and to short-cane red raspberries such as Sunrise and Latham, which tend to throw many suckers from the roots, making it difficult to maintain the plants in hills. Cuthbert, however, will have slender stems which are often cut back lightly in spring so they can better support their crop. Also, cultivars with weak or relatively tall canes are supported by different types of trellises.

The *linear* training system is more or less a modification of both the hill and hedgerow systems, in which no suckers are allowed to develop and the width of the row is restricted by cultivation to the parent plants. The field is cultivated one way only. Black and purple raspberries and some red raspberries are grown by this method. It is about the only system used in Washington where canes of the Willamette and Meeker are grown quite tall and trellises are used. In and near Moscow, Russia, it also is used.

Red raspberries are planted about 2 ft. apart in the row to get a quick stand and reduce the chance of skips and unproductive space.

The black raspberry has a spreading and drooping growth habit and thus requires somewhat more space than the red raspberries. They are set as an average 2½ to 3 ft. in rows 10 to 12 ft. apart (Mech. Harv.). Purple raspberries are more vigorous than the black varieties and should be set at 3 ft. between plants and 10 to 12 ft. between rows. The same is true for erect blackberries. Trailing blackberry is set 5 to 8 feet in the rows (6 ft. for higher yields) and 12 to 14 ft. between rows.

Planting Brambles. In large plantings, plow out a planting furrow in one direction, then cross-mark to spot planting holes. If plants are somewhat dry, soak in water over night; if very dry check with nursery, for recovery and "take" may be poor. Take plants to field in tub of muddy water, or cover with wet burlap *to keep moist until planted*. Cloudy days, no wind, are best. "Handles" or canes (on reds) can be pruned back by hand or band-saw to facilitate planting. Be careful not to break off soft white shoots; do not cover with soil the curled upward shoots on

---

[1] For specific recommendations for growing boysenberries and Olallie blackberries, secure a copy of Univ. of Calif. Leaflet 2441, Berkeley 94720, 16 p.

black and purple raspberries. In small plantings, cross-mark the field, use a spade, sink into soil, push forward, spread roots, plant, firm the soil, cross-cultivate prior to installing trellis the next year. Use only well-rooted plants (Figure 4). A modified vegetable planter (Chap. 21) will speed commercial plantings.

Soil management. After planting, cultivation may be necessary to move soil toward plants. Herbicides such as Surflan and Devrinol can be applied over the plants to control weeds. Incorporation of these herbicides by rainfall or irrigation aid in weed control. A herbicide strip of 2 ft. on each side of the plants (total 3 to 4 ft.) will reduce competition for nutrients and moisture. A grass sod drive row of creeping red fescue is suggested to reduce soil compaction by equipment and reduce weeds which harbor insects and nematodes.

Trickle irrigation is best installed by burying the line, either the bi-wall or twin wall hose with orifices at 12 inches on the outside and 60 to 72'' on the insde. This gives the most uniform watering pattern. The line should be buried 4 to 8 inches deep and the system should be turned on immediately after installation.

Any practice which increases or maintains moisture supply among brambles is an important factor in success with these crops. The brambles are shallow rooted and are the first to show the affects of drought. Cultivate only deep enough to destroy weeds.

Cultivation should cease around the first of September and the hoe used thereafter to eliminate weeds, except in the colder northern states where even hoe weeding may induce succulent cane growth susceptible to winter injury. Cultivated vegetables, except for the nightshades tomato, pepper, eggplant *(Verticillium* wilt), may be grown between the bramble rows the first year, but they should be removed before the end of the season for the same reason. The better the weeds are controlled the previous year, the less the difficulty with them during the fruiting season.

Most growers do not cultivate the row after the first season. Herbicides can be used in the row and mowing between rows (grass drive row). Rototillers are used to maintain row width of 18 to 24'' on red raspberries and erect blackberries to reduce plant vigor, increase sunlight and pesticide penetration and reduce diseases. Spring tooth harrows also can be used to reduce row width.

In home gardens, mulching with straw or leaves 6 to 8 inches deep each year frequently is practiced to maintain moisture supply. Where mulch is used, either manure or a nitrogen fertilizer should be applied to avoid a nitrogen deficiency. Manure with a high percentage of straw and free of weed seed makes an excellent mulch when available. Mulch may increase yields by three to five times, but it is a fire hazard in large commercial fields in dry seasons. Mulch, where economically available, cuts other costs.

Herbicides. Most states have herbicide recommendations. Suggestions for the midwest are rather typical. Funt and coworkers at Ohio State University found the purple raspberry, Brandywine, sensitive to Simazine. Based on their work with black, red and purple raspberries and blackberries, they make the following

Figure 6. (Above) Brambles grown in Maryland with a sod drive-strip in the middles, herbicides in the row and trickle irrigation located under the bramble row. Brambles are very sensitive to water shortage, even for short periods. (Below) Thornless blackberries on trellis showing cold damage, particularly at the terminals, after 9° F for 3 hrs. in Baltimore County, Maryland. (R.C. Funt, Ohio State University)

suggestions for commercial plantings.

At planting, over the plants: Surflan 75%, 3-4 lbs/A; or Devrinol 50%, 4-6 lbs/A; or Enide 50%, 8-10 lbs/A; or Enide 90% 5-7 lbs/A.

On *established planting* — in early spring on sandy soil less than 2% organic matter: Surflan 75%, 3-4 lbs/A; or Devrinol 50%, 4-6 lbs/A; or Surflan 75%, 3-4 lbs/A plus Karmex 80%, 2 lbs/A.

On *established planting,* early spring or late fall on loam soil and 2% or more organic matter: Simazine 80%, 1-2 lbs/A; or Karmex 80% 2-3 lbs/A; or Sinbar 80%, 1 lb/A; or Surflan 75%, 3-4 lbs/A plus Karmex 80% 2 lbs/A.

Irrigation. *Provision for irrigation is good insurance against drought in almost all regions. Continuous adequate soil moisture is probably the most important factor in high quality yields of brambles.* In the humid sections of the East, good crops may be grown without irrigation, but even in this area there are frequently periods when irrigation would increase the crop considerably. The furrow, portable sprinkler, or "trickle" systems as described for strawberries may be used. In Oregon, the equivalent of 4-5 acre inches will be needed 2-4 times a year, depending on rainfall and evaporation. Twin-walled drip tubing is located sub-surface 12-15 in. from plants, permitting irrigation during harvest, other advantages.

Trickle irrigation can be installed at planting as mentioned before or after establishment. It should be buried. The water pattern should be monitored by tensiometers which should utilize a 6, 12 and 18" probe. The 6" and 12" should give the best reading for plant growth while the 18" gives a reading of subsoil moisture reserve. Generally 1 to 4 hours per day to overcome the daily evaporation of .15 to .30 inch will allow sufficient moisture for optimal plant growth and fruit size. Except for immediate use after planting, the trickle system should start by June 1 and end September 1 (mid-Atlantic region) and be used everyday unless more than 1" of rainfall has occurred every 5 days. The best trickle system has a clock and solenoid value to allow daily water usage. Experiments on strawberries with injection of nitrogent through the trickle system look promising.

Fertilization. The importance of additions of large quantities of organic matter to bramble plantations cannot be overemphasized. The moisture-holding capacity, tilth, and aeration of the soil is improved greatly by organic matter. In addition to a heavy application of barnyard manure at the time the land is plowed and prepared, about eight to ten tons of manure, if available, applied per acre each year thereafter is one of the most effective means of maintaining vigorous growth and high fruit production.

Specific fertilizer recommendations for each bramble are difficult to make because soil conditions vary from location to location. Soil test and/or foliar analysis are important. It is highly recommended, also, that the grower maintain small test plots to determine the value of nitrogen, phosphorus, and potassium together and separately. It is known generally that black raspberries usually show the most response to fertility — the more fertile the soil, the stronger the growth and the larger the crop. Fertilizer requirements of purple raspberries are similar to those for the black cultivars. While red raspberries respond to a fertile soil, their fertilizer requirements are not so well understood. Michigan studies have indicated that the larger the cane diameter, the more productive the canes; branched canes produced more than unbranched canes. USDA reports that the best yields of red raspberries in the United States are obtained where annual application of two to 15 tons of stable manure per acre are made in addition to 400 to 500 pounds of a complete fertilizer. The Ohio Experiment Station shows a 20 to 40 percent increase in yield of Latham red raspberries receiving 500 pounds per acre of ammonium sulfate in the spring of each year. If manure is not available, 200 pounds of nitrate of soda per acre applied to black raspberry fields at blossom time is suggested for trial on medium loam soils. Five hundred pounds of cotton seed meal can be used in place of 10 to 15 tons of manure. A 5-10-10- with magnesium and trace elements (see Chapter XIV for suggested formula) may be needed on light sandy soils low in organic matter, and in humid regions.

In Oregon, Boysenberries require much less N than other trailers; flower buds may not form with 50 lbs N/A. With Loganberry, Marion and Thornless blackberries up to 80 lbs/A. are needed. P and K are applied every other year.

For trailing blackberries in North Carolina, two applications of fertilizer per season often are made after the first year, one immediately after the canes have been tied to stakes or the trellis in spring and the other shortly after the crop has been harvested and the old canes removed. First application consists of a low nitrogen (2-10-8) complete fertilizer applied at the rate of 500 to 700 pounds per acre. Second application usually consists of 500 to 800 pounds of cotton seed meal plus 100 pounds of nitrate of soda, or, if available, 10 to 20 tons of manure per acre.

Be aware that while brambles respond to boron when deficient, excessive amounts have been encountered when brambles follow a high B requirement crop as broccoli. One lb actual B/A/yr is suggested for soils showing need. Foliar analysis should be used to gauge kinds and amount of nutrients to apply. Amount and character of wood produced one season governs the size and quality of the crop next season.

A general recommendation is 15 to 20 lbs of actual nitrogen in the form of 5-10-10 (300 to 400 lbs) two weeks after planting. This should be broadcast or handled with care so as not to burn newly developing shoots. In the established planting 40 to 60 pounds of actual nitrogen as

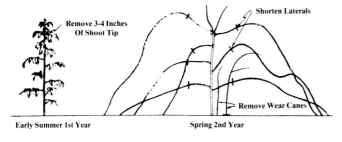

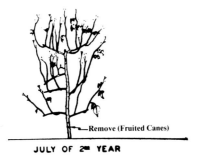

JULY OF 2ⁿᵈ YEAR

Figure 7. Black and purple raspberries produce shoots from the roots early in the growing season. When shoots attain proper height, summer pinching induces vigorous laterals which are shortened the following early spring. Bearing canes are removed immediately after harvest. Note tips of long laterals have taken root in center plant. New plants can be obtained by this means. Tips of laterals are covered in midsummer with two inches of soil to induce rooting, and they are removed from the mother plant the next spring, leaving about six inches of mother cane for convenience in transplanting. New shoots from the roots should complete the diagram below.

15-15-15 (250 to 400 lbs/acre) or 100 to 200 lbs of ammonium nitrate per acre is suggested in early spring March 15 to April 1. A split application of 20 to 30 pounds at this time and a second application 30 days later has been beneficial to berries which produce in July to August.

Training and pruning brambles. Fruit of brambles is borne on canes arising from roots or crowns one year, fruit the next, and die shortly after. Hence, after the planting year, there are two cane types: vegetative *primocanes* and fruiting *florocanes* present during the growing season. Shortly after harvest, remove the fruited canes together with weak late-developing new canes to admit light for better buds, thicker wood, better laterals. Dormant and summer pruning of shoots and canes may be needed, depending upon the bramble.

Black and purple (canes are headed back) raspberries, upright-growing blackberries require *summer "topping"* of the tips of new shoots (Figure 7). The top three or four inches of the new shoots are removed with gloved fingers or shears when they have attained a height of 18 to 24 inches for black raspberries, and 30 to 36 inches for purple raspberries and blackberries, depending upon vigor. This induces laterals to develop and results in a low stout plant resistant to snow breakage and flopping into row middles.

Tips of up-coming shoots should be "topped" at weekly intervals.

Red raspberries are *not* summer pinched (Figure 8). The *dormant pruning* should be done in spring after danger of freezing and before the buds begin to swell. *Red raspberries* in most plantations are given only light cutting back of tips to prevent canes from later becoming top-heavy with fruit and bending to the ground; the canes are headed back to 4-5½ ft. In areas such as the Northwest where conditions are favorable for tall growth of canes, trellises are needed and canes are headed to 5-5½ ft. Where no trellis is used, the least amount of heading required to keep the canes from bending into the rows and to the ground is the most desirable. Small spindly canes should be removed from the hedgerow, leaving the larger canes which are one-half-inch or more in diameter. From 8 to 14 canes (reds) should be left for hills or about ten canes for every four feet of the hedgerow. Canes in the hedgerow should be confined to a strip about 12 inches wide at the base. This is known as the narrow-hedgerow and is preferred to the wide-hedgerow which is 24 to 36 inches in width at the base. Two No. 12 gauge wires on either side of five and one-half foot posts spaced 15 to 30 feet apart in the row are sufficient for supporting tall or weak-cane varieties grown by this system. These canes may be braced further by tying them to the wires on either side allowing the new canes to grow up between.

In the Northwest, *Red raspberries* are supported by posts 15-20 ft apart with crossarms 20-24 in. wide, up to 4½ ft above ground, with No. 10 gauge wire secured at topside of crossarm ends (Figure 9). In fall after cane thinnng, half are tied to one wire, half to the other, providing room for new canes to grow in the center. Two wires 2 ft above ground attached to posts help guide new canes.

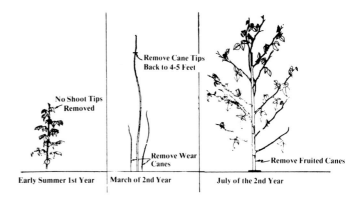

Figure 8. Red raspberry produces shoots from the roots; they require no summer pinching. Few, if any, laterals are formed. In spring of the following year, weak canes are removed and tips of remaining canes are cut back according to growth and cultivar. Growers in recent years are leaving the old canes till pruning time when they are removed; new shoots from the roots should complete the right diagram.

489

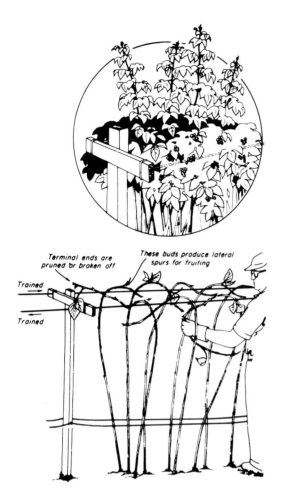

Figure 9. (Above) This is a midsummer view of the "Cross-Arm Trellis System" for training red raspberries in Oregon. Note the fruiting canes resting on the two wires and the new canes extending up between the wires. (Below) The following winter the fruited out and weak canes have been removed at the base. The remaining canes have been twisted over the wires, some tied. There is a long-handled sharp hooked blade tool for cutting and removing old canes. (W. Arden Sheets, Oregon University Extension Service, Hillsboro 97123)

In case of *black* and *purple raspberries* and *blackberries* which have been summer pinched, prune back the laterals rather heavily the next spring (Figure 7). For black raspberries, the size and the quality of the fruit is improved by leaving the stronger laterals with from eight to twelve buds on branches about eight inches long after pruning. In areas where drought periods are likely to occur, such as southern Michigan, only four to six buds are left per cane, resulting in larger better-quality fruit if no irrigation is provided. Shorter laterals may be cut shorter and very vigorous laterals left somewhat longer. The fruiting shoots will arise in spring from axillary buds along these laterals, a few on the main canes. Commercial *blackcaps* are not trellised in the northwestern United States.

Laterals of *purple raspberries* are pruned back to 10 and

Figure 10. This is a training system for mechanically harvesting raspberries in New Zealand. (Top) Raspberry primocanes trained to the Lincoln Canopy system. (Mid) Raspberries floracanes coming into flowering. (Lower) Lincoln N2AE1 harvester sweeping off ripe berries. Note new primocanes for next year's crop growing upright in the center of the row, left, untouched by harvester. (John S. Dunn, N. Z. Agr. Eng. Institute, Christchurch)

18 inches, depending upon their vigor (Figure 7). Longer laterals, about 5, are left for purple varieties because there is a tendency for the buds at the base of laterals to be vegetative. Small spindly laterals should be removed entirely. In the East, *black* and *purple raspberries* are not usually supported.

An interesting system for training raspberries for mechanical harvesting mainly for processing in New Zealand is shown in Figure 10. A report on this system and its relative cost and acceptance can be obtained by writing the N. Z. Agricultural Engineering Institute, Lincoln University, Christchurch, N. Z.

Laterals of *erect blackberries* which have been summer pinched should be left about 18 inches long. With blackberries, it is perhaps better to wait until the blossoms appear before the laterals are cut back. Some cultivars tend to bear fruit far out on the lateral and such a practice prevents cutting away too much of the crop. This is particularly true of the Eldorado which is still recommended in some regions. The strongest canes are thinned in the row to about ten inches apart. The plants sometimes are tied to a one-wire trellis two and one-half feet above the ground on low posts 15 to 30 feet apart. This holds the bushes in line and facilitates cultivating and harvesting. A two-wire vertical trellis may be employed for trailing blackberries as shown in Figure 11.

The *trailing blackberry* usually is planted in hills and trained to seven and one-half-foot stakes sunk in the ground about two feet. After the crop is harvested, old canes are removed and the planting is cultivated in one direction until the canes interfere seriously. Cultivation is then discontinued and the canes allowed to grow at random over the ground. The following spring, seven or eight

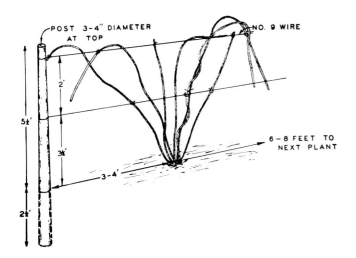

Figure 11. A two-wire trellis is convenient for training the trailing-type blackberry, Boysenberry, Youngberry, and dewberries. Trellis should be established before the beginning of the second year.

of the strongest canes in the hill are tied spirally around the stake at each hill and cut to a height of about five feet.

A special system of planting and pruning *trailing blackberries* is practiced in the Gulf States where no stakes are used. Plants are set 18 to 36 inches apart in the row and allowed to form a matted row. Before picking, the new shoots are mowed back to reduce interference with the picking operation. After harvest, the canes, old and new, are cut close to the ground with a mowing machine and burned where they lie after they have dried. Cultivation in one direction then is practiced while the new canes are developing for the crop the following year.

In the West, erect blackberries including the *Boysen, Logan and trailing blackberies* are trained to a single two- or three-wire trellis. Fruited canes are removed after harvest. New canes, one or two together are twisted spiral fashion (more rigid for mechanical harvesting), trained over the top wire then under the lower wire, completing the operation by early fall, or delayed to early spring to remove any winter damaged canes. In some areas of Willamette Valley (Ore.) the A/Y (alternate/year) system of management is used. Half a field is fruiting (on year) and half is developing canes (off year). In the field after fruiting, all canes are mowed off and shredded during the dormant season. Wires are tightened. Advantages are: (a) New canes are trellis-trained as they grow, reducing labor and damage to mixed-in fruiting cane; (b) cutting fruited canes after harvest is mechanized; (c) often 100% increase in yield; (d) grower has some control over fruit supply; (e) less pesticides and water (off-year needs are less). Other advantages are: Growth is stimulated with trellis-training during growing season, basal cane laterals are controlled with dinoseb herbicide and upper laterals are mechanically trimmed before touching ground. In early spring dinoseb sprays control lower laterals inaccessible to harvesters, killing back also new primocanes and weeds. Contact W. A. Sheets, Wash. Co. Ext. Agt., Hillsboro, Oregon for details.

Mechanical Pruning. To reduce hand-labor pruning costs, some growers are using a mower cutter bar to mow off the tops and sides of a bramble row, with followup hand-thinning as needed. Heavy duty electrical hedgers with portable generators also can be used.

With the Heritage fall-bearing system, plants can be harvested and then mechanically pruned to 1 inch above the soil with a rotary mower. According to research by M. A. Ellis at Ohio State University it is best to harvest and leave plants alone until early spring (March). Apply a dormant spray of lime sulfar while plants are erect and then mow off the canes. This allows old diseased canes to be covered with lime sulfur and reduce infection spread.

Controlling insects and diseases. Diseases and insects of brambles, although relatively few, may in some cases become serious. The following diseases are among the

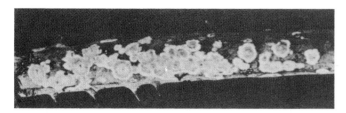

Figure 12. Anthracnose is a common disease affecting brambles, especially black raspberries. Disease may reduce yield markedly or kill the canes. It is controlled by a delayed dormant spray. (Ohio Agr. Exp. Sta.)

more common. *Anthracnose* (Figure 12) may be serious on purples, blacks, Boysens, Logans and less on reds. *Spur blight (Didymelia applanata)* can be serious, is seasonal, regional (in Poland, weakens canes to cold). *Crown gall,* a difficult disease to control, appears as "cauliflower" swellings on the roots, crown, or lower part of the cane. Blackberries are most susceptible. Bacteria enter in root wounds; use shallow cultivation, dig, burn galled plants. *Viruses* are serious on raspberries as *leaf curl* (deep green leaves curled downward and inward), *mosaic* (leaves green and yellowish-green mottled,) *streak* (reddish or purple stripes on canes) and *tomato ringspot* (spread by pollen, in-seed, soil nematodes). Black and purple raspberries are more fatally susceptible to viruses. Red raspberries may be damaged only slightly, but it is possible for the virus to be spread from red raspberry plants to purple or black raspberies by plant lice. *Orange* rust is destructive to blackberries and occasionally to black raspberries. *Double blossom* may affect blackberries seriously in southern regions. In Northwest USA, *Septoria* leaf and cane spot is bad on blackberry. On red raspberry, fruit rot is a problem on machine harvested fruit; root rot is the worst disease.

Best control of raspberry diseases is attained by observing the following precautions: (a) Plant the most disease-free plants obtainable. Seek only government-inspected plants. Heat-treated largely virus-free stock is available from reputable nurseries. (b) Keep plants growing vigorously by good cultural practices. (c) Immediately after planting, remove and burn handles or portions of the old cane on black and purple raspberry-tip

Figure 13. The top left photo and the left inset show larva and damage by raspberry cane-borer *(Oberea bimaculata).* The right-hand inset in the left photo shows the larva of Buprestid cane borer *(Agrilus* spp.). The top middle photo shows a cane injury due to larva of borer shown in left inset of top left photo. The top right photo shows leaf curl symptoms (a virus) on Cuthbert fruiting cane at left, and new shoot tip at right. The bottom photo shows tree cricket eggs which weaken or kill the raspberry canes. (New York Agr. Exp. Sta.)

plants. (d) Remove old diseased raspberry plantings to prevent spread of disease to new plantings. (e) Pull into the middle of the row and burn with a blow torch all plants showing such diseases as the viruses and rust. (f) Remove old fruiting canes immediately after harvest and burn in piles outside the patch. (g) Remove and burn all dead canes when pruning in spring. (h) Spray every spring for anthracnose.

The following insects are among the most troublesome (see also Figure 13 and your local spray schedule). *Spider mite* injury results in a grayish lusterless cast of the leaves. Spiders are tiny, a fraction the size of a pin head, more greenish than red, and move slowly over the leaf surface. In case of severe injury, leaves may become brown and die. Hot dry weather favors the pest. Check your local Agr. Exten. Serv. for recent recommendations.

The *tree cricket* (Figure 13) punctures the canes and lays eggs, stunting the canes; the *crown borer* may be destructive in some western bramble sections; the *cane borer* (Figure 13) girdles young canes and bores downward into roots. The *raspberry saw fly* larvae feed on leaves in eastern sections west of the Mississippi River. *Raspberry beetle* may cause numerous wormy red raspberries. The *tarnish plant bug* may injure berries (''nubbins''), reducing the crop appreciably. The *cane maggot* tunnels around shoot just under bark, ringing it; tips wilt in May. *Rose chafer* is yellowish brown, long-legged beetle ½-inch long; feed on leaves, buds. *Fruit worm* enters fruit and feed on receptacles, attacking red more than blackberries; tiny reddish-brown bettles skeletonize young leaves. Root diseases, including *Verticillium* wilt, are serious in the Pacific Northwest, U.S. Don't follow potato, tomato, pepper, eggplant with brambles. *Orange tortrix, oblique-branded leaf roller* larvae contaminate harvested fruit in NW USA: *red berry mite* can be a problem on some blackberries.

HARVESTING AND MARKETING BRAMBLES

Brambles, particularly red raspberries, are among the most perishable fruits. The harvesting season should be well organized with sufficient packages on hand, adequate pickers previously contacted, and the marketing channels defined clearly. Brambles reach a peak of maturity quickly and deteriorate fast. There is a very good market for bramble fruits.

Raspberries should be picked when dry and as soon as they separate easily from the clusters. At the peak of the season, they are harvested two or three times a week, sometimes more often if the weather is hot and dry. The thumb and two fingers are used with great care to avoid bruising. Only a few berries should be held in the hand at one time to avoid crushing. The berries are picked and placed, not dropped directly in the boxes in which they will

Figure 14. The trend in bramble culture commercially is to shift from a relatively costly hand operaton to machine operation almost totally from clearing the site, planting, hooded-boom spraying (Wash. Ext. Bull. 638) or planes, pruning, discing-herbicide weed control and harvesting. Arkansas blackberry harvester is shown above initially tested, 1961. Product quality is superior to hand picked later model. (Justin R. Morris, University of Arkansas, Fayetteville. 72701)

be marketed. Quart boxes are used for black and purple raspberries and for blackberries. Pint boxes are used for the more tender red raspberries to protect them against bruising and mashing. The picker should fill one box at a time to avoid excessive jarring and settling of the berries. Jarring not only injures the berries but reduces the volume yield and cash returns. The harvested berries should be handled as little as possible and kept in the shade of the bushes or shed.

Best period for picking is early morning (avoid dew) until about ten o'clock on sunny days; the hot midday period should be avoided. Cloudy cool days are ideal. Wet warm humid days hasten ripening, rotting. Local spray schedules are available from your county agricultural agent.

Pickers required per acre will vary from six to twelve, depending upon their efficiency, the yield, and other factors. Red raspberries are marketed in 12-pint cardboard, fiberboard or wood crates and other brambles are marketed also in pints and 8- to 16- qt. cartons.

A mechanical harvester has been developed for rapid picking of brambles (Figure 14). A motor-driven vibrator set of rubber fingers shakes the canes and jars loose the berries which fall on a belt canvas. The machine has the advantage of removing fruits of about the same maturity at more speed and less cost as compared with hand removal. In the 1970's, over 60% of the Oregon blackcap crop, 30% of the trailing blackberries, and 6% of the reds were harvested mechanically for processing, and these percentages are on the increase. Over 90% of the Pacific NW processing berries are being harvested mechanically.

Pre-cooling and refrigeration are recommended for shipment, or for a short holding period. A temperature of 31 to 32°F is suggested with a relative humidity of 90-95% for not more than 2-3 days. Red raspberries when handled properly can be shipped from the West Coast to the East. With the development of jet transportation, increasing quantities are being shipped by this means. Freezing preservation appears to be one of the most convenient and best ways of shipping and handling the brambles, particularly red raspberries.

Blackberries are picked when the berries are black and can be removed from the cluster while still firm. Eldorado blackberries can be picked soon after they turn black but most varieties are not ripe at this time. Berries which are black but difficult to remove from the cluster may be sour. Avoid exposing picked berries to sun as bitterness may develop. Pneumatic tires and vehicles with springs should be used in transportation to reduce jarring and settling to a minimum.

The same picking procedure and supervision as recommended for strawberries can be utilized with brambles. The picker's card is punched as containers are brought to the shelter. Change punches frequently to avoid fraud. Bonuses can be paid to pickers staying entire season, based on total volume picked. Best system may be to pay a picker each time he brings a carrier of baskets to shed, precluding later confusion.

Public picking of brambles is working satisfactorily in most areas. In the east where small acreages are scattered widely, mechanical harvest is expensive and mechanically harvested berries generally need to be processed immediately after harvest. Bramble crops are in high demand by the public who will pay good prices. See pick-your-own under strawberries Chapter 21 which also holds for brambles.

Uses. A large quantity of red raspberries, Loganberries and blackberries are made into wine; frozen yogurt flavored with a bramble is popular; ice creams are a favorite, particularly blackberry in the West. In recent years, however, raspberries, particularly the red varieties, are being frozen in large quantities. Brambles in general and blackberries in particular are made into jams, jellies,

TABLE 3. COMPARISON OF RASPBERRY VARIETIES FOR FREEZING IN NEW YORK (AFTER F. A. LEE AND THE LATE G. L. SLATE).

Good quality	Productivity	Fair quality	Productivity
		Red Varieties	
Willamette	Good	Marcy	Good
Cuthbert	Fair	Viking	Good
Milton	V. Good	June	Good
Taylor	Good	Heritage	Good
Newburgh	Good	Latham	Good
Sunrise	Good	Ontario	Good
Fairview	V. Good		
		Chief	Fair
		Black Varieties	
Allegheny	Good	Black Hawk	Good
Bristol	Good	Dundee	Good
Jewel	Good	Huron	Good
		Purple Varieties	
Sodus	Good	Columbian	Good
Marion	Good		
		Yellow Varieties	
Amber	Good		

[1]In Washington and the Pacific Northwest varieties suggested for freezing are: Willamette, Sumner, Meeker, Fairview, Canby and Matsqui.

and preserves and canned or frozen (Table 3).

Yields. Average yield for the United States is around 1000 quarts per acre, but this is a poor standard. In regions where brambles are adapted, the purple raspberries yield the best, followed by the black and red varieties in order. Under average to good care, purple varieties should yield about 4,000 to 5,000 quarts per acre; black varieties, 3,000 to 4,000 quarts; and the red raspberries from 2,000 to 2,500 quarts per acre. Yields in excess of these figures are common. In fact, in the Northwest, the Willamette and Meeker yield as much as 7,500 to 14,000 quarts per acre. Fall-bearing types may bring compensating prices, though bearing is ¼ - ⅓ summer fruiting types.

Under good management, favorable conditions, blackberries yield from 2300 to 5000 qts/A or more and with Himalayas and Evergreens in the Northwest yields are 1 to 2½ T/yr. A hot dry season can reduce yields appreciably, as they ripen later than raspberries.

In summary, raspberries now have a bright future with "virus-free" stock, greatly improved management techniques and cultivars, particularly the everbearing cultivar, Heritage.

COST COMPARISONS

Richard C. Funt, Univ. of Md., (later Ohio State University) made some interesting cost and return comparisons (see ref.) as follows: "PYO strawberries had the highest internal rate of return of crops studied. PYO thornless blackberries, red and black raspberries offer nearly equal returns. Higher prices for PYO grapes are needed to compete with above crops. PYO allows a highly perishable crop to be directly harvested and consumed in a short time. Hand harvested berries for sale had a much lower return. Strawberries and thornless blackberries offer good retuns if picked and sold at high quality at roadside stands. Thornless blackberries have a potentially large yield/A, but are not generally known by most people, so plantings should be made cautiously. Growers should consider other alternative crops than grapes if prospective returns appear no better than here. Growers with limited capital should try to PYO for strawberries and red raspberries. If capital and labor are not limiting, strawberries and thornless blackberries are logical choices. Black raspberries offer a continuous and diverse supply of berries between strawberry, red rasberry and thornless blackberry. Check reference for detailed yeild and cost data.

In 1981, Funt noted high interest rates became a major problem for growers. Growers who sold pick-your-own berries are more able to adjust price than those who sold to wholesalers or processors. An economic analysis using 1980 costs and a 20% return on investment which equals the rate of borrowed money, indicated that pick-your-own Heritage raspberries should be sold at 75¢ to 85¢ per pound and yield 3,500 to 3,700 lbs/acre while June-bearing types required $1.00 to $1.05 and 2,700 to 3,000 lbs/acre. The major difference between these two systems is the lower requirement for pruning and higher yields of Heritage than June-bearing red raspberries. Brandywine purple raspberries required the same price as June-bearing red raspberries. (Source: Funt, R.C. 1981. Summary of small fruit production systems, Ohio, 1980. Proc. Illinois Small Fruit School. Univ. of Ill. Coop. Est. Serv. Hort. Series 26. p. 15)

The annual cost of trickle irrigation in brambles was calculated in a 1978 study in Maryland by Funt. The study used a fruit planting of 45 acres of which 7.5 acres was planted to brambles. The initial cost per acre was $459 and the annual cost (includes repair, depreciation, interest and insurance) was $70 or an annual cost of 4ᶜ per plant.

BLUEBERRY CULTURE[1]

The blueberry, native to North America, grew wild before white settlers landed. Because there was an abundance of wild berries, no effort was made to develop improved varieties until 1906 when Dr. F. V. Coville of the U.S. Department of Agriculture initiated a cultural and varietal improvement program. Blueberries obtained either from the wild or from cultivated varieties are one of the most popular small fruits on the market. Most everyone

can eat and enjoy blueberries without allergies or digestive problems. They have wide culinary uses — fresh, frozen or canned. U.S. and world markets have not been exploited. The germ plasm is available for wide adaptation of the crop by breeding. An industry now is developing in Western Europe and Japan. Researchers in Australia, South Africa and New Zealand are developing the crop. the crop.

Different species of blueberries are found growing naturally from the low moist bog land in New Jersey to the high relatively dry uplands of Georgia and Maine. Florida, the Midwest and the Northwest have and are developing major industries. Blueberries are being cultivated on soil more or less acid, ranging from the sandy to clay types.

New Jersey has 7300 acres in cultivation; North Carolina, 3200; Michigan 8000, and other states including Washington, Oregon, Massachusettes and New York a total of around 1,000 acres. Value of the North American crop is approaching $100,000,000. These figures are likely to advance in future years in a rapidly expanding industry.

There are several commercially important wild species of blueberries distributed over the United States, six of which are shown in Figure 15. Selected cultivars from only two of these, the highbush and rabbiteye blueberries, are being propagated commercially, although similar progress is being made with other sorts and hybrids. Blueberries have many small soft seeds, as differentiated from the so-called huckleberries which have ten large bony seeds.

Lowbush blueberries are found growing wild in the northeastern states and Canada and are a very important commercial species. They grow from 6 to 18 inches high in upland areas, spreading by underground shoots. Fruit is harvested from July to September. The crop is harvested

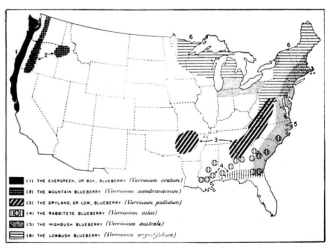

Figure 15. Distribution of six important species of wild blueberries in the United States. These are harvested extensively and marketed fresh, frozen, or canned. Plantings of the selected and cultivated highbush varieties are spreading and increasing in number.

[1]Dr. Paul Eck, Specialist in blueberry and cranberry culture, Rutgers University, New Brunswick, New Jersey 08903, assisted in this revision of this blueberry section.

largely for canneries. Mechanical harvesters that simulate the hand scooping and raking are being used, but irregular terrain is a problem. The entire crop is by no means ever harvested. Table 4 gives "production" in Maine and Canada, based on processed products.

TABLE 4. WILD BLUEBERRIES (LOWBUSH) PROCESSED IN MAINE AND CANADA, 1980-2. (NO. AMER. BLUEBERRY COUNCIL)

State or Province	1980	1981	1982
	millions of lbs		
Maine	21.2	19.0	36.9
Nova Scotia	8.3	12.8	14.1
Quebec	6.8	13.0	12.5
N. Bruns.	3.2	4.5	7.7
P.E. Island	0.45	0.8	0.7
N. Foundland	0.44	0.5	2.2
Total	40.4	50.6	74.1

The lowbush blueberry takes over after the forest is cut. In Maine in early spring, a third of a planting is burned over every third year to destroy weeds and prune the plants. The plants are rejuvenated from underground rhizomes. It is often necessary to control the blueberry fruit fly in these areas by extensive dusting.

In Canada, where much of the crop is produced, there are four types of lowbush, namely: velvet leaf *(V. myrtilloides)* from Nova Scotia to Vancouver Island, hairy lvs and stems, smooth leaf margins, sensitive to repeated burning; commom lowbush *(V. angustifolium)* from Newfoundland to Manitoba, shiny, smooth, toothed lvs with glands at points; black lowbush *(V. augustifolium* forma *nigrum),* blue-green lvs, black shiny berries found with common lowbush above. The Ground Hurst *(V. boreale)* is much branched, prostrate in headlands of Newfoundland, limited commercial use. Shoots develop from rhizomes, tips die, and vegetative or flower buds are set, the latter in greater numbers on new sprouts. Pollination is by bumble, solitary and introduced honey bees. Soils are light and well drained, pH 4.0-5.5. Abandoned farmland is easier to clear and develop. Pruning is done by burning in late fall, early spring on divided sections, one section a yr. Straw applied at about 1 T/A and scattered to assist burning. Oil burners and propane gas have been used but cost must be considered. Fields are divided into lanes 6-8 ft wide with a picker assigned to a lane, back to sun to see berries. A hand rake or scoop is used. Weeds are controlled by herbicides applied by special machines, some by hand. Pests are maggot, cutworm, chain-spotted geometer, flea beetle, casebeetle, thrips, fireworm. Diseases are mildew, rust, leaf spots. Government spray schedules are available. (See Agric. Canada Ottawa) Bul. 1477. 42 p. 1972 or update.)

Highbush blueberries grow wild from Florida to Maine and Ontario and west to southern Michigan (Table 5). The plant grows from 10 to 15 feet higher, performing best in swamps and moist fields at high elevations; it is subject to drought. Rubel, Adams, Harding, Brooks, Sooy, Chatsworth and Sam are highbush blueberries that have relatively large fruit size and have been selected from the wild. Most of the discussion on culture in this chapter is devoted to the highbush blueberry.

Dryland blueberries are of chief importance from northern Alabama and Georgia to Maryland and West Virginia. The plants are from one to three feet high, drought resistant, spread by underground shoots, and can thrive in relatively poor soils on ridges and hills. The light blueberries, of which there are no named varieties, have good flavor and ripen later than the lowbush and highbush sorts, but come on the market at good prices before the New Jersey blueberries.

Evergreen blueberries are gathered extensively and shipped in September and October from Oregon, Washington, and upper California. In addition to the fruit crop, large quantities of branches are shipped to the East as an "evergreen huckleberry" for decorative purposes. The plant reaches a height of 20 feet in open woods and can be used as an attractive ornamental shrub. Berries are shiny black with a strong flavor which makes them less desireable than other blueberries, but they are good in pies and for cooking.

Mountain blueberry, or "broad-leaf huckleberry," is found in the Northwest. This drought-resistant blueberry is three to five feet high. The berries, borne alone and in pairs, are pear-shaped, black or maroon, highly flavored, juicy and tart. No cultivated plantings are known.

Rabbiteye blueberry, grows wild in the Southeast in river valleys and at the edge of woods. It is less sensitive to soil acidity and more resistant to heat and drought than the highbush blueberry. Commercial fields have been propagated from selected high-quality, wild plants as well as cultivars improved by hybridization; with total acreage of more than 3,500, but the market value of the fruit is not known. The small black wild berries are sometimes of poor quality and coarse texture, receiving poor reception on the market. Propagation is by suckers of off-shoots arising near parent plants, although propagation from winter and summer cuttings, as for the highbush blueberry, is becoming increasingly popular. Cuttings are grown one year in the nursery before planting to the field in midwinter at a distance of 15 by 15 feet. Young plants grow rapidly and bear heavy crops beginning the third year. They respond well to mulching, cultivation and fertilization, and are pruned relatively little, although pruning as is practiced for highbush blueberry is desirable. Plants may bear an average of nine quarts, reaching 30 quarts in some years. Picking in Florida begins in May, the fruit ripening for some cultivars over a 30-day period, although others may ripen over a three-month period extending into September. Rabbiteye fruit withstands shipment well.

Callaway and Coastal, 1950, are no longer in production in quantity. Callaway and Tifblue, by taste panels, have the best flavor. Homebell, also a Myers x Black Giant cross, has large fruit and a highly productive bush. Southland, Briteblue Bluebelle, Climax and Delite are improved rabbiteyes that have been recently developed for The U.S. Gulf Coast and southeastern region, Menditoo, Woodward, and Morrow were released in the 1960's; Premier, Powderblue and Centurion in the late 1970s by Dr. Gene Galletta, USDA, for the Southern USA. Table 5 gives fruit characters of several cultivars.

Southern highbush. These cultivars have been and are being developed by Ralph Sharpe and Paul Lyrene from a cross between the hexaploid, *V. ashei* (rabbiteye) and a

TABLE 5. RATINGS OF RABBITEYE BLUEBERRIES FOR BUSH SIZE, SEASON, AND SOME BERRY CHARACTERISTICS (ADAPTED FROM DARROW AND MOORE, USDA).[1]

Variety	Bush Size	Season	Berry Size	Berry Color	Flavor	Scar
Bluebelle	7	7	10	10	10	10
Climax	6	10	8	6	8	9
Coastal	9	10	8	6	6	9
Garden Belle	10	10	6	8	9	9
Gallaway	7	9	8	8	10	10
Tifblue	9	9	7	10	10	10
Homebell	10	8	9	7	7	9
Menditoo	9	7	9	6	8	10
Woodward	8	10	9	10	9	7

[1]For bush size 1 = smallest, 10 = largest; for season 1 = latest, 10 = earliest; for other characters, 1 = poorest, 10 = best. Relative values in this table are not comparable with those for the highbush cultivars; e.g., 10 for bush size here does not indicate the same size as 10 for highbush blueberries. latest cultivar introductions and respective characters can be obtained from Dr. Paul Lyrene of Fruit Crops., Univ. of Florida, Gainesville 32611.

diploid type *V. darrowi*. Selections from these crosses have produced southern hexaploids with highbush fruit characters in plants with low chilling requirements. Flordablue, Sharpblue and Avonblue have been named and propagated for use from central Florida to southern Georgia (Table 5 and 6).

HIGHBUSH BLUEBERRY CULTURE

Climate and soil. The cold requirement of the highbush blueberry *(Vaccinium corymbosum)* is similar to that of the Elberta peach, 650 to 850 hrs. below 45 °F. It receives sufficient chilling in eastern North Carolina. The highbush types developed for Florida require only 250 hrs of chilling.

Plants may be killed at -20 °F or lower, but a blanket of snow and sites with good air drainage reduce this danger. The highbush blueberry grows best in a more or less continuously moist soil with a pH of 4.3 to 4.8, although

TABLE 6. BLUEBERRY CULTIVARS FOR VARIOUS PURPOSES IN FLORIDA OR SIMILAR CLIMATE AND SOILS, 1983. (PAUL LYRENE, UNIV. OF FL., GAINESVILLE).

	Rabbiteye or Highbush	Situation (see footnotes)*					
		1	2	3	4	5	Comments
Aliceblue	R	X	X	X		X	Use 2 cultivars
Beckyblue	R	X	X	X		X	in alternate rows
Climax	R	X	X			X	
Woodard	R	X	X				
Delite	R	X	X				
Bluebelle	R	X	X				
Premier	R	X	Test				
Powderblue	R	X	Test				Test only. See above.
Sharpblue	HB	X		X	X		well-drained
Flordablue	HB	X		X	X		soils only
Avonblue	HB	X		X	X		*(Phytophthera)*
		Situations					

*1. A few bushes in your backyard for yourself, your birds, and your friends.
 2. U-pick farm at a location where you have all the customers you need, now and well into the future, and located from Orlando north.
 3. Same as 2 but you are south of Orlando.
 4. Same as 2 but there is serious competition from other nearby U-picks and you cannot move.
 5. For mechanical harvest, packing and shipping fresh within and outside of Florida.
 6. Chaucer (3/16), Bonita (3/18) and Choice (3/25) have been named and introduced in 1983 for testing. The "3/16" is ripening date.

good crops have been seen in loam soils of about pH 5.5. Acidity should be raised or lowered to within this range by additions, respectively, of either lime or sulfur. It requires about a ton of lime per acre to raise the pH a half to one point, or, according to studies in New York, about 530 pounds of sulfur per acre to lower the pH one point on sandy soils and 650 to 1100 pounds on medium loams. Sulfur should be used on the more fertile loams to lower pH while ammonium sulfate serves the purpose better on sandy or poor soils where it also furnishes needed nitrogen.

Table 8 gives relative acreage and production of the cultivated highbush blueberry in the United States and Canada.

Cultivars. Most varieties now cultivated were bred by Drs. F.V. Coville, G.M. Darrow and D.H. Scott, USDA. Jersey is the leading commercial blueberry variety, comprising a high percentage of the U.S. acreage as noted in Table 9. Note that Rubel, a cultivar selected from the wild by Miss Elizabeth White of New Jersey, was used by early breeders to develop several of the cultivars grown today, including Jersey, the stable leader.

The following cultivars are suggested for different regions. For western North Carolina, Maryland, and New Jersey: Earliblue for early season; Blueray and Collins for early midseason; Bluecrop and Berkeley for midseason; and Jersey, Herbert, Elliott and Coville for late season are desirable. In eastern North Carolina: Angola, Wolcott, Croatan, and Morrow are suggested for early season, and Harrison and Murphy for midseason. Jersey is raised for late season in this area, but later varieties are considered

TABLE 7. CHARACTERISTICS OF STANDARD CULTIVARS IN FLORIDA AND PROPOSED RELEASES.[Y] (PAUL LYRENE, FRUIT CROPS, UNIV. OF FLA., GAINESVILLE, 32611) 1983.

	Ave. date in Gainesville				Fruit characteristics		
	50% Flowering	50% Ripening	Size	Color	Shipping quality (scar, firmness)	Ripening[z] span	Plant vigor
Aliceblue	Mar. 18	May 30	8	8	8	8	7
Beckyblue	Mar. 16	June 4	8	8	8	8	7
Climax	Mar. 18	May 31	8	7	9	9	7
Delite	Mar. 30	June 21	8	8	8	8	6
Bonita	Mar. 18	June 1	9	9	8	8	7
Choice	Mar. 25	June 20	7	9	8	8	8
Chaucer	Mar. 16	June 5	8	9	7	6	8

[y]10 = excellent, 6 = not very good.
[z]A high number for ripening span means all berries on the plant tend to ripen together.

less desirable than early ones. In Michigan and New England the standard variety is still Jersey, but Earliblue, Blueray, Bluecrop and Berkeley are good for early, early midseason, and midseason, respectively. Bluehaven is midseason, developed in Michigan; and Patriot is from New Hampshire. For late season, Herbert and Coville are recommended. In western Oregon and Washington, Stanley and Dixi succeed but Earliblue, Blueray, Bluecrop, Berkeley, Herbert, and Coville are worthy of trial. In W. Europe Bluecrop, Goldtraube H-1 and G-71 do well. In Florida, Floradablue and Sharpblue are early for top prices. Refer to Table 6 and 7. See Tables 9 and 10 and USDA Bull. 1951 for cultivar details.

Berries of a given variety attain higher flavor if the nights are cool during the ripening season; thus, as one would expect, flavor seems to be generally better in the northern regions. New blueberry cultivars from Florida, however, have highly acceptable quality.

Although large solid blocks of Rubel and other standard varieties have yielded well in Michigan, it is generally recommended to grow two varieties alongside to insure cross-pollination, larger earlier ripening berries, and good production.

The U.S. Department of Agriculture under the leadership of Dr. Arlen Draper is continuing its productive blueberry breeding program in cooperation with a number of state stations, particularly New Jersey, Michigan, Florida and North Carolina. Objectives of the program in

New Jersey, e.g., are (a) to develop varieties with greater winter hardiness, drought resistance and concentration of ripening; (b) expand the harvest season with new varieties earlier than Earliblue and later than Coville; also "plug" holes in the ripening season now open for lack of desirable varieties; (c) develop varieties with larger size, light powder blue color, small dry scars, and higher production and better flavor than some of the present leading varieties; (d) develop varieties resistant to mummy berry, anthracnose and (e) more dependable than present ones with respect to regular annual bearing. Unfortunately, we seem to have no germ plasm resistance to known viruses to develop a breeding program along this line.

Propagation. Although some wild highbush blueberries are being fertilized, sprayed and pruned, it is becoming increasingly desirable to propagate and cultivate the selected varieties for good yields of high-quality fruit. The blueberry can be propagated by hardwood or softwood cuttings, but exacting procedure is necessary for good results. Commercial propagation is done almost entirely by hardwood cuttings. In early spring, medium to medium-large hardwood cuttings, four to six inches long and from healthy dormant shoots of the previous season's growth, are cut just below a bud at the base and just above a bud at the top.

A mixture of peat and sand, half and half, to a depth of about six inches is used in the raised beds. The covered frame, as shown in Figure 16, is constructed 6 feet by 27

TABLE 8. CULTIVATED BLUEBERRY ACREAGE AND PRODUCTION, 1980-82. (NO. AMER. BLUEBERRY COUNCIL).

State[1]	Acreage Planted	Acreage Producing	Acres Planted/Yr.	Production Mil. lbs. 1980-1	Production Mil. lbs. 1981-2	Lbs Yield Per/A	Processed Mil. lbs.
Michigan	11,000	10,000	200	46.5	41.1	5200	32.2
New Jersey	8,200	8,000	Insignif.	27.0	30.0	3750	13.3
No. Carolina	4,000	3,000	350 & removed	6.5	3.7	2380	0.8
Georgia	3,000	1,500	500	1.0	—	670	—
Oregon	650	690	25	3.5	3.5	5830	1.6
Washington	700	700	20	5.5	5.6	6570	3.6
Br. Columbia	2,000	1,200	100	6.6	0.0	4200	5.2
Ontario	600	300	100	1.5	—	5000	—

[1]Other states producing (Mil. lbs.), acreage and lbs. yld./A, respectively; New York - 2.0, 600, 5000; Arkansas — 0.27, 157, 1500; Florida — 1.0, 100, 5000. Production in most states is showing an increase yr. by yr. Ozark blueberries totaled 298,000 lbs. in 1981, sold through ABGA.

TABLE 9. BLUEBERRY CULTIVARS ORIGINATED BY THE U.S. DEPT. OF AGRI. COOPERATIVE BREEDING PROGRAM. (ADAPTED FROM MOORE, J.N., 1956).

Variety	Parentage	Year Introduced	Estimated Per Cent of Acreage[a]
Pioneer	Brooks X Sooy	1920	0
Cabot	Brooks X Chatsworth	1920	0
Katharine	Brooks X Sooy	1920	0
Greenfield	Brooks X Russell	1926	0
Rancocas	(Brooks X Russell) X Rubel	1926	2
Jersey	Rubel X Grover	1928	28
Concord	Brooks X Rubel	1928	0
Stanley	Katharine X Rubel	1930	1
June	(Brooks X Russell) X Rubel	1930	1
Scammell	(Brooks X Chatsworth) X Rubel	1931	1
Redskin	Brooks X Russell (F_9)	1932	0
Catawba	Brooks X Russell (F_9)	1932	0
Wareham	Rubel X Harding	1936	0
Weymouth	June X Cabot	1936	12
Dixi	(Jersey X Pioneer) X Stanley	1936	1
Atlantic	Jersey X Pioneer	1939	0
Burlington	Rubel X Pioneer	1939	1
Pemberton	Katharine X Rubel	1939	1
Berkeley	Stanley X (Jersey X Pioneer)	1949	5
Coville	(Jersey X Pioneer) X Stanley	1949	8
Wolcott	Weymouth X (Stanley X Crabbe 4)	1950	9
Murphy	Weymouth X (Stanley X Crabbe 4)	1950	2
Angola	Weymouth X (Stanley X Crabbe 4)	1951	1
Ivanhoe	(Rancocas X Carter) X Stanley	1951	0
Bluecrop	(Jersey X Pioneer) X (Stanley X June)	1952	12
Earliblue	Stanley X Weymouth	1952	5
Herbert	Stanley X (Jersey X Pioneer)	1952	0
Croatan	Weymouth X (Stanley X Crabbe 4)	1954	1
Blueray	(Jersey X Pioneer) X (Stanley X June)	1955	4
Collins	Stanley X Weymouth	1959	0
Morrow	Angola X Adams	1964	0
Darrow	F-72 X Bluecrop	1965	0
Latablue	Herbert X Coville	1967	0
Bluehaven	Berkeley X 19H	1967	0
Northland	Berkeley X 19H	1967	0
Bluetta	North Sedgewick lowbush X Coville X Earliblue	1968	0
Meader	Earliblue X Bluecrop	1971	0
Elliott	Burlington X /Dixi X Jersey X Pioneer)/	1973	0
Bluebelle	Callaway X Ethel	1974	0
Harrison	Croton X US 11-93	1974	0
Patriot	US-3 (Dixi X Mich. LB-1) X Earliblue	1976	0
Flordablue	J. Ashei X V. darrowi	1976	0
Sharpblue	V. Ashei X V. darrowi	1976	0
Avonblue	Florida Selection 1-3 X E66 (V. Ashei X V. darrowi)	1977	0
Beckyblue	V. Ashei X V. Australe	1978	0
Aliceblue	Open pollinated seedlot of Beckyblue	1978	0
Bluechip	Croatan X US 11-93	1982	0

[a]Five percent of estimated acreage is planted to Rubel, a wild cultivar.

inches by 16 to 40 inches deep; it contains a tray four inches deep with a one-quarter-inch mesh hardware cloth bottom which rests on cleats about ten inches below the top of the frame. Cuttings are placed slanting about one inch apart in rows two inches apart in a peat medium. Coarse burlap about the texture of bran sacks may be used over the glass sash for shading the cuttings. Check the cuttings once every day or two to remove any dying cuttings and thus remove the source for fungus spread. The tray system of propagation has the advantage of being easily transported to the nursery row when the cuttings are ready to transplant.

Although the cuttings root by June, they are left in the beds or trays until the following spring. The shade is gradually removed with increased waterings until about September when the tray is sunk into the soil to ground level on a well-drained spot; it is protected from animals by a wire cloth over the top.

Cuttings are set in the nursery six to ten inches apart in rows 18 or more inches apart and grown for a year, as shown in Figure 16. They are sold as two-year plants. In the permanent location, plants are set one to two inches deeper than they grew in the nursery at a distance of four by ten feet when standard tractors are used in cultivation. A distance of five by eight feet is suggested where garden tractors will be used (Figure 16). Early spring planting is recommended, although in New Jersey blueberries are often planted in early fall; in North Carolina they may be

TABLE 10. RATINGS OF HIGHBUSH BLUEBERRIES FOR SOME BERRY CHARACTERISTICS.[a]
(ADAPTED FROM DARROW AND MOORE, 1966.)

Variety[b]	Season	Size	Color	Scar	Flavor	Remarks
Morrow	10	8	7	6	6	very early, canker-resistant
Angola	10	8	5	7	6	very fine bush, canker-resistant
Wolcott	9	8	6	9	6	very fine bush, canker-resistant
Croton	9	8	7	8	6	very fine bush, canker-resistant
Harrison	8	9	9	9	9	resistant to cone canker, bud mite
Bluechip	8	10	8	8	10	resistant to cone canker, excellent
Weymouth	9	8	5	6	5	poor bush, productive, poorest flavor
Earliblue	9	9	8	7	7	fine bush, won't drop
Collins	8	9		7	8	fine bush, won't drop
Murphy	8	8	6		7	spreading bush, canker-resistant
Cabot	8	5	7	6	5	spreading bush, berries crack
June	8	5	6	5	6	bush usually weak
Rancocas	7	6	7	6	6	berries crack, resistant to stunt
Ivanhoe	7	9	7	9	10	buds not hardy, hard to propagate
Stanley	7	6	7	4	9	easy to prune, berry size runs down
Blueray	7	10	8	7	9	bush hardy, easy to propagate
Bluecrop	6	9	9	9	7	drought-resistant, hardy, fine color
Concord	6	7	7	6	8	fine cluster size
Pioneer	6	6	6	6	9	berries crack
Scammell	6	7	6	6	7	sets too large clusters
Berkeley	5	10	10	8	7	berries drop some, lightest blue
Atlantic	4	8	7	7	8	berries drop some
Pemberton	4	8	6	4	7	bush very vigorous, most productive
Rubel	4	6	7	7	6	bush hardy, hard to prune
Jersey	4	7	7	7	6	bush hardy, long picking season
Dixi	4	10	6	5	9	berries crack, run down in size
Herbert	3	10	7	7	10	berries tender, bush hardy
Darrow	3	10	8	8	9	bush erect, vigorous, berries do not drop
Wareham	2	6	6	7	10	berries tender, bad mildew
Burlington	2	7	7	10	6	bush hardy, berries store well
Coville	2	10	7	6	9	berries won't drop, fine processed
Elliott	1	8	9	9	9	Adapt to machine harvest
Lateblue	2	9	9	10	9	Consistently productive, may be stemy

[a]For season, 1 = latest, 10 = earliest; for color, 1 = dark, 10 = light; for other characters, 1 = poorest, 10 = best.
[b]No ratings available for Redskin, Katharine, Catawba, and Greenfield.

planted in late fall or winter. Hand hoeing around the young plants is desirable.

Soft wood cuttings are made from the first and second flushes of new growth in the spring after cessation of growth as induced by the aborted terminal bud. A 4-inch cutting is stripped of all but 2 of its lvs and propagated on horticultural perlite under mist. The rooting is nearly 100% by this method. A rooting hormone is generally effective in the rooting of soft wood cuttings.

There are a number of *tissue culture* laboratories growing blueberry shoots successfully, which they then harvest and root on sphagnum. The University of Florida is conducting research in this area. It likely will be possible to propagate thousands of plants in a short time by this revolutionary technique.

Soil management. Shallow cultivation should be practiced until after harvest, when a locally suitable cover crop is sown. Spring oats and Sudan grass frequently are used in southern Michigan. Manure and leguminous mulch have been disastrous in some cases and should be avoided or thoroughly tested in small areas before generally used. Little or no fertilization may be needed on fertile soils, whereas poor soils may require large amounts for good yields. Nitrogen at 60 lbs. N/A has shown the best

response in New Jersey and North Carolina, Phosphorus, 67 lbs. P_2O_5 per acre, has given good results in Michigan, although 500 pounds per acre of a complete fertilizer usually has given better results. For sandy soils in Michigan, Stanley Johnston suggested an 8-8-8 formula, with potash derived from sulfate of potash, because muriate of potash (KCl) has caused injury to young plants. An 8-8-8 with 2 percent magnesium oxide is used in New Jersey. A 3-9-18 formula is recommended for muck soils in Michigan. One ounce per plant per year of age is suggested up to a maximum of eight ounces; more fertilizer might be used in rare instances. It is suggested that one application of 400 to 600 pounds per acre of a complete fertilizer, such as 5-10-5, be applied in spring when the buds start growth. If the soil is below pH 4.8, 150 pounds of nitrate of soda or calcium nitrate per acre should be applied six weeks later; or, if the soil is a little above pH 4.8, about 110 lbs. per acre of sulfate of ammonia should be used. On poor soils, this is followed by one or possibly two similar applications at six-week intervals. Magnesium (2 to 4% MgO), iron (Figure 17), and manganese may be needed on poor sandy soils. Where heavy mulches are used, more nitrogen should be applied, using instead 300 lbs. sulfate of ammonia per acre per application. The

Figure 16. (Top left) A blueberry nursery in Michigan. (Top right) Three-year Jersey blueberry bushes; left, a healthy plant; right, a plant with stunt disease (a virus). (Middle left) A low propagating frame with glass sash and burlap shade in place and two trays in front, one filled with root cuttings. Trays are placed in the top of the propagating frame and provide a convenient method for handling cuttings before they are sent to the nursery, shown in top left photo. (Middle center) Double spot is a serious leaf disease of cultivated highbush blueberry in the South. (Middle right) Blueberries grow best in acid soil; the pH of soil on left is 4.87 and on the right, 6.08. (Bottom left) A New Jersey double-disk harrow drawn by garden tractor; riding tractors are common in large plantings. Harrow will adjust itself to slope of ground. (Bottom center) Bush before pruning. (Bottom right) Four-year June blueberry after pruning. Buds were reduced by about 75 percent. A much larger number of buds may be left on plants in very fertile soil. (Bottom left) New Jersey Agr. Exp. Sta., (Middle center, bottom center, bottom right) G.M. Darrow, U.S.D.A., (Others) the late Stanley Johnston, Michigan Agr. Exp. Sta.

fertilizer is broadcast in the root zone six to twelve inches from the plants.

Moist soils are essential but the water table should not come higher than within about 18 inches of the surface. On low wet areas, tile or ditches of the proper depth will carry away excess water rapidly. The plants can be set on ridges in the low spots. If drought periods are a problem, mulching with sawdust six to eight inches deep is suggested; straw mulch requires the utmost precaution against fire. Trickle and sprinkler irrigation (Chap. XIX) are practiced today, with an application of one to two acre-inches at ten-day intervals during the picking season and possibly one or two applications later if needed. Trickle irrigation can make a marked difference in establishment of a blueberry planting, as shown in Figure. 18.

Some rotary hoes[1] are in use to cultivate 2 to 3 inches deep around the bushes. The hoe is tractor pulled and/or powered by a wheeled tractor. A metal-rod "whisker" rubs against the bush, activating a hydraulic system that

Figure 17. Iron deficiency is seen frequently on blueberry. It is characterized by a network of dark green veins on a background of light or yellowish green; tip leaves in more severe cases may be completely yellow with some marginal and tip burning of the leaves. Ammonium sulfate form of nitrogen will reduce or correct it if soil pH is relatively high. Iron chelate applied according to manufacturers' recommendation should be effective but it is expensive on a large scale.

---

[1]Contact Friday Tractor Co., Hartford, Michigan for catalogue descriptions of horticultural machinery.

Figure 18. Irrigation when needed, particularly on sandy soils, can make the difference between success and failure in establishing a blueberry planting, as shown here in North Carolina. Trickle irrigation was used during the first season in a test plot on the right, none on the left. (Courtesy Dan Finch, Bailey, Bx 699, N.C. 27807)

pulls the rotating hoe out and around the bush.

Chemical Weed Control. Growers still use the rotary PTO hoe to stir the soil about the bushes in spring and prepare for application of chemical weed control sprays in the row (Figure 19). Diuron, chlorpropham, dichlobenil, simazine, paraquat and terbacil are cleared for use on blueberries.

Write to the New Jersey Agricultural Experiment Station, New Brunswick, New Jersey, 08903, for the latest recommendations. See also Chapter 18, herbicide spray suggestions, for addition information.

Pruning blueberries. The blueberry bears fruit on wood of the previous season's growth, beginning the second year after planting. The largest and best berries are borne on the more vigorous wood. Inasmuch as most varieties tend to overbear, it becomes necessary to thin the bushes and prune off some of the excessive buds. Varieties, such as Cabot and Pioneer, which develop spreading bushes need more attention in removing the lower drooping branches, whereas upright growing varieties such as Rancocas, June, Rubel, Concord, and Scammell need more thinning at the center. Pruning consists of removing the weak branches and cuttng out wood older than 4 yrs. Heavy heading back of clusters is reported in Michigan to reduce the crop considerably, increase the size of the berries, and hasten ripening. The later-ripening somewhat smaller berries on lightly pruned bushes are desired in Michigan because they

Figure 19. A herbicide (Diuron) has been used in the blueberry row (above), applied with an off-center nozzle fan-tip (3 ft spread/side) that sprays overlap in the row, hitting the base of canes. Wider in-row control strips can be gotten by using an additional nozzle on the boom. Check row is shown in the center and below a field with this herbicide control. (W.V. Welker, USDA)

502

bring better prices as a result of less competition from wild blueberries and such fruits as raspberries, strawberries, and cherries.

Vigorous plants are able to carry a large crop of fruit and, therefore, should receive less pruning, provided soil moisture is adequate at all times. Somewhat more pruning is necessary on less vigorous plants growing on soils low in fertility and occasionally deficient in soil moisture.

No pruning is needed until after the third growing season when only the bushy growth is removed at the base of the plants. After the fourth season, remove the dead and broken branches. Confine the pruning as much as possible to a few large cuts in order to save labor, removing clusters of very thin bushy wood that tend to accumulate in mature bushes. Old stems which have lost their vigor and become very bushy may be removed at the ground, or, sometimes it is possible to cut them back to a vigorous side shoot. Branches drooping close to the ground should be removed. Concord, Rubel, and Rancocas bushes are more expensive to prune, because they require more thinning out of the small branches.

The fruiting shoots of varieties such as Cabot, Scammell, Pioneer, and Sam should be cut back to three to five fruit buds per shoot to increase berry size (Figure 20). Amount of cutting back varies with the number of fruit buds per shoot as influenced by growing conditions and variety. Varieties which require very little cutting back are Earliblue, Ivanhoe, Bluecrop, Blueray, Berkeley, Herbert, Rancocas, Concord, Stanley, Jersey, Rubel, and Weymouth. Scammell requires cutting back to about three to five fruit buds per shoot. The shoots should be cut back only after danger of winter injury is past.

Cost of pruning can be reduced and the job simplified by using short light lopping shears for the majority of the cuts. Pruning can be performed any time after the leaves drop until slightly after blossoming if necessary.

Harvesting and marketing. The harvesting season begins about May 20 for North Carolina, June 20 for New Jersey, and July 10 for southern Michigan (Table 11). Cultivars grown in North Carolina are the early to midseason sorts, in New Jersey the midseason to late cultivars (Figure 21), and in Michigan, the very late varieties. The picking season for any district may extend over a period of six to eight weeks, including early to late-ripening cultivars. Three to seven pickings are made at five- to seven-day intervals, depending upon the variety and weather. Blueberries hang on the bushes well and are not so perishable as raspberries. Only ripe berries are picked, since those having a reddish tinge are sour. Berries are picked directly into tightly constructed pint boxes in New Jersey, while in Michigan, small pails are used. Although some bloom is destroyed by more handling with the pails, the berries can be inspected and the leaves and green berries removed as they are poured gently from the pail into the pint boxes. If the crop

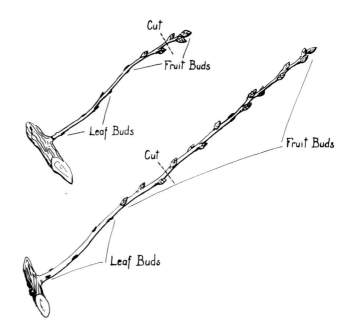

Figure 20. (Top) Lateral sprout of Cabot blueberry and (bottom) Sam showing amount of trimming back needed for varieties of these growth and fruiting characteristics.

is heavy, one picker can harvest from 60 to 80 pints in an eight-hour day.

Harvesting machines are available for blueberries and Michigan workers have devised equipment consisting of a gasoline powered electric generator and hand-operated electrically activated vibrators with rubber fingers that shake the ripe berries onto portable catching frames. Over the row, self-propelled harvesters (Figure 22). are being used extensively in Michigan and New Jersey; to a lesser extent in other areas. Pneumatic sorters are also in use which separate trash and small unripe berries from sound fruit by air-blast (essentially pea sorting machines). When prices are good, the early large berries are harvested by hand and the later smaller berries "cleaned up" by machine harvesting.

The crop is packed and marketed mostly by cooperatives and the berries are sold according to size grades, the larger the berry the higher the price. The grades in Michigan are as follows: Superior — 85 or fewer berries in a measuring cup; Golden Moon — 86 to 130 berries; Columbia — 131 to 190 berries; and Lake State—all marketable berries more than 190 to a measuring cup. Grading and sizing machines are being used (Figure 23) especially with the wild berries which may show more variation in size and grade than the named cultivated varieties. In Michigan, occasional sample cups of standard varieties are checked for number of berries; experienced people can estimate berry size almost at a glance. Polyethylene wrapped boxes (Figure 21) increase the attractiveness and holding period of the berries. A rubber

Figure 21. Harvestng Blueberries. (Top left) School children and instructors, as supervisors, are transported in early morning for blueberry picking. (Top right) Pint picking-baskets are fastened to the belt. (Middle left) Harvesting scene at Whitesbog, New Jersey, in July. (Top middle right) Late Elizabeth C. White, New Jersey pioneer in blueberry varieties and large commercial producer. (Bottom middle right) Twelve-pint trays are inspected by forewoman for any green and damaged berries; picker's card is punched if berries are satisfactory. (Bottom left) Most blueberries are marketed in crates and may be shipped long distances under refrigeration. Fiberboard and wood braced crates are used also. Polyethylene improves appearance and prolongs keeping. (Bottom right) Branch showing fruiting habit of blueberries. (Bottom left, Mich. State Univ.; others Curtis Publ. Co.)

TABLE 11. PERCENTAGE OF CROP PICKED EACH WEEK DURING THE RIPENING SEASON FOR SEVERAL BLUEBERRY VARIETIES IN EASTERN NORTH CAROLINA, SOUTHERN NEW JERSEY, AND MICHIGAN (AFTER DARROW).

State and Variety	Week of Season													
	1[a]	2	3	4	5	6	7	8	9	10	11	12	13	14
North Carolina														
Morrow	80	20	—	—	—	—	—	—	—	—	—	—	—	—
Angola	60	30	10	—	—	—	—	—	—	—	—	—	—	—
Wolcott	30	50	20	—	—	—	—	—	—	—	—	—	—	—
Weymouth	30	35	35	—	—	—	—	—	—	—	—	—	—	—
Croatan	20	50	30	—	—	—	—	—	—	—	—	—	—	—
Jersey	—	—	30	30	30	10	—	—	—	—	—	—	—	—
New Jersey														
Earliblue	—	—	—	—	40	60	—	—	—	—	—	—	—	—
Weymouth	—	—	—	—	50	35	15	—	—	—	—	—	—	—
Collins	—	—	—	—	—	50	50	—	—	—	—	—	—	—
Blueray	—	—	—	—	—	30	40	30	—	—	—	—	—	—
Bluecrop	—	—	—	—	—	20	40	30	10	—	—	—	—	—
Berkeley	—	—	—	—	—	—	20	30	30	20	—	—	—	—
Jersey	—	—	—	—	—	—	—	50	40	10	—	—	—	—
Herbert	—	—	—	—	—	—	—	20	40	30	10	—	—	—
Darrow	—	—	—	—	—	—	—	30	40	30	—	—	—	—
Coville	—	—	—	—	—	—	—	—	20	30	30	20	—	—
Michigan														
Earliblue	—	—	—	—	—	—	—	10	40	50	—	—	—	—
Stanley	—	—	—	—	—	—	—	—	20	30	40	10	—	—
Bluecrop	—	—	—	—	—	—	—	—	—	30	30	40	—	—
Berkeley	—	—	—	—	—	—	—	—	—	—	40	30	30	—
Herbert	—	—	—	—	—	—	—	—	—	—	40	30	20	10
Jersey	—	—	—	—	—	—	—	—	—	—	40	30	20	10

[a]May 15-22 in North Carolina.

band or a piece of sticker tape is used to hold the cellophane in place.

Experiments in New Jersey with precooling and use of fungicides has reduced molds and prolonged the freshness of berries from harvesting to the consumer. Big markets are developing outside blueberry areas; 1000s of crates have been going to W. Germany and Japan for top prices.

Figure 22. The Harvey Harvester, developed by USDA, Michigan State University and industry, harvests up to 3,000 lbs/hr of berries for processing, cutting costs to one forth as compared with hand-picked. First better berries may be picked by hand, later berries by machine. Panelling has been removed to show slappers, working parts. Berries are deposited in lugs at left.

Michigan yields on good soils will run from the second to sixth year, respectively, 50, 200, 2050, 4000, and 6000 pints per acre. A mature plant will bear an average of six to eight pints, but with proper soil management and medium pruning, it may produce 20 pints.

Most cultivated blueberries are marketed fresh, but increasing quantities are being frozen and canned. Frozen with or without a 50 percent sugar solution, the berries are used in pies or eaten with cream. Frozen berries are almost as good as fresh berries and superior to the canned variety; frozen Altantic, Coville, Cabot, and Concord have better flavor than Rancocas and Rubel. The texture and flavor is much better when frozen in a heavy syrup. Blueberries are high in vitamin C. A limited amount of blueberry juice has been produced commercially.

Costs. Data in Table 12 may be of assistance in setting up books for costs and returns in blueberry growing. Returns obviously will vary with price level, other factors.

Diseases and insects. *Stunt virus disease* (Figure 16) may appear on such susceptible varieties as Cabot, Pioneer, Concord, and Scammell in New Jersey and North Carolina and to a lesser extent in New York and Michigan. Rancocas is highly resistant. Other viruses as *shoe string* and *red ringspot* are under study. Rogue the infested bushes.

Mummy berry is an erratic fungus disease blighting blossoms and new shoot tips; mummified berries stick to the bush (Figure 25). The Michigan Experiment Station

Figure 23. (Top) The metal stack at the left is an air-specific gravity berry cleaner removing debris and immature berries. Remaining fruit is being graded on a belt. (Below) Berry packing line in South Jersey. Harvested berries in flats are dropped at left from field flatbed trucks, women hand-grade berries and cover pints with polyethylene and arrange in 12-pint flats for the cooler (foreground center).

recommends shallow plowing as early in the spring as possible (March or April) particularly in spots where infection has been severe. Then remove mummified berries from plant crowns and thoroughly hoe between plants. Cultivate at weekly intervals until after bloom. *Phomopsis twig blight* is usually not serious, entering fast-growing shoots causing them to wilt. Remove blighted wood during pruning. The *red ringspot* virus has become a serious problem in New Jersey on susceptible varieties such as Burlington, Coville, and Darrow. Control of the virus spread depends upon early diagnosis and thorough roguing of infected bushes. *Double spot* (Figure 16) may become serious in North Carolina, resulting in considerable defoliation in some years. Concord, June, Stanley, Rubel,

and Weymouth show resistance. Ferbam or Dyrene is effective control, using three applications starting after the blossming period; second application is made after harvest, followed by another 30 days later. *Stem* canker is a serious problem in North Carolina. Varieties resistant to the fungus, *Botryosphaeria corticis,* have been developed.

Figure 24. (Above) A lowbush blueberry field being dusted by helicopter which is better adapted to irregular ground and wooded adjacent areas than the airplane. Pest and disease control is good. (Courtesy of Bell Aircraft Corp.)

Table 12. Blueberry Production: Estimated Costs and Returns Per Acre Using Late 1970's Prices. (Rutgers University, New Jersey).

Item	Establishing	1st Yr.	2nd Yr.	3rd Yr.	4th Yr.	5th Yr.	6th Yr.	7th Yr.	8th Yr.
Land interest + tax	50.00	$50.	$50.	$50.	$50.	$50.	$50.	$50.	$50.
Land Preparation, Round Up herbicide + other	100.00								
Plants 1000 at 50c	500.00	50.							
Planting	50.00	10.							
Irrigation + labor	200.00	200.	200.	200.	200.	200.	200.	200.	200.
Fertilizer: Material, Sulfur + labor	25.00								
Cutting grass	20.00	50.	50.	50.	50.	50.	50.	50.	50.
Pruning	—	—	—	—	—	—	—	—	40.
Spraying insects — disease, weeds including labor, including Mesural (birds)	20.00	20.	20.	20.	50.	50.	70.	70.	70.
Interest & Depreciation	100.00	100.	100.	100.	100.	100.	100.	100.	100.
COSTS	1065.00	500.	440.	450.	480.	480.	540.	510.	550.
Advertising + oversers	—	—	—	—	50.	120.	210.	300.	360.
Prod. & Harvesting Costs	1065.00	500.	440.	450.	540.	600.	750.	810.	900.
Returns: Yield	—	—	—	—	1000 lbs.	2000 lbs.	3500 lbs.	5000 lbs.	7000 lbs.
Up-Pick Value at 40c lb.					400.	800.	1400.	2000.	2800.
Balance For the Year	-1065.00	-500.	-440.	-450.	-140.	+650.	+650.	+1190.	+1900.
Cumulative Balance to Date	-1065.00	-1565.	-2005.	-2455.	-2595.	-2395.	-1745.	-555.	+1345.

A *Blueberry maggot* (fruit fly) is serious, causing entire shipments to be condemned because of wormy berries. Airplane or power dusting with 4% Malathion or 2% rotenone is often used in New Jersey when adult flies first appear in numbers, but before egg laying starts, followed by a second application ten days later. Malathion is best but should not be used later than three days before harvest.

Cranberry fruit worms (and other fruit worms) cause relatively unimportant fruit damage, but a few of these worms crawling over the fruit under polyethylene packs is unsightly and may condemn sales. Dust with 1% parathion or 4% Malathion, 40 lbs. per acre about May 29 in New Jersey and 7-12 days later. *Cranberry weevil* may damage or destroy the blossoms, reducing the crop 50 percent in some blueberry areas. Other insects of less importance include the blueberry bud worm, forest tent caterpillar, fall webworm, Tatana worm, and leaf rollers, blueberry mite, scale insects, stem gall, stem borer, and cranberry root worm. For detailed descriptions and controls, call upon your local experiment station or county agricultural agent. Ask for local spray schedule from governmental agency. *Birds* are a pest in some areas; fire crackers on rope set to explode every 10 minutes or so, may be effective. Small plantings may be covered with screen or netting. Most states producing blueberries have secured state labels for use of Mesurol as a deterrent, which has been effective.

For detailed information on blueberry growing in North America, the reader is referred to *Blueberry Culture,* edited by Paul Eck and Norman F. Childers, 378 pp., Rutgers University Press, New Brunswick, New Jersey 08903 or Hort. Publ., 3906 NW 31 Pl., Gainesville, Fla., 32606.

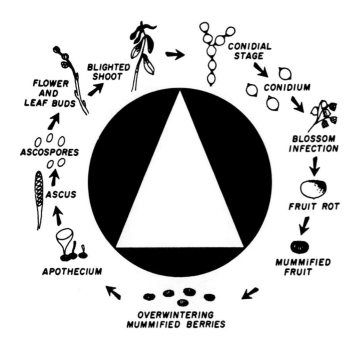

Figure 25. This is the life cycle of the mummy berry fungus on blueberry, one of the more troublesome diseases. (Michigan Agr. Exp. Sta.)

CURRANT AND GOOSEBERRY CULTURE

Currants *(Ribes rubrum L. red currant)* and gooseberries *(Ribes hirtellum Michx., American)* grow best in the northern United States and Europe where conditions are relatively moist and cool. In the warmer temperate

507

zone, the summers are too long and hot, and often too dry. In the Pacific Northwest and in the region of Colorado and Utah, they may grow satisfactorily provided irrigation is available. The main area for commercial currant production is in a line from southern Michigan to the Hudson River Valley of New York. Other favorable regions are around San Francisco, the Willamette Valley of Oregon, and the Puget Sound in Washington. Acreage of both currants and gooseberries in the U.S. is less than 1000 each.

Currants are easy to grow. They make fine juices, jellies and jelly combinations. Gooseberries are known for their jams, jellies, pies and sauces. Production generally over the United States has declined because of importation of these fruits at lower prices from foreign countries. Also, there is a lack of interest in the American public in using gooseberries in cooking. Be sure of local sales before making extensive plantings.

Black currants *(Ribes nigrum L)*, followed by red currants, gooseberries *(Ribes uva-crispall L.)* and white currants are popular in Europe. Much of the black currant is made into juice. Germany (FR) produces, in 000's of metric tons, about 110; United Kingdom, 30; and Poland, 30; followed by Netherlands, France, Belgium, Australia and New Zealand. Russia's plantings are largely in home gardens with some commercial plantings near large cities. *Ribes* grows wild in upper China but is not accepted in the diet.

Currants and gooseberries are extremely resistant to low temperature and with windbreaks will even survive in the northern Great Plains area. Gooseberries can be grown somewhat farther south than currants because they are more resistant to heat. The limits of currant and gooseberry growing can be extended or altered somewhat by higher altitudes or provision for irrigation.

Four main factors limit production of currants and gooseberries in the United States; namely, summer heat, lack of adequate soil moisture, the currant maggot which is difficult to control, and the white-pine blister rust. Before making a commercial or home planting of currants or gooseberries, the nursery inspection department of the local state department of agriculture should be consulted. The reason for this is because gooseberries and currants, particularly the black currants, are alternate hosts to the white-pine blister rust which is a very destructive disease of the five-leaf pines. If currants and gooseberries are destroyed in regions where the white pine is grown the disease is checked. In some areas of USA this regulation is easing since there are other forest tree species replacing the white pine. All citizens should cooperate.

Cultivars. Most desirable currants are the red cultivars which have an erect vigorous growth habit, are easy to cultivate and pick, and have large-sized firm compact clusters. Following cultivars are recommended in the

United States: Red Lake, Wilder and Stephens 9 for the northeastern section; Stephens 9, Wilder, Red Cross, Red Lake, Prince Albert, Perfection for Michigan, Middlewest; Perfection, London Market, Red Cross, Wilder, Fay, and Victoria for the Pacific Coast. Red Lake is tops in some regions and increasing in popularity in others. Red Lake has a larger cluster size and is easier to pick than Wilder, but the latter will yield better under most conditions. White and black currants receive limited attention because of color and the peculiar flavor of the blacks; the black currant also is highly susceptible to the white-pine blister rust. This rust disease may be largely responsible for the marked reduction in currant acreage since 1929. Black currants where grown are: Black Reward, Wellington XXX, Baldwin Hilltop (Eng.), Climax (Ont.), Kerry (Ont.), Boskoop Giant, Magnus, Naples (Eng.), Saunders (Ont.), Seabrook, Topsy. White Grape and White Imperial (better) are white currants. Red currants in W. Europe are Stanza and Jonkheer.

American varieties of gooseberries are most desired because they are more productive, hardier, and have better quality. European varieties are larger and sell better, but are more susceptible to mildew. The Poorman is widely planted in the North; Glenndale succeeds in Virginia, Tennessee, and Arkansas. Abundance, Perry, and Pixwell are recommended in the region of North Dakota. Welcome (Minn.) is nearly thornless, resistant to many diseases. Others: Clark (Ont), Fredonia (N.Y.), Oregon Champion and Captivator (Machine harvesting).

Establishing the plantation. Currants and gooseberries bloom very early in spring. Northern exposures are desirable, especially in the southern extensions of the industry. Air drainage and circulation are important against frost damage and also for disease control, especially with gooseberries. A deep fertile loam retentive of moisture is the best soil.

Currants and gooseberries should follow a cultivated crop, if possible; plow and disk the soil well, and add manure and fertilizer as recommended for raspberries. Fall planting is suggested for most areas because these fruits start growth so early in the spring. Spring planting is suggested in the northcentral area, in which case fall plowing is desirable.

The nursery is probably the best source for plants; they are shipped as one- or two-year plants in bundles of about 25 (Figure 26). If a grower desires to extend his planting of a preferred variety, this may be done by cuttings. Eight-inch cuttings from one-year wood are selected any time during the dormant season. They are tied in bundles of a dozen and placed base up in a box of moist sand or peat in a cool basement. In early spring, cuttings are set to the garden or nursery at a depth of six inches with a spacing of six inches in rows three feet apart. Gooseberries can be propagated by bending branches downward in the fall and

Figure 26. (Top left) Bundle of 27 vigorous gooseberry plants (currants are similar) as received from nursery. (Top right) Left rows in the currant plantation were sprayed with Bordeaux mixture with sticker-spreader for leaf spot; right rows unsprayed. (Bottom left) Imported currant worm may cause serious damage. (Bottom right) Curling of leaves caused by currant aphid on underside. (Top right) New York Agr. Exp. Sta., (Others) G.M. Darrow, U.S.D.A.

partly covering them with soil.

Gooseberries and currants also can be propagated by mound layerage; from 50 to 100 rooted cuttings can be obtained from a single plant. All branches are cut off about three inches above ground in early spring. In July, soil is mounded around the vigorous shoots, covering half their length. The rooted shoots are removed in fall or spring and set to the nursery for one year before planting permanently in the field.

These fruits are set four to five feet apart in rows five to ten feet apart, depending upon cultivation equipment available. In planting, damaged roots are removed, the branches cut back to five inches, and the plants set with the lowest branches just below the ground surface in order to encourage a bushlike plant. Dig holes for each plant in heavy soil; in light soil, a shovel may be inserted and moved back and forth to form a V-shaped opening into which the plant is set.

In home gardens, currants can be planted between and in grape rows, but cultivation must be done either by hand or by narrow machinery or herbicides, of course, can be used. Also, currants may be planted in tree rows, provided fertility and moisture are maintained sufficiently high for both crops.

Soil management. Frequent shallow cultivation should be practiced until shortly after picking when weeds are allowed to develop or a locally adapted cover crop is sown. These fruits respond well to a heavy mulch of straw or similar material. A double application of nitrogen fertilizer is needed with mulch to avoid nitrogen deficiency. A mouse poisoning program is necessary with mulching practice (Chapter V). No winter protection is needed, except perhaps to tie the bush in a bunch to prevent breakage from ice and snow. Currants are sensitive to chloride; use potassium sulfate instead of muriate (KC1).

Currants and gooseberries, like other bush fruits, respond well to drip irrigation or any type irrigation when drouths occur. In most regions where grown, much better growth and quality production can be had with regular water application when needed.

Currants and gooseberries respond well to a fertile soil and to additions of manure at the rate of 10 to 20 tons per acre. In the absence of manure, apply 200 pounds per acre

Figure 28. Multipurpose self-propelled concentrate sprayer useful in a small acreage of bush fruits, grapes and full dwarf trees. The 8 nozzles are independently adjustable. (KWH, Vandermolen Corp., Dorsa Ave., Livingston, N.J.)

of ammonium sulfate or nitrate of soda, or 150 pounds of ammonium nitrate. The manure or fertilizer should be applied as a side dressing early in spring about two or three weeks before growth starts. In the light sandy or low-fertility soils, it may be wise to establish small fertilizer test blocks, using N, P, K, and/or Mg and trace elements alone or in combination, particularly when the soil is sandy and low in organic matter. See Childers' *Fruit Nutrition* book, Chap. V, Bush Fruits, for leaf analysis data and techniques. Chemical weed control in the row can be practiced as described for blueberries.

Pruning. Plants are pruned to a bush form, varying in height from three to five feet. Best fruit with currants is produced on spurs of two- and three-year wood, although some fruit is borne near the base of one-year canes. Older wood produces inferior fruit. Prune in early spring before the buds begin to swell. The object is to remove branches over three years of age and, by thinning, select the proper kind and number of canes and branches to maintain a productive bush. Age of the wood can be judged by counting back annual growth rings from the tip (note change in color of bark and character of growth for each year). After pruning, the well-pruned dormant bush will have about three upright growths each of three-, two-, and one-year wood. With mature vigorous bushes, a few more upright growths of each age can be left (Figure 27). Thin the surplus slender weak wood. Branches growing horizontal and close to the ground should be removed to avoid dirty fruit. Pruning increases cluster size.

Gooseberries are often pruned similarly to currants, although they tend to bear heavier on one-year canes than do currants. Thus, the wood is sometimes removed after it is about two years old, or after is has borne a year from spurs.

Insects and diseases. *San Jose scale* appears as grayish

Figure 27. (Above) A Red Lake currant before pruning. (Below) After pruning. Tall growth was cut back; low horizontal branches and most of wood older than 3 years was eliminated. One-year canes were thinned to three or four vigorous canes.

crust formations on the older growth, resulting in a yellowish unthrifty dying condition. The *imported currant worm* (Figure 26) may appear shortly after the leaves expand in spring and destroy almost the entire foliage in a day or so. *Currant aphid* (Figure 26) attacks undersides of leaves, causing them oto curl. In order to hit aphids, spray should be applied before leaf curling is pronounced. *Currant fruit fly* or *maggot* is destructive to the berries, particularly in the West and Canada; no control is known. *Leaf spot* may result in defoliation (Figure 26), the leaves falling during mid- to late season, reducing production the following year. *Anthracnose* appears as numerous small brown spots on upper leaf surface causing foliage to turn yellow and drop. Other diseases include cane wilt, white-pine blister rust, viruses and powdery mildew which is particularly destructive on gooseberries. Contact your local government service station for spray recommendations.

Harvesting and marketing. Currants for jelly should be picked slightly underripe when the pectin content is high. Currants can be picked fully ripe over a long period of time if to be used for juice, spiced, or in jams. For the market, they should be picked with extreme care when an occasional berry on each bunch is slightly green. Pinch off the main cluster stem at the base, using the forefinger and thumb. Do not crush the berries. Injured berries exude juice which collects dust and dirt and may develop mold quickly, especially if they are held shortly under damp conditions. Currants can be stored for a short time under cool dry ventilated conditions.

A currant mechanical harvester is shown in Figure 29,

Figure 29. Currants are grown extensively in the cooler regions of West Europe. This is a "Hydrapick Twin" black currant harvester, built in cooperation with Britain's National Institute of Agricultural Engineering. Based on a 45 HP tractor, it twin harvests 150 lbs/minute, replacing 500 hand pickers. Black currant juice, cold, is a delicacy in Europe. (C. Rex Monigatti, Sales, P.O. Bx 3541, Wellington, N.Z.)

designed for rapid harvesting of the large acreages in Europe.

Gooseberries are mostly picked green at maximum size; harvesting may extend over a period of four to six weeks. For processing, berries can be stripped from the bushes with a cranberry scoop or heavy gloves, later separating the leaves by a grain-fanning mill. Gooseberries for the general market must be picked carefully to prevent injury and spoilage. Keep gooseberries in the shade to prevent sunscald. They can be held in storage much longer than currants.

Both goosberries and currants are marketed in 12-pint corrugated or fiberboard boxes and flats or 16-quart crates. Some wood containers are still in use. For the canner, six- to eight-pound grape baskets are standard.

Yields may average 100 bushels per acre for European gooseberries, and 300 bushels per acre for varieties of American or partly American parentage. In England, 1½ tons/A is average, but to "break even" a grower should get 2 tons, and for satisfactory profit, 3 tons/A of red currants. Higher yields, sales promotion and new products are needed to boost the industry.

For the processor, machine harvesting by suction is done with great care not to over-damage foliage. Ethephon is used to loosen berries. Special bush training is used. Pick-your-own is one of best ways to sell crops from small plantings.

CRANBERRY CULTURE[1]

The cranberry *(Vaccinium macrocarpon Ait.)* native to North America. It is consumed in the USA and Canada with few exports. Cranberry growing is a highly specialized industry confined to acid bog or swamp areas and, thus, limited to a few states. Massachusetts produces almost half of the world's supply, bringing the state $30 million or more in good years. The 1979-82 average production for the United States was 2,675,000 barrels (1 bbl = 100 lbs). Leading states, 1979-1982 period were: Massachusetts, 1,210,000 barrels; Wisconsin, 1,008,000; New Jersey, 245,000; Washington, 118,000 and Oregon, 94,000 barrels. There are nearly 23,000 acres being utilized to produce this crop in the United States. Scattered fields are in Maine, New Hampshire, Rhode Island, Connecticut, Virginia, Minnesota, Michigan, and Long Island. Canada has a limited acreage in Nova Scotia, New Brunswick, Prince Edward Island, Quebec and British Columbia. U.S. cranberry production and production and prices have increased markedly. In Europe, the cranberry-like

[1]Dr. Paul Eck, Specialist in Cranberry and Blueberry Culture, Rutgers University, New Brunswick, N.J., assisted in the cranberry section revision.

lingenberry *(V. vites ideae)* is made into jam, preserves, jelly, etc., and is preferred by many people to cranberries. European researchers, however, also are experimenting with the American cranberry.

Several factors should be considered before developing a cranberry bog. Cost per acre is rather high to clear and properly level and ditch the bog, install water pumping systems and dams, and to make the planting. There is also necessary upkeep for the first three years before the crop comes into bearing. Alkaline peat and ordinary garden and farm soils are not suitable. A large supply of water is needed for irrigation and flooding for protection against winter injury, untimely frosts, and insects. The site must permit drainage of the bog to a depth of 18 inches. A large supply of readily available clean sand is necessary. A climate, such as near Cape Cod, Massachusetts, and in

Figure 32. (Above) Biplanes and helicopters are a quick efficient method of applying fertilizers, herbicides and pesticides to cranberry bogs. Man at left is "flagging" the pilot to designate the "run". (Below) Sometimes we think the cranberry can grow and produce with almost no mineral nutrients: High nitrogen, left; low nitrogen, right. The plant, however, does respond to nitrogen as indicated in a greenhouse study. (Lower, courtesy Paul Eck, Rutgers University, New Jersey)

Figure 30. (Above) A long, narrow, well-kept cranberry bog on Cape Cod, Mass., showing proper grading and ditching with the sand supply banks on either side. (Mid) Early Black cranberries ready for harvest and, at right, an upright branch showing how the berries are borne. (Below) The old method of harvesting with a "snap" machine or scoop in a young planting. Obviously, many berries are lost and the vines trampled, vs the wet harvesting shown in accompanying photographs. (Mass. and N.J. Agr. Exp. Stas.)

Wisconsin is most desirable. A climate warmer than New Jersey induces more berry rotting and disease problems. Cranberry growing north of Nova Scotia is limited because the summers are too short and too cool. Cloudy weather during ripening, such as frequently occurs in Washington and Oregon, results in uneven maturity of berries. To establish cranberry fields in new sections, it requires years of work to develop new cultivars, to train local people in the business, and to learn the peculiarities of the industry.

A good bog site for cranberry growing is shown in Figure 30. Long narrow bogs are the most desirable with adequate air circulation on all sides, good sun exposure, and with potentialities of quick flooding and quick drainage of the field. Steps involved in the preparation of the field include: (a) clearing the field of trees and brush, (b) cutting the turf into squares, turning them over, and removing and burning roots of all weeds and obnoxious plants, (c) construction of ditches around and through the field, (d) grading the field level to facilitate quick flooding and drainage, (e) construction of dams for sectional flooding of the field if it is large or the grade is relatively marked, (f) construction of flood gates and installation of pumping equipment, (g) covering the field with three to four inches of white coarse sand free of small stones, (h)

Figure 33. Harvesting and processing of cranberries has become one of the most mechanized in the fruit industry. (a) Dry harvesting with Darlington picking machine; field boxes shown; (b) Motor-driven water beaters knock berries loose to float on flooded bog. (c) "Booming" berries after wet harvesting, using wooden booms to push berries toward shore sometimes with help of wind; (d) berries are pumped onto conveyor, removing the chaff; (e) berries are spewed through hose by powerful centrifugal pump into truck; (f) and this is a cranberry juice cocktail press in Ocean Spray plant where juice is thrown out by centrifugal force. Automatic bagging machine is used to weigh and bag the fresh berries for market. (Courtesy Ocean Spray cranberries, Inc., Hanson, Mass. 02341).

513

planting the cuttings in the early spring about a foot apart both ways, and (i) flooding the bog for a day or so immediately after planting.

Leading cultivars in Massachusetts are Early Black and Howes; in New Jersey, the Jersey, Howes, and Early Black (Figure 30); in Wisconsin, the McFarlin, Searles, and Stevens; and in Washington and Oregon, the McFarlin which comprises most of the crop. Improved carnberry Beckwith, Stevens, Wilcox, Bergman, Franklin and Pilgrim. Stevens is adapted to water harvesting (Figure 33).

Special attention to weeding is necessary for the first three years until the vines cover the ground. The bog is flooded to cover the vines with about 18 inches of water when the ground freezes in fall; it is drained about April 1 in Massachusetts, but may be left several weeks later if insects are a problem. Short floodings are necessary during the spring and fall for protection against frosts. Frost protection is being provided in some bogs with rotating sprinklers and overhead irrigation systems (Figure 34). Flooding is also timed during the early season to kill injurious insects, and is used occasionally for irrigation purposes during summer droughts. Some bogs are resanded periodically as needed, adding a one-quarter to one-inch layer for protection against frost, the girdler insect, the green spanworm, and the tip worm. This is done by hand from special wheelbarrows, or by dump trucks on the ice while the bog is frozen over. Special floating sand barges have been constructed for applying an even layer of sand durng the winter flood.

No fertilizer is usually needed for peat-bottom bogs unless growth becomes poor. Nitrate of soda and superphosphate are recommended on bogs in Massachusetts with sand or clay underneath, using 10 and 300 pounds per acre, respectively, applied when the vines are beginning to bloom in late spring. In New Jersey, an 8-8-8 fertilizer is used applying 150 lbs. in May and 150 lbs. about August 15 (Figure 32). Manures are likely to contain weed seed. Simazine (Princep 80W) can be applied in fall, winter or immediately after flood removal to control ferns, annuals and some grasses, rushes and sedges. Dalapon will control most weeds that are not killed by simazine, is applied after harvest, but bloom is lost for next year's crop in areas where used. Dalapon also is used in the ditches. Spot treatment with glyphosate has been effective in eliminating many weed species resistant to the traditional herbicides. See your local specialist for recommendations; follow them explicitly.

Berries may be harvested with the fingers, with hand scoops, mechanical scooping machines such as the Darlington (Figure 33), Western and Furford pickers, or by special water-harvesting (Figure 33). A foreman, 13 scoopers, and two helpers are needed in Massachusetts to harvest a 15-acre bog. Average acre-yields in recent years have been: 83, 105, 142, 106, and 109 barrels/acre for New

Figure 34. (a) Aerial view of processing and handling plant of Ocean Spray Cranberries, Inc., Middleboro, Mass. (b) Irrigation of sprinkler type is used for frost and drouth control. (c) Good berries are separated from bad berries by a bouncing (down steps) machine. Bad ones don't bounce well. (d) Small, light colored, bruised berries are sorted out before bagging fresh berries for sale. (e) Polybag machine prepares bags for cranberries as shown in 1 lb polybags at right (f). (Courtesy Ocean Spray Cranberries, Hanson, Mass.)

Jersey, Massachusetts, Wisconsin, Washington and Oregon, respectively. The field is flooded after harvest, and the floater berries are gathered and sold to the canneries. Water harvesting in large commercial bogs has become standard practice commercially (Figure 33).

Excessive runners are trimmed with a special knife-rake or pruner after harvest. On fertile bogs, the vines may need to be mowed if too deep and dense.

Cranberries can be stored in common storage in a screen house or in cold storage at 35°F., the latter being the better. The berries are first sent through a separator which removes chaff, then directed over bounding boards to separate decayed from sound fruits, and finally over grading belts for hand grading. Cranberries are sold by the hundredweight barrel box. Price per hundredweight varies from $25 to $50. Almost 80% of the crop is processed as sauce or made into beverages. Some cranberries are bagged (Figures 34, 35) others are quick frozen. There is a good demand for cranberries at Thanksgiving and Christmas and a much better year-round market has been developed

Figure 35. Fresh cranberries for store sales are being packaged in polybags in the Ocean Spray processing plant in Massachusetts. The machine forms, fills, cuts off and seals the bags, saving considerable hand labor. (Ocean Spray Cranberries, Inc., Hanson, Mass. 02341)

also for the cranberry fruit cocktail product sometimes mixed with apple juice. See Seelig and Roberts for review of growing, history, botany, processing and marketing of cranberries.

Diseases include *early rot* of the flowers, young berries, and stored berries and *false blossom* or rose bloom, a virus carried by the leafhopper. There are several troublesome insects. The *cranberry fruit worm* is sometimes found in a third of the crop; the *black-headed fireworm* feeds on the foliage; the *blunt-nosed leafhopper* carries false-blossom virus; the *root grub* causes dead spots over the field; the *gypsy moth* feeds on the foliage; and the *girdler* weakens or destroys plants by feeding on the underside of runners. The false army worm, brown spanworm, and other insects may become troublesome at times. For detail and up-dated control measures, see references at the end of this chapter and your local governmental service offices.

Well-managed cranberry fields are practically permanent.

Review Questions

Brambles

1. To what regions of the United States are the following brambles commercially adapted: red, black, and purple raspberries, erect and trailing blackberries, and loganberries? What generally is the world production situation?
2. Describe a suitable site and soil for red raspberries.
3. State briefly how the following brambles are propagated: red, black, and purple raspberries, blackberries, and dewberries.
4. How do the three main planting systems for brambles differ and to which bramble is each particularly adapted?
5. Outline a good soil management program for red raspberries in your locality. Would you include irrigation and, if so, why? Herbicides?
6. Which brambles are summer topped (pinched) and why?
7. How does dormant pruning of black raspberries differ from that for red raspberries?
8. When are trellises desirable for red raspberries and for blackberries?
9. How does dormant pruning for the upright blackberry differ from that for the trailing blackberry or dewberry?
10. Differentiate between anthracnose and a virus disease of raspberries.
11. At what stage of maturity should raspberries, blackberries, and dewberries be picked? Describe machine harvesting and its main value commercially.
12. Discuss mechanical harvesting of brambles. (Please check key references.)
13. For what brambles and in what regions is winter protection advisable? How is it provided?

Blueberries

14. What are the leading states in cultivated blueberry production?
15. Which of the blueberries are propagated of cultivation, and which is the most important commercially?
16. What are the climatic and soil requirements of the highbush blueberry?
17. List three leading varieties of the highbush blueberry.
18. How are blueberries propagated?
19. Outline a soil management program for a young and mature commercial planting of blueberries on a soil of medium to low fertility, having a pH of 5.0.
20. How would you prune a mature blueberry bush (a) with a spreading growth habit, (b) with an upright habit?
21. At what stage of maturity, how oftn, and over how long a period are highbush blueberries harvested in a given region? Discuss machine harvesting.
22. List an important insect and disease of blueberries.

Currants and Gooseberries

23. What are the soil and climatic requirements for gooseberries and currants?
24. Where in the United States and World are commercial currants largely grown? Where is the black currant grown and why? The red currant?
25. How are the gooseberry and currant propagated?
26. Give 2 leading varieties of gooseberry and currant.
27. On what type and age wood are currants and gooseberries largely borne?
28. Briefly describe how to prune a mature currant bush.
29. What is a leading disease and insect of currants and gooseberries?

Cranberries

30. Indicate where cranberries are grown in North America.
31. Briefly list the important factors to consider before establishing a cranberry planting.
32. What are the reasons for flooding a cranberry bog?
33. What varieties are most popular in the East, Midwest, and in the West?
34. Discuss methods and precautions for weed control in cranberries.
35. How are cranberries harvested, graded, and utilized?

Suggested Collateral Readings

(See earlier editions of this book for earlier literature)

BRAMBLES

ANON. Cane fruits. Ministry of Agriculture Bulletin 156, 40 pp. London, England. 1974.

BARRITT, B. H. and L. C. Torre. Fruit anthocyanin pigments of red raspberry cultivars. J. ASHS 100:98-100. 1975.

BARRITT, B. H. and L. C. Torre. Cold storage, handling red raspberry stock. HortSci. 9:344-346. 1974.

BARRITT, B. H. et al. Red raspberry clones resistant to root rot. Fruit Var. Jour. 35:(2) April 1981.

BARRITT, B. H. et al. Fruit firmness measurement in red raspberry. HortSci. 15(1):38-39. 1980.

BARRITT, B. H. et al. Breeding for root rot resistance in red raspberry. J. ASHS 104(1):92-94. 1979.

BARRITT, B. H. Fruit firmness selection, red raspberry. HortSci. 17(4). 648. 1982.

BOULD, C. Leaf analysis as a guide to the nutrition of fruit crops. VII. Sand culture NPK Mg experiments with red raspberry *(Rubus idaeus)*. J. Sci. Food & Agric. 19(8):457-464. 1968. (England).

BROOME, O.C. and R.H. Zimmerman. Tissue culture of thornless blackberry. Available at Fruit Lab., USDA, Beltsville, Md. 1980.

See also Bould's discussions in *Fruit Nutrition* by N. F. Childers, Hort. Publ. 888 pp. 1966. 3906 NW 31 Pl., Gainesville, Fl. 32606.

BORECKA, H. J. et al. Pruning on mortality, productivity of red raspberry infected with *Botrytis* and *Didymella*. HortSci. 10:403-404. 1975.

BOULD, C. Raspberry nutrition. In Plant Analysis and Fertilizer Problems. Publ. by ASHS. 54-67. 1964.

BOWEN, H. H. et al. 'Brison', 'Rosborough', and 'Womack' Blackberries. HortSci. 14:(6):762-763. Dec. 1979.

BRODEL, C. F. et al. Field evaluation of red raspberry resistance in *Aphis rubicola*. HortSci. 14(6):726-727. Dec. 1979.

CALDWELL, J.D. and Moore, J. N. Inheritance of fruit size in the cultivated tetraploid blackberry. (*Rubus* (Tourn.) *L.* subgenus *Eubatus)*. JASHS 107:(4) 628-631. 1982.

CONVERSE, R. H. Heat treatment on growth, fruiting of 'Thornless' Oregon Evergreen blackbery. HortSci. 16(3). June 1981.

CRAIG, D. L. Growing red raspberries in eastern Canada. Res. Sta. Kentville, Nova Scotia. Publ. 1196. 1974.

CRAIG, D. L. and L. E. Aalders. Response of 'Trent' and 'Canby' red raspberry to SADH applications. HortScience 8(4):313. August 1973.

CRAIG, D. L. and L. E. Aalders. Winter injury and yield of red raspberry under two culture systems, Nova Scotia. Can. Jour. Pl.Sci. 46:73-76. 1966.

CRANDALL, P. C. et al. Chemical primocane suppression on growth, yield, and chemical composition of red raspberries. J. ASHS 105(2):194-196. 1980.

CRANDALL, P. C. et al. Cane number, diameter, irrigation, carbohydrates on fruit number, red raspberry. J. ASHS 99:524-526. 1974.

CRANDALL, P. C. and J. D. L. Garth. Daminozide, Ethephon on raspberry. HortSci. 16:5. 654-5. 1981.

CZECH M. and Z. Krzywanski. Mg levels on resistance of red raspberry canes to *didymella applanata*/niessl./sacc. Fruit Sci. Rpts. Skierniewice, Poland. IV:(2)31-34. 1977.

DAUBENY, H. A. et al. Postharvest *Rhizopus* fruit rot resistance in red raspberry. HortSci. 15(1):35-37. 1980.

DAUBENY, H.A. et al. Occurrence and effects of raspberry bushy dwarf virus. J. ASHS 103(4): 519-522. 1978.

DAUBENY, H. A. and H. S. Pepin. Red raspberry cultivars and resistance to spur blight. HortSci. 10:404-405. 1975.

DAUBENY, H. A. Immunity to aphids in red raspberries. ASHS 88:346-351. 1966.

DAUBENY, H. and H.S. Pepin. *Botrytis* resistance in raspberry. ASHS 106(4): 423-6. 1981.

DAUBENY, H. A. et al. Red raspberry dwarf virus study. HortSci. 17(4) 645. 1982.

DAUBENY, H.A. Red raspberry varieties developed in B. Columbia. Fruit Var. Jan. 36 (3):87. 1982.

DAUBENY, H. A. and Stary, D. Resistance to *Amphorophora agathonica* in native North American red raspberry. J. ASHS 107:(4) 593-9. 1982.

DAVIES, F. S. and L. G. Albrigo. Water relations of small fruits. Ch. 3. 89-135. In water deficits and plant growth by T. T. Kozlowski. Academic Press, Inc. New York. 1983.

DENISEN, L. 'Liberty Raspberry'. HortSci. 11(4):433-4. 1976.

Disease control, brambles. USDA Farmers' Bull. No. 2208. 13 pp. 1971 or update.

DODGE, J. C. Growing raspberries in Wash. Ext. Bull. 401. 1971 or update.

EAVES, C.A., C.L. Lockhart, R. Stark and D.L. Craig. Influence of preharvest sprays of calcium salts on fruit quality of red raspberry. J. ASHS 97(6): 706. 1972.

FEAR, C. D. and B. H. Leonard. NAA on cane growth and yield of 'Boyne' red raspberry. HortSci. 17:(5)770. 1982.

FEJER, S. O. and L. P. S. Spangleo. Red raspberry yield components and relation to mechanical harvesting. J. ASHS 98(5):432. September 1973.

FUNT, R. C. Cost comparison small fruit production, harvest systems, Md. MP-922, Univ. of Md. 37 pp. 1975.

GARDINE, Kathleen D., et al. Extending the shelf-life of fresh raspberries. Plant Disease control, brambles, USDA Farmers' Bull. No. 2208. 13 pp. 1971.

GOUGH, R. E. and V. G. Shutak. Raspberry Culture for Homeowner. Univ. of R. I., Coop. Ext. Serv. Bul. 203. 12 p. up-date.

HALLOWAY, P. S. The arctic raspberry. Fruit Var. Jrn. 36(3):84-86. 1982.

HELLMAN, E. W. et al. Unilateral incompatibility between red and black raspberries. J. ASHS 107:(5) 781-4. 1982.

HOWARD, S. 'Pathfinder' and 'Trailblazer' everbearing raspberries. Fruit Varieties Jour. 30(3):94. 1976.

HUGHES, Megan et al. Mycorrhiza on nutrition of red raspberries. HortSci. 14(4):521-523. 1979.

HUGHES, Megan et al. Composition of red raspberry leaves as a function of time of season and position on cane. HortSci. 14(1):46-47. 1979.

HULL, J. W. and J. F. Lawrence. Blackberry growing USDA Farmers Bull. 2160. 1971.

IWAGAKI, Hayao. Fruits from USA, some promising new varieties. Bull. Hort. Exp. Sta., Iizaka, Fukushima, Japan, No. 1. 17 p. 1968.

JENNINGS, D. L. A hundred years of loganberries. Fruit Var. Journ. 35:(2) April 1981.

JENNINGS, D. L. Blackberries of South America - An unexplored reservior of germplasm. Frt. Var. J. 32:(3) 61-3. 1978.

JENNINGS, D.L. Two spine-free raspberries. FRuit Var. Journ. 37:(2). 34-6. 1983.

KNAPP, F.W. et al. Taste of processed Oklawaha and Flordagrand blackberries. Proc. Fla. State Hort. Soc. pp. 328-330. 1978.

KNIGHT, R. L. and Elizabeth Keep. Abstract Bibliography of Fruit Breeding and Genetics to 1955 for *Rubus* and *Ribes* — A survey. Tech. Comm. No. 25, Commonw. Bur. of Hort. and Plant. Crops, E. Malling, Maidstone, Kent, England.

LIPE, J. A. Daminozide, ethephon, and kikegulac on yield, harvest distribution, and ripening of blackberries. HortSci. 15(5):585-587. 1980.

LJONES, B. Bush fruits nutrition, Chap. V in Fruit Nutrition, Hort. Publ. 2nd Ed., 3906 NW 31 Pl., Gainesville, Fl. 32606, 1966.

LOCKSHIN, L. S. and D. C. Elving. Flowering of 'Heritage' raspberry, temperature and N. HortSci. 16(4) 527-8. 1981.

MARTIN, L.W. and R. Garren, Jr. Blackberry culture. Ore. Ext. Cir. 765. Jan. Update. Mechanical harvester field-freezes Boysunberries. Calif. Agr. Dec. 1970.

MARTIN, L.W. and F.J. Lawrence. Mechanical harvest of brambles in Oregon. HortSci. 18(2): 136. 1983.

MOORE, J.N. Blackberry Production and cultivar situation in North America. Fruit Var. Jour. 34(2): 36-42. 1980.

MOORE, J.N. et al. 'Cheyenne' blackberry. HortSci. 12(1): 77-8. 1977.

MOORE, N.J. et al. Inheritance of seed size in Blackberry. J. ASHS 100: 377-379. 1975.

MOORE, J.R. et al. Daminozide and ethephone on yield and quality of erect blackberries. J. ASHS. 103:(6) 804-6. 1978.

MORRIS, J. R. et al. Daminozide and ethephon on yield and quality of erect blackberries. J. ASHS. 103:(6) 804-6 806. 1978.

MORRIS, J. R. et al. Preharvest calcium sprays and postharvest holding on firmness and quality of machine-harvested blackberries. HortSci. 15:(1) 33-4. 1980.

MORRIS, J. R. et al. Quality of postharvest machine-harvested blackberries. J. ASHS 16:6 769-775. Nov. 1981.

MORRIS, J.R. et al. Developing a mechanized harvesting and production system for erect blackberries. HortSci. 13(3): 228-234. 1978.

OURECKY, D.K. Breeding brambles. In Jules Janick and J. Moore's "Advanced Plant Breeding," Purdue Univ. Press. 98-129. 1975.

OURECKY, D.K. 'Brandywine' purple raspberry. HortSci. 12(3): 268-9. 1977.

PYOTT, J.L. and R.H. Converse. In vitro propagation of heat-treated red raspberryt clones. HortSci. 16(3). 308-9. June 1981.

SANFORD, J.C. and D.K. Ourecky 'Royalty' purple raspberry. HortSci. 18(1): 109-110. 1983.

SHEETS, W. A. et al. Effects of plant density, training and pruning on blackberry yield. J. ASHS 97(2):262. March 1972.

SHEETS, W.A. Chemical pruning of cane berries with dinoseb. (Dow Chem. Co.) Down to Earth. 291:(4-7) Summer 1973.

SIMS, C. A. and Morris, J. R. Cultivar, irrigation, and ethephon in the yield, harvest distribution, and quality of machine-harvested blackberries. J. ASHS 107:(4) 542-7. 1982.

SKIRVIN, R.M. et al. Fireblight on thornless blackberries. HortSci. 13(4) 444. 1978.

SKIRVIN, R.M. and A.G. Otterbacher. Single and double-cropping on yields of fall bearing raspberries. Fruit Var. Jour. 33(4): 144-8. 1979.

SWARTZ, H.J., et al. Field performance and phenotypic stability of tissue culture-propagated thornless blackberries. J. ASHS. 108:(2). 285-290. 1983.

TODD, J. C. Brambles. Ministry of Agr. & Fish., N. Z. 19 p. 1974.

TORRE, C. and B. H. Barritt. Red raspberry establishment from root cuttings. J. ASHS. 104(1) 28-31.1979.

TORRE, L. C. et al. Rooting of young root-shoots of red raspberry in auxin solutions. HortSci. 15(2) 153-4. 1980.

WAISTER, P. D., M. R. Cormick, W. A. Sheets. Fruiting and vegetative competition in red raspberry. J. HortSci. 52:75-85. 1977.

WOOD, B. W. and J. N. Moore. Cane thorn density in tetraploid blackberries. J. ASHS 106:(6) 761-64. Nov. 1981.

Blueberries

AaLDERS, L. E. et al. Seed germination in lowbush blueberry. HortSci. 15(5):587-588. 1980.

AaLDERS, L. E. et al. Yields of native clones of lowbush blueberry. Frt. Var. J. Vol. 32, No. 3 64-67. July 1978.

ANDERSEN, P. C. et al. Yields of three rabbiteye blueberry cultivars with drip irrigation. J. Amer. Soc. Hort. Sci. 104(6):731-736. 1979.

ANDREWS, C. P. et al. Florida blueberry cultivars. Fruit South. 16-17. Oct. 1978.

AUSTIN, M. E. and J. S. Cundiff. Rabbiteye blueberry seed germination. J. ASHS 103(4):530-533. 1978.

AUSTIN, M. E., et al. Chilling on growth and flowering of rabbiteye blueberries. HortSci. 17:(5) 768-9. 1982.

AUSTIN, M. E. and W. T. Brightwell. Fertilizer on yield of rabbiteye blueberries. J. ASHS. 101(1):36-9. 1977.

AUSTIN, M. E. Difolitan on shelflife of rabbiteye blueberries. Fruit South 2:(2)62-5. 1978.

AUSTIN, M.E. Naphthaleneacetic acid and fruiting of rabbiteye blueberry 'Tifblue'. J. ASHS. 108:(2) 314-7. 1983.

BALLINGER, W. E. et al. Fruit anthocyanins in Vaccinium, Sub-genera Cyanococcus and Polycodium. J. ASHS 104(4):554-557. 1979.

BALLINGER, W. E. et al. Ripeness, holding temperature, and decay of blueberries. J. ASHS 103(1):130-4. 1978.

BALLINGTON, J. R. et al. Gibberellin on rabbiteye blueberry seed germination. HortSci. 11(4):410-11. 1976.

BALLINGTON, J. R. and G. J. Galletta. Fertility in diploid Vaccinium species. J. ASHS. 101(5):507-9. 1976.

BICE, C. Mississippi blueberry industry. Fruit South. pp. 8-9. Oct. 1978.

BIERMANN, J. et al. Freezing in cold-hardy blueberry flower buds. Jour. ASHS 104(4):444-449. 1979.

BITTENBENDER, H. C. and G. S. Howell, Jr. Predictive environmental, phenological components of flower bud hardiness, highbush blueberry. HortSci. 10:409-411. 1975.

BITTENBENDER, B. C. and G. S. Howell, Jr. Cold hardiness of flower buds from selected highbush blueberries. (Vaccinium australe Small). ASHS 101(2):135-9. March 1976.

Blueberry open house proceedings (published annually). N. J. Agr. Exp. Sta. New Brunswick, N.J. 08903.

BLOMMERS, J. et al. De Tellt van houtig kleinfruit. Publikatie no. 3 - 1976.

BLOMMERS, D. J. de teelt van blauwe bessen. Publikatie no. 4 - 1979.

BRIGHTWELL, W. T. and A. D. Draper. ''Bluebelle' and 'Climax' rabbiteye blueberries. Fruit Var. J. 29:44. 1975.

BROWN, J. C. and A. D. Draper. Response of blueberry (Vaccinium) progenies to pH, then iron. ASHS 105(1):20-24, 1980.

BYTHER, R. S. and Peter R. Bristow. No flavor changes detectible in Triforine-treated highbush blueberries. HortSci. 15(2):152. 1980.

CAIN, John C. and Paul Eck. Blueberry and cranberry nutrition. Chap. in Fruit Nutrition by N. F. Childers (Ed.), Hort. Publ., 3906 NW 31 Pl., Gainesville, Fla. 32606. 1966.

CAPPELLINI, R.A. et al. Market blueberry losses in New York City. HortSci. 17:1. 55. 1982.

CARKNER, R. W. et al. Blueberry establishment, production costs and returns, W. Wash. 15 p. 1981.

CHANDLER, C. K. and P. M. Lyrene. Guard cell length and ploidy in blueberry. HortSci. 17(1)53. 1982.

COCKERHAM, L. E. and G. J. Galletta. Pollen characteristics in certain Vaccinium species. J. ASHS. 101(6)671-676. 1976.

CUMMINGS, A., and J. P. Lilly. Fertilizer and lime rates on nutrient concentration in highbush blueberry fruit. HortSci. 15(6):752-754, 1980.

CUMMINGS, A. Plant and soil effects of fertilizer and lime on highbush blueberries. J. ASHS 103(3):302-305. 1978.

CUMMINGS, G. A. et al. Soil pH, sulfur, sawdust on rabbiteye blueberries. ASHS J. 106:6 783-5. Nov. 1981.

CUMMINGS, George, et al. Fertilizer and lime rates influence highbush blueberry growth and foliar elemental content during establishment. J. ASHS 96(2). March 1971.

DANA, M. N., and Mar H. Bigger. A population of Vaccinium corymbosum L. in Wisconsin. Fruit Var. Jour. 34(2):42-43. 1980.

DARROW, G. M. and J. N. Moore. Blueberry growing. USDA Farmers' Bull. 33 pp. Request recent edition.

DAVIES, F.S. et al. Yield, stomatal resistance, xylem pressure potential, and feeder root density in rabbiteye blueberry. HortSci. 14(6): 725-726. 1979.

DAVIES, F. S. and C. R. Johnson. Water stress with rabbiteye blueberries. J. ASHS 107:1. 6-8. 1982.

DEGNER, R. L. et al. Direct marketing blueberries in Florida. Industry Rpt. 81-2. 50p. 1981.

DOUGHTY, C. C. AND W. P. Scheer. Growth regulators increase yield, reduce bud hardiness. J. ASHS 100:115-118. 1975.

DRAPER, A. D. and John W. Nelson. 'Spartan' highbush blueberry. HortSci. 13(4):490. 1978.

DRAPER, A. D. et al. Breeding tetraploid blueberries. J. ASHS 107:1, 106-9. 1982.

ECK, Paul, and A. W. Stretch. Cutting wood from highbush blueberry mother block plants vs nitrogen and fungicides. HortSci. 14:(5) 599-600. 1979.

ECK, Paul. Nitrogen requirements of the highbush blueberry. J. ASHS 102(6):816-818. 1977.

ECK, Paul and N. F. Childers. Blueberry culture. (Technical and practical survey.) Rutgers Univ. Press, New Brunswick, N.J. 378 pp. 1966. (Obtainable at Hort. Publ., 3906 NW 31 Pl., Gainesville, Fla. 32606).

EDWARDS, T. W., Jr., W. B. Sherman, and R. H. Sharpe. Evaluation and inheritance of fruit color, size, scar, firmness and plant vigor in blueberry. HortScience 9(1):20. 1974.

EL-AGAMY, S. Z. A. et al. Fruit set, seed number of self- and cross-pollinated (4x) highbush and (6x) rabbiteye blueberries. ASHS 106(4).

443-5. 1981.

GALLETTA, G. Two to 5 A of berries can sweeten your income. USDA Yearbook. 1978.

GALLETTA, Gene. Breeding blueberries and cranberries. In Janick and Moore's, "Advances in Plant Breeding" pp. 154-196. Purdue Univ. Press. 1975.

GILREATH, P. and D. W. Buchanan. Chilling period of rabbiteye blueberry. ASHS 106:5. 625-28. 1981.

GOLDY, R.G. and P.M. Lyrene. Pollen germination in interspecific *Vaccinium* hybrids. HortSci. 18:(1) 54-5. 1983.

GOUGH, R. E. Roots of 'Coville' and 'Lateblue' highbush blueberry under sawdust mulch. J. ASHS 105(4):576-578. 1980.

GOUGH, R. E. et al. Growth and development of highbush blueberry. II. Reproductive growth, histological studies. J. ASHS 103(4):476-9. 1978.

GOUGH, R. E. et al. Highbush blueberry culture. R. I. Est. Serv. Bul. NE-248. 35p. 1981.

GOUGH, R. E. and G. Shutack. Highbush Blueberry Culture. Univ. of R. I. Coop. Ext. Serv. Bul. 143. 16 p. 1983.

GOUGH, R. E. and V. G. Shutak. SADH on leaves of cultivated highbush blueberry. HortSci. 11(5):514-5. 1976.

GOUGH, R. E. et al. Identification of highbush blueberry morphologically. HortSci. 11(5):512-4. 1976.

GOUGH, R. E. et al. Growth and development of highbush blueberry. I. J. ASHS 103(1):94-7. 1978.

HALL, I. V. et al. Lowbush blueberry production. Can. Dept. of Agr., Pub. 1477. 42 pp. 1972. (Very good).

HAMANN, D. D., L. J. Kushman and W. E. Ballinger. Sorting blueberries for quality by vibration. J. ASHS 98(6):572. Nov. 1973.

HANCOCK, J. F. et al. Aphid resistance in blueberry. HortSci. 17(3):362-363. 1982.

HANCOCK, J. F. and Siefker, J. H. Inbreeding highbush blueberry. HortSci. 17(3):363-366. 1982.

HAMMETT, Larry K., Walter E. Ballinger. Biochemical components of highbush blueberry fruit as influenced by nitrogen nutrition. J. ASHS 97(6):743. 1972.

HANEY, R. L. Rabbiteye production increase in Texas. Fruit South. 165. July 1978.

HEPLER, P. R. and A. D. Draper 'Patriot' blueberry. HortSci. 11(3):272-3. 1976.

HODGES, L. et al. Glyphosate on highbush blueberry *(Vaccinium corymbosum L.)* HortSci. 14(1):49-50. 1979.

HOWELL, G. S., Jr. et al. Ethephon and mechanical harvesting highbush blueberries. J. ASHS. 101(2):111-115. 1976.

HOWELL, Gordon S. et al. Rejuvenating highbush blueberries. J. ASHS 100:455. 1975.

HOWELL, G. S. et al. Mech. harvesting vibration on winter kill, highbush blueberry, HortSci. 10:85. 1975.

ISMAIL, A. A. and D. F. Yarborough. Glyphosate and 2, 4-D on Lambkill in lowbush blueberries. ASHS 106:3: 393-6. May 1981.

ISMAIL, A. A. and D. E. Yarborough. Flail mowing vs burning lowbush blueberries. HortSci. 16(3). 318-19. June 1981.

ISMAIL, Amr A. Selective thinning of black barrenberry fruit (a weed) in lowbush blueberry fields with ethephon. HortSci. 9:346-347. 1974.

ISMAIL, Amr. A. Terbacil, fertility effects on yield of lowbush blueberry. HortSci. 9:457. 1974.

JACOBS, L. A. et al. Mycorrhizal distribution in Florida rabbiteye blueberries. HortSci. 17:(6) 951-3. 1982.

JENSEN, K. I. N. Hexazinone herbicide for highbush blueberries. HortSci. 16(3). 315-17. June 1981.

KUSHIMA, T. and M. E. Austin. Seed number and size in rabbiteye blueberry fruit. HortSci. 14:(6):721-723. Dec. 1979.

KUSHMAN, L. J. and W. E. Ballinger. Blueberry quality and photoelectric measurement of anthocyanin content. J. ASHS 100:561. 1975.

KUSHMAN, L. J. and W. E. Ballinger. Season, location, cultivar, fruit size upon quality of light-sorted blueberries. J. ASHS 100:564. 1975.

LIPE, John A. Ethylene in fruits of blackberry and rabbiteye blueberry. J. ASHS 103(1):76-77. 1978.

Lowbush blueberry research information. Contact Univ. of Me., Orono and Canada Dept. of Agr., Charlottetown, Prince Edward Island, Canada, and Canada Res. Sta., Kentville, Nova Scotia.

LYRENE, P. M. Micropropagation of rabbiteye blueberries. HortSci. 15(1):80-81. 1980.

LYRENE, P. M. and W. B. Sherman. 'Aliceblue' and 'Beckyblue' blueberries. Fruit Var. Jour. 33(3):84. July 1979.

LYRENE, P. M. and W. B. Sherman. Occurrence and severity of cane canker *(Botryosphaeria corticis)* on *Vaccinium* species native to Florida. HortSci. 15(2):150-151. 1980.

LYRENE, P. M. Performance of fastrooting cuttings from blueberry shoot cultures. ASHS 106:3: 396-8. May 1981.

LYRENE, P.M. and W.B. Sherman. Mitotic instability and 2n gamete production in *Vaccinium corymbosum* x *V. elliottii* hybrids. J. ASHS. 108:(2) 339-42. 1983.

LYRENE, P. M. and W.B. Sherman. Breeding value of southern highbush blueberry. HortSci. 16(4) 528-9. Aug. 1981.

MAINLAND, M. Commercial Blueberry Production Guide for North Carolina. Agri. Ext. Ser. Bul. Request update.

MAINLAND, C. M. Stunt in rabbiteye blueberry. HortSci. 16(3). 313-4. June 1981.

MAINLAND, C. M. et al. Harvesting on yield, quality of fruit and bush damage, highbush blueberry. J. ASHS 100:129-134. 1975.

MAINLAND, C. M. and G. J. Galletta. The relationship of detachment characteristics of highbush blueberry fruit to mechanical vibration harvesting. HortSci. 8(4):309. August 1973.

MAKUS, D. J. and W. E. Ballinger. Characterization of anthocyanins during ripening of fruit of *Vaccinium corymbosum*. L. Cv. Wolcott. J. ASHS 98(1):99. 1973.

MATHIA, G. A. and R. A. Schrimper. Evaluation and measurement of characteristics affecting fresh market blueberry demand. J. ASHS 98(2):170. 1973.

MONACO, T. J. Effect of several herbicides on initial growth of highbush blueberry. HortSci. 8(4):308. August 1973.

MOULTON, J. E. et al. 'Tophat' blueberry. HortSci. 12(5):509. 1977.

MURPHY, Elizabeth F. et al. Effects of foreign edible berries on the flavor and texture of lowbush blueberry products. HortSci. 9(1):22. 1974.

MURPHY, Elizabeth F. et al. Effect of Trithion on the flavor of lowbush blueberries. HortSci. 8(1):42. 1973.

NORVELL, D. J. and J. N. Moore. Chilling and rest requirements for highbush blueberries. J. ASHS 107:(1) 54-6. 1982.

POWELL, C. L. and P. M. Bates. Ericoid mycorrhizas stimulate blueberry yields. HortSci. 16:5. 655-6. 1981.

REICH, L. A. et al. Mycorrhezal effects on blueberry at 2 pHs. HortSci. 17(4) 642. 1982.

ROBSON, M. G. and L. A. Miller. Small fruit production manual (includes blueberries). Rutgers University Ext. Bul. 432.48 p. 1981 (priced).

SHELTON, L. L. and J. N. Moore. Highbush blueberry propagatin in southern USA. HortSci. 16(3) 320-21. June 1981.

SHERMAN, W. B., R. H. Sharpe and Jules Janick. The fruiting nursery: ultrahigh density for evaluation of blueberry and peach seedlings. HortSci. 8(3):170. June 1973.

SHERMAN, W. B. and R. H. Sharpe. 'Avonblue' blueberry. HortSci. 12(5):510. 1977.

SHERMAN, W. B. and R. H. Sharpe. 'Beckyblue' blueberry. HortSci. 13(1):61. Feb. 1978.

SHERMAN, W. B. and R. H. Sharpe. 'Aliceblue' blueberry. HortSci. 13(1):62-63. Feb. 1978.

SMAGULA, J. M. and P. R. Helper. Urea and sulfur-coated urea as nitrogen sources for lowbush blueberries on a gravelly loam sand. J. ASHS. 103(6) 818-820. 1978.

SPIERS, J. M. Stage of bud development on cold injury in rabbiteye blueberry. J. ASHS. 103(4):452-455. 1978.

SPIERS, J. M. pH level and nitrogen source on elemental leaf content of 'Tifblue' rabbiteye blueberry. J. ASHS 103(6) 705-708.1978.

SPIERS, J. M. Freeze damage in rabbiteye blueberry cultivars. Fruit Var. Jour. 35:(2) April 1981

SPIERS, J. M. Fruit development in rabbiteye blueberry cultivars. HortSci. 16(2):175-6. 1981.

SPIERS, J. M. Ca and N nutrition of 'Tifblue' rabbiteye blueberry in sand culture. HortSci. 14(4):523-525. 1979.

SPIERS, J. M. Chilling and bud break in Tifblue rabbiteye blueberry. J. ASHS. 101:84-86. 1976.

SPIERS, J. M., W. A. Lewis and A. D. Draper. Hardwood propagation of rabbiteye blueberry. HortSci. 9(1):24. 1974.

SPIERS, J. M. and A. D. Draper. Chilling on Bud Break, rabbiteye blueberry. J. ASHS 99:398-399. 1974.

SWARTZ, H. J. and S. E. Gray. Annual chill-unit accumulation in USA. Fruit Var. Jrn. 36(3): 80-83. 1982.

TODD, J. C. Blueberries. Ministry of Agric. & Fish., N. Z. 8 p. 1973.

TERAMURA, A. H. et al. Comparative photosynthesis and transpiration in excised shoots of rabbiteye blueberry. HortSci. 14(6) 723-24. Dec. 1979.

TOMKINS, J. P. et al. Small fruits pest control and culture guides. Cornell Univ., Ithaca, N.Y. 1983 (yearly).

VASILAKAKIS, M. D. et al. Low temperature and flowering of primocane-fruiting red raspberries. HortSci. 15(6):750-751, 1980.

WARREN, J. M., W. E. Ballinger and C. M. Mainland. Ethephon on fruit development and ripening of highbush blueberries in the greenhouse. HortSci. 8(6):504. Dec. 1973.

WINDUS, D. et al. CO_2, C_2H_4 evolution by highbush blueberry fruit. HortSci. 11(5):515-17.

YARBOROUGH, D. E. and Amr A. Ismail. Barrenberry control in lowbush blueberry through selective application of 2, 4-D and glyphosate. J. ASHS 104(6) 786-89. 1979.

YOUNG, M. J. and W. B. Sherman. Duration of pistil receptivity, fruit set, and seed production in rabbiteye and tetraploid blueberries. HortSci. 13(3):278-9. 1978.

CRANBERRIES

BOYER, E. P., et al. Endomycorrhizae of *Vaccinium corymbosum L.* in North Carolina. JASHS 107:(5) 751-4. 1982.

BRAMLAGE, W. J. et al. Effects of preharvest application of ethephon on 'Early Black' cranberries. J. ASHS 97(5):625. 1972.

BRISTOW, P. R., and A. Y. Shawa. Fungicides on pollen and yield, cranberry. ASHS 106:3: 290-2. 1981 May.

Cranberries - Jewels from the Sand Bog. United Fresh Fruit & Vegetable Assn. Yearbook. 1973. Pp. 117-128.

Cranberry (In German). Guenther Liebster. Centrale. Marketinggesellschaft der Deutchen Agrarwartschaft MBH. To Service, 8, Munchen, Deutschland. 1972. 217 pp. illus.

CEPONIS, M. J., and A. W. Stretch. Water immersion at harvest on physiological breakdown of 'Early Black' cranberries in storage. HortSci. 16(1):60-61, 1981.

CHIRIBOGA, C. and F. J. Francis. An anthocyanin recovery system from cranberry pomace. J. ASHS 95(2):233-236. 1970.

DANA, M. N. and G. C. Klingbeil. Cranberry growing in Wisconsin. University of Wisconsin College of Agriculture Circ. 654. pp. 39. Update.

DEVLIN, R. M. et al. Abscissic Acid in Cranberry Seed Dormancy. HortSci. 11(4):412-13. 1976.

EATON, G. W. Floral induction and biennial bearing in the cranberry. Frt. Var. J. 32:(3) 58-60. 1978.

EATON, G. W. and T. R. Kyte. Yield component analysis in cranberry. J. Amer. Soc. Hort. Sci. 103(5):578-582. 1978.

EATON. G. W. and C. N. Meehan. Effects of N, P, and K fertilizer on leaf composition, yield and fruit quality of bearing "Ben Lear" cranberries. J. ASHS 98(1):89. 1973.

EATON, G. W. Effect of N, P, and K fertilizer applications on cranberry leaf nutrient composition, fruit color and yield in a mature bog. J. ASHS. 96(4):430. July 1971.

ECK, P. Nitrogen nutrition of 'Early Black' cranberry and vegetative growth, fruit yield and quality. J. ASHS., 101(4):375-7. 1976.

ECK, P. Cranberry growth and production in relation to water table depth. J. ASHS. 101(5):544-546. 1976.

ECK, P.Cranberry yield and anthocyanin content as influenced by ethephon, SADH, and malathion. J. ASHS. 97(2):213. March 1972.

FORSYTH, F. R., I. V. Hall and H. J. Lightfoot. Diffusion of CO_2, O_2, and ethylene in cranberry fruit. HortSci. 8(1):45. 1973.

GREIDANUS, Ted et al. Essentiality of ammonium for cranberry nutrition. J. ASHS 97(2):272. March 1972.

HALL, I. V. and R. Stark. Anthocyanin in cranberry, with cool temperature, low light. Hort. Res. 12:183-186. 1972.

HALL, I. V. et al. Growing cranberries. Canada Dept. of Ag. Publ. 1282. Res. Station, Kentville, Nova Scotia. Revised.

HOLLOWAY, P. S. et al. Gibberellic acid-induced fruiting of lingenberries, *Vaccinium vitis-idaea* L. spp. *minus* (Lodd.) Hult. HortSci. 17:(6) 953-4. 1982.

HOLLOWAY, P. S. et al. Chilling and budbreak in lingenberries, *Vaccinium vitis-idaea L.* J. ASHS 108:(1) 88-90. 1983.

LEES, D. H. and F. J. Francis. Standardization of pigment analyses in cranberries. HortSci. 7(1):83. Feb. 1972.

LENHARDT, P. L. and G. W. Eaton. Cranberry response to field applications of daminozide. HortSci. 11(6):599-600. 1976.

LUKE, Nai-chia et al. Dialysis extraction of gibberellin-like sustances from cranberry tissue. HortSci. 12(3):245-6. 1977.

LUKE, Nai-Chia and Paul Eck. Endogenous gibberellin-like activity in cranberry at different stages of development as influenced by nitrogen and daminozide. J. ASHS. 103(2):250-252. 1978.

MASSEY, L. M. et al. Impact-induced breakdown in cranberries. J. ASHS 106(2) 200-3. March 1981.

MASSEY, L. M. Jr. et al. Rough handling, CO_2 evolution, cranberries. HortSci. 17:1. 57. 1982.

PAPKE, A. M. et al. Airborne pollen above a cranberry bog. HortSci. 15(6):756, 1980.

SAPERS, G.M. et al. Cranberry quality: Selection Procedures for breeding programs. J. ASHS. 108:(2) 241-6. 1983.

SAPERS, G.M., et al. Recovery of juice and anthocyanin from cranberries. J. ASHS 108:(2) 246-9. 1983.

SEELIG, R.A. and Roberts. Cranberries (botany to marketing) U.S. Fresh Fruit and Vegetable Ass'n., 1019 19th St., NW, Wash., D.C. 20036. (Priced).

SHAWA, A. Y. Response of 'McFarlin' cranberry to N Sprays. HortSci. 17:(6) 949-50. 1982.

SHAWA, A. Y. Lime on yield and keeping quality of 'McFarlin' cranberries. HortSci. 14(1) 50-51. 1979.

SHAWA, A. et al. Cranberry yield components in NW USA. J. ASHS 106(4) 474-7. 1981.

SIECKMANN, S. and A. A. Boe. Low temperature on reducing and total sugar concentrations in leaves of Boxwood *(Buxus sempervirens L.)* and Cranberry *(Vaccinium macrocarpon Ait.)* HortSci. 13(4) 439-40. 1978.

SKIRVIN, R. M. et al. *In vitro* propagation of trailing thornless blackberry. HortSci. 16(3) 310-12. June 1981.

STONE, E. G. Cranberry seed germinatin in 3 media. HortSci. 17:1. 58. 1982.

Elderberry

RITTER, C. M. Elderberry Culture. Pa. Bull. 709, 22 pp. 1964.

WAY, Roger D. Elderberry Growing in New York State, N.Y. St. Coll. of Agri. and Life Sci. Ext. Bull. 1177:1-3. 1972.

(See additional references in former book editions)

a

b

c

d

e

f

g

RESEARCHERS IN SMALL FRUITS usually work in breeding and/or culture with more than one small fruit. While the researchers here work mainly with crops in Chapter XXII, they also may work with strawberries and grapes. Among those who have contributed to crops in Chapter XXII are: (a) Gene J. Galletta, blueberries, strawberries, general, USDA, MD; (b) Donald H. Scott, retired, blueberries, strawberries, USDA, MD; (c) Paul Eck, blueberries, cranberries, Rutgers University, New Jersey; (d) J. Wilson Courter, strawberries, general, University of Illinois; (e) James N. Moore, strawberries, blueberries, grapes, brambles, University of Arkansas; (f) Hayao Iwagaki, blueberries, Fukushima, Tokyo, Japan; and Richard C. Funt, strawberries, blueberries, brambles, general, Ohio State University. Others who have made key contributions include: G.M. Darrow, retired, USDA, Md.; the late G.L. Slate, N.Y. Exp. Sta., Geneva; Ralph H. Sharpe, Paul Lyrene and W.B. Sherman, University of Florida; H.S. Daubeny, B.C., Canada; W.A. Sheets, University of Oregon; R.E. Gough, University of R.I.; W.E. Ballinger and Charles Mainland, N.C. State University; J.M. Spiers, USDA, MS; and A.A. Ismail, University of Maine.

CHAPTER XXIII

Some Home Fruit Garden Tips

The home fruit garden may not only save on the food bill, but more important, it is a real source of enjoyment, can develop into a hobby and certainly is a healthful exercise. A little time on weekends and after dinner some evenings can bring you a lot of pride and satisfaction in a productive beautiful fruit garden. Some people have forgotten or never knew how good fresh fruits and vegetables can taste ripened to peak eating quality at harvest time (Figures 2-4).

Some things are key: (a) good sun exposure much of the day, (b) good soil drainage, and (c) a reasonably fertile soil with pH adjusted to around 6.0 by liming where needed. You can get your soil tested through your county agricultural agent usually located at the county seat Post Office or court building. A *regular* but not excessive supply of water to the plants is most important, either by

Figure 1. At the sunny side of your house a bed can be prepared for a few vegetables and several strawberry plants. This is protected from view in the front yard by a lattice fence. (Photo from Nevada, Missouri - Anne G. Barton).

sprinkling (eyelet hose or drip arrangement is good) or by 6-12 inch depth mulching with leaves, grass clippings, straw, peat moss, or by using poly strips. Grass clippings can be dumped from the mower catcher among the plants or under the trees during the growing season, and during the fall and winter the leaves can be spread over the garden area to decompose and be spaded under in spring as a source of organic matter. Some cultivation to loosen the soil and control weeds is desirable where feasible. Bear in mind that nitrogen fertilizer or fertilizer containing nitrogen must be applied to trees and plants that have been freshly mulched. Otherwise bacteria decomposing the mulch will get first draw on the nitrogen, causing a deficiency in the plant or tree. Fertilizer should be applied in spring before growth starts. In sandy soils one or two additional light fertilizer applications may be needed early in the season a month apart.

When selecting kinds of fruits and cultivars (varieties), check with your neighbors, maybe a commercial grower, your county agricultural agent, and perhaps a nursery catalogue which is representative of your area. Many home gardeners like to select the earlier ripening cultivars, but an extension of ripening season is frequently desirable. Most important, however, is to select the kinds of fruits you and your family like most. Apples and strawberries are among the most widely grown. Apricots, sweet cherries, peaches, nuts, almonds, blueberries, loganberries, for example, are somewhat more exacting. Pears and plums will succeed better than most fruits in the heavier moist soils. Tart cherries are good where adapted. Everbearing red raspberries and thornless blackberries are popular and productive if they can be grown in your area. Catalogues from the well supplied nurseries often can help.

As indicated in Figure 2, there are many fruit plants that can serve a double purpose in the landscape. Blueberries have beautiful red foliage in the fall and their bloom and berries are attractive. Some fruit trees have bloom even more attractive than dogwood. Strawberries can make an effective ground cover under trees and bushes in the more sunny locations. Blueberries, currants and gooseberries can grow in some shade provided they are watered and fertilized properly. Hanging baskets and window boxes of strawberries are somewhat of an oddity; pyramids and barrels of strawberries (see Chap. 21) can produce well in limited space. In Figure 4 is a tree trained fan-shape

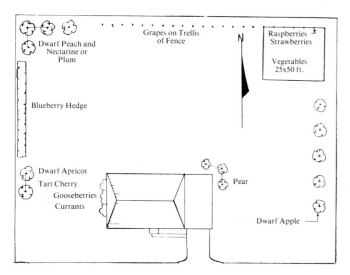

Figure 2. Above are suggested locations for fruit plants in the home landscape. If you wish, all fruit plants can be confined to upper right corner of plan. Size of entire lot is 130x160 ft. Ornamentals are to be added. Fruit plants can serve both as ornamentals and a source of food. (Plan by Jay H. Kirsh, Temple Univ., Ambler, Pa.)

againts a wall or you can use a trellis. Grapes can be grown on the border fence, a trellis or on an arbor (Chap. 20) for both shade and fruit.

If limited space permits only a tree or two of a kind of fruit, you can bud or graft cion wood of 2-5 different cultivars ripening at different periods on the tree(s) (See Chap. VIII). Some nurseries sell a tree with 4 or 5 cultivars on it.

Some problems you may encounter include: (a) winter cold damage to trunk, wood or roots; poor soil drainage, particularly standing water around the roots in spring; drouthy periods when you are on vacation; rabbit or mice bark or root damage; nutrient deficiencies in foliage and fruit; borers in peach trunk and other wood, aside from the usual insect and disease problems with specific fruits

(see Index and Chap. XVIII). You *must* plan on a spray program.

If you are an enthusiastic home horticulturist, you may want to seek the help of a local landscape designer to draw a professional landscape plan for your home and then follow his plan for well adapted flowering shrubs, trees, perennial and annual flowering plants as well as fruit and vegetable plants. Then seek a nurseryman to supply and perhaps plant the landscape. Installation of an automatic or manual sunken irrigation system is suggested in regions where drouths or short periods of no rainfall are likely to occur. Adequate and regular water supply with fertilizer added when needed are most important to successful home gardening. Timely irrigation of the lawn is most important also.

A Few References

Most state universities with agricultural colleges can supply home garden bulletins for local and climatic conditions. There will be separate bulletins for fruits, for vegetables and for lawn and ornamentals care. Ask for publications listing, prices.

1. Childers, Norman F. (Ed.) The Strawberry. Hort. Publ., 560 p. 3906 NW 31 Pl., Gainesville, Fl. 32606. 1981. (Priced).
2. Eck, Paul and N. F. Childers. Blueberry Culture. 450 p. Hort. Publ. 3906 NW 31 Pl., Gainesville, Fl. 32606. (Priced).
3. Klass, Carolyn and D. L. Pinnow. Disease and Insect Control In The Home Orchard (Color photos very good for identification) 16 p. N. Y. Agr. Exp. Sta., Bul. 124. 1977. (Priced).
4. Kolbe, Melvin H. Tree fruit production for home use. N. Car. Agri. Exten. Serv. Bull. AG 28. 20 p. Raleigh, N.C. 1978.
5. Rollins, Howard A. et al. Growing and using fruit at home. Cultural and pest management. Ohio Agric. Exten. Serv. Bull. 591. 54 p. 1980. (Priced).
6. Stebbins, R. L. and M. MacCaskey. Pruning - How-To Guide For Gardeners. 165 p. (Color). HP Books. P.O. Bx. 5367. Tuscon, Arizona 85703. (Priced).
7. Van der Zwet, Tom and Norman F. Childers. The Pear. Hort. Publ., 3906 NW 31 Pl., Gainesville, Fl. 32606. (Priced).

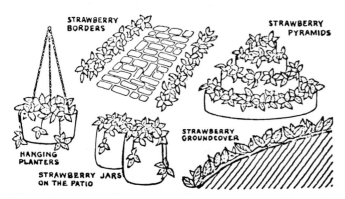

Figure 3. Strawberries are versatile — as a ground cover, in hanging baskets, in jars, lining the sidewalk, in a pyramid or barrel (see also Chap XXI). Courtesy Paul Stark, Jr., Stark Nursery, Louisiana, Mo. 63353.

Figure 4. Fruit trees on semi- or full-dwarfing rootstocks can be trained against a wall or fence *with good sun exposure.* They occupy but little space and will produce well. (See Chap. IV for training suggestions.) (From Eipeldauer, 1952).

522

Appendix

SUGGESTED POMOLOGY LABORATORY EXERCISES[1]

A "Modern Fruit Science Laboratory Manual" is available for use with this book. It has a color front cover, ring bound, lies flat on table, with 18 inside-outside basic pomology exercises.

There is an itinerary of advance jobs for the instructor to do in preparation for each laboratory.

Students are asked to complete diagrams, tables, study and interpret charts, plant material and chemical herbicide and pesticide samples, answer questions, and read and abstract outside references. There are a variety of exercises for a basic course in fruit science. See list of exercises below.

Copies of the Manual are available through Horticultural Publications, 3906 NW 31 Pl., Gainesville, Fla. 32606. A copy is mailed gratis to instructors of classes of 5 or more students. Cost has been under $10.

TEACHER EVALUATION BY STUDENTS

This teacher and course evaluation is used by Alpha Zeta, honorary fraternity of agriculture, on the Rutgers University campus to evaluate teachers and their courses (by their permission) a week to 10 days before the course is concluded. Summary evaluations are only circulated to teachers and students during the following semester. Answers to questions, A to D, are shown only to the respective teachers. A review of these desired characteristics here may help you as a teacher regardless of any evaluation by students.

Author of this text has had experience over some 25 yrs with student evaluations of their professors. There are some drawbacks. A young rather inexperienced teacher may be so criticised by his students that he becomes discouraged and switches to research or quits the job entirely when, with patience, he could develop into a valuable teacher, one of the best. Department heads usually know by comments coming to them (without a student evaluation) that a certain teacher is having problems. He can call him in and discuss how he could improve, give the teacher a chance and later make a decision what to do. Some good teachers just do not like to be criticised by students or anyone, and they would prefer not to be subjected to this, so they switch to research or extension, or! A disgruntled student can make it difficult for his teacher, which may not be justified, causing the teacher to skip a promotion. This markedly upsets the teacher.

Teaching is not easy. It is easier to NOT teach than to teach, so many professors in agriculture switch to total research where their time is more their own and they are not subjected to student problems. Unfortunately, promotions and salary raises often are based more on research accomplishments than on teaching. This must be changed and it is changing, but too slowly. The final overall result is that we are growing very short of good pomology teachers and thus, with fewer and fewer people to teach pomology, we have fewer students majoring in the field and less trained pomologists with MS and PhD degrees to take an interest in and train young pomologists. The industry suffers. And as a result we are hiring professionals in pomology jobs such as chemists, foresters, physiologists, botanists, physicists, engineers, mathematicians, etc., who know little or no horticulture or pomology. Some horticulture departments over the country are now over 50% not pomologists or horticulturists. The departments are losing contact with the growers for whom they are working to solve their problems which makes it difficult to get appropriations to support departmental teaching and research *for the industry*.

Student evaluation of their teachers is only one of a number of developments in the last few decades that may be interfering with efficient and productive management of a horticulture department in teaching and research.

INSTRUCTIONS TO STUDENTS:

Mark the answer sheet with a No. 2 pencil only (furnished each student by fraternity representative). Each evaluation characteristic is numbered for computer analysis. For each numbered characteristic you should select and mark a rating category from 1 to 5, e.g. 1 Excellent; 2 Good; 3 Average; 4 Fair; 5 Poor.

DO NOT MARK YOUR EVALUATIONS ON THESE SHEETS. USE THE ANSWER CARD (DESIGNED FOR

---

[1] See Chapter XIX in 1969 edition of Modern Fruit Science for instructions on training an apple judging team in cultivar identification and competition. Also, the ability to judge fruit at state or county fairs is stressed along with ability to judge sites and orchard value.

COMPUTER). (YOUR OWN CARD CAN BE DESIGNED FROM INFORMATION BELOW.)

PERSONAL TRAITS AND CHARACTERISTICS:

(1) fairness; (2) sympathy; (3) knowledge of subject; (4) firmness; (5) patience; (6) interesting; (7) enunciation; (8) willingness to help.

TEACHING ABILITY:

(17) preparation of lessons; (18) success in getting attention; (19) motivation—creating a need; (20) statement of lesson objectives; (21) use of varied techniques.

PRESENTATION:

(29) organization; (30) method of presentation; (31) ability to explain concepts; (32) extent and quality of questioning; (33) quality of review; (34) use of visual aids and devices; (35) ability to "stick to" topic.

ASSIGNMENTS:

(45) adequate time to complete; (46) understandable; (47) pertinence to lessons.

CLASS MANAGEMENT:

(57) care of physical conditions (lighting, ventilation, etc.); (58) ability to get things done; (59) fairness in grading.

LABORATORY MANAGEMENT (IF APPLICABLE):

(69) efficiency of organization; (70) fairness in grading; (71) preparation by laboratory instructor; (72) laboratory instructor's knowledge of subject

LABORATORY WORK (IF APPLICABLE):

(85) integration with text; (86) presentation of new and interesting ideas; (87) aid in better understanding course material; (88) encouragement to investigate on own.

LIBRARY AND CURRICULUM:

(97) Have you used the agricultural library relative to this course. If no, mark the 1. If yes, mark the 2 for one time, the 3 for two times, the 4 for three times, or the 5 for four or more times used: (101) Is this course required in your curriculum? If no, mark the 1; if yes, mark the 2.

OVERALL COURSE EVALUATION:

(113) My "learning experience" from the lectures; (114) My "learning experience" from the labs; (115) My "learning experience" from the course; (125) Expected grade: score 1, 2, 3, 4, or 5.

PLEASE ANSWER THE FOLLOWING ON THE BACK SIDE OF THE ANSWER SHEET.

A. Name one or two things which you especially like about this professor.
B. Give one or two suggestions for the improvement of this professor (objectionable, mannerisms, etc.)
C. Name one or two things you especially like about this course.
D. Give one or two suggestions for the improvement of this course.

Job Hunting

Suggestions to students from U.S. News and World Report Magazine

In order of importance, here are six things college recruiters look for when offering jobs to graduates:

1. Personal qualifications, such as maturity, initiative, enthusiasm, poise, appearance and the ability to work with other people. This is first in importance for candidates in all fields, from engineering to the liberal arts.

2. Scholastic grades—all fields.

3. Study in specialized courses relating to a particular area of work. True for every field except liberal arts, where this factor ranks fifth.

4. In all fields, kind and amount of part-time or summer employment.

5. Experience in campus activities, especially participation and leadersip in extracurricular life. For liberal-arts majors, this ranks third.

6. For all graduates, general or liberal-arts courses designed to impart a broad, cultural background.

This ranking comes from 215 corporations that responded to the 30th annual Endicott survey published by Northwestern University.

Note: "Merchandizing Your Job Talents," U.S. Dept. Labor, Manpower Admin., Wash., D.C. 20402 (Stock No. 2900-00220, Price 50ᶜ), Supt. Documents, gives pertinent information on job hunting, interviews, etc.

Glossary

The following word definitions may help in understanding terms used in this text and in horticulture in general. Webster's large or collegiate edition dictionaries are authoritative and also should be helpful in defining terms not found here. See also Zeilinski, Q. B. Modern Systematic Pomology. Wm. C. Brown Co., Dubuque, Iowa, 1955, for a glossary of varietal, propagation and taxonomic terms. Consult also: "A Technical Glossary of Horticultural and Landscape Terminology. Hort. Res. Inst., 835 So. Bldg., Wash., D. C., U.S.A., 20250.

Abrupt. Suddenly narrowed.
Abscisic Acid (ABA). A complex natural growth inhibitor, thought to be principal inhibitor in the dormant (resting) stage of buds.
Abscission. Dropping of fruit or leaves.

Absorption. Intake of water, other substances as by a cell, a root, or other plant organ.
Acaulescent. Apparently without a stem.
Achene. A hard dry one-seeded indehiscent fruit, especially one in which the pericarp very closely envelops the seed; the so-called strawberry "seed."
Acid. A condition in which the so-called acid elements (such as nitrogen, sulfur, or chlorine) in a solution overbalance the basic elements; associated with a great concentration of hydrogen and or hydroxyl ions.
Acuminate. Tapering at the end.
Acute. Terminating with a sharp angle.
Adjuvants. Correctives, stickers, spreaders, activators, flocculators and emulsifiers added to pesticides and herbicides to improve effectiveness or aid in correcting application problems.

Adnate. United with.

Adsorption. A surface phenomenon in which water or other substances become spread out on or otherwise attached to particles of some other substance.

Adventitious bud. A bud located out of the usual location. Shoots arising from these buds are known as adventitious shoots.

After-ripening. A kind of curing process required by the seed, bulb and related structure of certain plants before germination will take place.

Aggregate Fruit. A fruit consisting of a collection of carpels of one flower, e.g., blackberry or raspberry.

Air Layering. A form of propagation of plants in which a portion of a branch or stem, sometimes girdled, is kept covered with polyethylene enclosing moist peat moss over the girdle or rooting area until it forms roots and later may be detached from the mother plant and planted.

Alkali. Salts present in soils in amounts harmful to plants, such as sodium chloride, sodim sulfate or sodium carbonate.

Allopolyploid. A polyploid having dissimilar sets of chromosomes, usually differentiated in pairs.

Alternate (of leaves, etc.) (a) Not opposite on the stem axis, but arranged singly at different heights. (b) Alternate bearing is bearing fruit every other season. "Off-year" is the season of little or no bearing of fruit by a tree.

Alternate Leaves. Leaves placed singly on the stem (rather than opposite in pairs), or rather than whorled (if more than two).

Androecium. The stamens and their appendages collectively.

Annual. A plant whose normal life span does not exceed one year.

Anionic. Negatively charged molecules.

Antagonism. In relation to salts, a mutual counteraction of individual influence on plant cell permeability, eg.g., interaction of K+ and Mag++, high amounts of one interfering with entrance of another into a plant system.

Anther. Pollen (male)-bearing part of the stamen, borne at the top of the filament in the flower.

Anthesis. The state of full bloom in a flower; sometimes used to describe the period of flowering when pollen is shed from anthers.

Anthocyanin. Red pigment formed by some plants giving the fruit, leaves or other organs a red coloring.

Apomixis. Asexual seed production of reproduction budding in the ovary without fertilization.

Atriculate. Jointed.

Ascorbic Acid. A crystalline water soluble vitamin found in fruits and vegetables, commonly called Vitamin "C".

Asexual. Propagation other than by seed; budding, grafting, layering and use of cuttings are examples.

Autogamy. When a flower is pollinated by its own pollen.

Autonomic. A term referring to fruit which set without the stimulus of pollen; a part of parthenocarpy.

Auxins. Natural or synthetic substances which can regulate or stimulate plant growth and cell enlargement in plants.

Available water. That portion of the soil moisture supply, mainly the capillary fraction, which the plant can absorb.

Axil. Angle above the junction of a leaf-blade, petiole, peduncle, or pedicel, with the branch or stalk from which it springs.

Bacterial canker. An area of injury, often necrotic, of stems by bacteria; e.g., *Pseudomonas* sp.

Bark. Tough, external covering or investment of a woody perennial stem or root, consisting of tissues external to the cork cambium, which on being cut off from food supplies will soon die and dry.

Basic number. The number of chromosomes found in gametes of a diploid plant or a diploid ancestor of a polyploid plant.

Basin. The depression at the apex or blossom end (opposite the stem end) of fruits such as the apple.

Beaked. Ending in a prolonged tip.

Berry. A simple fruit derived from one flower, in which the parts remain succulent. The true berry is derived from an ovary (as is the grape); the false berry from an ovary plus receptacle tissue (as is the blueberry).

Berry. A pulpy, indehiscent fruit with few or many seeds. Technically, the pulpy or fleshy fruit resulting from a single pistil, containing one or more seeds, such as the blueberry or the orange.

Biennial. (a) Those plants which bear fruit only after two seasons of growth, as raspberry. (b) Biennial bearing of a tree is bearing heavy crops one year and little or none the next in a cycle.

Bifid. Two-cleft.

Bisexual. A plant or variety that produces both staminate (male) and pistalate (female) flowers.

Bitter Pit. Physiological disease appearing as small, round, dead depressions of the epidermis, hypodermis, and other first layers of the fruit, as in apple. Spots may have a bitter taste. Caused by calcium deficiency.

Black end (hard end). A physiological disorder of the calyx end of pear fruit caused by certain rootstocks (e.g., *Pyrus pyrifolia, P. ussuriensis*).

Blackheart. Physiological disease which causes the inner layers of woody stems to decay causing a loss in ability of all or part of the conducting tissue to perform their functions, often caused by low-winter temperatures.

Blade. The expanded portion of a leaf.

Blight. Disease causing general killing of stems, leaves or branches.

Bloom. The delicate white or powdery substance on the surface of some fruits, or on the canes of vine and bramble-fruits.

Blush. An unbroken red tint on the surface of a fruit.

Bog Soils. Soils arising from decay of swamp vegetation having very high organic matter content. Surface is usually muck or peat with underlying layer of peat, used, e.g., in cranberry production.

Boreal. Of or pertaining to the North; of northern latitudes.

†**Bound water.** Water held tenaciously in the form of extremely thin film surrounding very small solid particles.

Bract. Reduced or modified leaf which can be large and very showy in some flowers, as poinsettia, or small and inconspicuous as at base of an apple leaf petiole.

Branch. A shoot or secondary stem growing from the main stem. Or, a stem larger than a shoot growing on a tree or similar plant from the trunk or from a bough.

Breba. The first or spring crop of figs.

British Thermal Units (BTU). The quantity of heat required to raise the temperature of one avoirdupois pound of water one degree Fahrenheit at or near 39.2°F, the temperature at its maximum density.

Broadcast application. Application of agricultural chemicals over an entire area rather than in strips, beds or middles.

Brush. The bundle of fibers connecting the pedicel with the berry of the grape.

Bud scales. Scale-like leaf which forms the external covering of a bud in winter and may have dense coatings of hair, gum, or resin.

Bud Sport (Mutation). A branch, flower or fruit which arises from a bud differing genetically from the "mother" plant. Usually caused by a spontaneous mutation of cell genes.

Bulb. A large fleshy bud-like structure as e.g. head lettuce, onion, tulip.

Callus. Parenchyma tissue which grows over a wound or a graft, protecting it against drying or other damage.

Calorie. The amount of energy required to raise the temperature of one gram of water one degree Celsius. (1 food calorie = 1000 calories.)

Cambium. Undifferentiated meristematic tissue in the form of a very thin layer between bark and wood.

Cane. A shoot which bears but once, particularly one which arises from the crown or root, as in brambles.

Capillary. Hair-like.

Caprification. The process of pollination of the fig flower with pollen from the caprifig by the blastophaga wasp.

Capri Fig. The uncultivated wild fig, sometimes called the "male" fig.

Carbohydrate. A compound produced by plants containing chemically bonded energy composed of carbon, oxygen and hydrogen.

Carbon - Nitrogen Ratio (Relationship). Relative proportion, by weight, of carbon to nitrogen in the soil, organic matter or plant tissue.

Carotenoids. Yellow coloring pigments found in the leaves and fruits of plants. ($C_{26}H_{38}$.)

Carpel. A modified leaf forming the structure enclosing the seed.

Cationic. Having a positively charged molecule.

Catkin. A scaly cylindric floral spike.

Caulescent. Having a conspicuous stem.

Cellulose. Any of several fibrous compounds found in cell walls and fibrous products of plants; a complex polymeric carbohydrate $(C_6H_{10}O_5)x$.

Chalaza. The place where seed-coat and kernel of a seed connect.

Chamagamy. Pollination only after the opening of the flower.

Chemotropism. Movement of the plant by bending or twisting in response to a chemical stimulus.

Chimera. A mixture of tissues of different genetic constitution in the same plant. Peri-clinical chimera-tissues of one element completely encircles another, as in some thornless blackberries; once formed, is stable. **Mericlinal chimera -** the different tissue is one layer deep and may occur, e.g., as a wide dark red stripe on an apple, unstable, common. **Sectorial chimera -** the genetically different tissue penetrates all three meristematic layers or occurs as a large segment (pie shape) of the trunk or branches. Some may be graft-chimeras from a mixed adventituous bud at the union of stock and scion; uncommon unstable.

Chloroplast. Structure in a leaf called a plastid which contains chlorophyll.

Chlorosis. The yellowing of leaves; may be due to lime-induced iron deficiency.

Chromosome. Rod-like structures in the cell nucleus that contain the genes, the units of heredity.

Cleistogamy. Self pollination without the flower being open, as in violet.

Clone. A group of plants originating as parts of the same individual, from buds or cuttings or division.

Cluster base. Enlarged sections of a spur as in apple or pear to which the apple peduncle or flower pedicles were attached.

Coleoptile. A hollow living cylinder enclosing the epicotyl of a newly germinated grain seedling; it is attached to the seedling at the first node. Wheat and oat coleoptiles are used to study growth regulators and hormones.

Colloid. Usually an uncrystalline semisolid which is capable of slow diffusion through a membrane.

Compatibility. (a) In sex cells, the ability of male and female forms to unite to form a fertilized egg that will continue to grow to maturity. (b) Ability of the sclon and stock to unite in grafting and form a strong union.

Compound (leaf). Leaf which has the blade divided into separate leaflets.

Conduplicate. Folded upon itself lengthwise.

Connate organs. Organs congenitally more or less united.

Connivent. Coming into contact or to a point as the sepals on a Winesap apple.

Contact Herbicide. A chemical that kills the portion of the weed or plant upon coming in contact with it. A non-selective herbicide. Example is sodium arsenite.

Cordate. Heart-shaped, with the point upward.

Cork Spot (York Spot, drouth spot). Physiological (or virus?) disorder of apples appearing as slightly flattened areas on the apple having a water-soaked appearance, with deeper discoloration of the skin at the site of spot formation. Brown "corky" areas may form beneath the spotted skin. Boron, calcium and possibly other deficiencies or nutrient offbalances may be associated with the problem.

Corky Core. Disorder in apples, probably physiological, with symptoms of browning and corky textured areas around the core due to cell death; sometimes accompanied by a bitter taste. Boron deficiency is usually associated with the disorder.

Corymb. A flat-topped or convex open flower-cluster.

Cotyledons. The foliar portion or first leaves (one, two, or more) of the embryo as found in the seed.

Coulure. Failure of grape blossoms to set, resulting in premature drop.

Crenate. Dentate, with the teeth much rounded as on a leaf.

Crinkle. Apple disorder manifested by roughened skin on the fruit; a supposed form of drouth injury.

Cultivar. Technically, it is replacing the word, "variety".

Cuneate. Leaves that are wedge shaped at the base.

Cyme. A usually broad and flattish determinate inflorescence, with its central or terminal flowers blooming earliest.

Cytokinesis. Cytoplasmic changes involved in mitosis, meiosis, and fertilization, as distinguished from nuclear changes.

Cytokinins. A class of plant hormones that stimulate cell divisions and delay senescence; e.g., benzyl adenine, zeatin, kinetin.

Deciduous (leaves). Falling of leaves after one season of growth.

Degree-day. In pomology, a heat unit representing one degree of temperature above a given mean daily temperature on a given day. Since crops require a specific amount of energy in order to mature, the number of accumulated degree-days indicates how close a crop is to maturity.

Dehiscent. Opening regularly by valves, slits, etc., as a capsule or anther.

Dehorn. This refers to cutting of fruit trees back into 3- or 4-year wood during the dormant season to renew the top, usually following a freeze, as in case of peaches. Practice has not been encouraged in recent years.

Dentate. Toothed, usually with the teeth directed outward as in a leaf.

Determinate. With the terminal (center) flower of an inflorescence opening first, thus stopping terminal growth. The lateral flowers open somewhat later.

Dichogamy. When the stamens shed pollen and the pistils of a flower are receptive at different times; as in avacado.

Dicliny. The condition in which male and female organs are separate, in different flowers.

Dieback. A psysiological or pathological disorder of plants characterized by the death and/or failure of the younger areas of the plant to grow.

Dimorphism. Presence of two forms of leaves, flowers, or other organs upon the same plant, or upon other plants of the same species, such as pigmented or unpigmented fruit or deciduous or permanent branches.

Dioecious. Having the androecium (male flower) and gynoecium (female flower) on separate plants.

Diploid. A plant with two sets of chromosomes, as found normally in somatic cells of the sporophyte phase.

Dormant. Plants or buds which are not actively growing but can be made to grow with favorable environmental conditions.

Drought spot. *See* cork spot.

Drupe (Stone Fruit). A fruit developed from a single carpel with a fleshy exocarp and a hard stony endocarp containing a single seed. Some stone fruits are multicarpellate with one to several seeds, as in raspberry.

Drupelet. A diminutive drupe, as in a raspberry fruit.

Effective pollination period (EPP). The embryo-sac longevity minus the time required to complete pollination and pollen-tube growth.

Emarginate. Notched at the summit.

Emasculation. Removal of male parts of the flower by artificial means. Used by plant breeders to control pollination.

Embryo. The rudimentary plantlet within the seed.

Embryo Sac. Region of cell in the ovule where the embryo is formed.

Emulsion. Suspension of one liquid in another oil and water is a common emulsion.

Endocarp. The inner layer of the pericarp, ripened ovary or fruit, as the pit of a peach.

Endodermis. The innermost layer of the cortex which abuts the stele.

Endogenous. Originating within the plant.

Endosperm. The nourishment for the embryo, which surrounds the embryo in the plant seed.

Entire (leaves). Without any indentations or division.

Epicarp (exocarp). The outer layer of the pericarp, the ripened ovary or fruit coat, as the skin of a peach or apple.

Epicotyl. The stem above the cotyledons of a young seedling.

Epidermis. The thin layer of cells forming the outer covering of plants.

Epigynous (flowers). Attached to the surface of the ovary so as to be apparently inserted upon the top of it, as in case of the attachment of stamens, petals or sepals. The apple fruit is an example.

Epinasty. Downward bending or drooping of leaves caused by stresses at the petiole changing the direction of growth, as induced by some fruit thinning chemicals on a variety like Wealthy.

Erosion. Wearing away, or carrying away of the surface of land by agents of wind, water or other natural agents.

Etiolation. The condition of spindly white growth caused by excluding light.

Exanthema (fruit trees). A dieing back of younger wood in fruit trees due sometimes to copper deficiency which may be induced by excessive nitrogen fertilizer.

Exocarp. The outer layer of the pericarp, ripened ovary or the fruit coat, as the peel of an appricot.

Exocortis. A sluffing off of the bark of trees.

Exine. Outer layer of the pollen grain.

Eye. The calyx of a pome fruit; a compound bud of a grape; or the hole in an immature fig through which the wasp passes in pollination.

Family. A natural assemblage of plants placed together because of resemblances, as Rosaceae, which includes many pome fruits, rose, etc.

Fasciation. Flattening of the stem due to multiple terminal buds growing in the same place.

Fascicle. Condensed cluster.

Feather. In pomology, refers to branches of a nursery tree.

Fecundity. Ability of flowers to produce viable seed.

Feeder Roots. Fine roots and root branches with an unusually large absorbing area. Feeder roots are aided in uptake of water and minerals by their root hairs.

Fertility (in flowers). Ability to produce seeds that are viable (will germinate).

Fertilization. (a) In flowers, the fusion of the male and female gametes to form a zygote or new cell. (b) Also a term used to describe the process of applying fertilizers.

Filament. The anther supporting stalk in the flower.

Flaccid. Without rigidity. Wilted.

Floret. A small flower, usually one of a dense cluster, as in a sunflower.

Flower bud. A bud in which flower parts are contained. Better term than "fruit bud".

Foliar feeding. Act of mineral fertilization of a plant through the surface of the leaves, usually in sprays.

Forb. A herb other than grass, on which mice feed in the orchard floor.

Foxiness. The peculiar smell and taste in some grapes, particularly the native Labruscas.

Frenching. Physiological disease of leaves characterized by interveinal color loss.

Fruiting habit. Manner and location of fruit on a tree, bush or plant.

Fruit Set. Development of the parts of the ovary after fertilization of the egg(s) and swelling of the ovary is discernable.

Fulvous. Reddish-yellow, tawny.

Fungi. Organisms having no leaves, flowers or chlorophyll, and reproducing by means of spores.

Fungicide. Chemical agent used to control the infection and spread of fungi on crops.

Fusiform. Spindle-shaped; swollen in the middle and narrowing toward each end.

Gamete. A unisexual cell, male or female, which when fused with another gamete, forms a zygote, producing another individual.

Gene. The unit of heredity contained in the chromosome and is passed to the next generation via sexual reproduction.

Genotype. The entire genetic constitution of the organism.

Genus. A group of plants comprising a greater or less number of closely related species; plural is genera.

Gibberellic acid (GA3). Gibberellin A3, one of a related group of plant hormones found in fungi and higher plants.

Glabrous. Smooth; not rough, pubescent or hairy.

Glaucous. Covered with a bloom, as a McIntosh fruit before harvest (powdery covering).

Glucoside. One of a large group of natural compounds that yield glucose and some other substance on hydrolysis.

Glycoside. One of a group of compounds yielding a sugar and another substance on hydrolysis.

Graft. A form of asexual propagation in which a scion or bud of one plant is placed in intimate contact with another until they grow together.

Gram calorie. *See* Calorie.

Growth Regulator. A chemical substance capable of altering the growth characteristics of a plant. There are four groups of growth regulators recognized by plant scientists: auxins, gibberellins, kinins and inhibitors.

Gummosis. Disorder in citrus and stone fruits recognized by copious extrusions of sticky sappy substances on the stems and trunks of the tree.

Guttation. The exudation of water from the ends of the vascular system at the margins of leaves under humid conditions.

Gynoecium. The pistils collectively, or the aggregate of carpels.

Hairy Root. Excessive production and grouping of weak roots.

Haploid. Having only one set of chromosomes, as the gametophyte generation of plants.

Hard end. *See* Black end.

Hardpan. A subsoil horizon which has become hard or cemented by compaction. Minerals such as iron oxide, organic material, silica, calcium carbonate can be the cause of or associated with this cementing action. Compaction also may be associated with use of heavy machinery over the soil.

Heat of fusion. The heat released when a liquid freezes. For water, the heat of fusion is 80 calories per gram.

Heat of vaporization. The heat energy required to vaporize a liquid. For water, it is 540 calories per gram (at 100°C).

Herb. A plant with no persistent woody stem above ground.

Herbicide. A chemical which will kill plants on coming in contact with them, usually weeds, or slow their growth.

Hermaphrodite. Flower with both male (stamen) and female (pistil) parts.

Hesperdium. A berry of the type found in sectioned fruit like that of an orange.

Heterostyly. The presence of styles of two or more forms or lengths on a flower.

Hirsute. Pubescent with rather coarse or still hairs.

Homogamous. A condition of flowers all of one sex or two-sexed, having stamens and pistils that mature at the same time, allowing for self-pollination.

Hopperburn. Disorder of leaves which is manifested by curling, yellowing and browning of leaves, caused by leafhoppers.

Hormone. A chemical substance formed in cells which are produced in one area of a plant and transported or transferred to another where they affect the activity of those cells.

Horticulture. The art and science of growing fruits, vegetables and flowers or ornamental plants; a division of agriculture.

Hybrid. A cross-breed of two species.

Hybridizing. The operation or practice of crossing between species.

Hydrolysis. Decomposition of a compound into other compounds by the chemical addition of the elements of water (H + and OH-).

Hydrophyte. Those plants which grow naturally in water, as the water hyacinth or lily.

Hygroscopic. The ability of a substance to attract and hold moisture from the air.

Hygroscopic coefficient. The percentage of soil water retained in contact with a saturated atmosphere in the absence of any other source of water.

Hypanthium. The cup-shaped receptacle of a flower.

Hyphae. The interwoven hair-like growth of a fungus making up the mycelium.

Hypocotyl. The stem below the cotyledons and above the root of a young seedling.

Hypogynous (flowers). Refers to the structure of a flower where appendages such as sepals, petals and stamens are inserted upon the flower axis below the gynoecium or ovary and free from it. An example, orange.

Imbibition. Process of absorption of liquids by surface tension pull, usually by a solid such as blotting paper absorbing ink.

Imbricate. Overlapping.

Imperfect (flowers). Term referring to flowers in which either functionable stamens or pistils are present, not both.

Incompatibility. (a) Inability of sex cells to unite to form a fertilized egg that will grow to maturity. (b) Failure of the scion and stock to unite and form a strong union which will continue to grow.

Indehiscent. Not opening by halves.

Indeterminate. Continuing to grow. With inflorescences, the opening of the lower (lateral) flowers first, and the terminal ones opening later.

Indexing. A means of determining the presence of disease, such as a virus, in a stock by removing buds and grafting them into a readily susceptible variety of closely related species that readily "shows" the virus.

Indigenous. Original to the region.

Induction, floral. The condition required for floral initiation.

Inflorescence. The flowering part of a plant, flower-cluster. More accurately the mode of flowering.

Initiation, floral. The first discernible change from a vegetative bud to a floral primordium.

Integuments. The maternal layers (usually two) that grow around the ovule, eventually forming the seedcoat.

Interfertile. Two or more varieties that are able to cross-pollinate each other and produce seed.

Interfruitful. The ability of one variety to cross-pollinate another, resulting in either seeded or seedless fruit.

Internode. That portion of a stem between two nodes.

Intersterility. The inability of one variety of fruit to set fruit and produce seeds that will germinate when pollinized by another variety of the same fruit.

Intine. The inner layer of a pollen grain.

Intrasterile. The condition of a group of varieties in which none are cross compatible with each other.

Inversion temperature. The condition in which cold air settles beneath warm air on a clear night.

Involucre. A whorl of small leaves or bracts found below and very near to a flower or clusters of flowers as in all composites (sunflower).

Involute. Rolled inward.

June Drop. Abscission of partially mature fruit (usually occurring in June in Northeastern U. S.).

Juvenile stage. Early or vegetative phase of growth characterized by carbohydrate utilization.

Kilocalorie. One thousand calories, a food calorie.

King blossom. This is the first blossom to appear and is usually the strongest in a cluster of flowers, as for example in apple and pear.

Lamellate. Having a thin plate or layer.

Lanceolate. Lance-shaped.

Langley. A measure of radiant energy equal to one gram calorie per square centimeter.

Latent Bud. Dormant bud, usually hidden, which is over a year old and may remain dormant indefinitely.

Leaching. Washing of soluable nutrients downward through the soil or from a leaf.

Leaf area index (LAI). The total leaf area of a plant or plants divided by the land area covered by the plants.

Leaflet. One of the divisions of a compound leaf.

Lesion. A localized spot of diseased tissue.

Ligneous. Woody.

Locule. The cell or cavity of an ovary (or anther).

528

Long-day (plants). Period of daylight longer than 14 hours. Plants require a non-interrupted dark period of 12 hours or more to initiate flowering, as potato and spinach. Apple shows relatively little response to length of dark and light periods.

Low-Headed Tree. Trees which have primary branches low on the trunk.

Lumen. (1) The light emitted by one candle in a unit solid angle (*see* Lux). (2) The cavity enclosed by cell walls.

Lux. The illumination received from one candle on one square meter at a distance of one meter; one lumen per square meter; 0.0929 foot-candle. (*See* Foot candle.)

Mamme. First crop of the capri fig or "male fig" which matures early in the spring. Fruits usually overwinter as oversized fruit.

Maturity. Stage of development in fruit when eating or processing quality is at its maximum.

Measles. A physiological disorder of apple trees in which the bark of twigs and young branches becomes rough and scaly. May be caused by boron deficiency, manganese toxicity, or a virus.

Megasporophyll. A sporophyll or leaf or leaf-like appendage producing only megasporangia /give rise to gametophyte (female plant) as in ferns/.

Meristematic. Cells which are capable of division, or a region of plant where rapid cell division takes place.

Mesocarp. The middle layer of the pericarp, as the edible flesh of a peach between the exocarp (skin) and endocarp (pit).

Mesophyll. The cells of the middle portion of the leaf, containing chloroplasts.

Mesophyte. A plant species adapted to moderate moisture rather than to very wet or very dry conditions.

Metaxenia. Effect of pollen on tissue characteristics outside of the embryo.

Mildew. Plant disease (a fungus) coating the surface of plant parts, as powdery mildew.

Millerandage. A condition in grape, in which the ovary persists but the seeds remain small or do not attain the usual size.

Monecious. The male and female flowers are on the same plant, as in corn.

Monocotyledonous. A plant which produces seeds with a single cotyledon, e.g., corn, coconut.

Mulch. Materials placed on the soil surface or mixed in the soil such as straw to promote moisture retention, temperature control, provide cleaner fruit as in strawberries, weed control, and, if the mulch is plant material, supply nutrients as the mulch decomposes.

Multiple fruit. Formed by fusion of carpels from many flowers, plus stem axis and accessory tissues.

Mutation. Genetic change in a mother plant or stock which may influence the character of the offspring, buds or cions removed from the plants.

Mycorrhiza. Symbiotic association of the mycelium or hyphae of certain fungi (class **Basidiomycetes)** with the roots of the seed plant as in case of the cranberry and orchid. Research is underway with peach, apple and blueberry to determine any value of this association.

Neocrosis. Death of plant tissue due to psysiological, nutrient or pathological disorders or other causes.

Nectary. Any place or organ which secretes nectar.

Nematocide. Chemicals used to control nematodes.

Node. Area on a stem from which leaves and/or fruits develop.

Non-ionic. Having no electrical charge on the molecule, or it is commonly known as electrically neutral.

Nucleic acids. Organic compounds of high molecular weight found in the nucleus and cytoplasm of cells, containing the genetic information of the organism.

Nut. A hard indehiscent 1-celled and 1-seeded fruit, though usually resulting from a compound ovary.

Nutrients. Elements which are necessary and available for plant growth such as C, H, O and certain mineral elements.

Oblique. Unequal sided or slanting as a York Imperial fruit.

Obovate. Inverted ovate.

Obtuse. Blunt or rounded at the end.

Osmosis. Passage of materials through a semipermeable membrane from a higher to a lower concentration.

Ovary. In angiosperms, it is the enlarged (usually the basil) portion of the pistil or gynoecium containing ovules or seeds.

Ovate. Or ovoid. Egg-shaped.

Ovicide. A chemical used to destroy the eggs of insects.

Palmate. Leaflets of a compound leaf borne at the end of the petiole.

Panicle. A branching raceme.

Parthenocarpic. Physiological phenomena in fruit in which the fruit develops without seed production, as in the Thompson Seedless grape.

Pedate. Palmately parted leaf, or a leaf divided with lateral lobes cleft or divided.

Pedicel. The support of a single flower in a cluster.

Peduncle. A primary flower-stalk, supporting either a cluster or a solitary flower (the stem of an apple fruit).

Perfect flower. Having both male and female parts.

Perianth. The outer floral parts considered together.

Pericarp. The ripened and variously modified walls of the ovary. It sometimes exhibits three distinct structural layers, the endocarp, mesocarp and epicarp.

Perigynous (flowers). When stamens, petals and sepals, as an example, are attached to a ring or cup of the flower axis, which is loose from and surrounding the pistil, as in the peach, plum and cherry.

Pesticide Tolerance. Pre-determined quantity of a pesticide which may legally remain on the harvested crops and products sold in interstate commerce, USA.

Petals. Rather showy structures around the reproductive organs of the flower which help to attract insects.

pH. An expression of acidity or alkalinity as a scale of numbers from 1 (very acid) to 14 (alkaline); pH 7.0 is neutral representing the reciprocal of the hydrogen ion concentration and expressed in gram atoms per liter of a solution.

Phenotype. The observable hereditary traits of a plant which are the interactions of genotype and environment.

Phloem. Region of tissue in the plant, as in the stems or veins of leaves, composed of sieve tubes and parenchyma which translocate food elaborted by the leaves.

Photoperiodism. Response of plants in growth and flowering to varying quantities and qualities of light.

Photosynthesis. The synthesis, in the presence of light, of carbohydrates and other organic compounds from simple molecules through the aid of chlorophyll.

Phototropism. Directional growth in response to light.

Phyllociade. Leaf-like stem containing chlorophyll which performs photosynthetic action as in leaves.

Phyllody. A type of disorder in which the shoot or branch forms more leaves than is normal.

Phytotoxic. Poisonous to plants.

Pilose. Covered with soft slender hairs.

Pinnate (leaf). Compound, with the leaflets arranged on each side of a common petiole.

Pistil. Female part of the flower usually consisting of the ovules, ovary, style and stigma.

Pith. The tissue occupying the central part of stems, usually made up of soft parenchyma cells.

Pitted. Marked with small depressions or pits, as the fruit skin of some apple varieties.

Plumose. Feathery.

Plumule. The bud or growing point of the embryo.

Pollen. Spore-like particles which are in the anther and contain the male gametophyte.

Pollination. Transfer of pollen from the anther to the stigma as by bees, wind or rain.

Pollen tube. The growth extension in the style following the germination of the pollen grain (the male gametophyte is a part of the pollen tube).

Pollinator. The agent of pollen transfer, usually bees.

Pollinizer. The producer of pollen; the variety used as a source of pollen for cross-pollination.

Polyembryony. The production of two or more embryos from a single ovule.

Polygamous. Bearing both unisexual and perfect flowers on the same or different plants of the same species.

Polyploid. Containing one or more extra sets of chromosomes. Those plants having a 2N chromosome number or greater.

Polysaccharide. A carbohydrate containing three or more monosaccharide units (such as starch, cellulose, inulin).

Pome. Fleshy fruits, usually of a perennial woody plant, which have an embedded core and seeds such as the apple, pear, and quince.

Pomology. The science and practice of fruit growing.

Primordia. Area in plants as the tips of stems and roots where initials or beginnings of plant structures are formed.

Procumbent. Lying on the ground or trailing but without rooting at the nodes.

Profichi. One of the crops of the capri fig or "male" fig which is the second to mature during the growing season. The fruit appear to be very small "buttons" in the late fall or early winter months.

Proliferation. A rapid and repeated production of new parts or tissues.

Protandry. The shedding of pollen before the stigmas are receptive.

Protogyny. The stigmas being receptive before pollen is shed.

Pruning. The proper and judicious removal of such plant parts as leaves, twigs, shoots, buds, branches or roots of a plant to increase its usefulness.

Pseudohermaphrodite. Functional unisexualism in a plant that bears perfect flowers.

Pubescent. Covered with hairs, especially if short, soft and down-like.

Pyriform. Pear-shaped.

Q$_{10}$. Temperature coefficient. The rate of change in a process or reaction with each change of ten Celsius degrees in temperature.

Quarantine. A legal action preventing the sale or shipment of plants, seed, or reproductive parts to prevent the accompanying invasion and infestation of a disease or insect pest.

Raceme. A simple inflorescence of pediceled flowers upon a more or less elongated axis, opening from the base.

Rachis. Principal stem of a raceme.

Receptacle (torus). The apex of the pedicel or the stem of the flower, generally swollen, which bears the organs of a flower. If, for example, an apple forms, the pedicel becomes a peduncle or stem on the fruit.

Reflexed. Abruptly bent or turned downward as in calyx of apple.

Relative humidity (RH). The amount of water vapor in the air relative to the greatest amount that could be held at a given temperature. For example 50 percent RH at 20/ C is half the amount of water possible at that temperature.

Reniform. Kidney-shaped.

Respiration. The oxidation of food materials by plants and the release of energy in which oxygen is absorbed and carbon dioxide is released as a by-product.

Respiratory coefficient. The ratio of CO_2 given off the O_2 used in respiration.

Rest Period. Period of non-visible growth, controlled by internal factors, and when growth will not occur even when environmental conditions are favorable.

Reticulate. In the form of network; net-veined.

Revolute. Rolled backwards.

Rhizome. A rootlike stem under or along the ground, usually horizontal, which may send roots from its lower surface and leafy shoots from its upper surface.

Rib. A primary or prominent vein of a leaf; a ridge on a pome fruit.

Ringing. Removal of a narrow strip of bark of the stem, branch or trunk of a plant to prevent the downward translocation of food beyond the point of incision.

Root cap. The specialized structure at the tip of roots.

Root Hair. Lateral extension of an epidermal cell of a root.

Rootstock. Root material to which other varieties of fruit are grafted to produce a commercially acceptable tree or vine.

Rosette. Leaves having a bunched or clustered appearance due to a shortening of the internodes of leaves on a branch or stem, as in zinc and boron deficiencies.

Rugose. Wrinkled or uneven, as a leaf.

Salt. A compound produced by the reaction of a base with an acid, as sodium chloride or potassium nitrate.

Sapwood. Outer younger more porous region of the tree beneath the bark where there is active growth.

Scaffold branches. The larger branches arising from the central portion or trunk of a tree.

Scape. A leafless peduncle arising from the ground.

Scarf-skin. The roughened outer skin of a pome fruit; wax like and whitish.

Scarification. Injury by scratching, chemicals, cutting or removing of the seed coat to promote germination of seed.

Scarious. Thin, dry, and membranous.

Scion. (cion). Part of plant which is grafted or budded to an acceptable understock.

Seed. A fertilized and ripened ovule containing an embryo capable of developing by germination into an individual.

Seedling. A young plant grown from a seed without the intervention of any method of grafting.

Selective Herbicide. A chemical, which upon coming in contact with a weed or plant, is absorbed by it and translocated throughout the plant, causing it to succumb slowly. An example is 2, 4-D.

Self-fertilization. Pollination by pollen from the same flower or tree.

Self-Pollinated. Pollinated with the pollen of the same plant or a plant exactly like it.

Sepals. Leaf-like structures encasing a flower bud and later subtending the open flower.

Serrations. Teeth-like indentations at the margin of a leaf.

Sessile. Without footstalk of any kind.

Simple. Of one piece; not compound as in a leaf.

Shoot. Current season's stem growth which bears leaves and buds.

Short-Day (plants). Plants requiring at least 12 continuous hours of uninterruped dark period to induce flowering, such as poinsettia and salvia.

Shrub. A woody perennial, smaller than a tree, usually with several stems.

Slurry. A suspension made up of an insoluable material and water which is usually very thick in nature.

Sod Culture. Type of orchard management in which a permanent perennial ground cover is kept at all times. The cover, as grass, is mowed periodically during the growing season to keep the growth of the perennials in check.

Soft Fruits. Generally denotes those fruits which tend to be soft at maturity such as the stone fruits and brambles.

Soil sterilants or fumigants. Materials which prevent growth of plants when present in soils. It may also be of sufficient toxicity to destroy all other living organisms as well.

Somatic. In plants, the diploid body cells; vegetative rather than reproductive cells.

Soursap. Disorder characterized by a fermentation of tree sap associated with disorders of root and prolonged orchard wetting conditions.

Spore. Resting unicellular stage of a fungus capable of propagation.

Sporogenous. Producing spores.

Sporophyte. The diploid generation of a plant, arising from the fertilized egg (zygote).

Sport. A variety or strain arising from a bud mutation.

Spraydrift. Movement of airborne spray particles from area of origin to areas not intended to be covered.

Spur. Short woody stem or branch which is a principal fruiting area for most fruit trees, sometimes arbitrarily said to be 4 inches or less, a twig being 4'' or more.

Spur strain. Resembles parent as Red Delicious, but tree is ¾ its size, more open, fewer limbs, with numerous spurs. Characters permanent, apparently induced by extremes, as cold. Not available for all standard varieties.

Stamen. The male part of a flower consisting of an anther containing pollen and a filament.

Staminate (Flower). Flowers having stamens but no pistils; a male plant.

Starter Solution. A solution of soluable nutrients used to aid plants in surviving transplanting.

Stele. Group of vascular tissues in a stem, root and related plant part, including pericycle, phloem, xylem and pitch.

Stellate, stelliform. Star-shaped; said of star-like dots on the apple fruit.

Sterile flower. Without pistils or otherwise unable to accomplish fertilization.

Stigma. Upper surface of the pistil where the pollen grain settles and germinates.

Stion. Combined words, "stock" and "scion," indicating a specific combination gives a characteristic response, known as the "stion response".

Stipule. One of a pair of lateral appendages, often leaf-like, at the base of the petiole of many plants.

Stolon. Horizontal stem or shoot near the surface of the soil that gives rise to new plants at its tip, as in strawberry.

Stomach poisons. Insecticides or chemicals which are ingested by insects into the stomach, eventually killing them.

Stomate. Pore or opening in the epidermis of a leaf through which gases and water vapor pass.

Stratification (seeds). Process of subjecting seeds to an after-ripening period to break the rest period. The seeds are usually placed in layers of a well aerated media under varying temperatures.

Stone (Pit). The center portion of stone (drupel) fruits or the pit, endocarp or pyrene found in many of the prunus plants.

Suborbicular. Nearly round.

Subordination (pruning). A method of restoring apical dominance on a plant by heading back all but one of multiple leaders.

Succulent. Juicy; fleshy.

Sucker. Shoot arising from the roots or lower part of the plant stem.

Sulcate. Grooved longitudinally.

Sunscald. Injury or destruction of outer tissue due to excess sun heat, as on the exposed side of an apple. limbs or trunk.

Supercooling. Cooling hydrated tissue or a liquid below its freezing point without solidification occurring.

Superior. Said of the ovary when it is free; above, in position.

Surfactant. Materials wich tend to modify the surface tension of spray droplets, causing them, e.g., to spread out on a leaf forming a thin film; e.g. a detergent such as Tide.

Suture. A line formed by the union of two adjacent margins, as the suture line (union of folded fleshy modified leaf) on a peach fruit.

Syconium. The fruit of the fig, in which the inflorescence is borne on the inside of a balloon-like receptacle; a type of multiple fruit.

Syncarp. The fruit of the mulberry, composed of many druplets from many flowers plus the fleshy inflorescence axis; a type of multiple fruit.

Synergism. When two agencies act simultaneously to produce a total effect greater than the sum of their individual effects, as growth regulators and certain plant nutrients.

Systemic chemical. A compound which is translocated throughout a plant and may have effects on the pests or agents associated with the plant system, modifying its growth habit or killing it.

Tap-root. The perpendicular main root of a tree which is characteristic for the species and penetrates deeply into the ground and possesses but few laterals, as in case of the pecan. Relatively difficult to transplant.

Temperature coefficient. *See* Q_{10}.

Temperature inversion. Meteorological phenomenon whereby the air temperature becomes warmer with altitude instead of becoming cooler as is normal.

Tendril. The coiled thread-like organ by which some vines clasp an object.

Terminal. The end of a shoot, spur, stem or twig.

Testa. The outer commonly hard and brittle seed-coat.

Tetrad. A group of four pollen grains derived from a single microspore mother cell.

Tetraploid. An individual with four sets of chromosomes.

Topworking. Changing the variety of a tree by inserting buds or grafts of the new variety on its trunk and/or branches.

Torus. (1) The receptacle of a flower; part of the axis on which the flower parts are inserted. (2) A thickening in the membrane of a bordered pit.

Translocated herbicide. A chemical absorbed through one part of the plants and exerts toxic effects in other parts.

531

Translocation. Physical movement of water, nutrients, or chemicals such as a herbicide or elaborated food within a plant.

Transpiration. Water loss by evaporation from the internal surface of the leaves and through the stomata.

Triploid. An individual with three sets of chromosomes.

Tropism. An involuntary response in the form of movement of a plant, the direction of which is determined by the source of the stimulus.

Trunk. The main stem or body of a tree apart from limbs and roots.

Turgidity. Pressure caused by fluids in the cell pressing against the cell wall giving shape to the cell.

Twig. Small short shoot or branch; arbitrarily said to be more than 4 inches in length.

Vacuole. The cavity within the cell containing the cell sap.

Variety. A group of closely related plants of common origin which have characteristics not sufficiently different to form separate species. Horticulturally the term "cultivar" is preferred.

Vein (leaf). One of the vascular bundles forming the fibrous framework of a leaf and through which food, water and nutrients are translocated.

Vernation. The arrangement of leaves in the bud.

Villose. Having long soft hairs.

Viscid. Sticky material, such as sap.

Volatile. Property of liquids which allow it to change easily from a liquid to a gas. Some herbicides will do this, causing a drift problem on nearby unsprayed plants.

Water Berries. Grape disorder characterized by watery fruits and failure to ripen.

Water Core. A disorder of, e.g., apple, which gives the area near the core a watery or glassy appearance. It may disappear after a time in cold storage.

Water logged. Soil which has poor drainage and lacks the necessary O_2 for proper root functioning.

Watersprouts. Rapidly growing shoots or sprouts that grow from adventitious or latent buds on branches or trunks of trees.

Wilting Coefficient. Percentage of moisture in the soil when the permanent wilting of a plant is reached (plant will not recover when placed in atmosphere of 100% humidity).

Windburn. Disorder of leaves recognizable by dead, torn and browned margins and areas of leaves.

Woody (plants). Plant tissue having many xylem tubes and fiber which are resilient. A non-herbaceous plant.

Xenia. The physiological effect of foreign pollen on maternal fruit tissue. (This term formerly was applied to pollen effects on the embryo and endosperm).

Xerophyte. Plants which can endure extreme moisture stress, as in the desert. A cactus plant.

Xylem. Tough fibrous vessels formed from heavy walled elongated cells which are responsible for the upward movement of water and nutrient salts from roots to the entire plant.

Yield efficiency. Crop yield per unit of plant size or per unit of land area (e.g., kilograms of yield per square centimeter trunk, or yield per hectare.)

Zygote. A cell formed by the union of two gametes (male and female), or a fertilized egg or zygospore from which an individual will develop.

SCIENTIFIC NAMES OF SOME DECIDUOUS FRUITS[1]

COMMON NAME	SCIENTIFIC NAME
Almond	*Prunus amygdalus* Batsch. *(Amygdalus communis* L.)
Apple (Common)	*Malus pumila* Mill. (*Malus silvestris* Hort., *Pyrus malus* L.)
Apricot (Common)	*Prunus armeniaca* L. (*Armeniaca vulgaris* Lam.)
Apricot (Japanese)	*Prunus mume* Sieb. and Zucc. (*Armeniaca Mume* Sieb.)
Apricott, Siberian or Russian apricot	*Prunus sibirica* L. (*Armenica sibirica* Lam.)
Apricot, (Purple or Black)	*Prunus dasycarpa* Ehrh. (*Prunus armeniaca* var. *dasycarpa* K. Koch)
Blackberry (European)	*Rubus thyrsoideus* Wimm. (*Rubus candicans* Weihe)
Blackberry (Evergreen thornless)	*Rubus ulmifolius* var. *inermis* (Willd.) Focke
Blackberry (High or black-long berry or Allegheny or Mountain Blackberry)	*Rubus allegheniensis* Porter (*Rubus nigrobaccus* (Bailey)
Blackberry (Himalaya)	*Rubus procerus* P. J. Muell
Blueberry, (Highbush or Swamp blueberry or High blueberry)	*Vaccinium corymbosum* L.
Blueberry (Lowbush)	*Vaccinium angustifolium* Ait.
Blueberry (rabbiteye)	*Vaccinium ashei* Reade
Blueberry, (Evergreen or box)	*Vaccinium ovatum* Pursh
Blueberry (Mountain)	*Vaccinium membranaceaum* Dougl.
Blueberry, (Dryland or low)	*Vaccinium pallidum* Ait.
Blueberry, (European or Whortleberry or Billberry)	*Vaccinium myrtillus* L.
Butternut (or American butternut)	*Juglans cinerea* L.
Cherry, (Bird or Pin cherry or Wild red cherry)	*Prunus pensylvanica* L.
Cherry, (Flowering of Japan)	*Prunus pseudocerasus* Lindl.
Cherry, (Duke)	*Prunus effusa* (Host.) Schneid: P. gondouini (Poit. & Turpin Rehd.) (Hybrid between *Prunus avium* L. and *Prunus cerasus* Linn.)
Cherry, (Mahaleb or Saint Lucie cherry)	*Prunus mahaleb* Linn. (*Cerasus mahaleb* Mill.)
Cherry, (Manchu or Nanking cherry)	*Prunus tomentosa* Thunb. (*Cerasus tomentosa* Wall., *Cerasus trichocarpa* Bunge)
Cherry, (Sour or Pie cherry)	*Prunus cerasus* L. (*Cerasus caproniana* Ser.)
Cherry (Sweet or Mazzard)	*Prunus avium* L. (*Prunus cerasus* var. *avium* L.)
Cherry (Western sand)	*Prunus besseyi,* Bailey (Prunus pumila var. *besseyi* Waugh., *Prunus rosebudii* Reagan *Prunus prunella* Daniels)
Chestnut, (Allegheny chinkapin or Eastern chinkapin or Chinquapin)	*Castanea pumila* (L.) Mill.
Chestnut, (American)	*Castanea dentata* (Marsh.) Borkh. (*Castanea americana* Raf.)
Chestnut, (Chinese or Hairy chestnut)	*Castanea mollissima* Blume
Chestnut, (European or Spanish chestnut)	*Castanea sativa* Mill. (*Castanea vesca* Gaertn., *Castanea vulgaris* Lam.)
Chestnut, Japanese	*Castanea crenata* Sieb. and Zucc.
Cranberry, (Large or American)	*Vaccinium macrocarpon* Ait.
Cranberry, (Small or European)	*Vaccinium oxycoccos* L.
Currant, (Common red or Garden currant	*Ribes sativum* (Reichenb.) Syme (Ribes domesticum Jancz., *Ribes hortense* Hedland, *Ribes vulgare* Jancz.)
Currant, (European black)	*Ribes nigrum* L.
Currant, (Northern red)	*Ribes rubrum* L. (*Ribes sylvestre* DC.)

[1]Standardized Plant Names (Joint Committee), Second Edition, J. H. McFarland Co. 675 pp. Harrisburg, Pa. out-of-print but found in most university agricultural libraries; Manual of Cultivated trees and shrubs, The Macmillan Co., New York City, can be used as authorities.

To name and register a cultivar, consult "How to Name a New Plant", Bull. of Amer. Assn. of Nurserymen, Inc., 835 Southern Bldg., Wash., D. C. 20005.

Taxonomists at the Bailey Hortorium, Cornell University, Ithaca, N. Y. 14850, checked these names.

Dewberry (California or Western dewberry or Grapeleaf California dewberry)	*Rubus ursinus* Cham. and Schlecht.
Dewberry (Northern)	*Rubus flagellaris* Willd.
	(Rubus villosus Bailey,
	Rubus procumbens Muhl.,
	Rubus canadenis Torr.)*
Dewberry (Southern)	*Rubus trivialis* Michx.
	(Rubus carpinifolius Rydb.,
	Rubus continentalis Bailey)*
Elderberry	*Sambucus canadensis* L.
Fig, (Common)	*Ficus carica* L.
Filbert, (American Hazelnut)	*Corylus americana,* Marsh.
Filbert, (Beaked)	*Corylus cornuta* Marsh.
Filbert, (California or Western filbert)	*Corylus californica* Rose: (cornuta var. californica (A. DC.) Rose
Filbert, (European)	*Corylus avellana* L.
Filbert, (Giant)	*Corylus maxima* Mill.
Filbert, (Japanese or Siberian hazelnut)	*Corylus heterophylla* Fisch. ex Traut v.
Filbert, (Turkish)	*Corylus colurna* L.
Gooseberry, (American or Hairystem gooseberry	*Ribes hirtellum* Michx.
	(Grossularia hirtella Spach.)*
Gooseberry, (European, English)	*Ribes uva-crispa* L.,
	(Ribes grossularia L.,
	Ribes grossularia var. *pubescens* Koch.)*
	Ribes uva-crispa var. *reclinata*
Grape, (European or Wine grape)	*Vitis vinifera* L.
Grape, (Fox or Northern grape fox)	*Vitis labrusca* L.
Grape, (Muscadine or Bullace or Southern Fox Grape)	*Vitis rotundifolia* Michx.
Grape, (Mustang of Florida or Bird grape or Everbearing grape or Everlasting grape)	*Vitis munsoniana* Simson
Hickory, (Big shellbark)	*Carya laciniosa* (Michx. f.) Loudon
	(Carya sulcata Pursh
	Hicoria laciniosa (Michx. f.) Sarg.)*
Hickory, (Pignut)	*Cary glabra* (Mill.) Sweet.
	(Hicoria glabra Brit., *Carya porcina* Michx. f.)*
Hickory, (Red or Sweet pignut)	*Carya ovalis* (Wang.) Sarg.
	(Hicoria microcarps, Brit.,
	Hicoria ovalis Ashe.)*
Hickory (Shagbark)	*Carya ovata* (Mill.) K. Koch.
	(Hicoria ovata Brit., *Carya alba* Nutt.)*
Kiwi (Chinese Gooseberry)	*Actinidia chinensis* Planch.
Nectarine, (Smooth skinned peach, L. H. B., a single gene mutation from peach)	*Prunus persica* var. *nectarina* (ait.) Maxim.
	(Prunus persica var. *nucipersica* Borkh.)*
Peach, (Common)	*Prunus persica* (L.) Batsch
	(Amygdalus persica L.
	Persica vulgaris Mill.)*
Pear, (Chinese white)	*Pyrus bretschneideri* Rehd.
Pear, (European or Common)	*Pyrus communis* L.
Pear, (Sand)	*Pyrus pyrifolia* (Burm.) Nakai
Pear, (Snow or French Snow pear)	*Pyrus nivalis* Jacq.
Pear, (Manchurian or Ussurian)	*Pyrus ussuriensis* Maxim.
Pecan	*C. Illinoinensis* (Wang.) K. Koch
	(Carya pecan Engl. and Graebn.)*
Persimmon, (American)	*Diospyros virginiana* L.
Persimmon, (Kaki or Oriental)	*Diospyros Kaki* L.
	(Diospyros chinensis Blume, *Diospyros roxburghi* Carr.)*
Persimmon (Dateplum)	*Diospyros lotus* L.
Plum, (Beach)	*Prunus maritima* Marsh.
Plum, (Big tree)	*Prunus mexicana* S. Wats.
	(Prunus australis Munson ex Waugh,
	Prunus polyandra
	Prunus arkansana Sarg.)*
Plum, (Bullace or Damson plum)	*Prunus institia* L.
	(Prunus domestica var. *institia* Bailey,)*
Plum, (Canada)	*Prunus nigra* Ait.
	(Prunus pensylvanica L.
	Prunus mollis Torr.
	Prunus americana var. *nigra* Waugh.)*
Plum, (Chickawaw or Mountain cherry)	*Prunus angustifolia* Marsh.
	(Prunus chicasa Michx.
	Prunus stenophylla Raf.)*

Plum, (Common)	*Prunus domestica* L.
	(Prunus communis Huds.)*
Plum, (Common wild)	*Prunus americana* Marsh.
	(Prunus latifolia Moench.,
	Prunus hiemalis Michx.)*
Plum, (Hortulan)	*Prunus hortulana* Bailey
	(Prunus hortulana var. *waylandii* Bailey
Plum, (Japanese)	*Prunus salicina* Lindl.
	(Prunus triflora Roxburg.,
	Prunus japonica Hort.)*
Plum, (Myrobalan or Cherry plum)	*Prunus cerasifera* Ehrh.
	(Prunus domestica var. *myrobalan* L.*
Plum, (Oklahoma)	*Prunus gracilis* Engelm. and Gray
Plum, (Pacific)	*Prunus subcordata* Benth.
Plum, (Simon or Apricot plum)	*Prunus simonii* Carr.
	(Persica simonii Decne.)*
Plum, (Wild goose)	*Prunus munsoniana* Wight and Hedr.
Plumcots	Hybrids between *Prunus salicina* and *Prunus armeniaca*
Pomegranate, (Common)	*Punica granatum* L.
Quince	*Cydonia oblonga* Mill.
	(Cydonia vulgaris Pers.,
	Pyrus cydonia L.)*
Raspberry, (Black or Blackcap raspberry)	*Rubus occidentalis* L.
Raspberry (European red)	*Rubus idaeus* L.
Red Raspberry, (American)	*Rubus idaeus* var. *strigosus* Michx. Maxim.
Raspberry (Purple cane)	*Rubus neglectus* Peck.
	(A hybrid between *Rubus strigosus* and *Rubus occidentalis)*
Strawberry (Chilean or Beach Strawberry)	*Fragaria chiloensis* (L.) Duch.
Strawberry (Cultivated)	*Fragaria X ananassa* Duch.
	Hybrid between different *Fragaria* species, mostly between *Fragaria viginiana* Duch. and *Fragaria chiloensis* (L.) Duch.
Strawberry (Virginia or Wild Meadow Strawberry)	*Fragaria virginiana* Duch.
Walnut (Black or Eastern black walnut)	*Juglans nigra* L.
Walnut (Bolivian black)	*Juglans boliviana* Dode
Walnut (California black or Southern California black walnut)	*Juglans californica* S. Wats.
Walnut (Cathay or Chinese walnut)	*Juglans catheyensis* Dode.
Walnut (English or Persian walnut)	*Juglans regia* L.

FRUIT PUBLICATIONS

There is a list of publications which frequently or regularly contain articles pertaining to fruit growing obtainable from Bailey Hortorium, Cornell University, Ithaca, N. Y. 14850, entitled "Bibliography of Current Horticultural Publications." Request latest edition. Most of these publications, or records of them will be found at your nearest state or federal agricultural library.

Become a member or read regularly HortScience and the Journal of the American Society for Horticultural Science, 701 N. St. Asaph St., Alexandria, Va 22314, to keep up-to-date on latest research trends and findings. Read the Journ. of Pomology and Hort. Sci., London WC-2 for British work. Scientists should consult Horticultural Abstracts, P.O.B. 31, Farnham Royal, Bucks, England for world research summaries.

Most states have their own horticultural societies or associations and publish monthly, bimonthly, quarterly or annual reports of their annual meetings. The extension pomologist in the pomology or horticultural department of your state usually acts as secretary, or this person can refer you to the secretary for information. Become a member and receive the benefits for your business.

ABSTRACT JOURNALS

Many scientific publications are issued monthly, quarterly, or annually, which contain information pertaining to fruit growing. Results of most current publications are briefed into a paragraph or two and published in special abstract journals found in most university and college libraries.

Among them are the following:

Biological Abstracts (Plant Science section). 3815 Walnut St., University of Pennsylvania, Philadelphia, Pennsylvania. 19104.

Chemical Abstracts. Ohio State University, Columbus, Ohio. 43210

Horticultural Abstracts, Farnham Royal, Bucks, England. This is excellent for horticultural abstracts the world over (in English).

Review of Applied Mycology. Kew, Surrey, England.

A complete reference index to current agricultural publications for research workers is given in Bibliography of Agriculture, published monthly by the United States Department of Agriculture Library, Beltsville, Maryland 20705. Micro-film or photocopies of entire articles listed can be obtained through the United States Department of Agriculture at a nominal charge for both foreign and domestic publications.

SUGGESTED POMOLOGY BOOK LIST

Following is a partial list of pomology books and other books related to the fruit growing industry, which fruit growers and technical workers may wish to consider for their library. Books of possible interest only to professional workers are listed separately.

Anderson, H. W. Diseases of fruit crops. McGraw-Hill Book Co., Inc., N. Y. City, 501 pp. 1956.

Beach, S. A. The apples of New York. Vol. I, Vol. II. Out-of-print, available only from retiring horticulturists, second-hand stores. Color plates, history, variety descriptions. Early 1900's.

Brison, F. R. Pecan Culture. 292 pp. Capital Printing Co., Austin, Texas. 1974.

Chandler, W. H. Deciduous orchards. Lea & Febiger Co., Phila., Pa. 492 pp. 1957.

Chandler, W. H. Fruit growing (excellent literature review to 1925). Houghton Mifflin Co., N. Y. City, 777 pp. 1925.

Childers, N. F. (Editor) Fruit Nutrition — Temperate to Tropical (covers important deciduous and tropical woody plants and strawberries). Hort. Publ. 3906 NW 31 Pl., Gainesville, FL. 32606. 8x11 inches, 888 p. 1966.

Childers, Norman F., The peach — varieties, culture, marketing, pest control. Conf. Rpt. of 140 Researchers at Rutgers University. Out-of-print til 1986.

Childers, N. F. (Ed.) The Strawberry. By 60 US & Foreign Authorities. 600+ pp. 1981. Hort. Publ. 3906 NW 31st Pl., Gainesville, FL. 32606. Dom. $21.90; For. $25.00.

Childers, Norman F. Modern Fruit Science (In Spanish) Fruticultura Moderna, Vol. I & II, 457-525 p. Editorial Hemisferio Sur, Alzaibar, 1328, Montevideo, Uruguay, So. Amer. 1981.

Childers, N. F. and Hans Zutter. Modern Fruit Science Lab Manual for Modern Fruit Science book. Hort. Publ., 3906 NW 31 Pl., Gainesville, FL. 32606. 190 p. 1975.

Darrow, George M. The Strawberry — history breeding and physiology. Holt-Rinehart & Winston, N. Y. City. 447 pp. 1966.

Eck, Paul and Norman F. Childers. Blueberry Culture. Rutgers Univ. Press, New Brunswick, N. J. 378 pp. 1966. (Books also available at 3906 NW 31 Pl., Gainesville, FL. 32606). $25.00.

Fidler, J. C. et al. Biology of apple and pear storage, Research Rev. No. 3 Commonwealth Bur. of Hort., Farnham Royal, Slough, Eng. 235 pp. 1973.

Fruit Books from University of California (color). Ask for listings, prices. Agricultural Science Publications, Univ. of Ca., 1422 Harbour Way South, Rochmond, Ca. 94804.

Garner, R. J. The grafter's handbook. Faber and Faber Ltd., 24 Rosswell Sq., London, Eng., 260 pp. 1958.

Hartmann, H. T. and D. E. Kester. Plant propagation. 702 pp. Prentiss-Hall, Inc., Englewood Cliffs, N. J. 1975.

Hedrick, U. P. Peaches. Plums. Pears. Cherries. Small Fruits. (Separate books). Of New York. Color plates, history, variety descriptions. Available only from retiring horticulturists, second-hand stores. N. Y. Agr. Exp. Sta., Geneva. Early 1900's.

Jaynes, R. A. Northern Nut growing. About 400 pp. good book, Northern Nut Growers Ass'n., Univ. of Conn., Storrs. 1969.

Journal American Society for Horticultural Science and Hort-Science (Published bimonthly for the members), technical papers from 4,000 members. 701 N. Asaph St., Alexandria, Va. 22314.

Marshall, Roy E. Cherries and cherry products. Interscience Publ., Inc., N. Y., N. Y. 283 pp. 1954.

McGregor, S. E. Insect pollination of Cultivated Crops. USDA Hdbk. 496. 410 p. 1976.

Metcalf, R. L. and W. Luckmann. Insect Pest Management. John Wiley and Sons, Inc. 587 pp. New York, London. 1975.

Morettini, Alessandro. Frutticoltura — Generale Especials. (In Italian) Ramo Editoriele Degli Agricoltori, Publ., Rome, Italy. 692 pp. 1963.

Perkins, H. O. Espaliers and vines for the home gardener. B. Van Nostrand Co., Inc., Princeton, N. J. 206 pp. 1964.

Proceedings International Horticultural Congress (Published every 4 years). Excellent 4-volume set in 1966, XVII Congress at College Park, Md. (H. B. Tukey, Sr., Dept. Hort., Mich. State Univ., East Lansing, Mich.) See Proc. for '70, '74, '78, '82.

Shoemaker, J. S. Small fruit culture. Avi. Publ. Co., Westport, Conn., 4th Ed. 340 pp. 1975.

Smock, R. M. and A. M. Neubert. Apples and apple products. Interscience Publ., Inc., N. Y. City. 486 pp. 1950.

Thompson, Robert (Ed.) California Wine Country. Sunset books. 96 pp. Lane Books, Menlo, Calif. 1971.

Teskey, B. J. E. and J. S. Shoemaker. Tree Fruit Production (Deciduous), 2nd Ed. 336 pp. Avi Publ. Co., Westport, Conn. 1972.

Tukey, Harold B. Dwarfed fruit trees (an excellent book). The Macmillan Co., N. Y. City. 562 pp. 1964. Reprinted by Cornell University Press. Ithaca, N. Y. 1979.

Upshall, W. H. (Ed.) North American Apples — varieties, rootstocks outlook. Mich. State Univ. Press, E. Lansing. 197 pp. 1970.

Van der Swet, T. and N. F. Childers. The Pear, Cultivars to Marketing. By 85 world authorities. 500 p. Hort. Publ., 3906 NW 31 Pl., Gainesville, FL. 32606. 1982. Dom. $25.00; For. $30.00.

Wallace, T. Diagnosis of mineral deficiencies in plants by visual symptoms (color atlas and guide, 2nd Edition, Chemical Publ. Co., Inc., 212 5th Ave., N. Y. 1961.

Winkler, A. J. et al. General Viticulture. (A good book) Univ. of Calif. Press, Berkeley. 710 pp. 1974.

Westwood, W. N. Temperate Zone Pomology. W. H. Freeman & Co., San Francisco, Ca. 428 p. 1978.

Woodroof, J. G. Tree nuts — production, processing, products. Vol. I — Almond, Brazil nut, cashew, chestnut, filbert, macadamia, 35 pp. Vol. II — Pecan, pine nut, pistachio, black walnut, English walnut, 373 pp. The Avi Publ. Co., Inc., Westport, Conn. 1967. Available in one revised volume since 1979.

Woolrich, W. R. Handbook of refrigerating engineering. Vol. I, fundamentals; Vol. II, applications. 460 and 410 pp., resp. 1965, 1966.

Zielinski, Q. B. Modern systematic pomology. Wm. C. Brown Co., Dubuque, Iowa. 296 pp. 1955.

POMOLOGY BOOKS FOR PROFESSIONALS

Amerine, M. A., Technology of wine making. Avi Publ. Co., Westport, Conn., 799 pp. 1972.

Bailey, L. H. et al. Hortus Third. (Taxonomic Reference) Macmillan Publ. Co., London, New York. 1285 p. 1976.

Barfield, B. J. et al. Modification of Aerial Environment of Crops, Amer. Soc. Ag. Engin. 538 p. Niles Rd., St. Joseph, MI. 1979.

Brooks, R. D. and H. P. Olmo. Register of new fruit and nut varieties. 1920-1950, Univ. of Calif. Press, Berkeley. Supplements are available from Amer. Soc. Hort. Sci., 701 N. Saint Asaph St., Alexandria, Va. 22314.

Caillavet H. and J. Southy. Monograph of the principal varieties of peaches. (In French) Societe Bordelaise D'Imprimerie, Bordeau, France. 416 pp. 1950.

Chandler, W. H. Evergreen orchards. Lea & Febiger Co., Phila., Pa., 452 pp. 1950.

Chapman, H. D. (Editor). Diagnostic criteria for plants and soils. Univ. of Calif. Press, Berkeley. 1966.

Chatt, E. M. Cocoa — cultivation, processing analysis. Interscience Publ., Inc. N. Y., 300 pp. 1953.

Collins, J. L. The pineapple — botany, cultivation and utilization. Leonard Hill (books) Ltd., London, England, 296 pp. 1960.

Darlington, C. D. and A. P. Wylie. Chromosome Atlas. The Macmillan Co., New York City. 519 pp. 1956.

Dowson, V. H. W. and A. Aten. Dates — handling, processing and packing. Food and Agr. Org. of United Nations, Rome, Italy, 392 pp. 1962.

Esau, Katherine. Plant Anatomy. John Wiley & Son, Inc., New York City; Chapman & Hall, Ltd. London. 735 pp. 1953. A later smaller edition is available.

Frazier, N. W. et al. Viruses, small fruits, grapes, Univ. Calif. Agr. Sci., Berkeley, 290 pp. 1970.

Fogel, H.W. and H.F. Winters. No. Amer. & Europ. Fruit and Nut Germ Plasm Resources Inventory. USDA Misc. Publ. No. 1406. 732 p. June, 1981.

Free, J. B. Insect Pollination of Crops. Academic Press. New York, London. 544 p. 1970.

Gangolly, S. R. et al. The mango. Indian Counc. of Agr. Res., New Delhi, India, 530 pp. 1957.

Hewitt, E. J. Sand and water culture methods in plant nutrition studies. Commonwealth Agricultural Bureau, Maidstone, Kent, England. 547 pp. 1966.

Hilkenbaumer, F. Schnitt der Obstgehotze, Verlag J. Neumann—Neudamm, Melsungen, Germany. 145 pp. 1973. (Pruning fruit plants).

Horticultural Reviews. Covers horticultural specific subjects research in detail. Avi. Publ. Co., Westport, Ct. 500 p. 1979. 4 volumes available.

Hulme, A. C. Bio-chemistry of fruits and their products. Academic Press, London, N. Y. Vols. I & II, 620, 788 pp. 1970, 1971.

Janick, Jules and J. N. Moore. Advances in fruit breeding. Purdue Univ. Press. W. Lafayette, Ind. 623 pp. 1975.

Kolesnikov, V. Root systems of fruit plants (in English), Mir Publishers. Moscow, USSR. 269 pp. 1971.

Levitt, J. The hardiness of plants. Academic Press, Inc., Publishers. New York City, 274 pp. 1956.

Mathews, G. A. Pesticide Application Methods. 536 p. Longman Publ. Co., London. Repr. 1982 (1979).

Mengel, L. and E. A. Kirby. Principles of Plant Nutrition. Potash Institute. POB CH-3048, Worblaufen-Bern, Switzerland. 591 p. 1978.

Meyer, B. S. and D. B. Anderson. Plant physiology. D. Van Nostrand Co., Inc., Princeton, N. J. 785 pp. Request late edition.

Mortveldt, J. J. et al. Micronutrients in Agriculture. Soil Sci. Soc. of Amer., Inc., Univ. of Wis., Madison. 666 p. 1972.

Oberhofer, H. et al. Obstbau, Heute (Dwarf Tree Management) in German and Italian, Edizioni Agricole, 31, Emilia Levante, Bologne, Italy. 100 pp. 1974.

Planning your financial future - Investments, insurance, wills. 250 pp. U. S. News & World Rpt., 2300 N St., Wash., D. C. 20037.

Potter, N. N. Food science. Avi Publ. Co., Westport, Conn. 706 pp. 1973.

Reuther, Walter, L.D. Batchelor and H.J. Webber (Editors). The citrus industry, Vol. I-III, History, world distribution, botany, varieties, culture. Univ. of Calif. Press, Berkeley, Calif. 1967-72.

Ryall, A. L. and W. T. Pentzer. Handling, transportation, and storage of fruits and vegetables. Avi Publ. Co., Westport, Conn. Vols. I and II, 473 & 544 pp. 1972, 1974.

Simmonds, N. W. Bananas. Longmans, Green & Co., Inc., 119 W. 40th St., N. Y., N. Y. 1959.

Sinclair, W. B. The orange — its biochemistry and physiology. Univ. Calif. Press, Riverside, Calif. 1961.

Upshall, W. H. No. Amer. apples: varieties, rootstocks, outlook. Mich. St. Univ. Press, E. Lansing. 198 pp. 1970.

Urquhart, D. H. Cocoa. John Wiley & Sons, Inc., N. Y. City, 294 pp. 1961.

Virus diseases and other disorders with virus-like symptoms of stone fruits in North America, USDA Agr. Handbook 10, 276 pp. Apr. 1951.

Wilhelm, Steven and J. E. Sagen. History of the Strawberry. 300 p. Agr. Sci. Pub., Univ. of Ca., Berkeley 94720.

Woodroof, J. G. Coconuts: Production, processing, products. 241 pp. Avi Publ. Co., Westport, Conn. 1970.

Woodroof, J. G. and B. S. Luh. Commercial fruit processing. Avi Publ. Co., Westport, Conn. 710 pp. 1975.

Zielinski, Q. B. Modern systematic pomology. Wm. C. Brown Co., Dubuque, Iowa. 296 pp. 1955.

NOTE: The author of Modern Fruit Science book will appreciate copies of new books to consider listing here.

AGRICULTURAL EXPERIMENT STATIONS AND COLLEGES
IN THE UNITED STATES

A list of available bulletins, circulars, and other information regarding temperate fruit growing can be obtained by writing to the agricultural editor of your agricultural experiment station or college. If you want up-to-date economic or cost-of-production data on a given fruit crop, write to the department of agricultural economics at your state university or a university of a state that ranks high in that particular crop. If a pest problem, write to dept. of plant pathology (disease) or entomology (insects) or agricultural engineering if a machine problem, etc.

State	City	State	City
Alabama	Auburn 36830	New Jersey	New Brunswick 08903
Alaska	College 99701	New Mexico	State College 99701
Arizona	Tucson 85721	New York	
Arkansas	Fayetteville 72701	College and	
California	Berkeley 94720	station	Ithaca 14850
	Davis 95616	Station	Geneva 14456
	L. Angeles 90024		
	Riverside 92502		
Colorado	Fort Collins 80521		
Connecticut		North Carolina	Raleigh 27607
College and		North Dakota	Fargo 58102
Station	Storrs 06268	Ohio	
Station	New Haven 06504	College	Columbus 43210
Delaware	Newark 19711	Station	Wooster 44691
Florida	Gainesville 32601	Oklahoma	Stillwater 74074
	Tallahassee 32307		
	Lake Alfred 33850		
	Homestead 33030		
Georgia		Oregon	Corvallis 97331
College	Athens 30601	Pennsylvania	University Park 16802
Station	Experiment 30212	Puerto Rico	
Hawaii	Honolulu 96822	Insular Station	Rio Piedras 00928
Idaho	Moscow 83840	College and	
Illinois	Urbana 61801	Federal Station	Mayaguez 00708
Indiana	Lafayette 47907	Rhode Island	Kingston 02881
Iowa	Ames 50010	South Carolina	Clemson 29631
Kansas	Manhattan 66502	South Dakota	Brookings 57006
Kentucky	Lexington 40506	Tennessee	Knoxville 37901
Louisiana	University Station 70803	Texas	College Station 77843
Maine	Orono 04473	Utah	Logan 84321
Maryland	College Park 20740	Vermont	Burlington 05401
	Beltsville, USDA 20705		
Massachusetts	Amherst 01002	Virginia	Blacksburg 24061
			Winchester 22601
Michigan	East Lansing 48823	Washington	Long Beach 98631
		Puyallup 98371	Mt. Vernon 98273
		Vancouver 98660	Prosser 99350
		Wenatchee 98801	Pullman 99163
Minnesota	St. Paul 55101	West Virginia	Morgantown 26506
Mississippi	State College 39762	Wisconsin	Madison 53706
Missouri	Columbia 65201	Wyoming	Laramie 83070
Montana	Bozeman 59715	United States	
Nebraska	Lincoln 68503	Department of	Washington
Nevada	Reno 89507	Agriculture[1]	D.C. 20250
New Hampshire	Durham 03824		

[1] A list of Federal agricultural publications arranged by subjects can be obtained by requesting Miscellaneous Publication No. 60 from the Division of Publications, Office of Information, U.S. Department of Agriculture, Washington, D.C. 20250.

A published list of state and federal staff at the above experiment stations, Handbook No. 305, can be obtained from Cooperative State Research Service, U. S. Dept. of Agri., Washington, D. C. 20705 (priced). A Directory of institutions, staff, in 61 world countries, titled, "Horticultural Research International" is available (priced) from Ministry of Agriculture and Fisheries, P.O. Box 20401, The Hague, The Netherlands, 700 p., 1981. Am. Soc. Hort. Sci. also has over 4000 names, addresses, in its annual directory, 701 St. Asaph St., Alexandria, Va. 22314.

IMPROVING MANAGEMENT IN THE FRUIT BUSINESS

Management has been defined as containing elements of both an art and science. To argue the degree of each is pointless, but both must exist. Probably the most generally accepted definition is that management is the accomplishment of results through the efforts of other people. Managers have to decide what results are to be accomplished, and by what people. They must decide HOW and WHEN things should be done. They have to conclude whether the results have been obtained, and decide where to go from there.

Kinds of Managers

There are all kinds of managers—each with a unique personality. Some are harsh, some are lenient, some are disciplined, some are not. Some managers have organized work skills, some are casual, indefinite, and border on being confused.

Whatever a man's life style is, that style is quickly exposed to his employees through the daily contact of work supervision.

A manager cannot hide himself. His traits, characteristics, ambitions, fears and prejudices are all exposed. Try as we will to cover them, each of us exposes "bald spots," through our personal conduct—areas where improvement would be of benefit.

As a manager, the challenge is to improve his supervisory skill by improving himself in his dealings with others.

The Strong Manager

What does it take to work well through others? The following check-list is not all inclusive but outlines six characteristics of successful leadership.

1. Creative Ability: One who can think (also called vision) — imaginative. Must think creatively, constructively and clearly.
2. Judgment: Ability to judge justly or wisely, especially in matters which affect action.
3. Administrative Skills: Ability to forecast events and needs — to plan. An outward manifestation of orderliness — one's life, working quarters, desk, etc. Being organized.
4. Positive Attitude: Optimistic, one who can inspire others. The manager's behavior — facial expressions, droop of shoulders, etc. — all are closely watched by employees. Starts with good health.
5. Courage: Managers must be willing to gamble or take chances; courage to delegate — a manager can never abdicate responsibility.
6. Character: The previous five traits in varying degrees. But, on the question of integrity, there can be no comprise. A manager must have the confidence of his associates; his actions will be the same whether he is being observed or not. This is integrity!

The Weak Manager

By contrast, the weak manager inevitably lacks planning and organization with respect to supervising his people.

   a. He chooses people and makes assignments arbitrarily and emotionally rather than by an objective evaluation of their abilities and skills;

   b. He gives vague or incomplete instructions, showing he hasn't thoroughly analyzed the problem;

   c. He keeps subordinates in the dark about company policy;

   d. He is always too busy to train someone to fill his shoes.

Summary

With all the variety of orchard operations—both in scope and the wide range of management styles, each individual success is finally determined by the ability of each individual manager. His company becomes the lengthened shadow of himself. Since the subordinates are extensions of his own efforts, their errors are his errors, their successes his successes.

No matter how much work a man can do, no matter how engaging a personality he may be, he will not advance far in business if he cannot work through others.

How To Develop Leadership in Employees

Fruit growing normally does not attract employees highly skilled in sales motivation or work organization. Yet the fruit business depends upon these qualities for its very success.

It is apparent that chain stores, with centralized procedures, management-development programs and operating efficiencies can outdistance many of the independent orchard operations and their sales outlets.

Furthermore, it must be recognized that the chronic problem of low wages stems from the average low productivity of the workers involved.

One solution to this problem lies in the full development of latent abilities of employees. The challenge of the supervisor is to bring out the extra talents in his people.

It is enlightening to see the growth of people and the increased productivity of a work force when a supervisor, responding to leadership needs, develops a program of 1) training, 2) delegation, 3) correction, and 4) motivation. Ideas on how this can be done are as follows:

1. TRAINING. Sessions should be held on a regular basis and by the manager. This should not be delegated to an outsider or held away from the premises except for unusual circumstances or opportunities.

There is a psychology that works strongly in the manager's favor when the staff is brought together for training, discussion and commendation in the work environment. The feeling of acceptance and success that employees so badly need can only be conveyed by the person for whom they work. The core of these meetings should be information and training.

2. DELEGATION. If a manager organizes his operation into departments, usually by product lines or supporting functions, then delegating authority to his department heads naturally follows. However, there are some managers who go through the motions of delegation, but hug to themselves the essence of the job.

A manager with several orchard-block superintendents or department heads and still doing all the detail supervising is an example of this lack of real delegation. This often comes from the belief of some people that to have a job well done they must do it themselves. How are others going to be developed? Real delegation defines clearly in a job description the subordinate's area of responsibility and then grants him the full right for decision in that area.

The manager is still accountable for any errors of his subordinates and should accept the fault for such errors. That is the risk and the courage of delegation.

3. CORRECTION. A good supervisor should develop a technique for effective correction. Properly used, correction is the most important single device in leadership.

Here is a procedure abstracted from a publication of the

American Institute of Personnel Managers and modified to the needs of a farm manager.

    a. Acquaint yourself with all the facts so that you will be fair.

    b. Avoid correcting a person in the presence of anyone else.

    c. Always begin with a question — WHY — not an accusation. Give the person an opportunity to discuss the subject of the interview.

    d. Maintain your own calmness regardless of the other person's attitude.

    e. Never reprimand in anger.

    f. Always give reasons why you are making the correction.

    g. Be specific.

    h. Make suggestions as to how he can improve.

    i. Do not threaten.

    j. Try a "Criticism sandwich" (begin interview with a pleasant remark and close with a word of encouragement).

    k. Separate the man from the problem — correct the problem without demeaning the self-esteem of the person involved.

    l. Close interview pleasantly when all reasons for correction are throughly understood.

4. MOTIVATION — Motivation of subordinates is a most critical challenge to managers. Perhaps the most important to avoid are the three "C's."

    a. Don't Criticize.

    b. Don't Complain.

    c. Don't Condemn.

All too often a manager builds resentment and encourages inactivity through fault-finding. What employees need is an abundance of praise, recognition and encouragement.

A recent study by a leading psychologist listed five employee wants and asked 1,000 workers to rate them according to their importance. Here's how the motivators were ranked. Note that wages were last on the list of five.

    1. Recognition, appreciation for work well done.

    2. Feeling "in" on things.

    3. Help with personal problems.

    4. Job Security.

    5. Good wages.

It is such "psychic" values that managers must give their employees to achieve maximum productivity and good will.

In conclusion, an objective would be to strive to meet the increasing challenge to our market position by developing the latent capabilities of our employees through bolder and more aggressive leadership.

PROFIT SHARING

Helps avoid labor problems

Note: Following is a philosophy of orchard operation that may be of help to other orchard managers.

The key to a profitable orchard operation is a spirit of mutual trust, co-operation, and effort between management and labor. This is the philosophy of the late Henry Miller, Jr., Pres. of 1500-acre Consolidated Orchard Company of Paw Paw, W. Va. Beginning in 1939, Consolidated has encouraged a spirit of mutual interest through a profit-sharing plan for its employees. In addition to prevailing wages, paid semi-monthly, employees receive in cash, just before Christmas each year, a share of profits determined by the company's board of directors. Depending upon the market, production costs, and other economic factors, the plan has paid from 2 to 20% of each employee's yearly earnings during the over 40 years it has been in effect. The average has been about 10% extra pay to all regular employees.

What happens under profit sharing in a year when there are no profits? Consolidated made small year-end payments three times during the course of the plan when the company had not made an operating profit. After a heavy loss from hail storms, only 2% was paid and two of the years, small distriutions were made (6% and 5%) when the company just about broke even after being squeezed by a buyer's market, higher production costs, and adverse weather.

When year-end distributions are made, a personal letter from the company's president goes with each check, explaining in detail why it was possible to make the payment, how the enclosed check was figured, and how much the employee's friendly co-operation and good work has contributed to the success being shared by all.

To try to keep pace with changing trends in labor-management relations, Consolidated has from time to time also added some fringe benefits as the company became financially able to do so.

• The company covers a major part of the cost of a group insurance plan providing medical attention and hospitalization for employees and their families. Regular employees are eligible without examination after having worked with the company more than one year.

• After a year's service, employees are also entitled to a one-week vacation with pay at the company's convenience—generally Christmas week.

• The company owns and maintains 36 comfortable homes for foremen and other key personnel. These homes are rent free.

• After one year's service, regular employees with a good work record can borrow up to a specified limit without collateral or interest. Repayment is generally made by small payroll deductions later when the employee is better able to return the money.

Perhaps as important as the profit-sharing plan and fringe benefits at Consolidated is the company's attitude toward its employees. The manager felt strongly that employees should be treated as neighbors and friends. An employee visiting his office or home received the same pleasant and courteous consideration as a good customer. As Miller pointed out, a trained, interested employee is even more valuable to Consolidated than a good customer. Good employees under first-class management produce a good product, and a good product invariably attracts good customers—thus, the employee comes first.

As a result of close employee-management relationship at Consolidated, dissension and arguments between workers and management are practically non-existent and the company has thereby become known throughout the area as a good place to work. This is the major reason why the organization has never suffered from a shortage of good help. It has always been able to attract additional local help to harvest crops without resorting to the use of imported workers, even during World War II. All other large Appalachian orchardists have found it necessary to rely upon imported help to save their crops in recent years.

Occasionally someone indicates that Mr. Miller's plan is comparatively easy because the company operates in a depressed area where there is supposed to be a labor surplus. But Miller was quick to reply that this is an incorrect assumption because Consolidated orchards are located in northeastern West Virginia and western Maryland, in a highly developed industrial section.

The Organization

Consolidated Orchard Company now carries over 100 year-round employees, including labor and management to man the orchards, cold storages, packing plant, shops, and offices. In September and October about 100 more employees are added to the payroll in a normal season.

The company owns and operates four large orchards which are called divisions — Two in Allegheny County, Maryland, and one each in Morgan and Hampshire counties, West Virginia — for a total of 1500 acres. Each division has a superintendent and two foremen.

The central packing plant and cold storages are in Paw Paw and these facilities are used about nine months each year. The company produces a substantial tonnage of summer apples and peaches and the regular apple packing season generally lasts until late spring. All apples are packed fresh on order throughout the shipping season. Management in the plant consists of a packing superintendent and his assistant, plus a cold storage manager and his assistant.

A general workshop is maintained where all company machinery is kept in good working shape. During the winter months, four mechanics give trucks, tractors, sprayers, and other equipment a first-class overhauling. The shop foreman works full time at keeping up the equipment. However, his three wintertime helpers generally become truck, tractor, or fork-lift operators in the orchards and storages when the crop is being harvested.

After many years of experience with profit sharing, they are convinced that it is a sound business policy. They also are convinced that the plan has helped make it possible for Consolidated to produce and market a top-quality product that sells readily at premium prices. In their opinion there is no sounder moral or business investment than profit sharing.

How Profits Are Shared

All employees on the payroll during the pay period ending December 15 of each year are eligible. Seniority is not a factor in distribution under the plan. (Seasonal workers are not on the payroll when profit-sharing payments are made and, therefore, do not participate in the plan.)

The total number of dollars set up for distribution at the end of each 12-month period is voted by the Board of Directors. In determining the amount to be distributed in a given year, the Board first gives proper consideration to the company's general financial condition. When the company has had a financially satisfactory season, the Board then sets aside a safe and proper share of the net operating earnings, before taxes, for distribution to eligible employees.

Actual distribution is allocated to employees in proportion to the basic salaries received during the year for which a given distribution is made. The basic wage scale, before profit sharing, is maintained at or a bit above levels paid by other fruit producers in the area. All payments are made in cash.

CUSTOMERS ARE IMPORTANT!

A customer is the most important person in our business.
A customer is not dependent upon us.
A customer is not an interruption of our work.
He is the purpose of it.
A customer does us a favor when he comes in.
We are not doing him a favor by waiting on him.
A customer is part of our business — not an outsider.
A customer is not just cash in our cash register. He is a human being with feelings like our own.

A customer is a person who comes to us with his needs and his wants. It is our job to fill them.
A customer deserves the most courteous attention we can give him. He is the life blood of this and every business.
He pays our salary. Without him we would have to close our doors. Don't ever forget it.

Postmaster General, USA

FARM ACCOUNTING BY COMPUTER

Many growers, particularly large growers and grower-corporations, now are using electronic computer systems to save time, labor and money in their business and provide better accounting information. The service is furnished by companies over the world so-specializing. The service is confidential and economical. The mail-in forms require around 30 minutes of the bookkeeper's time a week. The service provides a wide range of information, including machinery costs, labor costs of each worker, income tax, social security, credit accounts, household expenses, depreciation records, etc. The service will indicate strengths and weaknesses in the operation and the manager will be able to spot areas needing improvement. Records can be kept by variety and block, e.g., indicating which blocks or varieties are paying and those that are a liability. Summary information is sent to the grower each month. The following column headings of a data sheet indicate the type of information recorded by day of the month and supplied at the end of the month to the service.

BASIC COMPUTER DATA SHEET

PAGE NO. 11

NAME: HORN-OF-PLENTY FRUITGROWER   ACCT. NUMBER:2987
ADDRESS: ORCHARDTOWN, N.J. 08850   MONTH: JANUARY 1974

Line No.	Day	Description and Source		Check No.	Item code	Credit code	Quantity		Dollar Amount
							Vol.	Unit	
1	3	Baskets returned	Pathmark Store		356		3	Bu	1.50
2	7	Labor	Bill Jones	43	374		1	wk	95.50
3	9	Soc. Security 9%	" "			802			8.60
4	9	Total trees			301		989	No	
5	10	Fertilizer	FCA	44	205		10	Tons	500.00

Note: Two additional column headings in table are (1) Enterprise code, (2) Allocation number.

Type of information received by the grower or corporation each month is: (a) a one-page summary of your business at a glance: breakdown of receipts and expenses, budget balance for the current month and year-to-date by general categories; (b) financial summary involving a classification of all receipts and expenses for the month (or report period) and cumulative totals for the year, quantities of items purchased and products sold for the period and year-to-date (lbs, hrs, numbers, etc.); (c) income and expense items separated for different enterprises and groups within enterprises if desired; (d) at the year-end you will receive (1) a tax summary of income and expense items for preparing your income tax form; (2) depreciation and credit investment and expense items for preparing your income tax reporting; (3) complete listing and classification of credit accounts (amounts paid, charged, borrowed and balances); (4) amount of income tax and social security withheld and deposits made with a running balance of liabilities; and (5) individual drawing accounts with special detail of household expenses to account for withdrawals and investments in the business. An annual summary analysis of the business is provided at the end of the year.

You can contact your local governmental agricultural extension service or Farm Bureau organization for information on how to obtain this service in your general area.

In order that the computer be of real service to the farmer, he must provide good management information. The computer can be no better than the information supplied to it. Good accounting information is not generally available from farmers and, hence, may be a good incentive to encourage fruit growers to keep better records.

WHAT IS AN ORCHARD WORTH?

The drastic changes in the fruit industry over the past several years and taking of land for public use have made the problem of orchard evaluation of considerable interest. The statement has been made that orchard owners have no basis of determining value. This statement in itself is suspect since all property has some value to someone although value may be lower or higher depending on circumstances.

There are two general problems: (a) Determining value to set for a sales price. (b) Determining value under condemnation or land-taking for public use.

The problem of determining a value for a sales price is usually a matter for an appraisal either by the owner, his representative, or by a trained appraiser. An appraisal is always an opinion. An appraisal by a trained and experienced appraiser is usually a composite based on observation of the property in its present condition and experience of the appraiser. It frequently is a composite of many opinions on parts of the farm and its setting.

The value of an orchard is determined by the production after development and the cost of maintaining that production. Any orchard will be in one of three conditions: (a) A developing orchard — on the way up in production; (b) a producing orchard — in full production; and (c) a declining orchard — going down in production.

When reaching a value for a developing orchard it is necessary to determine whether development can continue until the orchard is a producing one. If this seems likely then there are some requirements for a successful orchard: (a) The soil is important and it should be suitable for the varieties being grown as well as the type of fruit — apple — peach — pear; (b) The orchard should be located in a fruit area where there are other successful orchards; (c) Markets should be established; (d) Some plan for replacement should be indicated; (e) hazards of climate, drainage and requirements for irrigation should be minimum; (f) wild trees, abandoned orchards and other pest and disease sources should be few and control of orchard damaging animals should be established; (g) spacing and planting distances and varieties should meet accepted standards for the area; (h) orchard layout should permit use of labor saving equipment in orchard care, spraying and harvesting; (i) tree growth should be vigorous and evidence of good care should be present.

A producing orchard should meet all of the above tests plus having a record of high yields annually.

A declining orchard presents some additional problems. The property may have value for other uses. In this case the suitability of the soil for other crops becomes important and the cost of converting the orchard site for other uses becomes an item. If the reduced yields represent the start of a rather long period of declining yields, yield levels may still be such that continued operation is indicated and possible rehabilitation may be a consideration.

It is important in arriving at a value for a sales price to determine the stage of the orchard and then proceed to place a value on it by using all three of the generally accepted methods of determining value: (a) Values based on net income capitalization or "earning value"; (b) values based on comparison with other property which has changed hands or where values have been established; and (c) value based on reproduction cost.

Usually a sound answer to the question 'What is my orchard worth?' can be reached by considering all three of these and balancing them against each other to determine a basic value. The actual sales value then would be adjusted by comparison with sales prices of similar properties in the area.

The American Society of Farm Managers and Rural Appraisers has defined Present Market Value as follows: "It is the price at which, within a reasonable time and with a substantial down payment, the property may be expected to change hands from a willing, able and informed seller to a desirous, able and informed purchaser."

The problem of determining value under condemnation or land taking for public use is somewhat different from that of determining value for a sales price or present market value.

Taking private property for public use upon payment of just compensation is condemnation. The legal basis is called the "right of eminent domain." Under this procedure the people or the government take private property for public use when public needs cannot be provided for in some other manner.

The requirement that no person shall be deprived of private property without just compensation is a part of the "right of eminent domain." The courts by their decisions have varied in just what is "just compensation."

Under the "right of eminent domain" it follows that the injured party who is entitled to "just compensation" has the responsibility of determining values. The fact that the owner prefers the particular property to some other does not mean that he is thereby entitled to additional compensation. Legal precedent and usage have tended to favor the property owner.

In general, courts have held that market value is the guide to be followed in determining awards and further, again in general, the measure to be used in determining damages in condemnation cases is market value.

The courts have defined market value in these terms quite generally: "Market value is the highest price, estimated in terms of money, which the property will bring, if exposed for sale in the open market, with a reasonable time allowed to find a purchaser buying with knowledge of all uses and purposes to which it is best adapted, and for which it is capable of being used."

In some instances the term "fair market value" is used and then is defined as a situation where the sale can be made for cash or terms equivalent to cash, at a price agreed on by an informed seller willing but not obliged to sell to an informed buyer willing but not obliged to buy.

The attempt frequently made to value property taken under eminent domain or, for that matter, in attempting to arrive at a sales price by valuing the property by units and adding the unit values to get a value for the property, is likely to be very misleading. It is a good deal like trying to arrive at the value of a used car by placing values separately on the motor, the wheels, the tires, etc. and then adding the unit values together. The value needs to be determined for the whole property and it is the loss in value of the whole property as a result of the condemnation or partial sale, that needs to be determined. By Lawrence D. Rhoades, Department of Agricultural Economics, Univ. of Mass. Amherst.

ORCHARD CONDEMNATION VALUE SUGGESTIONS

. . . It should be emphasized that it is difficult to place a specific value on an individual fruit tree or group of trees killed by fire, or removed because of a highway or pipe line, or damaged or destroyed in other ways. Each case usually is different. Most important is the general effect on the grower's business. It takes 10 to 15 years to replace an apple, pear or cherry tree and 5-6 years for peach and dwarf trees. Trees removed from an orchard corner are not as serious to the business as those removed in a strip through the orchard. This cuts the orchard in two and makes it difficult to spray, harvest and conduct important operations. If his best block of trees is involved, his business is affected more than if his poorest block is involved. A grower who loses his trees during a prosperous period nationally may be affected more financially than if he lost trees driving a depression. Also, fruit trees are worth more during a period when the fruits in question are not over-planted nationally.

It should be taken into consideration that old untended fruit trees on the right-of-way are a liability rather than an asset to the buyer, who must pay for the cost of their removal, depending upon total number and method of removal.

Age of the trees may not be so important under some conditions. If they are in full bearing at a relatively young age, full value to the trees can be given. Trees may be rather old and still be in good production and thus would be worth the full value. Big apple trees may reach peak production at about 15 years, whereas peaches may reach top production between 6 and 8 years. Semi- and full-dwarf apple and pear may reach full bearing in 4-5 years.

In order to approach the problem of fruit tree appraisal, we have based decisions on one fact — a commercial grower who loses his fruit trees, by reason of condemnation proceedings for turnpikes or other reasons, not only loses the trees, but has his operations upset. His efficient use of men and equipment is reduced and the general plan of his orchard is changed. Therefore, we believe a grower is entitled to at least five years additional profit from each bearing tree destroyed for any reason if it is beyond his control. This figure will include full value of tree and consequential damages to orchard operations.

FRUIT-CROP-FROST-HAIL INSURANCE

By Paul W. Barden, Special Agent
Rain and Hail Insurance Bureau,
U.S. Rt. 15, Camp Hill, Pa. 17011

When your local agent quotes you the premium cost of hail coverage, your current Crop-Hail rate is determined by past loss experience on that crop in your locality. Records for all companies are tabulated on IBM cards by the Crop-Hail Insurance Actuarial Association in Chicago for the years 1936-on for each crop, and recorded by township, by county, and by state. Also there are accurate records for most fruit states as to premiums and losses for the years 1913-1936, so you can readily see that we have an excellent picture of what has happened concerning frequency and intensity of storms and the resulting cost to the insurance companies.

In New Jersey, e.g., our experience is not as conclusive as for some of our other states like Virginia, New York and Pennsylvania, but in 1969 crop hail rates were reduced by 20% in New Jersey which gives it the distinction of having the lowest crop-hail rates of any of the Northeastern states. The most frequently used contract is $4.00 per $100 of insurance per acre of apple in New Jersey as compared with $8.00 and $10 in New York State.

The all-time loss ratio on apples in several of our northeastern states is about 70%. Our administrative expense ratio was approximately 35% during this same period. From the preceding

figures you easily can see that our companies had had a median loss of about 5% by writing apples in the northeastern states and all insurance companies, like other businesses, must have some pleasure of profit as a goal. So with these percentages in mind, it is only practical for us to adjust our rates as conditions change. Therefore, we make a complete review of all crops in all areas at least every three years.

I have traveled the northeastern states for the past twenty-four years and we have tried to adapt our contracts to the needs of the various areas because we know that conditions in the Champlain Valley of New York are not the same as they are in Western New York, where the canning plants are principally located. We are attempting to improve our contract to secure a reduced rate for those growers who are primarily growers of canning apples.

Adjustment Procedure

In eastern New York, I still find growers who feel that we should pay 100% of a loss on all apples hit by hail irrespective for the degree of damage. Our adjustment procedure has always been based on U. S. standards for grades of apples, and our percentages have been based on a reduction in grade as follows:

U. S. No. 1 reduced to Utility 30%
U. S. No. 1 reduced to Canner. 50%
U.S. No. 1 reduced to Cider or Cull 100%

This provides an excellent yardstick from which to measure the loss.

After selecting two average trees in a ten acre block of apples and having picked 50 apples from each of four sides and the top of the tree, a typical weighted average adjustment for this block would be as follows:

$$
\begin{array}{rrr}
25 \times & 0 = & 0 \\
100 \times & 30 = & 3000 \\
225 \times & 50 = & 15000 \\
225 \times & 50 = & 11250 \\
150 \times & 100 = & 15000 \\
\hline
500 & & 29250
\end{array}
\qquad \frac{500}{29250} = 58.5\%
$$

If a grower had purchased X $ per acre of Crop-Hail Insurance (and he could have purchased up to X $), his return would be X $ x 58.5%.

By this method of adjustment our policy contract provides better coverage for partial losses than does the unit contract of the Federal Crop Corporation.

In our low rated areas, Federal Crop Insurance is about twice as expensive as our Crop-Hail policy because of the widely different methods of computing loss payments used by the two programs. By using a little arithmetic, many growers would find that our program would have saved them money.

Who adjusts our losses? Our adjusters are orchardists who have graduated from agricultural colleges, college professors, extension specialists, and other commercial men who have had many years of experience and are authorities in their field. They are fair-minded and impartial in their interpretation of the policy contract, but when a specific question arises the grower's interest is uppermost in their final decision.

When are losses adjusted? Preliminary inspections are made at the time of loss and final adjustment is completed prior to harvest.

Frost or Hail Loss

They say that people spend six days a week sowing wild oats and then go to church on Sunday and pray for a crop failure. I doubt that you will be praying for a crop failure, even though you have an "All Risk" Federal Crop policy, since 25% of the yield is deducted from coverage, thus removing the profit incentive. Also, in years with a relatively high yield, the percentage of damage must be severe before an indemnity is payable. Crop-Hail Insurance from stock companies may be purchased separately or in combination with Federal Crop Insurance in those areas where this is available. In the northeastern states, there are generally only two primary weather hazards: frost and hail. Once the frost-free date has passed, the only danger is from hail. You will have to decide which hazard reduces your profit the most. There is, I realize, a limit on the amount of protection you can afford to buy in a high-risk, high-rated area.

The Federal Crop Insurance Corporation, with unlimited resources of generous government subsidies, does have a value for all of us since they are able to accumulate statistics and experience which may be used in future years to encourage our stock companies to engage in the writing of All Risk crop insurance in this area. A Multiple Peril crop insurance program was approved and was introduced by private companies in five states on specific crops for 1969. The areas and crops are: Washington—wheat and barley; North Carolina—tobacco; and Illinois, Indiana and Iowa—corn and soybeans. The coverage parallels that previously offered only the Federal Crop Insurance Corporation.

Today we hear a lot about the "credit crunch, but apparently the Federal Crop Corporation, completely financed by your tax dollars, isn't particularly concerned because they do not require that premiums be paid until after harvest.

Credit is expensive and stock companies' Crop Hail Departments must operate in the black, especially when money can be invested at short term for relative high interest.

FARM DEFENSIVELY

By the late John Carew, Mich. State Univ., E. Lansing

Look for more environmental law suits against farmers. Livestock producers will be the hardest hit, but crop growers will also go to court. People no longer view farmers benevolently. Many regard farms as undesirable neighbors, sources of offensive odors and pollutants or competition for recreation land.

When the famous Michigan swine odor suit was settled, thousands of farmers smiled happily when the judge ruled in favor of the defendant whose farmer-neighbor claimed his pigs had a harmful smell. But the judge emphasized his decision was not to be regarded as a precedent. We can expect increased complaints against farm chemicals, odors, crop refuse, and noise.

Here are a few tips to individual growers for protecting against environmental law suits or court action:
• **Locate** all non-residential buildings, packing sheds, etc., in the middle of your property so as to provide wide buffer strips of land between you and your neighbors.
• **Pay attention** to state agricultural recommendations for building construction and the use of pesticides and fertilizers. The defense in the Michigan swine odor suit was strengthened considerably because the owner followed extension recommendations.
• **Train** employees to "Think and Act Environmentally": Pick up all pesticides and fertilizer containers. Do not spray in the wind. Dump nothing in streams. Burn only in compliance with local ordinances. Spread plant refuse on fields and disc it in.
• **Think . . .** before selling a home site on your farm. The man you sell to may be the one who takes you to court for polluting his air and water.
• **Develop** your personal public relations program. Deliberately, especially if they are not farmers, invite them to visit your farm. Show them what you do and why. Point out, diplomatically, how your business contributes to the community and the neighborhood; employment; your purchases of supplies and equipment; and the taxes you pay. Be certain to remind them that your crop-land is also open space with living plants that serve as air conditioners in the summer and soil acts as a water reservoir in the winter. You might gently remind them that the alternatives to your continued farming could be selling the land as real estate for housing or industrial development.
• Invite public school teachers to bring classes to your farm. Show the children your contribution to food production and to their environment. Do the same with members of your town council: some of them may never have been on a real farm.
• Become involved in all environmental and zoning law discussions. Our nation abounds with well-meaning but often misinformed laymen and government employees. Many seek to ban most pesticides and fertilizers. The most effective place to oppose them is at the community level.

In summary: "Drive Defensively" is sound advice for people who drive. The car coming toward you may not be completely under control.

"Farm Defensively" can be sound advice for men who earn their living on the land. Farming practices generally influence the environment adjacent to farms as well as on them. Operate your farm as though you might be called to defend it.

MICHIGAN'S RIGHT TO FARM LAW

This law became effective, 1981. It is the first such legislation in a major farm state in the United States. The bill provides that a farm or a farm operation shall not be a public or private nuisance if the operation conforms to generally accepted agricultural and management practices. Further, it will not be a nuisance if it existed before a change in the land use or occupancy of land within 1 mile of the farm land boundaries. The law takes into consideration changes in technology, and also allows an operation to change husbandry without becoming a nuisance. (The Great Lakes Fruit Growers News, July 1981.)

"U-PICK" STRAWBERRIES IN WISCONSIN

By G.C. Klingbeil, The University of Wisconsin, Madison

Not many years ago the commercial strawberry industry in Wisconsin had declined to near 1,000 acres and further reduction was imminent. Growers sales were at the mercy of a few fruit brokers, production costs were increasing, labor was high in cost and scarce in quantity due to laws that restricted the traditional use of women and children for harvest. Returns on investments were far from favorable. It was obvious that if strawberries were again to be a crop of economic significance in the state, a new and different approach to production and marketing must be developed.

Horticultural specialists from the College of Agricultural and Life Sciences and several key growers reviewed the problems facing the industry and then planned and implemented a program aimed at improving production and marketing. Two major projects developed—the Wisconsin Plant Improvement Program and the consumer harvest or "U-Pick" method of harvesting and marketing. In the years that followed, Wisconsin growers shifted to those essentially virus-free varieties that have proved to be reliable producers and most desirable for the "U-Pick" trade.

In 1967 we harvested about 2,000 acres and the acreage is continuing to increase. The major reason, however, for this vast improvement in the state's strawberry economy was the change in harvesting and marketing to the "U-Pick" program. Marketing procedures changed slowly at first but the obvious success of several growers in the "U-Pick" business encouraged others until the change was nearly complete. A decade ago, less than 10 percent of our berries were picked by consumers; today about 98 percent are harvested by the "U-Pick" method. From a few producing-shipping locations in the early 1950's, we have expanded to commercial plantings in every county in the state and the number of acres is increasing yearly.

Let's look more closely at the "U-Pick" harvestng and marketing program. What does it take to be successful? Success in the method can be assured by careful attention to planning, production, people, parking, policing, pricing, protection, public relations, patience and most of all, profit. Horticulturally, success requires a good site, good soil, adequate fertility, the best varieties, irrigation, pest control, and the production management skill to produce a good crop consistently. The location is not too important although close proximity to centers of population is most favorable. Records show that the greatest number of customers are within a 25-mile radius although it is not unusual for many to drive 75 to 100 miles for good fruit. Nearby customers come often and pick moderate quantities while those from greater distances may come only once but will take up to 100 pounds per customer. The average customer will take 20 quarts or around 28 pounds of berries each time. The amount harvested is generally in proportion to the kind of picking.

Productivity is a major criteria considered by all growers. Today, the main varieties in Wisconsin are Sparkle, Red Glow, Jerseybelle, Midway, Sunrise, and Badgerbelle with some Catskill and Robinson in localized plantings, but these are changing with experience and better cultivars. Growers should expect a minimum of 5,000 quarts per acre if they have irrigation. Some get 7,500 or more. Our yield trials indicate that 12,000 quarts per acre is not an unrealistic goal. The search for better varieties continues through variety trials and a breeding program aimed, in part, toward the development of varieties for the "U-Pick" trade.

One of the most important considerations for this kind of marketing is the provision for parking of customers' cars. Have plenty of space because many customers are senior citizens and women. They prefer not to walk far and will appreciate easy parking. A rule of thumb is to provide space for 200 cars for each 10 acres you expect to harvest. Provide a well-marked entrance and exit; one of each makes checkout easier. An early cut hay or mulch field is satisfactory.

It is desirable to have an area where youngsters can play. Youngsters supervised by a babysitter is an added incentive for many young housewives. Generally, children under 12 in the picking field are a liability. Post your rules such as picking hours and days, minimum age for pickers, prices and penalties. If customers know the rules, field supervision is easier. Customers tend to police themselves but a small battery powered portable loud speaker can be most helpful. Field supervisors, and you don't need many, should have a special hat or garb to identify them to the pickers.

We use a standard six-quart carrier. The use of quart cups and reliance on volume measurement is rapidly losing favor to a die-cut corrugated, fold-up box that is used in the carrier in place of quart cups. It will hold 10 to 12 pounds of fruit. The use of this liner-box and a weight measurement speeds checkout, eliminates the arguments that arise over the interpretation of "full quart" and encourages larger sales. Pricing is about the same throughout the area. An average (1983) is 60 to 70 cents per quart or 60 to 70 cents per pound.

Here are a few other suggestions:

(1) Protection — liability insurance for protection of the grower against personal injury and property damage claims is essential. We have had no difficulty with this problem yet, but an ounce of prevention is worth a pound of cure!

(2) Plan for a system of prompt banking and protection of cash receipts. Most all payments will be in cash and a large enterprise may collect several thousand dollars each day for several days.

(3) Establish and adhere to a daily time schedule for the picking operation. Most growers find 7:30 A.M. a convenient time to open the field for picking. Few growers find it necessary to continue daily picking after 3:00 P.M.

(4) Prepare a comprehensive plan of publicity and promotion through contact with communications media. A schedule of advertising rates for newspaper, radio and television outlets should be available to you. Our growers find that spot announcements on radio are an effective means of calling in customers and some have used this medium to discourage customers when the demand exceeded the supply of fruit. Roadside signs have not proven to be an effective means of reaching a mass audience for a short season of harvest.

(5) Develop a pleasant and patient approach to your customers. Your day as a hard-nosed independent farmer may return after the strawberry season, but for 3 weeks the public is your best friend and you better keep them contented and holding an easy hand on their pocketbook.

IN SUMMARY, let me say that growing strawberries is one of the most exacting kinds of agriculture. To aid in the decision-making that will result in maximum yields of high quality fruit, production management skills are needed in planting, pest control, irrigation, plant nutrition, and frost protection. Wisconsin growers have proven that a well-managed "U-Pick" strawberry enterprise can be profitable and in addition contribute to the recreational pleasure of a large group of people that enjoys getting into a rural area and have the pleasure of taking part in the berry harvest.

RENT-A-TREE

Rent-A-Tree is another way to move fruit. But Herbert T. Teichman of Eau Claire, southwestern Michigan, does this mainly for *public relations* with his best and reliable customers. He maintains the trees and makes only limited profit on this of many ventures he has underway. He maintains roadside stand sales, Pick-Your-Own, has a cherry "Pit Spitting" contest, accepts charter tours, and runs a large operation of nearly all fruits grown in Michigan except strawberries, where in his neighborhood there is too much U-Pick and price cutting. He has 100A of apples (5A Rent-A-Tree), 100A cherries, 50A peaches (all PYO), apricots, bush fruits (brambles, blueberries, currants), pears and grapes. His best customers (many rent-a-tree) start with the first of the season's fruits and come out almost weekly to harvest fruits through the season. In the fall they may arrange a family picnic around "their" tree, harvest and divide the fruit. In case of crop failure, they may be assigned another tree or trees.

In the early 1980s he was renting trees for $30-$50 each, depending upon the estimated yield per tree, cultivar and quality. Cultivars were mainly Delicious, Jonathan, Red Rome and Fenton. Customers may harvest 15-20 bushels or more.

Mr. Teichman, who owns and operates the "Tree-Mendus" fruit farm also has developed recreational areas around the apple trees that are available for the season to the renters. These include picnic areas, scenic hiking trails and tall pine trees.

Advantages cited for the grower in such an operation are that a sale is secured, less labor and housing is needed to pick the fruit and the program can be operated in conjunction with the farm's pick-your-own crops as well as a retail market.

Some disadvantages would include extra weekend work for the grower, maintaining a park-like atmosphere around the orchard and grounds, increase insurance costs and the problems associated with extra correspondence and record keeping.

For the customer Mr. Teichman said the advantages are a guarantee of tree ripe fruit, the chance to earn a little extra cash by selling the crop from his tree, and the experience of watching a tree develop from bloom through fruit.

The customer has no responsibility for care of the tree which is done by Mr. Teichman.

Here is how the "rent-a-tree" operation works.

The customer selects the tree he wishes to lease for the season and the tree is marked as "sold" and a contract is written between Mr. Teichman and the customer. A number is placed on the tree, which corresponds with an identification number-card given to the customer.

The customer must present his I. D. card upon entering the orchard when visiting his family tree. The card entitles the family to enter the grounds and any additional friends of the family will be charged 50ᶜ apiece to enter the grounds.

Persons who rent a tree are kept informed of its progress during the season, by postcard.

Mr. Teichman has maintained the Rent-A-Tree operation for over 10 years and is reasonably well satisfied with the good public relations he creates and the frequent media publicity.

In Germany, Gerhard Hopp of Baulkhausen (near Frankfurt) placed an ad several years ago offering to rent individual trees for a "fair" sum per year. After he had rented 1200 of his 3500 trees, he had to stop. His weekend traffic got so heavy, with whole families driving out to see their tree, he could not get anything else done. The idea is popular in Germany, where the cost of picking had reached an all time high. Apples belong to the renters, of course, and not all of them are harvested.

SEEKING RUSSET-FREE GOLDEN DELICIOUS

James N. Cummins, P.L. Forsline and R.D. Way of the N. Y. Agr. Exp. Sta., Geneva, 14456, compared Golden Delicious with several mutations on MM.106 rootstock, planted in 1970 and trained to the central leader system. Planting was located near Lake Ontario where humidity is higher and there is slower drying. Spray chemicals were used as captan that are relatively non-russet inducing. Apples at the end of the season were rated from 1 to 10, with a rating of 4.0 or more being too russetted for U. S. Fancy grade. Evaluations were made over 4 consecutive years 1973-6. The Smoothee cultivar gave about twice as many U. S. Fancy fruits as the regular Golden Delicious and they were

smoother to touch. Regular Goldens were better than any of the spur-types, which ripened about a week later. There were no differences in tree size or yield between Smoothee and the regular Goldens. Yellospur trees were the least efficient of the five tested. The accompanying table shows the differences in russet-ratings and percent U. S. Fancy fruits. (From HortScience **12**:(3) 241-2. June 1977.)

COMPARISON OF FRUITS FROM
GOLDEN DELICIOUS AND FOUR SUBCLONES
(MEAN VALUES FROM 4 YEARS OBSERVATIONS)

Cultivar	Percent U.S. Fancy fruits	Russet rating
Golden Delicious	38	4.13
Goldspur	5	5.69
Smoothee	81	2.72
Starkspur Golden Delicious	4	5.85
Yellowspur Delicious	5	5.60

TREE FRUIT FARM ACCIDENTS.
TABLE OF INJURIES AND COSTS ON THE FRUIT FARM (WASHINGTON STATE UNIV., EM-4513, 1979).

Type of Injury	Percent of Total Injuries	Percent of Total Cost	Cost Index
Fall from ladders	21	49.1	2.3
Struck by objects	22	11.5	0.5
Overexertion	14	9.1	0.6
Struck against	11	5.6	0.5
Rubbed or abraded	8	0.5	0.1
Fall from elevation	7	10.5	1.5
Fall on same level	6	6.8	1.1
Contact with caustic and toxic substance	6	0.9	0.2
Average	—	—	1.0

Suggestions

What can be done to cut down the rate of accidents? Costs are related to the number and severity of accidents. See Table below.

As you may know, your insurance base rate is determined each year by your class *compensable* claim record for a three-year previous period. The immediate past year is not used because those records were not completed in time.

Then your individual insurance can vary from the base rate as much as 200% above to 15% below depending on your individual compensable claim record and hours reported. The previous statement is an over-simplification of the rate formula and is mentioned to point out there is a monetary incentive to cut accidents. The key is the compensable claim records of you and your class group.

If you would like to check the details of this study, write for the bulletin cited above.

THE WEATHER

Weather is a major factor in successful farming and **particularly** in fruit growing. The fruit grower continuously is conscious and listening to weather predictions. His entire business is dependent upon how he can "swing" with the weather, controlling water supply by irrigation, controlling any freeze damage in the spring, fall and winter, dodging bad spraying and dusting days, adjusting his labor force to keep it busy indoors or outdoors, and to plan for or repair repairable damage due to a heavy snowfall, rainfall, hurricane winds, freeze damage, or other acts of the weather.

The United States Environmental Science Service Administration of the U. S. Department of Commerce, Washington, D.C. or your local governmental weather service can supply you with publications on details of past weather for many decades in your particular area. Also, in recent years, this Service is giving more detailed information on microclimate (near the soil surface) as well as other valuable information in local fruit crop areas. This information is quite valuable to individual growers in their immediate planning to save their crops or make any needed precautions.

The chart above shows frequency of destructive storms in the Atlantic Coast region of the United States. The hurricane that occurred in late summer of 1938 when leaves were on fruit trees in the New England area was heavily destructive and was "felt" for years afterward in weakened and/or dying trees. For details on this and other hurricanes from the seasons they occur to how they are "born" and perform can be found in "Hurricane — the Greatest Storm on Earth", ESSA/Pi 670009, Superintendent of Documents, U. S. Printing Office, Washington, D. C., 20402. 65 cents.

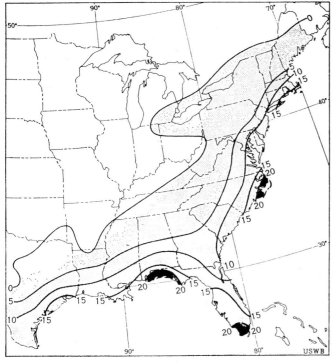

Number of times destruction was caused by tropical storms in Eastern United States, 1901-1955.

ORGANICALLY GROWN FRESH PRODUCE AS A NEW MARKET

Walter Androsko, Cooperative Extension Agent, Westchester County, N.Y.

"Organically" grown fresh produce offers a new market for some farm stand operators. There has always been a group of people interested in organic gardening and organically grown produce. With the emphasis on ecology, the concerns regarding the thousands of chemicals used in our society, and the new life style of the young, there is an increasing market for "organic foods." An examination of many home magazines will show glowing accounts and exotic recipes for "organic foods." Magazines and books have proliferated on the subject of natural foods, organic foods, the natural life, etc. Natural food stores are springing up in many communities.

Growers of fruits and vegetables have the opportunity of supplying some of these demands. All of you have used organic matter and organic fertilizers in the production of fruits and vegetables. It now becomes a management decision whether this market, with its possible premium prices, should be developed by you. This will mean some change in your farming practices. It may be that the organic fertilizers now used over the entire farm and then supplemented with commercial fertilizer will need be concentrated on one portion of the farm as the only nutrients used. It may be necessary that on some crops a change in pest control will be necessary. The term "organic foods" and organically produced foods mean different things to different people. It may be well for you to find out what is meant by these terms by your potential customers before you start a program of catering to this specific group.

Organic gardening and organic foods traditionally has meant the production of food without the use of commercial fertilizers. It may also mean the production of these foods without the use of pesticides of any kind. On the other hand, some organic gardeners feel that the use of plant type pesticides are in harmony with nature. These could be products such as rotenone, pyrethrum, tobacco products, Ryania, etc. There are other variations that could be mentioned but the point I make is that organic gardening and organic food does not mean the same to all people.

Roadstand operators have always been alert to the demands of their customers. If a certain portion of your customers are demanding organically grown foods and are willing to pay the price needed for you to produce them, it certainly behooves you to give consideration to these demands. It may also be that some of the "natural" food stores in your area would also be an outlet for these products.

There are pitfalls that should be considered by anyone contemplating the production of these organic foods. One consideration is the mentioned fact that your production methods, no matter how well intentioned, may not conform to the standard of organic food some customers desire. You would also need to adjust your own standards of perfection in production and harvesting as there will be imperfections that may be tolerated by the organic trade that you likely would not consider selling in your normal merchandising program.

You will also need to review your pricing policy carefully. The changes in production and the yield at harvest will be such that a different pricing policy will be necessary. This is a specialized trade and higher prices will be expected. Finally, it should be remembered that this is a new project for you. There is at least some fad element involved among the buyers. It may be that once the product is put onto your merchandising counter the appeal of it in comparison to your own product will be less and the demands lower than expected. On the other hand, we could hope that the demands would be above expectations; but either event caution and alertness should be followed with this new project. It will be an interesting departure for you. You will meet an entirely new clientele that will challenge you and I hope interest you.

You will find these customers for organically grown food different from your regular customers. Many of them are looking upon food purchases as an expression of their philosophy of living. They will question you and your practices, some will be overly zealous, others eager to learn. All will be interesting if you have the time and interest in their points of view. You must be alert to their wishes, to your cost of production and to the final figure that determines profit and loss which is so important to whether you continue this new enterprise, expand it or discontinue it. As with any new enterprise some patience will be necessary to allot time for the new products to catch on. Depending upon your own interests and enthusiasms, the growing of organic foods can present a challenge that will open up an entirely new farming experience for you.

INCOME TAX MANAGEMENT FOR THE FRUIT GROWER

By Timothy D. Hewitt
University of Florida, Agricultural
Research Center, Marianna

When the time approaches for filing income tax returns, all farmers are confronted with filling out many complicated forms. Knowing the options available and having records of the transactions of the farm operation are important. As a fruit or nut grower, you are confronted with several special provisions of the income tax regulations. Most of the provisions contain options or alternatives; thus understanding the tax regulations is important so you can make the best decisions concerning the options available to you.

A good detailed and easily read publication for farmers is: "Income Tax Management for Farmers", North Central Regional Publication No. 2. 24 p. Agr. Ext. Serv. of your state university or Purdue University, W. Lafayette, In. 47907, cooperating with USDA, up-dated every year, by P.E. Harris, R.E. Brown and W.A. Tinsley. IRS publication 225, "The Farmer's Tax Guide" is up-dated annually and gives a good treatment of the law but no managerial suggestions.

The purpose of this discussion is to cover the income tax provisions that apply to orchards or groves and some of the implications of these provisions. Also, the importance of farm records will be discussed and a method of estimating additional cost and financial loss in the planting due to tree loss will be discussed.

Farm Records

Maintaining up-to-date farm records is important in any type of farming operation and is the first step of income tax management. The purpose of farm records is to provide financial and physicial information concerning the farm operation and to supply information to use in decision making. Filling out tax returns is much easier when the grower has a good set of records. Farm records are also a necessity when you apply for a loan. Most lending agencies require certain farm records.

The Internal Revenue Service stresses the importance of good records in the Farmer's Tax Guide.* In the Guide, the main advantage of good records is listed as a savings in income taxes. The ways that good records help are:
1. Identify source of receipts
2. Prevent omissions of deductible expenses
3. Determine depreciation allowance
4. Take advantage of capital gain and loss provisions
5. Establish reportable earnings for self-employment social security taxes

6. Explain items reported in income tax return.

A helpful tool for farm planning for the grower is to develop an enterprise budget. These budgets provide estimates of the income, expenses and resource requirements of the planting. By developing these budgets, the grower may have an easier time in deciding the merits of expansion or any other decision that must be made.

An additional comment on farm records should be noted. Your farm records need proper protection from loss. The loss of your records could seriously jeopardize your farming operation. Duplicate copies of your records should be stored in a bank safe deposit box or a storage warehouse. Be sure to provide the storage facility you choose with the name of at least one person who can act either on your behalf or as an authorized representative.

Income Tax Management

In general, there are three stages in the life of a planting: preparatory, development and productive. Most expenses must be capitalized during the first or preparatory period. The grower has an option to capitalize or deduct ordinary business expenses during the development period. During the productive period the grower must deduct ordinary business expenses in connection with a fruit planting during the current year.

Preparatory Period

In the preparatory period, most expenses must be capitalized. However, some expenses may be deductible as soil and water conservation or land clearing expenses. If you have expenditures that qualify under this category you can elect to deduct these expenses in the current year.

Deductible soil and water conservation expenditures are those made on land used by you for farming at the time of the expenditures or before such expenditures are made. The treatment or movement of earth, such as leveling, grading, terracing, conditioning, or restoration of fertility are included as deductible expenses. Additionally, the construction of drainage ditches, earthen dams, diversion channels, ponds, the eradication of brush and planting of windbreaks qualify for this deduction.

It is important to remember that expenditures for depreciable soil and water conservation assets may not be deducted. You must capitalize your expenditures for structures or facilities such as water wells, pipe, and for wooden or concrete dams.

Another important point to remember is that if the soil and water expenditures are made to make the farmland suitable for a different use, as, for example, if you purchase pasture land and prepare it for use as a fruit planting, these expenditures will not qualify.

The total deduction in any tax year of expenditures of a capital nature for soil and water conservation is limited to 25 percent of your gross income from farming during the year. However, you may carry over any unused deduction to succeeding years.

You may also deduct expenditures for clearing land to make it suitable for farming. Your deduction in any year for land clearing expenditures cannot exceed $5,000 or 25 per cent of your taxable income from farming, which ever is less, and the balance must be capitalized.

The cost of fertilizer, lime and other materials used to enrich, neutralize or condition land that is to be used in establishing a planting may be deducted during the preparatory period.

During the preparatory period you can elect to capitalize taxes, interest and carrying charges. These items would normally be deductible in the current year.

The period of time after the trees are planted in a permanent

546

location and before a marketable crop of fruit or nuts is harvested is the development stage for a planting. In this period, you have the option of deducting or capitalizing expenses that are necessary for maintaining the trees. This option applies to amounts spent for upkeep, taxes, interest, irrigation costs, fertilization, control of undergrowth, cultivation and spraying trees. The election of the option is made at the end of the first tax year when the expenses are incurred. Once an election has been made for a particular group of trees planted in the same tax year all future expenses on these trees must be treated the same way.

Before deciding whether to deduct or capitalize expenses during this period you should consider some of the following factors:

1. Your income tax bracket during the development period
2. Your expected taxable income in future years when full production is reached
3. The amount of working capital needed for debt retirement.
4. The amount of investment that will qualify for investment credit.

Productive Period

The productive period is reached when a marketable crop is harvested. During this period all ordinary and necessary expenses must be deducted during the current tax year. You can also begin to depreciate the capitalized cost in the planting during this time.

Depreciation

The basis for computing depreciation is the cost of the trees at the time the orchard or grove reaches an income-producing stage, including initial cost and capitalized expenditures incurred in bringing the trees to production. The rate of depreciation is determined by the average productive life of the trees after the income-producing stage is reached.

If producing orchard or grove is purchased, the cost basis for the trees must be separated from the land since land cannot be depreciated. This allocation of the cost between the land and the trees is neccessary in order to determine the basis of the trees for depreciation. The allocation of the cost to each item should be made in proportion to its fair market value at the time of purchase.

Trees do no qualify for the additional first-year depreciation that is allowable for new or used tangible personal property.

Depreciation is a method of recovering the cost of a business capital item by deducting part of the cost each year. Depreciation records are used to record the original cost, useful life, depreciation method, and annual depreciation allowance for depreciable assests. The most critical decision to be made in using the depreciation schedule is the choice of a depreciation method.

An area where farmers have traditionally had a great deal of flexibility is selecting a depreciation method for newly purchased property. Even though the new Tax Bill presents an entire new set of depreciation rules, that flexibility remains. The present depreciation methods are replaced by new accelerated cost recovery system (ACRS). Under this system, all depreciable property purchased after December 31, 1980 is placed in one of four recovery period categories as follows:

— Three years. Includes autos used in the farm business, i.e. light trucks.
— Five years. Includes tractors, combines, machinery, single-purpose agricultural and horticultural structures, and office equipment and furniture.
— Ten years. Includes certain public utility property, railroad

tank cars, and residential manufactured houses (mobile home for employee or tenant).
— Fifteen years. General purpose farm buildings are included in this category.

In addition to these recovery periods, the Act offers an accelerated method for computing depreciation. The method is built into tables showing the percent of the cost that can be deducted in each year. The table showing the percentages for three- and five-year property placed in service 1981-1984 is shown below.

Recovery Year	Three-year	Five-year
1	25%	15%
2	38	22
3	37	21
4	—	21
5	—	21

In lieu of the above percentages, farmers may use the straight-line method. This method permits the cost to be spread evenly over the designated useful life. The following useful lives can be used:

ACRS Recovery Class	Optional Straight-line Useful Life
3-year property	3, 5, or 12 years
5-year property	5, 12, or 25 years
10-year property	10, 25, or 35 years
15-year property	15, 35, or 45 years

If the straight-line method is used for one piece of property in a recovery class, it must be used for all property in that class placed into service during that year. This means that if a farmer purchases a tractor and a plow in 1981, both must be depreciated the same manner.

Both methods use the half-year convention rule, thereby allowing only a half-year's depreciation in the year of purchase for personal property.

Salvage value is zero for both methods, which means the entire cost can be depreciated. The rules are the same for both new and old property. Property placed in service before 1981 will continue to be depreciated under the old rules.

Under the old rules, the three methods of depreciation most generally used are: (1) the straight line method, (2) the declining balance method, and (3) the sum of the years-digits method. The most commonly used method is the straight line method and this results in an equal amount of depreciation each year.

Although not as easy to compute as the straight line method, the declining balance and the sum of the years-digits methods have a definite advantage. These methods result in a larger depreciation deduction in the 1st year and gradually smaller deductions in each of the following years.

Investment Credit

Orchard trees established or purchased after January 21, 1975, qualify for the 10% investment credit. The credit is claimed the year in which the trees reach the productive stage. If the trees were already in production when they were purchased, the cost basis allocated to the trees is the amount of investment qualifying for the investment credit. In this case the trees would be considered as used property and there is a limit of $125,000 on the cost of used property that qualifies for credit in any one year.

If you establish a new planting your basis for investment credit would be the same as your basis for depreciation and includes the cost of the trees plus all capitalized expenses during the preparatory and development periods. These trees would qualify as a new property and there is no limit on the amount of new property which qualifies for the investment credit.

The investment credit is calculated on Form 3468 and then it is subtracted directly from tax due on Form 1040, thus it reduces tax dollar for dollar. For example, consider a planting that was purchased in 1982 with a cost basis in the trees of $20,000. The investment credit would be $2,000 (10 percent of $20,000. In this base the $2,000 would be subtracted from the tax due on the 1982 income tax return.

When using investment credit, remember that the useful life of property is determined at the time you place it in service. You must use the same useful life in determining the amount of the allowable investment credit that you use in computing depreciation.

The income tax provisions mentioned in this discussion are some guides and suggestions. Each grower should consult Farmers' Tax Guide or talk to an IRS representative to determine the options you may choose.

Additional Cost and Financial Loss Due to Tree Loss

Each year some trees are lost due to disease, accidents and lightning. The following is one idea for estimating additional cost and financial loss from tree loss. This is not intended to provide recommended details for determining tax deductible income loss for trees destroyed.

1. Inspect the trees and record the number of trees lost.
2. Determine the current level of production and estimate the future crop production of the lost trees.
3. Determine the current cost of tree replacement.
4. Determine the value of the current crop lost.
5. Discount additional cost and financial loss to present day values.
6. Sum the estimated replacement cost per tree and estimated loss of current yield to the present value of additional cost and future loss of income.

For example, you inspect your pecan grove and find two trees have died. One tree is 20 years old and the other tree is 10 years old.

The 10 year old tree is producing 38 lbs. of nuts at 80 cents/lb. The estimated loss of current yield is $30.40. Estimated replacement cost is $14.00. This totals $44.40. By using a 10 percent discount rate, the present value figure adds up to $136.53. Thus, the estimated additional cost and financial loss incurred in losing the pecan tree and replacing it is $180.93.

The 20 year old tree is producing 46 lbs. of nuts at 80 cents/lb. The estimated loss of current yield is $36.80. Estimated replacement cost is $14.00. This totals $50.80. By using a 10 percent discount rate again, the present value figure adds up to $152.21. You only discount for 12 years because you assume that it will only take 12 years for the replacement tree to reach the same production as the 20 year old tree. In this case, the additional cost and financial loss is $207.01.

The total additional cost and financial loss for the two trees is $387.94. (Pecan South, 1978, updated 1983).

Estate Law Changes

As a result of the Economic Recovery Act of 1981, some major changes have been made in the federal estate tax laws. These changes are particularly important to farmers and can result in tremendous tax savings for heirs. Under the new law the tax exempt portion of an estate will grow from $225,000 in 1982 to $600,000 in 1987. This means that under the law a person will be allowed to pass up to $600,000 to his or her heirs tax free. Further more there is no tax on any amount that is to be passed to a surviving spouse.

This is important legislation for farmers because, in the last 10 years, inflation has tremendously increased the value of most farm estates. It is important however, to remember that this new law affects only federal estate taxes, and does not apply to state inheritance taxes, at least not yet.

As an example, in 1982 two legislative proposals were introduced n the state legislature to conform New York estate laws to the changes made in the federal law. While both bills are similar in most respects, there is one major difference. The REP. bill S-8166 (Lombardi) and A-1)166 (Chesbro) would comply with the federal changes exactly, making the marital deduction unlimited. This would allow a decedent to leave his or her entire estate to the surviving spouse free of both state and federal estate taxes. A marital deduction also will be permitted where the surviving spouse is provided with an income interest in trust for life, with the remainder to be disposed of as the decedent has directed.

In the past, when the federal government has made changes in the federal estate law, New York State generally has followed and made changes to conform. By eliminating all the tax in the estate of the first spouse to die, the widow (er) will be able to maintain a level of lifestyle to which they have been accustomed for the balance of his or her lifetime.

It is well to keep in close contact with your CPA or lawyer to keep abreast with changes affecting your business and welfare.

Tax Planning In Buying And Selling a Farm

Note: Following information is from, "Income Tax Management For Farmers," North Central Regional Publication No. 2 by P.E. Harris et al., 1983 from Purdue University, W. Lafayette, Indiana 47907. Write for an updated copy, revised annually.

To insure maximum tax savings at the time of purchasing a farm, the buyer should allocate the total cost of the farm to: (1) growing crops, if any, (2) depreciable improvements, (3) dwelling and (4) land.

From a tax-management viewpoint, the amounts allocated to the different items are handled differently. The cost assigned to the growing crops is an offset (shown on Schedule F) against the selling price of the crop in the year of sale. The cost basis of the farm is reduced by the amount allocated to the growing crop.

The part of the cost allocated to land will not be recovered until the farm is sold, since land cannot be depreciated. So, too, the portion allocated to the dwelling is not depreciable if used solely as a personal residence. A tenant house is depreciable for tax purposes. Cost allocated to depreciable improvements will be recovered through depreciation. Investment credit can be claimed only on the part of the investment allocated to assets that qualify for the credit such as tile, grain bins, and fences.

For management and tax purposes, the cost must be broken down and allocated to each particular structure or improvement. In allocating cost to depreciable improvements the following procedure may be helpful: (1) figure the present cost of replacing the improvement, (2) estimate the number of years the improvement is normally used, (3) determine the age of the present improvement, (4) determine the remaining years the improvement will be used and (5) compute a value by dividing the remaining years the improvement will be used by the total years of normal use and multiplying the result by the replacement cost.

The following is an example of this procedure: (1) replacement cost of barn — $20,000, (2) number of years a new barn is normally used — 25, (3) age of present barn — 15 years, (4) remaining years the present barn will be used — 10, and (5) value of present barn — 10/25 of $20,000 = $8,000. The value of the lumber in the used-up barn does not have to be considered since the cost of removing the old barn will be about equal to the value of the lumber. (Note that the recovery period or useful life for depreciation purposes does not have to be the same as the estimate used for allocating the purchase price.)

Another guide in allocating costs is the reasonable insurance values of insurable property. Care should be taken to see that in the final allocation, the amount allocated to the bare land represents a reasonable value for similar land in the community.

The proper allocation of cost may help determine the price a buyer will pay for the farm. This is particularly true where the buyer is looking to future farm income after taxes to pay off the purchase price.

Closely related is the manner of payment of the purchase price. In computing taxable income, the buyer deducts interest payments, but not payments on principal. The seller treats interest as ordinary income, while principal payments in excess of cost basis are capital gains.

Managing Income For Maximum Social Security Benefits

In some cases, farmers may wish to increase their net farm income to the maximum amount subject to self-employment tax in order to secure larger social security benefits when they retire. The maximum amount of income subject to self-employment tax is $32,400 in 1982 and is scheduled to increase in future years. By increasing taxable income to boost social security benefits, you increase the amount of income tax and self-employment tax. However, it may be desirable to do so in order to gain additional retirement, disability and death benefits. Each individual must weigh the increased cost of obtaining the higher benefits against the value of the benefits.

Some of the methods for increasing income are: (1) renting and operating additional land, (2) intensifying and expanding present enterprises, (3) adding new enterprises, (4) electing to report sales of forest products as ordinary income, (5) selling more farm products and (6) doing custom work or other off-farm work.

Where choice of method of handling certain items of expense is optional, you may choose the method that gives the smaller deductions, such as: (1) using the alternate method of depreciation with long recovery periods, rather than the accelerated cost recovery system, (2) electing to treat soil and water conservation costs as capital investments rather than as current operating expenses, (3) disposing of some depreciable capital items to reduce the total depreciation deductions, and (4) in general, reducing operating costs to a minimum without impairing operating efficiency.

Farm rental payments are generally not considered to be self-employment income. However, if the landlord "materially participates" in the management of the farm, the income will qualify for self-employment. So if a landlord desires to increase social security coverage, the lease arrangement should be designed so that he or she "materially participates" in the management of the farm.

For years when farm income is low, there is an optional method of determining net earnings from self-employment. Under this method, a farmer whose gross income is more than $2,400 and whose net farm income is less than $1,600 may treat $1,600 as his or her net earnings from farm self-employment. This could help to increase social security coverage in a low income year or a year with a net operating loss. Also, under the optional method, a farmer whose gross income from farming is less than $2,400 may treat two-thirds of his or her gross income as net earnings from farm self-employment.

Tips

1. Pay cash wages to your children for farm work actually done by them and deduct as a farm business expense. In order to do this the wages should be reasonable and there should be a true employer - employee relationship. To establish this relationship, assign definite jobs, agree on wages ahead of time and pay the children regularly as you would any other employee. Wages paid to a child are included in his or her income and may result in the child having to file an income tax return. However, with the personal exemption and zero bracket amount, an unmarried person can now earn up to $3,300 without paying federal income taxes. The parents can also claim an exemption for the child as a dependent as long as they pay for over half of the child's support and as long as the child is either under age 19 or is a student. This makes possible two personal exemptions, one by the child and another as a dependent of the parents. Also, wages paid to children by parents are not subject to social security tax until the child reaches age 21.

2. Give income-producing property, such as: land, trees, livestock, and machinery to children and let them report income from their work and capital. Family partnerships and farm corporations through stock transfers are sometimes used to do this. It is another way to spread family income over the lower tax brackets. Remember, gifts and partnerships must be legally sound to achieve tax savings.

3. If you are age 63 or 64, postpone income to age 65 to take advantage of the double personal exemption. Persons approaching retirement, however, may want to maintain income as near as possible to the maximum for social security in these years ($32,400 in 1982).

4. Do not hold breeding stock used for production of market livestock too long. By selling sows after only one or a few litters, a higher percentage of hog sales will qualify for capital gain treatment over a period of years and reduce taxes.

5. Buy machinery and equipment in years of high income and take advantage of accelerated cost recovery, and possibly of the expensing option.

6. If you are selling timber, be sure to handle the sale so the gain can be reported as a capital gain.

7. Plan personal deductions. Some medical expenses or contributions that are normally spread over two years can be paid in one year and itemized as deductions. In the next year, the zero bracket amount (the old standard deduction) may be taken if higher than the total of actual itemized deductions. Be sure to choose the larger of the two.

8. Avoid wide fluctuations in income from one year to the next so you have enough income each year to take advantage of personal deductions and exemptions.

9. Installment sales of property can be used to spread income over a period of years and thus avoid high income.

10. Check for loss years in the past. Is there an unused net operating loss deduction? If so, file an amended return and obtain a refund on taxes paid in the past.

11. Be sure to claim the investment credit on all items that qualify.

12. To insure a record of all income and expenses, have a checking account in which to deposit all receipts and to pay all bills.

13. Be sure that CCC loans are not counted as income twice (in one year when borrowed and next year when crop is sold). Farmers can elect to report the loan as income in the year the loan is received or wait until the grain is either reclaimed and sold or forfeited to report the income. Farmers must report CCC loans in the same manner each year after the election is made for

the first CCC loan. Good inventory records will help ensure that the income is correctly reported.

14. If you are using the cash method, deduct cost of purchased livestock that was lost, stolen or that died during the year.

15. If you are using the accrual method, deduct all purchases of livestock. Make a livestock number check to see that the total number purchased and born plus the beginning inventory equals the total number sold, died and butchered plus the ending inventory.

16. Deduct as many auto, utilities, telephone, etc. expenses as actually used in the farm business (half is not enough in many cases). Make certain this use is well documented.

17. Keep records to insure deduction of easily overlooked items such as farm magazines, farm organization dues, bank service charges, business trips, portion of dwelling used for farm business, household supplies used for hired help and cash outlay to board hired workers.

18. Itemize on bank deposit slips all gifts, borrowings, etc., so that they will not be considered taxable income.

19. Keep records of all medical, dental and hospital bills, including premiums for accident and health insurance.

20. Establish a charge account at a hardware store, elevator or other places where considerable business is done during the year. Pay account by check upon receipt of monthly statements. This prevents omitting many small items which might otherwise be paid by cash.

21. Keep exact records of date of purchase, cost and date of sale on all items purchased for resale.

22. Pay bills by check whenever possible. Record all cash expenditures at once in an account book. Always get receipts for farm expenses paid by cash. Obtain a bank statement each month and check it aganst the farm account book.

23. Do not include in income any indemnity for diseased animals if payment has been or will be used to buy like or similar animals within two years.

24. Do not report capital gains on the sale of your dwelling as income if you plan within two years to buy and occupy another dwelling that will cost as much or more than the selling price of your present dwelling. Also, you have two years to build and occupy a newly constructed dwelling. In addition, if you are 55 or older, you may choose to take a once-in-a-lifetime exclusion of up to $125,000 of the gain on the sale of your personal dwelling, even though you don't reinvest in another house.

25. Remember that if you have income subject to tax, every dollar of cost not deducted will result in unnecessary income taxes.

BECOME A STOCKHOLDER — IT'S EDUCATIONAL

Reports to stockholders are often interesting reading. Especially when they contain very good or very bad news; or when they reflect major changes in company policy. For years, I have been suggesting that vegetable and fruit growers own at least one share of stock in every firm they sell to or buy from. You get the quarterly or annual reports without having to write for them; and sometimes you make a little money. But the greatest value is a glimpse into the economic health of the organization and occasionally a clear peek into the future of a firm in a related business. By the late John Carew, Michigan State University, East Lansing.

METRIC CONVERSION TABLE

Metric System		English	
Length			
Meter	= 1.093 yards	Yard	= 0.9144 meter
	= 3.281 feet	Foot	= 0.3048 meter
	= 39.370 inches	Inch	= 0.0254 meter
Kilometer	= 0.621 mile	Mile	= 1.609 kilometers
Surface			
Square meter	= 1.196 sq. yards	Square yard	= 0.836 sq. meter
	= 10.764 square feet	Square foot	= 0.092 sq. meter
Square centimeter	= 0.155 square in.	Square inch	= 6.45 sq. cms.
Square kilometer	= 0.386 square mile	Square mile	= 2.590 sq. kms.
Hectare	= 2.471 acres	Acre	= 0.405 hectare
Volume			
Cubic meter	= 1.308 cubic yards	Cubic yard	= 0.764 cubic meter
	= 35.314 cubic feet	Cubic foot	= 0.028 cubic meter
Cubic centimeter	= 0.061 cubic inch	Cubic inch	= 16.387 cu. cms.
Stere	= 0.275 cord (wood)	Cord	= 3.624 steres
Capacity			
Liter	= 1.056 U.S. liq. qts. or 0.880 Eng. liq. qts.	U.S. Liq. quart	= 0.946 liter
	= 0.908 dry quart	Dry quart	= 1.111 liters
	= 0.264 U.S. gal. or	U.S. gallon	= 3.785 liters
	= 0.22 Eng. gals.	English gallon	= 4.543 liters
Hectoliter	= 2.837 U.S bushels	U.S. bushel	= 0.352 heltoliter
	= 2.75 English bu.	English bushel	= 0.363 hectoliter
Weight			
Gram	= 15.432 grams	Grain	= 0.0648 gram
	= 0.032 troy ounce	Troy ounce	= 31.103 grams
	= 0.0352 avoirdupois ounce	Avoirdupois oz.	= 28.35 grams
Kilogram	= 2.2046 pounds av.	Pound	= 0.4536 kilogram
Metric ton	= 2204.62 pounds avoirdupois	Short ton	= 0.907 metric ton
Carat	= 3.08 grains avoirdupois		

WHAT THE FEDERAL GOVERNMENT (USA), YOUR BUSINESS, ETC., WILL PROVIDE ON YOUR DEATH
PREPARED BY DONALD S. SMITH, JR., CONN. GEN. LIFE INS. CO., HARTFORD, CONN., USA 06115

	Death	Disability	Education	Retirement
The Federal Government Will Provide ⌐—— Social Security & some service benefits	Odds are 1 out of 3 that you die before age 65.	Odds are 1 out of 3 that you will be disabled before age 65.	Odds are a certainty if you have children.	Odds are 2 out of 3 that you will reach age 65
	Monthly income for wife with dependent children under age 18.	Monthly income for self + for dependent children under 18.	Upon death of self, monthly income for children between ages 18-22 while still in college.	Monthly income for self and spouse to be paid for lifetime of both.
What the Business Will Do For You ⌐—— If Incorporated	Group life	Group accident & Sickness Blue	————	Pension Profit Sharing
└—— If Sole Proprietorship	————	Individual accident & sickness Blue Cross	————	HR-10 (Keogh Bill)
What You Are Doing For Yourself └—— Your Own Assets	1. Personal Life Ins. 2. Land 3. Stocks & bonds 4. Business	Personal accident & sickness contract to hedge against loss of income	Cash Value of life insurance Savings	Cash Value of life insurance Savings

REMINDERS:

1. Plan ahead for passing property on upon death. Distribution of assets will be controlled by the law of the state in which you reside or by the will drawn by your attorney.
2. Be sure to hand in social security benefit request card to be sure account is in order.
3. At age 65, you may wish to take advantage of the Keogh Bill RH-10, to deduct 10% or perhaps more under a new law, of your total or partial earnings, tax free. Equities may be purchased with the fund and is deductible from your earnings. Or, you can postpone your tax until a later date when your earnings are less.
4. After age 72 you are able to earn as much as you can and not lose Social Security benefits. (Law may be lowered to 70 years.)
5. Most of this information can be obtained from your local Social Security Office. Spend an hour or two; visit them. Rulings change.

Visit with consultants: Trust Officers, State Ag. Ext. Serv. people, attorneys, insurance counselors or accountants to obtain up-dated information.

Pension Plans: Do-It-Yourself

The so-called **Keogh plan** is ideal for farm operators. It was designed for self-employed people, either part time or full time. Allows you to salt away 15% of self-employed earnings up to $7500 a year. You can invest money many different ways, and earnings build tax free. Eventually, the tax is paid when you retire and begin the withdrawals. But note: If you set up a Keogh account, you MUST also include employees.

Individual Retirement Accounts are another type of program. Available only to those persons not covered by any pension arrangement. But the most you can put in an IRA is 15% of income up to $1500 a year.

The deadline for making your pension payments is Dec. 31, except that Keogh people can extend it to April 15 if they tell the IRS. For details, ask your insurance agent, banker, savings & loan or broker.

MINIMIZING ESTATE TAXES[1] [2]

Many times the impact of the estate tax problem is not recognized until too late. Being human, we all tend to delay facing or ignore discussion of what must be decided by plan or by default after we are gone. Planning can save many thousands of dollars that otherwise will be confiscated by the tax. More often than not the farm family is completely unaware of the fact that an estate tax problem exists. There are many situations in New Jersey where a farm has been owned by two or three generations. As the family grew, the needs of new families developed and adjoining land was purchased. What may have started as a farm of one hundred twenty acres may now be three hundred to five hundred acres. Urban development has crept in. The farm family has churches. In short, the roots of this family grow strong and deep in a community they consider their own. It would be expensive to replace the economic set-up. They have been offered high prices for the land, but they just do not want to sell, so they ignore the real estate man and go ahead planning for the children and grandchildren.

Grandfather bought one hundred twenty acres. Now that his three grandsons are farming, the acreage has expanded to 450 acres. Grandfather bought at $60 per acre. His son, the present owner, bought at $175, and for the last eight-five acres he paid $235 an acre in 1951. The boys, all married are living in homes on the land, have developed a fine system them $500 an acre for the land, but they did not want to sell. The land has increased in value since then, but they are reluctant to sell and, besides, Dad owns the land, and they do not want him to think they are trying to get things away from him.

Here is the position they are in, and sentiment will not change it. Unless something is planned, and carried out now, when the parents of these three married men go to their reward, the three men may have to give up their business, or spend the rest of their lives paying off a mortgage with after-income-tax dollars. They do not need to waste this productivity if they plan now. For instance, for estate tax purposes, let us value the land at $1500 per acre.

Land	$ 675.000
4 Homes	180,000
Equipment	200,000
Total	$1,055,000

We could add the value of storage, barns, bonds, etc.

The tax and settlement costs without planning could be about one-third or $105,700. by careful planning much or all of this cost can be eliminated.

There are four major methods of minimizing estate taxes:
1. Gifts
2. Consuming the estate during life
3. Sales of stock or land

4. Life insurance
A combination of these is the method many people decide to follow.

To give away too much and be sorry is not wise. It is important to be sure we will never really need what we give to others. However, if we have the desire, we can often save by transferring legal dollars to the persons we want to have them during our life time, rather than after we die.

To consume what we have created, to use it all up, is a plan that some may be willing to follow, but it could be dangerous. Not many of us want to take that chance.

To sell our land or our stock may be a good idea. However, some of us have a sentimental desire to keep in touch or hold onto what we have created. There are ways to do this through the use of corporate devices so we can maintain control and still reduce the gross taxable estate. However, it is important that competent legal advice be available in all of this planning.

Where life insurance fits, no other estate planning method conserves values better at less cost. It will accomplish things no other method can. Here, too, judgment and balance must play a major part. The planning team must be objective. To go off the deep end on the use of life insurance can become just as burdensome as doing too much for children or charities through gifts. In the end, a plan is a combination of opinion and judgment. There is no perfect plan.

A plan today that does an excellent job, may need serious revision two years from now. Children may be married, babies may be born, sales may occur, business may change, stocks may go down or up, people may die, or what we want today may be quite different from what we want two years hence.

One of the keys to any estate planning is a good will. It will cost you very little to have a will drawn up, but be sure to get a good lawyer. Do not do it yourself. Do you have a will?

In New Jersey, a man dying without a will leaves all his real estate to his children with a life interest in only ½ of the lands for the widow as dower. His personal property will go ⅓ to his wife and 2/3 to the children. If there are no children, the wife gets all the property purchased during the marriage, and only a life interest in half of any property purchased prior to the marriage. At her death, the residue goes to the husband's relations, brothers, sisters, parents. By these uncomplicated examples, you can see how important it is to write down what you want and have your lawyer put it into legal form. I cannot over-emphasize the importance of not doing it yourself.

You may have an estate tax problem and not know it. It is easy to find that the death costs will be as much as $300 of each $1,000 you thought were going to your heirs. You can save much or all of it by planning now. Get the best team you can. A good life insurance Estate Planner and a good lawyer can help.

BEAT THE UNION BY MAKING IT UNNECESSARY[1]

Note: Following are experiences with a farm union in California that could spread elsewhere in the USA.

It is suicidal not to make preparation in the form of worker relations to counter UFW's subtle organizing drives. If because you're far removed from California you feel that little if any impact is felt by your workers, I can only say that Cesar Chavez or his kind has not and will not go away as we thought in

---

[1]This discussion is based on a New Jersey Farmers Week talk by the late S.C. DeCou and applies to N.J. laws, but other states have similar laws.
[2]See also "A Will of Your Own" EM-3719, Dec. 1972. Pullman. Wash. Estate planning for Penna. families. Pa. St. Univ. Circular 557. 20 pp. 1973.

[1]Presented at the Michigan State Horticultural Ass'n Meetings, Jerry Hull, Secretary. 1981.

California. The UFW is an extremely sophisticated union today, not what it was in 1962. To those of you who make no effort to prepare your intermediate levels of management we say: "The union which you get is the one which you deserve."

We in California Agri-Industry have been dealt a devasting blow:

1. We have literally lost the right to manage our operation;
2. It is foreseeable that in the future many more farms will be driven out of business because of the outrageous contracts which are being forced on us at the threat of economic reprisal by the union (the boycott).

It is hoped that other predominately agricultural states have seen the writing on the wall and will take the appropriate steps both in worker relations as well as in the legislative halls.

It has become increasingly clear that the California's Labor Law is nothing but a sham and a fraud. Worker rights mean literally nothing under the Agricultural Labor Relations Act. The Law is merely a vehicle for the United Farms Workers of America—and any attempt to make it other than that is going to fail as long as we have "Brown Rot" (formerly Governor Jerry Brown) in California.

Case at hand: Six United Farmworker members in the Salinas area refused to contribute to the union's political fund known as the "Citizens Participation Day Fund (CPD)". The result: It was demanded of the employer that he terminate the worker who refused to give one day of work to the union, because they were members *not in good standing*. They, as many other workers, are in good standing as long as the union says they are.

Any member of the union who refuses to contribute one day of work to the union for political use loses his "good standing" and can be thrown out of the union. *Why?* Because the union is the sole judge of its membership on good standing. And this is precisely what happened to six workers in the Salinas area. The union held a kangaroo court and demanded that the company terminate the six workers, some of whom had been working with the company for as many as six years.

To explain: Here are some grounds for losing good standing in the union;

1. Conduct detrimental to the union.
2. Committing an act calculated to embarass or impare the dignity of the union, or committing such other offenses, equally as serious, which tend to bring the union into disrepute.

There are thirty other reasons cited under the constitutuion (UFW's) which can cause a member to be judged not in good standing.

Do workers have the right to defend themselves? Yes they do. Article 19 of the UFW Constitution reads as follows: "The trial shall be orderly, fair and impartial. The burden of proof shall be on the accuser. The accuser must be present. If the accused has been properly served and fails to appear, the trial shall proceed without the accused. The accused shall have the right to produce witnesses and present documentary evidence and to be heard on his or her own behalf. All witnesses shall testify under oath and the accused shall have the opportunity to cross examine witnesses. *No lawyers are permitted.* A prosecuter may be appointed, from among the membership, to assist the accuser in the trial and presentation of the evidence and the accused may select a member as counsel."

Senator Robert Nimo, R-Atascadero, introduced legislation to correct this abuse to worker rights. The assembly voted 46 to 30 in favor of passage of said bill. The bill went to the Governor's desk where it died with his veto. Workers literally have no rights in a state where an agricultural act was passed to help both workers and employers.

I pose a question to all of you. Can you beat the Union? The answer is a solid "NO". No one in California has beaten the union—they have made it unnecessary. It is extremely difficult to beat the UFW because it is the last remaining union that uses cultural class consciousness to emotionally tie workers to its ranks.

We find that todays workers aren't afraid to talk back to their foremen, it's the other way around; the foremen are frightened by the workers.

Agricultural employers traditionally work out their budget and set aside money for; entomology, pesticides, and other horticultural practices and what about your worker relations? Worker relations in Agriculture is a science and only in understanding this union and its use of the social movement can we effectively counter its campaigns.

UFW looks for issues that are basic, emotional, factual and shared by the majority of workers when preparing for organized drives. The union also thrives on horror cases and hard-line supervisors. The union does not invent issues; it finds and exploits the ones which already exist.

The following is a four step plan which employers should undertake to make unions unnecessary:

1. Understand what causes workers to seek unionization.
2. Thoroughly analize how UFW organizes farmworkers and understand the types of solutions which may provoke an organizing effort.
3. Recognize the early signals that the time is ready for an organizing drive and develop strategies to counter and correct the situation.
4. Develop and create ongoing attitudes aimed at fulfilling worker needs.

An effective worker relations program, such as the one which we use with our clients, covers a wide range of worker matters. The following eight points briefly outline a partial worker relations program:

1. Good supervision
2. Proper attitude toward workers
3. Clear communication
4. Proper hiring procedures
5. A worker complaint system
6. Sensible rules
7. Good working conditions
8. Fair wages and benefits

We as a consulting firm in California have made UFW unnecessary in every election. The reason: because we are in the business of helping employers effectively communicate with their workers. Our task is to teach supervisors and managers how to listen to problems effectively. Our victories are attributed to truly moving ahead of the union in workers understanding job security and dignity and in a continuing effort to bring employer relations as close as we can to our counter parts in industrial relations.

It is workers with needs and problems and the problems in your fields can best be addressed by you as the employers, not the union.

And for all this, the union calls us "union busters"! (Agricultural Communication Consultants, 5300 Calif. Ave., Suite 225, Bakersfield, Ca. 93309. 805-322-4844.)

FARM LABOR, PROTECTION OF PROPERTY RIGHTS

The following excerpts have been taken from McDermott, Frank X. "Guide to farm labor and the protection of property rights," circulated by the N. J. Farm Bureau, 168 W. State St.,

Trenton, 08608. The farm labor regulations and trends change. It should be recognized that these suggestions apply to the State of New Jersey and may vary elsewhere. They do give, however, a survey of the problems involved and suggested solutions.

Developing an Employee Program

"The most important thing you as a grower can do is to keep up with the prevailing wage rates and working conditions in your area and to have a personal awareness of the operation of your orchard. Keep abreast with the minimum wage from year to year.

A contract to pay less than the minimum wage is not enforceable, even if the worker signs a written agreement. However, reasonable deductions are permitted for the actual cost of food and lodging furnished. The grower who pays his employees the same wages which employees on neighboring farms receive and who provides comfortable living and working conditions is less likely to be singled out as the target of a strike or other union action on grounds that he is treating his employees in a substandard manner. In addition, the employer who knows the people who work for him and who shows an interest and awareness of their working conditions, is less likely to be organized by a union.

Check List For Good Employer-Employee Relations

This check list is designed to assist you in taking the pulse of employee morale. Questions which cannot be answered "yes" indicate areas where corrective action may be taken profitably.

Favoritism: Do you assign work to employees in a fair and equal manner? Are you impartial in your dealings with the people you supervise? Do you "play favorites"? Do you give some employees special privileges and deny them to others? Is overtime distributed fairly? Are your policies involving employee conduct administered in the same way to all employees?

Working Conditions: Have hazardous conditions been eliminated? Do working conditions compare favorably with other farms in the area? Are employees provided with convenient facilities which meet expected standards? Wash rooms? Fresh, cool water? Eating facilities? Are employees provided with proper work equipment and supplies?

Listening and Talking to Employees: Are employees kept informed on your plans, policies, "news," etc.? Do members of management make regular tours of the farm, and speak to employees? Are the suggestions and opinions of employees given careful consideration and, if not acted upon, the employees told why? Are employees encouraged to pass their thinking and reactions on to the supervisors? Does your announcement system scoop the employees? Is it by "grapevine"?

Employees Attitudes: Do you know what employees really think about you, the farm, their jobs, and their supervisors? Are employee attitudes friendly and cooperative? Are you constantly alert to conditions of possible employee unrest? Is employee turnover at a low level? Do you know the real reasons for the voluntary quits? Are they chargeable to poor supervision? Lack of complaints carefully noted and considered? Are "don't care" attitudes at a minimum? Is efficiency at satisfactory levels? Are supervisors alert for—and do they keep you informed of—any change in the attitudes of employees? Does your farm rate high as a place to work in the community? Do employees have a sense of pride in working for you? Do they have a feeling of belonging?

Relationship Of The Crew Leader To The Farmer

An increasing number of farmers have come to depend upon the use of migrant labor. As a rule, these laborers are supplied by crew leaders who round up the workers, transport them to and from the farm, and receive money from the farmer to pay their wages. Inquiries are frequently made about the status of the crew leader with respect to the farmer and the migrant laborer, and their respective liabilities for payment of wages and withholding taxes. Although both the State and Federal governments have laws requiring the crew leader to register and to conform to a certain standard of conduct, neither government has a policy sufficiently definite to provide clear answers to these and other questions that arise. The Federal law is revised and modified frequently. Therefore, the following observations ultimately may become the subject of court litigation before firm answers can be given in the current gray areas.

Who is the Employer? In the usual situation, the farm pays the crew leader who makes the necessary deductions and distributes the wages to the employees, keeping the balance as his fee. In this case, the crew leader should really be considered the employer because his relationship to the farmer is not unlike that of an independent contractor who employs laborers to do the work called for under the provisions of his contract with the owner. Therefore, the responsibility for payment of the minimum wage and for withholding social security taxes properly falls upon the crew leader and not upon the farmer. In fact, it is the administrative policy of the Federal Government that the crew leader occupies this status as an independent contractor, with the obligation to keep records and forward social security taxes, unless the crew leader enters into a written agreement with the farmer creating an employer-employee relationship between themselves. In such a case, the duty of record keeping and responsibility for social security taxes would fall upon the farmer as well, because the migrant laborers then would become the employees of the farmer. Obviously, so long as the Federal Government maintains this position, it is in the best interests of the farmer to avoid entering into a written agreement which might create an employer-employee relationship between himself and a crew leader, thereby protecting himself from liability in case of a default by a crew leader.

It must be remembered that the Crew Leader Registration Act is relatively new and will undoubtedly undergo certain changes, both in interpretation and application, before it becomes settled law. A farmer who "keeps his nose clean" by advising his crew leader that he expects compliance with the law, and by refusing, either actively or passively, to condone unscrupulous exploitation of migrant laborers, need not be alarmed when a Labor Department representative comes to make an investigation.

The Minimum Wage Law. The State Minimum' Wage Law, however, places responsibility upon a person who "suffers and permits" another person to work for him. On this basis, the State Department of Labor takes the position that the farmer as well as the crew leader may be responsible for payment of the minimum wage. The question is one of fact, and because a violation must be "knowing and willing," a farmer who acts honestly and in good faith, and not in collusion with a crew leader, cannot be prosecuted for criminal violation of the Wage and Hour Law where his violation is unintentional. As the New Jersey Minimum Wage Law is recent, there is little experience upon which the farmer may rely at this time. Undoubtedly, in the near future, there will be administrative and court decisions which will define and establish more clearly the legal relationship existing between crew leaders and farmers, and their respective responsibilities under the Act.

Workmen's Compensation Law. For purposes of workmen's compensation, the responsibility to provide coverage is upon the farmer. The fact that the crew leader makes wage payments to the laborers does not necessarily remove the farmer from responsibility. Under the totality of circumstances the farmer, who makes the decisions regarding when, where and how much work there shall be, is viewed as the employer.

Ordinarily, workmen's compensation coverage does not apply when the employee is going to or coming from work, but where transportation is furnished by the employer, it is considered to be incidental to and arising out of the course of employement and therefore covered. In this instance coverage begins at the moment the worker steps onto the bus. However, the crew leader is required under Federal Law to carry personal injury insurance for the protection of the workers while they are being transported to and from the farm.

The question of injuries to employees resulting from fights has been the subject of considerable litigation. Fights between fellow employees resulting from personal animosities are not compensable because they are not work-connected. Similarly, injuries sustained by employees as a result of "skylarking" or "horseplay" are not compensable. However, an innocent bystander injured as a rsult of "skylarking" or "horseplay" of others during working hours would be covered.

Injuries which occur during lunch hours or after the working day is over, whether from a fight or an accident, generally are not compensable. However, subject to the above-mentioned limitations there may be coverage for injuries sustained during a lunch hour if the employee is paid for his eating time, or if he remains under the control of the employer during his lunch hour. Under the Workmen's Compensation Law the decisions generally favored the payment of benefits to injured employees housed on a farm during either working or non-working hours.

How A Union Organizes Workers

Union attempts at organizing farm workers are inevitable and perhaps imminent. This does not mean that the farmer must sit back helplessly and allow the union to take over. The organizer has no right to come upon the farmer's property if he is unwanted, and he must leave if asked to do so. How, then, will the union attempt to organize the farm help?

The union organizer has two immediate objectives when he makes the first contacts with workers. He is looking for leadership for his campaign and information about the specific problems and complaints of the employees.

There is no blueprint for meeting individual workers and gaining their confidence—conversations can be started in restaurants and bars, through "leads" passed on by other union members, and by acquaintances made through social affairs. If there is any rule at all, it is that contacts are not made by suddenly appearing at the farm with a leaflet urging employees to sign a union authorization card and mail it to a post office box.

Most organizers are interested primarily in meeting with the type of employee who is respected by his fellow-workers and who has influence on the farm. Getting to know a few of these employees is more important—at this stage—than meeting with the maximum number of workers.

Developing Leadership. Once a potential leader has been contacted, it is important that the union organizer wins his confidence and trust. Time spent in developing this leader, answering his questions about the union, and explaining the benefits of collective bargaining will be well worthwhile after the organizing campaign gets underway and this leader becomes a union spokesman inside the company's premises.

Respected "inside leaders" are vital to any campaign. The union representative must be sure that they are not known as "gripers" or "soreheads" and that they are not motivated simply by a desire for revenge or a driving personal ambition.

In the "perfect" campaign, the organizer will find a leader in every group; a woman for the female workers, leaders within minority racial and national groupings, and spokesmen for the various work gangs. Since the "perfect" situation rarely exists, the union organizer must develop a leadership group as representative as possible.

If no potential leaders can be found, the union representative had better acknowledge the probability that he will not be able to wage a successful campaign. There is no sense wasting time and funds when all the influential employees are not interested in unionism or opposed to it.

Employees must have the desire to organize themselves and, in fact, must do the real job of building their own local union. The organizer can utilize his experience and knowledge to help workers win their rights, but he cannot forcibly organize them.

The Organizer Takes Over. Once the key leaders have been found, the organizer—who has gotten to know each of them as an individual—usually calls his people together for their first meeting. By pooling the knowledge of his leaders, the organizer will, at this meeting, get his first complete breakdown of employees in the potential bargaining unit and a picture of the company policies and practices that are responsible for worker discontent.

As the complaints are discussed, the organizer gains a good opportunity to describe how similar problems have been settled by the union in other places. This meeting usually ends with an agreed upon time for another discussion. The organizer may distrubute union membership cards to be given other employees who did not attend the meeting. The following meetings of the same group will be used to add new leaders selected by the organizer, to gain a more complete breakdown of the company's operations, and to secure the names of additional employees to be contacted.

Where will this meeting be? The most desirable place is on the farm itself, where the workers can be approached as a group. However, because the organizer would be trespassing if he simply walked up the main road to the farm in his normal business attire, and because the farmer would put him off the land quickly once his presence was discovered, it is reasonable to assume that the union organizer might try to disguise himself, perhaps as a hunter or as fisherman or even as a laborer, in order to get onto the property unnoticed. The farmer who follows the suggested procedure for protecting his property against trespassers and unwelcome visitors, to be discussed below, has his remedy available when the trespasser is found.

Property Rights Protections

By way of summary, it should be remembered that a property owner has the right to control who may and who may not come upon his property. He may place signs around his property forbidding trespassers to enter, or he may personally order trespassers off his land. He may permit people to come upon his property, giving permission either orally or in writing, and may revoke this permission whenever he chooses to do so. He is allowed to use a reasonable amount of self-help to eject trespassers or to take them into custody, and is given access to the Courts to protect his property rights. He must recognize, however, that certain government employees, in the exercise of their public duties, have a right to enter his property to perform that duty.

Points To Remember

1. You can and should deal with your own employees, but you are not compelled by law to deal with any union or other third party.
2. You do have the right to free speech and can freely discuss employment conditions with your employees. You can peacefully resist organizational union activity.
3. You can distribute and post information making your employees aware of the fact that they have a right to work. (See sample message below.)
4. You can effectively protect yourself against illegal trespassing, violence or threats of violence affecting you or your property. You have a civil right to collect for damages to your property.
5. You should always have the phone number of your local police to report instances of violence or threats of violence concerning your land or your produce, while it is still on the land or while it is being transported.
6. As soon as any union activity is noted, you should phone or visit the State Farm Labor Coordinating Committee and ask for information and advice.
7. You should consult with your own neighbors and help each other through the harvest period but notice should always be given to every employee if there is a labor dispute in progress.
8. You should take down license numbers of cars and take notes and pictures of any disputes occurring on the farm or affecting your produce off the farm.
9. Do not participate in unplanned discussions on farm labor conditions with outsiders or in labor negotiations with union officials unless you have competent advice. Check with State Farm Labor Coordinating Committee before proceeding.
10. You should cooperate with newspapers, radio and T. V. people whenever possible. They are performing a public service by keeping the people informed about items of general interest. On occasion, they have gained public support for the former if handled properly. Naturally, no one has to put up with unwarranted "newshounding" where it invades the right of privacy.

A Message To My Employees*

You Have A Right To Work
It is your American right to choose whether you want to work or not.

Don't Surrender That Right
No union pickets with a cardboard sign can stop you from working and earning a living for yourself and your family.

The Law Is On Your Side
Law enforcement agencies have sworn to protect you and your property. Don't hesitate to contact your County Prosecutor.

You Violate No Law When You Cross A Picket Line
Do not be frightened by the implications of threats.
Do not be fooled by union promises which cannot be fulfilled.
Work is available. The wages are good.

You Can Earn More Than The Union Wants Your Employer To Pay
You don't have to pay any union dues to get a job. All you have to do is present yourself and go to work.

....
Employer

*It is recommended that this type of message to employees not be used until difficulty is anticipated on your farm.

NOTE: For additional farm labor information and local laws, contact your Dept. of Labor, State Government offices and the Dept. of Labor, U. S. Government, Washington, D. C. for federal rulings. It is well to associate yourself now with a grower organization who will speak for growers in the formulation of future rulings.

ORCHARD LABOR MANAGEMENT

By John Giunco, Fruit Grower, Freehold, N. J.

My brother and I operate approximately 350 acres of orchard. We have our home farm of 250 acres, 50 in peaches of which 35 acres are in production. About 200 acres are in apples, 50 acres of which are in young trees and all of which are semi-dwarfs. We also rent 100 acres of apple trees which are 20 years old. We operate our own packing plant. While it is not worked steadily, it is in operation from 10 to 12 months a year. We have our own cold storage, half of which is CA and one-half mile from our packing house. Two years ago we went into the retail business and this opened a whole new field to us.

Labor—The Big Problem

Labor is of course a big problem, perhaps our biggest. I break down our labor into four types: (1) permanent employees, (2) packing house workers, (3) pickers and (4) the retail stand staff.

Each group is different and presents different problems. The permanent help are the people we depend upon the most. Without them we could not operate and we want them to know it. They present many problems. We have to build up a pride in their work and a sense of accomplishment. This sounds grand; but to do it, we have to hunt good workers and then try to keep them. To attract people we first have to pay them fairly well. All our steady help is paid on an hourly rate—6 paid holidays—time and a half after 45 hours—and paid vacation. I prefer our steady help to live off the farm but this does not always happen. We make adjustments to pay for those who live off the farm and those who live on the farm. The ones who live on the farm we try to give the best accommodations we have.

To build pride in work, give him a job, whether it be pruning, mowing, what have you, tell him what has to be done, let him decide how best to do it, then impress on him the importance of the job by checking constantly; I question how the job is going, offer suggestions on how to do it, listen to his ideas, and try not to "boss" him.

Often, especially during harvest season, we get our picking foreman, mechanic, tractor and truck drivers together, and discuss how things are going when we are running into difficulties. We also discuss the different pickers, who is good, who is bad. I try to give them an idea of how we are going to move from block to block. We believe this gives everyone a feeling of belonging and being a part of a team, because a farm operation is a team operation. Also, at some of these meetings we get some good ideas and suggestions. Incidently, a little praise, or even using a suggestion (even if you planted the idea yourself) can go a long way.

We always back up an orchard foreman 100% in a dispute with a picker—but in the same vein, we have to watch for favoritism of an individual picker by a foreman and attempt to adjust this before it causes trouble.

The second group, packing-house personnel, we consider our easiest group to get and to manage. The men during the summer and early fall are some of our steady people, together with school boys. The women are usually the wives and older daughters of some of our picking help. During late fall, winter, and spring, the men are our steady men. The women are all local housewives who want a part-time job.

We try to generate interest in the packing house operation by not running a secret service. We tell our people where and to whom the apples are going—if it is a special promotion of a supermarket.

Irregular Packing House Schedule

The biggest problem in the packing house is the irregular work schedule, which is necessary because we do not pack ahead except in special cases. Some of the larger promotional orders necessitate the build up of a fairly large stock of packed apples. This irregular work schedule has in the past cost us some of our best packers and will probably continue to cost us people. Because of this we are always hunting for new people. We prefer a woman whose children are in school and does not mind working one day one week and five days the next week. The irregularity of the work forces us into understanding appointments made and kept, sick children and all sorts of excuses when we would really like to have that person working in the packing house.

Picking Help

Our picking help certainly generates the most trouble and the most public interest. To understand the problem, let us try to understand them. These people are migrants, southern negroes. They generally travel in a family group. By that I mean a man and a woman. We do not encourage children in our camp because of the extra problems in housing, school, and damage to the camp and themselves when left unattended. These migrants like to display their independence, but depend on us for many things. We lend money to them, save for them, give them advice on anything from cars to baby cribs. For this, we carefully plan any weekend harvesting we want to do. We never demand that they work on a Saturday or Sunday. Why put yourself in a bad position? Your best picker may be the one that does not show up Sunday morning. I always plan to be in the best and fastest picking for the weekend, a place where even a slow picker can do well. Sometimes it is a nice medium-size tree where there is a big crop, other times it is a processing cultivar where careful handling can be forgotten for speed.

All our pickers work on a piece-work basis which is broken down into several rates for different jobs:

(1) Peaches—Open baskets for resale, field run, field crates for packing.

(2) Apples—Color or size picking—into 2 boxes—red—green—strip trees—most picking is special jobs with varying rate—large yellows—small yellows—small trees—light crop trees—all apples are picked in bulk bins except summer reds.

There are several rules I set for myself in handling the pickers:

(1) close supervision, constant irregular checks in the orchard; and do not form habits of time or routine; (2) never yell at a man without others hearing. If someone is doing a poor job the rest of them know it and want the wrong-doer to get yelled at. This also helps keep the others from getting into the same habits. I try never to yell at a really good picker.

Perhaps most important is to know your pickers. Know which ones can be trusted to do a good job, which one has to be watched, and which one wants reassurance, bad or good.

To minimize lost or wasted time I try to plan our picking moves several days in advance. I always attempt to make the shortest possible move, consequently, losing the least amount of time. Also, we try to move the pickers in the morning. A mid-afternoon move for some pickers is a signal for the end of the day. On Friday afternoon I am unavailable until 5:00 o'clock, because that money has to be spent and the faster the pickers get started the better job they can do spending it.

Retail Business

A retail business is an entirely new ball game. Here we need people who are cheerful, courteous, clean, neat, and who can think. A sour-faced clerk can drive customers away faster than the plague. I always encourage our people to answer all questions—they may not be 100% correct, but they probably know more than the questioner anyway. Neatness and cleanliness are important. This is the picture you want your customer to have. I demand that all arithmetic be done on paper or an adding machine—no matter how simple. The customer may be like some of my relatives—2 plus 2 is a major undertaking. The one thing I try to impress on everyone involved with our stand is that we need the customers. They do not need us. There is another place two or four miles down the road in every direction.

Recruiting boys and girls for the stand is fairly easy for us. We have three teenage children with lots of friends. Perhaps the best piece of luck with the stand is having a retired uncle and his wife who both enjoy working there. This also gives a certain sameness to the place, since my brother and I cannot devote too much time to the stand.

Generally speaking, there are several rules I try to maintain in managing our help. I try not to give a man a job he cannot handle. This does occur and when it does I try to get the man out of trouble without him losing face. At the same time I try to demand a high degree of success. Try not to lose your temper, but if you do lose it, do it at the right time and place. It can do a lot of good. I have several people, some migrants and some of our steady people with whom I have to get angry almost on schedule; they seem to be waiting for it.

I always try to sell a new machine or a new method to those who will be using it or doing it. Everyone ends up happier this way, including myself.

Incidentally, some of these machines or new concepts are going to take a better operator than we are accustomed to hiring. We have run into this with spraying. In the last few years we have gone from dilute spraying to 6x. The man who did the spraying for us for years just could not handle the more exacting ground speed and more care on turns and everything else that goes with concentrate spraying. We had to put him on a different job.

A part of the labor management and an important part is changing operations to fit the labor. We cannot do the impossible. Several years ago we switched from Puerto Rican to negro migrants. There were many reasons involved in this change. One of the biggest was that our apple plantings were growing up and our volume of apples was increasing with it. We were having trouble keeping enough help to finish apple harvest.

By changing, we solved the apple problem. But we started to get into a problem with peaches. The migrant workers, No. 1, did not like to pick peaches; No. 2, they could not make enough money picking them and we found we could not do the job we wanted to do with peaches.

Our solution was to cut down on the peach production and cut back on the number of varieties we were growing, hoping to have a break between varieties to rest the crew and ourselves. In the last several years we have ended up with a peach operation we can handle with the available labor. And more important, we make a profit at it.

Summary Statement

Changes are going to continue to occur in the fruit business and we will have to cope with them. One of our biggest problems will be to fit in our existing labor and recruit new types of labor to do their present jobs. Machines will be important and will help, but machines will only be as good as the people who operate them.

I believe that the single most important thing in the managing of labor is to figure out beforehand what we are going to do every day and know it with definiteness before the people are standing in front of you in the morning.

NUT TREE NURSERIES

Note: Pick a nursery for the nut you wish to grow in the area of the country where the nut predominates, or pick your neighboring nursery. For filbert trees, contact The Nut Growers Soc. of WA and OR, Bx 23126, Tigard, OR 97233.

Bass Pecan Co., MS 39455
Bear Creek Farms Nursery, POB 248, Northport, WA. 99157
Bountiful Ridge Nurseries, Inc., POB 250, Princess Anne, MD 21853
Boyd Nursery Co., Inc., POB 71, McMinnville, TN 37110
Buntings Nurseries, Selbyville, DE 19975
Burchhill Nursery, Inc., 4201 McHenry Ave., Modesto, CA 95356
Charter Co., Inc., 217 Bickett Blvd., POB 10938, Raleigh, N. C. 27605 (Carry Inertia nutcracker)
Contra Costs Nursery, Rt. 1, Bx 200, Brentwood, CA 94513
Cartright Nursery Co., TN 38017
Culver Nursery, POB 93, Fermersville, CA 93223
Driver Nursery Inc., 2737 North Ave., Modesto, CA 95351
Bill Erickson, 406 George St., Louisiana, MO 63353
Fiddymint Pistachios, 5010 Fiddymint Rd., Roseville, CA 95678
Forest Nursery Co., Inc., McMinnville, TN 37110
Dean Foster Nurseries, Rt. 2, Dept. AFG-L Hartford, MI 49057
Fowler Nurseries, Inc., 525 Fowler Rd., Newcastle, CA 95658
Green Tree Nursery Inc., 950 Highway 200 W., Plains, MT 59859
Gellatly, Bx 191, Westbank, B. C., Canada
Jersey Chestnut Farm, 58 Van Dyne Av., Wayne, N. J. 07470 (chestnuts)
Kelly Nurseries, 934 Maple St., Dansville, N. Y. 14437
Lakeland Nurseries, Hanover, Pa. 17331
Lawyer Nursery, Inc., 950 Highway 200 W., Plains, MT 59859
J. E. Miller Nursery, Canandaigua, N. Y. 14424
Musser Forest Nursery, Bx 151, IN, PA. 15701
N. Y. State Fruit Testing Ass'n, Geneva, N. Y. 14456
Pape's Pecan House, POB 1281, Sequin TX

Raynor Bros., POB 1617, Salisbury, MD 21801
Redwood Nursery, BX 32, Reedly, CA 93654
Simpson Nursery, POB 160, Monticello, FL 32344
Sierra Gold Nurseries, 5320 Garden Highway, Yuba City, CA 95991
Southern Nursery and Landsc. Nursery, Winchester, TN. 37398
Springhill Nurseries, Tipp City, OH 45371
Stark Nursery, Louisiana, MO 63353
Talbott Nursery, Rt. 3, Bx 212, Pinton, IN 47441
Traas Nursery, LTD, 24355 48 Av., Rt. 7 Langly, BC V3A 4R1
Van Well Nursery, POB 1339, Wenatchee, WA 98801
Waynesboro Nurseries, Inc., POB 987, Waynesboro, PA 22980
Leslie H. Wilmoth Nursery, Rt. 2, Bx 469, Elizabethtown, KY 42701
Dave Wilson Nursery, 112 Boulters Locke, Irmo, S. C. 29063
Zilke Bros. Nursery, Baroda, MI 49101

SUPPLEMENTAL LIST OF NURSERIES

NURSERYMEN (Outside U.S.)

NOTE: Following list of nurserymen will be expanded in future editions of this book.

ARGENTINA
Los Almos de Rosauer, Cipolletti, Rio Negro.
Estacion Experimental LAgric., Rama Caida, CC No. 79, San Rafael, Menooza.

AUSTRALIA
J. Brunning & Sons, Somerville. Vic. 3915.
W. A. Sheppard & Sons Pty. Ltd., Moorooduc Rd., Moorooduc, Vic. 3933
H. J. & J. H. Sparkes, Wandiligong, Vic. 3744 (Walnuts).
Premier Nurseries Pty. Ltd., P.O. Box 400, Griffith, NSW 2680.

BRAZIL
Instituto de Pesquisas Agropecuarias do Sul, Caixa Postal "C" 96100, Pelotas, R.G.S.

CHILE
Luis Castro Gonzalez Carrascal 4213, Santiago.
Santa Rosa, CC No. 32, Santiago.
Lindros, Av. Independencia 327, Santiago.

ENGLAND
Blackmoor Estate, Ltd,; Blackmoor, Liss, Hampshire, England.
Brinkman Bros., Lt., Walton Nurseries; Bosham, Chichester, Sussex, England.
East Malling Research Station; Maidstone, Kent, England.
Lauritzen, H., Epping Green Orchard; Epping, Essex, England.
F.D. Savage Jarmans Farm, Collier Street, Marden, Kent, England.
W. Seabrook & Sons Ltd., Boreham, Chelmsford, Essex, England.
K. A. Leech, Foxbro Parklane, Bulmertye, Sudberry, England.
Long Ashton Research Station; University of Bristol, Long Ashton, Bristol, England.
Matthews, F. P., Ltd., Berrington Court, Tenbury Well, Worchestershire, England.
Matthews Fruit Trees Ltd,; Thurston, Bury St. Edmunds, Suffolk, England.

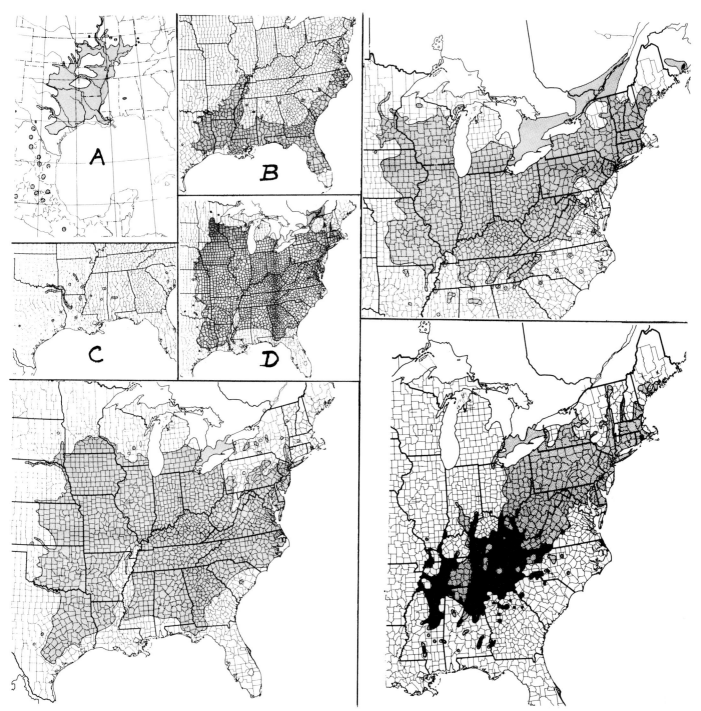

Natural ranges are shown above for the following nuts in the United States: (A) the pecan; (B) water hickory; (C) Nutmeg hickory; (D) Butternut hickory; (upper right) the butternut; (lower left) Black walnut; (lower right) the American chestnut. (USDA) Short pamphlets on each of these nuts can be obtained from the U.S. Printing Office, Washington, D.C. 20402, at a nominal price. Write for listings.

FRANCE

Languedoc: Pepinieres Cros Pierre-Emile a Herepian (34), France. Pepinieres J. et D. Toulemonde a Jonquieres (30), France.

Provence: Pepinieres Demol Henri a Mondragon (84), France. Pepinieres Meynaud a Noves (13), France.

Vallee Du Rhone: Pepinieres Noir Marceau a Manthes (26), France. Pepinieres Veauvy Marcel a Crest (26), France. Pepinieres Vernet Fernand a Valence (26), France.

Lepage Nurseries, BP 741, 49007 Angers Cedex, France.

Lambertin Nurseries, 90, Route d'Arles, 30000 Nimes, France.

Ch. Andre Nurseries, 02600 Villers Cotterets, France.

Darnaud Nurseries, 26200 Montelimar, France.

GERMANY

W. Bornholdt, Baumschulen; 2082 Tornesch, West Germany.

H. Cordes, Baumschulen; 2 Wedel/Holstein, West Germany.

H. Neuhoff, Baumschulen; 2084 Rellingen, Ellerbeker Weg 4-6, West Germany.

Claus Stahl, Baumschulen; 2082 Tornesch, Ahrenloher Strasse, West Germany.

G. Strobel & Co., Baumschulen; 20 Pinneberg, Wedeler Weg, West Germany.

F. Timmermann KG., Baumschulen; 2 Wedel/Holstein, West Germany.

Walther Uhl, Baumschulen; 208 Kummerfeld/Krs. Pinneberg, West Germany.

W. Walper, Baum- und Rosenschulen; 2082 Uetersen, Lesekampstr 11, West Germany.

Hans Wunderlich, Obstbaumschulen; 208 Pinneberg, Schulenhorn 10, West Germany.

ITALY

*Arturo Ansaloni, via Pontina 347,00100 Roma, Italy.

Monti F.LLI, 55010 Picciorana per Tempagnano (Lucca), Italy.

*Sgaravatti Benedetto, Grandi Vivai, 35020 Saonara (Padova), Italy.

Testi Cav. Ferdinando, Vivai, viale Carlo del Prete, 55100 Lucca, Italy.

*Vivai Cooperativi, 33095 Rauscedo (Pordenone), Grapes, Italy.

*Zanzi Vivai, 44040 Fossanova S. Marco (Ferrara), Italy.

　　*commercial growers also.

JAPAN

Fukushima Tenkoen Nursery, Kiyoshi OKADA, 2 Kamimachiura, Arai, Fukushimashi, 960-21, Japan.

Tsuchiya Nursery, (Grapes), Nagao TSUCHIYA, Todoriki, Katsunuma-Machi, Yamanashi-ken, 409-13, Japan.

Saikama Shokubutsuen Nursery, Tomezo IWASAWA, 4-23-3 Honmachi, Hatogavashi, Saitama-ken, 334, Japan.

Inazawa-shi Fruit Tree Producing Association, Yaichi IWASAWA, 383 Sakuramatsu, Shigemoto-cho, Inazawa-shi, Aichi-ken, 492, Japan.

Fukuoka-ken Tree Plants Agric. Co-op. Association, Masamori UCHIYAMA, Tanushimaru-machi, Ukihagun, Fukuoka-ken, 839-12, Japan.

NETHERLANDS

G. C. Arends, Opheusden, Netherlands. M.Th.W. Arts, Zandhoek 17, Oirlo, Netherlands.

N. V. Drayer Boomkwekerij, Heemstede Netherlands.

Fa. J. A. Driesprong, Boskoop, Netherlands.

Gebroeders Janssen, Nederweert, Limburg Netherlands.

W. Janssen, Groesbeek, Netherlands.

Fa. G. de Jong Pzn. & Zn., Boskoop, Netherlands

N.A.K.B., Groot Hertoginnelaan, 192, 's—Gravenhage, Netherlands.

Firma P. Slits-Brouns, Venray, Limburg, Netherlands.

Fa. G. Snel & Zn., Ceintuurbaan 14, Huizen, Netherlands.

YUGOSLAVIA

Neretva, Poljoprivredno Industrijski Kombinat Opuzen, Yugolsavia. (M.9 and M.26 apple and semi-wild peach pits for rootstocks).

Zavoda za Vocarstvo, Zagreb, Kaciceva-9, Yugoslavia.

CALIFORNIA SUGGESTED CRITICAL LEAF LEVELS FOR FRUIT AND NUT TREES[1]
(July Samples)

	% Nitrogen (N)[2]		% Potassium (K)[3]		% Calcium (Ca)	% Magnesium (Mg)	% Sodium (Na)	% Chloride (Cl)[4]	Boran (B) (ppm)			Zinc (Zn) (ppm)
	Defic. Below	Adequate	Defic. Below	Adequate Over	Adequate Over	Adequate Over	Excess Over	Excess Over	Defic. Below	Adequate	Excess	Defic. Below
Almonds	1.9	2.0-2.5	1.0	1.4	2.0	0.25	0.25	0.3	25	30-65	85	15
Apples	1.9	2.0-2.4	1.0	1.2	1.0	0.25	----	0.3	20	25-70	100	14
Apricots (ship)	1.8	2.0-2.5	2.0	2.5	2.0	----	0.1	0.2	15	20-70	90	12
Apricots (can)	2.0	2.5-3.0	2.0	2.5	2.0	----	0.1	0.2	15	20-70	90	12
Cherries (sweet)	---	2.0-3.0	0.9	---	---	----	---	---	20	-----	---	10
Figs	1.7	2.0-2.5	0.7	1.0	3.0	----	---	---	--	----	300	--
Olives	1.4	1.5-2.0	0.4	0.8	1.0	0.10	0.2	0.5	14	19-150	185	--
Nectarines and Peaches (freestone)	2.3	2.4-3.3	1.0	1.2	1.0	0.25	0.2	0.3	18	20-80	100	15
									18	20-80	100	15
Peaches (cling)	2.2	2.3-2.8	0.7	1.0	1.0	0.25	0.25	0.3	15	21-70	80	15
Pears	---	2.3-2.8	1.0	1.1	1.0	0.25	0.2	0.3	25	30-60	80	15
Plums (Japanese)	---	2.3-2.8	1.0	1.3	1.0	0.25	0.2	0.3	25	30-80	100	15
Prunes	2.1	2.2-3.2	0.9	1.2	1.0	0.3	0.1	0.3	20	36-200	300	15
Walnuts												

Adequate levels for all fruit and nut crops: Phosphorus (P) is 0.1-0.3%; Copper (Cu), over 4 ppm; Manganese (Mn), over 20 ppm.

[1]Leaves are from nonfruiting spurs on spur-bearing trees, fully expanded basal shoot leaves on peaches and olives, and terminal leaflet on walnut. (K. Uriu, J. Beutel, O. Lilland, and C. Hansen, University of California, Davis).

[2]N% in August and September samples can be 0.2-0.3% lower than July samples and still be equivalent. N Levels higher than underlined values will adversely affect fruit quality and tree growth. Maximum N for Blenheims should be 3.0% and for Tiltons, 3.5%

[3]K level between deficient and adequate is considered "low" and may cause reduced fruit sizes in some years. Potash applications are recommended for deficient orchards but test applications only for "low" K orchards.

[4]Excess Na or Cl cause reduced growth at levels shown. Leaf burn may or may not occur when levels are higher. Confirm salinity problems with soil or root samples.

Recent research at USDA, Beltsville, Md. by C. B. Shear and associates is indicating that a higher Ca level in apple leaves is needed, perhaps 1.5 to 1.8% to reduce or eliminate bitter pit, cork, other problems.

The following tables contain data on establishment costs, 1 to 5 yrs., 50A, red for semi-dwarf plantings in the Columbia Basin area of Central Washington. (H.R. Hinman, et al., Wash. State Ext. Bul. 0960, Pullman 99163. 1981)

Table 1. First Year Costs.[1]

	Unit	Price or Cost/Unit	Quantity	Value or Cost	Farm
Variable costs					
Nitrogen	lbs.	0.369	125.00	$ 46.13	_____
Machine hire	hr.	15.000	0.70	10.50	_____
Tractor driver	hr.	5.000	2.04	10.20	_____
Hand labor	hr.	5.000	6.90	34.50	_____
Stakes	acre	2.000	1.00	2.00	_____
Machine hire	acre.	22.500	1.00	22.50	_____
Trees	tree	4.100	250.00	1025.00	_____
Solican	acre	9.500	1.00	9.50	_____
Strychnine oats	lbs.	1.050	7.00	7.35	_____
Custom aerial	acre	4.500	1.00	4.50	_____
Rozol	lbs.	1.070	10.00	10.70	_____
Irrig. charge	acre	15.000	1.000	15.00	_____
Fuel for rented tractors	acre	1.230	6.75	8.30	_____
Machinery	acre	22.73	1.00	22.73	_____
Tractors	acre	26.30	1.00	26.30	_____
Irrigation machinery	acre	30.24	1.00	30.24	_____
Labor (tractor & machinery)	hour	5.00	12.29	61.47	_____
Labor (irrigation)	hour	5.00	0.88	4.40	_____
Interest on op. cap.	dol.	0.14	907.85	127.10	_____
Overhead cost	dol.	0.050	1478.41	73.92	_____
Total variable cost				$1552.33	
Fixed costs					
Machinery	acre	125.31	1.00	$ 125.31	_____
Tractors	acre	28.81	1.00	28.81	_____
Irrigation machinery	acre	115.25	1.00	115.25	_____
Taxes (land)	acre	12.00	1.00	12.00	_____
Land (net rent)	acre	0.08	2000.00	160.00	_____
Total fixed costs				$ 441.37	_____
Total costs				$1993.70	_____

Table 2. Second Year Costs (Continued)

	Unit	Price or Cost/Unit	Quantity	Value or Cost	Farm
Variable costs					
Custom aerial	acre	5.500	1.00	$ 5.50	_____
Thiodan	lbs.	4.420	2.00	8.84	_____
Trees	tree	4.100	14.25	58.43	_____
Hand labor	hr.	5.000	5.90	29.50	_____
Solican	acre	9.500	1.00	9.50	_____
Nitrogen	lbs.	0.369	125.00	46.13	_____
Strychnine oats	lbs.	1.050	7.00	7.35	_____
Custom aerial	acre	4.500	1.00	4.50	_____
Rozol	lbs.	1.070	10.00	10.70	_____
Irrig. charge	acre	15.000	1.00	15.00	_____
Machinery	acre	27.270	1.00	27.27	_____
Tractors	acre	23.200	1.00	23.20	_____
Irrigation machinery	acre	25.920	1.00	25.92	_____
Labor (tractor & machinery)	hour	5.000	12.59	62.97	_____
Labor (irrigation)	hour	5.000	0.88	4.40	_____
Interest on op. cap.	dol.	0.140	123.15	17.24	_____
Overhead cost	dol.	0.050	356.45	17.82	_____
Total variable cost				$ 374.27	_____
Fixed costs					
Machinery	acre	131.740	1.00	131.74	_____
Tractors	acre	25.410	1.00	25.41	_____
Irrigation machinery	acre	115.180	1.00	115.18	_____
Taxes (land)	acre	12.000	1.00	12.00	_____
Interest in accum estab cost	acre	1993.700	0.12	239.24	_____
Land (net rent)	acre	0.080	2000.00	160.00	_____
Total fixed costs				$ 683.57	_____
Total costs				$1057.84	_____

[1]**Note:** Figures given in this and the following 5 tables represent those of responsible well managed orchards, and not particularly an average. For other details, consult the respective Extension bulletins.

Table 3. Third Year Costs (Continued)

	Unit	Price or Cost/Unit	Quantity	Value or Cost	Farm
Variable costs					
Custom aerial	acre	5.500	1.00	$ 5.50	_____
Thiodan	lbs.	4.420	2.00	8.84	_____
Sinbar	lbs.	16.240	1.00	16.24	_____
Simazine	lbs.	3.500	2.00	7.00	_____
Spreaders	acre	60.000	1.00	60.00	_____
Hand Labor	hr.	5.000	13.50	67.50	_____
Roundup	acre	17.840	1.00	17.84	_____
Nitrogen	lbs.	0.369	155.00	57.20	_____
Strychnine oats	lbs.	1.050	7.00	7.35	_____
Custom aerial	acre	4.500	1.00	4.50	_____
Rozol	lbs.	1.070	10.00	10.70	_____
Irrig. charge	acre	15.000	1.00	15.00	_____
Machine hire	acre	5.000	1.00	5.00	_____
Machine hire	acre	10.000	1.00	10.00	_____
Red fescue seed	lbs.	1.5000	10.00	15.00	_____
Machinery	acre	22.540	1.00	22.54	_____
Tractors	acre	29.400	1.00	29.40	_____
Irrigation machinery	acre	25.920	1.00	25.92	_____
Labor (tractor & machinery)	hour	5.000	12.89	64.47	_____
Labor (irrigation)	hour	5.000	0.88	4.40	_____
Interest on op. cap.	dol.	0.140	170.43	23.86	_____
Overhead cost	dol.	0.050	478.26	23.91	_____
Total variable cost				$ 502.17	_____
Fixed costs					
Machinery	acre	131.830	1.00	$ 131.83	_____
Tractors	acre	32.200	1.00	32.20	_____
Irrigation machinery	acre	115.180	1.00	115.18	_____
Taxes (land)	acre	12.000	1.00	12.00	_____
Interest on accum estab cost	acre	3051.540	0.12	366.18	_____
Land (net rent)	acre	0.080	2000.00	160.00	_____
Total fixed costs				$ 817.39	_____
Total costs				$1319.56	_____

Table 4. Fourth Year Costs (Continued)

	Unit	Price Or Cost/Unit	Quantity	Value Or Cost	Your Farm
Variable Costs					
Preharvest					
Guthion	Lbs.	4.700	2.50	$ 11.74	_____
Sinbar	Lbs.	16.240	1.00	16.24	_____
Simazine	Lbs.	3.500	2.00	7.00	_____
Zinc Sulfate	Lbs.	1.350	12.00	16.20	_____
Hand Labor	Hr.	5.000	20.83	104.15	_____
Spreaders	Acre	50.000	1.00	50.00	_____
Solubor	Lbs.	0.570	5.00	2.85	_____
Nitrogen	Lbs.	0.369	125.00	46.13	_____
Strychnine Oats	lbs.	1.050	7.00	7.35	_____
Custom Aerial	Acre	4.500	1.00	4.50	_____
Rozol	Lbs.	1.070	10.00	10.70	_____
Irrig. Charge	Acre	15.000	1.00	15.00	_____
Superior Oil	Qt.	0.750	12.00	9.00	_____
Thiodan	Lbs.	4.420	2.00	8.84	_____
Parathion	Lbs.	1.120	3.00	3.36	_____
Machinery	Acre	32.90	1.00	32.90	_____
Tractors	Acre	23.21	1.00	23.21	_____
Irrigation Machinery	Acre	25.92	1.00	25.92	_____
Labor (Tractor & Machinery)	Hour	5.00	12.05	60.27	_____
Labor (Irrigation)	Hour	5.00	0.88	4.40	_____
Interest On Op. Cap.	Dol.	0.14	194.34	27.21	_____
Overhead Cost	Dol.	0.050	587.43	29.37	_____
Subtotal, Pre-Harvest				$516.35	_____
Harvest Costs					
Hand Labor	Bins	9.000	5.00	45.00	_____
Custom Hauling	Bins	4.500	5.00	22.50	_____
Machinery	Acre	0.06	1.00	0.06	_____
Tractors	Acre	14.89	1.00	14.89	_____
Labor (Tractor & Machinery)	Hour	5.00	3.60	18.00	_____
Subtotal, Harvest				$100.45	_____
Total Variable Cost				$616.80	_____

Fixed Costs

	Unit	Price Or Cost/Unit	Quantity	Value Or Cost	Your Farm
Machinery	Acre	154.59	1.00	$154.59	____
Tractors	Acre	43.70	1.00	43.70	____
Irrigation Machinery	Acre	115.18	1.00	115.18	____
Taxes (Land)	Acre	22.50	1.00	22.50	____
Interest On Accum. Estab. Cost	Acre	4371.10	0.12	524.53	____
Land (Net Rent)	Acre	0.08	2000.00	160.00	____
Total Fixed Costs				$1020.50	____
Total Costs				$1637.30	____

TABLE 5. FIFTH YEAR COSTS (CONTINUED)

	Unit	Price Or Cost/Unit	Quantity	Value Or Cost	Your Farm
Variable Costs					
Preharvest					
Thiodan	Lbs.	4.420	6.00	$ 26.52	____
Elgetol	Pt.	3.090	6.00	18.54	____
NAA	Oz.	0.070	3.00	0.21	____
Sevin	Lbs.	1.590	2.00	3.18	____
Guthion	Lbs.	4.700	2.50	11.74	____
Sinbar	Lbs.	16.240	1.00	16.24	____
Simazine	Lbs.	3.500	2.00	7.00	____
Zinc Kemin	Qt.	1.350	8.00	10.80	____
Solubor	Lbs.	0.570	5.00	2.85	____
Nitrogen	Lbs.	0.369	125.00	46.13	____
Strychnine Oats	Lbs.	1.050	7.00	7.35	____
Custom Aerial	Acre	4.500	1.00	4.50	____
Rozol	Lbs.	1.070	10.00	10.70	____
Irrig. Charge	Acre	15.000	1.00	15.00	____
Superior Oil	Qt.	0.750	12.00	9.00	____
Hand Labor	Hour	5.000	25.00	125.00	____
Parathion	Lbs.	1.120	3.00	3.36	____
Machinery	Acre	45.56	1.00	45.56	____
Tractors	Acre	29.72	1.00	29.72	____
Irrigation Machinery	Acre	25.92	1.00	25.92	____
Labor (Tractor & Machinery)	Hour	5.00	13.31	66.57	____
Labor (Irrigation) 1	Hour	5.00	0.88	4.40	____
Interest On Op. Cap.	Dol.	0.14	215.91	30.23	____
Overhead Cost	Dol.	0.050	720.86	36.04	____
Subtotal, Pre-Harvest				$556.57	____
Harvest Costs					
Supervisor	Bins	1.000	15.00	15.00	____
Hand Labor	Bins	9.000	15.00	135.00	____
Custom Hauling	Bins	4.500	15.00	67.50	____
Machinery	Acre	2.18	1.00	2.18	____
Tractors	Acre	31.65	1.00	31.65	____
Labor (Tractor & Machinery)	Hour	5.00	7.80	39.00	____
Subtotal, Harvest				$290.33	____
Total Variable Cost				$846.90	____
Fixed Costs					
Machinery	Acre	208.20	1.00	208.20	____
Tractors	Acre	70.93	1.00	70.93	____
Irrigation Machinery	Acre	115.18	1.00	115.18	____
Taxes (Land)	Acre	22.50	1.00	22.50	____
Interest On Accum. Estab. Cost	Acre	5508.40	0.12	661.01	____
Land (Net Rent)	Acre	0.08	2000.00	160.00	____
Total Fixed Costs				$1237.81	____
Total Costs				$2084.71	____

TABLE 6. SUMMARY OF PRODUCTION COSTS PER ACRE AFTER ESTABLISHMENT. (COLUMBIA BASIN; H.R. HINMAN ET AL. WASH. EXT. BUL. 1159. 1982)

	Unit	Price Or Cost/Unit	Quantity	Value Or Cost	Your Farm
Variable Costs					
Preharvest					
Enosulfan	Lbs.	4.420	8.00	$ 35.36	____
DNOC	Pt.	3.090	6.00	18.54	____
NAA	Oz.	0.070	4.00	0.28	____
Carbaryl	Lbs.	1.590	3.00	4.77	____
Azinphos Methyl	Lbs.	4.700	3.00	14.10	____
Liquid Zinc	Qt.	1.350	8.00	10.80	____
Solubor	Lbs.	0.570	5.00	2.85	____

	Unit	Price Or Cost/Unit	Quantity	Value Or Cost	Your Farm
Irrig. Charge	Acre	15.000	1.00	15.00	____
Superior Oil	Qt.	0.750	24.00	18.00	____
Parathion	Lbs.	1.120	3.00	3.36	____
Terbacil	Lbs.	16.240	1.00	16.24	____
Simazine	Lbs.	3.500	2.00	7.00	____
Nitrogen	Lbs.	0.369	125.00	46.13	____
Strychnine Oats	Lbs.	1.050	7.00	7.35	____
Chlorophacinone	Lbs.	1.070	10.00	10.70	____
Hand Labor	Hr.	5.000	85.00	425.00	____
Hand Labor	Tree	0.750	264.00	198.00	____
Supervisor	Hr.	5.000	2.69	13.44	____
Custom Aerial	Acre	4.500	1.00	4.50	____
Irrigation Electricity	Acre	12.72	1.00	12.72	____
Machinery Repair	Acre	95.27	1.00	95.27	____
Machinery Fuel & Lube	Acre	48.02	1.00	48.02	____
Labor (Irrigation)	Hour	5.00	0.88	4.40	____
Labor (Tractor & Machinery)	Hour	5.00	26.37	131.85	____
Interest On Op. Cap.	Dol.	0.14	613.01	85.82	____
Overhead Cost	Dol.	0.05	2231.85	111.59	____
Subtotal, Pre-Harvest				$1341.09	____
Harvest Costs					
Machine Hire	Acre	5.550	4.00	22.20	____
Machine Hire	Acre	2.775	2.00	5.55	____
Fuel (For Rented Tractor)	Gal.	1.495	27.00	40.36	____
Supervisor	Bins	0.500	60.00	30.00	____
Hand Labor	Bins	9.00	60.00	540.00	____
Custom Hauling	Bins	4.500	60.00	270.00	____
Machinery Repair	Acre	5.28	1.00	5.28	____
Machinery Fuel & Lube	Acre	24.93	1.00	24.93	____
Labor (Tractor & Machinery)	Hour	5.00	12.80	64.00	____
Subtotal, Harvest				$1002.33	____
Total Variable Cost				$2343.42	____
Fixed Costs					
Depre. On Mach. & Building	Acre	169.74	1.00	169.74	____
Ins. & Taxes On Mach. & Building	Acre	25.33	1.00	25.33	____
Interest On Equip. & Building	Acre	196.13	1.00	196.13	____
Taxes (Land)	Acre	22.50	1.00	22.50	____
Prorated Estab. Cost***	Acre	6093.11	0.13	815.87	____
Land (Net Rent)	Acre	0.08	2000.00	160.00	____
Total Fixed Costs				$1389.57	____
Total Costs				$3732.99	____

*Includes Fuel And Lube.
**14% Opportunity Cost On The Average Value Of Machinery And Buildings Over Their Useful Life.
***Amortized Over 20 Years At 12% Interest.

TABLE 8. PER ACRE RETURNS TO LAND AND MANAGEMENT FOR VARYING YIELDS AND PRICES. */ CENTRAL WASHINGTON.

	$60 Per Bin	$70 Per Bin	$80 Per Bin	$90 Per Bin	$100 Per Bin
Bins/A	$	$	$	$	$
40	-839	-439	- 39	361	761
45	-622	-172	278	728	1,178
50	-406	94	594	1,094	1,594
55	-189	361	911	1,461	2,011
60	27	627	1,227	1,827	2,427

*/ Assumes establishment cost as indicated in previous tables from Columbia Basin.

The following figures were collected by William Gerling, Regional Fruit Specialist in the Hudson Valley, P.O. Box 727, Highland 12528. Detailed copies are available. Orchards in the survey ranged in size from 42 to 593 acres. These figures should give you a comparison for your operation.

TABLE 1. APPLE GROWING COSTS IN DOLLARS/ACRE IN NEW YORK FOR SIX OPERATIONS, 1981. (WILLIAM GERLING, CORNELL UNIVERISTY, HIGHLAND, N.Y.)

	Average	Range
Orchard overhead		
Real estate tax	$ 15.19	$ 6.68 - 23.08
Return on investment	244.74	92.20 - 300.00
Rental	7.02	0 - 83.54
Other (insurance, short term interest, etc.)	57.77	5.79 - 195.40
Total	$324.72	$189.31 - 421.98
Management		
Salary	$ 74.77	$ 47.48 - 106.44
Accounting/secretarial	13.25	4.82 - 22.62
Office expense	4.80	.59 - 12.57
Total	$ 92.82	$ 54.94 - 127.94
Labor		
Pruning and brush removal	$119.64	$ 54.54 - 231.41
Spraying	32.92	8.92 - 49.77
Mowing	31.43	12.19 - 47.51
Other (spreading fertilizer, Herbicides, grubbing, irrigation)	39.01	4.92 - 179.15
Total	$223.00	$151.51 - 358.90
Equipment		
Depreciation	$ 45.53	$ 38.04 - 74.36
Return on investment	54.28	45.64 - 89.24
Fuel	57.25	28.82 - 77.41
Repairs and maintenance	74.98	31.79 - 117.89
Total	$232.04	$155.51 - 358.90
Materials		
Fungicides	$ 59.73	$ 37.43 - 86.34
Insecticides	44.57	24.38 - 61.05
Miticides	35.37	13.53 - 48.64
Spray oil	5.36	0 - 12.95
Growth regulators	16.85	11.76 - 27.25
Herbicides	7.33	1.47 - 13.93
Lime + fertilizer	22.28	11.43 - 30.15
Other (mouse baits, bees, etc.)	27.20	12.14 - 34.84
Total	$218.69	$122.50 - 279.61
Total growing cost per bearing acre	$1091.27	$826.36 - 12438.68
Yield per acre (bu.)	398	198 - 715
Cost per bushel	$ 2.74	$ 1.74 - 4.77

TABLE 2. COST PER BUSHEL OF APPLES AT DIFFERENT YIELDS AND GROWING COSTS IN DOLLARS. NEW YORK 1981.

Yield - bushel per bearing acre	Growing cost per acre Low $826	Average $1091	High $1244
150	$5.51	$7.27	$8.29
200	4.33	5.46	66.22
250	3.30	4.36	4.98
300	2.75	3.64	4.15
350	2.36	3.12	3.55
400	2.07	2.73	3.11
450	1.84	2.42	2.76
500	1.65	2.18	2.49
550	1.50	1.98	2.26
600	1.38	1.82	2.07
650	1.27	1.68	1.91
700	1.18	1.56	1.78
750	1.10	1.45	1.66

TABLE 3. HARVETING COSTS OF APPLES IN DOLLARS PER BUSHEL, SIX OPERATIONS. NEW YORK 1981.

	Average	Range
Equipment	$ .19	$ .12 - .25
Containers	.21	.10 - .42
Housing	.19	.07 - .41
Picking	.56	.48 - .76
Picker transportation	.08	.03 - .13
Other labor (supervision, handling, etc.)	.26	.11 - .40
Other (bad debts, interest on short term loans, advertisement, etc.)	.02	0 - .01
Total harvesting cost/bu.	$1.51	$1.08 - 2.01

TABLE 4. HARVESTING COSTS OF APPLES IN SELECTED YEARS IN DOLLARS PER BUSHEL. NEW YORK 1981.

	1971	1976	1980	1981
Equipment	$.03	$.07	$.13	$.19
Containers	.09	.14	.16	.21
Housing	.04	.06	.12	.19
Picking	.34	.46	.58	.56
Picker transp.	*	.04	.08	.08
Other labor (superv. & handling)	.08	.12	.18	.26
Other	.03	.01	.02	.02
Total harvest cost/bu.	$.61	$.90	$1.27	$1.51
Range, cost/bu.	$$.55-$.89	$.66-$1.33	$.98-$1.48	$1.08-$2.01

TABLE 5. APPLE GROWING COSTS IN DOLLARS/ACRE FOR SELECTED YEARS IN NEW YORK. 1981. 9W. GERLING, CORNELL UNIVERSITY, HIGHLAND, N.Y. 12528.

	1971	1976	1980	1981
Orchard overhead				
Real estate taxes	$ 14.93	$ 21.59	$ 21.90	$ 15.19
Return on investment	45.63	98.57	183.25	244.74
Rental	11.26	13.68	3.77	7.02
Other	&& -	1.11	36.29	57.77
Total	$ 71.82	$134.95	$245.21	$$324.72
Management				
Salary	$ 17.39	$ 71.64	$ 65.85	$ 74.77
Accounting/secretarial	3.15	1543	14.18	13.25
Office	1.47	4.37	6.28	4.80
Total	$ 22.01	$ 91.44	$ 86.31	$$ 92.82
Labor				
Pruning & brush removal	$ 35.67	$ 94.46	$ 94.71	$ 119.64
Spraying	7.73	17.26	32.36	32.92
Mowing	12.12	10.57	23.36	31.43
Other	17.66	28.77	30.68	39.01
Total	$ 73.18	$151.06	$181.11	$ 223.00
Equipment				
Depreciation	$ 15.01	$ 37.71	$ 46.84	$ 45.54
Return on investment	7.52	23.65	48.55	54.28
Fuel	13.34	21.39	46.66	57.25
Reapirs	14.93	46.38	70.25	74.98
Total	$ 50.80	$129.13	$212.30	$ 232.04
Materials				
Spray & dust	$ 53.74	$ 93.69	$106.81	$ 145.03
Lime & fertilizer	5.13	9.03	19.44	22.28
Growth regulators		11.56	18.85	16.85
Other	11.55	18.60	16.50	34.53
Total	$ 70.42	$132.88	$161.60	$ 218.69
Total cost per bearing acre	$288.23	$639.46	$886.53	$1091.27
Cost/bu. at average yield	$0.77	$1.85	$2.25	$2.74
Range in production cost per acre	$270-$408	$485-$905	$715-1097	$826-1244
Range in yield	307-634 bu/A	183-638 bu/A	406-630 bu/A	198-715 bu/A

WORLD APPLE PRODUCTION
UNIT - 1000 METRIC TONS
F - F.A.O. ESTIMATE

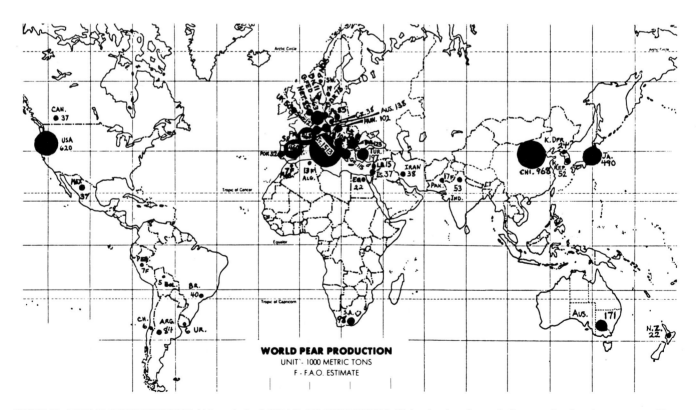

WORLD PEAR PRODUCTION
UNIT - 1000 METRIC TONS
F - F.A.O. ESTIMATE

WORLD APPLE PRODUCTION (Above) And PEAR PRODUCTION (Below), showing relative production by country. Heavy concentration is in Western and Eastern Europe. Data from FAO Production Yearbook, Rome, Italy.

564

The following Apple Data from California, which ranks high in Apple Production, comes from "Apple Production Costs — Santa Cruz County, California" by Ronald H. Tyler, Farm Advisor, Calif. Co-Op Ext. Serv., Watsonville 95076-2796. 8 P. 1982.

TABLE 1. USE AND VALUE OF APPLES, SANTA CRUZ COUNTY (AGRICULTURAL COMMISSIONER'S REPORT)

Use	Tons	% Of Total Tons	Value Per Ton	Total Value	% Of Total Value
Fresh	28,100	30.5	$316.50	$ 8,894,000	66.0
Dryer	5,200	5.6	76.00	395,000	2.9
Processing	22,000	23.9	91.90	2,022,000	15.0
Juice	36,900	40.0	59.00	2,177,000	16.1
All Uses	92,200	100.0%		$13,488,000	100.0%

TABLE 2. TREND OF APPLE ACREAGE

		Bearing Acres		Non-Bearing 1981	Total 1981
Major Varieties	1972	1976	1981		
Newton Pippin	3,337	3,404	3,118	211	3,329
Delicious - Red	3,376	3,319	3,108	106	3,214
McIntosh	223	234	225	59	284
Delicious - Std.	243	236	90	0	90
Winter Banana	106	120	89	0	89
Golden Delicious	78	83	83	0	83
W.W. Pearmain	73	66	61	0	61
Gravenstein	31	32	28	0	28
Other Varieties	79	101	97	5	28
Total	7,667	7,710	6,971	381	7,352

TABLE 3. APPLE TONNAGE AND PRICE PER TON, 1972-1981

	Fresh Tons	$/Ton	Dryer Tons	$/Ton	Processing Tons	$/Ton	Juice Tons	$/Ton
1972	43,210	208.60	11,470	67.75	36,990	85.71	34,050	56.53
1973	31,570	261.62	14,990	121.48	40,570	136.75	21,340	79.19
1974	37,570	249.07	15,710	110.11	36,760	99.56	33,070	81.94
1975	35,870	222.89	8,820	70.00	33,390	81.00	32,000	64.65
1976	31,450	261.11	6,910	90.50	36,530	111.85	28,810	75.60
1977	25,490	340.60	8,300	134.17	24,340	162.05	36,120	111.90
1978	38,040	361.25	11.600	155.20	19,610	197.95	38,700	140.95
1979	30,000	391.30	10,100	85.00	24,200	151.00	37,400	122.00
1980	33,300	339.00	7,000	159.00	24,600	90.50	33,400	73.00
1981	28,100	316.50	5,200	76.00	22,000	91.90	36,900	59.00
Average		$295.19		$106.92		$120.83		$ 86.48

See Tables 4 and 6 on following pages.

TABLE 5. COST/TON AT VARYING YEILDS/ACRE.

Yield: Tons	15	20	25	30
Cultural	$103	$ 77	$ 62	$ 51
Harvest	45	45	43	42
Overhead	23	17	14	12
Depreciation	20	15	12	10
Interest on Investment	25	19	15	12
Total Cost Per Ton	$216	$713	$146	$127

	Rate/Hr.	
(1)	$ 7.59	Equipment operator labor cost including benefits;
(2)	6.29	Other labor, including benefits;
(3)	9.53	Tractor, 50 Drawbar HP crawler diesel;
(4)	5.54	Tractor, 50 Drawbar Hp wheel diesel;
(5)	8.83	Sprayer, 500 gallon;
(6)	6.03	Brush chopper with wheel tractor;
(7)	5.72	Pipe trailer with wheel tractor;
(8)	6.98	Gopher machine with wheel tractor;
(9)	7.44	Forklift attached to wheel tractor;
(10)	6.15	Truck, ½ ton;
(11)	1.61	Disc, 8' offset;
(12)	1.47	Disc, 8' tandem, and
(13)	.92	Springtooth, 8'.

TABLE 7. COSTS/TON AT VARYING YIELDS PER ACRE

Yield: Tons	10	15	20	25
Cultural	$113	$ 75	$ 56	$ 45
Harvest	45	45	43	42
Overhead	27	18	14	11
Depreciation	32	21	16	13
Interest on Investment	40	27	20	16
Total Cost/Ton	$257	$186	$149	$127

TABLE 8. EQUIPMENT USED FOR 50 YEARS

	Cost	Years of Life
Tractor, 50 DBHP, crawler,	$ 50,000	15
Tractor, 50 DBHP, wheel,	12,500	10
Truck, ½ ton	18,000	8
Sprayer, air, 500 gallon	25,000	15
Disc, 8' offset	3,300	10
Disc, 8' tandem	1.500	10
Forklift attachment	7,000	10
Pipe trailer	1,000	10
Ladders	1,590	10
Props	500	10
Brush chopper, 6'	1,200	10
Other tools	2,300	10
Total	$126,890	

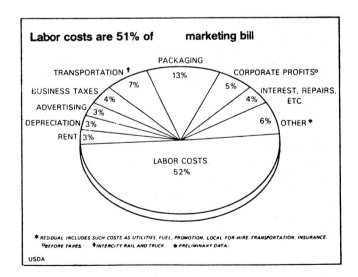

For the past several years labor costs have dominated the cost of marketing agricultural products, including fruit. Packaging ranks second in cost. USDA.

Table 4. Sample Cost to Produce Newtown Pippin Apples, Santa Cruz County. 1981

Based on a 50 acre mature orchard (25 acres Newtown Pippin and 25 acres Red Delicious) standard planting with 20-ton/acre production. (There are savings with semi-dwarfs MM-106, M-7)

Cultural Operations		Man Rate/ Hour	Cost	Machine Type/ Rate/Hours	Cost	Materials Kind	Cost	Total Cost per Acre
Prune	2/	60.0	$377.40					$ 377.40
Brush Disposal	1/	2.0	15.18	6/ 0.5	$12.06	80#N	$ 31.20	27.40
Fertilization	1/	0.5	3.80	4/ 0.5	2.77			37.77
Sprays, 3x @ ½hr.	1/	1.5	11.39	3/ 1.5	14.30	Insects,		
						Disease,	115.66	
4x @ ½hr.	1/	2.0	15.18	4/ 2.0	11.08	Thin		
				5/ 2.0	17.66			198.52
Irrigate 2x	2/	6.0	37.74	7/ 2.0	11.44	Power to pump	22.00	71.18
Cultivate 4x	1/	3.0	22.77	3/ 3.0	28.59	one acre ft		
				11/ 3.0	4.83			
4x	1/	3.0	22.77	4/ 2.0	11.08			
				12/ 2.0	2.94			
				4/ 1.0	5.54			
				13/ 1.0	.92			99.44
Thinning 2hrs./tree	2/	96.0	603.84					603.84
Propping Limbs	2/	6.0	37.74			Twine	3.00	40.74
Misc. Labor	1/	5.0	37.95	8/ 1.0	6.98	Gopher Bait,		
						Misc., other	10.50	86.88
Total Cultural Costs		190.0	1217.21	23.5	143.44		182.36	$1543.01
Harvest Operations								
Pick, 20T @$28/T			560.00					560.00
Move-Load Bins	1/	6.5	49.43	9/ 6.5	48.36			97.70
Haul	1/	5.0	37.95	10/ 5.0	30.75			68.70
Supervision	1/	7.0	53.13				$120.00	
Bin Rental						30 bins @ $4/90 days		120.00
Total Harvest Costs		18.5	700.42				$120.00	$ 899.53

Overhead Costs			
Taxes, Land:	$ 2,500	(1,072 tax rate)	$ 26.80
Taxes, Trees:	$ 550	" " "	5.90
Taxes, Equipment:	$ 1,269	" " "	13.60
Taxes, Building:	$ 240	" " "	2.57
Taxes, Irrig. System:	384	" " "	4.12
General overhead – 12% of cultural and harvest costs			293.10
Total Overhead Costs			$ 346.09
Total Cultural, Harvest, And Overhead			$2788.63

Depreciation Costs		
Trees: $550 – 30 yr bearing life		$ 18.33
Building for equipment: $240 – 25 yr life		9.60
Irrigation System: $384 – 20 yr life		19.20
Equipment, Cultural: $2538 – 10 yr life		253.80
Total Depreciation Costs		$ 300.93

Interest On Investment @ 12% on ½ of investment	
Land @ $2,500	$ 150.00
Trees @ $550	33.00
Equipment @ $2538	152.28
Irrigation system @ $384	23.04
Buildings for equipment @ $240	14.40
Total Interest On Investment	$ 372.72
Total Cost Of Production	$3,462.28

Note: Figure management costs at about 5%.

TABLE 6. SAMPLE COSTS TO PRODUCE RED DELICIOUS APPLES IN SANTA CRUZ COUNTY, 1981.

Based on 50 acre mature orchard (25 acres Red Delicious and 25 acres Newtown Pippin) standard planting, 55 trees/acre, with 15 ton per acre production.

Cultural Operations	Man Rate/	Man Hours	Cost	Machine Rate/Hours	Machine Cost	Materials Kind	Materials Cost	Total Cost per Acre
Prune	2/	42.0	$264.18					$ 264.18
Brush Disposal	1/	2.0	15.18	6/ 2.0	$ 12.06			27.24
Fertilization	1/	0.5	3.80	4/ 0.5	2.77	80#N	$ 31.20	37.77
Spray 2x @ ½hr.	1/	1.0	7.59	3/ 1.0	9.53	Insects,		
				5/ 1.0	8.83	Disease	108.92	
4x @ ½hr.	1/	2.0	15.18	4/ 2.0	11.08	Thin		
				5/ 2.0	17.66	Power to pump 1		178.79
Irrigate 2x	2/	6.0	37.74	7/ 2.0	11.44	acre ft.	22.00	71.18
Cultivate 4x	1/	3.0	22.77	3/ 3.0	28.59			
				11/ 3.0	4.83			
4x	1/	3.0	22.77	4/ 2.0	11.08			
				12/ 2.0	2.94			
				4/ 1.0	5.54			
				13/ 1.0	.92			99.44
Thin 1 hr./tree	2/	47.0	295.63					295.63
Propping Limbs	2/	10.0	62.90			Twine	3.20	66.10
Misc. Labor	1/	5.0	37.95	8/ 1.0	6.98	Gopher Bait		
								86.88
Total Cultural Costs		134.5	$817.14	23.5	$134.25		$175.82	$1127.21
Harvest Operations			405.00					
Pick, 15 T @ $27.00			405.00					$ 405.00
Move & Load Bins	1/	5.5	41.75	9/ 5.5	40.92			82.67
Haul	1/	4.0	30.36	10/ 4.0	24.60			54.96
Supervision	1/	6.0	45.54			23 bins $ 4.00		45.54
Bin Rental						90 days	92.00	92.00
Total Harvest Costs		15.5	$522.65	9.5	$65.52		$ 92.00	$ 680.17

Overhead Costs

		Total Cost per Acre
Taxes, Land: $2,500 (1.072 tax rate)		$ 26.80
Taxes, Trees: $ 970 " " "		10.40
Taxes, Equipment $1,269 " " "		13.60
Taxes, Building: $ 240 " " "		2.57
Taxes, Irrig. system: $384 " " "		4.12
General Overhead 12% of cultural and harvest costs		216.88
Total Overhead Costs		$ 274.37
Total Cultural, Harvest And Overhead Costs		$2081.75

Depreciation Costs

		Total Cost per Acre
Trees: @ $970 - 30 year bearing life		32.33
Building for equipment: $240 - 25 year life		9.60
Irrigation system: $384 - 20 year life		19.20
Equipment, cultural: $2,538 - 10 year life		253.80
Total Depreciation Costs		$ 314.93
Total Cash And Depreciation Costs		$2396.68

Interest On Investment @ 12% on ½ of investment

		Total Cost per Acre
Land @ $2,500		$ 150.00
Trees @ 970		58.20
Equipment @ $2,538		152.28
Irrigation system @ $ 384		23.04
Building for equipment @ $ 240		14.40
Total Interest On Investment		$ 397.92
Total Cost Of Production		$2794.60

The following tables give peach costs in South Carolina and Georgia. Data are from peach growers handbook by M.E. Ferree and P.F. Bertrand, Clemson University, So. Carolina and University of Georgia, Athens 30602; handbooks available from latter, priced, updated yearly, 1983.

TABLE 1. PER ACRE COST ESTIMATES FOR ESTABLISHMENT, DEVELOPMENT AND PRODUCTION OF PEACHES

A. ESTIMATED COSTS OF ESTABLISHMENT ON SOD — FIRST YEAR

Cost Items	Unit	Quantity	Price	Amount	Your Estimate
Land charge	acre	1	$60	$60	_____
Lime	ton	3	22	66	_____
Trees (18x20)	each	120	1.35	162	_____
Fertilizer(trees)	cwt.	4	8	32	_____
Nitrogen (32%)	cwt.	1	9	9	_____
Herbicides	-	-	-	-	_____
Pesticides	-		-	3	_____
Labor	hrs.	15.3	4	61	_____
Machinery	hrs.	5.1	15	77	_____
Miscellaneous	$	486	5%	24	_____
Interest on oper. cap.	$	510	14% (9 mo.)	54	_____
Management	$	564	10%	56	_____

TOTAL ESTABLISHMENT COSTS - FIRST YEAR $620 _____

Power and Labor Requirements for Establishment

Operations	Labor Hours	Machinery Hours
Subsoil or chisel	.6	.6
Disk(2)	.6	.6
Mark rows	.2	.2
Set trees	2.5	.3
Disk	.3	.3
Weed control	4.0	-
Stripping trees(2)	3.0	
Herbicide appl.	.6	.6
Pesticide appl.(2)	3.0	1.0
Mow sod(3)	1.5	1.5
Totals	15.3	5.1

B. ESTIMATED DEVELOPMENT COSTS — SECOND YEAR

Cost Items	Unit	Quantity	Price	Amount	Your Estimate
Land charge	acre	1	$60	$60	_____
Lime	ton	1.0	22	22	_____
Trees-replacement	each	4	1.50	6	_____
Fertilizer(trees) 10-10-10	cwt.	3.0	8	24	_____
Nitrogen(32%)	cwt.	2.2	9	20	_____
Herbicides	acre	-	-	20	_____
Pesticides	acre	-	-	25	_____
Custom prune & remove fruit	tree	120	.30	36	_____
Other labor	hrs.	10.2	4	41	_____
Machinery	hrs.	3.2	15	48	_____
Miscl.	$	302	5%	15	_____
Interest/Oper. Cap.	$	317	14% (8 mo.)	30	_____
Management	$	347	10%	35	

TOTAL DEVELOPMENT COST - SECOND YEAR $382 _____

C. ESTIMATED PRODUCTION COSTS — THIRD YEAR

Cost Items	Units	Quantity	Price	Amount	Your Estimate
Land charge	acre	1	$60	$60	_____
Trees,replacements	each	3	1.50	5	_____
Fertilizer: 10-10-10	cwt.	5.0	8	40	_____
Nitrogen(32%)	cwt.	2.0	9	18	_____
Herbicides	acre			20	_____
Pesticides	acre			50	_____
Custom Prune	tree	120	60	72	_____
Thin Fruit	tree	120	1.00	120	_____
Other Labor	hrs.	14	4	56	_____
Machinery	hrs.	7.1	15	107	_____
Misc.	$	548	5%	27	_____
Interest/Oper. Cap.	$	575	14% (8 mo.)	54	_____
Management	$	629	10%	63	_____

Total Pre-Harvest Production Cost $692 _____

Harvest Costs - Third Year

Cost Items	Units	Quantity	Price	Amount	Your Estimate
Picking and Handling	bus.	90	$ 1.50	$150	_____
Grading, packing, & Marketing	3/4 bus.	100	2.70	270	_____

	Harvesting Cost	$420
	Preharvest Cost	692
	Total Production Cost	$1112

Receipts:
100 3/4 bu. @ $8.00 = $800
 20 bus.   @ $3.00 =   60
   Total Receipts $860
NET PRODUCTION COSTS-THIRD YEAR $252

F. ESTIMATED PRODUCTION COSTS — FOURTH YEAR

Cost Items	Units	Quantity	Price	Amount	Your Estimate
Land charge	acre	1	$60	$60	_____
Lime	ton	1.0	22	22	_____
Trees,replacement	each	3	1.50	5	_____

Con't. above

Con't. next page

					Your
Fertilizer:					Estimate
10-10-10	cwt.	5	8	40	_____
Nitrogen	cwt.	2	9	18	_____
Herbicides	acre	-	-	20	_____
Pesticides	acre	-	-	50*	_____
Custom Pruning	tree	117	.60	70	_____
Custom Thinning	tree	117	1.50	176	_____
Other labor	hr.	8.6	4	34	_____
Machinery	hr.	7.1	15	107	_____
Miscl.	$	602	5%	30	_____
Interest	$	632	14% (8 mo.)	59	_____
Management	$	691	10%	69	_____

Sub Total Preharvest Production Costs:	$760
Amortization of Investment	329
Total Preharvest Production Cost	$989

Harvest Costs: - Fourth Year

Cost Items	Units	Quantity	Price	Amount	Your Estimate
Picking & Handling	bus.	200	1.50	$300	_____
Grading, packing & marketing	3/4 bus.	200	2.70	540	_____

Harvest Costs	$840
Preharvest Costs	989
TOTAL PRODUCTION COST - FOURTH YEAR	$1829

G. ESTIMATED PRODUCTION COSTS — FIFTH YEAR

Cost Items	Units	Quantity	Price	Amount	Your Estimate
Land charge	acre	1	$60	$60	_____
Lime	ton	1.0	22	22	_____
Trees, replacement	each	5	1.50	8	_____
Fertilizer					
10-10-10	cwt.	5	8	40	_____
Nitrogen (32%)	cwt.	3.0	9	27	_____
Herbicides	acre	-	-	20	_____
Pesticides	acre	-	-	50	_____
Custom Pruning(2)	tree	115	.75	86	_____
Custom Thinning	tree	115	1.50	173	_____
Other labor	hrs.	8.6	4	34	_____
Machinery	hrs.	7.8	15	107	_____
Miscl.	$	627	5%	31	_____
Interest on Oper. Cap.	$	658	14% (8 mo.)	61	_____
Management	$	719	10%	72	_____

Sub Total Preharvest Cost	$791
Amortization of Investment	329
Total Preharvest Production Costs	$1120

Harvest Costs - Fifth Year

Cost Items	Units	Quantity	Price	Amount	Your Estimate
Picking & Handling	bus.	250	$ 1.50	$375	_____
Grading, packing & marketing	3/4 bu.	250	2.70	675	_____

Harvesting Cost	$1050
Preharvest Production Cost	1120
Total Production Cost - Fifth Year	$2170

H. ESTIMATED ESTABLISHMENT, DEVELOPMENT & PRODUCTION COSTS OF PEACHES

Cost Items	Years				
	1	2	3	4	5+
Land charge	$60	$60	$60	$60	$60
Lime	66	22		22	22
Trees	162	6	5	5	8
Fertilizer, trees	32	24	40	40	40
Nitrogen	9	20	18	18	27
Herbicides	16	20	20	20	20
Pesticides	3	25	50	50	50
Pruning and Topping	-	36	72	70	86
Removing Fruit	-		120	176	173
Labor	61	41	56	34	34
Machinery	77	48	107	107	107
Miscl.	24	15	27	30	31
Interest/oper. cap.	54	30	54	59	61
Management	56	35	63	69	72
Sub Total Preharvest Costs	620	382	692	760	791
Investment Amortization	-	-	-	329	329
Total Preharvest Prod. Costs	$620	382	692	989	1120
Picking & Handling	-	-	150	300	375
Grading, packing & marketing	-	-	270	540	675
Total Production Costs	$620	$382	$1112	$1829	$2170

CASH FLOW — PEACH PRODUCTION

	Years							
	1	2	3	4	5	6	7	8
Total Production Costs	$620	$382	$1112	$1829	$2170	$2170	$2170	$2170
Gross Receipts	-	-	860	1590	2650	2650	2650	2650
Net Annual Differences	-620	-382	-252	-239	+480	+480	+480	+480
Accumulate Net Differences	-620	-1002	-1254	-1493	-1013	-533	-53	+427

The above computations are based on annual estimates of costs and yield estimates as shown in the budgets. Beginning with the fourth year the 3/4 bushel pack price is $10. The third year price is $8. It is assumed that a 3/4 bushel pack and .2 bushel of culls will be netted from each bushel yield. The price of culls is fixed at $3.00.

The contents of the above table indicate that a positive net annual difference between costs and receipts will be realized in the fifth year. However, it will be the eighth year before an accumulated net difference will be experienced. With variations in yield-price combinations the cash flow changes accordingly.

ECONOMICS OF IRRIGATION, PEACHES

Introduction, The capital investment requirements, annual fixed costs and operating costs will vary considerably. Factors contributing to this include: type of irrigation system, tree spacing, acreage involved, source of water and participation of the producer in the installation.

The annual fixed costs will also vary. Level of capital investment, interest rate and expected life are the major factors that influence annual fixed costs.

Operating costs consists primarily of repairs, labor and energy cost. The variability in operating costs rests heavily on the requirements for supplemental water.

Estimated Investment and Operating Costs for Trickle System

Cost installed and operational — $650
Useful life of system — 15 yrs.
Annual interest rate on av. invest. — 12%
   Estimated annual fixed cost per acre — $90
   Estimated annual operating cost per acre — $30
     Total Estimated Annual Cost Per Acre — $120

Yield Increases Required to Justify Irrigation Costs

Estimated Annual Irrigation Costs Per Acre	Breakeven Yields Required to Cover Added Irrigation Costs				
	Value of unharvested peaches ($/bu.)*				
	$3.00	$4.00	$5.00	$6.00	$7.00
$100	33	25	20	17	14
110	37	28	22	18	16
120	40	30	24	20	17
130	43	33	26	22	19
140	47	35	28	23	20

*The unharvested values are used since per bushel cost of harvesting, handling, packing and marketing are fixed and not influenced by the addition of irrigation.

SUMMARY COSTS OF REMOVING AND REPLACING DAMAGED FRUIT TREES

(FIGURES ADJUSTED FOR INFLATION, 1983, FROM WASHINGTON STATE UNIV. EM-4298. BY S.M. DORAN)

Item	Total	Per Tree
A. Tree replacement costs (5 T/A)	$ 56.70	$11.64
B. Plus present value of added establishment costs	+28.22	+5.64
C. Minus present value of reduced costs	−87.55	−17.17
D. Plus projected loss of income from replaced trees	+405.63	+81.13
E. Minus projected income from replacement trees	−73.91	−14.73
F. Equals subtotal (sum of above items)	$329.44	$66.46
G. Plus risk factor (25% of loss of Item C in Table 1 plus 25% of Item B above)	+12.70	+2.53
H. Equals expected Present Value of Costs of Removing and Replacing Tree(s). Sum of Items F and G.	$340.30	$68.69

Some Limitations of this Analysis Procedure

This analysis procedure was designed for those situations where only a limited number of trees in an orchard block are replaced. It is not suitable for determining the costs associated with:

1. Loss of a sufficiently large number of trees that an entire block has to be replanted.

2. Removal of part of an orchard for other land use.

3. Tree injury of a temporary nature that results in crop loss for only a few years.

4. Tree injury that results in permanently weakened trees or permanent loss of portions of trees.

Additionally, the procedure does not consider tax impacts associated with removing and replacing trees. The expected present value of costs are on a before-tax basis.

Finally, the proposed procedure considers only the time period for the expected life of the original planting; it assumes that all trees in the orchard block will be removed at the end of that time. Therefore, it does not properly reflect the costs for those orchard situations where the orchard block is renovated by interplanting young trees in an older planting.

FRUIT PRODUCTION COSTS IN CALIFORNIA
ALMOND ORCHARD ESTABLISHMENT COSTS. KERN COUNTY 1982.

Practices are representative of flood irrigation of the Valley floor. Costs are for a 24' x 24' planting with 75 trees/A. Labor costs of $6.25 and $5.25/hr. total costs to the grower. Medium wheel tractor per hour cash costs $9.86, depreciation $2.10 and interest $1.70. (Mario Viveros, POB 2509, Bakersfield, Ca. 93303)

Yield in nut meats: lbs. per acre	1st Year	2nd Year	3rd Year	4th Year
Pre-Harvest Cash Costs				
Land preparation	$ 76.00			
Level	118.00			
Trees: 75 @ $3.45	259.00			
Lay out field, plant, prune: 75 @ 95¢	71.00			
Replants: 2 @ $4.00		$ 8.00		
Tying		8.00	$ 25.00	
Irrigation preparation	7.00	7.00	28.00	$ 10.00
Fertilize: materials & application	12.00	20.00	27.00	43.00
Water: $50.00/ac. ft.	50.00	100.00	150.00	200.00
Irrigation labor	21.00	21.00	31.00	31.00
Spray materials	28.00	28.00	62.00	105.00
Spray application	10.00	10.00	30.00	50.00
Disc		24.00	24.00	
Mow centers, spray borders				73.00
Pollination service				25.00
Taxes	32.00	32.00	32.00	64.00
Misc. labor & field power	28.00	28.00	28.00	28.00
Misc. repairs	22.00	22.00	22.00	22.00
Supervision	20.00	20.00	20.00	20.00
Office & business costs	31.00	13.00	19.00	27.00
Interest on operating capital	65.00	26.00	40.00	56.00
Total Pre-Harvest Cash Costs	$ 874.00	$367.00	$ 538.00	$ 754.00
Harvest Costs:				
Knock, sweep, pick up, haul, hull @ 16¢/lb.				$ 72.00
Total Cash Costs	$ 874.00	$367.00	$ 538.00	$ 754.00
Depreciation	Investment per acre			
Irrigation systems	$422.00	$ 28.00	$ 28.00	$ 28.00	$ 28.00
Building & equipment	250.00	21.00	21.00	21.00	21.00
Total Depreciation		$ 49.00	49.00	49.00	49.00
Interest on Investment @ 14%:				
Irrigation system		$ 30.00	$ 30.00	$ 30.00	$ 30.00
Building & equipment, ½ cost $125.00	18.00	18.00	18.00	18.00
Land	$4500.00	630.00	6630.00	630.00	630.00
Interest on accumulated costs			224.00	409.00	643.00
Total Int. On Invest	$5172.00	$ 678.00	$903.00	$1087.00	$1321.00
Total Cost For The Year				
Credits for nut meats 90¢/lb.				$ 405.00
Net cost for the year	$1601.00	$1319.00	$1674.00	$1791.00
Accumulated net cost	$1601.00	$2920.00	$4595.00	$6384.00

ALMOND PRODUCTION COSTS KERN COUNTY 1982

Based on yield of 2200 lbs. (meats) per acre. Costs are for a 24' x 24' planting with 75 trees/A Labor. $5.25 per hour unskilled and $6.25 per hour skilled total cost to the grower. (Mario Viveros, Farm Advisor, POB 2509, Bakersfield, Ca. 93303)

	Total Costs	
	Per Acre	Per lb. (meats)
Pre-Harvest Costs:		
Pruning: 75 @ 65¢	$ 49.00	
Brush disposal	15.00	
Fertilizer: 225 lbs. N/ac. @ 32¢ + $5 appl.	72.00	
Spray 6x: materials and application	196.00	
Irrigation & frost protection: 4.5ac. ft. @$50	225.00	
labor: 6 hr.	32.00	
Weed control: strip spray 2x, materials & appl.	47.00	
Flail mow 8x	37.00	
Pollination service: 2½ hives @ $25	63.00	
Taxes	64.00	
Misc. labor & field power(includes replanting)	22.00	
Misc. repairs	20.00	

Con't. next page

Supervision		20.00		
Office & business costs		45.00		
Interest on operating capital @ 16%		94.00		
Total Pre-Harvest Costs		$1001.00	$ .46	

Harvesting Costs:

Shake. pole, sweep, pick up		$ 170.00	
Hulling: 4½¢/lb. meat basis		99.00	
Total Harvesting Costs		$ 269.00	$ .12
Total Cash Costs		$1270.00	$ .58

Depreciation:

Irrigation system, $422, 15 years		$ 28.00	
Buildings & equipment, $250, 12 years		21.00	
Trees, $6384, 20 years		320.00	
Total Depreciation		$ 369.00	$ .17

Increase on Investment @ 14%:

Irrigation system, $211		$ 30.00	
Buildings & equipment, $125		18.00	
Trees, $3192		447.00	
Land, $4500/acre		630.00	
Total Interest On Investment		$1125.00	$ .51
Total Cost Of Production		$2764.00	$ 1.26

Yield: Pounds/ac. meats	1200	1400	1600	1800	2000	2200	2400
Cash Costs/lb. meats	$1.02	$ .88	$ .78	$ .70	$ .63	$ .58	$ .53
Total Costs/lb. meats	2.26	1.95	1.71	1.52	1.37	1.26	1.16

RED RASPBERRIES

RED RASPBERRIES ESTABLISHMENT COSTS, YEAR ONE:

WESTERN WASHINGTON DATA, 10 ACRE ENTERPRISE — 1981. (R.W. CARKNER & W.P.A. SCHEER, WASH. STATE UNIV., PULLMAN 99163)

	Unit	Price Or Cost/Unit	Quantity	Value Or Cost	Your Farm
Variable Costs					
Soil Test	Acre	2.000	1.00	$ 2.00	____
Dolomite Lime	Tons	89.000	1.00	89.00	____
Roundup	Qt.	18.630	3.00	55.89	____
Custom Disc	Acre	7.500	2.00	15.00	____
Custom Plow	Acre	15.000	1.00	15.00	____
Fert. 10-20-20	Lbs.	0.125	800.00	100.00	____
Custom Disc	Acre	7.500	3.00	22.50	____
Hand Plant	Hr.	4.000	15.00	60.00	____
Raspberry Plants	100	20.000	20.00	400.00	____
Devrinol 50%WP	Lbs.	7.300	2.67	19.49	____
Hand Weed	Hr.	4.000	6.00	24.00	____
Hand Hoe	Hr.	4.000	4.00	16.00	____
Rented Spreader	Acre	2.500	1.00	2.50	____
Hole Digger Rent	Acre	5.000	1.00	5.00	____
Set Posts	Hr.	4.000	7.00	28.00	____
Wood End Posts	Each	3.000	18.00	54.00	____
Wood Center Posts	Each	1.600	160.00	256.00	____
Wiring Labor	Hr.	4.000	6.00	24.00	____
Nails & Staples	Lbs.	0.560	25.00	14.00	____
Overhead	Dol.	0.050	1618.09	80.90	____
Wire #12 & #14	Cwt.	56.000	3.51	196.56	____
Rented Spreader	Acre	2.500	1.00	2.50	____
Rent 1 BTM Plow	Acre	1.500	1.00	1.50	____
Rent 4 Row Cult.	Acre	2.500	1.00	2.50	____
Machinery Repairs	Acre	2.96	1.00	2.96	____
Tractor, Fuel,Lube,Repair	Acre	3.49	1.00	3.49	____
Irrigation Elec.&Repair	Acre	38.48	1.00	38.48	____
Labor(Tractor&Machinery)	Hour	6.00	18.86	113.16	____
Labor(Irrigation)	Hour	4.00	1.69	6.75	____
Interest On Op. Cap.	Dol.	0.12	405.17	48.62	____
Subtotal, Pre-Harvest				$1699.81	____
Total Variable Cost				$1699.81	____
Fixed Costs					
Machinery	Acre	76.03	1.00	76.03	____
Tractors	Acre	103.29	1.00	103.29	____
Irrigation Machinery	Acre	85.78	1.00	85.78	____
Taxes(Land)	Acre	100.00	1.00	100.00	____
Land(Net Rent)	Acre	0.12	4000.00	480.00	____
Interest On Estab. Investment	Acre			305.39	____
Total Fixed Costs				$1150.49	____
Total Costs				$2850.28	____

Con't.

Year	Production Cost[a/]	Returns/Acre[b/]	Net Establishment[c/] Cost/Acre
1	$2,850.28	0	$2,850.28
2	2,891.59	$2,400.00	491.58
Total			$3,341.86

[a]Production cost from Table(s) 2 include interest on the establishment investment.

[b]Yield in year two is approximately half of full production (4,000 pounds) and when valued at $.60 per pound, returns in year two are $2,400.00

[c]Net establishment costs are the sum of year one production cost, plus total production costs for year two less the value of production in year two.

RED RASPBERRY ESTABLISHMENT COSTS, YEAR TWO:

WESTERN WASHINGTON DATA, 10 ACRE ENTERPRISE — 1981. (R.W. CARKNER & W.P.A. SCHEER, WASH. STATE UNIV., PULLMAN 99163)

	Unit	Price Or Cost/Unit	Quantity	Value Or Cost	Your Farm
Variable Costs					
Preharvest					
Tie Canes	Hr.	4.000	30.00	$120.00	____
Baler Twine	Bale	55.000	0.30	16.50	____
Captan	Lbs.	2.230	10.00	22.30	____
Hand Hoe	Hr.	4.000	8.00	32.00	____
Lime-Sulfur	Gal	5.250	6.00	31.50	____
Simazine 80%WP	Lbs.	4.650	1.67	7.77	____
Paraquat	Pt.	5.860	1.33	7.79	____
Fert. 10-20-10	Lbs.	0.118	600.00	70.80	____
Diazinon 50%WP	Qt.	4.050	2.00	8.10	____
Banlate 50%WP	Lbs.	10.450	1.50	15.67	____
Train Canes	Hr.	4.000	4.00	16.00	____
Prune	Hr.	4.000	10.00	40.00	____
Flats	Each	5.000	5.00	25.00	____
Overhead	Dol.	0.050	1302.70	65.13	____
Machinery Repairs	Acre	5.13	1.00	5.13	____
Tractor Fuel,Lube, Repair	Acre	2.27	1.00	2.27	____
Irrigation Elec.&Repair	Acre	38.48	1.00	38.48	____
Labor(Tractor&Machinery)	Hour	6.00	12.31	73.83	____
Labor(Irrigation)	Hour	4.00	1.69	6.75	____
Interest On Op. Cap.	Dol.	0.12	192.15	23.06	____
Subtotal, Pre-Harvest				$ 628.09	____
Harvest Costs					
Hand Pick	Tons	300.00	2.00	600.00	____
Machinery	Acre	69.04	1.00	69.04	____
Labor(Tractor$Machinery)	Hour	6.00	12.00	72.00	____
Subtotal, Harvest				$ 741.04	____
Total Variable Cost				$1369.13	____
Fixed Costs					
Machinery	Acre	173.89	1.00	173.89	____
Tractors	Acre	67.23	1.00	67.23	____
Irrigation Machinery	Acre	85.78	1.00	85.78	____
Taxes(Land)	Acre	100.00	1.00	100.00	____
Land(Net Rent)	Acre	0.12	4000.00	480.00	____
Interest On Estab. Investment	Acre			615.06	____
Total Fixed Costs				$1521.97	____
Total Costs				$2891.59	____

FRUIT BOOKS

Ask for a listing of other fruit books published by Horticultural Publications, 3906 NW 31 Pl., Gainesville, FL. 32606.

Red Raspberry Production Costs — Years 3-10:

Western Washington Data, 10 Acre Enterprise — 1981.
(R.W. Carkner & W.P.A. Scheer, Wash. State Univ.,
Pullman 99163, Ext. Bul. 0930. 1981)

Variable Costs	Unit	Price Or Cost/Unit	Quantity	Value Or Cost	Your Farm
Preharvest					
Hand Prune	Hr.	4.000	10.00	$ 40.00	
Custom Subsoil	Acre	7.500	1.00	7.50	
40" Disk Drill Rent	Acre	1.500	1.00	1.50	
Rye Seed	Lbs.	0.170	30.00	5.10	
Tie Canes	Hr.	4.000	30.00	120.00	
Baler Twine	Bale	55.000	0.30	16.50	
Lime-Sulfur	Gal	5.750	6.00	34.50	
Top Canes	Hr.	4.000	6.00	24.00	
Hoe Shoots	Hr.	4.000	8.00	32.00	
Simazine 80%WP	Lbs.	3.250	1.67	5.43	
Parawuat	Pt.	5.860	1.33	7.79	
Dinoseb	Qt.	3.275	1.00	3.27	
Superior Spray Oil	Gal	2.950	0.50	1.47	
Diazinon 50%WP	Lbs.	4.050	2.00	8.10	
Benlate 50% WP	Lbs.	10.450	1.50	15.67	
Fert. 10-20-10	Lbs.	0.118	600.00	70.80	
Overhead	Dol.	0.050	2039.95	102.00	
Captan	Lbs.	2.230	10.00	22.30	
Train Canes	Hr.	4.000	4.00	16.00	
Machinery Repair	Acre	6.34	1.00	6.34	
Tractor Fuel,Lube,Repair	Acre	3.12	1.00	3.12	
Irrigation Elec.&Repair	Acre	38.48	1.00	38.48	
Labor(Tractor&Machinery)	Hour	6.00	16.87	101.24	
Labor(Irrigation)	Hour	4.00	1.69	6.75	
Interest On Op. Cap.	Dol.	0.12	237.13	28.46	
Subtotal, Pre-Harvest				$718.32	
Harvest Costs					
Hand Puck	Tons	300.00	4.00	$1200.00	
Machinery	Acre	110.47	1.00	110.47	
Labor(Tractor&Machinery)	Hour	6.00	19.20	115.20	
Subtotal, Harvest				$1425.67	
Total Variable Cost				$2143.99	
Breakeven Price, Variable Cost				535.997	
Fixed Costs					
Machinery	Acre	275.48	1.00	$275.48	
Tractors	Acre	92.24	1.00	92.24	
Irrigation Machinery	Acre	85.78	1.00	85.78	
Taxes(Land)	Acre	100.00	1.00	100.00	

Prorated Estab. Cost	Acre	3341.86	0.20	668.37	
Land(Net Rent)	Acre	0.12	4000.00	480.00	
Total Fixed Costs				$1701.88	
Total Costs				$3845.87	
Breakeven Price, Total Costs At		4.00	Tons/Ac	961.467	

ASIAN PEARS

As this book goes to press, we find there is considerable interest among pear growers in the Asian pears, which come mainly from China. Many of the cultivars are roundish, russeted, sweet and good eating out-of-hand. They have other valuable characteristics that could work into a breeding program. If interested write for the bulletin on "Asian Pears in California" by William H. Griggs, priced, University of California, Davis 95616. There also is an item in Calif. Agr., January 1977. 4 pp. "The Pear" book by over 100 world authorities also contains a chapter by Dr. Briggs, obtainable from Hort. Publ., 3906 NW 31 Pl., Gainesville, Fl. 500 pp. Edited by T. Van Der Zwet and N.F. Childers; $25 domestic; $30 foreign.

RINGING PEACHES

The practice of ringing peaches a few weeks after bloom is gaining interest in the United States. A ring is cut around the main trunk up to 2/8ths inch wide and the bark removed. The wound heals rather quickly. Benefits are earlier ripening peaches, larger size fruit and somewhat better color. A few growers in California claim satisfaction with the practice, but data are needed on long term effects on the trees and other problems that may develop. Contact your fruit extension agent.

Table 5 — Raspberry Returns Over Total Costs at Various Yields and Prices* (R.W. Carkner & W.P.A. Scheer, Wash. State Univ., Pullman 99163. Ext. Bul. 0930. 1981)

Yield Lbs.	30	35	40	45	50	55	60	65	70	75	80	85	90	95	1.00
4,000	-1932	-1732	-1532	-1332	-1132	-932	-732	-532	-332	-132	67	267	467	667	867
5,000	-1810	-1560	-1310	-1060	-810	-560	-310	-60	189	439	689	939	1189	1439	1689
6,000	-1688	-1388	-1088	-788	-488	-188	-111	411	711	1011	1311	1611	1911	2211	2511
7,000	-1566	-1216	-866	-516	-166	183	533	883	1233	1583	1933	2283	2633	2983	3333
8,000	-1444	-1044	-644	-244	155	555	955	1355	1755	2155	2555	2955	3355	3755	4155
9,000	-1322	-872	-422	27	477	927	1377	1827	2277	2727	3177	3627	4077	4527	4977
10,000	-1200	-700	-200	299	799	1299	1799	2299	2799	3299	3799	4299	4799	5299	5799
11,000	-1078	-528	21	571	1121	1671	2221	2771	3321	3871	4421	4971	5521	6071	6621
12,000	-956	-356	243	843	1443	2043	2643	3243	3843	4443	5043	5643	6243	6843	7443

CENTS PER POUND

*Positive returns for combinations of yield and price are indicated to the right of the heavy line, to the left show returns below total production costs. Those on the dark line indicate break even points.

PYO Irrigated Highbush Blueberry Costs

Note: The following figures are from R. Funt, Ohio State University, Columbus 43210. Value of the dollar is changing but the figures should give you an idea of relative costs.

TABLE 1. ESTIMATED COST PER ACRE FOR PICK-YOUR-OWN IRRIGATED HIGHBUSH BLUEBERRY PRODUCTION, OHIO, 1980

	Labor					Over-	Total
Year	Production	Supervisory	Total	Material[a]	Machine	Head	Cost
1	$332.75	$ 0.00	$322.75	$3,905.55	$202.97	$55.20	$4,526.47
2	35.75	0.00	35.75	142.00	134.68	85.20	397.63
3	110.55	55.00	165.55	171.83	160.15	85.20	502.73
4	114.10	110.00	254.00	192.20	192.31	85.20	723.71
5	217.00	132.00	349.00	175.82	141.97	85.20	751.99
6	327.65	132.00	459.65	285.02	141.97	85.20	971.84
7	382.09	132.00	514.09	247.60	141.97	85.20	938.86
8	438.64	132.00	570.64	228.02	141.97	85.20	1,025.83
9	493.19	132.00	625.64	265.20	141.97	85.20	1,118.01
10	646.00	132.00	778.00	331.82	141.97	85.20	1,336.99
11	646.00	132.00	778.00	227.40	141.97	85.20	1,282.57
12	646.00	132.00	778.00	245.22	141.97	85.20	1,250.39
13	646.00	132.00	778.00	283.20	141.97	85.20	1,288.27
14	646.00	132.00	778.00	248.82	141.97	85.20	1,253.99
15	646.00	132.00	778.00	381.19	141.97	85.20	1,386.36
16	646.00	132.00	778.00	253.83	141.97	85.20	1,258.38
17	646.00	132.00	778.00	283.91	141.97	85.20	1,288.46
18	646.00	132.00	778.00	274.61	141.97	85.20	1,249.00

[a]Includes cost for trickle irrigation system and well.

TABLE 2. ESTIMATED YIELD AND RETURN PER ACRE FOR PICK-YOUR-OWN IRRIGATED HIGHBUSH BLUEBERRY CULTURE, OHIO, 1980

		Five-year	Variation in returns according to price per pound[b]		
Year	Estimated yield[a]	moving average	$ .55/lb.	$ .65/lb.	$ .75/lb.
	pounds per acre		dollars per acre		
1	0	0	0.00	0.00	0.00
2	0	0	0.00	0.00	0.00
3	1,000	1,640	902.00	1,066.00	1,230.00
4	2,400	2,840	1,562.00	1,846.00	2,130.00
5	4,800	4,640	2,552.00	3,016.00	3,480.00
6	6,000	5,960	3,278.00	3,874.00	4,470.00
7	9,000	7,780	4,279.00	5,057.00	5,835.00
8	7,600	9,260	5,093.00	6,019.00	6,949.00
9	11,500	9,940	5,467.00	6,461.00	7,455.00
10	12,200	10,240	5,632.00	6,656.00	7,620.00
11	9,400	10,760	5,918.00	6,994.00	8,070.00
12	10,500	10,980	6,039.00	7,137.00	8,235.00
13	10,200	10,540	5,797.00	6,851.00	7,905.00
14	12,600	10,540	5,797.00	6,851.00	7,905.00
15	10,000	10,540	5,797.00	6,851.00	7,905.00
16	9,400	10,180	5,599.00	6,617.00	7,635.00
17	10,500	9,950	5,472.50	6,467.50	7,462.50
18	8,400	8,450	4,647.00	5,492.50	6,337.50

[a]Returns are based on five-year moving average.
[b]Plant spacing is six feet by twelve feet.

Table 3. Internal Rates of Return for 12 and 18 Years Production of Highbush Blueberries, Ohio, 1980

Planting life	Variation in rates of return according to price per pound		
	$ .55/lb.	$ .65/lb.	$ .75/lb.
	percent		
12 years	21.1	25.1	28.5
18 years	23.7	27.3	30.6

Blueberry growers should make management decisions based on rates of return that are greater than current interest rates. If the costs and returns are similar to those presented in the preceding tables, then the following ranges for price and yield are recommended.

Price (cents per pound)	Yield (pounds per acre)
$.65 - .70	7,000 - 8,000

PYO Irrigated Brandywine Purple Raspberry Costs

Brandywine purple raspberries ripen after black raspberries but before blackberries or blueberries. This gives them an advantage when few small fruits are available. Their disadvantage is the amount of labor in pruning. These results were published by Richard Funt, Ohio State University Extension Service, Columbus 43210. Dr. Funt can send a complete report if interested.

Table 1. Estimated Production Cost for Irrigated Brandywine Purple Raspberry Culture, Ohio, 1980

Year	Labor			Material[b]	Equipment[c]	Over-Head	Total Cost
	Production	Supervisory	Total				
1	$200.75	$ 0.00	$200.75	$2,394.50	$157.68	$85.20	$2,838.1
2	184.25	0.00	184.25	239.66	183.63	85.20	692.7
3	360.25	44.00	404.25	126.80	183.63	85.20	799.8
4	404.25	66.00	470.25	144.80	183.63	85.20	883.8
5	404.25	66.00	470.25	198.95	183.63	85.20	938.0
6	404.25	66.00	470.25	223.75	183.63	85.20	962.8
7	404.25	66.00	470.25	220.55	183.63	85.20	959.6
8	404.25	66.00	470.25	260.55	183.63	85.20	999.6
9	404.25	66.00	470.25	250.55	183.63	85.20	989.6
10	404.25	66.00	470.25	239.55	183.63	85.20	978.6
11	404.25	66.00	470.25	215.55	183.63	85.20	954.6
12	404.25	66.00	470.25	223.55	183.63	85.20	962.6

[a]All labor is calculated at $5.50 an hour.
[b]Includes cost of trickle irrigation and well.
[c]Equipment cost is prorated per acre.

Table 2. Estimated Yield and Return for Irrigated Brandywine Purple Raspberry Culture, Ohio. 1980. R.C. Funt.

Year	Estimated yield[a]	Five-year moving average	Variation in returns according to price per pound[b]		
			$.85/lb.	$.95/lb.	$1.05/lb.
	pounds per acre		dollars per acre		
1	0	0	$ 0	$ 0	$ 0
2	0	0	0	0	0
3	1,500	1,740	1,479	1,653	1,827
4	3,200	2,640	2,244	2,508	2,772
5	4,000	3,260	2,771	3,097	3,425
6	4,500	4,280	3,638	4,066	4,494
7	3.100	4,260	3,621	4,047	4,473

Con't. next page

Con't. from previous page

8	5,100	4,360	3,621	4,047	4,473
9	4.600	3,920	3,332	3,724	4,116
10	4,000	3,940	3,349	3,743	4,137
11	2,800	3,080	2,613	2,926	3,234
12	3,200	2,800	2,300	2,660	2,940

[a]Plant spacing is 3 feet by 12 feet.
[b]Returns are based on five-year moving yield average.

TABLE 3. INTERNAL RATES OF RETURN FOR TWELVE-YEAR LIFE OF IRRIGATED BRANDYWINE PURPLE RASPBERRY CULTURE, OHIO. 1980[A]. R.C. FUNT.

Price per pound	Rate of return
dollars	percent
.85	20.9
.95	24.2
1.05	27.3

Price (dollars per pound)	Yield (pounds per acre)
$1.00 - 1.05	3,000 - 3,400

If the costs and returns are similar to those presented in the preceding tables, then the following ranges for price and yield are recommended at right:

In order to make careful management decisions, I cannot emphasize enough how important it is to keep records of your own costs and returns.

COMPANIES HANDLING FRUIT GROWER SUPPLIES AND EQUIPMENT

Note: The categories of supplies and equipment are listed first, together with the numbers indicating which companies sell these items. Following these listings are the company names and addresses by number.

CATEGORIES

CHEMICALS

Antibiotics—1, 68, 77, 91.
Defoliants—25, 39.
Fertilizers, etc.
General—5, 25, 42, 72, 91.
Soil testing—62.
Spectrographic leaf analyses—73.
Trace elements—5, 27, 63, 91, 98.
Fumigants, nematicides — 25, 26, 39, 42, 85, 91.
Fungicides—5, 25, 26, 39, 42, 72, 84, 85, 91.
Growth regulators—1, 25, 68, 77, 91, 97.
Herbicides—25, 27, 39, 42, 72, 84, 85.
Insecticides—1, 5, 25, 26, 27, 42, 72, 84, 85, 91, 97.
Spreaders, stickers—26, 27, 42.

FROST PROTECTION

Alarms—65.
Foam—41a.
Heaters—17, 92.
Mulch, plastic—39, 41a.
Wind machines—44, 48.

FRUIT PROCESSING

Corers, pasteurizers, pressure cookers, slicers, sorting & trimming, tanks,—18, 28, 41, 44, 74.
Nut cracking—57.

GRAFTING

Knives—19, 35, 37, 43, 48.
Waxes—19, 39, 41.
Wound dressings—19, 35, 48, 53.

HARVESTING EQUIPMENT

Bins, carriers—11, 44, 47.
Harvesters
Berry—28, 52.
Grape—28.
Ladders, supplies, etc.—19, 35, 41, 50, 79, 104.
Nut—44, 79.
Pressure testers (fruit)—48, 65.
Refractometers—65.
Tree fruit—41.
Tree props—48.
Tree shakers—41, 48, 75, 79.

IRRIGATION AND DRAINAGE

Drip—18, 23, 102.
Engines—47, 59, 102.
Fertilizer injectors—2, 18
Jet—69.

Moisture meters—18.
Permanent (irrig.)—41a, 78, 102.
Pumps—41a, 71, 102.
Sub-irrig.—41a, 102.
Supplies—2, 18, 78, 102.

NURSERY STOCK

Grapes—21, 70, 45, 81.
Nuts—See index listing.
Rootstocks—3a, 30, 40, 65, 96, 90, 100.
Seed (Fruit)—21, 45.
Small fruits—4, 21, 33, 45, 82, 87.
Trees—3a, 15, 21, 33, 53, 60, 65, 90, 100.

PACKING HOUSE EQUIPMENT

Bin handlers, box dumpers, etc.—28, 29, 36, 41, 44.
Bulk shipping—8, 9, 34, 39, 76, 101.
Consumer packaging—9, 39, 42, 76.
Conveyors—10, 41, 44, 48, 102.
Cooling, hydrocoolers, icing—10, 44, 46.
Loaders, front end, truck—10, 29, 36, 44.
Packing machinery — 10, 41, 44, 59.
Roadside marketing—49, 50, 67 (plans), 74.
Waxers—41, 44.

PRUNING

Air compressors—48.
Brush disposal—43.
Hedging equipment—41, 44.
Platform lifts—43, 100a.
Pruners, pole, powers, rotary cutters, shears, saws,
   shredders—3a, 6, 24, 36, 43, 44, 48, 55, 99.
Tree guards—3a, 48.
Tree toppers—41.
Vineyard equipment—3a, 64.

RODENT, DEER, BIRD CONTROL

Birds—14, 32, 67.
Deer—42.
Netting—32.
Rodent—3a, 26, 53, 67, 74.

SPRAYERS

Concentrate—44, 2, 48, 51, 56, 71, 89, 99.
Foam applicators—56.
Hand mist sprayers—89.
Spraying supplies—44, 48, 51, 56, 89, 98, 99.
Weed sprayers—44, 48, 51, 71.

STORAGE EQUIPMENT

Blowers—12, 46, 56.
Buildings, storage—20, 61, 83, 84a.
CA Supplies, equipment—12, 38, 39, 46.
Machinery—38, 46, 84a, 105.

TRACTORS AND TILLAGE EQUIPMENT

Cultivators—6, 24, 36, 58, 66.
Drills—36, 44, 58, 66, 99.

Dry distributors—6, 36, 58, 66, 88.
Fertilizer applicators, liquid—2, 6, 36, 44, 58 89.
Fork lifts—36, 58, 66, 24, 43.
Fumigant, soil applicators—2.
Harrows—24, 36, 44 58, 66.
Hoes, grape—47.
Land levelers—36, 58.
Mowers—6. 24, 36, 44, 58, 66.
Mulchers—47, 102.
Plows—6, 36, 58.
Rotary—47, 58.
Stonepickers—36.
Tractors and equipment—6, 24, 36, 44, 47, 58.
Transplanters—54.

TRANSPORTATION & EQUIPMENT

Refrigeration units—84a.
Snowmobiles—36.
Two-Way radio—86.

COMPANIES (BY NUMBER) AND ADDRESSES

1. Abbott Laboratories, 14th & Sheridan Rd., No. Chicago, IL. 60064
2. Agrotec Serv. Inc., Box 215, Salisbury, MD. 21801
3. Ag-Rain, Inc., 600 S. Schrader, Havana, IL. 62644
3a. Amberg's Nursery, Inc., 3164 Whitney Rd., Stanley, N. Y. 14561
4. W. F. Allen Co., (Strawberries) P. O. Box 1577, Salisbury, MD. 21801
5. Allied Chemical Corp., Agr. Dept. P. O. Box 2064 R, Morristown, N. J. 07960
6. Allis-Chalmers Mfg. Co., Tractor Div. Box 512, Milwaukee, WI. 53201
8. American Box Co., P.O.B. 248, Fernwood, MS. 39635
9. American Can Co., American Lane, Greenwich, CT. 06830
10. American Conveyor Corp., 11340 S. W. 208 Dr., Miami, FL. 33189
11. American Plywood Ass'n., Tacoma, WA. 98401
12. American Standard Industries, 8111 Tireman, Detroit, MI 48204
13. Antles Pollen Supplies, Inc., Box 1243, Wenatchee, WA. 98801
14. Animal Repellants, Inc., Griffin, GA. 30223
15. Armstrong Nurseries, Box 473, Ontario, CA. 91764
16. Atlantic Berry Co., 4755 Chew Rd., Hammonton, N. J. 08037
17. Geo. J. Ball, Inc., Box 335, W. Chicago, IL. 60185
18. Ball Bros., Muncie, Ind. 47302
19. Bartlett Mfg. Co., 3044 E. Grand Blvd., Detroit, MI. 48202
20. Bestway Building Center, 505 S. 3rd Av., Yakima, WA. 98901
21 Bountiful Ridge Nurseries, Princess Anne, MD. 21853
22. Carrier Corp., P. O. Box 4800, Syracuse, N. Y. 13221
23. Chapin Watermatics, Inc., 740 Water St., Watertown, N. Y. 13601
24. J. I. Case Co., 700 State St., Racine, WI. 43403
25. Chemagro Div., P.O.B. 4913, Hawthorn Rd., Kansas

City, MO. 63120

26. Chevron Chem. Co., Ortho Div., 200 Bush St., Box 3744, San Francisco, CA. 94104
27. Ciba-Geigy Corp., Agric. Div., Box 18300, Greensboro, N. C. 27419
28. Chisholm-Ryder, Inc., 3800 Highland Ave., Niagara Falls, N. Y. 14035
29. Clark Equipment Co., Battle Creek, MI. 49106
30. Columbia Basin Nursery, Box 458, Quincy, WA. 98848
31. Compleat Winemaker, 1219 Main St., Helena, CA 94574
32. Conwed Corp., P. O. Box 43237, St. Paul, MN. 55164
33. C and O Nursery Co., Box 116, Wenatchee, WA. 98801
34. Container Corp. of America, 1 1St. Nat'l Plaza, Chicago, IL. 60670
35. Corona Clipper Co., 14200 6th St., Corona, CA. 91720
36. John Deere, Moline, IL. 61265
37. Disston Inc., 1030 W. Market St., Greensboro, N. C. 27401
38. Doub Engineering, Box 2080, Falls Church, VA. 22042
39. Dow Chemical Co., Ga-Organics Dept., Box 1706, Midland, MI. 48640
40. Dugan Nurseries, Center Rd., Perry, OH. 44081
41. Durand-Wayland Inc., P.O.B. 1404, La Grange, GA. 30241
41a. EECO, Inc., 4021 N. 6th St., Harrisburg, PA. 17110
42. E. I. Du Pont de Nemours, Co., Inc., Indust. & Biochem. Dept., Wilmington, DE. 19898
43. Edwards Equipment Co., 4312 Main St., Yakima, WA. 98902
44. FMC Corp., Agric. Mchny Div., Jonesboro, AR. 72401; San Jose, CA. 95103; Ocoee, FL. 32761
45. Foster Nursery Co., Inc., 69 Orchard Rd., Fredonia, N. Y. 14063
46. Frick Co., Waynesboro, PA. 17268
47. Friday Tractor Co., Rt. #2, Hartford, MI. 49057
48. Friend Mfg. Co., Prospect St., Gasport, N. Y. 14067
49. Fruit-O-Matic Mfg. Co., 10638 Painter Av., Cincinnati, OH. 45214
50. Gold Metals Products Co., 1837 Freeman Ave., Cincinnati, OH. 45214
51. Hardie Sprayers Div. Lockwood Corp., Gering, NE 09341
52. Harvey Harvesters, Inc. 17237 Van Wagoner Rd., Spring Lake, MI 49456
53. Hilltop Nurseries, Rt. 2, Hartford, MI. 49057
54. Holland Transplanter Co., Holland, MI. 49423
55. Homelite Div. of Textron, Inc., 14401 Carowinds Blvd., Charlotte, N. C. 28217
56. H. D. Hudson Mfg. Co., 500 N. Michigan Ave., Chicago, IL. 60611
57. IMP Nutcracker Co., 4214 Hamilton Rd., Columbus, GA. 31904
58. International Harvester Co., 401 No. Mich. Ave., Chicago, IL. 60611
59. International Staple & Machine Co., Box 629, Butler, PA. 16001
60. Kelly Bros. Nurseries, Dansville, N. Y. 14437
61. Kelly Klosure, Inc., P.O.B. 1058, Fremont, NE. 68025
62. LaMont Chemical Products Co., Chestertown, MD. 21610
63. Leffingwell Chem. Co., 111 So. Berry St., Brea, CA. 92621
64. Lewis Mfg. Co., North East, PA. 16428
65. McCormick Fruit Tree Co. (Effigi), 6111-A Englewood Ave., Yakima, WA. 98908
66. Massey-Ferguson Co., P.O.B. 977, 1901 Bell Ave., Des Moines, IA. 50315

67. Meister Publishing Co., 37841 Euclid Ave., Willoughby, OH. 44094
68. Merck Chemical Co., Rahway, N. J. 07065
69. Microjet International, Inc., P.O.B. 1125, Dundee, FL. 33838
70. Moser Farms, Rt. 1, Box 292, Coloma, MI. 49038
71. F.E. Myers & Bros. Co., Ashland, OH. 44805
72. Monsanto Chem. Co., Agric. Div., 800 No. Lindbergh Blvd., St. Louis, MO. 63166
73. National Spectrographic Sales Corp., 7650 Hub Pkway., Cleveland, OH. 44125
74. Orchard Equipment and Supply Co., Box 146, Conway, MA. 01341
75. Orchard Mchny. Corp., 2700 Colusa Hywy., Yuba City, CA. 95991
76. Packaging Corp. of America, Evanston, IL. 60204
77. Pfizer (Charles) and Co., 235 E. 42nd St., New York, N. Y. 10017
78. Rain Bird Sprinkler Mfg. Corp., 145 No. Grand Ave., Glendora, CA. 91740
79. Ramacher Mfg. Co., 5023 N. Flood Rd., Linden, CA. 95236
80. Ra-Pid-Gro Corp., P.O.B. 1370, Dansville, N. Y. 14437
81. Redwood Nursery Co., Box 12, Reedly, CA. 93654
82. Raynor Nursery, Salisbury, MD. 21801
83. Reynolds Metals Co., Box 27003, Richmond, VA. 23261
84. Rhom & Haas Co., Independence Mall West, Phila., PA. 19105
84a. Senico Mfg. Co., P.O. Dr. "H", Pharr, TX. 78577
85. Shell Chem. Co., Agric. Chem. Div., P. O. Box 3871, Houston, TX 77001
86. Std. Communications Corp., Box 92151, Los Angeles, CA. 90009
87. Stegmaier's Orchards, Inc., Rt. 8, Box 108, Cumberland, MD. 21501
88. Skibbe Mfg. Co., Sodus, MI. 49126
89. Solo Motors, Inc., Box 5030, Newport News, VA. 23605
90. Stark Bros. Nurseries and Orchard Co., Louisiana, MO. 63353
91. Stauffer Chem. Co., Agric. Div., Westport, CT. 06881
92. Spot Heaters Inc., 15552 Container Ln., Huntington Beach, CA. 92649
94. Taylor Instrument Co., Consumer Prod. Div., Sybron Corp., Arden, N. J. 28704
95. Thermo King, 314 W. 90th St., Minn., MN 55420
96. Traas Nursery Ltd., 24130 48th Av., Langley, B. C. Canada
97. Uniroyal, Inc., Chem. Div., Naugatuck, CT. 06770
98. U. S. Borax and Chemical Corp., Box 75128, Sanford Sta., Los Angeles, CA. 90010
99. Vandernolen Corp., 119 Dorsa Ave., Livingston, N. J. 07039
100. Van Well Nursery, P.O. Box 1339, Wenatchee, WA. 98801
100a. Weldcraft Industries, Inc., 10250 Highway 99E, Los Molinos, CA. 96055
101. Weyerhauser Co., Tacoma Bldg., Tacoma, WA. 98801
102. Williamstown Irrigation Co., Williamstown, N. Y. 13493
103. Wiss and Sons Co., 33 Littleton Av., Newark, N. J. 07107
104. Wells and Wade Hdw., P.O.B. 1161, Wenatchee, WA. 98801
105. York Industrial Products, P.O.B. 1592, York, PA. 17405

Index

DATE DUE

#12/04/11
8-25-04

#47-0108 Peel Off Pressure Sensitive